POLICY ISSUES FOR THE 1990s

POLICY ISSUES FOR THE 1990s

Policy Studies Review Annual

Volume 9

Edited by
Ray C. Rist

Transaction Publishers
New Brunswick (U.S.A.) and London (U.K.)

ISSN: 0163-108X
Library of Congress Catalog Number: 77-72938
ISBN: 0-88738-265-7 (cloth)
Printed in the United States of America

For Matthew—
who will come to adulthood in the 1990s
and inherit the issues written about here

Contents

Introduction
Declining Options/Increasing Needs:
The Policy Environment for the 1990s

Ray C. Rist

America is ready for change—but not much and not too fast. After eight years of a presidency characterized by considerable accomplishments and also considerable failures, the country stands ready to preserve the former and address the latter. The outstanding success of the Reagan administration in reducing unemployment and inflation, for example, represent two areas of economic policy where there is a national consensus to stay the course. But at the same time, and again in the economic policy arena, the failure of the Reagan administration to curb the dramatic growth of the national debt by not balancing the budget presents an area where changes in existing policy are clearly recognized as needed.

The list can continue. The twin options of continuity or change characterize current assessments across the spectrum of policy issues facing the country, be these health care, education, income security, environmental protection, or military preparedness, to name but a few. Indeed, it is one of the underlying intents of this volume to focus on these broadly sketched policy options and trace out their implications for the 1990s. Identifying the areas where we can anticipate continuity and where, in contrast, we can anticipate policy change will tell us much about what is going to crowd the policy agenda in the coming years.

The views expressed here are those of the author and no endorsement by the United States General Accounting Office is intended or should be inferred.

1

There are two ways in which the change that is underway in the United States can be characterized. One way is to focus on the immediate, the short term, the events that appear each day on the pages of the newspapers or on the evening news. Concerns over the federal budget, AIDS, the American addiction to chemicals, or our foreign policy toward the Persian Gulf are but a few examples of the topics that dominate public discourse. Tracking the day-to-day unfolding of these and many other situations facing the country is, without question, important. Each bears a direct impact on the country as well as on the lives of individual citizens. The need of governments at all levels to respond means that these issues must be clearly understood. Short-term policy responses will depend upon the clarity and breadth of these understandings.

But what is happening in the country is also to be understood by its undercurrents, the changes that are less perceptible and less evident on a short-term basis. These changes are over the horizon of a ninety-second-news-byte view of the world.

Tracking these undercurrents is no less important than having a good understanding of the events one sees continually on the surface. It is by going beneath the momentary realities that a sense of the movement of the country can be gained. It is at this level, for example, that one should look to understand the direction of race relations or the growing inequality among social classes. Only by looking to these longitudinal trends can one gain a sense retrospectively of where the country has been and prospectively where it appears to be headed.

Two such broad trends find themselves appearing and reappearing in the pages of this volume. It is important here to identify and discuss each of them so that when the various substantive sections are read, there is also an awareness of how these two trends underlie them. The first of these two underlying currents addresses the precarious capability of the United States to find sufficient institutional viability to solve our pressing problems. Stated differently, it is not self-evident that our current institutions have the skills and organizational structures appropriate to the problems they face. Successfully meeting the challenges, for example, in health, financial markets, or urban poverty cannot be assumed, a priori. There is no guarantee that the script has a happy ending.

The second of the undercurrents focuses on why it is that America seems to be sagging. The changes in the country in these past years— greatly increased national debt, a monthly multi-billion-dollar trade deficit, stagnant growth in productivity (a feeble 0.4 percent yearly throughout much of the 1980s), growing gaps in health care coverage for American citizens, and the solidification of a large underclass are but a few such examples that give pause to many about the direction the country is headed. Indeed, analyzing these undercurrents and their implications for the 1990s becomes of pressing importance if appropriate intermediate and long-term policy strategies are to be crafted.

Where Is America Going?

In trying to answer this alluring question, it is necessary to do two things. First, there is a need to assess retrospectively what has brought us to where we are. Thus each of the themes raised here has a historical dimension that is pivotal to our understanding of how we have come to our present condition. Second, and concurrent with this retrospective view, is the effort at prospective analysis, focusing on where the changes appear to be leading. This latter effort is understood as necessarily high risk. Prospective analysis is somewhere between good data and prophecy. Still, without careful consideration of the future implications of present conditions, the policy process is limited to a reactive mode, unable to anticipate and then plan a response, however tentative.

Institutional Capacity for Problem Solving

In reading across this collection of articles, one fundamental concern that emerges is the uncertainty as to whether or not the United States can any longer effectively respond to its present problems. Several of the authors here question the *political will* of the country to muster the energy necessary to take on, for example, the persistent and tough issues of poverty or the budget deficits. For each of them, the concern is whether sufficient mobilization of public commitment can be generated to instigate change. They worry, frankly, that the country has become so accustomed to these conditions that they are now taken as part of the status quo and are no longer seen as threats to the well-being of the society.

But for other authors, the most fundamental and insistent question is whether or not, regardless of good will and desire to bring change, the country any longer has the *institutional capacity* to effect the needed change. Here the concern is with the flexibility, adaptability, and vision that institutions will need to demonstrate in order to address present problems. Examples are cited in health care, defense procurement, international financial markets, urban economics, and government itself as to where basic problems appear to have grown beyond present capacities to respond effectively. It is this seeming mismatch between how our institutions are organized and what is needed to address present conditions that generates the alarm.

Raising concerns about institutional capacity quickly eliminates the possibility of focusing on short-term, quick-fix solutions. Creating new institutions or transforming present ones to meet the new demands and realities in American society means a concerted effort over years. Institution building will take time. The interim issue, however, is no less pressing, i.e., what to do now. While short-term fixes have reached a high state of political and organizational perfection in the United States, they will not suffice. Linking short and intermediate objectives to the overall strategy for building institutional capacity will be necessary.

Particularly intriguing about the strategy for building institutional capacity is that, in the end, institutions need to create their own self-generating means of change. Regardless of the institutional sector, the fundamental concern is with the passivity and acceptance of present circumstances as they are. (The authors make clear that this is not a new problem for the United States. They cite the many years that the United States auto industry cared little or nothing about quality in its products and the subsequent results for that industry in particular and the industrial health of the country overall. Near bankruptcy, like stock market crashes, captures people's attention.) Short-term profit motives, contentment with known organizational structures, and the self-interest of management all hinder flexibility and continuous adaptation. It is not easy to manage change; it is even less easy to predict exactly where the change will lead. Thus the low-risk posture of simply doing more of what one is already doing becomes extremely attractive. The solution that United States institutions have frequently settled for is working harder, not smarter.

Briefly, one encouraging but still tentative example at present of building new institutional capacity is the effort going into structuring the United States financial markets in the wake of the October 1987 stock market crash. New forms of regulation are recognized as needed. The various stock markets are talking to one another on strategy; the Securities and Exchange Commission is involved; large banks and brokerage houses are discussing ways better to preserve needed liquidity; and the outlines of some forms of cross-institutional cooperation are emerging. While it is much too soon to tell if these efforts will be successful, there is no doubt but that the events of October 1987 have generated a clear awareness that the institutional arrangements then in existence were inappropriate to the time and needs of a global, twenty-four-hour market system. The loss of nearly $700 billion in the value of American stocks in one month has not been without its consequences.

The current efforts in the Soviet Union to enhance institutional flexibility and adaptability through an emphasis on *perestroika* is but another indication that the problem is not simply one facing the United States. Indeed, the situation in Great Britain, discussed later in this volume, is also similar in this regard. Each country faces a set of problems more or less unique to its own circumstances and for which it has to seek its own solutions. (That some learning can occur from one another is also understood and finds expression in several papers included here.)

There are now multiple examples of problems that have grown over time in the United States and often in small increments. The end result of this creeping incremental growth in a problem is that it is often difficult to determine the cumulative impact. Three examples are discussed in this volume, each of which is in a different policy area. But all three are national in scope and central to the question of whether America is or is not going to be able to develop sufficient institutional capacity.

First, the United States has experienced the emergence of a true underclass that now numbers millions of persons. While there has been since the early 1960s a recognition that poverty was a persistent reality for tens of millions of Americans, there was also the parallel view that persons could be brought out of poverty with relatively straightforward programs and assistance strategies. That set of approaches and assumptions now is understood not to work for millions. They are the new underclass—a group not caught in any safety net, involved in no institutional programs, and living on the economic margins.

Second, the past decades have brought forth a Rube Goldberg tax system that is now incomprehensible to even the most sophisticated tax accountants and lawyers. The country has depended upon the conviction of the citizens that the tax laws were fair, understandable, and that what one paid was one's rightful share. The level of trust in the honesty of the citizens has been extremely high. But the system as it has come to be patched together erodes trust. Both the feeling that the laws are increasingly rigged to benefit the wealthy and that the present system is in total chaos leads to tax avoidance, cheating, and frustration. Now, when major accounting firms are no longer willing to certify their work for important clients because of the ambiguities and contradictions in the tax laws, the system is in deep trouble.

Finally, there is the growing recognition that the welfare state as it was conceived during the New Deal has proved a failure on its own terms. It is not because the impulse was wrong, but because the system as it has evolved no longer takes care of the poor. The poor have suffered from budget cuts and the elimination of programs in far greater proportion than have those in middle- and upper-income brackets. Indeed, the end result of the present system is that the poor are denied services and care while affluent Americans are not required to pay their own way. Of all the entitlement programs in the federal budget (entitlement being government commitments to assist financially certain target groups in the population, e.g., Social Security for those past a certain age, student loans, veterans compensations and military retirement, etc.) it is now estimated that only one dollar in five goes to the poor. The other four go to middle and affluent Americans. These nonmeans-tested, government handouts to those who do not need them draw valuable and scarce dollars away from education, nutrition, and employment training programs. So long as so many believe they are "entitled" to government support, even when they do not need it, those who do have real needs will never receive the necessary support. The welfare system has evolved to where the "haves" are in line ahead of the "have nots."

In reflecting on the means by which the United States can develop the necessary institutional capacity across various sectors to respond to these long-term trends and undercurrents, multiple authors conclude that the public sector has got to take the lead, period. As the country moves into the post-counterreform era of the 1990s, the bottom line is simply that the public sector has got to get involved, and get involved in a sustained way. Several authors have come to this conclusion from witnessing the results of efforts during the past decade to restrain the activities of government and seek private-sector solutions to the nation's problems. Deregulation, massive tax cuts, protecting wealth, the privatization of government services and functions, and reductions of 14 percent in federal support since 1979 for education are but some of the events that have occurred and the consequences of which have been observed. The belief by these authors is that the social costs paid for during the Reagan counterreform period have been out of proportion to the benefits.

Other authors in the articles to follow take the view that government ought to be involved in the efforts to develop new institutional capacity because it is singularly well placed to be a change agent. For these analysts, the status quo will give way only to concerted efforts to build and sustain change. Their view is that no single entity in the private sector can generate the necessary momentum or be a sufficient catalyst, given the magnitude of what has to be done. Further, the government has available to it such a wide variety of policy mechanisms and instruments—tax preferences, regulation, grants, laws, loans, loan guarantees, etc.—that it alone can effect the right mix and match to push for change.

This near unanimity of option among the authors that the government has a vital role to play in addressing the problems that the country is facing suggests a distinct difference between the 1980s and the 1990s. While it is, of course, too soon to see if this proposed reinvigorated role for government will emerge, one characteristic of those calling for this effort suggests that it will happen. Specifically, the call for greater government involvement cuts across traditional ideological perspectives. It is not only the liberals who are arguing for government involvement and leadership. It is coming as well from those on the conservative end of the spectrum. Consensus on this issue is provocative in its implications. It suggests that there could be broad-based support for a more targeted and proactive government. If this is so, there is then the potential for realignment on any number of politically charged issues such as defense procurement and Social Security.

But amidst this clamor for government leadership, there is a fundamental question that first must be addressed. The issue is the institutional capacity of government itself. While the calls for change ring out, the unexamined assumption is that the current institutional arrangements in government will allow for a response. Why, though, if other sectors of the society have not been self-renewing and adaptable to the changing circumstances of our day, might one suppose that it has taken place in government?

The reality is that it has not. If one looks to the Legislative Branch as an institutional setting from which leadership could come in addressing these emergent problems, one finds a terribly fractured organization where there are more than 250 committees and subcommittees, where the budget process has all but broken down, and where any coherence of a legislative agenda is entirely missing. In the Executive Branch, the circumstances are different, but the conditions are no better. Assistant secretaries play musical chairs among departments (average tenure in some departments for assistant secretaries is about eighteen months), there is frequently little or no coordination of policy efforts among key players, and the capacity to implement policies and programs effectively ranges from only some to almost none. The present conditions in government are themselves hindrances to renewal. How (and whether) the United States government changes during the 1990s and what institutional capacity it develops to respond to the issues facing the country will affect the quality of life for us all.

Is America in Decline?

Nearly a century ago, Woodrow Wilson wrote:

America is now sauntering through her resources and through the mazes of her politics with easy nonchalance; but presently there will come a time when she will be surprised to find herself grown old—a country crowded, strained, perplexed—when she will be obliged . . . to pull herself together, adopt a new regimen of life, husband her resources, concentrate her strength, steady her methods, sober her views, restrict her vagaries, [and] trust her best, not her average, members. That will be the time of change.

Authors in this volume say that the time is now. How the United States responds will determine not whether but how deeply this country continues to slide into a period of decline, both at home and abroad.

The notion that America is in serious trouble, (supported here by Peterson, Gilpin, and Calleo, among others), breaks out into two separate but interdependent arenas—foreign and domestic. Reading these authors makes clear their view that America cannot address its problems overseas without also addressing its problems here at home. For example, one cannot do something about foreign competition without also doing something about American productivity; one cannot argue for greater "burden sharing" among our allies without also doing something about our multibillion-dollar trade deficits, and it makes no sense to reduce the number of foreign graduate students allowed to enter our science programs if we fail to train our own students so that they could compete without protectionist quotas. Consequently, the analysis of decline, while focusing on different spheres of American influence and involvement, really is of a single thread. Treating our problems overseas as separate and distinct from those we are experiencing here at home is, in the end, a false dichotomy.

In addressing the issue of external or foreign decline, it is important to begin by stressing that the decline of the United States relative to its allies (and even to its adversaries) was inevitable. With respect to our allies, this decline has even been necessary. The global dominance of the United States in the years just after World War II was achieved largely through economic and technological superiority. Potential competitors at that time—Britain, Japan, Germany, France, and the Soviet Union—all had felt the ravages of war in ways that missed the United States. But as we have helped to rebuild the economic infrastructures and economies of friends and even former enemies (Germany and Japan), it was to be anticipated that they would increasingly become partners and not simply dependents. Our relative decline to their growth over these past years has been, in considerable part, our own doing. Stated differently, the outcomes of the North Atlantic Treaty Organization (NATO), the Marshall Plan, and the World Bank have met and even exceeded our expectations. But what has happened during the 1980s was that their growth and use of innovation surpassed ours. The complacency of American industry resulted in less productivity, less quality, and less attention to the economic foundations of the society. Today, the gross national product of the European Economic Community (EEC) exceeds our own.

Concurrent with these shifts in the economic relations among nations was the effort by the United States to sustain its military hegemony. In the forty-plus years since World War II, the United States has poured increasing amounts of its resources—material, intellectual, and financial—

into trying to maintain the military superiority that was unquestionably ours in the years immediately after the war. Yet our failure was to accept the shifting nature of global power relations and the fact that other countries would themselves develop military capabilities. The United States thus has been frantically trying to sustain its military positions simultaneously all over the globe. This overextension has profoundly upset the balance that is needed in a mature economy between foreign and domestic demands. Attending to our industrial infrastructure, education of the work force, support for research and development, and following up on basic research breakthroughs were all ignored in the pursuit of an ever more elusive military hegemony. The drain on the resources of this society have been enormous. A billion-dollar-a-day Pentagon budget does have its impacts.

What has happened domestically was not inevitable. The United States has declined internally as the result of our own failures. Relative to our allies, we have not invested in rebuilding our heavy industrial infrastructure, we have not encouraged savings as a source of capital for investment, we have pursued short-term paper profits, and we have chosen not to make the human capital investments we now need for the ever expanding technological competition we face. The 1980s thus witnessed, in spite of much political rhetoric that fogged the reality, a dramatic shift in economic conditions between the United States and its allies—especially Japan and Germany. For example, the United States began the decade with yearly productivity gains of approximately 3 percent. By the end, our productivity gains were less than 1 percent. For the past decade, our economic base has been shrinking relative to the growing economic bases of our main competitors. Their yearly productivity gains have been in the range of 3, 4, or even 5 percent.

With these understandings of the present situation, the question can be asked: Is America, like many other great nations before it, on a downward slope into becoming a second-tier nation, such as has already happened in this century to Britain and France? None of the authors in this volume takes this slide as either inevitable or irreversible. Indeed, the papers suggest a strong manifesto for reform that, if implemented, could reverse present trends. But they also believe present trends will continue at an accelerating pace if the United States does not fundamentally change its present policy priorities. The country must make concerted efforts to regain its balance, its sense of proportion between domestic and foreign demands, and reallocate its resources in ways that rebuild its economic foundations.

It is at this juncture where the earlier question on institutional capacity and the present question on American decline come together. Melding them generates the bottom line: *Does America have the institutional capacity to respond to the decline of the past decade, in both its domestic and its foreign components?* The authors in this volume are cautious. While no one of them takes on this question explicitly, they are hopeful that the United States can learn from its mistakes, chart a plan of action, and then muster the institutional capacity to follow through. But if the country falls short in developing and implementing reforms in the industrial and foreign-policy areas, if little new ground is turned, then they believe present trends will continue. Self-correcting responses do not come automatically. Without the necessary effort, America will defeat itself.

Postscript: Implications for Policy Studies

Working for the past decade in a counterreform environment has had its impacts upon those who labor in the vineyard of policy studies. It has also had its impacts upon the analytic developments of the field itself. Policy analysts are trained to consider and analyze options, assess their relative impacts, and link various options to costs and benefits. Conducting their craft in this way, during a period of tight budgets, clear ideological constraints on what alternatives would be considered, and a strong bias against government action, has taken its toll. The optimism of the late 1960s and the 1970s has given way to a more pragmatic and less proactive stance by the end of the 1980s.

In attempting to sketch broadly the current status of policy studies in the United States, there are several key points. First, the field appears to have become much more retrospective in its analysis. Looking backward to learn about what has happened to programs and policies seems to have overtaken efforts at framing future agendas and options. There is, overall, less attention to emerging issues and their implications. (The papers in this volume are then something of an anomaly for the field in general. They are here because of my intent to highlight and frame the emerging issues for the 1990s.) If a true cross-section of current writings were included, the preponderance of papers would not have the themes or scope found here.

Second, in this shift to retrospective analysis, there has also been a strong emphasis upon doing more "managerial" studies. Broader theoretical concerns as well as efforts to track long-term implications of policies have given way to shorter-term, management-oriented work. If counterreform policies tend to push for the reduction and withdrawal of government activity, then the kinds of information needs that managers working in this environment will have will not be those that are proactive or expansionist in nature. "Managing down" focuses on budgetary data, personnel ceilings, the tightness of eligibility criteria, transferring and eliminating program functions, etc. The task for policy analysis has been to help in this process, a responsibility that was inevitable but not welcomed.

Third, doing more and more of this work over the past ten years has remolded the craft. Linking policy analysis to budgeting, for example, has clearly emerged as one of the dominant themes of the field during the past decade. So also, for example, has the concern with policy implementation. By the end of the 1980s, the issues being addressed in the journals are infrequently those of whether policies are appropriate and likely to achieve stated goals. Rather, article after article focuses on how to implement effectively what one has. The concern with the processes, while not unimportant, tends not to lead to assessments of impacts or consequences. A stronger emphasis on neutrality has emerged. Analysts write less about results (good and bad), make fewer judgments about policy outcomes, and focus more on descriptive accounts of things as they are or as they were.

Finally, there appears to be a growing awareness of the limitations of policy analysis. These limitations are of two types. One focuses on the decisions that have to be made that cannot be captured in quantitative terms. The current situation of AIDS in the United States is instructive. There are moral and ethical dimensions to this problem that have to be addressed and for which policy analysis has very little to say. Providing condoms versus stressing sexual abstinence among teenagers is a case in point. The judgment on which way (or both) to go is basically a moral one. It has to be made on a level that is beyond the technical analysis of pros and cons.

The second limitation that has increasingly come to characterize policy analysis is the persistent deconstructionist nature of the American political system. Regardless of how thoughtful or how complete a particular piece of work might be, its distortion and abuse in the policy arena is inevitable, especially if it is on one of the politically sensitive topics of the day. The ways in which journalists, politicians, and the public-relations masters of "spin" take on an issue and remold it to suit their own needs leaves the policy analyst either decrying the changes or going with the flow, hoping that some splinter of the original analysis remains. But in neither instance has the analysis been able to stand its own ground. It has been picked up, swirled about, and spun off as something quite different. Such changes clearly delimit the impacts to be attributed to the original work.

The end result of these changes in the craft of policy studies over the past decade is that the work is now generally characterized as being retrospective, quantitatively rather mundane, limited in scope, focusing on processes, and driven by the information needs of program and project managers. The reality of conducting this kind of work is quite different from the rhetoric of the textbooks on the subject. The descriptions in these books simply no longer ring true of the analyst framing options for decisionmakers, bringing to bear a variety of sophisticated methodological tools for their work, and contributing to the larger understandings of the problems we face.

The policy studies community has also lowered its sights and expectations. With trimmed sails, students, professors, and practitioners alike are all wondering if they can ride out the wind that has blown them so far from their original course. But whether the original course should any longer be pursued is a question that begs for an answer. Stressing the rhetoric of doing work one way while, in reality, doing it quite differently is straining the credibility of the field.

Ironically, the changes in the methods and perspectives of the policy studies field that have taken root these past ten years are now themselves about to be called into question. As the country emerges from this counterreform period, there will be considerable demand for careful assessments of the current conditions in the society and what are the options for addressing our problems. Prospective analysis will again be in demand. Some in the field may argue that their keeping a candle in the window these many years has now been vindicated. Their vigil is now over; the textbooks were right. Policy studies can now go back to what it was in the 1970s, throwing off the constraints and contortions of the past ten years. Others will view these changes with less delight, given that they have retooled to work in the counterreform climate of the 1980s. They have found a niche in this new climate and they will not be happy to lose it.

Whether the policy studies field can again adjust its course and move toward making new contributions during the 1990s is an open question. Time will tell. But so too will the willingness of those in the community to take a fresh look at what has been learned in the 1980s that can be brought along into the discourse of the 1990s. Fiscal constraints will be a given. State and local governments are now permanent players on the field. Policy accountability is now a requirement. Ignoring these lessons and turning instead to the fond remembrances of the 1970s is a prescription for failure. Just as the country faces a set of changed realities, so too does the policy studies community. How it responds in the coming years will determine its relevance (or irrelevance) to the challenges at hand.

Part I:
FRAMING THE ISSUES

The Moral Dimension to Policy Analysis: The Case of AIDS

It is sobering to begin this book with a collection of papers on a topic where the clear limitations to policy analysis and policy making are so evident. The emergence of AIDS in the United States has compelled the country, in the words of Ronald Bayer, "to confront a challenge that is at once biological, social, and political." Further, it is a challenge where the empirical data are incomplete and open to multiple interpretations, where the medical aspects are only partially comprehended, and where the political options tend to be pulled into polar positions predicated on various moral, ethical, and legal values. The end result, at least for the foreseeable future, is that applications of conventional policy-analysis methods and techniques are woefully inadequate to the task and situation at hand. The policy response in America to the AIDS situation cannot be reduced to applications of cost-benefit studies, regression equations, or forecasting models.

Responding to the AIDS epidemic will involve bringing analysts who would work through policy formulations and options into contact with significant segments of the population who do not opt for or legitimate social science analysis as a framework for decision making. There are large numbers of persons in the society who would develop their policies on moral or ethical grounds, entirely independent of any data or analysis the social science community might provide. Further, there are those who would also argue for a response exclusively on the basis of medical evidence (or call only for more funds, because of the lack of definitive research). Others may also opt for the medical model strictly on the basis of their concerns about constitutional protections of privacy or the alternative pivot of the protection of society. Stated differently, the basis upon which AIDS policy can be formulated in a period of profound descensus

15

necessitates incorporating into the process many for whom the logic and assumptions of social science are irrelevant.

What further aggravates this situation, and is alluded to several times in the articles presented here, is that the AIDS epidemic generates concerted calls from many sectors of the society for "something" to be done. What such pressures precipitate are, of course, countless short-term, quick-fix responses to one sector or one component of the issue. That there are equally potent counterforces or counterreactions in other sectors of the issue are ignored in the rush to action. The articles by Horowitz and by Conrad both give multiple instances of attempts at formulating ad hoc public policies based on "ready, fire, aim."

The formulation of public policy in such a milieu is, obviously, extremely difficult. Deciding on a course of action (or actions) is but the first step on a journey that has to cross the rivers of multiple interest groups, climb the mountains of ideological fervor, and traverse the swamps of medical uncertainty. (And after all that, there is still the matter of funds. AIDS is a costly disease.) These efforts, it goes almost without saying, have then to be undertaken with a paucity of good scientific information.

The AIDS epidemic thus represents an important case study for those interested in the study and implementation of public policy. This is an instance where the disjuncture between policy analysis and policy formulation becomes so visible and so deep that the bridge between knowledge and action is held in place by a few thin threads. Where there are virtually few agreements on the moral basis of behavior, public policy is nigh unto impossible to formulate and implement—save in those rare instances where political power and control of the policy apparatus are so complete that one view among many can control the system. But this is not the case with AIDS. The checkmating among various groups is now so complete that the policy response is reduced to the least common denominator— push for more federal funding of medical research. A national health crisis is essentially left bereft of policy guidance.

The role for policy research in this context is all the more pressing and necessary. This is so even if few publicly call for it or acknowledge the present gaps in information on transmission and treatment, on the one hand, or clarification of the moral, ethical, and legal issues, on the other. As is noted by several authors, it is precisely these gaps in information that should give pause to those clamoring for new policy initiatives. The demand for policy in the absence of information is exceedingly risky. A modest but nonetheless vital role that policy researchers may fill in the coming years is to keep emphasizing all that is not known. For either until the sheer financial and medical magnitude of the crisis overwhelms the current political stalemate and the country breaks out of the political cul-de-sac, or until a political consensus is slowly forged on the directions various policy initiatives should take, caution on any bold initiatives seems prudent. The contribution of social science and policy analysis in such circumstances is both vital and thankless. Saving us from our own impulses is no small feat in an area such as AIDS.

All four of the articles to follow take up one aspect or another of this general theme. Each presents a careful and calibrated analysis of the AIDS crisis. Each attempts to assess the limits of what is known. There are also thoughtful reflections on what actions the country might wish to consider (as well as avoid). But running through all these analyses is the thread of caution, of lowering our expectations on what can be done with what we know. Solutions are partial, temporal, and tentative. They are cross-cut by ethical, moral, and legal concerns that define American society in general and specific constituencies in particular. And finally, they recognize that rationality, reason, and civility are precious components or ingredients in the overall mix of what the country chooses to do. Amidst the clamor for sweeping solutions and perfected policies, these authors calmly remind us that leaping before knowing is more likely to bring harm than help.

1

AIDS, Power, and Reason

Ronald Bayer

A T THE CONCLUSION OF HIS MAGISTERIAL HISTORY, *Plagues and People*, William McNeill (1976, 291) asserted:

> Ingenuity, knowledge and organization alter but cannot cancel humanity's vulnerability to invasion by parasitic forms of life. Infectious disease, which antedates the emergence of humankind, will last as long as humanity itself, and will surely remain as it has been hitherto one of the fundamental parameters and determinants of human history.

Written ten years ago, these observations seemed, at the time, somewhat overdrawn, especially with reference to the advanced technological societies. Now, in the fifth year of the AIDS epidemic, as American political and social institutions seek to fashion a response to the HTLV-III retrovirus, McNeill's observations seem prescient.

Since 1981, when the Centers for Disease Control determined that a pattern of extraordinary illnesses had begun to appear among young gay men on the West Coast, America has been compelled to confront a challenge that is at once biological, social, and political. What

From *The Milbank Quarterly*, Vol. 64, Supplement 1 (1986): 168–82.

some had believed might be a short-lived episode, like toxic shock syndrome or Legionnaires' disease, has proved to be quite otherwise, and no end is in sight. Predictions as to the ultimate toll over the next decade range into the hundreds of thousands. However this modern epidemic is brought under control, it is clear that no critical dimension of American social and political life will remain untouched. AIDS has become a "fundamental parameter" of contemporary history.

Like the epidemics of prior eras, AIDS has the potential for generating social disruption, for challenging the fabric of social life, the more so since it has been identified with those whose sexual practices and use of drugs place them outside the mainstream. As the disease spreads more rapidly among heroin users, the color of those who fall victim will darken, thus adding another dimension to the perceived threat to society posed by the bearers of the HTLV-III retrovirus.

In the face of an extended microparasitic siege, will American social institutions respond on the basis of reason guided by a scientific understanding of how HTLV-III transmission occurs, or will anxieties overwhelm the capacity for measured responses? Will the threat posed by AIDS elicit Draconian measures, or will fear of such measures immobilize those charged with the responsibility of acting to protect the public health? Will our capacity for social reason allow us to traverse a course threatened by irrational appeals to power and by irrational dread of public health measures? Will reason, balance, and the search for modest interventions fall victim to a rancorous din? At stake is not only the question of how and whether it will be possible to weaken, if not extirpate, the viral antagonist responsible for AIDS, but the kind of society America will become in the process.

Private Acts, Social Consequences

The central epidemiological and clinical feature of AIDS and the feature that makes the public health response to its spread so troubling for a liberal society, is that the transmission of HTLV-III occurs in the context of the most intimate social relationships, or in those contexts that have for nearly three-quarters of a century proven refractory to effective social controls. The transmission of AIDS occurs in the course of sexual relationships and in the course of intravenous drug use. In both realms, and fueled by struggles on the part of women, gays, and racial minorities, the evolution of our constitutional law tradition as well as our social ethos over the past two decades has increasingly underscored the importance of privacy and of limiting state authority—at times for reasons of practicality, at times for reasons of political philosophy.

It is no accident that the Supreme Court discovered the "penumbral rights of privacy" in a landmark case overturning Connecticut's efforts to prohibit the use of birth control devices[1]; that issues of privacy loomed so large in the early abortion decisions; that so many of the procedural rights of criminal suspects enunciated by the Warren court emerged out of drug control cases. In each instance, attempts to enforce the law required the intrusive reliance upon the police in ways that offended the liberal understanding of the appropriate limits of state authority. Furthermore, the very effort to enforce the criminal law in such private realms was held to be inherently corrupting of law enforcement agencies, the result a "crisis of overcriminalization" (Kadish 1968).

An ideology of tolerance emerged to reflect the new perspective on the limits of the criminal law (Packer 1968) and on the capacity of all agencies of social control to compel adherence to standards of personal behavior where no complainants existed. When framed in the diction of sociology, the ideology of tolerance focused on the impact of "labeling" upon deviants (Schur 1971); when framed by concerns of law enforcement, it centered upon "victimless crimes" (Schur 1965).

This was the legal-social context within which AIDS intruded upon America, forcing a consideration of how profoundly private acts, with dire implications for the commonweal, might be controlled.

The only effective public health strategy for limiting or slowing the further spread of HTLV-III infection is one that will produce dramatic, perhaps unprecedented changes in the behavior of millions of men and women in this country. Such changes will demand alterations in behaviors that are linked to deep biological and psychological drives and desires. They will demand acts of restraint and even deprivation for extended periods, if not for the lifetimes of those infected and those most at risk for becoming infected.

The transmission of HTLV-III has as its first and most obvious consequence a private tragedy: the infection of another human being.

---

[1] *Griswold v. Connecticut*, 381 U.S. 479 (1965).

But to conceive of such transmission between "consenting adults" as belonging to the private realm alone is a profound mistake (Mohr 1985). Each new carrier of HTLV-III infection is the potential locus of further social contamination. When few individuals in a community are infected the prospect of undertaking individual and collective measures designed to prevent the spread of AIDS is enhanced. When, however, the levels of infection begin to approach a critical mass, when a level of saturation is approached, the prospect for adopting programs of prophylaxis is diminished. At stake here is a matter of extraordinary social moment. It has been estimated, we cannot be sure with what degree of accuracy, that the levels of HTLV-III infection by mid-1986 among gay men in San Francisco were something over 50 percent. Similar levels of infection have been cited for New York City. (Among intravenous drug users in New York and New Jersey the figures are, if anything, more grim.) Therefore, in New York and San Francisco, the likelihood of a gay or bisexual man avoiding an encounter with an infected male partner has virtually disappeared (Kuller and Kingsley 1986). Only the practice of great care in the conduct of one's sexual behavior is left as a mode of protection against infection or reinfection. That is not now the case in many cities across the country, particularly in America's midsection. As a clinical intervention would seek to block viral replication, the public health challenge is to prevent the replication of New York and San Francisco.

In some important respects the problem posed by AIDS is like those problems posed by a host of behavior-related diseases, e.g., lung cancer, emphysema, cirrhosis, with which health policy has had to deal explicitly since the surgeon general issued his first report on smoking (U.S. Department of Health, Education, and Welfare 1964). Ironically, at the very moment that an ethos of privacy was being enunciated, founded on philosophical individualism, the collective significance of every individual's acts began to attain public recognition. Both in the Lalonde report issued in Canada and *Healthy People* (U.S. Department of Health, Education, and Welfare 1979), public officials have argued that many private acts have indisputably social consequences, and that public intervention to limit social costs—characterized by economists as negative externalities—was a matter of the highest priority.

In the debate that has raged over the past two decades about measures to promote health—particularly over mandatory seatbelt and helmet laws—the specter of "Big Brother" has been evoked in an effort to thwart public health regulations designed to limit morbidity through the modification of personal behavior (Moreno and Bayer 1985). But, in contrast to the difficulties that would be posed by efforts to limit the transmission of HTLV-III infection, those presented by attempts to modify smoking, alcohol consumption, and vehicular behavior are simple. In each of these cases we could, if we chose to, affect behavior through product design, through pricing and taxation mechanisms, through the regulation and control of essentially public acts. Invasions of privacy would be largely unnecessary. With the transmission of HTLV-III the public dimension of the acts that are critical for public health is exceedingly limited. Closing gay bathhouses in San Francisco or New York, the subject of acrimonious debate on both coasts—to the dismay of some traditional advocates of public health, who viewed such settings simply as "nuisances"—may have important symbolic meaning. But the bathhouse is not the Broad Street pump, so crucial in the history of the effort to control cholera in Great Britain. Attempts to control the public dimension of HTLV-III transmission, whether through bathhouse closings or the repression of male and female prostitution, even if successful, will have only the most limited impact on the spread of AIDS.

Public Policy, Civil Liberties, and the Modification of Behavior

The central public problem before us is how to alter behavior that occurs in the most private of settings. Can that be done? Can it be done in a way that will not involve levels of intrusion into privacy that are morally repugnant? Can it be done in ways that do not require surveillance of Orwellian proportions? Can it be done in ways that acknowledge the importance of civil liberties to the structure and fabric of American social life?

It is important to underscore at this point a matter of direct relevance to these questions. The ethos of public health and that of civil liberties are radically distinct. At the most fundamental level, the ethos of public health takes the well-being of the community as its highest good, and in the face of uncertainty, especially where the risks are high, would limit freedom or restrict, to the extent possible, the realm of privacy in order to prevent morbidity from taking its toll. The burden of proof against proceeding, from this perspective, rests upon those who assert that the harms to liberty would, from a social point of view, outweigh the health benefits to be obtained from a proposed course of action.

From the point of view of civil liberties the situation is quite the reverse. No civil libertarian denies the importance of protecting others from injury. The "harm principle," enunciated by John Stuart Mill, is in fact the universally acknowledged limiting standard circumscribing individual freedom. For twentieth-century liberals and civil libertarians, that principle has typically accorded considerable latitude to measures taken in the name of public health. But since the freedom of the individual is viewed as the highest good of a liberal society, from a libertarian point of view, measures designed to restrict personal freedom must be justified by a strong showing that no other path exists to protect the public health. The least-restrictive alternative, to use a term of great currency, is the standard against which any course of action must be measured. When there are doubts, the burden of proof is upon those who would impose restrictions.

These two great abstractions, liberty and communal welfare, are always in a state of tension in the realm of public health policy. How the balance is struck in a particular instance is, in part, a function of empirical matters—how virulent is a particular viral agent, with what degree of ease can it be transmitted, can therapeutic interventions blunt the consequence of infection—and in part a function of philosophical and political commitments. In the case of AIDS, the capacity of American culture to tolerate, over an extended period, the social stress engendered by the pattern of morbidity and mortality will determine how such empirical matters and philosophical concerns are brought to bear on the making of public health policy.

The Appeals and Limits of Power

Faced with the presence of a new infectious and deadly disease, one whose etiological agent has already infected one to two million individuals, there is an understandable tendency to believe that the public health response ought to reflect the gravity of the situation. A deadly disease demands a forceful and even a Draconian response. In fact, however, the public health departments in the two cities most affected by AIDS, New York and San Francisco, have responded over the past five years with considerable restraint. What better indication is there of the effort to balance a commitment to public health with an appreciation of the importance of civil liberties than the lengthy, perhaps tortured, discussion of whether or not to shut the gay bathhouses? At the federal level, the recommendations of the Centers for Disease Control (1985a, 1985b, 1985c) throughout the epidemic have been designed to limit the impulse toward rash and scientifically unfounded interventions. But to those who are alarmed, restraint appears as an apparent failure on the part of public health officials. The unwillingness to put forth "tough" policies on AIDS has provoked charges of timidity (Starr 1986), an unconscionable capitulation to gay political pressure, and the subversion of the ethos of public health by that of civil liberties (Restak 1985).

Accusations against public health officials for their failure to move aggressively against disease and for their capitulation to special interests are not new. Charles Rosenberg has noted that, in the nineteenth century, physicians who were too quick to discover the presence in their communities of epidemic diseases were often the targets of censure (Rosenberg 1962, 27). Since such diagnoses could well produce financial disaster for local commercial interests, public health officers sometimes sought to silence those who warned of the imminence of epidemics and to restrain the overzealous. A contemporary critic said of the New York Board of Health that "it was more afraid of merchants than of lying" (Rosenberg 1962, 19). In the case of AIDS—despite the professionalization in the twentieth century of those responsible for public health—anxiety has surfaced over whether political motivations have colored not only the willingness to press for forceful measures, but also prevailing official antialarmist pronouncements about the threats posed by HTLV-III. Have public health officials been too reassuring about the modes of transmission? Have they underplayed the potential role of female-to-male transmission? Have they failed to adopt standard venereal disease control measures like sexual contact tracing because of an unbalanced concern for civil liberties? Has a commitment to privacy and confidentiality thwarted sound public health practice, thus placing the community at risk?

Such AIDS-specific fears have merged with an undercurrent of populist distrust for scientific authority that has been amplified in recent years by the politically charged debates among scientists over

environmental and occupational health policy. These factors have contributed to the volatility of public opinion polls regarding matters
like quarantine and isolation. Eleanor Singer and Theresa Rogers
(1986) have found that as many as one-third of surveyed Americans
favor the use of quarantine against those with AIDS or those who
"carry AIDS," though they know a great deal about the modes of
HTLV-III transmission and appear to accept the findings of the Centers
for Disease Control on such matters.

Because of the potential abuse of power and authority that could
well attend the implementation of public policies designed to halt
the spread of HTLV-III infection, less attention has been given to
the ways in which a failure to take appropriate public health measures
could produce the popular basis for more drastic action. Writing
about the Black Death, McNeill (1976, 172) noted:

> In Northern Europe, the absence of well-defined public quarantine
> regulations and administrative routines—religious as well as medical—
> with which to deal with plagues and rumors of plagues gave scope
> for violent expression of popular hates and fears provoked by the
> disease. In particular, long-standing grievances of poor against rich
> often boiled to the surface.

We have, thus far, not experienced the kind of anomic outbursts
described by McNeill, though reported increases of assaults on gay
men (*New York Times* 1985) and strikes by parents seeking to keep
school children with AIDS from the classroom may be viewed as
functional (but pale) equivalents (Nelkin and Hilgartner 1986). More
to the point, however, have been the calls in the press, in state
legislatures, and from insurgent candidates for elective office—all still
restricted to the most extreme political right—for the quarantine of
all antibody-positive individuals (Intergovernmental Health Policy Project
1985). The most recent of such proposals is to be found in the March
1986 issue of the *American Spectator*:

> There are only three ways that the spread of lethal infectious disease
> stops: it may be too rapidly fatal, killing off all its victims before
> the disease can spread; the population affected may develop natural
> or medically applied immunity; it may not be able to spread because
> uninfected individuals are separated sufficiently well from those
> infected. [At this point the only way] to prevent the spread of the

disease is by making it physically impossible. This implies strict quarantine, as has always been used in the past when serious—not necessarily lethal—infections have been spreading. Quarantine in turn implies accurate testing.

The authors then lament the failure of nerve on the part of Americans:

Neither quarantine nor universal testing is palatable to the American public where AIDS is concerned, yet both have been used without hesitation in the past (Grutsch and Robertson 1986, 12).

What is so striking about such proposals is that they would enforce a deprivation of liberty upon vast numbers for an indefinite period (the duration of HTLV-III infection) because of how infected individuals might behave in the future. Unlike the transmission of some infections, where one's mere presence in public represents a social threat, the transmission of HTLV-III infection requires specific, well-defined acts. Hence, the quarantine of all HTLV-III-infected persons would rest upon a willingness to predict or assume future dangerousness and would be the medical equivalent of mass preventive detention. Even were such a vast and thoroughgoing rejection of our fundamental constitutional and moral values tolerable, and even if it were possible to gather broad-based political support for such measures, the prospects for so enormous and burdensome a disruption of social life make mass quarantine utterly unlikely.

Rarely do those who propose quarantines suggest how all antibody-positive individuals would be identified, how they would be removed to quarantine centers, how they would be fed and housed, how they would be forcibly contained. Indeed, it is one of the remarkable features of proposals for mass quarantine as a public health response to AIDS, and an indication of the profound irrationality of such suggestions, that they treat with abandon both matters of practicality and history. Because proponents of quarantine speak of mass removal as if it were an antiseptic surgical excision, they can assume that their ends could be achieved without grave social disruption. A vision of benign quarantine measures is informed by recent memories of health officers imposing isolation on those who suffered from diseases such as scarlet fever. But when quarantine has been imposed upon those who viewed themselves as unfairly targeted by the state's agents, the story has sometimes been quite different. Judith Leavitt's (1976, 559) description of how German immigrants in Milwaukee responded to efforts at the forced removal and isolation of those with smallpox provides ample evidence of what might be expected were even local and confined efforts to isolate large numbers of HTLV-III-infected individuals undertaken: "Daily crowds of people took to the streets, seeking out health officials to harass."

But the irrationality and potentially disruptive dimensions of quarantine are no guarantee against future impulsive efforts to move in such a direction were social anxiety over AIDS to continue to mount in the next several years. During the drug scares of the 1960s, both New York and California sought to meet that crisis by the establishment of mass civil commitment programs for addicts (Kittrie 1973). Such efforts failed to stop the spread of drug use, though many were incarcerated in the process. Folly by great states is not reserved to the international arena.

Apparently more tolerable and more practicable are calls for the mandatory screening and identification of all high-risk individuals so that they might be compelled to face their antibody status, adjusting their behavior accordingly. Since it is impossible to know who is, in fact, a member of a high-risk group, calls for mandatory screening of risk-group members would require universal screening. Such a program would, in turn, require the registration of the entire population to assure that none escaped the testing net. Finally, since one-time screening would be insufficient to detect new cases of infection, it would be necessary to track the movements of all individuals so that they might be repeatedly tested. The sheer magnitude of such an undertaking makes its adoption implausible. Modified versions of universal mass screening might take the form of governmentally mandated work-place testing. Though such efforts would eliminate the need for geographical dragnets, they would still pose enormous problems. To suggest that such mass screening might be undertaken, with the sole purpose of education and counseling, is inconceivable. The logic of universal mandatory screening for an infectious disease without cure leads ineluctably to mass quarantine.

Of a very different order are proposals for the quarantine of individuals—male and female prostitutes, for example—who though seropositive continue to behave publicly in a way that exposes others to the possibility of HTLV-III infection. Both criminal and health law provide ample authority for the control of such individuals. Though the moral, legal, and constitutional impediments to the imposition of state control over all antibody-positive individuals does not arise in such cases, it is abundantly clear that the strategy of isolating such persons could have very little impact on the spread of HTLV-III infection.

Though there is an historical precedent for such measures in the efforts to control venereal disease by the mass roundups of prostitutes during World War I in the United States (Brandt 1985), anyone who has examined the more finely tuned attempts to impose isolation or quarantine upon "recalcitrants" or "careless consumptives" (Musto 1986), for example, will attest to the administrative difficulties that are entailed when even a modicum of procedural fairness is employed. More important, such efforts, directed as they are at the most obvious sources of infection, would fail to identify and restrict the many hundreds of thousands of infected individuals who in the privacy of their bedrooms might be engaged in acts that involve the spread of HTLV-III infection. If the quarantine of all antibody-positive individuals is overinclusive, the quarantine of public recalcitrants is underinclusive. That is the price of living in a constitutional society committed to the rudimentary principles of law, privacy, and civil liberties. It is also a restriction placed upon us by reality.

The Appeals and Limits of Education

Confronted by the legal, moral, and practical costs of mass quarantine and the limited possibilities of selective quarantine, there has been an understandable embrace of education as the way of seeking to meet the social threat posed by AIDS. Teaching members of high-risk groups about how to reduce the prospect of infecting others, or of becoming infected, is viewed as the appropriate social strategy, one that is compatible with our legal, moral, and political institutions. Education must produce the critical and dramatic alteration in the sexual and drug-using practices of individuals, it is argued. That has been the program of gay rights and self-help groups, as well as of local and federal agencies (Silverman and Silverman 1985). What well-funded and aggressively pursued education might attain it is still too soon to know. Despite the paeans to education, governmental efforts have been limited by profound moralism. To speak directly and explicitly about "safe" or "safer" sexual practices would require a tacit toleration of homosexuality (Washington Report on Medicine and Health 1986). For those committed to a conservative social agenda, such a public stance is intolerable.

The turn to education is, of course, compatible with the liberal commitment to privacy, to voluntarism, and to the reluctance to employ coercive measures in the face of behavior that occurs in the private realm. But the commitment to education in the case of AIDS occurs against a background of controversy about the efficacy of efforts to achieve the modification of personal behavior by health-promotion campaigns. Attempts to encourage changes in vehicular behavior, smoking, and alcohol consumption by education alone have had only the most limited success. Campaigns to encourage seatbelt use in automobiles in the United States, Canada, Great Britain, and France all faltered, and ultimately necessitated the enactment of statutes mandating their use (Warner 1983). More to the point is the failure of sex education to affect demonstrably the levels of teenage pregnancy in many urban centers. Finally, the historical legacy of efforts to control venereal disease through moral education in the period prior to penicillin provides little basis for optimism (Brandt 1985). So skeptical are some about the prospects of health education, that they charge that such campaigns represent a diversion from the more complex and difficult choices that need to be made (Faden 1986).

Nevertheless, the shock wave sent through the gay community by the rising toll of AIDS cases, coupled with the extraordinary and inventive efforts by gay groups at reaching large numbers with information about "safer sex" and the transmission of HTLV-III have apparently had a dramatic effect, at least in the short run. Anecdotal reports, quasi-systematic surveys, and, most important, the declining incidence of rectal gonorrhea, all have suggested to some that in the face of AIDS an unprecedented change has occurred in sexual behavior in a relatively brief period. Not only have gay men reduced the extent to which they engage in sexual activity with strangers, but so, too, have they reduced the extent to which they engage in anal receptive intercourse, the most "risky" of risky behaviors.

A longitudinal study conducted at the New York Blood Center, however, provides a sobering antidote to such educational enthusiasm and is compatible with what we have come to expect from health promotion campaigns (Stevens et al. 1986). Though it, like other studies, found a dramatic change in the extent to which gay men engage in anal receptive intercourse, just less than half of those in the study population continued to engage in that practice. Needless to say, we know almost nothing about how education might affect the behavior of intravenous drug users, even were such efforts to be undertaken. In the absence of a natural social support constituency, the provision of education might well be utterly ineffective.

Conclusion

Faced with a fatal illness that has the potential for grave social disruption, the appeal of coercive state power as an approach to the interruption of the spread of HTLV-III infection is understandable. But to yield to its seduction would be socially catastrophic. Confronted with the unacceptable specter of gross violations of privacy and civil liberties, many have embraced the promise of education. Here, the risk is that the politically attractive will be confused with the socially efficacious. The illusions of both power and voluntarism must be rejected. Instead of the grand vision of stopping AIDS, we must settle for the more modest goal of slowing its spread. As we attempt to fashion policies directed at that goal it will be important, at each juncture, to acknowledge the fundamental limits of our capacity to fight an infectious disease like AIDS.

We are hostage to the advances of virology and immunology, and will be so for many years. As the AIDS-associated toll mounts, so, too, will the level of social distress. In this protracted encounter with a microparasitic threat, it will be critical to preserve a social capacity for reasoned analysis and public discourse. That is a capacity that may be subverted by those who would generate hysteria and repressive moves as well as by those whose fears of such a turn result in irrational charges of "totalitarianism" at the very mention of public health (Ortleb 1985, 1986). A failure to defend reason in the face of AIDS may not only hinder our efforts to limit the exactions taken by this epidemic, but will leave a dreadful imprint upon the social fabric. The history of earlier epidemics should serve as a warning.

References

Brandt, A. 1985. *No Magic Bullet: A Social History of Venereal Disease in the United States since 1880.* New York: Oxford University Press.

Centers for Disease Control. 1985a. Education and Foster Care of Children Infected with Human T-Lymphotropic Virus Type III/ Lymphadenopathy-associated Virus. *Morbidity and Mortality Weekly Reports* 34 (August 30):517–21.

————. 1985b. Recommendations for Preventing Transmission of Infection with Human T-Lymphotropic Virus Type III/Lympha-denopathy-associated Virus in the Workplace. *Morbidity and Mortality Weekly Reports* 34 (November):681–6.

————. 1985c. Recommendations for Assisting in the Prevention and Perinatal Transmission of HTLV-III/LAV and Acquired Im-munodeficiency Syndrome. *Morbidity and Mortality Weekly Reports* 34 (December):721–6.

Faden, R. 1986. Ethical Issues in Government-Sponsored Public Health Campaigns. *Health Education Quarterly* 13(4). (In press.)

Grutsch, J. F., and A. D. J. Robertson. 1986. The Coming of AIDS: It Didn't Start with Homosexuals and It Won't End with Them. *American Spectator* (March):12.

Intergovernmental Health Policy Project. 1985. *A Review of State and Local Government Initiatives Affecting AIDS.* Washington: George Washington University, Intergovernmental Health Policy Project.

Kadish, S. 1968. The Crisis of Overcriminalization. *American Criminal Law Quarterly* 7:17–34.

Kittrie, N. 1973. *The Right to Be Different.* Baltimore: Penguin Books.

Kuller, L., and L. Kingsley. 1986. The Epidemic of AIDS: A Failure of Public Health Policy. *Milbank Quarterly* 64 (Suppl. 1): 56–78.

Lalonde, M. 1975. *A New Perspective on the Health of Canadians.* Ottawa: Government of Canada.

Leavitt, J. 1976. Politics and Public Health: Smallpox in Milwaukee, 1894–5. *Bulletin of the History of Medicine* 50(4):553–68.

McNeill, W. 1976. *Plagues and People.* Garden City, N.Y.: Anchor Press.

Mohr, R. 1985. AIDS: What to Do—and What Not to Do. *Philosophy and Public Policy* 5(4):6–9.

Moreno, J., and R. Bayer. 1985. The Limits of the Ledger in Health Promotion. *Hastings Center Report* 15(6):37–41.

Musto, D. 1986. Quarantine and the Problem of AIDS. *Milbank Quarterly* 64 (Suppl. 1): 97–117.

Nelkin, D., and S. Hilgartner. 1986. Disputed Dimensions of Risk: A Public School Controversy over AIDS. *Milbank Quarterly* 64 (Suppl. 1): 118–142.

New York Times. 1985. New York City Gay and Lesbian Antiviolence Project. November 16.

Ortleb, C. 1985. The AIDS Prophet of Doom. *New York Native* (October 14–20):20.

———. 1986. Heil Bayer!! *New York Native* (June 2):4.

Packer, H. 1968. *The Limits of the Criminal Sanction.* Stanford: Stanford University Press.

Restak, C. 1985. Worry About Survival of Society First: AIDS Victims' Rights. *Washington Post,* September 8.

Rosenberg, C. 1962. *The Cholera Years.* Chicago: University of Chicago Press.

Schur, E. 1965. *Crimes without Victims.* Englewood Cliffs, N.J.: Prentice-Hall.

———. 1971. *Labeling Deviant Behavior.* New York: Harper and Row.

Silverman, M. F., and D. B. Silverman. 1985. AIDS and the Threat to Public Health. *Hastings Center Report* 15(4):19–22.

Singer, E. and T.F. Rogers. 1986. Public Opinion about AIDS. *AIDS and Public Policy Journal* 1(1):8–13.

Starr, P. 1986. Possible Social Consequences of the AIDS Epidemic. Paper presented at the American Association for the Advancement of Science meetings, Philadelphia, May.

Stevens, C., P. Taylor, E. Zang, J. M. Morrison, E. J. Harley, S. Rodriguez de Cordoba, C. Bacino, R. C. Y. Ting, A. J. Bodner, M. G. Sarngadharan, R. C. Gallo, and P. Rubenstein. 1986. Human T-Cell Lymphotropic Virus Type III Infection in a Cohort of Homosexual Men in New York City. *Journal of the American Medical Association* 255(16):2167–72.

U.S. Department of Health, Education, and Welfare. 1964. *Smoking and Health.* Washington.

———. 1979. *Healthy People: The Surgeon General's Report on Health Promotion and Disease Prevention.* Washington.

Warner, K. 1983. Bags, Buckles, Belts: The Debate over Mandatory Personal Restraints in Automobiles. *Journal of Health Policy, Politics and Law* 8(1):44–75.

Washington Report on Medicine and Health. 1986. No "Show & Tell" for AIDS Education, CDC Says. January 13.

Acknowledgments: The preparation of this paper was made possible by support to the Hastings Center Project on AIDS, Public Health, and Civil Liberties by the Field Foundation, the AIDS Medical Foundation, and the Pettus Crowe Foundation.

Address correspondence to: Ronald Bayer, Associate for Policy Studies, The Hastings Center, 360 Broadway, Hastings-on-Hudson, NY 10706.

2

The Limits of Policy and the Purposes of Research: The Case of AIDS

Irving Louis Horowitz

AIDS is considered a social as well as a medical problem. The AIDS epidemic is used to highlight a crisis in policymaking, a crisis in which prescription is based on the tentativeness of empirical evidence. Without wide consensus in this area and in the face of broad-ranging discussion, attempts at policymaking can only create more problems. This article argues that the social sciences must be utilized to view such a problem in the context of scientific, political, and moral considerations. The goal of problem solving may be difficult in this area, but evidence from the social and behavioral sciences must be advanced to provide knowledge as a guide for further action.

The epidemiology of AIDS illustrates a large and discomforting truth: that the sheer recognition of a major problem is far from a shared recognition of policy remedies. In the case of AIDS the most recent Gallup Poll indicates that more than two-thirds of the American people identify AIDS as the major disease of our time—far outstripping such major health problems as heart, cancer, drug abuse, pollution, and all others combined (Yang, 1987). Yet, there remains hardly any policy consensus on what should or even could be done. This disjunction

From *Knowledge in Society: An International Journal of Knowledge Transfer*, Vol. 1, No. 1 (1988).

between *knowledge as public awareness* and *knowledge as policy corrective* properly summarizes the basic message of this article.

At its most worthy level, the examination of a single policy quandary helps to illumine larger concerns. That, at any rate, is my aim in this brief excursion into the much-talked about AIDS epidemic. There is no need for a recitation of the medical aspects of AIDS, or even the broad demographic characteristics of populations that are most likely to contract or carry this newest dread and primarily fatal disease. Rather, I want to show how the epidemic of AIDS highlights a crisis in policy, one that the social sciences may clarify, and in so doing move the study of policy-making to some substantial higher ground.

There can no longer be an ounce of doubt that AIDS is no less a social than a medical problem. The best evidence for this, as indicated by Richard Rothenberg, an epidemiologist at the National Centers for Disease Control in Atlanta, is that although AIDS cases may have been introduced and reintroduced into the American population since the late 1960s, the disease spread widely only when a small number of carriers were able to engage in frequent intercourse with a large, sexually active population. Without such a transmission belt, the AIDS virus had scant opportunity to become a mass contagion (Kolata, 1987). In short, while the medical preconditions may have been present for many years, it was only when the social conditions became widespread that AIDS became a mass problem.

Whenever one poses the issue in terms of understanding rather than resolving, the risks in having social research denounced as irrelevant, if not downright obstructionist, are sure to follow. Yet such risks are minor compared to a bland acceptance of a presumed common wisdom that in fact often points to an uncommon folly. In the case of AIDS for example, a recitation of raw numbers of potential victims is of less importance for policy than the demographic, geographic, and sexual characteristics of those involved.

We need to begin then by a disaggregation of macro-policy from micro-policy. In one sense, the former is a bundle of issues comprised of the latter. But each has dynamics of its own. Affirmative action is a macro-policy. But it is derived in part from Executive Order No. 11246 issued during the Lyndon B. Johnson White House years. In its specifics, this order concerned government hiring. Now mandated quotas have been imposed on ever wider areas of the public and private sectors alike. At such a level, the concept of policy is a twentieth-century equivalent of the nineteenth-century notion of *geist* or *esprit*. Racial equity is not so much a crafted political position, but a broadly held felt need of the age. It exists across class no less than racial boundaries.

The issue of developing a policy toward AIDS is something else again. It is a specific disease, which afflicts a special segment of the social sector, for the most part urban homosexual communities, and to a far lesser degree, those who can acquire or transmit the infection through

IV drug usage. Further, it is an area in which a general policy consensus does not currently exist, and hence, the capacity to impose a policy on a society is more readily strained. Finally, it is an area in which neither the scientific nor medical parameters are entirely understood. For example, the length of the incubation period varies greatly, and only recently has it been brought to light that tests for AIDS may fail to indicate the presence of the dread disease for more than one year (Kolata, 1987). Hence, we can look at the AIDS problem as a relatively "pure" case of the extent to which policy is effective in contexts of both scientific doubt and intense social polarization.

These essentially policy differences between those who, like Education Secretary William J. Bennett, advocate teaching restraint as a virtue and avoiding premarital sex and illegal drugs as the safest and smartest way to prevent AIDS infection and those who, like Surgeon General C. Everett Koop (1987), emphasize the use of condoms and public health measures to reduce the risk of AIDS among the sexually active, are indicative of a general crisis in policy as such (Boffey, 1987). In the intensifying debate between the abstainists and pragmatists, and a corresponding decline as to what constitutes normative frameworks of behavior, it might well be that description rather than prescription is the order of the day.

That, at any rate, is what Hiatt and Essex (1987) claim in arguing the need for politicians to make clear their policy persuasions on such issues as: (1) conflicts between public health requirements and the right of the homosexual communities to privacy, (2) who should pay for treatment, (3) what ancillary programs should be introduced for drug users, (4) what programs should be supported for preventing AIDS in the newborn, (5) how can research be encouraged, (6) what educational programs should be advocated, (7) how can international cooperation be fostered in AIDS research and prevention, and (8) how should fiscal priorities be set, and at the expense of which current programs.

Before such a leap into policy considerations is made, it is important to state a few social truths about AIDS. In this epoch, it is precisely such "facts" that are dangerously obscured by phrases like "alternative life-styles" in contrast to "safe life-styles," and "high risk groups" in contrast to specific mention of homosexual populations or "homophobic bias," when the issue of victims is broached in a concrete fashion. This hapless way of avoiding the brute fact that approximately 75 per cent of the victims of AIDS are homosexuals (the figure would be even higher if one included those who sexual practices are not gender exclusive, the so-called bisexuals) is typical of those who want clear-cut policies even as they move to obscure clear-cut evidence.

It should be noted that at present no vaccine is available and no satisfactory antiviral drug preventative exists. In starkest terms the incidence of death in AIDS victims is very high (Dawson, 1987). The one drug that is being widely used, azidothymidine, or AZT, is so toxic that roughly fifty percent of AIDS patients cannot take it (Kingston, 1987; Kolata, 1987). We also know little about the origins of AIDS. It seems that the disease exists in a benign fashion in the green monkey of Africa, but that the same disease becomes virulent in humans. It can incubate for a long period of time, can be transmitted by the female no less than the male, and is infectious in carriers for years without people knowing it (Gross, 1987). We also have a situation in which testing for AIDS is not allowed, and in those rare instances when it is permissible, it is not always possible to identify specific individuals as carriers (Shilts, 1987).[1] Thus, generating policies for AIDS is at best a vague and general activity, one that comes hard against the granite wall of constitutional law no less than medical and chemical inadequacies.

What does exist is the development of long-term policies based on demands for increased funding for research on vaccines in order to avoid dealing with or bypassing short-term conditions. Thus, the policy of treating AIDS is also a metaphysical disposition to develop a policy in a context in which a social consensus does not exist, in which the scientific information base is limited, and in which moral premises are profoundly contradictory. A good example of this is the use of the AIDS epidemic by groups like the Planned Parenthood Federation of America to argue the need for "nationwide sexuality eduction," but with little, if any, commentary on the actual problem of AIDS as such (Wattleton, 1987). Given the nature of special interest groups in America, one can expect this sort of tendentious spinoff approach to become common currency among all sorts of secular and religious groups and on all sides of the issue.

Whenever a serious problem emerges in American society, the call for public action is sure to follow. One certain consequence of this is the formation of a presidential commission. And as we can see, this has already taken place, with the attendant politics of the composition of the commission taking up most of the time and energy of the presumed investigators and people dedicated to manufacturing a policy. At a more proximate level, a somewhat typical impassioned plea for a "do-something" approach was registered in a recent issue of The New Republic, which boldly presented "Our Cure for Aids." Arguing that we are in a condition similar to that of Father Paneloux's initial response to the plague, neutrality is culpable, judgment is a form of withdrawal and action becomes a moral necessity. So the first step toward a policy is to confront the moral trade-offs (i.e., private rights versus public goods), and move ahead from there.

Martin Peretz (1987) then moves rapidly from the general to the specific: (a) public educational campaigns that are explicit, colloquial, and geared less to restrictions on sexual pleasure than to guidelines for the possibility of safe and enjoyable sex, (b) the dispensing of condoms and their placement "in all bars and clubs," including "handing out condoms at the exit door of any club charging admission after 9 p.m. and at all rock concerts," and (c) reaching the neediest (i.e., black, Hispanic and poor people), the fastest growing group of AIDS victims, including dispensing and providing clean needles to drug addicts on demand.

At the conservative end of the spectrum, the concerns are less with a policy to protect the victims of the disease than to protect those innocents who may be exposed to the AIDS victims or the carriers. Thus, one might say that there is a set of demands for antipolicy (i.e., the cauterization and isolation of AIDS victims from the general society). To be sure, when efforts are made to impose the AIDS victims or their children on the general population, the revulsion is as violent as it seems complete. Fire-bombing, school boycotts, withdrawal of insurance premiums are now random, sporadic, but also frequent.

The philosophical foundations of such an antipolicy position are put forth by Adam Meyerson (1987) in the journal he edits, *Policy Review*, which under the circumstances is quixotic. It is his view that "with the AIDS scare and the death of prominent athletes and actors from cocaine, Nature has been confirming conventional morality by showing that there are certain things the human body is not supposed to do." It is clear that the use of the word "Nature" is precisely equivalent to the word "God." And if nature or God carry demonstrable proscriptions on action, on what one should not do, then clearly, policies intended to reverse such patterns can only be viewed as antinatural or worse, blasphemous.

A serious problem with the pure conservative approach is that even if one wants a laissez faire environment in which the victims of AIDS self-destruct as it were, the nature of the disease is such that a policy is still required for the consequences of AIDS for the general population. Thus, a society still needs a set of policies on how to quarantine the victims, how to identify the victims from nonvictims (i.e., medical clearance and surveillance for the population as a whole), on forms of indemnification for victims of AIDS and, no less, types of punishment for carriers who spread the disease knowingly. Only the most parochial view of policy identifies efforts at "doing something" exclusively with providing additional funds for medical research.

I have attempted to be fair in presenting the extremes in the matter of policy responses to AIDS. Let me hasten to add that this does not remotely exhaust approaches. The range of options between these two poles is extensive and largely put forth by serious people. But my concerns here are less the issue of AIDS than the problems that constantly, and in one field after another, beset the world of public policy. Indeed, it might be wiser to speak of the many worlds of public policy, since on a subject like AIDS, policy involves legislative supports, executive orders, judicial decisions, voluntary actions, and local agency funds. For built into the structure of policy, what invariably subjects specific recommendations to criticism and correction is the multiplicity of levels of organized life aimed at addressing even one specific problem area.

I would like then to briefly turn to what social science can contribute to this environment in which dissensus rather than consensus prevails, and in which good and honest people come to seemingly resolute and contradictory conclusions. For on a subject like AIDS, what one finds is broad agreement that a problem of widening contagion does exist, what one does not find is what, if anything, should be done, and by whom, to limit or ultimately overcome the problem. Berk (1987) in a provocative and able presentation notes that there are currently no experts on the long-range social consequences of AIDS. He proposes that social research produce experts; develop a crash program in social projections; develop the tools for such projections in short order, given the accelerated character of the AIDS epidemic; and finally, do so in the context of big science (i.e., many researchers draw from different fields working with relatively large budgets, or at least with minimal fiscal constraints) (Berk, 1987).

To do so signifies that we subject all efforts at policy to empirical scrutiny; that is to say, what are the scientific, political, and moral obstacles or impediments to new policy. Again, by no means do I suggest that what follows exhausts the information available. But it does raise a way of handling policy that gets beyond the pure optimism that a policy is always available to change existential reality and the equally undiluted pessimism in which prudence and natural law are invoked with impunity.

Since so much has been made of preventative medicine, at least during an interim period in which "cures" are simply unavailable (if indeed ever attainable), it is fair to hold our discussion to the impact of condoms on the AIDS population. While there is no question as to the prophylactic properties of condoms, and their capacity to minimize the spread of AIDS within homosexual populations, especially when used in connection with spermicides, serious questions exist in relation to the prevention or inhibition of AIDS.

Among the concerns raised are the following: (1) Among the sample batches tested, the Food and Drug Administration found that twenty percent of the latex condoms failed water leakage tests. This failure of 41 of 204 batches exceeded agency standards. (2) The failure rate for imported condoms is significantly higher than for domestic brands. (3) Latex condoms are less subject to microscopic damage than natural condoms made of lambs' intestines. Beyond the character of contraceptive devices are the human elements. (4) Anal intercourse is far more traumatic than vaginal intercourse, hence the wear and tear on condoms is much higher. (5) The potential for transmitting AIDS is higher than the possibility of pregnancy because female fertility exists only a few days each month, whereas the AIDS virus apparently can be spread all the time (Gruson, 1987).

Scientific studies of the impact of condom use in AIDS prevention are rare, given the ethical questions raised about establishing control groups in experimental situations. But in one survey of AIDS patients and their uninfected heterosexual partners, it was found that two out of twelve of the sexually active partners who claimed to regularly use condoms became infected with AIDS. Thus, without doubting the prophylactic values of condoms, the belief that a macro policy can be built upon condoms is obviously dubious. Beyond all such concerns is the obvious problem that the very belief that the use of condoms will prevent AIDS runs the risk of higher homosexual activity, and thus partially offsets their prophylactic value.

Rather than speak of political processes in general, it might, for present purposes, be best to simply restrict our discussion to public opinion surveys. The making of policy under conditions of dissensus is far more troublesome than under consensual conditions. And while 78 percent of Americans said that AIDS sufferers should be treated with compassion, once the Gallup poll questioning became more precisely worded, the actual gap in sentiment is seen as quite substantial (Gostin, 1987).

While 48 percent of those polled said AIDS victims should be allowed to live in the community unimpeded, 29 percent disagreed. On the issue of jobs, 33 percent said that employers should be permitted to dismiss those infected with the AIDS virus, while 43 percent said they should not. And on the question of responsibility, 45 percent of those surveyed agreed that most people with AIDS have only themselves to blame, while only 13 percent disagreed. And on the crucial statement: "I sometimes think that AIDS is a punishment for the decline in moral standards," 42 percent agreed with this proposition, while 43 percent disagreed, saying they did not sometimes hold that view (Senak, 1987).

At the other end of the political spectrum are the powerful forces mobilized in select urban centers by the homosexual community, for whom everything from closing bath houses to testing and identifying AIDS victims becomes anathema. Although estimates indicate that in a city like San Francisco there are perhaps 75,000 homosexual men, 10 percent of the city's population; and although half of them may be infected with the human immunodeficiency virus that causes AIDS, the prevalence of the disease has not been translated into specific policy recommendations. Local ordinances prevent San Franciscans with AIDS from being fired from their jobs. Nor can they be denied housing or evicted because of AIDS diagnosis. Insurance companies are not allowed access to results of the AIDS antibody test in assessing insurance premiums. In a city like San Francisco, it is anathema to raise a critique, however oblique, about homosexuality without being condemned as a homophile. Few politicians dare avoid support of "gay pride," much less advocate sexual abstinence. Thus, while a consensus does not exist at a macropolitical level, the operation of micropolitical

considerations further inhibit policy from being articulated, even tim-
idly (Bethell, 1987).

This public opinion division thus moves the issue of AIDS to a moral
center of gravity. But ethical parameters are hardly self-evident. The
utilitarian argument that self-interest is all-determining comes hard
upon those who argue that social interest must prevail. Further, self-
interest can be denied in terms of serving others as well as self. Ethical
slogans about the "greatest good for the greatest number" may tear at
the fabric of a system predicated on "no exploitation of a disadvantaged
minority for the benefit of an advantaged majority." The right to know
comes hard upon the right to privacy. Compassion comes upon retribution in arguments concerning capital punishment. The right to life
comes upon the right of the person to determine capabilities of support.

It is far simpler to discuss ethical concerns in terms of good versus
evil, truth versus error, or truth-telling versus lying. But these are less
ethical dilemmas than moral imperatives derived from the Western religious culture. And it is precisely the invocation of that culture which is
used by those who argue against an AIDS policy per se (Mars-Jones,
1987). In a world of ethics, and in a world of alternative goods, the
choice is between or among principles that can claim a wide number of
adherents. In this sense, the need to achieve a balance between pressures for reform, called policies, and compliance with long standing
standards, called ethics, is dramatically highlighted by the AIDS epidemic (Coleman, 1987).

One illustration may suffice: A majority of the population favors the
quarantine of AIDS victims. While this same public does not accept the
concept of quarantining people because of their sexual preferences,
they do assert that the risks to the uncontaminated public warrant such
severe measures. But of course to adopt such a policy is to deny a basic
set of civil liberties and personal rights to a special segment of the
American population. It raises also the specter of extending similar
harsh measures to other sectors of the population. There is a long gap
between an individual diagnosed as having AIDS and a cluster of AIDS
victims posing a community threat. Thus, we see the contradictions
between public policy and public morality in stark form in the emergence of AIDS as a broad national problem.

Moral discourse in the United States tends to be framed in terms of
notions of interest, purpose, and preference; that is, in structural terms.
But the exploration of phenomena like the AIDS epidemic is likely to
refocus our understanding of public morality in at least two respects:
one is to shift the center of gravity from moral codes or recipes to moral
decision-making and what policies are entailed (Edel, 1986). The experience with AIDS policies will also help to create a body of moral
knowledge, giving attention to the need to be innovative in resolving

problems and conflicts. Seen in this way, the appeals to normative structures are only one aspect of moral coding. The other is to reformulate the processes by which moral behavior is defined (Feldman, 1987). And this is a consequence of policy making about subjects like AIDS.

What we have then is a clear distinction between the development of social science and the manufacture of public policy. This does not imply a contradiction between the two, or an antagonistic relation, only that the realms of discourse are distinct, and that one cannot simply, in the name of policy, invoke social science. It is probably the case that in short-run terms, condom disbursement to a wide number of people would help to contain an AIDS epidemic that threatens to kill more people than any disease other than heart attack and cancer. At the same time, the cultural imperative underwriting such a short-term policy is that homosexuality is an alternative life style, criticism is homophobic or just plain neurotic (in contradistinction to earlier psychoanalytical traditions in which homosexuality was held to be a characteristic of neurosis).

The attitudes toward heart disease and acquired immune deficiency syndrome are radically different. There is no hue and cry for building massive numbers of JARVIK:7 artificial heart units. Rather, the call is for changes in personal life style: abstinence, no smoking, cutting down on the intake of caffeine and carbohydrates, less stressful modes of life. But in the case of AIDS, calls for abstinence are often met with derision and contempt. What we are faced with then is the power of a social movement rather than the worthiness or worthlessness of public policy.

Thus we come upon the limits of policy rather than the simple disenthrallment of policy. The cry to do something comes down to individuals doing something (i.e., as in the case of our heart patient urged to desist from smoking cigarettes, or the cry of society to do something, as in the case of our AIDS patient urged to demand social supports for correctives that would not entail a change in personal behavior). The thrust, the impulse, of policy is most often for governments to correct imbalances among populations; but in the case of AIDS, and in the absence of noticeable consensus or majorities in viewpoints at least, the issue of policies aimed at the elimination of a specific contagion or illness should be seen within a larger context of scientific, political and moral considerations. That panoply of concerns is what the social scientific study of public policy addresses.

There is a specific lesson in all of this for those whose chief concerns are the scientific study and practical implementation of public policy. Policy-making requires that either of two conditions be present to be successful: a broad-based public consensus on issues under consideration, or a narrow-based elite consensus on issues about which the public is either unconcerned or in which the technical knowledge requirements are so sophisticated as to lead to deferential behavior, which is equivalent to disinterest in the political arena.

Where there is a wide dissensus, and equally broad-ranging discussion, policy-making becomes extremely difficult, and is often reduced to a piecemeal or ad hoc set of considerations. Thus, the limits of policy-making can be seen quite clearly in the controversy over what should be done about AIDS. For the moment, and many moments to come, there is very little agreement on the need for information, hardly any consensus on the implications of the medical aspects of the AIDS issue, and virtually no agreement on the moral basis of behavior. When and if such a set of agreements are forthcoming, or perhaps, as is more likely in the matter of AIDS, when the medical aspects of the problem become so overwhelming as to defy common ideological proclivities, then policies will become possible. In the meantime, the demand for policy serves to acerbate rather than alleviate partisan considerations.

In his recent introduction to *The Art and Craft of Policy Analysis*, Aaron Wildavsky (1987) notes that under conditions of what he calls "elite polarization," policy analysis should become chastened, and seek to move from a one-sided emphasis on policy making to a search for the source of preferences and movements. I heartily endorse such a salutory sociology of knowledge approach, and would urge moving beyond it by indicating that under conditions of mass polarization, the potential for even this limited goal of problem finding may be hard to establish. At the moment, wisdom dictates that public policy in the matter of AIDS has been preempted by the need for social and behavioral science. This is perhaps a contemporary way of saying that knowledge is a guide for action, but in the absence of any consensus on the informational basis of an illness or contagion, demands for policy or for action become as dangerous, if not more so, than assertions or admissions of learned ignorance.

Our age tends to insist upon firm linkages between descriptive and prescriptive patterns of behavior. And while this may be an admirable ambition, we must not lose sight that there is a causal disjunction between the two. That is to say, accurate description must precede prescription if we are not to fall prey to the sort of fanaticisms and myth-making devices upon which scientists are fond of accusing others of basing their actions. It is this tentativeness at the empirical level, no less than dissensus at the ethical level, that should serve as a limiting test to those who would leap to policy recommendations without delay. If the wish is father to the act, then too, we should recognize that the fact is mother to the wish. Such homiletics may not lead us to instant solutions for such dread diseases as AIDS, but at least they will hold in check any approach that can only create more imperfect problems by immediate demands for more perfect policies.

The human confrontation with the AIDS epidemic is at rock bottom more a matter of values than of policies. The Latin American writer, Gabriel Garcia Marquez, well summarized this state of affairs when he said in a recent interview: "Plagues are like imponderable dangers that

surprise people. They seem to have a quality of destiny. It's the phenomenon of death on a mass scale. What I find curious is that the great
plagues have always produced great excesses. They make people want
to live more."[2]

Notes

Plenary address presented at the Conference on "Advances in Knowledge Utilization,"
sponsored by the University of Pittsburgh and the Howard R. Davis Society for Knowledge Utilization and Planned Change, held at the Pittsburgh Hilton Inn. October 8-10,
1987.

1. This volume makes a unique effort at tracking the path of one AIDS transmitter, and
   the victim, Gaetan Dugas, between 1979 and 1982. It is reported that at least 40 of
   the first 248 AIDS cases reported in the United States by April, 1982 either had
   sexual relations with Mr. Dugas or one of his sex partners. The accuracy of this
   claim remains to be determined.
2. Simons, M. (1988, February 21). García Márquez on love, plagues and politics, *New
   York Times Book Review*, p. 23.

References

Berk, R.A. (1987). Anticipating the social consequences of AIDS: A position paper. *The
    American Sociologist*, 18 (3), 3,23.
Bethell, T. (1987). Preaching to gay pride. *The Spectator*, 259 (8302), 15-16.
Boffey, P.M. (1987, October 7). U.S. AIDS guide for schools. *The New York Times*.
Coleman, J.S. (1987). The role of social policy research in society and in sociology. *The
    American Sociologist*, 18(2), 127-133.
Edel, A. (1986, December). *Naturalism and the Concept of Moral Change*. The First
    Annual Patrick Romanell Lecture on Philosophical Naturalism. American Philo-
    sophical Association, pp. 823-840.
Feldman, D. (1987). Ethical analysis in public policymaking. *Policy Studies*, 15(3),
    441-460.
Gostin, L. (1987). Traditional public health strategies. In L. Dalton and S. Burris (Eds.),
    Aids and the law, (pp. 47-65). New Haven and London: Yale University Press.
Gross, J. (1987, August 27). Bleak lives: Women carrying AIDS. *The New York Times*.
Gruson, L. (1987, August 18). Condoms: Experts for false sense of security. *The New
    York Times*.
Hiatt, H. H. and Essex, M. (1987, September 4). A test on AIDS for the candidates. *The
    New York Times*.
Kingston, T. (1987). Dying for dollars: The unhealthy profits of AZT. *The Nation*,
    245(12).
Kolata, G. (1987, September 25). No new drug for AIDS envisioned in next year. *The
    New York Times*.
Kolata, G. (1987, October 3). New finding made on AIDS detection. *The New York
    Times*.
Kolata, G. (1987, October 28). "Boy's 1969 death suggests AIDS invaded U.S. several
    times." *The New York Times*.
Mars-Jones, A. (1987), "Homosexual men as soft targets." *The Spectator*, 259 (Whole
    No. 8301), 13-15.

Meyerson, A. (1987). Ten years that shook the world. *Policy Review*. (Whole No. 41), 2-4.

Martin Peretz, M. (1987, August 31). Our cure for AIDS. *The New Republic*, 197(9), 7-9.

Senak, M.S. (1987). The lesbian and gay community. In L. Dalton and S. Burris (Eds.) *AIDS and the Law*, (pp. 290-300). New Haven and London: Yale University Press.

Shilts, R. (1987). *And the band played on: People, politics, and the AIDS epidemic.* New York: St. Martin's Press.

Wattleton, F. (1987, September 11). *Letter to special friends.* Planned Parenthood Federation of America, p. 5.

Wildavsky, A. (1987). *Speaking truth to power: The art and craft of policy analysis.* New Brunswick and Oxford: Transaction Books, 1987.

3

AIDS and the American Health Polity: The History and Prospects of a Crisis of Authority

Daniel M. Fox

IN 1981 WHEN AIDS WAS FIRST RECOGNIZED, THE American health polity was changing more rapidly than it had in a generation. The individuals and institutions that comprise the health polity had a growing sense of discontinuity between past and present. They were poorly prepared to take aggressive, confident action against a disease that was infectious, linked—in the majority of cases—to individual behavior, expensive to study and treat, and required a coordinated array of public and personal health services.

The unconventional phrase "health polity" encompasses more individuals, institutions, and ideas than the words usually used to describe health policies and politics. A polity is broader than a sector or an industry. It includes more people than providers and consumers of health services, more institutions than a health care delivery system, and it is more than an aggregation of policies. According to the *Oxford English Dictionary* (1978), a polity is "a particular form of political organization, a form of government . . . an organized society or community of men." I use the phrase health polity to describe the ways a community, in the broad sense of the OED definition, conceives of and organizes its response to health and illness.

My thesis is that, when the AIDS epidemic began, a profound crisis of authority was transforming the American health polity. The roots of this crisis reached back in time—some for decades, others

From *The Milbank Quarterly*, Vol. 64, Supplement 1 (1986): 7–33.

for just a few years. They included: changes in the causes of sickness and death and, therefore, concerted efforts to adapt facilities and payment mechanisms in order to address them; ambivalence about the recent progress of medical research, reflected in slower growth in research budgets and efforts to make scientists more accountable to their financial sponsors and the media; a growing belief that individuals should take more responsibility for their own health and that public health agencies should encourage them to do so; a sense that the cost of health care was rising uncontrollably and should be contained; and an increase in the power of the private sector and the states within the health polity. Everyone who worked in the health sector knew that a crisis was occurring; so did attentive consumers of print and television news. Uncertainty about priorities, resources, and, most important, leadership pervaded the health polity. The AIDS epidemic was an additional element in an ongoing crisis.

I write first as a historian and then as an advocate. This article has three parts. The first two analyze contemporary history. First, I describe the origins of the crisis of authority; then, I describe how the crisis has influenced the response of the polity to AIDS. In the third part, I identify shortcomings in how the American health polity responds to illness; these flaws have been revealed more clearly by this epidemic.

The Health Polity in 1981

The Declining Importance of Infectious Disease

The most profound change affecting the health polity in the late 1970s and early 1980s was a major shift in patterns of illness—a shift with consequences for every individual and institution within the polity. For more than a century, public health officials, physicians, medical researchers, and hospital managers had accorded priority to preventing, diagnosing, and treating infectious disease. Now, they were increasingly managing conditions that were chronic and degenerative. When priority had been accorded to infectious disease, most of the resources allocated to the health polity had been spent to manage acute episodes of illness. The new prominence of chronic degenerative disease was stimulating a profound reallocation of resources, new assumptions about the responsibilities of individuals and institutions, and considerable concern about rising costs.

In the 1970s, physicians, health officials, and journalists frequently described infectious diseases as problems that had been, or soon would be, solved by scientific progress and an improving standard of living. They usually defined the most pressing health problems as cancer, heart disease, mental illness, and infant mortality among the poor. In contrast, almost everyone knew the history of success in the struggle against infectious diseases during the past century. Smallpox would soon be the first infectious disease to be eradicated; measles would be the next target (Russell 1986). Controlling an infectious disease now seemed to be a routine process of discovering its cause and cure. It was no longer necessary, in the United States at least, to crusade for proper sanitation, housing, and diet in order to reduce the incidence of infectious disease. There was considerable evidence that, from the early nineteenth century until at least the 1930s, changes in diet and living conditions had been more important than medical intervention in bringing most infectious diseases under control (McKeown 1976). As a result of rapid scientific advance since the 1940s, moreover, many diseases that had once been leading causes of death had become brief, if unpleasant, episodes of illness. According to leading medical scientists, this success proved that research in basic science should have higher priority than efforts at care and cure (Thomas 1974). By the early 1980s, infectious disease accounted for "less than 5 percent of the costs estimated for all diseases in the United States" (Rice, Hodgson, and Kopstein 1986).

Sexually transmitted diseases were now accorded lower priority as threats to health. Syphilis and gonorrhea were amenable to drug therapy. In public health practice, treatment was now considered a method of controlling venereal disease. The availability of treatment, whether in public health clinics or the offices of private physicians, created opportunities for education as well as cure (Last et al. 1986). Although public health agencies still conducted vigilant surveillance, physicians reported a smaller number of their cases than they did in the past, in large measure because they perceived venereal disease as less of a threat to the community (Cleeve et al. 1967).

Just a few years later, some people would recall the general attitude toward infectious disease in the late 1970s. In 1986, for instance, a third-year resident, who had entered medical school at the end of the 1970s lamented that "many of today's residents spent their formative years in medical training during an era when the ability of the scientific community to solve health care problems seemed limitless" (Wachter 1986). The chief of the infectious disease bureau of a state health department recalled that, before the AIDS epidemic began, he had been considering a job with the World Health Organization because his work in the United States had become routine (see Acknowledgments).

Increasing Priority to Chronic Degenerative Disease

For more than half a century, a growing number of experts had urged that more attention and resources be allocated to chronic degenerative disease. In the 1920s and 1930s, a handful of medical specialists, clinical scientists, statisticians, and public health officials had insisted that chronic disease—then often called incurable illness—would become more important as average length of life increased. They urged their colleagues to accord higher prestige and priority to long-term and home care, but without much success (Boas 1940).

Chronic disease attracted increasing attention in the 1940s and 1950s. A privately organized Commission on Chronic Illness (1956–1959) issued what were later regarded as landmark studies. Some medical specialists began to shift their emphasis from infectious to chronic disease. Among the first to do so were specialists in tuberculosis, who broadened their emphasis to diseases of the respiratory system after streptomycin was introduced as a cure for tuberculosis in the late 1940s (Fye 1986). The new specialty of rehabilitation medicine gained widespread publicity as a result of its success during and after World War II and vigorous support throughout the 1950s from the Eisenhower administration and Congress (Berkowitz 1981). By the late 1950s the Hill-Burton Act had been amended to encourage the construction of facilities for long-term care and rehabilitation.

Nevertheless, priority within the health polity continued to be accorded to acute rather than long-term care—either for infectious disease or for acute episodes of chronic illness. There were several reasons for this. Physicians' prestige among both their colleagues and the general public continued to be a result of their ability to intervene in crises rather than their effectiveness as long-term managers of difficult cases. Moreover, most of the money to purchase health services was paid by Blue Cross and commercial insurers on behalf of employed workers and their dependents, whose greatest need was for acute care. Organized labor had little incentive to negotiate for fringe benefits for people too old or too sick to work. Since the inception of group prepayment for medical care in the 1930s, Blue Cross and commercial companies had resisted covering care for chronic illness, most likely because they feared that it would lead to adverse selection of risks and undesirably high premiums. A constituency for long-term care of chronic illness was, however, created in the 1950s by the campaign for Social Security Disability Insurance and then in the early 1960s by efforts to create what in 1965 became Medicare (Berkowitz and Fox 1986; David 1985).

In the 1960s, debates about national policy focused attention on unmet needs for health services in general and especially on care for chronic illness. Some advocates of health insurance for the elderly under Social Security, enacted as Medicare in 1965, emphasized the need for long-term as well as acute care. But Medicare insured more comprehensively against the costs of acute episodes of illness than for outpatient, nursing home, or home health care (Benjamin 1986). Medicaid, however, which had been conceived mainly as a program of acute care for recipients of categorical public assistance, quickly became a major payer for nursing home and home health care for the elderly. By 1965 there was little controversy about the inception of the Regional Medical Program of grants by the federal government to diffuse the results of academic research about the major chronic diseases—heart disease, cancer, and stroke (Fox 1986).

Federal leadership in shifting priority to chronic degenerative disease continued during the Nixon administration. In 1970 the president declared war on cancer (Rettig 1977). Two years later, an amendment to the Social Security Act nationalized the cost of treating end-stage renal disease by covering kidney transplants and dialysis under Medicare.

Individual Responsibility for Health

By the 1970s there was considerable evidence that progress in controlling and preventing disease, especially chronic disease, could be achieved by changing personal behavior—"lifestyles" was the euphemism. Accordingly, health professionals and the media admonished individuals to modify their behavior in order to prevent or delay the onset of heart disease, stroke, and some cancers. To the surprise of many cynics, these pleas were effective (Knowles 1977). Millions of people stopped smoking, drank less, exercised more, and ate less salt and fatty food. Preventing chronic illness had become a popular cause and, for some entrepreneurs, a lucrative one. For the first time since the nineteenth century, commercial food products were advertised as improving health, with the sanction of medical scientists. Manufacturers of healthier bread, cereals, and even stimulants, in turn, promoted exercise. Some of the new emphasis on individual behavior was a result of concern to reduce or shift the cost of health services. But much of it was associated with a spreading interest in fitness, and with the belief that individuals should exert more control over their own bodies.

The promotion of individual responsibility was linked to increasing emphasis on the rights of patients, particularly their right to be treated with dignity and after giving informed consent. Individuals were urged to take more responsibility for their own health status in part so that they could demand more timely and efficient attention from the individuals and institutions of the health polity (Levin, Katz, and Holst 1976). Critics of this point of view described it as another instance of "blaming the victim"; of making individuals responsible for the results of inadequate income and education (Crawford 1977). The new emphasis on individual responsibility for health strengthened existing oversimplifications of cause and effect in the spread of disease. Individuals could be held responsible for behavior they engaged in before it was known to be dangerous. Moreover, individuals could be artificially abstracted from the social groups that formed their values and influenced their behavior.

Reflecting the new emphasis on individual behavior, state and local public health agencies joined campaigns to persuade individuals to reduce smoking and substance abuse. Even vaccination became a matter of individual choice. Public health officials, who in the past had insisted that children be required by law to be vaccinated, now educated parents to make prudent choices.

Control of environmental pollution was an important exception to the increasing individualization of public health services. Public officials at the local, state, and federal levels exercised collective responsibility and evoked hostility from industry. Assisted and sometimes provoked by voluntary groups, public health officials called attention to the hazards of lead-based paint, fertilizers, chemical dumps, and atomic wastes. For reasons which are still obscure, the emphasis on collective rights and responsibilities in protecting people from diseases which had environmental origins was not translated into other areas of public health practice. Diseases were increasingly categorized as subject either to individual or to collective action.

The Unfulfilled Promise of Science

Another reason for urging individuals to take more responsibility for their own health was frustration at the inability of medical science to keep some of its implied promises of the 1940s and 1950s. The great advances against infectious disease of the 1940s, especially the development of effective antibiotic drugs, had been widely publicized as the beginning of a permanent revolution in medicine. During the 1950s, the budget of the National Institutes of Health and the expenditures of voluntary associations that sponsored research grew faster than ever before. Congressmen, philanthropists, the press, and the general public expected that the causes of and cures for chronic diseases would soon be found, as a result of research on basic biological processes (Strickland 1972). But medical scientists proved to be better at basic research and at devising new technologies for diagnosis and for keeping very sick patients alive than at finding cures. This technology was disseminated rapidly because third-party payers eagerly reimbursed hospitals for purchasing it, which they did at the request of growing numbers of physicians in each medical specialty. The Regional Medical Program, as it was originally conceived, proved to be redundant. But the vast expenditure for technology had little discernible impact on overall mortality from particular diseases. In the absence of new miracle drugs, the responsibility of individuals to reduce their risks was accorded greater importance.

By the 1970s, moreover, scientists were losing their privileged status within the health polity. Their success in the struggle against disease was no longer taken for granted. They were frequently admonished to propose ways to solve practical problems and to be more accessible and forthcoming to representatives of the press and television. Moreover, scientists were no longer assumed to be virtuous as well as effective. What was called the bioethics movement had begun a strenuous critique of medical scientists, especially clinical investigators, some years earlier. To many participants in this movement, protecting patients and research subjects from harm was the highest ethical goal. For some, autonomy took precedence over beneficence as goals (Pellegrino 1985). This concern was embodied in federal regulations for the protection of human subjects in research. Similarly, the venerable antivivisectionist controversy was reactivated by a new animal-rights movement. In part as a response to external criticism of science, but also because of general economic problems, research priorities and budgets were scrutinized more carefully than ever before by federal officials and congressmen.

For a generation, the resources allocated to the health polity grew because everyone assumed that the nation's health would improve if more money was spent for research, hospitals, physicians' services, and educating health professionals. Public subsidies helped to create an increasing supply of hospitals, professionals, and research facilities. Blue Cross/Blue Shield and commercial insurers, using the premiums paid by employers and employees, stimulated demand for care. After 1965, when Medicare and Medicaid were established, the federal government became the largest third-party payer. In the early and mid-1970s, there was broad agreement that access to basic medical care for the poor and the elderly was a diminishing problem (Anderson and Aday 1977), that the next problems to solve were improving the quality of care and expanding the coverage of insurance and public entitlement programs. But the consensus that had unified the health polity since World War II was now eroding.

From Comprehensive Services to Cost Control

The broad coalition that had dominated the health polity broke apart in the 1970s. The labor movement, weakened by declining membership, ceased to lobby forcefully on behalf of broad social policy. Executives of large corporations, who, for thirty years, had provided their employees with generous health insurance benefits, found it increasingly difficult in the economic conditions of the 1970s to pay the cost of health care by raising the price of goods and services. The comprehensive first-dollar insurance coverage available to workers in the largest industries began to be described as a luxury that must be sacrificed in order to avoid increasing unemployment. Community rating, which had been endorsed by labor and business leaders in the 1940s as a way to increase equitable access to comprehensive health care, had been sacrificed to experience rating, which shifted costs to the groups that could least afford to pay them. Moreover, generous health insurance benefits seemed to encourage unnecessary surgery and excessive hospital stays.

Evidence that numerous hospitals and physicians inflated their charges because third parties would pay them provided business, labor, and government leaders with additional justification for cost containment. As tax revenues declined in the recessions of the 1970s, the federal government and the states changed the emphasis of health policy from providing access to more comprehensive services to cost control.

Advocates of cost control also argued that generous subsidies and reimbursement policies had created an oversupply of physicians and hospitals. Many of them wanted to reallocate the resources of the health sector to take account of the increasing incidence and prevalence of chronic illness. They contrasted excess capacity to provide acute care with the lack of facilities for long-term care.

The Crisis of Authority

The new emphasis on cost control and reallocating resources was evidence of a profound change in the distribution of authority within the health polity. Since World War II, authority in health affairs, as in social policy generally, had been increasingly centralized in the federal government, though considerable power remained with state government and with employers. Centralized authority was frequently displayed in programs which required local initiative to meet federal standards; for example, the hospital construction program created by the Hill-Burton Act of 1945 and the community mental health and neighborhood health centers of the 1960s. In 1978 a political scientist, looking back at health policy since the mid-1960s, wrote that "in no other area of social policy has the federal government been so flexible, responsive and innovative" (Brown 1978).

But the federal role in social policy generally, and especially in health, narrowed after 1978. National health insurance, which many people believed to be imminent a few years earlier, was politically moribund by the late 1970s (Fox 1978). In Congress and federal agencies, there was active discussion about containing health care costs through tax policy and new reimbursement strategies that encouraged competition and offered incentives to physicians to use fewer resources (Meyer 1983). Prepaid group practices, which for half a century had been the favorite strategy of liberals for increasing access to medical care, were renamed health maintenance organizations (HMOs) by the federal government and used as a mechanism to control costs (Brown

1983). Diagnosis-related groups (DRGs), a mechanism to control hospital costs by setting prices based on the intensity of resource utilization, were devised by researchers at Yale in the mid-1970s and were initially implemented in New Jersey (Thompson 1978).

At the same time, many state health departments or rate-setting commissions were becoming, for the first time, active managers of the health industry. The goal of state and regional health planning changed from promoting rational growth to encouraging shrinkage or consolidation. Regulation, a word that had once been associated mainly with the responsibility of the states to implement health codes and license professionals, was now used more often to refer to setting reimbursement rates and issuing certificates of need for construction and new equipment.

Other states, however, chose to withdraw from active regulation of health affairs. Their leaders adopted the rhetoric of deregulation and competition that was heard with increasing frequency in discussions of national economic and social policy.

Business leaders began to claim new authority in the health polity. They perceived the cost of health benefits as an impediment to competition with foreign firms and a stimulus to dangerously high rates of inflation. In the United States, unlike other industrial nations, health insurance was linked to employment and was, therefore, a cost of production. A growing number of employers were choosing to self-insure in order to reduce costs. Many of them took advantage of a 1978 amendment to the Internal Revenue Code that permitted individual employees to select from a menu of benefits that often included less generous health insurance (Schmid et al. 1985). Responding to pressure from employers, Blue Cross and commercial insurance companies began to write policies with larger deductibles and copayments, to scrutinize claims more rigorously, to require second opinions and preadmission screening before hospital admissions, and to reduce beneficiaries' freedom to choose among physicians.

The health polity was experiencing a crisis of authority. Assumptions about the balance of power in the health polity that had been accepted, though often grudgingly, since the New Deal were now challenged. In health affairs, as in social policy generally, increasing centralization was no longer regarded as inevitable. Many congressmen and federal officials were eager to devolve authority over health affairs from the federal government to the states and the private sector. Business leaders were taking more initiative in health affairs. Devolution would soon be accelerated by the Reagan administration. The health polity in 1981, when AIDS was first recognized, was more fragmented than it had been at any time since the 1930s.

The Health Polity Responds to AIDS

The Modern Response to Epidemic Disease

The health polity had, however, devised a set of responses to epidemics during the twentieth century. These responses had been increasingly effective in controlling infectious disease (Dowling 1977). At the beginning of the AIDS epidemic there seemed no reason to doubt that the problems posed by this new infection could be solved promptly and efficiently by applying the well-tested methods of surveillance, research, prevention, and treatment. These methods had recently been used, with comforting success, to control Legionnaires' disease and toxic shock syndrome. In 1981, despite the crisis of authority in the health polity, AIDS did not seem to be an unusual challenge.

Widely shared assumptions about recent history generated confidence in these responses. For a generation, scientists had rapidly identified new infectious agents and devised tests for their presence, vaccines against them, and drugs to treat their victims. Most physicians and hospitals reported most cases of life-threatening disease, and public health officials held these reports in strict confidence. Although mass screening programs were sometimes controversial and were only partially effective in identifying new cases, there were widely accepted techniques for managing them. Since the early 1970s, moreover, it seemed possible to prevent disease through education and advertising, which had persuaded many people to modify their diets and habits of exercise and to stop smoking in order to reduce their risk of hypertension, heart disease, and lung cancer. Finally, despite the problems of high costs and fragmented authority, more Americans than ever before had access to medical care as a result of insurance or public subsidy.

Five years later, many public health officials remain confident that AIDS will eventually be controlled by the conventional techniques for responding to epidemic disease. In support of this position they note that there have been no documented breaches of confidentiality in reporting or screening; scientists have identified the infectious agent, devised a test for antibodies to it, and report progress in the search for a vaccine; many gay men have modified their sexual practices in response to education; no one is known to have been denied treatment for AIDS because of inability to pay for it; and, in several major cities, innovative programs of care are being offered to AIDS patients.

Other observers dispute this optimism, claiming that the conventional methods are inadequate to address AIDS (Altman 1986a). They point to events or policies that appear to be a result of hostility or insensitivity to gay men and intravenous drug users. Many gay men, for instance, fear that their privacy is threatened by reporting and screening policies that offer confidentiality, which could be breached, instead of guaranteeing anonymity. This administration, unlike earlier ones, has been reluctant to request funds from Congress for research and services during an epidemic; President Reagan did not even mention AIDS in public until January 1986. Despite education in "safe" sex, much of it financed by public funds, the percentage of gay men who have positive antibodies to HTLV-III virus continues to increase. Moreover, public agencies have been reluctant to reach out to drug users in illegal "shooting galleries" or to provide them with disposable needles. Many third parties are reluctant to pay the additional costs of treating patients with AIDS. Although programs to create separate hospital units and community facilities for AIDS patients have been presented by their sponsors as positive steps, some critics view them as the beginning of segregation, the modern equivalent of leper colonies.

Without denying the persistence of discrimination, I believe that the conventional responses to epidemics are now inadequate mainly because of the crisis of authority in the health polity. A polity that is focused on chronic degenerative disease, that embraces cost control as the chief goal of health policy, and in which central authority is diminishing cannot address this epidemic as it has others of the recent past. In the following paragraphs I describe how the crisis of authority has influenced the actions of the health polity in surveillance, research, paying the cost of treatment, and organizing services for AIDS patients.

Surveillance

Disagreements about policy for surveillance have highlighted problems of cost and fragmented authority. The definition of a reportable case of AIDS used by the Centers for Disease Control (CDC) excludes cases of AIDS-related complex (ARC). Since all but three states have adopted the CDC definition, the incidence and prevalence of ARC can only be conjectured. The absence of information about ARC has impeded accurate study of the onset and duration, as well as the cost, of the AIDS continuum. Reporting policy, on the surface a straightforward problem in public health practice, in fact understates the severity and the cost of the epidemic.

Moreover, legal standards for the confidentiality of case reports vary among the states. Four of them—Colorado, Wisconsin, Montana, and Minnesota—mandate that names of individuals who have antibodies to the AIDS virus be reported to state health departments (Intergovernmental Health Policy Project 1986). Moreover, because AIDS—as of the summer of 1986—is classified as a communicable disease everywhere except in Idaho and Puerto Rico, case reports are not protected as strongly by statutes as they are for sexually transmitted diseases. They can, for example, be subpoenaed, although there is no evidence that they have been.

The lack of uniformity among the states in standards of confidentiality is an old problem that is made worse by the absence of national leadership in health affairs. On the one hand, surveillance policy has always been the responsibility of state governments, except for Indians, immigrants, and the military. On the other, standards of confidentiality affect civil liberties, an area of policy over which all three branches of the federal government had, until recently, been exerting increasing authority for a generation.

The absence of encouragement to the states by federal officials to adopt common standards to protect confidentiality increases the fear of many gay men that they will be stigmatized and persecuted. This fear, already intense, grew after the publication of a survey commissioned by the *Los Angeles Times* according to which "most Americans favor some sort of legal discrimination against homosexuals as a result of AIDS" (Shipp 1986). Fear became rage when the columnist William F. Buckley wrote in the *New York Times* that "everyone detected with AIDS should be tattooed in the upper forearm, to protect common needle users, and in the buttocks, to prevent the victimization of other homosexuals" (Buckley 1986). The fear is so intense that it embraces the entire range of public policy: the irrational—Lyndon Larouche's proposal to screen every American for antibodies to the

HTLV-III virus; the dubiously effective—bills in several states to put AIDS patients in quarantine; the debatable—proposals to identify children or employees with AIDS to school officials; and the extension of traditional techniques of venereal disease control—tracing the sexual contacts of persons with AIDS.

Very little has been written or said to date about the effect of AIDS on the stigmatization of users of intravenous drugs. Unlike homosexuals, they do not organize to assert their rights, and they do not receive much public sympathy when they claim to do no harm by their private behavior. Drug users are generally stereotyped as pariahs who alternate between preying on innocent victims and receiving treatment and support at public expense. Moreover, many of them are also stigmatized because they are black. Addicts who die of AIDS may use fewer public funds than those who survive to receive treatment for their drug problems. Although several landmark civil liberties cases in the past have involved addicts, their rights—unlike those of gay men—have not yet been a subject of litigation during the AIDS epidemic.

Research

The brief history of research on AIDS has been influenced by the disinclination of the Reagan administration to assert central authority in the health polity (Arno and Lee 1985). In 1985 the Office of Technology Assessment, a congressional agency, reported that "increases in funding specifically for AIDS have come at the initiative of Congress, not the Administration." Moreover, "PHS agencies have had difficulties in planning their AIDS related activities because of uncertainties over budget and personnel allocations" (U.S. Congress. Office of Technology Assessment 1985). In January 1986, President Reagan called AIDS "one of the highest public health priorities," but at the same time proposed to reduce spending for AIDS research by considerably more than the amount mandated by the Gramm-Rudman-Hollings Act (Page 1986; *Blue Sheet* 1986; Norman 1986).

As a result, at least in part, of the administration's reluctance to fund research on AIDS, voluntary contributions and state appropriations for laboratory and clinical investigation have been more important than in other recent epidemics. Foundations to sponsor medical research established in New York City and, after Rock Hudson's death from AIDS, in Los Angeles have recently merged to form the American Foundation for AIDS Research. In several cities, community-based organizations began to raise funds for research within and outside gay communities using techniques similar to those invented many years earlier by the National Tuberculosis Association and the National Foundation for Infantile Paralysis. The states of California and New York appropriated funds for research. These appropriations may be the first significant state expenditures for research related to a particular disease—except, perhaps, mental illness—in a generation.

Similarly, state and local health departments, frequently in collaboration with community-based organizations, took the initiative in programs to prevent AIDS through public education. If the epidemic had occurred in the 1960s or even the early 1970s, the federal government might have established a program of grants for community action against AIDS. Consistent with the social policy of those years, such a program would have included guidelines for citizen participation. In the 1980s, in the absence of federal initiative, the leaders of community-based organizations in each major city combined goals and strategies from the gay rights, handicapped rights, and anti-poverty movements of the recent past. Because they do not receive federal funds, some community groups have been free to move beyond educational programs and mobilize political action on behalf of patients with AIDS (Needle et al. 1985). However, without a national program, community-based organizations are unlikely to emerge or to be influential in cities with small, politically weak gay populations.

Cost of Treatment

Because the epidemic began when government and private payers were restraining growth in the health sector, responsibility for the costs of treating patients with AIDS became a controversial issue. Many groups within the health polity had incentives to publicize and even to exaggerate high estimates of the costs of treating patients with AIDS. Prominent hospital managers were uncomfortable with the new price-based prospective reimbursement and were under pressure to offer discounts to health maintenance and preferred provider organizations.

They encouraged speculation by journalists that the cost of treating patients with AIDS was 40 to 100 percent higher per day than the average for patients in their institutions. Many insurance executives embraced the highest estimates, perhaps because they wanted the states or the federal government to assume the burden of payment. A few insurance companies tried to obtain permission from state regulatory agencies to deny initial coverage to persons at risk of AIDS (Shilts 1985). Officials of the federal Health Care Financing Administration have avoided discussing the cost of treating AIDS and have ignored suggestions that the two-year waiting period for Medicare eligibility be waived for persons with AIDS who qualify for Social Security Disability Insurance. When persons with AIDS qualify for the less generous disability provisions of the Supplemental Security Income program, they are eligible to receive Medicaid; the states have become the payers of last resort.

The actual costs of treating patients with AIDS are difficult to estimate because responses to the initial research on the subject are heavily political. The authors of a study conducted by the Centers for Disease Control in 1985 estimated that the cost of hospital care between diagnosis and death averaged $147,000 (Hardy et al. 1986). They derived this figure by using charges as a proxy for cost and multiplying them by an average length of stay that was unusually long because it was disproportionately weighted with data from New York City municipal hospitals, which treated large numbers of intravenous drug users who had multiple secondary infections and few home or community alternatives to hospitalization. Then, they compared hospital expenditures for AIDS with those for lung cancer and chronic obstructive pulmonary disease and found that they were "similar," despite the obvious differences in the course, duration, and incidence of these diseases. Whatever the authors intended, the exaggerated estimates alarmed insurers—now prohibited by insurance regulators in several states from denying coverage to victims of AIDS—public officials, hospital executives, and the media. Another study, conducted at San Francisco General Hospital in 1985, has alarmed some hospital executives because its estimate of the cost of hospitalization, between diagnosis and death, $27,857, was so low that it undercut their demand for higher reimbursement for AIDS patients (Scitovsky, Cline, and Lee 1985).

In the spring of 1986, two New York studies confirmed that most of the speculative earlier estimates were probably exaggerated. The state health department found that the cost of ancillary services for patients with AIDS in 1984 was 20 percent higher than for other patients whose diagnoses were classified in the same diagnosis-related group. A study conducted for the Greater New York Hospital Association by the consulting firm of Peat Marwick and Mitchell concluded, to the surprise of its sponsors, that routine costs for AIDS patients were only about 20 percent per day above the average for all patients.

Moreover, hospital managers complained less frequently about the cost of treating patients with AIDS as the institutions' occupancy fell, in large measure as a result of cost-control policies. For a variety of reasons—including reimbursement penalties for low occupancy and the desire to avoid layoffs—hospital leaders preferred expensively filled beds to empty ones.

Organizing Services

In no previous epidemic have variations in lengths of hospital stay for patients in different cities been discussed so widely. Most of the variation seems to be a result of the availability of nonhospital services—particularly ambulatory medical care, skilled nursing facility beds, housing, hospice, and home health care. A few city and state health departments have tried to coordinate services. In San Francisco, the city-county health department, allied with voluntary associations in the gay community, organized a network of inpatient, outpatient and supportive services (Arno and Hughes 1985; Arno 1986). In order to achieve similar goals in a different political environment—one that is larger, has more competition among institutions, and has no tradition of coordination by consensus—the New York State health department is establishing AIDS treatment centers. In this program, state officials will select hospitals that agree to meet specified criteria for managing a continuum of services (State of New York, Department of Health 1986). Each hospital will receive a higher reimbursement rate based on its proposal. Moreover, every hospital in the state will receive a 20 percent higher rate of reimbursement for each patient with AIDS treated since 1984.

The New York State health department requires that its AIDS Centers, like San Francisco General Hospital, dedicate beds for AIDS patients. The rationale for the requirement, according to a principal author of the New York program, is that patients will be treated better if they are clustered. He defined treated better to mean that, as in San Francisco, AIDS patients would be served by nursing and social service staff who had volunteered for their roles, and that there would be greater attention for continuity of care. Moreover, the dedicated beds in San Francisco seemed to be related to shorter lengths of stay and lower utilization of intensive care.

A substantial number of hospital administrators and physicians in New York were enraged by the requirement to dedicate beds. They insisted that segregated patients and their hospitals would be stigmatized. Moreover, dedicated beds created new burdens for overworked nurses. Perhaps most important, the health department was intruding on the domain of physicians and hospital staff. In the final regulations, a compromise was arranged which, health department officials hope, will lead most of the designated centers to dedicate beds. In fact, many teaching hospitals in New York already cluster their AIDS patients for convenience in managing them. This dispute, like so many others during the epidemic, was less about AIDS than about the changing distribution of authority in the health polity.

In October 1986, the Robert Wood Johnson Foundation made the first awards in a $17.2 million program to encourage case management for AIDS patients. Funds were granted to applicants from 10 of the 21 standard metropolitan statistical areas with the most cases of AIDS. Announcing the program, in January 1986, a foundation official described the federal government as if it were another philanthropic organization: "If an anticipated federal grants initiative for similar purposes materializes, the Foundation and the Department of Health and Human Services are planning to coordinate the two programs as closely as possible" (Altman 1986b). In 1985 Congress had appropriated $16 million for AIDS Health Services Projects in the four cities with the greatest number of cases. However, the administration sequestered these funds. For the first time since the 1950s, a foundation program may well serve as a surrogate for, rather than an example to, the federal government.

The absence of national policy to organize and finance treatment for patients with AIDS may be appreciated by state and local officials who prefer to avoid responsibility for treating these patients. After a generation in which barriers to access to health services were gradually lowered as a result of federal programs, geographic inequities may be increasing more rapidly for persons with AIDS than for victims of other diseases. AIDS patients in states or cities with relatively unresponsive health departments and no Robert Wood Johnson Foundation money may receive considerably less or lower quality care than patients in other jurisdictions. The programs funded by the Robert Wood Johnson Foundation may be emulated elsewhere because, according to evidence from San Francisco, coordination reduces the length of hospital stays and the utilization of intensive care. But earlier discharge from hospitals can also be combined with inadequate outpatient, nursing home, and home care. In many places, that is, superficial or cynical emulation of the policies of San Francisco or New York could produce results similar to what has happened when mental patients were deinstitutionalized.

There are many historical precedents for superficial acceptance or cynical distortion of strategies to improve health and social welfare in the United States. Since the 1930s, officials of many state and local agencies have accepted the policies urged by experts with national visibility only when adopting them was a precondition for receiving federal funds or under court order. The possibility that these officials will resist pleas and even incentives to coordinate services for AIDS patients is enhanced by the unwillingness of the Reagan administration to insist on particular actions by state governments and by the recent retreat of the federal courts from mandating states to improve the care of particular classes of patients.

The public officials and staff members of voluntary associations who coordinate treatment for patients with AIDS have benefited from the gradual reorganization of services to emphasize chronic illness. Like tuberculosis, the most lethal disease of the nineteenth century, AIDS is an infectious disease that requires services outside the hospital. Reimbursement incentives offered by Medicare and private insurance since 1981 have stimulated a substantial increase in the number of home health care agencies and skilled nursing facilities. Techniques for case management have been elaborated and tested in the past few years under waivers from the Health Care Financing Administration and by Blue Cross plans and commercial insurance companies. Moreover, recent interest in substituting palliative for heroic measures in treating patients whose illnesses are terminal has increased reimbursement for and thus the availability of hospice services.

AIDS is, to date, the only disease for which institutions are receiving grants and special reimbursement to coordinate inpatient and out-of-hospital services. The only comparable disease-specific case management is for end-stage renal disease—mainly for the procurement and distribution of organs. It is too soon to know if the interest groups organized around other diseases and conditions—people with multiple handicaps, for example—will demand similar services.

What is certain, however, is that the response to the AIDS epidemic by the American health polity has been shaped by fundamental changes that were occurring simultaneously. The most important of these changes, which I described in the first part of this paper, were according priority to chronic degenerative disease, emphasizing the responsibility of individuals for their own health, and controlling expenditures for health services. A crisis of authority was transforming the health polity. The future of the AIDS epidemic will be shaped, not only by the number and distribution of cases and by the results of research, but also—and perhaps most importantly—by how that crisis is resolved. If the polity responds to AIDS as it has done since 1981, it is likely that the epidemic will be another incident in the gradual decline of collective responsibility for the human condition in the United States. Because I hope for a different result, I describe next how the American health polity might reconsider its response to AIDS, or to any other life-threatening disease.

AIDS and the Future of the Health Polity

A Polemical Interpretation of Recent History

During the late 1970s and 1980s, the health polity broke sharply with long-term trends in American social policy. For most of the century, there was a gradual shift in assigning responsibility to care for the sick from individuals and families toward collective responsibility and entitlement. Individualism was regarded as a weak basis for social policy in an industrial society. For most of the century, authority in the health polity was gradually centralized in national institutions—notably the federal government, large insurance companies, international labor unions, and professional associations. Fragmentation was considered to be inconsistent with a just and efficient society. The centralization of authority in national institutions was never complete in any area of social policy. State and local institutions, both public and private, continued to exert enormous power. A health insurance system that was based almost entirely on employment and retirement from it created considerable insecurity and inequity. But the trend was clear; until the late 1970s those who opposed centralization, particularly the ideological right, considered themselves a minority group.

The AIDS epidemic coincided with a concerted effort within the polity to reverse the trends toward centralization in social policy. Authority within the polity was devolving from the federal government to the states and to private corporations.

The AIDS epidemic provides evidence that this reversal of social policy threatens the public interest in security against illness. I summarize that evidence and its implications in my concluding paragraphs.

The Persistence of the Unexpected

AIDS should provide convincing evidence that, despite the achievements of biomedical scientists, epidemics of diseases of mysterious origin and long latency will continue to occur, even in industrialized countries. Some of these diseases will be infectious; most will probably be linked in some way to behavior or location or work. Science will continue to comprehend nature incompletely. The individuals and institutions who comprise the health polity should, therefore, accept the need to study and treat a greater variety of diseases than anyone can now imagine. Pressure to contain costs should be offset by a sense that there are limits to how much the resources allocated to health care can be reduced in a society concerned about its survival.

The epidemic should also lead to better understanding of some practical implications of the platitude that all diseases are social as well as biological events. In the years before the AIDS epidemic, the health polity accorded priority to biological factors in disease because its members were optimistic about the progress of medical science. The social basis of disease was not so much denied, as some critics charged, as it was ignored because of enthusiasm in the health polity about the results of laboratory research. However precisely social factors in disease were identified, they did not contribute as effectively to diagnosis or therapy as the study of diseased tissue. The AIDS epidemic makes it difficult, however, to deny that many pathogens only cause disease when people facilitate their transmission. As a result of AIDS there may be increased willingness to speak openly about sexual behavior and to provide more systematic education about it. There is already evidence that, in some schools, teachers are being more explicit about the risks of sexual behavior in response to students' fears about AIDS (Rimer 1986). The media have been more explicit and accurate in reporting about AIDS than about any disease in the past that was linked to sexual behavior.

The Limits of Individual Responsibility

The epidemic also offers evidence that contradicts the assumption that it is desirable or even possible to substitute individual for collective responsibility for social welfare. For more than a decade it has been fashionable among some politicians and policy intellectuals of both the left and the right to assert that, if individuals are given proper incentives, they can provide adequately for their own health and welfare. A plausible extension of this argument is that removing people who have positive antibodies to the AIDS virus from insurance pools would, in the short run, save money for other people in those pools. Proponents of individualizing risk do not seem to care that removal would also prevent those with positive antibodies who do not get AIDS from subsidizing health care for other people.

Individualizing risk reinforces a short-sighted view of what is rational social policy. Consider a society in which everyone who is considered a poor risk is denied insurance or forced to enroll in a group composed entirely of people with expensive afflictions. In such a society, the premiums for the oldest and sickest people would be prohibitively high, forcing them to seek public assistance or charity. Since most people are likely to become very old, very sick, or both, the consequence of smaller, more homogeneous risk pools would be widespread pauperization. The political response to such a perverse policy might be broader support for a federally financed program of insurance against the catastrophic costs of illness.

AIDS also challenges the wisdom of offering incentives to apparently healthy young people to choose the least comprehensive health insurance.

The beginning of the epidemic coincided with the decision of many employers to offer their employees so-called flexible benefit plans. Under these plans, employees who considered themselves to be in excellent health could substitute other benefits or in some instances cash for the most expensive health insurance. There are no data about how many AIDS patients, most of them in their thirties and with no previous history of serious illness, chose such substitutions.

The epidemic emphasizes the limitations of social policy that links entitlement to health insurance to employment rather than to membership in society, and that provides benefits as a result of bargaining rather than entitlement. Since World War II, most Americans of working age have obtained health insurance from their employers or their unions. Federal income tax laws encouraged the link between insurance and employment and prohibited firms from discriminating among workers at different levels of pay in awarding benefits. The tax laws cannot, however, remedy disparities in the coverage offered by different firms. Moreover, state governments have been reluctant to mandate coverage and have done so mainly in response to pressure from members of new provider groups who wanted to be reimbursed. In addition, many employers now escape mandates by self-insuring. As a result, the extent and duration of coverage varies enormously among workers with different employers. A disease which, at the present time, mainly affects people of working age and drug abusers, many of whom do not work at all, reveals the limits of an insurance system that does not offer a set of uniform and adequate minimum benefits.

The epidemic has exposed the fragility of the networks of personal support that are frequently promoted as substitutes for services that are provided, at higher social cost, by insurance, philanthropy, or public policy. People who are at risk of contracting AIDS may be only slightly more isolated than everybody else. Americans increasingly live in small households, or alone; in the future, families and friends may be less frequently available during crises than ever before. Most of us may need sympathetic case management by professionals during our catastrophic illnesses.

The Reassertion of Central Authority

Finally, the AIDS epidemic may demonstrate that the American health polity best serves the public interest when institutions within it

struggle to assert central authority, when they do not accept fragmentation as the goal as well as the norm of health affairs. The
unwillingness of the federal government to exert strong leadership in
response to AIDS has been criticized by congressmen, journalists, and
victims since the beginning of the epidemic. In the absence of federal
assertiveness, however, the health departments of several cities and
states have coordinated the response of the health polity to the epidemic.
These health departments have tried, in different ways, to counter
fragmentation by linking their traditional responsibility for surveillance
with their more recent mandate to manage the health system. To the
extent that similar linkage of the responsibilities of public health
officers occurs elsewhere, it may be a partial substitute for the abdication
of federal leadership and, perhaps, a model for future national
administrations.

Such lessons could be drawn from the history to early 1986 of the
response to AIDS of the American health polity. If they are not, we
may recall the 1980s as a time when many Americans became increasingly
complacent about the consequences of dread disease and unwilling to
insist that the individuals and institutions of the health polity struggle
against them.

References

Altman, D. 1986a. *AIDS in the Mind of America.* Garden City, N.Y.:
    Anchor Press/Doubleday.
Altman, D. 1986b. Press release announcing the AIDS Health Services
    Program. Robert Wood Johnson Foundation. (Unpublished.)
Anderson, R., and L.A. Aday. 1977. *Health Care in the United States:
    Equitable for Whom?* Beverly Hills: Sage.
Arno, P.S. 1986. The Non-profit Sector's Response to the AIDS
    Epidemic: Community-based Services in San Francisco.
    (Unpublished.)
Arno, P.S., and R.G. Hughes. 1985. Local Policy Response to the
    AIDS Epidemic. (Unpublished.)
Arno, P.S., and P.R. Lee. 1985. The Federal Response to the AIDS
    Epidemic. (Unpublished.)
Benjamin, A.E. 1986. Reimbursement for Home Health Care: Methods

and Issues. New York State Center for Assessing Health Services.
(Unpublished.)

Berkowitz, E. 1981. The Federal Government and the Emergence of
Rehabilitation Medicine. *Historian* 43: 24–33.

Berkowitz, E., and D.M. Fox. 1986. *The Struggle for Compromise: Social
Security Disability Insurance, 1935–1986.* Washington: Institute
of Medicine, Committee on Pain, Disability and Chronic Illness
Behavior. (In press.)

Blue Sheet. 1986. AIDS Research Funding. February 26.

Boas, E.B. 1940. *The Unseen Plague: Chronic Disease.* New York:
J.J. Augustin.

Brown, L.D. 1978. The Formulation of Federal Health Care Policy.
Bulletin of the New York Academy of Medicine 54(1): 45–58.

Brown, L.D. 1983. *Politics and Health Care: HMOs as Federal Policy.*
Washington: Brookings Institution.

Buckley, W.F., Jr. 1986. Crucial Steps in Combating the AIDS
Epidemic: Identify All the Carriers. *New York Times,* March 18.

Cleeve, R.L., W.J. Dougherty, N.F. Fiumara, C. Jenike, J.W. Lentz,
and W.J. Rose. 1967. Physicians' Attitudes toward Venereal
Disease Reporting. *Journal of the American Medical Association* 202
(10): 941–46.

Commission on Chronic Illness. 1956–1959. *Chronic Illness in the
United States.* 4 vols. Cambridge: Harvard University Press.

Crawford, R. 1977. You Are Dangerous to Your Health: The Ideology
and Politics of Victim Blaming. *International Journal of Health
Services* 7(4): 663–80.

David, S.I. 1985. *With Dignity: The Search for Medicare and Medicaid.*
Westport, Conn.: Greenwood Press.

Dowling, H.F. 1977. *Fighting Infection: Conquests of the Twentieth Century.*
Cambridge: Harvard University Press.

Fox, D.M. 1978. Chances for Comprehensive NHI Are Slim in the
U.S. *Hospitals* 52 (Nov. 16): 77–80.

———. 1986. *Health Policies, Health Politics: The British and American
Experience, 1911–1965.* Princeton: Princeton University Press.

Fye, W.B. 1986. The Literature of Internal Medicine. Unpublished
Paper, Francis C. Wood Institute, College of Physicians of
Philadelphia.

Hardy, A.M., K. Rauch, D. Echenberg, W.M. Morgan, J.W. Curran.
1986. The Economic Impact of Acquired Immuno Deficiency
Syndrome in the United States. *Journal of the American Medical
Association* 255 (2): 209–11.

Intergovernmental Health Policy Project. 1986. *A Review of State and*

Local Government Initiatives Affecting AIDS. 2d ed. Washington: George Washington University, Intergovernmental Health Policy Project.

Knowles, J.H., ed. 1977. *Doing Better and Feeling Worse: Health in the United States.* New York: Norton.

Last, J.M., J. Chin, J. E. Fielding, A. L. Frank, J. Laslof, and R. B. Wallace, eds. 1986. *Maxcy-Rosenau Public Health and Preventive Medicine.* 12th ed. Norwalk, Conn.: Appleton-Century-Crofts.

Levin, L.S., A.H. Katz, and E. Holst. 1976. *Self-care: Lay Initiatives in Health.* New York: Prodist.

McKeown, T. 1976. *The Modern Rise of Population.* New York: Academic Press.

Meyer, J. A., ed. 1983. *Market Reforms in Health Care: Current Issues, New Directions, Strategic Decisions.* Washington: American Enterprise Institute.

Needle, R., F. Kroeger, M. Gorman, D. Sencer, B. Cassens, D. Toisma, W. Squires, and K. Mathews. 1985. *The Evolving Role of Health Education in the AIDS Epidemic: The Experience of Nine High Incidence Cities.* (Unpublished.)

Norman C. 1986. Congress Likely to Halt Shrinkage in AIDS Funds. *Science* 231:1364–65.

The Oxford English Dictionary. 1978. Oxford: Clarendon Press.

Page, S. 1986. Sharp Cuts in AIDS Funds Sought. *Newsday,* February 6.

Pellegrino, E.D. 1985. The Reconciliation of Technology and Humanism: A Flexnerian Task 75 Years Later. (Unpublished.)

Rettig, R.A. 1977. *Cancer Crusade: The Story of the National Cancer Act of 1971.* Princeton: Princeton University Press.

Rice, D.P., T.A. Hodgson, and A.W. Kopstein. 1986. The Economic Cost of Illness: A Replication and Update. *Health Care Financing Review.* (In press.)

Rimer, S. 1986. High School Course Is Shattering Myths about AIDS. *New York Times,* March 5.

Russell, L.B. 1986. *Is Prevention Better Than Cure?* Washington: Brookings Institution.

Scitovsky, A.A., M. Cline, and P.R. Lee. 1985. Medical Care Costs of AIDS Patients Treated in San Francisco. (Unpublished.)

Schmid, S., M. Holner, J. Mays, E. Moyer, and G. Trapnell. 1985. *A Study of Cafeteria Plans and Flexible Spending Accounts.* Washington: Department of Health and Human Services, Office of the Assistant Secretary for Planning and Evaluation.

Shilts, R. 1985. Insurance Denied? Industry May Screen for AIDS Virus. *Village Voice,* September 3.

Shipp, E.R. 1986. Physical Suffering Is Not the Only Pain That AIDS Can Inflict. *New York Times,* February 17.

State of New York, Department of Health. 1986. Request for Applications for Designation of AIDS Centers (March 24). Albany.

Strickland, S.P. 1972. *Politics, Science and Dread Disease: A Short History of United States Medical Research Policy.* Cambridge: Harvard University Press.

Thomas, L. 1974. *The Lives of a Cell: Notes of a Biology Watcher.* New York: Viking.

Thompson, J.D. 1978. Epidemiology and Health Services Administration: Future Relationships in Practice and Education. *Milbank Memorial Fund Quarterly/Health and Society* 56(3): 253–73.

U.S. Congress. Office of Technology Assessment. 1985. *Review of the Public Health Service Response to AIDS.* Washington.

Wachter, R.M. 1986. The Impact of the Acquired Immuno Deficiency Syndrome in Medical Residency Training. *New England Journal of Medicine* 314(3): 177–80.

Acknowledgments: This paper is based on published and unpublished sources, interviews, conversation, and observation. I have indicated my obligation to written sources in citations in the text. I have not, however, ascribed particular comments to particular people. Some of my interviews were formal, either on or off the record. On many occasions, however, I benefited from conversations that were not, at the time, regarded by the people I was talking to or by myself as data for an essay in contemporary history and advocacy of social policy. Sometimes the conversations were privileged as a result of my participation in research bearing on the making of policy. I list here, alphabetically, the names of some of the people who have, in conversations, helped to shape my views about the health polity's response to the AIDS epidemic: Dennis Altman, Drew Altman, Stephen Anderman, Peter Arno, David Axelrod, Ronald Bayer, Joseph Blount, Allen Brandt, Cyril Brosnan, Susan Brown, Brent Cassens, Ward Cates, James Chin, Mary Cline, James Curran, Peter Drottman, Ernest Drucker, Reuben Dworsky, Ann Hardy, Russell Havlack, Brian Hendricks, Robert Hummel, Mathilde Krim, Sheldon Landesman, Philip R. Lee, Richard Needle, Alvin Novick, Gerald Oppenheimer, Mel Rosen, Charles Rosenberg, Barbara G. Rosenkrantz, William Sabella, Stephen Schultz, and Ann A. Scitovsky.

4

The Social Meaning of AIDS

Peter Conrad

Disease and illness can be examined on different levels. Disease is understood best as a biophysiological phenomenon, a process or state that affects the body. Illness, by contrast, has more to do with the social and psychological phenomena that surround the disease. The world of illness is the subjective world of meaning and interpretation; how a culture defines an illness and how individuals experience their disorder.

In this article I am going to examine the social and cultural meanings of Acquired Immunodeficiency Syndrome or AIDS as it is manifested in late-20th-century America and relate these meanings to the social reaction that it has engendered. When I talk about the social meaning of AIDS, I am including what Susan Sontag has termed the metaphorical aspects of illness: those meanings of diseases that are used to reflect back on some morally suspect element of society.[1] As Sontag suggests, metaphorical aspects of illness are especially prevalent with dread diseases that have great unknowns about them. We need to look at AIDS not only as a biomedical entity, but as an illness that has a socially constructed image and engages particular attitudes. The social meanings of AIDS are simultaneously alarmingly simple and bafflingly complex, but are key to understanding the social reaction to AIDS.

The Social Reaction to AIDS

Five years ago virtually no one had heard of AIDS. In the past five years, however, AIDS has become a household term and a feared intruder in the society.

From *Social Policy,* Vol. 17, No. 1 (1986): 51–56.

The medical reality of AIDS, as we know it, remains puzzling but is becoming clearer. AIDS is a disease caused by a virus that breaks down the immune system and leaves the body unprotected against "opportunistic infections" that nearly invariably lead to death. The number of AIDS cases is growing dramatically and AIDS is considered an epidemic in the society. Over 19,000 cases have been diagnosed, with four or five times that many people having a chronic disorder called AIDS-Related Complex (ARC) and perhaps over a million individuals having an antibody-positive response to HTLV-III, the virus believed to cause AIDS. It is estimated that 5 to 20 percent of this exposed group will contract AIDS, but no one knows who they will be.

Over 90 percent of AIDS victims come from two risk groups: homosexual or bisexual men and intravenous drug users. (Hemophiliacs and others requiring frequent blood transfusions and infants born to mothers with AIDS are also considered risk groups.) The evidence is clear that the AIDS virus is transmitted through the direct exchange of bodily fluids, semen and blood; the most common mode of transmission is anal intercourse among male homosexuals and unsterile needle-sharing among intravenous drug users. There is virtually *no* evidence that the virus can be transmitted by everyday "casual contact," including kissing or shaking hands, or exposure to food, air, water, or whatever.[2] With the exception of very specific modes of semen or blood-related transmission, it does not appear that the AIDS virus is very easy to "catch."

Yet the public reaction to AIDS has bordered on hysteria. Below are a few examples of the reactions to AIDS or AIDS victims.

- 11,000 children were kept out of school in Queens, New York, as parents protested the decision to allow a 7-year-old girl with AIDS to attend second grade (despite no evidence of transmission by school children).
- Hospital workers in San Francisco refused to enter the room of an AIDS patient. When ordered to attend the patient, they appeared wearing masks, gowns, and goggles.
- A Baltimore policeman refused to enter the office of a patient with AIDS to investigate a death threat and donned rubber gloves to handle the evidence.
- A local school district in New Jersey tried to exclude a healthy 9-year-old boy whose sister has ARC (despite no sign of sibling transmission).
- An Amarillo, Texas, hospital fired a cafeteria worker who participated in a blood drive. This worker showed no signs of being ill or unable to perform his duties, but his blood had registered seropositive.
- In early 1985, Delta Airlines proposed a rule (later dropped) forbidding the carrying of AIDS patients.

• In New York, undertakers refused to embalm AIDS victims, householders fired their Haitian help, and subway riders wore gloves, all from fear of contracting AIDS.
• One child, hospitalized with AIDS, had a "do not touch" sign on her bed and was isolated from all physical contact with her parents.
• *The New York Times* reported cases of dentists who refused to treat gay patients (not just confirmed AIDS cases).
• In Dallas, a small group of doctors and dentists formed Dallas Doctors Against AIDS and began a campaign to reinstate Texas' sodomy laws.
• In a Boston corporation, employees threatened to quit en masse if the company forced them to work with an AIDS patient.
• Dade County, Florida, voted to require the county's 80,000 food workers to carry cards certifying they are free of communicable diseases, including AIDS, despite no known cases of AIDS transmitted through food and even though public health officials opposed this policy.
• The U.S. military is beginning to screen all new recruits for AIDS antibodies, with the likely result of declaring those who test seropositive ineligible for service.
• Several major life insurance companies are requiring certain applicants (young, single, male, living in certain areas) to undergo an HTLV-III antibody test.
• Public health officials in Texas passed a measure allowing quarantine of certain AIDS patients. A candidate with a platform calling for the quarantining of all people with AIDS won the Democratic party's nomination for lieutenant governor in Illinois.

The list could go on. There is clearly a great fear engendered by the spectre of AIDS, a fear that has led to an overreaction to the actual problem. This is in no way to say that AIDS is not a terrible and devastating disease—it is—or to infer that it is not a serious public health concern. What we are seeing is an overblown, often irrational, and pointless reaction to AIDS that makes the disease more difficult for those who have it and diverts attention from the real public health concerns.

The Social and Cultural Meanings of AIDS

To better understand the reaction to AIDS, it is necessary to examine particular social features of the disease: 1) the effect of marginal and stigmatized "risk groups"; 2) sexually-related transmission; 3) the role of contagion; and 4) the deadly nature of the disease.

The effect of marginal and stigmatized "risk groups." There are some illnesses that carry with them a certain moral devaluation, a stigma.

Leprosy, epilepsy, mental disorder, venereal disease, and by some accounts, cancer, all reflect moral shame on the individuals who had the ill luck to contract them. Stigmatized illnesses are usually diseases that in some fashion are connected to deviant behavior: either they are deemed to produce it as with epilepsy or are produced by it, as in the case of VD.

The effect of the early connection of AIDS to homosexual conduct cannot be underestimated in examining its stigmatized image. The early designation of the disorder was Gay Related Immune Deficiency Syndrome (GRID) and was publicly proclaimed as a "gay plague." It was first thought to be caused by the use of "poppers" (amylnitrate) and later by promiscuity.[3] Something those fast-track gays were doing was breaking down their immune system. However, AIDS is not and never was specifically related to homosexual conditions; viruses don't know homosexuals from heterosexuals.

Within a short time, other "risk" groups were identified for what was now called AIDS—intravenous drug users, Haitians, and hemophiliacs. With the exception of hemophiliacs (who made up less than two percent of the cases), AIDS' image in the public eye was intimately connected with marginal populations. It was a disease of "those deviants," considered by some a deserved punishment for their activities. In 1983 Patrick J. Buchanan, who later became a White House staffer, wrote: "Those poor homosexuals. They have declared war on nature, and nature is exacting an awful retribution."[4] It is certain that fear of AIDS was amplified by the widespread and deeply rooted "homophobia" in American society.

Sexually-related transmission. The dominant vector of transmission of AIDS is through sexual activity, particularly anal intercourse of male homosexuals. Although scientifically AIDS is better seen as a "blood disease" (since contact with blood is necessary for transmission), this common form of transmission has contributed to its image as a sexually transmitted disease.

Venereal diseases are by nature also stigmatized. They are deemed to be the fault of the victims and would not occur had people behaved better. As Allen Brandt points out, venereal diseases have become a symbol of pollution and contamination: "Venereal disease, the palpable evidence of unrestrained sexuality became a symbol for social disorder and moral decay—a metaphor of evil."[5]

AIDS, with its connection to multiple sex encounters and once-forbidden "sodomy," touches deep Puritanical concerns and revives alarms of promiscuity and "sexual permissiveness" that have become more muted in recent decades. The connection of AIDS to "sexual irresponsibility" has been made repeatedly.

Now that it appears AIDS can be transmitted through heterosexual intercourse as well, although apparently not as efficiently and rapidly, there is increasing concern among sexually active people that they may be betrayed in their most intimate moments. This connection with intimacy and sexuality amplifies our anxieties and creates fears that one sexual act may bring a lifetime of pollution and ultimately death.

The role of contagion. We have almost come to believe that large-scale deadly epidemics were a thing of the past. The polio panics of the early 1950s have receded far into our collective memory, and the wrath of tuberculosis, cholera, or diptheria have become, in American society at least, artifacts of the past. Everyday models for contagion are more limited to the likes of herpes, chicken pox, and hepatitis. When we encounter AIDS, which is contagious but apparently in a very specific way, our fear of contagion erupts almost without limits. When little is known about a disease's transmission, one could expect widespread apprehensions about contagion. But a great deal is known about AIDS' transmission—it appears only to be transmitted through the exchange of bodily fluids and in *no* cases through any type of casual contact. In fact, compared to other contagious diseases it has a relatively low infectivity. Yet the fear of contagion fuels the reaction to AIDS.

Given our extant medical knowledge, what are the sources of fear? We live in a society where medicine is expected to protect us from deadly contagious diseases, if not by vaccine, then by public health intervention. And when medicine does not do this, we feel we must rely on our own devices to protect ourselves and our loved ones. Contagion, even of minor disorders, can engender irrational responses. Several months ago my 5-year-old daughter was exposed to a playmate who came down with chicken pox. A good friend of mine, who happens to be a pediatrician, did not want his 4-year-old to ride in the car with my daughter to gymnastics class, even though he knew medically that she could not yet be infectious. He just did not want to take any chances. And so it is with us, our reactions to contagion are not always rational.

With AIDS, of course, the situation is much worse. When we read in the newspapers that the AIDS virus has been found in saliva or tears, though only occasionally, we imagine in our common-sense germ-theory models of contagion that we could "catch AIDS" in this manner. Reports that no transmission has ever occurred in this fashion become secondary. The public attitudes seem to be that exposure to the AIDS virus condemns one to the disease.

While AIDS is contagious, so is the fear and stigma. The fear of AIDS has outstripped the actual social impact of the disease. But, more importantly for families of people who suffer from AIDS, the stigma of AIDS becomes contagious. They develop what Erving Goffman has called a courtesy stigma, a taint that has spread from the stigmatized to his or her close connections.[6] Family members of people with AIDS are shunned and isolated by former friends and colleagues, for fear that they too might bring contagion.

A deadly disease. AIDS is a devastating and deadly disease. It is virtually 100 percent lethal: 75 percent of people with AIDS die within two years. There are few other diseases that, like AIDS, attack and kill people who are just reaching the prime of their lives. Currently, AIDS is incurable; since there are no treatments for it, to contract AIDS in the 1980s is to be served with a death warrant. Many sufferers waste away from Kaposi's sarcoma or some rare form of chronic pneumonia.

As various researchers have shown, caretakers and family alike tend to distance themselves from sufferers who are terminally ill with diseases that waste away their bodies.[7] The pain of suffering and the pollution of dying are difficult for many people to encounter directly in a society that has largely removed and isolated death from everyday life.

Taken together, these features form a cultural image of AIDS that is socially as well as medically devastating. It might even be said that AIDS is an illness with a triple stigma: it is connected to stigmatized groups (homosexuals and drug users); it is sexually transmitted; and, like cancer, it is a terminal, wasting disease. It would be difficult to imagine a scenario for a more stigmatizing disease, short of one that also makes those infected obviously visible.

The Effects of AIDS

The social meaning affects the consequences of AIDS, especially for AIDS sufferers and their families and the gay community but also for medicine and the public as well.

The greatest consequences of AIDS are of course for AIDS sufferers. They must contend with a ravaging disease and the stigmatized social response that can only make coping with it more difficult. In a time when social support is most needed, it may become least available. And in the context of the paucity of available medical treatments, those with AIDS must face the prospect of early death with little hope of survival.

People with ARC or those who test antibody-positive must live with the uncertainty of not knowing what the progression of their disorder will be. And living with this uncertainty, they must also live with the fear and stigma produced by the social meanings of AIDS. This may mean subtle disenfranchisement, overt discrimination, outright exclusion, or even total shunning. The talk of quarantine raises the anxiety of "why me?" Those symptomless seropositive individuals, who experts suggest have a 5 to 20 percent chance of developing full-blown AIDS, must live with the inner conflict of who to tell or not to tell, of how to manage their sexual and work lives, and the question of whether and how they might infect others. The social meanings of AIDS make this burden more difficult.

Families and lovers of people with AIDS, ARC, or an antibody-positive test are placed in an uncomfortable limbo status. Many live in constant fear that they might contract the AIDS virus, and thus limit their contact with the infected individual. Others wonder whether they too might be or become infectious. As mentioned earlier, families often share the AIDS stigma, as others see them as tainted, cease visiting their home, or even sever all contact with them. In one recent study of screening for AIDS among blood donors, the researchers noted they "have interviewed people in the pilot phase of [their] notification program who have been left by their spouses or significant others after telling them about their blood test results."[8]

The gay community has been profoundly affected by AIDS. The late 1960s and 1970s were an exciting and positive period of the American gay community. Thousands of gay men and women came "out of the closet" and proclaimed in a variety of ways that "gay is good." Many laws forbidding gay sexual activity were removed from the books. Gay people developed their own community institutions and more openly experimented and practiced alternative lifestyles. Although the celebration of anonymous sex among some gay males resulted in high rates of sexually-transmitted diseases and hepatitis B, the social atmosphere in the gay community remained overwhelmingly positive. While the attitudes toward homosexuality never became totally accepting, public moral opprobrium toward gays was perceptibly reduced.[9]

And along came AIDS. With its image as a "gay disease" related to a fast-track gay male lifestyle, the fear of AIDS tapped into a reservoir of existing moral fear of homosexuals. It was a catalyst to the reemergence of a latent "homophobia" that had never really disappeared. Now there was a new reason to discriminate against gays. Thus AIDS has led to a restigmatization of homosexuality. Every avowed male homosexual is a suspected carrier of AIDS and deemed potentially dangerous. This, of course, has pushed many gay men back into the closet, living their lives with new fears and anxieties. It is clear that AIDS threatens two decades of social advances for the gay community.

Concern about AIDS has also become the overriding social and political concern of the gay community, consuming energy that previously went toward other types of social and political work. The gay community was the first to bring the AIDS problem into the public arena and to urge the media, medicine, and government to take action. Action groups in the gay community have engaged in extensive AIDS educational campaigns. This was done out of concern, but not without a fear of government surveillance and invasion of privacy. There was also apprehension that the images of "bad blood" and depictions of gays as health risks might lead to new exclusions of gays.[10]

The scourge of AIDS in the gay community has led, on the one hand, to divisions among gays (e.g., should bath houses be closed) and, on the other, to unprecedented changes in sexual behavior (e.g., witness the dramatic drop in the number of sex partners and types of sexual encounters reported in several studies and indexed by the large decrease in new cases of rectal gonorrhea).[11]

There is also a great emotional toll from the AIDS epidemic in the gay community. Nearly everyone in the community has friends or acquaintances who have died from the disease. As one gay activist recently put it, many people in the gay community were suffering a "grief-overload" as a result of the losses from AIDS.[12]

The social image of AIDS has affected medical care and scientific research as well. In general, the medical voice concerning AIDS, at least in terms of describing it to the public and outlining its perils, has on the whole been cautious and even-handed. The tenor of information has been factual and not unduly emotional. The Center for Disease Control (CDC) has again and again declared that AIDS is not transmitted by casual contact and, although it is a major epidemic and a public health threat, it is one with specific risk groups.

However, some medical scientists have placed the dangers of AIDS in a highly negative light either to raise the public's concern or to elicit private or governmental research funds. For example, "Dr. Alvin Friedman-Kein, an AIDS researcher who saw the first cases, said that AIDS will probably be the plague of the century."[13] Dr. Mathilde Krim was quoted in *The New York Post* last September as saying that "it is only a matter of time before it afflicts heterosexuals on a large scale" while presenting no evidence or data to support the claim.[14] The media, of course, picks up these assertions, often highlighting them in headlines, which reinforces the public fear.

The stigma of AIDS in a few cases has affected medical practice. There have been some reports of doctors, health workers, or hospitals who have refused to treat AIDS patients. But fortunately, these extreme examples are rare and, for the most part, AIDS sufferers seem to have received at least adequate care from most medical facilities. But a mistrust of the ramifications of the public attitudes toward AIDS may well keep some "high risk" individuals from seeking medical diagnosis or care. The fear of being found seropositive and becoming a social pariah might well keep carriers of the AIDS virus from medical attention.

Finally, stigmatized attitudes toward a disease can constrain medical progress. As Allen Brandt points out, the negative social meanings attached to VD actually obstructed medical efforts. He noted that research funding was somewhat limited because the issue was thought to be best dealt with behaviorally. Among many VD researchers the discovery of penicillin was treated with ambivalence, since they were afraid a cure of syphilis would promote promiscuity.[15]

While medical scientists have recently gained a great deal of knowledge about AIDS, including isolating the virus, describing the modes of transmission, and developing a test for screening HTLV-III antibodies in blood (although it is imperfect for screening people[16]), the stigma AIDS presents has probably limited public funding for AIDS research and deterred some types of community research on AIDS natural history. Several commentators have noted that federal funding for research and prevention of AIDS was slow in emerging because AIDS was seen as a "gay disease." It was only when it threatened blood transfusions and blood products that public consciousness was aroused and federal support was forthcoming. Unfortunately, this increased support for research and education was "misinterpreted as an indicator that AIDS was a universal threat destined to work its way inexorably through all segments of society."[17]

One of the most striking aspects about the social reaction to AIDS is how fear and stigma have led to a resistance to information about AIDS. While at times the media has sensationalized AIDS, there has also been a great deal of information communicated concerning AIDS, its characteristics, and its modes of transmission. Yet study after study finds a small but substantial and consistent proportion of the population that exhibits profound misinformation about AIDS. An October, 1985, Harris Poll reported that 50 percent of those asked believed one could get AIDS from living in the same house with someone who had it or from "casual contact," and one-third of the respondents thought that one can catch it from "going to a party where someone with AIDS is."[18]

Another study of high school students in San Francisco found that 41.9 percent believed you could get AIDS if kissed by someone with the disease; 17.1 percent thought if you touched someone with the disease you could get AIDS; 15.3 percent believed just being around someone with AIDS can give you the disease; and 11.6 percent thought all gay men have AIDS.[19] In a study of adolescents in Ohio, fully 60 percent believed that touching or coming near a person with AIDS might transmit the disease.[20] These authors contend that low knowledge of AIDS is correlated with high perceived susceptibility.

In a survey in San Francisco, New York, and London, the researchers found that "more knowledge was significantly negatively correlated with general fear of AIDS and with anti-gay attitudes among risk groups."[21] It appears that rather than low knowledge creating fear, the social meaning of AIDS creates resistance and barriers to taking in accurate information about AIDS.

Such misinformation is also prevalent among health-care providers. In a Massachusetts study of the effect of AIDS educational programs on health-care providers, the researchers reported that before the program, "20.5 percent of providers thought AIDS could be transmitted by shaking hands and 17.2 percent thought it could be acquired simply by being in the same room with a patient."[22] Many of these beliefs seem resistant to change. In the Massachusetts study, "after the [educational] programs, 15 percent of the providers still thought AIDS could be transmitted by sneezing or coughing, and 11.3 percent thought it could be transmitted by shaking hands. [In addition] after the . . . programs, the majority (66.2 percent) still thought that gowns were always necessary and a substantial minority (46.3 percent) still considered quarantine necessary."[23] While the educational programs affected some change in knowledge about AIDS, the researchers found a strong resistance to changing knowledge and attitudes among a substantial minority of health-care providers. Such misinformation among health-care providers can only have negative effects on AIDS patients.

One of the social tragedies of the fear and stigma is that it has constrained compassion for AIDS sufferers. In our culture, we generally show caring and compassion for severely and terminally ill patients. The social meaning of AIDS mutes this compassion in families, among health-care providers, and with the public at large. It is a shame that a victim of any disease in our society must suffer the plight of Robert Doyle of Baltimore. After discovering he had pneumonia brought on by AIDS, no nursing home or hospice would take him. His family rejected him and his lover demanded that he move out of the apartment. With only months to live, he had no support, resources, or place to die. He finally rented a room in a run-down hotel, where the staff refused to enter the room and left food for him in the hallway. After a newspaper story, a stranger took him into her home, only to ask him to leave in a few days; next an elderly couple took him in, until threatening telephone calls and vandalism forced him to move again. He finally found a home with three other adults, one also an AIDS victim. Soon he was returned to the hospital where he died.[24] The fear of AIDS turned this sick and dying man into a social outcast.

Conclusion

The social meaning of AIDS has added to the victim-blaming response common to sexually and behaviorally-related diseases a powerful victim-fearing component. This has engendered an overreaction to the perils of AIDS and fueled the public fears of the disease. Some dangers and threats are, of course, very real, but the triple stigma of AIDS presents a frightening picture to the public, which leads to misguided attempts at "protection" and to resistance to contrary information. This only makes managing life more difficult for the sufferers and does not make the world "safer" from AIDS.

Since a medical cure or prevention for AIDS in the near future is unlikely, it is important that efforts be made to reduce the "hysteria" and overreaction surrounding this disease. We need to redouble our efforts to diffuse the unwarranted aspects of the fear of AIDS and to reduce its stigma. There are several strategies for attempting to accomplish this.

AIDS appears to be "out of control." If some type of medical intervention emerged that could limit the spread and/or symptoms of the disease, this sense of lack of control might be decreased and the public expectations of medicine's protective function might be somewhat restored. But given the historical examples of epilepsy and syphilis, available and efficacious medical treatments do not in themselves alter the image of a disorder. The stigma of these diseases, while perhaps reduced, are still prevalent in our society.

Activists, policymakers, and medical personnel must directly attempt to change the image of the disease. Sometimes a disease's stigmatized image is reinforced by incorrect information. A classic example is the notion that leprosy was highly contagious and sufferers needed to be placed in isolated colonies. We know now that leprosy is not easily communicable. With epilepsy, myths developed that both emerged from and sustained the stigma, including notions like epilepsy is an inherited disease or it causes crime. These myths often gained professional support and led to misguided public policies such as forbidding marriage or immigration.[25] Such incorrect information and mythology must be unmasked and not be allowed to become the basis for social policies.

Another strategy to reduce stigma is to "normalize" the illness; that is, to demonstrate that not only "deviants" get the disease. It is important to show that conventional people can suffer the disease and, to the extent possible, lead normal lives. For example, Rock Hudson's belated public disclosure of his AIDS was an important symbol. He was identified as a solid, clean-cut American man, almost an ideal. He was also a movie hero with whom many people had made some kind of vicarious relationship. To a certain extent Rock Hudson helped bring AIDS out of the closet. An important public policy strategy should be to "normalize" AIDS as much as possible—to present exemplars of people who still can live relatively normal, if difficult, lives, with positive antibodies, ARC, or even AIDS. The media has done this to a degree with children—depicted as innocent victims of the disease—but we need to bring other AIDS sufferers back into our world and recreate our compassion for them.

We need to develop policies that focus on changing the image of AIDS and confront directly the stigma, resistance to information, and the unnecessary fears of the disease. Given the social meaning of AIDS, this won't be easy. While studies have shown us how difficult it is to change public attitudes toward illnesses,[26] images of diseases like leprosy (Hanson's disease) and, to a lesser degree, epilepsy have changed. We must develop the professional and public resolve to change the social meanings and response to AIDS and make this a high priority, along with the control, treatment, and eventual eradication of the disease. It is incumbent upon us to reduce the social as well as the physical suffering from AIDS.

Notes

1. Susan Sontag, *Illness as Metaphor* (New York: Farrar, Straus and Giroux, 1978).
2. Merle A. Sande, "The Transmission of AIDS: The Case Against Casual Contagion," *New England Journal of Medicine,* vol. 314 (1986), pp. 380–82. See also, June E. Osborn, "The AIDS Epidemic: An Overview of the Science," *Issues in Science and Technology* (Winter, 1986), pp. 40–55.
3. Jacques Liebowitch, *A Strange Virus of Unknown Origin* (New York: Ballantine, 1985), pp. 3–4.
4. Cited in Matt Clark et al., "AIDS," *Newsweek* (October 12, 1984), pp. 20–24, 26–27.
5. Allen M. Brandt, *No Magic Bullet* (New York: Oxford University Press, 1985), p. 92.
6. Erving Goffman, *Stigma* (Englewood Cliffs, NJ: Prentice-Hall, 1963), pp. 30–31.
7. Sontag, 1978. See also, Anselm Strauss and Barney Glaser, *Awareness of Dying* (Chicago: Aldine, 1965).
8. Paul D. Cleary et al., "Theoretical Issues in Health Education about AIDS Risk." Unpublished paper, Department of Social Medicine and Health Policy, Harvard Medical School, 1986.
9. Peter Conrad and Joseph W. Schneider, *Deviance and Medicalization: From Badness to Sickness* (St. Louis: C. V. Mosby, 1980).
10. Ronald Bayer, "AIDS and The Gay Community: Between the Specter and the Promise of Medicine," *Social Research* (Autumn, 1985), pp. 581–606.
11. Donald E. Riesenberg, "AIDS-Prompted Behavior Changes Reported," *Journal of the American Medical Association* (January 10, 1986), pp. 171–72;

Ronald Stall, "The Behavioral Epidemiology of AIDS: A Call for Anthropological Contributions," *Medical Anthropology Quarterly* (February, 1986), pp. 36–37; Jonathan Lieberson, "The Reality of AIDS," *New York Review of Books* (January 16, 1986), p. 47.

12. Christopher Collins, "Homosexuals and AIDS: An Inside View." Paper presented to the American Society of Law and Medicine conference on "AIDS: A Modern Plague?" Boston, April, 1986.
13. Lieberson, 1986, p. 45.
14. Ibid., p. 46.
15. Brandt, 1985, p. 137.
16. Carol Levine and Ronald Bayer, "Screening Blood: Public Health and Medical Uncertainty," *Hastings Center Report* (August, 1985), pp. 8–11.
17. George F. Grady, "A Practitioner's Guide to AIDS," *Massachusetts Medicine* (January/February, 1986), pp. 44–50. See also, Kenneth W. Payne and Stephen J. Risch, "The Politics of AIDS," *Science for the People* (September/October, 1984), pp. 17–24.
18. Cited in Lieberson, 1986, p. 44.
19. Ralph J. DiClemente, Jim Zorn, and Lydia Temoshok, "A Large-Scale Survey of Adolescents' Knowledge, Attitudes, and Beliefs About AIDS in San Francisco: A Needs Assessment." Paper presented at the meetings of the Society for Behavioral Medicine, March, 1986.
20. Cited in ibid., p. 4.
21. Lydia Temoshok, David M. Sweet, and Jane Zich, "A Cross-Cultural Analysis of Reactions to the AIDS Epidemic." Paper presented at the meetings of the Society for Behavioral Medicine, March, 1986.
22. Dorothy C. Wertz et al., "Research on the Educational Programs of the AIDS Action Committee of the Fenway Community Health Center: Final Report." Submitted to the Massachusetts Department of Public Health, AIDS Research Program, 1985, p. 11.
23. Ibid., p. 12.
24. Jean Seligman and Nikki Fink Greenberg, "Only Months to Live and No Place to Die," *Newsweek* (August 12, 1985), p. 26.
25. Joseph W. Schneider and Peter Conrad, *Having Epilepsy: The Experience and Control of Illness* (Philadelphia: Temple University Press, 1983), pp. 22–46.
26. Elaine Cumming and John Cumming, *Closed Ranks* (Cambridge: Harvard University Press, 1957).

Looking Forward: Framing the Issues for the 1990s

With the departure of one president and the inauguration of another, there is the frequently espoused view that the country is ready for new leadership and a fresh start. The moment is at hand, it is said, for moving away from the outmoded perspectives and policies of the past and into new and invigorated efforts to make things over. And while there is a certain illusion (or even conceit) that the time is come for those new energies and ideas, there is also in the changing of power a certain dynamic that suggests the status quo cannot hold. Indeed, it can be argued that the change in the presidency is but an effort by the political system to catch up to changes that have already occurred in other arenas.

If there is a middle ground between the rhetoric of "new beginnings" and the reality that presidents do not always lead, it is in an understanding of the continuities of American life. The United States is not now in the midst of a true crisis that would argue we have reached a watershed in our national life. Rather, for most citizens in most parts of the country, the transition from one president to another has no impact on their daily lives. They go on living, business as usual.

Yet, it is true that the United States is being forced to change and adapt to a set of both domestic and international conditions that are different from those experienced twenty years ago. Indeed, the changes during the eight years of the Reagan presidency have in many ways been quite profound. But they have not been either unanticipated or completely without explanation. Further, these changes have evolved and been watched as they did so. Huge trade and budget deficits do affect our national economy, reductions in the availability and accessibility of social services will affect the poor and the aged, and locking in defense spending

89

at the rate of nearly $1 billion every day has a clear ripple effect throughout the society.

The articles in this section seek to explore the ways in which that tension between continuity and change is working itself out in America. What makes these papers noteworthy is that the proclivity of the American policy community to respond is based on how the issues get defined. Tinkering and playing on the margins with pressing issues of the day are more politically safe. Yet they in some instances may simply not be enough; more systematic and thorough changes are needed.

The four articles in this section work through the matter of issue formulation and the subsequent implications for policy in the 1990s. Each of them can be analyzed around the pivot of continuity versus change. The first three pieces, by Palmer; Rabe; and Weidenbaum, Burr, and Cook, all stress that the adaptations and changes needed in the United States in this new decade can be accommodated within existing policy assumptions and systems. Each would argue that the status quo is not likely to persist, but each would also see the present systems being able to accommodate to the necessary change. The final article, by Peterson, takes a quite different view. Here the argument is that the present conditions in the American economy are so severe that trying to tinker with an increase in interest rates here or some tax credits there will not suffice. America is late in paying its economic dues for its behavior during the 1980s and the time for collection is now.

One other point to note in examining these four articles is that all agree that the economic choices of the 1980s in the United States have set the stage for what will be happening in the 1990s. There is little to no disagreement as to what the economic contours are as the United States moves into the new decade. The disagreement is over whether the present system can absorb the coming changes without vast dislocations and upheavals.

The first piece, by John Palmer of the Urban Institute, addresses income-security policies in the United States and what they portend to be in the 1990s. Palmer concludes his thoughtful assessment with the judgment that American income-security policies are likely neither to contract further, nor to resume their expansion as they did in the 1960s and 1970s. Rather, he posits that the retrenchment of the 1980s will continue into the 1990s, resulting in only marginal changes and few commitments to expanding the public resources devoted to this area. It is, as it were, that United States policy will be moving sideways regarding income security—refining target populations, leaving admitted gaps in coverage, and recognizing the limitations on policy options.

For Barry Rabe, the role of the United States government in health care during the 1990s is one of finding its niche among those providing both funds and services. Rabe's conclusion is that the government is likely to withdraw still further from service providing or even service specification, but will continue to find itself at the center of debates on funding the system. The scenario may play out that the federal government will take responsibility for the "floor" of health care costs and that the state and local governments along with the private sector will have to put up the walls and roof. Further, as budget pressures persist, the federal government may face heavy pressure to redistribute health care resources among competing target populations, particularly away from the elderly. If such reallocations do occur, existing political compromises and resource allocation policies will crumble.

Murray Weidenbaum and his colleagues are decidedly optimistic that the economic dislocations and turmoils of the 1980s have had one important benefit—the United States is making the necessary efforts and changes to turn the tide. They see present efforts as resulting in "a period of sustained prosperity in the 1990s." For them, the party was over some time ago; now everyone realizes the need for cleaning up and getting on with the tasks at hand. American efforts at enhancing quality, reducing costs, accelerating funds for research and development, and continually stressing strategies of greater productivity have all come together to lay the foundation for sustained economic growth into the 1990s. The task now is not to assume discontinuities, but to stress the continuation of those efforts already underway.

Finally, a New York investment financier and a former secretary of commerce under Richard Nixon finds himself in the presumably unaccustomed position of being a prophet calling United States economic policy into question. Peter Peterson's provocative piece from the *Atlantic Monthly* (which ironically or maybe prophetically) appeared the same month as the severe October 1987 stock market crash. He argues that a "business as usual" approach to current United States economic conditions is simply unacceptable and indeed destructive to the future well-being of the country. Here he clearly disagrees with the conclusions of the previous article by Weidenbaum et al.

For Peterson, the conditions are now so serious that there is no longer any room to pretend that we can continue to muddle along and eventually get ourselves free of the present problems. Further, he stresses that we shall be forced to respond, even if we are not willing to do so, because the pressures and currents of change are no longer under the control of the United States. The United States is part of a global economy, a network of international banks, corporations, and financial interdependencies that will pull the country along, willing or not. And the more the United States resists the changes that Peterson sees as necessary, the greater the decline in the United States economy and the greater the loss of jobs, income, and industry from America. The reckoning is at hand. The speculative bubble of greed and borrowed prosperity blown up during the 1980s has burst.

5

Income Security Policies in the United States: The Inevitability and Consequences of Retrenchment

John L. Palmer

ABSTRACT

During the 1960s and early 1970s, strong economic growth and highly expansionary income security policies led to considerable progress for the entire American population with respect to major income security goals. However, in the last fifteen years much of this progress has been either arrested or reversed, particularly for the non-aged, as economic growth slowed and income security policies ceased to expand and, in some cases, contracted. This retrenchment was the inevitable consequence of numerous phenomena which preceded, and were reinforced by the Reagan era. American income security policies are not likely to contract generally in the future, nor to resume expanding in a direction characteristic of many Western European welfare states. Rather, the prospects are for slow economic growth, higher targeting of programs by income in some areas, and marginal expansions requiring minimal new commitments of public resources in others. Major income security problems, especially among the lower income population, will remain.

* The author wishes to thank Emily Andrews, Richard Rose, Patricia Ruggles, Ray Struyk, Barbara Torrey and M. Peter van der Hoek for their comments on an earlier draft, and Gregory Frenzel and Sue Poppink for their research assistance. Any opinions expressed herein are his own and do not necessarily represent the view of The Urban Institute or its sponsors.

From *Journal of Public Policy*, Vol. 7, No. 1 (1988): 1–32.

Elaborate conceptual arguments about comparative welfare state developments are beyond the scope of the paper. However, since many other OECD countries seem to be moving in the direction of restraint, if not retrenchment, it may be useful to examine in an American setting the practical evolution of income security policies, which are at the heart of all modern welfare states. To this end, I first provide a general orientation to American income security policies and programs over the past three decades, followed by a documentation of the consequences of these policies, and economic and demographic trends, affecting the achievement of income security goals. In the third section I argue that we are witnessing neither the unravelling of the American welfare state nor simply a respite before its continued expansion in the manner of Western Europe. Rather, it is a consolidation which will be marked by marginal adjustments in income security policies for the foreseeable future. I conclude with an observation about the relevance of the future of American policies to other OECD countries.

The Changing Federal Role in Income Security

American income security policies have three primary goals: (1) the alleviation of poverty; (2) the prevention of precipitous declines in economic well-being due to largely involuntary disruptions of earnings; and (3) the assurance of financial access to an adequate level of certain goods and services that society deems indispensable. A fourth goal, that of narrowing income differentials, has sometimes been advocated, but never gained popular acceptance as an explicit motivation of public policies, although the distributional impacts of such policies have often been taken into account by policy makers. These four concerns are distinct but highly interrelated; policies designed to promote one are likely to promote others. For example, the subsidization of health care expenditures narrows effective income differentials. Similarly, programs that replace part or all of the earnings lost by a family through the unemployment, disability, retirement or death of a breadwinner also prevent millions of people from falling into poverty.

The four income security concerns are often perceived to conflict with other values and goals of our economy or society. Policies altering the market-determined distribution of command over goods and services necessarily abridge individual freedom and cause some people to be treated differently from others. Sometimes they offend our work ethic – the idea that monetary rewards ought to be tied to productive activities. Also, the growth of the economy may be slowed by the disincentive effects of certain tax or transfer policies. Such concerns contribute to our reluctance as a society to adapt a more aggressive stance toward income inequality, and they also affect our willingness to pursue the three primary goals.

The government, in its pursuit of income security objectives, can alter the distribution of income both directly and indirectly. Here we are concerned with direct methods: tax collection, transfers, either of cash or by the financing or provision of certain goods and services intended primarily for current consumption; and subsidized employment in the public sector. And among these direct methods, we are primarily concerned with transfer programs, which is what Americans usually mean by the term income security policy. The indirect methods are numerous and too complex and diffuse to be examined within the scope of this paper.

The tax system's potential to affect income security objectives has grown with the size of the public sector, with annual tax revenues of nearly $1.5 trillion, or about 34 percent of GNP. The rates, structure and other provisions of the tax code directly affect the amount and distribution of after-tax income available to individuals and families, and the specific provisions of the tax law create various incentives that, in turn, affect the level, composition and distribution of various sources of income.

The subsidization of earnings and employment has been undertaken only sparingly since the Depression. Beginning in the 1970s, however, expanded use was made of tax credits, both for low-income workers and their employers as well as of public service employment. (The earned income tax credit offsets a large portion of the payroll tax burdens for low income families and tax credits have been extended to employers for hiring certain classes of disadvantaged workers.) The total amounts of money involved in the tax credits have never been more than a few billion dollars annually. Public service employment, on the other hand, became a sizeable program (peaking at nearly $7 billion in 1978), before its elimination in the early 1980s.

The major public transfer programs serving income security purposes and the corresponding federal expenditures for 1985 are shown in Table 1. The cash programs are of two types: means-tested programs designed to put a floor under the income of recipients, thus alleviating or eliminating their income poverty; and non means-tested ones that generally have eligibility criteria related to employment history and current labor force status and are intended to replace some of a disrupted flow of earnings for people at all income levels. The non cash, or in-kind, programs support three types of consumption – food, housing, and health care – and are predominantly means-tested. Many of these programs are administered at the state and local level, and several involve partial state and local, as well as federal, financing. However, the aggregate of state and locally financed expenditures for income security purposes is relatively quite

TABLE 1 : *Federal Expenditures and Reductions from Pre-Reagan Policy Baseline for Income Security Programs, Fiscal Year 1985*

Program	Expenditures ($ billions)	Increase or Reduction from Pre-Reagan Baseline[a] (%)
Cash Programs		
Means-tested		
Aid-to-Families with Dependent Children[b]	8.4	−14.3
Supplemental Security Income[c]	8.6	8.6
Non Means-tested		
Social Security[c, d]	194.3	−4.6
Income Security for Veterans[c, e]	14.1	−1.4
Unemployment Compensation[b]	20.4	−17.4
Public Service Employment[f]		
Subtotal	245.8	−5.3
In-kind Programs		
Means-tested		
Food Stamps[f]	11.8	−13.8
Medicaid[b]	21.8	−2.8
Child Nutrition[f, h]	5.4	−17.5
Housing Assistance[f]	10.6	−11.4
Non Means-tested		
Medicare	70.2	−6.8
Subtotal	119.8	−7.6
Subtotals		
Means-tested programs	66.4	−7.3
Non Means-tested programs	298.9	−5.8
Total	365.41	−6.1
Total as a percentage of GNP	9.2	
Total as a percentage of the federal budget	38.6	

Sources: Baseline cuts from D. Lee Bawden and John L. Palmer, "Social Policy: Challenging the Welfare State," (Table 6.1, pp. 185–86) in John L. Palmer and Isabel V. Sawhill, editors, *The Reagan Record: An Assessment of America's Changing Domestic Priorities*, Cambridge, MA: Ballinger Publishing Company, 1984. 1985 expenditures from Office of Management and Budget, *Historical Tables: Budget of the United States Government, Fiscal year 1986*, February 1985.

a Reductions are measured relative to what expenditures would have been in FY 85 under FY 81 policies. They are probably overestimates of the actual effects of program reductions since they are based on projections of inflation made in 1982–83 that turned out to be too high.

b State and local administration and cost sharing. Includes total expenditures for unemployment compensation and the federal share (about 55 percent of the total) for AFDC and Medicaid.

c Full federal financing and administration, though several states supplement the federal SSI benefits with their own funds.

d Includes railroad retirement.

e Includes veterans insurance programs, plus 'and black lung'. A small portion of this is means-tested.

f State and local administration, full federal financing.

g Public service employment was funded at 3.1 billion in 1981 and then phased out in 1982 and 1983.

h Includes special milk program; women, infants and children programs; and child nutrition programs.

small – less than 10 percent of coreesponding federal expenditures – and mostly for the Medicaid and aid-to-families with dependent children (AFDC) programs for which the federal, state and local governments share costs.

Fueled by the fiscal abundance resulting from the strong economic growth of the 1960s and 1970s and the growing public support for governmental efforts to assist the disadvantaged (The Great Society), these income transfer programs grew extremely rapidly throughout the 1960s and much of the 1970s. As a result, spending for social programs (of which income transfer programs constitute the vast bulk) more than doubled as a percentage both of total federal outlays and of GNP. (See Figure 1, where the 'social insurance and other' and 'low income assistance' categories in this figure correspond roughly to the non means-tested and means-tested income security programs in Table 1.) Growth came in three distinct forms. Of greatest importance was the creation of new programs – most notably Medicare, Medicaid and Food Stamps – and legislated expansions of eligibility for old ones, such as AFDC, SSI and housing assistance. Secondly, increases in the real value of the benefits received by typical recipients in most programs resulted from numerous explicit legislative decisions to raise benefit levels, as well as from adjustments built into the basic structure of some programs – most notably Social Security, where benefit levels for new retirees reflect rising real wage rates, and Medicare and Medicaid, where benefit levels reflect changing medical practices and costs. The third form of expenditure growth came from the faster rate of growth of recipient populations than of the general population. This occurred because demographic change (e.g., the growth of single parent families and population aging) led to a growing percentage of the population being comprised of categorically eligible groups (the aged and single parent families), because an increasing number of the aged had extensive years of Social Security covered earnings, and because a much greater proportion of the eligible populations choose to participate in some programs (e.g., AFDC).

By the late 1970s, several factors had coalesced to produce a substantial shift in the previous expansionary trend of public income security programs. Chief among these were the major slowdown in economic growth, the growing public acceptance of conservative critiques of the course of the American version of the welfare state, and the maturation of many of the key programs of this welfare state. This maturation would have produced a natural slowing of the growth of federal spending for income security programs in any event, but the other two factors contributed strongly to a major change in the political climate. Because of the economy, Democratic President Jimmy Carter could find little room in the federal budget for new expenditures for social programs without

FIGURE 1: *Federal Social Program Spending as a Percentage of GNP*

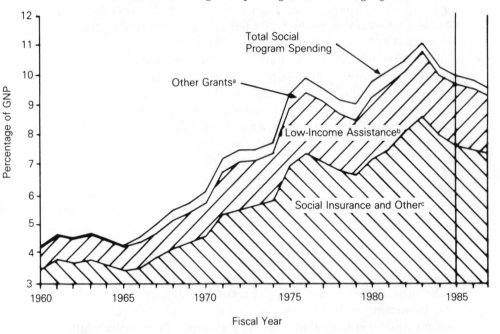

Source: *Historical Tables: Budget of the United States Government, Fiscal Year 1986.* Office of Management
and Budget; unpublished tabulations; and author's calculations.

Notes: Figures for 1986 and 1987 are projections based on 1985 policies.

a. Includes Compensatory, Vocational, and Adult Education, Education for the Handicapped,
Rehabilitation Services, Health and Social Services, Refugee and Entrant Assistance, and
Employment and Training Programs.

b. Includes Medicaid, Aid to Families with Dependent Children (AFDC), Veterans' Pensions,
Supplemental Security Income (SSI), Food Stamps, Student Financial Assistance, Housing
Assistance, Child Nutrition, Special Supplemental Feeding Program for Women, Infants, and
Children (WIC), and Low-Income Energy Assistance.

c. Includes Medicare, Social Security, Unemployment Insurance, Guaranteed Student Loans,
Veterans' Compensation, Medical Care, and Readjustment Benefits.

raising taxes, and the public's fiscal generosity was waning with stagnant
disposable incomes and growing skepticism of the efficacy of many social
programs. To be sure, some expansions of income security programs did
occur. For example, temporary increases in unemployment insurance and
public service employment were legislated in response to high unemployment rates at the beginning of Carter's term, and the federal commitment
to housing assistance was considerably expanded (although this involved
raising the budget authority for future spending much more than it did
raising current spending). But much more important was what did not
happen. In particular, President Carter's proposals for national health
insurance and welfare reform, which in the late 1960s and early 1970s had

appeared logical major next steps in the expansion of federal income security policies, were rejected by Congress. In consequence, the growth in federal spending for income security programs slowed markedly in the second half of the 1970s to little more than that of GNP.

The shift in income security policy was furthered with the election of Ronald Reagan as president. Social programs were targeted for sizeable reductions by his administration, not only to make room in the budget for an accelerated defense build-up and large tax cut, but also because their previous growth was identified by President Reagan as a major contributor to US economic woes, through the undermining of incentives for self-reliance and material advancement. In his first term President Reagan proposed cuts in income security programs amounting to about 13 percent, relative to what such spending would have been under the policies he inherited. Congress, in fact, granted him reductions of somewhat less than half this amount. (Table 1) As discussed in Bawden and Palmer (1984), the resulting cuts were proportionately greater in the means-tested programs, where they were largely designed to restrict benefits to the lowest income recipients. The reductions in non means-tested programs similarly trimmed benefits for many of the most well-off recipients, but also reduced coverage for many recipients who might be considered to exercise some choice about whether to work. Although the cuts were not large enough in the aggregate to arrest the real growth of federal spending for income security purpose, it was further slowed. In consequence, outlays for the programs ceased to grow relative to GNP.[1] Congressional action, so far in the second term of the Reagan administration, in response to concerns about the federal budget deficit (which has averaged in excess of 5 percent of GNP since 1982), has consolidated this new trend.

The Consequences

The effect of the changing patterns of federal expenditures discussed above on the actual income security of individuals and families is the subject of heated debate in the United States. Here we survey the best available data on progress toward income security policy goals with an eye toward assessing the contribution of particular public policies.

Poverty

The simplest approach to measuring progress against poverty in the United States is the movement of the official poverty rate, the proportion of the total population living in households whose money income falls below a designated poverty threshold which varies with household size and is adjusted over time to inflation. The poverty threshold in 1985 was about $5,600 for a single individual and $11,000 for a family of four. The official poverty rate declined markedly from above 20 percent in the early 1960s, when it first became a focus of attention, to 11 percent in the early 1970s, with the gains widely shared among all demographic groups. Poverty rates for the non-aged then remained relatively stable through 1979 and rose rapidly thereafter to a peak in 1983, from which they have fallen only modestly in the subsequent three years. However, poverty among the aged continued to decline steadily throughout the 1970s and so far in the 1980s. It is clear that changes in public transfers, in the economy, and in the demographic composition of the population all have played an important role in determining this pattern, although it is difficult to sort out precisely their respective roles.

The antipoverty effectiveness of the various public transfer programs is often understated. First, since only money income is considered in calculating the official poverty rate, in-kind programs do not affect it. If all in-kind benefits were counted as income at their cost to the government, the poverty rate by 1979 would have been under 7 percent rather than the official rate of 11.7 percent.[2] Second, the poverty rate is strongly affected by demographic change – in particular, by the increase in the proportion of the low-income population that has little potential for earnings or other sources of private income. (See Table 2.) Most notably, between 1960 and

TABLE 2: *The Poverty Population for Selected Years*

Poverty Measure	1960[a] %	1970 %	1980 %	1985 %
Incidence of Poverty[b]				
All persons age 65 or over	35.2	24.5	15.7	12.6
Persons less than 65 in households with female heads	50.4	37.4	35.2	35.9
Persons less than 65 in households with male heads	17.8	7.5	7.9	9.1
All persons	22.2	12.6	13.0	14.0
Composition of the Poverty Population				
All persons age 65 or over	13.9	18.5	13.2	10.5
Persons less than 65 in households with female heads	21.2	34.0	42.2	43.1
Persons less than 65 in households with male heads	65.0	47.5	44.6	46.5
Total	100.0	100.0	100.0	100.0

Source: US Department of Commerce, Bureau of the Census, *Money Income and Poverty Status of Families and Persons in the United States: 1985*, Current Population Report, Series P–60, No. 154, Table 16.

[a] Based on 1960 household composition and 1959 income data.
[b] Incidence refers to the proportion of the total population in each age–household category that is classified as poor.

1985 the proportion of the poverty population living in female-headed households below age 65 more than doubled, reflecting a similar increase in the share of female-headed families among all families over the same period. The official poverty rate would have been an estimated two percentage points lower in 1979 were it not for these and other changes in the demographic composition of the population since the mid 1960s (Gottschalk and Danziger, 1984).

The influence of these factors is illustrated in Figure 2, which shows poverty rates since 1965 based on three different measures – pre-transfer income, money income, and adjusted income (which includes in-kind benefits received and nets out taxes paid). Comparison of these rates demonstrates that the sharp reductions in poverty in the 1960s were caused by the combination of rising pre-transfer income growth resulting from the strong economy and rapidly growing transfers, whereas the

FIGURE 2: *Trends in the Percentage Poor Among All Persons*

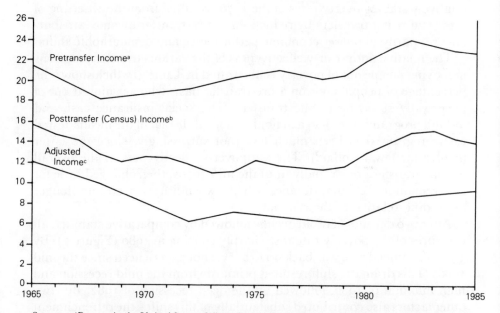

Sources: 'Poverty in the United States: Where Do We Stand Now?' Focus, Winter 1984, Institute for Research on Poverty, University of Wisconsin; unpublished data from Sheldon Danziger (Institute for Research on Poverty, University of Wisconsin), and author's estimates.

a. Pretransfer income or market income. Excludes government transfers, but includes private transfers such as gifts, alimony, child support, and private pensions.
b. Posttransfer income. The official income definition includes market income and cash transfers; does not subtract taxes.
c. Adjusted income. Includes in-kind benefits, subtracts direct taxes and adjusts for under-reporting of cash benefits.

TABLE 3: *Antipoverty Effectiveness of Major Income Transfers, Selected Years, 1965–1984*

		Percent of Pretransfer Poor Moved Out of Poverty by			
Year	Cash Social Insurance Transfers	Cash Means-Tested Transfers	All Cash Transfers	In-Kind Transfers	All Transfers
1965	23.5	3.3	26.8	16.4	43.2
1976	37.6	6.2	43.8	28.1	71.9
1978	37.6	5.9	43.5	NA	NA
1980	35.2	8.5	43.7	NA	NA
1982	33.8	3.8	37.6	25.8	63.3
1984	33.2	3.9	37.1	22.7	59.8
1985	33.5	4.0	37.5	NA	NA

Source: Tabulations from the relevant Current Population Survey data tapes prepared by Christine Ross and extended by George Slotsve of the Institute for Research on Poverty at the University of Wisconsin.

NA = not available

relatively stable poverty rates of the 1970s resulted from the offsetting of these still rising transfers by reductions in pre-transfer income, attributable primarily to poorer economic performance and demographic shifts.

The relative antipoverty effectiveness of the various transfer programs in moving people out of poverty is illustrated in Table 3, which shows the percentage of people poor on a pre-transfer basis who are moved out of poverty by receiving public transfers. The social insurance cash and in-kind programs have had a major impact, while that of the means-tested cash programs has been much less (not surprisingly, since the latter involve far fewer dollars). The antipoverty effectiveness of the overall income transfer grew rapidly until the mid 1970s, then changed little for the remainder of the decade, when expenditures were no longer expanding relative to the economy.

After two decades of rapid decline followed by comparative stability, all measures of the poverty rate rose sharply starting in 1980 (Figure 2). By 1983, the official rate was back up to a level not experienced since the mid 1960s. This dramatic shift resulted primarily from the mild recession and high inflation of 1980, followed by the deep recession of 1982. But two other factors also contributed substantially to this shift – the retrenchment in income security programs and a marked trend towards greater inequality in the earnings of non-aged families (as discussed later). Program retrenchment accounted for about one-quarter of this increase in the poverty rate; however, the precise impact of the growing, pre-transfer inequality is hard to disentangle from cyclical effects. So far, the policy changes and growing pre-transfer inequality have proven more permanent than the recession and are the major reasons why the poverty rate has declined only modestly since 1983, despite the strong recovery from the 1982 recession and subsequent economic growth (Danziger, Gottschalk, and Smolensky, 1985). Also because of them, there has been a reduction in the antipoverty effectiveness of income security programs in the 1980s, as shown in Table 3.

But just as the antipoverty effectiveness of the programs is often underestimated for reasons we discussed above, so it is overestimated by the measures reported in Table 3, which assume that the pre-transfer poverty rate would be the same regardless of the size of the public transfer system, whereas the growth of the system itself may have caused some increase in pre-transfer poverty by reducing incentives for work and savings and increasing incentives for family splitting. In fact, some critics of the American welfare state have gone so far as to argue that, due to these factors, the official poverty rate is actually higher than it would be in the absence of income security programs. While the evidence does not support anywhere nearly this strong a conclusion, it does suggest that the measures in Table 3 generally overstate the true antipoverty effectiveness of income transfer programs, as well as indicate more growth in this effectiveness during their expansionary period and less decline during their recent contraction than actually occurred. There is considerable conclusive evidence showing modest negative labor supply effects (Plotnick, 1984); however, that on family splitting and savings is much more ambiguous Danziger et al., 1981). In any event the trends shown in Table 3 would be the same.

Earnings Replacement

The earnings of individuals and families can be sharply curtailed by a number of events, chief among which are retirement, disability, unemployment, and death. Numerous public programs have been developed over the years in the United States to moderate the effects of these events on the incomes of individuals and families. These programs are not means-tested: entitlement to benefits depends principally on employment history, and thus people at all income levels can be eligible.

Social Security – old age, survivors, and disability insurance (OASDI) and unemployment insurance (UI) are by far the largest public earnings replacement programs, but they are only part of a large matrix of both public and private sources of such income support, as shown in Table 4. The federal role in this area is extremely complex, because it involves not only the specific structure of federal programs but also the provision of incentives for and regulation of both state programs (e.g., workman's compensation) and certain private activities (e.g., private pensions).

Because of the complexity of these activities, there is no simple way to measure progress toward fuller earnings replacement. We can, however, note that the increase in expenditures in this area prior to the late 1970s is indicative of rapidly expanding protection for workers and their families. For example, expenditures under the public programs shown in Table 4 grew from 2.6 percent of GNP in 1950 to 7.8 percent in 1975; for the corresponding years, private employee benefits grew from 0.4 to 1.5 percent of GNP. Interestingly, payments under the public programs grew somewhat more slowly than private payments over the period, indicating an increasing relative role in earnings replacement for the private sector. The major component of this private sector earnings replacement is private pensions, where growth has been encouraged by favorable tax treatment. All employer and most employee contributions to private pension programs are deductible from current income for tax purposes and any returns they earn are also tax exempt. Only when pension income is finally received in retirement is it taxed. This tax deferment is the largest and fastest growing tax expenditure at the federal level, rising from a little over $5 billion in 1975 to about $53 billion in 1985. Data on expenditure in more recent years for all the activities in Table 4 are not available, but it is apparent that total spending is no longer growing relative to GNP.

TABLE 4: *Major Provisions for Earnings Replacement in the United States, 1985*

Reason for Earnings Loss	Earnings Replacement Source[a]	Jurisdiction
Temporary unemployment[b]	Unemployment insurance	State, federal
Disability		
Resulting from work only,	Workmen's compensation	State
total and partial	Veterans compensation	Federal
	Black lung program	Federal
Other	Sick leave	Public and private employees
Short-term,	Temporary disability insurance	State, private
Long-term, total	Social security (disability insurance)	Federal
	Long-term disability insurance	Private
	Early retirement pensions	Most public and private pensions
Retirement and death		
Low-to-middle income	Social security (old age and	Federal
classes	survivors insurance)	
Middle-to-upper income	Social security (old age and	Federal
classes	survivors insurance)	
	Pensions	Most employers
	Annuities, life insurance, and other savings	Private

[a] In addition there are many favored tax treatments that support the earnings replacement function.
[b] Public service employment was also a source of earnings replacement in the late 1960s and 1970s; it was virtually eliminated in the early 1980s.

Retirement and Social Security. The degree of protection against lost earnings provided by unemployment insurance and Social Security can be measured more precisely. Over the past 40 years Social Security has increased its coverage of the private labor force from 65 percent to virtual saturation. Table 5 shows the amount of earnings replacement Social Security currently provides for various types of workers and their families. The replacement rate is the ratio of the initial year's benefits to the worker's gross earnings in the year just prior to eligibility. It provides a useful measure of the extent to which Social Security benefits alone will permit a family to maintain the standard of living achieved just prior to eligibility. The estimated rate necessary for full maintenance ranges from about 60 percent for high wage workers to 80 percent for low wage workers.

Current Social Security replacement rates are considerably higher than those prior to the 1970s, although they have declined substantially from their peak in 1981. After fluctuating between 45 to 50 percent in the late 1950s and 1960s, replacement rates for the typical married workers steadily increased by 75 percent over the next eleven years and then lost over half this gain in the past five years. The increases in the first half of the 1970s were a result of conscious legislative decisions, but those in the latter half were the unintended result of a technical flaw in the formula for automatically adjusting to inflation the wage histories and, therefore, the benefits of new retirees that was initiated in 1975. The combination of both this problem and the slowdown in economic growth forced Congress to pass major ligislation in both 1977 and 1983 to improve the solvency of the Social Security trust funds through a combination of benefit reductions and tax increases. The recent decline in replacement rates is one consequence of these changes; the legislative intent was to stabilise them for the remainder of this century at their mid-1970 level, which has now more or less been accomplished.

Examination of Table 5 suggests that nearly adequate replacement rates have been achieved through Social Security alone for fully covered low-to-medium wage workers who do not retire early and their families. And, although Social Security replacement rates fall far short of the levels required to maintain prior standards of living as workers' wage histories exceed the median, most of these workers have private pensions and other private resources that result in adequate total replacement rates. Over one-third of all aged individuals or couples receive a pension or annuity in addition to Social Security, and a majority have income from assets. Both of these sources of income are highly concentrated among the higher income aged.

At one time it appeared that employer-based pensions might continue to increase in importance relative to Social Security in providing earnings

TABLE 5: *1985 Replacement Rates under Old Age and Survivors Insurance by Age of Retirement*

Retirement Age and spouse's Age	Replacement Rate[a] for Worker with		
	Low Earnings[b]	Median Earnings[c]	Maximum Earnings[d]
Worker retiring at			
Age 65	.638	.409	.228
Age 62	.510	.327	.182
Worker retiring at age 65 with spouse			
Aged 65	.956	.613	.341
Aged 62	.877	.562	.313
Worker retiring at age 62 with spouse			
Aged 65	.830	.532	.296
Aged 62	.750	.481	.268
Surviving spouse aged 65 with deceased spouse retiring in 1985 at			
Age 65	.638	.409	.228
Age 62	.526	.337	.188
Surviving spouse aged 62 with deceased spouse retiring in 1985 at			
Age 65	.529	.339	.189
Age 62	.526	.337	.188
Surviving spouse aged with deceased spouse retiring in 1985 at			
Age 65	.455	.292	.163

Sources: Based on tabulations provided by the U.S. Department of Health, Education, and Welfare, Office of the Assistant Secretary for Planning and Evaluation.
[a] The replacement rate is the constant dollar value of 1985 benefit divided by the constant dollar value of the 1984 wage.
[b] Minimum wage pay over a continuous work history.
[c] Median for all male wage and salary workers with earnings subject to the Social Security tax over a continuous work history.
[d] Worker earning at or above the maximum wage subject to the old age, survivors, and disability insurance payroll tax over a continuous work history.

replacement, but recent events have cast some doubt upon this. The portion of the labor force that was covered by employer-based pensions grew rapidly in the post World War II era from very little to a peak of 56 percent in 1979, but since then it has declined to 52 percent. Much of the decline undoubtedly was due to the recessions of 1980 and 1982, but the fact that the recent recovery has not reversed it raises questions about whether the 1979 high will again be achieved or surpassed (Andrews, 1985). The proportion of aged households actually receiving employer based pensions has held steady at about one-third in recent years after climbing rapidly for several decades. The growing labor force participation of women and new federal requirements for vesting eventually should lead once again to some increase in these recipiency rates; however, they will ultimately be constrained by the pattern of coverage.

While discussion of earnings replacement in retirement indicates considerable achievement of the desired goal despite recent declines in employer-based pension coverage and Social Security replacement rates, some caveats need to be kept in mind. There are still sizeable numbers of aged whose standard of living falls considerably in retirement and who live near or below the poverty level. Older retirees, widows and divorcees without a substantial earnings history, and workers who were disabled are especially vulnerable. And catastrophic medical expenses for acute or long term care pose a serious and widespread threat to the income security of all but the most affluent aged.

Unemployment Insurance. The unemployment insurance (UI) system has followed a similar course as OASDI over recent decades, expanding its earnings replacement capacity throughout most of the post World War II era, and then retreating substantially in the 1980s from the previous peak. Coverage of the basic state program has expanded from under 60 percent of all wage and salary earners in the early 1950s to nearly the entire labor force now. States gradually increased maximum benefit durations (the number of weeks of unemployment per year for which covered workers could claim benefits) until the current norm of 26 weeks became widespread in the 1960s. Statutory replacement rates were gradually increased, so that by 1980 the ratio of benefits paid to average covered weekly wages (in the base period for calculating the benefit) ranged between 50 and 60 percent across the vast majority of states, reflecting the intent to replace half of the lost income due to unemployment. However, more sophisticated measures of replacement rates, which adjust for such things as weekly benefit minimums and maximums, benefit exhaustion, taxes, work expenses, and fringe benefits, indicate that the actual replacement rates for typical workers in 1980 were more on the order of 40 percent.[3]

In addition to this 26 weeks basic state program, two tiers for extending the duration of benefits with federal financing were added in the 1970s, in response to concern about widespread benefit exhaustions. The previous ad hoc practice of temporarily extending benefits an additional 13 weeks in recessions was made an automatic feature in 1970, with coverage triggered when unemployment rates exceeded predetermined thresholds; and temporary, ad hoc expansions of another additional 13 and 26 weeks of benefit eligibility were made during the 1972–73 and 1975–77 economic downturns respectively.

By the end of the 1970s, several states were experiencing financial difficulties in their UI programs because of the sluggish economy and had begun to restrict eligibility for benefits through various means. Steps taken at the federal level in 1981 then greatly increased this tendency towards retrenchment by: (1) imposing much greater costs on those states that were borrowing from the federal government to help finance their basic programs, thus encouraging further state tightening; (2) sharply restricting worker access to extended benefits under the 13 weeks state-federal program by tightening the unemployment 'trigger' provisions; and (3) curtailing the availability of federally-funded UI benefits to certain special groups.

In response to the subsequent deep recession, and against the wishes of the Reagan administration, Congress took a series of steps in 1982 and 1983 to ease the UI financial burden of borrowing on some states and to temporarily provide longer term UI benefits without altering the earlier changes in the trigger. The resulting UI system that is now in place, however, is still considerably less generous than that of the 1970s.

There is no simple way to measure the degree of reduction in earnings replacement by the UI system from its peak in the late 1970s, since no comprehensive study of replacement rates has been undertaken since 1980 and many of the recent changes have served to restrict benefit eligibility rather than to reduce benefit levels, per se. However, two more general indicators are available. First, estimates suggest that aggregate expenditures for basic state UI in the 1982–84 period were 30 to 40 percent less than they would have been under the previously prevailing policies and that the corresponding reduction for extended benefits was more than 50 percent. Second, insured unemployment (claimants for regular state UI benefits), which averaged about 50 percent of total unemployment in the three recessions between 1970–81, did not even rise above 40 percent during the much deeper recession of 1982 (Vroman, 1985). The recent reduction in earnings replacement provided by the UI system clearly has been quite large overall and particularly concentrated among the longer term unemployed.

Financial Access to Certain Goods and Services

The federal government has long promoted financial access to certain widely valued goods and services, but only in the past two decades has this policy been vigorously pursued. In fact direct in-kind programs for food, low-income housing, and financing of medical care barely existed before the beginning of President Johnson's War on Poverty in the mid 1960s, while they have been the fastest growing component of federal expenditures for social purposes since then.

Food. Although there are no reliable time series measures of the degree of hunger and malnutrition among the population, it is clear that both declined steadily throughout the 1960s and 1970s as a result of economic growth and public programs. Hunger became a major national issue in the late 1960s and early 1970s, when a series of reports documented its continued pervasiveness, despite a decade of unprecedented economic prosperity that had undoubtedly resulted in major dietary improvements. These reports prompted a series of actions at the federal level, including a sizeable expansion of specialized feeding and nutrition programs targeted on pregnant women, infants and school children and the emergence of a new national program (food stamps) to provide financial assistance to low-income families and individuals for routine purchase of food.

The food stamp program is by far the most important of federal programs for promoting a nutritionally adequate diet. Since 1974 all households in the United States have been eligible to receive food stamps, which can be redeemed for groceries at most stores, under nationally uniform criteria, if their income and assets fall below prescribed levels. The value of the food stamps for which a family is eligible is determined by what the Department of Agriculture considers sufficient to purchase a minimally adequate diet and varies with family size and is adjusted for changes in food prices over time (In 1986 it amounted to about $3,200 a year for a family of four). Initially, most households had to pay between 20 to 30 percent of their monthly income (after some deductions for such things as work-related expenses) to receive food stamps adequate to purchase the government-determined minimally adequate diet. This purchase requirement was subsequently eliminated in order to remove a possible barrier to participation so that the value of the food stamps actually provided is now the difference between the prior level and 30 percent of income after deductions.

By the end of the 1970s participation in the food stamp program had grown to over 20 million persons, about 60 percent of those estimated to be income-eligible, including two-thirds of the official poverty population and several million near-poor persons. Total spending on this and other food and nutrition programs totalled well in excess of $10 billion annually, in contrast to less than $500 million in the early 1960s. Follow-up studies show that these programs and other public and private efforts had made a huge difference. Despite the slowdown in economic growth beginning in the mid 1970s, evidence of widespread hunger and malnutrition could not be found (Physician Task Force on Hunger in America, 1985).

However, more than a dozen reports have appeared over the past three years documenting sizeable increases in hunger and malnutrition in the 1980s and concluding that America once again has a serious hunger problem, though not so serious as twenty years ago. Although these reports vary considerably in their degree of rigor and objectivity, the better ones leave little doubt that the problems has grown worse in the early 1980s. Some explanations for this increase in hunger emphasize worsened economic conditions, while others blame cutbacks in public assistance. Both have undoubtedly played a role, but the relative degree of their importance is a matter of dispute. The higher poverty rates since

1979 clearly attest to a growing financial squeeze on lower income families. Also, starting in 1979, several steps were taken to limit eligibility and benefits for food and nutrition programs, culminating in sizeable reductions, in 1981. These were aimed at the least poor recipients; however, many of those affected were near to or below the poverty level at least temporarily. In consequence, while 68 percent of the officially defined poor participated in Food Stamps in 1980, this number had declined to only 59 percent of a much larger population in 1985 (Urban Institute, 1985).

Housing. The incidence of people living in physically substandard housing or overcrowded conditions has declined continuously and dramatically in the United States over the past four decades. By one criteria of physical adequacy, between 1940 and 1970 the percentage of all occupied housing units which were 'lacking complete plumbing facilities and/or dilapidated' decreased from 48.6 to 7.4. According to more recent surveys that entailed a broader and more stringent set of 'adequacy' criteria, about 11 percent of all occupied units were physically inadequate in 1975 and less than 9 percent by 1983. In 1940 over one in five households lived in units that provided less than one room per person. By 1970 the corresponding figure was less than one in twelve, and overcrowding has continued to decline as a problem since then (Congressional Budget Office, 1978; Irby, 1986).

Despite these remarkable gains in housing adequacy, serious problems remain for many low-income families and individuals and continue to grow worse in one important respect. Since the remaining physically inadequate housing is concentrated among low-income households, about one-fifth of the housing occupied by this population is still substandard or overcrowded. And a large and growing share of those who are able to live in physically adequate and uncrowded units (currently nearly half of the households in the bottom income quintile) do so only by spending more than 30 percent of their income on housing – a share that the federal Department of Housing and Urban Development (HUD) defines as 'excessive.'

The overall gains in housing adequacy over the past four decades were due largely to general income growth; however, federal policies have also contributed considerably through their role in the housing finance system, tax incentives for investment in housing, and the provision of direct housing assistance. Until recently all three federal policy approaches had been on an expansionary path for several decades; now all have been or are being curtailed. Tax incentives and the housing finance system, which overwhelmingly benefit middle and upper income households, have been of far greater overall significance in terms of fiscal and social consequences, than direct housing assistance, which is targeted on lower income households. For example, federal outlays on all housing assistance programs in 1985 totalled somewhat under $14 billion, whereas the estimated revenue loss from major housing-related tax expenditures was about $46 billion. The federal government has largely deregulated the housing finance system over the past decade and is in the process of reducing its role in housing loans and loan guarantees. Tax reform acts in 1981 and 1986 restricted the tax breaks for investment in housing in numerous ways. But it is the recent curtailment of direct housing assistance that is of greatest current concern, since serious housing problems are now essentially only a low-income phenomenon and concentrated particularly among the longer term, as opposed to the temporarily poor (Newman and Struyk, 1983).

Grounds for this concern can be seen in Figure 3. Before 1968, housing assistance to the lower income population was meagre, but from then through the 1970s it expanded rapidly. Numerous programs were involved but the important ones had two common characteristics: the subsidies were applied largely to units newly constructed to house low income tenants, and they were designed to limit the housing costs of eligible families and individuals to 20 to 25 percent of income. Unlike most other income security programs, this housing assistance has never been an entitlement. Sufficient funds were never budgeted to cover more than a small fraction, about one-sixth, of the eligible population. However, by the late 1970s, nearly five million urban and rural households were benefiting from such assistance programs, and an average of 400,000 to 500,000 new units were being added to this assisted group each year. In consequence, the portion of the eligible population being served was growing rapidly, and the growth in the number of low income households with housing problems slowed markedly. However, several chnages have occurred to housing assistance programs in the 1980s: the number of net new annual commitments has been sharply cut to about 150,000; they have been more tightly targeted to the poorest of households; and they have been shifted almost exclusively to existing units (i.e., the much more expensive new production is no longer being subsidized).[4] Although the latter two steps have lowered the average cost per household assisted, the dramatic cutback in new commitments means that the growth in assisted units has barely kept pace with that of the eligible population and has fallen behind the growth rate of low income households having to pay an excessive amount of their income for housing.

This discussion of housing so far has focused on occupied units. But not all Americans have a home. In the past few years there has been growing attention to the plight of the homeless. Various studies have estimated the size of this population to be from one-tenth of one percent to a full one percent of the total population – with the lower end of the range most likely

FIGURE 3: *Numbers of Very Low Income Household[a] with Housing Problems and of Total Housing Assistance Commitments Outstanding (millions of units)*

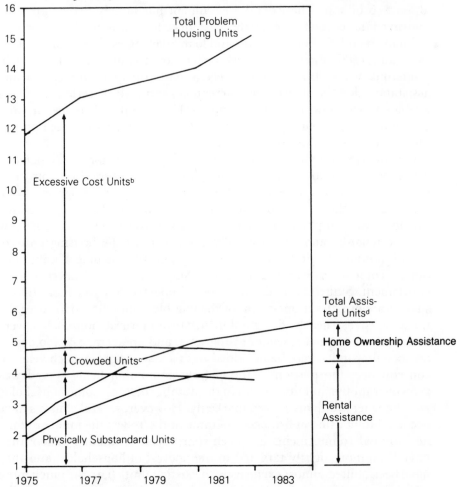

Sources: Iredia Irby, 'Attaining the Housing Goal?' Housing and Demographic Analysis Division, Office of Economic Affairs, Federal Department of Housing and Urban Development, July 1986. Marin D. Levine, Statement Before the Subcommittee on Housing and Consumer Interests, Select Committee on Aging, US House of Representatives.

a. Income at or below 50 percent of the median.
b. Units that cost more than 30 percent of monthly income if rented or 40 percent if owned. Does not include substandard or crowded units.
c. More than one person per room. Does not include physically substandard units.
d. This is the gross level of outstanding housing assistance commitments each year, not the net number of new commitments in the year. A small and declining portion of total assisted units are between 50 and 80 percent of median income level as new commitments are restricted to those under 50 percent.

correct (250,000 to 350,000 people) – but all agree that the numbers of homeless have grown rapidly over the past five years (United States General Accounting Office, 1985). Until recently the homeless appeared to be largely transients, alcoholics, addicts, and mentally ill persons; however, now a significant and growing portion appear to be less deviant personalities, including families with children, who simply cannot find affordable housing.

Health care. The best single measure of improvement in the population's financial access to health care is the extent of coverage of health insurance, whether it be publicly or privately provided. There are numerous public programs for financing (or providing) medical services, but Medicare and Medicaid, which were initiated in the late 1960s, are by far the most important. The Medicare program now provides basic hospital insurance for all people who are disabled or sixty-five or over and covered by Social Security and offers a highly subsidized supplemental medical insurance plan covering physicians services and certain other benefits. Under the Medicaid program, the states and the federal government share the costs of providing basic medical coverage to welfare recipients and, in many states, to the 'medically indigent' – those categorically eligible for cash welfare, but with incomes somewhat too high to receive payments.

A large majority of the population not covered by these two programs has private health insurance, generally provided through employers. The federal government subsidizes the purchase of this private health insurance through the tax system, primarily by exempting employers' contributions from taxation. The value of this exemption is substantial and has been growing rapidly in recent years with the expansion of employer-provided insurance. In 1985 it was over $20 billion, nearly the amount of federal expenditures under Medicaid. In contrast to Medicare and Medicaid, the vast bulk of these subsidies do not go to aged or low-income people.

The rapid expansion of Medicare, Medicaid and private insurance in the 1960s and 1970s resulted in a large decline in the share of the population that remained uncovered. By the mid 1970s virtually all of the aged had one or more of these types of health insurance, and the portion of the non-aged who did not dropped from over 30 percent in the early 1960s to just under 14 percent by the mid 1970s. Not only the coverage, but also the value of this health insurance increased enormously during this period, as a wider range of services and incresingly sophisticated medical technologies were covered.

In contrast to the "minimal adequacy only" aims of federal policies in the housing assistance and food areas, federal health care policy has long reflected higher public expectations: in particular, that the federal government ensure financial access for all to mainstream health care.

Despite these expectations, however, and despite the very substantial progress in the preceding decade, the country still fell far short of this goal in the late 1970s. The most glaring problems were: some 30 million people not covered by any health insurance plan, most of whom were in families with low incomes and/or unemployed heads, for Medicaid has never covered more than half the poverty population; the general lack of protection for catastrophic illnesses and for long term care except for the financially destitute under Medicaid; and financially burdensome out-of-pocket costs for even basic expenses under Medicare. But soaring public and private medical care costs were receiving increasingly political attention, and health cost containment superseded national health insurance as a public concern.

The subsequent cutbacks in Medicare and Medicaid have successfully slowed the growth rate of public expenditures on health care (though not the real rate of growth of overall health care costs), but they, in combination with events in the private sector, also have led to reduced financial access to medical services in the 1980s. For example, states have tightened up considerably on Medicaid coverage of the non-aged, and a higher percentage of the labor force is either unemployed or in jobs that do not offer health insurance. As a result, after holding steady at just under 14 percent from 1976–78, the proportion of the non-aged population without any health insurance has crept steadily upward every year since – to a current level of about 17 percent. Although Medicare and Medicaid continue to provide very substantial protection to the aged, the share of their income the aged have had to spend on medical care has also risen significantly.

Income Distribution

The degree of overall money income inequality in the US has followed a pattern somewhat similar to that of the poverty rate over the last 20 years. It decreased in the late 1960s (though far more modestly than the poverty rate), fluctuated in a narrow range through the first half of the 1970s and crept upward in the second half of the 1970s, then rose sharply in the early 1980s. This recent rise has resulted in an overall degree of money income inequality in the mid 1980s that is significantly higher than twenty years ago and which has not abated since the last recession.

The overall trend in income inequality also masks a very different experience for the aged and the non-aged since the late 1960s, mirroring the poverty story. Although the income of a typical aged family unit is still below that of the non-aged, the gap has been considerably narrowed. The ratio of aged to non-aged median income rose from .53 to .71 between 1967 and 1983. And although the degree of income inequality within the aged is still greater, it has declined dramatically over the past twenty years, while income inequality has increased to a nearly commensurate degree among the non-aged. Table 6 documents the changes between 1967 and 1983 in the quintile shares of aggregate income and a conventional measure (the Gini coefficient) of the overall concentration of income for the total aged and non-aged populations. Since these measures do not typically vary much over time, the shifts shown in the aged and non-aged measures are very large by historical standards.

What lies behind these remarkable shifts, and what role have income security policies played? Ignoring the possible effects of income security policies on the pre-transfer distribution of income, which are far more complex and ambiguous than the effects on pre-transfer poverty discussed earlier, we can answer these questions with a mix of facts and speculation. The relative income gains of the aged vis-à-vis the non-aged were clearly due to the strong growth over the entire period in non-earnings income on which the aged primarily rely, in contrast to the weak growth of earnings, on which the non-aged primarily rely, over much of the period. Income security programs were critical to this growth in non earnings income, since it was largely a result of the rapid expansion of Social Security. (High interest rates also played an important role, because the aged are the primary recipients of interest income.) The weak growth in earnings was due in part to the slow overall growth of the economy since 1973; however, the extremely large relative size of the baby boom age cohorts, who have been entering the labor market since the mid 1960s, also appears to have constrained their earnings potential (Levy and Michel, 1986).

TABLE 6: *Relative Income Shares and Index of Income Concentration for Family Units by Age of Unit Head, 1967 and 1983*[a]

Age of Unit Head	Year	Income Quintiles (Percent)						Index of Income Concentration[b]	
		Lowest	2	3	4	Highest	Total	Level	Percent Change
All ages	1967	4.7	11.0	16.9	24.1	43.0	100.0	.382	
	1983	4.2	10.4	16.6	24.5	44.3	100.0	.398	4.2
Under 65	1967	5.3	12.1	17.4	23.8	41.4	100.0	.355	
	1983	3.9	10.8	17.1	24.7	43.5	100.0	.392	10.4
65 and over	1967	4.6	8.8	13.3	21.5	51.8	100.0	.458	
	1983	5.6	9.9	14.9	22.7	47.0	100.0	.406	−11.4

Source: 'Changes in the Money Income of the Aged and NonAged', *Studies in Income Distribution*, Social Security Administration, 1986.

[a] The incomes underlying these data are adjusted for size of family unit (using the poverty thresholds equivalence scale) and change in the age distribution of family unit heads between 1967 and 1983.
[b] Gini-coefficient.

The reasons for the changes in the income distribution within each group are easy to explain for the aged, but more elusive for the non-aged. The greatly reduced inequality among the aged is the result of the decline in the importance of earnings, which are extremely unequally distributed, and the increase in the importance of Social Security, which is far less unequally distributed. The growing inequality among the non-aged reflects a growing inequality of earnings that outweighed the offsetting influence of cash transfers during their expansionary phase and was then reinforced by the reduction of cash transfers in the 1980s. The puzzle, however, is exactly what accounts for this pattern in earnings. While it is impossible to quantify the relative contributions, some of it appears to be grounded in demographic change – e.g., the rapid growth in younger workers and female family heads whose earnings are low – and some of it in the generally slack labor market, since lower wage workers tend to do relatively worse in periods of higher unemployment. But these two factors do not seem sufficient; there is also some evidence of growing inequality in earnings that *may* be related to structural change in the American economy, such as the increased foreign competition for goods and services produced by low-wage workers and the related shift in employment from the manufacturing to the services sector.

Our discussion so far on the distribution of income has been based on pre-tax, post-transfer cash incomes. How would our previous conclusions be modified by taking into account taxes and in-kind transfers? The short answer is little. The distribution of total tax burdens in the US is relatively equal and has not changed much over time. Depending upon what assumptions are made about the incidence of property and corporate income taxes, the distributional effects of the tax system in 1980 ranged from very mildly regressive to mildly progressive – causing an adjustment in the index of income concentration of from only −0.9 to 2.5 percent, in contrast to the distributional effect of cash transfers, which probably had an equalizing effect on the order of 15 percent or more (Pechman, 1985). More importantly, what small shift there was in distributing the tax burden over the past 20 years reinforced the trends in the pre-tax cash income distribution discussed above. The major change over the past twenty years has been decreased reliance upon the progressive property and corporate income taxes, which are more important for the aged, and increased reliance on the regressive payroll tax which is more important for the non-aged. Also, the large 1981 income tax cut was regressive. Going in the other direction is the fact that the 1986 tax reform largely relieves those below the poverty level from income taxations – but this just reinstates a condition that existed in the mid 1970s before inflation greatly eroded the value of the personal exemptions and standard deduction.

The inclusion in income of some measures of in-kind benefits makes more of a difference than consideration of taxes, but still does little to modify the earlier conclusions. By 1980 in-kind benefits had a significant equalizing effect on the overall distribution of income – probably about half that of cash transfers – and one that had grown over time. But most of this effect was on aged incomes; the aged receive the vast bulk of all in-kind benefits, as most of Medicare, about half of Medicaid and a sizable portion of housing assistance and Food Stamps expenditures are spent on them. Thus, it reinforces both the reduced inequality among aged households and the gain in the income of the aged vis-à-vis the non-aged reflected in the income statistics. In contrast, the equalizing effects of the expansion of in-kind benefits for the non-aged in the late 1960s and 1970s were quite small, and these are the benefits that have been cut the most in the 1980s.

The Prospects

When one stands back from the specifics in each area of income security, a broad pattern is evident. Strong progress was generally made with respect to all income security measures in the late 1960s and early 1970s, when there was both strong economic growth and highly expansionary public policies. This progress then slowed or stalled in the mid-to-late 1970s, as both economic growth and program spending slowed markedly. Finally, in the first half of the 1980s, with continued sluggish economic growth and contractionary policies, income security measures evidenced deterioration on virtually all fronts. Only when the aged and non-aged are considered separately is there significant variation from this pattern. The trends in poverty and income distribution for the aged were highly favorable over the entire period, whereas income inequality (though not poverty) grew within the non-aged population throughout the 1970s as well as in the early 1980s.

So much for the record. Now we consider the prospects over the next decade, both for income security policies and for the achievement of income security goals. The latter, of course, is critically dependent not only upon the former, but also upon the future course of the economy. And given the very pragmatic orientation of Americans to these affairs, the future of income security policies will be determined as much by what Americans, as a body politic, feel we can afford to do as by what we might desire to do.

On the one hand, if economic growth is as weak for the next decade as it has been so far in the 1980s (about 2 percent annually on average), there are hard times ahead for income security policies and goals. Such a rate of growth would not only be insufficient (in the absence of policy changes) to reverse the general deterioration in measures of income security in the first half of the 1980s, but undoubtedly would result in the continuation of this deterioration in most respects (replacement rates being the most notable exception, since they are fixed by law). Furthermore, severe fiscal austerity would continue to be the dominant theme for federal spending through the 1990s, since there would be virtually no growth in per capita real incomes and the currently large federal deficit (about 4 percent of GNP) would only decline appreciably with both major additional spending cuts and tax increases. Under these circumstances, further retrenchment in income security policies appears probable. Of course, a prolonged period of economic stagnation or recession could conceivably trigger a major expansion in the role of the state, as it did in the 1930s, but that is beyond the bounds of speculation here.

On the other hand, a return to the halcyon days of sustained strong economic growth, as in the 1960s and early 1970s (when annual real GNP growth averaged nearly 4.5 percent), would by itself reverse many of the undesirable recent trends in income security measures. In addition, there would soon be ample room once again in the federal budget for considerable expansion of income security policies without having to raise tax burdens. Such a prospect, however, currently appears well beyond the reach of the American economy. Most economists believe that the unprecedented accumulation of public and private foreign and domestic debt in the United States over the past five years poses continued problems for the economy in the immediate years ahead, and estimates of the growth rate of potential GNP tend to cluster under 3 percent per year.

The most likely outcome is that the economy will follow a modest growth path that is insufficient by itself to reverse the recent trends in income security measures. Under these circumstances, what can we expect to be the fate of income security policy? If history is any guide, we should not expect a return to the 1960's era of highly expansionary policies, nor further major contractions in the interest of promoting the 'rugged individualism' of an earlier era. Enduring characteristics of the American social and political landscape place very real constraints on our ability to move very far in either direction. The past decade has amounted to a testing of these constraints, and the verdict appears conclusive: the United States cannot swallow the colectivist notions of the public good embodied in Western European welfare states, but neither is it prepared to sacrifice the guarantees of primarily middle class economic security embodied in the New Deal and post New Deal programs.

The former proposition – that the United States is not, and never was, headed ultimately toward a true welfare state – I have argued extensively elsewhere (Palmer, 1986). Here let it suffice to note some of the abiding verities of American public life that preclude such a course: to wit, the widespread belief in the 'American dream' of individual opportunity, rejection of class-based politics and collectively orchestrated schemes of redistribution, suspicion of government power, and identification of personal freedom with private enterprise (Heclo, 1986). These distinctively American characteristics have conditioned public support for income security policies for decades and, in consequence, the political foundation for those policies is largely pragmatic, not ideological. Policies have been developed *ad hoc*, in response to particular social and economic problems, rather than in reflection of any widely shared vision of the just society. Even during the extremely liberal 1960s, successful politicians generally eschewed collectivist visions of the public good in favor of arguments that particular policies would help every individual and group to get ahead in a growing economy.

Thus, what is new about the Reagan era is not the President's credo: he has tapped an enduring current in the American public philosophy, and we should expect this current to continue to influence social policy in the United States after Reagan's departure. What has changed, however – and what makes any resumption of very expansionary social policies unlikely – is the terms of debate. What had been a matter of philosophical inclination has now acquired the lustre of practical wisdom, so that future advocates of expansionary social welfare policies will face a much heavier and more pragmatic burden of proof.

There are two prominent reasons for this shift in terms of debate. First, although still subject to considerable controversy, arguments and evidence that income security programs have undesirable incentive effects, which reduce their effectiveness in achieving income security goals and impose significant efficiency costs on the economy, have gained considerable credibility over the past decade. Even many of those who believe that the benefits of the income security system now in place greatly exceed the costs acknowledge that continued expansions will yield substantially diminishing benefits relative to costs. (For example, see Danziger et al., 1981.) Second, the federal budget deficit will still be a strong fiscal constraint with only moderate economic growth – and, much more than a constraint if there is slow economic growth. For example, even if there were to be no real growth in the defense budget, achieving federal budgetary balance in the early 1990s (as Congress is committed to do) would still require a combination of domestic spending cuts and/or tax increases of several percentage points of GNP relative to current policies (Palmer, 1987).

There are philosophical and economic reasons why there would not be a continuing overall retreat in income security policies under a regime of moderate economic growth. Simply put, Americans want the type of income security made possible by the public policies that they now have, and they feel they can afford it. These programs have been under an attack of growing intensity for more than a decade. What is most remarkable is not that they were finally cut back in the 1980s after expanding for so long, but how little they were cut back, given President Reagan's immense popularity, the generally artful orchestration of his administration's pursuit of its domestic policy agenda, and the ensuing strong fiscal pressures for retrenchment. *In fact, the basic structure of the income security system Reagan inherited is intact, with only some of the more dubious expansions of the past two decades trimmed away.*

One can conclude from all this that the conservative challenge of the past decade has served to clarify and consolidate a substantial consensus regarding the role of the federal government in income security. As a result, a broad scale reversal of that role appears even less likely now than it might have before the advent of the Reagan administration. Nor will the budgetary pressure accompanying moderate economic growth be sufficient to force this reversal. Congressional behavior over the past two years strongly indicates that the burden of eliminating the remaining deficit will fall primarily on the defense build-up and other parts of the domestic budget – and eventually a tax increase – and not on income security programs.

Having made these general observations about the broad boundaries for income security policies in the near future in the United States, I want to sketch briefly the concrete implications for particular policies and policy proposals. As usual, it is easier to spot the negative implications – that is, to rule out certain possibilities – than it is to predict positive outcomes. Thus, for example, we can say with some confidence that a re-emergence on the public agenda of national health insurance proposals is unlikely, as is the creation of entitlement programs for housing assistance (comparable to food stamps) or for long-term care (comparable to acute care under Medicare). Also improbable is the replacement of AFDC with a broader based income maintenance program (such as a negative or credit income tax or children's allowance) and anything approaching the-government-as-employer-of-last-resort. All of these issues were prominent on the liberal agenda at one point or another in 1960s and 1970s, and several were closely contested in Congress. Similarly, as far as contraction is concerned, we are unlikely to see wholesale delegation of the AFDC program to the states; the imposition of mandatory 'workforce' on all able-bodied welfare recipients; the total cessation of new federal commitments to housing assistance; or means-testing of Social Security and/or Medicare. These are all ideas that have been advanced in conservative quarters in recent years and, in some cases, recommended in Reagan Administration budget proposals.

Much more plausible than either of these sets of extremes are selective adjustments to existing programs in response to increasing public concern about the deteriorating conditions identified herein. Some of these adjustments may entail the modest commitment of new public resources. However, given the fiscal stringencies, they clearly will also involve a reorientation of priorities and a greater emphasis on the use of private resources, such as employer-based fringe benefits. In any event, the specifics of the changes will be far more reflective of traditional conservative concerns than were those of the 1960s and 1970s, and selective program contractions that do not appear to compromise vital income security goals will be necessary to help finance them.

The specific possibilities for new policy initiatives are obviously too numerous and complex to be examined in any detail here; the following list provides representative sampling of proposals already in circulation. It should be kept in mind that these initiatives raise many thorny issues – regarding the public vs. private responsibility, federal vs. state and local roles and the use of direct expenditures vs. incentives and regulation.

— Greater emphasis on work/training/retraining rather than income maintenance for the longer term unemployed and welfare recipients.
— Greater emphasis on initial family, rather than immediate public, responsibility for potential welfare recipients, such as strengthening legal obligations and enforcement for support of children by parents and grandparents (where the parents are minors), and for aged parents on the part of their children.
— Alterations in Medicaid, AFDC, and/or SSI to provide a more nationally uniform and adequate floor of income and health care protection to poor children and the aged.
— Greater emphasis on assisting the working poor and near poor through the tax system and other mechanism than 'welfare' programs.
— Federally-mandated provision of health insurance by all private employers which meets specific standards of adequacy.
— Modest expansion of new commitments to federal housing assistance, continuing the new emphasis on vouchers for existing units as opposed to new construction.
— Insured availability of catastrophic health insurance for acute care (and possibly some limited long term care) for the broad middle class.

Because many programs have already been pared to the publicly acceptable limits, there are far fewer candidates for contraction than for new initiatives in income security policies. Nevertheless, general budgetary pressures and the desire to free up resources for limited expansions may result in some continued cutbacks. The prime candidates here are reductions in public subsidies of pensions and health insurance for better off workers and retirees – i.e., greater targeting – and reductions in provider (i.e., hospitals and doctors) reimbursement in health care. Some major steps in this direction have been taken in the past two years, in response not only to general budgetary pressures but also to the perceived improvement in the economic status of the aged, the continued escalation of health care costs, and increasingly widely voiced concern about the impending fiscal burden of population aging. But more tightening could be in the cards for both public programs (e.g., Medicare, veterans programs, and possibly Social Security) and tax expenditures (e.g., employer contributions to health insurance) (Palmer and Gould, 1986).

Conclusion

Assuming my scenario for the next decade is more or less borne out, what does it imply for income security in the United States as the twentieth century draws to a close? Despite the very considerable progress in this century, it would still leave America with major problems, especially among the lower income population, and little consensus about how to deal with them. While we can hope that a resurgence of economic growth akin to the 1960s will eventually bring marked improvement in the underlying conditions, as well as facilitate more of a political consensus, this is only a hope. Meanwhile, we are likely to find ourselves in the painful process of accumulating problems faster than solutions.

Ironically, the United States, which has usually been characterized as laggard among OECD countries as far as social welfare policies are concerned, may find itself becoming a leader in some respects. Richard Rose has argued that American 'exceptionalism' should more appropriately be viewed as American 'distinctiveness,' since we share with other 'Pacific outlook' countries the common trait of relatively high wealth and relatively low (as a percentage GNP) public expenditures (Rose, 1985). In a recent analysis of income security issues, Colin Gillion documents that other major OECD countries also now share with us many of the deteriorating conditions identified earlier in this paper – e.g., slow economic growth, increased inequality of employment outcomes, highly constrained public budgets, and growing gaps in the present structure of support of income security programs – as well as growing concerns about the effects of high levels of public transfers on economic incentives and performance (Gillion, 1987). Gillion concludes by pointing out that, under these circumstances,

The policy options thus appear fairly limited. Some constraint on the growth of real benefits appears inevitable, coupled with a greater degree of discrimination, targeting or means-testing towards those in need and perhaps linked also with a greater degree of reliance on non-government pensions as a form of retirement provision.

If he is right (and I expect he is), then the United States experience may provide some useful lessons for other OECD countries about how and how not to respond to these new circumstances.

NOTES

1. It is difficult to discern the trends discussed in the text for the late 1970s and early 1980s in Figure 1, because they are obscured by periods of recession or very slow economic growth (in 1974–75, 1980 and 1982), which temporarily inflate income security program spending relative to GNP (since GNP drops below its trend growth rate and income security outlays rise in response to higher unemployment and lower incomes). Nevertheless, they are clearly evident when average real growth rates of spending are computed over multiyear time periods.
2. Some argue that in-kind benefits should not be counted, because the poverty threshold was originally established on the basis of cash income only; if in-kind income had been considered, the threshold would have been set higher. There are also difficulties in measuring the value of in-kind benefits, since they are often of less value to the recipient than their cost to the government. For a discussion of these issues and estimates of alternative methods of evaluating in-kind benefits, see Smeeding (1982).
3. The mean replacement rate considering only unemployed weeks in which benefits were received was 45.7 percent. When uncompensated weeks of unemployment (due to the time lag between application and receipt of benefits or benefit exhaustion) are also considered the mean rate drops to 39.1 percent (Vroman, 1980).
4. The eligibility standard for rental assistance was lowered from 80 percent of medium income 'low income' in the Department of Housing and Urban Development terminology) to 50 percent 'very low income'), with the subsidy only paying housing costs in excess of 30 percent of income. (Homeownership assistance standards are somewhat higher.) This shrinkage in the definition of the eligible population increased the proportion being served from about 15 to 25 percent.

REFERENCES

Andrews, E. (1985) *The Changing Profile of Pensions in America*, Washington: Employee Benefits Research Institute.
Bawden, D. L. and Palmer, J. (1984) Social Policy: Challenging the Welfare State. In J. Palmer and I. Sawhill (eds.), *The Reagan Record: An Assessment of America's Changing Domestic Priorities*. Cambridge, Massachusetts: Ballinger Publishing Company.
Congressional Budget Office (1978) 'Federal Housing Policy: Current Programs and Recurrent Issues,' Background Paper, Washington: Government Printing Office.
Danziger, S., Gottschalk, P. and Smolensky, E. (1985) The Effects of Unemployment and Policy Changes on America's Poor, *Journal of Social Policy*, 14(Part 3), July.
Danziger, S., Haveman, R., and Plotnick R. (1981) How Income Transfer Programs Affect Work, Saving, and the Income Distribution: A Critical Review, *The Journal of Economic Literature*, XIX, September, 975–1028.
Gillion, C. (1987) Social Security, Employment and Income Support in OECD Countries: Developments Since the Mid-1970s. Paris, Organisation for Economic Co-operation and Development (processed).
Gottschalk, P. and Danziger, S. (1984) Macroeconomic Conditions, Income Transfers, and the Trend in Poverty. In Bawden, D. L. (ed.), *The Social Contract Revisited: Aims and Outcomes of President Reagan's Social Welfare Policy*. Washington: The Urban Institute Press.
Heclo, H. (1986) 'Reaganism and the Search for a Public Philosophy,' In Palmer, J. (ed.), *Perspectives on the Reagan Years*, Washington: The Urban Institute.
Irby, I. (1986) Attaining the Housing Goal? Washington: Department of Housing and Urban Development, Office of Economic Affairs, (processed).
Levy, F. and Michael, R. (1986) An Economic Bust for the Baby Boom, *Challenge*, 29(1), March–April.

Newman, S. and Struyk, R. (1983) Housing and Poverty, *Review of Economics and Statistics*, 65(2), May.
Palmer, J. (1987) The Changing Structure of the Deficit, *The National Tax Journal*, Volume XXXIX(3), 1987.
Palmer, J. and Gould, S. (1986) The Economic Consequences of Population Aging, *Daedalus*, 115(1), Winter.
Palmer, J. (1986) Philosophy, Policy, and Politics: Integrating Themes. In Palmer, J. (ed.), *Perspectives on the Reagan Years*, Washington: The Urban Institute.
Pechman, J. (1985) *Who Paid the Taxes, 1965–85*. Washington: The Brookings Institution.
Physician Task Force on Hunger in America (1985) *Hunger in America: The Growing Epidemic*, Cambridge: Harvard University School of Public Health.
Plotnick, R. (1984) The Redistributive Impact of Cash Transfers, *Public Finance Quarterly*, 12(1), January.
Rose, R. (1985) *How Exceptional is American Government?* Glasgow, Scotland: Strathclyde. Studies in Public Policy Number 150.
Smeeding, T. (1982) *Alternative Methods for Valuing Selected In-Kind Transfer Benefits and Measuring their Effects on Poverty*. Bureau of the Census Technical Paper 50. Washington: Government Printing Office.
US General Accounting Office (1985) Homelessness: A Complex Problem and the Federal Response, Washington: Government Printing Office.
Urban Institute (1985) *The Effects of Legislative Changes in 1981 and 1982 on the Food Stamp Program*, Volume I. Washington: The Urban Institute.
Vroman, W. (1980) State Replacement Rates in 1980. In *Unemployment Compensation: Studies and Research Volume 1*. Washington: National Commission on Unemployment Compensation.
Vroman, W. (1985) The Aggregate Performance of Unemployment Insurance, Washington: The Urban Institute (processed).

6

The Refederalization of American Health Care

Barry G. Rabe

The endurance of a significant federal government role in health care into the late 1980s is remarkable, given the factors which seemed so likely to herald a new era of reduced central government involvement in health and countless other areas of domestic policy. Quite aside from the prospects for realignment and the overwhelming political success of a president with an abiding personal commitment to just such a "defederalization" strategy, spiraling health care costs and federal budget deficits seemed to augur not only a reduced role for the public sector in health care but, in particular, a reduced role for the central government. Health care was not a dominant issue in either the 1980 or 1984 election campaigns, but one congressional leader declared in 1981 that "Ronald Reagan's selection may have its most radical impact on the health care industry." This assertion may ultimately prove true, but if so it will be attributable to a transformation—and in some respects an intensification—of the federal role in health care, rather than a decided step away from federal involvement in the American health care system.

This resiliency of the federal government role in health care extends to all aspects of its relation with the nation's health care system, state and local governments, and health-related social and economic activity. This pattern encompasses federally funded and regulated categorical and block

From *Medical Care Review*, Vol. 44, No. 1 (1987): 37–63.

grant programs in health care, as well as direct federal regulation of health care delivery and public health functions such as environmental protection. It suggests an enduring role for the central government in health policy, albeit one that increasingly emphasizes cost containment rather than service expansion or equalization.

ATTEMPTING TO DEFEDERALIZE

The Reagan strategy to defederalize American health care consisted of three general lines of attack that, if fully accepted and implemented, would indeed have shriveled the involvement of the central government in the system. Each portion of the strategy succeeded in certain respects, but, as we shall see, the overall impact was reduced by a variety of institutional, political, and philosophical factors. Nonetheless, the very emergence of such a concerted effort to defederalize American health care constituted an unprecedented challenge to a concentration of central government authority that had accumulated gradually over almost a half-century.

DECENTRALIZATION

One aspect of this defederalization strategy stemmed from a perception that, to the extent the public sector could play an appropriate role in health care at all, its activities should be concentrated at subnational levels of government. In particular, many politicians and policy analysts in the late 1970s and early 1980s increasingly perceived states to be linchpins of the federal system and the logical focal point for public sector involvement in health care. The Reagan era version of decentralization thus differed from the local government orientation of the earlier Nixon administration decentralization efforts. This transfer of authority to state governments could be accomplished through a number of legislative changes, including outright dismantling of existing federal categorical programs and consolidating multiple categoricals into broadly defined block grants that states could allocate for multiple purposes. There was no more enthusiastic proponent of this multifaceted approach to decentralization than President Reagan, who explained in 1981:

> I have a dream of my own. I think block grants are only the intermediate step. I dream of the day when the federal government can substitute for [block grants] the turning back to local and state governments of the tax sources we ourselves have preempted at the federal level so that you would have those tax sources. (Cannon and Dewar 1981)

A variety of decentralization proposals were made during the first Reagan administration, including one recommendation for a grand swap of control over various grant-in-aid and entitlement programs accompanied by tax turnbacks, that was the centerpiece of his 1982 State of the Union address (McKay 1985, pp. 183–89). All of these were consistent with what David Walker, formerly of the U.S. Advisory Commission on Intergovernmental Relations, has characterized as "an almost wholly devolutionary approach . . . to achieving its prescribed cure of intergovernmental decongestion" (Walker 1983, p. 3). Health care programs were important components in all of these proposals, but they were not necessarily slated for the most far-reaching decentralization.

DEREGULATION

The Reagan defederalization strategy called for far more than shifting authority over programs of the central government to the states. Numerous proposals were made to weaken the capacity of federal bureaus and agencies that regulated both health care delivery and the social and economic activity which threatened public health. Health Systems Agencies and the certificate-of-need process as well as the health-related regulatory activities of such bodies as the Food and Drug Administration, the Occupational Safety and Health Administration, the Environmental Protection Agency, and the Federal Trade Commission faced a series of assaults. Vice-President Bush directed a task force charged with reversing or weakening those regulations perceived as most onerous to business and industry; individuals opposed to the basic mission of certain bureaus or agencies were appointed to leadership positions; and proposals were made to reduce dramatically funding for many organizational operations. All of these actions constituted an effort to reduce or eliminate the regulatory burden on many industries, including regulatory activity with a direct role in health care or with a direct impact on public health.

DEDISTRIBUTION

Both the decentralization and deregulation proposals had fairly lengthy periods of incubation. They were buttressed by a growing body of highly critical policy research and increasing public skepticism concerning the federal role in domestic policy that created a context in which far-reaching changes could be proposed by a popular national leader. Various decentralization proposals, calling for a shift from central to local government control, had been offered and some had been accepted during the Nixon administration, and deregulation was a popular topic during the Carter years. But the third aspect of the Reagan strategy was perhaps most novel and radical. Indeed, the mere mention of the idea of taking away benefits or entitlement to health care services for such politically potent constituencies as senior citizens was almost revolutionary. Governments are generally adept at creating and distributing governmental benefits, whether direct subsidies or services. The central government has no rival in the American context in this regard.

It is almost wholly inexperienced, by contrast, in "dedistributing" such benefits and services, particularly the transfer of them from politically important constituencies to such broad efforts as national defense improvement or deficit reduction (Light 1985). It is one thing, for example, to shift responsibility for a specific health care program from the federal government to state government (decentralization) or to weaken restrictions on the research and promotional activities of pharmaceutical companies (deregulation). It is another step entirely, however, to openly discuss reducing or eliminating direct forms of central government assistance to individuals through entitlement programs such as Medicare or Social Security. Although these types of alternatives were advanced more gingerly than other aspects of their defederalization strategy, various efforts of the Reagan administration attempted to legitimize serious consideration of dedistribution, whether through increasing the eligibility age for receiving Medicare and Social Security benefits or through even more radical proposals such as privatization of Social Security or transforming Medicare into a catastrophic-oriented or voucher-based program.

STEPS TOWARD DEFEDERALIZATION

The Reagan administration strategy to reduce the federal government role in health care has not been easy to adopt. Some decentralization, deregulation and dedistribution has occurred, but what is most striking about the federal system of the mid-1980s is how much it continues to resemble the system of the late 1970s. Although the first half of the 1980s was dominated by talk of fundamental political realignment and by the seemingly inexhaustible popularity of a president with an abiding commitment to transfer authority to state governments and the private sector, the central government role in health care remains substantial.

Defederalization efforts have not been entirely sidetracked. A number of changes have occurred during the 1980s, particularly in the first half of the first Reagan term, that reduced certain aspects of the central government role and seemed to set the stage for additional alteration of the federal role in health care. Some decentralization was accomplished, for example, through the consolidation of numerous categorical programs, many of which were highly restrictive, into new block grants that were intended to maximize state discretion in the use of central government dollars for health-related services. These changes paralleled in many respects the decentralization efforts of the Nixon years, in which General Revenue Sharing was established and major block grants were created for employment training and community development. The number of federal categorical programs shrank from 539 in fiscal year 1980 to 404 in fiscal year 1984. Health care categoricals were not exempt from this process: 21 programs were compressed into four new block grants that received significantly less funding than the combined costs of the earlier programs. Programs that had focused on high blood pressure, risk reduction and health education, venereal disease, immunization, fluoridation, rat control, lead-based paint poisoning prevention, and family planning services, for example, were consolidated into a Preventive Health Services Block Grant.

Many of the programs that survived consolidation were altered so as to give states greater influence over their operation. States gained considerable new authority over Medicaid, as federal policy changes enabled them to contract with less expensive hospitals and physicians; limit the service choices of program recipients; reimburse hospitals differently and at lower levels than before; decide who should receive coverage under optional eligibility categories; offer various community-based services in place of nursing home care; and more easily acquire waivers to experiment with alternative methods for service delivery (Altman and Morgan 1983; Freund 1984). The central government role in Medicaid funding also declined, as the federal share of program costs was reduced by 3.0 to 4.5 percent annually between fiscal years 1982 and 1985, and more than one million people were declared ineligible for Medicaid through legislated rule changes. Moreover, some have argued that the decentralization efforts of the Reagan administration have gone so far as to have "largely broken the link between the distribution of Medicaid funds and state compliance with federal Medicaid requirements" (Mashaw and Rose-Ackerman 1984, p. 114).

Some degree of deregulation was also achieved in the early 1980s. Health Systems Agencies were rendered impotent by substantial funding cuts, halting a major experiment in central government-sponsored health planning. The Reagan administration also took full advantage of its appointment powers to stock regulatory agencies and bureaus holding health-related duties with officials who were devoted to the cause of deregulation. This strategy had its most dramatic impact on environmental policy with the appointment of controversial figures such as Anne Gorsuch and

Rita Lavelle to the Environmental Protection Agency, but it also resulted in significant changes in the interpretation and enforcement of regulatory responsibilities in numerous other agencies and bureaus. The Office of Management and Budget gained unprecedented authority over the activities of health-related regulatory agencies in 1981 through Reagan's Executive Order 12291 that provided it with superagency stature and mandated cost-benefit analysis in the agencies.

Furthermore, seemingly impregnable entitlement programs of the central government such as Social Security and Medicare, which directly assist formidable political constituencies, were exposed to unprecedented dedistributive pressures. Policy change was particularly extensive in Social Security: the 1981 Omnibus Budget Reconciliation Act eliminated the minimum benefit for both new and current recipients and phased out benefits for postsecondary students 18 years or older, and the legislative package developed by the 1983 Bipartisan Commission on Social Security Reform authorized a gradual increase in the standard retirement age to 67 beginning in the year 2000 and the taxation of program benefits for high-income individuals and couples. The Medicare program escaped such extensive dedistributive changes, but both the hospital and physician deductibles were increased in 1982, among other modifications. In addition, the recommendation of the Bowen Commission on Medicare to raise the eligibility age to 67 and the mounting concern over the adequacy of the program's trust fund suggest continuing pressure for change. As R. Kent Weaver has noted, "the direction of entitlement policy choices has shifted; a long-term trend toward expanded eligibility has been reversed" (Weaver 1985, pp. 307–8). Health care entitlements were consistent with this pattern.

LIMITS TO DEFEDERALIZATION

These changes produced an American health care system that, in certain respects, was less central government-oriented but hardly transformed by the late 1980s. Despite all the forces that seemed to indicate not only health care defederalization but fundamental political realignment, the kinds of changes that have occurred are more the stuff of incrementalism than policy revolution. On the whole, relatively little shift of authority from Washington to state governments and the private sector occurred, and a number of developments suggest that the future role of the federal government in health care may stabilize or gradually increase rather than be decisively reduced. After exploring the failure to transform the federal role in health care, I shall consider the complicated set of factors that must converge for major shifts in policy to occur and how these factors did not converge (and are unlikely to do so) in this policy area.

LIMITS TO DECENTRALIZATION

There has been no grand transfer of authority or resources from the federal to subfederal levels of government in health care or in many other areas of domestic policy. Block grant creation, categorical program tinkering, and certain funding reductions notwithstanding, most of the major federal activities in health care have changed surprisingly little since 1980. This is consistent with the overall pattern of federal grants, since more than 80 percent of federal aid remains in categorical programs (Lovell 1985, p. 613) and the vast majority of regulatory provisions previously attached to those programs remain in force. David Beam, formerly of the U.S. Advisory Commission on Intergovernmental Relations, concludes that "the basic contours of the federal system are not markedly different. No real devolution of power has been accomplished" (Beam 1985, p. 589).

After early efforts at decentralization either trimmed, eliminated, or consolidated the most politically vulnerable and smallest health care programs, further changes proved more difficult to achieve. The health block grants encompassed fewer categorical programs, contained more funding, and featured far more regulatory restrictions than originally proposed. Many regulatory provisions normally attached to categorical programs were ultimately affixed to one or more of the new health care block grants, including "maintenance of effort" and "supplement not supplant" restrictions on funding usage, matching and reporting requirements, limits on expenditures for administrative costs, and citizen participation requirements. Although designed as vehicles for decentralization, these block grants borrowed heavily from their categorical, federally oriented predecessors.

Nor were these initial changes stepping-stones to more profound alterations of federal grants. The most ambitious decentralization strategy, the "New Federalism" proposed by Reagan, was not particularly threatening to the federal role in health care and, moreover, was politically stillborn. This proposal called for a swap of three major programs, with the federal government assuming full responsibility for Medicaid while states would take full responsibility for AFDC and food stamps. This component would actually have increased the federal role in health care, but would have been offset by a turnback to the states of some 61 federal programs as well as some of the revenues (tax sources) to pay for them. However, the proposal quickly dropped from political sight and no equally comprehensive scheme of decentralization has been forthcoming.

LIMITS TO DEREGULATION

The deregulatory fervor that transformed telecommunications, aviation, trucking, and other industries in the late 1970s and early 1980s had little transferability to social regulation. Health Systems Agencies and Professional Standards Review Organizations were phased out, but new and more forceful central government regulatory programs emerged at the same time. The federal government terminated subsidies to Health Maintenance Organizations, but continued to evaluate those seeking federal qualification status and devised new measures to stimulate enrollment in HMOs by Medicare and Medicaid recipients. The number of HMOs deemed federally qualified soared from 42 in 1977 to 128 in 1981 to 310 in 1985. Moreover, most aspects of social regulation linked to health remain largely unchanged. As the decade nears its end, any deregulatory momentum seems to have been reversed in favor of continued or intensified federal regulatory efforts.

Reducing regulatory competence through budget cuts and weakening commitment to regulation through appointment of officials opposed to the basic mission of their bureau or agency proved to be the principal Reagan approach to health-related deregulation. The Occupational Safety and Health Administration and the Environmental Protection Agency were particularly affected by this strategy. But, in the process, most of the legislation underlying the social regulatory activity of the federal government was never seriously challenged. Moreover, the adverse publicity attracted by some of the actions of controversial officials and the seemingly resilient public commitment to strong social and health regulatory policy triggered a political backlash that appears to have pushed serious discussion of health-related deregulation off the political agenda. Rather than being a "watershed in social regulation", this period has been characterized as "a detour on the road to regulatory reform" (Eads and Fix 1984, p. xiv).

LIMITS TO DEDISTRIBUTION

The steps toward dedistribution were profound in that they began to withdraw previously authorized federal entitlement benefits but were modest in impact. Some entitlement programs were significantly reduced during the first Reagan term, such as trade adjustment assistance, guaranteed student loans, child nutrition, and food stamps, but health care entitlements emerged relatively unscathed. During the period from 1975 to 1984, described by R. Kent Weaver as a time of entitlement "consolidation and retrenchment", health care entitlements continued to increase their share of the total federal budget, although at a declining rate from the prior decade (Weaver 1985).

Overall health spending by the central government has continued to increase since the late 1970s, driven by the growth of Medicare, Medicaid, veterans' care, and health research. It soared from $73 billion in 1981 to $109 billion in 1985, well above the inflation rate during this period. Even as national defense, Social Security, and interest payments consumed an ever growing percentage of total federal government outlays during the 1980s, the percentage of the budget devoted to health programs continued to climb. It grew from 10.1 percent in 1977 to 10.8 percent in 1981, reached a record 11.5 percent in 1985, and is expected to attain even higher levels in the late 1980s (Table 1).

TABLE 1   Health Program and Overall Federal Budget Outlays, and Health Program Outlays as Percentage of Overall Outlays, 1977–1986 (billions of current dollars)

	1977	1978	1979	1980	1981	1982	1983	1984	1985	1986[a]
Health care services	13.0	13.9	16.0	18.0	21.2	21.8	23.0	24.5	27.0	28.6
Health research	2.5	2.8	3.0	3.4	3.8	3.9	4.0	4.4	4.9	5.5
Education & training of health care work force	1.0	0.9	0.6	0.7	0.8	0.7	0.6	0.4	0.5	0.5
Consumer & occupational health and safety	0.7	0.8	0.9	1.0	1.0	1.0	1.1	1.1	1.2	1.2
Medicare	19.3	22.8	26.5	32.1	39.2	46.6	52.6	57.5	65.9	68.7
Hospital and medical care for veterans	4.7	5.3	5.6	6.5	7.0	7.5	8.3	8.9	9.5	9.9
Total health program outlays	41.2	46.5	52.6	61.7	73.0	81.5	89.6	96.8	109.0	114.4
Overall budget outlays	409.2	458.7	503.5	590.9	678.2	745.7	808.3	851.8	946.3	979.9
Health program outlays as percentage of overall budget outlays	10.1	10.1	10.4	10.4	10.8	10.9	11.1	11.4	11.5	11.7

Source: U.S. Office of Management and Budget, Budget of the United States Government, Fiscal Year 1987 (Washington, D.C.: Government Printing Office, 1986).
[a]Estimated outlays.

SIGNS OF REFEDERALIZATION

Defederalization was further mitigated by a number of developments that called for a greater central government role in health care. At the very time that decentralization, deregulation, and dedistribution initiatives were moving slowly if at all through the political system, federal involvement in health care was expanded or intensified in certain respects. This refederalization of American health care constituted yet another twist on what Thomas Anton has characterized as a "gradual augmentation of national government power" that has occurred since the New Deal (Anton 1984, p. 23). Rather than simply expand federal responsibility for health care service delivery or health regulation on an incremental basis, the federal government in the 1980s latched onto a significant new tool for guiding the health care system and assumed new areas of regulatory involvement.

The most profound development was the creation of prospective payment based on Diagnosis-Related Groups (DRGs) in the Medicare program in 1983. This regulatory tool gives the federal bureaucracy, subject to congressional oversight, the authority to establish in advance rates of reimbursement for hospitals that serve Medicare patients. Rather than transfer rate-setting authority to the marketplace (as would a deregulatory strategy) or to state government (as would many decentralization strategies), the DRG process gives unprecedented authority to the central government. The Department of Health and Human Services has used DRGs as the principal component of its strategy to contain Medicare costs. That strategy eschews withdrawing benefits from recipients in favor of applying pressure on service providers to make them work more efficiently. This new tool might have been used cautiously given the general anticentral government climate and Washington's traditional reluctance to disrupt providers, but DRGs have quickly become a cornerstone of the federal health care regulatory effort. James Morone and Andrew Dunham have noted that it "is striking how quickly federal officials began squeezing DRG payments to hospitals" (Morone and Dunham 1985, p. 277).

The long-term potential of DRGs for expanding and intensifying the central government role in health care does not lie merely in its current application to hospitals under the Medicare program. Morone and Dunham even suggest that DRGs could constitute a "slouching towards national health insurance", with this approach being gradually expanded to other areas, such as Medicare physician payments, Medicaid and, conceivably, all reimbursement to hospitals and physicians (Morone and Dunham 1985, p. 277). This would be entirely consistent with the gradual expansion of the central government role in health care over recent decades, with a new round of incrementalism launched from the starting point of DRGs now that the more traditional focus on expanding delivery of health care services to populations with special needs seems to have ended. DRGs may, in fact, epitomize a new form of health care regulation that involves both federal and state governments, in which regulatory approaches are designed to foster greater competition among service providers while relying heavily on governmental rules to establish and governmental officials to interpret the conditions under which competition may take place. They closely resemble many of the hospital regulatory programs devised by many state governments in the past decade (Brown, forthcoming).

The advent of DRGs has been accompanied by federal sponsorship of Peer Review Organizations (PROs) to monitor the quality of care provided to Medicare beneficiaries. Rather than simply peel away the procedures established previously through Professional Standards Review Organizations in pursuit of a reduced regulatory role, the federal government has established a more rigorous peer review process whereby PROs may refuse to authorize Medicare funding for hospital services deemed unnecessary and may determine in advance whether surgical procedures are appropriate for a patient.

Other new federal government regulatory efforts in health care extend beyond Medicare. Legislation signed into law in early 1986 established new federal requirements that prevent hospitals from rejecting emergency room patients or "dumping" them on other institutions out of fear that these individuals will be unable to pay their bills. Another provision of the same legislation requires an 18-month continuation of health insurance coverage for laid-off workers in firms with 20 or more employees. It also requires a three-year extension of coverage for families of workers who die. The recipients of the extended coverage would pay the premiums, but would do so at the lower group rate. Proposals to expand these new provisions will be considered in the One Hundredth Congress.

The federal government has also expanded its involvement in a number of regulatory areas related to health. Congress has been particularly emphatic about maintaining or intensifying the rigor of national environmental legislation such as the Comprehensive Environmental Response, Compensation, and Liability Act (Superfund), the Toxic Substances Control Act, the Resource Conservation and Recovery Act, and the Clean Air Act. Such legislation is drafted with increasingly specific deadlines and requirements and is routinely exposed to detailed interpretation by the federal judiciary.

Even the Reagan administration in some instances has abetted an expansion of regulatory authority. Among those efforts related to health, the administration has sought to expand federal authority over abortion, care of handicapped infants, interstate transport of hazardous products, and commercial use of hazardous substances such as lead and asbestos. It has also supported legislation to link full allocation of federal highway construction funds to states' acceptance of a 21-year-old drinking age. Additional central government involvement may be forthcoming in regulation of physician fees, organ transplants, medical liability, drug abuse control, and restrictions on the tobacco industry. And, in a move almost unthinkable in an era purportedly devoted to seeking noncentral government solutions to health care and health-related problems, President Reagan in February 1987 embraced a proposal to expand Medicare to cover the "catastrophic" costs of acute illness, and members of Congress have begun to explore even more expansive program alternatives. Alongside the generally modest results of decentralization, deregulation and dedistribution efforts, these efforts to increase the central government role further deterred any shift toward a defederalized American health care system.

THE IMPEDIMENTS
TO DEFEDERALIZATION

The signs of refederalization of American health care are all the more striking in contrast to the era of defederalization that appeared so likely in the early 1980s. Few periods in the twentieth century have loomed as such promising "windows of opportunity" for far-reaching change in public policy. The New Deal and Great Society were created when such windows opened, and the defederalized society envisioned by Ronald Reagan seemed within striking distance in early 1981 when he assumed office.

But policy formation, particularly when it involves major shifts of direction, is a complicated and difficult process. Analysts of this process have emphasized that various conditions must converge before policy formation can occur; a popular president with a popular message is not necessarily sufficient. Instead, political factors must augur well for new policy, ideas that are well grounded and widely accepted must be available for translation into specific policy proposals, a problem or crisis must exist to which a policy proposal can be attached and thereby legitimized, and skillful policy entrepreneurs must embrace the policy proposal and shepherd it through the formation process (Kingdon 1984). Without a convergence of such factors, policy formation is likely to be confined to tinkering with existing policies rather than making major shifts in course and taking dramatic new initiatives. In the case of the Reagan defederalization strategy, no such convergence took place. By contrast, it did

occur in the formation of the most significant federal health care innovation of the 1980s to date, the DRG-based Prospective Payment System
that may lead to an expanded central government involvement in health
care.

POLITICS

The principal political force behind defederalization was Ronald Reagan, but even his exceptional political popularity and skill were insufficient to defederalize American health policy. A president enjoys
considerable authority, especially early in a term, but that authority can
be extended to only so many policy priorities. And since that authority
normally wanes during a term of office, those priorities must be carefully
selected and adroitly pursued (Light 1982). Sensitive to these realities,
Reagan emphasized tax cuts, defense spending increases, and domestic
spending reductions. The last of these goals had some impact on health
care, particularly through program cuts made in the 1981 Omnibus Budget Reconciliation Act, but it also inspired the search for new regulatory
tools such as DRGs and PROs. Nonetheless, the defederalization strategy
was generally treated as a lesser overall priority, especially as applied to
health care. By the time Reagan proposed a New Federalism in his 1982
State of the Union address, he was engulfed in controversy over proposed
dedistribution of Social Security benefits, beginning to slide in public
opinion polls, facing a weakening economy, and about to lose his working majority in the House of Representatives. And even this sweeping
proposal would have traded a reduced federal role in certain health care
programs for a more dominant role in Medicaid.

Reagan remained supportive of defederalization, but more on the
margins than as a central policy priority. Even after the restoration of his
political popularity and his resounding reelection, Reagan did not place
defederalization high on his agenda. Not only had earlier attempts in this
area largely fizzled, but the president established other priorities such as
income tax reform and arms reduction negotiations with the Soviet Union.
He also faced a number of political setbacks, including the Iran-Contra
scandal, that impaired his capacity to set the national agenda as forcefully
as he had during his first term.

With less than robust political backing from the executive branch,
defederalization faced formidable political opposition. One of the most
important developments in American public policy in the last quarter-
century has been "the relative autonomy of political institutions" (March
and Olsen 1984). These institutions need not be dependent on social and
political developments such as electoral support or public opinion, and

can exercise considerable political influence, particularly in specialized areas where their expertise is unrivaled.

Whether one chooses to call the structured alliance of these institutions "subgovernments", "iron triangles", or "issue networks", they have proven to be well entrenched in federal health care policy. These health care institutions include congressional committees and subcommittees, federal and subfederal bureaucracies, and relevant pressure groups. After the policy breakthrough that facilitated the enactment of Medicare and Medicaid in 1965, "policy making in health became placid and routinized, with low public visibility and few disruptive controversies," according to Edward Laumann and his colleagues (Laumann, Knoke, and Kim 1985, p. 5). This pattern was particularly evident when these authors compared the process of policy formation in health care to the less institutionalized and more turbulent process of policy formation in energy, and it suggests that the health care policy process may be unusually resistant to significant change.

Congress proved to be a particularly formidable ally to the federal bureaucracy and pressure groups. The split-level nature of the political realignment in the 1980s left the House of Representatives in Democratic hands, assuring at least some continued commitment to the central government approaches that the Reagan administration found so unacceptable. But more important, the enduring fragmentation of congressional authority into dozens of committees and subcommittees in both chambers provided considerable protection for existing health care programs, institutions, and regulatory approaches (Davidson 1981). After committees had developed particular expertise in and influence over focused areas of health care policy, they were extremely reluctant to transform those areas and perhaps eliminate them outright. By the mid-1980s, the most influential federal policymakers in health care included congressional leaders of both parties, such as David Durenberger, John Heinz, Fortney Stark, and Henry Waxman, who used the committees and subcommittees that they chaired to offer policy alternatives that deviated significantly from those supported by the Reagan administration.

Many congressional committees minimized the impact of defederalization by accepting only those changes that were emphasized early by the Reagan administration. Granting the political imperative of cutting domestic spending in 1981, many committees used their authority under the budget reconciliation process to stretch required cuts over a large number of programs and agencies. In the process, they retained the authority to preserve most of the basic procedures and regulations for these programs. For many programs thus protected structurally in 1981 and 1982, Congress managed to restore in 1983, 1984, and 1985 some of the funding that had been cut and reinserted certain regulatory provisions that had been removed. The Ninety-eighth Congress proved particularly adept at using hearings to rally opposition to further cutbacks of health care programs designed to assist low-income groups.

The Reagan budget victory in 1981, therefore, was "more a triumph in his war against overall federal domestic spending than a successful strike against centralized federalism and the congressional structure that supports it" (Chubb 1985, p. 290). This was particularly true in health policy. And after Reagan's early domestic triumphs had had little impact on defederalization, the natural forces of declining presidential influence, congressional resilience to nonincremental change, Democratic gains in the 1982 and 1986 elections, and bureaucratic preferences for the prevailing order deflated any subsequent plans for decentralization, deregulation, or dedistribution in American health care.

IDEAS

The absence of ideas that were well accepted and readily transferable into viable policy proposals also undermined defederalization. Although critics of the prevailing federal order found it relatively easy to offer condemnation, they were much less effective in articulating comprehensible and politically acceptable alternatives. No clear strategy emerged that outlined the ways in which the Reagan administration intended to redirect the federal system. This was in marked contrast to the more careful idea development that guided Nixon administration efforts in redesigning federal grants and that brought issues of federalism to "a high point of conceptualization" (Palmer 1984, p. 21). Instead, defederalization Reagan-style was pursued in ad hoc fashion, using available political tools to scrape away federal authority where possible, whether trimming budgets of health care programs with the least political support or stocking regulatory agencies with officials who shared the administration's antipathy toward the existing system.

The importance of well-defined ideas in policy formation for defederalization is illustrated by the breakthroughs in federal economic deregulation that occurred in the late 1970s. Decades of research by political scientists and economists had revealed fundamental shortcomings in federal efforts to regulate various industries. This provided a solid base of ideas that legitimized radical deregulation of industries such as aviation, telecommunications, and trucking (Derthick and Quirk 1985; Page 1983). These changes had little if any impact on health care, but did illustrate that substantial defederalization was possible in which federal regulatory authority was eliminated in favor of competition.

It proved much more difficult to chart a federal social deregulatory course for public or semipublic goods such as health care and public health protection. Whereas the deregulated market could be relied on to provide an adequate supply of telecommunication services, the outcomes of health-related deregulation were much more unpredictable and potentially dangerous for society. It remains unclear just how a deregulated health care system or environment would function, largely because few coherent ideas have emerged that would explain or guide that change. There has been extensive discussion about devising market-based strategies to facilitate social deregulation, but most proposals remain opaque at best. As George Eads and Michael Fix (1984) of the Urban Institute observed:

> The problem is that no one knows what such legislation would look like. Economists have not yet met the challenge of specifying where and how their proposals could be implemented in sufficient detail to permit legislative changes to be drawn up. Neither have economists seriously addressed the ethical and political objections that have been raised to the use of market-like mechanisms. (P. 260)

And in the few instances in which such approaches have been attempted, such as emissions trading under the Clean Air Act, they have not performed as smoothly or effectively as theory would suggest (Liroff 1986). A number of years after federal economic deregulation has been implemented, drawing heavily on the ideas of social scientists, the ideas used to support social deregulation proposals remain too murky to be translated readily into policy.

The generation of mature ideas that would foster either decentralization or dedistribution has been similarly slow. Despite periodic discussion of a grand "sorting out" of intergovernmental responsibilities in health care and other areas of domestic policy, the analysis of intergovernmental relations and the proper distribution of authority among federal, state, and local levels of government have generally lacked any guiding theory or principles. Numerous reform proposals were developed in the late 1970s and early 1980s, including those advanced by the National Governors Association and the U.S. Advisory Commission on Intergovernmental Relations. Many of these advocated some sort of decentralization, but none offered a compelling set of alternatives. In an exhaustive review of the research on American federalism, Thomas Anton concluded, "To the extent that recent authors have contributed anything innovative, it is a new mood of pessimism, derived from largely implicit images of despair" (Anton 1984, p. 16).

The Reagan administration was generally sympathetic to many of these decentralization proposals, but its own pronouncements on federalism lacked, according to Claude Barfield of the American Enterprise Institute, "a set of guiding principles or criteria that add up to a coherent theory of federalism". Barfield, a leading advocate of decentralization, also emphasized that the Reagan administration "has proceeded in a piecemeal fashion and has not set forth . . . its long-range goals concerning federalism in any detail" (Barfield 1981, p. 62). Even the New Federalism Reagan proposed in 1982 did not deviate from this pattern, as the suggested set of changes were "simply another device for reducing federal spending" rather than a coherent effort to reorient intergovernmental responsibilities according to "criteria of economic efficiency, increased accountability, administrative rationality or equity" (McKay 1985, p. 202; Peterson, Rabe, and Wong 1986, chapter 1). The proposal treated health care and welfare policy as divisible among governments, concentrating responsibility for Medicaid in Washington, D.C. and authority for dozens of other closely related programs in state governments.

The emergence of ideas based on such criteria would not, of course, automatically lead to policy formation that reflected them, since so many other factors are involved in that process. But the absence of ideas that could be reshaped into viable policy proposals limited any potential impact for decentralization or deregulation. Ideas that might shape and facilitate dedistribution were also poorly conceptualized, as little systematic thought has been devoted to the ways in which well-established central governmental benefits are best reduced.

The approach to Social Security dedistribution in 1983 may offer some lessons, in that a fairly straightforward set of options consisting primarily of different ways to reduce benefits or increase taxes had been examined, their impact was readily quantified, and they were made available to a bipartisan national commission. This body received a clear charge to do something about the program's serious funding problem and included an unusually powerful array of elected and appointed officials of the executive and legislative branches, who were allowed to forge a compromise during proceedings that were unusually secretive for the post-Watergate era (Light 1985). Although this may be a more effective method for dedistribution than simply hacking federal spending in certain programs, it does not provide a clear understanding of who deserves what from the federal government. Without coherent, well-accepted ideas to guide those decisions, dedistribution, like deregulation and decentralization, is not likely to go far.

PROBLEMS

Policy formation also requires the emergence of serious problems, often a crisis, to which ideas can be offered as a solution and around which political forces can coalesce. Kingdon has characterized such problems as "triggering events" that lead to a search for solutions and often result in new policy (Kingdon 1984). Just as problems of communicable disease triggered an expanded governmental role in public health in prior generations, new problems such as the alarming spread of acquired immune deficiency syndrome (AIDS) today prompt considerable governmental activity at federal, state, and local levels.

But what was the problem that would trigger an effort to defederalize American health care? The cost of health care was indeed high and growing rapidly, attributable in part to federal programs such as Medicare and Medicaid. But the very nature of the American health care system obscured many of these costs to the consumer. And while public opinion surveys showed considerable concern about the cost of health care, the American public has repeatedly demonstrated satisfaction with the care that it receives and has not perceived rising costs as a leading national problem. Opinion surveys also indicate that the public does not want any government-sponsored changes in the system to disrupt the care that is available (Blendon and Altman 1984). They further suggest that most Americans are opposed to deregulation in areas such as environmental health and dedistribution in popular programs such as Medicare and Social Security (Mitchell 1984).

It is difficult to discern any widespread perception that health care is a problem-laden area in need of extensive defederalization. In fact, since national health insurance has ceased to be a seriously considered issue, there has not been a single, attention-riveting problem in health care or federal health care policy that would trigger far-reaching defederalization. Those who bemoan "supermarbleization and hyperintergovernmentalization", deem the federal system to be "out of control" (Walker 1981) and advocate defederalization may strike a responsive chord with those who have to fill out complicated forms to obtain funding through federal programs or to comply with program regulations. Likewise, those who deem federal budget deficits to be long-term threats to economic well-being may be supportive of dedistribution. But these problems have not proved sufficient to attract extensive political support, to launch a search for policy ideas, or to culminate in far-reaching new steps in health policy formation.

To the extent that major problems or crises have emerged since 1980, they are likely to lead to greater or continued federal and subfederal authority rather than less. Insofar as policy has changed at all in response to the continuing growth of total health care costs and government budget pressures, it has involved expanded and intensified regulation at both the central and state government levels. The mounting environmental health concern triggered by toxic substances and hazardous wastes has put enormous pressure on legislators and regulatory officials to expand and intensify central government involvement. This problem has led to extensive state and local activity too. Furthermore, the widely publicized problems of America's poor, particularly the homeless and unemployed, have made it politically difficult to consider further reductions in federal health care and other programs that assist them. Even the leading grants-in-aid reform proposal currently on the national legislative agenda, the proposed Federalism Act of 1987 that follows the recommendations of the Committee on Federalism and National Purpose, would give the central government virtually complete responsibility for funding Medicaid, expand the scope of services and eligibility for the program, and also create a major new program in long-term care. In turn, many programs would be eliminated or consolidated, but the vast majority of these do not involve health care.

POLICY ENTREPRENEURS

A fourth component of policy formation—skillful and influential policy entrepreneurs who can pull together politics, ideas and problems into new policy—was also lacking in the case of defederalization in American health care. Whereas the formation of Medicare was attributable in part to entrepreneurs such as Lyndon Johnson and Wilbur Cohen and airline deregulation was attributable in part to the entrepreneurial talents of Alfred Kahn, no such leaders emerged to guide the various components of defederalization.

The most obvious and potentially influential entrepreneurs were too occupied with other business to champion such change. President Reagan was the most likely entrepreneur, given his long-standing opposition to a substantial central government role in health care and most areas of domestic policy. Having opposed the enactment of Medicare in the 1960s, for example, Reagan supported radical revision of the program as an off-and-on presidential candidate in the 1970s. But Reagan was too devoted to the leading issues on his agenda, particularly income tax cuts and a national defense buildup, to focus consistently and intensely on health care defederalization. To the extent that domestic budget cuts became a political necessity as the budget deficit soared, Reagan was somewhat more involved. But he was never willing to risk much political capital in such an unpopular area, particularly when it came to cutting popular programs with large middle-class support, including Medicare, Veterans Administration health care, and medical research.

At the same time, those Reagan lieutenants directly responsible for advancing defederalization were among the least politically effective members of the administration. Potential entrepreneurs of defederalization in health care, such as cabinet-level officials and regulatory agency heads, lacked the stature and political skill necessary for the task. Department of Health and Human Services secretaries Richard Schweiker, Margaret Heckler, and Otis Bowen were not particularly influential members of the Reagan cabinet. Among leaders of health-related federal agencies and bureaus, Anne Gorsuch at EPA, Frank Young at FDA, and Thomas Auchter at OSHA had neither the political credibility nor the skill to guide a deregulation revolution. By contrast, the real policy entrepreneurs of the Reagan administration, such as James Baker and David Stockman, devoted relatively little effort to health care. As discussed earlier, the most influential entrepreneurs in federal health care policy during the 1980s were congressional leaders of both parties who did not share the president's defederalization vision.

Policy entrepreneurship for defederalization was similarly lacking at the state level. A chorus of senators, representatives, governors, and state government associations had long railed at the strings attached to federal programs in health care and other areas of domestic policy, as well as the central government role in health-related regulation. But, with the possible exception of former Arizona Governor Bruce Babbitt, who proposed a grandiose swap of federal and state functions rather than an across-the-board reduction of federal responsibility, no particularly influential entrepreneurs emerged to steer a defederalization strategy to formation. Dedistribution was particularly unpopular once discussion shifted from generalities to specific program cuts, and state political leaders— potential entrepreneurs—were chary about staking their careers on proposals to accumulate new health program and regulatory responsibilities at their level of government. Governors played a particularly decisive role in scuttling the Reagan New Federalism proposal, deeming it to be fiscally disadvantageous to the states.

Ambitious state programs in hospital cost containment, which could ultimately be meshed with Medicare DRGs, were the biggest exception to this pattern. Indeed, the policy process that produced DRGs, initially as a Medicare demonstration project in New Jersey and later on a nationwide basis, was driven by a convergence of the very factors that were missing in defederalization. Policy entrepreneurs in state and federal governments, including legislators and bureaucrats, were skillful in transforming the basic ideas in DRG-type reimbursement into a workable policy proposal that might improve on the dismal track record of past governmental efforts to contain costs. Officials of the New Jersey Department of Health during the Brendan Byrne administration, particularly

Commissioner Joanne Finley, were instrumental in developing the DRG proposal and acquiring the federal agency and state legislative support needed to put it into operation.

In 1982, Congress ordered the Department of Health and Human Services through the Tax Equity and Fiscal Responsibility Act to devise a prospective Medicare reimbursement reform that responded to the mounting problem of program costs. The Health Care Financing Administration within HHS proposed a variant of the New Jersey DRG experiment that it had funded in the 1970s, and Congress acceded in remarkably short order (Morone and Dunham 1985). HHS Secretary Richard Schweiker quietly gained the support of key congressional leaders and moved the proposal quickly past a hospital industry that was divided on the issue. The House Ways and Means Committee, with the leadership of chairman Dan Rostenkowski, drafted the bill and gained full committee and House approval in one day. The Senate Finance Committee and then the Senate also approved a similar bill, which was signed by the president in April 1983, less than two months after the House action. There was minimal discussion and controversy in either chamber of Congress over this far-reaching reform, and a handful of legislators, working closely with HHS officials, were instrumental in this rapid policy formation process. In short order, the political, idea, and problem factors crucial to policy formation converged, pulled together by both elected and nonelected health care officials who demonstrated considerable political acumen and influence.

RAMIFICATIONS OF REFEDERALIZATION

The failure to defederalize American health care serves as a reminder that far-reaching institutional change is more easily said than done in American politics. It also suggests that health care occupies a distinct place on the national political agenda that may protect it from rapid policy shifts. Health care rarely emerges as the dominant domestic priority of the president or the Congress. It is unlikely that any president or major congressional leader will risk his or her reputation with an all-out effort to transform the federal role in health care, given other pressing issues. Thus, it will be rare for health care to receive the kind of political attention, and the devotion of scarce political resources, necessary to facilitate far-reaching policy change, except under very unusual conditions, such as those that led to the creation of DRGs.

At the same time, even if health care were emphasized as a high-priority agenda item, perhaps central to some future effort to slash the budget deficit, it retains sufficient independent prominence on the national political agenda to resist substantial change. If not such a high policy priority as to be vulnerable to far-reaching change, health care is not such a low policy priority as to be easily swept away when political currents reverse. Indeed, most areas of federal government involvement in health care retain substantial legislative, bureaucratic, pressure group, and general public support. It is not surprising, therefore, that defederalization initiatives may have had the greatest impact in those areas of domestic policy with lower standing on the national political agenda, such as housing, transportation and nonnuclear energy, and those areas within health care with the weakest political support, such as small categorical programs for the disadvantaged (Peterson, Rabe, and Wong 1986, chapter 9). By contrast, the basic components of the federal government role in health care are likely to endure given its prominent but not preeminent place on the national political agenda.

If slow to change, federal policy toward health care should not be thought of as impervious to defederalization efforts. It may, in fact, be permanently influenced by the developments of the early and mid-1980s. These can be viewed as a series of opportunities lost as well as opportunities gained.

OPPORTUNITIES LOST: FAILURE TO
SORT OUT THE SYSTEM

The political mood of the early 1980s has not stimulated a thorough examination of the myriad activities of federal, state, and local governments in health care or rearranged them in a more orderly fashion. Even a clear shift of authority away from the central government is not evident. Lawrence Brown observed in 1984 that "no endorsement of devolution is sweeping American political culture" and "no orderly and principled devolution of federal activities is in prospect" (Brown 1984, p. 107). Such an assessment remains especially accurate in the context of health care policy. Where defederalization did occur it was not attributable to any careful examination of the ways in which central government resources and regulatory efforts might best be focused. Instead, defederalization advanced farthest where political opposition to change was weakest. The principal criteria for decentralizing categorical programs into new block grants was a minimum of political resistance rather than whether or not they were efficiently and effectively operated; deregulation was advanced primarily in those instances where political appointees could slow or impede regulatory activity rather than where Congress revised regulatory legislation; dedistribution was accomplished in those programs that were deemed politically vulnerable or for which a politically acceptable compromise could be struck rather than in those that were proven inefficacious. And, similarly, any steps toward an expanded and intensified federal government role in health care have occurred on an ad hoc basis rather than as part of any coherent strategy to redefine federal, state, and local responsibilities.

Without such a sorting out of functions, many aspects of the central government role in health care may have been cemented in, at least for the rest of this century. Many of the most pressing problems have received little attention. For example, rather than a period of sorting out responsibilities for Medicaid and more general consideration of providing health care for the indigent, the 1980s have been a period in which the federal and state governments remain at loggerheads over such matters. Neither level seems to know what to do differently, although the program has many serious shortcomings, including tremendous state-by-state disparities and huge gaps in eligibility among the lower-income population.

Future prospects for sorting out intergovernmental responsibilities for health care in a more rational way are dimmed not only by the missed opportunities of the early 1980s but also by the fiscal realities imposed by the enormous federal budget deficits. Deficit reduction is likely to dominate the national political agenda for at least the balance of the decade, and the pressures on the central government to contain spending place it in a poor bargaining position to entice state and local governments to explore ways to reorder intergovernmental relations. State government officials scorned the Reagan New Federalism proposals, for example, when they recognized that the plan was intended primarily to transfer numerous federal program responsibilities and relatively modest revenue sources.

OPPORTUNITIES GAINED: THE PRESSURE TO DEDISTRIBUTE AND THE SEARCH FOR INNOVATION

The impact of enormous budget deficits on the federal role in health care may, however, have far greater long-run consequences than complicating efforts to sort out intergovernmental responsibilities for various aspects of health care. They may eventually place unprecedented pressure on the president and Congress to dedistribute extensively. Such pressure, whether triggered by a Gramm-Rudman-Hollings type procedure, a Constitutional amendment to balance the budget, or an economic decline attributed to the deficits, may not hit all areas of the budget equally but will certainly not bypass health care totally. And the prospect of looming $100 billion deficits in the Medicare trust fund by the late 1990s may even make health care programs more vulnerable than other areas of domestic spending.

But while such pressure might ultimately open a window of opportunity to extensive dedistribution, including outright reductions in federal expenditures, it may also result in a more prudent central government role in health care. The federal government will have less money to spend, but political leaders are unlikely to extricate themselves from responsibility for popular programs such as health care for the elderly, less-popular but enduring programs such as health care for the poor, or social regulatory activities that are designed to protect health. This will trigger a search for new procedures that will maintain the quality of existing services and the intensity of current regulations, but at a reduced cost to the federal government. In particular, this more mature federal role may emphasize reduced deference to the providers of health care services while protecting the service needs of special populations.

The DRG system for Medicare may be a prototype of the future federal role in health care. Acknowledging limits to its resources, the federal government has deployed a mechanism that gives it unprecedented leverage to set priorities—and to influence the direction—in American health care on the basis of the reimbursement levels it chooses to establish for various medical procedures. DRGs give the federal government unprecedented authority to ration health care, which has hitherto been unthinkable in the American political context (Aaron and Schwartz 1984). Already applied to hospitals that serve Medicare patients, further use of DRGs by the federal government in the future could lead to a far-reaching expansion of its role in health care. States could further increase their involvement in this process, whether through continued innovation in hospital cost-containment programs or adoption of DRGs in Medicaid. But without an exclusively state-funded health care activity that rivals Medicare in scope, and given the fact that combined state and local expenditures per capita for health are less than half of federal per capita expenditures, states will lack the leverage of the federal government in this area.

DRGs are not the only possible tool for refederalization in American health care, however. What is striking about virtually all of the major proposals for far-reaching change in health care is that they call for an extensive, and often expanded and intensified, role for the federal government. Quite aside from more traditional proposals to expand the coverage of populations with special needs, even those proposals explicitly intended to foster individual choice among service consumers and competition among service providers are heavily dependent on the federal government to determine the rules of the game. The various versions of the health care voucher plan proposed in the early 1980s by David Stockman and Richard Gephardt, for example, would have the federal government prescribe the number and kinds of services that would be required in a minimum health plan, and establish eligibility requirements and funding levels for vouchers. Similarly, Alain Enthoven's Consumer Choice Health Plan for universal health insurance also established a procompetitive strategy on the basis of "more intelligent use of government". Under this plan, the federal government or states under federal standards would oversee a system with open enrollment and community-rating procedures, minimum service packages, premium rates set by market area, catastrophic expense protection, and mandatory disclosure of information (Enthoven 1980, pp. 126–30). Such a system, or others like it, might indeed foster competitive efficiency and ease the pressures of dedistribution, but it would rely heavily on the regulatory skill of the federal government. Other options include prevention-oriented strategies, including new or expanded forms of health-related regulation. It is not clear, however, that any of these are likely in the short term to meet the conditions necessary for policy formation, as long as political obstacles are particularly substantial.

As the federal government searches for new mechanisms to carry out dedistribution, it will also have to address the issue of intergenerational transfer of resources. The reduction in the proportion of the elderly population below the poverty line is widely acknowledged as one of the great triumphs of programs such as Social Security and Medicare. Some have argued that this achievement has come at considerable cost to younger Americans, with public sector funding that might have been directed to the health care, education, and social welfare needs of children and young adults transferred into entitlement programs for the elderly that are indexed to the inflation rate (Preston 1984). As the Baby Boom generation matures, an extraordinary imbalance could occur with too few workers to support too many retirees while maintaining economic growth. In this situation, the federal government may have to devise new mechanisms for continuing to assist the elderly while spending less in the process. Rather than achieving a bigger or smaller federal role in health care, the ultimate challenge increasingly will be to find the most effective federal role.

ACKNOWLEDGEMENTS

I would like to thank Lawrence D. Brown, Paul E. Peterson, and two anonymous reviewers for their comments on earlier versions of this article.

REFERENCES

Aaron, H. J., and Schwartz, W. B. (1984). *The Painful Prescription: Rationing Hospital Care.* Washington, D.C.: Brookings Institution.

Altman, D. E., and Morgan, D. H. (1983). "The Role of State and Local Government in Health," *Health Affairs* 4 (Winter): 7–31.

Anton, T. J. (1984). "Intergovernmental Change in the United States: An Assessment of the Literature." In *Public Sector Performance: A Conceptual Turning Point,* ed. T. C. Miller, 15–64. Baltimore: Johns Hopkins University Press.

Barfield, C. E. (1981). *Rethinking Federalism: Block Grants and Federal, State and Local Responsibilities.* Washington, D.C.: American Enterprise Institute for Public Policy Research.

Beam, D. R. (1985). "After New Federalism, What?" *Policy Studies J.* 13 (March): 584–90.

Blendon, R. J., and Altman, D. E. (1984). "Public Attitudes about Health-Care Costs: A Lesson in National Schizophrenia," *New England J. of Medicine* 311 (August 30): 613–16.

Brown, L. D. (1984). "The Politics of Devolution in Nixon's New Federalism." In *The Changing Politics of Federal Grants,* by L. D. Brown, J. W. Fossett, and K. T. Palmer, 54–107. Washington, D.C.: Brookings Institution.

———. (forthcoming). *Health Regulatory Politics.* Washington, D.C.: Brookings Institution.

Cannon, L., and Dewar, H. (1981). "Reagan Asks $48 Billion Budget Curb," *Washington Post* (March 10).

Chubb, J. E. (1985). "Federalism and the Bias for Centralization." In *The New Direction in American Politics,* eds. J. E. Chubb and P. E. Peterson, 273–306. Washington, D.C.: Brookings Institution.

Davidson, R. H. (1981). "Subcommittee Government: New Channels for Policymaking." In *The New Congress,* eds. T. E. Mann and N. J. Ornstein, 99–133. Washington, D.C.: American Enterprise Institute for Public Policy Research.

Derthick, M., and Quirk, P. (1985). *The Politics of Deregulation.* Washington, D.C.: Brookings Institution.

Eads, G. C., and Fix, M. (1984). *Relief of Reform? Reagan's Regulatory Dilemma.* Washington, D.C.: Urban Institute.

Enthoven, A. C. (1980). *Health Plan: The Only Practical Solution to the Soaring Cost of Medical Care.* Reading, Mass.: Addison-Wesley.

Freund, D. A. (1984). *Medicaid Reform: Four Studies of Case Management.* Washington, D.C.: American Enterprise Institute for Public Policy Research.

Kingdon, J. W. (1984). *Agendas, Alternatives, and Public Policies.* Boston: Little, Brown.

Laumann, E. O.; Knoke, D.; and Kim, Y-H. (1985). "An Organizational Approach to State Policy Formation: A Comparative Study of Energy and Health Domains," *American Sociological Review* 50 (February): 1–19.

Light, P. (1982). *The President's Agenda.* Baltimore: Johns Hopkins University Press.

————. (1985). *Artful Work: The Politics of Social Security Reform.* New York: Random House.
Liroff, R. A. (1986). *Reforming Air Pollution: The Toil and Trouble of EPA's Bubble.* Washington, D.C.: Conservation Foundation.
Lovell, C. H. (1985). "Deregulation of State and Local Government," *Policy Studies J.* 13 (March): 607–15.
McKay, D. (1985). "Theory and Practice in Public Policy: The Case of the New Federalism," *Political Studies* 33 (June): 181–202.
March, J. G., and Olsen, J. P. (1984). "The New Institutionalism: Organizational Factors in Political Life," *American Political Science Review* 78 (September): 734–49.
Mashaw, J. L., and Rose-Ackerman, S. (1984). "Federalism and Regulation." In *The Reagan Regulatory Strategy: An Assessment,* eds. G. C. Eads and M. Fix, 111–45. Washington, D.C.: Urban Institute.
Mitchell, R. C. (1984). "Public Opinion and Environmental Politics in the 1970s and 1980s." In *Environmental Policy in the 1980s: Reagan's New Agenda,* eds. N. J. Vig and M. E. Kraft, 51–74. Washington, D.C.: Congressional Quarterly.
Morone, J. A., and Dunham, A. B. (1985). "Slouching Towards National Health Insurance: The New Health Care Politics," *Yale J. on Regulation* 2 (No. 2): 263–91.
Page, B. I. (1983). *Who Gets What from Government?* Berkeley: University of California Press.
Palmer, K. T. (1984). "The Evolution of Grant Policies." In *The Changing Politics of Federal Grants,* by L. D. Brown, J. W. Fossett, and K. T. Palmer, 5–53. Washington, D.C.: Brookings Institution.
Peterson, P. E.; Rabe, B. G.; and Wong, K. K. (1986). *When Federalism Works.* Washington, D.C.: Brookings Institution.
Preston, S. H. (1984). "Children and the Elderly: Divergent Paths for America's Dependents," *Demography* 21 (November): 435–57.
Walker, D. B. (1981). *Toward a Functioning Federalism.* Cambridge, Mass.: Winthrop Publishers.
————. (1983). "A Perspective on Intergovernmental Relations." In *Intergovernmental Relations in the 1980s,* ed. R. H. Leach, 1–13. New York: Marcel Dekker.
Weaver, R. K. (1985). "Controlling Entitlements." In *The New Direction in American Politics,* eds. J. E. Chubb and P. E. Peterson, 307–41. Washington, D.C.: Brookings Institution.

7

The Pedagogy of Competition

Murray L. Weidenbaum,
with Richard Burr and Richard Cook

During hard times, steps are often taken that provide the basis for future expansion. These include cost-cutting, product and process innovations, and other productivity-raising moves that help to turn the tide. The United States is experiencing such a period right now, and there are three key forces that make a period of sustained prosperity in the 1990s more likely: (1) a variety of actions that reduce the cost of producing goods and services in the United States; (2) new awareness of personal responsibility for the quality of what Americans produce, and (3) more rapid growth in investments in research and development, the basic fuel for innovation and technical progress.

Reducing Costs

For a variety of sensible reasons—most notably to keep up with foreign competition—many American business firms have taken actions during the past several years that reduce the domestic cost of production. These actions range from simple changes in production methods to a basic restructuring of the business firm. Since compensation of employees constitutes about two-thirds of the cost of producing the nation's output, labor costs are a natural starting point for cost cutting.

The measurable changes that are occurring in the labor market are dramatic. For example, the 54 strikes involving 1,000 or more workers in

From *Society*, Vol. 25, No. 1 (November/December 1987): 46–54.

the United States during 1985 were the fewest since 1947, when the Labor Department first began compiling such statistics. In addition, the 324,000 workers involved in the strikes was the lowest number of strikers on record. While the history of labor-management disputes in the United States since the end of World War II has shown both ups and downs, the American economy is now enjoying a sustained period of domestic labor peace.

More fundamentally, competitiveness has been enhanced by the substantial slowing of the rise in nominal wage costs. In 1980, the average worker in the private sector in this country received a 9.0 percent wage increase. By 1984, the average annual increase was down to 4.1 percent. Perhaps surprising to the proverbial man in the street, this change also turns out to be beneficial from the workers' viewpoint. In real terms (after boiling out the effects of inflation), the average worker in 1980 suffered a 0.2 percent decline in real wage rates. In contrast, 1984 witnessed a real increase of 0.3 percent—a modest change but in the desired direction. The downward trend in nominal wage costs was similar in both manufacturing and nonmanufacturing sectors.

The pace of negotiated wage increases in union agreements has slowed visibly. During the past four years, some groups of workers have actually experienced wage cuts. For example, in 1980, 71 percent of the workers covered in major collective bargaining settlements received an annual wage increase of 8 percent or more. By 1985, only 4 percent of the workers were in that category—and 26 percent received no increase or actually suffered a decrease. Looking ahead, the Conference Board's Labor Outlook Panel is forecasting a modest 3.6 percent overall increase in average hourly earnings in 1986.

Some analysts see a further shift in the relative bargaining power of management and labor resulting from greater use of contingent employees. For example, companies that are trying to respond to rapid market changes, especially those caused by foreign competition, are increasingly using temporary and employee-leasing arrangements. Contingent employees also serve as a buffer to protect the security of regular employees.

While management negotiations with unions are stabilizing labor costs, import penetration has sparked a war on other costs. In addition to holding down the cost of labor, firms are attempting to get more for the labor dollars they do spend by improving productivity. More flexible work rules and improved worker attitudes are two of the more important methods being used.

Loosened work rules can generate important savings in the production process. The traditional way was to have narrow job classifications, with each employee performing one task. With new agreements to perform a number of different tasks, fewer workers are required, or the same number of workers can produce more. Also, there is less downtime due to waiting for a worker with the right classification. This illustrates one among many efficiencies—large and small—which, in the aggregate, can result in substantial increases in productivity and hence competitiveness. For example, a Chrysler plant in Indiana has reduced labor costs by 30 percent or $2.8 million a year by getting workers to agree to perform tasks outside their crafts. Goodyear has signed a pact that allows the 429 craftsmen at its Alabama plant to work outside their trade as much as 25 percent of the time if necessary. General Motors successfully negotiated with its Manville, Ohio, union to eliminate jobs such as machinists' "tool chasers." Having machinists get their own tools and other changes raised productivity in one stamping plant by 26 percent.

Work-rule changes also have saved money in the petroleum industry, where refiners report that output per worker increased by more than 10 percent in recent years. One oil company, American Petrofina, merged six classifications into two at one refinery, cutting the work force by 25 percent. The move saved $4 million a year.

Some companies have attempted to improve worker attitudes on the reasonable assumption that more motivated workers do better quality work. At Jones & Laughlin, a major steel maker, a labor-management participation team analyzes production problems and suggests ways of improving efficiency. The company saved $75 million in 1982 largely because of employee suggestions and work force cutbacks that resulted in the remaining workers being assigned more duties.

The Harley-Davidson Motor Company is also making great strides. Although the motorcycle maker has been protected by high tariffs, those tariff rates will decline automatically to 4 percent in 1988 from the 24 percent level levied in 1985. The prospect of dwindling protection has caused the company to adopt Japanese management techniques that are partially responsible for making it profitable again. Indeed, Harley-Davidson has attracted executives from other companies to its monthly seminars on efficient management. The firm has sharply decreased absenteeism by maintaining an open-door policy with workers and discussing employee complaints. Costs of fixing motorcycles on warranty have plummeted as a result of a new commitment to quality, the company says. This experience is not unique in American industry.

Tough negotiations with labor can cause backlashes. United Airlines pilots, angry because they believe the company tried to break the Air Line Pilots Association during a twenty-day strike in 1985, are reportedly wasting fuel. A veteran United pilot told a reporter that an "awful lot of pilots are burning more gas. We're not interested in saving money for the company any more."

Several American companies have adopted the Japanese just-in-time inventory system in which components are provided as needed instead of having large batches made in advance and stored. Harley-Davidson, for example, reports that the system freed $22 million previously tied up in inventory at a York, Pennsylvania, plant alone and dramatically reduced reorder lead times.

A Chrysler plant in Fenton, Missouri, also is using the just-in-time approach. The system cut its inventory to $20 million from $29 million, resulting in about $1 million a year of savings in interest costs. Reduced inventory also has meant less damage to parts from overcrowded storage conditions.

One of the most ambitious production improvement efforts to date is the General Motors Flint Assembly project, which is converting a sixty-year-old complex of unrelated component manufacturing and auto assembly plants into a 500-acre integrated production facility. The Flint Assembly Complex builds, virtually under one roof, most of the major components needed for the front-wheel drive vehicles that replace the Buick LeSabre and the Olds Delta 88. The work performed includes engines, transmission components, and complete bodies. In effect, steel blanks for body construction enter at one end of the plant and finished cars leave at the other. Previously, partially completed automobile bodies were built at a body plant on the other side of town and shipped to the final assembly location.

A key element at Flint is the just-in-time system of inventory management. The complex operates without the usual safety net in a conscious effort to force discipline into a manufacturing system that formerly operated with convenient, but expensive, fallback positions. If a quality problem now arises in any part of the system, it must be corrected immediately. Otherwise, the entire production operation may grind to a halt.

As might be expected, considerable investment is required, especially in the company's work force. Between 4,000 and 5,000 employees are receiving training in new technical skills in three Flint-area educational institutions. Building on the on-going Quality of Work Life program, union officials participated in the planning of Flint Assembly throughout its development.

Each of the major auto producers is pursuing joint ventures with Japanese and South Korean companies as a long-term way of cutting costs on small cars. Proponents of this approach defend it as a way of saving some American jobs, while opponents view such out-sourcing as "exporting" of jobs. General Motors has at least four separate agreements with

Japanese and South Korean affiliates to supply up to 500,000 cars a year to its United States dealers. Ford has contracts pending with Japan's Mazda Motor Corporation and Korea's Kia Industrial Company. Chrysler has signed ventures with Mitsubishi Motors and Samsung Corporation.

The American steel industry is seeing the benefits in a similar arrangement. National Steel Corporation, which is half-owned by Nippon Kolan, has enhanced its productivity. In the first year of Japanese involvement, National Steel increased the amount of prime finished product made from molten steel by 3 percent. National Steel's president, Robert McBride, estimates that a 1 percent increase in product yield adds $20 million to the company's profitability.

Caterpillar Tractor Company, the world's largest manufacturer of heavy construction equipment, also has learned this lesson. The company reached its goal of slashing costs by more than 20 percent by the end of 1985, a year ahead of schedule. It has reduced its work force by one-third and increased the number of parts it acquires from outside. Caterpillar's efforts seem to be paying off. The company reported a fourth-quarter 1985 pretax profit of $87 million, compared with a loss of $251 million for the same period in 1984.

Simultaneously, the composition of new capital spending by American industrial firms has shifted away in large measure from additions to productive capacity and toward replacement of existing machinery and facilities with more efficient equipment. For example, the outlays for new plant and equipment devoted to computers and instruments rose from $28 billion in 1970 to $142 billion in 1983. Such changes curb the unit cost of production rather than expand the total amount of product.

In some cases, the use of new technology can result in products manufactured more efficiently than at modern foreign plants. One ton of steel production at Chaparral Steel is estimated to use 1.8 man-hours, whereas the Japanese on average require 2.3 man-hours. Another steel maker, Timken Company, invested $500 million in an advanced mill in the midst of the last recession. The new facility makes better quality steel for its tapered roller bearings, the antifriction devices Timken invented.

Price reductions forcing cost containment have emerged as the dominant way that American firms respond to import pressures, but it is clear that they rely on other approaches simultaneously. In addition, there are many variations on the price or economizing approach to meeting foreign competition. For example, in the auto manufacturing industry for many years operations had been based on achieving economies of scale via high-volume, long-running production with fairly rigid product specifications. Because economies of scale emphasized large factories and standard product design, changes in the product could become expensive. Today, as a result of a shift to computer-based manufacturing, production can be based on economies of scope. This newer approach allows for low-cost, flexible production of a variety of products on the same automated equipment.

An extension of this economizing strategy is leading to important structural changes in a great many of the larger American corporations. The horizontally integrated firm, producing virtually every product in the markets in which it operates, is becoming less prevalent. Many companies are preferring to specialize, focusing on specific product niches that are secure against foreign competition. On reflection, this is to be expected as United States firms find themselves competing more fully in a global economy. Surely far fewer of our domestic markets can be properly thought of as part of a closed economy.

In an ambitious restructuring effort, General Electric raised about $5 billion since 1981 by selling off 155 divisions. Among them were their small appliance operation, which manufactures toasters and irons, and Utah International, a natural resource subsidiary. The company's new strategy is to move gradually away from traditional manufacturing and to focus instead on growth industries such as electronics and financial services. The $5 billion proceeds from its restructuring activities helped to finance its acquisition of RCA, a move strengthening General Electric's position in electronics and services.

The Union Carbide Corporation, a firm under severe pressure for many reasons in addition to foreign competition, also has undergone extensive restructuring. It has divested $500 million in what it now views as non-strategic assets and businesses, including its commodity-metals business and its European bulk-chemical, plastics, and polyethylene businesses. Carbide also wrote down other assets totaling $865 million, including petrochemicals, metals, and carbons segments. At the same time, the company built an industrial gases plant in Spain, acquired a consumer products business in France, and entered an industrial gases joint venture in Italy.

Companies also are combating imports with innovations in financing. Major United States car manufacturers have increased sales by providing low-interest-rate financing on new cars. In effect, this means squeezing profit margins in an effort to remain competitive.

A rapid rate of product innovation has also been emphasized. American shoe firms such as Timberland Company, Reebok International, and Rockport Company have responded with stylish footwear to ward off foreign competition. Even apparel manufacturing, one of the most import-affected industries, is using style to compete with low-cost foreign products. Companies such as RJMJ Inc. continue to make a profit selling women's pants and shorts through improved timing and greater flexibility of production. Whereas foreign apparel makers need at least six months of lead time to coordinate manufacturing with retail sales, RJMJ's president says his company "can turn on a dime. We can get piece goods to [our plants] in a day or two and produce products for the shelves in three to four weeks. That enables us to catch a trend."

Government actions to reduce the value of the dollar in world currency markets are helping American firms to compete more effectively both at home and abroad. Despite some softening in the dollar in 1985, the average value of the dollar in relation to other major currencies (the "trade-weighted" dollar) remains almost 40 percent higher than the level in 1980. This is the equivalent of a special 40 percent tax levied on American producers, exacerbating other cost differences with their foreign competitors.

There are many reasons for the strong dollar. Some of these are inherently favorable, such as the worldwide view that the American economy is a major safe haven for investors. There is little concern here about expropriation or the other arbitrary governmental actions that have occurred so frequently overseas and have increased the relative risk of investing in many other countries. But some of the reasons for the strong dollar are not so benign, such as the massive budget deficits whose financing has forced real interest rates up so high. That, in turn, has increased the foreign demand for dollars and in the process raised the "price" (or exchange rate) of dollars.

Recent governmental policies and actions have attempted to restore the United States dollar to its earlier exchange rate relationships. The passage of the Gramm-Rudman-Hollings bill represents a congressional and presidential commitment to eliminate the federal budget deficit by 1991. The specific budget cuts needed to achieve that goal have not yet been designated by the Congress or the White House.

Simultaneously, Secretary of the Treasury James Baker has embarked on an international cooperative effort to encourage the downward movement of the dollar in foreign exchange markets. A significant weakening of the dollar would enhance the effectiveness of the various private-sector strategies to restore the competitiveness of American firms and of the goods and services that they produce and sell. But lasting changes in exchange rates require more substantive actions than merely financial intervention by governments in international currency markets. Sustained improvements in monetary and fiscal policies are required.

Improving Quality

An important lesson that American companies have learned in recent years is that "Made in Japan" (or South Korea or Taiwan) is no longer synonymous with shoddy quality. In fact, the inroads of foreign competition into United States domestic markets have frequently been caused by the superior quality of the import rather than just lower cost. As a result, unprecedented pressure has been generated for improving the quality of products that American businesses manufacture.

A 1985 poll on product quality showed mixed results. In many product categories, American-made items were rated as being of higher quality than the corresponding import. Important examples of perceived United States superiority in quality included furniture, clothing, personal computers, appliances, and—by a smaller margin—automobiles. The survey also showed that 45 percent of the respondents viewed imported consumer electronics goods (televisions, radios, and video cassette recorders) as being of higher quality, while only 40 percent thought the same goods made in the United States were of higher quality. Many recent actions by United States companies to deal with the quality challenge demonstrate the feedback effects of our nonlinear economy.

Many United States firms are responding positively to the consumer preference for quality. For example, Steinway & Sons, the well-known piano manufacturer, facing rising competition from Yamaha and Kawai, has improved the quality of its pianos, which remain popular with concert pianists. The company proudly recalls that at a recent international competition, thirty-five of the thirty-seven Asian contestants performed on Steinway grand pianos. Despite increased imports, Steinway & Sons is forecasting increased sales. Steinway's president, Lloyd Meyer, contends that American manufacturers generally have rested too long on their laurels and allowed importers to equal them in quality—"I blame management for losing the quality edge."

Ignoring or deemphasizing quality can indeed be costly, as a Harvard Business School study of the air-conditioning industry demonstrated. David A. Garvin, in the 1983 *Harvard Business Review,* found that the failure rates of room air conditioners from the lowest-quality producers were between 500 and 1,000 times greater than those from the highest-quality producers. Garvin analyzed Japanese and American firms in an industry in which practically the same assembly-line processes and manufacturing equipment are used to make an essentially standardized product. Therefore, the staggering differences in performance between Japanese and American firms could not be attributed to differences in technology or capital.

Japanese companies were reported to be far superior to their United States counterparts in many measurable ways. The average United States assembly-line defect rate was almost seventy times that of the Japanese, and their average first-year service-call rate was nearly seventeen times the Japanese service-call rate. Products made by the worst Japanese company had an average failure rate of less than half that of the best United States manufacturer.

The key payoff of higher quality comes from the savings realized by avoiding the costs of reworking defective products or replacing defective parts. Garvin noted that "failures are much more expensive to fix after a unit has been assembled than before." In addition, customer complaints about products—even when they are subsequently replaced—often result in the long-term erosion of a company's customer base.

Westinghouse Electric is an example of a corporation that can show benefits as a result of emphasizing quality. It has established 2,000 quality circles involving 20,000 employees and a Quality College to foster participative management and quality training. The result has been that Westinghouse has averaged real productivity gains of 7 percent a year for three years in a row, 1982 through 1984. Thomas Murrin, president of Westinghouse's energy and advanced technology group, says such a result "means that every ten years you double your output without adding any resources."

Emphasizing quality has also profited Harley-Davidson. Management places more responsibility on the individual worker, coaching employees to evaluate their own work and improve the quality of the components. All employees receive forty hours of training in statistics so they better understand how to measure the quality of their output and improvements in it. These moves have caused a rise in defect-free motorcycles coming off the assembly line. Whereas 50 percent of the motorcycles were free of defects five years ago, 99 percent are now reported to be flawless.

High technology industry also is concentrating on quality. In 1980, Hewlett-Packard tested semiconductors from three American companies and three Japanese firms and found that the Japanese failure rate was one-sixth that of the United States producers. When the same test was made two years later, the American firms virtually had closed the gap.

America's automakers, long regarded as the epitome of old-line industry, are also making substantial strides. On a crash program to close the quality gap with their foreign counterparts, particularly the Japanese, domestic automobile manufacturers have been pressuring American steel manufacturers to improve their performance. Three years ago, for example, Ford was rejecting and returning nearly 9 percent of the steel it purchased from suppliers because of surface defects or faulty chemistry. Now that rate has been reduced to less than 2 percent.

One way of improving quality is to iron out the bugs in the assembly process before shipping the product. General Motors took this step in its new Wentzville, Missouri, facility. The announcement was unusual apparently because the company's—and the industry's—previous practice was to iron out these problems while continuing production. Quality problems in the past were thus passed on to the dealers and customers to avoid the huge cost of halting production.

Something similar occurred in the fall of 1985 in Ford's automotive operations in Dearborn, Michigan. Production was delayed because the rear doors were not meeting the rear fenders correctly. Ford executive Lou Ross was quoted as saying, "Ten years ago, confronted with the same problem, we would have built on the appointed day. Today . . . we start when we meet the standard."

The scene was repeated at a Detroit-area General Motors plant, where faulty Cadillacs and Chevrolet Caprices remained in the repair lots instead of being shipped to the dealers. "What really blows the mind of people today is that we won't ship cars if we don't have the quality right," says General Motors spokesman Clifford Merriott. Unintentionally repeating Ford's estimate, he adds, "There's no doubt that ten years ago we would have shipped those cars." "Ha! Ten years ago?" says M.L. Douglas, president of the United Auto Workers Local 22. "It's more like two years ago. . . . But people are beginning to realize that we just can't do things like that anymore." In retrospect, how could the average worker on the production floor have been expected to really care about quality when management appeared to be so indifferent?

Pushing faulty cars out the factory door also can be expensive. Chrysler learned that lesson when it tried to meet a deadline on the Plymouth Volare/Dodge Aspen models in the mid-1970s. "Not doing any galvanizing on the Aspen/Volare cost us $100 million because of rust," Chrysler's chairman, Lee Iacocca, says. The rest of the industry seems to have learned the lesson. Ford now allows thirty-six months from car design to production instead of the former twenty-eight months.

Auto companies also have improved quality through quick response to defects in parts. Chrysler's Fenton, Missouri, plant now corrects problems with parts in two days. A decade ago, the turnaround time could have been as much as twenty days.

Quality is not only important to American consumers, but especially to foreign consumers, notably the Japanese. Ocean Foods of Astoria, Inc., in Oregon has capitalized on the Japanese consumers' characteristic concern for higher-quality products, making Japan one of its principal markets. "They'll pay top dollar for your product, but only if it's of absolute top quality," says Grant Larson, vice president of Ocean Foods. "They are unmovable when it comes to quality control." Ocean Foods pays special attention to detail in its food processing to ensure mandatory quality control for the finicky Japanese. In the words of one senior executive of the firm:

When we catch the fish, they are eviscerated and stacked a precise way. Then the fish are flash-frozen. If the salmon aren't arranged this way prior to freezing, some of them will freeze at uneven temperatures. The flesh can become slightly discolored, or part of a tail will stick to the salmon below or above it and break off. If there is the slightest discoloration of the fish, or if part of the tail is broken off, forget it. You just won't sell that salmon [to the Japanese].

Other United States companies are apparently realizing the appreciation that the Japanese have for quality: the average consumer in Japan spends about $600 a year on American-made goods (the average United States consumer spends only $290 a year on Japanese products). Although few people in Japan had heard of Cross pens a decade or so ago, they have become a status symbol and are considered a most desirable business gift. Comparable results have occurred for other overseas competitors in Japan. Bondhus Corporation hand tools command 80 percent of the Japanese market even though five Japanese firms have lower prices.

The enhanced concern with improving quality in American industry has not been primarily a matter of setting up new quality-control departments or even expanding existing ones. After all, companies in the United States traditionally devoted far more resources to quality-control efforts than did their foreign counterparts. But quality assurance is more than just a collection of expensive scientific and professional personnel checking, reviewing and improving production practices. Producing quality requires emphasizing this aspect of the production process throughout the firm.

The air conditioner industry study we cited confirms this point. Japanese companies pay more attention to quality than many of their American competitors by means of such innovations as creating internal consumer review boards to evaluate the products. Another way the Japanese foster quality is by having top management hold daily review meetings about quality. In contrast, American firms with the lowest assembly defect rates meet ten times a month; the worst-quality United States companies average four such meetings a month.

Management's message was reflected on the front lines of production. First-line supervisors at four of six Japanese air conditioner manufacturers surveyed said quality was most important to management; their counterparts at nine out of eleven United States companies surveyed said meeting the production schedule was the highest priority. Management can communicate its emphasis on quality by paying attention even to small details. For instance, National Steel now requires workers to clean their work stations instead of leaving the task for janitors. The Japanese coowners, who suggested the policy, reasoned that if workers have enough pride to take care of their work stations, they might also care more for their product.

There is more to improving quality than just providing an example. For instance, Chaparral Steel Company uses an unusual but no longer novel approach to employee relations to ensure that workers put into practice what the company preaches: it practices egalitarianism in many aspects of its activities in an effort to improve output and quality. "We consider everyone to be line, there are no staff positions per se," says Chaparral's president, Gordon Forward. The company has no customer service representatives, for example. Production managers answer customer complaints. Forward says, "You ought to see how motivated they are to fix the problem when they come back."

The most effective quality controls involve, in effect, a shift in the locus of responsibility—from the inspectors in the quality control department to the employees who actually do the work. Pushed by foreign competition and the nonlinear nature of America's free market economy, many United States companies are discovering this way to achieve higher quality production.

Accelerating Research and Development

Even though many government officials occasionally wax eloquent about the science policy of the federal government, the United States lacks a comprehensive policy on the subject. Others can debate whether that is good or bad. What is relevant to this analysis is that the great bulk of research and development financed and sponsored by the federal government is not a result of deliberate actions to carry out a policy on "science." Rather, in most instances, it is more a matter of happenstance. Yet a shift in science funding has powerful effects on the competitiveness of American industry.

In the haphazard nature of science policy, the completion of the Man on the Moon project by the National Aeronautics and Space Administration (NASA) meant a reduction in that agency's budget. NASA devotes one of the highest percentages of expenditures to research and development among the federal agencies. NASA spent one-half of its budget on research and development in 1981, while the figure for the federal government as a whole was less than 5 percent. Thus, a shift in emphasis in the federal budget away from space exploration was simultaneously a move to downgrade the importance of science in the federal government.

Similarly, and of greater consequence because of its overwhelming size, the post-Vietnam cutbacks in the military budget meant a major decline in the volume of federal research and development funding—but not as a deliberate policy. The shift in emphasis in the federal budget during the 1970s from, so to speak, warfare to welfare meant a shift of resources away from the most research-and-development-intensive sectors of the budget. Simultaneously, a rapid expansion occurred in federal spending programs that involve the least amount of outlays for science and technology, notably the Department of Health and Human Services (in the form of transfer payments) and the Department of Agriculture (primarily price-support subsidies).

The massive buildup in United States defense spending begun in 1981 has ended the slowdown of federal research and development outlays that occurred in the 1970s. Now the largest dollar increases in federal expenditures are budgeted for the Pentagon, a part of the government that spends more than twice the proportion of its budget on research and development than the typical civilian agency. There is considerable controversy about the extent to which research and development spending by the military establishment benefits the civilian economy. Certainly not all military research and development has commercial applications. The United States has considerable negative experience with past attempts to apply defense technology directly to civilian uses.

A recent analysis of approximately 1,000 large United States manufacturing firms concluded that company financed spending on research and development is more productive than federally financed research. Presumably, the firm spends money on research and development to raise its productivity and profits, while government financed research and development is undertaken primarily to fulfill specific research contracts for which the firm is remunerated directly.

It does seem that subcontractors and supplying firms in the electronics and instruments industries, for example, have enjoyed considerable success in commercializing their defense financed technology. In contrast, the large aerospace firms have demonstrated only limited ability to diversify outside of aviation.

All in all, when the Department of Defense devotes an additional $100 million to applications of science and engineering in a half-decade, there is a great possibility that a larger stream of product and process innovation will occur in the years ahead. That possibility is reinforced by the Pentagon's current tendency to support technological advancement in areas having civilian applications, such as computers. For example, the Department of Defense recently awarded Carnegie-Mellon University a $103 million contract to develop and operate a software engineering institute. The bulk of the institute's work will be original, unclassified research, including development of better education processes for teaching software.

Although its main customers will be defense contractors, a second tier will include companies that build such commercial items as telecommunications and air traffic control systems. Moreover, some analysts contend that the Pentagon's Strategic Defense Initiative (SDI) (popularly known as Star Wars) will yield commercial applications in such areas as supercomputers, software, sophisticated sensors, and space technology.

High-yield supercomputers are useful in a wide range of scientific and industrial applications, including telecommunications, weather forecasting, medical research, and aircraft design. The need to automate SDI systems is also expected to advance commercial applications in the emerging field of artificial intelligence. Likewise, in order to meet the tracking requirements of the SDI, developments will take place in optical design and manufacturing that can have important civilian uses.

There is no need to jump to the conclusion that the most effective way of promoting scientific progress in the United States is to encourage a military buildup. Surely, the direct expenditure of these funds on civilian-oriented research and development, especially of a commercial orientation, would be expected to be far more productive; but the only time Congress will appropriate tens of billions of dollars on research and development in a half-decade is when it elevates national defense and such other research-and-development-intensive functions of government as space exploration and energy development to the top of the priority list. In 1984, for example, the Department of Defense spent $23.6 billion for research and development, the Department of Energy $4.7 billion, and NASA $3.5 billion.

In striking contrast, when Congress decides to be generous to science and technology per se, it expands the budgets of the major science agencies by only tens of millions or, at best, by several hundred million dollars. In 1984, the total budget of the National Science Foundation came to $1.2 billion. That year the Department of Commerce spent about $300 million on the Bureau of Standards and all of its other scientific activities. The Department of the Interior devoted approximately $400 million to the Coast and Geodetic Survey and other research and development bureaus. Also, federal funding for research and development tends to fall when income transfer programs are elevated to higher priority in the budget. In the case of the Department of Health and Human Services, research and development expenditures in 1984 comprised 1.5 percent of its budget (mainly for the National Institutes of Health).

It is far easier to measure inputs than outputs in science and technology. That is, we can more readily quantify the resources going into the performance of research and development than the new or improved products or processes that result. Nevertheless, several economists have attempted to estimate the overall rate of return from research and development performed in the United States in recent years. Estimates of its payoffs range widely. The lower figures usually are limited to benefits to the company performing the research and development, while the higher estimates include uses by the customers of the company and other firms. Surely, we would expect individual analysts to differ in their calculations. What is reassuring is that virtually all of the measured returns to research and development are impressively high.

The tax reforms of 1981 included a new tax credit for incremental research and development, an incentive in addition to direct federal spending in this area. Preliminary evaluations showed limited effects in terms of added private-sector research and development undertakings; however, the temporary nature of the tax credit was cited as an important limitation. The House of Representatives voted in December 1985 to extend the life of the tax credit but not to make it a permanent feature of the Internal Revenue Code.

Data published by the National Science Foundation show a rapid upturn in growth rates of both federal and private expenditures on research and development in recent years and thus an acceleration in total spending on it in the United States. During the four-year period from 1980 to 1984, federal spending on research and development in real terms (adjusted for inflation) rose 12.2 percent a year. This was a significantly more rapid growth rate than the 9.4 percent average for the preceding four years. During the same periods, private-sector-financed research and development spending rose at a greater rate—14.2 percent a year since 1980 and 13.9 percent annually in the prior four years.

Some of the specific instances of recent state and local investments in research and development are noteworthy. Since 1983, Michigan has invested more than $50 million in small, new companies. Three other states—Ohio, Illinois, and Indiana—have spent more than $250 million on programs for new, high technology entrepreneurs. In addition, the thirteen states of the Midwest Governors Conference each have contributed $250,000 to open the Midwest Technology Development Institute in Minneapolis.

There are already some promising indicators of the effects of the stepped up investments in research and development. According to the Federal Reserve Bank of Chicago, more than 15,000 companies make high technology equipment in the eight states bordering on the Great Lakes. At least 100 new companies specializing in biomedicine and computer software have located within fifty miles of the Mayo Clinic in Rochester, Minnesota. Based on experience, we can expect that recent investments in research and development will create some new product lines and perhaps even new industries with high growth potential.

This process of "creative destruction" described by Schumpeter implies that some industries will likely decline while others take their place. As pointed out by Sven Arndt of the American Enterprise Institute, in 1984 in *The AEI Economist,* domestic products that incorporate substantial amounts of research and development become competitive while more mature items are increasingly replaced by imports.

Thus, products with well-established design and production technology often can be manufactured more economically abroad by producers who acquire blueprints, technological know-how, and even factories in world markets. Their quality control is frequently superior, and a large part of the production costs is relatively cheap factory labor. High-priced workers in the United States using technologies that are available to their lower-cost competitors find it increasingly difficult to compete.

Investments in research and development constitute an important way in which American industry can hold its own in the face of virulent foreign competition. Improving process technology or offering new and superior products is a far more positive—and essentially more effective—approach than seeking government protection.

In many industries, designing and marketing new and better goods makes the future bright for an advanced economy such as the United States. That is, this country frequently maintains its competitive advantage in research-and-development-intensive industries. In most cases, product development and technological skills are listed by the Japanese as the keys to sales penetration by American firms. Thus, increased application of the fruits of science and technology to American industry is an important reason for expecting that today's gloom-and-doom expectations will turn into tomorrow's nonlinear economic recovery.

Outlook for the 1990s

The often-painful changes provoked by greater competition, at home and abroad, range from out-sourcing to reducing labor costs to fundamental corporate restructuring. Simultaneously, many United States firms are discovering that product quality rests primarily with the workers on the front lines of production rather than in quality control departments. At the same time, the expansion of military spending has resulted in an upturn in federal research and development that has powerful spillover effects in the civilian economy.

None of these three factors yields quick or dramatic changes. Yet the cumulative and interactive effects that they generate are likely to endure and to reinforce each other. Virtually all of the changes work in the same direction—toward generating new and better products that will result in more new orders; production; employment; income and profits for American investors, managers, and workers. These changes surely will not prevent the possibility of another recession during the second half of the 1980s; but they do make for a brighter outlook for the period beyond, that is, for the decade of the 1990s.

There is a reasonable basis for expecting that the ability of American firms to compete in world markets in the years ahead will be substantially improved. Likewise, the relative attractiveness of domestically produced products to American consumers should increase significantly. In the process, the real standard of living of the American people should rise noticeably.

We need to realize that the industrial sector of the American economy is far from being in the sad shape that many fear. In a journalistic version of Gresham's Law, it sometimes seems that bad news drives out good. It is not widely known that industrial production in the United States hit a new high in 1984 when the Federal Reserve's index reached 122 (1977 = 100). During 1985, the Index of Industrial Production reached a plateau averaging 124. In fact, manufacturing's share of the real gross domestic production has held steady for the last thirty years—at about 25 percent. Economic nay-sayers do not have a factual basis for their unallayed pessimism. Manufacturing in the United States is not going down the tubes, nor are we becoming a nation whose major employers are hamburger stands and clothing stores.

On the other hand, the positive developments we stress are not foregone conclusions. For one thing, foreign competitors can improve on their current strategies while United States companies try to catch up. Signs of such a development are showing in the automobile industry. While a *Wall Street Journal*/NBC News poll in November 1985 reported that the percentage of Americans choosing to buy foreign-made cars had declined from 25 percent to 21 percent, it also found that one-third of college-educated Americans and 30 percent of Americans under thirty-five years of age said they would purchase a foreign car. Automakers emphasize the importance of those groups: college-educated Americans tend to buy the most expensive cars and acquire them more frequently. Auto companies have also learned the hard way that if a young American's first car is foreign-made, it is harder to convince him or her to "buy American" in the future.

There is no certainty that America's Big Three car makers will succeed in closing the gap. Simultaneous with the improvements in United States automaking, Japanese motor vehicle manufacturers are becoming very different and more dangerous competitors. They are doing so by differentiating their products according to function, price, and appearance as well as size, attacking the American Big Three from many directions at once. The Japanese have increased the twenty-one nameplates and forty-six separate models made in 1980 to thirty-four nameplates and seventy-four separate models last year. "It won't be enough to have both fuel-efficient and high-quality cars," says Gerald Hirshberg, director of design at Nissan in California. "What's left is sheer creativity and agility that will dictate success and failure of new entries."

The Japanese are not the only competitors with whom American companies must deal. The South Koreans are pinning their hopes of opening United States markets to Korean brand products on the Excel, a subcompact car introduced in 1985. If the Excel is successful, it will add to the quieter successes of Korean-made products such as the Leading Edge D personal computer, which was the fastest-selling product in its industry during the last Christmas shopping season. In fact, Korean companies also have entered many United States consumer-goods markets, such as color televisions, as manufacturers for American brand distributors. "As the Japanese keep moving 'upmarket,' " says David Cole, Far East specialist at the Harvard Institute for International Development, "the Koreans can move in and take over."

Other countries also are improving their competitive positions, and the changing relationships at times may be indicative of future trends. For example, Korean construction companies—who have increasingly been giving their American counterparts tough competition in bidding on overseas projects—are now complaining about the low-cost rivalry from Turkish and Indian firms.

Further public policy changes that may not all be benign may hurt the chances of an improved economy in the 1990s. Pressures to reduce the budget deficit, for example, may result in raising the tax burden on saving and investment, reducing these basic factors for economic growth. Indeed, the tax reform bill that the House of Representatives passed in December 1985 eliminates the investment tax credit, reduces the research and development credit, and tightens up on depreciation allowances.

Should protectionist pressures succeed in leading to the erection of additional trade barriers, much of the resultant burden would be borne in the form of higher costs imposed on the industries using higher-priced protected inputs. United States export industries would be especially hard hit—and would be vulnerable to retaliation.

A new round of burdensome domestic government regulation would both raise the cost of compliance and deter companies from investment and innovation. Moreover, another shift in federal budget priorities—from defense to transfer payments—could dampen the upward trend of research and development spending. Yet the three key forces for enhanced competitiveness identified here appear to have considerable momentum, and the prospects for their durability are bright.

Our upbeat conclusion does more than merely take an optimistic position for the future. It relies on the powerful importance of feedback effects. The 1990s look good because downward trends tend, after a while, to be reversed in the nonlinear American economy. But that phenomenon also alerts us to another, related fact that is likely to be more germaine for the following decade: upward trends breed a complacency that erodes the progress made during the doldrums. That underscores a far more basic point: in change there is both opportunity and challenge.

8

The Morning After

Peter G. Peterson

In 1981 Ronald Reagan took the helm of a nation whose economy was reeling, with inflation in double digits, the prime rate hurtling past 20 percent, and the national spirit sagging into bewilderment. Today other countries gaze enviously over an American economic landscape that shows little trace of past convulsions and, indeed, seems to burst with new businesses, new jobs, new Dow Jones records, and a newfound confidence.

Yet, six years after the radical reforms of Reaganomics got under way, Americans are about to wake up to reality: for some time now the foundations of their economic future have been insidiously weakening. This awakening is currently being delayed by the widespread preoccupation with "competitiveness." Under the prodding of a trade balance in manufactured goods that collapsed from a $17 billion *surplus* in 1980 to a $139 billion *deficit* in 1986, including the first deficit ever in high-technology goods, and with additional shoves from a shaky dollar, from nervous financial markets, and from stagnating real wages, the so-called competitiveness problem is quickly climbing to the top of American's political agenda.

What does *competitiveness* mean? In many American households today it means worry about future living standards and about whether one's children, ten to fifteen years into their careers, will be able to out-earn their parents. In corporate boardrooms *competitiveness* means the executive nightmare of seeing Americans gorge themselves on goods from foreign firms.

From *The Atlantic Monthly*, October 1987, pp. 43–69. Reprinted with permission of author.

For many blue-collar workers *competitiveness* has an even crueler meaning: layoffs and the understandable desire to get even with the anonymous forces behind them. Over the past three years America's import deluge has resulted in pink slips for one to two million domestic manufacturing workers each year. More than a third of them remain indefinitely out of work; more than half the rest have taken pay cuts of 30 to 50 percent in new jobs that cannot make use of their experience. Economists are looking closely at this dislocation for signs of structural disintegration in U.S. communities, and of the decay of skills and habits that once made manufacturing an engine of U.S. comparative advantage in world trade.

In Washington *competitiveness* seems to mean both nothing and everything. Some senators advocated a speed limit of sixty-five miles an hour on rural highways as a "competitiveness" measure. House members are justifying yesteryear's jobs bills by renaming them "competitive adjustment programs." And lobbyists are arguing for stricter world cartels on everything from shoes to semiconductors on the grounds that such agreements will improve our "competitiveness." After announcing in its 1987 Economic Report of the President that recent U.S. performance in manufacturing has vindicated our competitiveness, the White House has refused to be upstaged on the issue, even going so far as to claim that the Strategic Defense Initiative is "pro-competitive."

Democrats are demanding that the Administration get back America's "rightful share" of jobs and wages through protectionist measures. If imports are cut back, they say, the jobs and income generated by producing for American consumers will be miraculously transferred from foreign to U.S. firms. Get tough on the *other* guys and *our* situation will improve—that seems to be the general idea. What all public statements on "getting back" our competitiveness neglect to mention is that Americans will have to give up something to get it back. Over the next few years policymakers will wake up to the true cause of our "competitiveness" predicament: the incalculable damage we have inflicted on our economy in recent years.

An x-ray of the damage would show its antecedents stretching far back in the past, across several Administrations. Our national preference for consumption over investment—the root malady—did not begin with the Reagan Administration. Still, that set of policies loosely known as Reaganomics has certainly worsened the damage. In the finest tradition of Euripidean irony, measures meant to save us have worked in the end to afflict us, so much so that even our nation's non-economic hopes—cultural, social, and strategic—have been clouded by our disastrous fiscal mismanagement. It has been a hard lesson in the law of unintended results.

Intent: From a decade of feeble productivity growth (0.6 percent yearly in the 1970s) and early signs of rising poverty rates, we entered the 1980s flush with expectations of "supply-side" prosperity. *Result:* We have ended up with still feebler productivity growth (0.4 percent yearly from 1979 to 1986) and, despite a debt-financed rise in personal income, with an upward leap in every measure of overall poverty. More important, we have witnessed a widening split between the elderly, among whom poverty is still declining, and children and young families, among whom poverty rates have exploded—a development with dire implications for our *future* productivity.

Intent: After a decade of worry about our low level of net private domestic investment (6.9 percent of GNP from 1970 to 1979) and an unsustainable real decline in the construction of public infrastructure, we wanted the 1980s to be a farsighted decade of thrift, healthy balance sheets, and accelerating capital formation. *Result:* We have ended up with by far the weakest net investment effort in our postwar history (averaging 4.7 percent of GNP from 1980 to 1986) and have acquiesced in the crumbling of our infrastructure. Moreover, far from renewing our saving habits or our balance sheets, or bolstering the "supply side" of our economy, the 1980s have turned out to be the most consumption-biased "demand-side" decade experienced by *any* major industrial country during the postwar era.

Intent: In 1980 American voters decisively endorsed a smaller and leaner federal government, with special exceptions for defense spending and for poverty-related "safety-net" benefits. *Result:* We ended up with a significantly higher level of federal spending in 1986 (23.8 percent of GNP) than we had in 1979 (20.5 percent of GNP)—with most of the growth concentrated in precisely what needed to be controlled: interest costs and entitlement benefits unrelated to poverty (or, to put it bluntly, welfare for the middle class and up). Federal interest payments on the national debt, $136 billion in 1986, are now equivalent to the total taxpayer savings originally projected from the 1981 income-tax cut. As for federal benefits doled out regardless of financial need, these have grown from about $200 billion in 1979 to $400 billion in 1986. They totaled $46 billion in 1968.

Intent: Entering the 1980s, we acknowledged that it was bad policy to allow federal outlays to exceed federal revenues (with deficits averaging 1.7 percent of GNP from 1970 to 1979). We promised ourselves to do better. *Result:* We made the gap between spending and taxes wide beyond precedent (with deficits averaging 4.1 percent of GNP from 1980 to 1986, and rising to 4.9 percent of GNP, or 90 percent of all private-sector net savings, in 1986). Our publicly held federal debt is nearly three times larger now than it was in 1980. The projected deficit numbers have improved somewhat, but the much heralded future declines are premised on very rosy assumptions—no recession, for example, and an interest rate of 4.0 percent.

Intent: Americans voted in 1980 for leadership that emphasized greater global competitiveness and freer world markets as the most advantageous means of achieving balanced economic growth. *Result:* America's steep decline in savings during the 1980s has precisely reversed our intentions. We were promised a $65 billion trade *surplus* by 1984; instead we suffered a $123 billion trade deficit. Today, despite four years of extraordinary luck on the energy front, we have managed to twist the global economy into the most lopsided imbalance between saving (foreign) and spending (American) ever witnessed in the industrialized era. In the process—as we all know—we have transformed ourselves from the world's largest creditor into the world's largest debtor. In reaction to this shift the rest was inevitable: a more than tripling (from about five percent to 18 percent) in the share of U.S. imports subject to quotas, a colossal about-face in public opinion away from free trade, and the appearance of the most blatantly protectionist bills before Congress since the days of Senator Reed Smoot and Congressman Willis C. Hawley—despite the President's free-trade convictions.

Intent: America came into the 1980s longing to strengthen its military defenses and to project its power abroad more effectively. *Result:* We now find that budget deficits and an evaporation of the public's pro-defense consensus are drawing an ever tighter circle around all our strategic options. Not only must we now replay the wasteful 1970s by cutting short production runs on dozens of weapons systems, but once again we are about to demonstrate to the rest of the world that America is incapable of sustainable long-term defense planning.

Intent: More than just a defense build-up, Americans wanted a more assertive, unilateral foreign policy, a way to make ourselves stand tall again in our leadership of the free world. *Result:* Our fast-growing debt to the other industrial countries has diverted our diplomatic energy into placating foreign central banks with exchange-rate agreements (already by May of this year the interventions to support the dollar amounted to a staggering $70 billion), into jawboning foreign governments to get their people to buy more of our exports, and into pawning off our Third World financial leadership onto more solvent economies. When action requires money, we now scrape our "discretionary" budget to procure the most meager support. We spend virtually nothing to try to avert the growing risk of social, economic, and political chaos right at our doorstep in Mexico. An additional $50 million was nearly considered too much to send to the Philippines after the 1986 democratic election of Cory Aquino. Even the Administration now publicly declares that our "foreign-affairs funding crisis" could mean "the end of U.S. global leadership." Eight years ago no one imagined an austerity-led shift toward U.S. isolationism. Now we're seeing it: an attempt to stand tall on bended knees.

Intent: Going into the 1980s, America's deepest wish was that renewed economic strength might foster a renewed cultural and ideological strength and an ethic of saving, hard work, and productivity. We wanted to replace malaise with a confident sense of forward motion. *Result:* As the ideological enthusiasm of 1981 has gradually been worn down by economic reality, this wish, too, has foundered, leaving many of our political leaders as defensive and uncertain as those of a decade ago—and almost relieved to have us fixated on public and private scandals.

While many in the Administration believe or act as if there is no problem—and hence no need for a solution—others want to avoid all association with the dreaded next act of the economy. The Democrats' fears show up in a darkly humorous story told by Democratic leaders: On January 20, 1989, after the inauguration, President Reagan flies off to Santa Barbara. While he is in the air, the stock and bond markets crash, the dollar plunges, and interest rates soar. When Reagan lands in Santa Barbara, he announces to a swarm of reporters, "See, I told you the Democrats would screw up the economy!"

For the time being, the competitiveness issue remains a sort of curtain that Americans have hung between Reaganomics and the future. Neither political party dares to disturb it, for it allows every policy leader to keep our attention fixed on the trivial. For example, we are told to get furious about the trade effects of Japanese "dumping" of semiconductors or enthusiastic about the federal sale of loan assets as a way to plug the budget deficit, even though every expert denies that such things make much difference one way or the other.

The truth is that the most astonishing success of Reaganomics has been the myth of our own invincibility. This myth rests upon an enduring, bipartisan principle of American political life which in the 1980s has become gospel: never admit the possibility of unpleasantness—especially when it appears inevitable.

If you allow for unpleasantness, the mechanics of our trade deficit cease to be confusing. America runs a deficit because it buys more than it produces. By systematically discouraging measures that would boost its anemic net savings rate, the United States has acquired a structural deficit economy, meaning that at no stage of the business cycle can we generate the amount of savings necessary for minimally adequate investment. In 1986, in fact, nearly two thirds of our net investment in housing and in business plant and equipment would not have occurred without dollars saved by foreigners. (This level of investment was, to be sure, very low by historical standards, but without the capital inflows that accompanied our trade deficit in 1986 it would have been at the rock-bottom level of a severe recession year—lower, in fact, than during the recession years of 1980, 1975, 1970, and 1958.)

Washington debate over trade policy invariably neglects this elementary fact about our balance of payments: dollars that flow abroad to buy imports always flow back. (Since foreigners don't use dollars, they spend them as soon as they get them.) The only question is how our dollars flow back—to buy our goods and services or to buy our IOUs. During the 1980s we have decided that our biggest "export" should be IOUs. In 1986 we sold to foreigners, net, a total of $143 billion in U.S. financial assets. Most of this consisted of stocks, bonds, T-bills, repos, bank balances, and other assorted paper, but a steeply increasing proportion of it was in real estate and other direct investment. This financial surplus was the flip side of our trade deficit, and if we had invested more at home, our surplus (in selling IOUs) and deficit (in selling trade goods) would have been even greater. As long as we cannot function without dollars saved abroad, exchange rates will fluctuate and interest rates will go up until we can attract those dollars back as loans. America must learn the basic distinction between capital flows for investment, which produce future return, and capital flows for consumption-related debt (for example, inflows to fund the budget deficit), which simply produce future debt service.

Correcting the current imbalance assumes that America can embark on an enormous shift from consumption to savings, and that this shift will not throw the world's economy into a tailspin, either by trade-led recessions in the other industrialized countries or by a chain of debt defaults among the less-developed countries (against whom we will be competing for trade surpluses). The alternative to this daunting scenario, of course, is the crash: a huge plunge in the dollar, unaffordable imports, a long recession, garrison protectionism, rampant inflation, and a marked decline in American living standards. The crash alternative prescribes that we pay off our debts through indefinite poverty. Can we avoid the crash? Yes, but doing so will require Americans to produce more while consuming less, and very close macro-economic coordination among nations.

A European critic is reported to have said this about the link between America's fiscal and international deficits: "Your policies in the 1980s remind me of Christopher Columbus's travels. Like you, he didn't know where he was going. He didn't know where he was when he got there. And he didn't know where he'd been when he got back. All he knew for sure was that the whole trip had been financed with foreign money." Or, as Fred Bergsten, the director of the Institute for International Economics, recently quipped, "We finally understand the true meaning of supply-side economics: foreigners supply most of the goods and all of the money."

How America has reached the end of an avenue with no pleasant exit is too long a story to be told here. But it is worth mentioning the key contribution made by two sweeping institutional developments that have taken place since the beginning of the 1970s. Both are what might be called changes in the rules of the game, rules that used to protect us from our own folly.

The first change has been in how we legislate federal budgets. Until fifteen years ago most federal spending was discretionary and unindexed, and federal tax policy still functioned under the very strong presumption that federal dollars spent should be paid for out of revenue. Large deficits, therefore, were difficult to achieve, because so many easy corrective options were available, both in spending and in taxing. The spending rule was eliminated in the early 1970s by our decision to transform most non-poverty benefit programs into untouchable and inflation-proof entitlements. The taxing rule was eliminated in the early 1980s by the jihad prayers of supply-side economists. Our deficit has thus become no one's responsibility. It is subject to "projection" but no longer to control.

The second big change has been the transformation of the world financial system. Back in the early 1970s we all accepted the basic postulates of the postwar Bretton Woods arrangements: fixed exchange rates and relatively little mobility of capital between nations. But the problem with fixed exchange rates was that they led to inconvenient balance-of-payment crises and didn't allow us the freedom to determine our own macroeconomic fate. So we closed the gold window in 1971 and shook ourselves loose from fixed parities by 1973. By the late 1970s and early 1980s, as the dollar sloshed up and down in ever larger waves, the world financial community accommodated our proud creation, the "float," and greatly liberalized the flow of capital across borders. The inevitable result has been to give every nation—especially the United States, as the owner of the world's reserve currency—much greater latitude to borrow as it pleases, with few restrictions other than the specter of national bankruptcy in the mind of the creditor. Fifteen years ago if the United States had begun to borrow the equivalent of 3.5 percent of its GNP from abroad, that would have created a national emergency, with Churchillian presidential addresses and wartime austerity measures. Today it creates—well, nothing, really. It's a number you can read about toward the end of the business section of your newspaper.

Most of these rule changes, with the exception of the new revenue-ignorant tax policy, took place before Ronald Reagan assumed office. Countless commentators have decided that Reaganomics represents a total reversal in inherited economic policy. But not so many years from now historians may simply be calling it an acceleration of inherited policy.

For staying the course while double-digit inflation was tamed—the only Reagan, or Reagan-Volcker, measure that seriously tested our threshold of pain—President Reagan deserves credit, as he does for courageously taking on the air-traffic controllers (which helped moderate the wage binge of the 1970s). He deserves credit as well for helping renew the popularity of markets and of entrepreneurial risk, here and abroad, and for persuading us to abandon the worst vices of regulation in such industries as airlines, banking, and energy. And he was surely correct in advocating cuts in marginal tax rates. We now know, for instance, that a maximum tax rate of 50 percent actually generates more revenue from the wealthy than a maximum tax rate of 70 percent, and provides real incentives for budding entrepreneurs. And for now, at least, Reagan has swept off the agenda such policies as national planning, wage-and-price controls, and wide-scale jobs programs.

We need, though, to be honest: as far as the basic allocation of our economy's resources is concerned, Reaganomics has either opted for or acquiesced in some of the worst, future-averting choices America has ever made, the full implications of which will not be known for years.

Vicious-Circle Economics

To begin to grasp what Reaganomics has wrought, go back to the presidential campaign of 1980. It was the evening of October 28, and the eyes of many American voters were fixed on the television debate between Ronald Reagan and Jimmy Carter. Facing the camera squarely, Reagan posed his famous question: "Are you better off than you were four years ago?" The next day newspaper polls began to report a surge of support for Reagan, which led to a Reagan landslide one week later.

Now, imagine that Reagan had immediately followed up his question with this guarantee: "I promise to make you feel better. While real personal consumption per fully employed American hardly budged during the Carter presidency, I will make it rise by about $300 per worker every year over the next six years. I'm also going to kick in another $140 per worker per year that we in government will be spending mainly to repair the fall in our defense budget during the seventies.

"How will I do it? Well, let me tell you. I will not do it by increasing the quantity of real goods and services produced per working American to any appreciable degree. Instead, I will do it by diverting to consumption, between last year and 1986, about three quarters of the resources per worker now devoted to savings. Half of the money will be obtained by simply cutting domestic investment, and to do this we will run enormous federal deficits—so big that the federal debt the public has bought since the time of the Founding Fathers, about $645 billion at the end of 1979, will have nearly tripled by the end of 1986. The other half will come from borrowing abroad. By 1986, in fact, our foreign borrowing alone will fund all of our net housing investment and a good 40 percent of our declining level of net business investment—freeing up by that year a fantastic $2,100 of extra personal consumption per employed American. From the end of last year to the end of 1986 our national per-worker balance with foreigners will fall from a credit of $989 to a debt of $2,500; and our federal per-worker balance with creditors, wherever they are, will plunge from a debt of $6,750 to a debt of $16,562. I'll bet you're feeling better already. Thank you and good night.''

This speech might not have won the presidency for Reagan. But it would have forecast precisely the performance of the economy during the candidate's subsequent term of office.

Reagan was right in the debate with Carter: the 1970s *were* tough by comparison with the 1960s. He was also right in observing that lower productivity growth and higher federal-benefit growth during the 1970s "squeezed out" defense spending in favor of privately earned spending on consumption. What looks quite significant in retrospect, however, is that at least the squeezing did take place. Few Americans watching the debate in 1980 ever imagined that over the coming decade we would just decide to ignore the law that limits consumption to production.

This is, quite simply, the dirty little secret of Reaganomics: behind the pleasurable observation that real U.S. consumption per worker has risen by $3,100 over the current decade lies the unpleasant reality that only $950 of this extra annual consumption has been paid for by growth in what each of us produces; the other $2,150 has been funded by cuts in domestic investment and by a widening river of foreign debt. From 1979 to 1986 the total annual increase in workers' production amounted to about $100 billion (in 1986 dollars). The comparable total for increases in personal consumption plus government purchases was about $300 billion. That leaves a difference of a bit more than $200 billion—just slightly more than the increase in annual federal deficits over the past six years. Deficit spending, of course, has been the primary engine behind this consumption bacchanalia—a superhot and super-Keynesian demand-side tilt that replaced the reviled "Tax and spend" motto of the 1970s with the new motto "Borrow and spend." In every previous decade we consumed slightly less than 90 percent of our increase in production; since the beginning of the 1980s we have consumed 325 percent of it—the extra 235 percent being reflected in an unprecedented increase in per-worker debt abroad and a decline in per-worker investment at home. This is how we have managed to create a make-believe 1960s—a decade of "feeling good" and "having it all"—without the bother of producing a real one.

We cannot, of course, go on borrowing from foreigners indefinitely to finance our consumption. Soon we must stop and, at that point, decide whether to repay them the principal or to forever commit ourselves (and our children) to pay annual interest to foreigners as the price for our 1980s binge. Nor can we go on starving domestic investment to finance our consumption. Soon we must stop and replenish the factories, bridges, and schools we have forgone or else forever relegate ourselves (and our children) to slower growth in our standard of living. Supply-side economics without the "supply" can have only one sequel—something we may soon call vicious-circle economics.

It is therefore all but inevitable that our level of consumption must slow its climb, or even fall, while our level of production catches up. But of course the speed with which it can catch up depends in turn on how much we can invest, which depends on how much we can save.

The connection between exploding public deficits and a lower national saving rate is not absolute and unbreakable. Conceivably, we might have left overall national savings untouched if we had engineered a huge rise in private-sector savings at the same time that we embarked on a huge rise in deficit spending. In fact, however, *net private savings*—the net income saved by private households and firms—has been declining very sharply over the past decade (from 8.1 percent of GNP in the 1970s to 6.1 percent of GNP in the 1980s). Consequently, *net national savings,* which equals net private savings minus public-sector dissaving, has been declining over the past decade, from 7.1 percent of GNP in the 1970s to 3.4 percent in the 1980s. In fact, during three of the past six years—1982, 1983, and 1986—U.S. net national savings has dipped below two percent of GNP. Huge capital inflows from abroad have thus been inevitable.

The conservative stewards of Reaganomics, ironically, have themselves created the Keynesian nightmare—large and permanent deficits—they so much feared. And Americans have endured it with remarkably little protest, because, after all, if conservative Keynes-haters didn't know the dangers of deficits, who did?

Apologists for Reaganomics once claimed that "rational expectations" would lead people to increase private savings to compensate for public deficits and that the tax cut of the early 1980s would lead to a savings surge. The latter line of reasoning is legitimate and important—at the margin and over the long haul. Unfortunately, it is an idea that works well only when we tax saving less and consumption more. Most of the 1981 tax cut was simply an across-the-board cut in personal income-tax rates and thus did little to alter the *relative* tax burden on savings versus consumption. In any case, what is truly inexcusable is the expectation that we could come out ahead simply by cutting the *overall* level of taxation while still allowing federal spending to grow. When tax cuts go unmatched by spending cuts, they must be accompanied by additional public borrowing from households and firms—thus by a dollar-for-dollar reduction in otherwise investable private savings. Therefore, in a near-full-employment economy only a tiny fraction of the cut is likely to show up as additional private savings. If families and firms treat the tax cut just as they treat other income, the savings might be six or seven cents on the dollar—a tiny margin that can disappear entirely if there is a negative shift in the private sector's overall inclination to save. As we have already observed, there was such a negative shift.

Other apologists for the 1980s "boom" have claimed that there is no historical correlation between public-sector deficits in bust years and negative trade balances. Even after budget deficits had soaked up some private savings, they point out, there was still enough left over for Americans to be net investors abroad; that's why bust years typically brought us an improvement in our trade balance. Evidence that this time-tested pattern no longer obtained, however, was already surfacing in 1982, when the steepest recession in thirty years was accompanied by such large-scale federal borrowing that our current account—the ledger of our financial transactions with foreigners—did not break even. Since then we have been sailing in uncharted waters: a cyclical recovery accompanied by enormous and widening foreign-capital inflows.

Some apologists for the 1980s have gotten so carried away with the idea of market expectations—Reaganomics is all about psychology and expectations—that they can justify any catastrophe by references to a rosy future. Alan Reynolds, the supply-side guru, believes that heavy foreign borrowing is a sign of economic strength. He has compared our huge current-account deficit today to Japan's big trade deficits in the 1950s, claiming that what the two situations clearly have in common is buoyant growth expectations. Although some U.S. observers in the 1950s were dubious about the wisdom of Japan's foreign imbalance, "in retrospect, U.S. worries about Japan's trade deficits look rather foolish." Likewise for the United States today. "What has happened in the 1980s," Reynolds writes, "looks like a reversal of roles, with the U.S. becoming the relatively vigorous tax haven, attracting foreign capital and goods, while Europe and Japan slip into the stagnant, export-dependent role that the U.S. experienced in the Eisenhower years."

The argument is half right. Japan *was* a capital importer in the 1950s, because it was a rapidly growing economy—more than that, it was a country literally reconstructing itself after a war that had largely wiped out its industrial base. It borrowed abroad to finance a higher investment level than would have been possible by relying on its already hefty savings rate alone. The result was an incredible net investment rate of well over 20 percent of GNP. Did such capital inflows make sense? Of course, for they rapidly paid for themselves in increased economic output. From 1950 to 1960 the Japanese economy grew at an average real rate of nearly 10 percent a year; real net output per worker grew at the extraordinary rate of 6.6 percent a year. The relative burden of financing the nation's foreign-capital inflows (which ceased by the mid-1960s) thus fell over time.

The parallel between the United States and Japan, however, utterly escapes me. Over the course of the 1980s the U.S. investment rate has been the second-lowest in the industrialized world (just above Britain); meanwhile, the rate of growth in our real net output per worker, absolutely the lowest, has averaged about 0.4 percent a year. That is less than *one fifteenth* of what the Japanese were experiencing thirty years ago. Japanese productivity in the 1950s, in other words, grew more in nine months than ours now grows over ten years. And unlike Japan, we have been borrowing abroad for consumption, not investment.

To find the proper historical parallel for the United States in the 1980s we should not look to Japan in the 1950s, nor should we look to our previous experience with heavy borrowing from foreigners. That was in the 1870s, when we issued bonds (at half the current interest rate) to Europeans in order to finance our huge investment in railroads and heavy industry. Instead, we must look to those rare historical occasions when an economy's large size, its world-class currency, and its open capital markets have allowed it to borrow immense sums primarily for the purpose of consumption and without regard to productive return. The illustrations of lumbering, deficit-hobbled, low-growth economies that come most easily to mind are Spain's in the late sixteenth century, France's in the 1780s, and Britain's in the 1920s.

So there we have it: a conservative Republican Administration that promised us a high-savings, high-productivity, highly competitive economy, with trade surpluses, and gave us instead a torrid consumption boom financed by foreign borrowing, an overvalued currency, and cuts in private investment, with debt-financed hikes in public spending and huge balance-of-payments deficits. It's the same script, proceeding toward the same woeful finale, that we have seen played out over the years by many a Latin American debtor. As one wit has put it, just as the 1970s saw the "greening" of America, the 1980s is seeing the "Argentining" of America.

Now let us examine the pieces of this fiscal debacle in more detail. We will turn first to the critical near- and medium-term challenge of reducing our foreign-credit inflow—and, at the same time, of coping with the harsh policy choices and the danger of global crisis that must accompany such a reduction. Then we will take a longer-term view of the inexorable link between investment and living standards. Finally, we will discuss the manner in which American public policy treats our future. If before the 1980s this manner was one of neglect, today it borders on open contempt.

"Owing It to Ourselves" No Longer

How much, exactly, do we now owe the rest of the world? Officially, our net position (what we are owed minus what we owe) at the end of 1986 was a *negative* $264 billion. By the end of 1987 we will be closing in on a negative $400 billion. The incredible speed of America's transformation from creditor to debtor can hardly be exaggerated. Only six years ago, at the end of 1981, the United States had achieved its all-time apogee as a net creditor, with an official position of a positive $141 billion. Over the past six years, in other words, the United States has burned up more than $500 billion, net, by liquidating our foreign assets and by borrowing from abroad. That's an immense flow of capital, even in global terms. By 1986 our net borrowing had dwarfed the fabled bank recycling of OPEC surpluses after the oil price hikes of 1973 and 1979. The sum was twice the size of all foreign interest payments by all the less-developed debtor nations, and about half the approximate dollar value of total net investment in all less-developed countries combined.

What does the future have in store for a nation that is borrowing such sums from foreigners? As a net debtor of growing proportions, the United States must inevitably become a sizable net exporter of goods and services. (I repeat: exporter.) This proposition is just a matter of arithmetic. Since our indebtedness cannot grow indefinitely as a share of our GNP— beyond some point, foreign creditors will regard us as a growing credit risk, a risk that must be compensated for by prohibitively high interest rates—our current-account deficit must eventually decline substantially. And when that happens, we will have to export more than we import in order to service our deficits on interest and dividend payments to foreigners. Just to say that something is inevitable, of course, does not tell you when it will happen. But I think it's fair to say that the growth of America's foreign debt may push us—painfully—to a current-account balance and a trade surplus by the mid-1990s, and almost certainly will do so by the year 2000.

Our opportunity for a relatively smooth readjustment is perilously narrow. On the one hand, it seems likely that the rest of the world will grow reluctant to keep lending to the United States once our net indebtedness rises much beyond 35 percent of our GNP, or a bit more than $1 trillion at today's prices. Some experts suggest that this debt may entail net U.S. debt-service payments equivalent, as a share of exports, to those of many developing nations and about on a par with Germany's reparations burden following the First World War. The experts agree that it is quite impossible for the United States to go on indefinitely borrowing principal at or near its current rate of 3.4 percent of GNP per year. Such borrowing, combined with accumulating debt-service costs, would dictate an absurd $3 trillion in net debt by the end of the century, and foreign investors would close down the pipeline long before we got there.

On the other hand, it is practically inevitable that our net debt will reach the $1 trillion mark by the early 1990s no matter how vigorously we act to stem the inflow of foreign savings. Obviously, there are limits to the speed with which the United States can curtail consumption and generate growth in net exports. Consider, for instance, a scenario in which the United States, starting next year, makes steady additions to the value of its net exports such that its current account reaches zero by 1994 and its net debt is reduced to today's level by the year 2000. That sounds like a rather modest achievement. Yet it will still lead to a net debt of about $1 trillion by 1994 and will require a real improvement in U.S. net exports of more than $20 billion a year, each year, for the next ten years, or a total positive shift of more than $200 billion. As Fred Bergsten has observed, the magnitude of the necessary adjustment facing us is equivalent to about two thirds of our entire defense budget and is several times larger than the total shift resulting in the United States from the 1970s oil shocks.

According to the adjustment scenario above, we need to reduce our foreign borrowing stream by $20 billion yearly, or $200 yearly for each of our 100 million workers. Yet real net product per worker has been growing each year by just $135. Further, our continuing debt growth will mean that about $40 per worker per year must be devoted to rising foreign debt-service payments. And to increase productivity sufficiently to raise net exports will require at least our 1970s level of net investment at home—an additional $60 per worker per year over a decade.

So where are we going to find, each year, the extra $20 billion in unconsumed exportable production necessary to make this readjustment scenario work? Over the next decade, with only $35 per worker available ($135, minus $40, minus $60), consumption per worker in the United States may have to decline by $165 each year. That's $1,650 overall for the average worker, and of course we can expect those Americans with the most vulnerable incomes—minority workers, young adults laboring under two-tier contracts, and service employees who receive no benefits—to suffer losses rhat are far greater than average. Neither the American public nor the nation's politicians have even begun to face this prospect. In comparison, during the 1970s—a decade now known to most of us as "hard times"—U.S. consumption per worker nonetheless rose by $200 each year. What the early 1980s gave us, the 1990s may well take away.

In what exports, specifically, is the United States going to see the enormous gains it must achieve to lower its trade deficit? First of all, we can forget about any major contributions from the 22 percent of our trade exports now composed of agricultural goods and raw materials. The $25 billion trade surplus we had in agricultural exports in 1981 shrank to $3 billion last year. Over the past decade the European Economic Community has raised its grain balance, improbably enough, from a deficit of 25 million tons to a surplus of 16 million tons. India, Pakistan, and China have all become net farm-product exporters. Even the Soviet Union now seriously asserts the breath-taking goal of becoming a net food exporter by the year 2000. We will therefore be lucky to slow the current decline in our agricultural balance. Much the same goes for raw materials.

As for oil imports, nearly all experts expect that declining U.S. production will push our current 25 to 30 percent dependence on oil imports to 50 to 60 percent during the 1990s, and at higher prices. Philip Verleger, Jr., a visiting fellow at the Institute for International Economics, estimates that the value of our oil imports will rise from $44 billion in 1985 to $120 billion or $130 billion by the mid-1990s. The 1980s have been happy, quiescent years from an energy standpoint, but we may, in the 1990s, again face some of the energy turbulence of the 1970s. The $70 billion real improvement (in 1986 dollars) in the energy balance that Americans have enjoyed since 1980, in other words, will reverse direction. Let's be optimistic and assume that our annual total farm and raw-materials balance for the foreseeable future will decline by only $10 billion per year. That means we need a good $30 billion yearly improvement in the remaining 75 percent of our exports—namely, manufacturing.

Some critics balk at this point and complain that this logic unfairly omits our exports in services. According to a recent *Fortune* article titled "The Economy of the 1990s," the United States will improve its balance on services by $125 billion between now and the year 2000. This service surplus, like some deus ex machina, is supposed to more than pay the debt service on what *Fortune* admits will be a "debt mountain" of some $1 trillion by the mid-1990s. This analysis confuses a large flow of services that are actually debt service (for example, the payment of interest and dividends) with a much smaller flow of services that are actually current production (for example, travel, shipping, and insurance). We already know what will happen to the balance on the former type—it's going to go deep into the red. And U.S. exports of the latter type, unfortunately, are both too small (a total of $49 billion in 1986) and too inflexible to make much difference. Two thirds of these exports consist of shipping, transportation, and travel; the rest consist of business services that usually accompany trade exports. In fact, since so many of our high-tech service exports are linked to manufacturing exports, it strikes me as virtually meaningless to project one without the other.

Let's be optimistic and assume that service exports will eventually grow by fifty percent. That still leaves us with a need to increase our manufacturing exports by $275 billion, or achieve a real annual growth rate of 10 percent over the next decade. Can we emulate Japan and sustain such a prodigious performance in manufacturing over so many years? Perhaps we can, but the prospect seems daunting. So far in this decade our manufactured exports have actually *declined* in real terms, but over the coming decade we will be aiming for a higher export growth rate than we have yet achieved in the twentieth century. In every respect the achievement would be unprecedented: we would have not only to break our earlier record but to do it with a lower average level of domestic business investment, with a complete freeze on imports, and with steadily declining living standards.

Any way one looks at it, the arithmetic is cruel and inescapable. It's hard to imagine huge growth in our manufacturing output, for instance, without a very large increase in domestic business investment. But to further increase investment at home we may have to undergo a further decline in consumption, in order to hold constant our net export improvement. And, clearly, we are not going to see any decline in consumption in favor of saving unless there is a radical change in our public policy, especially our fiscal policy (something I will discuss later on), and in our politics as well.

There remains, moreover, yet another problematic assumption in our readjustment scenario: the willingness, or even the ability, of the rest of the world to absorb our proposed huge increase in manufacturing exports. Current thinking on this problem seems to grow out of two separate theories. One theory emphasizes foreign economic growth, the other exchange rates.

The foremost proponent of the first theory is the Reagan Administration, which has repeatedly insisted that higher rates of growth abroad—particularly in the stagnant-demand economies of West Germany and Japan— will solve our problem. This is a worthy idea but hardly a solution. Consider, for instance, a sustained one percent real increase in economic growth in the rest of the world—say, from about the current 2.5 percent to 3.5 percent (surely we cannot expect more). Then imagine that all this growth is purely domestic. Using rosy "multiplier" assumptions, we could get a two- or even four-percent real increase in exports. Recall, however, that we need a *10* percent real increase.

The second theory, to which many economists subscribe, is that any level of net export improvement is possible as long as we endure a "sufficient" decline in the exchange rate—that is, a continued fall in the value of the dollar relative to other currencies which will make our goods more attractive to foreign buyers.

Experience demonstrates, however, that exchange-rate adjustment also has its difficulties. Over the past few years nearly all economists have been humbled by how far they had overstated the extent to which world trade balances would adjust to the recent fall in the dollar. Given this track record, it is cause for deep reflection that forecasts now being made in major think tanks say that even a 25 percent further devaluation of the dollar will be lucky to push the annual U.S. current-account deficit much below $100 billion over the next few years. The underlying problem might be posed as follows: even if we accept a lower dollar, which I believe to be virtually inevitable, will economies in the rest of the world accept it? The challenge facing America—generating a $275 billion positive swing in manufactured exports over the next decade—sounds tough enough without worrying about whether our trading partners will accommodate our necessities. Yet we often forget that our objective of huge yearly increases in U.S. net exports translates directly into decreases in the net exports of our major trading partners (recently the very source of much of their growth). It's not just a question of our resolve; it's also a question of their resolve, something over which we have little or no control.

What we hope, of course, is that our trading partners will accept our agenda. In general, we want them to raise the demand for goods and services in their countries at the same pace at which we are suppressing demand, with smaller fiscal deficits and higher private savings rates, in our own country. Specifically, we hope they will stimulate their domestic demand with looser fiscal policy, keep their currency strong with restrained monetary policy, and pull down import barriers so that U.S. exports can expand with minimal pressure on exchange rates. Our unspoken assumption is that once we decide to act, they can be expected to cooperate.

In reality, foreign economies may be otherwise inclined. Instead of loosening fiscal policy, they may continue to tighten—raising their own national savings rates in tandem with ours even at the risk of a collapse in global demand. And instead of embracing a lower dollar, they may continue to resist it, either by pushing their exports harder (with price cuts and aggressive marketing) or by discouraging imports (with official or unofficial import barriers or simply a social consensus not to "buy Ameri-

can''). Either way, readjustment may entail risks that persuade all parties
to abandon the effort. In the former case the risk is worldwide economic
stagnation. In the latter the risk is a precipitous fall in the dollar and the
danger of financial panic.

Why might our trading partners not want to cooperate? For one thing,
foreign leaders may be slow to believe that the United States will do what
it says it intends to. Look at it from their point of view. Ever since 1983
the United States has been assuring the rest of the world that it is just
about to cut back on its budget and current-account deficits and that other
countries should therefore immediately begin stimulating their domestic
demand in order to "pick up the slack." Other countries have responded
with caution, and in retrospect—the U.S. deficits having grown rather than
shrunk—their leaders must now be glad they were cautious. They still
have their exports, they still have their productivity growth, and they still
have stable prices.

Given the recent sharp fall in the dollar, many Americans figure that our
trading partners have begun to see the handwriting on the wall. Surely, we
think, Europe and Japan must soon opt for large-scale domestic stimulus
in their own interest—especially when it means the instant pleasure for
their own citizens of more disposable income and more consumption. Yet
here we confront a deeper issue—the vast differences in culture, history,
and politics which make it just as hard for other industrial countries to do
what we find natural (stimulate consumption) as it is for us to do what they
find natural (stimulate savings). We find inflation worth risking, but the
West Germans, scarred by the memory of the 1920s, would rather risk
recession. We find it easy to sacrifice exports on the altar of the high
dollar, but the Japanese, who have spent generations fighting to earn
dollars to pay for their food, raw materials, and oil, find the equivalent
idea tantamount to economic surrender (particularly considering their
long-sought, stunning manufacturing trade surplus of $150 billion, or about
eight percent of their GNP). The necessary reversals in national economic
direction are profound. If we assign Japan one third of the needed adjustment, for example, or $50 billion annually by 1994, this would amount to
eight percent of its total manufacturing output (in a negative direction). To
those who argue that Japan adjusted successfully to two oil shocks, and so
can handle this challenge, I argue that those shocks required the Japanese
to do *more* of what they had always been doing (namely, exporting), while
the present predicament will require them to do *less*. American leaders
think that stimulating domestic demand is child's play. Most leaders
abroad do not. They are, in fact, extremely doubtful that their consumers
will be able to pick up where exports to America leave off.

To allay doubts about our intentions, we must change our policy in credible and irrevocable ways, and announce these changes ahead of time. Readjustment becomes sticky when, even in the face of changing prices, foreign exporters hope to preserve their sunk costs, their hard-won market shares, and their relentless productivity and cost-reduction efforts—as Americans hooked on imports hope to preserve their buying habits. Those hopes are our enemy. We cannot cloud the air with chatter about painless global growth when in fact we are asking exporters abroad and importers at home to endure inevitable hardships.

Second, to eliminate uncertainty about the implications of our policy, we must talk realistically about a genuine transformation of the world's major political economies. "Fair trade" (whatever that means) isn't really the point. Our objective is to raise U.S. exports so that we avert a tragedy that threatens everyone—a global crash. Finally, to encourage political as well as economic balance in the world, we must renounce our recent policy of "global Keynesianism"—the policy of being everyone's buyer of last resort. The mercantilist aggressions bred by such a policy, including retaliatory protection and games of "chicken" with exchange rates, have themselves become a major obstacle to readjustment. Confidence, not fear, is the best way to get foreigners to retool their export plants for their own domestic markets.

If we simply proceed with the "business as usual" approach to the world's growing imbalance, America's foreign creditors will ultimately become aware that the situation is unsustainable. At that point anything, from a small decrease in the value of the dollar to a mild political crisis, could cause investors around the world to decide to rid themselves of dollar-denominated assets. If the resulting plunge in the dollar's exchange rate persuades ever larger numbers of investors to follow suit, the "dollar overhang" might at last turn into the worst freefall nightmare of Paul Volcker, the former Federal Reserve chairman: an avalanche pouring down on the dollar's financial capitals, from London to San Francisco.

The United States, in response, would have little choice but to raise interest rates sky-high, in order to attract at least some investors to the dollar to finance our budget deficits. We would also have to acquiesce in a long and almost deliberate recession, both to shut down most of our foreign borrowing (in a matter of months rather than years) and to suppress U.S. demand for imports. Actually, the recession is likely to be of the "stagflation" variety, since higher import prices may double our inflation rate even before we prime the pump. The peak-to-trough downturn could be quite steep indeed and could easily become our most severe economic crisis since the 1930s. Nor have I yet mentioned how the razor-edge plight of many less-developed debtor nations will add to the danger. Every forecast I have seen warns that the largest South American debtors will be pushed from illiquidity to insolvency by a far milder recession, and far smaller interest-rate hikes, than those envisioned here. Many have even suggested that spreading defaults among less-developed countries may precipitate the crisis.

No one knows, of course, how long such a hard landing would last. It is possible, I hope, that it would be limited to a financial crunch followed by a severe but brief recession, rather than a lengthy depression. The economy could recover with relatively moderate increases in world unemployment, but surely the value of the dollar would be much lower and U.S. import levels would be much reduced. This is what I call the "bumpy start-and-stop" scenario—the one that has afflicted postwar Great Britain. Under this scenario the standard of living in the United States would have dropped, its indebtedness would be little changed (but no longer growing), its international responsibilities would be necessarily curtailed, and its people would be aware, through occasional jumps in interest rates and the yo-yo behavior of the dollar, that their economic fate was hostage to the tenuous and nervous confidence of outsiders. The British economist Michael Stewart recently observed that "anyone who has lived through our 40 years of balance of payments crises, and seen the constraints they have imposed on domestic policies, must stand amazed at the insouciance with which the United States is piling up external debt." These constraints, of course, were not only domestic; they also hobbled British foreign policy—most dramatically in the Suez crisis of 1956, when the United States, which held reserves of British sterling as foreigners hold our dollars today, warned the British that we would declare war on the pound if they did not stop their invasion of Egypt. So much for the perils of dependence on foreign investors.

Should we have the worst hard landing—a lengthy U.S. depression—let us simply be forewarned that our traditional policy responses would be of limited use. Hardship-bloated budget deficits would prevent us from applying more fiscal stimulus; a low and skittish dollar would defy our attempts to loosen monetary policy. Whereas the "start-and-stop" landing presumes that Americans could pay for their debts by a one-time shock in living standards, and thereafter by slower productivity growth and reduced international leadership, the true-depression hard landing presumes that Americans would service and pay off their debts through indefinite impoverishment. Either scenario could, of course, lead to a resurgence in state control over the economy (on a scale that might put Jimmy Carter's credit controls to shame)—an ironic last act in an opera that opened with the chorus singing praises to laissez-faire.

Some observers play down the possibility of such a crisis. They point to the apparent ease with which the world has so far endured a substantial decline in the dollar's value. Clearly, however, the easy stage is now coming to an end. In trade, the dollar has now reached the point at which further declines can no longer be absorbed by exporters' profit margins and will leave no foreign alternative other than structural change or economic stagnation. Just as the American economy has since 1980 suffered the trauma of de-industrialization, so the Japanese economy has begun to suffer from what some Japanese call the "hollowing out" of their industries—worker layoffs, unused capacity, and a scramble toward off-shore assembly. In finance, further dollar declines are likely to be accompanied not by lower U.S. interest rates, as in the past, but by unchanged or even higher interest rates, as we experienced last spring. This will present the Fed with a no-win choice between defending the dollar and loosening credit. And it will hit foreign investors with the double whammy of further exchange-rate losses compounded by losses in bond-market values. The preconditions for a dollar-dump panic, in short, may already be moving into place.

Of course, one hopes that Americans will never have to live through these dismal outcomes. But avoiding them will take great effort—not just in changing policy but ultimately in changing our very self-image and in persuading our trading partners to change theirs. Japan's problem, a senior official there told me recently, is global-asset management; ours, alas, is global-debt management.

The financial expert David Hale has written, "The U.S. is a debtor nation with the habits of a creditor nation while Germany and Japan are creditor nations with the habits of debtor nations." Needless to say, America must soon change its habits, including its fixation on creative consumption. Our ability to do so safely, however, will depend on more than just our own hard work and determination. It will also depend on whether we can persuade our trading partners to change their habits, at the same speed and at the same time that we are changing ours.

Turning Away From Posterity

Our growing foreign debt and trade deficit not only threaten a sacrifice in our consumption levels but also symptomize our unwillingness to acknowledge a deeper and more long-standing disease: a steady thinning out of those activities and attitudes that tend to generate, over the long term, a rising level of productive efficiency. When the seriousness of this problem became increasingly apparent, during the 1970s, we should logically have chosen to allocate fewer of our resources toward consumption and more toward investing in productive physical and human capital.

Instead, under a supply-side banner, we have blindly chosen to do the opposite.

Does it matter that our productivity is growing only a fraction as fast as it was in the 1950s or 1960s? Indeed it does. To recognize some of the consequences, we have only to consider that to end foreign borrowing with no change in per-worker consumption or domestic investment will take us *twelve years* of productivity growth at the current rate. The same task would take us only a bit more than three years at the growth rate of the 1960s or only a bit more than two years at the rate of the 1950s. To put it another way: Our per-worker flow of foreign borrowing, as we have seen, is now running at about $1,350 a year. But whereas the net product per worker that is left after we service our debt, and that we can apply to reducing our current-account deficit, is rising by only $95 a year now, it would be rising by $630 a year at 1960s growth rates and by $985 a year at 1950s growth rates.

Yet it would be wrong to see productivity differences solely in terms of our foreign balances. Far more important is the role such differences must play in determining long-term growth in our future living standards. The cumulative impact of small differences in yearly growth rates cannot be underestimated. Consider the year 2020, when those who are now infants will be in the prime of their working life. If productivity growth proceeds at its 1980s rate (and does not decline still further), the average worker in 2020 will be producing $40,100 worth of real goods and services, only about 14 percent more than his or her parents are producing today ($35,300). Under the smoothest-possible-readjustment scenario already described, which would result in declining per-worker consumption through most of the rest of this century, even by 2020 his or her yearly consumption will have risen only eight percent above the 1986 level.

America's standard of living, for the first time in its history, will have hardly budged for a span of forty years. The 1980s and 1990s may be remembered, with bitterness, as a turning point in America's fortunes—a period of transition when we took the British route to second-class economic status. Britain's decline took seventy-five years of productivity-growth rates that were half a percentage point lower than those of its industrial competitors. Because America's corresponding gap is more than three times as large, its relative decline is proceeding far more swiftly.

If, however, U.S. productivity now started growing again at the 2.4 percent average rate that prevailed during the 1950s and 1960s, miraculous though that would seem, our sons and daughters in 2020 would each be producing $77,200 worth of real goods and services—some 120 percent more than their parents are each producing today. Consumption standards would rise by nearly as much, since we would have been able both to close our foreign-borrowing gap and to recoup our foreign liabilities by the early 1990s. In this case our grandchildren would look back on us as relative paupers, and by 2020 Americans would be enjoying buoyant prosperity and widening social opportunities in a nation that would still be a leading force in the world's economic and political affairs.

Understandably, most Americans do not want to confront the painful idea that we are headed toward the wrong future. Yet that is the melancholy fact of the matter. What is less understandable is the strident defense that so many opinion leaders offer for our present course. We hear time and again that the U.S. economy in the present decade has grown "as fast as" or "faster than" the collective economy of the rest of the industrial world. So far as this claim goes, it is correct. From 1979 through 1986 real U.S. GNP grew by a rate of 2.1 percent a year—about the same growth rate as that of the collective GNP of all other industrial nations. However, in the United States most of the growth (70 percent) was due to increases in the number of workers, while in the other countries most of the growth (85 percent) was due to increases in output per worker.

The rapid growth in U.S. employment has partly been the consequence of an entrepreneurial and new-business surge, the flexibility of our labor markets, and several booms (for example, a consumption boom, providing jobs in distribution; the health-care-for-the-elderly boom; the home-services and eating-out boom; and the postwar Baby Boom, which has no counterpart in other countries). According to a recent Commerce Department report, from 1981 to 1986 the equivalent of nine million full-time jobs were created. And yet, contrary to the widespread impression, this represents a job-creation slowdown; over the previous six years the equivalent of 14 million full-time jobs were created.

In any case, this kind of growth must cease within a few years, when all the Baby Boomers are employed, and reverse itself in future decades, when young adults will be scarce and retiring workers ever more plentiful. More important, it is not the kind of growth that raises our standard of living. Augmenting production by adding more working bodies (what classical economists used to call the "dismal" Asian model) does not enhance the standard of living. Only augmenting production per working person does that, and Europe and Japan do that far more successfully than we do. The employment of the largest and best-educated generation of Americans in history should have caused U.S. GNP to rise far faster than GNP in any other country—as it should also have pushed up our savings rate, since presumably this working generation of young adults will want to allocate some of the extra production to provide for their children and their own retirement (as the Baby Boom becomes the Senior Boom). Instead, with the part-time nature and much lower value-added character of many of the new jobs, we have barely managed to keep pace with the GNPs of our competitors, and our savings rate has declined. This is not success but a large-scale admission of failure.

Yet it is surely true, the optimists say, that productivity growth and investment performance in the other industrial countries have declined sharply over the past fifteen years, and this must mean that we are doing better than they are. Not really. Because the performance of the other countries was so superior to begin with, and because our own performance has also fallen, product per worker is still growing considerably faster abroad than here in the United States.

How have these economies managed? The most apparent factor has been much higher investment levels. Here, Japan is the leader. From the 1960s to the 1980s its total net investment as a share of GNP (including investment in public infrastructure as well as in all private structures and equipment) has fallen from 22.6 percent to 16.1 percent; the latter figure, however, is still three times larger than the equivalent U.S. figure for the 1980s (5.3 percent). In fact, at 1986 exchange rates (as the dollar falls, the comparison is getting worse) Japanese net investment in 1986 amounted to $300 billion, while U.S. investment amounted to only $270 billion. (This has been the result, in part, of a cost of capital in Japan that has consistently been less than half ours—a situation not at all helped by the 1986 Tax Reform Act.) It is a spectacle that ought to shock Americans: a population half the size of our own, living on a group of islands the size of California, is adding more each year to its stock of factories, houses, bridges, and laboratories—in absolute terms—than we are to ours. And Japan still has savings left over, about $80 billion in 1986, to lend to thriftless foreigners. (About $50 billion of that sum was lent to us.) Between the two countries, therefore, the 1986 disparity in net savings ($380 billion in Japan versus only $125 billion in the United States, a six-to-one per capita difference) was even more lopsided.

For years many U.S. experts have been predicting that the relative productivity-growth advantage of the other industrial countries would soon slow down. Back in the 1960s and early 1970s such predictions were based on the "postwar reconstruction" thesis. Industrial phenomena like Japan and West Germany, it was said, were growing faster merely because they still had to "replace" the capital stock they had lost in the Second World War. More recently this line of reasoning has been abandoned, because it obviously cannot explain why these countries have replaced most of their business plant and equipment several times over since the early 1950s. In Japan, to take the extreme example, there is hardly a single factory now standing that has not been built, rebuilt, or entirely re-equipped since the mid-1970s. Indeed, each Japanese worker is supported by more than twice the plant and equipment that supports his or her American counterpart. A new argument, therefore, has become popular. This is the so-called convergence thesis, according to which other countries are getting a free ride by copying American technological breakthroughs. Once the other countries reach our level, it is said, their productivity growth must slow down sharply. At that point they will have to do the same tough "pioneer" work that we do.

The convergence thesis makes sense only if we assume that the other countries' overall disadvantage relative to the United States is spread about equally across every economic sector, and that it is especially marked in manufacturing, where technology presumably is most important. Unfortunately, this assumption isn't plausible. Most economists agree that America's remaining absolute advantage is due mostly to superior productivity in agriculture, raw materials, and services, and that little if any of it is now due to superior productivity in manufacturing.

Instead of hoping for convergence, we Americans ought to recognize that we are already getting beaten in manufacturing. We must also recognize that over the foreseeable future the biggest productivity-growth opportunities in Europe and Japan will lie in improving efficiency in agriculture and services—something that requires no big research-and-development breakthroughs and could occur with disquieting suddenness.

The defenders of Reaganomics, of course, protest against any such conclusions. The growth of U.S. manufacturing productivity, they claim, has been one of our great achievements in the 1980s. And now that the dollar is back down where it was when President Reagan took office, American exporters will no longer have to compete against absurdly cheap foreign labor costs. The future, then, looks bright.

But does it really? True enough, U.S. manufacturing productivity has recently run against our economy's declining trend. For example, from 1979 to 1985 Ford reduced its global employment by nearly 30 percent while reducing its car and truck output by only about five percent. Overall growth in manufacturing productivity rose from a yearly average of 2.3 percent in the 1970s to nearly 3.2 percent in the 1980s. What the optimists do not point out, however, is that such numbers are the perverse if procompetitive result of seven catastrophic years for U.S. manufacturers— two domestic recessions (1980 and 1982–1983) followed by a high dollar export recession (1984–1986).

Still less do the defenders of the 1980s want to point out that U.S. manufacturing productivity, even with the help of its recent job-slashing acceleration, grew more slowly during the 1980s than the average for our major industrial competitors. And far from granting slower real pay raises, foreign manufacturing exporters have been using their productivity advantage to grant their workers much larger pay raises than firms in the United States have done. Since 1969 real manufacturing pay has risen by only 17 percent in the United States, but by a colossal 115 percent in Japan.

The fact that U.S. wages have grown even more slowly than U.S. productivity certainly reflects the adverse exchange-rate climb of the dollar during the early 1980s. But since the gap in wage growth was already apparent at the end of the 1970s—before the dollar's long climb—some experts suggest that it may also reflect a negative shift in the image of U.S. goods for quality and reliability. Our decline in underlying competitiveness, in other words, may be even greater than what the output-per-worker numbers indicate. For this reason the recent emphasis on quality by many U.S. manufacturers can only be regarded as gratifying.

A final defense of our economic performance in the 1980s rests on the sweeping claim that none of this "smokestack" productivity matters anymore because our economy will henceforth thrive on our alleged global monopoly on information and inventions. Pure products of the mind have limited appeal as final consumer products, however, and so one wonders how they can generate wealth unless we have the capability—the plants, tools, and production skills—to turn them into salable goods and services. Perhaps, it is said, we could sell this intellectual property directly to foreigners. A good idea, but the numbers hardly indicate that such sales could ever drive our economy by themselves. In 1986 our total net receipts from royalty and licensing contracts with unaffiliated foreigners (including movie and TV rights) amounted to about $1.5 billion, or about four ten-thousandths of our GNP. And in inflation-adjusted dollars our receipts of this kind have actually been declining over the past decade.

Knowledge and innovation, to be sure, are an absolutely vital precondition for long-term economic growth. But we Americans tend to overrate the significance of our leadership here. We forget that intellectual glitz and scientific glory do not always translate into the humble, wealth-generating chores of commercial innovation. Although we like to point out that we lead the world in the share of GNP that we devote to research and development, we neglect to add that much of this is devoted to obscure weapons R&D that leads to few commercial spinoffs. In civilian R&D we lag behind both Japan and West Germany. We should be pleased with the rapid growth of venture and equity financing for small high-tech businesses during the 1980s, but we should also be cautious: thus far we have seen no comparable surge in small-business R&D, no reversal in the downward trend in U.S. patent applications, and no resurgence in high-tech exports. As for U.S. universities, they are indeed a global showcase for Nobel laureates and pathbreaking research. Yet most of the brilliance emanating from our universities is as freely available to foreigners as it is to our own citizens.

More important, it is hard to imagine any long-term economic renaissance—especially one built on "working smarter"—without a determined investment in the most precious of our assets: the skills, intellect, work habits, health, and character of our children. Yet this is precisely where we may be courting our most catastrophic failure. In the words of one analyst cited by the 1983 National Commission on Excellence in Education, "For the first time in the history of our country, the educational skills of one generation will not surpass, will not equal, will not even approach, those of their parents." Recent trends indicate that each year the typical American child is increasingly likely to be born in poverty and to grow up in a broken family. And a study by the Committee for Economic Development points out that without major educational change, by the year 2000 we will have turned out close to 20 million young people with no productive place in our society. The CED study continues, "Solutions to the problems of the educationally disadvantaged must include a fundamental restructuring of the school system. But they must also reach beyond the traditional boundaries of schooling to improve the environment of the child. An early and sustained intervention in the lives of disadvantaged children both in school and out is our only hope for breaking the cycle of disaffection and despair." Our children represent the furthest living reach of posterity, the only compelling reason that we have to be serious about investing in the future. And we are failing them.

The Politics of Debt

There is no question that federal fiscal policy deserves much of the blame for our national failure to invest during the 1980s; recall that the 1986 federal deficit consumed the equivalent of 90 percent of all private-sector savings that year. On the one hand, opinion polls consistently show that the American public overwhelmingly favors, in theory, a balanced budget. On the other hand, serious attempts to reduce the deficit continue to encounter, in practice, enormous bipartisan resistance. Congress and the Administration invent countless reasons why solving the problem can be postponed just a bit longer or why the deficit can't really be doing us that much harm.

We have little time left to get beyond such rationalizations. It is sometimes asserted that our economy's saving behavior would be pretty much the same today without a federal deficit. But, again, consider the numbers. During the 1980s we have succeeded in nearly tripling the national debt, from $645 billion (at the end of fiscal year 1979) to $1.745 trillion (at the end of fiscal year 1986). We have, in addition, saddled ourselves with an informal debt of nearly $10 trillion in unfunded liabilities in Social Security, Medicare, and federal pensions. That astronomical figure is the difference between the benefits today's workers are now scheduled to receive and the future taxes today's workers are slated to pay for them. It amounts to a hidden tax of $100,000 on every American worker, and its toll will be exacted on our children.

For Americans to believe that their national balance sheet is in the same shape now as it used to be, they would have to believe that the enduring investments made by the federal government during the past seven years are comparable to all those made during the preceding two centuries—including the taming of the frontier, victories in several wars, the Marshall Plan, miracle vaccines, the Apollo missions, Grand Coulee Dam, and the interstate highway system.

From fiscal year 1979 to 1986 federal revenue fell from 18.9 percent to 18.5 percent of GNP, while federal outlays rose from 20.5 percent to 23.8 percent of GNP. Why has federal spending risen? The big growth areas over the past seven years have been defense, entitlement benefits, and interest on our national debt; all other spending has been cut back dramatically. Over the longer term, however, entitlement benefits dominate the picture. Since 1965 they have grown from 5.4 percent to 11.5 percent of GNP; all other spending excluding interest (which simply represents the permanent cost of cumulative deficits) has declined from 11.0 percent to 9.5 percent of GNP. This growth in entitlements over the past twenty-one years is equivalent to 6.1 percent of GNP—an amount greater than the entire investment we currently make in all business plant and equipment, plus all civilian R&D, plus all public infrastructure. Even defense spending, as a share of GNP, has risen only half as much during the 1980s as it declined during the 1970s. At 6.6 percent of GNP in 1986, defense spending is still lower than it was in any year from 1950 to 1973.

Our budget-cutting efforts during the 1980s have failed because they have allowed continued growth in the one type of spending—for entitlement benefits—that had already risen to unprecedented heights. Even where the 1980s budget ax has fallen hard, the major victims have been precisely those rare federal programs whose purpose is physical or human investment rather than consumption.

This last point is worth emphasizing, for it explains the unique vulnerability in recent years of that small area of the federal budget called discretionary non-defense spending. That's the old-fashioned type of spending in which Congress—unconstrained by automatic-indexing formulas and prior-year contracts—votes on bills each year, presumably for the best interest of our national future. Unfortunately, since the future has no lobby, no formula, and no contract, the Administration and Congress have found this the perfect place to demonstrate their budget-cutting zeal publicly even while allowing all other types of spending to keep rising. By 1986 discretionary non-defense spending had been cut to 4.09 percent of GNP, its lowest level since 1961.

This spending category includes that bellwether of federal investment activity, the maintenance and construction of America's public infrastructure. Net real investment in roads, bridges, mass transit, and other public works has dropped by 75 percent over the past two decades; much of our infrastructure is wearing out far more rapidly than it is being replaced. We do not have a new generation of infrastructure technology, from high-speed trains to underwater tunnels, because we have chosen not to pay for it.

But the steep decline in federal investment during the 1980s has not been limited to infrastructure. Investment in our environment and in human capital—research, education, job skills, and remedial social services—has also plummeted. These, too, have now been deemed superfluous. From 1979 to 1986, in real dollars, federal spending on natural resources has been cut by 24 percent, non-defense R&D by 25 percent, aid to schools by 14 percent, and energy preparedness by 65 percent.

Far from forcing a "revolution" in the role of the federal government, the 1980s have instead seen the federal budget become an ever larger and more efficient consumption machine. In the mid-1960s checks mailed out automatically (to bond owners, health insurers, retirees, state and local benefit administrators) accounted for about 58 percent of all federal non-defense spending. By 1979 their share stood at 68 percent; today it has grown to nearly 80 percent. We have now reached the point, in fact, where even if we eliminated all discretionary non-defense spending (imagine that we could fire all civil-service employees and replace them with a giant check-writing machine), the federal budget would *still* be running a deficit. Our government's function as an investor, a steward of our collective future, is small and shrinking. Its function as a consumer, a switchboard for income transfers, is large and growing.

Surely, it is argued in defense of the growth in entitlements, the alleviation of poverty also constitutes "investment" of a sort—an investment in the long-term social and economic benefits of preventing serious material hardship. If the premise were valid—that federal entitlements go to the poor—this would be a worthy argument. Unfortunately, the facts seem to be otherwise. In 1986 the U.S. public sector spent about $525 billion, or 12.5 percent of GNP, in benefit payments to individuals. Of this total, about $455 billion was financed at the federal level: about $360 billion consisted of cash payments, and the rest consisted of in-kind payments (for example, health care, food stamps, and rental assistance). How much of all this went toward alleviating poverty? No one knows for certain, but probably no more than about 20 percent of the total, or approximately $100 billion. The rest represents income transfers from non-poor taxpayers to non-poor beneficiaries (and, increasingly, to non-poor purchasers of federal debt).

This result should not be surprising, considering that of the $455 billion dispensed from the federal budget, 85 percent was not means-tested—in other words, was not targeted to people living in poverty. These non-means-tested benefits went, by and large, to those groups least likely to be poor. The lion's share, $271 billion, consisted of Social Security and Medicare payments, which went indiscriminately to nearly every elderly person. The elderly now enjoy the lowest poverty rate—less than three percent when the calculation includes total benefit income—of any age group. Far from targeting the poor, Social Security cash benefits are actually regressive, in the sense that those with the highest lifetime incomes receive the highest monthly payments. Another $47 billion was spent on the two most generous pension systems in America: civil-service and military retirement programs. Among the beneficiaries of these programs poverty is practically unheard of; most are not "retired" at all but working at another job and earning a second pension. The average annual income for a federal pensioner is now more than $35,000. Still another $26 billion went to agricultural subsidies. Though this is equivalent to about $18,000 per person working in agriculture, it doesn't help many farm workers. Instead it goes primarily to the owners of the farms with the largest sales, and to banks to service farm debt. Finally, about $43 billion was spent on assorted other non-means-tested programs, such as veterans' health care (going mostly to elderly people with higher-than-average incomes and without service-related illnesses). Unemployment compensation, amounting to less than $18 billion, almost gets lost in this sea of money.

Many of these programs, and especially Social Security, provide invaluable income support to millions of people who would be in poverty without them. This is true especially for members of what Stephen Crystal, in *America's Old Age Crisis,* calls the "multiple jeopardy" groups—those who can be characterized in two or more of these ways: over seventy-five (a group expected to grow by more than 50 percent by the year 2000), widowed, single, divorced, in poor health, without a private pension, and nonwhite. For example, the mean income of the black elderly was only 54 percent of the mean income of the white elderly in 1980. But these people are helped mainly by dint of the enormous sums of money spent, not by virtue of any rational allocation scheme.

It is also argued that federal retirement benefits "belong" to the recipient—despite the consensus among experts that the benefits payback for Social Security and Medicare is five to ten times greater than the actuarial value of prior contributions; plainly put, even middle- and upper-income groups get back vastly more than they put in (including interest and employers' contributions). As for civil-service retirement, we are told that it is a genuine pension system, under which federal workers and federal agencies each contribute seven percent of payroll to a "trust fund" in behalf of every worker's retirement or disability. Yet the pension level is so high (averaging 56 percent of pre-retirement pay), the retirement age so young (age fifty-five after thirty years of service), and the disability criteria so easy (one quarter of all civil-service pensioners are "disabled") that every outside actuary has found, here too, that benefits far exceed contributions. Most say that recipients get somewhere between two and three extra dollars for every dollar they contribute. Unlike any private pension, moreover, civil-service pensions are 100 percent indexed to the Consumer Price Index—with the absurd result that federal pensioners often outearn their successors in office.

As for military retirement, here we confront the ultimate bonanza. The serviceman contributes nothing to a trust fund, but upon reaching a median age of forty-one (and completing at least twenty years of service), he is entitled to 50 to 75 percent of pre-retirement pay, indexed yearly, for life. Typically, military pensioners—including many of the most valuable members of our Armed Forces, who are induced to quit by the retirement bonanza—spend more years collecting benefits than they ever spend in the service. Only one quarter are over age sixty-five, all are eligible for Social Security, and most pursue second careers to achieve a "triple-dip" private pension.

The Administration and Congress have often boasted of "cutting back" on excessive benefit spending. Unfortunately, nearly all the painful and high-visibility cuts have been made in the 15 percent of all benefit programs that are means-tested. One result is that means-tested benefits have hardly grown at all as a share of GNP during the 1980s (in fact, excluding Medicaid, they have actually shrunk; hardly any poverty cash benefits are indexed). Another result is that such benefits target the poor even better now than they did in the 1970s, since most of the cuts have effectively excluded many near-poor beneficiaries, those whom we do not consider truly needy. Meanwhile, the tremendous non-means-tested programs—protected by powerful middle-class lobbies and automatic 100-percent-of-CPI indexing—have burgeoned.

Over the past generation federal benefits have grown roughly twice as fast as our economy. What is most ominous about the long-term trend in the cost of non-means-tested benefits, however, is that these benefits will necessarily continue to grow faster than our economy even if we do nothing explicit to increase benefit levels. Just leaving the budget on "automatic pilot" will lead to fiscal disaster. The forces guaranteeing this result are threefold: the aging of America, the hyperinflation in health care, and the uncontrollability of benefit indexing.

The aging of America: Well over half (about 56 percent) of all federal benefits now go to the 12 percent of our population who are age sixty-five and over. We now direct, on average, about $9,500 a year in federal benefits to each elderly American (largely consumption). In contrast, we direct less than $950 in federal benefits, including aid to education, to each American child (largely investment). In fact, *total* federal spending on net infrastructure investment and non-defense R&D, the benefits of which will last several generations, amounted to only $357 per child in 1986. That's equivalent to the *increase* in federal benefits per elderly person that now occurs every six months.

But even if benefits per elderly person henceforth grow no faster than our economy, we can be certain that the total cost burden will. By about the year 2015 the age composition of the entire United States will be the same as that of Florida today. By 2040 there may be more Americans over age eighty than there are American today over age sixty-five. Over the next fifty years, depending on future fertility and longevity, our working-age population will grow by two to 18 percent, while our elderly population will grow by 139 to 165 percent.

The more "pessimistic" projection (to use the strange term applied by the Social Security Administration to the projection involving longer life-spans) implies that our labor force will grow by only six million people while our elderly population will grow by 46 million. Today each retired Social Security beneficiary is supported by the payroll taxes of 3.3 work-ers. By the year 2020 the ratio will have declined to at most 1:2.3. The official pessimistic picture shows the cost of all FICA-funded Social Security benefits rising to an obviously unacceptable 36 percent of every worker's taxable pay by 2040, from 13 percent today.

Health-care hyperinflation: The novel cost-saving reforms introduced four years ago to Medicare and Medicaid (such as the new prospective pricing now used by Hospital Insurance) stirred widespread hope that we had turned the corner on the rapid growth of health-care spending. Today such hope has faded. Although total U.S. health-care spending as a share of GNP fell slightly in 1984 (from 10.5 percent to 10.3 percent), it rose anew, to an unprecedented 10.7 percent, in 1985, and further, to 10.9 percent, last year. We already know that the rate of inflation for medical care was 7.9 percent in 1986, a rate about seven times higher than the rise in the Consumer Price Index. Optimistic projections made by federal health officials just two years ago are already in shreds. As the Health Care Financing Administration admitted in its report last year, "Little relief appears to be in sight. . . . The decline in the share of GNP going to health in 1984 appears to be a one-time blip in the historic trend rather than the start of a new trend." Health-care benefits as a share of the federal budget, meanwhile, did not experience even a one-year dip. They have risen every year of the 1980s and now amount to about $120 billion annually, or 25 percent of all federal benefit spending.

The underlying causes of America's health-care cost explosion have been discussed at length elsewhere: the rapid climb in real technological and labor costs per treatment, the impressive increase in the number of treatable acute and chronic illnesses, and, of course, the stubborn persistence, in both the public and private sectors, of inefficient health-care regulations and perverse, cost-plus reimbursement systems that insulate both health-care professionals and patients from the cost of treatment. Amazingly—even with the federal reforms enacted in this decade—Medicare has shown nearly the same real rate of annual growth in the 1980s (8.2 percent from 1979 to 1986) as it did in the 1970s (8.7 percent from 1969 to 1979). As recently as 1975 Medicare's total cost was only $14 billion. Last year it was $74 billion, and it may well hit $100 billion by 1990. By 1991 outlays for Hospital Insurance, which account for two thirds of Medicare benefits, may already start to exceed payroll-tax revenue. Thus, without further reform the Hospital Insurance trust fund will almost certainly go bankrupt by the end of the 1990s.

Why have the reforms thus far proved ineffective? A large part of the problem is that *per capita* health-care costs are rising much faster for the elderly than for the population as a whole. Longer life expectancy means disproportionate growth in the oldest age groups, and it is well documented that every measure of health-care utilization rises steeply from age sixty-five on. In 1982, for instance, the average reimbursed hospital cost for Medicare enrollees over age eighty-five was two thirds higher than that for enrollees aged sixty-five to seventy-five. The average per capita cost of long-term care is ten times higher for the "old" elderly than for the "young" elderly, and the high cost of long-term nursing care for the elderly, which is not covered by Medicare, is steadily encroaching on means-tested public benefits not primarily designed for the elderly. In 1984, for instance, though the elderly made up only 10 percent of Medicaid's beneficiaries, they accounted for nearly one third of Medicaid's total spending.

Experts at the Health Care Financing Administration now project that health-care spending in the United States will hit 15 percent of GNP by the year 2000. Do we really think we can become competitive in trade while allocating a still larger proportion of our scarce supply of capital and skilled labor to health-care consumption? According to Lee Iacocca, the Chrysler Corporation pays more money to Blue Cross/Blue Shield every year than it does to any other supplier. Sooner or later we must debate health-care spending in terms of affordability. We must ask why, for instance, we continue to devote so many resources to comforting us at the end of life (more than half of an American's lifetime health-care costs are incurred after age sixty-five), while we pay a Head Start teacher less than $10,000 annually to prepare us at the beginning of life. Other industrial countries are facing such questions with both common-sense humanity and a steady eye on the future. We alone are not.

Uncontrollable indexing: The history of the indexing of non-means-tested benefits is one of the sorriest stories in federal policy-making. Perhaps the most flagrant case in point was the egregious "double-indexing" of Social Security cash benefits enacted in 1972, which essentially pushed up the benefits for new retirees by two CPI indexes at once. This was a colossal error that caused the average retiree benefit to grow far faster than either prices or average wages during the mid-to-late 1970s. The error was apparent to nearly every policy expert as soon as the legislation was passed. But though Congress took only several weeks to debate and pass the 1972 Social Security amendments, it required several years to correct the mistake. In the late 1960s only six percent of all benefits were indexed; today 78 percent of all benefits are indexed to one price index or another, including nearly every non-means-tested cash benefit. The result, quite simply, has been to render outlays for benefits uncontrollable by either Congress or the President.

Most important, indexing makes it impossible for elected policy-makers to reorder their spending priorities by gradually allowing real benefit levels in some programs to fall behind inflation while committing new resources to new problems. This perversity is highlighted by the names that we give to these two types of spending ("discretionary" to outlays earmarked for national investment, and "entitlements" to outlays earmarked for personal consumption).

Back in the early 1970s, when most federal benefit programs were first indexed, none of these problems seemed to matter much. Back then, after all, real federal spending, real GNP, and real wage levels were all still growing rapidly. Today such problems obviously do matter. Facing the prospect of declining or (at best) stagnant real consumption per worker over the next ten or fifteen years as we do, it follows almost by definition that during many of these years we will see prices rising faster than after-tax wages. Each year this occurs, indexing will automatically cause benefit spending to grow faster than wages are growing. The very nature of indexing will then pose genuine questions of equity: to what extent should beneficiaries not in poverty be "held harmless" from downward jolts in the standard of living that affect all other Americans?

To say that the fundamental forces driving up federally financed consumption are aging, health-care inflation, and indexing is not, of course, to say that there is any painless way to avoid them. They cannot be avoided, precisely because all three forces are so closely connected to the shape of our population, as well as our technology, expectations, and political culture. We can, however, speculate on the consequences of trying to avoid them. Recently I asked James Capra, an expert on the federal budget (an unequaled forecaster of our current deficits), to make a forty-year projection of the federal budget—given no change in defense or domestic policy and using the same long-term economic and demographic assumptions that are used by the Social Security Administration.

The results? Using the official pessimistic assumptions, total non-means-tested benefit spending—in the absence of any new benefit provisions—will rise by an amazing 9.6 percent of GNP by 2025, as the retiring Baby Boom generation claims its health-care and cash retirement benefits. By then the explosion in Medicaid-funded nursing care will add another 1.2 percent of GNP. All told, assuming that the totality of other federal costs grows no faster than our economy, the total projected federal outlays for fiscal year 2025 will amount to about 35.4 percent of GNP. Outlays for benefits will consume 22.3 percent of GNP—a sum nearly equal to the entire federal budget today—and outlays for Social Security and Medicare alone will consume more than 31 percent of workers' taxable payroll. These incredible results are most certainly not *predictions;* instead they are *projections* of the future of our present policies. That these outcomes seem impossible is a virtual guarantee that they will be just that. What they mean is that today's policies are unsustainable. They will be radically changed. The only question is how—whether in a political spasm or gradually, allowing those affected to plan ways of coping.

From Denial to Reconstruction

We face a future of economic choices that are far less pleasant than any set of choices we have confronted in living memory. What, concretely, will these choices entail? Looking into the future is always a dangerous task, but here is my attempt to sketch a sequence of future economic issues that will change our lives. My sketch follows the probable chronological order—near-term, medium-term, and long-term—in which reality will impose these issues on us.

The near term (1988 to 1992): Over the near term (a period that already exceeds the "long-term" time horizon of almost every legislator and executive policy-maker) America's primary economic challenge will be to extricate itself from growing foreign indebtedness without touching off a global crisis. The single most important step toward a successful outcome will be for America to generate steady, large, and predictable increases in its net national savings rate over the next several years. This, in turn, cannot be accomplished without steps to eliminate the federal-deficit drain on private savings. Fiscal balance is thus the cornerstone of any plan to cut our trade deficit.

So long as the U.S. demand for foreign savings remains insatiable, any attempt to force-feed U.S. exports to foreigners in any one sector or to any one country will simply be vitiated by a stronger dollar, which will tend to worsen the U.S. trade balance in all other sectors or with all other countries. It's like placing a few sandbags on top of an overflowing dam: you can change where the water will spill over, but you can't change the fact that it will spill over somewhere. If there is little action on the federal budget over the next five years, therefore, the odds of a global crash landing will certainly grow.

As we have seen, a successful escape from our foreign-sector imbalance (barring an improbable near-term leap in U.S. productivity growth) could be accompanied by a decline in real consumption per U.S. worker. Over the next five years, in other words, we must be prepared for a perceptible fall in real after-tax employee compensation combined with a similar decline, or at best a stagnation, in real government spending—both in benefit payments and in defense spending. On the positive side, we can look forward to a rapid expansion in U.S. manufacturing output and employment, a steady improvement in our trade balance, and a steady decline in the rate of foreign-capital inflows (slowing, though not stopping, the deterioration of the net U.S. investment position by 1992). But, in order to avoid the crash scenarios, there is plenty that we must also prepare for on the negative side: a further (though modest) decline in the exchange rate of the dollar, considerable inflationary import-price pressure, and a very tough assignment for the Federal Reserve Bank and its new chairman, Alan Greenspan—finding an interest rate high enough to control inflation and keep the dollar from collapsing, yet low enough to avoid a serious U.S. recession. Most likely, the Fed will have to strike a balance between bad news on both fronts: some accommodation to inflation (as import prices rise) and some accommodation to higher interest rates (as foreign lenders get finicky).

For most working Americans the coming decline in the growth of real household consumption will probably be felt not in any marked change in dollar salary raises but rather in the erosion of real dollar income caused by unavoidably swifter inflation. Wages in manufacturing, exportable business services, and energy will climb much more steeply than wages in other sectors—a trend reversal from the early and middle 1980s which many Americans will welcome. The indexing of federal benefits, meanwhile, will become a major political issue. Not only will steady reductions in budget deficits be difficult to sustain without a major reform of indexing, but 100 percent cost-of-living adjustments for middle- and upper-class federal beneficiaries during years of declining real income for most American workers will raise reform as a stark question of equity. The cost-effectiveness of defense and foreign-aid spending will also come under increasing scrutiny. Since we know full well that it will take a heroic effort to find the resources for economic investment alone, it is totally incredible that we could fund both our domestic obligations and our current global military obligations. By the end of this decade, therefore, it is likely that the United States will raise strategic "burden-sharing" as a routine point of discussion in our economic summits with other industrialized powers.

The medium term (1992 to 2007): The fifteen years that follow our near-term period promise to be a crossroads in our nation's future. As Americans enter this era, five years from now, they may still be uncertain whether the United States has successfully worked its way out of its foreign-sector imbalance. Ironically, it will probably be a signal of impending disaster if real per-worker U.S. consumption is significantly higher in 1992 than it is today, and it would almost certainly be a symptom of worsening global imbalance. Other symptoms would include minimal reductions in our budget deficits and in our credit inflows, further cuts in our net domestic investment, high interest rates, and special ad hoc arrangements to keep our creditors happy—such as yen-denominated Treasury bonds or de facto foreign veto power over U.S. monetary policy. More likely, we will see a considerable dampening in real per-worker consumption, and we will be worrying about (or trying to recover from) a long recession characterized by stagnant global demand.

But twenty years from now, when young adults currently entering the work force are approaching the peak of their careers and when the oldest Baby Boomers are contemplating retirement, the foreign-imbalance problem will have been resolved, one way or the other. By then we may have entered one of the prolonged crash scenarios sketched earlier—the decline of the bumpy British variety or the indefinite depression of the 1930s variety. If, on the other hand, we have resolved the problem successfully, we can expect that our current-account deficit will have declined steadily during the early 1990s and will be turning into a modest surplus by the late 1990s. As that happens, the focus of our policy debates will likely shift from the problem of reducing our foreign borrowing to the challenge of raising our level of domestic investment. Over the near term most of our extra savings must be focused on raising net exports, which is our sole means of weaning ourselves away from foreign creditors. Only later will we be able to concentrate on the more rewarding task of reconstructing our future. Only after paying off our credit-card bills, so to speak, can we think of buying a new home.

The long term (2007 on): Should America not make investment its number-one policy priority in the medium term, it will surely have to pay the price in the long term. It will not be a price denominated solely in terms of labor productivity, real wages, and global political influence. The price will also include an utter lack of preparation for the most stunning demographic transformation—from workers to dependents—in American history. In the fifteen years between 2010 and 2025 the number of Americans who are of working age will decline by perhaps as many as 12 million (from 174 million to 162 million). Meanwhile, assuming that current longevity trends persist, the population of elderly will grow from 42 million to 65 million. If investment, retirement, and health care for the elderly seem unaffordable to our society today and for the next twenty years, when a "boom" generation is working and a "bust" generation is retiring, we can only imagine how unaffordable they will be thirty years from now, when the situation is reversed.

If in the medium term the Baby Boom has channeled a sufficient share of its income into education, training, tools, and infrastructure to permit a quantum leap in productivity by the next generation of workers, it may enjoy a prosperous and contented old age. But if the flow of invested endowments from each generation to the next has ceased—and if each generation instead insists on its "right" to consume all its own product and part of the next generation's as well—then we can count on a meager and strife-torn future.

In any summary discussion of America's prospects in the near, the medium, and the long term, there is one theme that must be emphasized above all others: the indissoluble bond between the economic behavior of one decade or generation and the economic well-being of the next decade or generation. Over the near term we must accept the punishment we are inheriting from the ill-fated gamble of Reaganomics. Similarly, over the medium term we must overcome the low-investment heritage we have received from thirty years of postwar preoccupation with "demand management." Both tasks will require a determined effort to save. We will have to raise our net national savings rate, now somewhere between two and three percent of GNP, to between six and seven percent of GNP in the coming five years (a level still beneath our level in the 1970s) and to between 10 and 12 percent of GNP within twenty years (a level far beneath that of Japan's, but just about on par with the average for today's industrial countries). By the first decade of the twenty-first century, in other words, we will have to be rechanneling yearly into investment some $450 billion that we now spend on private and public consumption.

This broad prescription has implications not only for action but also for understanding. The question is not the easy and popular one of where to invest but the brute one, ignored by both political parties, of where to find the resources. Thus, in the coming election year we need to apply a critical yardstick to the policy proposals of the presidential candidates: Does this proposal face up to the long-term problems caused by our neglect of investment in favor of consumption?

Our problems are not, at bottom, economic. We are stymied by our lack of *political* consensus on economic policy—something unimaginable to our Japanese and German trading partners, for whom national consensus (born of national crisis) informs decisions on savings, investment, productivity-related wage increases, exports, and money-supply growth.

With the proviso that we must put a very large question mark over the capacity of our political system to deal with the nation's economic problems, I offer these brief policy suggestions.

First, we must tame the federal budget deficit. Real defense spending has been effectively frozen for the past couple of years, and we may be at a crossroads in foreign policy which will allow us to make substantial future savings in security expenditures. Greater sharing of the burden by our NATO allies is clearly on the horizon; it should proceed proactively, not reactively (that is, not simply in response to one financial crisis or another). I believe the time is also right for a historic arms treaty with General Secretary Mikhail Gorbachev, whose nation's resources are far more severely constrained than ours and who desperately needs breathing space. The deal I envision would cover the more costly and, when one considers the size of the Soviet tank armies, more plausibly threatening conventional forces, as well as strategic weapons. A new international division of labor remains to be worked out with Japan. The agreement that I think is needed would have Japan provide, for example, far more World Bank support, aid not tied to its exports, and more incentives for major capital flows to Third World countries; further, it would forge a U.S.-Japan strategic-economic partnership in areas of the world critical to both countries—Latin America, say. In turn, the United States would continue to provide military assistance to Japan. Finally, the newly industrializing countries can no longer simply be beneficiaries of an open world economy. They must now join the club of the industrial countries and pay their dues, including aid to the poorer countries.

As for domestic spending, we must above all slow the growth in non-means-tested entitlements, starting with a reform of benefit indexing. Cutting the non-poverty-benefit cost-of-living adjustment, or COLA, to 60 percent of the CPI (a "diet COLA"), for instance, would save about $150 billion in federal outlays annually by the year 2000. Gradually raising the retirement age and lowering initial benefits to the relatively well off (for example, those with histories of high wages) should be combined with the taxation of all benefits in excess of contributions, which could save well over $50 billion annually by the year 2000. Note that under this proposal the progressivity of the tax system would leave intact benefits that go to the poor. There are those who protest the "humiliation" of the means test; however, these reforms go far toward honoring the principle of need, doing so implicitly rather than explicitly.

We should also take a more serious look not simply at the unfunded liabilities of our federal retirement programs but at all the various elements of a grievously costly fringe-benefit pension program. Civil-service and military retirement programs should be made part of a *total* compensation package comparable to those in the private sector. They should gradually be made self-supporting (that is, funded as our corporate pension plans are), through a combination of benefit reductions (with special emphasis on lower initial benefits and later retirement, as well, of course, as reductions in COLA indexing) and higher contribution rates.

Second, we must act decisively to put a lid on America's excessive and wasteful consumption of health care, three quarters of which is either funded directly from public budgets or paid through publicly regulated insurance systems. This is not the place to enter the thicket of specific health-care reforms, but we must begin to experiment in earnest with various means by which to replace the horrendous, indeed perverse, inefficiencies of the current "cost-plus" system with the discipline of market forces (for example, greater cost-sharing, or the use of medical vouchers).

Third, to the extent that our federal deficits cannot be eliminated in the near term by simply deciding to spend less, we must increase federal revenue. The Reagan Administration has steadfastly opposed tax hikes by claiming that they would permanently sanction an increased "tax burden." But surely the alternative is worse: to sanction permanently an increased "debt burden." My choice among revenue options is some form of consumption-based tax. A phased-in tax on gasoline of twenty-five cents a gallon, for instance, would generate about $25 billion a year by 1990—and also serve to depress world energy prices and moderate the now-rapid rise in our oil trade deficit, without destroying the global competitive position of critical export products such as petrochemicals. A broad-based five-percent value-added tax on all products would of course generate considerably more revenue—more than $100 billion in 1990, or enough to halve the federal deficit.

Fourth, over the longer term we should encourage higher private-sector savings rates by trading off increases in consumption-based taxes for reductions in investment-based taxes. Our industrial competitors, after all, have already adopted the principle that people should be taxed more according to what they take out of the pot than according to what they put in. Most of those countries do not tax corporate income twice; most of them do not tax interest, dividends, and capital gains as ordinary income; and most of them do not allow sweeping personal exemptions for home-mortgage interest, for employer-paid health care, and for unearned public retirement benefits. At the same time, all our industrial competitors have much higher household and corporate savings rates than we do. It's time our policy-makers put two and two together.

The least productive enterprise Americans can engage in—though it is virtually second nature—is trying to place the blame for what has happened to our economy in the 1980s on one political party or ideology. Blame is beside the point, for it is something we all share. To be sure, it is easy to find fault with the conservative fiscal leadership of the current Administration. (Indeed, I will confidently predict that in the years to come President Reagan will lament his May, 1985, decision not to support his own party's leadership in its effort to freeze entitlement COLAs. President Richard Nixon, after all, has come to lament his decision to sign those COLAs into law.)

But, clearly, the liberals and the Democrats are equally to blame. Long before Reagan entered the White House, liberal opinion leaders persuaded the public to regard the budget and the tax code as engines of free national consumption. It was a Democratic Congress that argued in favor of deficit spending for so many years that no one could recall (with only one budget surplus since 1960) the rationale behind fiscal balance. And it was a Democratic President who pioneered the art of disingenuous forecasts (when President Johnson signed the Medicare Act, he said that an extra $500 million in federal spending would present "no problem"; today Medicare costs 150 times more than estimated). The very success that the Democrats enjoyed in promoting consumption, in fact, persuaded Reagan's conservative backers to dish the Whigs and beat the opposition at their own game.

Reaganomics was founded on a bold new vision for America, yet today—another irony—we hear every politician who is warming up for the 1988 campaign, Republican and Democrat alike, complaining about the lack of vision in America. The reason we feel adrift is that we are waking up to the fact that blind and self-indulgent gusto is not vision at all but denial. True vision requires the forging of a farsighted and realistic connection between our present and our future. It means recognizing in today's choices the sacrifices all of us must make for posterity. America's unfettered individualism has endowed our people with enormous energy and great aspirations. It has not, however, given us license to do anything we please so long as we do it with conviction.

1980s Decisions; 1990s Consequences

As the policy issues are framed for the 1990s, agendas for action articulated and refined, and as political careers are hitched to various causes, there is the nagging reality that "fresh starts" are few and far between. What policymakers and their constituencies will confront is the fact that prior administrations, prior policy agendas, and prior decisions have established the context within which the present actions can be contemplated. Parameters are in place. Some are simply continuations of a long-standing consensus, e.g., ten-year-old children should not be working like adults, and others may be the result of much more recent vintage, e.g., health care costs cannot be allowed to move upward unchecked by government action.

In either event, the end result is that future policy possibilities take their clues from what is already in place. Further, there is a sometimes rather rough cost-effectiveness calculation undertaken where the benefits of change have to be weighed against the efforts necessary to make that change happen at all. Continuity and bureaucratic stability have, almost uniformly, all the advantages in their corner. "Making the effort" needs to have some encouragement that the end result will occur and that it will be worthwhile.

The three papers in this section all address the consequences of what policy decisions made during the 1980s will have on the policy options of the 1990s. Each of them stresses that while the decisions made earlier were perhaps justifiable in terms of the political and ideology agenda of those in power, the results can outlast them by a considerable time. Stated differently, having been successful in actually effecting change, the weight of this new-found institutionalization as the "way things are" means that any new efforts in a different direction have to face significant resistance. First, there is the need to overcome the resistance of those who have succeeded in getting the new system in place—even if they do function from the position of "loyal opposition." The successes of the previous group will not be yielded meekly. Second, the level of effort has to be sufficient to go beyond existing resistance (or inertia) to be able to put new perspectives and policies in place. And finally, those who have new efforts in place have to give sustained attention and time literally to driving the policies and practices deep into the system. If the changes remain superficial, their staying power will be marginal.

Articles here reflect something of what staying power can accomplish. The focus here is on those changes brought about by two political leaders who have had long tenures—President Ronald Reagan and Prime Minister Margaret Thatcher. The first article, analyzing the state of science and technology in Great Britain, makes clear that the manner in which the Thatcher government has allocated resources over the past decade has had a profound impact on the capability of the United Kingdom any longer to compete at the cutting edge of scientific research. Of particular salience is the emphasis on economic cost containment having consequences that further hinder economic recovery—in this instance the ability of the United Kingdom to use an advanced scientific infrastructure to develop industries and jobs. For those who would wish to reinvigorate scientific research during the 1990s, they will face the cumulative shortcomings of the 1980s—be they the absence of trained staff, the lack of necessary facilities, or prolonged levels of low funding that have undercut the willingness of British researchers to stay in Britain and make the sacrifices necessary to do their research.

The second article, focusing on the Reagan administration initiatives to reduce federal support for urban areas, stresses that the consequences do not just stay at the federal level, but filter down almost immediately to the state and local levels of government as well. Thus, state and local government officials are increasingly facing the decision to cut back on fiscal support. Further, larger levels of government are trying to push the consequences through to smaller levels of government. States are trying to force fiscal changes on counties and localities, while the individual local level frequently tries to manage a smaller pie by cutting services, raising taxes, and when all else fails, going back to the federal government for assistance. The possibilities of local cities going bankrupt are there. The issue is whether the Reagan initiatives and perspectives are now so ingrained that the political process will allow such a condition to unfold across the country.

The final article, by Schlesinger, focuses on the consequences of a newly competitive health care system for the poor in general and minorities in particular. As he notes, "American medicine of the 1980s, though, has seemingly neared a consensus favoring a greater role for market forces and private enterprise. These views have strongly shaped the health policies pursued by the Reagan administration.'' By tracing out these views as they were transformed into a political agenda and subsequent policies, this paper makes clear that not all groups in the population were impacted equally. Nor, it might be added, were all equal participants in coming to this new consensus. Some have clearly borne the burden more than have others.

These policies were not necessarily created to punish one group more than another but, rather, to satisfy broader, more ideological impulses. It was in the translation from macro policies to the micro consequences that impacts for individuals were differentially distributed. Schlesinger makes clear that the least advantaged among minorities have been made even worse off under the system put in place during the 1980s. Consequently, any thought at change of their worsened condition will have to recognize the organizational and policy obstacles they now face. Both a new consensus and a new set of institutional arrangements will have to be forged if those who are least well off in the American medical system are to have their condition changed for the better.

9

The State of Science and Technology in Great Britain

David Phillips

Prologue: The struggle to maintain an adequate level of funding for science in an era of inflation, budgetary constraints, and competing demands on finite resources is not confined to the United States. To build, equip, staff, and maintain a world-class research institute today, whether under university or government auspices, is extraordinarily expensive for every country.

Nowhere is this appreciated more painfully than in Great Britain, where the tradition of scientific research rests on centuries of achievement. In the following essay Sir David Phillips, professor of molecular biophysics and fellow of Corpus Christi College at the University of Oxford, describes the straitened state of British science and the efforts now being made to keep it alive. The transition from steady growth in government-funded research to spending levels more closely tied to changes in gross domestic product, he says, has hit Great Britain ahead of other industrialized countries, but technological competitors, including the United States, are also beginning to feel the pinch.

Without a strong economy, he observes, it is difficult to compete internationally in science. But failure to compete may perpetuate that economic weakness. Great Britain, which has never had an explicit science policy, may now require a national plan for science that provides

Reprinted with permission from David Phillips, "The State of Science and Technology in Great Britain," *Issues in Science and Technology*, Vol. 3, No. 2 (Winter 1987). Copyright 1987 by the National Academy of Sciences, Washington, D.C.

*a more balanced set of national R&D priorities, if only to stem the outflow
of talented British scientists to other countries.*

Science tends to grow exponentially. Money to pay for research does
not. Although the rate of growth in the civil sicence budget in Great Britain
began to tail off in the 1960s (see Figure 9.1), it is only in recent years that
the real strains on the system have begun to show. The strains are reflected
in the contrary positions taken on science funding: Government officials
argue that their stated policy of maintaining level funding for science has
been upheld, whereas the group of researchers mobilized in 1985 under
the banner "Save British Science" believes a once great scientific tradition
is facing calamitous decline.

From the perspective of the Advisory Board for the Research Councils,
which each year frames proposals for the government science budget

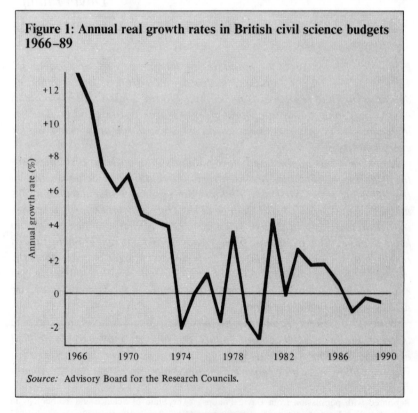

FIGURE 9.1
Annual Real Growth Rates in British Civil Science Budgets 1966–89

covering five research councils, the two views are not inconsistent. The research councils are the main granting agencies for academic and academically related research in Great Britain. The secretary of state for education and science almost always accepts the advisory board's advice on the allocation of funds to the councils, even if the board's overall budget demands are not met. Thus, in 1986–87, the total £614.6 million ($891.1 million) science budget of the Department of Education and Science was divided as follows:

* Science and Engineering Research Council—£315.5 million ($457.5 million)
* Medical Research Council—£128.3 million ($186 million)
* Agricultural and Food Research Council—£52.7 million ($75.4 million)
* Natural Environment Research Council—£70.3 million ($101.9 million)
* Economic and Social Research Council—£23.6 million ($34.2 million)

In addition, there were smaller allocations to the Royal Society and other entities. The five research councils can point to expansions in scientific opportunity. The Science and Engineering Research Council, for example, which funds particle physics and astronomy as well as basic chemistry, biology and mathematics, and engineering research, is also responsible for such increasingly important areas as computer science, molecular electronics, and new materials. Finding the funds to promote such research, however, is increasingly difficult.

The cash value of the science budget has been roughly maintained in real terms over the last five years, although often by last-minute additions grudgingly granted. For several reasons, however, cash parity is not sufficient to maintain the volume of research. Some of these are peculiar to Great Britain, some exist worldwide. Together, they add up to a research system in rapid change, trying to promote important new areas of science while balancing the books.

Some of the roots of British researchers' disquiet lie in key differences between funding arrangements on the two sides of the Atlantic. Great Britain operates a so-called dual support system in which most government-backed civil research is supported cooperatively by the 40 or so British universities and the research councils. (The major source of university funding is an annual government allocation of £1.2 billion [$1.7 billion] for higher education.) Table 9.1 shows that universities and research councils together account for just over a quarter of total government-funded R&D. Table 9.2, taken from a study performed for the Advisory Board for the Research Councils by the science policy research unit at Sussex University, shows government spending in different fields in 1982.

TABLE 9.1
British government R&D expenditures (in £ million, constant 1983–84 prices)

	1981–82	1983–84	1985–86	1987–88 planned
Civil departments	953.6 ($1,382)	907.3 ($1,315)	930.5 ($1,348)	787.4 ($1,141)
Research councils	469.3 ($680)	479.8 ($696)	494.6 ($718)	491.8 ($713)
Universities	539.0 ($781)	551.0 ($799)	530.6 ($770)	520.0 ($754)
Total civil	1961.9 ($2,845)	1938.2 ($2,810)	1955.8 ($2,836)	1799.2 ($2,609)
Total defense	1942.8 ($2,817)	1984.0 ($2,877)	2181.3 ($3,162)	2181.3 ($3,162)
TOTAL	3904.7 ($5,662)	3923.0 ($5,688)	4137.0 ($5,999)	3980.6 ($5,772)

Source: Annual Review of Government Funded R&D, Her Majesty's Stationery Office, 1985.

In 1982, in absolute terms, Great Britain was behind all the other countries studied except the Netherlands. The relative position of Great Britain has almost certainly worsened since then.[1]

The University Grants Committee distributes the annual £1.2 billion government allocation for higher education. In theory, part of the block grants to individual universities from the committee goes toward basic scientific equipment and laboratory overhead and pays for some research. Larger projects are then funded by grants from the research councils or elsewhere. In this system, which is both more centralized and more dependent on government funds than that in the United States, the nation's overall research capability depends crucially on general university funding.

Furthermore, while research council budgets have stayed roughly level since 1981, university funds have been cut. The estimated research contribution from the overall university grant declined by some 3.5 percent in real terms between 1981–82 and 1987–88, according to official figures. However, most believe the decline has been greater because universities have protected teaching at the expense of research as budget pressures have grown.

On the research councils' side, the purchasing power of the money granted has also declined because of increases in salaries and retirement benefit costs. The international weakness of the pound has made it harder to pay subscriptions to overseas scientific organizations, such as CERN (European Center for Nuclear Research) in Geneva, and there have been perennial increases in the cost of laboratory instrumentation—dubbed the "sophistication factor" in Great Britain. Overall, the Advisory Board for the Research Councils estimates that the volume of research funded through the science budget, as opposed to general university funding, will shrink by more than 10 percent over the next decade.[2]

TABLE 9.2
Comparative funding for academic research, by field, 1982 ($ million)

Field	Great Britain	West Germany	France	Nether-lands	United States	Japan
Engineering	304.6	409.6	205.6	90.0	1,135.8	683.4
	(15.8%)	(12.4%)	(8.0%)	(10.1%)	(12.1%)	(21.6%)
Physical sciences	415.7	835.5	843.8	175.5	1,416.2	451.5
	(21.6%)	(25.3%)	(32.6%)	(19.6%)	(15.1%)	(14.3%)
Environmental sciences	127.8	153.8	119.2	21.8	591.9	101.2
	(6.6%)	(4.7%)	(4.6%)	(2.4%)	(6.3%)	(3.2%)
Mathematics and computing	86.0	114.6	136.4	32.6	281.3	72.5
	(4.5%)	(3.5%)	(5.3%)	(3.6%)	(3.0%)	(2.3%)
Life sciences	662.4	1,192.4	935.2	345.8	4,629.8	1,046.8
	(34.4%)	(36.2%)	(36.2%)	(38.6%)	(49.4%)	(33.1%)
Social sciences (includes psychology)	112.3	163.9	119.2	98.2	592.2	132.0
	(5.8%)	(5.0%)	(4.6%)	(11.0%)	(6.3%)	(4.2%)
Professional and vocational	96.7	175.4	60.0	57.3	269.3	334.2
	(5.0%)	(5.3%)	(2.3%)	(6.4%)	(2.9%)	(10.6%)
Arts and humanities	119.7	228.4	165.6	72.6	286.7	344.0
	(6.2%)	(6.9%)	(6.4%)	(8.1%)	(3.1%)	(10.9%)
Multidisciplinary	—	23.2	0.5	0.8	169.4	—
		(0.7%)	(0.0%)	(0.1%)	(1.8%)	
TOTAL	1,925.4	3,296.6	2,585.4	894.9	9,372.7	3,165.6
	(100.0%)	(100.0%)	(100.0%)	(100.0%)	(100.0%)	(100.0%)

Source: Science policy research unit, Sussex University.

This decrease is in part a sign of an inevitable transition from the exponential growth of government-funded research, which has characterized the economies of members of the Organization for Economic Cooperation and Development since World War II, to spending levels linked more tightly to movements in gross domestic product—the transition that science historian Derek DeSolla Price foresaw more than 20 years ago. But if so, Great Britain's relatively poor economic performance has brought about this transition ahead of other countries. At least until 1986, our main economic competitors were still increasing their research budgets. In consequence Great Britain lags on most international indices of research spending, especially for civil research. There looms a painful double bind. Our economic weakness makes it hard to compete internationally in science. But a failure to compete may perpetuate that weakness.

As chairman of the Advisory Board for the Research Councils, I believe that the board must argue for real budget increases. At the same time, though, the board must convince researchers that they can expect something much closer to steady state funding than they became used to in the 1960s, when the budget was still doubling every 10 or 15 years. In addition, any extra money the board can win from government will be in return for stronger assurances that the money will be spent wisely. Advisers such as those on my board have to find new ways of answering the key policy questions: How do we back the best quality research? How do we promote selectivity between program areas and institutions? How do we strike a balance between funding people and instrumentation? How do we ensure that strategic research fields are selected with an eye to future economic potential? In short, how do we select and structure our research portfolio to justify our claims on the taxpayer?

Selectivity in research support is not new in Great Britain, as befits a country that accounts for only around 5 percent of global R&D. As long ago as 1970 the Science and Engineering Research Council—the largest spender—announced a policy of selectivity and concentration in research grants, in response to a decline in the annual rate of growth of its budget. Even then, in many areas, 10 percent of grant applicants received half the available money, although the selectivity then applied was more in terms of institutions than disciplines.

However, the demand for selectivity is undoubtedly increasing in response to the new pressures, notably on the university side of the system. The University Grants Committee is moving toward designating sheep and goats among its flock of 42 institutions, at least as far as research goes, with the consequent redistribution of funds. According to Peter Swinnerton-Dyer, chairman of the committee, "If the best research is to be adequately supported, the less good research will suffer more: but this is better than a policy of inadequate support for everybody."[3]

The committee now allocates part of each institution's grant specifically on research-based criteria, although universities are still free to spend the money as they wish. The teaching component, which accounts for most of the committee's £1.2 billion budget, is fixed solely by student numbers, as before. The research component has four subsidiary elements:

1. A sum equivalent to 40 percent of an institution's income from research council grants, to make dual support more explicit.
2. A sum related to student numbers and academic staff, for general research overhead.

3. A sum related to external contract research income.
4. A sum determined by judgment of an institution's research strengths—as weighed by individual subject committees with advice from research councils and others.

One result has been, in effect, a ranking of British universities by scientific department and discipline—although this was not the University Grants Committee's intent. There has been much unhappiness in many departments that failed to achieve a "star" in the committee's research rankings, and the recently published results will likely affect student choices to some extent. In May 1986 Keith Joseph, then secretary of state for education and science, told the House of Commons that the overall funding allocation exercise was a "landmark" in university policy. The committee's allocations for each discipline were fixed before the calculations about institutional distribution were made, and the total sums moved around will be relatively small in the first years. Nevertheless, the long-term effect will be to shift the cash to universities that are successful at winning external grants and that the committee judges to be strong research centers—presumably the same set. The procedure marks a step toward a possible stratification of universities into high-level research centers and institutions mainly concerned with teaching, much more like the existing U.S. system.

Meanwhile, the research councils are grappling with their own agenda for selectivity. For some of them this has involved large-scale restructuring of programs and heavy staff losses. The Agricultural and Food Research Council, for example, has shed 2,000 staff from the original total of 6,000 employed in its own institutes while managing a shift from farming to food processing research on a declining overall budget.[4]

For others, such as the Science and Engineering Research Council, a larger proportion of university grant applications has been rejected, and spending on central facilities for university research has been cut.

The research councils and the advisory board are also interested in selecting areas of strategic research for support in those scientific disciplines most likely underpin future industrial expansion. The Advisory Board for the Research Councils' sister committee, the Advisory Council for Applied Research and Development, which advises the prime minister on R&D and innovation policy but has no specific budgetary or executive responsibilities, published a report earlier in 1986 calling for an effort to identify "exploitable areas of science." The advisory council argued that strategic research, concerned with both advancing fundamental knowledge and developing new technological possibilities, is assuming more importance in a climate of stronger international industrial competition.

The council's report suggested that the United States is probably the only country that can afford to fund basic research across the board, treating the commercial exploitation of science as a random process. For the less healthy, judicious selection is essential. The council looked to Japan's extensive system for scientific and technical forecasting for inspiration in outlining a process to help Great Britain formulate national R&D priorities geared to industrial growth. The intent would be to try to identify exploitable areas of science, defined as areas "in which the body of scientific understanding supports a generic (or enabling) area of technological knowledge; a body of knowledge from which many specific products and processes may emerge in the future." In other words, the advisory council would go beyond the broad emphasis—now shared by many countries—on biotechnology, information technology, and new materials and would select promising areas in more detail. However, the council also recognized that Great Britain does not have the systematic data collection needed for such an effort. If the preliminary studies begun in the wake of this report bear fruit, which will depend partly on industry putting up the bulk of the money, they could have important results for development of British science policy.[5]

To round off this brief description of moves by research funding agencies toward greater selectivity, I must mention the further pressures—also familiar in the United States—that force those who hold the purse strings to think deeply about the distribution of funds. A striking example of these pressures comes from the United States, in fact—namely the discussion of instrument needs in the National Academy of Sciences survey entitled *Opportunities in Chemistry*.[6]

There are important implications for Great Britain in the academy panel's conclusion that a university chemistry department with the broadest research capability must maintain six out of a possible eight state-of-the-art laboratory instruments—and that at current U.S. funding levels only 20 out of 198 Ph.D.-granting institutions in the United States can expect to operate at this level.[7]

The academy report also envisages a further 40 second-tier and 60 third-tier institutions whose financial needs are part of a general case for additional funding. This analysis points up issues that British research administrators have scarcely recognized. It is widely assumed in Great Britain that every university worthy of the name must have a chemistry teaching department and that every teaching department must do some front-rank research. The Advisory Board for the Research Councils must now ask if our relatively small funding can support anything like the same number of research departments in chemistry as there are universities. If not, there will be hard decisions on location and selection of the real research centers. These questions, and the analogous set in other disciplines, raise long-term, strategic issues that the advisory board will address later this year and in 1987. Great Britain, which has long muddled through without any explicit overall science policy, may now need something like a national plan for science—at least in the academic sector.

A plan for science, if such a thing is possible, will be merely a bureaucratic exercise unless its authors address how to maximize the benefits from research. It is often alleged that Great Britain is brilliant at basic research but inept at translating ideas into hard cash—a perception manifested in attitudes like those of U.S. companies who keep abreast of basic science by "renting a Brit." At home, many compare our record unfavorably with our competitors in Asia; in caricature, the British invented radar and the Japanese adapted the same technology to sell microwave ovens to the world.

In reality, of course, the British preoccupation with improving links between academic research and industry is shared today by many other countries, including Japan. And we have some very good examples of how to succeed, as well as some less auspicious cases. The growth of high-technology industry around Cambridge University does not exactly rival that of Silicon Valley, but the area can boast more than 300 start-up companies over the last 25 years—the vast majority in the last decade. The lessons we have learned from both the successes and the failures are now beginning to feed through into policymaking.[8]

My own feeling is that much earlier policy thinking, in Great Britain at any rate, was hampered by allegiance to a misleadingly simple linear, or assembly line, model of the innovation process. This model, in which inputs into basic research lead through a sequence of stages—applied research, development, design, and marketing—to product or process innovations, was sold to the British government after World War II, just as Vannevar Bush sold it to the Truman administration. But it does not bear close examination.

Great Britain has expended much effort over the years on trying to make its exploitation of science fit the linear model, with often disastrous results. Organizations such as the former National Research Development Corporation had a disappointing history of unsuccessful attempts to introduce innovations based on clever scientific ideas. For example, it turned out that there was no significant world market for the Hovercraft.

We are now nearer to recognizing a more complex, interactive model of innovation, in which contact between academic research and industry is needed at all levels to create the most fruitful coupling between the research base and the market. One implication is that there is no single most favorable institutional model for expediting profitable innovation.

And Great Britain is currently home to as diverse a range of experiments in technology transfer as any country. We have university science parks, industrial liaison teams, private-sector technology transfer agencies funding the development of promising ideas, computer data bases of academic research, and collaborative research schemes linking research councils, universities, government departments, and industry. Much of this is new and untried. As a working group of the Advisory Board for the Research Councils reported in May 1986, "A ferment of activity is in progress, the results of which will not be known for some years."[9] The rationale for most such schemes is to bring academe and industry closer together and give each side more knowledge of the other's priorities, rather than simply to speed up the movement of ideas from the laboratory to the factory.

This is all promising, but there are still tensions among different priorities. Government pronouncements sometimes give the impression that universities should do more research of direct, immediate relevance to industry—and the pressures on college funds have certainly induced some campus researchers to move this way. But there are real fears that this shift could undermine the long-term future of basic research.

Government is more likely to heed this message from industry than from bodies such as the Advisory Board for the Research Councils (although the board has industrial members). And there are encouraging signs of British industrialists rallying in support of public funding for basic research. For example, John Harvey-Jones, chairman of ICI, the British chemicals giant, put the point uncompromisingly in a broadcast lecture earlier in 1986: "We are in danger of failing to recognize that our science is a major strength, is a capacity uniquely suited to the modern world and ought to be a cornerstone of future competitiveness. The Government must ensure that our national intellectual and scientific assets are effectively sustained by its support of fundamental research."[10] Statements like this are commonplace in the United States, but it has hitherto been relatively rare for British business to recognize the importance of novel science and technology.

The domestic picture in Great Britain is thus one of rapid change. Nevertheless, in a small country, policy for science tends to be more and more shaped by developments abroad, and this is especially true for Great Britain, which often is torn between throwing in its lot with European partners and forming stronger links with the United States. Current issues such as the future of high-energy particle physics, participation in the Strategic Defense Initiative (SDI) research program, and establishment of the pan-European Eureka (European Research Coordination Agency) civil research program exemplify this conflict.

In some areas Great Britain's focus is firmly European. In particular, officials of the governments concerned are moving to internationalize Europe's admirable facilities for condensed-matter research. The Science and Engineering Research Council's new neutron source, called ISIS, is to be offered to French, Italian and, probably, West German researchers, in return for British researchers having access to the planned European synchrotron radiation facility in France. ISIS, at the Rutherford Laboratory in Oxfordshire, is the world's most intense source of pulsed neutrons and will be widely used by biologists, chemists, and physicists investigating everything from surface effects to protein structures. It will complement the X-ray beams from synchrotron sources. Great Britain is also a founding member of the European Space Agency and takes part in such European Economic Community programs as ESPRIT (European Strategic Program for R&D in Information Technologies), as well as in numerous smaller scientific exchange schemes. In particle physics Great Britain has a particular interest in future relations between the cooperative European laboratory at CERN in Geneva and similar research centers in the United States because the British government is seeking a 25 percent reduction in its contribution to CERN. On the face of it, particle physics is ripe for the final stage of evolution toward intercontinental, if not global, collaboration to construct the next generation of accelerators. However, there is a widespread perception in Europe that the spirit behind current U.S. proposals for the Superconducting Supercollider is emphatically competitive, rather than cooperative—a spirit sharpened by the spectacular successes at CERN in the early 1980s, when the W and Z particles were characterized.

In my view all governments should now ask why they support high-energy physics. If it is for pure scientific interest, wider cooperation must be the way to go. The promise of applications in fields such as energy technology should be no bar to collaboration—any more than in further development of fusion power. If, however, there is now military interest in particle beams and new accelerator technology, wider collaboration will be harder to achieve. The spirit of CERN is certainly opposed to any weapons-related applications of the laboratory's expertise.

That opposition is also reflected in attitudes among British scientists to participation in SDI research. Although the British government was the first to agree formally to collaborate with the United States in this area, a significant number of British researchers in key disciplines—notably computer science and physics—have opposed any involvement in what they regard as a dangerous and misguided program. This, of course, will not deter others from applying for funds. When they do, there will still be residual British concerns about whether Great Britain can retain control of the intellectual property rights accruing from SDI research—and also about the implications for the balance of the British effort in a few crucial fields. The needs of the SDI program in software engineering, for example, may not be the same as those of civil industry.

In addition, many feel it would be unfortunate if the prospect of support for Brisih researchers from the SDI budget drew an even larger proportion of Great Britain's best R&D people into defense-related work. Great Britain is the only Western country that spends anything approaching the U.S. percentage of its government R&D budget on defense work—more than 50 percent at present. And the fact that most of the basic research associated with British defense programs goes on in Ministry of Defence establishments, in contrast to the U.S. model of university-administered laboratories, has limited private-sector commercial exploitation of this work.

A number of related efforts are under way to break down the barriers around British defense research. They include a company specially formed to assist commercialization of selected promising ideas from Ministry of Defence laboratories, a joint research councils/Ministry of Defence grants program for university research launched in 1985, and discussions about joint planning of large experimental facilities involving civil and defense research programs. But none of these efforts changes the fact that while Great Britain's civil science is losing funds—and international standing—the country continues to spend more than £2 billion ($2.9 billion) a year on defense R&D. True, much of this is development work that might be classified as weapons procurement, but most members of the civil science community believe the defense program must be trimmed to give a more balanced set of national R&D priorities.

As suggested already, those priorities will also have to be framed while keeping a close eye on European R&D. In research programs designed to produce innovations for industrial development in the relatively short term, for example, the full fruits can be realized only by collaboration between firms that can address the European market as a whole—thus benefiting from the same advantages as U.S. firms that can launch their initial sales efforts in a large, homogeneous domestic market.

Thus, there is a growing British consensus that a second phase of the joint academic/industry program for artificial intelligence and computer science research must be "Europeanized" when the first five years and £200 million ($290 million) of state funds come to an end in 1988. This program, launched in answer to the Japanese fifth-generation computer effort, is known as the Alvey program—after John Alvey, the author of a report to the government that proposed it. This program is designed to promote research and industrial development in advanced information technology and computer science, and it brings together universities, research councils, companies, and the departments of education and science, trade and industry, and defense. But it is restricted to British companies, unlike the similar European Economic Community program ESPRIT, in which firms from two or more countries are involved in each project. A further phase of the Alvey effort will have to be linked closely with ESPRIT.

Related to this aim is the broader, and less well-defined, European initiative known as Eureka. This is shaping up to be strongly market driven, partly at Great Britain's behest, and it will be a vehicle for European firms to develop collaborative R&D with the blessing and, possibly, some financial encouragement from participating governments. Eurkea is supposed to promote the application of new technologies in European-wide markets and overcome the disadvantages of markets divided among relatively small countries. The official British position at present is that there will not be new money for Eureka, but British firms will be able to put Eureka projects forward for support under existing schemes to promote industrial innovation supervised by the British Department of Trade and Industry.

SDI, seen not as a defense program but as a massive U.S. government subsidy for new technologies of significant industrial potential, again looms in the background for Eureka. In this sense Eureka was conceived in part as a response to SDI, although the Eureka proposals have also crystallized a feeling that Europe must get its own act together in high-technology R&D.

In any event the core technologies that figure in both programs overlap heavily, especially in such areas as computer architecture, software, sensors, and new materials. Great Britain's position of signing up for both now looks more likely to be shared by other major European countries following the West German agreement on SDI and France's recent change of government.

A final, highly visible issue in Great Britain, and one that affects British thinking on science matters, is the outflow of talented scientists to other countries—most often the sunnier parts of the United States. The so-called brain drain has been an important part of the case for more civil research funds in the last couple of years, as the flow appears to be increasing. Great Britain already contributes more scientists and engineers—around 1,000 a year—to the U.S. technical work force than all other European countries put together, and there is serious concern in Great Britain about the effects of this in key fields. The Advisory Board for the Research Councils is studying the volume and character of the outflow to see what may be done to induce the more able researchers to stay home.

British institutions cannot possibly compete with the salaries offered by some U.S. employers, but the advisory board may be able to cater to those prospective emigrants whose concerns focus more on research opportunities and standards of laboratory instrumentation. For example, a special addition of some millions of pounds to the universities' equipment budget in 1985 was allocated to a very few groups, to ensure they had state-of-the-art instruments. We may see more of this selective extravagance as a matter of advisory board policy.

Anyone contemplating the state of science and technology in Great Britain must consider where the next generations of researchers will come from, especially if we continue to lose so many early in their careers. Science can reproduce itself only if there is a steady supply of aspiring researchers coming out of the schools and seeking an apprenticeship at the laboratory bench. This is a serious cause for concern in Great Britain. Demands from industry for highly qualified scientists and technologists are revealing shortages in such key skills as computing, which raise salary levels beyond universities' means.

Efforts to meet these shortages are being hampered by the condition of British primary and secondary education. School teaching does not have high status in Great Britain, and a loss of morale among teachers combined with low salaries has drastically curtailed recruitment of the mathematics and physics teachers essential to bringing students up to university entrance level in science. Government policy calls for curriculum changes that will ensure that all students take some science subjects, but they may well be supervised by teachers unqualified in science unless measures such as use of differential salaries can raise the numbers of qualified teachers. Great Britain appears on the verge of a renewed debate about educational standards, with special emphasis on the quality of technical and vocational education, but the results will take a long time to affect the numbers of qualified teachers.

Related to this is a wider debate familiar in the U.S. context about the level of public understanding of science, or scientific literacy. This concerns many scientists partly because of worries over economic performance and attitudes regarding new technology, but also because of some currents of public opinion that come closer to the laboratory. Examples of the latter include strong opposition to in vitro fertilization research—a bill that would have outlawed all experiments on human embryos went through several stages of debate in Parliament before being filibustered and so defeated—and criticism of experiments using animals. Militant animal liberation groups have raided laboratories, threatened researchers, and damaged the researchers' property up and down the country. They regard new British legislation regulating animal research as a charter for vivisectionists.

British researchers naturally regard these currents of opposition as stemming from a failure to appreciate the merits of their work. A 1985 report from the Royal Society rightly concluded that education must be the main target for action on this front.[11] But the Royal Society also urged working scientists to take more responsibility for explaining their research to lay audiences. This is a difficult responsibility to place on researchers already trying to keep pace with fast developing fields on tight budgets. However, perhaps if it comes to be taken more seriously in Great Britain, as it already is in the United States, making the case for science funding would also become easier. That in turn may help achieve long-term security of funding instead of an annual uncertainty about next year's budget.

NOTES:

1. Ben R. Martin and John Irvine with Nigel Minchin, *An International Comparison of Government Funding of Academic and Academically Related Research,* ABRC Science Policy Studies No. 2 (Brighton, England: Sussex University, Science Policy Research Unit, Oct. 1986).
2. Department of Education and Science, *Science and Public Expenditure 1986: A Report to the Secretary of State for Education and Science from the Advisory Board for the Research Councils* (London: ABRC, July 1986).
3. Peter Swinnerton-Dyer, "Weighing Out the Pots of Gold," *Times Higher Educational Supplement,* Nov. 15, 1985.
4. Agricultural and Food Research Council Corporate Plan, 1986–1991 (London: AFRC, March 1986).
5. *Exploitable Areas of Science: A Report by the Advisory Council for Applied Research and Development* (London: Her Majesty's Stationery Office, 1986).
6. National Research Council, *Opportunities in Chemistry* (Washington, D.C.: National Academy Press, 1985).
7. National Research Council, *Opportunities in Chemistry,* 303–5.
8. *The Cambridge Phenomenon: The Growth of High Technology Industry in a University Town* (Cambridge: Segal Quince and Associates, 1985).
9. Advisory Board for the Research Councils/Department of Education and Science, *Report of the Working Party on the Private Sector Funding of Scientific Research* (London: ABRC, May 1986).
10. John Harvey-Jones, "Does Industry Matter?" *The Listener,* Apr. 10, 1986.
11. *The Public Understanding of Science: Report of a Royal Society Working Party* (London: Royal Society, 1985).

10

A New Urban Crisis in the Making

Thomas R. Swartz

In October of 1972, President Nixon signed into law the "State and Local Fiscal Assistance Act." This act of legislation, popularly known as General Revenue Sharing, exemplified the generosity bestowed on local governments by both the federal and state governments. This legislation was also the cornerstone of President Nixon's "New Federalism," a policy designed to give state and local governments greater decision-making responsibilities while at the same time giving the federal government greater revenue responsibility for funding local needs.

These were the "golden years" for local governments. This fifteen-year period—1964 to 1978—was an era of new programs: The Economic Opportunity Act, Medicaid, Title I and II of the Elementary and Secondary Education Act, Manpower Training and Development Act, Comprehensive Employment and Training Act (CETA), Community Development Block Grants, Law Enforcement Assistance Administration, and the Economic Development Administration.

These were years of rapid growth for state and local governments: State and local spending increased from 10.7 percent of GNP in 1964 to 13.7 percent of GNP in 1978—a 28 percent increase; federal aid to state and local governments increased from 17.3 percent of their own tax receipts to 32.1 percent—an 85.5 percent increase; state and local expenditures per capita increased from $491 to $888—an 80.8 percent increase; and state and local employment increased from 7.5 million to 12.7 million—a 69.9

Reprinted with permission of publisher, M. E. Sharp, Inc., 80 Business Park Drive, Armonk, New York, 10504, USA, from the September–October 1987 issue of *Challenge,* pp. 34–41.

percent increase. Thus, as Table 10.1 indicates, state and local governments grew at an almost uncontrollable rate during this period.

The Tax Revolt

However, the growth of state and local government expenditures (particularly the latter) came to an abrupt halt on the morning of June 7, 1978,
when Americans awoke to discover that the voters in California had passed
Proposition 13. Voters across the nation were quick to follow California's
lead. They called on their local governments to "pull in their belts" and to
get the "fat out of government." They demanded "a smaller, more
efficient government which would not compete with the interests of the
private sector."

This 389-word addendum to the California Constitution, known as the
Jarvis-Gunn Amendment, set in motion a radical shift in our system of
fiscal federalism. In a single stroke it reduced the most important source
of local government revenue in California by 57 percent and saved California nearly $7 billion in property taxes. It established a property tax rate of
1 percent for all real property—houses, farms, factories, businesses, and
vacant lots. It rolled back 1978 assessments to levels that existed in 1975–
76 (California reassessed all real property on an annual basis prior to
Proposition 13) and froze them at these levels until a time when the
property was sold or improved. It limited increases in the property tax
levy to a mere 2 percent a year. And it mandated that the state legislature
obtain a two-thirds majority of both houses to increase any other tax in
California.

Hindsight suggests that voters in California supported Proposition 13
because of a set of circumstances that were unique to their state, not
because they were dissatisfied with government in general and therefore in
a "tax revolt." (There were four unique circumstances in California: (1)
the presence of a $7 billion state surplus; (2) a property tax levy that
increased 20 percent a year for the two years prior to Proposition 13; (3) a
high tax effort and expenditure pattern compared to other states; and most
important, (4) a school finance formula that reduced the state share of
education costs and increased the local share each time local assessments
increased.)

Even though voters in California may not have intended to participate in
a tax revolt, the fact of the matter is that this action was perceived as a tax
revolt by the rest of the country. It was also perceived as the beginning of
a national tax revolt. Within four short months, state after state followed
California's lead. The print and electronic media rushed to tell us about
the Headlee Amendment in Michigan, Proposition 2½ in Massachusetts,

TABLE 10.1
The Golden Years of State and Local Government Finance

Years	State/local expenditures (after transfers) as % of GNP	State expenditures (after transfers) as % of GNP	Local expenditures (after transfers) as % of GNP	Federal aid as a % of state/local general revenue	State/local expenditures per capita (1972 $)	State expenditures per capita (1972 $)	Local expenditures per capita (1972 $)	State employment (000)	Local employment (000)
1954	8.2	2.9	5.3	11.4	311	110	200	1,149	3,710
1964	10.7	3.8	7.0	17.3	491	172	319	1,873	5,663
1969	12.6	4.5	8.0	20.4	675	243	432	2,614	7,102
1978	13.7	5.1	8.6	32.1	888	330	558	3,539	9,204

Source: U.S. Advisory Commission on Intergovernmental Relations, *Significant Features of Fiscal Federalism, 1985–86 Edition* (Washington, D.C.: Government Printing Office, February 1986) Tables 2, 44, and 79.

and Florida's Proposition 1. The media also followed Howard Jarvis as he stomped across mid-America and up and down the Eastern Seaboard seeking support for new controls on state and local tax and spending authority.

When the dust finally settled, 51 new fiscal controls or restrictions were placed on state and local government tax and expenditure powers. As Table 10.2 on the next page shows, most of the controls, 35 out of 51, were imposed on local governments and a vast majority of these local controls were aimed at limiting local government taxing authority. Only 16 of these 51 new controls were directed toward state expenditure and tax authority. Half of these state controls were mandated by constitutional provision and half statutorily.

It is important to note that although the post-1978 period witnessed a frenzy of activity in the control area, all but two of the state controls and almost all of the local controls occurred in 1978, 1979, and 1980. In part as a result of the wave of fiscal controls enacted in this period, and in part as a result of independent legislative action, many state governments systematically reduced their broad-based sales and income taxes. These actions represented major policy reversals. In the "golden years" prior to Proposition 13, thirteen states adopted the personal income tax and twelve states adopted a general retail sales tax. This same period witnessed 75 personal income tax rate or base increases and 76 rate or base increases for the retail sales tax. However, during the "tax revolt years," not only were there no new state adoptions of sales or income taxes, but there were 35 personal income tax decreases and 19 sales tax reductions.

Congress Gets the Picture

The fiscal controls that states rushed to place on their local governments and their own fiscal powers were not the only legacy of Proposition 13. As fiscal conservatism swept across the country, federal policymakers soon began to sense a shift in public opinion. In 1978, Democrats joined their Republican colleagues in a call to re-examine the growth of domestic spending programs, including the entitlement programs. Federal spending, and the entitlement programs in particular, had taken on a life of their own. They continued into the future without a "sunset provision" and, more important, they continued on an ever larger scale. The result was a growing intrusion of the federal government into the economy. During the 1960s and 1970s, federal expenditures fluctuated between 16.9 percent and 18.8 percent of GNP. By fiscal 1980, federal expenditures as a percent of GNP were expected to rise to 19.5 percent and they were projected to inch upward at a steady rate during the decade of the 1980s. (Even with the

TABLE 10.2
Revenue and Expenditure Controls on State and Local Governments

Period	Local Government Limits					State Government Limits*			
	Total number of controls	Number of states with revenue controls	Number of revenue controls	Number of states with expenditure controls	Number of expenditure controls	Number of controls	Number of states with expenditure controls	Type of control Constitutional limit	Statutory limits
Enacted prior to 1930	33	33	25	0	0	0	0	0	0
Enacted between 1970 and 1977	24	18	10	4	4	2	2	0	2
Enacted after 1978	51	33	21	2	2	16	2	8	8

*In addition to these controls, every state with the exception of Vermont has some constitutional or statutory provision to maintain a balanced state budget.

Source: U.S. Advisory Commission on Intergovernmental Relations, *Significant Features of Fiscal Federalism, 1985–86 Edition* (Washington, D.C.: Government Printing Office, February 1986) Table 91.

fiscal restraints imposed by Presidents Carter and Reagan, federal expenditures on the national income accounts budgets were estimated to be 24.3 percent of GNP in 1986.)

A national consensus began to take shape in 1978. Programs such as CETA, subsidized housing programs, AFDC, child nutrition programs, food stamps, and mass transit aid were no longer looked upon with favor. Now even the "sacred cows" came under close scrutiny: extended unemployment benefits, veterans programs, and SSI. The call from Capitol Hill sounded much like the call from statehouse after statehouse: "Pull in your belts," "Get the fat out of government," and "Let's strive for a smaller, more efficient government which does not compete with the interests of the private sector."

Congress didn't wait for the arrival of President Reagan. Instead, a Congress controlled by Democrats and led by a Democratic President took the first steps toward cutting federal government expenditures. In President Carter's 1978 State of the Union address, he declared:

> This budget for fiscal year 1980 is *lean and austere*. It recommends a spending level well below that suggested by the recent momentum of federal spending. It will disappoint those who seek expanded federal effort across the board. It meets my commitment to a deficit of $30 billion or less.

President Carter's call for deep cuts in domestic spending was not limited to a few high-profile programs; it extended all the way through the budget to programs such as general revenue sharing. For the first time since its enactment in 1972, the legitimacy of this program was challenged. As Table 10.1 suggested, federal aid as a percent of state and local general revenue had increased at a remarkable rate. In 1954 it was only 11.4 percent of state and local general revenue; by 1978 federal aid had increased to 32.1 percent. This means that in less than twenty-five years federal support for state and local programs had nearly tripled. Confronted with this reality, many in Congress began to wonder whether state and local governments could be fiscally responsible when one out of every three dollars they spent was a gift from the federal government.

With the support of Congress, President Carter targeted general revenue sharing. He proposed a renewal of this program, but a renewal with several distinct modifications. Although the 1980 legislation renewed revenue sharing for another three years (it was subsequently renewed again for three years in 1983, and quietly killed in the fall of 1986), this 1980 legislation reduced it from $6 billion a year to $4.5 billion a year and limited the sharing to local governments alone, bypassing the state. Carter did not stop with recommendations for cuts in this program; he went on to recommend reducing grants for local public works projects, public service unemployment, and counter-cyclical revenue sharing. The bottom line was clear: The federal government was no longer going to underwrite a larger and larger share of state and local expenditures. To the contrary, the tide had turned. The federal government would now only be committed to a progressively smaller share of future state and local expenditures.

The Reagan Years

The "lean and austere" budgets of President Carter seem pleasantly plump compared to those offered by President Reagan. When this new President swept into office pulling with him many first-term conservative members of the House and Senate, he claimed a mandate that he meant to use.

No one should have wondered about the course of public policy under the Reagan Administration. The newly elected President had repeatedly stated his intentions during his campaign for office. In the event that doubts remained, he restated his goals with forthright clarity in his inaugural address. He called for: (1) reduced federal taxes and regulation; (2) a balanced budget; (3) increased defense spending; (4) a renewal of national pride; and (5) a policy that would return power to the states.

Of course it is this fifth goal that is of great importance in a discussion of the new urban crisis. However, do not lose sight of the fact that other policy prescriptions of the Reagan Administration had very direct and immediate implications for state and local governments. Many of the budget cuts engineered by this administration impacted state and local governments just as certainly as his $11.6 billion reduction in grants to state and local government.

Therefore, while Table 10.3 tells an important story, it does not tell the whole story. The federal government could and did slow the flow of funds to these programs, but this did not necessarily mean that there was a corresponding reduction in the demand for these programs. Indeed, as fall turned to winter in 1981, and the economy slid into the worst recession in the post-Depression era, a *growing* number of individuals, not a declining number, needed food stamps, trade adjustment assistance, and help in paying their utility bills.

There is a curious irony here. The Reagan policies were designed to reduce federal support for a number of domestic social programs. However, because Reagan's macroeconomic policies threw the economy into a severe recession, federal expenditures for these domestic social programs actually increased. Take care not to be misled by these aggregate figures. Although total federal expenditures increased, the federal share fell. Of

TABLE 10.3

Federal Aid to State/Local Governments as a Percentage of State/Local Revenue and by Major Expenditure Category

($ in millions)

Fiscal Year	Amount	As % of state/local revenue	Education	Highways	Public welfare	Housing and urban development	All other—including revenue sharing
1954	$ 2,967	11.4	$ 475	$ 530	$ 1,439	$ 90	$ 433
1964	10,097	17.3	1,371	3,628	2,973	564	1,561
1969	19,421	20.4	4,960	4,314	6,358	921	2,868
1978	79,172	32.1	11,620	6,197	20,051	2,969	38,353
1980	90,836	30.4	12,889	9,457	28,494	6,093	33,903
1981	94,609	28.4	12,708	9,253	34,405	6,065	32,178
1982	86,014	23.3	11,971	8,000	34,414	5,716	25,913
1983	88,539	22.3	12,528	8,851	36,282	5,583	25,295
1984	99,015	22.2	13,608	10,204	40,054	8,817	26,332

Source: U.S. Advisory Commission on Intergovernmental Relations, *Significant Features of Fiscal Federalism, 1985–86 Edition* (Washington, D.C.: Government Printing Office, February 1986) Table 44.

course this means that the state and local share of the fiscal burden of
these programs increased and the actual dollars spent on these programs
increased dramatically.

The States Tax Again

As the Reagan years wore on and Administration macroeconomic policies continued to hamper growth, states were forced to reverse the policy
of tax reductions that was established in the 1978–1980 "tax revolt period." Instead of 54 reductions in rates or bases of state sales and income
taxes, state governments enacted 58 increases in these taxes! The search
for additional revenue did not stop with income and sales tax increases. A
total of 177 other tax increases were passed by our state legislators. The
scramble for new sources of revenue was on. Thirty-four states increased
taxes in 1981, twenty-five states increased taxes in 1982, and forty-one
states raised at least one tax in 1983.

It is interesting to note that in their attempts to close the revenue gap,
many states at first thought they could cover the revenue shortfall with a
Band-Aid solution. In 1981, 69.2 percent of all tax increases were excise
tax increases, often on such products as alcohol and motor fuel. However,
as the severity of the revenue gap became more obvious, state governments were forced to increase their broad-based sales and income taxes.

There is little wonder why states felt it necessary to engage in this
hailstorm of tax increases. The Omnibus Budget Reconciliation Act, the
tax/expenditure bill that incorporated most of President Reagan's domestic
policy initiatives, was passed by Congress in August of 1981, but the real
impact of this legislation was not felt until 1982. From 1981 to 1982 the
absolute value of federal aid to state and local government fell by $8.6
billion or 9.1 percent. Thus, the trend established by the Carter Administration was brought into sharp focus by the Reagan Administration. In
1978, federal aid as a percent of state and local general revenue was 32.1
percent. This fell to 30.4 percent in 1980 and to 28.4 percent in 1981.
However, in 1982 a new pattern was established. Instead of providing state
and local governments with one of every three dollars they spent, the
federal government would begin to move toward a one-of-five-dollar level.
Athough the cuts came across the board, highway grants (13.5 percent)
and the "other" category (19 percent) were hardest hit.

Finally the economy broke out of the 1981–82 Reagan recession and by
mid-1983 was growing at a very rapid rate. In real terms, the growth rate
was 6.8 percent in 1983. Once the ground that was lost in the 1981–82
recession was recovered, however, the economy settled into a lackluster
growth rate of 2.5 percent annually. This pattern is reflected in both

industrial production data and in employment data. Industrial production burst forth from the recession at a 16.4 percent rate of growth for 1983. This slowed to a 6.6 percent growth rate for the first three quarters of 1984 and has since declined to 1 percent. The same is true for the unemployment rate. From 1982 to early 1984 it fell from 10.8 percent to about 7.2 percent; since that time unemployment has only recently dropped below the 7 percent level.

These growth rates have been disappointing and perhaps even alarming. The fact that industrial production has remained virtually unchanged since August of 1984 does not bode well for those of us in the Great Lakes states or in the Northeast where there is a high level of industrialization. In part, this sluggish economy explains the recent pattern of state tax policy. The slow rate of growth meant that the tax base in many states (and therefore their tax receipts) was not growing, forcing some to raise rates or redefine their tax base. Others were more optimistic and have moved to reduce their taxes in anticipation of future economic growth. Thus, no clear new tax pattern was established in the 1984–85 period.

Federal Tax Reform

Enactment of the 1986 federal tax program added to the ambiguity. Although Congress intended this legislation to reform the federal personal income tax by broadening the tax base and reducing marginal tax rates, this tax program also immediately impacts those states that coordinate the administration of their state income tax with the federal income tax.

Currently, only six of the forty states that employ a significant personal income tax (three additional states impose a very limited tax) do not synchronize their tax with the federal tax. Of the remaining thirty-four states and the District of Columbia, there are degrees of cooperation. In the most extreme cases, four states eliminate nearly all of their tax auditing responsibilities by defining state tax liability as a simple percentage of the federal tax liability. For example, state income tax in Nebraska is 19 percent of federal tax liability. In other words, a resident of Nebraska with a federal tax bill of $1000 knows that the state tax bill is $190, or 19 percent of $1000. At the other end of the spectrum, seven states begin calculation of state tax liability by asking taxpayers to report adjusted gross income as it appears on their federal income tax returns. Thus, if a resident of Arizona reports $50,000 on line 32 of form 1040, the State of Arizona accepts that dollar amount as adjusted gross income for state tax purposes. Arizona then applies its own exemptions, deductions, and rate schedule to this base income.

Because of the differences in the linkage between the federal tax and the various state taxes, states are affected differently by the tax reform package. Three broad groups can be identified: (1) states that are expected to experience a revenue loss; (2) states that are expected to be unaffected; and (3) states that are expected to experience a windfall gain. As Table 10.4 suggests, four states will be negatively impacted, twenty-three states will be unaffected, and twenty-three states plus the District of Columbia will experience a windfall. In the first case, a revenue loss is expected because the federal tax reform will reduce the tax receipts of the personal income tax. (In order to keep the total tax package revenue-neutral, corporate taxes were increased.) Since Nebraska, North Dakota, Rhode Island, and Vermont determine state tax liability by taking a percentage of federal tax liability, these states are expected to experience a revenue loss. The twenty-three states expected to be unaffected by the federal tax reform either have a very limited personal income tax or no state income tax at all; have a personal income tax but do not coordinate that tax with the federal income tax; or limit the coordination of their income tax to accepting adjusted gross income as calculated for federal tax purposes. The third group of states, which are expected to experience a windfall gain, benefit from the broadened tax base that is not automatically offset by tax rate reductions. That is, those states that accept federal definitions of taxable income (or most of these definitions in terms of exemptions and deductions from adjusted gross income) but have retained their own state tax rate schedules will see their income tax receipts increase in 1987 unless they take steps to adjust their tax rates downward.

However, there is no guarantee that these fortunate twenty-three states receiving an unintended benefit from the recent federal tax reform will share this largess with their cities. Nine of these states have already moved to cut their 1987 budgets, apparently with the full knowledge that their tax receipts will increase in future years because of the federal tax changes. Four of these states plus an additional five states placed expenditure/tax controls on their state systems in the aftermath of Proposition 13; thus, these states have revealed a conservative fiscal posture. Lastly, in at least a few of the state legislatures of those nine states that have not cut their budgets for 1987 or recently enacted control legislation, legislators are debating the merits of passing this bonus back to taxpayers by cutting state tax rates. This is most notably the case in New York. It can only be concluded that few states will be in a position to support the activities of their local governments and fewer still will be so inclined.

This rather pessimistic picture is consistent with the results of the latest annual survey of the fiscal vitality of our cities which was undertaken by the National League of Cities. Their survey of 660 municipalities reveals the following: (1) 56 percent of the cities sampled anticipate their expendi-

TABLE 10.4
The Impact of Federal Personal Income Tax Reform on State Personal Income Tax Revenue

| | States expected to be unaffected | | | States expected to experience a windfall gain | |
| | States with no or a limited income tax | States with a personal income tax | | States that use federal taxable income as base | State that use federal adjusted gross plus most federal deductions |
States expected to experience a revenue loss		No coordination with federal tax	Use federal adjusted gross income only		
1. Nebraska[a,b]	Alaska[a,b]	Alabama[a]	Arizona[a,b]	Hawaii[b]	California[a,b]
2. North Dakota[a]	Connecticut	Arkansas[a]	Illinois	Idaho[b]	Colorado[a]
3. Rhode Island	Florida	Mississippi	Indiana[a]	New Mexico[a]	Delaware
4. Vermont	Nevada[b]	New Jersey	Massachusetts	Oklahoma	District of Columbia
5.	New Hampshire	North Carolina	Michigan[b]	Oregon[b]	Georgia
6.	South Dakota[a]	Pennsylvania	Ohio	South Carolina[a,b]	Iowa
7.	Tennessee[b]		Wisconsin[a]	Utah[b]	Kansas[a]
8.	Texas[a,b]				Kentucky[a]
9.	Washington[b]				Louisiana[a,b]
10.	Wyoming[a]				Maine
11.					Maryland
12.					Minnesota[a]
13.					Missouri[b]
14.					Montana[a,b]
15.					New York
16.					Virginia
17.					West Virginia

[a]These are states that have made cuts in their 1987 state budgets because actual tax revenue is assumed to be less than projected tax revenue due to the sluggish economy.

[b]States that have imposed new fiscal controls on their state governments since 1978.

Source: U.S. Advisory Commission on Intergovernmental Relations, Significant Features of Fiscal Federalism, 1985–86 Edition (Washington, D.C.: Government Printing Office, February 1986) Tables 60 and 91; Government Finance Review, Vol. 3, no. 1 (February 1987) p. 4.

tures to exceed revenues this year; (2) because many cities have been forced to fund current deficits out of general fund balances, these balances were lower at the end of 1986 than they were at the beginning of 1986 for nearly 60 percent of the cities and towns sampled; and (3) more than 50 percent of the sample did not expand or actually reduced their municipal workforce during 1986. Thus recent data suggest that hard times are ahead for our urban places.

The Future

One fact emerges quite starkly: President Reagan has been successful in implementing his promise to return power to state and local governments. This is true even though Congress explicitly rejected his 1982 policy initiative in this area. That legislation would have had the federal government assume full responsibility for Medicaid if the states would assume full responsibility for AFDC and about 40 other programs in the areas of education, community development, transportation, and social services. States would have been subsidized for their efforts by a temporary trust fund backed by the tax receipts of the federal excises.

It must be remembered that President Reagan's notion of decentralization, or returning power to the state and local government level, is a far cry from President Nixon's call for a New Federalism. Both Nixon's and Reagan's policies assume that it is right and just for local governments to make decisions that affect them directly; however, President Nixon intended to share in the cost of these activities through general revenue sharing, while President Reagan intends for state and local governments to pay for these programs themselves.

Given the limited fiscal capacity of many states and localities, the effect of Reagan's policy is preordained. State and local expenditures as a percent of GNP must fall, and fall they did from the 13.7 percent level of 1978 to 13.2 percent in 1985. What is surprising is the fact that states have reversed the stand they took during the tax revolt years. Instead of limiting the activity of their local governments, they have begun to shift more fiscal responsibility toward them. This is apparent in Table 10.5. Although state aid to local governments has increased in nominal terms, state aid as a percent of local government general revenues has fallen markedly since the late 1970s. In 1979, state aid as a percent of local government general revenue was equal to 63.5 percent. By 1984, the state share had fallen to 54.3 percent. This represent a 15 percent reduction.

The combined impact of federal and state participation in the fiscal affairs of local governments has resulted in a radical shift in the nature of our fiscal federalism. Local governments across the country—particularly

TABLE 10.5
States Shift Fiscal Responsibility
to Their Local Governments

Year	State aid to local governments ($ in millions)	State aid as a percentage of local general revenue
1978	$ 65,815	59.4%
1979	74,461	63.5
1980	82,758	63.6
1981	91,307	62.7
1982	96,980	59.4
1983	99,544	55.6
1984	106,651	54.3

Source: U.S. Advisory Commission on Intergovernmental Relations, *Significant Features of Fiscal Federalism, 1985–86 Edition* (Washington, D.C.: Government Printing Office, February 1986) Table 45.

county and city governments—are far more dependent on their own sources of revenue in 1987 than they have been in recent memory. From 1978 to 1984, the relative importance of grants-in-aid to our county governments fell by more than 20 percent, while the relative importance of grants-in-aid for city governments fell by more than 30 percent. This means that local governments must be more dependent on their own sources of revenues.

Since local governments are to provide for their current and future needs, they must take advantage of all opportunities that their state governments make available. The golden days are over. Local governments can no longer depend on the state and federal government to bail them out. They must analyze their long-term needs and adopt a long-term program that fits those needs. This is the message of the new New Federalism.

If local governments are to share a larger and larger portion of the cost of providing basic government services, we must expect that over time a larger and larger number of these local governments will encounter difficulties in meeting these new responsibilities. Indeed, the very reason why states and the federal government became deeply involved in funding the activities of local government was the recognition that these local governments had widely disparate fiscal capacities.

Public policy is about to complete a grand full cycle. We are about to return to the days when city after city faced the reality of major service reductions and even bankruptcy. This is the implied intent of Reagan's policies: pit region against region and city against city. That is, for the sake of some abstract notion of economic efficiency, subject our local communities to the same market discipline to which we subject our business community. Unless public policy changes, we will pursue a "survival of the fittest" strategy for the 1990s. Those towns and cities that are strong will survive, those that are weaker will wither. With the demise of these communities will go an irreplaceable part of the America we know today: the stability and certainty of each of our hometowns.

11

Paying the Price: Medical Care, Minorities, and the Newly Competitive Health-Care System

Mark Schlesinger

> I took one Draught of Life —
> I'll tell you what I paid —
> Precisely an existence —
> The market price, they say.

Emily Dickinson, poem no. 1725

T HERE HAS LONG BEEN A TENSION IN AMERICAN policy making between reliance on government and reliance on the market to allocate socially valued services such as health care, education, and social services. Nowhere has this tension been more pronounced than for those services used by racial and ethnic minorities.

The market has been portrayed by its advocates as preserving free choice, safeguarding minorities from the oft-times insensitive will of the majority (Friedman 1962). But these safeguards clearly have their limits. Minorities who lack financial resources will have little voice in the market. With a poverty rate for black families that is three times that of white households, much of the black community is economically disenfranchised (Jones and Rice 1987). Nor are all choices in the market freely made. Those who face discrimination lose much of their free choice. Under some circumstances, discrimination based

From *The Milbank Quarterly*, Vol. 65, Supplement 2 (1987): 1–27.

on race is not only possible, but virtually inevitable in a market system (Spence 1974).

If the market only imperfectly reflects minority interests, the same is certainly true for government. When a representative government inadequately represents blacks, it will not be fully responsive to their concerns. And despite two decades of voting-rights legislation and registration campaigns, blacks continue to be underrepresented, particularly in Congress and most state legislatures (Persons 1987).

For those who would promote minority interests, there are, therefore, no obvious choices between public and private sectors, between markets and the political process. Equally thoughtful observers reach diametrically opposed conclusions, some favoring the market (Sowell 1981), others government action (Winn 1987).

American medicine of the 1980s, though, has seemingly neared a concensus favoring a greater role for market forces and private enterprise (Goldsmith 1984; Schlesinger et al. 1987). These views have strongly shaped the health policies pursued by the Reagan administration (Dobson et al. 1986). They have been encouraged by large employers and other private purchasers of health services. Virtually all observers agree that the United States health care system of the 1990s will be far more "competitive" than at any period in recent history (Arthur Anderson & Co. 1984).

But those who advocate these changes often do so on the basis of very broad generalizations, arguing that the "average" purchaser of health care services is almost certain to benefit (Kindig, Sidel, and Birnbaum 1977). Relatively little attention has been paid to the fate of individuals and groups that are in some manner not "typical," either because of their health care needs or the options open to them as consumers of health care (Anderson and Fox 1987; Schlesinger 1986, 1987). Receiving perhaps the least attention are the racial minorities of this country, who are likely to face some important disadvantages in the newly competitive markets for health services (Winn 1987).

This article assesses the effects of competition on the health care of black Americans. Because there has been relatively little empirical research on this topic, the evidence presented below is often fragmented and incomplete, drawn in large part from research intended for other purposes. In some instances, no data are available at all, and it becomes necessary to reason by analogy. Though the inadequacy of this data makes clear the need for additional research, it does not in my assessment undermine the basic conclusions of the article—that while some black Americans will benefit from a more competitive health care system, the least advantaged will likely be made even worse off.

The article is divided into four sections. The first describes in detail the various changes in American medicine that are often grouped together under the label of "increasing competition." The second identifies subsets of the black population that may fare more or less well under competition. The third section reviews recent evidence on the actual costs and benefits of competition to black communities, evidence used in the final section to discuss the appropriate future role of public policy in this area.

Competition in the Health Care System

American medicine, like the rest of our society, has always contained a strong element of competition (Vladeck 1985). Labeling ongoing changes in the health care system as "increased competition" is thus to some degree a misnomer. What is changing is the nature, as well as the extent, of competition among health care providers.

Historically, health care providers competed to attract patients—in particular, to attract patients with the resources or insurance to pay for their health care. Following the post-World War II expansion of hospital facilities, the most aggressive competition occurred in the market for hospital services. To attract patients, hospital administrators believed that they had to attract physicians. Hospitals could do this by offering physicians more supportive environments for their practices, with a larger nursing staff as well as more elaborate and accessible technologies. Consequently, competition during this period tended to increase costs. Studies of hospital markets during the 1970s found that the more competitive the local market for hospital services, the higher the hospitals' operating costs (Noether 1987; Robinson and Luft 1985; D. Farley 1985). Increased competition and higher costs were associated with more full-time-equivalent staff per bed and a broader range of diagnostic and therapeutic services (Noether 1987; D. Farley 1985).

Sharp declines in hospital use over the past few years—occupancy rates fell from 76 percent in 1981 to 65 percent in 1985—have increased pressures for hospitals to find additional patients. Their methods for doing this, though, have changed from the strategies of the 1970s.

The nature of the relation between hospitals and physicians has changed. The expansion of medical schools in the 1960s and 1970s has led to what many perceive to be a "glut" of physicians (Harris 1986). Consequently, hospitals have become less concerned with attracting medical staff, and have increasingly sought to market directly to potential patients (Seay et al. 1986). At the same time, private practitioners have become more entrepreneurial, establishing a host of free-standing facilities such as ambulatory surgery centers and emergency medical centers (Ermann and Gabel 1985). These directly compete with hospitals, and many observers believe that this competition will intensify in the future (Seay et al. 1986; Arthur Anderson & Co. 1984).

In addition, purchasers of health care have become far more sensitive to the price of services. Faced with the rapidly rising costs of health care benefits, private employers and public agencies have developed purchasing systems that encourage or require enrollees to seek lower-cost providers. In the private sector, these have most often taken the form of "preferred provider arrangements" (PPAs). In a PPA, enrollees pay lower copayments if they obtain health care from providers who have established reduced-price contracts with the employer or insurer (Lissovoy et al. 1986). In the public sector, these innovative arrangements are generally termed "competitive bidding" systems. In a number of Medicaid programs, for example, providers bid for the right to treat Medicaid enrollees, and the state selects the low-cost bidder or bidders in each region (Anderson and Fox 1987; Freund and Neuschler 1986).

These changes in the market for health services can significantly alter the behavior of providers, and thus the accessibility and quality of health care. How these changes will affect blacks is discussed in some detail below. But changes in market conditions are not the only potentially important consequences of the new competitiveness in health care. Market conditions are to some extent a reflection of, and to some extent reflected by, what could be termed a new "competitive ethos," a shift in popular perceptions about the appropriate roles of health providers in the community and public policy in the health care system.

For hospitals and other institutional providers, this ethos represents a change in expectations. Increasingly, health care facilities are being perceived and portrayed as commercial enterprises, rather than as institutions with a fiduciary responsibility to the community in which they are located. This changes the expectations of and incentives for the administrators of the facility.

Any hospital administrator who doesn't do all he can to fend off as many general assistance patients as he can . . . just isn't being "businesslike" and will be so judged by his board of trustees. The word "businesslike" poses the problem in a larger context. The chorus of criticism of the not-for-profit hospital now coming from business leaders and government alike and much abetted by the present editorial content of many hospital journals is that they need to be "better managed." Not surprisingly, many CEOs are taking this to mean that you shouldn't treat many patients who represent bad debts, free care, or oversized "contractual allowances" (Kinzer 1984, 8).

These changes undoubtedly go beyond admissions policies. The more health care facilities are viewed as commercial operations, the more their governing structure is likely to become like that of any other business. One would thus expect the board of directors to include fewer "members of the community" and more representatives of the professionals with which the facility does business—physicians, large employers, and officers of local financial institutions.

The growing competitive ethos in health care is also shaping public policy. Most evident have been policies promoting "deregulation," allowing market forces to work unfettered (Winn 1987; Davis and Millman 1983). A dozen states, for example, have discontinued their certificate-of-need programs to encourage the entry of new health care facilities (Polchow 1986). Less obvious, but potentially more significant, have been changes in public subsidies to health care agencies. Proponents of competition typically call for "a level playing field," that is, for the elimination of subsidies that are available only to some providers. Their rationale is that "fair play" in the market requires that all competitors begin on an even footing.

Whatever the merits of this argument on ethical grounds, it can have important consequences for the delivery of health services. Preferential subsidies, including tax exemption, are made available primarily to public and private nonprofit agencies (Clark 1980). But with subsidies there comes an expectation of community service. The Hill-Burton program, for instance, subsidized the construction of a number of public and nonprofit hospitals (Lave and Lave 1974). In return, hospitals receiving funds were required to make services available to the medically indigent.

Not all subsidies explicitly require community service, and those that do may not be effectively enforced (Silver 1974). Nonetheless, subsidies have provided both a legal and, to some extent, a moral basis for encouraging private providers to take actions in the public interest (Blumstein 1986). Eliminating subsidies would inhibit the extent to which policy makers and public advocates can influence the delivery system in this manner. Making subsidies available to all providers would diffuse their effectiveness, since it is the public and larger private nonprofit facilities that are disproportionately located in the most disadvantaged communities of our country (Vladeck 1985; Davis and Millman 1983).

As this discussion suggests, the changes wrought by competition will be reflected in both the market and public policy. Competition will alter access to care, but it will also change the nature and extent of public influence on private health care providers. The consequences for blacks, and other groups, will thus involve their role as members of the community as well as consumers of health care. Before assessing whether these changes will be for good or ill, it is useful to review briefly some of the important factors that have historically affected blacks' use of health services.

Black Americans as Consumers of Health Care Services

The benefits of competitive health care markets depend to a large extent on the potential for patients to purchase treatment suited to their health needs, choosing among alternative sources of care. Two important hindrances exist for many black Americans.

First, many lack the purchasing power to voice effectively their preferences in the market. A disproportionate number of blacks live in low-income households. A third of all black households have incomes below the poverty line, and almost half of all black children live in these families (Jones and Rice 1987; U.S. Congressional Budget Office 1985). With such limited resources, many blacks cannot afford to purchase private health insurance. Only 5ᴜ percent of all black respondents under the age of 65 reported on the 1984 National Health Interview Survey that they had private insurance coverage (Andersen et al. 1987). Respondents without private coverage were divided evenly between those enrolled in Medicaid and those with no insurance coverage. Blacks are thus 50 percent more likely than whites to have no health insurance and 5 times as likely to be covered by Medicaid.

These financial factors have a number of important consequences for use of health care. Blacks will be disproportionately affected by experiments that introduce competitive bidding to the Medicaid program—40 percent of all Medicaid enrollees are black. Many other black Americans face significant financial barriers when seeking needed health care. Nine percent reported in 1986 that they did not receive health care for "economic reasons" (Freeman et al. 1987). Blacks who reported themselves to be in "poor or fair health" had one-third fewer visits to a doctor than did whites with comparable health status; a quarter of all blacks with chronic illnesses did not see a physician at all in the previous year (Freeman et al. 1987).

Black Americans thus are often less "connected" than are whites to the health care system. Twenty percent reported that they had no "regular source of care" in 1986; for many of the others, their regular source of care was a hospital emergency room or outpatient department, where they had only limited continuity of contact with a particular provider (Leon 1987; Okada and Sparer 1976). This limited contact affects the options and choices available to blacks as patients.

The second important consideration for blacks as consumers of health services is that, apart from differences in income, they have fewer alternative sources of health care. This is true for several reasons. Black communities are much more likely to have a limited number of health care providers. This includes both inner cities and rural areas in relatively poor states (Foley and Johnson 1987; Ruiz and Herbert 1984). As of 1985, for example, one-third of the 750 American counties with the highest proportion of black population had been designated by the federal government as "critical shortage areas" for primary care physicians; this is half again as common as for all other counties in the country. Consequently, a disproportionate number of blacks rely on hospitals and community health centers to provide primary care (Davis et al. 1987; Hanft 1977). Black overall health care utilization in these communities is lower than that of whites with comparable incomes (Okada and Sparer 1976).

Even when services are geographically accessible, blacks may face racial discrimination that makes it difficult for them to obtain care or limits their choices among health care providers (Jones and Rice 1987; Holliman 1983; Windle 1980). This discrimination may simply be the result of irrational racial prejudice, but may also reflect a more calculated judgment that black patients will be more difficult or expensive to treat. The origins of this expectation are discussed in detail later in this article.

Lack of information prevents many blacks from becoming effective consumers of health care. Surveys have shown that minority Americans are less informed than are whites about both the services available in their community and the provisions of their health insurance policies (Holmes, Teresi, and Holmes 1983; Marquis 1983). There are several possible explanations for these differences. As noted above, blacks tend to be less closely tied to a particular health care provider and thus are less likely to have a physician who fully understands their health needs and can adequately advise them. And communication between provider and patient may be further impeded by barriers of culture and language (Foley and Johnson 1987). The episodic employment history of many black workers makes it less likely that they will have contact with benefits managers at the companies that employ them (Jones and Rice 1987). All these problems are compounded by lack of education—minority Americans are three times as likely to have less than five years of formal education (Rudov and Santangelo 1979).

For many blacks the changes in competition among health care providers discussed above will have much the same costs and benefits as they do for the rest of the country. Assessing the consequences of competition for this broader population is an important task, but it is one that has been discussed extensively elsewhere (Meyer 1983; Luft 1985; Willis 1986). The remainder of this article will focus instead on those black communities—urban and rural—that in the past have lacked the financial and medical resources for adequate access to health care. The critical question is thus whether the changing nature of health care competition will ameliorate or exacerbate these problems.

Disadvantaged Minorities and Competition in American Medicine

As discussed above, a number of shifts in health care and health policy are often associated with increasing health care competition. For simplicity, these will be combined here into three general categories. The first set of changes are reflected in the private market for health care, affecting blacks in their role as consumers. The second involves reforms designed to introduce competitive bidding to the Medicaid program, affecting the 5 million blacks enrolled in that program. The third involves the set of changes in public expectations and public policy associated with the growth of a competitive ethos in health care, affecting blacks by reducing the influence that they, and the general body politic, have over the delivery of health care.

Competition in Private Markets for Health Services

Two ongoing trends have altered competition among health providers: first, the apparently growing excess supply of both hospital beds and physicians; and second, the increased price sensitivity of private insurers and employers. One would expect that these trends would work in offsetting directions, the first enhancing, the second reducing, the accessibility of health care in low-income black communities.

The more empty hospital beds and physicians' waiting rooms, the greater the financial incentive for health care providers to treat patients they would previously have viewed as undesirable (Vladeck 1985). These conditions may induce providers to overlook racial prejudice. It may encourage them to locate practices in areas that they would otherwise have considered unsuitable (Lewis 1976).

The effects of increased price competition are likely to be more problematic. On the positive side, if price-based competition causes providers to become more efficient, they will profitably be able to treat more patients with limited insurance or financial resources. Disadvantaged black communities would clearly benefit (P. Farley 1985). On the other hand, competitive pressures are likely to lead to larger reductions in prices than in operating costs (Schlesinger, Blumenthal, and Schlesinger 1986). This reduces the profits generated by treating privately insured patients, and providers become less able to cross-subsidize care of the uninsured or provide services that do not yield sufficient revenues to cover costs (Schlesinger et al. 1987; Shortell et al. 1986). Low-income communities, which have disproportionately black populations, will bear the brunt of these cutbacks.

The net effect on access depends on the relative magnitudes of these various changes. Unfortunately, there has been too little research in this area to identify conclusively the effects of competition on access in general, let alone for specific racial groups. The expanding supply of physicians does appear to have had some positive effects. In 1980, 41 percent of the counties in the highest quartile for the proportion of inhabitants who were black had been designated critical shortage areas for primary care physicians. By 1985 this had declined to 34 percent.

This greater availability of providers, however, seems to have been offset by other changes. Prior to 1980 racial differences in health care use had been steadily declining over time (Leon 1987). Since 1980, as competitive pressures in health care have been building, black overall access to health care has clearly declined. Studies have found that financially motivated transfers of patients from private to public hospitals—up to 90 percent involving minority patients in some cities—increased significantly during this period (Schiff et al. 1986). Between 1982 and 1986 the gap in physician use between blacks and whites in poor or fair health grew by more than a quarter (Freeman et al. 1987). The proportion of blacks without a regular source of care rose from 13 to 20 percent (Leon 1987).

Competition alone did not cause these outcomes. Other important changes in the health care system have occurred during this period that also may have hindered black access to care, including state cutbacks in Medicaid eligibility and benefits as well as changes in the coverage and practices of private insurers (Goldsmith 1984; Munnell 1985). Without further research, it is impossible to identify the separate effects of competition. It seems very likely, however, that the blacks who benefit from increasing competition are those with at least limited insurance coverage, making them marginally profitable to treat. Those lacking any insurance are likely to find it increasingly difficult to find private health providers who are willing or able to provide them with care.

Competition in Public Programs: Competitive Bidding in Medicaid

Corresponding to the growing emphasis on competition for the privately insured, there has been greater interest in competitive reforms for public programs like Medicare and Medicaid (Willis 1986). This interest has been embodied in a series of demonstration projects and several more permanent program changes. As noted above, because one in five black Americans is enrolled in Medicaid, representing 40 percent of the program's recipients, changes in Medicaid have a particularly pronounced effect on low-income black communities.

The specific nature of these Medicaid experiments varies from state to state. Some have focused on reducing charges paid to hospitals, others on enhancing the role of primary care physicians (Anderson and Fox 1987; Freund and Neuschler 1986). Because many of these programs involve a fixed annual payment to an HMO or other prepaid health provider, I will focus here on this approach.

Most of these programs have several common features. Providers wishing to treat Medicaid enrollees must submit a "bid," stating the price at which they are willing to provide services. State officials (or an organization acting at their behest) select one or more of the bidders to be the designated Medicaid provider in each community. These are typically chosen on the basis of cost, though other criteria may also affect the selection (Christianson et al. 1983). If there are several designated providers in an area, Medicaid recipients are generally given the option of selecting their preferred provider—those who do not make a choice within a specified period are assigned to a provider. Most programs periodically permit beneficiaries who are dissatisfied with a provider to switch to another in the area.

The potential advantages and disadvantages of these competitive models reflect in part the competitive bidding process, in part the requirement that providers be prepaid for the care they provide. Competitive bidding arrangements reduce program costs, at least in the short run (Christianson et al. 1983; Freund and Neuschler 1987). They do so by restricting enrollee choices to a limited number of lower-cost providers. This would seem to reduce access to care and potentially to threaten quality, since it restricts the alternatives for enrollees if they are dissatisfied with the care that they receive.

In practice, however, these may be small liabilities. Historically, many states have had difficulty convincing providers, particularly physicians, to participate in their traditional Medicaid programs, because they are paid relatively little for medical services (Sloan, Mitchell, and Cromwell 1978; Davidson et al. 1983). As a result, Medicaid recipients often had few real choices for obtaining treatment, so that being limited in the future to choosing among a small number of participating HMOs may not seriously restrict their options, though it may reduce somewhat their access to minority physicians (Foley and Johnson 1987; Kindig et al. 1977; McDaniel 1985). In fact, accessibility and quality of care may be enhanced because patients are formally linked to a particular provider or group of providers. If significant numbers of enrollees go without needed treatment, it becomes easier to assign responsibility to those providers.

It is often argued that this sense of responsibility is augmented when providers are prepaid for the care that they provide. To the extent that prepayment places providers at financial risk for illness, it creates an inducement for them to identify illness at an early stage when it is less expensive to treat. This is thought to be a particularly important consideration for minorities from low-income communities, who often lack a regular source of care and may thus require outreach to bring them into the health care system (Wolfe 1977).

Not all the consequences of competitive bidding, however, are likely to be favorable. Although competitive bidding systems increase the probability that Medicaid recipients will be formally tied to a particular provider, they do not guarantee that the recipients will actually receive treatment. Prepaid plans must operate within a fixed budget. The more effective the competitive bidding system is in cutting costs, the smaller this budget will be. To keep within budget, prepaid plans have adopted a variety of administrative procedures for rationing care (Luft 1982).

It remains a matter of considerable debate whether enrollees with lower incomes and less education are able to negotiate effectively these administrative requirements and obtain needed health care (Foley and Johnson 1987; Luft 1981). Studies of HMOs operating in predominantly black, low-income communities have also reached somewhat mixed results, but generally suggest that access and quality of care in prepaid plans is at least as high as, and often higher than, that for solo practitioners (Dutton and Silber 1980; Gaus, Cooper, and Hirschman 1976).

Less recognized, however, is the extent to which operating under limited budgets may encourage a form of economic discrimination against black enrollees. HMOs participating in competitive bidding programs receive a fixed payment for each member. Plans that enroll relatively healthy Medicaid recipients will prosper under this system; those with unusually sick and therefore expensive enrollees will face financial difficulties. Race serves as an effective predictor of future health care costs. In part as a legacy of past restrictions on access, blacks are 50 percent more likely than whites to be in fair and poor health (Freeman et al. 1987). As a result, when given greater access to care, they tend to have longer stays in the hospital and higher overall health care costs (Andersen et al. 1987; Heyssel 1981). Providers concerned with limiting their expenditures can thus be expected to discourage enrollment by black Medicaid recipients and perhaps to focus their cost-containment efforts on this group.

Because Medicaid competitive bidding programs are new, we have relatively little hard evidence to determine the consequences for black participants. Preliminary evidence suggests that in urban areas, at least, the programs have been reasonably successful at attracting a number of participating plans and satisfying Medicaid recipients (Anderson and Fox 1987). In Arizona, for example, 79 percent of black enrollees reported that they found health care more accessible under the competitive bidding program than under previous arrangements (Flinn Foundation 1986). Over two-thirds preferred the care they received under the program to that available previously (Flinn Foundation 1986). (It should be remembered, however, that prior to adopting the competitive bidding system Arizona was the only state without a Medicaid program and thus represented a rather low standard of comparison.)

Several caveats, however, should be added to this basically positive assessment. First, competitive bidding systems are likely to be less effective in rural areas, in which the number of bidders is fewer and geographic barriers to access greater (Turner 1985; Christianson, Hillman, and Smith 1983; Martin 1977). It is, therefore, not surprising that the native American population in Arizona was significantly less satisfied with the competitive bidding program than was the more urban black population (Flinn Foundation 1986). Second, these programs generally offer less choice than is initially apparent. Even in areas in which there are a significant number of participating providers, the most popular typically reach their enrollment capacity fairly quickly, leaving few attractive options for many Medicaid recipients (Rowland and Lyons 1987). Third, few if any of the existing competitive bidding programs have developed the administrative capacity to monitor effectively provision of services, and thus to hold providers responsible if health needs are going unmet (Anderson and Fox 1987). This is perhaps natural in new programs, but it is unclear how long it will take for their administrative capabilities to improve.

Finally, whatever the impact of competitive bidding on Medicaid recipients, it is likely to have a decidedly adverse effect on health care for the uninsured living in the same community. Providers who treat substantial numbers of Medicaid recipients also often have many uninsured patients. Consequently, as competitive bidding cuts payments for Medicaid enrollees, it further reduces provider ability to cross-subsidize unprofitable patients. Under these conditions, providers become less willing to treat the uninsured (Schlesinger et al. 1987). In addition, competitive bidding programs induce providers to join HMOs, few of which encourage their medical staff to treat uninsured patients (Anderson and Fox 1987).

Evidence from Arizona documents the loss of access for the non-Medicaid poor after a competitive bidding program has been established. The proportion of low-income blacks who did not have a regular source of care increased by over 60 percent (Flinn Foundation 1986). The proportion of low-income families not in Medicaid who were refused care for financial reasons also increased; the proportion unable to obtain care for a sick child more than doubled (Kirkman-Liff 1986).

The Competitive Ethos and Control over the Health Care System

Although most discussions of competition focus on the market for health care, more significant consequences for black communities may lie outside the direct delivery of services. With the growth of a competitive ethos, and the corresponding perception of health facilities as commercial enterprises, have come changes in popular expectations of providers and the extent of public influence over their performance. These changes can be seen in both the internal governance of health care organizations and the public policies that shape their behavior.

Competition and the Governance of Health Care Facilities. One potentially important influence on the services provided at a health care facility is its sense of commitment to the local community and the influence of community members on its governance (Dorwart and Meyers 1981). Although nonprofit organizations are generally expected to encourage community participation, actual practices have been highly variable (Middleton 1987). In general, representation of minority interests appears to be weakest in larger institutions, such as general hospitals, in which boards of directors tend to be dominated by community elites (Kindig et al. 1977; McDaniel 1985). Minorities seem to have greater influence in facilities such as community health and mental health centers, which operate under more explicit federal guidelines governing participation on boards of directors (Dorwart and Meyers 1981). As one review of these organizations observed:

> The ability of some minority community groups to build leadership and power via the federally funded community health center program served to defuse conflict over health services as well as to bring services into congruence with community perceptions of need (Davis and Millman 1983, 75).

To the extent that health facilities are seen as commercial enterprises, however, they are less likely to be required or pressured to maintain this community participation in governance. There are, as yet, no studies of this outgrowth of competition. Comparisons between for-profit and nonprofit hospitals, however, seem analogous, since the public generally perceives the former as more commercially oriented than their private nonprofit counterparts (Jackson and Jensen 1984).

Surveys of hospital boards of directors indicate that there is less potential for broad community representation on the boards of for-profit facilities. In part, this is simply because these boards are significantly smaller than those of comparable-sized nonprofit hospitals (Sloan 1980). The composition of the boards is also rather different. In the average private nonprofit hospital, just over half of the board is composed of physicians and representatives of the business community. In the average for-profit hospital, these groups represent between 80 and 85 percent of the board (Sloan 1980). It is, therefore, likely that the governance of these more commercial facilities is shaped to a greater extent by professional concerns (Alexander, Morrisey, and Shortell 1986). Broader community interests may be given less attention.

Competition and Community Influence over Health Care Facilities.   The practices of health care providers are also shaped by political pressures and government regulation. These can work to the benefit of otherwise disadvantaged communities, particularly in those public programs that explicitly require participation by members of the community. Provider behavior may be changed by either formal regulatory requirements or more informal moral suasion.

The certificate-of-need (CON) program represents a good example of these benefits. In many states, health care institutions intent on substantial new capital acquisitions or construction projects are required to seek approval from a local health systems agency (HSA). In 27 of the 39 states with CON programs, approval of a CON request is contingent on the willingness of the facility to provide care to the medically indigent. In 22 of these states this is required by law or administrative regulation, in 5 states it has emerged as a practice of the committees reviewing CON applications (Polchow 1986).

To the extent that a competitive ethos is associated with deregulation of the health care system, this source of leverage over facility behavior will be lost. The consequences of this loss for disadvantaged black communities are difficult to assess accurately. On one hand, blacks have been well represented in the health planning and regulatory system (Altman, Greene, and Sapolsky 1981). Nationwide, 15 percent of the board members of local HSAs have been black (Institute of Medicine 1981).

On the other hand, many observers have questioned whether participants in these public programs actually represent the interests of the less advantaged members of their communities (Morone 1981; Lewis 1976). Those on HSA boards were rarely from low-income households. In communities in which blacks were most likely to face racial discrimination when seeking health care, they were also least likely to participate in the CON program (Checkoway 1981). Even these critics acknowledge, however, that HSAs have often provided effective political leverage to encourage providers to treat more low-income patients (Checkoway 1981).

It therefore seems likely that the growing competitive ethos in American medicine will be associated with a decline in black influence over the performance of health care facilities. More generally, it will reduce public pressures for private facilities to act in the interests of disadvantaged communities. The consequences of these changes, being indirect, are more difficult to quantify and document than are some of the market-based changes discussed earlier. It would be a mistake, however, to equate quantifiability with importance. It seems very likely that the long-term responsiveness of the health care system to the needs of black communities will depend at least as much on the ability of community members to participate and influence the governance of medical institutions as on the willingness of providers to see black patients as profitable customers.

Conclusion: Competitive Markets and Competing Health Policies

Owing to the recency of competitive pressures in health and the dearth of research on their implications for minorities, much of the foregoing discussion was necessarily speculative. Nonetheless, it seems clear that a more competitive health care system will have mixed, but predominantly negative, effects on less-advantaged black Americans. Competition does offer some benefits to the partially insured who should gain in access because a larger number of providers become willing to offer them care. Since somewhere between 18 and 25 percent of the black population can be classified in this group, this is not an insignificant benefit (P. Farley 1985). But it is likely to be overshadowed by questions about the care of blacks enrolled in competitive bidding programs under Medicaid and by the almost certainly large losses of access for the 5 million blacks who have no health insurance. Perhaps more important in the long term will be the accompanying reduction in influence over the governance and performance of health facilities located in black communities.

This assessment assumes a continued incremental expansion of price-based competition and a competitive ethos in American medicine. Were policy makers to adopt some of the more comprehensive proposals for competitive reform, though, the implications for minorities might be quite different. Proponents of these competitive plans generally acknowledge most of the problems discussed above. To overcome these liabilities, they propose large-scale redistributions of income to increase the ability of low-income households to purchase adequate health care. For example, Enthoven's proposed "Consumer Choice Health Plan" (CCHP) would provide low-income families with a voucher worth

$1,350 in 1978 dollars ($2,250 in 1985 dollars) toward the purchase of prepaid health care:

> One of the goals of any national health insurance proposal is to redistribute resources so that the poor will have access to good care. The most effective way to redistribute income is to do it directly, i.e., to take the money from the well-to-do and pay it in cash or vouchers to the poor. . . . Purchasing power is the most effective way to command resources. A low-income family with a voucher worth $1350 to shop around in a competitive market is much more likely to receive good quality services willingly provided than in any other system (Enthoven 1977, 5).

Faced by discrimination and limited geographic access to health care providers, disadvantaged black families may not fare as well as the average low-income household. Nonetheless, these concerns should be addressable, and a proposal such as Enthoven's clearly holds appeal for many black families with limited financial resources. Of course, so would any proposal that redistributes income to this extent—in 1985 dollars, CCHP would entail a payment of well over $15 billion annually to low-income black families. The advantages and disadvantages of competition, relative to other resource allocation systems, are trivial compared to the consequences of payments this size.

Unfortunately, the redistributive aspects of the program are likely to be the weak political link in the proposal. Historical experience with policy making in this country suggests that the redistributive provisions of public policies tend to be lost somewhere between the initial program conception and its eventual implementation (Ripley and Franklin 1982). The risk seems particularly great in this case. Not only would many blacks receive large vouchers as a result of their limited incomes, but their vouchers would have to be additionally augmented to compensate providers for agreeing to treat a population with below-average health status (and thus above-average future health care expenses) (Winn 1987). A second rather bitter lesson of history is that programs or provisions targeted explicitly to blacks in this manner rarely have the political support to assure their continued survival (Jones and Rice 1987; Kieser 1987). Realistically then, the rather ambiguous benefits of procompetition provisions are far more likely to survive to become law than are the certainly beneficial redistributive aspects of the proposal.

But if a comprehensive plan that promotes competition and redistributes income is beyond the reach of contemporary policy makers, how then should they respond to concerns about the consequences of competition for disadvantaged black communities? To address this question, it is helpful to introduce a simple conceptual framework for considering policy interventions of this type.

Generally speaking, policy makers have available three strategies for addressing the needs of groups who are adversely affected by broad societal changes: separation, adaptation, or compensation. Under the first approach, policies could be designed to isolate, or shield, disadvantaged communities from competitive pressures. Under the second strategy, competitive models could be adapted to meet the special needs of black participants. Finally, competitive influences could be allowed to fully evolve in the health care system, but compensation would be provided to those made worse off by competition.

A complete and detailed assessment of these strategies is beyond the scope of this article. Political circumstances and historical experience suggest, however, that some of these strategies can be more fruitfully pursued than can others. First, the history of racial tensions and segregation in this country makes it difficult to initiate and maintain a program that differentiates, even in a positive sense, one racial group from another. This limits the extent to which compensatory programs can be explicitly targeted to black families. For example, a recent review of programs designed to reduce the disparity between black and white infant mortality questioned the value of racially targeted programs on the grounds that they would be perceived as either "labelling the beneficiaries as different in a negative sense" or would polarize other racial groups who "might perceive their needs to be just as great" (Howze 1987, 131–2). For similar reasons, it may prove difficult, or even impossible, to shield minority groups from society-wide competitive pressures that policy makers wish to encourage in order to limit the growth of health care costs.

> Anyone who believes that rich white people are prepared to absorb increased costs of medicine for black people is living in a fool's paradise. . . . It is necessary, therefore, for blacks to be in the forefront of alternative methods for managing medicine. . . . They must recognize the inevitable fact that medical expenditures will be managed and must seek strategies that minimize the impact on the black community (McDaniel 1985, 110).

Whether or not racial polarization in policy making is in fact this extreme, concerns of this sort will certainly limit the range of politically feasible responses to the adverse by-products of competition. These considerations suggest that a conversion or adaptation strategy may be more effective than separation or compensation strategies, which carry greater overtones of racial discrimination.

This approach could take several forms. Several seemingly promising reforms involve better adapting competitive bidding systems to fit the needs of black communities. For example, these programs could be made more suitable for potentially high-cost patients by incorporating health status adjustments into provider payments or by offering publicly funded reinsurance to providers to pay for very high-cost cases. Modifications of this type would reduce the incentive for participating plans to discriminate against black patients on economic grounds. Competitive bidding systems could also adopt provisions to mitigate the adverse effects for the uninsured of expanding the role of HMOs in low-income communities. Participating plans could, for example, be required to provide a minimum amount of care to the medically indigent living in the area.

It may not, however, prove necessary to abandon completely the compensation strategy. Although it may prove politically difficult to tie compensatory programs to particular racial groups, it may be feasible to link these programs to geographic areas or communities in which there are a disproportionate number of disadvantaged black residents. Congressional precedents exist for this approach. Programs that "forgive" medical school loans for physicians who practice in medically underserved areas work on this principle. More recently, to cope with some of the consequences of Medicare's shift to prospective payment for hospital care, Congress authorized the Health Care Financing Administration to develop more generous provisions for so-called "disproportionate share" hospitals. These are facilities located in areas with an unusually large number of low-income patients. Indirectly, such provisions disproportionately benefit disadvantaged minority groups.

The two greatest problems created by increased competition in many black communities are the reduced ability of providers to treat the uninsured and the reduced influence of the community over facility performance. These could be simultaneously addressed with a single compensating program. By authorizing a program that provided a pool of funds to pay for uncompensated care in particularly disadvantaged communities, policy makers could reduce the incentive to avoid treating the uninsured (Lewin and Lewin 1987; Rice and Payne 1981). By channeling these funds through a local board composed of community representatives, the program could restore some of the community's leverage over the health care institutions located within their boundaries.

These proposed strategies for public policy are simply meant to be suggestive. Defining effective and politically resilient reforms clearly requires far more detailed analysis. The overall strategy or particular proposals offered here can be further refined as we gain a better understanding of how system-wide changes in competition among health care providers affect particular groups of patients and communities. But it is important that policy makers begin to consider these issues. They must develop ways of constructively addressing the growing variations in health system performance that are related to race. Political action and public policy in this area will obviously raise some sensitive questions. But continued inaction will only guarantee that groups that have in the past lacked adequate access to health care will in the future face even greater barriers and threats to their well-being.

References

Alexander, J., M. Morrisey, and S. Shortell. 1986. Physician Participation in the Administration and Governance of System and Freestanding Hospitals: A Comparison by Type of Ownership. In *For-Profit Enterprise in Health Care*, ed. B.H. Gray, 402–21. Washington: National Academy Press.

Altman, D., R. Greene, and H. Sapolsky. 1981. *Health Planning and Regulation: The Decision-Making Process*. Washington: AUPHA Press.

Andersen, R., M. Chen, L. Aday, and L. Cornelius. 1987. Health Status and Medical Care Utilization. *Health Affairs* 6(1):136–56.

Anderson, M., and Fox, P. 1987. Lessons Learned from Medicaid Managed Care Approaches. *Health Affairs* 6(1):71–86.

Arthur Anderson & Co. 1984. *Health Care in the 1990s: Trends and Strategies*. Chicago.

Blumstein, J. 1986. Providing Hospital Care to Indigent Patients: Hill-Burton as a Case Study and a Paradigm. In *Uncompensated Hospital Care, Rights and Responsibilities*, ed. F. Sloan, J. Blumstein, and J. Perrin, 94–107. Baltimore: Johns Hopkins Press.

Checkoway, B. 1981. Consumer Movements in Health Planning. In *Health Planning in the United States: Selected Policy Issues*, ed. Committee on Health Planning Goals and Standards, Institute of Medicine, vol. 1, 184–203. Washington: National Academy Press.

Christianson, J., D. Hillman, and K. Smith. 1983. The Arizona Experiment: Competitive Bidding for Indigent Medical Care. *Health Affairs* 2(3):88–102.

Clark, R. 1980. Does the Nonprofit Form Fit the Hospital Industry? *Harvard Law Review* 93:1416–89.

Davidson, S., J. Perloff, P. Kletke, D. Schiff, and J. Connelly. 1983. Full and Limited Medicaid Participation among Pediatricians. *Pediatrics* 72(4):552–59.

Davis, K., M. Lillie–Blanton, B. Lyons, F. Mullan, N. Powe, and D. Rowland. 1987. Health Care for Black Americans: The Public Sector Role. *Milbank Quarterly* 65(Suppl. 1):213–47.

Davis, E., and M. Millman. 1983. *Health Care for the Urban Poor: Directions for Policy,* Totowa, N.J.: Rowman and Allanheld.

Dobson, A., J. Langenbrunner, S. Pelovitz, and J. Willis. 1986. The Future of Medicare Policy Reform: Priorities for Research and Demonstrations. *Health Care Financing Review* 1986 annual supplement: 1–7.

Dorwart, R., and W. Meyers. 1981. *Citizen Participation in Mental Health.* Springfield, Ill.: Charles C. Thomas.

Dutton, D., and R. Silber. 1980. Children's Health Outcomes in Six Different Ambulatory Care Delivery Systems. *Medical Care* 18:693–714.

Enthoven, A. 1977. The Consumer Choice Approach to National Health Insurance: Equity, the Market Place, and the Legitimacy of the Decision-making Process. In *Effects of the Payment Mechanism on the Health Care Delivery System,* ed. W. Roy, 4–10. DHEW pub. no. (PHS) 78–3227. Washington.

Ermann, D., and J. Gabel. 1985. The Changing Face of American Health Care: Multihospital Systems, Emergency Centers, and Surgery Centers. *Medical Care* 23(5):401–20.

Farley, D. 1985. *Competition among Hospitals: Market Structure and Its Relation to Utilization, Costs and Financial Position.* DHHS pub. no. (PHS) 85–3353. Washington.

Farley, P. 1985. Who are the Uninsured? *Milbank Memorial Fund Quarterly/Health and Society* 63(3):476–503.

Flinn Foundation. 1986. *Health Care for Arizona's Poor, 1982–1984.* Phoenix.

Foley, M., and G. Johnson. 1987. Health Care of Blacks in American Inner Cities. In *Health Care Issues in Black America,* ed. W. Jones, Jr., and M.F. Rice, 211–32. New York: Greenwood Press.

Freeman, H., R. Blendon, L. Aiken, S. Sudman, C. Mullinix, and

C. Corey. 1987. Americans Report Their Access to Health Care. *Health Affairs* 6(1):6–18.

Freund, D., and E. Neuschler. 1986. Overview of Medicaid Capitation and Case-management Initiatives. *Health Care Financing Review* annual supplement:21–30.

Friedman, M. 1962. *Capitalism and Freedom,* Chicago: University of Chicago Press.

Gaus, C., B. Cooper, and C. Hirschman. 1976. Contrasts in HMO and Fee-For-Service Performance. *Social Security Bulletin* 39(5):3–14.

Goldsmith, J. 1984. Death of a Paradigm: The Challenge of Competition. *Health Affairs* 3:5–19.

Hanft, R. 1977. Problems and Issues in the Financing of Health Care. Paper presented at a National Conference on Health Policy, Planning, and Financing the Future of Health Care for Blacks in America, Washington, October 28–29.

Harris, J. 1986. How Many Doctors Are Enough? *Health Affairs* 5(4):73–83.

Heyssel, R. 1981. Competition and the Marketplace for Health Care—It Won't Be Problem Free. *Hospitals* 55(22):107–14.

Holliman, J. 1983. Access to Health Care. In *Securing Access to Health Care: Ethical Implications of Differences in the Availability of Health Services,* President's Commission for the Study of Ethical Problems in Medicine, 79–106. Washington.

Holmes, D., J. Teresi, and M. Holmes. 1983. Differences among Black, Hispanic and White People in Knowledge about Long-term Care Services. *Health Care Financing Review* 5:51–65.

Howze, D. 1987. Closing the Gap between Black and White Infant Mortality Rates: An Analysis of Policy Options. In *Health Care Issues in Black America,* ed, W. Jones, Jr., and M.F. Rice, 119–39. New York: Greenwood Press.

Institute of Medicine. 1981. *Health Planning in the United States: Selected Policy Issues.* Vol. 1. Washington: National Academy Press.

Jackson, B., and Jensen, J. 1984. Consumers See Chain Ownership as Minus for Hospitals: Survey. *Modern Healthcare* 14:176–78.

Johns, L. 1983. Selective Contracting in California: Early Effects and Policy Implications. *Inquiry* 22:24–32.

Jones, W., and M. Rice. 1987. Black Health Care: An Overview. In *Health Care Issues in Black America,* ed. W. Jones, Jr., and M.F. Rice, 1–20. New York: Greenwood Press.

Kieser, K. 1987. Congress and Black Health: Dynamics and Strategies. In *Health Care Issues in Black America,* ed. W. Jones, Jr., and M.F. Rice, 59–77. New York: Greenwood Press.

Kindig, D., V. Sidel, and I. Birnbaum. 1977. National Health

Insurance for Inner City Underserved Areas: General Criteria and Analysis of a Proposed Administrative Mechanism. In *Effects of the Payment Mechanism on the Health Care Delivery System*, ed. W. Roy, 60–75. DHEW pub. no. (PHS) 78–3227. Washington.

Kinzer, D. 1984. Care of the Poor Revisited. *Inquiry* 21:5–16.

Kirkmann-Liff, B. 1986. Refusal of Care: Evidence from Arizona. *Health Affairs* 5(4):15–24.

Lave, J., and L. Lave. 1974. *The Hospital Construction Act*. Washington: American Enterprise Institute.

Leon, M. 1987. *Access to Health Care in the United States: Results of a 1986 Survey*. Robert Wood Johnson Foundation Special Report no. 2. Princeton: Robert Wood Johnson Foundation.

Lewin, L., and Lewin, M. 1987. Financing Charity Care in an Era of Competition. *Health Affairs* (6)1:47–60.

Lewis, C. 1976. Efforts to Increase the Number of Physicians: Impact on Access to Medical Care. In *A Right to Health: The Problem of Access to Primary Medical Care*, ed. C. Lewis, R. Fein, and D. Mechanic, 92–110. New York: John Wiley.

Lissovoy, G., T. Rice, D. Ermann, and J. Gabel. 1986. Preferred Provider Organizations: Today's Models and Tomorrow's Prospects. *Inquiry* 23(1):7–15.

Luft, H. 1981. *Health Maintenance Organizations: Dimensions of Performance*. New York: John Wiley.

———. 1982. Health Maintenance Organizations and the Rationing of Medical Care. *Milbank Memorial Fund Quarterly/Health and Society* 60:268–306.

———. 1985. Competition and Regulation. *Medical Care* 23(5):383–400.

Marquis, M. 1983. Consumers' Knowledge about Their Health Insurance Coverage. *Health Care Financing Review* 5(1):65–80.

Martin, E. 1977. Consumer Choice Health Plan Impact on Rural America. In *Effects of the Payment Mechanism on the Health Care Delivery System*, ed. W. Roy, 45–50. DHEW pub. no. (PHS) 78–3227. Washington.

McDaniel, R. 1985. Management and Medicine, Never the Twain Shall Meet. *Journal of the National Medical Association* 77(2):107–12.

Meyer, J.A. 1983. Introduction. In *Market Reforms in Health Care*, ed. J. Meyer, 1–11. Washington: Enterprise Institute for Public Policy Research.

Middleton, M. 1987. Nonprofit Board of Directors: Beyond the Governance Function. In *The Nonprofit Sector*, ed. W. Powell, 141–53. New Haven: Yale University Press.

Morone, J. 1981. The Real World of Representation and the HSAs.

In *Health Planning in the United States: Selected Policy Issues,* ed. Committee on Health Planning Goals and Standards, Institute of Medicine, vol. 2, 257–89. Washington: National Academy Press.

Munnell, A. 1985. Ensuring Entitlement to Health Care Services. *New England Economic Review* November/December:30–40.

Noether, M. 1987. *Competition among Hospitals.* Staff Report of the Bureau of Economics, Federal Trade Commission. Washington.

Okada, L., and G. Sparer. 1976. Access to Usual Source of Care by Race and Income in Ten Urban Areas. *Journal of Community Health* 1(3):163–75.

Persons, G. 1987. Blacks in State and Local Government: Progress and Constraints. In *The State of Black America,* ed. Janet Dewart, 167–92. New York: National Urban League.

Polchow, M. 1986. *State Efforts at Health Cost Containment: 1986 Update.* Washington: National Conference of State Legislatures.

Rice, H., and L. Payne. 1981. Health Issues for the Eighties. In *The State of Black America,* ed. National Urban League, 119–51. New York: National Urban League.

Ripley, R., and G. Franklin. 1982. *Bureaucracy and Policy Implementation.* Homewood, Ill.: Dorsey.

Robinson, J., and Luft, H. 1985. The Impact of Hospital Market Structure on Patient Volume, Average Length of Stay, and the Cost of Care. *Journal of Health Economics* 4:333–56.

Rowland, D., and B. Lyons. 1987. Mandatory HMO Care for Milwaukee's Poor. *Health Affairs* 6(1):87–100.

Rudov, M., and N. Santangelo. 1979. Health Status of Minorities and Low-income Groups. DHEW pub. no. (HRA) 79–627. Washington.

Ruiz, D., and Herbert, T. 1984. The Economics of Health Care for Elderly Blacks. *Journal of the National Medical Association* 76(9):849–53.

Schiff, R., D. Ansell, J. Schlosser, A. Idris, A. Morrison, and S. Whitman. 1986. Transfers to a Public Hospital: A Prospective of 467 Patients. *New England Journal of Medicine* 314(9):552–57.

Schlesinger, M. 1986. On the Limits of Expanding Health Care Reform: Chronic Care in Prepaid Settings. *Milbank Quarterly* 64(2):189–215.

———. 1987. Children's Health Services and the Changing Organization of the Health Care System. In *Children in a Changing Health Care System: Prospects and Proposals for Reform,* ed. M. Schlesinger and L. Eisenberg. Baltimore: Johns Hopkins University Press. (Forthcoming.)

Schlesinger, M., J. Bentkover, D. Blumenthal, R. Musacchio, and

J. Willer. 1987. The Privatization of Health Care and Physicians' Perceptions of Access to Hospital Services. *Milbank Quarterly* 65(2):1–33.

Schlesinger, M., D. Blumenthal, and E. Schlesinger. 1986. Profits under Pressure: The Economic Performance of Investor-owned and Nonprofit Health Maintenance Organizations. *Medical Care* 24(7):615–27.

Seay, J., B. Vladeck, P. Kramer, D. Gould, and J. McCormack. 1986. Holding Fast to the Good: The Future of the Voluntary Hospital. *Inquiry* 23(3):253–60.

Shortell, S., E. Morrison, S. Hughes, B. Friedman, J. Coverdill, and L. Berg. 1986. The Effects of Hospital Ownership on Nontraditional Services. *Health Affairs* 5(4):97–111.

Silver, L. 1974. The Legal Accountability of Nonprofit Hospitals. In *Regulating Health Facilities Construction*, ed. C. Havighurst, 76–89. Washington: American Enterprise Institute.

Sloan, F. 1980. The Internal Organization of Hospitals: A Descriptive Study. *Health Services Research* 15(3):203–30.

Sloan, F., J. Mitchell, and J. Cromwell. 1978. Physician Participation in State Medicaid Programs. *Journal of Human Resources* 13:211–45.

Sloan, F., J. Valvano, and R. Mullner. 1986. Identifying the Issues: A Statistical Profile. In *Uncompensated Hospital Care, Rights and Responsibilities*, ed. F. Sloan, J. Blumstein, and J. Perrin. Baltimore: Johns Hopkins Press.

Sowell, T. 1981. *Markets and Minorities*. New York: Basic Books.

Spence, A.M. 1974. *Market Signaling: Informational Transfer in Hiring and Related Screening Processes*. Cambridge: Harvard University Press.

Turner, T. 1985. Health Care Issues in Southern Rural Black America. *Urban League Review* 9(2):47–51.

U.S. Congressional Budget Office. 1985. *Reducing Poverty among Children*. Washington.

Vladeck, B. 1985. The Dilemma between Competition and Community Service. *Inquiry* 22:115–21.

Willis, J. 1986. Preface. *Health Care Financing Review* 1986 annual supplement. 1–2.

Windle, C. 1980. Correlates of Community Mental Health Centers' Underservice to Non-Whites. *Journal of Community Psychology* 8:140–46,

Winn, M. 1987. Competitive Health Care: Assessing an Alternative Solution for Health Care Problems. In *Health Care Issues in America*, ed. W. Jones, Jr., and M.F. Rice, 233–44. New York: Greenwood Press.

Wolfe, S. 1977. Problems and Issues in the Financing of Health Care. Paper presented at the National Conference on Health Policy, Planning and Financing the Future of Health Care for Blacks in America, Washington, October 28–29.

The Use and Abuse of Economic Policy Instruments

The roller-coaster aspects of macro economic conditions in the United States have captured our national attention. The turmoil in our economy has been the basis for countless television specials, articles, books, commissions, and legislative initiatives. But with all this attention to the "big issues," there has been less attention in the policy arena to smaller-scale economic policies and their consequences. The fixation on such large-scale situations as the budget deficit, trade deficit, stock market volatility, and the precarious financial condition of literally hundreds of American banks has diminished the attention paid to less grand, but nonetheless critical economic policies now in place. Indeed, the cumulative consequences of these "mid-range" economic policies can come to exert major influences upon the macro conditions noted above.

It is to the use and abuse of these mid-range policies that this present section is devoted. Further, a number of the authors here are able to track the consequences of these policies both down into smaller economic sectors as well as up to the half-dozen or so clearly national economic issues facing the country. While the topics may not, at first glance, appear especially intriguing or be the basis for cocktail and dinner discussions, each one of them involves major allocations of the country's economic resources. As but one example, discussions of employee stock-ownership plans may not frequently come up in classrooms or on the evening news, but the cumulative costs (lost revenue) to the federal government over the past ten years has been nearly $12 billion. Clearly, it does not take too many policies of this type to begin to exert a critical influence on the course of economic events.

What further distinguishes this collection of papers is that there are two quite distinct and, indeed, contrary impulses to the policies discussed

279

here. Three of the papers (Daneke; Fox and Schaffer; and Russell) stress that the economic policies in question all began with the impulse to do well for large numbers of American citizens—attract high-tech investment into an individual state, provide workers with alternative benefit packages, or allow workers to share in the capital and profits of their companies. That each of these efforts has had serious—and seemingly unanticipated—consequences is part of the analysis that unfolds here. Two other papers (Aldous; and Levitan and Shapiro) emphasize various economic decisions made with the clear understanding that there would be relatively clear winners and losers—and the losers would be the traditional powerless and poor groups in the country. Whether it was to address inflation by deliberately driving up unemployment or whether it has been to hold down the wages of the poor and marginal groups by keeping the minimum wage extremely low (and even so 3.3 million American workers were working for wages below the minimum wage in 1986), these were not policies of economic inclusion, but of economic exclusion.

The first paper in this group, by Daneke, addresses the multiple efforts being made by state and local governments across the country to attract "high-tech" industries, either by raiding companies from other states with the lure of reduced taxes, help with start-up costs, etc., or by attempting to "home grow" such companies. Daneke uses the term "short-stack chasing" to emphasize the intent of the states to encourage small, innovative, technologically oriented companies as opposed to the large manufacturing firms so eagerly sought in earlier times. But he stresses that much of the effort to date is more symbolic than substantive. What has occurred has frequently been conceived in a period of hysteria and high anxiety regarding economic competitiveness among regions. The present "greenhouse" efforts to build new centers comparable to Silicon Valley (which took thirty years to develop) in extremely short time frames are running directly into constraints that have to be addressed. That the complete cost-benefit equation is not known should produce some caution in those now pressing so hard for state support of such initiatives.

The second article traces out a 1978 change in the tax law that was conceived with the intent to give employers more flexibility in the benefit packages they offered to employees. Concurrently, the law also gives the employees more choices in the type of benefit package suited to their individual needs. But almost from the moment of passing the legislation, the Department of the Treasury changed its mind and started working to rescind the very legislation it had originally supported. The reasons for this abrupt change of position, the implications for basic assumptions about the tax law, and the relation of tax policy to social policy are all detailed in the paper by Fox and Schaffer. They focus specifically on the ways in which tax laws can be used to make social policy in the health area. But as they also stress, the United States uses its tax laws to make social policy in housing, education, income security, and countless other areas. Their paper raises important questions about using the tax law to achieve explicit social policies via implicit (or at least indirect) means.

Raymond Russell examines the manner in which the United States government has supported employee stock-ownership plans (ESOPs), both because of presumed desirable social outcomes (increased worker productivity, sharing capital with workers, saving distressed firms, etc.) and because of some extremely powerful political support on the Senate Finance Committee. Since legislation was passed in 1974, the federal government has been encouraging the formation of ESOPs by offering very generous tax-credit incentives to companies who will provide stock to their employees. This paper provides an excellent analysis of yet another instance where public policy was established, significant funds were spent (or in this case tax liability was reduced), and little systematic understanding or analysis either preceded, accompanied, or even followed the policy initiative. All that essentially happened for a decade was that an unexamined social policy was put in place, let be, and resulted in the loss of more than $12 billion to the government.

As noted earlier, if the three former instances of the uses of economic policy emerged from the proactive impulse of the government to do well by its citizens, the two latter analyses provide counterpoints. The paper by Aldous examines the various economic policies used during the 1970s and early 1980s to combat inflation and the consequences of these policies on different groups in the society. What is particularly intriguing about her analysis is the finding that the inflation itself was less detrimental to middle- and low-income groups than were the strategies used to combat that inflation. In the pursuit of stable prices, the deliberate increase in interest rates had a whole cluster of consequences for low- and middle-income persons that were clearly detrimental. Most dramatic was the increase in unemployment. As Aldous notes, unemployment is a much harder fate than is inflation—if one must necessarily choose between the two. She argues that when the next round of inflation hits the United States, policies that attempt to reduce inflation should also address the negative impacts upon the groups vulnerable to such policies.

Finally, Levitan and Shapiro address United States policy with respect to the minimum wage. The appropriate level for the minimum wage has been a point of constant controversy and heated dispute. But amidst all the debate, the wage itself has stayed exceedingly low and did not change appreciably throughout the 1980s. Concurrent with no real increase in the minimum wage was an increase in taxes for those in poverty. Thus by the end of the 1980s, low-wage workers had less net real income than at the end of the 1970s. (This takes into account as well the tax revisions of 1986 that did reduce the amount of taxes paid by the poor.)

The authors note that raising the minimum wage would have appreciable positive effects for almost all groups currently working at or below the minimum wage. The one group where an increase in the wage would have a disincentive would be for the young, though even here impacts are modest. They argue that raising the minimum wage is preferable in its assistance to the working poor over changes in tax policy that reduce the taxes they pay. Increasing the minimum wage would have positive effects for literally millions of American workers. Why it does not happen deserves careful understanding.

12

Short-Stack Chasing: The Perils and Prospects of State and Local High-Tech Development

Gregory A. Daneke

Introduction

Amid the national industrial policy paralysis (see Daneke, 1984), the various states parlayed their continuing interest with economic develop-ment into a vanguard position. As a recent publication of the prestigious Committee for Economic Development (Fosler, 1986, p. 3) suggests:

> States have become leaders in confronting the global challenge to American competitiveness. Considered by some people to be Constitutional anachronisms not too many years ago, states have reasserted their traditional roles as experi-menters and first-line managers in regional governance. In today's interdepen-dent world economy, they are not so much the traditional "laboratories of democracy" as fifty bubbling crucibles in an American national laboratory that is seeking a new formula for global economic success.

Despite this enthusiasm, recognizing this leadership role may merely present another case of the blind leading the infirm. While certain states or regions have been successful in upgrading antiquated, single-industry economies (e.g., tobacco in North Carolina; copper in Arizona), it remains

This discussion draws upon pieces of research supported by Stanford University and the Small Business Administration, and the following publications: "Small Business Policy Amid State and Local Industrial Planning," *Policy Studies Journal* Spring 1985), and "Economic Devel-opment and Technological Entrepreneurship: A Review of Recent Experience and Implications for Sunbelt States," *The Western Governmental Researcher* (Winter 1987).

to be seen if they will achieve a "globally competitive" economic base. Such status requires cutting-edge technologies and a start-up environment. While nearly every state economic development plan mentions elements of technological entrepreneurship, this is often much more rhetoric than reality. Moreover, actual policy initiatives have yet to demonstrate much in the way of effectiveness. This lack of performance is partially explained by the relative newness and largely symbolic nature of many programs. Yet future performance will probably fall short of expectations given the generally ill-conceived nature of most initiatives. Such a judgment does not suggest that the basic idea of stimulating "home-grown" high-tech industries is wrong-headed but, rather, that the critical dynamics of technological innovation are very ill-understood, and that growing evidence from major high-tech centers does not support current emphases.

The loose case analysis that follows was chosen in lieu of a more systematic approach, given the relative newness of most state and local programs and the general lack of specific performance indicators. Even where assessments were underway, baseline information was weak and programmatic outputs were rarely measured in commensurate terms. For such studies relationships between interventions and results will be subject to serious question. Isolating high-tech economic development from aggregate data is difficult and start-ups are often indistinguishable from expansions. Moreover, controlling for differences in regional endowments, etc., is nearly impossible. A few quantified studies (see Hansen, 1984; Luger, 1985; Daneke, 1987) have managed to draw tentative observations about the basic elements of successful economic development generally. But with regard to high-tech industrial policy, it is perhaps best qualitatively to suggest some cautionary notes regarding underlying concepts and misconceptions.

The Short-Stack Solution?

While local governments have always supported small business (usually through the nebulous maintenance of a "favorable business climate"), it is a fairly recent phenomenon for state-level economic development plans to place much emphasis on new start-ups. Such an emphasis constitutes a significant departure from the previous focal point of both state and local policy—"smoke-stack chasing" (enticing large manufacturing firms to the region). It is even distinct from "chip chasing," which emphasizes attracting medium-sized high-tech firms. This new focus on nascent industries is a function of a rather convoluted logic and is related to the frenzy over high-tech development. Much of the effort, so far, is more symbolic than substantive. Nonetheless, to the extent that subnational governments are beginning to explore the husbandry of innovation and entrepreneurship, their experience may contribute to the vaguely understood political economy of technology generally (for an example of diverse initiatives see appendix to this article).

"Chip Chasing" amid Start-Up Hysteria

The desire to replicate the experience of regions such as Silicon Valley and Boston's Route 128 is born of the frustration of accelerating economic transition. This transition is not so much the once reported "de-industrialization" as it is a complex "restructuring" of the economic base, in which the forces of decay and rejuvenation collide and contradict one another. This confusing confluence of forces causes increasing havoc for those who would attempt to plan for orderly economic development. Traditionally, policy instruments have been vague and multifaceted, and range from low property and corporate taxes, and "right-to-work" laws, to low-cost services designed to lure major manufacturing investment. Such inducements, while not as significant as natural endowments (e.g., rivers, harbors, raw materials, etc.) have and continue to play a major role in plant-location decisions. Moreover, changes associated with the rise of the so-called information society may reduce the importance of natural endowments and increase the significance of policy-sensitive elements (e.g., research universities). These changes in the technological character of industry, however, also make the design of policy far more difficult.

From both a national and a subnational perspective, the panacea for the mounting economic ills brought on by increased global competition has become the pursuit of the ill-understood phenomenon of technological innovation. In turn, this pursuit has placed unprecedented emphasis on the start-up, rather than the established firm. This emphasis stems from the realization that most United States advances in technology grow out of small firms and/or semiautonomous research shops (or "skunk works") within larger firms (see Peters and Waterman, 1982; Tornatzky et al., 1983). Small innovative firms tend to spawn, cluster, and thrive within certain highly entrepreneurial environments where there is ready access to seed- and venture-capital markets, large defense contractors and/or top-flight universities, and skilled labor pools (Armington, et al., 1983; Dorfman, 1983; Premus, 1982).

But these naturally occurring high-tech hotbeds (e.g., Silicon Valley) grew very slowly over time (sometimes thirty years); and largely without direct state and local government assistance. Merely replicating the critical elements above is not necessarily a guarantee of success. Intense start-up activity may be a function of the given state of a technology, during which the relative newness, lack of standardization, and/or specialty markets greatly reduce "economies of scale." Moreover, start-ups are highly sensitive to the "cost of capital," something that the 1986 tax reforms have adversely affected. Also, the impacts upon the national investment climate of the mounting "debt crisis," while difficult to predict, may well retard capital mobility as new ventures compete with the federal government for declining levels of savings. Even if the current macro-economic misfortunes precipitate major changes in national strategy, it is not immediately clear what role start-ups will play. Consider for example the most radical proprosals such as Gary Hart's "strategic investment initiative" (shifting defense spending into advanced technologies and retraining programs), the primary beneficiaries of which would probably be established firms. Meanwhile, "down-sizing" and "redesign" of existing corporate conglomerates is providing a number of mid-sized competitors for venture capital. In sum, the intricacies of technological entrepreneurship are becoming increasingly uncertain, especially the evolving institutional dynamics. As noted by Irwin Feller (1984, p. 381): "The euphoria associated with bold new ventures by the states to initiate high technology and development can obscure many political and economic realities that condition and constrain them."

Since primary justification for nearly all economic development effort remains job generation, smoke-stack chasing has merely been replaced with "chip chasing" in most regions. While a certain critical mass of high-tech activity is important to a start-up milieu, plant attraction has yet to produce much in the way of the desired entrepreneurial environment. Several regions of the country (largely in the Sunbelt) have found it fairly easy, given "right-to-work" laws, etc., to attract relatively mature high-tech manufacturing assembly plants. They have been considerably less successful in gaining the research and/or headquarters facilities. These hub activities tend to remain in established high-tech and/or commercial centers. With the manufacturing (e.g., chip fabrication), communities get many of the associated problems such as environmental degradation, but not necessarily the spinoff potential of research intensiveness. Contrary to popular beliefs, few high-tech operations are environmentally clean, and many regularly use and dispose of large quantities of toxic chemicals (see Seigel and Markoff, 1985). Sunbelt regions highly dependent upon ground water may find these operations a mixed blessing indeed.

Small Is Beautiful?

Enthusiasm over high tech, and the belief that many technological innovations originate in small firms have combined with the recent reification of "the entrepreneurial spirit" (see Guilder, 1984) to generate even greater policy confusion. Programs to aid small business are assumed to impact high-tech start-ups equally. This assumption ignores studies that describe the character and circumstances of high-tech entrepreneurship (e.g., Moore, 1986). High-tech people are often very reluctant entrepreneurs who merely want to do their research. If the state of a given technology overwhelms a single firm or forces the firm to ignore its particular stream of research, it might be coerced into starting its own research firm—that is, if it is near to a superheated new-ventures culture, which dictates that those with "something on the ball should be their own boss." There are, of course, weekend inventors, but these are much more rare than displaced corporate types, and given the culture of academia, university researchers are even more reluctant. Moreover, unlike true entrepreneurs these individuals are far more risk-averse, and far less likely to make the dozen or so attempts required to develop a successful company. Home growing high-tech companies is, therefore, much more difficult than mere small business creation. Like creating life, all the chemical elements of the primordial seas can be isolated, but without that magical spark, nothing combines.

As global pressures intensify, the scale of innovativeness may gradually move up, in terms of firm size. Studies which suggest that small firms are "24 times more innovative per research dollar than large firms" (Tornatzsky, 1983) may prove transitory as major United States firms move to mirror in-house research and development (R&D) practices of their global competitors (especially Japan). Moreover, the newly emerging pattern of joint-venturing between large and small suggests that established firms may become a prime mover in the process of innovation.

Likewise, the job-generating potential of small businesses may be somewhat overstated. For example, when Massachusetts Institute of Technology (MIT) researchers suggest that 80 percent of all the new jobs come from firms with fewer than 100 employees (Dorfman, 1983) they do not necessarily imply that small firms will supplant major corporate employers anytime soon.

The real beauty of small firms, for those regions fortunate enough to be able to inspire them, is actually much more subtle. To begin, an entrepreneurial milieu is likely to foster enhanced performance from its corporate inventory—both large and small. Like a diversified portfolio, the presence of a start-up environment provides a distinct hedge against the accelerating cycles of decline in mercurial global markets. Those regions with only high-tech assembly plants may find that these operations will withdraw to their base communities or move "offshore," once a particular product life cycle has run its course or labor costs increase. Finally, and perhaps more important, those states and localities that can stimulate home-grown industries have been the beneficiaries of the socially responsive corporate citizenship that tends to coincide with a sense of having a stake in the community (see Ouchi, 1984; Norris, 1984).

A Tentative Review

A preliminary assessment of the panoply of state and local initiatives suggests that not all policies are equally likely to succeed. A significant measure of effort is primarily symbolic, designed to make governors look progressive (see OTA, 1984, p. 11). Other initiatives, while more substantial, are only tangentially related to the goal of enhancing technological entrepreneurship. As alluded to above, many programs generate positive, yet unintended, consequences; however, in the dark economic times that lie ahead, tolerance for these tangents is likely to be quite low.

For lack of a more concise evaluation scheme, it may be possible to distinguish three broad categories. As the titles indicate, a certain policy priority is provided in reverse, starting with the least advantageous. These are: *big-ticket tangents* (costly efforts, which may or may not impact technological entrepreneurship); *focused frivolity* (costly efforts, which appear well-designed and purposeful but which have little impact in the short run); and, *bargain building blocks* (low-cost efforts, which immediately improve the start-up milieu and may provide significant payoffs over time).

Much Effort, Minimal Success

A vast variety of state and local economic development activities are mistakenly associated with high-tech entrepreneurship when they are tangential, at best. As the Office of Technological Assessment concluded, the term "high-tech" is very vaguely applied. The humorous story is told of a rural community that attracted a Frito Lay factory, and called it high-tech "because they make chips." With so many corporate CEOs considering themselves entrepreneurs, the association with firm creation is even less well established. As suggested above, several states have assumed that merely securing the relocation of a sophisticated assembly plant is nearly as important as fostering infant industries. As a result, regions such as the Research Triangle Park in North Carolina, which actually has few start-ups (Luger, 1984), are mistakenly looked upon as exemplars of successful high-tech development policies. It is true that successful "chip chasing" adds to a region's technical infrastructure and human capital. Moreover, as studies suggest, the human-resource base of a region is the single most important indicator of economic development potential (see CFED, 1987; and Daneke, 1987). Nonetheless, these conditions in and of themselves are not sufficient to stimulate technological entrepreneurship. Furthermore, the resources expended in attracting auxiliary or manufacturing facilities are not inconsequential.

Likewise, the contributions to the overall technical base of other big-ticket facilities are often enormously overstated. Consider the current clamor over the location of the new "supercollider," an expensive investment, which the scientific community itself labeled as "least instrumental" in terms of technological payoffs (see GAO, 1985). Yet these outpourings of the dwindling public largess into pure-science facilities are probably not nearly so wasteful as the vast number of defense technology projects. Here again, given the importance of generic defense funding to regions such as Silicon Valley, any defense installation is usually welcomed. State and local planners drastically overestimate the potential for civilian spin-offs. This is especially true of the current generation of highly specific defense research projects.

Perhaps the most promising of these big-ticket tangents are the various investments made in upgrading university research facilities. Such investments at the University of Texas, Austin, are credited with stimulating the growth of technological activity in the region (Smilor et al., 1987). This experience notwithstanding, states cannot hope to generate world-class research universities overnight. With numerous states bidding for a diminishing pool of top scholars, the price tag of academic excellence is becoming prohibitive. Moreover, the mere presence of such academic establishments does not guarantee success in technological innovation.

A more pragmatic approach appears to be the provision of space and facilities for a university-related research park. However, the proliferation of these entities across the country may also set forth the best example of focused frivolity. Few of these parks actually establish enduring linkages between academic and commercial research, and many firms that avail themselves of these subsidized facilities would have located in the region anyway. Essentially, parks contribute to the critical mass of technically trained individuals in a fixed space; few parks have become the "spawning grounds" they were designed to be.

Some research park environments have combined with "incubators" to enter the start-up business. The park at Rensselaer Polytechnic in Troy, New York, for example, has pursued this approach with some success (Abetti et al., 1987). Nonetheless, for many states and localities, incubators are a separate enterprise in which any type of small business can gain assistance. Thus the technological contributions of incubators, in themselves, have been very slight. With regard to economic development generally, incubators are gaining a reputation for being "flake factories," where the corpses of ill-conceived ideas are kept on display.

The only clear winner in this category is a tactic that might be called "consortia capturing." Given recent adjustments of antitrust provisions, and the realization that so many of the United States's global competitors collude on generic research problems, a few multifirm research consortia have formed of late. The most famous of these is the Microelectronics Computer Technology Corporation (MCC). Several states fought tooth and claw to become its home; but the highly aggressive "give-away-the-store" approach of Texas ultimately won out. Whether or not their level of effort and resources were well spent remains an open question. A couple of regional scientists (Farley and Glickman, 1986) have concluded that attraction of MCC to Austin was hardly a bargain. While basically supportive of Austin's long-term strategy, they do illustrate some adverse impacts, and suggest that the short-term economic benefits "will be slight" (p. 407).

Once again, however, the long-term benefits of acquiring research-intensive activities can be considerable, and Austin's recent success with also attracting the semiconductor consortium "Semitech" is testimony to the type of "snowballing effect" that can occur once a region establishes itself as a research bastion. Unfortunately, there are too few of these consortia to go around, and for most states the costs of mounting a consortia-capturing campaign are barely worth the gamble. A more prudent strategy might be to allow university research teams to solicit subscribers to highly applied, nonproprietory types of in-house consortia. Stanford University has been extremely successful in these arrangements, which involve some 100 firms giving rather modest ($100,000) tax-deductible contributions to a particular campus center (e.g., the Center for Integrated Systems) in exchange for being privy (along with all other subscribers) to any finding. This strategy is, of course, contingent upon having a state-of-the-art research facility in place, as well as a good deal of corporate contacting—neither of which is cheap.

Building Up Institutional Support Systems

Furthermore, most of the approaches above rely upon a high level of institutional support. If a state or community is without them, it is a logical place to begin, and building these systems is relatively inexpensive. Also, the various bargain-basement entrepreneurial and financial networks, if successful, become conduits for expanding the resource base of a region. Several state and local governments have recognized the need to form entrepreneurial networks, and most state-level industrial plans provide at least rhetorical support for the concept of coordinating a network of individuals interested in new ventures. Despite the low level of resources required to implement such networks, many of these plans remain more rhetoric than reality. Systematic programs for identifying and involving "reluctant entrepreneurs" and remote investors are among the vital prerequisites that are often overlooked. Resistance, both overt and covert, on the part of established industries in the region may explain some of the failure to establish effective networks.

Fortunately such resistance is not universal. In fact, in those areas where networks seem to work best (such as Minneapolis), major firms are the prime movers in the networking process (see Ouchi, 1984, pp. 199–209). Curiously enough, executives from these firms provide their expertise to assist small start-ups. Of course some of these new ventures will eventually be linked back into these major firms through product development or merely marketing. However, some of these start-ups may become independent competitors. The attitude of these corporate godfathers appears to be that the entire regional environment will be enriched through such competition, and that this attitude keeps their own R&D staff on their toes as well as giving them colleagues to talk to (see Norris, 1984). This interfirm cross-fertilization is somewhat alien to the traditional competitive ethos, yet it seems to be common to the new high-tech development centers. In any case, aspiring regions must discover ways to effectively involve both large and small firms in networking systems.

Providing support to high-tech entrepreneurship (both managerial and financial) is not the only direct by-product of these networks. As suggested earlier, these networks provide a forum for addressing a variety of community concerns, especially those related to general "life-quality," an integral element in attracting new research firms. It may well be that these new community-level institutional dynamics explain much of the economic development success of a particular region. OTA (1984, p. 8) described the following characteristics of high-tech centers:

> An organizational culture that promotes a common civic perspective and a positive attitude about the region's attributes and prospects;
>
> An environment that nurtures leaders, both public and private, who combine an established track record for innovation with a broad view of their community's resources and promise; and,
>
> A network of business/civic advocacy organizations that attracts the membership of top officers of major companies and receives from them the commitment of time and effort to work on issues of mutual concern, including cooperation with the public sector.

Once the foregoing types of community institutions begin to evolve, they might be directed toward bringing established financial institutions into the process of new-ventures generation. Viable seed- and venture-capital markets are obviously important ingredients to have; however, state-level policies may be overemphasizing their importance. Venture capital is less than 20 percent of the investment economy, and relatively few businesses depend upon it. It is the regulated financial institutions, banks, thrifts, insurance companies, and pension funds that control most of the available capital (over $5 trillion). Commercial banks alone control assets worth over $2 trillion, or approximately $40 billion per average-sized state (CASLP, 1983, p. 39).

Many start-ups rely heavily upon these traditional institutions, but access, at reasonable interest rates, poses real problems for many a small firm. Commercial banks, pension funds, and other regulated financial institutions are very conservative, largely as a result of stringent federal and state requirements. While prudent in the short run, the long-term effect of this conservatism is to exacerbate the general economic malaise, which in turn leads to poor performance and increased conservatism.

Those small firms who utilize short-term, bank-financed debt are placed in the extreme squeeze of interest rates amid low cash flows. Unlike their large competitors, they cannot completely pass on the high cost of debt management or absorb it through diverse product lines. The increasing rate of small business failures (up 500 percent from 1981) is attributable in large measure to debt-load problems in a sluggish economy (CASLP, 1983, p. 39).

Small research firms are in even worse shape when it comes to financing. Federal grants and contracts tend to go to large corporations and universities. With no products to market and thus no profits, investment tax credits are hardly of much use. If they get venture capital, they may be forced to go public sooner than is prudent and suffer at the whims of a mercurial stock market, or they may merely be bought up by a large firm. Even if they are successful in securing manageable financing, they may be encouraged to emphasize "Mickey Mouse," short-term product development over more promising long-term research.

State and local governments can do much to brighten the financial picture through supplemental financial institutions. To begin, networks (mentioned above) should include representatives from large and small lending institutions. Collectively these groups could establish new small business loan-and-performance criteria and encourage the development of more favorable debt-to-equity terms. These special loan programs could be linked to state and local deposits or to public employee pension funds.

Pension funds are a particularly promising start-up resource; however, at present these abundant pools of patience funding go largely to well-established firms and/or merely serve to displace existing investments.

Lawrence Litvak (1983) suggests that pension funds could be reoriented to fill the "capital gaps" for "undervalued" growth companies, without making financial concessions, with higher returns than many Fortune 500 firms, and with no more risk than existing investments. Of course, institutional mores must also be reoriented to facilitate these investments. Pension funds offer the "long-time horizons" needed for research-intensive investments given their partially indexed liabilities and their ability to trade reduced liquidity for higher fixed rates. Yet these assets are usually diverted to purchase home mortgages or fund large firms that don't necessarily need the long-term provisions. Working through private placement debt financing or appropriate intermediaries, state and local government pension funds could be mixed with private pensions to extend the venture-capital pool of a region. Most venture-capital firms earn more than 25 percent return on their portfolios and rarely expose themselves to undue risk. Moreover, there is potential for even greater returns once small firms go public. Litvak (1983) cites recent studies that point out that the stock of the smallest publicly traded companies have long offered rates of return far in excess of that required to offset their level of risk. A few states have explored the use of pension funds for new ventures, but the missing link is the technical and entrepreneurial expertise required to insure reasonable investments. By drawing advisory teams from the financial business entrepreneurial networks, these funds could be more carefully targeted.

Conclusions

In concert, the efforts above may still not bring a bumper crop of innovative ventures, but these steps may give start-ups a fighting chance amid the onslaught of major corporations intent on maintaining their market share. The key is greater appreciation for the role that small businesses play in energizing the United States economy. Eventually, large firms may come to view their counterparts more as partners and less as competitors or ready prey. Minneapolis and other cities are beginning to teach the rest of the nation that such a symbiotic relationship between large and small businesses is indeed possible and mutually profitable.

The more difficult matter may be to prove that government can effectively intervene to accelerate these evolutionary dynamics. Whether or not public officials can discover the optimal mix of public and private institutions, they are certainly going to continue to try. Thus it is incumbent upon the applied social scientist to aid in this process. As alluded to earlier, many of these infant initiatives afford golden opportunities for quasi-experimental (time-series) evaluations, and policy researchers

APPENDIX
A Sampling of State and Local Initiatives

State	Description of Initiative	Initiated in	Resources
Arizona	In Phoenix, the U.S. Small Business Administration Loan Program makes loans to small business under its Section 503 program. This program also aids small businesses in applying for government contracts. Community Development & Urban Development Action Block Grants have also been used to finance portions of several projects.	1982	Total budget for the overhead of the operation is $250,000 annually.
Connecticut	The Innovation Development Loan Funds were generated to match EDA grants, which are used to provide financial, managerial, and technical assistance to inventors and small high-tech businesses.	Unknown	Unknown.
Georgia	Georgia Tech, in connection with its incubator facility and entrepreneurial assistance program, supports formation of seed-capital funds for new start-ups.	1980	$2 million in plant and $750,000 in operating funds.
Kansas	Over 50 local businesses support the Center for Entrepreneurialship and Small Business Management at Wichita State University.	1977	Operating budget of $175,000.
Massachusetts	The Massachusetts Small Business Development Center was developed to obtain U.S. Small Business Administration funding and establish five centers to assist small businesses.	1980	For every state dollar, the SBA matches it 2 to 1 and local universities put up $1 worth of space—i.e., xeroxing, office space. For Fiscal Year 1985 the state's contribution was approximately $450,000; SBA's was about $900,000.

Michigan	The Massachusetts High Technology Council (MHTC) is an advocacy group for high-tech entrepreneurs.		In December 1982, they met their $15 million goal of raising their level of support for higher education to 2% of their R&D expenditures.
	State regulators have identified for elimination unnecessary regulations on small businesses.	1984	Not applicable.
	Michigan Tech formed the first university-based Small Business Investment Corporation.	1984	SBA 6 to 1, original budget of $2 million.
	The University of Michigan's Innovation Center helps both small and large firms improve productivity by adopting new manufacturing techniques.	1983	Initial operating budget in the millions.
Minnesota	The City of St. Paul, in connection with the Port Authority, has plans to set aside 10% for the new downtown World Trade Center as an incubator space for small businesses and spinoffs that will generate exports.	Construction began in 1985.	Private investment in the park will exceed $100 million. Public costs include: UDACs of $15.5 million, EDA public works grant of $2.3 million, plus $31 million in IDBs issued by the city.
	The Minnesota legislature has targeted tax credits to encourage equity investment in start-up companies, and to promote individual and corporate contributions to nonprofit organizations that provide management assistance to entrepreneurs.	1983	Unknown.
	State legislation provides tax credits for technology transfers or investments in qualified small businesses.	1983 (authorized)	Unknown.
	The Minnesota Businesses Partnership, in cooperation with the University of Minnesota and state and local governments sponsor StarCo (Start-a-Company), a program in which	1983	The seed-capital fund has attracted capitalization of $10 million from pension funds and individual investors.

	established firms assist in the creation of new small businesses through technology spinoff, management consulting, and/or equity investments. The Minnesota Seed Capital Fund was an outgrowth of the MBP.		
	The Minnesota Project Innovation helps the state's small high-tech firms compete for grants under the federal government's new Small Business Innovation Research (SBIR) program.	November 1983	Funding is from state legislation and private sources. In 1984, the state legislature gave $750,400; private sources, $61,520.
Nebraska	LB 1117, a state economic bill signed by Governor Robert Kerry, created a Small Business Development Authority, which includes a program that focuses on stimulating new small business start-ups.	1984 (signed into law in April)	Funding sources are yet to be determined.
New York	State University of New York at Binghamton grants many technical degrees. Broome County Industrial Development Agency owns a 27,000 sq. ft. incubator in Binghamton.	Mid-1970s (BCIDA has owned the building since then)	Unknown.
Pennsylvania	A referendum was passed in bonding authority for an incubator program for small businesses. The funding will be used for building acquisition and renovation, operating costs, and capital assistance.	1984 (referendum passed in April)	Out of the $190 million passed, $20 million will be used for the small business incubator program.
Tennessee	In connection with the U.S. Department of Energy and Union Carbide, the city of Oak Ridge has built a 12,000 sq. ft. incubator. It has led to the development of at least two companies that employ a total of 110 people.	1982 (incubator has been in operation since then)	Incubators cost $300,000 to build; the Appalachian Regional Commission recently gave the city a $96,000 grant to construct a new building.

| Texas | The Texas business community, the state of Texas, the city of Austin, and the University of Texas pooled their resources to provide an overwhelmingly attractive package of support facilities, endowed university chairs, etc., to MCC, a consortium of small microelectronic research firms. | 1984 (agreement signed) | Total package is over $25 million. |

should avail themselves. In the absence of these empirical tests, policy-makers should proceed cautiously and focus most of their energies on fostering cooperative institutions through which private investors are the prime movers.

Building this new set of supportive relationships is really the crux of industrial policy, and it is this type of business-government-society partnership that, on a national scale, explains much of the success of nations like Japan (Ouchi, 1984). However, unlike Japan, the genius and competitive advantage of the United States system is in the creativity of its small-scale entrepreneurs. Building institutions that inspire cooperation but do not stifle innovation is the challenge for the 1990s and beyond.

References

Abetti et al. 1987. "Developing Centers." Presentation at the "Technopoleis" Conference, Ic² Institute, University of Texas (March 12).

Armington, C., et al. 1983. *Formation and Growth in High Tech Firms: A Regional Assessment*. Washington, D.C.: The Brookings Institution.

CASLP. 1983. *America's State: A Citizen Agenda*. Washington, D.C.: Conference on Alternative State and Local Policies.

CCD. 1983. *Small Business and State Economic Development*. Cambridge, Mass.: Counsel for Community Development.

CFED. 1987. *Making the Grade: The Development Report for the States*. Washington, D.C.: The Corporation for Enterprise Development.

Daneke, G. A. 1984. "Why Sam Can't Plan: Industrial Policy and the Perils of a Nonadaptive Political Economy," *Business Horizons* November/December: 50–56.

———. (1987). "Crosstabulations of Factors Affecting Economic Development Ratings." Working Paper, School of Public Affairs, Arizona State University.

DES. 1984. "Small vs. Large Firms and Job Generation," *Arizona Labor Market Newsletter*, 7, no. 14. Phoenix: Arizona Department of Economic Security.

Dorfman, N. S. 1983. "Route 128: The Development of a Regional High Technology Center," *Research Policy 12:* 299–316.

Farley, J., and N. J. Glicksman. 1986. "R&D as an Economic Development Strategy," *American Planning Association Journal* (Autumn): 407–18.

Feller, I. 1984. "Political and Administrative Aspects of State High Technology Programs," *Policy Studies Review* (May).

Fosler, R. S., ed. 1986. *The New Economic Role of American States*. New York: Oxford University Press.

GAO. 1985. *DOE's Physics Accelerators: Their Costs and Benefits*. Washington, D.C.: U.S. General Accounting Office, RCED–85–96 (April).

Guilder, G. 1984. *The Spirit of Enterprise*. Reading, Mass.: Addison-Wesley.

Hansen, S. B. 1984. "The Effects of State Industrial Policies on Economic Growth." Paper Presented at the Meeting of the American Political Science Association (September 2).

Litvak, L. 1983. "Pension Funds for Economic Renewal." In M. Barker, ed.,

Financing State and Local Economic Development. Durham, N.C.: Duke Policy Studies Press.

Luger, M. 1985. "Explaining Differences in the Use and Effectiveness of State Industrial Policies." Working Paper, Institute of Policy Sciences and Public Affairs, Duke University.

Luger, M. 1984. "Does North Carolina's High Tech Development Program Work?" *Journal of the American Planning Association* 50, no. 3: 280–90 (Summer).

Moore, G. E. 1986. "Entrepreneurship and Innovation: The Electronics." In R. Landau and N. Rosenberg, eds., *The Positive Sum Strategy*, pp. 423–28. Washington, D.C.: The National Academy Press.

Norris, W. 1984. "Only Big Business Has Resources to Address Unmet Social Needs." *Woodlands Forum*, no. 2.

OTA. 1984. *Technology, Innovation and Regional Economic Development*. Washington, D.C.: Office of Technology Assessment, U.S. Congress.

Ouchi, W. 1984. *The M-Form Society: How American Teamwork Can Recapture the Competitive Edge*. Reading, Mass.: Addison-Wesley.

Peters, T. J., and R. H. Waterman. 1982. *In Search of Excellence: Lessons from America's Best-Run Companies*. New York: Harper & Row.

Premus, R. 1982. *Location of High Technology Firms and Regional Economic Development*. Washington, D.C.: Joint Economic Committee, U.S. Congress.

Seigel, L., and J. Markoff. 1985. *The High Cost of High Tech*. New York: Harper & Row.

Smilor, R., et al. 1987. "Emerging Centers." Presentation at the "Technopoleis" Conference, Ic² Institute, University of Texas (March 12).

Tornatzky, L. G., et al. 1983. *The Process of Technological Innovation: Reviewing the Literature*. Washington, D.C.: National Science Foundation (May).

13

Tax Policy as Social Policy:
Cafeteria Plans, 1978–1985

Daniel M. Fox and Daniel C. Schaffer

In 1987 Congress amended the Internal Revenue Code to permit employers to offer employees a choice betwen nontaxable fringe benefits or cash. These so-called cafeteria plans were a minor issue in 1978. But they subsequently stimulated controversy about fundamental issues of tax law and about the relationship between tax and social—especially health—policy.

Treasury officials and probably most tax lawyers soon came to regard the enactment of Code Section 125, which authorized cafeteria plans and a variation called flexible spending accounts, as a mistake. As the Treasury's regrets intensified, it tried to reclaim through regulation the revenue and the fundamental principles of tax law it had inadvertently asked Congress to give away in 1978.

Cafeteria plans have been popular with employers and employees— much more popular than the Treasury anticipated. Some people think that they will become universal. The *Wall Street Journal* reported in 1986 that 20 percent of "major corporations" have flexible benefit plans.[1] As we shall see, that is part of the failure from the Treasury's point of view.

This paper is a history of Section 125, emphasizing its relationship to health policy. Cafeteria plans offer employees a choice of tax-free fringe benefits, of which medical insurance or reimbursement directly by one's

This is a revised and abridged version of a paper that first appeared in the *Journal of Health Politics, Policy, and Law* 12, no. 4 (1987): 609–64. The abridgment omits many technical legal issues, clarifying examples, a glossary, and the statute as enacted and amended.

employer for medical expenses is only one. The plans have implications for several areas of social policy, including child care and pensions. We chose health policy rather than other fringe benefits because the quarrel over cafeteria plans as tax policy turned into a debate (still unresolved) over whether cafeteria plans contain or promote spending for health services.

Most people who are interested in health policy or in tax policy would probably agree that parts of the Internal Revenue Code deeply affect how health care is provided in the United States, to whom it is provided, and who provides it. The impact of tax law on health care goes back at least to 1942, when Congress first permitted deductions for medical expenses, and even to 1918, when Congress first exempted medical insurance payments from taxes.[2]

This history is based on published primary sources and interviews with some of the people who helped to formulate policy about cafeteria plans. We did not have access to documents in the files of the Treasury.

What the Treasury Wanted in 1978

The Internal Revenue Code has long provided that an employer's payment of an employee's health insurance premiums (or simply payment of the employee's medical expenses) is not income to the employee.[3] This is one of several exceptions to the general rule that all compensation for services is taxable. The Treasury's view in 1978 was that these exceptions had serious disadvantages.[4]

The only justification for leaving employer-provided benefits untaxed was that it encouraged the use of health insurance, disability insurance, and pension schemes "so that individuals, particularly lower income employees, will be assured of protection against certain contingencies—sickness, disability, retirement—which are particularly difficult to plan for at low income levels."[5] This justification failed if employers provided tax-free benefits only to their more highly paid employees. The one exception was tax-free pension and profit-sharing plans. Since 1942 these had been subject to rules forbidding discrimination[6] against lower-paid workers, but even these rules were relatively ineffective. What the Treasury wanted in 1978 was new statutory rules requiring employers who provided tax-free benefits like medical insurance to their more highly paid employees to provide similar benefits to all of their employees.

The Treasury's proposals in 1978 were ambivalent and ambiguous. They were ambivalent in that the Treasury made a powerful case against the tax-free status of employer-provided benefits, then asked Congress to extend tax-free benefits to more employees. As we shall describe, the Treasury had recognized that there was no political support for abolishing the tax-free status of fringe benefits and had chosen the second-best solution for improving them.

The proposals were ambiguous in that they implied different health policies—and, at times, no health policy at all, but instead the prevention of tax avoidance. Sometimes the Treasury seemed to be saying that its purpose was social policy, encouraging employers to provide a basic minimum of health insurance for more employees. It was equally plausible that the goal of policy was not greater social welfare but finer adjustment of the tax incentive. According to this latter interpretation, Congress has given up tax revenue in order to encourage employers to provide health insurance to employees who would not otherwise provide for themselves, and so the Treasury would propose antidiscrimination rules so that revenue would be foregone only for plans of the type Congress was trying to encourage. The first approach would cost the Treasury revenue; the second would bring in revenue.

Another plausible interpretation was that the Treasury was mainly concerned with abuse of the tax system. The Treasury's proposal to Congress argued that "current law had led to . . . particularly abusive situations."[7] All four of the examples of abuse that the Treasury used were cases of reimbursing the medical expenses of the shareholder-officers of closely held corporations.[8] At this point the Treasury seemed more worried that shareholders of such corporations had found a way to distribute disguised dividends to themselves. Dividends are supposed to be taxable to the recipients and not deductible by the distributing corporation, but these medical reimbursements were tax-free to the recipients and deductible by the corporation. This attack on tax avoidance contradicts a concern that all employees should have access to medical care. The Treasury would appear to be satisfied if an employer offered no health insurance at all or if employer-provided health benefits were fully taxable to employees.

Thus the Treasury had several policies at the same time. When the Treasury came to consider cafeteria plans, it tried and failed to impose a rigorous antidiscrimination requirement as the price of its consent. Perhaps one reason for the failure was that the Treasury had never explained clearly to Congress the difference among its various policies. Treasury officials may not have perceived the ambivalence and ambiguity of their policies. In discussions with us, for instance, they did not draw the distinctions we make here.

What Health Policymakers Wanted in 1978

While the Treasury was preoccupied with its proposals for requiring more equitable distribution of fringe benefits, including medical care and insurance, the nation's health policy was being rethought by experts inside and outside the federal government (Brown, 1978). For years, the principal goal of national health policy had been to make medical care more "accessible." Now the important question was how to contain the high price of medical care.

Health costs, particularly hospital costs, were rising more rapidly than the rate of inflation. Most hospital costs were paid by insurance linked to employment, either as a fringe benefit or after retirement as entitlement to Medicare. Business leaders complained for the first time that the cost of health insurance for their workers could no longer be passed on to consumers in higher prices because of the challenge of foreign competition. Prominent federal officials worried that the cost of Medicare would bankrupt the Social Security trust funds. Increasing numbers of the elderly were receiving nursing home and home health care under Medicaid at enormous expense to the federal government and the states because of the limits of Medicare coverage.

By 1978 most economists agreed that health insurance contributed to the rising cost of health services. Their theory was that the increasing numbers of workers whose health benefits offered low deductibles, coinsurance, or even first-dollar coverage had little personal experience with the cost of services. Hospitals were reimbursed on the basis of costs, so physicians were inhibited from spending freely on behalf of their patients only by their professional ethics and peer review. In this theory, tax law helped to inflate costs. Because employer-provided health insurance was tax-free, workers had reason to prefer health insurance to other goods and services, which they could purchase only out of after-tax income. When private health insurance had been universally regarded as a good thing, its favored tax status was uncontroversial. Now it was viewed as too much of a good thing.

Many congressmen, federal officials, and officials of state regulatory agencies accepted this interpretation of the results of making health insurance more comprehensive for more people. But there were dissenters. Some experts believed that the way to control the rising cost of medical care was to regulate supply, not demand. In this view (which found favor in the Carter administration, at least at first) the better policy would be some combination of government regulation of hospital rates, national health insurance, and encouraging competition between alternative systems of health care. Others argued that if employers bought more "shallow" health insurance for their employees, the first coverage to go would be preventive and primary care, thus stimulating use of hospitals and leading to a more expensive health care system rather than a cheaper one.

Even if one believed that not taxing employer-provided health insurance as income drove up the price of medical care, the virtues of the policy might still outweigh the evils. As it became clear that national health insurance would not be enacted in the 1970s, the choice for health policy might seem to have been between wider and better private coverage and leaving many people without proper (or any) insurance.

In 1978 there were plainly a variety of opinions about whether it was good health policy for tax law to encourage employers to provide health insurance to their employees. Only a handful of liberals still advocated achieving national health insurance by making it a public utility or subsidizing the extension of private insurance to all workers, children, and the unemployed. Moreover, tax law that encouraged employer-provided health insurance was for the first time controversial as health policy. It was into this changing climate of opinion that the Treasury threw its proposals to forbid discrimination in employer-provided health insurance and to permit cafeteria plans.

What Employers Wanted in 1978

At least one private employer and an increasing number of state and local governments had different problems that were not obviously related to "antidiscrimination" rules. TRW, Inc. had found a way to attract skilled workers in the competitive labor market of northern California. For some years TRW had been offering its California employees the opportunity to select nontaxable benefits from what was in effect a menu. Now TRW wanted to add cash to the menu, giving its employees a full-fledged "cafeteria" plan with a choice of nontaxable benefits or taxable cash.[9] At the same time, state and local governments were adopting benefit plans in which employees could choose to reduce their taxable salaries in return for a tax-free contribution of an equivalent amount to a public employees' retirement fund.

Constructive Receipt

Both practices raised the issue of what in tax law is called constructive receipt. The problem of constructive receipt touches on an array of arrangements in which there is choice between cash and tax-free benefits or between immediate and deferred payment. For the Treasury in 1978, cafeteria plans were a very small part of the problem of constructive receipt.

Finding constructive receipt is usually a way of determining the year in which a taxpayer should be treated as having received income. A taxpayer who has the choice of receiving money now or later is often taxable on it now even if he chooses to defer the receipt until later. If he could have received it if he had wished, he may be treated as having received it. (When the law treats a person as if he had done something because he could have or should have done it, lawyers use the word "constructive." A person who should have inquired about a fact will often be treated as if he knew it: he has "constructive notice.")[10] When state and local governments gave their employees a choice of full salary or a reduced salary plus a contribution to the employee's retirement account, the Treasury had to decide whether the employers' contributions were taxable immediately rather than upon retirement because the employees had chosen to defer their compensation. Private employers had been allowed to do this for years, but for technical reasons it was much less useful to them than it would be to state and local governments.

In other cases, the doctrine of constructive receipt is used to decide not *when* a taxpayer has income but *whether* a taxpayer has income or not. This happens when the employer purchases a benefit (like health insurance) for an employee at the employee's request. The basic legal issue, stripped of subissues and technical detail, is whether or not the employee who chooses nontaxable benefits rather than cash should be treated as having received the (taxable) cash and having purchased the benefits with it. Before Section 125 was enacted the answer was Yes, the employee is taxed. Section 125 changed the answer to No, the employee is not taxed. What makes the question so important in practice is that the American income-tax system strongly favors benefits provided by employers to employees, but not benefits that employees purchase for themselves.

Since 1972 first the Treasury and then Congress had provided that under the rule of constructive receipt the availability of cash as a possible choice would make taxable not only cash if an employee chose it, but the value of any benefit received by any employee under the plan, including benefits (like health insurance) ordinarily not included in income, up to the amount of the cash the employee could have chosen. Like the state governments' deferred salary plans, TRW's appeal to Congress raised an issue of constructive receipt. But TRW's plan posed an additional policy question: Should the Treasury ask Congress to allow a benefit plan that offered choices to employees if the more highly paid workers might take greater advantage of it—that is, if the highly paid workers might choose nontaxable benefits while the lower-paid workers chose taxable cash? That was, of course, one more variation on the problem of "discrimination" in tax-free benefits.

The Internal Revenue Service (IRS) had been struggling since at least 1956 to answer similar questions. In that year the IRS had ruled that an employer who maintained a qualified profit-sharing plan could offer its employees a choice between a taxable year-end cash bonus or a nontaxable contribution to the plan. In tax jargon, this is a "cash or deferred arrangement" (CODA). This ruling treated the question as whether or not in practice the choice caused discrimination against lower-paid workers without asking about constructive receipt at all. In later rulings, the Revenue Service insisted that not very onerous rules of constructive receipt be followed.

Allowing employee choice (which is to say, using an easygoing rule of constructive receipt) in these rulings made it likely that the higher-paid employees would choose the nontaxable benefit and the lower-paid employees would choose taxable cash. The link between employee choice and discrimination is that higher-paid workers would tend to defer their income more frequently than those who are paid less because their marginal tax rates are higher and because they do not need all their income for immediate consumption.

It may have been to limit such discrimination that the Treasury in 1972 proposed a regulation[11] that would require the employee to count as income the amount the employer had contributed. There would be no offsetting deduction for the employee, since employee contributions to pension and profit plans are not deductible.

Congress responded to this proposed regulation with a mixture of sympathy and indecision. In 1974 it provided that the proposed regulation should apply to CODA plans created after June 1974 and before 1 January 1977.[12] Thus the Treasury got its way on the new plans for the next three years. On the other hand, firms that had created CODA plans before 1974 were made exempt from the proposed regulations until 1 January 1977, giving them at least three more years of favorable treatment. Congress later extended this freeze on new plans through 1 January 1978, and the House of Representatives and the Senate Finance Committee voted in early 1978 to extend it again.[13]

This legislation (including the extension through 1977 and the proposed extension through 1978) applied not only to CODAs but also to cafeteria plans.[14] Unlike CODAs, cafeteria plans had never been the subject of a public ruling or proposed regulation. We were told that only one company, TRW, had received a private ruling in 1970 in favor of its cafeteria plan, and that it sought congressional help because it feared that the regulations proposed in 1972 might eventually be applied against it.

Exchanging Constructive Receipt for Antidiscrimination

On 30 January and 2 February 1978, the Treasury proposed contradictory actions that, as we reconstruct their purpose, became the basis for the subsequent history of cafeteria plans and, in particular, for their curious relationship with health policy. On 30 January, the Treasury sent Congress, as part of the president's 1978 tax legislation, a proposal to allow cafeteria plans.[15] This proposal undid the rule of constructive receipt as it would apply to these plans. Three days later, the Treasury proposed regulations that would make much stricter the rules of constructive receipt promulgated in rulings over two decades.[16] An employee would be taxed in the present year on a salary deferred until a later year if the salary were fixed by contract or statute and the deferral was at the employee's option. (That is, the salary to be paid in a later year would be "constructively received" in the year earned.) The regulation, though inspired by the salary reduction plans adopted by state and local governments, also forbade private deferred income plans. CODA arrangements would become ineffective whether the deferred salary was contributed to a retirement plan or the employer simply promised to pay the deferred salary to the employee in a later year. The latter was, as we have said, a common arrangement in industry for highly paid employees, and one which the Treasury had previously allowed.

We believe the contradiction was deliberate. The regulations and the legislation were part of an elaborate strategy to further the goals of liberal social policy. A principal author of this strategy was Daniel Halperin, a distinguished academic tax lawyer who served as tax legislative counsel and later as deputy assistant secretary of the Treasury for tax legislation in the Carter administration. The purpose of the strategy was to improve the benefits, including health benefits, available to lower-paid workers. Halperin proposed to achieve this goal by giving up a strict interpretation of constructive receipt in return for a broader definition of discrimination. This exchange, though it would apply to cafeteria plans, was aimed at a much larger and more important class of benefits. In addition to allowing cafeteria plans, the Treasury proposed to make employer-provided benefits like health and life insurance subject to antidiscrimination rules for the first time and to tighten the rules that already applied to qualified pension and profit-sharing plans. The regulations of 2 February were intended to be dropped if the legislation included a strong antidiscrimination provision. Such a strategy made sense considering that, as one of our informants recalled, "Congress wasn't interested in antidiscrimination rules in 1978."

We base our interpretation on four types of evidence: what was said at hearings on the legislation in 1978, what Halperin subsequently wrote about cafeteria plans (Halperin, 1983), what he said to us in a lengthy interview, and a letter from Halperin commenting on a draft of this article.[17] Halperin was explicit in his 1978 testimony that the Treasury wanted to trade strict rules of constructive receipt for strict rules against discrimination. Testifying about cafeteria plans on 15 March, he asserted that "it seems to us that a uniform system could be developed in which amounts set aside at the employees' election are deductible or excludible if the arrangements are nondiscriminatory with respect to both coverages and contributions of the employees." In case his point was not clear, he added, "In other words, we would say let us forget the constructive receipt issue if the actual participation in the plan is on a nondiscriminatory basis."[18]

Several years later Halperin offered three reasons for his decision to "forget the constructive receipt issue" even though he believed that constructive receipt was a way to achieve nondiscrimination. The first was that neither the Treasury's past rulings nor case law supported so strict a rule of constructive receipt (Halperin, 1983: 39–5). This was true: the preface to the proposed regulations of 2 February listed administrative rulings that would no longer stand and judicial decisions that the government might now have to challenge. The second reason, which Halperin considered "most important," was that a strict standard was unenforceable. When compensation is established in private negotiations, the IRS cannot tell if the employee had a choice. Yet constructive receipt turns on a determination that the employee rather than the employer made the decision that determined how much salary would be paid.[19] This is also believable. The Revenue Service's traditional reason for permitting employees who arrange for part of their pay to be deferred until a later year to be taxed in the later year was that "The statute cannot be administered by speculating on whether the payor would have been willing to agree to an earlier payment."[20]

A third reason for forgetting constructive receipt was that employers were "putting increased emphasis on the flexibility provided by employee choice" (Halperin, 1983: 39–5). The argument, which the Treasury seems to have found persuasive, is that the employee is the best judge of what fringe benefit he needs, or whether he needs cash instead of a fringe benefit.

It may not seem unusual for policymakers to respect individual choice. But the Treasury also believed that the only justification for making employer-provided benefits excludible from income was that employees needed an incentive to provide for their retirement, sickness, disability, etc.—in other words, that left to themselves, employees might not make the right choices. Treasury officials have never seemed to feel the need to explain how they could believe both at the same time. It is, of course, reasonable to believe both at the same time and to see the problem as how to strike a balance between the two imperatives rather than as which one should prevail. In 1978 TRW's plan may have been seen as balanced in this sense because it required employees to accept a minimum amount of health insurance, leaving them a choice only as to "deeper" insurance. TRW wanted to be able to offer its employees cash instead of fringe benefits, but said they "would require all participants to take the minimum level in each benefit category. This requirement would be used to prevent employees from neglecting important long-range benefits in order to build up current income."[21] And Section 125 required that health benefits in a cafeteria plan be relatively equal for all employees. According to this interpretation, the balance struck between consumer sovereignty and paternalism would be to allow firms to define an appropriate minimum level of health insurance, and then allow choice above that level but not below it.[22]

In his testimony of March 1978 Halperin implied an explanation for the breadth of the proposed regulations that is different from ours, seeming to suggest that the Treasury had acted inadvertently.[23] It was certainly true that the proposed regulations were written so broadly that they threatened a larger group than was necessary if they were really aimed only at people like state employees, whose salaries were matters of public record. But that this action was inadvertent is hard to believe. These proposed regulations turned upside down an important area of tax law. The Treasury said as much in listing the rulings that the regulations would overturn and the judicial decisions in which the Treasury "would have to reconsider its acquiescence."[24] It is more likely that they were issued in order to be bargained away in negotiations with lobbyists and congressional staff. Treasury would not issue the regulations if Congress agreed to a broader antidiscrimination standard.

Cafeteria plans stand out because, along with CODAs, they are the surviving remnant (in modified form) of the preferred bargain. Congress rejected most of the Carter administration's 1978 tax program. Among the casualties was the proposal for a general prohibition on discrimination in fringe benefits.

We were told the plausible story that Section 125 survived because of astute lobbying on behalf of TRW. In the February hearings on the president's proposals, a TRW vice president claimed that his company had "pioneered this cafeteria approach." The TRW plan offered "group hospitalization, life insurance, accident insurance, sickness or long-range disability and vacation." TRW now wanted to add a "cash option" in which employees could choose "to increase their income in lieu of a full benefit package which they may not need."[25] But if an employee were allowed to choose between taxable cash and nontaxable benefits, he would be taxed even if he chose the nontaxable benefit. Under the strict rules of constructive receipt, which the Treasury had proposed in 1970 and which

Congress had explicitly made applicable to cafeteria plans through 1976, then through 1977, and which were about to be extended again, TRW could add its cash option only if the Treasury's proposal to allow cafeteria plans was enacted.

Carroll Savage, the lawyer for TRW, told us that his client persuaded the Treasury to include the cafeteria plan proposal in the 30 January legislative package. He then worked to persuade congressional staff to pass it no matter what happened to the rest of the administration's tax program. We conjecture that the allure of the TRW proposal was that it was a miniature version of the sort of deal that the Treasury was seeking for employer-provided benefits in general. TRW wanted freedom from the existing rules of constructive receipt, which Congress was about to extend. In exchange, the corporation was glad enough to include a nondiscrimination rule in what became Section 125 because, as its vice president had said in February 1978, "TRW's cafeteria program is completely nondiscriminatory."[26]

The Treasury could have asked Congress for antidiscrimination rules without also proposing to allow cafeteria plans. There was no necessary or logical connection between the two, and they were of very different degrees of importance. The two became linked fortuitously. The Treasury was willing to give way on the general subject of constructive receipt in return for general and uniform antidiscrimination rules that would apply to all fringe benefits. Cafeteria plans were at the time seen as an exotic and unimportant variety of fringe benefit, a minor part of both the problems of constructive receipt and of discrimination in employer-provided benefits. Still, it was only on cafeteria plans that the deal could be struck.

But the antidiscrimination provisions of Section 125 were more ambiguous than those which Halperin and his colleagues at the Treasury had been advocating. The Treasury had feared that under cafeteria plans the higher-paid employees would select nontaxable benefits while the lower-paid employees chose taxable cash. To prevent this, Treasury wanted the test of nondiscrimination to be whether lower-paid employees actually used the available nontaxable benefits, not whether those benefits were merely available to them.[27] The statute as actually written did not impose such a "usage" test of nondiscrimination. At best, the statutory language was ambiguous. The Treasury itself has never asserted that Section 125, properly interpreted, imposes a "usage" test.

If our overall interpretation is valid, the Treasury wanted but failed to make a deal by which Congress would change the law to permit cafeteria plans in exchange for rigid and clear requirements that lower-paid employees would get tax-free benefits from those plans. How the failure occurred is not easy to say. We conjecture that Treasury officials either made an agreement or thought they had made an agreement and then failed to protect its essence. We do not mean that Savage double-crossed Treasury officials at the last moment. One reason to reject this explanation is that the Treasury officials to whom we spoke made no such complaint; another is that he and they play by the same rules. What is likely is that Treasury officials either did not explain adequately to the staff of the congressional committee the precise terms on which they consented to the legislation that TRW wanted, or they failed to reach a complete understanding with Savage.

Our speculation fits in with the general way the Treasury treated cafeteria plans in 1978. First, we can say with hindsight that Treasury officials did not think out the implications of permitting cafeteria plans; in particular, they did not see that Section 125 could be read to permit what came to be called "flexible spending accounts," about which more will be said later. Second, neither the Treasury nor anyone else thought that the taxation of cafeteria plans was of general importance. Only TRW testified in favor of cafeteria plans at the congressional hearings on the president's tax program. Halperin remarked to us in 1985 that he could not even remember why in 1978 the Treasury had decided to make a legislative proposal about cafeteria plans. The congressional committee reports on what was to become Section 125 said that "this provision will have no effect upon budget receipts."[28] Perhaps the reason that the Treasury did not consider thoroughly the implications of Section 125 and failed to get an unambiguous antidiscrimination rule written into it was that it considered the whole matter a mere sideshow.

We are not saying that the Treasury had no policy. The Treasury was pushing hard for its antidiscrimination rules for fringe benefits. It had also decided that it could not enforce the rules of constructive receipt and asked Congress to ease them substantially. It hoped that it could trade the first for the second. Rather, we are saying that once the Treasury found that Congress would not give it what it wanted generally, it mistakenly treated the remaining question of cafeteria plans as a minor matter.

Cafeteria Plans in Congress

Congressional staff played only a technical role in drafting this legislation. Seven years later neither Halperin nor his aide could remember who on the staff of the tax-writing committees had worked on cafeteria plans in 1978. A lawyer who served on the congressional staff in 1978 and specialized in the taxation of fringe benefits remembers that the Treasury and Carroll Savage worked out the principles of Section 125 together. Savage says that the Treasury and the congressional drafting staff (the latter responsible only for drafting, not formulating policy) wrote the statutory language.

The simplest explanation of why Section 125 was enacted is that in 1978 no one was against it and the Treasury was for it. When Congress had temporarily forbidden new cafeteria plans while permitting existing plans to continue in 1974, it was a compromise between what certain employers had wanted and what the Treasury had asserted to be the law. Once the Treasury changed its mind and proposed that cafeteria plans be allowed, the ensuing political situation was that employers wanted cafeteria plans, the Treasury agreed, and no one opposed them.

Cafeteria Plans and Health Policy in 1978

The Treasury does not seem to have asked itself what kind of health policy it was making when it proposed that cafeteria plans be allowed. In 1978 health insurance was the most important benefit on the menus of cafeteria plans. Other benefits were minor in comparison. CODAs, for instance, were not originally in the Treasury's recommendation, and Congress did not make employer-provided child care a tax-free benefit until 1982.

By 1978, as we have said, there was an extensive literature purporting to show that public and private health insurance was an important cause of the rising cost of health care. In this view, tax law was one of the villains: by making employer-provided health insurance a nontaxable form of compensation, it reduced the effective price of health insurance and gave employees an incentive to purchase it instead of other goods and services. Indeed, there was more than an extensive literature—this view was widely held among health economists, who in turn convinced many members of Congress as well as federal and state officials (Ginsburg, 1981).

Where cafeteria plans of the type envisioned in 1978 fit into this analysis is still not clear. There has been a good deal of theorizing on the subject. In principle, it is possible that an employee allowed to choose between taxable cash, medical insurance, and other tax-free benefits may skimp on medical insurance in order to get some other tax-free benefit. Emil Sunley, a prominent tax economist who was also a deputy assistant secretary of the Treasury for tax policy, testified in 1979 that one way to induce workers to choose alternative and cheaper health insurance plans would be to give the worker who chose a cheaper plan other fringe benefits or taxable cash.[29] On the other hand, in 1978 the Treasury assumed exactly the opposite: that workers would choose health insurance before any other benefits. There is a type of cafeteria plan that allows an employee to reduce his (taxable) salary by the amount he chooses to increase his (tax-free) employer-provided insurance, with no other benefit on the menu. That choice presumably pushes in the direction of more comprehensive health insurance. Even today no one knows whether flexible benefit plans encourage or discourage the use of "rich" health insurance as compensation, much less by how much.

Yet the Treasury officials who worked on the cafeteria plan proposals for 1978 seemed to be uninterested in how cafeteria plans might affect tax-induced inflation of health care costs, or in any other effect they might have on health policy. How this happened is not easy to explain. There were individuals within the Treasury who were thinking about the problem of tax-induced inflation in health care. Cafeteria plans were Halperin's project, however, and he remembers that he did not talk about the possible connection between cafeteria plans and health policy with experts outside the Treasury, and Sunley and Halperin both say that they did not talk to each other about it.

Antidiscrimination Rules and Health Policy in 1978

Nobody seems to have regarded the cafeteria plan proposal as even related to health policy. The Treasury did understand that its more general and (as it then thought) more important proposal to impose antidiscrimination rules on employer-provided fringe benefits (including health insurance) would affect how much health insurance workers would receive. But senior Treasury officials disagreed among themselves in their goals in proposing antidiscrimination rules for health insurance and other benefits.

Halperin's purpose in proposing antidiscrimination rules was to provide rank-and-file workers with more fringe benefits, including health insurance. This was his purpose in 1978, and has remained his purpose. In 1985 he told us that he was concerned that employees given a choice of taxable cash or tax-favored retirement benefits were choosing cash. When in the 1980s the Reagan administration's Treasury warned that an explosion of tax-free benefits was eroding revenues, Halperin justified the trend as, in effect, a reduction in the tax rates on income from labor. In 1984 he testified that if antidiscrimination rules in pension plans failed to provide rank-and-file workers with adequate retirement incomes, Congress should turn to a more direct approach.[30]

Emil Sunley, on the other hand, insists that the Treasury in 1978 expected antidiscrimination rules to reduce employer-provided health insurance. He cites the Treasury's "Tax Reform Option Paper No. VI," sent to the president, which predicted an increase in revenue of $30 million per year if the proposal to forbid discrimination in health insurance was adopted.[31] For him, the Treasury's purpose was to insure that benefits be available at the bottom if they were available at the top, but not to increase the amount of health insurance for lower-paid workers.

Eugene Steurle, then an economist in the Treasury's Office of Tax Analysis, suggests that the 1978 Treasury is best understood as an institution looking for a way to reconcile conflicting goals. The Internal Revenue Code provided an incentive to employers to provide health insurance to employees who might not otherwise buy it. On the other hand, the Treasury also wanted to avoid losing revenue. Antidiscrimination rules reconciled these goals to a degree by denying income-tax exclusion to health insurance that an employer makes available only to highly paid employees. The Treasury's object was to get "more bang per buck" of lost revenue. Health insurance plans limited to top employees may cost the government little in lost revenue, but that revenue is wasted because such plans do not extend health insurance to employees who need it but would not buy it without a tax incentive.

The Treasury's View of Itself as a Maker of Health Policy

The task of drafting regulations for Section 125 and for the limited antidiscrimination rules for health insurance that Congress had enacted in 1978 was delegated to officials below Halperin's level. We asked some of them if they had thought of themselves as making health policy. They had not.

This fact may explain a lapse in the Treasury's process. The Treasury apparently never discussed cafeteria plans with health policy professionals until 1984, six years after Section 125 was passed. In 1978 it would have learned from such discussions that while some officials in the Carter administration were still pushing national health insurance, many health policy experts had concluded, often reluctantly, that it was dead, at least for the moment. It would have learned that cost containment was the wave of the future. The Treasury did start to talk about cafeteria plans to health policy specialists in 1984, perhaps because employers were then insisting that a new kind of cafeteria plan called flexible spending accounts helped to contain health costs. Or perhaps it was because the president in 1983 proposed to tax employer-provided health insurance to hold down health costs. Health policy and tax law had finally come together explicitly.

Halperin's thinking about the Treasury's role in making health policy was more complicated. He says he believes that tax law is a poor substitute for explicit social policy. There is no reason to doubt this; it is probably the dominant option among Treasury officials, academic tax lawyers, and tax economists.

This predominant view is associated with the late Stanley Surrey, professor at the Harvard Law School and assistant secretary of the Treasury for tax policy under Kennedy and Johnson. In speeches and articles beginning in the late 1960s, Surrey convinced many lawyers and economists that the great flaw in the American tax system was that it was being used to achieve ends extrinsic to taxation. He pointed to the prevalent tendency to give exclusions, deductions, and credits against tax to achieve social ends, and urged that appropriated funds be used instead for these purposes (Surrey, 1973).

How then does Halperin explain what he was doing in 1978 when he pressed for tax law that he hoped would bring increased fringe benefits (including health benefits) for lower-paid workers? His answer is:

> I do not think it is correct to say Treasury was trying to use tax law to make health policy in 1978 or ever believed it should be part of their job to make health policy. It is fair, I think, to say that the Treasury took the policy of the tax law to encourage spending on health insurance and health care as a given (which could not be changed despite repeated efforts to do so) and was trying to implement it more equitably. . . . Perhaps Treasury (and me) [sic] too often takes a tax preference as a given (which should be improved if possible) without continually reminding people that such improvement is only a "second best" solution.[32]

There is no reason to doubt that this was indeed what Halperin believed in 1978. It was, as we have said, what most senior Treasury officials and most academic lawyers believed. Emil Sunley gave us an almost identical explanation of Treasury policy. It is confirmed by the language with which the Treasury in 1978 justified its proposal to Congress for stricter antidiscrimination rules. This is the language of a Treasury that deplores the tax-free status of employer-provided health insurance but knows that Congress will not make a fundamental change. It is a succinct statement of why these provisions should not be in the Internal Revenue Code, followed by a proposal that assumes that these provisions will stay in the Internal Revenue Code.

We can say, then, that senior Treasury officials had a health policy of their own, that they derived the content of this policy from the Internal Revenue Code, and that they felt a responsibility to propose legislation that would carry out that policy more perfectly. At the same time, they believed that it would be better if health policy were left to other departments and taken out of the Internal Revenue Code, but they did not try to bring the health policy in tax law closer to that of other departments, or even try to find out what other departments' health policy might be. Finally, we can say that two officials whose purposes in recommending antidiscrimination rules for health insurance were very different could nonetheless both believe they were implementing and perfecting the health policy of the Internal Revenue Code. Apparently there is more than one interpretation of the health policy implicit in excluding employer-provided health insurance from income.

The Treasury's tax legislative staff did not include experts on the many subjects touched by tax policy (e.g., health, housing, and energy). Toward the end of his term, Halperin says, he "became convinced that this was probably a mistake and that the Treasury should explicitly develop this expertise in-house." Looking back on 1978, Halperin now argues simultaneously, and in a very sophisticated form, that the Treasury was not trying to use tax law to make health policy, that it should not use tax law to make health policy, that tax law contained a health policy which it was the Treasury's duty to make more equitable, and that the Treasury must strengthen its ability to make good health policy.

Autonomy of the Treasury in 1978

The Treasury was able to put forward its proposals to allow cafeteria plans and to forbid discrimination in fringe benefits without consulting other agencies concerned with health policy. None of the Treasury officials with whom we spoke mentioned "legislative clearance" or coordination, formal or informal, with other departments, nor does Halperin's own written narrative of how the Treasury came to ask Congress to permit cafeteria plans (Halperin, 1983). After reading an early draft of this paper, Halperin suggested that the most useful suggestion we could make was either that the Treasury develop more procedures to coordinate tax policy with other departments when tax law touches on matters within their jurisdiction or that it develop its own expertise on issues of social policy.

According to OMB Circular A–19, no department or agency may propose legislation to Congress until it has been "cleared" by the Office of Management and Budget.[33] The purpose of "legislative clearance" is to ensure that departments carry out the president's policy and to coordinate the work of the several departments so they do not work at cross-purposes. To this end, a department seeking legislative clearance must submit to OMB "an identification of other agencies that have an interest in the proposal" and "an indication of any consultation with other agencies in the development of the proposal."[34]

In practice, we were told, legislative clearance was easy to get for tax proposals that seemed minor in their impact and whose relationship to the work of another department was not obvious. Our informants guessed that OMB simply lacked the staff to give more than cursory review to any but the most important proposals or to see the need for coordination between departments when it was not apparent on its face. One Treasury official guessed that OMB decided which tax legislative proposals were important by looking at the revenue estimate attached to each proposal. Cafeteria plans were supposed to have no effect on revenue.

Sometimes tax proposals are so obviously a way of making health policy that there is no lack of coordination between the Treasury and the Department of Health and Human Services (HHS). Sunley assures us that this was true during the Carter administration when the issue was whether to impose a "cap" on the exclusion from income of employer-provided health insurance. One assumes that was also true when the Reagan administration actually made such a proposal. Now that these episodes are in the past, old ways may be reasserting themselves. A Treasury official who reviewed a preliminary draft of this paper wrote a thoughtful explanation of the health policy found in the Internal Revenue Code without mentioning any health policy of the Reagan administration.

Innovation without Regulation, 1978–84

Between 1978 and 1984, Treasury officials struggled to write regulations that would implement their health policy despite the ambiguity of the nondiscrimination language in Section 125. According to the officials who spoke to us, there were two impediments to issuing regulations, one technical and one political.

The technical problem is the difficulty of constructing a test of nondiscriminatory usage of benefits. The statute and legislative history require that benefits (not just contributions) "bear a uniform relationship" to compensation. In a cafeteria plan, different employees receive different benefits. No one has quite determined how to compute and compare the value of the different kinds of benefits a cafeteria plan can offer.

The political impediment was that Treasury officials believed that Congress would not accept a usage test even if one could be devised. Treasury had insisted on such a test in 1978 without success. Half a decade later, officials were still insisting, on behalf of an administration that had a vastly different tax policy, that they were unwilling to settle for an availability test of discrimination.

In late 1982 Assistant Secretary of the Treasury John Chapoton had given a different explanation for the delay in writing the regulations. In early 1982 and again in the fall of that year, Senator Durenberger of the Senate Finance Committee wrote to the Treasury asking when regulations to Section 125 would be proposed, stressing the need for regulations to guide employers who wished to set up cafeteria plans, and asking that the

issuance of regulations be expedited.[35] Assistant Secretary Chapoton's
reply was that two issues were making the regulations hard to write. The
first was that "many employers wish to use salary reduction to implement
cafeteria plans." The Treasury and Revenue Service had been wrestling
with the question of "whether salary cafeteria plans are consistent with
congressional intent that such plans be nondiscriminatory." The second
was that Section 125 required relatively equal medical benefits for all
employees, but neither the statute "nor the legislative history provide
guidance concerning the application of this section to contributory health
care plans, to health maintenance organizations, or to other programs
designed to lower health care costs."[36]

Both Savage and Halperin believe in retrospect that the Treasury should
have issued regulations. Savage recalls that employers who used flexible
benefit plans were urging the Treasury to provide them with guidance
either by issuing regulations or by asking Congress for amendments to the
statute. He remembers that when Section 125 was enacted in 1978, he
expected that the Treasury would promptly issue regulations interpreting
its nondiscrimination rules. He has no doubt that the Treasury had the
authority to impose a "usage" test, and he believes that they should have
done so. Halperin also believed that the statute would support such
regulations, and both thought that if the statutory authority was lacking,
the Treasury should have asked for it and Congress given it (Halperin,
1983: 39–10, 39–11).

In the absence of regulations, cafeteria plans spread slowly. Benefit
consultants, eager to promote new plans, were the major source of information about the extent of their adoption. But many tax lawyers advised
their clients to be cautious in the absence of a regulation interpreting
Section 125 to permit employees to reduce their salaries in order to choose
untaxed benefits. In 1981, however, the Treasury proposed regulations that
would allow salary reduction under Section 401(k). This was a companion
statute to Section 125 permitting CODAs. These regulations specified that
a Section 401(k) plan could be paid for from salary reduction.[37] Because of
the similarity between 401(k) and cafeteria plans, many members of the
tax bar assumed that cafeteria plans could be financed in the same way.

Growing confidence that salary reduction would be permitted for cafeteria plans coincided with the invention of flexible spending accounts
(FSAs). It was flexible spending accounts that made cafeteria plans controversial. The essence of an FSA is that the employee accepts a reduced
salary and buys benefits like medical care himself. The employer reim-
burses him in cash up to the amount of the reduction in salary. The benefit
must be one which would be tax-free if provided by the employer (for
example, child care, health insurance, or payment of an employee's

medical expenses). The inventors of FSAs hoped that the cash reimbursement would be tax-free to the employee because it would be seen as the employer's provision of a nontaxable benefit. Two features made the FSA a potent and popular method of tax avoidance: it was funded out of salary reduction (so it cost the employer nothing), and any amount not used was refunded to the employee as (taxable) cash, so it cost the employee nothing if he elected to reduce his salary and then did not fully use his flexible spending account.

The first flexible spending accounts were of a type called "benefit banks." Each employee could elect to reduce his salary by some amount up to a set maximum, and in return have an account of the same amount in the "benefit bank." When the employee showed that he had made a qualifying expenditure he could claim reimbursement from his account in the benefit bank. These were, it was believed, tax-free. If the employee did not use up his account in the benefit bank, the unused portion was returned to him in cash, which was taxable.

Then some employers began to pay eligible expenses without setting up an account for each employee. Each month, the employer would reimburse employees for these expenses and reduce their salaries by the same amount. Consultants who recommended these plans argued that the reimbursement was excluded from gross income. This practice was called the zero balance reimbursement account (ZEBRA). With ZEBRAs there is no question of whether the employee gets back the unused amount of his account; he has never put anything into an account.

The final step in the elaboration of FSAs was to pay employees their full salaries and invite them to submit receipts for qualifying expenses at the end of the year for certification as benefits excluded from taxable income. From the tax lawyer's point of view, this was bold indeed. Here the employee was not given a choice of salary or tax-free benefits, but had already received his taxable salary and was trying to recharacterize it retroactively. In tax jargon, this was called the "ultimate ZEBRA" (or more fondly, "call Karen," after a personnel officer in some unknown firm).

In June 1983, before the IRS even learned about FSAs, Assistant Secretary of the Treasury for Tax Policy John Chapoton proposed to restrict cafeteria plans (which he still thought of as flexible benefit plans) as part of a general strategy to increase revenue by taxing fringe benefits.[38] The Treasury was worried that an increasing proportion of compensation was being paid in tax-free benefits. Chapoton saw the problem mainly as one of revenue loss. The tax reductions of 1981 had created a great revenue famine. (The very name of 1984's revenue act was the Deficit Reduction Act of 1984.) Others opposed tax-free compensation on grounds of equity;

their basic argument was that taxpayers receiving the same amount of compensation should pay the same tax, without regard to the form of the compensation (Student Note, 1976). The problem was made worse because not only were there fringe benefits that Congress had explicitly excluded from income, but there were also fringe benefits whose taxation was not defined by statute and which taxpayers were increasingly tending to assume were tax-free (free parking, merchandise discounts, and free travel for airline employees, for example). The Treasury had been trying to issue regulations about this latter category for years, but Congress had forbidden it.

Chapoton believed that flexible benefit plans made tax-free benefits even more attractive. He argued that the plans removed what he aptly called "employee jealousy" as a constraint on the growth of fringe benefits. When fringe benefits had been uniform among employees, with no choice allowed, benefit plans had been a compromise among the competing interests of employees. Some employees would want one benefit, some another, and some would prefer cash to any fringe benefit. Cafeteria plans eliminated this conflict among employees because they allowed each employee who wanted a tax-free benefit to choose it without reducing the cash salary or affecting the fringe benefits of any other employee. Chapoton proposed that Congress take nonstatutory benefits out of cafeteria plans and limit salary reduction.

Cafeteria Plans Transformed

The year 1984 was the most eventful year since 1978 in the brief history of cafeteria plans. Early in February the IRS announced that flexible spending accounts did not qualify under Section 125. Two weeks later, employers and lobbyists appeared before the House Ways and Means Committee to argue that flexible spending accounts should be preserved because they held down the cost of health care. In May the Treasury proposed regulations to Section 125, which allowed flexible spending accounts only if the unused portion of the account was forfeited, not refunded. In the Revenue Act of 1984 Congress again took up the issue of cafeteria plans, with only limited success. It defined for the first time the kinds of tax-free benefits that could be offered as part of a cafeteria plan. It added a new antidiscrimination rule, but did not require a "usage" test of discrimination. It also in effect ratified the proposed regulations. Unable to resolve the quarrel over whether flexible spending accounts increase the cost of health care or help to control it, Congress ordered the secretary of Health and Human Services to study the issue.

By the end of 1984 cafeteria plans were very different from either what

Daniel Halperin and his colleagues had wanted in 1978 or what the most adventurous firms had tried to make them be. Barber Conable, then the ranking Republican member of the Ways and Means Committee, caught the importance of the events of 1984 when he joked while receiving an award from the Employers' Council on Flexible Compensation that his views were "consistent with Congressional intent in enacting Section 125—though I've forgotten what that intent was" (Sheppard, 1984a). We now turn to the events of 1984.

The Attack on Flexible Spending Accounts, 1984

The Internal Revenue Service was irate when it learned about flexible spending accounts late in 1983. One official recalled that work on regulations for Section 125 had more or less stopped, because "we couldn't write discrimination rules and there wasn't any pressure to do it." Then, he continued, "A friend in private practice told me about 'Call Karen.' We had a good laugh at the idea that anyone could expect so outrageous a scheme to work. Then we began to hear from field units that it was used all over . . . so we had to decide." Moreover, Commmissioner Egger himself was "offended."

According to this account the Revenue Service acted promptly after it learned of flexible spending accounts. Halperin, however, now back in academia, had raised the question of how such arrangements should be taxed at an important professional meeting in 1982 (Halperin, 1983: 39–28, 39–29, 39–30). As one of our informants remarked, "He always seems to be a year ahead of the rest of us." We have no reason to doubt that the Revenue Service learned of flexible spending accounts only in late 1983, but we have no explanation of why Halperin's speech in 1982 did not put them on notice.

The date of 1983 is important because by then a substantial number of firms had adopted flexible spending accounts and had a stake in defending them. Carroll Savage criticizes the Treasury and Revenue Service for not issuing regulations forbidding flexible spending plans before their use became widespread. He goes so far as to say that the fiasco of flexible spending accounts had its origin not in the 1978 legislation but in the later failure of the Reagan administration's Treasury to administer the statute properly.

The commissioner himself began the attack in February 1984 by announcing at the midwinter meeting of the Tax Section of the American Bar Association that the Revenue Service considered FSAs invalid. Next came a more formal notice that "so-called 'reimbursement' and 'flexible spending' arrangements are without substance and do not reduce employees' taxable income."[39] The Revenue Service's view was that these plans did not reimburse the employee for expenses at all because the amount the employer paid and the amount the employee received did not change according to whether or not the employee had qualifying expenses; all that changed was the label attached to the employee's salary. What this came down to was that the Revenue Service would respect flexible spending accounts financed out of salary reduction only if the employee who chose to reduce his salary in return for tax-free benefits ran a risk of receiving less because of making the election. The ZEBRA and ultimate ZEBRA could never qualify under this rule. The benefit bank could if it were changed in one crucial way: the employee who did not incur sufficient expenses to use up the amount he had "deposited" in his account must forfeit the unused amount instead of receiving it as a refund. A flexible spending account had to provide that the employee "use it or lose it." The flexible benefit plans that the Treasury had in mind in 1978 when it agreed to permit cafeteria plans always meet this test, and the Revenue Service was careful to make clear that it was not attacking them.

At the 1984 hearings before the House Ways and Means Committee,[40] cafeteria plans were for the first time recognized as bearing on health policy and discussed as such. Employers and their lobbyists defended cafeteria plans as a tool to contain health care costs. The Reagan administration had accepted the thesis that health insurance contributed to rising costs, especially when it provided first-dollar coverage and when payers reimbursed providers without insisting on stringent utilization controls. It had also accepted that the tax-free status of employer-provided health insurance increased this tendency by artificially reducing the price of insurance, making it all the more popular. It had even proposed taxing employer payment of health insurance premiums for employers. Now the employers told the committee that flexible spending plans enabled them to wean their employees from inflationary health insurance. The director of compensation at Pepsico, for instance, explained that "we have offered our employees, on a voluntary basis, insurance-type protection with some of the highest deductibles and copayments in the country."[41] For these employees, the company set aside the money it saved on premiums "in an account for each participating employee."[42] Employees who became sick or injured drew on the money in this account to pay medical bills. As an incentive to reduce spending for medical care, Pepsico gave employees any money "not spent on medical care during the year . . . as a taxable cash payment."[43] The result was a 23 percent decline in total expenditures for medical insurance premiums. Other witnesses gave similar testimony. A leading benefit consultant added that many companies believed that their employees would have gone on strike if they had been asked to accept reduced "basic medical coverage without adding a reimbursement account."[44]

These were really two arguments being made at the same time. The first was that a refundable flexible spending account provided a desirable incentive. It gave the employee reason to think about the cost of medical care before he bought it. This argument did not work for the ZEBRA, and most employers were careful to say that they neither used nor could defend that device. The other argument was that introducing flexible spending accounts made employees less resentful as employers reduced the value of the health insurance they provided. The FSA was the candy coating on a bitter but necessary pill.

The administration challenged the thesis that flexible spending accounts helped to contain health care costs in an exchange of letters between Chapoton and Robert Rubin, assistant secretary of Health and Human Services (HHS) for planning and evaluation. In a letter dated 10 April, Chapoton said that cafeteria plans which reimbursed employees with taxable cash for unused health benefits would most likely increase premiums for health insurance.[45] Two kinds of employers offered flexible spending accounts, he said. The first were those like Pepsico who had been offering very expensive medical coverage—"Cadillac plans"—and who wanted to reduce that burden. The second and larger group were employers who had never paid for expensive insurance. Chapoton conceded that flexible spending accounts might help the employers in the first group to reduce the amount their employees spent on health care. But flexible spending arrangements would enable most employees to pay more of their medical expenses from before-tax dollars, and would therefore encourage the purchase of more health care by reducing its effective price. In a reply just one day later, Rubin agreed and added that health costs might increase even more because "all employees" might eventually take advantage of flexible spending accounts.[46]

The question of the impact of FSAs on health cost was argued within rigid ideological boundaries. Both sides in this debate assumed that the United States devotes too much of its resources to health care, that it is acceptable to contain health costs by limiting access to medical care, and that one way to do this is to make consumers bear a greater part of the cost of health care.

Not everyone in Congress accepted these boundaries, however. Senator Packwood, for example, was firmly convinced that there should be no tax on employer-provided health insurance, and the administration eventually had to give way to him. Perhaps this explains why the employers were not fully successful in their effort to save flexible spending accounts.

Early in May the Treasury officials rushed out proposed regulations to forbid flexible spending accounts.[47] Rather than resolving the problem of what discrimination against lower-paid workers was forbidden, they ignored it, except for a lame appeal for advice. As the Revenue Service's announcement had warned, the regulations condemned refundable flexible spending accounts (that is, it treated reimbursements paid under them as taxable). The only flexible spending accounts permitted were the forfeitable kind.

The Treasury's intense dislike of flexible spending accounts was based on reasons of tax policy, not health policy. The most important reason was the need to retain revenue. In the politics of 1984, the federal deficit was a great issue, perhaps the supreme issue. A year earlier Assistant Secretary Chapoton had warned about the expansion of fringe benefits in general plans, and in cafeteria plans in particular. Now his estimate was that getting rid of flexible spending accounts would save $10 billion in revenue over the next six years.[48]

Other officials had different reasons. An attorney in the Treasury's Office of Tax Legislative Counsel, for example, emphasized to us that the Treasury was defending important policies of the Internal Revenue Code. A person who has medical expenses may deduct them only to the extent that they exceed 7.5 percent (at that time 5 percent) of adjusted gross income.[49] This policy has a purpose. It separates extraordinary medical expenses, which are seen as a hardship, from those which are predictable and for which the taxpayer can budget. As this official said to us, "We see the 5 percent floor as drawing a line around budgetable items." Flexible spending accounts undo the 5 percent floor on medical expenses. An employee who has a medical deduction of $1,000 may not be able to deduct it because it does not exceed 5 percent of his adjusted gross income. But if he has a flexible spending account, he can pay the $1,000, reduce his (taxable) salary by $1,000, and receive $1,000 as an untaxed reimbursement. For this employee, the limitation on deduction of medical expenses has disappeared.

Finally, there was a collective memory in the Treasury of what cafeteria plans in 1978 were supposed to be about. They were supposed to be about insurance: life insurance, medical insurance, disability insurance. Sometimes this meant encouraging employer-provided insurance, and sometimes is meant eliminating double insurance coverage in families where both spouses had insurance on the job. Refundable flexible spending accounts were not insurance. The employer paid the employee the same amount whether the employee had medical expenses or not; only the label on the payment changed. From the Treasury's point of view, confining the statute to insurance did not misinterpret it but, rather, restored its original purpose, although that purpose was not expressed in the statute's words or legislative history.[50]

Whether the Treasury achieved its aims is another question. Although Assistant Secretary Chapoton seemed confident that forbidding refundable FSAs was the same as forbidding all FSAs, others have doubts. Flexible spending accounts that are forfeitable may at first seem to be unattractive to employees. An employee can choose to reduce his taxable salary by $1,000 in return for his employer's promise to reimburse him (without tax) for up to $1,000 in, say, uninsured medical expenses and day care. But what if he should have the misfortune of good health? Then he has lost $1,000 of salary and gotten nothing for it (because his flexible spending account is not refundable).

Yet it may be that flexible spending accounts will remain popular even if they have to be forfeitable. Some kinds of expenditures are predictable. An employee who knows that he will have to pay for nursery school for one child, after-school day care for a second, and summer day camp for both should be able to estimate how much to choose for his flexible spending account without concern that he will forfeit the part that he does not use. Perhaps taxpayers can even guess rather accurately that they will have some minimum of uninsured medical expenses. After all, the reason for disallowing the deduction of medical expenses which do not exceed 5 percent of adjusted gross income is that some medical expenses are not "extraordinary" in amount. They are predictable enough that we expect the taxpayer to budget for them. Then there are medical expenses extraordinary in amount but still predictable, like the cost of nursing home care for a parent or surgery that can be postponed until the next year of the cafeteria plan.

In the Revenue Act of 1984, Congress implicitly ratified the proposed regulations and prohibited a method of discrimination in cafeteria plans that was not foreseen in 1978. But it ignored the deeper problem of defining precisely what kind of discrimination the 1978 legislation was intended to prevent. The proposed regulations seemed to receive congressional approval because the act provided an intricate scheme of retroactive relief for firms and their employees who had been using flexible spending accounts of the type forbidden by the regulations. Congress also clarified the law by defining which fringe benefits could be offered through a cafeteria plan and which could not. As the administration had urged, it provided that only benefits excluded from gross income "by reason of an express provision of this chapter" could be offered, and even some of those were excluded. Free parking, for example, could no longer be part of a cafeteria plan.

The new antidiscrimination rule was not one that would accomplish

Halperin's original purpose or resolve the issue of whether the standard for finding discrimination should be usage or availability. The 1984 amendment mostly prohibited plans that grossly favored the highest-paid officers and owners of a firm. The discrimination rules of Section 125, ambiguous as they were, had seemed to provide clearly enough that benefits (other than health insurance) could be provided in proportion to salary. In a small firm with a flexible benefit plan, this allowed a significant advantage to higher-paid employees, as Chapoton had pointed out in 1983. To remove this advantage, the 1984 amendment denies the use of Section 125 for a benefit "attributable to a plan for which the statutory nontaxable benefits provided to key employees exceed 25 percent of the aggregate of such benefits provided for all employees under the plan."[51]

The 1984 amendment achieved its purpose, but had its effect mainly on small firms. In a large company, the key employees would be such a small fraction of the total that their cafeteria plan benefits would be in no danger of exceeding 25 percent of the benefits provided to all of the employees.

This new antidiscrimination rule will not accomplish the original purpose of providing fringe benefits to lower-paid employees, and was not meant to do so. It merely forbade cafeteria plans that were a system of tax benefits for only the highly paid. By 1984 lawmakers seemed uninterested in the original dream of providing more fringe benefits for rank-and-file workers and measuring discrimination by comparing tax-free benefits. Halperin told Congress in 1984 that "discrimination" must be defined in terms of "usage," not mere "availability," in order to ensure that rank-and-file workers got their fair share of employer-provided benefits.[52] In 1983 and 1984, however, neither Congress nor the Treasury even discussed this issue in public.

Instead, Congress wanted rules that would contain health costs. At one point during the drafting of the bill, Representative Conable even said that the purpose of *the 1978 legislation* was to contain health care costs.[53] The employers had apparently made an impression with their argument that refundable FSAs would induce workers to choose the least expensive health insurance. But Treasury's rebuttal (in which Assistant Secretary Rubin of HHS had concurred) was also plausible. Congress therefore ordered the secretary of HHS to study the effect of cafeteria plans on the containment of health care costs.[54]

Since 1984

The publication of the HHS study in the summer of 1985 is the final event in our history of the transformation of the belief of federal officials that cafeteria plans would increase the access of lower-paid workers to health benefits into the fear that they are an inflationary challenge to a national cost-containment policy. The report's predictions were sensational. It forecast that revenue losses from flexible spending accounts would eventually reach $12 billion per year in 1983 dollars, even though employers were now restricted to forfeitable FSAs.[55] (And this is only the revenue loss to be expected from the use of FSAs to pay for health care; the HHS mandate did not extend to studying the use of FSAs to pay for child care, life insurance, and other benefits.) The authors of the HHS report expected the increase in health expenditures resulting from FSAs to be about 5 percent, although 5 percent of what was not clear.

The HHS report reflected the extent to which the nation's health policy had changed since 1978. When Halperin and his colleagues ignored cost containment in order to provide access to benefits, they were consistent with part of the policy of the Carter administration. In 1984 very few experts on health policy—and nobody in power in Washington—talked about combining cost control with better access for the un- or under-insured.

Ideology seems to have had a strong influence on the HHS report. The HHS staff made assumptions that were arbitrary and that, once made, could only result in a conclusion that Chapoton and Rubin had been right in 1984 in predicting that flexible spending accounts would drive up health costs. The staff conceded that some employers used FSAs as a way of making their employees feel better about sharing the cost of health care.[56] Nevertheless, the staff excluded this effect from their calculations. Their reason was that only some companies—those with "Cadillac" health plans—could reduce health costs this way, and the data needed to calculate the number of firms (and employees) that fell into this category were not available: "There does not appear to be any way to test [this effect] at the aggregate level."[57] Thus the staff agreed that the employers' strongest argument had some weight but that the amount was unknown, and then left it out of their calculations.

More important, the authors assumed that a very large number of employees would eventually have cafeteria plans with flexible spending accounts. They did not say precisely how many employees they assumed would have plans, but working backwards from their data we estimated that they assumed the number was 73 million. The principal author confirmed to us that they had "assumed that nearly everyone would have a flexible spending account."

This assumption converted the HHS study into a fantasy of a future in which the federal government simultaneously spurns tax revenue and increases the cost of health care. There is no way to know if forfeitable flexible spending accounts will some day be universally popular. At the moment it is only the best guess of informed people that forfeitable FSAs will even be a usable substitute for refundable FSAs. Moreover, the authors of the study assumed that every worker will have available sophisticated fringe benefits, when in fact many employees do not get any kind of medical insurance at all. They also assumed, contrary to considerable evidence, that every taxpayer seizes every opportunity to avoid taxes. And because they tried to predict only the ultimate effect of FSAs on health care and taxes without estimating how long it would be before that point was reached, their study is of no use in estimating the current effect of these plans. As the principal author acknowledged, "We took an extreme position to make our point." In a subsequent conversation, he said, "We are very discouraged that the House Ways and Means Committee has not gotten rid of flexible spending accounts." When asked why he felt so strongly, he replied that FSAs would lead to overutilization of health services because they would lower prices to consumers. Then he added that "the depth of our concern is much greater because of our concern for the tax base."

The last comment reveals a curious pattern of policymaking. The HHS staff made tax policy the major subject of their study. Their report makes dire predictions of revenue loss. Yet the authorizing statute called for a study "of the effects of cafeteria plans on the containment of health costs," not for a study of tax policy or revenue loss.[58] The conference report confines the study to questions of health costs and "other health care policy goals." The only reference to taxation in the conference report is that "The *conferees* intend to examine [in the future] . . . the effect [of nondiscrimination rules and forfeitability requirements in cafeteria plans] on the federal tax base" (emphasis added).[59] In the Treasury, officials from Halperin to Chapoton tried to make health policy through tax law. Now officials charged to make health policy were making a judgment about proper tax policy.

Meanwhile, Daniel Halperin himself, along with other experts, had come to believe that there were inherent limitations on the degree to which strict nondiscrimination rules can help lower-paid workers, and his new skepticism was influential in the Treasury. In an article about retirement as a tax-free fringe benefit, Bruce Wolk had argued that antidiscrimination rules could be self-defeating (Wolk, 1984). Wolk's analysis was that employers provide tax-free benefits because highly paid employees are willing to accept less total compensation if part of their compensation is tax-free. Lower-paid workers, on the other hand, may prefer cash, even though it is taxable. One reason is that in their lower tax brackets, tax savings are insignificant. Another reason is that they may be pressed for cash. If so, the employer must pay these workers more total compensation if part is in

the form of, say, a contribution to a retirement plan than if all is in cash
(Wolk, 1984: 430–33, 466). The need for antidiscrimination rules confirms
this. If lower-paid workers were content to accept fringe benefits as the
equivalent of cash, employers would not keep trying to provide only the
highly paid employees with tax-free fringe benefits. Halperin himself had
said as much in the past. What Wolk added was that antidiscrimination
rules might do more harm than good: "For any given employer, the cost
may eventually exceed the benefits of covering the highly paid employees.
At that point, the employer would decline to establish or contrive a
retirement plan" (Wolk, 1984: 432–33). The same argument would apply
to health insurance or any other benefit.

In more recent testimony on proposed changes in the discrimination
rules governing pension plans, Halperin repeated his belief that tax law
should be used to bring benefits to lower-paid employees, but showed a
new pessimism about the inherent limits of that approach. He had always
seen tax law in general as a second-best and imperfect substitute for direct
social policy. Now Wolk's reasoning had convinced him that antidiscrimination rules might become less and less useful.[60]

Congress, however, has become more willing to legislate antidiscrimination rules at the same time that experts like Halperin and Wolk were
warning that they may not always be the best solution. The Tax Reform
Act of 1986 imposes a whole new set of antidiscrimination rules on fringe
benefit plans, repealing the rules discussed in this paper, although it is too
early to say how effective they will be.[61] A new chapter in the history of
tax policy as social policy has just begun.

A member of the congressional staff mused that Halperin's liberal views
have gradually impressed conservative legislators. Many conservative
members of Congress believe in a voluntary approach to providing health
care, retirement plans, and other benefits. In particular, Senator Packwood
has been a determined and successful defender of tax-free fringe benefits.
These legislators know that part of the liberal critique of a voluntary
approach is that tax-free benefits in practice benefit mainly higher-paid
employees. They have come around to Halperin's view that the special
status of employer-provided benefits in tax law cannot be defended unless
the rank-and-file receive more of those benefits. No one can say whether a
Finance Committee that is again controlled by Democrats will be as
interested in forbidding discrimination in tax-free benefits.

Speculation on the Failure of the Treasury

We believe the history of Section 125 is a story of the failure of Treasury
officials in making both tax policy and health policy. The Treasury did not

foresee fringe benefits paid for out of salary reduction. Still less did it foresee flexible spending accounts paid for out of salary reduction. We here consider and reject three explanations for the failure of the Treasury: (1) the Treasury's lawyers were inadequate; (2) tax expenditures are likely to lead to this kind of failure; and (3) Treasury officials mismanaged the administration of sound legislation.

The simplest explanation is that the Treasury's lawyers made a mistake; the way to avoid lawyers' mistakes is to get better lawyers. But the Treasury had fine lawyers. This was Daniel Halperin's project. Halperin is widely admired among law professors and in the legislative and executive branches of the federal government. There is no use saying the Treasury needed a better lawyer; they were lucky to have a very good one indeed. The question is why the system worked badly when the people running it were so very able.

The second explanation is that health policy, and indeed any social policy made through tax law, is likely to be badly made. According to this fashionable point of view, the only policy tax law should carry out is tax policy. We have already discussed this theory briefly because it was part of the ideology of Treasury officials, including Daniel Halperin. We return to it here because many tax lawyers and economists would probably use it to explain what went wrong.

Tax-expenditure theory may be a splendid guide to the best solution to certain problems, but it is not of much help to an official who has to choose between leaving a tax expenditure unchanged and tinkering with it to improve it a bit. The Treasury could press for fairer, less discriminatory employer-provided plans or not, try for a better "tax expenditure" or not. That was its choice. The Treasury, of course, knew all about tax-expenditure theory, but felt itself responsible for a tax law that provided health benefits until direct expenditures—such as national health insurance—were enacted. Treasury officials understood they were choosing a second-best policy.

Carroll Savage offers the third explanation of why things went wrong: the Treasury mismanaged a sound policy and a sound piece of legislation. He argues that neither Halperin nor anyone else made a mistake in 1978. Flexible benefit plans are a good thing, and Section 125 was both wise and technically sound. The fiasco came later, when under a new administration in the early 1980s the Treasury failed to issue regulations.[62] Regulations could have interpreted the antidiscrimination language of the statute to include a "usage" standard. The Revenue Service and Treasury should have learned about flexible spending accounts earlier and forbidden them before they became widely used. Savage would add that if the revenue loss from all tax-free fringe benefits is intolerable, the solution is a cap on the amount allowed to each taxpayer (whether through a cafeteria plan or not). He recognizes that Congress refused a cap when the Treasury has asked for it, but reasons that the Treasury is hardly to blame for that.

This argument oversimplifies the problems of the officials who had to write regulations. Treasury officials complained that this was a statute that presented "tremendous problems," both technical and political. When the Treasury issued regulations on flexible spending accounts in 1984, it asked the bar and other interested parties for guidance in constructing nondiscrimination tests. None was forthcoming. In addition, we heard claims that it would not have been politically feasible for the Treasury to issue regulations (or get legislation) imposing a "usage" standard on flexible benefit plans.

More fundamentally, Savage argues that a particular rule of tax law is good tax policy. He, and others, believe that "the need to offer choice was compelling in 1978 and is even more compelling today." It was "an inevitable trend which had to be dealt with."[63] This is a question on which reasonable people can and do differ. But it is neither the question that we set out to answer nor a question that we have answered, and answering it would not bring us closer to our goal. Our purpose has been to ask how in one particular case the Treasury made tax policy which was also health policy.

In this paper we have offered two explanations for the Treasury's failures. One was that Halperin and his colleagues made a less than rigorous assessment of the impact of cafeteria plans because they were preoccupied with a larger agenda of making tax-free benefits more equitable. The other was that Treasury officials saw no reason to look beyond themselves to plan this agenda and therefore ignored important issues in health policy.

Treasury officials saw no reason to look beyond themselves for a health policy in 1978 because they saw themselves as implementing and perfecting a health policy already in the Internal Revenue Code. Senior Treasury officials drew a sharp line between asking Congress for tax legislation in order to carry out social policy (which they regarded as bad) and asking Congress for legislation that would improve an already existing use of tax law to carry out social policy (which they considered necessary). When the question of putting a cap on tax-free employer-provided health insurance came up, there was no lack of coordination with other departments. Perhaps the difference was between perfecting the health policy found in the Internal Revenue Code, which the Treasury saw as purely its own problem, and explicitly rejecting the health policy of the Code for reasons extrinsic to tax law, which was more obviously an affair for other departments.

Looking back in 1987, Halperin himself agrees that "there was insufficient thought to whether the tax law was consistent with [administration] health policy on cost containment," but points out that this might just as reasonably be seen as the fault of HHS as of the Treasury. More generally, he thinks that the Treasury is inevitably going to find itself proposing improvements in tax laws that Congress has enacted to achieve social and economic goals extrinsic to tax policy. He suggests that the Treasury's opposition to such "tax expenditures" may be one reason that the tax legislative staff "is very small by any standards and has never explicitly included experts on health policy, energy, housing policy, etc." He says that toward the end of his tenure he became convinced that the Treasury should build up in-house expertise, and he now suggests that an alternative might be to develop procedures of coordination with other departments.

This raises a dilemma. It is hard to be against the suggestion that the Treasury should know what it is talking about when it faces proposals for tax legislation meant to be part of health policy, housing policy, and other social policies. On the other hand, many Treasury officials are dedicated to the proposition that the way to improve tax law is to remove from it "tax expenditures." A Treasury crammed with experts in social policy might find it even harder to resist making tax proposals meant to achieve nontax goals. Experts like to use their expertise. Halperin himself understands this. He calls his approach, "If you can't beat them, join them." Yet so strong is the ideology that tax expenditures are bad that he was indignant when we mistakenly suggested that he had not been an adherent.

There are many omissions and conjectures in our story. One mystery is different in kind and more important than the others. In 1978 the Treasury not only was making health policy through tax law, but seems to have had no doubt that this was its normal and natural function. One might say the Treasury had been doing so since 1942, when it proposed the medical deduction now found in Section 213. How did the Treasury first decide that this was proper? What is the history of its interaction with the people who make explicit health policy? How did the legislative clearance process operate to permit the Treasury to make health policy through tax law? For those who believe we cannot understand where we are without understanding how we got here, the episode of cafeteria plans raises these broad and as yet unanswered questions.

Notes

1. *Wall Street Journal*, 13 May 1986, p. 1.
2. Revenue Act of 1918, sec. 213(b), 40 Stat. 1066.
3. I.R.C., sec. 106.

4. Department of the Treasury, "The President's 1978 Tax Program: Detailed Descriptions and Supporting Analysis of the Proposals," 145 (30 January 1978), reprinted in "The President's 1978 Tax Reduction and Reform Proposals: Hearings before the House Committee on Ways and Means," 95th Cong., 2d Sess. 160, 304 (1978) [hereinafter cited as "The President's 1978 Tax Program"].

5. Id.

6. In tax law, "discrimination" does not refer to racial discrimination, sex discrimination, age discrimination, or to any of the other kinds of discrimination that preoccupy the civil rights lawyer. "Discrimination" in tax law has to do with tax-free fringe benefits, and the question is always whether the benefits are dispensed in a way that discriminates unduly "in favor of employees who are officers, shareholders, or highly compensated." Internal Revenue Code, sec. 410(b)(1).

7. "The President's 1978 Tax Program," supra note 4, at 164.

8. Id. at 164–54.

9. "The President's 1978 Tax Reduction and Reform Proposals: Hearings before the House Committee on Ways and Means," 95th Cong., 2d Sess. 5626 (1978) [hereinafter cited as House 1978 Hearings] (statement of Michael Monroney).

10. We use the masculine pronoun in examples in order to avoid both the awkwardness of repeating "he or she" and the random use of the feminine pronoun. Rev. Rul. 60–31, 1960–1 C.B. 174, 178.

11. Prop. Reg. sec. 1.042(a)–1(a)(1)(i), 37 Fed. Reg. 25938 (6 December 1972). The suggested link between the regulation's ostensible subject of constructive receipt and discrimination is suggested in Halperin (1983: 39–8).

12. Employee Retirement Income Security Act of 1974. Pub. L. No. 93–406, 93rd Cong., 2d Sess. sec. 2006, 1974–3 C.B. 161.

13. H.R. Rep. No. 95–1445, 95th Cong., 2d Sess. 63, 66 (1978); 1978–3 Cum. Bull. 237, 240.

14. The 1974 legislation described cafeteria plans as arrangements "under which an employee was permitted to elect to receive part of his compensation in one or more alternative forms if one of such forms results in the inclusion of amounts in income under the Internal Revenue Code of 1954." The House Ways and Means Committee saw "no difference between this type of plan and salary reduction plans," a judgment with which most tax lawyers would probably agree.

15. "The President's 1978 Tax Program," supra note 4, at 170–30.

16. Prop. Reg. sec 1.61–16, 43 Fed. Reg. 4368 (3 February 1978) (filed 31 January 1978).

17. Letter from Daniel I. Halperin to the authors, 8 January 1987; Tax Shelters, Accounting Abuses, and Corporate and Securities Reforms: Hearings before the House Committee on Ways and Means, 98th Cong., 2d Sess. 196 (1984) (Statement of Daniel Halperin) [hereinafter cited as House 1984 Hearings].

18. Reporting Requirements for State and Local Government Pension Plans and Tax Treatment of Deferred Amounts under Qualified Deferred Compensation Plans: Hearings before the Senate Committee on Finance, 95th Cong., 2d Sess. 25 (1978) [hereinafter cited as Senate 1978 Hearings] (statement of Daniel Halperin).

19. Id. at 39–5; House 1984 Hearings, supra note 17.

20. Rev. Rul. 60–31, 1960–1 C.B. 174, 178.

21. House 1978 Hearings, supra note 9, at 5626, 5627 (statement of Michael Monroney).
22. We are grateful to James Mays for this suggestion.
23. Senate 1978 Hearings, supra note 18, at 26.
24. 43 Fed. Reg. at 4638–39.
25. House 1978 Hearings, supra note 9, at 5626–31 (statement of Michael Monroney).
26. Id. at 5629.
27. Senate 1978 Hearings, supra note 18, at 25. The Treasury's proposal to permit cafeteria plans had been explicit about this from the beginning: "Rank-and-file employees could not disproportionately elect to receive taxable benefits in cash or otherwise." "The President's 1978 Tax Program," supra note 4, at 171.
28. S. Rep. No. 95–1263, 95th Cong., 2d Sess. 76 (1978).
29. Hearings on Tax Expenditures for Health Care, Committees on the Budget and on Ways and Means, 96th Cong., 1st Sess. 71 (1979) [hereinafter cited as House 1979 Hearings].
30. Retirement Income Security in the United States, Hearings before the House Committee on Ways and Means, 99th Cong., 1st Sess., ser. 99–50, at 246, 281, 283 (1985) [hereinafter cited as House 1985 Hearings].
31. Provided by Mr. Sunley to the authors. The congressional committee reports on the much more limited antidiscrimination rules actually enacted in 1978 (which applied only to employers who self-insured) also predicted an increase in revenue, albeit a smaller one. S. Rep. 95–1263, 95th Cong., 2d Sess. 187 (1978).
32. Letter from Halperin to the authors, 8 January 1987.
33. The rule in force during the Carter administration was that "In the case of proposed legislation, the originating agency shall not submit to Congress any proposal that OMB has advised is in conflict with the program of the President." Executive Office of the President, Office of Management and Budget, Legislative Coordination and Clearance, Circular No. A–19, Revised 10 (September 1979).
34. Id. at 6f(1)(e) and (f).
35. The letters are summarized at 13 Tax Notes 96 (1982) and XV Tax Notes 183 (1982).
36. Letter dated 7 December 1982 from Chapoton to Durenberger, 13 Tax Notes 1038 (1982).
37. Proposed Treas. Reg. sec 1.401(k)–1, 46 Fed. Reg. 55546 (10 November 1981).
38. Senate 1978 Hearings, supra note 18, at 28, 38–39.
39. IR–84–22, [1984] 10 Stand. Fed. Tax Rep. (C.C.H.) 6383.
40. House 1984 Hearings, supra note 17.
41. Id. at 200, 203.
42. Id.
43. Id.
44. Id. at 208, 211 (statement of Susan Koralik).
45. Letter from John E. Chapoton to Robert J. Rubin, M.D. (10 April 1984), reprinted in 23 Tax Notes 308 (1984).
46. Letter from Robert J. Rubin, M.D., to John E. Chapoton (11 April 1984), reprinted in 23 Tax Notes 547 (1984).
47. Proposed Treas. Reg. sec 1.125–1 (1984), 49 Fed. Reg. 19322 (7 May 1984).
48. Fringe Benefits: Hearings before the Senate Committee on Finance, 98th Cong., 2d Sess. 30, 32 (statement of John E. Chapoton).

49. Three percent under the law in 1978, later raised to 5 percent, and to 7.5 percent after 1986.
50. Halperin made the same points in testimony at the House 1984 hearings, House 1984 Hearings, supra note 17, at 195–96 (statement of Daniel Halperin).
51. I.R.C. sec. 125(b)(2). Section 125 as amended by the Revenue Act of 1984, sec. 531, is set out in Appendix B.
52. House 1984 Hearings, supra note 17, at 191, 196.
53. Letter from Barber B. Conable to John E. Chapoton (21 May 1984), reprinted in 23 Tax Notes 1107 (984).
54. Tax Reform Act of 1984, sec. 531(b)(6).
55. U.S. Department of Health and Human Services (1985).
56. Id. at 25.
57. Id. at 21.
58. Tax Reform Act of 1984, supra note 54, sec. 531(b)(6) (1984).
59. H.R. 98–861, 98th Cong., 2d Sess. 1177 (1984).
60. House 1985 Hearings, supra note 30, at 280–81, 283.
61. I.R.C. sec. 89, added by Tax Reform Act of 1986, Pub. L. 99–514, at 1151 (1986).
62. Letter from Mr. Savage to the authors, dated 16 January 1987.
63. Id.

References

Bittker, B. 1981. *Federal Taxation of Income, Estates and Gifts.* Boston, Mass.: Warren, Gorham and Lamont.

Brown, L. 1978. "The Formulation of Federal Health Care Policy." *Bulletin of the New York Academy of Medicine* 54: 45–58.

Ginsburg, P. 1981. "Altering the Tax Treatment of Employment-Based Health Plans." *Milbank Memorial Quarterly* 59: 224–55.

Halperin, D. 1983. "Cash or Deferred Profit-Sharing Plans and Cafeteria Plans." Annual New York University Tax Institute 41: chapter 31.

Irish, L. 1984. "Cafeteria Plans in Transition." *Tax Notes* 25: 1127–41.

Lubick, D. 1980. "The Treasury Department and Tax Legislation." In *Tax Legislative Procedures,* ed. J. Colvin. Washington, D.C.: Federal Bar Association.

Sheppard, L. 1984a. "Employers Conference on Flexible Compensation Bestows the Mr. Flex Award on Packwood and Conable." *Tax Notes* 23: 1129–30.

————. 1984b. "Zebras on the Loose in the All-You-Can-Eat-Cafeteria." *Tax Notes* 23: 565–70.

Student Note. 1976. "Federal Income Taxation of Employee Fringe Benefits." *Harvard Law Review* 89: 1141–73.

Surrey, S. 1973. *Pathways to Tax Reform.* Cambridge, Mass.: Harvard University Press.

U.S. Department of Health and Human Services. Office of the Assistant Secretary for Planning and Evaluation. 1985. *A Study of Cafeteria Plans and Flexible Spending Accounts.* Washington, D.C.: DHHS.

Wolk, B. 1984. "Discrimination Rules for Qualified Retirement Plans: Good Intentions Confront Economic Reality." *Virginia Law Review* 70: 419–71.

14

U.S. Government Support for Employee Stock Ownership Plans

Raymond Russell

Since 1974 the U.S. government has been encouraging the formation of "Employee Stock Ownership Plans" (ESOPs) through a wide variety of means. There are probably very few programs in recent American history that provide better examples of the casual and offhand manner in which billions of dollars in federal revenues can be spent. By 1983 the U.S. General Accounting Office estimates that the federal government had spent more than $12 billion to encourage the formation of ESOPs, without making any effort to find out how many of these plans had actually been formed, how many employees were covered by them, or what the impact of the plans on the firms that had adopted them had been (U.S. General Accounting Office, 1986b: 26–32).

This paper will attempt to shed some light on both the causes and the consequences of this federal generosity toward the ESOPs. It will trace the evolving uses and advantages that have been associated with the ESOPs, it will review the most significant ESOP policy debates, and it will weigh the best available evidence concerning the ESOP program's actual benefits and costs. It will begin, however, with a consideration of the factors that contributed to the establishment of the federal ESOP program in 1974.

This is an original contribution prepared for this volume.

Origin of the ESOPs

The credit for initially proposing that the United States government should become involved in promoting employee stock ownership undoubtedly belongs to San Francisco attorney Louis Kelso. Kelso has advocated such measures in a series of publications dating back to 1958 (Kelso and Adler, 1958, 1961; Kelson and Hetter, 1967; Kelso and Kelso, 1986). For Kelso, the need for a federal employee ownership policy was fundamental, and the benefits to be expected from such a policy were equally broad. Kelso entitled his first work on this subject *The Capitalist Manifesto* to underline the economic and political significance that he attached to his plans.

For Kelso, the most important thing wrong with the United States today is that American workers earn too little income in the form of profit and too much in the form of a wage. As a result, American workers take too little interest in corporate profits, and are all too ready to press for constant increases in the size of their wage. The specific problems that Kelso sees as emerging from this situation are almost too numerous to list. They include union militance, inflation, economic stagnation, and a decline in United States competitiveness overseas.

Kelso's early works recommended a wide range of measures for dealing with these problems. They included the encouragement of "equity-sharing plans" that make stockholders of employees, plus a number of other measures designed to maximize the amount of income that every stockholder derived from owning stock. Such measures included the abolition of the corporate income tax and the passage of legislation that would require mature corporations to pay out all of their earnings in the form of dividends to stockholders rather than retaining them in the treasury of the firm. The goal of all these policies would be to provide every American worker with a "second income" derived from corporate profits that would compare favorably with the income that comes in the form of a wage.

In 1967 Kelson and his future wife, Patricia Hetter, proposed a new technique for promoting employee ownership in the United States that would not require any amendments in existing federal law. Entitled *How to Turn Eighty Million Workers into Capitalists on Borrowed Money*, the work offered American corporations a way to promote employee ownership and save money on taxes at the very same time. The key to these tax savings was for a corporation in need of money to have its employee benefit plan take out a loan, and then to use the loan proceeds to purchase an equivalent amount of company stock. The stock thus purchased serves as collateral for the loan, and the company then makes annual contributions to the plan sufficient to cover the payments on the loan. The tax savings that result derive from the fact that the corporation is thereby permitted to deduct the principal in addition to the interest as it repays the loan.

Kelso's proposals went nowhere for a number of years. Academic economists either ignored him entirely or called attention to a number of errors in the theoretical portions of his work (Jochim, 1982: 12–16). Politicians occasionally gave his ideas a sympathetic reception (Speiser, 1977), but it was not until Kelso was introduced to Senator Russell Long in 1973 that his ideas really got off the ground.

When Senator Long met Louis Kelso in 1973, Long was serving as chair of the powerful Senate Committee on Finance, which was then in the process of drafting the Employee Retirement Income Security Act (ERISA) of 1974. The ERISA legislation was initially conceived as an attempt at pension reform, and most of its provisions were intended to enhance the security of employees' retirement accounts. Early drafts of the act would have strongly discouraged employee benefit plans from investing their assets in their company's own stock, and would also have explicitly prohibited corporations from using their employees' pension assets as security for any loans. Thanks to Senator Long's efforts, however, the final draft of this legislation gave explicit encouragement to the formation of Employee Stock Ownership Plans, or ESOPs, and established the ESOPs as the only employee benefit plans that had the right to use their assets as security for a loan.

From 1974 until his retirement from the Congress in January 1987, Senator Long remained the ESOPs' best friend in Congress and sought to encourage the spread of the ESOPs through a broad range of means. Since Long's support has been so crucial for the ESOPs, there has been a good deal of speculation about the considerations that may or may not have led him to become such an enthusiastic supporter of these plans. Some analysts have looked back to the legacy of Russell Long's father, the populist Louisiana governor, Huey Long. Huey Long had announced that his goal was to make "every man a king." With the aid of the ESOPs, Russell Long is now helping to make every person a capitalist, if not a king (Speiser, 1977; Sloan, 1981).

In the speeches he has given on behalf of the ESOPs, Long often calls attention to the economic benefits of employee ownership that feature so prominently in Kelso's work. For example, he is particularly fond of citing cases and studies that indicate that a transition to employee ownership improves the productivity or profitability of a firm. It is also clear from his speeches, however, that in his case the reforms proposed in Kelso's *Capitalist Manifesto* have as much a *political* as an economic rationale. In May 1981, for example, Long argued in the Senate that employee ownership will "help create a stronger political base for our endangered private property system" (U.S. Congress, 1981b). Two months previously, Long had stated even more explicitly that "Capitalism really needs a broader constituency. It needs more people who regard themselves as capitalists if this system is going to survive . . ." (U.S. Congress, 1981a).

New Uses for the ESOPs

By the time of its origination in 1974, the federal ESOP program had thus already been directed toward a wide range of goals. Their inclusion in ERISA meant that the ESOPs, like all other employee benefit plans, must be established for the exclusive benefit of employees. But in addition, both Louis Kelso and Russell Long hoped that the ESOPs would motivate employees to become more productive and to increase the profits of their firms. Both for Kelso and for Long, the ESOPs had the potential to serve much grander ends than these, such as restoring prosperity to the nation and renewing American capitalism's faith in itself. In the years after 1974, however, a number of American corporations began to find some new uses for the ESOPs that had little or nothing to do with any of these initial goals.

Tax Advantages of ESOPs

Having succeeded in establishing the federal ESOP program in 1974, Senator Long spent many of the following years offering American corporations a number of additional inducements for establishing these plans. Most prominent of these inducements was a tax credit for ESOPs that Long had incorporated into the Tax Reduction Act of 1975. Subject to certain limitations, this tax credit reimbursed corporations dollar for dollar for gifts of stock they made to an employee stock ownership plan. ESOPs that qualified for this tax credit were originally known as Tax Reduction Act ESOPs (TRASOPs), but in 1980 their name was officially changed to Tax Credit ESOPs. Since 1983 the Tax Credit ESOPs have also frequently been referred to as PAYSOPs, in recognition of the fact that the tax credit for ESOPs in that year became "payroll-based."

In addition to this tax credit for ESOPs, Long was able to enact a number of other tax advantages for ESOPs before his retirement in 1987. For example, the Deficit Reduction Act of 1984 included a provision that permits banks to exclude from their taxable income 50 percent of the interest that they earn on loans to an ESOP. That same act contained other benefits for ESOPs that will be discussed in greater detail below.

In 1980 the Human Resources Division of the U.S. General Accounting

Office (GAO) brought to light another tax advantage of the ESOPs that had never been intended by any federal law. In closely held corporations, where no market mechanism exists to place a fair valuation on a company's stock, the GAO concluded that firm owners were often inflating the tax deductions or tax credits associated with their gifts to their ESOPs by assigning unreasonably high values to their stock. Of the thirteen closely held corporations whose records the GAO examined, the GAO found reason to question the values that all of them had assigned to their gifts of stock, and called particular attention to the case of one company in which IRS investigators concluded that stock contributed to an ESOP had been overvalued by 632 percent (U.S. General Accounting Office, 1980: 16).

ESOPs and Divestitures

In Louis Kelso and Russell Long's initial vision for the ESOPs, their intent was clearly to make employees minority owners of otherwise conventionally owned firms. But once the ESOP program with its accompanying tax advantages had been established, it did not take long for many people to begin to realize that the ESOPs would make outstanding vehicles for the divestiture of entire firms. For a retiring owner, a gradual sale to an ESOP offered an attractive opportunity to liquidate his investment without allowing his life's work to become just another branch of some nationwide firm. And for the firm itself after the retiring owner would be gone, if Kelso and Long were right in thinking that a little employee ownership would be good for a firm, would not a lot of employee ownership be even better?

As news of the attractiveness of this use for ESOPs filtered back to Washington, Long was soon adding new provisions to the tax code to encourage its use. In 1984 employers obtained the right to defer capital gains on stock that they sold to an ESOP, provided that the transaction would result in the ESOP owning 30 percent or more of the company's stock. Two other provisions were intended to make it easier for an ESOP to acquire the stock of a firm owner after the owner had died. The first, passed in 1984, gave ESOPs the right to assume the tax liability of a deceased owner's estate, provided that the estate contributed to the ESOP an equivalent amount of stock. The second, enacted as Long was retiring late in 1986, permitted the estate of a deceased owner to exclude from the estate's value 50 percent of the proceeds resulting from the sale of stock to an ESOP.

The Use of an ESOP to Save a Closing Firm

In the late 1970s and early 1980s, the worsening competitive position of the United States in international markets gave rise to another new and unanticipated use of the ESOPs, namely, the purchase of a firm by an ESOP to prevent the closure of the firm. In most of these cases, the ESOP's beneficiaries were unionized employees, and the sale of the firm to its ESOP was the only condition under which the employees' representatives would agree to the wage concessions that appeared to be needed to keep the firm alive. The first major instance of this practice was the purchase of the Rath meat packing plant in Waterloo, Iowa, by more than 2,000 of its employees in 1979. Another well-publicized example occurred in 1981, when 750 New Jersey roller-bearing makers purchased General Motors' Hyatt Clark plant. In March 1983 the largest of these deals on record occurred when 7,000 steelmakers used an ESOP to purchase National Steel's Weirton, West Virginia, plant.

This use of ESOPs to avert plant closures has attracted a great deal of publicity, and is therefore probably the best-known use of ESOPs in the United States today. The ESOPs' principal backers, however, have resisted the popular impression that ESOPs are primarily in the business of saving failing companies, and often point out that the proportion of ESOPs that are formed for this purpose has always been rather small. In recent years the failure of the Rath and Hyatt Clark ventures appears to have helped to discourage this practice, but Weirton Steel continues to stand out as its largest and most conspicuous success.

The "Management Entrenchment" Stock Ownership Plan

In the 1980s two even more controversial uses of ESOPs began to receive prominent attention in the nation's business press. These are the use of ESOPs to protect a publicly traded corporation against takeover attempts, and to turn a publicly traded corporation into a privately traded one.

The appeal of an ESOP as a form of takeover defense lies in the fact that it increases the number of shares that are in "friendly" hands, and that can therefore be expected to support a firm's existing management in any takeover fight. So-called leveraged shares in ESOPs that are being used as security for a loan are voted by the ESOPs' trustees, who are appointed by management and can therefore normally be expected to side with management in a takeover fight. All other shares in ESOPs would be voted by the employees in a takeover fight, but it is normally expected that a firm's employees will cast their votes with management rather than running the risk of turning the firm over to an unknown buyer from outside. The use of an ESOP to make a public corporation private provides an even more effective defense, as it completely eliminates the possibility that a hostile suitor will begin buying up the company's shares.

Some of the most prominent instances of these uses of ESOPs have included the role of ESOPs in resisting takeovers of Phillips Petroleum, Carter Hawley Hale, and Harcourt Brace Jovanovich, and the use of ESOPs to turn such corporations as Dan River, U.S. Sugar, and Avis Rent-a-Car into privately traded firms. The Department of Labor (DOL) has occasionally objected to some of these transactions on the grounds that the ESOPs in these cases are not being administered as ERISA requires for the exclusive benefit of employees. The DOL has been particularly likely to intervene in cases in which an ESOP pays inflated prices to purchase company stock in the heat of a takeover fight, or in which the terms of a proposed leveraged buyout appear too favorable to management. But provided that the most obvious sins have been avoided, these deals have generally been allowed to go through. This in turn led Corey Rosen of the National Center for Employee Ownership to remark in 1984 that the nation's "Employee Stock Ownership Plans" were in danger of being transformed into "Management Entrenchment Stock Ownership Plans" (Williams, 1984).

The Politics of ESOPs

When he entitled his first work *The Capitalist Manifesto,* in 1958, Louis Kelso left no doubt about the ultimate target against whom his proposals were aimed. A nationwide system of employee stock ownership would provide America's ultimate refutation of the work of Karl Marx. The future President Ronald Reagan made this point even more explicitly in commenting on the ESOPs in 1975. "Could there be a better answer to the stupidity of Karl Marx," he asked, "than millions of workers individually sharing in the ownership of the means of production?" (U.S. Congress, 1981b).

Marxists, for their part, have long understood the political significance of ESOP-like reforms. More than a hundred years before the ESOP program was established, Engels had quoted with approval an Italian Marxist's comment that "the cleverest leaders of the ruling class have always directed their efforts toward increasing the number of small property owners in order to build for themselves an army against the proletariat" (McClaughry, 1972: 89). But the ESOPs also help to shed light on a more recent Marxist debate, namely, that between advocates of "structuralist" and "instrumental" models of the capitalist state. "Instrumentalists" see the state as an explicit tool or "instrument" of the capitalist class, and call attention to direct ties between business and government in the form of lobbying, campaign contributions, etc., as proof of their point. "Structuralist" Marxists, on the other hand, emphasize the "relative autonomy'' of the state, and call attention to the state's capacity to take actions that serve the interests of capitalism in the absence of any lobbying, or even over the objections of individual capitalists who are required to foot the bill for the state's cosmetic reforms. (For a particularly pithy and influential discussion of this debate, see Gold, Lo, and Wright, 1975.)

In its inception and the early years of its development, the federal ESOP program provided a textbook example of a purely "structuralist" reform. The program in those years was by no means entirely free of controversy, but those debates that did take place arose almost entirely within the federal government. Thus the ESOPs' most important political battles took place between the ESOPs' advocates in Congress and officials in such executive agencies as the departments of Labor and of the Treasury who bear primary responsibility for making sure that employees' pension assets are not abused.

As the ESOP program has matured, however, more and more ESOP legislation has taken on the characteristics of an "instrumental" reform, as it becomes more and more likely to be the result of active lobbying by groups most affected by these laws. In this regard the ESOPs appear to be repeating a pattern that was first described years ago in Philip Selznick's classic study of *The TVA and the Grass Roots* (1949). What Selznick showed there was that reforms initially implemented in the absence of any political constituency eventually generate their own constituency in the form of the beneficiaries of these reforms. Selznick showed how this process had occurred after the creation of the Agricultural Extension Service in the early part of this century, and again after the creation of the Tennessee Valley Authority in the 1930s and 1940s; and the pattern appears to have been repeated once again as a result of the establishment of the federal ESOP program in 1974.

The ESOP Voting Rights Debate

Both the oldest and the most enduring of the controversies surrounding the ESOPs has revolved around the voting rights associated with employees' ESOP stock. The issue first surfaced in 1976, when the Treasury Department released the first draft of the regulations that it would use to administer the ESOP program. Among the requirements that these regulations would have imposed on the ESOPs was a stipulation that stock in the ESOPs should include voting rights that would be "passed through" to the individual employees who participated in the plans. A number of firm owners who were in the process of setting up ESOPs objected to this provision, because they did not want the ESOPs to diminish in any way their control of their firms. These owners appealed to Senator Long and other friends in the Congress, and persuaded them to intervene on their behalf. Their congressional allies inserted the following statement about the federal ESOP program into the Tax Reform Act of 1976:

> . . . the objectives sought by this series of laws will be made unattainable by regulations and rulings which treat employee stock ownership plans as conventional retirement plans, which reduce the freedom of the employee trusts and employers to take the necessary steps to implement the plans, and which otherwise block the establishment and success of these plans.

In the Conference Committee report that accompanied this law, Congress explicitly identified the proposed voting rights provision as one of the draft regulations that most threatened to "frustrate Congressional intent." When the final version of the Treasury regulations was published in 1977, it no longer contained any mention of ESOP voting rights.

The ESOP voting rights issue resurfaced in 1978, when that year's Revenue Act created a uniform set of standards that would be equally applicable to the original ERISA ESOPs and to the new tax credit ESOPs. The law that created the tax credit ESOPs in 1975 had initially required that stock in TRASOPs must carry full voting rights, and that these voting rights should be "passed through" the trust to individual employees. In the Revenue Act of 1978, this full voting rights pass-through requirement was retained only for ESOPs in publicly traded firms. In privately traded corporations, voting rights could be more limited, but the act imposed a minimum voting rights requirement even on these firms. Closely held corporations would henceforth be required to pass through voting rights on all issues that state law required to be approved by more than a majority vote. These are typically such issues as mergers, acquisitions, relocations, and liquidations.

Modest as this limited voting rights pass-through for closely held firms might appear to be, it upset the owners of many firms with ESOPs, and a campaign was soon launched for its repeal. Lobbying for the ESOP firm owners was handled by the newly formed ESOP Association, with headquarters in Washington, D.C. At the association's urging, more than a half-dozen bills or amendments that would have repealed this provision were introduced in either the House or the Senate in the early 1980s. One such amendment passed the Senate by a vote of 94 to 3 in 1981, but was vetoed by the House negotiators when the bill was in conference.

When the Tax Reform Act of 1986 was initially being prepared, both the White House and the House of Representatives offered versions that would have required employees in all ESOPs to receive full voting rights. Washington insiders attributed these proposals not to pressure from constituents

but, rather, to the staffs of executive agencies and congressional committees who felt responsible for protecting employees' pension rights. It has
also been argued that the House has occasionally passed provisions that
take a harsh stance toward ESOPs in order to use those provisions as
"bargaining chips" in their negotiations with the Senate, and in particular
with Russell Long. Sure enough, the Senate version of the 1986 tax bill
imposed no new conditions regarding ESOP voting rights, and the bill's
final version contained only one minor provision affecting ESOP voting
rights. That provision explicitly defined, without increasing the range of,
issues on which employees in closely held ESOPs must receive voting
rights.

Employee Incentives or Retirement Plans?

Another perennial source of controversy associated with the ESOPs is
the plans' dual and often contradictory nature as both employee incentives
and retirement plans. That ESOPs would have to attempt to be both of
these things is a consequence of the ESOPs' inclusion in the ERISA
legislation in 1974. But in practice it has not turned out to be easy to
pursue both of these goals at once. Insofar as employee stock ownership
is supposed to act as an incentive, for example, it has often been argued
that its motivational effects will be maximized if employees receive direct
title to their shares and earn frequent cash dividends on their stock.
Treating the ESOPs as pension plans, on the other hand, requires employees' stockholdings to be accumulated in the plan until they are ready to
leave the firm, and makes it likely that the earnings on those stockholdings
will be held in the plan as well. Insofar as one does view the ESOPs as
pension plans, moreover, they always look inferior to more conventional
arrangements that invest their assets in diversified portfolios of stocks and
bonds.

On a number of occasions, Senator Long and his allies have sponsored
amendments to the ESOP program intended to make it easier for employers to use their ESOPs to motivate employees. For example, the Tax
Reform Act of 1976 explicitly authorized ESOPs to pay cash dividends to
employees, rather than simply adding these dividends to employees'
retirement accounts. And in 1984 corporations received the right to take a
deduction for dividends that they pay on shares in ESOPs, provided that
those dividends are "passed through" as cash payments to the individual
employees. Data released by the General Accounting Office in 1986,
however, indicate that neither of these measures had had much effect. Of
firms with ESOPs that the GAO surveyed in the latter half of 1985, 58
percent had never paid dividends, and of the remaining 42 percent that did

pay dividends, 86 percent were in the habit of merely adding dividends to the balances in employees' ESOP accounts (U.S. General Accounting Office, 1986b: 36–37).

When the Tax Reform Act of 1986 was initially being drafted early in 1985, the White House proposed that the ESOP program should be redesigned in a way that would completely end the treatment of the ESOPs as employee retirement accounts. The White House recommended that the ESOPs should issue shares directly to employees, and called for employees to have the right to sell their shares after holding them for three years. The ESOPs' backers were quick to denounce these proposals as alterations that had the appearance of being offered as friendly improvements in the program, but that would in practice be so onerous for employers that they would essentially kill the program.

When the House of Representatives began preparing its own version of the tax reform bill in September 1985, it proposed to continue treating ESOPs as employee retirement plans, but retained one element from the president's "direct ownership" proposal in the form of a provision that would have given employees the right to "cash out" of an ESOP after they had participated in the plan for a minimum of seven years. It was at this point that the ESOP Association's new allies in the Congress rallied to their defense. On October 25, Representative Beryl Anthony of Arkansas introduced an amendment at a meeting of the House Ways and Means Committee that would replace this provision with a much milder one that merely permitted employees with more than ten years' participation in their plans to "diversify" 25 percent of their investments when they reach the age of fifty-five, or 33⅓ percent (later changed to 50 percent) when they reach the age of sixty. Other Ways and Means Committee members who joined Representative Anthony in speaking out in favor of the ESOPs included Representatives Pickle, Rangel, and Crane; and with their help, his amendment was made part of the version of the tax bill that won the endorsement of the full House of Representatives in December 1985.

On the Senate side, in the meantime, Senator Long continued to lead the pro-ESOP forces, and soon prepared a major counterattack on their behalf. On June 19, 1986, Long introduced an amendment to the tax bill that would add a number of new tax incentives for the ESOPs, and that contained language explicitly rejecting the various recent efforts to redesign or discourage the use of the plans. In words reminiscent of the Tax Reform Act of 1976, Long's amendment said of the ESOPs:

> It is the policy of the Congress that such plans be used in a wide variety of corporate financing transactions as a means of encouraging employees as beneficiaries of such transactions. The Congress is deeply concerned that the

objectives sought by the series of applicable laws and this Act will be made unattainable by regulations and rulings which treat employee stock ownership plans as conventional retirement plans under the Employee Retirement Income Security Act of 1974, which reduce the freedom of employee stock ownership plans and employers to take the necessary steps to utilize employee stock ownership plans in a wide variety of corporate transactions, and which otherwise impede the establishment and success of these plans.

In the debate on Long's amendment that took place on the floor of the Senate on June 19, one senator after another rose to praise the ESOPs and Long's role in promoting them. Particularly vociferous in their support for the ESOPs were Senators Baucus of Montana, Matsunaga of Hawaii, Byrd and Rockefeller from West Virginia, Hatfield and Packwood of Oregon, and Kennedy from Massachusetts. Not a single senator spoke out against the Long amendment, and the measure was adopted by a vote of 99–0.

Despite this strong showing of Senate support, House negotiators on the Conference Committee continued to insist on the special problems raised by using employer securities in retirement plans, and in the end it was they rather than Senator Long who prevailed on this point. Thus the bill's final version omitted the "intent of Congress" statement that had been proposed by Senator Long, and included the "diversification" requirement that had been passed by the House. In his remarks to the House on the ESOP-related provisions contained in the new tax bill, on September 25, Ways and Means Chairman Dan Rostenkowski took explicit note of the House negotiators' rejection of Senator Long's statement on congressional intent, and reaffirmed that the potential conflicts of interest inherent in the ESOPs' dual nature would continue to subject them to special scrutiny from both the Department of Labor and the House.

ESOPs after Long

While the ESOPs' backers may have lost this one battle in preparing the Tax Reform Act of 1986, they appear generally to have won the war. The redraft of the tax code in 1985–86 was perhaps the ESOPs' greatest political test. The period had opened with proposals that would have virtually dismantled these plans, and it ended with a tax bill that did more to strengthen than to weaken the plans.

Of greatest importance to the ESOPs' principal backers, the 1986 Tax Reform Act retained all the incentives that had been added in 1984, and contributed several new ones to the set. The most important of these new incentives was the provision referred to earlier that allowed estates that sell stock to an ESOP to deduct from the value of the estate 50 percent of the proceeds they receive from the sale. In addition, "leveraged" ESOPs received the right to take a deduction for dividends that are used to repay an ESOP loan, and the 50 percent interest exclusion for lenders was made available to mutual funds in addition to banks.

Possibly even more significant than the tax bill's specific provisions was the new political muscle that the ESOPs had shown. Henceforth, it appeared, the ESOPs would no longer depend solely on the good will of ideologically committed backers like Senator Long; in the future, they could expect increasing support from a new generation of legislators who had ESOPs in their districts, and who saw support for the ESOPs as a good way to increase their own political backing at home. Thus, for example, the successful worker buyout of Weirton Steel had helped to make both Senators Byrd and Rockefeller of West Virginia enthusiastic backers of these plans. Other ESOPs in the constituencies of Representative Anthony in the House and of Senators Baucus and Matsunaga in the Senate have helped propel all of them into their current positions of leadership within the ESOP movement.

Clearly the ESOP lobby has grown powerful, but is not so powerful as to have things all its own way. The ESOPs have been with us long enough to have attracted a few enemies as well as friends. In addition to being concerned about the deficiencies of the ESOPs as retirement plans, legislators in 1985–86 had also become quite concerned about the costs of the ESOP program, and this was another area in which the ESOPs' backers had to give. By far the biggest cost associated with the federal ESOP program has been the tax credit for ESOPs. This tax credit had already been scheduled to expire at the end of 1987, but under the terms of the 1986 Tax Reform Act the tax credit for ESOP was terminated one year early, on December 31, 1986.

It is most enlightening about the new politics of ESOPs to note that no one even attempted to defend the tax credit for ESOPs when its demise was being contemplated in 1985–86. The tax credit for ESOPs had always been a surprisingly weak incentive for forming ESOPs, despite the apparent generosity of its terms. Unless they had other, more compelling reasons for forming ESOPs, most employers apparently felt that the administrative costs associated with the ESOPs outweighed the tax credits they would receive for them. Thus the GAO found that not much more than 1,000 American corporations had established tax credit ESOPs by the end of 1983, and these tax credit ESOPs were generally the most superficial of all ESOPs, with the fewest assets per participating employee (U.S. General Accounting Office, 1986a: 9, 23). The employers who have made use of the tax credit for ESOPs also appear to have found their ESOPs more trouble than they are worth, and therefore never bothered to join the ESOP Association, and made no effort to speak out on behalf of this benefit when it was slated for elimination as part of the Tax Reform Act of 1986.

The expiration of the ESOP tax credit in 1986 brought an end to an incentive that through 1983 had accounted for nearly 80 percent of all ESOP assets and for more than 90 percent of ESOP participants (U.S. General Accounting Office, 1986a: 23). It nevertheless appeared that the ESOP movement would be stronger without these plans. The pruning of the tax credit for ESOPs meant that employers would henceforth be less likely to use the ESOPs for superficial purposes, and would be more likely to use them to control the destinies of entire firms. With the 1984 and 1986 incentives and with their new friends in Congress, the ESOPs would appear to be well equipped to serve such a purpose in the future.

Evaluating the ESOPs

It is interesting to note that these momentous decisions about the future of the ESOPs were decided in the absence of virtually any reliable data about the number or actual impact of these plans. Senator Long had requested the GAO to conduct a comprehensive evaluation of the ESOPs in the summer of 1984, but the GAO's study required more than three years to complete, and its most important findings were not released until after the Tax Reform Act of 1986 had become law. Since the GAO study did provide answers to some of the most policy-relevant questions about the purposes and impact of these plans, a few of its most significant findings will be briefly reviewed here.

What Are ESOPs Really For?

The GAO study dealt only with ESOPs that had been established by the end of 1983, and can therefore tell us only about the impact of the incentives that had become effective prior to 1984. The GAO estimates that nearly 5,000 ESOPs had been established in the first decade of the federal ESOP program, of which more than 4,000 plans were still active as of 1985 (U.S. General Accounting Office, 1986a: 9).

The GAO found that many of the most highly publicized uses of ESOPs had actually played a surprisingly modest role in encouraging the spread of these plans. Only 15 percent of all ESOPs, for example, had ever used their assets as security for a loan. Another 25 percent of ESOPs had taken the ESOP tax credit, but this still means that the two best-known incentives for forming ESOPs prior to 1984 had together accounted for only 40 percent of all plans. Other highly publicized uses of ESOPs had led to the creation of even smaller numbers of plans. Only 4 percent of ESOPs had been formed to save a failing company. Only 5 percent acknowledged the desire to make a firm less vulnerable to takeovers as being among the reasons for forming their plans, and only 1 percent had been used to turn a publicly traded company into a privately traded one (U.S. General Accounting Office, 1986b: 20).

If the spread of the ESOPs had so little to do with any of these purposes, why had the plans been formed? Fully 91 percent of plans told the GAO that they had been formed "to provide a benefit for employees"—a not particularly revealing finding, given that ERISA requires that this be among the purposes for forming a plan. Another 74 percent reported that "tax advantages" of one kind or another had led them to set up their plans. Of more specific purposes, many of the most popular choices involved the potential effects of ESOPs on employees—i.e., "improve productivity" (70 percent); "reduce turnover" (36 percent); "decrease absenteeism" (14 percent); and "avoid unionization" (8 percent).

Perhaps the biggest surprise in the GAO's findings is the frequency with which the ESOPs were being used as vehicles for the divestiture of healthy firms. Fully 38 percent of ESOPs reported that they had been formed to purchase the stock of a major owner, and 32 percent said they were in the process of transferring majority ownership of their firms to their employees. This is a use of the ESOPs that appears not to have been anticipated either in the works of Louis Kelso or in the early legislative efforts of Russell Long. But with the demise of the ESOP tax credit and as the effects of the 1984 and 1986 incentives make themselves felt, it seems likely that ESOPs formed for purposes of divestitures will become increasingly common, and that the future of the ESOPs will lie with these firms.

ESOP Benefits and Costs

Another major theme of the GAO evaluation concerned the question of how the ESOPs' benefits stack up against their costs. The GAO documented that by far the lion's share of the costs attributable to the ESOP program through 1983 could be charged against the tax credit ESOPs, which cost the federal government $11.8 billion between 1977 and 1983. The remaining ESOPs could be held responsible for revenue losses over this period ranging from an upper limit of $1.5 billion down to as little as $227 million, depending on what assumptions one made about these plans (U.S. General Accounting Office, 1986b: 26–31).

In return for these expenditures, what did the U.S. government gain? The GAO estimates that the more than 4,000 ESOPs formed through 1983 had by 1985 accumulated $18.66 billion in assets in the names of more than 7 million employees (U.S. General Accounting Office, 1986a: 23). Thus the

ESOPs had indeed succeeded in conferring stock ownership on a quite substantial fraction of the American labor force. But since the U.S. government had paid more than $12 billion to encourage employers to make these gifts of stock, this represents an appallingly unproductive application of federal largesse. The ESOPs look even more disappointing when one considers that they held an average account balance of only $2,635 per participating employee, and included only 51 percent of the labor force of the firms that had these plans (U.S. General Accounting Office, 1986a: 33).

Clearly the most disappointing of the ESOPs were the tax credit ESOPs. They had accounted for by far the largest share of the ESOPs' expenses, and held average account balances of just $2,316 per participating employee. The remaining ESOPs consisted of about 3,000 plans with only about 700,000 participating employees, but they had much more significant average balances of $5,589 per participating employee. The real stars by this criterion were Kelso's favorites, the leveraged ESOPs, which had average account balances of $9,166 per participating employee (calculated from U.S. General Accounting Office, 1986a: 9, 23).

Minus the tax credit ESOPs, the ESOPs do appear capable over time of amassing quite substantial stockholdings in the names of at least a modest number of American employees. But so what? What about the broader goals and claims that have been associated with the ESOP movement? Can the ESOPs really revitalize American capitalism and make the nation's economy more competitive by increasing the productivity and profitability of the firms that adopt them?

A number of previous studies have addressed themselves to this issue (Conte and Tannenbaum, 1978; Marsh and McAllister, 1981; Rosen and Klein, 1983; Wagner and Rosen, 1985; Trachman, 1985; Cohen and Quarrey, 1986; Quarrey, 1986), and all but two of them (Tannenbaum, Cook, and Lohmann, 1984; Bloom, 1985) have concluded that the ESOPs have favorable economic effects. Almost all of these previous studies, however, have had to rely on self-reported data from self-selected samples of ESOPs, or have put together their samples of ESOPs through some sort of reputational approach. It is very likely, therefore, that the samples of ESOPs employed in these studies were unintentionally skewed in favor of the more successful firms, while the "non-ESOP" comparison data used in these studies were typically collected through methods that did not introduce such a bias. Also, most of these previous studies were not in a position to collect data from the ESOP firms covering periods before their ESOPs were introduced, so they leave open the possibility that economic success makes firms more likely to adopt ESOPs rather than the adoption of an ESOP causing a firm to become a success.

In preparing its own test of this question, the GAO was in a better position than any previous researchers to draw a random sample of ESOPs and to compare their performance to that of a well-matched sample of non-ESOP firms. With the aid of the IRS, the GAO was able to take data on the economic performance of both sets of firms directly off their corporate income tax returns. And to control for preselection effects, the GAO collected data running from two years before through three years after the year in which each ESOP was introduced.

Applying this design to a sample of 111 ESOP firms, the GAO concluded that the ESOPs had had no impact on either the profitability or the productivity of their firms. This finding of no effect, moreover, applied both to tax credit and to nontax credit plans, and was also unaffected by the average amount of assets per participant that had been accumulated by each plan (U.S. General Accounting Office, 1987: 14–31).

Does Employee Ownership Need the Federal Government's Help?

In 1983, when the nation's 4,000 ESOPs were covering 7 million employees, the New York Stock Exchange estimated that more than 10 million Americans were direct owners of stock that they had purchased at a discount from their employers through employee stock purchase plans (New York Stock Exchange, 1984: 12). Millions of other American workers were participants in corporate profit-sharing or stock-bonus plans. In addition, it was not difficult to identify entire industries and occupations in which some form of ownership, profit-sharing, or bonuses tied to performance routinely formed a part of most employees' pay. For example, corporate managers, outside sales representatives, cab drivers, hairdressers, lawyers, and practitioners of many other professions are among the numerous occupations of which this is true (see Russell, 1984a, 1984b).

Are the ESOPs so far superior to these alternative forms of employee ownership and profit-sharing that they should be entitled to special subsidies that these other arrangements do not receive? We have yet to see any persuasive evidence indicating that they are. Comparisons of the ESOPs to these other programs instead suggests that insofar as the idea of employee ownership has any merit at all, it can get along fine without the government's help; and insofar as the federal government does insist on getting into this act, its chief accomplishment so far has been to promote employee ownership in some of its most wasteful and ineffective forms.

Despite this dismal record, chances appear excellent that the federal government will continue to offer encouragement to these plans—not because there is any evidence that they do any good, but simply because they have so many political factors working on their side. The ESOPs currently have many friends and few enemies. Congressmen seem to like ESOPs not only because the ESOPs now have a modest lobby working on their behalf, but also because the lawmakers themselves continue to be autonomously attracted to the idea, as support for the ESOPs allows a legislator to feel and to claim that he is doing something to help American businesses and their employees at the very same time.

The ESOPs have yet to play a major role in any political campaign, but someday they might. In 1988 Arizona Governor Bruce Babbitt made support for the ESOPs one of the themes of his presidential campaign, and several other candidates had favorable things to say about the ESOPs as well. Should the ESOPs ever emerge as a major issue in any national campaign, they should withstand that test as well. Richard Nixon is said to have told Louis Kelso in 1965 that "I'm no economist, but I do think I understand politics, and I will say politically that I could sell this to the American people in six months" (Speiser, 1977: 156). Since support for the ESOPs is not a matter of economics, but politics, the ESOPs appear likely to be with us for many years to come.

References

Bloom, S. M. 1985. "Employee Ownership and Firm Performance." Doctoral dissertation, Harvard University.
Cohen, Alan, and Michael Quarrey. 1986. "Employee Ownership Companies after the Founder Retires." *Journal of Small Business Management* (June).
Conte, Michael, and Arnold S. Tannenbaum. 1978. "Employee Owned Companies: Is the Difference Measurable?" *Monthly Labor Review* 101: 23–28.
Gold, David A.; Clarence Y. H. Lo; and Erik Olin Wright. 1975. "Recent Developments in Marxist Theories of the Capitalist State." *Monthly Review* 27, no. 5 (October): 29–43.
Jochim, Timothy C. 1982. *Employee Stock Ownership and Related Plans: Analysis and Practice.* Westport, Conn.: Quorum Books.
Kelso, Louis O., and Mortimer J. Adler. 1958. *The Capitalist Manifesto.* New York: Random House.
———. 1961. *The New Capitalists: A Proposal to Free Economic Growth from the Slavery of Savings.* New York: Random House.
Kelso, Louis O., and Patricia Hetter. 1967. *How to Turn Eighty Million Workers into Capitalists on Borrowed Money.* New York: Random House.
Kelso, Louis O., and Patricia Hetter Kelso. 1986. *Democracy and Economic Power: Extending the ESOP Revolution.* Cambridge, Mass.: Ballinger.
Marsh, Thomas R., and Dale E. McAllister. 1981. "ESOPs Tables: A Survey of Companies with Employee Stock Ownership Plans." *Journal of Corporation Law* 6, no. 3 (Spring): 551–623.
McClaughry, John. 1972. *Expanded Ownership.* Fond du Lac, Wisc.: Sabre Foundation.
New York Stock Exchange. 1984. *Shareownership 1983.* New York: New York Stock Exchange.

Quarrey, Michael. 1986. *Employee Ownership and Corporate Performance*. National Center for Employee Ownership, 927 S. Walter Reed Drive, Suite 1, Arlington, Va. 22204.

Rosen, Corey, and Katherine Klein. 1983. "Job-Creating Performance of Employee-Owned Firms." *Monthly Labor Review* 106 (August): 15–19.

Russell, Raymond. 1984a. *Sharing Ownership in the Workplace*. Albany, N.Y.: State University of New York Press.

———. 1984b. "Employee Ownership and Internal Governance." *Journal of Economic Behavior and Organization* 6: 217–41.

Selznick, Philip. 1949. *TVA and the Grass Roots*. Berkeley, Calif.: University of California Press.

Sloan, Allan. 1981. "An Idea Whose Time Has Come?" *Forbes* 128, no. 2 (July 20): 75–78.

Speiser, Stuart M. 1977. *A Piece of the Action: The Quest for Universal Capitalism*. New York: Van Nostrand Reinhold.

Tannenbaum, Arnold S.; Harold Cook; and Jack Lohmann. 1984. *The Relationship of Employee Ownership to the Technological Adaptiveness and Performance of Companies*. NSF Research Report. Ann Arbor, Mich.: Institute for Social Research.

Trachman, Matthew. 1985. *Employee Ownership and Corporate Growth in High Technology Companies*. National Center for Employee Ownership, Arlington, Va.

U.S. Congress, Senate. 1981a. Senator Long speaking on "Expanded Ownership—Its Importance to the Free Enterprise System." An address initially delivered on March 16, 1981, to the Government Affairs Committee of the ESOP Association of America, 97th Cong., 1st Sess., 27 March, *Congressional Record* 127, no. 50.

———. 1981b. Senator Long speaking for the Expanded Ownership Act of 1981, S. Res. 1162, 97th Cong., 1st Sess., 12 May, *Congressional Record* 127, no. 72.

U.S. General Accounting Office. 1980. *Employee Stock Ownership Plans: Who Benefits Most in Closely Held Companies?* HRD–80–88. Washington, D.C.: U.S. General Accounting Office.

———. 1986a. *Employee Stock Ownership Plans: Interim Report on a Survey and Related Economic Trends*. GAO–PEMD–86–4BR. Washington, D.C.: U.S. General Accounting Office.

———. 1986b. *Employee Stock Ownership Plans: Benefits and Costs of ESOP Tax Incentives for Broadening Stock Ownership*. GAO/PEMD–87–8. Washington, D.C.: U.S. General Accounting Office.

———. 1987. *Employee Stock Ownership Plans: Little Evidence of Effects on Corporate Performance*. GAO/PEMD–88–1. Washington, D.C.: U.S. General Accounting Office.

Wagner, Ira, and Corey Rosen. 1985. "Employee Ownership: Its Effect on Corporate Performance." *Employment Relations Today*. Spring, pp. 77–82.

Williams, John D. 1984. "Buyouts Made with ESOPs Are Criticized." *Wall Street Journal*, February 21, pp. 35, 53.

15

If Inflation Returns: Hard Lessons from the Past

Joan Aldous

Since World War II, inflation appears to be a chronic danger for developed countries. It was less than a decade ago that the United States was grappling with a bout of double-digit inflation. A period of high inflation rates characterized the 1970s, with the 1974 Arab oil embargo adding upward pressure to the already higher trend in the Consumer Price Index (CPI). In the years 1973 through 1981, only the bicentennial year of 1976 saw the CPI inflation rate fall below 6 percent. In four of the nine years, the rate reached double-digit proportions. Thus it is not too long ago that the United States was living with inflation rates considerably higher than the 3 percent once considered a not unreasonable goal, or the 5 to 6 percent labeled a "substantial" inflation rate (Maynard and van Ryckeghem, 1975, p. 248; Haberler, 1976, p. 164). Governmental concern with inflation, however, tends to vary along with changes in the Consumer Price Index. After 1981's 10.4 percent rate, inflation began falling to levels low enough to allow United States policymakers to turn their attention elsewhere.

A new element has entered and complicated the inflation picture. There has been a fundamental shift in the United States economy in the last eight years, and this shift suggests we may be in for a period of higher inflation rates. The United States no longer enjoys foreign trade surpluses, but, today, is on the short end with trading partners. Citizens are doing less

This is an original contribution prepared for this volume.

saving and more consuming, so that large federal deficits resulting from tax cuts and continued high federal spending have had to be financed outside United States borders. The United States has lost its status of being the world's largest creditor nation and, instead, has become its largest debtor nation. As a consequence, the value of the dollar is under downward pressure, and inflation again may become a central political issue (Wren-Lewis and Eastwood, 1987; Peterson, 1987).

This article will look at what we have learned from our past experience with inflation in terms of who got caught in the inflationary squeeze and what might be done to ease the squeeze and to control inflation. The answer to the question of who was hurt by inflation is fairly easy to obtain. A number of studies have focused on the characteristics of those most affected in the high inflation decade of the 1970s. There are fewer reports on strategies to lessen inflation taking into account the impact of inflation and its deflationary aftermath on the vulnerable. The following discussion will cover what was actually done to lower inflation and to bring about a more stable price level. There will be an assessment of the individual costs of these inflation-fighting strategies, and a discussion of how these past lessons on handling inflation may have to be modified in the future, given the changed economic position of the country.

Who Was Affected by the Last Inflation Period?

Conventional wisdom has it that the families who lost out in the 1970s inflation more often consisted of the retired and the poor, while the "professional middle class" was largely insulated from the effects of recession (Kowinski, 1980). They and other groups receiving yearly salary increments could count upon some measure of inflation relief, which often surpassed the rising living costs. Better-off working people with debts would also be able to pay off their loans for houses and other consumer purchases with cheaper money. Continued inflation, however, could lead to higher interest rates benefiting persons with money to lend and hurting borrowers. Thus, in this view, inflation sharpens social class differences.

Yet there were some challenges to the conventional wisdom. For example, research done on the earlier inflation period of 1972–74, showed the elderly not to be adversely affected. After looking at the effects of inflation in this period on various subgroups among the elderly, investigators reported that the incomes of retired families, with the exception of the oldest married couples, actually increased in real terms during this period (Barnes and Zedlewski, 1981). The elderly's level of living depends mainly on Social Security and Supplemental Security Income payments. Both sources, through being tied to the Consumer Price Index (CPI), were protected from the effects of inflation. Thus, due to the strategy of indexing, rising prices were not likely to threaten the elderly's level of living.

It also appears that, contrary to popular belief, the wealthy may not have benefited unduly from inflation in the early 1970s. One economist, who estimated changes in household wealth holdings during the period 1969 to 1975, concluded that "the overall distributional effects of this particular inflationary period was to induce a fairly substantial drop in the level of wealth inequality" (Wolff, 1979, p. 207). Whites, persons who were married, the middle-aged, and, particularly, homeowners gained relative to their opposite numbers, and the middle class advanced in comparison with the poor and the rich. These results suggested that the middle groups whether in age or class were winners in the early experience with inflation, and in this respect conventional wisdom was correct.

Both the study of the elderly and the study of wealth changes, one could argue, are restricted to the inflationary period associated with the Vietnam War. Only the household wealth study covers the 1974 OPEC oil crisis when changes in the cost of living resulted in a CPI jump from 6.2 in 1973 to 11 percent in 1974 (U.S. Bureau of the Census, 1982: Table 758). Neither research includes years in the latter part of the decade with its high inflation. But even in 1979, when inflation was running at 11.3 percent, Gallup Poll interviewers found that three-fourths (76 percent) of the persons they interviewed felt "somewhat" or "very" financially "fit" (Anonymous, 1980, p. 9).

It would seem that at least some of these respondents were experiencing "monetary illusion." Because their wages had gone up, they assumed they were doing well despite erosion of their real wages (Niemi and Lloyd, 1981, p. 71). Not all of the persons surveyed by Gallup in 1979, however, were suffering from monetary illusions. The financial lot of many of them had improved in the course of the decade. Economist L. Thurow (1981, p. 48), noted that real per-capita disposable incomes actually increased by 16 percent in the years 1972 to 1978. He concluded (p. 53) that "inflation seems to have had little, if any, impact on the distribution of income" in this country. Some individuals had been hurt, but no "significant group" had experienced a real income drop.

However, timing is everything in research on inflation as in entertainment. To determine the effects of inflation on households, it is necessary to go beyond the early inflation years and include the period when inflation-fighting strategies are taking effect in the period being studied. We can then see whether the tactics used to bring about more stable prices disproportionately aid or harm particular segments of society. We know, for example, that unexpected inflation can benefit debtors who can pay off fixed monetary loans with cheaper money. When, however, interest rates go up as an inflation-fighting strategy, popular beliefs are right. The consequence of that strategy is to sharpen socioeconomic inequality. More of the near poor who must borrow slide into poverty while the wealthy with money to lend benefit from the higher interest rates. Thus, if we compare median family income figures for 1976, a recovery year, but one with inflation over 5 percent, and 1982, a recession year, due in part to inflation-fighting measures, but with continued high inflation at 6 percent, we see a decline in constant dollars from $23,147 to $19,446 (Avery, et al., 1984, pp. 680–81).[1]

The years 1973 to 1982 cover the necessary broader time period for looking at the effects of inflation. In this period, families experienced the 1970s when inflation was in full swing along with the beginning of the 1980s when it was being brought under control. My own research, using the Panel Study of Income Dynamics (PSID) data from households contacted yearly in that period, indicated that just about every household in this national sample had incomes that failed to keep up with the inflation rate at least one year. Half the sample (49 percent) fell behind five or more years, with only 5.3 percent affected less than three years. A comparison of the households whose incomes kept up with the inflation rate for two-thirds or more of the nine years with households whose incomes fell behind two-thirds or more of the years showed the characteristics of the inflation winners and losers to be more as conventional wisdom would have it.

By 1981, when inflation-fighting monetary policies were taking effect, the two groups differed significantly on their characteristics, particularly those related to employment status. A higher proportion of the more consistent losers to inflation were those with minor or no attachment to the labor force. These included the retired, the permanently disabled, and female household heads who were also more likely to be full-time home-makers. Conversely, household heads who worked longer hours along with larger families, who presumably had a greater number of adults to be employed, were more often found in the winners' group. As a result, average real income in 1981 differed expectably between the two groups. It was $10,252 among the households generally matching or surpassing inflation and $5,225 among the households generally falling behind. Home ownership differences were not large enough to differentiate the two groups in 1981, nor did race, although there was a nonsignificant trend for nonowners and blacks to be more often found among the losers.

We can tease out more specifically how different household groups fared in real income over the full-swing inflation years and the inflation-fighting years through looking at the years 1973, 1978, and 1981. The first provides a rough base-line year, while 1978 was a year in the middle of the high-inflation years before inflation-fighting strategies began. The year 1981 was at the end of the high-inflation period when the strategies were in place. Table 15.1 shows what happened with respect to all white households in each of those years in the PSID sample where the major earner was of retirement age or younger and was either a man or a woman.[2] To provide a graphic standard of comparison, I have set the 1973 income of under-sixty-five, white males at 100, since they are apt to be employed full time.

As can be seen from table 15.1, each of the groups did somewhat better proportionately in 1978 as compared with 1973. By 1981, when deflationary strategies were underway, households headed by nonretired persons had lost real income relative to 1978. Younger women heads responsible for others' support, as shown by their mean family size, even fell behind their starting point in 1973. When working, they generally received less pay than their male counterparts. They were also more apt to be out of the labor market and financially dependent on welfare payments not indexed to inflation. Thus nonretired women were less well-off in 1981 than in 1973. In contrast, their male elders, more protected from financial reverses by Social Security payments adjusted for inflation, did better relative to their initial income levels than even the employed younger white males. Thus

TABLE 15.1
Average Real Income of White Household Heads by Selected Year, Gender, Age, and Family Size

Gender	Male		Female	
Age	Under 65 years	65 years and over	Under 65 years	65 years and over
Real Income	$13,839	$7,708	$7,394	$3,993
1973 Index	100.00[a]	55.70	53.43	28.85
Mean Family Size	3.6	2.1	2.1	1.3
Per Capita	$3,844	$3,670	$3,521	$3,072
N =	1,519	207	263	106
Real Income	$15,562	$7,905	$7,651	$4,046
1978 Index	112.46	57.12	55.28	29.23
Mean Family Size	3.6	2.0	1.9	1.1
Per Capita	$4,323	$3,952	$4,027	$3,678
N =	1,408	264	238	187
Real Income	$14,344	$8,884	$6,762	$4,506
1981 Index	103.65	64.20	48.86	32.56
Mean Family Size	3.5	2.0	2.0	1.2
Per Capita	$4,098	$4,442	$3,381	$3,755
N =	1,335	304	227	235

[a]100 = 1973 average real income of white, male household heads under 65 years of age.

this review of which groups were most affected by the high-inflation and inflation-fighting years of the 1970s and early 1980s underlines the importance of employment for economic well-being. If a household head is out of the labor market due to retirement, lack of job skills, or child-care responsibilities, indexing of transfer payments can serve as a security net. Those whose incomes are not indexed through wage or welfare increments are the primary sufferers from inflation.

The Different Beneficiaries of Inflation and Inflation-Fighting Strategies

The evidence on who got hurt in the 1970s inflation reviewed above indicates that it was initially less hard on middle- and low-income groups than many expected. There was even a bit of a "blip" in real income, as table 15.1 shows for male earners in the high inflation year of 1978. Inflation, after all, when it was relatively uncontrolled tended to result in the transfer of wealth from the few to the many, or from creditors to debtors. The better-off, those whose incomes depended upon interest on investments, lost out to inflation as the money they received cheapened in value. In contrast, middle- and lower-income groups dependent upon wages for their sustenance and the paying-off of house mortgages and consumer debts, benefited as inflation eased the burden of loans and made borrowing less costly.

Moreover, rising house values added substantially to their assets as cheaper dollars lightened their debts. Borrowing money to buy houses with government subsidies had been the means whereby the overwhelming majority of American families had been able to build up real assets as opposed to their day-to-day dependence on current income from wages and salaries. Houses constituted a form of wealth that could be borrowed against, and could be cashed in, in old age, and the money passed on to the next generation. Inflation with its built-in debt reduction speeded up the wealth-accumulation policy for any family able to make a housing down payment. Thus the years of high inflation saw a transfer of wealth from the fewer, more affluent, and older persons who had money to loan to the less well-off who had to borrow to pay for consumer goods including houses and cars. It was also a transfer across the generations from the elderly who had already purchased the standard consumer package and now had savings to loan to the young, who were presently amassing consumer goods (Greider, 1987a, pp. 69–70).

Even the less well-off do not suffer unduly from inflation if labor demand holds up (Maynard and van Ryckeghem, 1975, p. 246). With the sizable exception of Aid to Families with Dependent Children (AFDC), most government transfer payments to the poor after an initial lag generally tended to keep up with inflation (Blank and Blinder, 1986, p. 197). The poor were also somewhat shielded from skyrocketing health and housing costs by Medicaid coverage and public housing (Greider, 1987a, p. 69).

But this progressive change in wealth distribution that the 1970s, years of high inflation, brought about could not continue. Investors with money to lend were threatening not to lend it other than for short periods of time. Rather than committing their money for long-range economy-building investments like construction, industry modernization, and product development, they were buying tangible wealth in the form of gold coins, antiques, and art objects whose value would increase with the inflation rate. The middle- and working-class short-run beneficiaries of higher inflation-driven wages and lower long-term borrowing costs were also unhappy. They found their higher wages made them subject to higher income taxes (Greider, 1987a, p. 73).

As one economist noted, income redistribution due to inflation leads to personal insecurity and dissatisfaction (Ackley, 1978, p. 51). Even persons who keep up with, or do better than, inflation resent the higher prices they have to pay. Their income gains, they feel, would have occurred regardless of inflation, but the spiraling living costs they experience due to inflation they view as unjust. So the many who were generally benefiting from inflation's cheap money joined the comparatively few money-holders losing out through its value erosion in demanding that something be done to stop it. The public wanted an answer to what it perceived as a problem (Thurow, 1983, p. 103).

Ironically, the strategies used to fight inflation were harder on the economic well-being of middle- and low-income groups than the inflation had been. The strategies centered on monetary policy, specifically the policy of the Federal Reserve Board beginning in late 1979 to raise interest rates (Greider, 1987b, p. 68). The higher cost of money made it harder for people to get loans for "big-ticket" items like automobiles and houses. Past loans easy to pay off in ever cheapening money became onerous as installments were made in appreciating dollars. Repossession of consumer goods and house and farm foreclosures became more common. Sales in these areas of the economy went down, and consumers, hard pressed for credit, cut back purchases in other areas. Exports also declined as harder dollars and harder credit terms priced American products out of the reach of consumers in other countries. Workers in the automobile, construction, and other industries, affected in a chain reaction of falling demand, were laid off (Greider, 1987b, p. 66). Inflation declined during the recession of 1981–82, but unemployment rose to 12 million in December 1982, a figure not seen since the days of the Great Depression. The trade-off for lower inflation using the strategy of high interest rates was decreased production and increased unemployment.

For the poor, the trade-off between deflation and inflation was especially costly. Unemployment, not inflation, is the harder fate, since it affects them more. And, as we earlier saw, inflation is hardest on those younger household heads who are out of the labor market. Economists Blank and Blinder (1986, p. 188), have estimated the differential costs of the two threats to economic well-being. Their calculations show that a 1 percent increase in unemployment among men in the active working years increases the poverty rate by 0.7 points in the same year, with a "final net effect" of 1.1 points if the higher jobless rate endures. A comparable yearly rise in the inflation rate results in an increased poverty rate only one-seventh as large.

With unemployment and anticipated inflation data for the months January 1955 to May 1984, these economists also determined just which groups were hurt by unemployment and inflation. Nonwhite males and younger workers, sixteen to thirty-four years of age, were most threatened by unemployment (Blank and Blinder, 1986, pp. 190–91). These are persons likely to be forming their own families or already parents with children to support. Females and workers over sixty-five were least affected. They were the groups most apt to be in families with other wage-earners responsible for their well-being or to be receiving government transfer payments. With respect to inflation, the results were different. Workers twenty-five to thirty-four years of age, those again who were in the prime years for marrying and having children, tended to benefit from inflation and its higher wages, while younger workers presumably just starting out in the work and family worlds generally were negatively affected. This was also true of older workers on a wage plateau.

As far as shares of income were concerned, as we have already noted, inflation had a mildly progressive effect. The rich rather than the poor tend to lose because their income on property after taxes goes down with inflation (Blinder and Esaki, 1978). High unemployment results in loss of income for the bottom two quintiles and increases in the top quintile (Blank and Blinder, 1986, p. 197). It is a bad bargain for the less well-off to exchange lower inflation for rising unemployment rates. This judgment is especially true for the low-wage, more often jobless workers who are most frequently not covered by unemployment insurance (Blank and Blinder, 1986, p. 192). And even those covered by unemployment benefits suffer from low payments that have not kept up with inflation (Aldous and Tuttle, 1988).

Inflation and unemployment, the evidence shows, tend to be especially hard on those just starting out, whether in an occupation or setting up housekeeping and raising a family. Unemployment, however, has the greatest negative effect. In both instances, it is the generation whose job productivity and child-rearing responsibilities are critical to the future welfare of the nation who are most affected. Thus inflation-fighting strategies that are accompanied by high unemployment are necessarily a concern in policy making.

Lessons from Past Inflation-Fighting Strategies

If inflation proved a wealth-redistribution agency from those having money to sell to those needing money to buy in the 1970s, the interest-raising strategies used to fight it in the early 1980s tipped the balance the other way. For inflation was a political issue in which the economic interest of the many tended to be at odds with that of the few. Less affluent groups, who along with wealth-holders feared inflation in the 1980s, may be more wary in the future of high interest rates as a means for fighting it. They were the ones who lost jobs, houses, and farms as a consequence of deflation's harder money. But as economist George L. Perry (1986, p. 128) writes, the postwar period has shown that inflation is difficult to fight. "Once well-established, it is extremely costly to get rid of."

This difficulty in fighting inflation, particularly in ways less harmful to the more vulnerable, is compounded by the change in the global economic standing of the United States in the low-inflation years of the 1980s. As noted earlier, the United States is no longer in complete control of its own economy. Its large budget deficit and continuing trade imbalances have led to its debt being held outside the country. Foreign creditors concerned about their loans can exercise constraints on fiscal policy. In the worst-case scenario, according to some thinking, uncontrolled deficits could lead to creditors trying to get rid of dollars and thus to a "free fall" in the price of the dollar. Rising import prices would trigger high inflation. To get foreigners to finance the U.S. debt, the Federal Reserve would have to raise interest rates. A long and "almost deliberate" recession would result to cut down imports and foreign borrowing (Peterson, 1987, p. 57). We have already seen that such a policy can lead to higher unemployment, as was true in the 1982 recession.

In a better-case scenario, according to this thinking, by cutting the federal deficit and its drain on personal savings, people would gradually increase their savings to be used for investment in the U.S. economy. To do this, deficit reduction would require a "stagnation" in government spending, a decline in the value of the dollar, and "considerable inflation-ary" import price increases. Thus the Federal Reserve would have to find an interest rate high enough to keep foreign investors content but low enough to avoid a recession (Peterson, 1987, p. 67). Even if both these projections are too pessimistic, high federal debts and trade imbalances will limit how much the federal government can afford to do for the victims of inflation-control tactics. As far back as 1974, economists like Milton Friedman (1974, p. 94) were warning that "ending" a period of inflation, would lead to a varying period of recession and "relatively high unemployment."

In the light of these fiscal constraints, let us evaluate strategies suggested or used in the past to do something about inflation and to ameliorate its effects on the vulnerable. It is well to note that the discussion does not cover strategies to cope with continued hyperinflation such as Germany experienced after World War I. When money becomes virtually worthless, there are few winners and it is hard to stave off economic collapse. It is this past experience that has made it difficult for West Germans to consider risking inflation through buying more consumer goods (Peterson, 1987, p. 53).

Economists like Milton Friedman (1974) have argued for a general policy of indexing wages, prices, and interest payments, a strategy heretofore largely restricted in this country to wages in private industries with strong unions. When the cause of inflation is the excessive creation of money, according to this argument, indexing should not exacerbate inflation. Higher wages would follow higher prices, not create them. The advantage of such a policy is that it would soften hardships resulting from a fall in the inflation rate, hardships the country did have to live through in 1982 and beyond. Inflation-swollen wages that employers pay will decline as deflation occurs. Borrowers will not be repaying debts in appreciating dollars, as interest costs will also lessen. There will be less tendency for businesses to put off investment that would create jobs in the expectation of lower prices for the goods they would need (Friedman, 1974, p. 176). Other economists would want in addition to indexation a wage policy limiting total wage increases to the inflation rate. Usual productivity growth rates would then gradually reduce the inflation rate (Maynard and van Ryckeghem, 1975, p. 241).

Problems associated with indexation strategy include the difficulty of indexing all contracts and the "cumbersome" nature of such widespread escalation (Friedman, 1974, p. 96). More important, if the pessimists with respect to the future of the U.S. economy are correct, "most" workers will experience a decline in real income due to higher inflation (Peterson, 1987, p. 67). There will be a smaller economic pie to share, as we have to consume less and export more to pay our debts. Under these conditions, indexing will not protect individuals from a fall in real income, nor will it save the country from higher inflation. Indexing would not serve the various competing groups pressing for higher proportional returns from a smaller economic base in addition to inflation increments, returns that could come only at the expense of other groups' economic payoffs (Maynard and van Ryckeghem, 1975, p. 242).

However, as an inflation-ameliorating strategy for vulnerable victims of inflation, indexing of transfer payments to the cost of living can be helpful. Experience in the 1970s showed that economically more vulnerable groups like the poor and the elderly widows can be protected from devastating cuts in income if some welfare payments are indexed. The failure of AFDC payments to keep up with inflation, in contrast to the indexing of Social Security payments, is one of the reasons children have replaced the elderly as a sizable proportion of the poor (Preston, 1984; Peterson, 1987). Since Social Security payments are nonmeans-tested, these indexing additions go in large part to benefit the non-needy. Moreover, it is apparent that the so-called COLAs (cost of living allowances), when added to Social Security checks, increase the payroll taxes that wage earners must pay to keep the system solvent. Thus the COLAs lessen the amount of money that workers can save for investment in the economy.

There are increasing worries over the regressive effects of indexing transfer payments. Such a policy of automatic inflation adjustments also removes substantial portions of federal expenditures from the control of elected officials. These worries can be assuaged by making such transfer income taxable at the individual recipient's tax rate. And recent better targeting of means-tested transfer payments like AFDC ensures that these benefits go only to the poor. Moreover, these payments are the mainstay of women household heads, often with children to support, who, we have seen, are most likely to be adversely affected by inflation.

Another inflation-fighting policy that was tried and abandoned in the early 1970s was wage-price guidelines. Economists thought the guidelines would counter the upward "flexibility" of higher wages and prices that could threaten high employment with its threat to the less well-off. Experience in the early 1970s showed it to be difficult to craft an income policy in a politically palatable way. The guidelines in various countries were also often abandoned in response to supply shocks like the oil price increases in 1974. Wage "explosions" tended to follow, as expectations of higher inflation occurred, thereby increasing inflationary pressures (Perry, 1986, pp. 146–48). Thus the guidelines, like general indexing, do not operate well, even if wisely designed, when business and labor groups are competing for portions of an economy's diminishing output.

So far, the discussion of possible inflation-fighting strategies has largely focused on easing the costs of deflating the economy to households with job-holders. The one exception was the proposal to index transfer payments to the needy. But none of the other plans addresses the problems of the poor in times of high inflation, and the plans do not claim to control the unemployment accompanying a return to more stable price levels. Proponents of a general indexing policy believe it will lessen the extent and duration of unemployment but not eliminate it when inflation tapers off. Wage and price guidelines are attempts to hold down but not deal with inflation's side effects or the costs of deflation.

In the past, there has been some support for government-supported public works programs to assist those losing their jobs because of the cooling-off of the inflation-heated economy. Public works counter deflation's regressive character of generally harming the needy and benefiting the more affluent (Heberler, 1976, p. 162). Since the high costs of such a program would work at cross-purposes to fighting inflation, they could be justified only as a means to make deflation more politically acceptable. The unfavorable economic situation of the United States, however, with its heavy debt and nondiscretionary budget allocations, makes pump-priming less feasible. Rather than putting inflation pressures on an already weakened dollar through large-scale, national job-creation initiatives, limited employment programs geared to specific groups liable to high unemployment like young workers appear to be the most feasible alternatives (Bendick, Jr., 1987, p. 459).

Final Thoughts on Responses to Inflation

There seems to be some agreement that the United States is unlikely to continue to enjoy the comparatively stable price level of the last several years. Under these circumstances, policymakers face the unenviable task of getting the domestic economy in better order within the constraints set by foreign creditors worried about a fall in the value of their loans through a weaker dollar. None of the inflation-fighting strategies outlined above is designed to shield the less well-off from their deflationary costs. Whether higher interest rates directed to money-holders, and interest, wage, and price indexing or wage and price guidelines, two policies directed to employers, employees, and investors, they are not concerned with the unemployed or those likely to be so through their policies. Thus indexing means-tested transfer payments to the needy seems a minimum safety-net protection response. Some consideration of specific programs to upgrade the job skills of youths likely to be in the labor market for a long time and in the process of family formation would also appear to be a reasonable and limited concession to the harm inflation-control policies bring to the less well-off. Such a policy protects those liable to unemployment resulting from inflation-control strategies and represents an investment in a more productive future labor force. Thus thoughtful policymakers operating in the present and near future economic climate can seek to ameliorate the ill effects of their inflation-fighting strategies through restricted jobs programs and indexing means-tested transfer payments. Their main concern, however, will necessarily need to be to keep inflation comparatively quiescent along with our foreign creditors while strengthening the economy.

Notes

1. Part of the decline, Avery and his associates (1984, p. 680) point out, is due not only to differences in economic activity but to changes in household composition in the two periods when the Federal Reserve System Surveys of Consumer Finances were taken. The number of smaller families, which include unmarried and single-person units with potentially lower incomes, was larger in 1982.
2. The black household sample divided by age and gender was too small to provide other than suggestions as to changes in their incomes during the period. These data indicate, however, that the gap between the incomes of younger black-household female heads and their white counterparts diminished over the years as black women obtained more comparable education and jobs or received similar welfare payments. Their larger families, however, continued to put them at a disadvantage. Black males showed relatively little change in real income over the years 1973, 1978, and 1981. The number of black elderly women, less that twenty-five in each year, are too few to make the data worth reporting.

References

Ackley, G. 1978. "The Goals of Stabilization Policy: The Costs of Inflation." *American Economics Review* 68: 149–54.

Aldous, J., and R. Tuttle. 1988. "Unemployment and the Family." In Catherine Chilman and Fred Cox, eds., *Families with Problems of Work and Financial Resources*. Vol. 1. Beverly Hills, Calif.: Sage.

Anonymous. 1980. "Gallup Poll Finds Americans Feel Financially Fit." CUNA Annual Report. Madison, Wisc.: CUNA Foundation.

Avery, P. B.; G. E. Elbehausen; G. B. Canner; and T. A. Gustafson. 1984. "Survey of Consumer Finances: 1983," *Federal Reserve Bulletin* 70: 679–92.

Barnes, R., and S. Zedlewski. 1981. "The Impact of Inflation on Elderly Families." Washington, D.C.: The Urban Institute.

Bendick, Marc, Jr., 1987. "Improving Employment Opportunities for Minority and Disadvantaged Youth." In Ray Rist, ed., *Policy Studies Review Annual*. Vol. 8. New Brunswick, N.J.: Transaction Books; pp. 452–65.

Blank, R. M., and A. S. Blinder. 1986. "Macroeconomics, Income Distribution, and Poverty." In S. H. Danziger and D. H. Weinberg, eds., *Fighting Poverty: What Works and What Doesn't*. Cambridge, Mass.: Harvard University Press; pp. 180–209.

Blinder, Alan S., and Howard Y. Esaki. 1978. "Macroeconomic Activity and Income Distribution in the Postwar United States. *Review of Economics and Statistics* 60: 604–9.

Friedman, Milton. 1974. "Using Escalators to Fight Inflation." *Fortune* 91: 94–98.

Greider W. 1987a. "The Fed." *New Yorker* 63 (November 9): 54–112.

———. 1987b. "The Fed." *New Yorker* 63 (November 23): 49–105.

Haberler, G. 1976. "Some Current Suggested Explanations and Cures for Inflation." In K. Brunner and A. H. Meltzer, eds., *Institutional Arrangements and the Inflation Problem*. Vol. 3. New York: North-Holland Publishing; pp. 143–77.

Kowlinski, W. S. 1980. "The Squeeze on the Middle Class." *New York Times Magazine* (July 13): 27–29.

Maynard G., and W. van Ryckeghem. 1975. *A World of Inflation*. New York: Harper & Row.

Niemi, B. T., and C. B. Lloyd. 1981. "Female Labor Supply in the Context of Inflation." *American Economic Review* 71: 70–80.

Perry, George L. 1986. "Policy Lessons from the Post-War Period." In Wilfred Beckerman, ed., *Wage, Rigidity, and Unemployment*. London: Gerald Duckworth and Company.

Peterson, Peter G. 1987. "The Morning After." *Atlantic Monthly* 160: 43–69.

Preston, S. 1984. "Children and the Elderly in the U.S." *Scientific American* 251: 44–50.

Thurow, L. 1983. *Dangerous Currents*. New York: Random House.

U.S. Bureau of the Census. 1982. *U.S. Bureau of the Census Statistical Abstract of the United States, 1982–1983*. 103d ed. Washington, D.C.: U.S. Government Printing Office.

Wolff, E. N. 1979. "The Distributional Effects of the 1969–1975 Inflation on Holdings of Household Wealth in the United States." *Review of Income and Wealth*. Series 25, no. 2.

Wren-Lewis, S., and F. Eastwood. 1987. "Chapter II: The World Economy." *National Institute Economic Review* 120: 21–38.

16

Making Work Pay

Sar A. Levitan and Issac Shapiro

The federal government directly influences working conditions through its minimum-wage and tax policies. The minimum wage helps workers earn adequate levels of income, and tax policies determine how much of that income they retain. The judicious application of these policies increases the net income of low-wage workers, alleviates deprivation, and sustains the incentive to work.

The working poor and other low-wage workers who lack bargaining power must rely on government action to set a floor under their wages. In the 1980s this floor dropped considerably. Minimum-wage earnings in 1986 for a full-time year-round worker provided income equivalent to only four-fifths of the poverty line for a family of three.

Federal policies in the first half of the 1980s had a negative effect on the position of the working poor. Not only did inflation erode the value of the minimum wage, but the working poor had to pay substantially more in taxes. The 1986 tax reform bill provided substantial relief to the working poor: the standard deduction, the personal exemption, and the earned income tax credit were each raised, thus reducing or eliminating the taxes of millions of the working poor.

Minimum Wage

The need for a federal minimum-wage floor became clear during the first few decades of this century. The unregulated market sys-

From *Working But Poor: America's Contradiction,* by Sar Levitan and Isaac Shapiro, The Johns Hopkins University Press. Copyright, The Johns Hopkins University Press, 1987.

tem did not lead to minimally acceptable living standards for significant numbers of the work force. Existing state regulation of wages was limited and ineffective. These factors resulted in the passage of the Fair Labor Standards Act of 1938 which set a national wage standard for the first time in American history. Since then, Congress has increased the minimum-wage level on six occasions and coverage has been extended to the bulk of all nonsupervisory employees. Congress passed the latest round of minimum-wage amendments in 1977, when it raised the hourly rate in four steps, reaching $3.35 in 1981. It remained at the same level six years later.

The minimum-wage law directly and indirectly affects millions of workers. In 1986, about 1.6 million salaried and 5.1 million hourly workers earned the minimum wage or less. Almost six million more workers received wages just above this level. Some low-wage employers who pay above the minimum link raises to the level of the federal standard.

Hourly earnings, 1986

	Total	*Below minimum*	*At minimum*	*$3.36–3.99*
Workers (in millions)	96.9	3.3	3.5	5.8

Minimum-wage workers tend to be part-time workers and women; almost two-thirds of minimum-wage workers are in either category. As a result, the level of the minimum wage often directly influences female-headed households. Although a disproportionately high number of minimum-wage workers are black, more than four in five minimum-wage workers are white.[1] Contrary to a common misconception, most minimum-wage workers are not teenagers in their first job. Only 31 percent are teenagers, another 21 percent are twenty to twenty-four years old, and 48 percent are twenty-five years or older. Twenty-eight percent of all minimum-wage workers are heads of household and another 28 percent are spouses. Millions of minimum-wage workers play a central role in providing a decent standard of living for their families.

Minimum-wage workers are found in a broad array of occupations, although they tend to be concentrated in the service industries, agriculture, and retail trade—all industries that employ a high proportion of the working poor. Three of every four private household workers earn the minimum or less, and one of every three service workers (other than private household) is employed at or below the minimum, as are nearly half of all farm laborers and one in five of all sales workers.[2] Some employers or occupations remain exempt from minimum-wage requirements.

The earnings of poor workers tend to cluster around minimum-wage levels. One in four impoverished workers receiving hourly rates in March 1985 earned the minimum wage or less. Another one in three of these workers earned between $3.36 and $4.35 an hour. However, four out of five workers earning the minimum wage escape poverty, primarily because other earners supplement family income.[3] Most working poor earn near the minimum wage but most minimum-wage workers are not poor. The appropriate level of the minimum wage must be judged in light of its effects on workers from both poverty and nonpoverty families.

A Sinking Floor

By any measure, the 1986 minimum wage provided a historically low level of support. Adjusted for inflation, the statutory hourly wage rate was at its lowest level since 1955. The minimum wage rose in real terms until 1968, stabilized in the 1970s, and fell sharply after 1979. In 1986, the real wage was 20 percent less than its average in the 1970s and a third less than its peak in 1968 (Figure 6).

The Reagan administration opposed increasing the minimum wage and Congress followed its lead, despite the fact that prices rose by 27 percent during the six years following the 1981 increase. As a result, the minimum wage slipped below 40 percent of the average hourly wage for nonsupervisory private, nonagricultural workers for the first time since 1949. In the 1950s and the 1960s, Congress generally set the minimum wage at about 50 percent of the average wage in private industry.

Minimum-wage income is only enough to raise some individuals above the poverty threshold. In 1986 a full-time year-round minimum-wage worker earned $6,968 in a year—$1,800 less than the poverty threshold of $8,738 for a family of three and $4,200 less than the poverty threshold of $11,200 for a family of four. In contrast, throughout most of the 1960s and the 1970s, the minimum

Figure 6. The real value of the minimum wage has declined sharply in the 1980s.

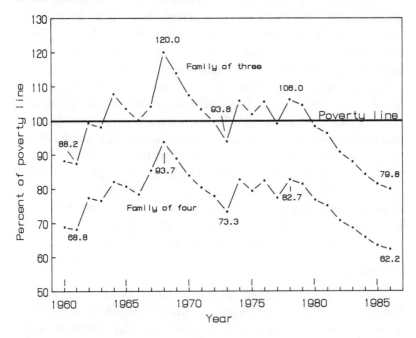

Source: U.S. Department of Labor

wage was sufficient to bring a family of three out of poverty (Figure 7). As the real value of the minimum wage declined since 1978, it is no surprise that the number of working poor rose.

As the federal minimum sank to historic lows, seven states and the District of Columbia raised their minimums above $3.35 an hour. These actions have affected only a small minority of minimum-wage workers. Moreover, in real terms, the statutory minimum wage in these states is still below historic levels. Federal action strengthening the minimum wage would provide more substantial support for the working poor and other low-wage workers.

A Cracked Floor

As testified to by the 3.3 million workers who earned less than the minimum wage in 1986, the wage floor does not protect all workers. The self-employed are not covered; in addition, exemp-

Figure 7. Minimum wage earnings for a full-time year-round worker have fallen well below the poverty line for a three-member family.

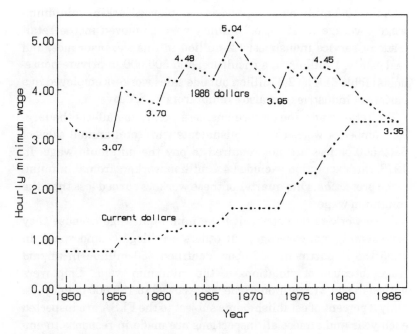

Source: U.S. Department of Labor

tions in the law apply to ten million private nonsupervisory employees. Many employees are denied minimum-wage earnings not because of exemptions, but because of employer noncompliance. Poor workers are presumably highly represented among these groups, although precise breakouts of the number employed in uncovered sectors or who are illegally paid less than the minimum wage are unavailable. Moreover, with the exception of the self-employed who may be experiencing a low-earnings year, below-minimum wage positions are unlikely to provide opportunities for future earnings growth.

The proportion of workers covered by the minimum wage has increased considerably since the law's inception. The 1938 Fair Labor Standards Act covered only one in four workers, compared with 87 percent of all private nonsupervisory employees in 1985. As a result of a 1985 Supreme Court decision in *Garcia v. San*

Antonio Metropolitan Transit Authority, state and local employees
are now covered by the federal minimum-wage standard.

Of the 10.5 million nonsupervisory employees lacking minimum-
wage coverage in 1985, 6.3 million were employed in the retail
trade or service industries; 1.2 million in finance, insurance, and
real estate; 1 million in agriculture; and 500,000 in private households (Table 5). The 2.6 million outside sales workers employed in a
variety of industries are also exempt from FLSA coverage.

The retail trade and service business exemption affects the largest number of workers. Establishments with total annual sales of
$362,500 or less are not required to pay the minimum wage. In
1978, this exemption excluded 4.2 million workers from minimum-
wage protection. One-quarter of these workers earned less than the
minimum wage.[4]

Some workers do not receive the minimum wage because they
are exempt from coverage, but others are illegally underpaid. In
1985 the Department of Labor identified $30 million in unpaid
wages because of violations of the minimum wage. Employers
agreed to pay $19 million of the wages owed to 139,000 employees.
Only 3 percent of establishments subject to the FLSA are inspected
each year and almost all inspections are made in response to employee complaints. Fines are mere slaps on the wrist; in most cases,

Table 5. Nonsupervisory private-sector employees, September 1985
(in millions)

	Covered by FLSA	Exempt
Total	63.0	10.5
Agriculture	.6	1.0
Manufacturing	16.8	.5
Wholesale trade	4.0	1.0
Retail trade	13.4	2.5
Finance, insurance, and real estate	3.9	1.2
Service industries	13.2	3.8
Private household	1.1	.5
Other	10.1	.1

Source: U.S. Department of Labor, Employment Standards Administration
Note: Details do not add to totals because of rounding off.

an employer is obliged to pay only the difference between the actual amount paid and the amount that is due under the minimum wage. In rare instances, employers are required to pay double that amount.

The Minimum Wage Study Commission estimated that in 1979 only about one-fifth of the underpayments resulting from FLSA violations were detected. Over 70 percent of total minimum-wage violations occurred under the provision that allows employers to deduct costs of meals, lodging, and other expenses customarily provided to minimum-wage workers. These violations are sometimes due to technical mistakes in calculating wages and not to willful violations of the law.[5] The percentage of violations currently detected is probably even lower, as both the number of man-hours spent on enforcement and the level of fines dropped in the 1980s.

Although some of the violations of the minimum wage are trivial in nature, other violations should be cause for concern. In 1982, the Labor Standards Subcommittee of the House Education and Labor Committee found widespread evidence of sweatshops in the needle trades. The subcommittee chairman described an employee-employer relationship in these sweatshops as follows: "An under-educated, underskilled, usually illegal worker is compelled by economic desperation to work under intolerable, less than subsistence conditions, abused and unprotected from the most fundamental forms of industrial exploitation."[6] In addition to the effect on workers, legitimate employers are placed at a competitive disadvantage when other employers illegally pay less than the minimum wage.

The extent of sweatshops and the size of their employment force is unknown. Presumably many of these workers are poor, but they are not reflected in official statistics because they are not legal residents of the United States. Sweatshop workers usually do not report the illegal and inadequate conditions under which they work because they lack knowledge about labor laws, because they are afraid of losing their jobs, or because they fear deportation.

The increased use of workers at home, either in the needle trades or in newly developed arrangements in which a worker may be employed at home but be hooked up to the office via computer, compounds enforcement problems. Current staffing levels prevent federal officials from inspecting most businesses, let alone individual households. Enforcement could be strengthened if a greater effort was made to inspect potentially egregious offenders.

A Help or a Hindrance?

The appropriate level of the minimum wage has been the subject of intense dispute. Proponents argue that the minimum wage increases the standard of living and enhances the work ethic. Opponents argue that the minimum wage hurts low-wage employees because increases of hourly rates by government fiat reduce demand for workers and results in loss of jobs. The acid test is whether the benefits of high wages outweigh the negative effects of lost employment opportunities.

At the most fundamental level, the minimum wage is a statement by society that work conditions below a given standard are unacceptable. The need for government intervention to mandate a minimal standard of living for workers reflects the reality that low-wage laborers are normally not in a position themselves to bargain for better working conditions. Most employees are protected from unreasonable work conditions either by unions, their own special skills, or benign employer practices. This is not often the case in low-wage labor markets which lack unions, in which workers lack skills and political clout, and in which employers are unlikely to adopt beneficent standard labor practices. Federal intervention helps to bring the work conditions in these labor markets up to socially required standards.

Many individuals and families benefit from the higher wages that result from the mandated minimum. The wage floor helps some escape poverty and lessens its impact on others. For minimum-wage earners who are not poor, the extra income is often essential. A teenager can save more money to pay for rising school costs or a multi-earner family may scrape together enough money to purchase more than the bare necessities.

Studies of the minimum wage tend to focus on its employment effects and ignore its equally important income effects. The limited evidence that is available does indicate, however, that the income effects have been substantial, and that especially among adult females, they overshadow the expected job loss.[7] In 1981, when the hourly minimum wage was raised from $3.10 to $3.35, the Department of Labor estimated that the potential aggregate annual increase amounted to $2.2 billion, and that 5.5 million workers were eligible to receive raises. The income effects in other years were of equivalent size.

Another salutary impact of the minimum wage is that it encourages individuals to work rather than depend on welfare. When individuals earn income instead of relying on government support, they not only benefit from the satisfaction of helping themselves, but their possibilities for future advancement are enhanced. Society benefits both from the increased output and the reduction in welfare costs. An inadequate statutory minimum wage may discourage the poor from seeking employment. When the working poor toil for little gain, work can be seen as a less desirable and futile alternative to welfare.

Statutory increases in the minimum wage do result in some job losses; workers can be priced out of the market when the wage is set by government fiat. However, minimum-wage opponents tend to overstate both the extent of job loss and the applicability of free market theory to the functioning of low-wage labor markets. Economists have attempted to measure the employment loss from the statutory minimum wage, but because of the complexity of economic interactions, the quantitative results from these studies are subject to considerable imprecision. Nevertheless, a few general conclusions are warranted.

The minimum wage has the largest disemployment effect on young workers. The Minimum Wage Study Commission estimated that a 10 percent increase in the minimum wage decreases teenage employment opportunities by about 1 percent.[8] More recent analyses have supported this estimate.[9] The effect is greatest for those youths whose earnings are close to the minimum wage. Of course, the employment effect varies with economic conditions and demographic trends. The job loss among adults is less than that among youths. Adult labor markets are not so sensitive to minimum-wage changes as youth labor markets, both because youth workers are likely to be laid off before adult workers and because a smaller proportion of adults work at the minimum.

Quantitative estimates of job losses caused by the minimum wage are ballpark guesses. Objections to a statutory floor under wages are grounded more in free market theory than in empirical evidence. According to that theory, by arbitrarily setting the minimum wage above the wage workers would otherwise receive, the demand for workers drops and the supply of workers rises because potentially higher earnings induce more workers to seek jobs. The inevitable result, according to the opponents of a standard minimum wage, is that fewer workers are employed and the unemployment rate rises.

In practice, this theory may not be reflected in the actions of either employers or employees. Higher wages may enhance job stability and commitment among workers. Employers, in turn, may respond by reorganizing production processes to make better use of their existing employees. As a result of increased productivity, the actual cost of labor may not rise so much as the cost of the minimum wage. Also, since minimum-wage firms compete with one another, raising the minimum wage for all firms, as long as coverage is complete and enforcement is effective, will not give one firm a competitive advantage over another.

Some firms set their pay scales at the minimum wage which in some areas may be below the market clearing price. In these cases, raising the wage would actually increase employment because workers who would turn down jobs at lower wages might accept them at a higher pay. At least to some extent, firms have adjusted their wages upward in the absence of a minimum-wage increase,[10] but market reactions are not so quick and smooth as predicted by free market theorists. Minimum-wage employers are reluctant to raise their pay scales absent a federally mandated requirement.

The minimum wage has scant impact on overall economic conditions. Little noticeable effect on unemployment has followed increases in the hourly rate. In the 1950s and the 1960s, when the minimum wage rose in real terms, the unemployment rate remained low. In the 1970s and the first half of the 1980s, the wage floor sank but the sinking did not prevent high levels of unemployment. Similarly, since the vast majority of workers earn considerably more than the minimum wage, it has only a minuscule effect on the inflation rate. In any event, workers who earn the minimum wage should not shoulder a disproportionate financial burden in the fight against inflation.

A prudent minimum wage policy must balance the prevention of job losses with the benefits of eliminating unacceptably low rewards for labor. If the minimum wage is too high, the working poor and other minimum-wage workers may indeed suffer more than they gain. Nearly a half century of federal experience with the minimum wage offers persuasive evidence that if the floor under wages is set at one-half of the average hourly pay of nonsupervisory workers, the resulting disemployment effects remain insignificant and the accompanying income boosts are instrumental in alleviating deprivation and in encouraging economic self-sufficiency. The task for Congress is to strike the right balance between employment and income effects.

Youth Subminimum

A subminimum wage for teenagers has been proposed in an effort to drive down the high youth unemployment rate. Advocates of this approach argue that the minimum wage has its highest disemployment effect on the young, preventing them from acquiring essential employment experience. Teenagers, it is argued, do not require wages as high as adults. The Reagan administration proposed a "youth opportunity wage" equal to 75 percent of the minimum wage. The administration estimated that lowering the cost of hiring youths would create 400,000 jobs for youths. By April 1987, the real value of the minimum wage was 30 percent lower than when President Reagan took office and the number of youths entering the labor market had also declined. Yet teenage unemployment remained at high levels, creating doubts that further cuts in the minimum wage would in fact generate added employment opportunities.

A subminimum is already in effect for some young workers. Since 1961, employers have been able to obtain Department of Labor certification to hire full-time students at 85 percent of the minimum wage as long as these students work less than twenty hours a week. In fiscal 1985, an estimated 195,800 students were certified for employment under this program.

Employers of economically disadvantaged youths are also eligible for a 40 percent wage subsidy under the Targeted Jobs Tax Credit. For disadvantaged sixteen to seventeen year olds in summer employment, the subsidy is substantially more generous and amounts to an 85 percent tax credit. If lower wages are essential to induce employers to hire economically disadvantaged youths,

the TJTC not only reduces wages more than a youth subminimum wage would, but has the advantage of providing more income to the targeted youths. Furthermore, youths from poor families who have trouble breaking into the labor force tend to lack
skills and connections to the job market. Lower wages will not
necessarily induce employers to hire these youths; they need to
master the three Rs and they require specialized programs, such
as the Job Corps, to prepare them for the job market.

Not only would the subminimum result in an income loss for
many youths, it could well harm the working poor and other
adults who work at the minimum wage, because some young
workers would be substituted for older workers. The Minimum
Wage Study Commission, which opposed a youth subminimum
wage, speculated that a youth subminimum set at 75 percent of
the adult minimum would create 400,000 to 450,000 jobs for
youths but would also displace 50,000 to 150,000 adult workers.
The commission noted that this displacement estimate is low because its analysis implicitly examined the possibility of youth
replacing average adult workers instead of examining the more
likely effect that adult workers earning the minimum wage or
slightly higher would be displaced.[11] Additionally, the job creation figures must be viewed with some skepticism because youths
have alternative uses for their time. In some labor markets, there
is mounting evidence that their reservation wage is higher than
the current minimum wage, let alone the proposed subminimum.

Reforms

Restoring the minimum wage to its traditional level of
support—50 percent of the average nonsupervisory private hourly
wage—would require as of early 1987 a 32 percent increase or
about $1.07 per hour. At whatever level the minimum wage is set,
its protection is sharply diminished if exemptions are common
and if the law is not enforced. Strengthening the minimum-wage
standard will not lift all of the working poor out of poverty. A
sizable proportion of the full-time year-round working poor are
self-employed or otherwise uncovered by the minimum-wage law
and part-time minimum-wage workers may still have annual
earnings below the poverty line. Nevertheless, some individuals
would be raised above the poverty threshold by a higher mini-

mum wage and others, though remaining in poverty, would receive necessary additional income. Though most minimum-wage workers are not poor, they, too, would benefit from a raise.

Federal Taxes

The disposable income of the working poor depends, of course, not only on the wages they receive but on their tax burden. In the first half of the 1980s, federal tax policy contributed to the deteriorating situation of the working poor. The minimum wage declined considerably whereas the taxes of low-wage workers rose substantially. The 1986 tax bill, however, provided relief to low-income workers; it restored the effective federal tax rate of low earners to the level of the late 1970s.

Structure

The three largest components of the federal tax system are the personal income tax, the social security tax, and the corporate income tax. A goal of the progressive structure of the personal income tax has been to minimize the obligations of low-wage earners. The social security tax has been a greater burden on the poor. This rate has risen considerably over time and, in addition, workers pay the same rate from the first dollar they earn annually up to the $43,800 they earn. (The maximum social security tax base of $43,800 in 1987 is adjusted annually for inflation.) The corporate income tax affects the poor only indirectly through goods consumption, but it is generally considered to be a progressive tax; its costs are borne more by the owners of the business than by the less well-to-do.[12]

In addition to the tax rate, three aspects of the federal personal income tax system significantly affect the poor. The first, the standard deduction, is the amount of earned income which is exempt from any taxation. The standard deduction is available to all taxpayers who do not itemize their deductions. A second aspect of the system that influences the amount of taxes paid by low-wage workers is the personal exemption given for each individual covered by a tax return. A third key element of the tax system for the poor is the earned income tax credit (EITC), enacted in 1975. In contrast to the standard deduction and personal exemption which can be used by filers at all income levels, the EITC can be used only by low-income households with children. A tax credit is earned on a percentage of initial earnings and is phased out as earnings rise. If the credit exceeds personal income tax liability, the difference is refundable. The credit can, therefore, also offset the social security tax paid by low-wage workers.

Trends

Taxes are not considered in the calculation of the official poverty thresholds. Individuals and families who drop into poverty because of tax payments are not counted among the poor. The increase in the number of the officially counted working poor between 1979 and 1985 cannot be attributed to the higher taxes on low earners. Though taxes do not affect official poverty status, they obviously do affect the purchasing power of low earners.

Federal taxes paid by low-wage workers soared in the 1980s as social security taxes rose and as provisions benefiting low-wage workers failed to keep pace with inflation. When a deduction remains static, while both the cost of living and wages rise, the value of the deduction falls, thus increasing the effective tax rate at the poverty income level.

In 1979 a family of four was liable for the federal personal income tax when its income exceeded the poverty line by 16 percent; in 1986, the income tax threshold for this family was 17 percent *below* the poverty line. Combining the personal income tax with the social security payroll tax, the 1986 effective federal tax rate for a family of four with an annual income equal to the poverty threshold jumped nearly sixfold, from 1.8 percent to an estimated 10.6 percent. From 1979 to 1984 (the last year for which figures are available), the number of individuals whose incomes fell below the poverty line after payment of federal taxes increased from 675,000 to 2.4 million.[13]

Politicians of all stripes supported the 1986 tax bill with its beneficial provisions for the working poor. The tax bill raised the standard deduction, the personal exemption, and the earned income tax credit, and indexed the latter to inflation. The standard deduction and personal exemptions had been indexed to inflation as of 1985. For those earning less than $10,000 the 1986 bill cut

Table 6. Effective tax rate for family of four with poverty-level earnings

Year	Rate
1965	4.4%
1969	7.6
1973	6.6
1977	2.9
1979	1.8
1981	8.5
1983	9.8
1985	10.4
1988 (est).	2.1

Source: Center on Budget and Policy Priorities

the expected federal income tax liability by 57 percent in 1987 and 65 percent in 1988.[14] The percentage of income the poor must pay in personal income and payroll taxes returned to the levels of the late 1970s (Table 6).[15] The Center on Budget and Policy Priorities estimated that the tax cut would raise the income of a four-person family at the poverty level by greater than $1,000 or over 10 percent.[16]

The 1986 tax law also increased the standard deduction. The biggest effect was on single persons heading households.

	1986	1988
Joint return	$3,670	$5,000
Single heads of household	2,480	4,400
Single individual	2,480	3,000

The value of each personal exemption was almost doubled, increasing the $1,080 exemption in 1986 to $2,000 in 1989, and the earned income tax credit for low-wage workers was raised. In 1986, the EITC was equal to 11 percent of the first $5,000 in earnings (or a maximum credit of $550) and was phased out as earnings rose from $6,500 to $11,000. The credit benefited an estimated 6 million families to the tune of $2.1 billion, $1.4 billion of which was received as income tax refunds. Under the new tax law, the credit was increased to 14 percent of the first $5,714 in earnings (for a maximum credit of $800), and starts to phase out when earnings reach $9,000—its value declines to zero when earnings equal $17,000.

The 1986 tax law left unchanged many deductions that benefit middle-and upper-income filers, but that tend to be of little benefit to low-wage workers. For example, the generous mortgage interest deduction (totaling an estimated $27.6 billion in 1986) helps few low-income individuals because most working poor are unlikely to own their homes. The poor are also hardly in a position to take advantage of tax code provisions that encourage workers to save for the future; the poor need that money now. Whatever the merits of these deductions, they offer little assistance to the poor.

The 1986 tax act extended some assistance to low-wage workers in other areas. It included provisions that encourage employers to provide pension and health insurance benefits to low-wage workers. Under the new law, pension plans must cover a higher percentage of a firm's workers and the vesting period was reduced. A new tax credit was created for owners who lease units to low-income renters although other changes in the law may decrease investment in housing.

The 1986 tax bill provided tremendous benefits to the working poor, and because key provisions were indexed, the working poor will have low effective federal tax rates for the foreseeable future. A possible additional reform is extension of the EITC to single individuals or childless couples with low incomes who would benefit from a tax credit to offset their payroll taxes. The tax reform debate may now shift to the state and local level, where the poor are burdened by regressive state and local property and sales taxes.

Net Compensation

During the first half of the 1980s, two concurrent trends reduced the real income of the working poor. The minimum wage remained unchanged while taxes on those in poverty rose to historically high levels, increasing by almost 10 percent for a family of four with poverty level earnings. As of 1985, the net real income of low-wage workers was dramatically lower than in the late 1970s.

The 1986 tax bill reversed one of these trends by lowering taxes for the poor who will now keep almost all of the wages they earn. The challenge for the balance of the 1980s and beyond is to raise the real value of their earnings. If the minimum wage is raised to its traditional level, and thereupon is indexed and strictly enforced, the fruits of labor will be considerably more positive.

In lieu of raising the minimum wage, some analysts have proposed raising the earned income tax credit. This option would be targeted to the working poor; it would only increase the income of low-wage workers from poor families. Moreover, it would not discourage hiring because the direct cost of labor to employers would remain the same. The size of the credit could also vary by family size.[17]

Although a further expansion of the EITC would benefit the working poor, there would still be advantages to raising the minimum wage instead. First, low-wage workers who are not in poverty would also benefit from a raise in the minimum wage. Second, given the high federal deficit, increasing federal outlays and reducing revenues both present serious policy drawbacks. Raising the minimum wage, a private sector approach, also would provide the poor with more *earned* income, which is preferable to a large government income transfer. Third, and finally, a tax credit gives income at the end of the year but the poor require that income throughout the year.

Establishing labor conditions that will provide incentives to help lift workers out of poverty as a result of their own initiative is the best mechanism to improve the lot of the working poor. It is more preferable for workers to earn their way out of poverty than for the government to provide additional income support or in-kind benefits. The right mix of low federal taxes and an adequate federal minimum wage will establish labor conditions in which more workers can escape poverty on their own.

Notes

1. Earl F. Mellor and Steven E. Haugen, "Hourly Paid Workers: Who They are and What They Earn," *Monthly Labor Review*, February 1986, p. 25.

2. *Report of the Minimum Wage Study Commission*, vol. 1 (Washington, D.C.: U.S. Government Printing Office, 1981), pp. 19–21.

3. Congressional Budget Office, *The Minimum Wage: Its Relationship to Incomes and Poverty*, Staff Working Paper, June 1986, pp. 16–18.

4. *Study Commission*, p. 121.

5. Ibid., pp. 156, 158.

6. Statement of Congressman George Miller, *The Reemergence of Sweatshops and the Enforcement of Wage and Hour Standards of the Committee on Education and Labor*, U.S. House of Representatives, Subcommittee on Labor Standards of the Committee on Education and Labor, 1982, p. 4.

7. Edward M. Gramlich, "Impact of Minimum Wage on Other Wages, Employment, and Family Incomes," *Brookings Papers on Economic Activity*, 1976:2, pp. 419–52.

8. *Study Commission*, p. 38.

9. Gary Solon, "The Minimum Wage and Teenage Employment: A Reanalysis with Attention to Serial Correlation and Seasonality," *Journal of Human Resources*, Spring 1985, pp. 292–97.

10. Martha Brannigan, "A Shortage of Youths Brings Wide Changes to the Labor Market," *Wall Street Journal*, September 3, 1986, p. 11.

11. *Study Commission*, p. 47.

12. Rebecca M. Blank and Alan S. Blinder, "Macroeconomics, Income Distribution, and Poverty," in *Fighting Poverty: What Works and What Doesn't*, ed. Sheldon H. Danziger and Daniel H. Weinberg (Cambridge, Mass.: Harvard University Press, 1986), p. 198.

13. U.S. Congress, House Committee on Ways and Means, *Background Material and Data on Programs within the Jurisdiction of the Committee on Ways and Means*, March 3, 1986, p. 565.

14. U.S. Congress, Staff of the Joint Committee on Taxation, "Data on Distribution by Income Class of Effects of the Tax Reform Act of 1986," JCX-28-86, October 1, 1986, Tables 1 and 8.

15. Sheldon Danziger and Peter Gottschalk, Testimony, *Work and Poverty: The Special Problems of the Working Poor*, Hearing, U.S. Congress, Committee on Government Operations, December 12, 1985, p. 22; Center

on Budget and Policy Priorities, "Taxes on Working Poor Rise for Sixth Straight Year," Washington, D.C., April 9, 1986, p. 1.

16. Center on Budget and Policy Priorities, "Conference Agreement on Tax Reform of Major Benefit to Working Poor," Washington, D.C., September 18, 1986, pp. 1–3.

17. Robert D. Reischauer, "Welfare Reform and the Working Poor," in *Reducing Poverty and Dependence* (Washington, D.C.: Center for National Policy, 1987).

Part II
NATIONAL SECURITY AND FOREIGN POLICY

Commitments and Capabilities: The New Realities in American Defense Policy

The Reagan administration rhetoric of its being "Morning in America" now seems antiquated and strangely out of place with current conditions. There is a growing consensus that with the departure of President Ronald Reagan, his unique approach to foreign policy will have come to an end. His successor faces a set of problems and dilemmas that no longer can be indefinitely avoided. Whereas Reagan presided over what Arthur Schlesinger, Jr., termed a "messianic foreign policy," the new realities of America's capabilities vis-à-vis its commitments and aspirations will not go away.

Succinctly, the United States now faces a period where there are deep and profound concerns about its ability to meet present security and defense commitments, given the tightening constraints on its economic system. There is simply no longer the latitude to maintain the present level of military spending in the country and still keep up the current commitments. The choices essentially come down to two: reduce the commitments to get more in line with current capabilities, or increase expenditures to meet current commitments. The political feasibility of the latter is almost nil. Thus the discussion on "burden-sharing" and troop withdrawals from Europe as ways of reducing the United States military overextension.

The high-water mark of the Reagan administration military buildup came in Fiscal Year (FY) 1985, culminating a 55 percent real increase in defense funding over six years, FY 1980 to FY 1985. In the years since, the defense budget declined in real terms by almost 10 percent during the years from FY 1986 to FY 1988. When the funds were flowing freely into defense projects of all types, the notion that the United States was overextended seemed silly. The building of a 600-ship navy, for example, was stated national policy. But with the downturn in funding during the second term of President Reagan, the gap between promises and ability to keep same has begun to show.

This reduction in growth coupled with the clear economic vulnerability arising from the trade imbalances and budget deficits has called into question our ability to balance our security considerations and our economic well-being. It is as if the United States has suddenly and dramatically gone from being a country vigorous in its foreign policy and economically self-confident to one where it is now vulnerable, overextended, and unable to meet present commitments. That these changes have caught American policymakers off guard cannot be doubted. (This is the charitable conclusion. That they knew what was happening and chose not to respond is the more disquieting view.) Whether the country can thoughtfully and carefully respond to the new circumstances is now the question that no longer can be put off.

As noted in the introduction to this volume, one of the current themes pervading policy discussion in the United States is whether the country is on the downside of a historical curve. Has the United States, as is now baldly phrased, gone into a period of decline? The discussion around this question—and heated it is—focuses essentially on two concerns, the economic health of the country and the military capability to defend ourselves and those allies who look to us for protection. The answer to these twin concerns necessarily needs to address them simultaneously. The economics are driving questions of foreign policy and national security. The reverse is also true: foreign policy considerations are having considerable impacts on America's economic well-being.

The articles in this present section take on the issue directly. There are authors here who agree with the thesis of American decline and others who do not. Likewise, there are authors on both sides of the question of whether the United States must keep current security commitments and agreements or whether the present conditions necessitate a new formulation of the Western security partnership. Finally, the positions here split over whether the economic conditions in the United States suggest the country is essentially healthy or, alternatively, there is a cancer in the economic vitals that has to be removed.

The first four articles in this section can be read together as an informed and lively debate regarding the issues discussed above. Brzezinski, in the lead article taken from an issue of *Foreign Affairs,* makes essentially two key points. First, America is not in decline. He notes that such rumors are "premature." But having said that, he also recognizes that the status quo will not hold. The issue then is the direction and intensity of the change that is already underway. Brzezinski calls for the United States to develop, in a term taken from the title of the article, a "new geostrategy." In such a new strategic view, the United States could expect more assistance from its European allies, a stronger partnership with Japan including even a free-trade zone, a Marshall Plan for Latin America, and support for a more active spirit of cooperation and consensus-building among the Western economies.

Robert Gilpin is much more pessimistic about the problem-solving capability of the United States at present. He believes that the country is entering a new era where fundamental changes in "global, diplomatic, economic, and strategic relationships" have occurred. The crisis for the United States comes in refusing to recognize and appropriately respond to a changed reality where there is no longer a consensus in the West on what is meant by the "Soviet Threat." The consequence is a fracturing of the allies on how they ought to respond. This growing descensus among members of the North Atlantic Treaty Organization (NATO) has further ramifications in the economic area. The uneven economic strength of the various members, the views on appropriate burden-sharing, and the strength of the commitments made to one another have also resulted in a pulling apart of the alliance. Gilpin traces the origins of these problems to the condition of the American economy and the unwillingness of policy-makers and public alike to confront them seriously. To do so will require urgent economic reforms and it is precisely the flight from such efforts that generates his pessimism.

Christopher Layne, in his "Requiem for the Reagan Doctrine," argues that the Reagan policy of global containment was bankrupt from the very beginning. The roots of this doctrine come from the Cold War and the more recent incarnation being the effort to build anew an "assertive America" that was out from under the guilt and ambivalence of Vietnam. Layne argues that the efforts of the Reagan administration to reverse America's declining global influence were doomed to fail. They were doomed to fail, not only because of an incoherent understanding of events, but because we did not have the means to reach the desired ends. Here the argument coincides with that of Gilpin. America has overreached in its capabilities to do all that it sought to do under the Reagan Doctrine. The successes of this approach have been few and far between and many of the presumed victories were "hollow," to use Layne's term. That there were massive failures, Layne takes to be self-evident. Layne also questions the willingness of the United States to tailor the domestic and foreign policies it needs to reverse its present decline. As he concludes, "It is hardly certain that things will turn out well."

The fourth article in this section, and one that rounds out the first cluster, is by Alton Frye. His paper addresses a specific aspect of the changing world in which the United States must conduct its foreign policy. Frye analyzes the current conditions for the development of a treaty that would place restraints on the strategic nuclear weapons of both the United States and the USSR. Frye believes that we are in a unique period when far-reaching and substantive arms-control agreements are, in his words, "in sight—but not in hand." With careful planning and sustained commitment, the two countries have a window of opportunity to develop a mutual agreement to reverse the ever growing arsenals on both sides. Frye lays out the contours of a compromise that would respect the interests of both countries—and it is axiomatic that both countries will have to see advantages to themselves if they are going to sign. Frye's concern is that the opportunity to craft this compromise will not last long. Failure to act at the present may mean that we shall then have to wait some considerable time before the opportunity to develop such a treaty will again present itself. And all the while, both sides are moving toward substantially larger and more lethal forces.

David Robertson, in his original contribution prepared for this volume, reminds us that the United States is not the only Western country facing important trade-offs and limitations in the exercise of its security policy. His analysis of the current situation in Britain provides an important comparative perspective in that the British face many of the same constraints, albeit on a less global level. Nonetheless, British defense policy is undergoing a review and reconsideration that will have ramifications well into the twenty-first century. Given the political and economic constraints on its defense policy, Britain has essentially two options: redefine its roles and contributions or start cutting everywhere while admitting to no reduction and no lower level of readiness. Robertson ends with revisiting the nuclear deterrence question in light of the constraints on British defense policy. Such deterrence, all of a sudden, starts to seem plausible once again.

The final two articles in this section address the relation of defense policy to available (or hoped for) technologies. The Strategic Defense Initiative (SDI) is but the largest and most widely discussed of a whole array of technological efforts now being supported.

David Calleo, director of European Studies at the School of Advanced International Studies, Johns Hopkins University, shares the view noted earlier that United States strategic capabilities are in need of serious reconsideration. It is his view that reliance on SDI is misplaced and misguided. Geopolitical and economic problems are not going to be solved by reliance on technology—especially on a technology that is so uncertain in its capability. Rather than turn to technological fixes, Calleo argues that the United States can get out of its current bind only by moving away from being the nuclear protector of Europe and instead becoming part of a nuclear alliance. Further, it is his view, shared by others in this section, that Europe must begin to take the chief responsibility for its own defense. It no longer makes political or strategic sense for the countries of Western Europe to presume that the United States nuclear umbrella is a sufficient deterrent.

The last article, written by Jean-François Delpech, explores the continuing emergence of new technologies and the implications of these technologies on the stability of the NATO alliance. In his view, defense expenditures cannot continue to grow indefinitely. Consequently, there will be an even greater need to optimize security interests with those funds that are made available. Delpech believes that there is tremendous potential within the NATO countries for greater use of technologies. These technologies, if managed in a flexible and decentralized fashion, could provide the edge the West will need to stay credible in its defense posture. He foresees the possibility of NATO becoming something of a clearinghouse for cooperative technological efforts among the allies—in contrast to presuming any one country (read here the United States) can any longer afford to fund large-scale technological developments alone. The present chaos of SDI should be instructive in this regard. Cooperative R&D efforts could both strengthen the alliance and build new economic vitality into the various national economies. These are no small consequences in comparison to the disarray within NATO at present over the introduction and use of various single-country technological options. They are also no small benefits to the United States at a time when the Reagan Doctrine is in shambles, SDI is crumbling, and a new set of relations with our allies is needed.

17

America's New Geostrategy

Zbigniew Brzezinski

The rumors of America's imminent imperial decline are somewhat premature. They are, however, quite fashionable. Particularly within some intellectual circles a decided preference has taken hold for Spenglerian handwringing, which barely conceals a measure of schadenfreude over the anticipated end of the imperial phase in the history of this somewhat crass, materialistic, chaotic, libertarian and vaguely religious mass democracy. America's assumption of the imperial role after World War II—with U.S. power and influence projected around the world—was never popular either within America's intellectual class or more recently within its mass media. Hence the anticipatory gloating over the allegedly inevitable demise of the world's current number-one power.

To debate the accuracy of such a prognosis may be futile. The future is inherently full of discontinuities, and lessons of the past must be applied with enormous caution. Some recent scholarly studies have attempted to do so in a searching and comprehensive fashion, and without the dogmatic assumption of any kind of inevitability. This has greatly helped to raise the level of thoughtful discussion. From the political point of view, moreover, there is even some genuine benefit to be derived from the fact that doubts have been raised regarding America's future. Posing the issue so starkly focuses attention on the definition of the actions needed to maintain a constructive American world role, the essentials of American security, the core American interests, and the effects on the foregoing of the inexorable geopolitical and technological changes.

In other words, the intellectual debate over a possibly inevitable decline can become a political deliberation on how to avoid it, how to reinvigorate America's global power and how to redefine it in the context of a changing world. That can be the objectively positive result of posing the issue. Accordingly,

Excerpted by permission of *Foreign Affairs*, Spring 1988. Copyright 1988 by the Council on Foreign Relations, Inc. Vol. 66, No. 4 (1988): 680–99.

the task of responsible statesmanship is to define more precisely the policy implications of the geopolitical and technological changes for the U.S. relationship with the world over the remaining years of this millennium, bearing in mind that such changes are significantly altering the setting within which U.S. interests and national security must be protected. Out of such an examination one can derive better guidance regarding the very character of America's world role in the years ahead.

In any such analysis three clusters of issues are central, namely: (1) strategic doctrine, which bears on how the United States can best promote its national security; (2) geopolitical imperatives, which determine the central foci of American regional involvements; and (3) the U.S. global role, which pertains to the manner in which America should wield its worldwide influence.

Over the last forty years the United States has relied heavily, indeed, predominantly, on nuclear deterrence to check much-feared Soviet expansion, particularly in central Europe. In the late 1940s and early 1950s, when it in effect possessed a monopoly on the capability to deliver nuclear weapons at intercontinental range, the United States went so far as to postulate the doctrine of massive nuclear retaliation as a response to even conventional Soviet aggression. But as Soviet strategic capabilities grew, adjustments in doctrine became necessary. By the 1960s U.S. strategic doctrine was embracing the concept of flexible response to a Soviet military challenge, though it still lacked to a considerable extent the targeting capabilities and the weapons needed for sustaining such a strategy.

The increased vulnerability of American society to a Soviet strategic attack, however, gave rise to the publicly compelling view that the condition of mutual assured destruction (known as MAD) had now become the basis for reciprocal deterrence. The resulting strategic dilemma was that this transformed deterrence into an essentially apocalyptic threat to commit suicide, a threat that could be credible only to deter a similarly suicidal attack by the enemy. Short of that extreme eventuality, U.S. strategic policy started to lose its credibility in deterring less than a total attack—while concurrent technological refinements have at the same time given rise to altogether novel opportunities for far more selective and strictly military uses of nuclear weaponry. A doctrinal readjustment, with significant force posture implications, was thus becoming due in order to close the consequent deterrence gap.

Over the last four decades, U.S. geopolitical imperatives have been largely preoccupied with the defense of both the far western and the far eastern extremities of the Eurasian continent against Soviet political and military domination. With the recovery of both Western Europe and Japan, which enhanced their capacity for more effective self-defense, and with the felicitous consolidation of a new, stabilizing relationship between the United States and the People's Republic of China, Americans have come to see the Soviet threat as less ominous. At the same time, American geopolitical concerns are being refocused on other critical regions, heretofore not major sources of U.S. security or political concerns.

The American global role has also been undergoing a profound transmutation. Throughout much of the last forty years, American political leadership has rested on a solid base of economic and military preeminence, and much of the motivation for the exercise of that primacy stemmed from a concern that the Soviet Union was seeking to dethrone and to replace the United States in the exercise of that special role. Today, the economic basis of American primacy is clearly much weaker and is likely to become weaker still in relation to the growth of other economic centers. At the same time, however, the Soviet Union has clearly failed as an economic rival. It has been revealed to be at best a one-dimensional power, a challenger in the military realm alone but not a serious rival socially, economically or ideologically. In other words, the Soviet Union poses a threat to American security and geopolitical interests, but does not represent a challenge to American global primacy as such.

Thus on the strategic, geopolitical and global levels the need exists for significant adjustments in the way the United States participates in the global political process and promotes its fundamental national interests. Let us examine the policy implications that follow in each of the above three broad clusters.

II

In strategic doctrine, the United States needs to shift away from its long-standing preoccupation with the threat of a nuclear war between the superpowers or a massive Soviet conventional attack in central Europe. Neither danger can be dismissed as impossible, but a central nuclear war is not likely to be initiated deliberately; America certainly has the means to maintain a military posture that precludes any rational Soviet decision-making process from reaching a suicidally erroneous conclusion. Much the same can be said about the possibility of a massive conventional Soviet attack on Western Europe, given not only the complexities of calculating intelligently the real battle trade-offs between existing NATO and Warsaw Pact forces but also the high risk of nuclear escalation.

It must be hastily added that the reassessment of the level of the threat does not imply in the least any decline in the U.S. interest in the security of Western Europe or any significant U.S. disengagement from the defense of Europe. Indeed, the specific adjustments in strategic doctrine and in force posture that are proposed below focus on the central goal of reinforcing the overall credibility of the American strategic and conventional deterrent, of which Western Europe and also Japan are the principal beneficiaries.

To enhance deterrence in the current and foreseeable conditions, a doctrine and a force posture are needed that will enable the United States to respond more selectively to a large number of possible security threats, ranging from the strategic to the conventional.[1] On the strategic level it must be recognized that technological changes have wrought a revolution in the way nuclear weapons may be used in the future. They are no longer just crude instruments for inflicting massive societal devastation but can be used with precision for more specific military missions, with relatively limited collateral societal damage. The increased versatility of nuclear weapons is the consequence of the interaction between smaller warheads and highly accurate delivery systems. The result is that nuclear weapons are no longer primarily blunt instruments of deterrence but can also serve as potentially decisive instruments of discriminating violence.

As a result, in the future the United States should rely to a greater extent on a more flexible mix of nuclear and even non-nuclear strategic forces capable of executing more selective military missions. The central purpose of the strategy of discriminate deterrence is to heighten the credibility of American threats to respond to aggression by increasing the spectrum of

---

[1] For more on these recommendations see *Discriminate Deterrence*, Report of The Commission On Integrated Long-Term Strategy, Fred C. Iklé and Albert Wohlstetter, co-chairmen, Washington: G.P.O., January 1988.

effective responses to such aggression, short of the inherently improbable option of simply committing national suicide. More specifically, this calls for greater reliance on highly accurate but less destructive long-range strategic weaponry, including procurement of the now-feasible non-nuclear strategic weapons. In addition, in order to deny to the potential aggressor the temptation of preemptively destroying U.S. strategic forces, it is also recommended that U.S. strategic forces be based on a prudent mix of both offensive and defensive systems, thus assimilating into U.S. force posture some initial elements of the much-debated Strategic Defense Initiative, marking an important break with the notions of MAD.

Space control is likely to become tantamount to earth control. There are striking parallels between the role of the navy in the emergence of American global power and today's incipient competition for a dominant position in space. The earlier competition among the Great Powers for maritime primacy involved rivalry for effective control over strategic space between the key continents. Control over such space was central to territorial preponderance. That is why the United States, in the phase of its geostrategic expansion, placed such an emphasis on the acquisition of dominant Atlantic and Pacific fleets, linked through direct U.S. control over the Panama Canal.

Today the equivalent of that naval rivalry is the competition in space. At the very minimum it must be the U.S. strategic objective to make certain that no hostile power can deny the United States, while retaining for itself, the means for using space for intelligence, early warning, reconnaissance, targeting, and command and control. Modern military operations are highly dependent on space assets performing these functions, and U.S. vulnerability in this area could be crippling. Thus, even short of seeking to exploit space control for offensive purposes against an enemy (e.g., by the use of weaponry deployed in space), the capacity to protect its nonlethal military space assets, or to inflict a denial of the use of space to the enemy, has become essential to an effective U.S. military posture.

On the conventional level similarly important adjustments are becoming necessary. The most probable threat stems from what are called low-intensity conflicts in areas where American forces are not permanently deployed. Thus, the United States must place less emphasis on prepositioned heavy forces in foreign bases and more on lighter forces, supported by enhanced air- and sea-lift capabilities, poised for a prompt long-distance response. This would reduce the risk that in a crisis (such as during the 1973 Middle East war or the U.S. air raid in Libya in 1986) the freedom to use American forces stationed abroad would be restricted by political inhibitions on the part of U.S. allies.

More generally, the United States in the years ahead must take advantage of its enormous capacity for technological innovation to enhance its military flexibility. Over the last several decades the United States has gradually become a military Gulliver, enormously powerful yet clumsy and inert. Technology is certainly not a "silver bullet" for solving a variety of deficiencies. Neither is it a substitute for well-trained and motivated manpower. But it does provide the basis for effective and rapid coordination, for precision in operations, for enhanced intelligence and for prompt concentration of destructive power. America is almost uniquely equipped to exploit these technological capabilities.

These adjustments in our military strategy and posture will have to be pursued in the context of unavoidable budgetary restraint. It follows, therefore, that some standing priorities will have to be revised. It also follows from the foregoing analysis that the targets for budgetary reallocation will have to fall within three broad categories: less emphasis on offensive central strategic nuclear weapons; less concentration on the funding of new major systems for the individual branches of the armed services and more on technological force-multipliers for existing weaponry; and a reallocation of expenditures and heavy forces away from Europe-oriented missions toward greater flexibility and longer-range mobility in conventional responses to conflicts in regions where no U.S. forces are prepositioned.

The underlying purpose of these adjustments will be to sustain a strategy of more selective commitment and more flexible capacity for action. The era of the big stick is over, but the reality of violence in international affairs is still with us. Under these circumstances, while retaining a residual capacity for an all-out nuclear war to avoid being blackmailed by its threat, U.S. military power must be designed for more limited, prompt and even preemptive actions in areas clearly defined not only as vital but also as not capable of adequate self-defense. In brief, instead of planning to be able to fight two-and-a-half major wars (as not long ago was the case), the United States must be ready to deter one major war by having the means to fight it while also being able to respond effectively to more varied but less apocalyptic security threats.

III

These needed strategic adjustments go hand in hand with changing U.S. geopolitical imperatives. In the years ahead, three regions other than the far western and far eastern extremities of Eurasia are likely to become the central foci of American concerns. For much of the cold war the major U.S. fear was the possible Soviet domination of Western Europe. It now appears likely, however, that in Europe for the next decade the Soviet Union will be increasingly on the defensive ideologically and politically. The internal communist threat to Western Europe has passed, while the vitality of Western Europe's development stands in sharp contrast to the stagnation to the east. Western Europe's economic and political recovery represents a monumental success for America's postwar policy.

The next phase should therefore involve an increased assumption by Western Europe of the costs of its defense. The U.S. commitment to Europe's security is sacrosanct, but there is nothing sacrosanct about the level of U.S. military manpower in Europe or the proportion of the U.S. defense budget dedicated to Europe's security. Since Europe can and should do more for its defense, and since the United States has to make more of a defense effort elsewhere but cannot afford to do so, it follows that a gradual but significant readjustment in burden-sharing is necessary and will occur.

In the meantime, Eastern Europe is rapidly emerging as Europe's region of potentially explosive instability, with five countries already in a classic prerevolutionary situation. Economic failure and political unrest are becoming the dominant characteristics of life in Poland, Romania, Hungary, Czechoslovakia and in non-Soviet-dominated but geopolitically important Yugoslavia. In any one, or even in several at once, a spark could set off a major explosion, given the intensity of popular dissatisfaction. Indeed, there are suggestive parallels between the current state of affairs in the region and the historic Spring of Nations of 1848.

Given the volatile state of the *perestroika* (restructuring) program in the Soviet Union itself, it is even conceivable that the systemic crisis of Eastern Europe will become a more general crisis of communism itself. Unrest has already surfaced in the Soviet-occupied Baltic republics, in western Ukraine, in Central Asia and elsewhere. Moreover, it could become more acute if current Soviet reform initiatives do not yield positive and tangible results but instead prompt, as is in fact likely, major economic dislocations, higher food prices, inflation and even large-scale unemployment.

In that context, a major eruption in Eastern Europe would almost certainly precipitate not only a Soviet intervention but the end of the *perestroika* itself. What could happen, therefore, is a matter of some importance to the West as a whole. It is not clear that the West has given sufficient thought to the longer-range implications of East European unrest. Gradual change in the region is certainly desirable, especially change involving the progressive self-emancipation of peoples who have long desired to be part of a larger Europe free of Soviet domination. But a large-scale explosion could have tragic consequences, not only for the region itself but also for East-West relations, by prompting a lasting revival of the most negative attributes of the Soviet system.

As a result the United States and its European allies should focus actively on an effort to forge a more stable relationship with Eastern Europe. A more coordinated Western policy of political and economic engagement should be designed to facilitate the evolutionary dismantling of the Stalinist relics in the region. But such a strategic approach is strikingly absent. Failure to develop one could confront the United States, and its allies, with explosive and eventually very dangerous circumstances.

The region's renewed geopolitical salience is likely to be maximized by growing speculation regarding Germany's future orientation. Already today in Paris and even in London the topic of concerned conversations is focused as much on the future of Germany as on the future of *perestroika* or the likely outcome of the American elections. Some of this may be dismissed as an outdated obsession with "the German question." But some of it does reflect an intelligent appreciation of the German angst over the country's unnatural division and of the traditional German yearning for a grand deal with Moscow.

Any major alteration in the German-Russian relationship would parallel in its geopolitical consequences the earlier American-Chinese accord that so shook the world and so gripped the Russians with the fear of strategic encirclement. It is, therefore, likely to be tempting to Soviet strategists. Moreover, it can only make Soviet economic planners salivate, for in one stroke a new German-Russian relationship would help to resolve the Soviet cravings for both investment and technological innovation.

Fortunately, however, the scope of any potential Soviet initiative toward Germany is constrained by the scope of the East European systemic crisis. In the present circumstances, releasing East Germany—as the price of seducing West Germany— would deprive the Soviet Union of its key bastion for the exercise of effective Soviet military and political control over Poland, Czechoslovakia and Hungary. A neutralized Germany on the edge of an economically stagnant but politically restless Eastern Europe would be disruptive not only for NATO but for the Warsaw Pact as well.

In any case, because of the region's centrality to East-West relations, Eastern Europe is now likely to become increasingly an object of international anxiety and thus of America's concern. Its economic problems are so deep-rooted, its political structures so weak and its geopolitical moorings so shallow that for the next decade at least the region's problems are likely to be high on the statesman's agenda.

The second major regional focus of American concern will continue to be the Persian Gulf/Middle Eastern area. America's deep involvement in the problems of this part of the world stems from two major developments over the last two decades. One involved the emergence since about the mid-1960s of a tight American-Israeli connection; the second involved the gradual replacement "east of Suez" of Great Britain by the United States. The first has been, by and large, the product of domestic impulses in the United States itself, spurred on by very successful lobbying of Congress on behalf of Israel. The second was the result of the need to fill the geopolitical vacuum left by Britain and by the collapse of its U.S.-sponsored would-be regional successor, Iran.

The consequence was that the region's troubles have become America's burden: America is to prevent the Soviet Union from dominating the Persian Gulf region and also to preserve Israel's security. There is no reason to believe that in the years ahead these obligations will recede, and there is much cause to expect continued or even intensified conflicts in the area as a whole. Protection, mediation and deterrence will remain predominantly American responsibilities.

The Carter Doctrine, deliberately drafted to echo the words

of the Truman Doctrine, was subsequently reiterated by President Reagan. It represents an unequivocal commitment to respond, in whatever fashion necessary, to any Soviet effort to gain a geopolitical presence in the Gulf. That Soviet goal, expressly confirmed by Stalin to Hitler in 1940 and implicitly by Brezhnev's invasion of Afghanistan in 1979, can only be denied if America possesses the forces for rapid counterintervention. Only this capability would pose the prospect for Moscow of a direct American-Soviet collision. And U.S. ability to exploit this capability in turn depends on at least a minimal political relationship between the United States and the two geopolitically key barriers to Soviet expansion, Pakistan and Iran.

The creation of the Rapid Deployment Force was meant to meet the first need, and its further expansion has already been justified in the preceding discussion of changes in strategic doctrine. The second requirement was met in part by the extensive American-Pakistani collaboration that developed in the wake of the Soviet invasion of Afghanistan. It is important to register here the proposition that this collaboration should continue even if the Soviet forces are eventually withdrawn from Afghanistan. At that stage, the inclination is likely to arise, especially in the Congress, for a contraction of some aspects of the American-Pakistani relationship, particularly as some of the more contentious but lately repressed issues resurface (such as the Pakistani nuclear program or the question of internal democracy). In addition, there will be the temptation to sacrifice some aspects of the U.S.-Pakistani connection for the sake of a better relationship with India. Yet it is important not to lose sight of the simple fact that an isolated and hence weakened Pakistan could yield the Soviets geopolitical benefits that Soviet arms have not been able to gain in Afghanistan.

Equally important to the stability of the region, and to key U.S. interests, is the independence and territorial integrity of Iran. For the time being, and probably not until the Iranian-Iraqi war wanes or Ayatollah Khomeini dies, American-Iranian relations will remain antagonistic. But in the longer run some reconstitution of a more normal relationship is in the interest of both countries and thus is likely to take place. For most Iranians, current sloganeering to the contrary, the truly threatening "Satan" is the one to the north and immediately contiguous to Iranian territory. All Iranians know that over the last century and a half the principal hostile designs on their soil and independence have originated from Russia. Rhetorical fanaticism does not obliterate historical memory.

Under these circumstances, some eventual accommodation is likely and will carry opportunities for renewed economic American-Iranian cooperation and perhaps even some military connection. The latter will depend on how the Iranians perceive future Soviet policy and also on the nature of Iranian-Arab relations after Khomeini. One of the major tasks of American diplomacy in this area will be to seek to relieve some of the current antagonism, although the scope for any genuine regional accommodation will probably be quite limited for a long time to come. Much will depend on how long-lasting and dynamic the current wave of Islamic fundamentalism proves to be.

Until then, the more immediate task of the United States will be to make certain that the more moderate Arab states in the region are not destabilized. As events have already shown, this will require both active diplomacy and a significant military presence. There is no reason to believe that the need for either will significantly recede, and thus the American preoccupation with this region is likely to be prolonged, risky and costly.

Much the same can be said of the American involvement in the Israeli-Arab issue, given the incompatible views of the local parties on the Palestinian problem (the West Bank and Gaza) and regarding the Golan Heights. Even if the peace process is revived, it will require extremely absorbing and frustrating mediation. In brief, for America the prospect is a grim one: a continuing and seemingly endless involvement in a messy and dangerous conundrum of ethnic and geopolitical conflicts, in the realization that American disinvolvement from them would create even more dangerous consequences.

The foregoing two geopolitical concerns, as taxing as they are, may yet, and before too long, yield in priority to a third one much closer to home. Unless the United States can soon fashion a bipartisan and comprehensive response to the mushrooming Central American crisis, it is quite likely that in the years ahead the region will pose for the American public the most preoccupying challenge, diverting America from its other global concerns. Fashioning such a response may well become the most urgent foreign priority for the next president, especially since on the other critical strategic and geopolitical issues some ongoing strands of policy exist and some degree of national consensus supports them.

The sad fact is that for the last 15 years the United States has been attempting to respond to the region's simultaneously nationalist and social revolution, and to the Soviet-communist exploitation of it, by partial measures and through proxies. It has sought solutions on the cheap. Though President Kennedy proclaimed the creation of a communist regime in Cuba to be an intolerable security threat to the United States, his response was to send three thousand Cuban patriots to solve America's problem—and then to abandon them promptly when the going got tough. Two decades later, another president, Ronald Reagan, similarly proclaimed the Nicaraguan Sandinista regime to represent a mortal threat to the United States. He turned to proxies for a resolution of the problem, with the U.S. Congress then abandoning them.

Neither response was worthy of a Great Power, especially when its vital interests were said to be involved. Kennedy failed to exploit the Soviet collapse of will during the subsequent Cuban missile crisis to insist on a neutralized status for Cuba. Reagan failed to define an equally legitimate U.S. goal regarding a neutralized status for Nicaragua. Both shrank from backing such limited objectives with U.S. national power. Instead, their reliance on proxies to achieve more ambitious goals for an otherwise passive America proved in the end to be self-defeating. In Nicaragua, moreover, the Congress failed to back military leverage with the needed economic development aid programs for the region, as recommended by the Kissinger Commission, with the result that the American capacity to use either positive or negative leverage became severely restricted.

It therefore appears altogether likely that in the years ahead political instability, and more assertively anti-U.S. nationalism, will surface more prominently also in other Central American countries. In Panama, instability will pose an immediate threat to a vital security installation. Moreover, just north of Central America and immediately south of the continental United States, Mexico has the makings of a political as well as economic crisis that could impinge most directly on America. Already Mexico's serious financial and demographic problems are increasingly becoming America's nightmares.

Inherent in this mushrooming crisis is an even larger danger: a direct, immediate impact on American society that could prompt a mood of panic and even isolationism. This is why the issue deserves a high priority, and this is also why the most recent conflict on the matter between the president and Congress was so destructive. The disturbing fact was that both sides adopted escapist stances, each avoiding a confrontation with bitter realities. The first chose indirect and evasive means to achieve a forced solution to a problem that went deeper than the presence of Soviet-backed communism. The second preferred to rely on wishful thinking regarding a solution to the real problem posed by the undeniable presence of a Soviet-communist regional challenge. The present political stalemate in Washington does not augur well for the emergence of the needed comprehensive regional strategy, one that combines attainable and legitimate goals with a determination to act effectively on both the geopolitical and the economic levels.

IV

America's capacity to cope on both the strategic and the geopolitical planes will depend ultimately on America's overall global position. The undeniable relative decline in American economic primacy, especially given the American-sponsored recovery of Western Europe and Japan, has already led some to suggest that the United States resembles Great Britain in the early twentieth century. Even more ominously, it is postulated that America is doomed to replicate the experience of other imperial powers, and that the painful process of degeneration is already under way.

It would be historical blindness to disregard warning signs based on past experience. Moreover, there is, alas, some justification for historical pessimism. It is, for example, disturbing to recall that in the initial phase of their decline the Roman, French and Ottoman empires were characterized by economic inflation and budgetary deficits, by a preoccupation with gold, by costly external (over)expansion, by domestic fatigue and political gridlock, by cultural hedonism and conspicuous materialistic self-gratification, and even by monumental architectural self-glorification. (The manner in which corporate and governmental America splurges on ostentatious monumentalism is strikingly reminiscent of the pompous architectural explosions in Paris, London and Vienna in their late imperial phases.)

But the differences between those circumstances and America's position today are equally important and are perhaps more suggestive of future trends. In almost all cases of imperial decline, economic attrition through war—leading to truly significant demographic depletion and eventually even to the collapse of the ruling political elite—was the major precipitating cause. This has not been the case with the United States. Even the recent massive expansion of defense spending did not raise its level above seven percent of the GNP. Though prompting for a while extensive social demoralization, the war in Vietnam did not cause massive casualties. In fact, the last several decades have seen a remarkable infusion of new and creative blood into the American social and political leadership previously dominated by the more traditional elite, notably first from the Jewish community and more lately through the remarkable attainments of first-generation Asian Americans. The dynamics of social renewal are still at work in America, with their impulses for creativity, innovation and sheer drive.

Even more important are two major external differences. The relative decline in American global economic preeminence occurred not in spite of America but because of America. It was the consequence of a deliberate and sustained American policy, pursued with strategic constancy over several decades. It was the American goal to further the recovery of Western Europe and Japan, and the current situation is the consequence of the successful attainment of that central goal.

To be sure, it can be argued that the above does not alter the fact of America's relative decline, and that it is the fact of decline that counts and not its origins or motivations. This is undeniably true. But it ignores an important aspect. The change in America's global economic position is neither the consequence of an antagonistic competition nor the result of a hostile rival for global primacy gradually attaining success in displacing America. Instead, it is the outcome of a cooperative policy initiated and sustained by the United States itself. That creates a rather different web of global relations.

Moreover, it leads directly to the other major and perhaps even more important difference. In the past the displacement of a dominant power usually led to the emergence of a replacement power, which then assumed the attributes of wide leadership. A decline and fall of one was part of a cycle involving also a rise and a peak by another. This time the United States does not have a rival that could be a successor. Western Europe simply will not become in the near future a united center of political power capable of filling America's global shoes. Japan's aspirations for military-political power are also modest. Thus, neither of the two principal economic beneficiaries of the progressive redistribution of global economic power is America's political rival for global primacy.

Neither is the Soviet Union—as this analysis has shown, it is a one-dimensional rival. It is a credible challenger in the military realm alone. But the price paid for that awesome military might is that as a result the Soviet Union is not competitive politically, ideologically, economically or socially. In fact, it is becoming even less of a rival in these domains, and that is the principal reason for the currently desperate efforts of the Soviet leadership at a *perestroika*.

Since it is unlikely that the Kremlin can greatly diminish its military exertions, it is quite probable that over the next two or three decades the Soviet Union will fade even further. As a result the global economic hierarchy by the year 2010 might be the following: first, the United States (with a GNP just under $8 trillion); second, the European Economic Community (with a similar or perhaps even larger GNP but lacking the attributes of a single political power); third, China (with a GNP of just under $4 trillion); fourth, Japan (with roughly the same GNP); and then only fifth in rank, the Soviet Union (with a GNP of just under $3 trillion).

The Soviet Union thus cannot replace the United States. The most it can do is displace it through the use of its military power, prompting a decisive geopolitical upheaval. But Moscow is simply incapable of becoming the world's financial center or the source of global economic manipulation. This has important implications. Given the fact that the international system cannot operate on the basis of goodwill and sheer spontaneity alone but needs some center of cooperative initiative, financial control and even political power, it follows that the only alternative to American leadership is global anarchy and international chaos. This would have the most destructive political and cultural consequences for those countries that are doing reasonably well in their socioeconomic development.

These considerations, in turn, underline the salience of the point made earlier: the relative decline in America's global primacy is in part the result of America's own policies and was effected cooperatively. This reality enhances the stake that other successful states will continue to have in an America that is able to exercise a constructive and cooperative global role. In effect, the fact that the only alternative to America is anarchy generates the vested interest that both Western Europe and

Japan will continue to have in the preservation of some kind of a central American role.

Admittedly, that also implies major adjustments in both the style and substance of that role, as well as some significant efforts at revitalizing the American capacity to act. It is evident that in the years to come the United States will have to exercise its special world responsibilities by increasingly subtle, cooperative and even indirect means. The effective exercise of that role will depend on the cooperative stake of others in a reasonably controlled international environment. The analogy that readily comes to mind is not that of states intimidated by a global policeman but rather that of airliners cooperating with their air traffic controller.

That change has already been occurring, with the United States today sharing to a very considerable extent with West Germany and Japan the responsibility for international financial policy. The annual economic summit, despite its meager output in recent years, provides a further example of essentially indirect policy direction. In the military realm the required strategic changes will also enhance the role of the key European countries in NATO decision-making, with the American role becoming relatively less decisive. Consensual leadership, although still based on a central American role, is thus already becoming a fact.

The positive management of the East-West relationship is also likely to become a more collective affair. It is most improbable that a grand American-Soviet accommodation can take place. The interests of the two sides are simply too conflicting. The notion of a global U.S.-Soviet partnership for peace and development is even more illusory. More probable are partial accords on issues where the two sides do have reciprocal interests, in a setting of both continued geostrategic competition and some cooperation. In contrast our European friends, notably Germany, are likely to move further than the United States in exploring various forms of political and economic collaboration with Moscow.

Nonetheless, it is likely that in the foreseeable future the Soviet sphere will be preoccupied with a protracted systemic crisis, including major economic upheavals and perhaps even political unrest. Thus, the Soviet Union will remain internally too weak to become a partner for peace and externally too strong to be satisfied with the status quo. Under these conditions the East-West relationship will continue to represent the

negative aspect of the global agenda—i.e., how to avoid growing tensions or conflicts—rather than its more positive, cooperative side.

The emergence in the meantime of a greater degree of
pluralism in the West's decision-making is all to the good. It is
also in keeping with long-standing American aspirations. But
such consensual leadership still requires a vital, dynamic and
powerful America. All concerned are aware that consensual
leadership can otherwise easily degenerate into a gridlock.
Thus even America's economic rivals have a fundamentally
positive interest in America's economic health.

V

This is particularly true in the American-Japanese relationship. A greatly revitalized America can be nurtured by policies
that exploit the special complementarity of American and
Japanese interests, while also providing Japan with the safest
route to continued growth. It is really quite striking how much
the two countries' needs and interests match. The strengths of
one compensate for the weaknesses of the other. Each needs
the other; indeed, each is likely to falter without the other.
Working together ever more closely, they can assure for themselves unrivaled global economic, financial and technological
leadership, while reinforcing the protective umbrella of American global military power.

America needs Japanese capital to finance its industrial renovation and technological innovation; it needs Japanese cooperation in protecting its still significant global lead in creative
R&D and in opening up new scientific frontiers for both
peaceful and military uses; it needs Japanese participation in
securing through enhanced economic development such geopolitically threatened yet vital areas as the Philippines, Pakistan,
Egypt, Central America and Mexico. Japan needs American
security protection for its homeland; it needs open access to
the American market for its continued economic well-being
and, through cooperation with America, secure access to a
stable and expanding world market; it needs to maintain and
even expand its collaborative participation in the vast American
corporate and academic research facilities that are so central
to Japan's continued innovation.

With Japanese investment in America growing, the Japanese
stake in a healthy America will continue to grow. Japan for
many years to come will be heavily dependent on American

security protection, obtained by an American willingness to spend on defense a share of its GNP more than three times larger than Japan's; hence the Japanese stake in a globally engaged America will remain great. With America heavily indebted, the American stake in a productive and prosperous Japanese partner will also grow—but so will resentments over the trade imbalance and probably also over the increasing Japanese buyouts of American corporations and properties. Conflict between the two thus could grow even as the need for a joint partnership becomes more obvious.

While it is impossible to quantify the importance of the relationship to either of the two sides, over the last several years the American economic situation, given both the trade and the budget deficits, might have become untenable without the inflow from Japan of well over $100 billion. Even that rough figure does not account for the various other tangible and intangible benefits to America of the good political relationship that it has with the new economic giant across the Pacific. It is simply central to America's global geostrategic position.

For Japan, these incalculable considerations are even more important; indeed, they are quite literally a matter of life or death. Japan would simply not be—nor would it remain—what it is without the American connection. At the same time, on the narrow level of military expenditures, it can be roughly estimated that without American protection Japan would probably have to spend on its defense some additional $50 billion a year in order to feel truly secure (while at the same time alienating and frightening by such expenditures many of its neighbors).

It is important to restate these verities, for there is the possibility that in the foreseeable future domestic political pressures, especially in America, could damage the relationship—at the very stage when it is ripe for further development. Only through the deliberate fostering of a more cooperative, politically more intimate, economically more organic partnership—in effect, through the gradual and informal emergence on the world scene of a de facto new player—can these two major countries not only avoid a debilitating collision but also ensure that America continues to play the role the world system requires. In brief, the upgrading of the U.S.-Japanese relationship from a transpacific alliance into a global partnership is needed not only for the sake of the two countries concerned but also for the sake of the stability and prosperity of the international order as a whole.

Seeking a more organic partnership of global consequence will require overcoming the obvious cultural and institutional obstacles on both sides, penetrating the tight insularity of the Japanese society and rising above the inherent shortsightedness of the American political process. It will call for a series of sustained, minor steps toward an ever closer relationship, as well as perhaps one or two major acts designed to propel the process more significantly forward.

In the first category one might include the deliberate nurturing of a cross-participation of Japanese and Americans on respective boards of directors of major enterprises, mergers by major business institutions or banks, much expanded exchanges of scientific talent, joint investment schemes and widened collaboration in high technology innovation. Some of that is happening already, but much more could be done, especially as the linguistic barriers fade with the greater familiarity with English on the part of the emerging Japanese elites and also with the forthcoming availability of computerized pocket translating devices.

Perhaps even more significant in fostering the needed global partnership—which one can perhaps call "Amerippon"— would be some major, farsighted acts of statesmanship that in themselves would be beneficial to the international community while advancing the special interests of the partnership itself. While such efforts would require a very major initiative and a great act of political will, they are feasible.

One effort could entail a joint, comprehensive strategy for the development of either the Latin American economy as a whole, or at least its Central American and Mexican portions. Japanese leaders have at times spoken of a possible Japanese initiative on this front. A joint American-Japanese undertaking not only would give the effort greater dimension, but would also significantly upgrade the level of ongoing American-Japanese cooperation. In any case, the need for a major international effort in the region is well established, and the benefits, strategic and economic, to "Amerippon" of a major joint regional initiative—in an area of great potential importance to both—are also self-evident.

An even more ambitious goal might involve jointly setting a target date for an American-Japanese free-trade zone. This would involve a commitment by both sides to a relationship

that moves deliberately in the opposite direction from protectionism. In today's climate it may appear utopian even to invoke
this notion, yet the more farsighted thinkers on both sides
recognize that movement in such a direction would greatly
enhance the prospects of global multilateral cooperation while
directly benefiting the two economies involved. This is why
such a seemingly farfetched notion was quietly whispered about
during the Japanese prime minister's visit to Washington in
early 1988. It would be the logical outcome of a process that
deliberately exploits the objective complementarity of the respective interests and needs of the two sides. The result would
be not only the creation of the world's paramount economic
unit but also inevitably enhanced global political consultations
and joint strategizing.

VI

In the years to come no alternative to a leading American
world role is likely to develop, and America's partners will
continue to want the United States to play that role. But in
addition, there will be creative opportunities for a renewed
and revitalized American contribution to a more cooperative
world system. That makes our historical context rather different from the experience of other major powers whose historical
trajectories entered irreversible declines.

To seize these opportunities America will have to be guided
by a geostrategic vision that accepts the need for more consensual leadership, that purposely shapes a new global partnership
with Japan while also coping in the meantime on its own with
new geopolitical and security challenges. All of this will call for
major adjustments in the American global geostrategy, on a
scale perhaps as great as took place in the late 1940s. That is
the likely challenge facing America during the last decade of
the second millennium. It is also a challenge that can be met.

18

American Policy in the Post-Reagan Era

Robert Gilpin

T HE POSTWAR ERA of international relations has ended and a
new era has commenced. The intensity of the Cold War,
begun in 1946 with the conflict over the futures of Poland
and Germany, was considerably lessened at the Helsinki Conference
in 1975. While the East–West confrontation in Central Europe
continues, American interests in the Pacific, the Middle East, and
other areas have become more and more important. Political, economic, and strategic relations have been transformed during the past
decade and a half. Today, an increasingly nationalistic and regionalized world economy is displacing the liberal world economy based on
American leadership and free trade. Although the American alliance
system and bilateral American–Soviet negotiations continue to be of
concern, issues of a multipolar world are rapidly overtaking them.

The importance of these changes in international affairs, and their
implications for America's place in the world and for its policies, have
not yet been sufficiently appreciated. Policymakers generally assume
continuity in international affairs and base their actions on this
assumption. Indeed, the Reagan years have masked the profound
developments that have occurred and the challenges they have posed.
The United States has been living on borrowed time—and borrowed
money—for much of the last decade; this has enabled the United

This article, in a slightly modified form, was originally presented on May 30, 1987 at a
symposium at the University of Washington, sponsored by the Henry M. Jackson School of
International Studies and the Henry M. Jackson Foundation to commemorate the 75th
birthday of the late United States senator. The author's most recent book, *The Political
Economy of International Relations* (Princeton University Press, 1987), develops many of the
themes in this article.

Reprinted by permission of *Daedalus,* Journal of the American Academy of Arts and Sciences,
Cambridge, Mass. "Futures," Vol. 116, No. 3 (Summer 1987).

States to postpone the inevitable and painful adjustments to the new realities in global diplomatic, economic, and strategic relationships.

In order to appreciate the magnitude of the changes that have taken place, especially during the Reagan tenure, and the challenges posed for the United States, one must understand what I shall call the American System; that is, the political, economic, and security ties forged between the United States and its major European and Japanese allies in the early postwar era. This System is in serious trouble. In the short term, decisive actions are required by the United States to shore up the System. In the long term, the United States and its allies undoubtedly must move beyond the System, at least in its present form, to more stable political and economic relations.

THE AMERICAN SYSTEM

The United States emerged from the Second World War with a clear vision of the new international order that it wished to create: a universal economic and political system. The United Nations, and in particular the Security Council composed of the five permanent members, would be responsible for guaranteeing the peace. A constellation of novel institutions, including the International Monetary Fund (IMF) and the International Bank for Reconstruction and Development (World Bank)—that is, the Bretton Woods system—would administer an open and multilateral world economy. The victors would build the peace that had eluded mankind after the First World War.

Within a brief period, the American conception of "one world" was shattered. The American–Soviet confrontation over the territorial settlement in Eastern and Central Europe destroyed the wartime spirit of collaboration. The ideal of a reunited world economy collided with the realities of the economic devastation wrought by the war and what would become known as the Cold War. The United States set about the task of formulating a new foreign policy and of fashioning an economic and political bloc that would restore the economies of its allies, provide military security, and contain the expansionist Soviet Union. The American System emerged from this effort.

After four decades, the economic and political structure created by the United States and its allies between 1946 and 1950 still stands, having survived numerous severe crises and intense conflicts of national interests. The trauma of the Vietnam War, the dramatic reversal of American foreign economic policy by President Richard Nixon in 1971, and periodic clashes over nuclear strategy and arms control have strained Allied unity. The foundations of the American System have seriously eroded, although it still constitutes the dominant feature of world politics. It is a weakened structure, one unprepared to withstand the earthquake that is bound to come in the post-Reagan era. If it is to survive or to be transformed in a way that conforms to American interests, the United States must construct a new and more secure foundation for its relations with other countries, especially its allies.

Components of the System

The American System has had two basic components: the American relationship with Western Europe and American ties with Japan. Although these two quite separate alliances have certain common features, they also have several differences that have become more pronounced over time, causing strains in the System, and making it more difficult for the United States to reconcile these tensions.

The American–West European component. As relations with the Soviet Union deteriorated after 1945, the United States realized that there were fundamental problems related to Western Europe that required solution. The most pressing need was to assist the revival of the West European economy while also finding a way to guarantee the military security of the West Europeans against the threat of the Soviet Union. To achieve an American commitment to the pursuit of these goals, the American people had to be linked psychologically to Western Europe. A retreat into isolationism, like that which followed the First World War and contributed to the outbreak of the Second World War, had to be prevented.

The Marshall Plan (which encouraged intra-European cooperation) and the formation of the European Economic Community (EEC, or Common Market) were together regarded as the solution to the economic problem of a devastated and fragmented Europe. The creation of a huge market in Western Europe would give the West

Europeans the strength to resist native communist parties and the blandishments of the Soviet Union. Although the Common Market represented a violation of the American ideal of a multilateral world and entailed discrimination against American exports, American policymakers assumed that the Common Market, with its external tariff and protective Common Agricultural Policy, was a necessary stepping-stone to an eventual multilateral system rather than an end in itself. It was expected that once Western Europe had regained its economic strength and confidence, it would lower its external barriers and participate in the open world economy envisioned by the United States at Bretton Woods in 1944. Meanwhile, the United States required an economic quid pro quo in the form of access to the EEC for American multinational corporations. Thus, the United States tolerated what it assumed would be temporary discrimination against American exports in order to rebuild Western Europe and thwart Soviet expansionist designs.

The North Atlantic Treaty Organization (NATO) was formed in 1949 to link the two sides of the Atlantic and bring Western Europe under the American nuclear umbrella. Through the strategy of extended deterrence, the United States communicated to the Soviet Union that an attack on Western Europe would be tantamount to an attack on the United States itself. The stationing of American troops on European soil has been a visible sign of this commitment. The NATO Treaty identified and legitimated for Americans and West Europeans alike the linking of their security.

The American–Japanese component. In Asia, the United States also found itself facing a political, economic, and strategic challenge because the Second World War and its aftermath had strengthened the position of the Soviet Union in East Asia. The Red Army had gained advanced positions in the region, the Japanese economy had been even more devastated than had initially been appreciated, and North Korea and China had become communist and part of the Soviet bloc. The traditional markets of Japan were now in hostile hands. There was thus an intense concern that the forces of economic gravity would pull Japan toward the Soviet Union and its Chinese ally. Today, it is difficult to understand that thirty-five years ago American officials despaired over the problem of ensuring Japanese economic survival.

The United States wanted to integrate Japan into a larger framework of economic relationships and thereby remove the attractiveness of the communist-dominated Asian market. However, there were no large neighboring noncommunist economies to which the Japanese economy could be attached. In order to overcome this problem of an isolated and vulnerable Japan, the United States took several initiatives. One was to expedite the decolonization of Southeast Asia; after all, one cause of the Pacific War had been that European colonizers had closed Southeast Asian economies to the Japanese. The United States also sponsored Japanese membership in the "Western Club." Despite strong West European resistance based on intense fear of Japanese economic competition, the United States secured Japanese participation in the IMF, the World Bank, and other international economic organizations. In addition, the United States gave Japan relatively free access to the American market and American technology without an economic quid pro quo, although it did require strategic concessions (i.e., air and naval bases) from the Japanese.

In order to guarantee Japanese security, the United States also spread its nuclear umbrella over Japan. The American–Japanese Mutual Security Treaty (MST), however, differs fundamentally from the NATO alliance. Under the NATO treaty, an external attack on any member obliges the others to consider measures of mutual defense. In the MST, the United States agrees to defend Japan if it is attacked, but the Japanese are not obligated to defend the United States. Also, whereas the NATO agreement applies only to the territory of its members, the MST refers to the outbreak of hostilities in the entire Pacific region. Through this agreement, the United States obtained the right to use air and naval bases in Japan to defend and secure its position in the Western Pacific. The Japanese were given access to the American market; in exchange, America gained the right to anchor its strategic East Asian position in Japan.

Foundations of the System

The United States is the fulcrum of the American System; the American–West European and the American–Japanese components of the system have little to do with one another. The lines of cooperation run through Washington, D.C. Although Japan and Western Europe are equal participants in the annual "Western" summits, Japanese–West European diplomatic relations are primarily a function of their ties to the United States. In the economic area, Japanese–West European commerce is relatively minor compared to the commerce of either with the United States. While the Japanese would very much like to expand these commercial relations, the Europeans prefer to keep the Japanese at bay. With respect to security, almost no military connections exist between Western Europe and Japan, despite Prime Minister Yasuhiro Nakasone's pronouncement at the Williamsburg Summit in 1983 that Japan is part of the Western security system. Soviet stationing of intermediate-range nuclear weapons in Asia and the increasing deployment of the Soviet strategic missile force in and around the Sea of Okhotsk could, however, change this situation significantly. For the moment, in security as in diplomatic and economic relations, the American System rests squarely on American leadership, or what many scholars call American hegemony.

Common interests and understandings have enabled the structure to withstand innumerable attacks from without and serious differences within the alliances themselves, even though important differences between the United States and its allies have existed from the very beginning. International conditions have changed dramatically, and the basic assumptions upon which the American System was founded have become less valid. What one might call the internal "contradictions" within the System have grown, and the foundations have eroded. The differences among the allies over the nature of the Soviet threat, over nuclear issues, and over economic problems have increased and threaten to cause a rupture of the System.

A shared perception of the Soviet threat has been central to the unity of the System. The Western policy of containment was based on the assumption that the West faced an expansionistic and monolithic Communist bloc. It was also generally believed that diplomatic resolution of East–West differences could not be achieved until the Soviet Union and international communism were transformed. The Western "negotiation from strength" position meant that serious negotiations had to await Soviet recognition of Western military superiority. The United States assumed that there was a global communist military threat; its allies tended to consider the problem more of a regional political challenge.

Differences in perception among the allies have grown over the years due to political and economic changes. The unified Communist bloc no longer exists, West European communist parties have ceased to be a serious problem, and the Soviet Union faces an independent and potentially dangerous China in the East. Despite its military might, the Soviet Union's serious economic problems and the economic strength of Western Europe have reduced the fear that the Eastern market might ensnare the West Europeans. The Helsinki Agreement (1975) reduced the confrontation in Central Europe and commenced what many Europeans believe (or want to believe) is a gradual internal "liberalization" of the Soviet Union, a belief fostered by the diplomacy and reforms of Mikhail Gorbachev.

These and other changes have accentuated inter-allied political differences between the United States and Western Europe. In the words of Denis Healey, former British minister of defense, "it is difficult [for Europeans] to believe that the Soviet superiority is sufficient to tempt the Kremlin into a deliberate attack on Western Europe. . . ."[1] West Europeans resist the American desire to extend the scope of the NATO alliance, arguing that NATO applies only to the security of its members and cannot be extended to the Middle East or other regions, despite U.S. pressures for strong actions against Soviet aggression in Afghanistan and Soviet support of Marxist regimes elsewhere. Powerful groups in Western Europe hope for an easing of the division of Europe as a result of Gorbachev's policies; some consider Western Europe to be only a middleman needed to moderate the clash between two equally irresponsible superpowers. Although the West Europeans remain committed to the alliance, interests have diverged considerably and the political tie has surely been attenuated.

Differences among the allies on the issue of defense have also grown. The American commitment to the defense of Western Europe, assumed to be temporary, was never intended to result in the stationing of tens of thousands of American troops in Western Europe or to reach an annual cost of over $100 billion forty years after the founding of NATO. The Europeans were expected to be able to defend themselves, at least in the conventional sphere, and the United States to be able to reduce its commitment; this crucial assumption was undermined by the unanticipated growth of Soviet power and by European refusal to finance the necessary conventional buildup because of its costs and because of concerns that a buildup might weaken the American nuclear guarantee. The Europeans alternate between worrying that the immature and pugnacious Americans will trigger a fight with the Russians on European soil (as they did when the intermediate-range missiles were deployed in the early 1980s) and fearing that the United States will abandon them. This latter concern has increased as the United States and the Soviet Union have begun negotiations over the removal of these same weapons. Meanwhile, American citizens are more and more frequently asking whether they are really willing to put their own society at risk in order to deter an attack on West Europeans, who are unwilling to make the sacrifices necessary to defend themselves.

The Chinese conventional threat and the Soviet nuclear threat were the foci of security concerns in East Asia. The American rapprochement with China and the Soviet nuclear, naval, and conventional buildup in that strategic theater have transformed that situation. American–Japanese political relations have greatly improved because the Japanese no longer fear that the United States will drag them into an American–Chinese conflict. However, with the growth of Soviet power in Asia, the United States has become increasingly impatient over the Japanese "free ride" with respect to their security and their resistance to extensive rearmament. American pressure on the Japanese to rearm more rapidly has caused great resentment in Japan. The Japanese vehemently resist a linkage of economics and security; the United States, on the other hand, links past economic concessions to increased Japanese cooperation in the security realm. Intensification of the defense/economic conflict has stimulated nationalistic reactions in the Japanese and a tendency for Americans to feel that they have been "used."

Economic ties have complemented the political and security foundations of the American System. Even though the trading and monetary system established at the end of the Second World War has facilitated an unprecedented era of economic growth and world commerce, differences over economic matters have always existed among the allies. Important changes in economic strengths and relationships during the past decade and a half have accentuated inter-allied economic conflicts and today seriously threaten the stability of the international economic system.

The United States and Western Europe have very different conceptions of the European Economic Community. The United States tolerated EEC discrimination against American exports primarily for security reasons and assumed that the Europeans would soon reopen their markets to American exports, thus creating the multilateral trading system. For many Europeans, the EEC, with its tariff barriers and its agricultural price supports, constitutes an end in itself. This concept of Western Europe as a protected regional bloc has been strengthened as the number of nations in the Community has grown. Although the United States initially gained politically and economically from the creation of the EEC, the economic costs to American businesses and farmers have greatly escalated in recent years.

The other assumption on which the postwar world economy was established was that Japan was economically vulnerable. How could an overpopulated archipelago devoid of indigenous resources possibly survive? The American policy (described earlier) of supporting Japanese economic development has been so successful that Japan, after Canada, has become the primary economic partner of the United States; the American–Japanese economic nexus has become a central economic relationship for both countries. With the growth of the Japanese economy, the United States has demanded a more open Japan and the same access for American firms to the Japanese economy that Japanese firms have to the American economy. These pressures for greater liberalization, however, run directly counter to important aspects of Japanese society and have become a major source of conflict. Despite its competitive strengths and huge capital accumulation, Japan remains a highly vulnerable economy. It has no large, developed neighbors with which it can trade and it continues to be overly dependent on the American market; it has yet to find a secure niche in the world economy. So, for their own reasons, the United States and Japan have formed a close but basically unstable symbiotic relationship.

Erosion of the economic foundations of these Atlantic and Pacific relationships is the most problematic and troublesome of the issues now affecting the American System. Because the economic differences among the allies raise immediate and fundamental challenges for American domestic and foreign policy, this essay will stress the economic dimensions of this complex alliance structure and examine the potential for serious conflict in this area among the allies. Yet all foundations of the System are intimately joined and affect one another. For example, the continued stationing of large numbers of American troops in Western Europe and the building of a 600-ship Navy are contributing factors to the problems of the American economy. This analysis of American policy will begin with a careful look at the economic crisis of the System.

THE RELATIVE DECLINE OF AMERICAN POWER

The economic crisis of the American System is a consequence of the long-term relative decline of the American economy and, more immediately, the policies of the Reagan Administration. Although the American economy is still the largest and most powerful in the world, it has declined relative to its competitors and, most importantly, with respect to what Americans and others expect from it. At the same time that the United States has assumed the largest portion of the burden of financing the American System and of confronting the growth of Soviet power, the American people have demanded both an ever-rising standard of living and improved government services. Government expenditures have risen faster than the gross national product (GNP); these expenditures have financed Social Security (including Medicare), congressional "pork barrels," and weapons systems. American leaders, Democrats and Republicans alike, have failed to educate the American people to the stark choices confronting the nation and the trade-offs that we face. Instead, Americans have simultaneously had a massive defense buildup, expensive programs like Social Security, and rising domestic consumption.

In the early 1950s, the United States accounted for approximately 40 percent of the gross world product; by 1980 the American share had dropped by half to approximately 22 percent. Whereas the United States produced 30 percent of world manufacturing exports in the early postwar period, by 1986 its share had dropped to a mere 13 percent. American productivity growth, having outpaced the rest of the world for decades, declined dramatically from a growth rate of 3 percent annually in the early postwar years to an incredible low of .8 percent in the 1970s.[2] As American productivity growth has fallen behind that of other economies, particularly Japan, West Germany, and the newly industrializing countries (NICs) of East Asia, the economy has become less competitive and the American standard of living has been lowered. In capital formation, technological leadership, and the quality of the labor force (human capital), the United States has not kept pace. Sadly, the international competitiveness of the U.S. economy is increasingly based on "cheap labor." If this trend is to be reversed, the United States must increase its level of investment in plants and people in order to raise its rate of productivity growth.

In the closing decades of the twentieth century, the United States faces an imbalance between its commitments and its decreased economic base. To keep pace with what it considers to be expanding Soviet military power, the United States has assumed increased costs to maintain its global political and military position; simultaneously, the rise of new industrial competitors and the loss of dominant positions in energy, technology, and agriculture have decreased the capacity of the United States to finance its many commitments. With a decreased rate of economic growth and a low rate of national savings, the United States has lived far beyond its means and has also maintained domestic and international commitments that it can no longer afford.

THE REAGAN LEGACY

Despite its superficial success, the Reagan administration has failed to reverse the relative decline of the American economy. On the contrary, the long-term problem of relative economic decline has been greatly compounded by its policies—policies that have largely been abetted by Congress. The administration's theory of supply-side economics, its military buildup, and its massive tax cut were geared to restore American power and prestige (after the humiliations of the Carter years) by rebuilding American military power and renovating the American economy, while simultaneously achieving domestic prosperity.

Despite its notable achievements in restoring self-confidence in the American population, reducing the rate of domestic inflation, and reviving economic growth, the Reagan administration has not solved the important problems of the relative decline of the American economy and of a nation living beyond its means. Instead, the policies of the administration have masked the underlying problem of the weakening economic foundations of American power. Indeed, its policies have further undermined the competitiveness of the American economy, transformed the United States into the greatest debtor in world history, and made the United States increasingly dependent on foreign capital to maintain its domestic prosperity and global position. In the short term, this transformation of the American economic position has profound implications for America's relations with its allies, especially the Japanese. In the long term, it will force the United States to make drastic changes in its economic and foreign policies.

The primary force behind these developments has been the massive tax cut and the resulting budget deficit. Anticipating the need to finance the deficit, American interest rates rose and led to a large capital flow into the American economy; this in turn raised the value of the dollar. With an overvalued dollar, American exports dropped and imports rose dramatically. The primary beneficiaries of this radical shift in macroeconomic policy were American consumers and foreign exporters, especially the West Germans, the Japanese, and the NICs of East Asia. These economies prospered as they shifted to an aggressive strategy of export-led growth, while American industry lost markets everywhere. The rapidly expanding American market in Latin America was destroyed because of the debt crisis, the severity of which was accentuated by the rise of global interest rates; these countries had to restrain their economies and cut back on American imports. The Reagan administration's economic policies have resulted in the loss of foreign markets for American exporters, the deindustrialization of the economy, and the decline of the United States to the status of a "net debtor" nation (i.e., its international liabilities exceed its international assets).

This shift of the United States from creditor to debtor nation is an event of immense historical significance because of its effect on American trade, industry, and power. The budget deficit and the resulting greatly-overvalued dollar reversed the favorable trends of the late 1970s. The American trade balance deteriorated and, by the mid-1980s, the annual trade deficit had reached the unbelievable figure of $170 billion. The huge net earnings on foreign investments ($34 billion in 1981) have been greatly reduced. Although foreign protectionism and the economic policies of other countries have been partially responsible for the deterioration of the American trading and payments situation, the basic explanation for this turnaround is to be found in simple economic relationships, which tell us that the budget deficit *is* the trade deficit.

American macroeconomic policies, resulting in a greatly overvalued dollar—not the machinations of the Japanese—constitute the underlying cause of the trade deficit. The trade deficit is caused in Washington, D.C., and it is there that the problem must be solved. A distinguished economist and expert on these macroeconomic relationships states:

Macroeconomics impinges on the trade deficit through two laws of economic arithmetic. First, our net national dissaving—that is, the shortfall of savings in relation to the demand for them at home—must be financed by funds generated at home or abroad. Second, our account deficit equals the net capital inflow from abroad. This simply says that if the money foreigners get by selling us goods and services is not being spent to buy goods and services from us, then it must be spent in buying our assets [real estate, securities and Treasury bonds].

If, at the prevailing exchange rates and interest rates, people's willingness to buy and sell, borrow and lend, is not compatible with these two equations, then the prices will change until the balances are restored.

The U.S. has a large national dissaving because the public-sector dissaving (the Federal budget deficit) exceeds the net saving of the private sector. This raises our interest rates until foreign funds flow in to close the gap. That, in turn, raises the value of the dollar and increases our trade deficit by an equal amount.[3]

In oversimplified terms, the causal relationship between the budget deficit and the trade deficit is as follows:

Budget deficit → Need to finance deficit → Rise in interest rate → Capital inflow → Overvalued dollar → Decreased exports, increased imports → Trade deficit

The macroeconomic policies of the administration not only had a devastating impact on American trade, but also failed to raise the rate of national savings and domestic investment; indeed, both declined dramatically, and the ratio of total debt to GNP has reached an unprecedented and disturbing level. Between 1980 and 1985, the necessity of financing annual budget deficits of $200 billion or more caused the American savings rate to drop from approximately 17 percent to 12 percent; during this same period the personal savings rate plunged to postwar lows of 4 percent and less. (In contrast, the Japanese national savings rate has continued to be closer to 20 percent and, by some estimates, as high as 30 per cent.) This approximately $200 billion reduction of national savings per year has been balanced by reduced domestic investment and by foreign borrowing.

The budget deficit also means a relative decline in capital accumulation and domestic investment.[4] As the deficit has absorbed more than half of all national savings, it has raised interest rates and "crowded out" domestic investment; the rate of capital accumulation declined from about 17.5 percent of the GNP in 1979 to 16.2 percent in 1985. The long-term effect of the $1.6 trillion decline in capital accumulation has meant "a loss of $160 billion a year in perpetuity."[5] It should be pointed out that throughout the postwar period, the United States has invested at home far less than its competitors; in contrast to 17 percent or so for the United States, the West German rate of domestic investment is close to 25 percent and the Japanese rate is well over 30 percent.[6] Lowered capital accumulation has meant lower productivity growth and accelerated deindustrialization of the American economy; it portends a significantly lowered standard of living in the future. In effect, Americans have been able to consume more in the 1980s by paying lower taxes and by borrowing abroad, but they will one day have to pay the bill through increased exporting, higher taxes, renewed inflation, or (most likely) some combination of the three.

During the first five years of the Reagan administration, the national debt doubled, exceeding the $2.0 trillion level.[7] By the year 1990 the debt could reach approximately $2.3 trillion, or 40 percent of the GNP; assuming 1986 interest rates, the interest payments will increase by $200 billion and take 40 percent of all personal income taxes by 1990.[8] At 1987 exchange rates, the foreign debt (net obligations to foreigners) is $200 billion and will be approximately $800 billion by the beginning of the next decade.[9] The United States has been mortgaging its future to a degree unprecedented in world history.

The level of private, public, and foreign debt of the American people and the costs of servicing this debt have become, in the words of the president of the Federal Reserve Bank of New York, "threatening to the financial stability of the United States and the rest of the

The World Economic Cycle Under the Reagan Administration

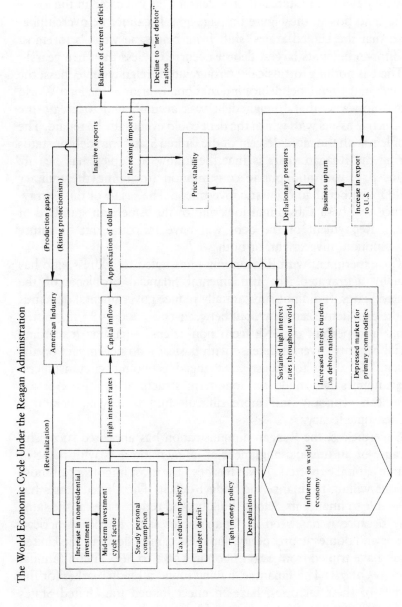

world."[10] Like other declining powers in the past, the United States has been indulging itself in overconsumption and underinvestment for too long. The result of this profligate behavior is the decline of the United States to the status of "net debtor" (as indicated in the lower right-hand box in the Figure on page 47). It cannot be overemphasized that the United States' shift from being the world's foremost creditor to being its largest debtor occurred in less than five years!

There is nothing intrinsically wrong with foreign indebtedness; the United States was a net debtor internationally prior to the First World War. However, that foreign debt was accumulated to create the productive assets with which the debt could eventually be repaid. The problem with the rapid descent of the United States into debtor status during the Reagan years is that the inflow of capital has heavily financed private and public consumption (including the military buildup) rather than domestic investment. The result of this extravagance will be a substantial lowering of the American standard of living. Repayment of the debt will have to come out of future consumption, investment, or both.

The experiment with Reaganomics has failed to address, and has actually aggravated, the fundamental financial problems of the United States. It did not substantially reduce governmental demands on the productive economy, but between 1980 and 1985 it "shifted about 1.5 percent of GNP from non-defense spending (excluding Social Security) over to defense with basically no net impact on the deficit."[12] Failing to adjust to changed economic circumstances, Reaganomics has made the long-term structural problems of the American economy still more difficult and is leaving behind a burdensome legacy.[13]

Nevertheless, the Reagan administration has appeared successful because of an unusual alignment of its own interests with those of certain capital exporters. Japan has been the most important of those nations willing to finance the budget deficit. The United States has been able to finance its defense buildup and reduce taxes at the same time because it has been in Japan's interest to finance American power and domestic prosperity. Japanese capital flows to the United States have tripled from $20 billion in 1982 to $60 billion (annual rate) in 1987.[14] The Japanese, having found a ready market for the output of their factories, have in effect loaned the United States money to sustain Japan's strategy of export-led growth, to maintain a high level of domestic employment, and to help finance the American military buildup on which the security of Japan rests.

As the economic and financial positions of the United States and Japan have been reversed, the political and economic relations of these countries have been transformed. Each, for its own reasons, has entered into an intimate relationship in which the Japanese have become the principal underwriters of President Reagan's policies. If Japanese capital flows were to stop, there would be a devastating impact on the American economy. In fact, it would be very difficult for the United States to fight another war on the same scale as the Korean or Vietnamese conflicts without Japanese permission and financial support of the dollar. However, this crucial symbiotic relationship between the United States and Japan, which has developed during the Reagan years, is highly vulnerable. When it disappears or is at least attenuated, both the United States and Japan will be faced with difficult choices.

The global "good times" generated by the Reagan budget deficit appear to be over. American capacity and willingness to tolerate a massive trade deficit, borrow funds to pay for imports, and plunge deeper into national debt have resulted in a potentially serious deindustrialization of the American economy and a historically unprecedented national indebtedness; now there is a threat of a congressional revolt through protectionist actions. As the United States retreats from its role as the primary engine of growth for the world economy, growth rates everywhere are slowing and the specter of a worldwide recession looms. The United States must quickly reverse its continuing economic and political decline.

The dollar has been the keystone of the American world position; as the dominant currency in the international monetary system, it has cemented the American System of global alliances and has been the foundation of American hegemony. With the dollar providing the base of the monetary system, the United States has been able to fight foreign wars, maintain troops abroad, and finance its hegemonic position without placing substantial economic costs on the American taxpayer. This crucial role of the dollar and the "exorbitant privileges" (to use the term of Charles de Gaulle) that it has conferred on the United States (e.g., to fight the Vietnam War by printing dollars) have required a foreign partner to help support it.

In the early postwar period, the American position in the world and the support of the dollar were based on American and British cooperation; this "special relationship," begun in the interwar years, had been solidified by World War II. Together, the Anglo-Saxon powers framed the Bretton Woods system and reestablished the liberal international economy. In 1967, the decline of their economy forced the British to devalue their currency and pull away from the United States.

West Germany replaced Great Britain in the late 1960s as the foremost economic partner of the United States and supporter of the dollar. Throughout the Vietnam War and into the 1970s, the Germans supported American hegemony by holding dollars and buying American government securities. This special relationship was weakened in 1973 by its inflationary cost to the Germans; it was dissolved in 1979 when the Germans refused to support the expansionary economic policy of President Carter.

During the Reagan administration, the Germans have been replaced by the Japanese, who have provided the financial backing for President Reagan's economic and military policies. Today, this special American–Japanese relationship is under severe strain due to American pressures on the Japanese to stimulate their economy, the devaluation of the dollar, and protectionist legislation in Congress. A collapse of this relationship would destroy a crucial underpinning of American power and domestic prosperity; its fragility makes it imperative for the United States to put its financial house in order, and to do so quickly.

POLICY PROPOSALS

The Reagan years have been years of lost opportunity. The belief that "America is back" (to quote the president in one of his more exuberant moments) is simply not true and never will be—at least not if this means that the United States has regained the unchallenged preeminence it enjoyed in the early postwar years when the American System was established. America, and by implication its allies, must adjust to new economic, political, and military realities. Such adjustments have been made more difficult by the extravagant and debt-driven policies of the Reagan administration, but they are not yet impossible. To succeed, the United States must adopt new economic and foreign policies. In the short term, it must arrest the rapid deterioration of the American economy. In the long term, it must address the larger problems of the American economy, and of America's relations with its allies and other countries.

Restore Fiscal Solvency Through a Temporary Surcharge on American Imports

The United States must restore fiscal solvency as rapidly as possible. Unless this is done quickly, the economic and political consequences of protectionist efforts in Congress will be devastating. Putting America's financial house in order will require the solution of three problems that have been attacked separately, but that are, in reality, closely linked: the federal budget deficit, the trade deficit, and repayment of the accumulating foreign debt. Let us briefly examine current proposals and their limitations before proposing a workable solution.

Raise taxes and reduce expenditures. The most sensible solution to these problems is to raise taxes substantially and cut federal spending drastically. The resulting elimination of the budget deficit, which will be approximately $130 billion in the next fiscal year, would in time lead to the gain of a trade surplus and the foreign earnings needed to repay the debt. Unfortunately, this solution appears to be unfeasible for domestic political reasons: neither major political party wants to bear the onus of advocating higher taxes, or major cuts in defense spending or Social Security.

Elimination of the "Growth Gap." The position of the Reagan administration is that these fiscal and trade problems would go away if only West Germany, Japan, and some other countries adopted supply-side economics and followed the example of American economic success. If these other countries stimulated their economies, opened their markets, and thereby imported more goods, the American trade deficit would disappear. Such actions on the part of other economies would surely help, but they would have only a small impact on the trade imbalance as long as the American budget deficit persists. More importantly, the growth option is largely irrelevant: for domestic economic and political reasons, neither the West Germans nor the Japanese are at all likely to increase their rates of economic growth sufficiently.

Devaluation of the dollar. While this has been a crucially important step, it has been too little and too late relative to the rapid growth of protectionist pressures in Congress. Moreover, for it to be effective, the dollar's value would have to fall substantially below its present level, perhaps as low as 120 yen to the dollar. Such a drastic devaluation would be strongly (and probably effectively) resisted by other countries that pursue export-led growth policies. While the devaluation of the dollar over the past year or so has had an impact on Japanese export, it has not adequately affected the exports of other countries that also have a huge trade imbalance with the United States—countries such as Canada and South Korea, which peg their undervalued currencies to the dollar.

Voluntary export restraints. One of the worst solutions to the trade deficit, this is also the most popular. It raises the price to American consumers for imported goods and greatly benefits a small number of American and foreign firms. While it may reduce the trade deficit somewhat, it does nothing about the budget deficit and debt problem.

Bilateral balancing. Congressman Richard Gephardt's 1987 proposal to retaliate against countries that have a large trade surplus with the United States (such as Canada, Japan, and South Korea) would seriously damage both America's economy and its foreign relations. While some relief might be achieved through imposing import restrictions or forcing open other markets, this policy would have only limited effect and would not eliminate the true cause of the American trade imbalance (i.e., the budget deficit). Its major consequences would be to (1) shift the trade surplus to different exporters, (2) eliminate Japanese financing of the American budget deficit, and thereby (3) raise interest rates and slow the American economy.

Protectionism. Many in Congress seem to consider outright protectionism, particularly against the Japanese, to be the most attractive solution. While high tariffs and import quotas would benefit a few American industries, the closure of the American economy would invite foreign retaliation and worsen all the other problems afflicting the American economy, such as the productivity slowdown and decreasing international competitiveness. Equally important, as with the Gephardt proposal, capital imports from Japan would decline and—unless the budget deficit is solved—inflation and interest rates would escalate with a devastating impact on the economy. Protectionism would also destroy the economic foundations of the American System and isolate the United States from its allies.

Attack the cause of the problem. The problem with all the above proposals (except the first) is that they do not really address the crux of the problem: the American budget deficit. The solution to the trade problem must begin with the realization that it is primarily a consequence of American macroeconomic policies. Although the economic policies and protectionism of European nations, Japan, and other countries are also factors, they account for only about 20 percent of the trade deficit.[15] Americans must realize that the trade and payments deficits are primarily of their own making; with the tax cut and resulting budget deficit, the United States has achieved the impossible: an unprecedented trade deficit with almost everyone.

However, it is simply not the case, as many popular journals and commentators allege, that the American economy has become inherently noncompetitive and must therefore be protected. We must remember that the United States had a current account surplus in 1981 and that the devaluation of the dollar and other economic measures were then showing results. The United States had recovered from the balance-of-payments difficulties of the 1970s, American exports were expanding, the income on foreign investments was substantial, and American industry was beginning a major structural adaptation. While the United States was running a trade deficit in consumer durables, especially with Japan, it had a growing trade surplus in agricultural products and high-technology industries. The industrializing less-developed countries (LDCs), particularly those in the Pacific and Latin America, were becoming increasingly important markets for American exports.[16] The American economy was competitive; it will be again when the dollar is sufficiently devalued for a long enough period. Unfortunately, Reaganomics and the global debt crisis destroyed the promising developments of the late 1970s and early 1980s.

Impose a temporary import surcharge on certain imports. The simplest, fastest, and, most politically feasible way to move toward a solution of the budget and trade deficits, as well as to stop the accumulation of foreign debt, would be to place a temporary surcharge of approximately 20 percent on American imports (excluding, perhaps, component parts and raw materials), similar to the one President Nixon imposed in 1971.[17] In effect, this would be a revenue-raising or taxation measure that would reduce the budget deficit. It would also bring down global interest rates, thereby helping the LDC debtors and stimulating American exports to those countries. It would cause a further devaluation of the dollar, which would give another boost to American exports. The trade deficit would be reduced and eventually eliminated. American businesses, workers, and farmers would be benefited. On the negative side, it could trigger inflation if monetary growth is not controlled; American consumers would obviously suffer. But every conceivable solution to the economic plight of the United States risks inflation and necessitates a relative reduction in the American standard of living; having lived beyond their means on other people's money for so long, the American people must of necessity suffer the consequences. While a surcharge would be resented abroad and might even invite retaliation, its impact on foreign exporters would be somewhat moderated in that it would apply equally to all countries, would lower global interest rates, and would be presented as a temporary expedient. It would be a stopgap measure that would buy time and provide an opportunity to turn things around through tax and expenditure changes. It could easily be removed once its purpose of restoring an internal and external fiscal balance in America's accounts had been achieved.

While a surcharge should be the first and most important step in restoring fiscal responsibility, the United States must also take strong measures to liquidate its huge accumulated foreign debt. This task will require a trade surplus of approximately $100 billion annually.[18] William Branson points out that in order to create this trade surplus, the dollar would have to drop below its 1981 level relative to other currencies. This severe devaluation is necessary because the United States, by becoming a debtor, has lost earnings on foreign investment; it therefore requires a sufficiently large trade surplus to compensate for these lost foreign earnings while also servicing its debt. The high dollar's long-term effect on the competitiveness of American industries necessitates an additional devaluation.[19]

An American trade turnaround of the magnitude required to achieve these objectives would cause serious difficulties abroad and would raise questions as to where export markets would be found and whose exports would be displaced. It would produce powerful reactions in countries that have been pursuing export-led growth policies, such as Japan and West Germany. The adjustments they would have to make as they shifted to a domestic-led growth strategy would be huge and difficult, which explains their strong resistance to stimulating their economies in response to present American demands. Any American policy to reverse its trade deficit and repay its debt could easily trigger a severe trade war. Yet the United States must eliminate its huge trade deficit and foreign debt, lest the service charges weigh it down and further undermine American economic strength. The choices facing the United States and its allies are stark, and the range of choices is narrowing.

Until and unless the United States reduces its federal budget deficit and eliminates the deficit's effects on the value of the dollar, it will find itself in a debilitating dilemma. On the one hand, an overvalued dollar means a massive trade deficit, continued industrial decline, and further descent into debtor status. On the other hand, the devaluation of the dollar means higher interest rates, rising inflation, and a slowing of economic growth. If Congress and the president are unwilling to raise taxes or cut expenditures to remove the deficit, then the only practical solution is a temporary import surcharge. It should be enacted quickly before more foolish remedies are tried—and once it has achieved its purpose of restoring fiscal solvency, it should be just as quickly removed.

Deemphasize the Goal of Global Multilateralism and Emphasize the LDC Economies

The United States must also acknowledge that its postwar commitment to a liberal, multilateral world economy is unrealistic. Recent efforts of the administration to achieve this through pressures on other economies have become increasingly counterproductive. American foreign economic policy should be based on realities: increasing regionalization of the world economy, politicization of economic relations, and the waning of the liberal trade regime of the postwar era. However, the Reagan administration and most American economists cling to the Bretton Woods ideal of an open, multilateral trading system. The concerted attempts of the United States to force open West European, Japanese, and other economies to American trade, investment, and multinational corporations are of limited utility. These countries, responding to American demands, reluctantly entered the GATT (General Agreement on Tariffs and Trade) Uruguay Round of trade negotiations on agriculture and services (e.g., insurance, finance, and telecommunications). However, chances for success in these complex negotiations are minimal, the potential benefits for American industry are small, and the probable political costs to relationships among the allies are substantial.

American foreign economic policy should deemphasize its efforts to create a multilateral system and acknowledge that both the EEC and Japan are and always will be relatively closed economies. They have never accepted the American commitment to an open, liberal system or the goal of a multilateral system. Instead, each prefers state control over trading relations and close state–business relations, as in the case of the European Airbus or the Japanese practice of "administrative guidance." Each is becoming the focus of a developing regionalized economy. Moreover, the Europeans have never wanted extensive trade with Japan; this, of course, intensifies Japanese export pressures on the United States. Furthermore, the larger LDCs will not accept the American position. The world economy will be based increasingly on bilateralism or trilateral negotiations among the world's centers of economic power rather than on global multilateralism.

The EEC is not a stepping-stone to a global multilateral system, but an end in itself. The intra-European alliance is based on economic, political, and security ties that its members will not surrender: West German subsidies for French agriculture, assurance of continued West German–French friendship, and a combined weight that enables the West Europeans to counterbalance the superpowers. West Europeans believe that the costs to domestic social peace of competing against the low-wage NICs and the high-technology Americans and Japanese have become too great. The EEC, having expanded from six to a dozen members, is now a more self-contained economic bloc, and it will resist any American effort to weaken it.

Japan does not accept the Western liberal ideal of an open economy in which the government severely limits its intervention in market relations. U.S. demands that the Japanese adopt American economic practices, open their economy to American corporations, and deregulate their economy are deeply resented and are stimulating powerful nationalistic reactions. Whereas the United States quite correctly regards these aspects of Japanese culture as barriers to commerce and exerts pressure on the Japanese to eradicate them, the Japanese, in the words of one Japanese business executive, also correctly regard these American demands as "tantamount to raising objections to Japan's social structure"; he continues, "there is little possibility that those requests will be met."[20] Intensification of resentment on both sides will be the primary outcome of this political and cultural impasse, in which the Americans see the Japanese as the principal cause of their economic problems and the Japanese see themselves as scapegoats because American leaders will not eliminate the budget deficit.

This argument does not imply that the United States is virtuous in trade matters. In important respects, it is even more protectionist than the Europeans or the Japanese: witness its extensive use of voluntary export restraints. Rather, the argument is that current attempts by the United States to force open and reform West European, Japanese, and other economies have been counterproductive, and a new approach to international trading relations is required. For example, it would be far better for the United States to follow the West European example of protecting specific industrial sectors than to attempt to force open the Japanese economy. As two leading American experts on the Japanese economy have pointed out, the Japanese could more easily learn to live with such so-called "sectoral protectionism" than with external pressure to open their economy.[21] A return to the extensive liberalization effort of the early postwar era is not a real alternative; intensification of Japanese nationalism is the most likely consequence.

In place of the present strong emphasis on the GATT ideal of global multilateralism, the agreements of the so-called Tokyo Round (1973–1979) of trade negotiations could provide the basic framework of trading relations.[22] These agreements apply to a world in which bilateral arrangements, government intervention, and domestic policies have become increasingly important determinants of international economic relations; they attempt to establish codes of conduct governing a more politicized world economy. While this effort has just begun, it is more promising than the path of multilateral negotiations chosen by the Reagan administration.

As the world economy moves into an era of intense trade competition and negotiated arrangements, the United States will have to decide with whom to ally itself economically and to whom priority access to the American market should be granted. Should it be the Europeans, the Japanese, or perhaps America's near neighbors? The United States has given such "political economy" questions very little attention, but it must find answers soon. The United States would be wise to avoid the temptation of favoring one component or the other of the American System. In classic balance-of-power terms, the maneuverability and leverage of the United States in economic negotiations will be greatest if it continues to give approximately equal weight to its European and Japanese allies.

The United States does have to give greater prominence to the developing world, especially Latin America and the Pacific Rim. As noted above, the interdependence of the United States and these countries was rapidly expanding until Reaganomics and the debt crisis. If this potentially huge market for American agriculture and manufactures is to be revived, the global debt problem must be attacked more aggressively. The administration's approach of encouraging growth in the debtor nations has failed miserably. How can a Latin America that has become a net exporter of capital possibly grow? Whatever the solution to this exceedingly difficult and complex problem, it must entail the recommencing of capital exports to these economies. The recent Japanese initiative proposing a $30 billion transfer of capital to Latin America is a modest but important step in this direction.

Link Nuclear Disarmament, Conventional Disarmament, and Political Agreements

The third immediate issue facing the American System is raised by the negotiations over the removal of intermediate-range (and possibly other) missiles from Western Europe. The crisis in alliance relations caused by these American–Soviet discussions arises from the fact that postwar Western security and disarmament policies have been based on a fundamental contradiction. On the one hand, the defense of the American System, primarily for economic reasons, has been based on the use of nuclear weapons to counter the Soviet geographical advantage and its perceived superiority in conventional forces. On the other hand, the highest priority in disarmament and arms control negotiations from the Baruch Plan (1946) to the present has been the elimination of this nuclear deterrent. This inherent conflict between Western security needs and arms control policies was of little consequence when the Soviet Union engaged in meaningless propagandistic proposals for total disarmament. However, Gorbachev's shift (now that his concern over SDI has apparently diminished) to a strategy of eliminating specific nuclear systems, beginning with intermediate-range missiles in Western Europe, confronts the West with the consequences of this contradiction.

In general, the disarmament policy of the West has ignored lessons from prior successful arms reduction agreements such as the demilitarization of the Great Lakes (1817) and the Washington Conference (1922). In these agreements, political differences were settled in conjunction with arms limitation. In the mid-1970s the United States (under President Nixon) and the Soviet Union followed this pattern when they agreed to SALT I as part of the larger effort to settle East–West political differences that culminated in the Helsinki Agreement (1975). Steps can and should be taken to reduce the risks of accidental war; yet there is danger in pursuing policies that lead to disarmament prior to the settlement of the political disputes that are responsible for the armaments in the first place.

The arms control effort has rested on a questionable and perhaps even dangerous premise. From the Surprise Attack Conference (1958) to the present, it has been assumed that the risk of a nuclear war arises mainly from the mutual fear of a nuclear attack. The emphasis in negotiations, therefore, has been to reduce this risk through such measures as restrictions on the size and composition of nuclear forces. The problem with this fixation on nuclear weapons, however, is that it ignores the greatest danger in the contemporary situation: the possibility that a political crisis and conventional confrontation could escalate into a nuclear one. Unfortunately, little has been done to reduce this possibility. The Vienna negotiations on conventional disarmament have dragged on for years and have been given a very low priority. Ironically, arms control in the nuclear area might actually increase the probability of a conventional conflict, and a conventional war between the superpowers could easily escalate into a nuclear conflict. The nuclear, conventional, and political realms are intimately linked; they must not be separated.

The West could actually compound the problem if it accepts extensive nuclear disarmament agreements, such as the removal of all short-range or battlefield nuclear weapons from Western Europe, without commensurate reductions in conventional armaments and prior to a settlement of those political differences that could lead to a conventional conflict. As long as it is overly dependent on nuclear weapons and as long as political differences exist, the West should be wary of agreements that strip Western Europe or other areas of nuclear weapons. The elimination of nuclear weapons should be tied more closely to reduction of Soviet conventional forces and establishment of political agreements reducing potential sources of conflict. If not, the military balance in Western Europe and elsewhere will shift against the West, and the risk of a nuclear war resulting from the escalation of a conventional conflict in Europe or other regions will increase.

Reverse Industrial and Productivity Decline

The United States must also reverse deindustrialization and the severe decline in productivity growth, and begin the long-term process of reindustrialization. Some scaling-down of America's traditional industrial base was inevitable with the shift toward high technology and the postwar revival of other economies. However, the budget deficit and high interest rates depressed domestic investment and accelerated the decline of many industries; the 60 percent appreciation of the dollar during President Reagan's first term is estimated to have caused a 13 percent reduction in manufacturing employment.[23] In addition, the high dollar shifted American consumer tastes toward imported goods; this "leakage" of domestic demand to other countries further decreased investment in American industrial plants and encouraged foreigners, especially Japan and the NICs, to produce goods in which the United States formerly had a comparative advantage. It also encouraged American firms to set up production facilities abroad to serve both American and foreign markets. To compensate for all this, the United States must accelerate domestic investment in order to modernize its plants, reverse its productivity decline, and develop new industries for domestic and export markets.

As Lester Thurow has convincingly argued, the decline in the growth of productivity is a critical weakness of the American economy.[24] As a result, competitiveness has disappeared from many industries where America was once the world leader; the great American automobile no longer exists but is a mélange of imported components. While there are many causes of this industrial decline, the most important, according to one recent study, is a drop in capital investment in the United States.[25] The United States has also failed to understand that a key component of Japanese economic success has been Japan's emphasis on an educated and skilled work force. The United States has underinvested in education, as well as in civilian research and development, relative to its major economic competitors. While some spillover does take place from military projects into commercial applications, military research and development more frequently drive out civilian work. Indeed, if the Strategic Defense Initiative is not properly managed, it could have a strong negative impact on American industry.

Reduce the Costs of Overseas Commitments

The other long-term problem for the United States is to reduce the costs of the American System and thereby scale down its defense expenditures. It must face up to the hard fact that the maintenance of the American System has imposed a heavy burden on the American economy. The deterioration in the economic position of the United States relative to its domestic and international commitments will force the United States to make some difficult choices. If the United States cannot continue to borrow abroad to finance its military power and social programs, will not decrease domestic consumption, and can no longer afford to slight capital formation, then it will have no other choice than to reduce the costs of its overseas commitments in Western Europe, East Asia, and elsewhere. Unless major efficiencies are achieved in the Pentagon, as foreseen by Richard Halloran and other reformers, the United States will be forced to cut back its commitments.[26] Expenditures for maintenance of the American System will have to be reduced in order to balance national resources with national objectives.

Opportunities for scaling down these costs appear to exist. Consider, for example, the situation in Europe. While the Soviet Union continues to have a preponderance of conventional forces, the capacity of the West Europeans to resist has increased and the likelihood of a successful attack is low.[27] West German tank and

antitank forces are considerable; battlefield nuclear weapons constitute a formidable deterrent to a conventional attack. Modernization
of the British and especially the French nuclear deterrents is revolu-
tionizing their significance; they will soon pose a much more serious
threat to the Soviet Union. In the words of one study, "the levels of
damage approach, if they do not exceed, the 'assured destruction'
criteria set for U.S. strategic forces in the 1960s."[28] This qualitative
change in the European nuclear balance may be a significant factor in
renewed Soviet interest in arms control, beginning with the
intermediate-range missiles deployed in Western Europe. While the
Soviet conventional challenge continues to be formidable, these
changes permit one to question whether the United States still needs
to keep its forces in Western Europe at their present level in order to
maintain the credibility of its nuclear umbrella. Meanwhile, greater
cooperation among the three major West European powers should be
encouraged.

   While the precise expenditures to be reduced obviously cannot be
addressed in this essay, the general approach can be. The primary
responsibility for the security of America's allies must be shifted from
the United States to them; they are no longer impoverished. How this
shift is to be accomplished cannot be spelled out here either, but it
must begin with a change in attitude on both sides. The United States
should cease behaving as if the security of its allies is primarily an
American responsibility. In the decision to deploy intermediate-range
missiles, and on other occasions, American policy has been counterproductive; it has reduced the incentive for its allies to take greater
responsibility for their own security. It is worth noting that the
decision of the United States to negotiate the removal of these same
intermediate-range missiles from Western Europe has greatly concentrated the attention of West European leaders on the need for defense
cooperation.

   Whether or not Gorbachev's ostensible desire to reduce armaments
through arms control agreements also provides an opportunity for
the United States to cut back its commitments and defense expenditures cannot be determined at this juncture. For reasons that cannot
be discussed in detail here, strategic nuclear and conventional forces
probably cannot be cut drastically through arms control agreements
without a simultaneous settlement of the serious political and ideological issues dividing the United States and the Soviet Union. On the

other hand, it is imperative that the search continue for ways to reduce the burdens imposed on the American economy by its costly global commitments. This must be done slowly and deliberately, either through unilateral steps taken by the United States or, preferably, through agreement with America's allies. Considering the relative decline of American economic power, if the reduction of American commitments does not take place through a planned and orderly retrenchment, it could one day be forced upon the United States by a major fiscal crisis.

Keep the Deterrent But Decrease Reliance on Nuclear Weapons

It is nothing less than insanity for the United States to rely on a military strategy committed to the inevitable use of nuclear weapons, which could mean the end of American society and perhaps of all higher forms of life.[29] In the long run, the United States must reduce its postwar overreliance on nuclear weapons at the same time that it keeps the nuclear deterrent. Such a controversial departure from current American policies would obviously be difficult and would take many years to achieve, but steps toward such a change should be taken.

The primary purpose of the American nuclear deterrent should be to prevent an attack on the United States or its allies. The idea that nuclear weapons can be used to fight wars is extremely dangerous. Rather than restrict ourselves to the objective of deterring a war with the Soviet Union, we have become overly dependent on nuclear weapons for war-fighting and have integrated them into almost every aspect of the defense of American interests around the world. This nuclear-first strategy has involved the United States' dispersion of nuclear weapons into every potential theater of war and down the chain of command to very low levels, thus increasing the possibility of their theft by terrorists, their inadvertent employment, and the escalation of any conflict into a major nuclear war.

Reducing the reliance on nuclear weapons would require several initiatives. The most important would be to increase the capacity of the West to defend itself with conventional forces; this would obviously require a much greater effort by America's allies. Conventional and nuclear weapons must be separated more completely than at present, and the latter must be placed under centralized control that is directly responsible to the president of the United States. While the United States should not foreswear the possibility of the first use of nuclear weapons to "communicate" a threat or to deter aggression, military strategy must be predicated on the exercise of maximum discretion regarding use of the nuclear option.[30]

A deliberate policy of reducing the American nuclear umbrella over Western Europe and Japan would obviously lead to intense resistance, especially by the Europeans. There is no way, however, that Western Europe or Japan will assume a greater responsibility for its own defense if the United States continues to base its military strategy almost totally on nuclear weapons. If it is believed and proclaimed that Europe can never be defended with conventional forces and therefore must always depend on American nuclear weapons, the Europeans will strongly resist doing anything to reduce their dependence on the American nuclear guarantee. This self-reinforcing situation must be changed.

While a deemphasis on nuclear weapons is a long-term objective, the nuclear deterrent itself constitutes a necessary basis of world peace and must be maintained. From this perspective, it is ironic that Ronald Reagan may one day be seen as the American president who did more than anyone else to undermine the nuclear deterrent. As Robert W. Tucker has pointed out, the president's Strategic Defense Initiative challenges the legitimacy of nuclear weapons and signifies a loss of faith in nuclear deterrence as the principal means of keeping the peace.[31] The president's agreement with Gorbachev at Reykjavik to eliminate all nuclear missiles (however impractical this may be) and his decision to remove from Western Europe the intermediate-range missiles that he had earlier worked so hard to place there, are further indications that his commitment to the utility of the nuclear deterrent is shifting. Nevertheless, until the political differences between the United States and the Soviet Union are greatly decreased, the nuclear deterrent will help maintain the peace and must be kept at the ready.

CONCLUSION

Despite the cries of a few Cassandras, the indebted prosperity of the Reagan "economic miracle" and the soaring stock market have hidden from the American people the reality of their situation and the fact that they have been prospering, in part, on other people's money. The country has failed to appreciate the historic meaning of the relative decline of American power, the long-term corrosive effects of the budget deficit, and the severe implications of these developments for American domestic welfare and the United States' place in the world. While these problems need not cause despair, both immediate and long-term solutions should be implemented.

This essay has put forth several proposals that would facilitate adjustment to the reduced economic and political position of the United States. Their purpose is not to abandon the principle of collective security or the goal of an open world economy, but to place these objectives on a more firm and realistic basis. The choices before the United States are unpleasant, and the proposed solutions would cause immense difficulties with America's allies. Both the West Europeans and the Japanese would react bitterly to an import surcharge. They would tenaciously resist any American effort to achieve an export surplus, rebuild its industrial base, and acquire the earnings with which to repay the accumulated U.S. foreign debt. These economies have pursued a mercantilist, export-led growth strategy for over a decade. The internal adjustments that would be required of these economies to reduce their exports, increase their imports, and become more dependent on domestic-led growth would cause serious political and social upheavals in their societies. Deemphasis of the seemingly futile effort to create a liberal, multinational world economy also holds dangers and could cause a decrease in global wealth and living standards.

The West Europeans and Japanese are extremely reluctant to assume greater responsibility for their own defense. The associated costs would mean reduced domestic prosperity and increased political dissension in these societies. Unless the Soviet Union is willing to play a more constructive role in solving international political problems and to scale down its large conventional forces considerably, reduction of the American commitment in Western Europe and elsewhere could lead more countries to develop their own nuclear deterrents. This disturbing scenario might stir the Soviet Union to settle its differences with the West and to negotiate conventional disarmament more earnestly.

Perhaps the economic, political, and strategic adjustments required in the relations between the United States and its allies can be made, and differences resolved through negotiations and compromise. If not, the United States must take action unilaterally. Its choices will narrow as the relative decline of its economy continues and as it goes deeper into debt. Whatever the process by which these changes are effected, the United States can no longer afford to pay the heavy costs of maintaining the American System in its present form. The goal of American policy should be to establish a new relationship among the United States, Western Europe, and Japan that reflects contemporary political, economic, and strategic realities.

The postwar era is over, and the conditions underlying American policies for several decades have dramatically changed, partially as a result of American success. Although Western Europe remains militarily vulnerable and suffers from some real economic difficulties, the effort that began with the formation of NATO and the Marshall Plan has largely succeeded. Japan, despite its economic success, does continue to be vulnerable and overly dependent on the United States, but it no longer faces a hostile China. In East Asia, the Soviet Union confronts a quasi-alliance of the United States, Japan, and China. What was once seen as a monolithic Communist bloc has disintegrated, and the economic failure of the Soviet system is forcing it, however slowly and reluctantly, to abandon many of its abhorrent features. The United States continues to behave as if its power and wealth were inexhaustible. However, the fact of relative decline can no longer be denied; new policies must be shaped for a world in which neither the United States nor the Soviet Union is an unchallengeable superpower. The multipolar world foreseen by President Richard Nixon appears, at long last, to be coming into existence.[32] If the United States is to assume its rightful place in this multipolar system, it must act to solve the problems posed by reduced power and extended commitments.

ENDNOTES

[1]Denis Healey, "A Labour Britain, NATO and the Bomb," *Foreign Affairs* 65 (1987), pp. 716–29.
[2]Isabel V. Sawhill and Charles F. Stone, "The Economy," Chapter 3 in *The Reagan Record: An Assessment of America's Changing Domestic Priorities*, John L. Palmer and Isabel V. Sawhill, eds. (Cambridge, MA: Ballinger, 1984), p. 73.
[3]Avinash Dixit, *New York Times*, 15 July 1985, p. A18.
[4]Martin Feldstein, "The Future of Economic Policy." (The Janeway Lectures, Princeton University, unpublished), pp. 2–3.
[5]Ibid., p. 3.
[6]Uwe E. Reinhardt, "Enjoy the Party—For Tomorrow Somebody Will Have to Pay," *Princeton Alumni Weekly* (25 February 1987), pp. 13–19.

[7]*New York Times*, 22 September 1985, p. E5.

[8]Feldstein, "Future of Economic Policy," p. 2.

[9]Martin Feldstein, "Correcting the Trade Deficit," *Foreign Affairs* 65 (1987), pp. 795–806.

[10]E. Gerald Corrigan, "Public and Private Debt Accumulation: A Perspective." Federal Reserve Bank of New York, *Quarterly Review* 10 (1985), pp. 1–5.

[11]Robert Gilpin, *The Political Economy of International Relations* (Princeton: Princeton University Press, 1987), p. 146. Original source: *White Paper on International Trade—Japan 1985* (Tokyo: Japan External Trade Organization, 1985), p. 8.

[12]Feldstein, "Future of Economic Policy," p. 7.

[13]Robert O. Keohane, "The World Political Economy and the Crisis of Embedded Liberalism," Chapter 1 in *Order and Conflict in Contemporary Capitalism: Studies in the Political Economy of Western European Nations*, ed. John H. Goldthorpe (Oxford: Clarendon Press, 1984), p. 37.

[14]William H. Branson, "Capital Flows from Japan to the U.S.: Another False Alarm." (Unpublished, 16 March 1987), p. 1.

[15]Gerald Marks, *New York Times*, 18 April 1987, p. 19.

[16]William H. Branson, "Trends in United States International Trade and Investment Since World War II," in *The American Economy in Transition*, ed. Martin Feldstein. (Chicago: The University of Chicago Press, 1980) pp. 183–257.

[17]For the economic rationale for a surcharge, see William H. Branson and J. Pearce, "The Case for an Import Surcharge." (Unpublished, March 1985).

[18]Feldstein, "Future of Economic Policy," p. 4.

[19]William H. Branson, "The Limits of Monetary Coordination as Exchange-Rate Policy." (Unpublished, 3 and 4 April 1986).

[20]Quoted in Murray Sayle, "Victory for Japan," *New York Review of Books* 32 (1985), pp. 33–40.

[21]Hugh Patrick and Henry Rosovsky, "The End of Eras? Japan and the Western World in the 1970–1980s." (Unpublished, 1983, p. IV.)

[22]Gilbert W. Winham, *International Trade and the Tokyo Round Negotiations* (Princeton: Princeton University Press, 1987).

[23]Branson, "Limits of Monetary Coordination," p. 3.

[24]Lester Thurow, "A Time to Dismantle the World Economy," *The Economist* (9 November 1985), pp. 21–26.

[25]William J. Baumol and Kenneth McLennan, eds., *Productivity Growth and U.S. Competitiveness* (New York: Oxford University Press, 1985).

[26]Richard Halloran, *To Arm a Nation: Rebuilding America's Endangered Defenses* (New York: Macmillan, 1986).

[27]John J. Mearsheimer, "Nuclear Weapons and Deterrence in Western Europe," *International Security* 9 (1984–85), pp. 19–46.

[28]John Prados, Joel S. Wit, and Michael J. Zagurek, Jr., "The Strategic Nuclear Forces of Britain and France," *Scientific American* 255 (1986), pp. 33–41.

[29]Robert Jervis, *The Illogic of American Nuclear Strategy* (Ithaca: Cornell University Press, 1984).

[30]Morton H. Halperin, *Nuclear Fallacy: Dispelling the Myth of Nuclear Strategy* (Cambridge, MA: Ballinger, 1987).

[31]Robert W. Tucker, *The Nuclear Debate: Deterrence and the Lapse of Faith* (New York: Holmes and Meier, 1985).

[32]Richard M. Nixon, quoted in *New York Times*, 7 July 1971, p. 16.

19

Requiem for the Reagan Doctrine

Christopher Layne

Predictably, the Reagan Doctrine led the administration into a political and moral morass. Far more than a set of specific policy prescriptions, the Reagan Doctrine provided the intellectual framework—the *Weltanschauung*—that shaped the administration's external policies. As events proved, the Reagan Doctrine was an unsuitable basis for a viable post-Vietnam foreign policy because it failed to mobilize sustained support for American engagement abroad; it could not be implemented without circumventing established constitutional and political norms, and it ignored the shifting balance of world forces that underscored the continuing erosion of the United States' postwar political and economic hegemony.

Ronald Reagan's 1980 victory rested in large measure on his pledge to arrest the country's declining prestige and to conduct a tough-minded foreign policy backed by a restored consensus. Yet, when the Iran-*Contra* scandal broke—severely crippling Reagan's presidency two years before his term expired—friends and adversaries alike regarded the United States as not only weak but also hypocritical. The administration's grasp of world politics, in its own way, was as flawed as the Carter administration's. The Iran-*Contra* hearings highlighted the administration's failure to rebuild the postwar foreign policy consensus that Vietnam had shattered.

What was the Reagan Doctrine? How did it compare with the policies of other postwar administrations? What was wrong with it? The answers

Reprinted by permission of the *SAIS Review*, Vol. 8, No. 1. Copyright 1988 by The Johns Hopkins Foreign Policy Institute, SAIS.

to these questions hinge in part on events that transpired before the Reagan administration took office.

In 1976 an America disillusioned by Vietnam and Watergate sent Jimmy Carter to the White House. He brought with him a new foreign policy elite whose members were relatively young, with roots in the Democratic party's McGovern wing and a view of the world far different from that of the postwar establishment that had been broken by Vietnam. Carter's election symbolized the liberals' response to the costs of American intervention abroad; it reflected their determination never to pay such a price again. The United States, Carter believed, was a status quo power that needed to get on the right side of change by promoting human rights and supporting progressive movements that would deal with the root cause of Third World revolutions. Because the administration placed indigenous causes, not the East-West power struggle, at the root of Third World conflicts, U.S. military force was seen as an ineffective tool. In Carter's view the way to deal with such problems was to act in concert with others, to seek diplomatic solutions, and to provide economic aid.

The Carter approach was not entirely without useful insights, but it was neither a viable nor a politically acceptable foreign policy. It overlooked Moscow's imperial ambitions — not the sole cause of regional conflicts, to be sure, but sometimes a relevant factor. Although vital U.S. interests were seldom at stake in Third World disputes, neither U.S. policymakers — including, ultimately, Carter himself — nor the public were willing to hold to Carter's laissez-faire approach in the face of the expansion of Soviet power and influence worldwide. The Iranian revolution undermined Carter's critical assumption that the forces of change could be managed and that change of a non-Marxist character would always be advantageous to the United States. Repeated crises reminded the United States that it indeed had national interests that could not always — or even often — be subordinated to the requirements of multilateral diplomacy and Alliance solidarity.

Echoing neoconservative calls for rearmament, revitalization of containment, and renewed vigilance, Reagan's 1980 campaign caught the mood of an "assertive America" fed up with the Vietnam syndrome (which all but ruled out the use of military force to defend U.S. interests abroad) and disillusioned by the string of foreign policy setbacks that began with Angola and ended with Desert One. The election gave Reagan a clear mandate to halt the erosion of U.S. military power and self-respect that had occurred during the 1970s. Beyond that, however, it was unclear how far the administration's mandate extended or what the scope of its policy would be.

Washington would have to choose between "a policy of a resurgent America intent once again on containing Soviet influence — as well as the expansion of communism generally — or a policy of moderate containment," wrote Robert W. Tucker in *Foreign Affairs* in the winter of 1979-80. Both courses entailed risks. Moderate containment might fail to secure important U.S. interests and would require Washington's adjustment to America's declining global influence. Moreover, a more circumscribed approach would break sharply with the United States' postwar commitment to building a stable world order reflecting liberal, democratic values. Serious questions arose, however, about the United States' ability to sustain a more ambitious policy. Global containment in the 1980s—essentially a return to the Truman Doctrine—would be a far different affair from what it had been in the period from 1947 to 1965. In 1981, in *Foreign Affairs*, the late Robert E. Osgood pointed out that the new administration faced "unprecedented constraints on the effective exercise of American power in its economic, diplomatic, and military dimensions." The loss of strategic nuclear superiority, the Soviet Union's emergence as a global power, and the relative decline of U.S. economic power had transformed the geopolitical situation, tilting it to America's disadvantage.

Neoconservatives quickly gained the leading role in shaping and articulating the Reagan administration's foreign policy. Betraying no concern about adverse international systemic trends—and no post-Vietnam ambivalence about America's world role—they pushed hard for a return to global containment, rechristened the Reagan Doctrine.

Though the Reagan Doctrine has never definitively been outlined, its content can be inferred from statements made by President Reagan, Secretary of State George Shultz, and from the writings of neoconservative foreign policy theorists, such as Charles Krauthammer, Irving Kristol, and Norman Podhoretz. As it came to be commonly understood, the Reagan Doctrine committed the United States to resisting Soviet and Soviet-supported aggression wherever it arose, to building American-style democracies in Third World countries, and to rolling back communism by aiding anticommunist insurgencies. The Reagan Doctrine assumed that U.S. security required nothing less than the ideologically congenial world it sought to create. For some neoconservatives, moreover, the doctrine's objectives expanded to include the breakup of the Soviet empire and, ultimately, the collapse of the Soviet state itself. The Soviets would be vanquished by a series of "small defeats" in the Third World (which would presumably undermine the Soviet regime's domestic legitimacy), by failure in the high-technology arms race, and by debilitating economic pressure imposed by Washington in concert with its security partners.

The Questionable Inheritance

The aspirations, underlying assumptions, and rhetoric of the Reagan Doctrine echoed those of the post–World War II Truman Doctrine. In fact, the Reagan Doctrine's intellectual architects were the rightful political heirs of the cold war liberalism championed by Democratic presidents Harry S. Truman, John F. Kennedy, and Lyndon B. Johnson, and by senators Hubert H. Humphrey and Henry M. "Scoop" Jackson. The experience with Vietnam had cast the cold war liberals out of their own party and transformed them into "neoconservatives." Though still nominal Democrats (in most instances), they voted for Ronald Reagan in 1980 and 1984, served in his administration, and vigorously advocated his policies.

The Truman Doctrine was based on the Wilsonian premise that the world would be both better and safer if it adopted the United States' political values and structures. According to the Wilsonian vision, the world would be peaceful and harmonious if only nondemocratic states (inherently bad) become democratic states (inherently good). The Truman Doctrine also reflected the purported geopolitical "lesson" of Munich — that totalitarian states are insatiably aggressive, that peace is indivisible, that aggression must be resisted everywhere, and that failure to do so is foolhardy "appeasement." In Daniel Yergin's words, Munich stands for "the assumption that all international events moved in simple chain reactions, that all points on a map were equally close, and that every event was of equal importance."[1] When fused, these assumptions produced a foreign policy that committed the United States to a messianic, global crusade against communism. In a September 1946 memorandum to Truman, presidential adviser Clark Clifford recommended that "the United States should support and assist *all* democratic countries which are in *any way* menaced by the Soviet Union," emphasizing that U.S. policies should be "global in scope."[2] Heeding Clifford's advice, the president's now famous March 1947 speech announced the Truman Doctrine to the world: "It must be the policy of the United States to support free peoples who are resisting subjugation by armed minorities or by outside pressures." He said, "We must assist free peoples to work out their destinies in their own way."

Cold war liberalism found perhaps its clearest expression in NSC-68: the national security study prepared by the Truman administration in early 1950 to set forth U.S. global strategy for "containing" the Soviet Union. The document depicted U.S.-Soviet competition as a "basic conflict between the idea of freedom under a government of laws, and the

1. Daniel Yergin, *Shattered Peace: The Origins of the Cold War and the National Security State* (Boston, Mass.: Houghton Mifflin, 1978).

2. "American Relations with the Soviet Union: A Report to the President by the Special Counsel to the President," in Thomas H. Etzold and John Lewis Gaddis, eds., *Containment: Documents on American Policy and Strategy, 1945–1950* (New York: Columbia University Press, 1978), emphasis added.

idea of slavery under a grim oligarchy of the Kremlin." In this worldwide ideological struggle the United States could not afford to be vanquished anywhere because "the assault on free institutions is worldwide and a defeat anywhere *is a defeat everywhere*" (emphasis added).

In its official statements the Reagan administration simply recycled these now familiar tunes from the cold war era. Echoing Truman's 1947 remarks, President Reagan stated in his 1985 State of the Union speech, "We must stand by our democratic allies. And we must not break faith with those who are risking their lives—on every continent, from Afghanistan to Nicaragua—to defy Soviet-supported aggression and secure rights which have been ours from birth." Secretary of State Shultz hit the same notes, proclaiming in a February 1985 speech to San Francisco's Commonwealth Club the existence of a worldwide "democratic revolution" that America had to support in "word and deed" by standing for "freedom and democracy not only for ourselves but for others." These remarks elaborated on themes Shultz had presented the previous year to the Trilateral Commission. At that time he had said, "Our security, and our alliances can be affected by threats to security in many parts of the world; and the fate of our fellow human beings will always impinge on our moral consciousness." The United States, though not the world's policeman, had a responsibility as the free world's strongest power. "The preservation of our values, our principles, and our hopes for a better world rests in a great measure, inevitably, on our shoulders," Shultz said.

The Truman Doctrine left an unfortunate inheritance to the Reagan administration. As Hans Morgenthau wrote in 1951, "The Truman Doctrine transformed a concrete interest of the United States in a geographically defined part of the world (Greece and Turkey) into a moral principle of worldwide validity, to be applied regardless of the limits of American interest and power."[3] The Reagan Doctrine simply perpetuated this inability to distinguish between vital and peripheral interests. As a result, both doctrines defined American interests in ideological rather than tangible terms, committing the United States to opposing communism and defending democracy everywhere. Such was the logical implication of a foreign policy that held other nations to be threats to America's security because of their internal political structures and not their external policies. According to both doctrines, any failure of U.S. resolve or any curtailment of its commitments could undermine U.S. security.

Both doctrines also raised critical questions. Were U.S. interests menaced by communist ideology itself or only by the expansion of Soviet political and military power? (After all, Yugoslavia's 1948 break with Moscow and the Sino-Soviet split showed that nationalism can impel even

3. Hans Morgenthau, *In Defense of the National Interest* (New York: Alfred A. Knopf, 1951).

communist states to follow anti-Soviet foreign policies.) Could American-style democracy be successfully transplanted to the Third World, and at what cost? How could an expansive definition of U.S. national interests be reconciled with the imperative of balancing resources and commitments, thereby ensuring that excessive security burdens would not damage the economy? What effect would a crusading, anticommunist foreign policy have on the United States' domestic political structures and its constitutional processes?

In 1980 Americans opted for a policy of strength but, in an apparent paradox, retained their skepticism about U.S. involvement overseas. As public opinion analyst William Schneider observed in 1984, Americans were "suspicious of international involvements of any kind [and] predisposed against U.S. involvement in other countries' affairs unless national interests or national security [was] at stake."[4] For its architects, the Reagan Doctrine's emphasis on the ideological component of the U.S.-Soviet rivalry was a tool to overcome public recalcitrance and to mobilize support for a reinvigorated global containment policy. Because it was thought Americans would not make the material or psychological sacrifices the Reagan Doctrine required simply to maintain a cynical balance of power policy, it was necessary, Norman Podhoretz wrote, to infuse the superpower rivalry with a "moral and political dimension for which sacrifices could be intelligently demanded by government and willingly made by the people."[5]

The neoconservatives believed that embarking on an ideological crusade would arouse the nation's fervor and persuade it to accept the Reagan Doctrine's domestic political and economic costs. Here again the doctrine had returned to its roots in the Truman Doctrine. Senate Foreign Relations Committee chairman Arthur Vandenberg had told then-undersecretary of state Dean Acheson in 1947 that the way to gain support for the Truman Doctrine was "to scare the hell out of the American people" about the communist threat. Throughout the cold war — until Vietnam — U.S. leaders won backing for global containment by following Vandenberg's advice.[6] But in the 1980s Americans did not answer the Reagan Doctrine's call to battle. Neoconservatives could resurrect the rhetorical framework of global containment, but they could not turn the clock back to the cold war mind-set of the 1950s.

4. William Schneider, "Public Opinion," in Joseph S. Nye, Jr., ed., *The Making of America's Soviet Policy* (New Haven, Conn.: Yale University Press, 1984).

5. Norman Podhoretz, "The Future Danger," *Commentary* (April 1981).

6. Walter Isaacson and Evan Thomas, *The Wise Men: Six Friends and the World They Made* (New York: Simon and Schuster, 1986), 395.

The Failure of the Reagan Ideology

The Reagan Doctrine's strident rhetoric backfired, making Americans less, not more, willing to support an active policy abroad. The doctrine raised twin fears of a superpower confrontation and indiscriminate U.S. involvement in foreign conflicts where U.S. vital interests were not at stake. The overblown rhetoric — the call for a "worldwide democratic revolution" — made Americans skeptical rather than supportive of the Reagan Doctrine. Concerning Nicaragua, for example, few doubted that the Sandinistas really were very bad, but most Americans found it hard to believe the *Contras* were much better — not to mention that they were the "moral equivalent" of America's own founding fathers, as the Reagan administration had tried to sell them to Congress and the public.

In fact, the failure of the administration's foreign policy is most dramatically underscored in Central America. There it had a compelling geopolitical case to make for its Nicaraguan policy. Even the administration's liberal critics acknowledged that America's vital security interests required excluding Soviet military bases from, or advanced weapons sales to, Nicaragua as well as preventing the Sandinistas from exporting their revolution.

But this was not the case the administration took to the nation. For the Reagan Doctrine's neoconservative architects — and for Ronald Reagan himself — Nicaragua's Sandinista government was an ideological threat. More concerned with Nicaragua's domestic political structure than with its foreign policy, the White House could not tolerate a Marxist regime in Managua. For Reagan and the neoconservatives, the objective of U.S. Central American policy was never in doubt: the Sandinistas had to be removed from power.

Neither Congress nor the American people endorsed these ambitious ideological objectives, partly because of the obvious gap between the administration's professed ends and the chosen instrument of its policy. Few really believed the *Contras* could overthrow the Sandinistas; full-scale U.S. military intervention ultimately would be required to achieve that goal. Therein lay the problem. Americans had no enthusiasm for going to war to change Nicaragua's internal political system. The Reagan Doctrine's crusading rhetoric defeated itself. Instead of focusing on Nicaragua's special importance because of America's geopolitical and historical regional interests, Washington presented its Central American policy as the centerpiece of the global crusade against communism. Americans had not forgotten Vietnam; in light of the Reagan Doctrine's rationale, Nicaragua looked like the first step down the slippery slope to U.S. involvements in Third World quagmires.

The administration's failure to adopt a Nicaragua policy with realistic objectives had baleful consequences. The House Democratic leadership and the Central American governments, led by Costa Rican President Oscar Arias Sanchez, outmaneuvered the administration, filling the policy vacuum. The resulting Central American peace proposal did not take account of U.S. security concerns and rested on the dubious premise that the Sandinistas would risk their hard-won political position by democratizing Nicaragua. As the Reagan administration entered its final year, it was unclear whether its Central American policy could be salvaged. A new approach was urgently needed. To deal with Nicaragua, Washington should have bypassed the Arias plan and struck a deal with the Sandinistas exchanging U.S. noninterference in their internal affairs for limits on the size and strength of Nicaragua's armed forces, an end to Sandinista subversion of other regional governments, and the withdrawal from Nicaragua of Soviet bloc military personnel. As Alan Tonelson wrote, Washington should handle "the Sandinistas and other potential threats in Central America the way that great powers have always dealt with pesty, puny neighbors: by laying down the law unilaterally and enforcing our will through intimidation and direct uses of military force."[7]

A new U.S.-Central American policy would renounce any attempts by Washington to shape the domestic structures of the region's countries. At the same time, the United States should be prepared to use air and naval power to enforce its agreement with the Sandinistas, to prevent outside powers from establishing a military presence in Central America, and to keep the Panama Canal open. Such a policy has several attractive features. By eschewing the use of ground troops, the United States can avoid the domestic consequences of a protracted military stalemate. By staying out of Central America's internal politics and confining itself to using only air and naval power, Washington would avoid most of the pitfalls of *Yanqui* imperialism. A new U.S. policy would put to the test the Central Americans' claims that they recognize and accept America's legitimate regional security interests. As Tonelson said, "This back-to-basics approach would satisfy America's needs in Central America, if not all of our wants. And it suffers none of the fatal flaws of the major alternatives"—continuing U.S. support for the *Contras* or embracing the toothless Arias peace plan.[8]

Elsewhere in the world the Reagan Doctrine required the United States to choose between equally unsavory groups whose brutality often was distinguishable only by whether it was used to preserve power or seize it. It was hard to see how such choices advanced democratic principles, making it difficult to accept the Reagan Doctrine's claims that the United States was helping to spread democracy in the Third World. Although

7. Alan Tonelson, "Give 'em Hell," *The New Republic*, October 5, 1987, 21.
8. Ibid.

Jonas Savimbi's National Union for the Total Independence of Angola (UNITA) forces and Afghanistan's Islamic fundamentalist rebels might have usefully tied down Soviet and Soviet proxy forces, it was clear that they were not fighting for democracy. Although the distinction between totalitarian and authoritarian governments may be academically interesting, there was no credibility in a global democratic revolution whose supporters apologized for Chile, South Africa, and (nearly to the end) the Marcos-ruled Philippines.

Anticommunism successfully mobilized public support during the cold war years when the United States was still adjusting to its newly inherited global responsibilities. By the early 1980s, however, Americans had a more realistic view of the world and saw international politics in shades of gray rather than black and white. Afghanistan, Lebanon, and Vietnam, the Persian Gulf war, and other upheavals suggested that Third World nationalism had reduced the ability of both superpowers to influence the outcome of regional conflicts. Americans had rightfully learned to be wary when summoned by their leaders to an ideological crusade to make the world safe for democracy, and they had learned the hard way that the United States lacked the psychological and material resources to remake the world in its image. Not surprisingly, then, the Reagan Doctrine's militant anticommunism had little resonance with public opinion. Indeed, in 1981—when the mood of assertive America supposedly was at its peak—a public opinion survey found that "anticommunism as a national slogan or marching theme is increasingly on the wane, despite the Reagan Administration's attempts to emphasize it."[9] Perhaps—as the disciples of the Reagan Doctrine claimed—Americans were unwilling to sacrifice the nation's blood and treasure merely to uphold the balance of power. Vietnam had already demonstrated conclusively their unwillingness to sacrifice for ideology alone. The Reagan Doctrine ignored a basic lesson of American history: only when Americans believe that ideological aspirations and national security coincide does the domestic consensus needed to sustain overseas involvements emerge. The Reagan Doctrine failed to convince Americans that the United States should become involved in regional disputes that, at most, were only peripherally connected to its national security. The Reagan Doctrine also ran counter to Americans' desire for peace, to their instinctive and wise aversion to overseas adventures, and—most painfully and paradoxically for the doctrine's architects—to their most cherished democratic values. The Iran-*Contra* debacle made this failing all too obvious.

9. Daniel Yankelovich, "New Rules in American Life: Searching for Self-Fulfillment in a World Turned Upside Down," *Psychology Today*, April 1981, 35-91.

The Iran-*Contra* affair raised a basic issue: could a democracy be a superpower without compromising its domestic political principles? It was not the first time this issue had surfaced in American history. Those who believed the United States' pursuit of world power advanced the cause of liberty always disagreed sharply with those who believed a foreign policy of restraint was essential to preserving constitutional government at home. Although the worst fears — the suppression of liberty and the alteration of the constitutional system of checks and balances — of those who advocated restraint had not been realized, Vietnam, Watergate, and the Iran-*Contra* affair demonstrated that their concerns were not unfounded.

In this respect the implications of the Iran-*Contra* affair were especially disturbing. Despite having a valid case against a Sandinista regime that even a prudent, restrained America could not allow to become a Soviet military outpost, the administration was unable to rally public support for the *Contras'* cause and was able to gain only sporadic and tenuous congressional backing for its Central American policy. The illegal diversion of funds from the Iranian arms sales to the *Contras* happened because the Reagan Doctrine's backers were not willing to heed the stop sign erected by the democratic process.

The Iran-*Contra* case was not an aberration in the administration's record. It was a scandal waiting to happen from the beginning, because the Reagan Doctrine's underlying ideological ethos led its adherents to believe they had a monopoly on defining the "true" national interest. They viewed world politics as a Manichaean struggle between democracy and communism in which the United States was already at war in all but name. To prevail, the executive branch needed freedom to conduct diplomacy and covert actions unhampered by congressional or public oversight. Believing that their goals legitimated the use of any means, the doctrine's architects also believed they were justified in arrogating the right to ignore political and legal norms in pursuit of these so-called transcendent, moral objectives. The crusade against communism was deemed so vital it could not be constrained by abstract notions, such as the popular will or constitutional propriety. These attitudes have dangerous implications for the American governmental system.

When caught, the men who put the Reagan Doctrine into action — such as Rear Admiral John Poindexter and Lieutenant Colonel Oliver North — did not deny that the administration had ignored legal and constitutional norms and that it had lied to Congress and the American people about the Iran-*Contra* affair. On the contrary, they justified their actions, proudly painting themselves as clear-eyed "realists" who alone knew what was right for the country. Impatient with constitutional constraints, the Reagan Doctrine's defenders muttered darkly about an alleged conflict between the country's global responsibilities and its democratic system. They embraced Alexis de Tocqueville's indictment that "foreign policies demand scarcely any of those qualities which are peculiar to democracy [and] require, on the contrary, the perfect use of almost all those in which it is deficient."[10]

De Tocqueville's observation cannot simply be dismissed. The United States does not exist in isolation; as a great power in an anarchic international system, it lives, as all nations live, in the shadow of the perennial security dilemma. Granted, American freedom can be dramatically affected by outside events; at a certain point, external threats dictate the moment when foreign policy must take priority over domestic policy. Thus in 1940–41 president Franklin D. Roosevelt was justified in acting without congressional or public approval to make the United States a de facto belligerent — a Nazi victory would have posed a clear and present danger to U.S. security. But those who would make foreign policy paramount bear a heavy burden of proof. Only an extraordinarily compelling end justifies a foreign policy whose means require the circumvention of established political and constitutional processes.

The Reagan Doctrine's backers never met this burden of proof. This is largely because they fundamentally misperceived America's geostrategic relationship to external events. Historically, most great powers have had little choice about either the objectives or the means of their foreign policies. The geographical proximity of threatening rivals, a geopolitical reality for Europe's great powers, necessarily defined security as their overriding national objective, thereby subordinating domestic objectives to the requirement of protection from external attack. The United States, however, has seldom been compelled to subordinate domestic concerns to its foreign policy goals because of its relative immunity to external danger. The United States has built on its geographical advantage, maintaining invulnerability through nuclear weapons and superior military and economic capabilities.

Few events abroad truly affect U.S. security. Therefore, while the United States cannot be indifferent to overseas developments, it can invariably afford to react deliberately to them. This is a luxury denied to less powerful and less fortunate states. Ironically, the Reagan Doctrine's obsession with communism (something quite different from the geostrategic advance of Soviet power) led its adherents to choose a foreign policy that undermined America's own political institutions — even though they knew America's safety was not tangibly threatened.

The Iran-*Contra* scandal serves as a pointed reminder that Americans should treat with suspicion arguments that "national security" justifies a presidential detour around Congress and the Constitution. With its combination of Bismarck's cynicism and Wilson's self-righteous zeal, the Reagan

10. Alexis de Tocqueville, *Democracy in America* (New York: Vintage Books, 1954).

Doctrine was a prescription for political and moral disaster. The neo-conservatives' blend of an assertive, hard-edged "realism" with a messianic commitment to defeating communism everywhere with whatever means resulted in a dangerous brew.

Ideologically driven foreign policies such as the Reagan Doctrine have serious effects on domestic institutions. They instill in policymakers an "end justifies the means" mentality that places personal convictions above constitutional responsibilities. Such policies also disturb the considered allocation of power between branches of the government and encourage an intolerance that coarsens the quality of political discourse. (The McCarthy years offer the most dramatic example of this. Some Reagan Doctrine advocates showed signs of a McCarthy-like mentality, for example, when a former senior White House official accused congressional opponents of *Contra* aid of being communist sympathizers.) Moralistic, crusading foreign policies foster in decisionmakers a hubris from whence such disasters as Watergate and Iran-*Contra* spring. There was a sad and bitter irony in a foreign policy that, as had the Reagan Doctrine, sought to promote democracy abroad by subverting it at home.

The Gamble with Power

The Reagan Doctrine—a policy based on restoring U.S. power—had the perversely paradoxical effect of accelerating the United States' geopolitical decline. America's power had begun to erode well before Ronald Reagan took office. But instead of adjusting to adverse trends, the Reagan administration exacerbated them. At a time when prudence dictated that America reduce its global responsibilities, the United States incurred additional strategic obligations, further overtaxing U.S. resources and imperiling the nation's long-term economic prospects.

The signs of latent economic distress were evident everywhere. Even those who pretended all was well had their eyes opened by the stock market crash of October 19, 1987. It could no longer be denied that massive budget and trade deficits would eventually pose a Hobson's choice between high taxes or high inflation. The budget deficit grew with the Reagan Doctrine's large appetite for defense outlays, and the trade deficit was linked to America's global military burdens. Moreover, in a dazzlingly short time the United States had gone from being the world's leading creditor to being its leading debtor. America's share of total world manufacturing output had fallen from 50 percent in 1945 to 31.5 percent in 1980 and was projected to drop to 20 percent by the end of the century.[11]

11. Paul Kennedy, "The First World War and the International Power System," *International Security* (Summer 1984): 36–39.

Apart from its quantifiable direct costs (such as the nearly 60 percent of the U.S. defense budget consumed by America's NATO commitment), America, in its superpower role, had serious hidden costs that helped put the United States at a disadvantage in the global economy. While American capital and technology were diverted from the private to the military sector, Western Europe and Japan took advantage of U.S. security guarantees by enhancing their international competitiveness with resources that otherwise might have been spent on defense. Not surprisingly, it appeared there was a significant correlation between high military spending and slowed national growth. Thus, in 1983 Japan had devoted 1 percent of its gross national product to defense; in 1973–83 its national economic productivity improved 2.8 percent. The comparable figures for West Germany were 3.4 percent and 2.3 percent; France, 4.2 percent and 2.2 percent; the United States, 6.9 percent and 0.3 percent.[12]

Contrary to its supporters' assertions, the Reagan Doctrine was not a cheap means of countering communism. The best illustration of the Reagan Doctrine's likely ultimate costs is the fact that, notwithstanding the administration's seven-year buildup, studies have indicated that the gap between America's power and its strategic responsibilities has actually grown worse during the Reagan years. Unless this gap is closed, the United States risks political embarrassments and military setbacks abroad. By trying to close the power/interests gap through its own efforts, however, the United States risks crippling its increasingly fragile economy—the ultimate foundation of its national power. Unlike true conservatives, the administration and its neoconservative supporters failed to recognize that achieving a harmony between America's ambitions and its resources is a moral as well as strategic imperative: states that tolerate a persistent imbalance between the ends and means of policy inevitably run the risk of national ruin.

Hollow Triumphs: The Reagan Legacy

The Reagan years were not without some real foreign policy successes. Reagan did help restore a national pride and self-confidence damaged by Vietnam and the 1979–80 Iran hostage crisis; his administration also halted the adverse shift in the global balance of forces that occurred during the 1970s. The administration emphasized rightly that arms control was largely a symbolic issue and not the real centerpiece of U.S.-Soviet relations. At the same time, along with the Strategic Defense Initiative, the Reykjavík summit and the "double zero" arms accord with

12. Rich Atkinson and Fred Hiatt, "The Hidden Costs of the Defense Buildup," *The Washington Post*, December 16, 1985, national weekly edition, 10.

Moscow (removing from Europe intermediate- and short-range nuclear forces) implicitly acknowledged that American strategists had finally recognized that extended deterrence could not be credible in an age of nuclear parity.

Notwithstanding these pluses, history's overall verdict on the Reagan administration's foreign policy seems destined to be negative. Its successes have been incomplete and contain the seeds of their own undoing. For example, the short-term benefits of the administration's military buildup have to be evaluated against the long-term damage that the administration's strategic and budgetary policies will inflict on the economy. And although the administration understood that an obsessive focus on arms control anesthetized Americans (and West Europeans) to the Soviet threat, it failed to offer a politically salable alternative. The administration's early attempts to offer such an alternative by shifting the superpower agenda from arms control to regional conflicts and human rights did not work because these issues, though not unimportant, were essentially peripheral to the central aspects of the U.S.-Soviet competition.

Further, where an opportunity did exist to change the focus from arms control to more substantive issues, the administration apparently missed an important opening to make political and diplomatic progress in Europe. There, generational change in the Kremlin, intriguing hints of new flexibility in Soviet policies, and shifts in European attitudes all suggested the time was ripe for Washington to link superpower military disengagement to a political solution for Europe's division. But the administration's militant ideological bent blinded it to this possibility; instead, the administration remained wedded to the cold war objectives of "rollback" and "liberation." The unfortunate upshot of this rigidity was to leave Soviet leader Mikhail Gorbachev with the initiative in the political struggle to shape West European public opinion. Similarly, the effects of Reykjavík and the double-zero option cut to the heart of NATO's strategy, putting in question the Alliance's very raison d'être. Yet the administration made no attempt to initiate the long overdue restructuring of Atlantic relations that would relieve the United States of the disproportionate share of NATO's strategic risks and economic burdens it has shouldered for the past four decades.

With the close of the Reagan era eight more years have passed without the formation of a post-Vietnam foreign policy consensus. The American foreign policy debate continues to be dominated by the same two badly discredited paradigms—the Vietnam syndrome and the Munich analogy—that have been shaping policy dialogue for at least fifteen years. On the eve of the 1988 presidential primary season, political discourse remains polarized between those who want to see the United States as omnipotent and capable of opposing communist aggression everywhere and those who regard the use of force abroad with the profoundest skepticism. At least as far as foreign policy is concerned, the political center destroyed by Vietnam has yet to be rebuilt.

A new foreign policy synthesis is urgently needed. The halcyon days of American hegemony, when it seemed that the United States could pursue all its international objectives without immediate sacrifice or long-term economic consequences, are gone forever. America is still undergoing a difficult transition from a postwar to a post-hegemonic world. Yet, the Reagan administration acted as if it could turn the clock back to the 1950s, when America was at the zenith of its power. It did not understand that the end of American hegemony involves complex, objective geopolitical factors and cannot be reversed merely by an assertion of national will or by stirring, but hollow, references to a new "morning for America." The administration did not come to grips with the fundamental paradox of postwar U.S. foreign policy: America's globalist aspirations had the perverse effect of undercutting the very foundations of national power that had enabled Washington to pursue such an ambitious foreign policy in the first place. Similar to previous imperial powers, the United States has reached a critical point at which its world order aspirations are no longer compatible with its national interests.

By pursuing a foreign policy that further overstretched U.S. resources, the Reagan administration bequeathed a somber legacy to its successors. The next administration inevitably has no choice but to face the difficult task of launching a strategic retrenchment. Although a formidable undertaking, this process will complete America's postwar foreign policy agenda. Immediately after World War II Washington actively encouraged the diffusion of world economic power with the expectation that it would eventually result in a parallel diffusion of military power, thereby relieving the United States of many of containment's burdens. Only after the Korean War did U.S. policymakers become enamored with an "imperial" foreign policy; since that time U.S. foreign policy has manifested an ambivalence between pursuing the ideal of a more plural world versus maintaining America's hegemonic prerogatives.

Surprisingly, the Reagan administration—in which nationalist and unilateralist views have been well entrenched—did not begin the process of strategic readjustment that would have returned the country to the 1945-49 vision of America's world role. Its failure to do so showed just how far its foreign policy had departed from traditional Republican concepts. After all, such traditional conservatives as president Eisenhower and senator Robert Taft (R-OH) had been deeply concerned about the strains a globalist foreign policy would place on the national economy (concerns that were also shared by some Truman administration policymakers before the outbreak of the Korean War).[13] President Nixon and secretary of state Henry Kissinger were acutely aware of the United States' strategic overcommitment. They moved, though somewhat tentatively, to resolve America's overextension by devolving strategic responsibilities to U.S. security partners (the "Nixon Doctrine") and erecting a more multipolar world political structure (the "pentagonal balance of power").

For a moment, in November 1984, it appeared that the Reagan administration had finally awakened to the growing constraints on U.S. foreign policy. In a widely discussed speech, secretary of defense Caspar Weinberger stated that the United States no longer could afford to defend the Western world unilaterally. He outlined a rigorous set of guidelines, which, if followed, would have sharply curtailed America's involvement in the Third World. The moment passed. Administration policy remained as before. The United States would contribute more, not less, to its partners' security (through the U.S. defense buildup) and would not draw back from Third World commitments. By mid-1987 the "Weinberger Doctrine" had sunk beneath the waves of the Persian Gulf.

In the Persian Gulf the United States allowed itself to be drawn into a quintessential Third World struggle fueled by religious fundamentalism and nationalism, not by Soviet expansionism or communist ideology. The open-ended U.S. commitment seemed to steer Washington toward either war or another setback, as in Lebanon. Other than in protecting oil routes for Japan and Western Europe, a task for which those nations showed no enthusiasm, it was hard to see how America would benefit from its gulf commitment. The risks were plainly visible. U.S. intervention threatened to push Iran closer to the Soviet Union, an ironic result considering that the original impulse behind the events culminating in the Iran-*Contra* scandal was Washington's desire to open a possible rapprochement with post-Khomeini Iran. No matter how strong, the U.S. naval presence in the gulf cannot save the area's shaky conservative regimes from Islamic fundamentalist subversion. On the contrary, the U.S. presence incites even more turmoil. And, short of direct intervention, the United States cannot ensure Bagdad's ability to stave off military collapse in the Iran-Iraq War. Although Americans may wish to punish Iran for past transgressions, the desire for vengeance is likely to fade quickly if the U.S. foray in the gulf degenerates into a protracted and costly military venture. As 1987 drew to a close, it seemed that only the return of the now legendary luck of Ronald Reagan's first term would allow the United States to escape a serious political setback in the gulf.

13. See John Lewis Gaddis, *Strategies of Containment: A Critical Reappraisal of Postwar American Security Policy* (New York: Oxford University Press, 1982), chaps. 2 and 3.

As the United States prepares to enter the 1990s the successor generation — the first group of Americans in this century to have experienced something other than U.S. omnipotence in world politics — will have to formulate a new foreign policy synthesis. Theirs should be a policy of realism, not isolation; of restraint, not withdrawal. It should reflect an appreciation of both the possibilities and the limits of power and be based on a balance between resources and commitments. It should be a policy that protects the integrity of America's democratic institutions, preserves national strength, and husbands resources and expands them wisely.

Although Ronald Reagan ignored the consequences of the United States' geopolitical decline, his successors will not have this luxury. Unless U.S. policy is tailored to fit America's economic circumstances and the shifts in world political forces, the United States risks the kind of imperial decline experienced by Great Britain earlier this century.

There is room for optimism, however. Although America's power relative to the rest of the world has slipped markedly, the United States remains very powerful in absolute terms and retains formidable military and economic assets. Washington's ability to shape international political outcomes has diminished sharply, but America still plays a leading role on the world stage. With diplomatic skill and flexibility, the United States can manage the transition from crumbling bipolarity to a multipolar system in which the United States could occupy an enviable position as "holder" of the balance of power.

It is hardly certain that things will turn out well. The United States is not the first great power to shed an empire and seek a new world role — the historical record is not encouraging. The danger for a nation with deeply imbedded isolationist impulses is that what may begin as an orderly retrenchment could turn into a wholesale abandonment of international obligations. The United States' experience has been one of power and freedom of action. It will be painful for Americans and their leaders to acknowledge the growing constraints on national policy and to accept reduced status in world affairs. Yet if they wait too long, it may be too late. A series of major policy challenges await the emerging leaders of the next generation. Their success in holding back the deluge will determine whether or not history remembers Ronald Reagan as America's Louis XV.

20

Crafting a Strategic Compromise

Alton Frye

The long search for negotiated restraint on strategic nuclear weapons has now reached a decisive juncture. At no time since the strategic arms negotiations began in 1969 has there been such dramatic and substantial movement in Moscow's diplomatic positions. Mikhail Gorbachev has more than matched the important changes Ronald Reagan began to introduce in American proposals in 1983. The United States and the Soviet Union have worthwhile agreements in sight—but not in hand.

There are obvious pitfalls and barbs in recent Soviet proposals, just as some American proposals are, as Alexander Haig has said, clearly "nonnegotiable." At the same time the surprising surge toward an agreement on the so-called zero solution for intermediate nuclear forces (INF) is a caution against hard and fast assumptions about what is negotiable. Preoccupation with the relatively modest INF prospects should not, however, divert attention from the more compelling question: Are there fresh elements in the positions of the two sides which, blended with previously negotiated arrangements, could meet President Reagan's goal of deep cuts in offensive forces while strengthening strategic stability? There are, but it will take more creative statecraft than either government has yet shown to achieve that goal.

Both governments enter this phase of negotiations with a good deal of leverage—and a great many problems. United States technological prowess gives Moscow real concern about long-term trends, particularly when we recognize that excessive concentration on land-based intercontinental ballistic missiles (ICBMs) creates a relatively greater Soviet vulnerability than the United States has in its force structure. The Soviets' hot produc-

From *Society*, Vol. 24, No. 5 (July/August 1987): 44–50.

tion base must concern Americans. Indeed, if they were free to multiply warheads on individual missiles they could field more additional warheads on existing launchers than the entire United States ballistic missile modernization program will provide. That would be a foolish gesture in many ways but, if the two sides enter upon a peacock game of displaying strategic potential, one may expect some rather foolish attempts at intimidation.

At present, the United States and the Soviet Union are each headed toward substantially larger forces in the next decade. Unless interrupted by mutual agreement, current trends could move strategic force levels to 15,000 or more weapons on each side in the 1990s. There would be a degree of inertial stability at such force levels as neither side could expect to conduct an attack without incurring intolerable retaliation. But even if stability in the narrow sense persisted, movement toward ever higher force levels implies a degree of political tension that is itself a profound source of potential instability. It also suggests a declining confidence in the fragile regime of nonproliferation as other states judge the superpowers to have welched on their commitments under the nonproliferation treaty to curb their own nuclear deployments. It would further diminish the already slender prospects for an agreed transition to some measure of reliance on strategic defenses as a component of mutual stability.

The enormity of expenditures involved in this course would further compound the chronic budgetary pressures of the late 1980s. The American economy can surely outlast the Soviet in an expanded competition to produce arms, but Americans can no longer take comfort in the notion that they can spend the Soviets into the ground without unacceptable damage to their own economic well-being. Our own stake in a robust prosperity, no less than Moscow's severe economic distresses, argues for avoiding an open-ended strategic contest. By contrast, these problems could become more manageable in the context of declining force levels. It is reasonable to believe that political frictions could be modulated, although not eliminated, by successful collaboration in regulating the strategic competition. These considerations all reinforce the importance Reagan attributed to seeking genuine force reductions—and they highlight the necessity to compare possible outcomes in the negotiations not only with current force postures, but, more significantly, with those likely to evolve in the absence of diplomatic intervention. We cannot expect to solve all our strategic problems at the bargaining table. The realistic objective for diplomacy is to make those problems more soluble than they would be in a totally unregulated relationship.

For some time to come, both Soviet and American ICBMs are going to be theoretically vulnerable. While retaining the survivability advantages of the present triad, as the Scowcroft Commission described them in 1983, it is possible to use the reductions process to create incentives to move toward more stabilizing forces in the course of modernization. On that point, there is now a fair measure of agreement with strategic analysts in the Soviet Union. For example, there is a shared interest in the possibility of diminished reliance on fixed-base MIRVed missiles and in a gradual movement toward smaller, single-warhead missiles. Such missiles, even if mobile, could have difficulty surviving in an environment of continuing force growth. By contrast, at the numbers of warheads and force levels now being advocated by both Moscow and Washington as goals for reductions, the prospects for such so-called *Midgetman* missiles look increasingly promising.

Among other things, reductions of the scale now being mentioned would have major implications for the long-standing disparity between the two sides in missile throw-weight. Reagan and Gorbachev agreed at Reykjavik on numbers—6,000 warheads and 1,600 strategic launchers—that would have a powerful impact on relative throw-weight. That result was confirmed in Secretary of State Shultz's visit to Moscow in April 1987, when the Soviets agreed to trim their heavy ICBMs by 50 percent. Any plausible force the Soviets might field at the proposed levels would significantly narrow the gap in throw-weight between the United States and the Soviet Union, and it would sharply curtail the capacity of the Soviets to barrage deployment areas chosen for a *Midgetman* system. Senior Soviet analysts do not believe they can or should forestall United States pursuit of a smaller ICBM to assist the de-MIRVing option, although there is bound to be a considerable wrangle over the *Trident D-5* submarine-launched ballistic missile, designed to give submarines a precise counterforce capability for the first time.

A useful way to frame the current negotiating issues is to ask: What are the opportunities to shape a constructive agreement by splitting the difference between Soviet and American positions? Any such approach must always remain subject to a careful judgment about the impact of the result on stability and deterrence. There is no one right solution to the complex simultaneous equation relating Soviet and American forces. Within the bargaining possibilities that appear to be open, there are a wide range of outcomes that would serve American security better than the alternative which would pit increased United States deployments against massively augmented Soviet forces. Many roads lead to Damascus.

The focus here is on the immediate tasks in the central strategic negotiations. The analysis does not address the more visionary goal of the total abolition of nuclear weapons, adumbrated by President Reagan and General Secretary Gorbachev. Hasty discussions of such radical notions gave Reykjavik an air of recklessness that damaged confidence in the two sides' capacity to conduct more sober proceedings. Nor does this essay treat the tangled arguments over intermediate nuclear forces (INF), although successful negotiations on that front could lubricate the sticky wheels still jamming strategic diplomacy.

One can illustrate the opportunities to split the difference between Soviet and American positions by addressing three critical questions: (1) How can the two sides now make the "fair trade-offs" Reagan promised in 1983 between United States strategic advantages, mainly in bombers, and Soviet strategic advantages, mainly in ballistic missile throw-weight? (2) How can they relate a Soviet-American deal for reductions to the forces of other nuclear powers? (3) How can offensive reductions be related to the antiballistic missile (ABM) treaty and future possibilities for strategic defense?

The movement in the Soviet negotiating position, with all its problematic aspects, represents an adjustment of historic scale. It opens the way to a variety of trade-offs of the sort implied by the president. To begin with, even before the two leaders met in Iceland, explicit Soviet acceptance of the concept of a reduced ceiling on warheads or "charges" constituted a basic accommodation to Reagan's demands. It confirmed the position expressed by Deputy Foreign Minister Gyorgy Kornienko to Republican Senator William Cohen of Maine in early 1984. Kornienko made clear at that time that the Soviet Union accepted the need to reduce warheads as well as delivery vehicles.

To be fair, the Soviet suggestion of a reduction to 6,000 charges or weapons in some respects trumps prior United States offers. The American Strategic Arms Reduction Talks (START) proposal originally called for a limit of 5,000 ballistic missile reentry vehicles (RVs), but bombers were to be left free to deploy up to 8,000 air-launched cruise missiles (ALCMs). In that sense, the proposal was not a true reductions scheme, since it would have left the United States (and possibly the Soviet Union) with more strategic nuclear weapons than it currently deploys.

In light of the continued growth in Soviet forces since 1981, by virtually any interpretation the Soviets now offer to cut a larger number of weapons from their force than the United States then demanded. That is, to achieve a 5,000 RV limit in 1981, the Soviets would only have had to eliminate about 2,500 warheads from their arsenal; to achieve the 6,000 warhead level today, even if they used their entire quota for ballistic missiles and had no aircraft, they would have to take out over 3,000 RVs. More likely, they would allocate some weapons to the modern aircraft presently in development, meaning that reductions in ballistic missile RVs would be still larger.

The offer of a further sublimit on the fraction of weapons that could be deployed in any one category of delivery vehicle goes a considerable distance toward the president's previous insistence that no more than 2,500 warheads be deployed on ICBMs. In principle, the Soviets could deploy up to 3,600 warheads in that mode—a difference of little military meaning. Frankly, neither the Soviet nor the American proposal offered significant relief for the hypothetical vulnerability of ICBMs; depending on how concentrated the ICBM force was, either 2,500 or 3,600 hard-target killers would pose a substantial threat against them.

Shortly before meeting Gorbachev at Geneva in 1985, President Reagan signaled his interest in a compromise on this point and the two sides have continued to scout for common ground on the issue. It would probably be wise to avoid too stringent a rule, for the simple reason that the United States may prefer a larger deployment in the submarine missile force. In the course of reductions the Soviet Union would move toward a more dispersed and hence more stable ICBM force since it defies reason to believe that they would concentrate their weapons in a few increasingly vulnerable silos by retaining the bulk of their SS-18 force. That is the logic of their recent agreement to lower warheads on heavy missiles from over 3,000 to 1,500.

The most crucial difficulty in attempting to accommodate Soviet and American positions, as so far outlined, may concern the relationship of bomber-carried weapons to those on ballistic missiles. As a practical matter, the United States attempt to protect an option to deploy up to 400 heavy bombers and 8,000 ALCMs bore little resemblance to the probable shape of the American bomber force. It now stands at little more than 250 platforms, and programs now in view look toward further phasing out of B-52s as the air force completes the B-1 program and moves forward with the Advanced Technology Bomber, dubbed *Stealth*. Cost factors alone argue strongly against the numbers originally advanced at START. More plausible deployment totals for ALCMs fell in the 2,500 to 3,000 range.

In one of his most dramatic departures, Reagan altered the American demand for an almost open-ended ALCM quota. With the concurrence of the Joint Chiefs of Staff, the president conveyed to the Soviets a willingness to meet the 6,000 warhead total by restraining ALCMs to 1,500. Yet, despite professions of interest in eliminating all nuclear weapons, the United States could not absorb reductions to the level of 6,000 weapons if all bomber weapons were counted as equal to those on missiles. That is why the decisive event at Reykjavik may well have been Gorbachev's acceptance of a more lenient standard to account for weapons carried on bombers.

Several factors justify treating bomber weapons differently from missile warheads—and there are equitable principles on which to base an accord. The first such principle is that limits on warheads should apply to those which are independently deliverable. To contribute to stable deterrence, bombers must be capable not only of escaping attacks on their bases but of penetrating the heavy Soviet air defenses. (The proliferation of Soviet air defenses has not induced a tendency to cut back on the number of weapons carried by American bombers—quite the contrary. There is a lesson in that experience.) So far as gravity bombs and short-range attack missiles are concerned, the platforms have to reach each of their targets in sequence to deliver their weapons. In light of these factors it makes sense to discount those weapons substantially in any inventory of "charges" against a reduced ceiling.

Fortunately, we already have a precedent for doing so. In the SALT II agreement, bombers without air-launched cruise missiles are equated with single-warhead ballistic missiles. In presentations before the Soviet Academy of Sciences in 1984, Senator Cohen, Democratic Senator Joseph Biden of Delaware, and I argued that this should be the principle for counting non-ALCM aircraft in any reductions agreement. Then, and in many subsequent discussions with Soviet officials and analysts, no one challenged this concept. The Soviets' preoccupation is with the mounting inventory of cruise missiles, and there a very different standard is in order.

In the previous negotiations we discover a suggestive counting rule for cruise-missile carriers. The parties agreed that they would not initially deploy more than twenty ALCMs on each heavy bomber, although they reserved the right to install up to twenty-eight ALCMs at a later date. They also agreed that any aircraft equipped to carry long-range ALCMs would be defined as a heavy bomber for purposes of the delivery vehicle limitations. In those negotiations the Soviets yielded on their demand to ban all cruise missiles. They now have begun a limited ALCM program of their own, although it is not clear that they need it against the exceedingly limited air defenses deployed in North America.

The asymmetries in United States and Soviet forces can be accommodated in a reduction regime by building on the previous negotiations to establish counting rules for bombers comparable to those SALT II applied for ballistic missile warheads. Retaining the precedent treating non-ALCM bombers as equal to single-warhead missiles (and devising ways to distinguish them from ALCM-carriers), and setting an ALCM-bomber counting rule at 20 or so, the parties could make reductions to a nominal 6,000 weapons without precluding a robust bomber force. Depending on how one chose to use the quota, one could field 50 to 100 cruise missile carriers and 100 to 200 other bombers, a force not too different from that currently deployed. The Soviets would probably field a smaller number of ALCM carriers, taking a slightly larger fraction of their quota in ballistic missiles.

Other Nations' Nuclear Forces

These precedents also have a bearing on another key controversy. The United States has often raised the *Backfire* bomber issue, which the parties had set aside in 1979, just as the Soviets frequently press for counting United States planes deployed in Europe as strategic systems. Yet under the precedent all of these aircraft would be counted as only one unit, for purposes of warhead accounting. If the *Backfire* were deployed with ALCMs it would be defined as a heavy bomber and captured by both the delivery vehicle limitations as the costly warhead charge of twenty per platform proposed here. Without ALCMs these systems are relatively light weights in the overall accounts. All of them have limited capability against the other country's heartland, but they represent trivial factors at the force levels now being considered. For that reason it makes little sense for either side to press its position adamantly. It should be possible to split the difference by both sides receding on these demands. The United States should relax its insistence on counting the *Backfire* as a central strategic system and the Soviets should do the same with regard to our forward-based aircraft. This seems to mesh with the inclinations expressed during and since the encounter at Reykjavik.

These suggestions illustrate some of the central possibilities for balanced trade-offs between bomber and missile forces. There is bountiful room for argument about details, but if there is to be agreement on these issues, it almost surely lies somewhere in the zone described.

The protracted deadlock over INF has been broken by a Soviet decision to abandon the long-standing demand that British and French systems should be included and to accept an INF accord separate from strategic limitations. Yet the existence of these countries' nuclear capabilities lurks in the background as a future complication, even if the superpowers make their way toward initial reductions of strategic forces.

Over the longer term a Soviet-American deal is unlikely to endure unless they can devise a tolerable stance regarding the nuclear forces of other countries. We cannot negotiate about the nuclear deterrents of our British and French allies, but we cannot expect to bargain conclusively with Moscow unless we take account of the existence of those forces. Gorbachev's interesting overture for separate negotiations with Britain and France remains on the table. It has profound political implications, but it also reflects a reality with which we must contend: superpower reductions will not continue for long if other states increase their forces without restraint.

We come to this dilemma: we and the Soviets cannot negotiate limits on other countries but, for understandable reasons, they presently decline to enter negotiations. We cannot allow attempts at superpower restraint to be hostage to the policies of other states, however friendly they may be. Accordingly, the time has come to shift the focus of discussion with Moscow and to lay down a clear marker linking superpower reductions goals to other governments' deployment plans. To be specific, the United States and the Soviet Union should declare that if any other state increases its deployments above a stated level—perhaps 15 percent of the lower levels to which the superpowers are moving—each reserves the right to adjust its forces proportionately. If, for example, a third country deploys 16 percent of the warhead level agreed upon by Moscow and Washington, we and the Soviets would be free to deploy an additional 1 percent of that level.

Reserving the right does not necessarily mean exercising the right. That would depend on a prudential judgment to be made under the circumstances at the time. The purpose of the rule is to signal to other states that they, too, have a stake in superpower restraint. It seeks to discipline decisions elsewhere by making clear in advance that excessive buildups on their part will jeopardize the process of superpower arms reductions. It would pose for other governments the hard political choice of whether they would prefer to exercise reasonable self-restraint in their programs or to legitimize countervailing deployments by one or both superpowers.

The United Kingdom has already indicated a sympathetic view of the need to display commensurate restraint in its nuclear programs if the United States and the Soviet Union actually embark upon major reductions. More equivocally, the French have stated a contingent willingness to participate in future arms discussions if Moscow and Washington actually cut back their forces. The Chinese have also begun to hint at interest in the arms control process; Beijing has already stated its desire for Soviet INF reductions in Europe to be matched by elimination of similar systems in Asia. An understanding of the sort proposed is a straightforward method for addressing one of the most intractable obstacles to meaningful reductions in superpower arsenals. It would help make possible an agreement now and, without presuming to bind any state in advance, would create a wholesome context for intra-alliance consultations for future nuclear deployments.

Americans and Soviets are not going to be able to agree on curbing other countries' nuclear forces. The most that they can do is agree on how they will react if those forces grow so large as to undermine the reductions regime they are trying to establish.

ABM Treaty and Strategic Defense

The impasse in Iceland made evident that all prospects for offensive force reductions hinge critically on the ABM treaty and, more generally, on what the two sides do about strategic defenses. It is also evident that Reagan's vigorous interest in such defenses has simultaneously energized and immensely complicated the negotiating process. Can we sort out those complications and craft a bargain that meets the contending objectives set forth by Reagan and Gorbachev? It depends a great deal on which of the several themes struck by the two leaders gain priority.

Is the American aim to end the erosion of the AMB treaty, as Secretary of State Shultz emphasized to former Soviet Foreign Minister Andrei Gromyko in January 1985? Is the United States government, in Robert McFarlane's words to the British shortly thereafter, "under no illusions" that it would be possible to make a unilateral transition to a defense-dominant world? Are the criteria stated by Paul Nitze—feasibility, cost-effectiveness, survivability, and cooperation in any transition—to govern the Strategic Defense Initiative (SDI)? Will the SDI, as Reagan has repeatedly assured allies and citizens, be limited to research within the boundaries of the ABM treaty as interpreted since its inception? Will the United States be willing to share defensive technology with the Soviet Union? From the answers to these questions flow certain consequences for relating defensive programs to offensive reductions.

Much confusion continues to surround these topics, but some elements are growing clearer. The thorough and persuasive analyses by Democratic Senator Sam Nunn of Georgia have rebutted the ill-considered claims by administration officials that the president has an option to interpret the ABM treaty "broadly," effectively amending out of existence some of its central constraints. Congressional cutbacks in funding for the SDI reveal persistent doubts about the program's concept, pace, and direction, reflecting particular concern that the SDI conform to the original interpretation of the ABM treaty. The Soviets have begun to concede, notably during Shultz's mission to Moscow, that the treaty affords considerable latitude for testing certain kinds of advanced defensive technologies at fixed sites on the ground.

Diplomacy cannot proceed unless it has a clear view of the context in which it must function. Three aspects of that context deserve emphasis. First, whatever the SDI program turns out to be, it is also an anti-SDI program. For every strategic defense concept yet identified promising countermeasures are already described, often exploiting the same technologies. As Harold Brown has written, many of the lethal technologies being contemplated are even more promising for suppressing the defenses than for defending against ballistic missiles. For the pursuit of SDI is not an exercise in unopposed science. It is a contest of man against man, not man against nature.

To paraphrase Malcolm Muggeridge, even a great success in SDI could prove to be the hallmark of failure. The problem is not only that unilateral efforts to erect heavy defenses will increase pressures on the other side to expand its offenses. There is also a grim and poorly understood paradox: rising defenses are likely to compel greater targeting of cities, not less. In order to maintain deterrence in the face of such defenses, the military targeter must ensure that he holds the other side's most valuable targets hostage. Faced with declining confidence in the number of his weapons likely to penetrate, he must assign a larger fraction of his force to the highest value targets. Thus, an imperfect defense may be good enough to erode the opponent's capacity to mount a counterforce attack; unless it is perfect, deterrence will require increased targeting of population centers, the opposite of Reagan's goal.

More reassuring, Soviets and Americans should recognize that they have a long time to refine controls over strategic defenses. Pressures for early deployment of some SDI elements enjoy little support beyond a narrow faction. The hypothetical technologies of most concern lie well in the future. There may be a role for discriminating applications of defensive technologies, if the two sides find that advantageous. If there is any possibility for an agreed transition to partial reliance on such systems, it depends almost entirely on how the two sides manage their intense offensive competition.

For Reagan, the fundamental fact is that he can improve his successors' options for strategic defenses only if he achieves a meaningful start on offensive force reductions as the basis for a cooperative transition to a different regime. For Gorbachev, the fundamental fact is that the most potent guarantee against a unilateral American attempt to break out of current restraints on strategic defense would be an ongoing process of offensive reductions—a contribution to strategic stability few would wish to jeopardize in a risky and costly spurt toward reliance on SDI. The collapse of hopes for progress on arms reductions, on the other hand, could swing sentiment in favor of the premature commitment to partial SDI deployment which was rejected in the United States administration in early 1987.

Logically, reductions in the threat have an intrinsic priority over defenses against the threat. It is better to eliminate one thousand weapons from the other side's forces than to attempt to destroy them after they are launched. In that sense Reagan was on solid ground when he began his approach to these questions with his speech at Eureka College.

Recent changes in the Soviet position offer dramatic new opportunities for pursuing the president's first priority. They also reveal a considerably more reasonable approach to the question of research on strategic defenses. Well before the latest glimpses of the Soviet attitude, analysts close to Gorbachev and the Soviet Defense Ministry were suggesting welcome movement on their part. Not only does one hear a recognition that the basic research authorized by the ABM treaty can proceed; there is even the suggestion that many aspects of the SDI as now defined would be acceptable. For example, the bulk of activities now funded in the so-called SATKA elements of the SDI—technologies for surveillance, acquisition, tracking, and kill assessment—could be acceptable to the Soviets. These include a number of space-based technologies, several of which could serve multiple purposes.

What would not be acceptable would be development, testing, and deployment of such components and systems as lethal space-based lasers. But, as Democratic Senator Henry Jackson of Washington emphasized to his colleagues in the Armed Services Committee before deciding to vote for the ABM treaty in 1972, the treaty clearly prohibits those activities. That is the conclusion reiterated by Senator Nunn. Unless the United States elects to withdraw from the treaty, which is contrary to Reagan's stated purpose, what is needed at this stage is a definitional negotiation to specify more fully those development and testing activities that would infringe the treaty. That same discussion would have to redress the Soviet effort to exploit the space tracking loophole in the treaty to justify the early warning radar being installed at Krasnoyarsk. Moscow has now invited negotiations of this nature.

Thos technical, definitional negotiations might best take place in the Standing Consultative Commission (SCC) established by the Salt I agreements, which has in earlier years worked very productively to handle similar problems. They could focus primarily on precluding the introduction into space of weapons-grade lasers and particle beams above certain output potentials, of large mirrors, and of power sources above certain scales. Action on those issues could be sufficient to assuage Soviet concerns that the United States' true intention is to break out of the ABM treaty. It would permit both sides to continue substantial research under the rubric of strategic defense, as the president is determined to do.

Even if the treaty provisions are clarified and tightened, there will remain a chasm of mistrust between the two sides. If additional assurances of good-faith compliance with ABM treaty obligations are forthcoming, how can the two sides make them credible enough to accept the risks of beginning offensive force reductions? One possibility would be to phase down the offensive systems through a kind of escrow procedure. The procedure could build upon and vary the precedents established in the SCC for dismantlement and destruction of strategic weapons.

The two sides would remove missiles from operation and make their silos or submarines accessible to national means of observation. Silo roofs would be removed, perhaps other fixtures dismantled; submarines would be beached with conning towers and other critical components removed; aircraft would be mothballed without engines and possibly with control surfaces detached. Each side would carry out these measures in ways permitting the observer to determine that the launchers contained no operable weapons and that they could not function without significant, detectable refurbishment.

Missiles taken out of service would be diassembled, under surveillance, and their stages stored in separate, identified locations at agreed distances from each other. Storage sites would be accessible to independent monitoring, either by roofs removable on demand, continuous television and seismic monitors, or other agreed methods, not excluding on-site inspection. The purpose would be to reduce operational capabilities in ways which, if either country crosses the threshold to impermissible defensive deployments, would permit the other to reverse its offensive reductions in a timely manner. The lead time for reintroducing such weapons into the operational forces would be much less than required to install significant defenses.

Escrow, as distinct from elimination, would have some costs and risks of its own. Mothballing and storage of segregated components are not cheap, and we would have to contend with the problem of preventing other missiles which have been produced and assembled clandestinely from being installed in existing launchers. Those problems should be manageable by strict requirements to place launchers in a condition from which they could not function without substantial, time-consuming, and detectable reconstruction. As an intermediate form of force reduction, the escrow concept could enable reductions of deployed forces now, even in the midst of great suspicion between the parties. It could contribute immediately to relieving problems of crisis instability. Procedures of this type may be necessary, given the need both governments feel to hedge against an ABM breakout on the other side.

This discussion treats only a few of the important disputes that will have to be resolved if there is to be a Soviet-American agreement reducing nuclear weapons on a meaningful scale. Its purpose is only to illustrate that there are practical approaches to bridging the gap between the two sides. The recent exchanges between the two governments invite the effort to do so.

In diplomacy there are two cardinal virtues: patience and a sense of timing. During his first term, Reagan displayed the first virtue in abundance. He has been rewarded with the most forthcoming Soviet counterproposals in the history of arms control negotiations. The question now is whether the administration has the sense of timing and the skill to seize upon this opportunity.

Many have lampooned the president's performance at Reykjavik as suggesting amateurism and impatience. It undoubtedly alarmed allies and Americans alike. Yet there is a fine line between the reckless and the bold, and it is fair to note that the erratic course of events at the Iceland summit did generate movement on many fronts. The president's behavior may owe a great deal to his sense that the moment is at hand for reaping the harvest from his investment in steadfastness toward Moscow.

Even a critic of that summit must acknowledge that it elicited extraordinary shifts in the negotiations. To paraphrase Donald Regan, "the United States put its proposals on the table, the Soviets gave in on everything—and then they linked it to SDI." That is not a bad summary, and it underscores the fact that Reykjavik created a new context in which major reductions actually seem achievable and a sharper focus on resolving the differences over SDI as the prerequisite to deep cuts. Most important, the stream of initiatives and concessions put forward by Gorbachev leave no question that he places high value on striking a bargain with Reagan, knowing that this president is uniquely situated to provide the legitimacy needed for an arms control process that must continue for many years beyond his term in office.

In considering the end game in Reagan's diplomacy with Moscow, it is vital to realize that the capacity to wait it out, the option to exercise patience, has shifted to the new leadership in Moscow. Politically, Gorbachev's style and initiative are bound to buy him something in Western opinion. The West will no longer have the free ride associated with the images of inept or unappealing leaders of our principal adversary. Psychologically, the arrival of a young politician at the top of the Soviet regime creates very different expectations and time horizons in Moscow.

When Reagan completes his second term, he will have presided over almost one-fifth of the entire nuclear age. But Gorbachev will be younger in the year 2,000 than Reagan is now. He may well preside over one-third of the nuclear era. That is a change of the utmost significance in gauging the current diplomatic window. If our sense of timing fails us, if we respond without imagination to the opening that now appears, the patience and steadfastness we have shown may avail us little.

21

When Budget Cuts Count: Conventional Defense and British Strategy

David Robertson

... it is difficult for anyone not in the know to discuss how changes in strategy would affect the spending pattern in the future. That pattern is closely guarded; the public has no access to the long-term costings.

—Admiral of the Fleet Lord Hill-Norton, former Chief of the Defence Staff

The General Strategic Context

People often talk about Britain's "strategic choices." Britain has few choices to make at the conventional level, and even fewer are grand enough to warrant the adjective "strategic." There are policy choices, but they are perhaps more aptly described by the Soviet conception of decisions at the operational level.[1] These are decisions about how to organize and structure forces for operations within only one theatre, and against a background of preordained political goals.[2] The reason is that the United Kingdom's conventional forces are far too closely integrated into the North Atlantic Treaty Organization (NATO), and too much designed for the single purpose of fighting Central Europe's next world war to leave room for genuinely strategic problems to occur.

Unlike both the United States and France, where there is a real element of choice about actual full intervention on the central front, British conventional forces are more akin to West Germany's, and one does not easily talk about the Federal Republic's "strategies."[3]

This is an original contribution prepared for this volume.

There are two genuinely "strategic" choices that are talked of in the United Kingdom, by which I mean policy decisions that could be made, changing a long-term consensus. These would have radical implications for what 90 percent of men, machines, and money are currently occupied with, but they are not "conventional" decisions in either the ordinary or the jargon sense of that word. The best known of these strategic preoccupations is the whole question of Britain's nuclear role.

As an aside, it is necessary here to make a comment on which political parties are to be taken seriously in the United Kingdom at the moment. After the huge Conservative victory in 1987 two facts were obvious. One was that their main contender, the Labour Party, would not soon recover from its third defeat in less than ten years. But the second point was that the would-be third force, the Liberal-Social Democrat Alliance, was in even worse shape. Subsequent events have only served to strengthen this impression. By the spring of 1988 the Labour Party was facing yet another internecine battle between the left and right wings for the leadership. The Social Democrat Party (SDP) and the Liberal Party had just bungled an attempt to merge into one party, which attempt had already lost the SDP their leader, David Owen. However, British politics is in such turmoil that no one can be discounted. Consequently this paper still treats all four parties as important, and on the whole treats them as wedded to the policies they were last clearly identified with, in the 1987 election.

It is generally accepted that the Labour Party's policy of unilateral nuclear disarmament (with or without the sub-policy of removing American nuclear bases from the United Kingdom) would have profound implications for Britain's purely NATO role. This is held to be true for two distinct reasons. On the one hand, those who, like the Conservatives and the Social Democrats, are committed to a nuclear role believe this to *be* part of the United Kingdom's contribution to NATO. If this is true, it must follow that removal of such a contribution will rebound on other forces tasked to NATO.

Others, possibly again including the SDP but not, officially anyway, the Conservatives, argue that the Trident replacement for Polaris is so expensive that it is *buying it* that will rebound on the United Kingdom's conventional contribution. This paper is not an appropriate place to discuss Trident. No effort will be made to judge the merits of the policy. Nonetheless, the cost implications are believed by many to be great, and these are treated later.

The other genuinely strategic issue is perhaps only a live option in restricted circles; it revolves round the question of Britain's force-projection capacity "out of theatre." It is uncontroversial to say that this is not large. Estimates of how much of the defence budget can be attributed to the out-of-theatre role vary because of definitional problems, but there is a rough consensus. David Greenwood, perhaps Britain's most respected defence economist, puts the out-of-theatre costs for 1986–87 at around 5 percent; this author sets them at nearer 7 percent, but the order of magnitude is the same.[4] What is also uncontroversial is that the capacity would be even smaller had it not been for the Falklands' conflict, which temporarily halted a policy of winding down such force-projection assets even further.

Partisan politics exaggerate the real policy differences in this area. The Labour Party likes to pick on a tendency in the first years of the first Thatcher administration (1979–83) to increase funding for this task, and to make much of the annual cost of "Fortress Falklands." In fact none of her four defence secretaries since 1981 has seriously believed that Britain could afford a real out-of-theatre role, and no other political party disagrees with them. It is not even clear that the one serious force-projection task the United Kingdom has *inside the NATO commitment,* to reinforce the northern flank in Norway with the Royal Marines, is safely catered for, given the hesitancy of the government to replace the aging amphibious warfare ships properly.

The only effective domestic lobby for out-of-theatre provision is, unsurprisingly, the Royal Navy, whose political wings have probably been clipped by organizational changes inside the Ministry of Defence (MOD) since 1981. Their most extreme advocates, it is true, would like to see a major reversal of Britain's postwar conventional strategy towards what they call, echoing an American debate, Britain's *traditional* maritime strategy. No one can seriously deny that a move to such a strategy could not be contained within any conceivable defence budget without very major cuts to Britain's prime Central European NATO commitment.

Hill-Norton, perhaps the most outspoken supporter of naval power (including Trident) is particularly keen to stress that force structure must be tailored to real national interests and that doctrine should derive from these perceptions, and not be written to defend what actually exists. His major theme is the need for out-of-area force projection and a worldwide naval presence. Unfortunately he clearly commits his own sin. "Such a capability, out to the limits of our economic sphere of interest, requires sea- and air-portable 'all arms' force, including naval, marine, army and air elements, at about reinforced-brigade-group strength with appropriate logistic support."[5]

But nowhere does Hill-Norton begin to explain why this force size, which just happens to be almost exactly what the United Kingdom does have in five Infantry Brigade plus Royal Marine Commando units, is just the right size. Indeed from the grandiose account he gives of the United

Kingdom's far-flung economic interests and intervention needs, it is obviously too small.[6] Though there is very little likelihood of this change in strategy occurring, it cannot be dismissed. Even the MOD was sufficiently worried by its advocates to include a strong rebuttal of the argument in the 1986 *Statement on the Defence Estimates*.[7]

Nonetheless there is an argument for force projection. It has less to do with the practical protection of United Kingdom interests in the short term. The argument is that the leading nation in the NATO Alliance, the United States, has for many years complained at the failure of European NATO countries to take their share of the burden of defending general Western interests in areas like the Persian Gulf and the Indian Ocean. It is hard to know how strongly this problem of alliance management weighs with the British government, but it must act to reinforce whatever vestigial attachment there is to a world police role.

These questions, of Britain's nuclear role, and of its out-of-theatre role, can best be seen as highlighting the strategic background against which the actual working out of conventional defence policy over the rest of this century will take place. Defence policy in Britain has been deeply consensual for most of the postwar period. The consensus, since the East-of-Suez decision of the Labour government in the mid-1960s has essentially been that Britain would have a strategic nuclear force and would not otherwise expend serious money on anything except the NATO commitment.

We shall assume that the second part of the consensus holds. As far as the nuclear issue goes, we shall argue that the cost implications for conventional force structures are much less than is often believed, and that we can safely consider the conventional future as though *both* of these elements in the long-term consensus remain valid. This does not mean that radical changes may not have to be made in the size and nature of the United Kingdom's NATO contribution, but that they are unlikely to arise because of major strategic rethinking. Consequently the rest of this paper will focus on three questions: (1) economic constraints on defence expenditure; (2) political constraints on conventional defence; (3) operational consequences of these constraints.

The Alliance Context

It is obvious that one cannot discuss the future defence policy of a NATO member state, especially one for whom the NATO commitment is as central as Britain's, as though the other member states did not exist. Unless something is badly wrong with NATO, developments in the other two major partners, the United States and the Federal Republic of Germany (West Germany), must impact on Britain. Let us very briefly look at two or three trends facing these alliance partners, which may seriously affect the background against which the United Kingdom has to plan for the rest of this century.

The United States is facing much the same budgetary freeze on military expenditure over the next few years as is the United Kingdom. No congressional leaders believe that the Department of Defense can hope for more than inflation adjustment to their budget, and some doubt even this will be forthcoming fully.[8] This financial squeeze has started somewhat too early, as it has in Britain, for the full fruits of the 1979–80 defence build-up to be achieved. Targets like the "600 ship" navy will be achieved only, if at all, by cheating.[9]

There are regular reports of important new arms projects being cancelled or held up. These typically involve projects deemed necessary for the modernized warfare planned for the central front: new army helicopters, joint radar and target acquisition research, and so on. In general the army seems to be suffering. Recent reports in the *Washington Post* on "The Reagan Build Up," for example, show how much of the modernization programme for main battle tanks and armored fighting vehicles is way behind schedule.[10]

All of this has to be seen against a background of (largely civilian) enthusiasm for the Emerging Technology (ET) weaponry, which is supposed to make Deep Strike not only viable but a way of lowering the nuclear threshold. Many circles in the U.S. Army in fact fear that the quasi-commitment to Deep Strike may lower the nuclear threshold if the doctrine gets firmly entrenched but the super-conventional weapons to carry it out do not appear, leaving commanders with *only* tactical nuclear weapons with which to apply it.[11]

From NATO's viewpoint financial shortages in United States military planning have an even more sinister implication. The ever slumbering fear of serious United States troop withdrawals from Europe is fully awake again. It is not only the media, in Europe as much as in America, who think troop withdrawals are on the way.[12] Informed sources inside the Pentagon can be heard to predict withdrawals, not for re-deployment, but to be brought back to the United States and just "let go" within a short period. Indeed, unless U.S. military commanders ignore all their other commitments, there seems no way of avoiding this, given that the army in 1988–89 cannot afford to recruit up to its authorized totals.

A situation where the U.S. Army and Air Force in Europe are both less well equipped than their doctrine calls for, and slimmer in numbers, would have two different consequences for Britain. On the one hand, the political attraction of withdrawing some of the British contingent from West Germany would be much greater because the American action would serve as a face-saving precedent. On the other hand, the operational problems for what remained of the British Army of the Rhine (BAOR), if not supported by United States troops to the same extent as in the past, would be even more severe.

Such problems will be exacerbated by any weakening in West Germany's ability to protect itself. Yet such a weakening is almost inevitable. The demographic problems facing the Federal Republic's conscription system are well known. Some estimates suggest that the pool from which conscripts are drawn may be cut by as much as 50 percent by the end of the century.[13] There is very little the Federal Republic's government can do about this. The problem cannot be solved by increased spending on equipment to act as a force multiplier; even if the old Lanchester Law is not exactly right, "force multiplication" would have to involve huge costs, if possible at all, to remedy this situation.

Nor is it clear that there is the political will in West Germany to support much of an increase in defense expenditure. The richest European member state was one of the majority that failed to meet the 1977 3 percent annual defence-increase figure, and has never spent as much as either France or the United Kingdom as a percentage of its gross national product (GNP). Currently it spends even less than the United Kingdom *in absolute terms,* though its GDP is half again as much as that of the United Kingdom.[14] This is not to deny that there are many good justifications for West Germany's degree of burden sharing, but simply to note that even if more money could solve the demographic problem, it probably would not be forthcoming.

To put these figures into context, it can be noted that the West German regular army of 335,600 would suffer a 16 percent cut if its numbers fell by the total size of the BAOR—and 16 percent is most certainly within the parameters of the demographic cuts. Similarly a cut the size of the whole BAOR in the U.S. Army in Europe would represent less than a 27 percent troop withdrawal—and if the U.S. Senate is at all serious about troop withdrawals, such a proportion could be in the cards. In other words, likely, perhaps unstoppable, trends could lead the BAOR to fight alongside armies that had been reduced by *twice* its own regular strength. Any serious inadequacies the BAOR itself suffers or may come to suffer from will be multiplied tremendously by these trends.

Economic Constraints on Defence Expenditure

The Situation

Since 1979 Britain has experienced an unprecedented peacetime increase in defence expenditure, so that 1985 expenditure was at least 20 percent higher in real terms than 1979 expenditure. Heady though they may have been, these days are already over. The defence expenditure plans announced in spring 1986 involve at least a 6 percent cut in real terms between 1986–87 and 1988–89. As early as 1981 the government admitted that the defence budget was overstretched, even assuming the continuance of the 3 percent per year real increase. In the controversial White Paper *The Way Forward* it was stated that "even the increased resources we plan to allocate cannot adequately fund all the force structures and all the plans for their improvement we now have."[15]

Since then two factors have come into play. First, the defence review of 1981 *was never carried out*. The Falklands intervened, saving the Royal Navy from the 30 percent cut in surface vessels planned. Secondly, the 3 percent increase has been abandoned. It is not only radical critics or academic defence economists who believe that the defence plans even as they were in the early 1980s, let alone what might need to be planned for in the future, simply cannot be achieved within existing financial constraints. The House of Commons Select Committee on Defence is dominated by defence-minded Tory MPs. Yet they have repeatedly called attention to this underfunding. The committee has stated on record that it does not believe the government can manage the procurement plans it has on the projected nongrowth figures.

These include not only Trident (perhaps £10 billion between 1985 and 1995) but also the European Fighter Aircraft (EFA). It is not yet clear quite what the cost of this program will be. The Tornado will have cost £17 billion in 1985 prices. Cost growth in each generation of modern aircraft is accepted as huge, and it is not thinkable that the EFA can realistically be costed at much less than Trident. The most recent estimate prices the aircraft at £25 million, and reports the Royal Air Force (RAF) as requiring around 240 of them. So without allowing for the almost inevitable price escalation, the cost will be some £6 billion, to be spent over the same period as the major Trident expenditure.

Just these two projects will account for an average 10 percent of the total defence budget, and well over 20 percent of the procurement budget each year for the next decade. Ten percent of this year's equipment budget would be over £900 million. But *the total* equipment budget for all land forces is to be only £1.7 billion. Where are the new Challenger main battle tanks, the Multiple Launch Rocket System, the new Warrior (MCV 80) armored personnel carriers coming from?[16]

They are not all going to come, is the answer. In fact, between the spring of 1986, when the defence estimates were published, and the end of the year an entirely unplanned extra expenditure of around £800 million was added to the Ministry of Defence's (MOD) problems. Though it is hardly a recurring expenditure, it illustrates the haywire nature of British defence budgeting. The government was forced to drop General Electric Corporation's efforts to make the Nimrod radar surveillance programme and buy Boeing AWACs instead. Immediately the army lost, amongst other things, its entitlement to reequip one of its West German-based armored regiments with the new Challenger Main Battle Tank (MBT). (There are only eleven such regiments in the whole BAOR. As of 1986 only six of them had been refitted in the whole 1979–86 period.) Yet for months before the Nimrod fiasco, MOD had been working in secret to find a way of trimming the expenditure plans for 1986–87 of a billion pounds just to bring existing procurement plans into line with the budget, because of over-spends by all services.

There is abundant evidence that existing reequipment plans cannot be met within budgets as set even by this most defence-minded of all British governments. Indeed no one outside the government even pretends they can.[17] At this point we need to ask what the chances are, therefore, of a serious improvement in conventional weaponry by utilizing the "emerging technologies" to produce for Britain the level of force multiplication advocated in some versions of the 1985 NATO Conventional Defence Improvement plan.

The British army has not announced, and probably does not have any wide-ranging plans for buying, these technologies. We can make a simple heuristic estimate by comparison with the U.S. Army's published Conventional Defense Enhancement plans. These call for using a variety of technologies, ranging from new infantry antitank weapons via sophisticated radar and other target-acquisition mechanisms to reactive armor for tanks and precision-guided munitions for tube and MLRS artillery. The program is costed at between £55 and £70 billion over five years, and probably entails an expenditure about half that rate for the following five years to deal with Soviet countermeasures.

There is no automatic formula for translating the costs of a known United States program to a hypothetical British one. The U.S. Army is roughly five times bigger than the British army, but simply dividing the United States costs by five would produce an excessive estimate. The United Kingdom does not need to be quite so modern, and it does not need to modernize so large a portion of its army. Entirely arbitrarily we can suggest that the United Kingdom could not, however, bring the BAOR up to near-American levels of military technology for less than 10 percent of the United States costs. At a *minimum* we can set $1 billion a year for five years as the British army technological modernization cost, of £600 million. This would involve an increase of 3 percent-plus in each of these years on just one service or, in other terms, increasing the army procurement budget by 35 percent. And these are minimum costings: the true figure could easily be double, making army modernization as expensive as Trident. It is quite inconceivable that any British government will go ahead with a program like this (and indeed, by no means certain that the U.S. Congress will).

The Trident Question

Most critics of this budgetary situation blame the decision to replace the Polaris fleet with Trident, at a cost of between £9 and £11 billion (depending on whose figures one accepts), for the major part of the strain on the budget. This may be so, though it is interesting to note that when the 1981 defence review was formulated, Trident was expected to cost only £5 billion. Even now MOD insists that over the ten-year procurement period Trident will have cost only 3 percent of total defence expenditure and 6 percent of procurement expenditure. It is certainly true that Trident will cost less than did the Tornado reequipment programme for the RAF, which will come in at a minimum of £17 billion.

The purpose of this paper is not to make policy judgments. The only relevant question for us is whether or not the budgetary crunch may be solved by the abolition of Trident. There are endless conflicts about what the opportunity cost of Trident is, that is, what could the United Kingdom buy if it did not buy Trident? It is quite impossible to know this, but the range of answers indicates the inherent confusion. The semi-official government answer is that abolishing Trident would only allow it to create, staff, and equip two new armored divisions (roughly 300 tanks).

An estimate from the Bradford University School of Peace Studies claims that 2,500 Challenger tanks could be bought. (The total tank inventory of the British army is currently only 1,180, of all types.) One might just as well say that as the unit cost of a kinetic energy round for the British Main Battle Tank (MBT) is £1,000, the United Kingdom could fill its arsenals to overflowing with 10 million such rounds. The comparisons are absurd, because they involve comparing unlikes. Trident is a very expensive capital project with an in-service life of over thirty years and very low manpower and running costs. Less than 1 percent of British servicemen are required to run the Strategic Nuclear Force, which takes about 2.5 percent of the annual defence budget.

Armored divisions, in the ungenerated state, have about 11,000 men with about 150 tanks and all the associated running costs of an all-volunteer force trying to attract skilled men to an unpopular posting. Furthermore, armored divisions require continuing upgrading and development to face enemy weapons developments. The division you buy in 1990 as part of not buying a strategic force is going to need considerable and expensive upgrading in 1999. (And that ignores the fact that the majority of Britain's tank force is twenty-five years old, with such inadequate optics and gun-laying technology that it regularly comes last in NATO competitions.)

The relevant question is not whether there is some hypothetical way of funding the conventional forces out of earmarked Trident money, but whether there is any realistic chance of this happening. It is actually very unlikely that this money will be freed. In February 1987 the government announced it was about to place the order for the second of the fleet of four Trident submarines. It also announced that by then £3 billion had been legally committed to the project, and £1 billion actually spent. It rather pointedly added that this meant that an incoming government with an alternative plan for replacing Polaris would therefore have to add £3 billion to their costings![18] The outcome of the 1987 general election, as far as Trident goes, could have been one of three things: (1) a Conservative victory, in which case Trident goes on; (2) a Labour victory, in which case Trident is cancelled and not replaced; (3) a result in which the SDP-Liberal Alliance could have exerted control over defence policy. Theoretically this would have meant that Trident was scrapped and some other Polaris replacement was undertaken.

Although there are, again, vast disagreements about the costs of alternatives to Trident, it is very unlikely that Polaris could have been replaced much more cheaply. Certainly if sunk costs on Trident cannot be ignored, it is impossible to see how any significant amount of money can be freed for conventional defence unless the British nuclear deterrent is indeed scrapped.[19] This is not the place to debate the Labour Party's long-term electoral chances, though it is commonly agreed that their defence policy did not help their electoral performance. What one must do is to ask how high the probability is that any significant sum saved by cancelling Trident would in fact be put into conventional arms improvements.

The Labour Party's social and economic programme is not cheap. Just before the election a job-creation programme was announced that, by Labour's own accounting, cost almost the same as Trident. There must be at least a chance that any future Labour government would come under enormous financial pressure, particularly if the economy goes into another downturn. Will it, in those conditions, actually not announce a defence review and reduce military expenditure? (It should be explained that the term "defence review" in British politics is code language for "abolishing some military capacity.")

For the scrapping of Trident to have any effect on the defence budget, it must stay at its current level (around £18 billion for 1986–87) in real terms. Even a Conservative government may not be able or willing to do that.

And even staying real-money-constant will in fact involve a reduction in purchasing power, because military expenditure rises by at least 1 percent more than the general rate of inflation every year. However sincerely they mean it, it is simply very improbable that a Labour government could, whether from Trident savings or otherwise, maintain the defence budget. This is especially problematic because of another question: What *sort* of conventional defence would a Labour government wish to spend money on?

In sum, then, it does not look at all likely that Trident's future will unstick the defence budget. The expectation must be that a budget that was known to be underfunded in 1981 will get steadily if slowly more so year by year unless a drastic redefinition of Britain's military tasks takes place. What this might be, and whether it will be, is the subject of a further section.

Political Constraints on Conventional Defence

There is nothing cynical about suggesting that a Labour government would not keep up, still less increase, the defence budget. There is a perfectly good case to be made, and one that usually *is* made by the Labour Party, that British defence expenditure is way out of line with its economic capacity. Why on earth should the country with only the eighth highest GNP per capita in Europe spend the largest absolute amount of money on defence? Why *should* a detente-oriented party, which would be elected to revivify Britain's deeply ailing social and education services, not put defence in its traditional low rank as an expenditure claimant? It was only the curious dynamics of the 1987 election season that even began to raise the possibility of there not being defence expenditure cuts under a Labour government. (Essentially the Labour Party was unable to get itself off the hook of its unpopular anti-nuclear stance, and sought to make up for this by actually outdoing the other parties in the purity of its pro-NATO *conventional* defence policy. It succeeded in convincing no one of this, either.)

The point is not just whether a Labour government would continue defence spending at its recent level, but whether any future British government would do so. Public expenditure remains a very high proportion of total expenditure in the British economy despite eight years of determined cost cutting under Mrs. Thatcher's administrations. An equally important fact, from the viewpoint of reinvigorating the economy, is that defence R&D accounts for 55 percent of all government-funded R&D, vastly higher than any of its economic competitors. The economy shows no sign of a return even to the modest 2.5 percent annual growth of the 1960s and 1970s.

The nonpartisanship of the felt need not to continue higher defence spending is well shown by the fact that within one week of winning the 1983 general election, Mrs. Thatcher's cabinet refused an MOD request to continue the 1977 annual 3 percent increase policy, though that election was widely thought to have been won in part through the Conservative's popularity after the Falklands.

Nor is there any sign of public-opinion support for a high salience to defence expenditure. Opinion polls in the months leading up to the last election, a time when defence issues had an unprecedented airing in public, did indeed regularly show that defence was the second most pressing issue in the public mind. But while 78 percent put unemployment as the major issue, only 17 percent ranked defence there. There is no historical reason to expect electoral pressure for high defence expenditure—with the possible exception of 1987, no election in postwar Britain has been seriously affected by such issues.[20] Public attitudes towards the Soviet Union do not demonstrate any great fear; indeed, polls regularly demonstrate that when asked, "Which is more likely to start a nuclear attack in Europe, the United States or Russia," not more than 50 percent say the USSR, and as much as 30 percent say the United States. Though the increased salience of defence politics has raised the general perception of war probability, in an "ordinary" year, 1979, less than 10 percent of the population thought a third world war was probable.[21]

Apart from a general financial restriction on defence policy that is very likely to come from any government, there is one other, deeply partisan, view that may cause serious restrictions on future conventional operational policy. The Labour Party has started taking its defence policy much more seriously in recent years, and has produced some military thinkers, from the left of the party, for whom simply scrapping nuclear weapons is not enough. This school of thought, summarized as "a genuinely defensive defence," has not yet been fully integrated into official party policy. However, influential publications, the most notable being *Defence without the Bomb*,[22] have argued that the whole NATO posture is overly offensive, not only its reliance on nuclear weapons. Some aspects of this report found their way into the last two official party defence policy statements. Since then the Warsaw Treaty Organization (WTO) has adopted many of the demands for "nonprovocative defence," thus making Labour policy much nearer the mainstream of European thought.

Of particular relevance is a sense that the American Deep Strike and Airland Battle, and NATO's Follow on Forces Attack (FOFA) are aggressive doctrines that increase tensions in Europe and could not be supported by a Labour government. This is combined with a distrust of high-technology weapons both because of their cost and reliability and because of the associated doctrines. The Labour Party's view of Britain's NATO posture is that it should "mount forces which are designed, as unambiguously as possible, for defensive purposes only."[23] Similarly, discussing possible changes to improve NATO's conventional capacity, they insist: "But changes in NATO's conventional force posture must be carried out in a defensive manner without leading to a conventional arms race."[24]

On the Deep Strike/FOFA posture, the party's opposition is summed up:

> It would also be inappropriate because, from the Soviet viewpoint, the ability of NATO to seize terrain well into Eastern European territory would be perceived as part of a political and military offensive strategy for NATO.
>
> Defence policy should not send the wrong political signals to a potential enemy. A policy of defensive deterrence is not compatible with an offensive military posture such as proposed in the new "deep strike" strategies.[25]

Other signals have been sent recently as the party struggles to make credible its claim to be pro-NATO yet opposed to the nuclear base of flexible response. Curiously they sound familiar to an American-attuned ear, because they stress options like greater use of reserves (by West Germany and other European countries—the United Kingdom has none!), the reliance on "defence in depth," and the fortification of the inner West German border. These are all arguments of the military reform group in America, in such authors as Jeffrey Record and Steven Canby, put to an ideologically different use.[26]

The general point is that a Labour government would be very unlikely to allow or fund any moves by the BAOR and RAF in West Germany to reorganize and reequip themselves to fight in a way that might make up for numerical inferiority. As *no* British government is going to find money for high technology defence, and will indeed not find much for more conventional defence improvements, the future of Britain's NATO commitment is fairly clear—it is very much a matter of "less of the same"! We can now turn to what coping mechanisms are available for the United Kingdom in the next ten to twenty years.[27]

Operational Consequences of These Constraints

There are only two ways Britain can cope with the economic and political constraints on its defence posture from now onwards. These are:

(1) a major and formal redefinition of its defence tasks; (2) a hidden reduction in its defence capability.

A Major Formal Redefinition

A major and formal redefinition would have to go at least as far as, and most probably much further than, the aborted 1981 defence review. But what is there to give up? It became apparent in early 1988 that actual strength of the Royal Navy, because of failure to order replacements and because extended refit times had sunk, de facto, at least as low as the de jure levels recommended in the Nott report, despite official statements that the pre-Nott level would be adhered to. There are four official tasks set to the British military: (1) a major anti-submarine warfare (ASW) role in the Channel and Eastern Atlantic; (2) defence of the United Kingdom land and air space; (3) a "minimum deterrent" strategic nuclear force; (4) a major air and land contribution to the central and northern flanks on the European continent.

The 1981 review attempted to square the defence circle by restricting the Royal Navy entirely to the first task, and restructuring its posture even for that, by putting very much more emphasis on submarines and United Kingdom-based air assets. Even if it had gone through fully, it would probably not have been enough of a cut in the long run. Of the 1986 total defence budget of £18,500 billion, probably only 17 percent, or £3,117 billion, goes on the NATO ASW role. Other figures put it no higher than 23 percent. With this relatively modest share of the budget, the United Kingdom carries 70 percent of the ASW work in these areas.

Obviously we cannot consider the various options without some baseline for how much the United Kingdom can or should continue to spend on defence. There is no value-free answer to this. One simple way is to argue that the United Kingdom can and should be able to afford an expenditure in line with a comparable European country. Many analysts suggest France as the obvious comparison, which makes sense because France is the only other European NATO country that tries to carry out the full range of defence functions of a major power with a medium power's economy. This would mean a defence budget of around 4 percent of GDP. The cut in the 1986 budget implied by this would have been on the order of 20 percent, or £3.7 billion. That is, the *entire* NATO ASW function would have to be given up to produce the sort of defence budget Britain might be able to live with.

Obviously no government would announce and immediately carry out a policy of reducing defence expenditure to this level. More likely would be a slow and steady but unannounced process in which small cuts in money figures were allowed (or could not be prevented from reaching such a figure) as a long-term sustainable plateau. Where could such cuts come, given that nothing as absurd as abandoning the whole Royal Navy is even remotely in question? Table 21.1, below, gives the 1986 breakdown of expenditure on the major defence functions.

As the basic position of the current government is to keep the budget steady in real terms for the next several years, we can take this as a baseline for a projection. We know the nuclear force will increase, possibly to something like 8 percent of the budget in most of the next ten years, which effectively means that the other categories have to take the whole £3 billion-plus cut. Of course, the cuts could be applied, as so often has happened, across the board, reducing the degree to which all functions are fulfilled. We turn to this later. A defence review, however, would have to try to carry out real surgery on commitments. Probably the position espoused by John Nott in 1981 will reemerge, and the navy will take a considerable part of the cuts, especially in the surface fleet.

The 1981 White Paper never actually gave a figure for what was to be achieved in money terms by the reform, but it certainly cannot have been an annual saving of even remotely the order of magnitude we are discussing here. The *total* cost of surface units, including manpower in 1986, was only £935 million. Perhaps a third of that might be saved, but this would not begin to make a real contribution to the long-term cost problem. Nor, in a sense, is it the radical surgery required in any case. Altering the posture under which a commitment is undertaken is never going to achieve as much as actually cutting out a commitment.

Assuming that only marginal savings can be made in the ASW role, what remains? The out-of-area function is slightly misleading because most of the units contained in it have other roles. Were all force projection capacity abandoned, it would actually amount to denying a NATO commitment—the northern flank reinforcement role. This is a possibility; from time to time the disbanding of the Royal Marines is canvassed as a possibility.[28]

TABLE 21.1
Estimated Functional Costs of the United Kingdom Defence Budget 1986–87 in
£ Millions, 1986 Prices

West German Commitment	NATO ASW	United Kingdom Defence	Out of Area	Nuclear Force	Total
8018	3117	5243	1259	862	18500
43%	17%	28%	7%	5%	100%

Source: Author's calculations based on United Kingdom Government Defence Expenditure Reports.

Doubtless some trimming in out-of-theatre capacity would be part of a review, but the long-term savings on what is largely a light infantry force would not be very great.

It is to be presumed that no British government would, publicly at least, abandon the defence of the homeland as a major United Kingdom defence policy goal. The real prize is obvious—the continental commitment of the British Army of the Rhine and RAF in West Germany. Since the late 1950s the United Kingdom has kept 55,000 army personnel and over 10,000 of the RAF in West Germany—over a third of the entire army. Yet these figures, though they are the way the issue is usually presented, actually underplay the real centrality of the West German commitment. Table 21.2, showing deployment of army and RAF units, makes it much clearer.

The table can be summarized in an interesting way. A modern army, such as the West German or the U.S. Army, has a roughly equal number of infantry and armored battalions (a British Armored "Regiment" is a

TABLE 21.2
Major Unit Deployment 1986

	Regular Army West Germany	Regular Army Elsewhere	Territorials
Corps HQ	1		
Div HQs	3	1	
Brigade HQs	11	16	
Armored Regiments	11	3[a]	
Armored Reccon. Rgts.	2	3	5
Artillery:			
Field Rgts.	8	6	2
Heavy Rgts.	1		
Missile Rgts.	1		
Depth Fire Rgts.	2		
Air Defence Rgts.	2	1	4
Engineers:			
Engineer Rgts.	5	6	7
Armored E Rgts.	1		
Amphib E Rgts.	1		
Infantry:			
Battalions	16	34	40
Army Air Corps Regiments	3	1	

[a]Two of these are training regiments.

battalion). The BAOR is a modern army. But the rest of the British army, the 110,000 or so, is an almost purely infantry force. The only formed division of the army *not* in Europe is an infantry division. Over 70 percent of the regular artillery is in West Germany. Over 50 percent of the regular engineering units are in West Germany. Their principal role, as also that of the Territorial Army, is of course to reinforce the BAOR come a war. On mobilization the British force in Europe will rise to 150,000, but this will be terribly "infantry-heavy," unlike the reinforcements the United States will send to Europe, and unlike the army the French may decide to deploy in NATO's support.

The Air Force picture is not dissimilar. There are sixteen RAF squadrons defined as "Strike/Attack" or "Offensive Support." Eight of these, including six of the nine Tornado squadrons in service, are in Germany. The others are mainly tasked for Strategic Air Command—Europe's (SACEUR) purposes either to fly out of English bases or to reinforce the RAF in West Germany directly.[29]

It is legitimate to ask whether, absent the obligation to help defend West Germany, Britain would have any need for its modern army at all. Territorial defence inside the United Kingdom, police duties, even out-of-theatre tasks would never call for those armored divisions, and arguably would not require the same artillery structure, certainly not the new Multiple Launch Rocket System (MLRS) regiments scheduled to be bought. The RAF's situation is even worse. Not only would the ground attack capacity of the Tornado squadrons not be needed, but buying them has diminished the United Kingdom's own air defence. That is principally why the RAF now has to ask for the money for the European Fighter Aircraft (EFA), thus asking, in the second time in a decade, for historically unprecedented project costs.

The point of this rather unusual look at the structure of the Rhine army is to demonstrate that the European commitment offers a splendid target for a defence review because it is so single purpose. If a United Kingdom government decided that a land commitment in Europe could no longer be supported, it could save an enormous amount of money because the army it would retain would be not only smaller, but disproportionately cheaper. The suggestion of removing or reducing the BAOR is often met with the claim that it would save no money to bring the troops home. Nor would it. But to disband them, to give up the NATO land commitment, would save. In fact it would save even more, since the United Kingdom infantry force is larger than it need be because it is principally tasked for the Federal Republic of Germany as well.

No United Kingdom government is going to abandon entirely the NATO land-war commitment. But any serious cut in the Rhine army—not in the forward deployment, but in the total effort promised to that front before *or after* mobilization—would be the easiest way of bringing demands into line with finance. One factor making this argument plausible is that the BAOR accounts, at most, for 20 percent, more probably only for 10 percent, of the total NATO effort on the central front, but it takes up over 40 percent of the defence budget. Contrast this, as the Royal Navy loves to do, with 70 percent of the ASW role carried out for around 20 percent of the British budget. There seems no good argument why the European central-front role should not be the one that a serious defence review decided to axe or reduce. This would be all the more pressing under either of two suppositions: (1) that the United States made similar cuts; (2) that other European armies organized themselves around technology and as-sociated doctrines of mobility warfare and Deep-Strike-style operations calling for weaponry the United Kingdom cannot begin to afford.

These two suppositions may be contradictory, which only makes the point stronger. They may be compatible—the United States will withdraw troops and the Federal Republic will lose troops, but both will try to make up for this by investment in expensive and sophisticated weapons. Britain could not match such force-multiplier investment. Just how is SACEUR going to handle slimmed but high-tech United States and West German units fighting alongside a BAOR of 150,000, of which all but twelve or so battalions are infantry, with ill-equipped supporting artillery? It must seem that there are few arguments against the United Kingdom's bowing out of the land conflict, though it *might* continue to make a major tactical air effort as long as Tornado exists and remains adequate.

A Hidden Reduction

Will any United Kingdom government abandon or seriously curtail the central-front task? Almost certainly not. The political importance of the Rhine army and RAF West Germany is enormous as symoblism to the small elite who care about defence and foreign policy in the United Kingdom. One can see this by the way the traditional figure of 55,000 for the BAOR is treated as though it were a treaty obligation. In fact, it is not. Until the late 1950s the BAOR was set at 77,000, and there was little trouble in negotiating this down to 55,000. Even that figure is set in no stone. Nor is the idea that Britain is obliged to protect a specified sixty-five miles of the inner West German border. Nonetheless the force of Europeanism is so strong that, combined with military traditionalism, an outright statement that Britain just will not do anything to carry out these tasks is unthinkable to most people, of any party and none, in the policy-making circles.

Furthermore, the entrenched service interests and lobbies would be outraged. How would the army recruit if it could offer only a humdrum garrison life inside the United Kingdom? Anyone who has witnessed the ability of the army to whip up public and Parliamentary support over an emotional issue such as disbanding the entirely redundant Ghurka battalions, or the amalgamation of a couple of infantry battalions representing historic county regiments, will see this.

But much less publicity would be stirred up if the last regiments do not get the Challenger MBT to replace the Chieftain for an extra few years, if the MLRS regiments never get smart warheads, if infantry companies slip to two platoons from three and many do not get the MCV 80 carrier, if war stocks slip further, and training days, practice shoots, and armored track miles all decline until the troops would not know what to do in a hot war. After all, the defence estimates simply tell us, in a table boasting of what has been bought, that by 1985–86 the supply of "New 120mm ammunition" for main battle tanks was "operational stocks completed"—but no member of the British public (or House of Commons) is going to be told just how many days these stocks will actually last!

Implications

1. The implications are either that the United Kingdom will have to withdraw from its West German commitment or that it will become a very different army from that of its allies. In many ways it already is. The 150,000 men the BAOR will field on full mobilization are well trained and equipped to fight the last theoretical war of NATO planning. They will fight well an infantry/anti-tank linear defence. They will not engage in manoeuvre warfare, they will not interdict the second echelon 100 miles into East Germany. An increasingly high proportion will be Territorial Army, not regulars. The armored force will be less and less modernized, and probably a smaller and smaller portion of the whole. Whoever commands the Br(I) Corps will husband his dozen or so armored regiments with loving care. So will the British Air Commander protect his Tornado squadrons, because he will have less aircraft year by year than the scanty few he now has. How many of the second-generation Harriers will be have?

And what doctrine will the British troops fight by? The U.S. FM 100–5 Field Manual and its West German counterpart will have little to say to the British army.

2. Or has the whole debate and effort been misplaced? Should there ever have been an attempt to "go conventional"? A much cheaper and smaller BAOR and RAF West Germany would suffice to play its part in a nuclear tripwire. In some cosmic sense the United Kingdom *can* afford to

pay its way to a conventional defence against a Soviet threat. But in no real sense can it, or will it, invest in such insurance. Could it possibly be that the whole stress of NATO defence policy from McNamara onwards has been mistaken, and the nuclear deterrence against fighting any war in Europe again is the correct answer? Such arguments fit badly with the new era after the Intermediate Nuclear Forces (INF) Treaty. But we can already see the British government reacting; it is the most enthusiastic of all NATO members for effectively *undoing* INF by modernizing battlefield nuclear weapons. A government that is seriously trying to develop a new-generation nuclear stand-off bomb for its air force while making no moves to expand its conventional forces has fairly clearly decided how it will meet its unmeetable obligations.

Notes

1. See Edward N. Luttwack, "The Operational Level of War." In Steven E. Miller, ed., *Conventional Forces and American Defense Policy* (Princeton, N.J.: Princeton University Press, 1986).
2. The "Operational Level," ironically, is accepted as a term of art by most major armies *except* the British army. For a good discussion of the relevance to the term in the NATO context, see Chris Bellamy, "Trends in Land Warfare: The Operational Art of the European Theatre." In *Rusi and Brassey's Defence Yearbook 1985* (London: Brassey's Defence Publishers, 1985), p. 228.
3. It may not be well known, but the training of most of the British army is so concentrated on central-front tactics that units have to undergo lengthy special training before they can be sent to Ulster on "aid to the civil power" tours.
4. All such estimates are unofficial. The Ministry of Defence refuses ever to publish genuinely "functional" cost estimates. David Greenwood, "Economic Constraints and Political Preferences." In John Baylis, ed., *Alternative Approaches to British Defence Policy*, p. 36. See also David Robertson, "Defence Policy Options for Britain in the New Cold War." In Steven Smith, ed., *The New Cold War* (London: Allen & Unwin, 1987), p. 247.
5. Hill-Norton, "Return to a National Strategy." In John Baylis, ed., *Alternative Approaches to British Defence Policy* (New York: St. Martin's Press, 1983).
6. Ibid.
7. *Statement on the Defence Estimates 1986.* Vol. 1. Cmnd 9763-1. (London: HMSO, 1986), p. 7.
8. In fact, very serious cuts have been imposed on DOD's procurement for 1988–89 already. See *Jane's Defence Weekly,* January 19, 1988 (London).
9. See "The Reagan Build Up," *Washington Post,* March 16, 1987. Note also the resignation of the secretary of the navy on this issue in March 1988.
10. Ibid., February 22, 1987. Note that even the badly needed new howitzer, the M198, has been cancelled in the 1988–89 budget.
11. The Intermediate Nuclear Forces (INF) Treaty of January 1988 makes no difference to this analysis, because the tactical nuclear force will not only *not* be cut, but may well be modernized in important ways.
12. *Sunday Times* (London), February 22, 1987, reports Senator Carl Levin touring

Europe and warning of impending troop cuts. The article suggests a figure of some 100,000 as likely cuts.
13. Susan Clarke has written an excellent account of the whole demographic problem for NATO.
14. See David Robertson, "Fair Shares in NATO." *Rusi and Brassey's Defence Yearbook 1986* (London: Brassey's Defence Publishers, 1986).
15. *The United Kingdom Defence Programme: The Way Forward.* Cmnd 8288 (London: HMSO).
16. In December 1987 the MOD admitted that the Army Staff was seeking funds to replace 900 of Britain's 1,200 tanks. The 900 Chieftain-model tanks are over twenty-five years old. As a ballpark figure, the newest United States tank, the M1, costs $2.2 million. So, just to replace the *existing* United Kingdom force, long before rearmament is considered, would cost another £1.1 billion from that same over-committed procurement budget.
17. For assessments, see Robertson, "Defence Policy Options," and Greenwood, "Economic Constraints." See also David Robertson and Robin Laird, "The Future of British Defence Policy," *Orbis,* Autumn 1987. For a more theoretical analysis, see K. Hartley, "UK Defence Policy: Seeking Better Value for Money." In *Rusi and Brassey's Defence Yearbook 1985* (London: Brassey's Defence Publishers, 1985), pp. 105–19.
18. *Daily Telegraph* (London), January 28, 1987.
19. The government published an Open Government Document, *Trident and Its Alternatives,* on January 30, 1987, arguing that a cruise missile alternative, as favored by the SDP, would cost twice Trident. The analysis is contested by other experts.
20. Even the "Falklands Factor" in 1983 probably existed more in the minds of the media and politicians. Recent academic research has failed to find any significant impact on actual voting decisions. David Sanders, "The Falklands Factor," *British Journal of Political Science,* Summer 1987.
21. David Robertson, *Class and the British Electorate* (Oxford: Basil Blackwell, 1984).
22. *Defence without the Bomb: The Report of the Alternative Defence Commission* (London: Taylor & Francis, 1983).
23. *Defence and Security for Britain* (London: Labour Party, 1984), p. 5. Though not the latest policy statement, it has not been overruled by any subsequent one, and is the most detailed statement.
24. Ibid., p. 12.
25. Ibid., p. 14.
26. See, for example, Steven L. Canby, "The Conventional Defense of Europe," in Lars B. Wallin, ed., *Military Doctrines for Central Europe* (Stockholm: Swedish Defence Research Institute, 1984.)
27. A very full discussion of force levels and conventional coping mechanisms for the whole of NATO is contained in David Robertson, *The Conventional Defense of Europe in the Post-INF Era* (New York: Institute for East-West Security Studies, forthcoming).
28. As it happens, a similar commitment, by Canada, has recently been dropped. See *Naval Institute Proceedings,* March 1988, Washington, D.C.
29. All of the figures in table 21.2, or otherwise quoted, refer to 1986 and are to be found in *Statement on the Defence Estimates 1986,* vol. 1 (London: HMSO, Cmnd 9763–1, 1986), pp. 73–76.

22

SDI, Europe, and the American
Strategic Dilemma

David P. Calleo

Many Europeans look upon SDI as a strange religious frenzy that has somehow overtaken their distant imperial court. Cast in the role of conservative provincials, they have had trouble grasping the new faith. They have been able neither to figure out what President Reagan's vision was meant to be nor to develop any clear idea about what it is likely to become. As first revealed, the president's program seemed designed to make nuclear deterrence obsolete. Authoritative disciples soon described it as an enhancement of deterrence.[1] Reading between the lines, Europeans thought SDI might be primarily a bargaining chip for forcing the Soviets into an arms agreement. Or they saw it as another great technological boondoggle to keep the United States' scientific and strategic communities well provisioned beyond the end of the century.

Even if the program's original intent had been crystal clear, great uncertainties about its likely evolution would still exist. The president's continental bubble to cover American cities would require space-based weapons, which, even if they could be developed, would remain highly vulnerable to preemptive attack.[2] Such a defensive regime, to be stable, would appear to require so intense a degree of cooperation between the superpowers as to constitute a sort of world government, a project that would seem highly fanciful even if among the Western allies, let alone between rival superpowers. If the bubble is almost certainly infeasible for the United States, as nearly everyone except the president apparently concedes,

From Robert W. Tucker et al., *SDI and U.S. Foreign Policy*. Reprinted with permission from Westview Press and the Foreign Policy Institute, The Johns Hopkins University, 1987.

it seems absolutely impossible for Western Europe.[3] Since Russia is, after all, part of Europe, there seems to be no remotely conceivable technology to insulate West European territory from Soviet missiles, let alone other means of nuclear and conventional attack.

A more limited ballistic missile defense (BMD) for "point" defense—to cover such targets as U.S. missiles, command centers, bases, and even specific cities—is more feasible technically and could also be deployed to cover similar targets in Europe. Several studies believe point defense of missiles could be effective strategically, particularly if combined with mobile and deceptive basing, because any preemptive attack might well have to use up many more missiles than the attacker could expect to destroy on the ground. But many other studies suggest that point defense, even for missile sites, would be either unnecessary, because of the great diversity of U.S. retaliatory capabilities, or not cost-effective, because such a defense would cost more overall to develop and install than the additional or adapted offensive missiles required to overwhelm it.[4] Moreover, the Russians, with an ample supply of heavy missiles, are particularly well fixed to increase their number of warheads drastically. Under the circumstances many Americans find it hard to see any national advantage in taking the lead to deploy such weapons. Europeans, with their additional geographical disadvantages, seem even less-favorably situated for deployment.

Insofar as BMD could be effective, many analysts worry about its possible destabilizing consequences. If only one superpower achieved an operative space-based bubble, it would have achieved strategic hegemony. The other might feel compelled to strike before such a system could be deployed. If both had bubbles, total victory would follow from a successful strike against the space bases of the other. More plausibly, a superpower well-endowed with point missile defenses might strike first on the grounds that its own BMD could easily contain whatever retaliatory force remained to the opponent.[5] Each side, fearful of being disarmed by a first strike, would feel compelled to strike first to preempt. Many American analysts wonder if it will ever make sense to initiate deployments that will result in such mutually unfavorable circumstances. Many Europeans agree.

Low expectations for SDI have begun to extend even to SDI's diplomatic usefulness. Europeans applauded SDI's apparent role in bringing the Soviets back to arms talks. They keep hoping that Reagan's subsequent unwillingness to negotiate over SDI is gamesmanship rather than obduracy. As time goes on, the hope proves difficult to sustain without more positive reinforcement than it has yet received. Europeans have begun to suspect that even if the Americans never deploy SDI, they will prove incapable of parlaying it into a serious arms agreement.

Europeans were immediately impressed by the possibilities of SDI as an industrial boondoggle. The scale of the proposed research funding seemed highly promising for the branches of science and technology involved. European firms have feared the spinoff would greatly favor their American industrial rivals and have therefore been eager to pick up whatever business—and information—they can get. The Pentagon has vigorously promoted sanguine expectations. Past and recent experience, however, has discouraged any excessive or unguarded optimism about sharing in U.S. military research and procurement. After years of wrangling over Eastern trade and technology transfer, Europeans have grown attentive to the pitfalls of cooperation.[6]

Europeans have now had over three years to wrestle with what SDI means for them. As they now see it, any actual program is likely to be far less disturbing than the initial rhetoric. As they look at the manifold strategic risks and ambiguities, the preposterous costs and the manifest disagreements within the American political and strategic communities, including the Reagan administration itself, they cannot make themselves believe that SDI will ever fulfill either Reagan's revolutionary hopes or their own corresponding fears.

Europeans, to be sure, may be allowing their particular interests to cloud their general judgment. Their own military interests strongly predispose them against heavy superpower investment in missile defense. Defensive systems might have a disproportionately weighty effect on Europe's own nuclear deterrents. The upgrading planned for British and French nuclear forces by the mid-1990s might, in theory, be robbed of much of its effectiveness. The French have declared themselves confident about their ability to penetrate missile defenses with modified and more numerous warheads.[7] But the French cannot be enthusiastic about the resources this will take— resources to be wrested from the civilian sector or, more probably, from other parts of their military budget. Depleting conventional arms, including normal air defense, may reduce security overall. Europe is, after all, highly vulnerable to nonballistic air attack, not to mention the Red Army's tanks.[8]

Europeans also fear SDI's effects on the U.S. military budget. The French problem with budgets is a miniature version of the American. If SDI proceeds to even limited deployment, a vast sum will have to be attracted away from a combination of U.S. civilian and other military programs.[9] Given the current state of U.S. budgetary politics, other military programs are likely to be a prime source. Particularly vulnerable will be the large, very expensive conventional forces the United States justifies chiefly by their role in the defense of Western Europe. Since up to half the U.S. defense budget can be attributed to such forces, SDI is likely to make the long-gestating American inclination to withdraw conventional forces from Europe increasingly difficult to resist.[10] A substantial diminishing of U.S. forces for NATO that leads to a notable improvement in the American fiscal situation could have substantial compensating benefits for Europe, particularly if a significant Europeanization of the alliance was the result. In due course, a reduced U.S. fiscal deficit could certainly have highly beneficial long-term effects for the world economy. But SDI seems an unlikely way to lower the U.S. military budget and fiscal deficit, even if it does reduce the American conventional commitment to Europe.

Many Europeans, of course, fear that the urge to "decouple" from the risks of extended nuclear deterrence has been, all along, a principal driving force behind SDI. What has been so disturbing to them about Reagan's dream, which calls for a total defense against missiles shared by European allies and Soviets alike, is that it implies the end of U.S. or any other nuclear deterrence for Europe.[11] Its technological implausibility for Europe is not what arouses the Europeans' objections. On the contrary, only the general implausibility of SDI reconciles European governments to it. While the goal of a world free from offensive nuclear weapons doubtless appeals to publics in Europe as in the United States, it has no appeal at all to NATO governments, all of which have firmly embraced the strategy of nuclear deterrence. When the issues have been clearly posed, moreover, these governments have been sustained by their publics.[12]

No one should be surprised at European support for the strategic status quo. Since 1945 Europe has enjoyed a peace nearly as long as between 1870 and 1914, and in much less promising political circumstances. Given the division of Germany and the failure of the Russians to consolidate their hold over major East European countries, so enduring a peace would be difficult to imagine under the prenuclear military conditions of 1939.

This is not simply another way of saying that, without nuclear deterrence, the Soviets would have conquered the rest of the continent. A nonnuclear Europe would not necessarily have become a Soviet-dominated Europe. But had there been a European military balance in a nonnuclear world, the Europeans, rather than the Americans, would have had to maintain it. U.S. forces are unlikely to have stayed mobilized for four decades in order to match the Soviets in Eurasia. It is certainly conceivable that, in time, a Western Europe encouraged by the United States could have mobilized its own immense resources to build conventional forces to match the Soviets'. But it is far less conceivable that such forces would have sat immobile for four decades in the absence of any viable political settlement.

Compared to the likely alternatives, the nuclear balance of terror has given West Europeans a very comfortable time. Not only have they been preserved from a war, but the cost to them of their security has been rather low. Since the late 1960s, particularly, they have devoted a substantially smaller proportion of their resources to military costs than in the years before World War I or during the interwar period.[13] The benefits have been manifest for their economic systems and standards of living. Europeans have used their abundance to build political-economic systems that are not without problems, to be sure, but in which the age-old tensions that wracked their societies in the past have been greatly mitigated.

Their security has cost the Europeans so little not only because nuclear deterrence has been much cheaper than conventional forces, but also because the essential nuclear forces for Europe have been provided mainly by the Americans. To this day NATO remains essentially a nuclear protectorate of the United States.

As everyone knows, "extended deterrence" has grown increasingly difficult. Until the 1960s NATO and U.S. strategic predominance went hand in hand. NATO provided the forward bases that gave the United States its ability to strike the Soviets. Even with nuclear weapons, the Soviets, lacking similar bases, could retaliate only on U.S. allies. The development of intercontinental missiles effectively ended U.S. invulnerability and, eventually, U.S. strategic superiority as well. Under the circumstances, the risks for the United States of extended deterrence have, in theory at least, increased dramatically.

Discussions of U.S.-Soviet strategic balance often tend to ignore the critical role of America's extended deterrence for Europe. It is, however, the crux of the nation's strategic problem. Strategists and their computers can dream up innumerable scenarios for confrontation. But given the heroic risks and uncertainties, an unprovoked Soviet nuclear attack on the United States seems a remote possibility. No doubt both sides could work themselves into such a state of collective hysteria that such extremities begin to seem imaginable. But whatever the fantasies and terrors of the target planners, the nuclear balance is extremely robust. Europe aside, no direct conflict between Americans and Soviets could remotely justify running such risks.

In Europe, however, the superpowers do have a point of direct contact over a geopolitical stake so vital to both that an intercontinental nuclear war does become imaginable. Despite forty years of peace, Europe's political conditions still seem fundamentally unstable. The continent's artificial division remains. The Red Army still sits over a restive Eastern Europe. Germany remains split down the middle. In this nuclear era hardly anyone imagines any European state deliberately starting a war to change the status quo. All the same, it is not easy to imagine Europe going on forever in its present state. The basic political instability is attested to by the large military forces that continue to confront each other on both sides. In recent years, despite some apparent progress in reaching a more comfortable pan-European modus vivendi, these forces have not diminished but increased substantially.[14] The United States, meanwhile, remains the principal guarantor of West European security.

The clear and present danger to U.S. security, in short, has been that a war might start over Europe. How to deter such a war, and what to do if it occurs, has been the chief driving concern of U.S. nuclear strategy since the 1950s.

Since strategic superiority began to fade, the United States has never been able to find a satisfactory resolution.[15] While technological reality imposed the doctrine of mutual assured destruction, it was the European commitment that inspired flexible response and, later, counterforce strategy. The essential point of the strategy is that any engagement over Europe should be limited as much as possible to the minimum needed to stop the Soviet thrust. While the logic of flexible response called for a genuine balance of conventional forces, in reality the Europeans have been unwilling and the Americans incapable of providing such forces. Instead, they have compromised on a NATO with just enough conventional forces to prevent an easy Soviet conventional victory on the ground. Any Soviet attack will mean a major battle, with several hundred thousand American soldiers involved. Such a prospect makes a U.S. resort to nuclear weapons probable, and thus makes more plausible the nuclear deterrence upon which NATO's defense really depends.

In effect, Americans have had to content themselves with a very expensive NATO that nevertheless falls short of providing a real conventional balance. A NATO first use of nuclear weapons has therefore never been far in the background. The thrust of American strategic thinking, as opposed to European, has been to limit the scope of nuclear use as tightly as possible. From the 1950s on, NATO has planned on using small-yield nuclear weapons to stop numerically superior advancing Soviet forces. Over the years flexible response has been elaborated into a hierarchy of specific target sets designed to raise the level of nuclear force just sufficiently to stop the Soviet thrust without precipitating an all-out intercontinental war.

Once multiple independently targeted reentry vehicle (MIRV) technology created the possibility of a greatly expanded number of highly accurate warheads, flexible response evolved into counterforce strategy. With such a strategy, even a European war that escalated into an intercontinental exchange could be spun out into a protracted and strictly limited test of will. Precise attacks and counterattacks could be directed at enemy missiles, moreover, rather than at enemy cities.

The U.S. lead in MIRVs provided the technology that made a counterforce strategy plausible. America's consequent and very substantial lead in warheads gave it "escalation dominance," which meant that the United States could, at various limited stages of nuclear escalation, reasonably hope to present the Soviets with a calculus of punishment and gain that made it more rational for them to back down than to escalate.

Counterforce strategy, however, has not been a satisfactory resolution for America's strategic problem of extended deterrence. The technological lead upon which the strategy was based has not proved stable. The Soviets have gradually acquired MIRV technology of their own. Since they have always concentrated on comparatively large land-based missiles, MIRVing has allowed the Soviets to catch up rapidly, threatening to surpass the Americans in numbers of land-based warheads.[16] This, in turn, has led to American apprehensions about a "window of vulnerability." A Soviet first strike could, in theory, destroy the bulk of U.S. land-based missiles. Thus disarmed, America might decline to retaliate. Hence, the pressure for mobile missiles, ballistic missile defense, and now SDI.[17]

The whole situation has its ironic side. The MIRV technology that was to have permitted a limited first strike by the United States to stop a conventional attack on Western Europe has now led to widespread American fears of a Soviet first strike on the United States. Technology has escaped from its original strategic context and now threatens both sides with a manic arms race undisciplined by any real strategic interest other than countering the most recent innovations of the other. As a practical matter, the United States has now grown more directly and acutely vulnerable than ever before.

All of this would be easier to dismiss as merely a strategist's fantasy were it not for the continuing U.S. protectorate for Western Europe. That commitment, still nuclear-based because Western Europe will not build an adequate conventional deterrent, holds despite the radical deterioration in the United States' own strategic position. The United States' strategic dilemma is that the obligation to Europe requires America to prepare for an early first use of nuclear weapons, but it no longer has sufficient technological dominance to rely comfortably on making such a threat.[18]

From this perspective SDI has a double meaning. In theory, it could be seen as a way to escape from this strategic dilemma over the European protectorate. A United States once more invulnerable to nuclear attack, or whose deterrent is far more effectively protected, would be in a much better position to confirm its extended geopolitical engagements. But the president's rhetoric embodies a purely defensive strategy for SDI. It proposes to abolish offensive nuclear weapons and share the SDI technology with the Soviets. The president's rhetoric seems, in effect, a renunciation of extended deterrence for Europe. Thus, the rhetoric troubles Europeans far more than any actual military program.

European unhappiness with U.S. fashions in deterrence is hardly new. Europeans have always been intellectually uneasy with flexible response and counterforce strategies.[19] Limiting escalation in a European war has always been a predominantly American concern. European strategists have generally argued that deterrence is greater when the threat of all-out war is most immediate. If Europe is to be destroyed, in other words, why not the United States and Russia, too? The certain prospect that a war in Europe would automatically ruin both superpowers seems, in European perspectives, the best defense against such a war ever occurring. For Europeans, plans for a limited nuclear war in Europe conjure up visions of a superpower nuclear tournament, with Eastern and Western Europe the playing field. Early in the postwar era the British and French thought it prudent to develop their own nuclear forces, conceived of as "triggers" to turn an attack on themselves into a nuclear war by attacking the Soviet homeland regardless of what the Americans were doing. European and American strategic views are fundamentally different mainly because the two sides of the Atlantic are in different geopolitical situations when it comes to European deterrence. Europe's own limited nuclear forces exist to retaliate against an attack on themselves, not on their allies. While it is even doubtful, for example, that French nuclear forces would engage themselves in the defense of Germany, unless France also saw itself as being under attack, no one imagines the French force being used if the Soviets attacked the United States but left Europe alone.

All Europeans, of course, are not in the same situation. Of the West European powers, only Britain and France have nuclear weapons of their own. West Germany and Italy, along with the smaller NATO powers, rely entirely on the United States. The

British nuclear deterrent depends on U.S. technology and is integrated in NATO, although it is subject to national control in a supreme emergency.[20] The French deterrent is completely national in origin and control. But its only unambiguous purpose, according to declared French strategy, is to retaliate if France itself is attacked by nuclear forces or is about to be overrun by conventional forces. French strategy has long contemplated using tactical nuclear forces against advancing Soviet forces in Germany, not so much to defend Germany as to demonstrate a willingness to proceed to an all-out nuclear attack against Soviet cities to defend France. An all-out threat obviously seems most plausible, and therefore is most deterring, when a country is defending its own territory and independence. It grows less so, and therefore is less deterring, in defense of an ally. It seems weaker still when meant to cover an ally against a conventional, not a nuclear, attack. In other words, France, with its limited force, can threaten a massive attack on Soviet cities to defend itself, while the United States cannot so plausibly threaten massive retaliation for a Soviet conventional invasion of Germany. Since the Americans could not, and the Europeans would not provide NATO with an adequate conventional deterrent, the U.S. commitment rests upon an early NATO use of nuclear weapons. Under the circumstances, the United States has looked for a way to use these nuclear forces in a selective and limited fashion. This explains the American predilection for flexible response and counterforce strategies, as opposed to French enthusiasm for massive retaliation.[21]

Despite their intellectual disagreements with the Americans, the French have found a very comfortable position within the American protectorate. Given their own diffidence about extending their deterrent, they have never had any trouble understanding American uneasiness. It was precisely because of doubts about whether the United States—or any other country—would sustain the risks of extended deterrence that the French insisted upon pressing ahead with their own nuclear force. Their *force de dissuasion* was designed to ensure that if France were devastated, the Soviet Union itself would not escape devastation regardless of the U.S. reaction. The Soviets in turn would be unlikely to suffer the grievous damage of a French attack without retaliating against their principal nuclear adversary, the United States. Thus, any major European war involving France was likely to be both nuclear and intercontinental. As the French saw it, their force not only reduced the likelihood of a nuclear contest between the superpowers conducted in Europe alone but also enhanced U.S. deterrence for Europe. Thanks to the French "trigger," the Soviets would not start any confrontation in Europe unless they were prepared for mutual suicide.

To some extent the French deterrent can be seen to benefit Western Europe as a whole. While the French have never yet promised a nuclear riposte to an attack on their West German ally, French ground forces remain in Germany and are equipped with nuclear weapons. A second nuclear force among Germany's allies, in itself, increases "uncertainty," and hence, according to French doctrine, it increases deterrence. The French now and then have described their nuclear force as being held "in reserve for Europe." They have, nevertheless, carefully refrained from making precise commitments to their German neighbors, despite extensive bilateral discussion during the past several years. To underscore their complete self-determination of their own obligations and interests, they have kept their forces independent from the NATO command since 1966. They remain within the Atlantic alliance but cooperate only selectively with its integrated military structure.

In effect, the French have their cake and eat it, too. They can avoid any more intimate and committed involvement in the collective continental defense because they can presume a U.S. defense that covers France as well. The French have thus greatly reduced the price and enhanced the quality of their national security. With a proportional defense budget regularly one-half to two-thirds of the American, they have managed to build a respectable strategic force, including nuclear submarines, as well as formidable conventional forces for global interventions.[22] Forces for conventional defense still receive a relatively low priority, not, presumably, because the French are uninterested in the territorial defense of Europe, but because they believe this task can be left mainly to the Germans and Americans. One consequence is to make a genuine conventional balance impossible. With their faith in nuclear deterrence, the French do not believe that one is needed.

Like the Germans, and in strained but durable cooperation with them, the French have mounted a persistent campaign to improve Europe's general political relations with the Soviets.[23] The French

have also promoted West European economic and political cooperation, and a special Franco-German relationship in particular, to speed
modernization of the French economy and to provide a reasonably
effective counterweight to the giant U.S. economy. In short, within
the present nuclear and geopolitical dispensation, France has managed to achieve a high degree both of security and prosperity.

Among the major European countries, Germany is geopolitically the least comfortable. The border between its two halves constitutes the front line between Western and Eastern systems. It is
among the West Germans that the notion of transatlantic "coupling" has received its most elaborate development. Lacking nuclear
weapons of their own, German strategic theorists argue that the
alliance rests, in effect, on the European perception that the United
States and Western Europe share an equivalent vulnerability.[24]
Thanks to that perception, Germans can tolerate U.S. missiles based
on their soil and can control their twin fears: that the United States
will not defend them or that it will involve them in a limited war
having little to do with Germany's own interests. SDI, German
analysts insist, inevitably emphasizes the unequal vulnerability of
Europe and its U.S. protector, thus threatening the psychological
constitution of the Atlantic alliance. Needless to say, this view of
the alliance has never had wide currency in the United States. If
it did, the United States would probably leave NATO.

In a more realistic vein, the Germans have taken serious steps
to assuage American worries about the growing vulnerabilities of
extended deterrence. One palliative is stronger NATO conventional
forces to give greater credibility to flexible response. The Germans
have long provided the backbone of NATO's conventional forces,
and thanks to them, the United States is not likely to be called upon
to use nuclear weapons to stop a limited thrust across the frontier.[25]

At the same time, the West Germans have improved the European diplomatic and political atmosphere. Mostly on their own initiative, they took advantage of the superpower détente of the late
1960s and 1970s to reach a broad political modus vivendi with the
Soviets, the East Germans, and the rest of Eastern Europe. They
recognized the status quo, including the existence of a separate East
German state, and renounced the use of force to change that status
quo. In their own complicated formula they accepted the notion
of "two states in one German nation." While they have not

renounced hopes that "peaceful change" may bring some eventual national reunification, the prevalent formula for that reunification is not the old Bismarckian Reich, which was a centralized imperial state. Instead it is something closer to the confederal models that predated the Bismarckian creation. In effect, as is commonly said, German unification can take place only in the context of peaceful European unification—a long-range vision designed to keep alive hope for the future without arousing fears in the present.[26]

German diplomatic concepts have been successful not only in improving and stabilizing relations with the East but also in enlisting the support of the West European allies—most notably France, which had its own vision of a "Europe from the Atlantic to the Urals." Thanks to robust West European support for this German-crafted pan-European détente, the deteriorating superpower relations of the 1980s have not brought about a comparable degeneration of East-West relations within Europe itself. One reason is undoubtedly the shared stake—on both sides—in East-West trade. German money has greatly aided German diplomacy. Despite Eastern Europe's severe economic problems in the depressed 1980s, the long-term political-economic prospects have seemed sufficiently promising for Western Europe to resist stoutly the strong American pressures to limit economic relations. West European governments will be on their guard that SDI not become a powerful U.S. lever to control their Eastern trade.[27]

Given their painful historical situation, the Germans have made themselves comfortable within the present strategic arrangement. In the face of unpromising geopolitical circumstances, the U.S. deterrent has given them more military security than they have enjoyed since well before World War I, and at an economic cost greatly inferior to their military burdens of the past. In addition, they have parlayed their military dependence into a promising diplomatic accommodation with the East that increases their present security without decreasing their future prospects.

Not surprisingly, neither the French nor the German political elites, nor those of any other NATO country, wish to see radical changes in the current transatlantic security relationship or strategy. Extended deterrence under the American protectorate has suited them well enough. Other West Europeans are like the Germans. They have never known invulnerability at any period of their history, and they do not expect it now. They rate the actual risks to their security exceptionally low by comparison with nearly any other modern period. This high security, moreover, comes exceptionally cheap. They are nearly all spending a relatively low proportion of their national incomes on defense, compared to present U.S. or their own historical standards. Considering the Europeans' dependence on it, U.S. military protection does not unbearably constrain their economic or diplomatic independence. In the French case it hardly limits their military independence.

Pressure for change is naturally much stronger on the American side. For a country accustomed to invulnerability, the risks of extended deterrence have grown increasingly hard to bear. Weak NATO conventional forces mean that the United States must be prepared for a first use of nuclear weapons to fulfill its NATO commitment. Only possession of clear strategic superiority, if not outright invulnerability, can make the United States truly comfortable with such a commitment.

It may be argued that the United States must and can learn to live with this burden. Considering the stake, the United States cannot disengage from European defense, and the existing NATO arrangement is less uncomfortable than any conceivable alternative. This view might have been held more complacently before the Reagan administration and SDI. It seems less easy to hold it now. Even if the Reagan administration's strategic views seem highly idiosyncratic, they have behind them a decade of mounting U.S. dissatisfaction with the country's strategic posture. The widespread clamor against the "window of vulnerability," the disillusionment with arms control, and the pressures for "no first use," upgrading conventional forces, and European burden-sharing all suggest the growing instability of any American strategic consensus, including, implicitly, the commitment to extended deterrence for Europe.

In effect, counterforce strategy—designed to preserve the plausibility of American first use for Europe—requires U.S. superiority. Once the Soviets acquired MIRV technology, and hence parity, it became impossible to stabilize the nuclear balance in a fashion adequate for U.S. purposes. No arms agreement was satisfactory because no arms negotiator could reasonably expect the Soviets to concede to Americans the superiority needed to keep extended deterrence safe for the United States.

Is SDI a solution for extended deterrence? In theory it might be. If the United States were invulnerable to the Soviets while the Soviets remained vulnerable to U.S. nuclear forces, a U.S. nuclear commitment to Western Europe could be sustained with impunity. If SDI also made Western Europe invulnerable to nuclear attack while leaving the Soviets vulnerable, NATO's problems with extended deterrence would presumably be over. If the United States were invulnerable but Western Europe and the Soviets were not, then the old problems of the 1950s and 1960s would reappear. Those Europeans without effective nuclear deterrents of their own would feel that they were Soviet hostages for American good behavior. An invulnerable United States might grow too bellicose, and Europe would feel Soviet retaliation. But these fears were manageable before and doubtless could be managed again.

None of this speculation is very realistic because it is all based on technological fantasy. Few analysts expect SDI to give the United States anything approaching invulnerability. At best, SDI may give U.S. land-based ICBMs better protection, which is still unlikely to provide a stable margin of superiority. And since Western Europe is open to so many kinds of nuclear attack, not to mention an overwhelming conventional invasion, expectations are still lower for what SDI can offer European security. By taking funds away from conventional defense or by increasing the cost of Europe's own nuclear deterrents, SDI's net military effects are likely to be harmful. Politically, by raising all the thorny issues of extended deterrence and decoupling, without offering any real chance of improvement, the net effect is also harmful.

Similarly, insofar as SDI blocks progress on arms control and further deteriorates superpower relations, or appears to do so, it may undermine the political modus vivendi in Europe itself. Most Europeans see pan-European political understandings as a major component for their security. Insofar as SDI seems to defeat the apparent efforts of the Gorbachev regime to cool the arms race and proceed with modernization of the Soviet economy, Europeans are likely to blame the United States for missing a historic opportunity for a radical improvement of pan-European security.[28] In short, SDI is unlikely to resolve the dilemmas of extended deterrence. Instead, it will make them worse.

Quite apart from the intellectual instability of American deterrence theory, another powerful solvent is now dissolving the strategic status quo: America's structural and fiscal deficit and its heavy, rapidly growing foreign indebtedness. The fiscal imbalance and consequent monetary gyrations and external imbalances have seriously disturbed both domestic and world economies. In due course, powerful pressures arising from the fiscal situation seem bound to force a reconsideration of military priorities. Enthusiasm for a new and expensive strategic program like SDI would only intensify the squeeze. The very high cost of maintaining standing conventional forces for Western Europe obviously makes existing NATO arrangements a ripe target. Moreover, U.S. pressure for European burden-sharing has been swelling for over a decade.

That the transatlantic military relationship has grown unjustifiably lopsided has long been widely admitted. The American nuclear protectorate over Europe, undertaken in the conditions of the late 1940s and early 1950s, clearly stands in need of revision in the very different strategic and economic conditions of the 1980s. If all SDI did was to precipitate that revision, it would be no bad thing.[29] Unfortunately, it also threatens to deteriorate superpower relations, highlight insoluble strategic questions within the alliance, and undermine further the alliance's conventional forces. On the face of it, none of this sets a propitious climate for successful revisions in the alliance.

Obviously, so long as the future shape of SDI remains so indefinable, predicting its consequences for the alliance is conjectural. In the worst case the United States, having spent a great deal of money for a marginal improvement in the survivability of its land-based missiles, would diminish its conventional commitment to Europe without any corresponding economic benefit. As the Soviets deployed their own defensive systems, European nuclear deterrents would seem devalued. For France and Britain, demands for increased spending on conventional forces would be paralleled by demands for strategic upgrading. Europeans, feeling beleaguered, would blame the Americans for spoiling the opportunity for a more solid détente in order to ratchet up the arms race. Not even the usual ham-fisted Soviet diplomacy would quell a powerful European impulse toward accommodation with the Soviets—and from a position of military weakness and alienation from the United States. Such conditions are unlikely, moreover, to encourage much solidarity among the West Europeans themselves.

A best case can be imagined from the obverse of the worst. The strategic and budgetary effects of SDI might finally precipitate the fundamental and long-needed reorganization of the alliance. Europeans at last would be provoked into creating a more balanced and autonomous defense. To sustain it, France, Germany, and perhaps even Britain would reach a more serious political and military consensus among themselves. Such an evolution would not break the American link or end extended deterrence. Europeans would assume primary responsibility for organizing conventional defense, but some U.S. forces would continue to be involved. A stronger European nuclear force would be created, but the U.S. commitment would remain. The emphasis would merely shift from extended to multiple deterrence.

Logically, a more indigenous defense should not lessen European security, particularly if fiscal pressures reduce the U.S. contribution in any event. A more Europeanized NATO could greatly improve the general psychological mood of transatlantic relations. American resentments and pretensions should decline with American hegemony, and a less dependent Europe should also grow less pusillanimous. The primordial common interest in containing Soviet power in Eurasia should be less encumbered on both sides.

At the same time, a militarily more self-sufficient Europe should also be in a better position to pursue containment through cooperative diplomacy with the East. A long-term strategy of trying to domesticate the Soviet regime within a pan-European system is certainly not bad in itself provided it is based on West European strength and unity rather than despairing weakness and disunity. Further insulating détente in Europe from the vagaries of U.S.-Soviet relations should actually strengthen the Atlantic alliance.

A new equilibrium within NATO should also help superpower relations. With the United States relieved of its too exclusive responsibility for European defense, the pressure for the arms race ought logically to diminish. In short, in the best case SDI will provoke devolution, and it is only devolution, rather than SDI, that can relieve the problems of extended deterrence.

Successful devolution within NATO, however, may seem even more fantastic than President Reagan's dreams for SDI. A common view sees Europe incapable of rising to such an occasion. The alleged feebleness of the European states, however, has been greatly exaggerated, as well as manipulated, to dampen any initiative for change. Europeans have all along behaved logically, given the U.S. commitment, with no sign of diminished concern for self-interest or self-preservation. Since SDI cannot resolve the problems of extended deterrence, but may well leave the United States still less able to sustain the present arrangements, devolution seems NATO's only real option, short of an end to the Atlantic alliance altogether.

Such conclusions about Europe suggest a different direction for U.S. strategic thought and policy than is customary among either advocates or opponents of SDI. It is true that the old faith in deterrence and arms control has shown considerable powers of resistance. Those faithful to the traditional doctrines form a large part of the U.S. political establishment and are in a broad conspiracy to withstand the SDI frenzy. Considering SDI in relation to Europe, however, suggests that preserving deterrence requires a bolder strategy than simply clinging to the traditional formulas. The strategic instability that drives the arms race and inspires SDI stems, in good part, from the U.S. nuclear commitment to Europe. It is the tension inherent in extended deterrence that has goaded counterforce strategy to its present manic extreme. Relief cannot come merely from well-intentioned efforts to promote U.S.-Soviet self-restraint and agreement. Something must also reduce the too heavy burden that extended deterrence lays on U.S. nuclear strategy. So long as Europe's defense rests so exclusively on a U.S. first use of nuclear weapons, nothing short of superiority will ever soothe American anxieties and nothing short of Soviet capitulation will end the arms race.

Devolution of European defense is not, of course, a panacea. For a start, it can only be partial. Realistically, the United States probably cannot, and certainly should not, escape engagement in European defense. But the American strategic burden would be far more manageable if the Europeans took over the primary responsibility for running their own defense and NATO evolved from a nuclear protectorate into a nuclear alliance. Such an evolution would bring U.S. commitments into some reasonable relation with U.S. resources. Today's stubbornly bipolar strategic culture would begin to come to terms with the world's pluralistic economic and political system.

How is it that so much of U.S. strategic thought ignores the real problems of American security? Why has a vision as improbable and disruptive as the original SDI been taken so seriously? All branches of specialized learning have a tendency to become a sort of cult, cut off from any broader historical, political, or philosophical foundation that might keep them anchored to the real world. Postwar economics, for example, has increasingly become a sort of faddish technology for producing miracles.[30] And industrial technology has too often embraced technical improvements in efficiency that carry much heavier long-term environmental or social costs.

Part of the explanation for this narrowness is doubtless sociological. Specialization seems natural to mass-produced, upwardly mobile elites who, as "experts," can feel confident without the need for any broader and more comprehensive education, even in their own specialties. Thus, for example, economists can become technicians, reared narrowly in one sect or another, with little knowledge of economic history or the development of economic theory. The same process has characterized nuclear strategy, which has gradually isolated itself not only from politics and economics but from any comprehensive view of military strategy itself. When a society as a whole loses its capacity to resist these cults, when, in other words, it loses its common sense, then the nation is headed for trouble. The administration's freakish enthusiasm for SDI as a technological remedy for all our geopolitical problems, not to mention the lemming-like conversion of much of the strategic and technological elites, seems a symptom of a certain cultural decadence afflicting our society. It is an unhappy reversal of stereotypes that the Europeans seem so much more robust in their common sense. It would be a happy irony to have Europe bring us back to our senses.

NOTES

1. See the March 23, 1983 "Address to the Nation by President Ronald Reagan: Peace and National Security," *Department of State Bulletin* 83, no. 2073 (Washington, D.C.: GPO, 1983), 8–14. See also Reagan arms-control adviser Paul Nitze's caution that BMD systems should not be deployed unless "cost-effective at the margin...that is, they must be cheap enough to add additional defensive capability

528 Policy Issues for the 1990s

so that the other side nas no incentive to add additional offensive capacity to over-come the defense." *The New York Times,* February 21, 1985. The president himself, after the October 1986 U.S.-Soviet summit in Iceland, described the strategic defense effort merely as "insurance" against Soviet cheating on arms agreements. *The New York Times,* October 14, 1986.

For the ambivalent conclusions of the president's own expert panels, see "Strategic Defense and Anti-Satellite Weapons," hearings before the Commit-tee on Foreign Relations, U.S. Senate, 98th Cong., 2d sess., April 25, 1984, 94–175; Donald L. Hafner, "Assessing the President's Vision: The Fletcher, Miller, and Hoffman Panels," in *Weapons in Space,* vol. 1 ("Concepts and Technologies"), *Daedalus* 114, no. 2 (Spring 1985), 91–107; and John C. Toomay, a member of the Fletcher panel, "The Case for Ballistic Missile Defense," in *Weapons in Space,* vol. 2 ("Implications for Security"), *Daedalus* 114, no. 3 (Summer 1985), 219–37. For the uneasy intellectual coexistence between Reagan's original exalted vision and the more prosaic rationales offered by most SDI proponents, see former secretary of defense James R. Schlesinger, "Rhetoric and Reality in Star Wars," *International Security* 10, no. 1 (Summer 1985), 6, or George Rathjens and Jack Ruina, "BMD and Strategic Instability," *Weapons in Space,* vol. 2, 255.

2. For a sampling of arguments against the continental bubble, see Schles-inger, "Rhetoric and Reality in Star Wars"; Rathjens and Ruina, "BMD and Strategic Instability"; or Hans A. Bethe, Jeffrey Boutwell, and Richard L. Gar-win, "BMD Technologies and Concepts in the 1980s," in *Weapons in Space,* vol. 1, 53–72. For the vulnerability of satellites, see Ashton B. Carter, "The Relation-ship of ASAT and BMD Systems," in *Weapons in Space,* vol. 1, 171–89; Kurt Gott-fried and Richard Ned Lebow, "Anti-Satellite Weapons: Weighing the Risks," in *Weapons in Space,* vol. 1, 147–70; and Harold Brown, "Is SDI Technically Feasi-ble?" *Foreign Affairs* ("America and the World 1985"), 64, no. 3, 442–47.

3. Europe, much closer to the Soviets, is far more vulnerable to cruise missiles, bombers, nuclear artillery, and so on. Shorter-range missiles, moreover, have a much shallower trajectory that makes them correspondingly more difficult to in-tercept. Paul Gallis, Mark Lowenthal, and Marcia Smith, *The Strategic Defense Initiative and United States Alliance Strategy* (Washington, D.C.: Congressional Research Service Report No. 85–48F, 1985).

4. A distinction must be made between costs at the margin for offensive and defensive systems already built and overall costs of developing and deploying the systems in the first place. Opponents of the bubble argue that even marginal exchange costs favor offense, whereas many admit that the reckoning of marginal exchange costs for point defense is less clear-cut. For example, "preferential" point defense—secretly choosing a fraction of offensive missile silos to defend—might obtain improved marginal exchange costs. This is because the enemy, not knowing which silos are defended, would be forced to throw additional warheads against all of them to have any reasonable chance of preventing a retaliatory second strike. The overall costs of the bubble are, of course, enormous, although the value of what is being defended, for example, the entire U.S. population, is priceless. Point defense, with far less overall cost, also covers targets, for example, missiles or bases, whose own value is far less. Its cost, therefore, must be weighed against the cost of ensuring a second-strike ability by other means—for instance, deploy-ing additional offensive missiles. For definitions, estimates, and arguments, see

Barry M. Blechman and Victor A. Utgoff, *Fiscal and Economic Implications of Strategic Defenses* (Boulder, Colo.: Copublished by Westview Press and The Johns Hopkins Foreign Policy Institute, 1986), 25; Rathjens and Ruina, "BMD and Strategic Instability," 242–50; Brown, "Is SDI Technically Feasible?" 444–45; Toomay, "The Case for Ballistic Missile Defense," 224–25; and Schlesinger, "Rhetoric and Reality in Star Wars," 7.

5. John C. Toomay, supposedly advocating BMD, in fact renders a most damning indictment along these lines. ("The Case for Ballistic Missile Defense," 232.) See also the chapter by Robert W. Tucker in this book; Schlesinger, "Rhetoric and Reality in Star Wars," 10; and Jerry Hough, "Soviet Interpretation and Response," in *Arms Control and the Strategic Defense Initiative: Three Perspectives* (Muscatine, Iowa: The Stanley Foundation, Occasional Paper 36, 1985). Rathjens and Ruina, because they deprecate the feasibility of the bubble, are not worried about instability in a crisis but rather about the tremendous new impetus to the U.S.-Soviet arms race. See "BMD and Strategic Instability."

6. See Thierry de Montbrial, "The European Dimension," *Foreign Affairs* ("America and the World 1985"), 64, no. 3, and Samuel F. Wells, Jr., "The United States and European Defense Cooperation," *Survival* 27, no. 4 (July/August 1985), 162–65.

7. Both Britain and France prefer today's barring of nationwide BMD systems by the ABM treaty but do not depend on it for the viability of their deterrence. See the interview with then French defense minister M. Paul Quilès, "La défense spatiale ne rend pas caduque l'arme nucléaire," *Le Monde*, December 18, 1985; and Benoît d'Aboville (French Ministry for Foreign Affairs) and M. Guionnet (French National Space Agency), "How BMD and ASAT New Developments Could Affect Third Countries," unpublished paper (Paris: June 1985), 16. See also Lawrence Freedman, "The Small Nuclear Powers," in Ashton B. Carter and David N. Schwartz, eds., *Ballistic Missile Defense* (Washington, D.C.: The Brookings Institution, 1984). For the current and planned configurations of British nuclear forces, see Secretary of State for Defence (U.K.), *Statement on the Defence Estimates 1985*, no. 1 (London: Her Majesty's Stationery Office, 1985), 19–21, 54. For France, see David S. Yost, "France's Deterrent Posture and Security in Europe, Part 1: Capabilities and Doctrine," *Adelphi Papers*, no. 194 (London: International Institute for Strategic Studies, Winter 1984/85), 19–29.

8. See *Strengthening Conventional Deterrence in Europe, Proposals for the 1980s*, Report of the European Security Study (Boston, Mass.: American Academy of Arts and Sciences, 1983), 7–36, 153–54.

9. Most analysts decline to estimate the potential cost in any specific manner. The oft-cited figure of $1 trillion seems intended to convey only an order of magnitude. A major exception is found in Blechman and Utgoff, *Fiscal and Economic Implications of Strategic Defenses*. For various versions of strategic defense, their figures range from $160 billion to $770 billion. But the authors concede that their estimates are based on some optimistic assumptions that become more questionable as the systems projected become more advanced. For instance, while some Soviet countermeasures are projected, increasing the number of Russian ICBMs is not. The authors themselves appear to rebut their own most important

assumption: "that the Soviet Union's antisatellite effort could be countered effectively for costs on the order of those described for the satellites used in the systems. *There is little basis for this assumption.* The potential vulnerability of defense satellites to attacks appears to be perhaps the largest unsolved problem for strategic defenses, and we are unaware of any promising solutions to it" (101, emphasis added).

10. It is not possible to make a precise calculation of the share of the U.S. military budget that is devoted to defending Europe. Brief reflection, however, can suggest the magnitude. Roughly 40 percent of the defense budget is manpower cost. Roughly one-third of the army's standing divisions are in Europe; another third have European defense as their primary mission. These "heavy" divisions have enormous associated capital expenditures, including major equipment and ammunition. In addition to the army divisions stationed in the United States but with Europe as their primary mission, the United States is obligated to supply eighty-eight air force squadrons and one marine amphibious brigade as reinforcements within ten days of the outbreak of hostilities. See *The Military Balance: 1985–86* (London: International Institute for Strategic Studies. 1985), 13; U.S. Department of Defense, *Report on Allied Contributions to the Common Defense* (citation), 76, 81; and Caspar Weinberger, *Annual Report to the Congress, Fiscal Year 1986* (Washington, D.C.: Department of Defense, 1985), 224.

Earl Ravenal has estimated the annual cost of the U.S. force commitment to Europe, for general purpose forces, to be $134 billion. ("Europe Without America: The Erosion of NATO," *Foreign Affairs* 63, no. 5 [Summer 1985].) For an extended but older version of this argument, see Earl C. Ravenal, *Defining Defense: The 1985 Military Budget* (Washington, D.C.: CATO Institute, 1984). Reduction of the U.S. commitment to European ground defense might also imply considerable reductions in the Reagan plans for a 600-ship navy. For the official justification of a 600-ship navy, see the statement of John F. Lehman, Jr., secretary of the navy, hearings before the Committee on Armed Services, U.S. Senate, 97th Cong., 2d sess. (Washington, D.C.: GPO, 1982), part 2, 1054–72. For a critique, see Joshua M. Epstein, *The 1987 Defense Budget* (Washington, D.C.: The Brookings Institution, 1986), 41–45.

11. See Christoph Bertram, "Strategic Defense and the Western Alliance," in *Weapons in Space*, vol. 2, 276–96.

12. For the views and prospects of various peace movements, see Werner Kaltefleiter and Robert L. Pfaltzgraff, eds., *The Peace Movements in Europe and the United States* (New York: St. Martin's Press, 1983). For recent polls of European opinion, see *SIPRI Yearbook 1986* (Oxford: Oxford University Press, 1986), 28–32. For an analysis of the West German elections of 1983, in which missile deployment was a key issue, see Arthur M. Hanhardt, "International Politics and the 1983 Election," in H. G. Peter Wallach and George K. Romoser, eds., *West German Politics in the Mid-Eighties, Crisis and Continuity* (New York: Praeger, 1985), 219–34.

13.

DEFENSE EXPENDITURE AS A PERCENTAGE OF GNP

	1914[a]	1938[b]	1949	1954	1965	1969	1974	1977	1980[c]	1983[c]
USA	—	1.5	5.1	12.7	8.3	9.6	6.6	6.0	5.6	7.4
FRG	4.6	—	—	4.7	5.0	4.1	4.1	3.4	3.3	3.4
France	4.8	6.6	6.2	8.5	6.1	4.9	4.1	3.6	4.0	4.2
U.K.	3.4	5.8	7.0	9.9	6.6	5.8	5.8	5.0	5.0	5.5
Italy	3.5	—	3.9	4.5	3.7	3.0	3.0	2.4	2.4	2.8

Source: Except where otherwise noted, data is from Kenneth A. Myers, ed., *NATO: The Next Thirty Years* (Boulder, Colo.: Westview Press, 1980), 406.
[a]A.J.P. Taylor, *The Struggle for Mastery in Europe* (Oxford: Oxford University Press, 1954), xxix.
[b]Study for the Joint Committee on the Economic Report, *Trends in Economic Growth* (Washington, D.C.: GPO, 1955), 276.
[c]*The Military Balance: 1985-86* (London: International Institute for Strategic Studies, 1985), 170.

14.

NATO AND WARSAW PACT FORCES IN EUROPE

	1976		1985	
	NATO	Warsaw Pact	NATO	Warsaw Pact
Combat and Direct Support Troops[a]	1,175,000	1,305,000	2,088,000	2,685,000
Tanks	11,000	26,500	20,333	52,600
Tactical Aircraft	2,960	5,300	4,056	6,159[b]
IRBMs	18[c]	—	18[c]	381
MRBMs	—	—	54	—
GLCMs	—	—	64	—
SRBMs	262	300	261	1,396

Source: Data from *The Military Balance: 1976-77* (London: International Institute for Strategic Studies, 1980), 76, 99, 101, 102; and *The Military Balance: 1985-86*, 186-87, 165-66.

[a]Recent inclusion of previously excluded support troops in the calculation of troop strength makes year-to-year comparisons difficult. However, the figures for missiles, aircraft, and tanks demonstrate the buildup.
[b]Estimated.
[c]French IRBMs.

15. For a general history of U.S. strategic problems and doctrines, see Lawrence Freedman, *The Evolution of Nuclear Strategy* (New York: St. Martin's Press, 1981).

16. Ibid., 345–47.

17. Fears of a U.S. "window of vulnerability" were popularized by the "Committee on the Present Danger," a group formed in the late 1970s by conservative critics of U.S. nuclear policy in general and the SALT II treaty in particular. See Charles Tyroller II, ed., *Alerting America, The Papers of the Committee on The Present Danger* (Washington, D.C.: Pergamon-Brassey's International Defense Publishers, 1984). The thesis was perhaps most notably challenged by President Reagan's own Commission on Strategic Forces, chaired by General Brent Scowcroft. See *Report of the President's Commission on Strategic Forces* (Washington, D.C.: President's Commission on Strategic Forces, April 1983), 7–8, 16–18. For a general account, see Freedman, *The Evolution of Nuclear Strategy*, 372–95. For a similar argument on the link between extended deterrence and the pressure for SDI, see the chapter by Robert W. Tucker in this book; on the link between extended deterrence and counterforce doctrine, see Steven Canby, "The Nuclear Weapons Debate: Is the Framework Right?" chapter in a forthcoming book.

18. Then defense secretary Robert McNamara provided an early and succinct statement of this dilemma when he unveiled "flexible response" as its solution. See "Ann Arbor Speech," June 16, 1962, Department of Defense News Release no. 980.

19. See Michael M. Harrison, *The Reluctant Ally: France and Atlantic Security* (Baltimore, Md.: The Johns Hopkins University Press, 1981), 72–76, 128, and Freedman, *The Evolution of Nuclear Strategy*, 313–29.

20. Lawrence Freedman, "Britain: The First Ex-Nuclear Power?" in *International Security* 6, no. 2 (Fall 1981), 80–104. See also Lawrence Freedman, *Britain and Nuclear Weapons* (London: Macmillan, 1980).

21. For arguments that NATO's conventional forces could or should be improved sufficiently to render a NATO first use or U.S. strategic superiority unnecessary, see Steven Canby and Ingemar Dorfer, "More Troops, Fewer Missiles," *Foreign Policy*, no. 53 (Winter 1983–84), 3–17, or McGeorge Bundy, George F. Kennan, Robert S. McNamara, Gerard Smith, Morton J. Halperin, William W. Kaufmann, Madalene O'Donnell, Leon V. Sigal, Richard H. Ullman, and Paul C. Warnke, "Back From the Brink," *The Atlantic* 258, no. 2 (August 1986), 35–41.

22. For an admirable summary of French doctrines and policies, see Harrison, *The Reluctant Ally*, 134–69. For a concise review of strategy under François Mitterrand, see Robert S. Rudney, "Mitterrand's Defense Concepts: Some Unsocialist Remarks," *Strategic Review* vol. 11, no. 2 (Spring 1983), 20–35; Michael M. Harrison and Simon Serfaty, "A Socialist France and Western Security" (Washington, D.C.: The Johns Hopkins Foreign Policy Institute, 1981), 27–35; or Yost, "France's Deterrent Posture and Security in Europe, Part 1," and "France's Deterrent Posture and Security in Europe, Part 2: Strategic and Arms Control Implications," *Adelphi Papers* no. 195 (London: International Institute for Strategic Studies, Winter 1984/85).

23. For my own analysis of de Gaulle's *Ostpolitik*, see *The Atlantic Fantasy: The U.S., NATO and Europe* (Baltimore, Md.: The Johns Hopkins University Press, 1970). For an update, see my forthcoming study for the Twentieth Century Fund, *America and the Defense of Europe*, chap. 10 and 11.

24. For an example of this view, see Bertram, "Strategic Defense and the Western Alliance."

25.

NATO FORCES IN WEST GERMANY

Belgium	1 corps HQ, 2/3 mechanized division
Canada	1 mechanized brigade
Denmark	None
France	1 corps HQ, 3 armored divisions[a]
Great Britain	1 corps HQ, 4 armored divisions, 1 infantry brigade
The Netherlands	1/3 mechanized division
U.S.	2 corps HQ, 2 armored cavalry regiments, 2 armored divisions, 2 mechanized divisions, 1 armored brigade, 2 mechanized brigades[b]
West Germany	3 corps HQ, 6 armored divisions, 5 mechanized divisions, 3 airborne brigades[c]

Source: Data from William P. Mako, *U.S. Ground Forces and the Defense of Central Europe* (Washington, D.C.: The Brookings Institution, 1983), 50–51.

[a]Excludes a brigade in West Berlin.
[b]Excludes an infantry brigade in West Berlin.
[c]Includes 1 mountain division counted as a mechanized division.

In the mid-1980s, the Bundeswehr has actually been expanding its wartime mobilization level. After 1987, when the Wartime Host Nation Support Programme is fully implemented, wartime strength is to rise to 1.34 million men. Federal Minister of Defense, *The Situation and the Development of the Federal Armed Forces, White Paper 1985* (Bonn: Federal Ministry of Defense, 1985), 236.

26. For Konrad Adenauer's insistence on a Western alliance over a neutralist reunification, see his early collection of speeches, *World Indivisible* (New York: Harper & Brothers, 1955), 49–104. As vice chancellor and foreign minister, Willy Brandt laid out his views on *Ostpolitik*, reunification, and ties to the West in *A Peace Policy for Europe* (New York: Holt, Rinehart and Winston, 1969), especially 94–155. For examples of Chancellor Helmut Kohl's speeches before the Bundestag on the subject of reunification, see "State of the Nation in Divided Germany," *Statements and Speeches* 8, no. 4 (March 5, 1985), and 9, no. 5 (March 18, 1986).

27.

TRADE WITH WARSAW PACT COUNTRIES
(as a percentage of total trade)

	1984		1985	
	Imports	Exports	Imports	Exports
France	3.68	3.17	3.48	2.99
FRG[a]	5.34	4.15	5.09	4.00
Italy	7.20	3.37	5.44	3.33
U.K.	2.23	1.85	1.86	1.51
U.S.	.66	1.92	.56	1.50

Note: Warsaw Pact = Bulgaria, Czechoslovakia, German Democratic Republic, Hungary, Poland, Rumania, and the Soviet Union.

Source: Data from *Monthly Statistics of Foreign Trade* (Washington, D.C.: Organization for Economic Cooperation and Development, August 1986), 50–51, 64–67, 74–75, 90–91.

[a]Excludes trade with the German Democratic Republic.

WEST GERMAN TRADE WITH THE GDR
(as percentage of combined trade with GDR and world)

	1984		1985	
	Imports	Exports	Imports	Exports
FRG	1.75	1.30	1.62	1.45

Source: Calculated from *Country Profile: West Germany 1986–87* (London: The Economist Intelligence Unit, 1986), 31–32.

28. For Soviet economic reform as a principal imperative behind current Soviet arms diplomacy, see Bruce Parrott, *The Soviet Union and Ballistic Missile Defense* (Boulder, Colo.: Copublished by Westview Press and The Johns Hopkins Foreign Policy Institute, 1987). For U.S. SDI as a needed threat to spur advances in Soviet technological capabilities, see Hough, "Soviet Interpretation and Response."

29. For my extended case for devolution of NATO burdens, see *America and the Defense of Europe.*

30. For the gimcrackery of U.S. economic policy, see the conclusion of my *The Imperious Economy* (Cambridge, Mass.: Harvard University Press, 1982).

23

New Technologies, the United States and Europe: Implications for Western Security and Economic Growth

Jean-François Delpech

Effective use of new military technologies is a recurrent theme throughout history; it has always had a very high priority for any group anxious for survival. However because of the strengthening pressure of the Warsaw Pact and the rapid emergence of new technologies, there is something essentially new in the trends we are now witnessing within both the Pact and the Atlantic Alliance. New technologies are particularly critical today because progress has been extremely rapid in many fields. For example, some claim that new sensors, coupled to high performance data acquisition and handling systems, may now make it possible to identify, acquire, and destroy moving, elusive targets at distances of 100–250 kilometers. If confirmed and implemented into actual weapon systems this would certainly have decisive consequences in the way armies are supposed to operate on NATO's central front.

JEAN-FRANÇOIS DELPECH is directeur de recherche au CNRS, CREST, École Polytechnique, Paris. Research for this paper was completed at the Woodrow Wilson International Center for Scholars, Washington, D.C. The author wishes to express appreciation to officials of United States government departments and agencies, and to colleagues at the French ministries of defense and scientific research for their assistance, and also special thanks to Dr. Samuel F. Wells, Jr., associate director of the Wilson Center. The article expresses the views of the author alone.

Reprinted with permission from *The Atlantic Community Quarterly,* Vol. 25, No. 1 (Spring 1987): 47–64.

Of course the Strategic Defense Initiative is a prime example of the potential integration of new technologies into a new military system with novel, ambitious goals, obviously with strategic implications. It is also unfortunately a prime example of the tensions induced between allies by unilateral technological enthusiasm. One feels that on each side closer attention to the needs of others might have been more productive. While Europeans have serious misgivings about a possible negative impact on military doctrine and on the credibility of the United States guarantee, they are often quite eager to seize this opportunity for improving their research capabilities in high technology areas in coordination with the United States.

Problems related to the introduction of new technologies are compounded by the fact that the development-production cycle in the field of armaments, which started with World War II and rebounded in the sixties, has now brought us near the end of the production phase of systems designed fifteen to twenty-five years ago. We are again at a stage where many decisions have to be made in the development of new systems. These decisions will undoubtedly define the status of our defense well into the first decades of the next century, given the long operational life of weapon systems.

Despite common basic security needs among nations of the Alliance, divergences of opinion stem in part from the fact that our economies are involved in a healthy but highly competitive economic struggle. Lack of complete agreement is to be expected in an alliance of free nations. This is why we need to understand thoroughly the varying needs which arise from complementary and sometimes quite different national viewpoints.

What Are New Technologies?

There have been many important technological breakthroughs in the last decades, and it seems safe to assume that there will be many more in the future. To avoid *a priori* definitions we shall simply remark that in high technology industries, scientists, engineers, and their research and development efforts play a very important or even a central role. According to this criterion, most would agree on the following list of at least ten groups of industries which make very extensive use of high technologies:

1. guided missiles and spacecraft
2. communication equipment and electronic components
3. aircraft and parts
4. office, computing, and accounting machines
5. biotechnologies
6. drugs and medicines
7. industrial inorganic chemicals

8. professional and scientific instruments
9. engines, turbines, and parts
10. plastics, resins, composite materials

To a large extent each of these groups of industries relies not on one single technology but rather on a broad front of basic technologies: electronics, computer science, new materials, biotechnologies. Progress in these basic technologies, like progress in the related industries, often depends on progress made in other high technology industries.

Thus the first essential characteristic of modern technologies is that they are closely interrelated: their development feeds on that of other technologies. Breakthroughs occur simultaneously over a broad front of applications. They overlap in ways that are largely unanticipated, reinforcing each other and making more progress possible through *cross-fertilization*. Hence the development of new technologies is not a linear process. It depends very much on the size of the economy and on the efficiency of socioeconomic processes that put a premium on interaction and exchange of information.

Modern technologies also tend to be *highly fragmented*, because a better understanding of small parts of a larger process, or the availability of higher performance materials for a particular function in a large ensemble often give a decisive edge over the competition.

Finally, modern technologies often have *finite, comparatively short lifetimes* because of the rapid pace of scientific and technical progress and also in consequence of the above-mentioned fragmentation. New techniques are developed all the time and are incorporated into the end product on an evolutionary basis (although revolutionary end products may appear from time to time, as was the case with the microcomputer revolution).

These general characteristics of modern technologies have two closely related consequences: technologies are not necessarily produced and used within the same company, group, or nation; and they are by their very nature highly tradable. There is an international market for high technologies. Their ease of trade has also the unfortunate consequence that they may be difficult to secure.

The center of gravity of the market for high technology—as well as its precise nature—has substantially shifted over time. Initially and until the second part of the nineteenth century the development and use of high technologies was centered in Europe, mainly Britain, France and Germany. But even before the First World War the United States had begun playing an increasingly important role. The United States was critically helped between the two World Wars by the flow of refugees from Nazi-controlled Europe and also by the openness, the dynamism, and the competitive nature of its laboratories and institutions, where these refugees rapidly became very productive. In cooperation with their American colleagues they served the needs of a society that put a large premium on innovation. By 1945 only the United States was in a position to make complete and adequate use of this huge technology base, which had considerably expanded during the war. Also the United States was learning how to manage it effectively, instead of more or less "letting it happen." This situation raised grave concerns in Europe; many felt that the "brain drain" was unduly beneficial to the United States, which was freely using the great potential created in Europe by decades of investment in basic research and giving little in return.

In retrospect it seems quite clear that the only sensible and effective solution for Europe was to do exactly what she did: rebuild a competitive scientific, technical, and industrial base and ensure that the social conditions for innovation were once again fully operative. With the remarkable economic recovery of Europe, followed by Japan and by the development of the Newly Industrialized Countries (NICs), especially of East Asia, the situation has once again shifted. There are many buyers and sellers in the high technology marketplace, and United States and/or European temporary monopolies have come to an end—probably forever. In fact, in the first five years of the current decade, according to United States Department of Commerce statistics, the surplus enjoyed by the United States in trade in high technology manufactures (roughly corresponding to the ten industry groups listed above) dwindled from $26.6 billion to only $6.2 billion. This balance became negative in 1986. Still more impressive is the fact that by far the largest negative contribution (as seen from the United States point of view) is due to group 2, communication equipment and electronic components, where the United States had a huge lead until very recently.

This trend may perhaps have some healthy consequences in that it reflects a broadening of the marketplace related to increasing overall co-prosperity. As already noted, a larger technological base is in our common interest because it increases the possibilities of cross-fertilization. Furthermore, competition is very effective in keeping complacency down. However it is on the whole a very sobering trend, and concerns are again raised in some quarters (especially in the United States) about the fairness of the current situation.

A related problem is that weapon design has become less national and more cooperative. According to a recent report from the United States National Academy of Engineering, United States-made missile guidance systems, radars, communications gear, satellites, air navigation instruments, and other sensitive devices have become increasingly dependent on foreign parts and manufacturing expertise. Similar conclusions are no doubt reached within other NATO countries, and the associated risks are carefully weighed. Even when (as is generally the case) suppliers are located in friendly countries, they may be more vulnerable than local suppliers, and shipments may very well be interrupted or slowed even under low-intensity crisis conditions, or because of unilateral decisions. It may also be more difficult to obtain state-of-the-art technology from a foreign supplier who may not be particularly inclined to help outside competitors, or who may be discouraged from doing so by discreet external interventions. The exportation of military systems using foreign-made parts (even marginally) may also pose specific difficulties. For example even for exports between NATO members a specific license is needed whenever a military product contains a component included in the United States Military Critical Technologies list.

An even more serious problem, albeit not one reflected in trade balance figures, is that the Soviet Union is evidently using Western technology to increase its political and military power base. Not only do they "legitimately" tap into the Western marketplace, but they also use more devious means. These are now well documented in the open literature since French intelligence published in the early 1980s cost-efficiency evaluations drawn up by the Soviet VPK, the interministerial body assessing technology transfers from the West.

The question of how to keep our technological edge has thus become of central importance. The collective security of the West largely depends on it. But concerns, however legitimate, do not easily translate into sensible policies. There are no simple solutions to this very complex set of interrelated problems. Some measure of protection is probably unavoidable in trade within the Alliance. But it should at least be consistent with the very finite lifetime of many of these technologies, and it is essential that the common, overriding security interests of the Alliance should never be forgotten. Common sense and history both indicate that in the long run the most effective policy for the Alliance would not be technological protectionism, but rather striving to remain ahead of the competition by strengthening the scientific and technical establishments of member states and increasing cooperation. We certainly still have the capabilities to do so, in terms of organization and manpower.

Military Implications of New Technologies

A Short List of "Military" Technologies

The high technology industries discussed above were listed without attempting to distinguish between their military or civilian importance. In fact, they are all clearly essential both for military and for civilian applications. Some examples of military uses of these technologies might be useful, however, to give a practical feel to the discussion which follows.

Advanced composite material technology provides high-strength, lightweight, survivable, corrosion-resistant component materials. They may furthermore be producible more economically, faster, and from domestically available materials.

Genetic engineering can be used to develop chemical and biological detection systems, vaccine antidotes, and other compounds for prevention and treatment of casualties. An important long-term goal would be to make chemical/biological warfare as unattractive as possible to the Soviets.

Advanced visible and infrared sensor technology greatly improves our capabilities passively to detect and identify targets at night or under adverse observation conditions. Developments in focal plane arrays, charge-coupled devices, and other detector technologies will permit achievement of these capabilities in the near future.

Millimeter wave technology will permit us to "see" through battlefield smoke, fog, and dust, with applications to terminal homing missiles and to self-guided artillery ammunitions.

Very high speed integrated circuits are the building blocks for the computers and/or the processors needed for intermediate-level tasks like automatic target recognition (using data produced by the above-mentioned sensors) and also for higher-level tasks like analyzing and integrating battlefield data, and to aid in battle management and tactical decision making. Development of new semiconductor materials such as Gallium Arsenide will permit similar capabilities to be realized with smaller systems that have lower power and cooling requirements and better environmental properties (e.g., radiation hardening).

Robotic/artificial intelligence systems may help us to analyze data and organize their presentation, and also to optimize the results that human operators can obtain from machines. They should also permit remote-controlled hazardous operations, which may someday become much cheaper without the constraints of maintaining a suitable environment for man.

Progress along most of these lines depends heavily on continuing progress in *basic and applied computer science*: directly, through the development of new, more reliable, much faster, and more systematic ways of writing software—perhaps using standard building blocks and interfaces—and also indirectly, across an even broader field, by the development of computer-aided design techniques, manufacturing, and inspection procedures to produce lighter-weight, more reliable combat and support vehicles with enhanced mobility and needing less logistic support. One will note throughout most of this list the obvious, close relationship that exists between civilian and military applications. But while still playing a very important role as a large customer and strongly motivated promoter of high technologies, the military sector is not the leader anymore in the West. As perhaps never before, the civilian and the military sectors reinforce each other and make good use of the cross-fertilization potentialities of high technologies. This gives us a reason for some cautious optimism in the West, with our strong civilian sector, in contrast with the central role of the military in the economies of the Warsaw Pact, which seem particularly ill adapted to the present situation.

However, the fact that the nature of the innovation process is changing to some extent should not make us too complacent in the West. A top-down approach used to be fashionable in the sixties and early seventies, when a few highly competent and skilled bureaucrats would launch spectacular technical projects with innovations coming from government or big corporations. This approach meshes well with the military conception of a well-run, orderly system and may still be favored in many military procurement agencies throughout the world. Nevertheless, while it may still be useful in some situations, other approaches may be more effective now in the late eighties. After all, the microcomputer revolution resulted largely from a "bottom-up" approach, when many independent, small-scale actors decided to try to apply microprocessor "intelligence" to all kinds of activities, spreading it through the economy and through the society with spectacular success.

The Integration of New Technologies into Military Systems

How eagerly should we pursue the development of military applications of new technologies? How fast will new weapons incorporating them have a sizable impact on battlefield situations?

Not surprisingly in view of the many potentialities of new technologies, the expectations of many of their proponents have tended to be very sanguine. This is not a new phenomenon, as evidenced by this pronouncement made in 1969 by General William C. Westmoreland, then United States Army chief of staff:

> On the battlefield of the future, enemy forces will be located, tracked and targeted almost instantaneously through the use of data links, computer-assisted intelligence evaluation, and automated fire control. With first-round kill probabilities approaching certainty, and with surveillance devices that can continually track the enemy, the need for large forces to fix the opposition physically will be less important.

Seventeen years later, although much progress has certainly been made, it is obvious that active or passive countermeasures have also made much progress in the forces of the Warsaw Pact, and that the situation has not been radically altered. The need for numbers both in manpower and in equipment is still keenly felt. In particular, the possibility of automatically acquiring, tracking, targeting and destroying militarily significant mobile targets on the ground at distances over 100 kilometers is still very far from obvious under real battlefield conditions, particularly in Europe.

Even at the end of a successful research phase new technologies may still require much development and are often extremely expensive to implement. Also, as our Western space programs have painfully reminded us in the last year, high technologies are not necessarily synonymous with high reliability. In fact recent events have led many to wonder if we should not borrow from the relatively low-tech approach of the Russians and be slightly more interested in quantity and a "natural" reliability associated with simplicity, and less in textbook performance. This is why it would be most dangerous at this point to be carried away by technical enthusiasm and forget that there is usually a long way from the laboratory to the application. Even though progress may be very fast on the basic "building blocks" described above, it is generally safe to assume that technologies normally take a long time to mature into systems, except in cases where there is tremendous pressure, either from a national emergency (e.g., the Manhattan Project—but the goal was only a demonstration, not really a system) or from market forces (e.g., the microcomputer revolution—but the technology was partially there).

Even an apparently simple system may require very complicated software, particularly when high reliability is desired (as is often the case for military applications). It took about fifteen years to develop the Franco-Belgian RITA Multiple Subscriber Equipment system (a kind of battlefield phone system), and the United States Army had to abandon its own effort within the Triservice Tactical Communications Program because it found it too expensive and too time demanding. Such difficulties may thus have positive consequences, as they sometimes lead to improved cooperation.

Will new high technologies reduce the manpower needs of NATO armies? Such claims are frequently made (as in General Westmoreland's quotation above), and might be partially true for fighting forces: more advanced equipment should lead to increased efficiency, as in the civilian sector of the economy. However, a portion of the manpower saved will certainly be shifted from fighting to support, particularly maintenance. While it is difficult to predict the extent of this shift, current experience with various new weapon systems is not particularly encouraging. Furthermore, the required technical personnel must be highly qualified, particularly in electronics. There will thus be a fierce competition for talented people, already in short supply throughout our economies, while unskilled labor, still relatively abundant, will have less and less use. Economic benefits stemming from manpower changes related to high technologies would thus seem dubious. Still more highly trained engineers and technicians will be needed in the defense industries of the Alliance if there is a determined push towards high technologies, and the economic and social consequences are uncertain. There will be spin-offs, to be sure, but there will also be shortages in some fields, which may be very important to the economy as a whole.

A Balanced Evolution of Forces

As our goal of common defense through adequate military preparation can only be achieved if we maintain substantial political cohesion, we have to be very careful in balancing the evolution of our forces. The complexity and variety of the problems created by the introduction of new technologies in weapon systems make them already extremely difficult to manage even within a single country, however powerful. It is no surprise that they should prove particularly vexing inside an alliance, where appreciations, capabilities, and needs are vastly different.

Obviously, NATO forces must evolve (as do Warsaw Pact forces) in response to the new technical environment, which is very far from being under the control of the military establishment, at least in the West. New ideas have to be formulated, like the mission of Follow-on Forces Attack (FOFA) of NATO, like the AirLand Battle doctrine of the United States Army, or perhaps even the Counter Air 90 concepts under discussion in NATO circles. Some will slowly gain acceptance. Still, even if we are able to keep balanced forces within the Alliance, the question remains whether we should try to accelerate or to slow down this evolution.

We know that nuclear deterrence is basic to our defense posture and that conventional forces are necessary. The initial question thus turns into two related questions: how fast should new technologies replace older technologies in our conventional defense? and to what extent should they supplement or even partially replace our nuclear forces?

The Balance between "Old" and New Technologies

In fact "old" technologies interact with and benefit from new technologies. Think for example of aircraft and high-precision standoff missiles, or of tanks, laser rangers, and electronic fire control systems. As already noted, new technologies are often used in components of systems relying also on well-proven technologies. Furthermore, the Soviets have made substantial technical progress in the last decade or so. It would probably be dangerous and unrealistic to assume that they would not be able to do about as well as we do—albeit perhaps differently. We may have better technical abilities, but it is not completely obvious that we are able to exploit them much better.

There remains however a very real uncertainty as to what should be the best mix between old, field-proven systems and promising new technologies. From a military point of view, high technology conventional weapons suffer from the obvious drawback of being of very uncertain effectiveness as long as they have not been extensively tested under real battle-field conditions. It is clear that it would take an unusual degree of confidence to rely extensively on such weapons.

Also, there is unfortunately one thing very certain about new technologies: they are and will remain very expensive, at least in the medium run. This is a basic consideration at a time when budgets are at near saturation. Some slight increase may still be possible in some countries but most probably not in the United States. Claims that NATO should increase expenses substantially faster, perhaps by one or two percentage points above 3 percent, are thus most likely to remain unheeded, and may well be counterproductive. Despite their obvious utility in United States internal politics, they may ultimately put in jeopardy the basic political asset of the Alliance, its unity. Furthermore they may well foster public suspicions of inadequate defenses and encourage pacifism. The balance between old and new technologies will thus no doubt be strongly influenced by budgetary considerations. The stimulus the Soviets gave us unwittingly in the late 1970s with the invasion of Afghanistan and the Polish crises may not be forthcoming in the future.

And the Balance between Nuclear and New Technologies

The famous Lisbon force goals—that NATO forces should be a rough match to the Soviet and East European forces confronting them then and now—were set by NATO ministers in 1952 at the height of the Korean War, and embodied in MC 14/1. Since then NATO has been committed in principle to increasing conventional defenses. In practice, of course, no real effort was made to reach these goals, which were probably quite unrealistic, and which were in any event soon made obsolete by the "new look" strategy of the Eisenhower administration. Since the early sixties the tension between American preferences for European conventional defenses and the European interest in preservation of American nuclear deterrence has been chronic, and has been far from being entirely resolved by the adoption of the "flexible response" strategy in 1967.

This drive toward increased conventional defenses has been complemented by assertions that new technologies could change qualitatively the *rapport de forces* between NATO and the Warsaw Pact. Some for example believe that new conventional high-precision weapons will more or less replace tactical nuclear weapons. On a strategic level President Reagan in his famous March 1983 SDI speech extolled his dream of a world where nuclear weapons had become "impotent and obsolete," that is, where technology had in effect succeeded in eliminating any benefit that might accrue from the threat of nuclear weapons. In fact, as already noted, it is far from clear that the West would be in a position to exploit its technological lead at little cost to drive back a Soviet attack by nonnuclear means. Furthermore, while it is fortunate that mankind has such an extreme fear of nuclear war, this should not blind us to the real issue—avoiding war. Nuclear weapons are a fact, and they will not be disinvented. They have the advantage of using largely proven technologies. Their effects on tactical targets are large enough to be assured even if their delivery is not very precise. The corresponding disadvantage is that their collateral effects will often be larger than for conventional weapons—except in such borderline cases as chemical weapons used on extensive targets (the Soviets are known to be well equipped in chemical weapons).

There is a great diversity of opinions within any NATO country, as is to be expected in democracies. But I think it is fair to say that to a majority of Europeans it is not just *nuclear war*, but *any kind of war*, which must be avoided. Past experience has shown us that even a purely conventional war can be highly destructive. Events of the last forty years lead many of us to believe in the deterrent effect of nuclear weapons. Any policy which makes their use—and even their first use—by NATO forces less likely in case of war, thus raising the "nuclear threshold," is bound to be met in Europe by fears that it may thereby make war appear a more reasonable proposition to the Soviets and give them a very substantial and perhaps decisive advantage in the balance of forces.

After more than twenty years, many Europeans would still subscribe to the remark of Bernard Brodie that Europeans are sensitive to the fact that "(nuclear) weapons have vastly affected the expectations of major war in Europe, and it is absurd not to make the most of that change. It is illogical to propose that the NATO powers should add substantially to their defense burdens in order to exploit a probably slim chance for moderating a possible future European war—which however the present dispositions make highly improbable." It is obvious that geography and politics are such that a purely conventional defense of Europe is not now possible. Nuclear weapons are necessary both in the course of a conflict and as a strategic deterrent.

Because of our different geostrategic situations things may superficially appear different from a United States point of view. War may not look completely lost to Americans if it is lost only in Europe, and if no nuclear weapons were used the continental United States would emerge unscathed. However if the West were winning a conventional war in Europe, would the Soviets accept defeat without resorting to nuclear weapons? And in the long run, if Europe were lost, how viable would America be, confronted by a vastly expanded Soviet empire in complete control of Eurasia and Africa?

What is then the suitable balance between nuclear and conventional forces in Europe? The answer is not quite the same for deterrence (where a rational enemy tends to consider the upper limit of risk) and for war fighting (where actual capabilities as effectively deployed are tested). Nuclear weapons are essential for deterrence and chances are that they will remain so in the foreseeable future.

If deterrence should fail, better conventional capabilities to stop an invasion early would be welcome—for example with "smart" antitank weapons. However, let us not forget that the main reason why NATO authorities would very quickly face the decision to release theater nuclear weapons in case of a conventional attack is today's lack of sustainability with trained manpower, ammunition, and war reserve matériel. Efforts are clearly necessary in all these domains, perhaps along lines similar to the Long Term Defense Plan of 1978. But the budgetary constraints mentioned above would make it extremely unlikely that a marked shift to high technologies would have a positive effect on sustainability. In fact it may turn out to have quite the contrary effect and, to quote Lenin, "quantity has a quality of its own." To talk now of replacing nuclear weapons with conventional ones, when economic and political realities alone make it almost impossible, and when techniques are still at best very uncertain, is thus most dangerous. In fact it can only reinforce public perceptions of an inadequate defense and play into the hands of pacifists. This is certainly not in the interest of the West.

New Technologies: For Better or for Worse?

Even if there were general agreement about the military importance and urgency of new technologies (and this is far from being the case), their introduction would have to be handled in quite different ways on both sides of the Atlantic, and also in different European countries, because of unavoidable divergences in national appreciations, of their large impact on technology bases and economic power and well-being, and of the varying roles of internal pressure groups. All these considerations are generating substantial political pressure. Despite its current state of fairly reasonable health, exclusive or even excessive attention to narrowly defined military problems would be just as self-defeating for the Alliance as fixation on economic considerations because it is its *political cohesion* which is of paramount importance. Other questions should always be kept in a broader political perspective.

An Uneasy Relationship between the United States and Europe

Although many attempts have been made to rationalize programs and encourage transatlantic exchanges, they have not always met with success. Relations between the United States and its European partners are often uneasy, especially so far as research, production, and weapons acquisition are concerned. Europeans have traditionally been wary of United States good intentions in favor of increased transatlantic cooperation. They are afraid of losing technological or industrial independence. Even those who are most in favor of strong cooperative efforts may be hindered by United States attitudes (witness Secretary Weinberger's letter on SDI cooperation in April 1985, written no doubt with the best intentions, but resented as an ultimatum in many European capitals). Europeans are also keenly aware of the extent of the "NIH syndrome" in the United States: the tendency to reject what is Not Invented Here. The ultimate failure of the *Roland* missile adaptation in the United States is a good case in point.

Many also fear that cooperation in United States-led programs could undermine their own attempts to start rationalizing their defense industry through joint research efforts, a goal currently being pursued through the IEPG (Independent European Program Group). They feel that the recent Nunn initiative (see below) is a potential distraction from intra-European cooperation, which remains essential if Europe is to strengthen its own technological capabilities.

On the United States side there is a strong feeling that European countries should do more toward overall support of NATO. This is of course the line of reasoning behind the 1984 Nunn amendment, which was defeated but is still being kept visibly on the shelf. (And needless to say this United States viewpoint is hotly disputed by most Europeans, this author included.) Another important but far less explicit consideration is a fear in Washington that a technologically strong but independently oriented Europe would not necessarily be in the best interest of the United States and would in fact weaken the political coherence of the NATO alliance. There is also a renewed consciousness in the United States of the critical importance of keeping a keen technical edge to the United States economy. This is of course somewhat inimical to the necessity to use new technologies for the balanced development of the Alliance.

Other realities must also be considered: the United States enjoys a dominant position. In many cases technological, financial, or industrial considerations make buying American weapons a necessity for Europeans. This explains the present strong disequilibrium of the military trade balance of most of European countries in favor of the United States. There have been some successes, such as the Durandal, Dauphin, and RITA programs, but most would agree that the celebrated two-way street needs serious improvements!

Despite these misgivings on both sides, most Western observers agree that a stronger European pillar is a necessity for our security in the long run, not only for Europe, but also for the United States. The very real problems posed by cooperative action must be examined anew and from the ground up. They warrant a very patient, progressive effort, and close attention to the best near- and long-term interests of all parties concerned. Indications are that under the pressure of necessity practical and successful compromise positions may be found acceptable.

A New Awareness within the Alliance

Particularly in times of budgetary restraint there are compelling, purely economic arguments in favor of cooperation. A better value for the dollar and a more effective defense system would result from better harmonizing the military hardware produced by the sixteen members of NATO. This is part of the rationale for the recent important Quayle and Nunn-Roth-Warner amendments. The Quayle amendment gives the secretary of defense far greater latitude in structuring cooperative programs with NATO allies by removing constraints which had been shown to have negative consequences in earlier cases. In particular, the Department of Defense may now enter into work sharing agreements, where it formerly had to insist on open competition. The amendment also removes some restrictions on contracting for goods and services from a project partner and provides that the United States may now enter into cooperative agreements entailing ownership and disposal of joint property.

An amendment to the 1986 defense authorization bill, sponsored by Senator Nunn and cosponsored by Senators Roth and Warner, earmarks $200 million specifically for NATO cooperative R&D projects. The money is to be divided into four equal parts: $50 million to each of the three services and $50 million to Defense Department agencies. The amendment also authorizes expenditure of an additional $50 million for side-by-side testing of allied and American systems. Finally, and this may have far-reaching consequences, it directs that the Department of Defense identify and consider cooperative development or existing systems of allies as alternatives to United States development or systems at every step of the acquisition process. The money has to be spent in the United States. In order to encourage allied contributions United States money cannot be spent without a cooperative program governed by a formal agreement. However, while European partners must make equitable contributions to the program, they do not have to match the United States contribution. There is a firm deadline of September 1987 by which formal contracts must be negotiated in order to qualify for Nunn amendment funding.

This development has had positive consequences for the Alliance. Letters of intent for six multinational development projects have already been signed by armament directors of twelve NATO countries, with partial financing by funds authorized by the Nunn-Roth-Warner amendment:

- a standoff airborne radar demonstrator system for surveillance and target acquisition programs

- an autonomous, terminally guided 155 mm munition program
- question and answer components for the NATO identification system, which includes IFF (Identification Friend or Foe) equipment
- a multifunction information distribution system
- a modular standoff weapons program
- a support environment for the ADA high-level computer language

These projects have been under discussion for some time at various levels and within the IEPG. Development had already been started independently by several nations on a few of these projects. France and Germany included corresponding line items in their respective 1986 budgets. Signatory nations also provide experts to participate in the initial planning stages of what are provisionally called "Nunn Cooperative Projects."

Problems and potential hurdles abound: Will adequate funding be provided? How can development and purchasing cycles be coordinated in the various nations? Will it be possible to overcome the opposition of vested interests? In particular, the satisfactory resolution of technology transfer problems may turn out to be difficult. However, United States officials are optimistic that this offer will prove an important step toward closer cooperation in weapons-related research. The United States budget for FY 1987 also contains interesting new provisions such as the Senate's Balanced Technology Initiative and the House's Conventional Defense Initiative, and also a Senate proposal to earmark $50 million in SDI funds for exploration of antitactical ballistic missile systems on a cooperative basis with allies. It remains to be seen what practical impact such measures will have. But they soften to some extent the blow felt in NATO capitals after the Senate's positive vote on the Glenn amendment, which would have made SDI cooperation with the closest American allies all but impossible (that amendment was fortunately dropped from the final language of the authorization act).

On a strictly European level there is no coordination of military R&D, although there are several bi- or multilateral development projects. Europeans are acutely conscious of their current technology lag behind Japan and the United States—which many ascribe primarily to excessive fragmentation, leading to wasteful duplication of efforts both among countries and among research centers and enterprises within a single country—and are trying to remedy it.

In the last few years, the European Economic Community (EEC) has devoted an increasing proportion of its budget to cooperative research programs; ESPRIT (European Strategic Program for Research in Information Technology) is the most visible of these. A total of 750 million ECU was allocated by the EEC to ESPRIT for the period 1984–1988 (one ECU is roughly one dollar). Funding by participating organizations should match this amount. Although many feel that ESPRIT falls far short of the need, it is clearly a success. Its specific action areas are

- advanced microelectronics, including VLSI and high-speed circuits
- software technologies: theories, methods and tools
- computer architecture and advanced information processing
- "bureautique," including office and factory information technologies
- computer-integrated design and manufacturing

Two other cooperative programs have been launched by the EEC: RACE (Research into Advanced Communications technologies in Europe) addresses the growing concern that Europe lags in maintaining an efficient telecommunications network, with the goal of uniting all of the EEC by 1995 in a single, integrated broadband communications network. This program is in its definition stage and should be on a scale similar to that of ESPRIT. BRITE (Basic Research in Industrial Technologies for Europe) aims to stimulate cooperative, precompetitive R&D in areas not already covered by industry.

Quite independently of the EEC Framework Program, France proposed in early 1985 that Europe should coordinate its efforts in high technologies expected to yield major economic benefits, thus launching *Eureka* (In deference to Archimedes I use lower case letters. One is free to read EUrope and REsearch; some even claim that the *k* stands for Koordination and the *a* for Agency!). The originality of *Eureka* is that it is primarily market oriented, and also that its structure is very light and informal. It is coordinated by seven persons and has nineteen member countries. Important decisions are left to the *Eureka* council of ministers—the ministers of research of all 11 participating countries, assisted by high representatives of participating states, as well as the European Commission. Its total budget at the end of 1986, including private funding, was over $2 billion, shared among sixty-two projects covering most high technology areas. *Eureka* is gathering momentum and both its budget and the number of projects are growing rapidly. Widely viewed at its inception as a response to the SDI program, it is in fact purely civilian in its conception and organization, although civilian research may clearly have military spin-offs.

Mention should also be made of the European Space Agency (ESA), which has been very successful in putting Europe into the space business, with a current budget of $830 million (about 10 percent of NASA's budget).

There is a common thread running through most of the programs discussed above: it was recognized that it would not be possible to produce common equipment and that agreement would only be reached by focusing on components rather than systems. The fact that the programs were still at an early stage paved the way for cooperation on common components that can be incorporated into the systems of more than one nation. The advantage of starting at the research end is that it is relatively inexpensive. But when it involves United States companies it also raises in the minds of many Europeans a strong fear of a new kind of brain drain, with the United States trying to procure "on the cheap" new and promising ideas.

Conclusion

We are faced with the difficult problem of maintaining the cohesion of the Alliance while making its military posture more efficient. While most acknowledge our obvious common, long-term interests, short-term difficulties arise from the search for competitive advantages, from divergent economic interests, and from different geopolitical appreciations. Such tensions are normal within a free alliance of free countries. They must be accepted, but their importance should not be exaggerated. And they must be prevented from interfering with our basic goals.

After all, we should still be collectively able to strike an acceptable balance between the partially contradictory requirements detailed in this article. A real political will to succeed is becoming apparent on both sides of the Atlantic. The overriding importance of the Alliance is broadly recognized, and our long-term concerns are fortunately reinforced by more immediate considerations: Military expenditures cannot increase indefinitely. New technologies are amenable to a flexible and decentralized management style.

Military expenditures cannot increase indefinitely. With defense resources stationary or even decreasing in many countries, and with costs increasing, cooperation becomes a necessity. Even the United States can no longer afford the cost of developing independently all the systems it needs. A good case in point is the Mobile Subscriber Equipment discussed above, which led to the signing of a multibillion-dollar United States-French contract for the RITA system last year.

New technologies can be managed more flexibly. The relationship between the military and civilian sectors is changing. The degree of overlap is certainly growing, with their common entrepreneurial emphasis, their rapid exploitation of basic research, and their orientation toward components. NATO already takes on an increasing role in creating a framework for the integration of subsystems and in having the responsibility for the interoperability of the elements. Because high technologies are now as much linked to national competitive advantages in global markets as to military security, due attention must be paid to legitimate national concerns. But NATO should explore new management approaches, akin to ESPRIT or *Eureka*, within a framework which might be reminiscent of the Long Term Defense Plan of the late seventies. Within a balanced evolution of forces we should simultaneously aim to protect emerging technologies in the national R&D phase and to promote competitive innovation for the many components that will make up the conventional systems of the next decade.

Recent advances both in transatlantic and intraeuropean cooperation point the way. New, carefully handled programs to facilitate the cooperative introduction of new technologies in our defense systems at a reasonable pace will contribute to a real and lasting strengthening of the Alliance, if we pay simultaneous attention to economic and defense considerations and are properly sensitive to the implications of different political perceptions in NATO's sixteen countries.

Part III
DOMESTIC ISSUES THAT WON'T GO AWAY

Health Care Policy: Understanding the Emerging Medical-Corporate Complex

Each of the four papers in this section carries a common theme: health care in the United States is increasingly to be understood as a commodity controlled by financial and corporate interests. Indeed, much of the health care in the United States is now delivered by corporations, be they corporations that own large numbers of hospitals, control networks of nursing homes, or establish health maintenance organizations. This rapid and profound transformation of the health care system in the United States, furthermore, has had government support and encouragement. Several of the articles here detail the ways in which the Reagan administration pushed the privatization of health care delivery as well as emphasized deregulation and market forces in the allocation of this care. The end result is that the country enters the 1990s with a health care system substantially different from the one in place a decade earlier.

In this changed system, there are those for whom health care is and will be readily available and of high quality. Simply stated, if one can afford privately to pay for health care or if one can gain access through employment to health care coverage as part of the benefit package, then sufficient health care can be taken as a given. It is an available resource to be drawn upon as needed. But there are two key groups in the society for whom such assumptions or presumptions do not hold—the uninsured and the elderly. Further, the policies of the last decade have not sought to include them.

As the data in several of the articles make clear, there are literally millions of Americans who are working in the labor force but have no health care coverage. These persons are often in low-wage, low-skill, frequently temporary positions (agriculture, day laborers, hotel maids, restaurant workers, etc.) where the only employer-granted benefit may be

555

the mandated payments into the Social Security system. Health care coverage is nonexistent. Other groups in the working population who frequently lack coverage are those who are self-employed (house painters, truck drivers, beauticians, etc.) and who cannot afford the premiums to purchase private health insurance on $15,000, $20,000 or $25,000 a year and for whom health care insurance is out of the question. They live with the continual risk of illness and wish for health.

The second large group for whom health care cannot be taken as a given is the elderly. While many in this group had had insurance when working, the move into retirement drastically reduced their coverage and protection. For those who had never had such coverage, the fact of being aged means more risk and more likelihood of facing the need for health care with no coverage other than that provided by the government through Medicare. To compound being old by also being poor is to ensure that access to health care will be tenuous at best. Several of the following articles devote themselves to the situation of the elderly and the conditions they face in attempting to find health care. The situation is not encouraging. The prospects are dim that access and protection will grow in the coming years.

The growth in the number of aged and thus the growth in demand for health care over the coming years portends a period of contentious political struggle—a struggle over the breadth and level of publicly funded health care coverage to be offered the elderly. Health care for the elderly is going to be one among many competing demands for public-sector support. That the elderly will be organized to pressure the political system on their own behalf can be taken as a given; it is already the case. How far the political system can go in response, given the competing demands, is uncertain. But that there will be a struggle over the available public monies is inevitable.

If there must be a rationing of health care, especially that which is reliant on expensive advanced medical technologies, the consensus on when and how that rationing should occur needs to be developed through extensive political discourse. The policy arena will confront a need for clear and explicit trade-offs—something presently avoided as much as possible. The just initiated policy in the state of Oregon of no longer publicly funding kidney transplants and instead using those dollars for prenatal care is but an opening round in this profound struggle. Persons who need kidney transplants in Oregon and who cannot privately afford to pay for them are now dying. The decision has been made explicitly to shift the funds elsewhere. It is a crass form of cost-benefit analysis, trading off kidney transplants for prenatal care, but it is nonetheless a resource allocation and rationing question that was made after extensive political discussion on the matter.

The first article in this section, written by Vincente Navarro of Johns Hopkins University, explores the question of why President Reagan could receive such strong electoral support from those who at the same time deeply disagreed with his policies. The question of whether the Reagan election was a mandate for specific policy and programmatic changes in health, among other areas, is answered in the negative. For Navarro, "Electoral behavior and popular opinion are not synonymous." Thus he argues that there was no evidence to support the notion that the health care policies of the Reagan administration were responding to a popular mandate. What happened instead, he argues, was a more profound struggle among the social classes in American society—specifically between the 60 percent of Americans who are in the working class and the 1½ percent who are in the capitalist class. For Navarro, understanding the policies of the Reagan years is to understand the capitalist class working in its own behalf (via its corporate-controlled systems) and against the interests of other classes in the society. It is a provocative analysis that merits careful attention.

The second of the papers, by Steven Wallace and Carroll Estes, specifically addresses health care policy for the elderly. In this original contribution to the volume, they systematically lay out for this population the policy issues confronting the country. Among the central points of their analysis is that the aged cannot be considered a homogeneous population. There are now "young old" and "old old," for example, and the needs of these two groups are quite dissimilar—especially in the need for such services as nursing homes or home health care. Wallace and Estes do an outstanding job of tracing the policy changes brought about during the Reagan years and the consequences of these changes for the country during the 1990s. In broad terms, the Reagan policies fundamentally reshaped the policy assumptions and approaches to health care for the elderly. Whether these new policies will be adequate to the demands and needs of the 1990s is yet an open question. The authors are not optimistic.

Returning again to a central theme of this section, Bovbjerg, Held, and Pauly address the Reagan administration efforts to privatize health care delivery in the United States. Their analysis focuses on the consequences of the policies in place to hold down the costs of public-sector funding of health care via a renewal of budgetary control. This squeeze on costs has had a number of consequences for those making decisions in the health care systems about the level, intensity, and duration of health care provided under public sponsorship. The authors stress that, while the budget cutbacks have occurred, there has been no concurrent redefinition of

558   Policy Issues for the 1990s

priorities or policies to apply to the new situation of rationing. Consequently, those who have to make the choices are frequently doing so in ways that they hope will not call attention to themselves or to the policy vacuum in which they have to operate. (Oregon, by exception, reinforces the general premise.) The authors provide a comparative perspective with their contention that in many non-American systems, the choice would be made publicly and as a result of understood trade-offs. The United States, they note, has been hesitant to specify standards of access or either the quality or quantity of care to be received. Thus decisions are not formally announced, trade-offs are postponed or obscured, and the effort continues to do as much as possible with fewer resources. The end result is, no doubt, less access, less quality, and less quantity of care, if only because spreading the cuts across all three dimension avoids decisions as to relative importance.

Two British policy analysts, Patricia Day and Rudolf Klein, devote their article to a comparative analysis of how it is that both the United States and the United Kingdom develop means of regulating their nursing homes. Their emphasis is on developing an appropriate and sensitive process of regulation, not on specific models of how to regulate. Indeed, they take the position that the two countries experience a striking degree of similarity in the regulatory process, even as they use quite dissimilar systems and models. They stress that the regulation of nursing homes needs to attend to the social environment of these homes, places where both societies have unresolved and nasty problems. Failing to recognize that nursing home environments are not like other health care sectors, nor like schools or factories, means that inappropriate regulatory procedures and perspectives aggravate already poor situations. Thus the problems become worse, the impulse grows to regulate still further, and the cycle spirals downward. Following the present path much further, argue the authors, will create serious conditions for the elderly in both countries. The aged face a situation of needing the care and fearing the care givers.

24

Federal Health Policies in the United States: An Alternative Explanation

Vincente Navarro

ONE OF THE MOST IMPORTANT CHARACTERISTICS of the policies of the current Republican federal administration has been an unprecedented (in peace time) growth of military expenditures and an equally unprecedented reduction of social (including health) expenditures. From 1980 to 1985, the federal military expenditures rose from 7.2 percent to 9.9 percent of the gross national product (GNP), with a projected rise to 10.5 percent of the GNP in 1988. By 1990, the United States government will have spent, during the period of 1980 to 1990, $2,500 billion, which is more than the whole United States military expenditure from 1946 to 1980 ($2,001 billion) (Melman 1985, 11). On the other hand, federal social expenditures (including Social Security) declined for the period of 1980 to 1985 from 11.2 percent to 10.4 percent of the GNP. Federal funds for health and medical programs have also been reduced from 44.9 percent of all social welfare expenditures in 1980 to 42.4 percent in 1983. And the rate of growth of federal health expenditures has fallen from 16.5 percent per year in 1980 to 10.1 percent in 1983. The U.S. Council of Economic Advisors in its 1984 report to the president refers to such shifts of federal resources as "absolutely unprecedented" (U.S. Council of Economic Advisors, 1984; see also *Social Security Bulletin* 1986 and *Health Care Financing Review* 1984).

From *The Milbank Quarterly*, Vol. 65, No. 1 (1987): 81–111.

The explanations given for these federal policies are many. A widely held interpretation attributes these policies to a popular mandate received by the Republican administration in the 1980 and 1984 presidential and congressional elections. Instances of this interpretation in the health and medical care bibliography are many. For example, the leaders of the Robert Wood Johnson Foundation, in an article in the *New England Journal of Medicine*, referred to the 1980 election as a "powerful mandate to decrease taxes and non-defense expenditures" (Rogers, Blendon, and Maloney 1982). In the same issue, J.K. Iglehart (1982), reporting on a major conference attended by leading exponents of the medical establishment, wrote of a quasi-consensus among participants that cuts in federal health expenditures had to be made in response to a popular mandate.

That popular mandate was perceived to be a result of popular disenchantment with government, and a popular desire to reduce government intervention in the health sector. Again, examples of this interpretation of the popular-mandate argument in the medical care bibliography are many. For instance, Paul Starr (1984, 419) in his influential *The Social Transformation of American Medicine*, interprets the victory of Reagan in 1980 as a result of people's belief that the government was *the* problem (for a critique of Starr see Navarro 1984b). This popular belief was based on the perception that, as David Mechanic (1984) approvingly put it, "the heavy hand of government causes more problems than it solves." Consequently, and as indicated by the publisher (W.B. Walsh [1985]) and the editor (J.K. Iglehart [1985]) of *Health Affairs*, a major health policy forum in the United States, Americans wanted the size of their government reduced and its interventions in the health sector diminished. These are not solitary voices. Far from it. These are representative voices of prevalent interpretations of current federal health policies.

The accumulated evidence for all of these years does not, however, support this interpretation of a popular mandate for these federal health policies. Quite to the contrary, a survey of all major opinion polls from 1976 to the present shows that there has been a constant and undiminished support for an expansion rather than a reduction of health and social expenditures (and for keeping and/or strengthening government interventions to protect workers, consumers, and the environment). Similar evidence exists to show that the reduction of social expenditures, as well as other domestic policies carried out by the current administration, such as the transfer of federal funds from the social to the military sector, are not popular policies (Navarro 1982, 1985b; see also Ferguson and Rogers 1986, 1–39). Even Senator Paul Laxalt, a close friend of President Reagan and the chairman of the Republican National Committee, has recently referred to "the strange phenomenon that most Americans express approval of Ronald Reagan, although they are opposed to much of what the President supports" (cited in Lipset 1985). Lipset (1983) and Ferguson and Rogers (1986, 1–39) have shown that the majority of Americans remain more liberal than the president on economics, defense, foreign policy, and social questions. A survey of popular opinion regarding federal health policies shows that the same is true for health questions (Navarro 1985b).

In light of this evidence, a question that needs to be raised and answered is why did people vote both in 1980 and in 1984 for a candidate whose commitment to carry out those unpopular policies was clearly stated? Indeed, a major assumption made by the authors who believe in the popular mandate as the force behind those federal social policies is that *electoral behavior and popular opinion are synonymous*. The answer to the question needs to be given at different levels. One explanation is that the overwhelming majority of United States presidents have been elected by a minority, not a majority, of potential voters. And President Reagan, elected by 32.3 percent of the potential electorate in 1984 and 27.2 percent in 1980, was no exception to this reality.

Still, the question may be asked again. How is it that so many people voted for candidate Reagan despite the fact that they did not support his social (including health) policies? The answer involves the nature of Western democracy and its limitations. The act of voting is based on a totalizing interpretation of policy. In other words, in the act of voting (except in referendums), people are asked to vote for totalities, not for sectional choices. One votes either Republican or Democratic. But one cannot vote selectively, i.e., one is not offered the chance of voting for the many components of those policies (such as education, health services, transport, and employment policies). The vote is everything or nothing. In Walter Lippman's (1925, 56–57) words:

We call an election an expression of the popular will. But is it? We go into the polling booths and make a cross on a piece of paper for one or two or perhaps three or four names. Have we expressed our thoughts on the public policy of the United States? Presumably, we have a number of thoughts on this and that with many buts and ifs and sos. Surely the cross on a piece of paper has not expressed them.

Thus, representative democracy is insufficient. It does not measure, nor does it reflect, the popular will on the many dimensions of public life. *Electoral behavior and popular opinion are not synonymous*. Consequently, there is no contradiction or schizophrenia involved in Reagan's winning the election while the majority of the people (including his voters) have different and even opposite views on many and even the majority of Reagan's policies (for a debate on popular opinion see Blendon and Altman 1984; Navarro 1985a, 1985d; Altman 1985). The paradox of the last elections—that the majority of the electorate seemed to be in disagreement with many of the Reagan positions, yet still the majority of those who went to the polls voted for him—is not incomprehensible. Polls (including exit polls) in 1980 and in 1984 show that the majority of people were in disagreement with many of Reagan's social policies. This disagreement appears even among Reagan's voters. In 1980, voters preferred Reagan over Carter primarily because of Carter's perceived unpopularity, and in 1984, voters preferred Reagan over Mondale primarily because they identified the economic recovery (and primarily the decline of inflation) with his policies (Nelson 1985). Moreover, no incumbent president has been defeated when economic growth in the election year has exceeded 3.8 percent; in 1984 economic growth exceeded 6 percent (Quirk 1985).

In summary, there is no evidence to support the thesis that the current federal social (including health) policies respond to a popular mandate. Thus, the original question of why these policies remains. I postulate that in order to answer this question we have to analyze these policies within the social, political, and economic context in which they take place. In other words, in order to understand these federal health policies—the tree—we have to understand the actual distribution of social, economic, and political power in the United States today—the forest.

Class as Explanatory Value in Health Policy

One of the most striking areas of silence in the analysis of health policy in the United States is the absence of class as a category of power. Class, in health care bibliography, seems to be an "un-American" category. In most of this bibliography, the citizens and residents of the United States are divided according to biological (e.g., gender, race) or cultural (e.g., Hispanic, ethnic) categories, but rarely, if ever, according to class categories. Thus, the United States is the only major country in the Western industrialized world in which health and social statistics are not recorded according to class. An elementary observation needs to be made, however. The United States has classes. This observation bears repeating in light of dominant discourse in which class as a category of analysis and bearer of power relations is rarely mentioned. Aside from references to the United States as a middle-class society (a society in which the majority of United States citizens are supposed to be in the middle, between the rich and the poor), the power category of class never, or very rarely, appears in the major media in general or in the medical literature in particular. This definition of the United States as a middle-class society takes place, incidentally, in spite of the fact that more United States citizens define themselves as members of the working class (48 percent) than of the middle class (43 percent) (*Public Opinion* 1984) (see Appendix note 1).

Actually, the size of the working class is even larger than that based on people's self perception of themselves as part of the working class. Erik O. Wright (1985) has shown how the actual size of the working class is over 60 percent of the United States population. The middle class, which has always been smaller in size than the working class, has been further reduced in size recently owing to the changes in the occupational structure of the United States (Thurow 1985, 60–66). Most of the major media, however—including the medical media— never refer to the majority of the United States population as working class. Rather, they define it as middle class. Just as the members of the working class are never or rarely referred to as such, so those "on the top" are never presented, discussed, applauded, or denounced as the capitalist class, a term usually dismissed as "rhetorical" and/or "doctrinaire." (Contrary to prevalent belief, United States academic discourse and United States culture are heavily ideological. It is sufficient

to use certain unacceptable terms in that discourse to trigger unresponsive, if not plainly hostile, responses.) Here, a second observation
needs to be made. The United States capitalist class is the most
powerful capitalist class in today's world. In a truly Gramscian fashion,
the interests of this class have been presented (and accepted) as the
universal interest. To be anticapitalist, for example, is to be perceived
as anti-American. Indicative of the power of this class to define the
dominant discourse is the fact that classes never appear in that discourse.
The capitalist class, however, is the most class conscious of all classes
in the United States. And the current leadership of the Republican
administration represents the most "class conscious" stratum within
that class. In the unrestrained pursuit of its interests, it has exhibited
a clear class behavior. One of its most substantial class achievements
has been the weakening of the base of government support for organized
labor in its dealings with management. This has been accomplished
through sharp reductions in unemployment insurance, through the
dismantling of the public service job program, through the weakening
of the Occupational Safety and Health Administration, through the
appointment of persons hostile to organized labor both to the National
Labor Relations Board and to the Department of Labor, and through
the reduction of social (including health) expenditures (Edsall 1984,
229). Similarly, Reagan's tax and economic policies have benefited
primarily the capitalist and upper middle classes and have hurt the
lower middle and working classes (Bawden 1984; Moon and Sawhill
1984).

The effect of these policies has a clear class base. According to the
Economic Report of the President, 1985 the following changes have occurred
between 1979 and 1984 (as I have indicated elsewhere [Navarro
1985b] some of the social policies of austerity started under the Carter
administration in the 1979 and 1980 federal budgets): (1) before tax
profits and interest (correcting for inflation) grew 3.6 percent per year;
(2) real wages of nonsupervisory workers fell by 5 percent; and (3)
net farm income fell by 36 percent (U.S. President 1985, table B2,
234). In 1983, employers' health payments as a percentage of the
GNP declined for the first time in recent history (*Medical Benefits*
1986a). Also, and as reported by the U.S. Bureau of the Census, the
median income of those in the bottom 40 percent—a largely Democratic
constituency—fell by $477 (from $12,966 to $12,489) between 1980
and 1984, in constant 1984 dollars, while the income of those in the

top 10 percent—a largely Republican constituency—rose by $5,085 (from $68,145 in 1980 to $73,230 in 1984) (U.S. Bureau of the Census 1984). Similarly, the Congressional Budget Office has found that the net effect of spending and tax cuts has resulted in a loss of $1,100 between 1983 and 1985 for those making less than $10,000, while those making more than $80,000 annually have gained $24,200 as a result of government policy (U.S. Congressional Budget Office 1984). It is this class behavior that also explains the shift of federal resources from the social to the military areas. The reduction of social expenditures and interventions does weaken the working population in its bargaining with the class of employers (e.g., an unemployed worker without health and/or unemployment insurance is more likely to accept a low-paying job than if he or she had insurance). As David Stockman (a main spokesperson for the Reagan administration) indicated, a main purpose of the reduction of social expenditures was to discipline labor, a policy that has been largely successful. (David Stockman refers to that process of disciplining labor—that included increased unemployment in the years 1980 to 1983 and cuts of social expenditures—as "part of the cure, not the problem" [cited in Ferguson and Rogers 1986, 49].) The number of strikes reached a long-time low in 1982 and the rate of salary growth was the smallest ever.

The opposition party—the Democratic party—however, does not represent any form of class behavior in general or working class behavior in particular. Not even a semblance of class discourse appears. Actually, one of the most successful capitalist class interventions in the United States was to outlaw any form of class behavior on the part of its antagonists: the working class (see Appendix note 2). The Taft-Hartley Act forbade American labor to act as a class and forced it to function as just another "interest group" (Milton 1982, 159). The steel workers cannot strike in support of the coal miners, for example. They can only take care of their own. No other major Western capitalist country has faced this situation. This splitting of the working class into different interest groups dramatically redefined all elements of political, economic, and sociocultural behaviors and possibilities. Class has disappeared from reasonable discourse; terms such as "capitalist class," "petit bourgeois," and "working class" are dismissed as ideological. Instead, the new terms of political discourse are "the rich," "the middle class," and "the poor," all defined in the area of consumption rather than in terms of the relation of people to the means of producing wealth and income. Language, however, is not innocent. It does, indeed, reflect the power relations in society. The working class and the United States population have been redefined in terms of biological categories (black, white, women, men, the aged) and in terms of consumption (rich, middle, and poor). The political, economic, and social consequences of that redefinition of the working class into interest groups are enormous, as is their importance for understanding today's United States health policies. For example, United States health services are largely paid for by work-related health benefits achieved through a bargaining process in which each sector of labor tries to get as much as possible for its own constituency. As a result of this situation, we find that different sectors of the working population in the United States have different types of health coverage, with manufacturing having better coverage than other workers, and sales and service workers being the least protected (*Medical Benefits* 1985, table 1, 3; Root 1985, 101–18). Table 1 records the relation between health benefits coverage in two major sectors of employment in the United States. Even within the same sector of employment, the degree of coverage depends on the strength of labor via unionization (Black 1986).

The consequence of this "interest group" behavior is that, while the coverage is comprehensive for some sectors of the working population, the coverage for the whole class is rather limited. As an average,

TABLE 1

Percentage of Workers Who Are Unionized in Certain Types of
Employment and Percentage of Coverage in Specific Types
of Health Insurance

Industry	Percentage unionized	Percentage uninsured all year	Dental services coverage	Vision or hearing
Manufacturing	46%	4.8%	30.9%	15.6%
Personal Services	13	16.0	17.0	5.0

Sources: Bureau of Labor Statistics, Unionization. Directory of National Unions and Employment Associations, 1975; and Employment Associations, 1975; and Employment and Earnings, January 1979, table 1: Coverage of the privately insured population less than age 65 for selected health services: percent insured by type of insurance and identity of primary insured in *Medical Benefits* 1985, table 3: Employment and Health Insurance Coverage in Monheit et al. 1985.

United States citizens still pay in out-of-pocket and in direct expenses larger percentages for health benefits than any other Western industrialized nation (Maxwell 1981, table 4.1). Another consequence of relating health benefits to employment (besides reinforcing the resource disparities arising from pay differentials) is that it weakens the popular demand for improving governmental programs. Thus, those who remain unprotected through the work place are more isolated politically, decreasing the popular pressure for government to meet their needs.

This focus on work-related benefits (assured by collective private bargaining) rather than benefits assured by the state (which may be paid through general revenues or payroll taxes) is the primary difference between the expansion of health services coverage in the United States and in western Europe (Navarro 1985c). While the working class in western Europe has conducted its struggle for expanding health services coverage primarily through the state, its counterpart in the United States has struggled (not as a class but as an interest group) primarily through the bargaining table at the work place. A major objective of the labor movements in western Europe has been to achieve the universalization of health benefits covering all the population. A main goal of these European health services (both in the national health service or in the national health insurance varieties) is that the health benefits received by the individual or citizen do not depend on the amount of payment he or she makes as a worker. The struggle for that goal has occurred not only in the collective-bargaining arenas but primarily in the forums of the state (Esping-Andersen 1985). In the United States, the "interest group" behavior (each segment of labor looking out for its own) rather than class behavior (labor struggling with class solidarity for all sectors of labor) explains the enormous diversity of health benefits within the working class and the population.

In describing this situation, there is a need for four clarifications. First, this situation in which labor acts as an interest group rather than class and in which health benefits are work related rather than state provided is not, as Starr (1984, 312–13) indicates, an outcome of labor's choice or American values. He assumes that whatever happens in the medical sector is, in the final analysis, an outcome of what the majority of Americans want. Empirical information shows that this is not the case (see Navarro 1984b). Rather, this "interest group" type of behavior has been imposed on labor as the outcome of enormous struggles in the 1950s when labor was forced by the Taft-Hartley

Act not to behave as a class. Prior to that act, sectors of labor could strike in support of other sectors. That power of class mobilization represented a clear threat to the dominant sectors of the business community or capitalist class. The dominant sector of that class (particularly the employers of the labor-intensive sectors of industry) was afraid that that possibility of acting as a class could threaten their own class interests. They could remember an instance of that class mobilization during the New Deal, a program that they strongly opposed. Consequently, an important component of the Cold War and the repressive regime known as McCarthyism was to purge labor unions of that segment of the leadership that emphasized class practices rather than interest group practices within labor. Thus, an enormous struggle was carried out at all economic, political, and ideological levels of American society aimed at weakening labor and forcing on it this "interest group" type of behavior. Labor, through its major federation, the AFL-CIO, has fought the Taft-Hartley Act since its very beginnings (Milton 1982, 159).

The second clarification is that the majority of the poor and the majority of the uninsured are members of the working class (workers, retired workers, potential workers, and their dependents) (Stallard, Ehrenreich, and Sklar 1983; Harrington 1984; Monheit et al. 1985). In this respect, the problems of the poor and uninsured (high costs and limited coverage) are not dissimilar to the problems of the majority of the working population; the differences are primarily in degree rather than substance. According to popular opinion polls, high costs and limited coverage are still among the major problems faced by the United States population. In 1984 the reduction of social—including health—expenditures was one of the top three issues in the country about which the majority of Americans expressed concern (Shriver 1984; Altman 1985). This clarification bears repeating in light of the existing "dichotomy" between the middle class and the poor. This dichotomy seems to indicate that the problems of the poor are of a different type than the problems of the middle class. They are not.

The third point of clarification is that this interest-group type of behavior weakens the whole of the class. Witness how vulnerable labor is today to the current antilabor avalanche from the class of employers usually referred to as the business community. One result of this weakness is that one of the most prevalent health-cost-control measures among employers has been to increase the coinsurance and deductibles among employees, which is frequently accompanied by the establishment of two layers of benefits, one for the already employed and another for the newly employed (*Medical Benefits* 1986b). These two layers of benefits weaken considerably the class solidarity among workers.

The fourth point of clarification is that the institutional structures that have arisen in the implementation of work-related benefits have strengthened a set of private vested interests that present great resistance to change. For example, the growth of private work-related benefits among the employed population is partially responsible for the growing dependency of life insurance companies on health insurance premiums. As L. Root (1985, 114) has indicated:

> The income of life insurance companies has become increasingly dependent upon health insurance premiums and, to a lesser extent, upon retirement funds. In 1960, life insurance premiums accounted for 52.2 percent of the income of the 1,441 life insurance companies then operating. At that time, health insurance represented less than 18 percent of income, and annuity considerations only 6 percent. Twenty years later, life insurance premiums were only 31 percent of income, while health insurance and annuities contributed 40 percent—22 percent and 18 percent, respectively.

The life insurance industry has been one of the major forces lobbying against the establishment of a national health program in the United States (Navarro 1976, 151).

Class, Taxes, and Health Legislation

United States labor has not always followed corporativist or interest group practices. The most important elements of social legislation— the New Deal—responded to the class practices of American labor. The New Deal (e.g., Social Security) benefited, for the most part, the majority of the working population. It was an enormous working-class mobilization that forced the establishment of the New Deal (Milton 1982; see also Huberman 1947, 351). Needless to say, other sectors of the population, such as farmers and small entrepreneurs and even sectors of the capitalist class (particularly the supporters of capital intensive industries) also benefited from these New Deal programs. It bears repeating that the New Deal did benefit the whole of the working class, rather than just one segment. The programs were the result of class pressure and the establishment of the New Deal strengthened that class (e.g., a worker can stand up to his or her employer better with unemployment insurance than without it).

The breaking of class into interest-group behavior (that occurred primarily in the 1950s) explains why social legislation after the 1950s took place as a response to sectors of the working class (the Great Society type of programs) rather than to the whole class. (The United States welfare state includes two types of social programs: (1) non-means test programs that benefit the majority of the working population [e.g., Social Security], and (2) means test programs that benefit specially vulnerable sectors of the population [e.g., Medicaid]. The majority of the New Deal programs correspond to the first type of programs while the majority of the Great Society programs correspond to the second type. Medicare corresponds more to a New Deal type of program than a Great Society one. It is non-means tested and benefits the majority of the working population since the majority will age and become elderly.)

During the last forty years the expansion of social expenditures has affected both types of programs, although the overwhelming growth of these expenditures has been in New Deal or non-means test types of programs. (Only 8 percent of all federal social expenditures are of the Great Society variety. Charles Murray in his *Losing Ground: Social Policy 1950–80*, refers to the assumed failures of the Great Society type of programs—a minority of social programs—to support his policy conclusion of eliminating the majority of social policy interventions by the federal government. For a detailed analysis of the success of the Great Society type of programs see Schwarz 1983.) As I have shown elsewhere, there has been undiminished popular support for both types of programs, although support for existing New Deal programs is higher (95 percent of the people) than for the Great Society programs (68 to 72 percent, depending on the program) (Navarro 1985b).

These programs are funded primarily with taxes paid by wage and salary earners. Table 2 records that while income taxes and, in particular, social security taxes (as a percentage of all taxes) increased during the period of 1960 to 1984, corporate taxes declined dramatically (and, in particular, during the Reagan administration, which halved them in its first four years).

TABLE 2
Sources of Federal Revenues, by Percentage

Fiscal year	Individual income tax	Social insurance tax	Corporate income tax	Excise, state and other
1960	44.0%	15.9%	23.2%	16.8%
1965	41.8	19.1	21.8	17.4
1970	46.9	23.0	17.0	13.0
1975	43.9	30.3	14.6	11.3
1980	47.2	30.5	12.5	9.8
1984 (est.)	44.8	36.8	7.8	10.5

Source: Adapted from table 6.4 in Edsall 1984, 212.

The shift of revenues becomes even more significant when we analyze the increased differentials in taxes paid between wealthy and nonwealthy income earners (Kuttner 1984, 53):

Between 1953 and 1974, direct taxes paid by the average income family doubled, from 11.8% of income to 23.4% of income, while the tax burden of a family with four times the average income went from 20.2 percent to 29.5 percent, an increase of less than half. Between 1969 and 1980, social security taxes applied to only the first $37,700 of wages; the major portion of this increase was on the non-wealthy. During the same period, corporate income tax collections fell 14 percent, and capital gains rates were cut by 20 percent.

This shift of fiscal responsibilities is justified by conservative forces by the need to stimulate capital investment. The benefits for the corporate class, it is claimed, will eventually trickle down to the rest of the population. Even on its own terrain, however, this argument does not hold much credibility. The United States was one of the low-performance economies in the 1970s in spite of very low tax burdens on capital (far lower than in Japan and West Germany, defined as good performance economies, which had the highest and second highest reliance on capital taxes) (Kuttner 1984, 187).

In summary, the point that needs to be emphasized is that federal expenditures (including health expenditures) are based on taxes coming from labor rather than from capital, i.e., the welfare state is paid for to a very large degree by the working population. Here, it is important to clarify a much debated and misunderstood issue: the overall level of taxation. It is true that the total United States tax level is relatively low compared with other countries. In 1974 it was 27.5 percent of the GNP, placing the United States 14th out of 17 major industrial capitalist nations. Only Switzerland, Japan, and Australia had lower overall tax levels. But, if instead of looking at overall levels one focuses on levels of taxation by occupational groups, it then emerges that for an average production worker the United States ranked 8th highest in the tax burden (Kuttner 1984, 190). The American tax system is indeed highly regressive.

This regressiveness is further highlighted if we look at what the average citizen gets in return for his or her taxes. The average European gets more from government than does the United States citizen. For the most part, the European citizen gets free or almost free health care (very low out-of-pocket expenses), generous family allowances, and better unemployment insurance, pensions, and disabilities than his or her American counterpart, as well as many other social benefits that increase individual income. The United States welfare state is underdeveloped compared with western Europe. In the health sector, for example, the United States citizen still pays 27 percent in direct costs compared with 8 percent in Sweden, 5 percent in Great Britain, 12 percent in West Germany, and 19 percent in France (Maxwell 1981, table 4.1). And no other country among Western industrialized nations has 38 million inhabitants (representing 16 percent) uncovered by any kind of insurance (*Medical Care Review* 1984). Fifty-six million people under the age of 65 are either uninsured for health care during the entire year, uninsured for a part of the year, or significantly underinsured (Farley 1985). For the 30 million people over the age of 65, Medicare covers only 49 percent of total health care costs, costs which average $4,200 per year (*Washington Report on Medicine and Health* 1985, 1986). The average American taxpayer gets comparatively little from his or her taxes. A large percentage of taxes goes for military expenditures that return very little economic benefit to the average citizen. In 1983, government health expenditures represented only 4.5 percent of the GNP in the United States, compared with 8.8 percent in Sweden, 6.6 percent in West Germany, 6.6 percent in France, 6.2 percent in Canada, and 5.5 percent in the United

Kingdom (OECD Directorate for Social Affairs 1985). In brief, the average American taxpayer pays more and gets less back than his or her counterpart in other developed industrialized countries.

This measure of regressiveness explains why the average citizen feels under a heavy tax burden and strongly opposes increasing taxes. People are against increasing taxes because they are not getting much in return. But (and it is an extremely important but), they are willing to pay higher taxes if they are assured that they will benefit from them. This explains why: (1) Social Security taxes (the taxes that have increased most rapidly in the last ten years) are the least unpopular taxes (Peretz 1982); (2) the majority of Americans would be willing to pay higher taxes if they could be assured that those revenues would pay for health services (such as a national and comprehensive health program) from which *all* citizens would benefit (Navarro 1982). People are not willing to increase taxes, however, to resolve the deficit problem. Their anti-tax sentiment is highly selective. Thus, it is wrong to state, as is frequently done, that people are against paying taxes. How people feel about paying taxes depends on what they will get in return. It is as simple and logical as that; and (3) there is more support for New Deal types of programs (aimed at the whole population) than for Great Society programs (aimed at specific populations).

In brief, the average United States citizen is getting less in return for his or her taxes than the average citizen in major western European countries, a situation that is in large degree explained by the highly skewed nature of the tax system of the United States (falling heavily on the middle- and low-income levels of the working population) and by the large proportion that military expenditures represent within federal government expenditures. Since social expenditures are, for the most part, financed by taxes imposed on the working population, these transfers of government funds have not had a redistributive effect from the capitalist class to the working class. Rather, there has been a redistributive effect within the working population, with some sectors of the working class paying for others. This situation explains why Great Society programs have been somewhat less popular than New Deal types of programs. They have frequently been used to divide the working class, pitting whites against blacks, men against women, young against old, the middle-income families against low-income families, and so on. The identification of the Democratic party with the Great Society (e.g., Medicaid) rather than the New Deal (e.g., Medicare and Social Security) has contributed to the weakening of the popularity of the party. As Edsall (1984, 39) has written,

> The two tiered structure of social programs has functioned in practice to divide the working class Democrats from poor Democrats. . . . The formulation of mechanisms to reduce the divisions between these two sets of programs, if not to integrate them, remains essential to the Democratic Party if it is to lessen this conflict within its own constituencies.

In summary, the electoral history of the United States shows that the Democratic party has been more popular in periods when it has been perceived as the party of the entire working population, not just the party of its different components or interest groups. (The main reason given by Democrats in the summer of 1985 to explain why "they considered themselves Democrats" was that "the Democratic Party is the party of the working people." And 80 percent of voting Democrats who did not vote in 1984 for Mondale indicated that "if Mondale were more of a strong Democrat like JFK or FDR who'd fight for working people, I'd be more inclined to vote for him" [poll results quoted in Fingerhut 1985, 25, 23].) One of the most popular Democratic administrations in the United States was the New Deal administration. Under the New Deal, the working population fought for and won Social Security, the Work Projects Administration, the National Labor Relations Act, and an enactment of a system of progressive taxation (low for the working class and high for the wealthy)—all programs and interventions that actually or potentially benefited the whole working population. One of the missing pieces was a national health program, dropped by New Dealers because of opposition from the insurance industry and the medical profession. It bears repeating again that the Democratic party has been most popular when it has been perceived as committed to the expansion of social expenditures that would benefit the whole working population. (Contrary to widely held belief, Ferguson and Rogers [1986, 35–36] have shown that the weakening of the Democratic party's commitment to the New Deal was partially responsible for their defeat in the 1980 and 1984 Presidential elections.) In brief, class practices with a demand for programs that benefit the majority of the population rather than interest group practice is what has put Democrats in power. Let me stress here that this situation is not unique to the United States. Countries such as Finland and Sweden, where parties are perceived to have clear class practices, have higher rates of electoral involvement, higher voter turnout, and more extensive welfare states than countries that do not have these practices. Indeed, Edsall (1984, 146) and Korpi (1983, 39) have shown that societies (such as Sweden) in which the political and economic instruments of labor are perceived as class instruments have less income inequality between the top and the bottom layers, a higher percentage of the GNP allocated to social expenditures, and a higher level of overall progressive taxation than those countries where labor is weak and does not follow class practices (such as West Germany, France, and the United States). Similarly, the first group of countries has higher coverage for health services, a smaller for-profit sector in the health sector, and less out-of-pocket expenditures in the health sector than the second one (Navarro 1985c). Table 3 records this situation for two countries at opposite poles, Sweden and the United States. In Sweden, labor follows class practices, with (1) a central labor federation that defends the interests of all sectors of labor and bargains centrally and collectively, (2) 88 percent of the working population unionized, and (3) a major political party, the Social Democratic party, that sees itself primarily (but not exclusively) as a working-class party. In the United States, labor follows a corporativist practice with (1) each union defending the interests of its own constituency, (2) 18 percent of the working people unionized, and (3) no parties with congressional representation that define themselves as working-class parties.

It is in those countries in which class practices within the working class do not exist and in which labor operates as one more interest group (highly divided into different subgroups, each one looking out for its own), that we also find a depoliticization of the population, with low voter turnout and a fragmentation of politics (Edsall 1984, 197). This is precisely what is happening in the United States today.

The lack of polarization of American politics and the conventional wisdom that parties have to move to the center to attract the middle class are producing a depoliticization of American life, with increasing disenchantment toward the two major political parties. In 1980, between 60 and 70 percent of the population (depending on the problem area) indicated that it did not perceive much of a difference

TABLE 3

The Consequences of Labor Practices in Social and Health Policy: Sweden and the U.S.

Labor practices		Average turnout in national elections 1965–80 (percentage)	Income inequity*	Public social expenditures as percentage of GNP	Tax revenue as percentage of GDP	Uninsured population (percentage)	Size of for-profit sector** (percentage of total health expenditures)	Direct out-of-pocket (percentage of total expenditure)
Sweden	Class	90%	28	33.8%	44.0%	0%	17%	8.4%
U.S.	Interest group	56	38	14.2	31.5	16	44	27.1

* The higher the number, the larger the disparity in income between the top 20% and the bottom 20% of the population. The index represents the difference between the proportion of income earned by the top 20% and the bottom 20%.
** For-profit sector includes payments to physicians and others in private practice or working as independent contractors, to pharmaceutical companies, and to other medical and hospital suppliers. The figure for the U.S. is the lowest within a range estimated by R.J. Maxwell.
Sources: Cameron 1981; Magasiner and Reich 1982; Maxwell 1981, tables 4-1 and 4-2; Organization for Economic Cooperation and Development Directorate for Social Affairs 1985; Korpi 1983, 56.

between the two major parties (Ladd 1985, 223). The weakening of the New Deal commitments in 1984 (e.g., the Democratic party did not include a commitment to establish a national health program) also led the *New York Times* (1984) to editorialize that the programmatic differences between the two parties were uncomfortably narrow. It is not surprising then that, in 1980, 40 percent of Americans defined themselves as Independent, followed by 37 percent as Democrats, and 24 percent as Republicans (Ladd 1985, 222), a considerable increase in the number of Independents and dramatic decline in both Democratic and Republican party adherents. A similar situation has been reported by T.J. Lowi (1985) for 1984 (also Zald 1985). More than a realignment, what we have seen in the United States is a dealignment from the two major parties. The similarity between the two parties has also led to an increase in the number abstaining from electoral politics. The United States has the highest abstention rate in the Western world (Manatos 1984); 50 million eligible citizens did not register in 1984 and 35 million of those who registered did not vote. Another characteristic of American politics is that the working class votes less than the other classes. In 1980, 77 percent of white-collar professionals voted compared with only 44 percent of blue-collar workers. This class abstention hurts the Democrats more than the Republicans (Edsall 1984, 184), since the working class tends to vote more Democratic than Republican, and nonvoters tend to be more progressive than voters. Workers support larger social expenditures in larger percentages than do employers (Wolfinger and Rosentone 1980, 109–10). The declassing of American politics and the absence of class polarization, together with the recycling of politics through interest groups, has thus led to depoliticization and abstention, particularly among the lower echelons of the working class that do not see much meaning in their electoral participation.

In the United States, union membership (an important but not exclusive component of class practice) climbed from 3.8 million in 1935 to 10.2 million in 1942 (the largest growth of union membership took place during the New Deal years) and continued growing until the late 1950s (Troy 1965, table 1; cited in Root 1985, 104). It was after the anti-working-class legislation (the Taft-Hartley Act) that union membership started declining, a process that has been further accelerated during the Reagan years. This decline is not unrelated to the "interest group" practices followed by labor, also responsible for the decline of electoral participation that has occurred since the late 1950s in the United States. Since 1960 the percentage of nonvoters among the adult population has increased from 37 percent to 47 percent in 1980. During this period the level of popularity of the New Deal type of programs has not declined, not even during the Reagan years of 1981 to 1986. But the level of support of the Democratic party among its supporters has declined (Ferguson and Rogers 1986, 3–39; Abramson, Aldrich, and Rohde 1986, 122–24). This weakening of support is not unrelated to a weakening of that party's commitment to the New Deal.

As I indicated before, this relation between class practices and electoral participation is not unique to the United States. The international experience shows that political diversity and class polarization is a condition both for active democratic participation and expansion of the welfare state. The further expansion of the welfare state, centered around the New Deal, has as a prerequisite the political polarization of the Democratic party and the development of class practices.

An Example of a New Deal Program: A Comprehensive and Universal Tax-based Health Program

Let me give an example of what I mean by this emphasis on a New Deal program. There is today a large problem in the health care sector of the United States. By whatever health indicator one can think of (infant mortality, low birth weight, life expectancy, etc.), indicators in the United States do not compare favorably with those in other developed industrialized countries. And the situation is deteriorating in many important areas. For example, the decline of infant mortality has slowed down since 1981 (Shapiro 1984). This is a result, among other factors, of the 1979 to 1982 recession and of the reduction of social expenditures, a reduction that affected primarily but not exclusively the low-income groups within the working class. Those cuts were carried out with bipartisan support, following a nonexistent popular mandate. This reduction of social expenditures further increased the number of people who did not have any form of private or public insurance coverage. This problem also affected the majority of the population that did have some form of coverage, since the most common form of coverage is not comprehensive and still requires substantial payments by the patient.

These major problems explain why people in the United States want to see changes in the health sector. In 1983, 50 percent of polled Americans indicated that "fundamental changes are needed to make the health care system work better" and another 25 percent felt that "the American health care system has so much wrong with it that we need to completely rebuild it." These percentages increased in 1984 to 51 percent and 31 percent respectively (Louis Harris and Associates 1985; Schneider 1985).

If the United States does not have a national health program it is not, as Victor Fuchs (1986, 269) wrongly indicates, because Americans do not want it. Nor is it because, as Reinhardt has indicated (Reinhardt and Relman 1968, 8), we Americans face a moral crisis, "an apparent unwillingness of society's will to pay for the economic and medical maintenance of the poor." (Reinhardt assumes, as many others do, that whatever occurs in federal health policy is the outcome of people's wishes. This assumption perceives the American political system as fully responsive to people's wishes. This assumption ignores the accumulated evidence that shows that popular opinion is not always the determinant of federal executive and legislative behavior.) Actually, in a 1984 ABC News-*Washington Post* poll, an unprecedented 75 percent of the respondents indicated that "the government should institute and operate a national health program," a demand preferred by the majority of the American population for the last fifteen years (Schneider 1985; Navarro 1982).

Nor is the absence of such a program due to lack of resources; the United States spends 10.8 percent of the GNP on health services (Gibson et al. 1984). The problem is in the channels (i.e., the institutions) through which those resources are being spent. Indeed, the problems of insufficient coverage and high costs are rooted in the private, for-profit character of American medicine. An international analysis of health services shows that those countries with government control of the funding and administration of health services have better coverage, lower costs, and better distribution of health resources than those countries that have large for-profit private sectors in the health services—such as the United States (Navarro 1985c).

Meanwhile, this unfinished business of the New Deal—the national health program—continues to be wanted by the majority of the population, to the extent, I repeat again, of their being willing to pay even higher taxes. The issue, however, is not higher taxes for the working population. It is the fact that the majority of working people (the social group with a heavier tax burden) are willing to pay even higher taxes, which shows how much they want that program. Yet, the establishment of such a program should not be based on further taxation for that sector of the population. The funding of a comprehensive and universal health program could be based on different but highly popular interventions:

1. Changed priorities within the health sector, not only through incentives but also active government interventions. The current reliance on highly technological medicine is neither good medical care nor good health care. Although high-technology curative medicine has a role to play, it should not be the dominant form of intervention. For example, the state of North Carolina has about the same number of deliveries per year as Sweden, but twice as many low-birth-weight babies and neonatal deaths, due to poverty and malnutrition. In 1978 and 1979 there were only 30 ventilator-equipped neonatal intensive-care-unit beds in Sweden compared to 60 or so in North Carolina, where even further expansions are now proposed (David and Siegel 1983). It would be cheaper and more humane to provide food and other social services rather than curative technology. The laissez-faire approach to medical care enables and stimulates a sophisticated technological approach to medical problems, but does not serve well a broadly based preventive approach capable of diminishing both the problems and the need for expensive technology. In summary, there is a need to shift the priorities away from hospital, curative, personal, and highly technological medicine toward preventive, community, environmental, occupational, and social interventions. This shift of priorities will not occur by continuing reliance on the for-profit private sector; it requires an active government intervention and active popular participation.

2. A shift of resources within the public sector, away from the military and back to social expenditures, reversing a trend that threatens the survival of the United States population. According to the 1986 Reagan budget proposal, the military budget will have further increased by a staggering 239 percent over the 1980 level by the year 1990. These funds are spent, in official rhetoric, to make American children more "secure" from external

enemies. Meanwhile, from 1980 to 1985, during the Reagan administration, more American children died from poverty than the total number of American battle deaths in the Vietnam War. It is estimated that, until 1990, 22,000 American babies will die per year because of low birth weight. Poverty is the greatest child killer in 1985 in the affluent United States. None other than President Eisenhower indicated that "the problem in defense is how far you can go without destroying from within what you are trying to defend from without" (Children's Defense Fund 1985). Here again, we find that Americans do support the reversal of this trend, with the shifting of resources from military to social and health expenditures. The level of popular support for health and social expenditures is much, much higher than the level of support for military expenditures (*Washington Post*-ABC News Poll 1985).

3. Increases in the level of taxation of the corporate class and upper-middle class, a level that has declined dramatically and is even imperiling the functioning of the American economy. The overall size of tax cuts aimed at the corporate class was $220 billion in 1984 (*UAW Washington Report* 1981). The entire federal cost of a comprehensive health program was estimated by the Carter administration to be $20 billion for 1984, less than 10 percent of the revenues lost to the federal government because of tax cuts for the corporate class (U.S. Department of Health and Human Resources 1974). A comprehensive health program has to be redistributive, based on authentically progressive revenues. It should increasingly rely on general revenues rather than Social Security taxes, which would also allow for shifting revenues among sectors. This situation is particularly important in light of the demographic transition, which is usually presented as a major reason for the rise of health expenditures. To have more elderly means to have more health consumption. The absolute and percentage growth of the numbers of the elderly is presented as one of the reasons for the crisis in the Western systems of health care. Due to the repetitiveness of this argument, let me clarify two points. First, the enormous growth of expenditures in the federal program for the elderly—Medicare—for the period 1978 to 1982 was not caused primarily by an increase in the numbers of elderly. The major cause of that growth of expenditures

was price inflation, i.e., price inflation of hospital and medical services that benefits providers and suppliers but not the patients. Second, the same demographic transition leads to fewer young people, with a freeing up of public funds for education, transportation, and recreation that could be shifted to health services. For example, the Organization for Economic Cooperation and Development (1985) secretariat has shown that, in the seven major industrialized countries, the estimated saving for public education due to the demographic transition could ensure a 0.7 percent annual growth of real social expenditures until 1990, more than sufficient to cover the expanding demands of the elderly in health services.

4. Government funding and administration of the health care services and institutions, with active worker and community participation in the running of these institutions. Himmelstein and Woolhandler (1986) have documented the ideological biases of most cost-control measures that are being researched in the United States, and that are being implemented by the American government. A majority of these measures involved a cut of benefits to the working population. A progressive agenda will have to focus on cost controls that enlarge these health benefits and further empower the patient and potential patient population, i.e., the citizenry. These authors estimated that if the United States had had a national health insurance in 1983, it would have saved the population $42.6 billion annually ($29.2 billion in health administration and insurance overhead, $4.9 billion in profits, $3.9 billion in marketing, and $4.6 billion in physicians' income). If the United States had had a national health service, the population would have saved $65.8 billion ($38.4 billion in health administration and insurance overhead, $4.9 billion in profits, $3.9 billion in marketing, and $18.6 billion in physicians' income). Complete nationalization of the health services, with nationalization of the drug and supplies industries, would save $85.3 billion (one third of all health expenditures). And most important, these savings would occur while expanding rather than reducing the health benefits for the whole population (Himmelstein and Woolhandler 1986).

All of the points presented in this article bear repeating in light of current arguments about the "crisis" of the welfare state and the health and social austerity policies that are being followed, which attribute that crisis to the growth of public expenditures (assumed to be out of control), and which explain and justify those austerity policies as responding to a popular mandate. Evidence presented in this article questions each one of these positions. These policies of austerity respond to the correlation of forces, including class forces, that exists in the United States today. The resolution of the major health problems, such as insufficient coverage and high costs, requires a change in the political practices and assumptions of the two major parties, with further development of the New Deal by the establishment of a national health program. Contrary to what is widely reported, there is, indeed, evidence of popular support for this health policy intervention by the federal government. The creation of such a program depends not only on that popular support but on the practices of the political and economic instruments through which class interests are expressed.

Appendix note 1

Class is an objective category defined by the position of the individual within the social relations of production. (For an analysis of competing definitions of class see Wright 1985, 17–30.) According to Wright the capitalist class includes those individuals who, by virtue of owning substantial quantities of the means of production need not themselves work. Capitalists own sufficient capital such that they are able to obtain at least the socially average standard of living without working at all—they are able to reproduce themselves and their families entirely on the labor of others. This does not imply that capitalists always refrain from work but simply that they need not work to obtain the socially average standard of living (Wright 1985, 149, 188). They represent 1.9 percent of the United States population. The working class includes the nonskilled wage earner plus the semicredentialed workers and the uncredentialed supervisor. It does represent 60 percent of the United States population. Besides these two polar classes there are other classes, including the class of small employers, the petty bourgeoisie, managers and supervisors, nonmanagerial experts (including professionals), and skilled employees (including school teachers and craft workers, sales persons, and clericals with college degrees and

584   Policy Issues for the 1990s

whose jobs have real autonomy). Middle classes are the nonworking class wage earners (Wright 1985, 187). Regarding the class structure there are two points of clarification that need to be made. One is that this class structure responds to objective and not to subjective conditions. People who objectively are part of the working class may not *feel* part of that class. Another point is that most social (including health) statistics are not collected according to class. Rather, other indicators such as income and education are used as proxies for class. These indicators, however, are not the determinants of class; rather, they are the symptoms of class. Because of the absence of class statistics in the United States, I, too, use income as a proxy for class in this article, in spite of the inherent limitations of such an approach.

Appendix note 2

I want to clarify that working-class behavior and anticapitalist behavior are two different things. Swedish labor follows class practices that are not anticapitalist (see Navarro 1984a for an expansion of this important distinction). Working-class practices appear when there is (1) one major union formation that unites labor and that sees itself as representing the whole class rather than specific sectors of that class, (2) a high degree of unionization among major sectors of employment, and (3) a major political party that represents labor. The opposite to class practice is "interest group" practice in which (1) each sector of labor defends its own specific interests independently of other sectors of that class and frequently in competition among themselves, and (2) there is not a political party that represents labor. Within the Western world, the northern European countries are the ones in which labor follows more closely class practices while the United States is the country in which labor follows interest group practices (for a further expansion of this point see Korpi 1980; 1983, 39). United States labor has historically followed interest group practices although there have been historical periods (like the New Deal) in which there have been elements of class practices in labor's behavior, i.e., large sectors of labor were mobilized in support of working class interests and labor was strongly influential in the Democratic Party.

References

Abramson, P.R., J.H. Aldrich, and D.W. Rohde. 1986. *Change and Continuity in the 1984 Elections.* Washington: Congressional Quarterly Press.

Altman, D.E. 1985. What Do Americans Really Want? *International Journal of Health Services* 15(3):514–15.

Bawden, D.L. 1984. *The Social Contract Revisited: Aims and Outcomes of President Reagan's Social Welfare Policy.* Washington: Urban Institute.

Black, J.T. 1986. Comments on "The Employed Uninsured and the Role of Public Policy." *Inquiry* 23(2):209–12.

Blendon, R.T., and D.E. Altman. 1984. Special Report: Public Attitudes about Health Care Costs: A Lesson in National Schizophrenia. *New England Journal of Medicine* 311(9):613–16.

Cameron, R.D. 1981. *Politics, Public Policy, and Economic Inequality: A Comparative Analysis.* Paper presented at a conference on the Role of Government in Shaping Economic Performance, University of Wisconsin, Madison.

Children's Defense Fund. 1985. *A Children's Defense Budget: An Analysis of the President's FY 1986 Budget and Children.* Washington.

David, R.J., and E. Siegel. 1983. Decline in Neonatal Mortality 1968–1977: Better Babies or Better Care. *Pediatrics* 71:531–40.

Edsall, T.B. 1984. *The New Politics of Inequality.* New York: W.W. Norton.

Esping-Andersen, G. 1985. Power and Distributional Regimes. *Politics and Society* 14(2):223–56.

Farley, P. 1985. Who Are the Underinsured? *Milbank Memorial Fund Quarterly/Health and Society* 63(3):476–503.

Ferguson, T., and J. Rogers. 1986. *The Decline of the Democrats and the Future of American Politics.* New York: Hill and Wang.

Fingerhut, V. 1985. Misunderstanding the 1984 Presidential Elections: Myths About the Democrats. *Campaigns and Elections* 1:21–28.

Fuchs, V. 1986. *The Health Economy.* Cambridge: Harvard University Press.

Gibson, R.M., K.R. Levitt, H. Lazenby, and D.R. Waldo. 1984. National Health Expenditures, 1983. *Health Care Financing Review* 6(2):1–29.

Harrington, M. 1984. *The New American Poverty.* New York: Holt, Rinehart, and Winston.

Health Care Financing Review. 1984. Aggregate and Per Capita National

Health Expenditures by Source of Funds and of Gross National Product, Selected Years 1929–1983. 6(2):3, table 1.

Himmelstein, D., and S. Woolhandler. 1986. Socialized Medicine: A Solution to the Cost Crisis in Health Care in the United States. *International Journal of Health Services* 16(3):339–54.

Huberman, L. 1947. *We the People: The Dream of America*. New York: Monthly Review Press.

Iglehart, J.K. 1982. Special Report: Report on the Duke University Medical Center Private Sector Conference. *New England Journal of Medicine* 307(1):68.

―――. 1985. From the Editor. *Health Affairs* 4(2):4.

Korpi, W. 1980. Strikes, Power, and Politics in the Western Nations, 1900–1976. In *Political Power and Social Theory*, ed. M. Zeitlin, volume 1, 301–34. New York: JAI Press.

―――. 1983. *The Democratic Class Struggle*. Boston: Routledge and Kegan Paul.

Kuttner, R. 1984. *The Economic Illusion*. Boston: Houghton Mifflin.

Ladd, E.C. 1985. The Reagan Phenomenon and Public Attitudes toward Government: In *The Reagan Presidency*, ed. L.M. Salmon and M.S. Lund, 221–49. Washington: Urban Institute.

Lippman, W. 1925. *The Phantom Public*. New York: Harcourt Brace.

Lipset, S.M. 1983. The Economy, Elections, and Public Opinion. *Tocqueville Review* 21(1):432–71.

―――. 1985. Feeling Better: Measuring the Nation's Confidence. *Public Opinion* 8(2):6–9.

Louis Harris and Associates. 1985. 1983 Equitable Health Care Survey. Washington.

Lowi, T.J. 1985. An Aligning Election: A Presidential Plebescite. In *The Elections of 1984*, ed. M. Nelson, 278–301. Washington: Congressional Quarterly, Inc.

Magasiner, I.C., and R.B. Reich. 1982. *Minding America's Business*. New York: Harcourt Brace.

Manatos, A. 1984. U.S. Voter Turnout: Now World's Worst. *New York Times*, December 1.

Maxwell, R.J. 1981. *Health and Wealth. An International Survey of Health Care Spending*. Lexington, Mass.: Lexington Books.

Mechanic, D. 1984. The Transformation of Health Providers. *Health Affairs* 3(1):65–75.

Medical Benefits. 1985. Coverage of the Privately Insured Population Less Than Age 65 for Selected Health Services: Percent Insured by Type of Insurance and Industry of Primary Insurance. U.S. 1977. 2(12):1–3.

————. 1986a. Employer Health Care Spending Drops as Percent of GNP for First Time. 3(4):4.

————. 1986b. Survey of Cost Containment among 861 Corporations. 3(3):1–2.

Medical Care Review. 1984. Number of Uninsured Americans Increases. 41(2):72–73.

Melman, S. 1985. *The Permanent War Economy.* New York: Simon and Schuster.

Milton, D. 1982. *The Politics of U.S. Labor: From the Great Depression to the New Deal.* New York: Monthly Review Press.

Monheit, A.C., M.M. Hagan, M.L. Berck, and P.J. Farley. 1985. The Employed Uninsured and the Role of Public Policy. *Inquiry* 22(4):348–64.

Moon, M., and I.V. Sawhill. 1984. Family Incomes: Gainers and Losers. In *The Reagan Record,* ed. J.L. Palmer and I.V. Sawhill, 317–46. Washington: Urban Institute.

Navarro, V. 1976. *Medicine under Capitalism.* New York: Neale Watson.

————. 1982. Where is the Popular Mandate? *New England Journal of Medicine* 307:1516–18.

————. 1984a. The Determinants of Health Policy: A Case Study: Regulating Health and Safety at the Workplace in Sweden. *Journal of Health Politics, Policy and Law* 9(1):137–66.

————. 1984b. Medical History as Justification Rather Than Explanation: A Critique of Starr's "The Social Transformation of American Medicine." *International Journal of Health Services* 14(4):511–28.

————. 1985a. In Defense of American People: Americans Are Not Schizophrenic. *International Journal of Health Services* 15(3):515–19.

————. 1985b. The 1984 Presidential Elections and the New Deal: An Alternative Explanation. Part 1. *Social Policy* 15(4):3–10.

————. 1985c. The Public/Private Mix in the Funding and Delivery of Health Services: An International Survey. *American Journal of Public Health* 75(11):1318–20.

————. 1985d. A Response to Conventional Wisdom. *International Journal of Health Services* 15(3):511–13.

Nelson, M. 1985. *The Elections of 1984.* Washington: Congressional Quarterly Inc.

New York Times. 1984. Happy Days Are Here Again. August 26.

Organization for Economic Cooperation and Development. 1985. *Social Expenditures 1960–1990. Problems of Growth and Control.* OECD Social Policy Studies. Paris.

Organization for Economic Cooperation and Development. Directorate for Social Affairs. 1985. *Measuring Health Care 1960–1983*. Paris.

Peretz, P. 1982. There Was No Tax Revolt. *Politics and Society* 11(2):231–49.

Public Opinion. 1984. Social Class. 8(7):21–22.

Quirk, J.P. 1985. The Economy: Economists, Electoral Politics and Reagan Economics. In *The Elections of 1984*, ed. M. Nelson, 155–88. Washington: Congressional Quarterly Inc.

Reinhardt, U.E., and A.S. Relman. 1968. Debating For-profit Health Care and the Ethics of Physicians. *Health Affairs* 5(2):8–31.

Rogers, D.E., R.J. Blendon, and T.W. Maloney. 1982. Who Needs Medicaid? *New England Journal of Medicine* 307(1):13–18.

Root, L.S. 1985. Employee Benefits and Social Welfare. *Annals of the American Academy of Political and Social Science* 479:101–18.

Schneider, W. 1985. Public Ready for Real Change in Health Care. *National Journal* 3(3):664–65.

Schwarz, T.E. 1983. *America's Hidden Success: A Reassessment of Twenty Years of Public Policy.* New York: W.W. Norton.

Shapiro, S. 1984. Sociodemographic Risk Factors in Infant Mortality and Low Birth Weight. Health Policy Forum, Harvard University, October 15. (Unpublished.)

Shriver, T. 1984. The Most Important Problem. *Gallup Report* 220–221:28–29.

Social Security Bulletin. 1986. Social Welfare Expenditures under Public Programs: Federal Funds as Percent of Total Expenditures, Selected Fiscal Years 1950–1963. 49(2):19, table 5.

Stallard, K., B. Ehrenreich, and H. Sklar. 1983. *Poverty in the American Dream.* Boston: South End Press.

Starr, P. 1984. *The Social Transformation of American Medicine.* Cambridge: Harvard University Press.

Thurow, L.C. 1985. *The Zero Sum Solution: Building a World-Class American Economy.* New York: Simon and Schuster.

Troy, L. 1965. *Trade Union Membership 1817–1962.* Occasional Papers 92. Washington: National Bureau of Economic Research.

UAW Washington Report. 1981. The Winners and the Losers under Reaganomics. 21(33):2–3.

U.S. Bureau of the Census. 1984. *Money, Income and Poverty Status of Families and Persons in the U.S., 1984.* Washington.

U.S. Congressional Budget Office. 1984. *Staff Memorandum: The Combined Effects of Major Changes in Federal Taxes and Spending Programs since 1981.* Washington.

U.S. Council of Economic Advisors. 1984. *1984 Economic Report to the President of the Council of Economic Advisors.* Washington.

U.S. Department of Health and Human Resources. 1974. National Health Insurance: Working Papers, Volumes I and II. Office of Assistant Secretary for Planning and Evaluation. Washington.

U.S. President. 1985. *Economic Report of the President, 1985.* Washington.

Walsh, W.B. 1985. Publisher's Letter. *Health Affairs* 4(2):3.

Washington Post. 1985. *Washington Post*-ABC News Poll. January 20.

Washington Report on Medicine and Health. 1985. July 22.

————. 1986. March 31.

Wolfinger, R., and S. Rosentone. 1980. *Who Votes?* New Haven: Yale University Press.

Wright, E.O. 1985. *Classes.* New York: Verso.

Zald, N.M. 1985. Political Change, Citizens Rights, and the Welfare State. *Annals of the American Academy of Political and Social Science* 479:48–66.

25

Health Policy for the Elderly: Federal Policy and Institutional Change

Steven P. Wallace and Carroll L. Estes

Present Trends in Health Policy

When Ronald Reagan assumed the presidency, both conservative and liberal analysts predicted revolutionary changes in the health and welfare system of the country (Heritage Foundation, 1982; Piven and Cloward, 1982). As Reagan leaves office eight years later, major programs affecting the elderly that had been targeted for radical modification or elimination still exist. Medicare continues as a federal program that pays half of the medical bills of the elderly. Medicaid remains a joint federal-state program that pays the medical bills of a large number of elderly poor. Social Security offers federally administered income support, while other programs provide federal funds for social services, food, and other needs.

While the Reagan years did not revolutionize health policy for the elderly, significant structural trends were initiated and/or reinforced. These trends could have long-lasting consequences for the elderly. As the number of elderly grows dramatically over the next fifty years, the federal health policy for the aged will reflect the heritage of New Federalism, fiscal crisis, and austerity, and deregulation. These will affect health policy for the elderly by their encouragement of the continued medicalization and commodification of health care, and of the continued growth of the medical-industrial complex.

This is an original contribution prepared for this volume.

The Demographic "Imperative"

Two factors cause policymakers to worry about the future of health policy for the elderly: the growing number of the elderly and their health status. It is possible to estimate reliably the health care demands of the elderly at the turn of the century because of two factors. All of those who will be elderly have already been born, and the health of the elderly as a group changes gradually.

The number of elderly in the United States will grow rapidly over the next forty years. In 1980 there were 25.5 million persons aged sixty-five and over in the United States, accounting for 11.3 percent of the population. That number will double by the early part of the next century; those aged sixty-five and over will number 51.4 million by the year 2020. During this time the "oldest-old," those aged eighty-five and over, will increase threefold, from 2.2 million to 7.1 million (U.S. BOC, 1984).

Because the elderly are more likely to suffer from chronic illnesses than younger age groups, the growth in the number of elderly raises concerns. Table 25.1 shows that the elderly are much more likely to suffer from chronic conditions than the general population, even though they are less susceptible to common acute conditions.

Chronic conditions often lead to limitations in the activities of daily living among the elderly, such as dressing, bathing, or walking. Of the younger elderly (ages sixty-five to seventy-four), 37 percent are limited in some way in their activities. For the oldest-old (ages 85 and up), almost 60 percent have limitations. About one-third of the oldest-old with limitations are totally unable to carry out one or more activities (U.S. NCHS, 1987).

Most of the elderly who have activity limitations remain in their com-

TABLE 25.1
Acute and Chronic Illness Rates for the Elderly, 1983

	Total Population	65 Years and Over
Acute Conditions (Rate/100 Population)		
infective and parasitic	20.3	7.3
upper respiratory	40.6	18.1
digestive system	7.6	7.2
Chronic Conditions (Rate/1,000 Population)		
heart conditions	82.8	303.0
hypertension	121.3	387.9
arthritis and rheumatism	131.3	471.6

Source: U.S. Bureau of the Census, 1986, Tables 164 and 166.

munities. Only about 5 percent of those aged sixty-five and over reside in nursing homes, although this percentage rises sharply to almost 22 percent of those aged eighty-five and over. Studies have estimated that about 80 percent of all caretaking needs of the elderly are provided by their families (U.S. NCHS, 1987).

Chronic activity limitations require long-term care for some, while acute episodes of underlying diseases generate hospital costs. For 1987, United States expenditures for health care were projected to total almost $500 billion for the entire population, exceeding 11 percent of the gross national product (GNP). Over half of that total will be spent on hospital and nursing home care (HCFA, 1987). While the elderly comprise 12 percent of the population, they account for 31 percent of those expenditures. Actually, a small proportion of the elderly are responsible for the lion's share of health care expenses. The last year of life is typically the sickest—only about 6 percent of the elderly who die in a given year account for 28 percent of all Medicare expenses (Waldo and Lazenby, 1984).

Demographic and health trends are not independent forces on federal health policy for the elderly. Political and economic conditions that frame these trends shape the policy response. The central structural constraints on future health policy for the elderly include the health care system, the changing shape of federalism, the fiscal crisis of the state, and deregulation.

The Health Care System and the Biomedical Model

While chronic illness has become the nation's primary health problem, the medical care system remains biased toward acute care. The biomedical model is oriented toward treating individuals who have short-term conditions that can be fully reversed. Chronic illnesses, on the other hand, are usually long-term conditions that require supportive and palliative care, and environmental modifications. Federal health policy virtually ignores these needs as it spends the majority of its "health" funds on institutional and acute care.

Some of the most significant health problems of the elderly are more sensitive to social and environmental interventions. The reduction in mortality due to heart disease can be attributed to changes in diet and smoking patterns. The large increase in lung cancer deaths is attributable almost entirely to the increased percentage of smokers in the aging population (U.S. NCHS, 1985). Functionally impaired elderly frequently use low-technology equipment to adapt to their illnesses, such as special grab bars or raised toilet seats (Macken, 1986).

The medical care system individualizes problems of living. Illness and functional disability are typically addressed with little attention to the family, community, or social context. Medical research and treatment for the problems of the elderly focuses on the human organism, even though social forces such as poverty, widowhood, or housing conditions may be equally significant.

Changing Shape of Federalism

Federalism denotes the relationships among different levels of government. Since the depression and the New Deal, the federal government has taken an increasingly large responsibility for the health and welfare of the population. The federal government has assumed full responsibility for some programs that address needs of the elderly, such as Social Security for income and Medicare for acute medical care. For other programs, such as Medicaid, which provides health care for the poor, the federal government has developed cooperative relationships with states and localities.

In the 1970s President Richard Nixon initiated policies that increased state and local discretion and responsibilities; President Reagan has vigorously followed this lead by limiting the federal role in health and welfare through block grants, program cuts, and increased state responsibility. Havighurst (1982) reflects New Federalism's ideology that the individual in an open market should be unaffected by government. He states that "the competitive process, precisely because it is based on choice, validates the outcome whatever it may turn out to be. . . . [A]n intensely personal matter as what to do about disease should be kept within the realm of private choice" (p. 7). This ideology resulted in proposals to eliminate direct federal involvement in most major health and welfare programs, including Medicare, Social Security, and even the National Institutes of Health (Pear, 1987; Moore, 1986). In its most basic form, New Federalism challenges the idea that there is any societal responsibility for meeting basic human needs in health, income, housing, or welfare (Estes, Gerard, Zones, and Swan, 1984).

New Federalism's goals have been more far-reaching than its achievements. While the Reagan administration has proposed various program changes that would have sharply limited the federal role in the health and welfare of the population, actual changes have followed a historically incremental course. Dramatic changes, such as placing Medicare recipients in the market for private health insurance, have not been successful in Congress. Concurrent policy changes, however, are significantly restructuring the health care system for the elderly.

The *ideology* of the proper federal role has shifted dramatically. The federal government was viewed as the key agent for solving the nation's problems under President Lyndon Johnson's New Society. Under Reagan's New Federalism it is seen as a source of the nation's problems. The ideological shift away from a strong federal role provides a powerful constraint on future policy initiatives. This will be significant for the elderly because of their dependence, along with the poor, on federal programs for their health and welfare. While the ideology of New Federalism is to reduce the involvement of the federal government in the lives of citizens, demographic changes in society will increase the pressure on the federal government to take a larger role in the health and welfare of the elderly.

The reliance of the elderly on federal programs is most evident in the importance of Social Security and Medicare to the elderly. If Social Security were eliminated, the poverty rate among the elderly would soar from 12.4 percent to 47.6 percent. Many of those helped out of poverty by Social Security are not far from falling into poverty. Congressional Budget Office analyses of a proposed cost-of-living-adjustment freeze in 1985 estimated that a one-year freeze would have dropped between 420,000 and 470,000 elderly into poverty (Villers, 1987). The dependence of the poor and near poor on Social Security is shown in table 25.2. Low-income couples depend on Social Security for 82 percent of their income, while high-income couples have assets as their primary source of income.

The elderly's dependence on Medicare and Medicaid is similarly large. Medicare paid almost half the medical expenses of the aged in 1984; Medicaid paid an additional 13 percent. Despite these programs, each elderly person had an average of $1,059 in out-of-pocket health expenses, not including insurance premiums (U.S. Senate, 1986). This is a substantial sum, particularly for those living in or near poverty. When the elderly

TABLE 25.2
Comparisons of Sources of Income Between High- and Low-Income Elderly, 1984

| | Percentage of Total Income | | | |
| | Couples | | Individuals | |
Source	Less than $10,100	$30,100 and up	Less than $4,200	$13,700 and up
Social Security	82	18	75	22
Pension	5	17	1	16
Income from assets	6	38	3	49
Earnings	2	26	1	12
Means-tested cash transfer	3	0	18	0
Other	2	1	2	1
Total	100	100	100	100

Source: U.S. GAO, 1986.

need long-term care for a chronic illness they are particularly vulnerable because Medicare pays for limited nursing home or home health care. The only way for the elderly to get assistance with prolonged long-term-care bills is to spend themselves into poverty and qualify for Medicaid. This threatens the independence of the elderly, since few have resources to remain out of poverty after paying for as little as thirteen weeks of nursing home care (U.S. House Select Committee on Aging, 1987).

As a result of their reliance on federal programs for income and health care, the elderly are particularly vulnerable to changes in federal policy that affect the health and welfare of the nation. The needs of the growing number of elderly persons conflict with the antigovernment ideology of New Federalism. While it is unlikely that the federal government will repudiate all responsibility for the health care of the elderly, the legitimation of New Federalism may limit federal government growth to a level below what is necessary to keep up with the needs of the growing number of elderly.

Fiscal Crisis

There are two ways to define a condition of fiscal crisis. One is the objective deficit between revenues and expenditures. This is particularly critical for state governments, since they must normally have balanced budgets. There is also a subjective element to fiscal crises, since a "crisis" implies that there are no easy solutions to the fiscal imbalance. The level of taxation that a jurisdiction can support, or the level of program reduction that citizens are willing to suffer, is a political issue. For there to be a crisis, therefore, policymakers and the public must perceive a lack of politically legitimate options.

The objective aspects of a fiscal crisis can be observed in local, state, and federal budgets since the late 1970s. The crises have been brought to a head by taxpayer revolts, federal tax cuts, and economic recession. Just as economic crisis provided the context for government expansion during the New Deal, the fiscal crisis of the 1980s is a driving force of New Federalism's attack on government. At the federal level, declining revenues have been caused by massive tax cuts enacted in 1981 and the largest peacetime military buildup ever. This reordering of budget priorities has also led to national debt levels of historic size, both in dollar amounts and as a percentage of the GNP (U.S. House Committee on the Budget, 1987).

The subjective component of fiscal crisis is present in the belief that federal spending on the elderly and the poor is a major cause of United States economic problems. This belief legitimates proposals to decrease the federal deficit by reducing programs for the elderly and the poor, even though over half of the current deficit can be traced directly to the 1981 tax cuts (U.S. House Committee on the Budget, 1987). While the tax burden in the United States is lower than in almost all other industrialized nations, austerity is presented as the only possible response to declining revenues. As a result, Social Security and Medicare expenditures, which are funded by a special tax and trust fund, have been used as a political maneuver to reduce the size of the general revenue deficit. In fiscal year 1988, Social Security alone is projected to have a *surplus* of up to $38 billion, with the accumulated surplus growing to an estimated $12 trillion by 2020 when baby boomers will begin to draw it down (*New York Times,* 1987). Medicare's surplus for 1988 is projected to be approximately $20 billion (U.S. OMB, 1987). On paper this reduces the federal deficit, even though Social Security and Medicare funds can be used only for those programs. The fiscal crisis has entrenched austerity in the public debate, as evidenced by austerity (versus equity) becoming the driving ideology behind health and social policy for the elderly.

Austerity hits the elderly particularly hard because it focuses on governmental finances rather than on total social effort. Attention to the total social effort notes that the number of dependents in society (children under eighteen plus the aged) has been *decreasing* since the mid-1960s. Children, however, are largely supported by their parents and local programs, while the elderly are most dependent on federal programs for their health and welfare. As the aged segment of society grows, and the child segment declines, an increasing proportion of society's support for dependent populations will be channeled through the government rather than through the family economy. The dependence on family caused by 65.7 children per 100 adults in 1965 shifted toward the government by 1985 as the *total* dependency ratio (aged plus children) fell to 62.1. As the total dependency ratio falls through the end of this century, the proportion of dependents who rely on the federal government will continue to rise (U.S. BOC, 1984).

The elderly are also frequently assigned blame for the increasing costs of the medical system. Recent data, however, show that factors other than the increasing number of the elderly are much more important. A study of 1985 health expenditures (Waldo, Levit, and Lazenby, 1986) and spending projections to the year 2000 (U.S. HCFA, 1987) indicate that health care costs are rising primarily because of rising prices in the medical care system itself (e.g., rising hospital and physician charges, 55.6 percent of increase), and secondarily because of increased intensity of care (higher technology, services, 22.9 percent of increase). Increased utilization of services and the much heralded demographic changes have contributed far less to rising health expenditures. Population growth has contributed less than 8 percent to the rising cost of care, and changes in utilization have no effect. The net result of blaming the elderly for contributing to the fiscal crisis questions the deservedness of those receiving the medical care (the aged) rather than the deservedness of those receiving payments and making profits from providing medical services to the aged.

The politics of fiscal austerity define health and welfare expenditures for the elderly as involved in a zero-sum competition with other sectors of the economy. The argument assumes that if the country is in a fiscal crisis, someone *has* to lose out. An alternate way of conceptualizing expenditures on the elderly is to include those expenditures as part of a "citizens' wage." This approach views payment to the elderly as part of delayed wages, rewarding the recipient for previous work. During the post-World War II period, increased health and pension benefits were given to workers as a part of wage compensation to promote labor peace and productivity (Myles, 1984). The broad social benefits of delayed compensation are reconceptualized as burdens on business and society by the politics of austerity. As long as fiscal crisis is the focus of public policy, this dynamic of austerity will continue to define the parameters of the possible.

Deregulation

Deregulation is a hallmark of New Federalism policy. Minimizing government influence on markets is a key goal of New Federalism, since competition and other market forces are seen as maximizing socially valued ends. This approach incorporates the view of people as primarily economic beings (Wallace, Bowers, and Chico, 1984). In health care, this approach assumes that health can be treated as a commodity, with the consumer making fully informed rational decisions about the costs and benefits of treatments to prevent pain, illness, and death. A deregulated health market would have little incentive to address the social and environmental bases of many illnesses (Salmon, 1982).

An important example of the impact of deregulation in health care is the eradication of federal restrictions that precluded the entry of for-profit firms in government-financed programs. We are witnessing a federal health policy shift from a concern with benevolence to a concern with economics. With United States personal health care expenditures exceeding $400 billion per year (29 percent spent for the elderly), corporate attraction to for-profit markets in medical care for the elderly is obvious (U.S. HCFA, 1987). Four proprietary hospital chains already own or manage 12 percent of United States hospitals, and some experts predict that in a competitive environment ten giant national firms will capture 50 percent of the medical market in the next ten years (*Wall Street Journal,* 1985).

Deregulation is also giving increased discretion to states in joint federal-state programs. In 1981, for example, federal funds given to the states for social services (Title XX) were reorganized into a block grant with the elimination of most targeting and reporting requirements. Federal regulations have also been relaxed in state-run programs that affect the elderly such as Medicaid and other health programs.

Deregulation is supposed to foster efficiency in the market of services, and give states discretion to shape programs to local needs. The increasing concentration of power in the medical care industry, however, may simply shift the power from the government to corporate board rooms rather than to the market. While some states have a history of providing adequate benefits to their citizens, states' ability to fund and their commitment to health and welfare programs vary widely and are increasingly disparate (Thompson, 1987).

Future Trends in Health Policy for the Elderly

The structure of the health care system, the ideology of New Federalism, the fiscal crisis of the state, and deregulation are all influences on health policy that have developed or been shaped during the Reagan years. In the years ahead we suggest that these forces will result in further changes in the medical system and health policy, including medicalization, the commodification of health, and the continued growth of the medical-industrial complex.

Medicalization

Medicalization involves the expansion of the power of medicine over social problems. The cost-containment strategies under New Federalism have created conditions that further the medicalization of health services for the elderly. As noted earlier, the major health problem of the elderly is chronic illness that creates needs for supportive care and social services. Families currently provide the majority of the assistance needed by the chronically ill, resorting to institutions only when they are unable to provide the needed care at home (Doty, 1986). For those without families, services similar to nonmedical family care are necessary to maintain the elder in the community.

In contrast, cost containment has focused on limiting the use of costly medical services and reducing services for the least disabled. One of the most significant cost-containment actions has been changing Medicare hospital reimbursement to fixed rates based on diagnosis (DRGs). By fixing reimbursement by diagnosis, hospitals now have an incentive to discharge elderly patients as early as possible, resulting in a decrease in the average length of a hospital stay for the elderly by two days. The release of sicker people into the community has increased the demand for higher technology and skilled services in the community. This increased demand is accompanied by a narrow interpretation of Medicare's home health benefit in an attempt to keep those costs under control. The result is that the skilled nursing paid for by Medicare is being directed toward only the sickest in the community (Estes, 1988).

The reductions under New Federalism of federal funding for social services (down 42 percent between 1982 and 1988) have forced agencies to reorient their services to be able to obtain reimbursement from other sources, such as Medicare and Medicaid. By shifting their services from social programs to medical support, the agencies reduce their commitment to providing a "continuum of care" that can offer services at the least restrictive (and least medical) level needed (Wood and Estes, 1988).

The biomedical model defines the needs of the aged around a medical services strategy, as individual medical problems rather than as a result of societal treatment of the elderly, inadequate income, or other social problems. Similarly, the government's response to the needs of the elderly as primarily medical rather than social (e.g., housing, social services, and family care allowances) reinforces the mistaken view that rising health care costs are attributable to the elderly. Contemporary health policies attempt to "solve" the health care cost crisis by addressing only symptoms through medically based management strategies (Estes, Gerard, Zones, and Swan, 1984).

There does not appear to be any movement away from the trend of treating the problems of the elderly as primarily medical in nature. Because of the politics of austerity, the expansion of nonmedical community services can be legitimated only if they cost no more than the current medically oriented system. A recent review of demonstration projects that provide community care concludes that programs designed to reduce nursing home use fail to save government money. Noninstitutional care does improve the quality of life of the recipients, but advocating for community care based on reducing costs does not appear viable (Kemper, Applebaum, and Harrigan, 1987). As long as fiscal crisis defines policy options, it will be difficult to include quality of life as a cost or a benefit. Thus the fiscal crisis, New Federalism, deregulation, and the health care system all support the continuation of health policy that emphasizes an acute medical model in its treatment of the chronic illness and support needs of the elderly.

Commodification

Rather than treating the health of the aged as a public good that is provided and enjoyed collectively, health is increasingly accessed through the market like other goods and services. Providers of health care to the aged are being forced to abandon charitable goals in the face of the economic "realities" of the market (Gray, 1986).

The shift of health care into a competitive market is a central aspect of New Federalism. The federal government now allows states to award contracts based on competitive bids to providers of medical care for the poor, with California and Arizona taking the lead in implementing this approach. Other states are using competitive bidding to select providers of community care services for the elderly and social services under Title XX (Dyckman and Anderson, 1986). Entry into the market is typically justified as a cost-containment measure and is made possible by loosening public program regulations.

As health is treated more as a commodity, health providers come to operate increasingly like other businesses. We shift from "outreach" programs designed to bring needed services to the community, to "marketing" strategies designed to attract paying customers. This is apparent even in the nonprofit sector, as strategic planning and other business practices become necessary for the economic survival of health care providers (Salmon, 1983). Concern has been raised about what will happen to those unable to pay for their care, an important issue since only one-third of noninstitutionalized poor elderly are covered by the medical care program for the poor, Medicaid (Villers, 1987).

As a commodity, health care relies on the market where access and distribution are based on the ability to pay. As commodification increases, hospitals are shifting their goals from institutions that provide services for those in need, to ones that offer services to customers (Robinette, 1985). Rather than satisfying a need, medical providers are increasingly in the position of trying to attract profitable patients while avoiding others who may be even more needy (Relman, 1980). The structure of medicine as a commodity puts physicians in a particular dilemma, since they must balance their role as patient advocates with their role as fiscal agents of hospitals and other health care organizations (Veatch, 1983). As social good (health) becomes a commodity that is valued for its ability to create profit, many of the conditions that maximized the well-being of the elderly are weakened. The growing reliance on the market has intensified a perennial and profound health care question: Should health care be provided as a "market good" that is purchased as a commodity by those who can afford to pay, or should it be provided as a "merit good" that is available as a right or collective good, regardless of ability to pay (Estes, Gerard, Zones, and Swan, 1984)? The ideology of New Federalism, politics of austerity, and deregulation are all fostering a situation where health care for the elderly is increasingly treated as a commodity.

The Medical-Industrial Complex

The medical-industrial complex consists of the growing concentration of private for-profit hospitals, nursing homes, and other medical care organizations, along with businesses related to medical goods and services (Wohl, 1984). By 1980 the growth of the medical-industrial complex had become a significant enough force in American medicine to cause the editor of the *New England Journal of Medicine* to warn of its impact on the shape of American medicine (Relman, 1980). In his Pulitizer Prize-winning book, Paul Starr (1982) notes that medicine is losing its basis in voluntarism and local control as a result of the growth of the complex. Not only are an increasing number of hospital beds and other medical services becoming profit-oriented, but even nonprofit hospitals are often establishing for-profit subsidiaries to help generate revenues. Both proprietary and nonprofit hospitals are also integrating horizontally into multihospital chains across the country, and integrating vertically by establishing a host of lab, supply, home health, and other services so the patient's medical dollars stay entirely within one company.

The medical-industrial complex has been able to grow because medical care programs for the elderly and the poor have bought into the existing medical system rather than establishing a national health service. Since Medicare and Medicaid were designed to provide equal access to "mainstream medicine," government clinics were established only in areas that were unattractive to private providers (via community health centers, Indian Health Service, etc.). While the government philosophy of Johnson's Great Society was expansionist, new programs worked to help the elderly participate in the medical market rather than change or eliminate the market to meet the needs of the elderly. Publicly funded medical assistance thus greatly enlarged the market for medical providers. The increased number of paying customers for services, and guaranteed profits in some sectors, fueled the expansion and consolidation of medical services (Brown, 1984).

The medical-industrial complex is best organized to survive and even thrive during a period of austerity. Proprietary facilities are organized around costs, while public and religious facilities are traditionally organized to provide care to needy populations (Henriot, 1985). Profit-oriented providers are therefore more able to respond quickly to cost-cutting policies, as well as to expand into the most lucrative new areas.

New Federalism's emphasis on the market gives the medical-industrial complex an advantage, since proprietary-hospital chains are the best positioned to take advantage of a market-oriented system. Hospital chains are moving to "multiclustering" where a hospital serves as the core of a regional health care network owned by one corporation. These networks can include skilled nursing facilities, home health agencies, durable medical equipment center, and psychiatric, substance-abuse, and rehabilitation units. One large chain, National Medical Enterprises (NME) is already establishing such multis in Tampa–St. Petersburg, Miami, St. Louis, New Orleans, Dallas, San Diego, and Long Beach. American Medical International, Inc. (AMI) and Hospital Corporation of America (HCA) have targeted fifteen other cities for their multis (Hospitals, 1986). Private nonprofits are also moving in this direction, but they have neither the capital nor the institutional size to create comparable networks nationwide.

With the growing aging population and a concern with costs, there is an increasing move toward home care services. As with institutional providers, there are strong incentives for profit-making companies to expand in this area. In 1985 nine profit-making companies, including giants like Upjohn Health Care Services, operated over 1,000 full-service home health care offices across the country (Reuben and Hamilton, 1986). Some of these companies, like American Hospital Supply, have integrated their services vertically so that they not only manufacture supplies for hospitals but also deliver those same supplies in individuals' homes.

The linkage that will give proprietaries the largest advantage is their merging with or starting insurance divisions. AMI already has its own group health plan, AMICARE, that offers integrated services at its own facilities. NME is also preparing to enter the insurance arena (Hospitals, 1986). With insurance companies already among the largest sources of capital in the United States, proprietary chains will be able to strengthen further their market position by accessing the capital made available through their insurance subsidiaries. In contrast, nonprofits face possibly worsening problems in obtaining capital for maintaining their facilities and modernizing care (Morris, 1985). In addition, "brand-name medicine" is being promoted by Humana and other chains through putting their corporate names on all of the facilities they own (*Wall Street Journal*, 1985). To the extent that health care is deregulated and commodified, providers will do the best by marketing brand-name medicine and insurance rather than by pushing intangibles like public service.

One of the hazards of a large medical-industrial complex is that the power concentrated within such an industry can shape the direction of health policy to the benefit of the industry, which does not necessarily coincide with the needs of the elderly. A recent example of this is the attempt by the drug industry to defeat the inclusion of drug coverage in a proposed Medicare expansion to cover catastrophic illnesses (*Washington Post Weekly*, 1987). Since Medicare has not covered outpatient drug costs, they have been a major burden on the resources of the elderly. Drug companies worried that the inclusion of drugs as a Medicare benefit would lead to a limiting of the costs of drugs, pinching profits.

It should be noted that the growth of the medical-industrial complex is not a unique process. During the Reagan years, a deregulatory approach to mergers facilitated the increased concentration of ownership in a variety of sectors, from transportation to industrials (Eads and Fix, 1984). While this article focuses on the plight of health policy for the elderly, it is important to keep in mind that many of the structural conditions discussed in this paper extend beyond medicine to affect other sectors of the economy as well.

Hospital Reimbursement for the Elderly

Federal changes in hospital reimbursement for the elderly under Medicare demonstrate how New Federalism, fiscal crisis, and deregulation result in increased medicalization and commodification and the growth of the medical-industrial complex. When Medicare began in 1966 it paid hospitals retrospectively, i.e., hospitals were paid, after providing care, for all "reasonable" expenses incurred in treating a patient (including construction costs and profits). In 1983 the federal government began to set limits on the amount Medicare would pay per hospital admission for illness groupings, called diagnosis related groups (DRGs). Establishing payment rates per diagnosis (DRG) before services are provided creates significant incentives for hospitals to reduce in-patient days by discharging elders "sicker and quicker." Introduced as an austerity measure to reduce federal Medicare costs, DRGs have indirectly raised new discussion about quality of care and access to medical care, both of which were major issues during the 1960s (Estes, Wallace, and Binney, 1989).

The shifting concept of federalism is reflected in the early discharge of ill Medicare patients, shifting care into the community where Medicare pays a smaller proportion of the costs, and state and local governments and individuals pay a larger share. Increasing copayments and deductibles for individuals have accompanied DRG-based reimbursement. Out-of-pocket health care costs for the elderly averaged 15 percent of their median income in 1984 (U.S. Senate, 1987), while elder blacks paid 23 percent of their income for health care expenditures in 1981 (Estes, 1985). States and localities also shoulder increased responsibility for expenses not covered by Medicare incurred by the elderly poor.

Although the DRG regulates payment by diagnosis, decisions about how to cut costs are left entirely to providers, reflecting their deregulatory aspect. Tax laws and deregulation have also encouraged the increased entry of for-profit corporations into medical markets (including both hospital and home health care).

The medical-industrial complex is uniquely positioned to take advantage of DRG-based reimbursements. Proprietary hospital chains, linked to supply companies and post-hospital care services, benefit from economies of scale, mass marketing, and the ability to cost-shift. Proprietary chains have pioneered new services to maximize profits, such as freestanding emergency rooms, sports medicine clinics, and drug/alcohol abuse programs which are well reimbursed or which draw the middle class, who can pay the fees. Hospitals have reacted swiftly to the new system, *increasing* their profits after the introduction of DRG-based payment. Investor-owned hospitals made the highest returns on their investments (see Waldo, Levit, and Lazenby, 1986). At the same time, some public hospitals are being closed or bought by investors.

By focusing on the issue of hospital costs, the major component of Medicare expenditures, DRGs perpetuate Medicare's bias toward medically oriented institutional care of the acutely ill. Federal interest in developing an integrated long-term care system that adequately addresses the chronic-illness problems of the elderly remains low, since ensuring a continuum of care is not likely to reduce costs, reduce federal responsibilities, or result from deregulation.

The Future of Austerity and Cost Containment

A recent survey of the nation's health system leaders found that those most influential in health care and health policy are divided as to whether cost containment or quality of care will be the most important issue at the turn of the century. These leaders primarily wanted to improve service delivery and financing within the current health system. One in five, however, felt more fundamental changes are needed, including the creation of a national health service or an insurance plan involving federal resource allocation (Policy Research Institute and Project HOPE, 1985).

Continuing efforts to balance the federal budget indicate that cost containment will remain the central feature of health policy in the near future. Continuing austerity at the federal level was institutionalized by the Gramm-Rudman-Hollings Balanced Budget Act (or simply "Gramm-

Rudman'') in 1985, and revised in 1987. This act required that the federal budget be balanced by decreasing the deficit each year. If Congress does not make budget changes that reduce the deficit by a predetermined amount, automatic expenditure cuts occur. In contrast to tax surcharges that were used in the 1960s to compensate for a growing deficit, this bill embodies an austerity approach to the budget by addressing only spending. The automatic cuts are across-the-board, with the dollar reduction split between military and nonmilitary spending (U.S. House Committee on the Budget, 1987). Program changes are not mandated, only spending levels. This budget-led planning typifies the politics of austerity that is driving health policy.

There are a set of ''protected'' programs exempt from the cuts, including basic entitlement programs. Inflation and/or increased needs would still create de facto cuts in these programs. Medicare and other health programs were semiprotected by a ceiling on the amount they could be cut automatically. In 1987 Congress avoided the automatic cuts by passing spending and revenue bills that lowered the deficit. Included in the package were increased premiums and deductibles for Medicare recipients, further increasing the out-of-pocket medical expenses of the elderly without modifying the system that generates rising medical costs.

The continued viability of a budget centered around the issue of the deficit ensures that federalism, austerity, and deregulation will remain at the forefront of the policy agenda. Policy concern over medicalization, commodification, and the growth of the medical-industrial complex have to wait until the focus of policy concern returns to the health care system and the health of the elderly and others.

Just as the focus of health policy shifted from access in the 1960s to cost containment in the 1970s, the economics of austerity is leading health and aging policy into retrenchment for the 1980s and 1990s. Retrenchment fits into the ideology of New Federalism, where the federal government is considered responsible primarily for only the national defense (Wallace, Bowers, and Chico, 1984). Forcing cutbacks in social programs to help balance the budget would further move the burden of aiding the elderly and disadvantaged citizens to states and localities. The nonprofit health sector will also continue to face increased demand. While about 35 percent of free health care is provided in public institutions, almost all of the balance is provided in nonprofit institutions (Relman, 1985).

Program changes can only be justified if they save money under the politics of austerity. Unmet needs or inequitable distribution, key arguments for program changes before New Federalism, will continue to be insufficient rationale. Within the last ten years, attention has shifted from a proactive discussion of the government's role in insuring the nation's health via national health insurance to a reactive debate about whether the government should stop regulating health care and let the market control decisions. This debate directs attention away from an adequate assessment of the needs of the elderly and others in society.

The next significant step likely to be taken in providing health care for the elderly within the framework of New Federalism's limits, the politics of austerity, and deregulation is the further contracting out of services and programs that the government currently provides (Moore, 1986; Dobson, et al., 1986). Medicare is a likely candidate for contracting out, since private companies already play a significant role in administering the program by acting as fiscal intermediaries. Demonstration projects can be implemented under current law to give contracts to insurers like Blue Cross to be responsible for all Medicare recipients in defined geographic areas. These contracts could either be competitively bid, as California did with MediCal (Medicaid) hospital contracts, or they could be offered at a fixed sum (such as current Medicare expenditures). While the private insurer would have to offer recipients the option of keeping their same Medicare benefits, the private insurer could also offer cost-saving options. Options might include offering recipients reduced copayments if they agreed to go only to specified providers. Contracting out gives private insurers the responsibility of designing options, assuming some underwriting risks, and negotiating with and regulating medical providers. This can be seen as a step toward deregulation, since the insurers would be given discretion over program options. The prospect of keeping some or all of any savings (profits) would provide an incentive for the insurers to focus their efforts on costs. A smaller-scale effort in this direction is occurring with the federal interest in increasing HMO and other prepaid group practice use.

One of the consequences of contracting out is that it removes the program from the political process. This can be seen as a benefit because it weakens the hands of special interests (Moore, 1986), or it can be seen as a disadvantage because it makes the program less sensitive to those affected by it (Estes, 1979). In the case of a contracted-out Medicare, politicians could depoliticize increases in deductibles and copayments by blaming them on insurers' decisions, while the insurers could blame increasing costs on their contracts. The end result would be to defuse the ability of the elderly and other advocates to shape the costs and benefits of Medicare.

Deregulation assumes that the marketplace is the most efficient and effective distributor in society. This implies, a priori, that there is no need to discuss what policies could be enacted to foster the health of the elderly, nor is there a need to evaluate carefully the consequences of deregulation.

Thus, to the degree that deregulation is embodied in public policy, it obviates the need for program data or debate about public policy for the elderly.

Another challenge will come from the special health needs of elderly women and minorities in the next century, many of whom will be among those least able to pay for it. The feminization of poverty, coupled with the longer life-spans of women, results in older women comprising a higher share of those needing health care while having fewer resources (Arendell and Estes, 1987). Similarly, blacks, Hispanics, and other disadvantaged minorities have poorer health, more chronic illnesses, and lower income than whites, as well as inferior access to health care (U.S. HRSA, 1986). The proportions of minority communities that are elderly, historically small in number, are increasing faster than the proportion of whites who are elderly (U.S. Senate, 1987). Minority elders will need expanded, culturally relevant, low-cost health care.

If the nation continues to be influenced by New Federalism, austerity, and deregulation, health policies will continue to contribute to the medicalization, commodification, and corporatization of health care. Who will pay for the costs of these "unprofitable" patients is likely to be a growing question. Relegating health care distribution to the market assumes that consumers will be sufficiently informed to make the best choices. Fostering public knowledge of costs, quality, and optimal treatments is problematic.

Unless precautions are instituted, severe fragmentation of health care will occur as companies are drawn to the most profitable sectors of care and unbundled services for the elderly, neglecting unprofitable treatments and populations. This growing fragmentation will decrease the possibility for policies that rationalize the system along criteria of need. Fragmentation of less powerful interest groups is possible as they are pitted against each other for shrinking government resources. Finally, with federal reimbursements made primarily in medical services to the elderly and with the reduced social service expenditures, broadly conceived "health" care will be a low priority.

Scenarios for Change

The two competing approaches to health-policy challenges for the elderly have been based on models of market competition and government regulation (Mechanic, 1986). While New Federalism emphasizes market-oriented policies, a return to more regulatory approaches would not necessarily change the trends of the Reagan years. The growth of the medical-industrial complex, for example, may have given it sufficiently concentrated power that it could effectively control local attempts at health planning and regulation (Chesney, 1982). Rather than reforming the present system at the margins through regulation or competition, a substantial restructuring of the health system is needed to best confront the basic problems that affect health of the elderly.

Because of the power of the medical profession and the medical-industrial complex, restructuring health care for the elderly will require forming coalitions that transcend age and unite groups with common interests (e.g., the elderly and the disabled [see Institute for Health and Aging, 1986]). These groups could advocate redefining health care away from a strict medical model toward the organization, financing, and delivery of health care along a continuum. This continuum would range from respite care for relieving families who already provide most of the nation's caretaking, to adequate incomes, to acute medical services. In place of austerity and New Federalism, health policy will have to treat health care as part of the Constitution's federal mandate to "promote the general welfare" rather than as a private commodity.

It should be noted that children and the poor do not compete with the elderly in the challenges of health policy, but share these concerns. The medicalization of health care deflects concern with health issues of inner-city children such as lead poisoning, nutrition, and maternal and child health promotion. The commodification of health threatens to widen the gap between the care available to those who can pay and those who cannot, regardless of age. Comparisons between the economic status of the elderly and children are typically made to assert that the elderly have too much, implying that poverty among the elderly should be as shamefully common as it is among children. On the other hand, since the government has been successful in reducing poverty among the elderly, it could be argued that the government should now do the same for children, whether through guaranteed jobs for parents, increased minimum wages, or other income-enhancement policies. If adequate and appropriate health care and an adequate income become federal-policy priorities, citizens of all ages would benefit.

In sum, the Reagan years have redirected the course of health policy for the elderly. This change in course has not been the sharp turn hoped for by advocates of the Reagan agenda, but the changes have set up limits to the directions that health policy can take in the coming years. As currently structured, health care for the aged will become increasingly medicalized, commodified, and provided by corporations. Coalition-building is needed between the elderly and others concerned with the direction that health policy is taking us if the medical care system is to be reoriented by public policy.

Health policy debate and action for the elderly in the future need to be indivisible from struggles to:

(a) redress restrictions to access to health care that have grown markedly in the 1980s as a result of funding cuts and an increased un- and under-insured population. The uninsured population of 30 to 35 million includes 3 million persons aged fifty-five to sixty-four and almost 400,000 persons over age sixty-five (U.S. Senate, 1985). Rising out-of-pocket costs to the elderly will further contribute to access problems as health care increasingly moves out of the hospital since 60 percent of the elderly's physician charges, for example, are paid out-of-pocket. These statistics challenge the concept that the elderly can bear increased cost shifting and continue to have any reasonable access.

(b) develop workable alternatives in providing long-term-care services and in preventing the need for institutionalization. The challenge is to strengthen ambulatory care, the continuum of community-based services (e.g., adult day care, congregate meals) and in-home services, and to find mechanisms to bolster the role (acknowledging the limits and personal costs) of family caretaking and other vital sources of personal and social support.

(c) refocus attempts at health care cost containment from the ill to the structure of the medical care system itself. It will be difficult and expensive to target appropriate health services to those most in need as long as health care is increasingly commodified and medicalized. The government needs to reshape the medical care system rather than simply buying into the medical-industrial complex.

Given the scope and costs involved, long-term care and acute care can no longer continue to be financed and developed separately. Piecemeal development of policies based on either market reforms or regulatory cost-containment strategies that leave the basic health care financing system and medical system intact are inadequate. Developing a system that provides universal quality care at an affordable cost will require concerted federal leadership and a federal role.

References

Arendell, Terry, and Carroll L. Estes. 1987. "Unsettled Future: Older Women, Economics and Health." *Feminist Studies* 7:3–25.

Brown, E. Richard. 1984. "Medicare and Medicaid: Band-Aids for the Old and Poor." In V. Sidel and R. Sidel, eds., *Reforming Medicine*. New York: Pantheon Books, pp. 50–76.

Chesney, James D. 1982. "The Politics of Regulation: An Assessment of Winners and Losers." *Inquiry* 19:235–45.

Dobson, Allen; John C. Langenbrunner; Steven A. Pelovitz; and Judith B. Willis.

1986. "The Future of Medicare Policy Reform: Priorities for Research and Demonstrations." *Health Care Financing Review. 1986 Annual Supplement,* pp. 1–8.

Doty, Pamela. 1986. "Family Care of the Elderly: The Role of Public Policy." *Milbank Quarterly* 64, no. 1:34–75.

Dyckman, Zachary, and Judy Anderson. 1986. "Competitive Bidding for Health Care Services." *Health Care Financing Extramural Report.* Washington, D.C.: Health Care Financing Administration.

Eads, George, and Michael Fix. 1984. *The Reagan Regulatory Strategy: An Assessment.* Washington, D.C.: Urban Institute.

Estes, Carroll L. 1979. *The Aging Enterprise.* San Francisco, Calif.: Jossey-Bass.

———. 1985. "Long Term Care and Public Policy in an Era of Austerity." *Journal of Public Health* 6, no. 4:464–75.

———. 1988. "Cost Containment and the Elderly: Conflict or Challenge." *Journal of the American Geriatrics Society* 36:1.

Estes, Carroll L.; Lenore E. Gerard; Jane Zones; and James Swan. 1984. *Political Economy, Health, and Aging.* Boston, Mass.: Little, Brown.

Estes, Carroll L.; Steven P. Wallace; and Elizabeth A. Binney. 1989. "Health, Aging, and Medical Sociology." In H. E. Freeman and S. Levine, eds., *Handbook of Medical Sociology.* 4th ed. New York: Prentice-Hall, pp. 400–18.

Gray, Bradford, ed. 1986. *For-Profit Enterprise in Health Care.* Washington, D.C.: National Academy Press.

Havighurst, Clark C. 1982. *Deregulating the Health Care Industry, Planning for Competition.* Cambridge, Mass.: Ballinger Publishing Co.

Henriot, Peter J. 1985. "Catholic Health Care: Competing and Complementary Models." *Hospital Progress* 66, no. 7:36–40.

Heritage Foundation. 1982. *Understanding Reaganomics.* Washington, D.C.: Heritage Foundation.

Hospitals. 1986. "Multi Clustering: A Natural Evolution," 60, no. 5 (March 5):56ff.

Institute for Health and Aging. 1986. *Executive Summary: Towards a Unified Agenda, A National Conference on Disability and Aging.* San Francisco, Calif.: Institute for Health and Aging, University of California.

Kemper, Peter; Robert Applebaum; and Margaret Harrigan. 1987. "Community Care Demonstrations: What Have We Learned?" *Health Care Financing Review* 8:87–100.

Macken, Candice L. 1986. "A Profile of Functionally Impaired Elderly Persons Living in the Community." *Health Care Financing Review* 7, no. 4:33–49.

Mechanic, David. 1986. *From Advocacy to Allocation.* New York: Free Press.

Moore, Stephen, ed. 1986. *Slashing the Deficit Fiscal Year 1987: A $122 Billion Savings Strategy to Avoid the Gramm-Rudman Ax.* Washington, D.C.: Heritage Foundation.

Morris, Stephen M. 1985. "The Not-for-Profit Dilemma." *Hospital and Health Services Administration* 30, no. 4:47–54.

Myles, John. 1984. *Old Age in the Welfare State.* Boston, Mass.: Little, Brown.

New York Times. 1987. "Social Security Taxes to Increase This Week." December 28, p. 13.

Pear, Robert. 1987. "Budget Plan Would Privatize National Institutes of Health." *New York Times,* December 16, p. 1.

Piven, Frances Fox, and Richard A. Cloward. 1982. *The New Class War: Reagan's Attack on the Welfare State and Its Consequences.* New York: Pantheon Books.

Policy Research Institute and Project HOPE. 1985. *Health Prospects 1983/2002.* Baltimore, Md.

Relman, Arnold S. 1980. "The New Medical-Industrial Complex." *New England Journal of Medicine* 303, no. 17:963–70.

———. 1985. "Selling to the For-Profits, Undermining the Mission." *Health Progress* 66, no. 7:81–85.

Reuben, Ellen B., and Robert D. Hamilton III. 1986. "Entry and Competition in the Home Health Care Industry." *Health Care Strategic Management* 4, no. 1:4–9.

Robinette, Tasker K. 1985. "Adapting to the Age of Competition: A Paradigm Shift for Voluntary Hospitals." *Hospital and Health Services Administration* 30, no. 3:8–19.

Salmon, J. Warren. 1982. "The Competitive Health Strategy: Fighting for Your Health." *Health and Medicine* 1, no. 2:21–30.

Starr, Paul. 1982. *The Social Transformation of American Medicine.* New York: Basic Books.

Thompson, Frank J. 1987. "New Federalism and Health Care Policy: States and the Old Questions." In L. D. Brown, ed., *Health Policy in Transition.* Durham, N.C.: Duke University Press, pp. 79–102.

U.S. BOC (Bureau of the Census). 1984. *Projections of the Population of the United States, by Age, Sex, and Race: 1983 to 2080.* Current Population Reports. Series P-25, no. 952.

U.S. GOA (General Accounting Office). 1986. *An Aging Society, Meeting the Needs of the Elderly While Responding to Rising Federal Costs.* Washington, D.C.: U.S. Government Printing Office.

U.S. HCFA (Health Care Financing Administration), Division of National Cost Estimates. 1987. "National Health Expenditures, 1986–2000." *Health Care Financing Review* 8:1–36.

U.S. HRSA (Health Resources and Services Administration). 1986. *Health Status of the Disadvantaged, Chart Book 1986.* Washington, D.C.: U.S. Government Printing Office.

U.S. NCHS (National Center for Health Statistics). 1985. *Health United States, 1985.* Washington, D.C.: U.S. Government Printing Office.

———. 1987. *Health Statistics on Older Persons, United States, 1986.* Vital and Health Statistics, Series 3, no. 25.

U.S. OMB (Office of Management and Budget). 1987. Budget of the United States Government, FY1988. Washington, D.C.: U.S. Government Printing Office.

U.S. House, Committee on the Budget. 1987. *President Reagan's Fiscal Year 1988 Budget.* Washington, D.C.: U.S. Government Printing Office.

U.S. House, Select Committee on Aging. 1987. *Long Term Care and Personal Impoverishment: Seven in Ten Elderly Living Alone Are at Risk.* Committee Print. Washington, D.C.: U.S. Government Printing Office.

U.S. Senate, Special Committee on Aging. 1985. *Americans At Risk: The Case of the Medically Uninsured.* Washington, D.C.: U.S. Government Printing Office.

———. 1987. *Developments in Aging: 1986.* Vol. 3. Washington, D.C.: U.S. Government Printing Office.

Veatch, Robert. 1983. "Ethical Dilemmas of For-Profit Enterprise in Health Care." In B. H. Gray, ed., *The New Health Care for Profit.* Washington, D.C.: National Academy Press, pp. 125–52.

Villers Foundation. 1987. *On the Other Side of Easy Street.* Washington, D.C.: Villers Foundation.

Waldo, Daniel R., and Helen C. Lazenby. 1984. "Demographic Characteristics and Health Care Use and Expenditures by the Aged in the United States: 1977–1984." *Health Care Financing Review* 6:1–29.

Waldo, Daniel; Katharine Levit; and Helen Lazenby. 1986. "National Health Expenditures, 1985." *Health Care Financing Review* 8:1–31.

Wall Street Journal. 1985. "Four Hospital Chains, Facing Lower Profits, Adopt New Strategies." October 10, p. 1.

Wallace, S. P.; B. Bowers; and N. P. Chico. 1984. "Ideology and Policies of New Federalism: The Case of Health Policy." Unpublished manuscript. San Francisco, Calif.: Department of Social and Behavioral Sciences, University of California.

Washington Post Weekly. 1987. "An Insurance Plan for Major Illnesses Is Now in Trouble." September 28, p. 34.

Wohl, S. 1984. *The Medical-Industrial Complex.* New York: Harmony.

Wood, Juanita B., and Carroll L. Estes. 1988. "The Medicalization of Community Services for the Elderly." *Health and Social Work,* pp. 35–42.

26

Privatization and Bidding in the Health-Care Sector

Randall R. Bovbjerg, Philip J. Held, and Mark V. Pauly

Public provision of health care, as under Medicare and Medicaid, traditionally "privatized" major production decisions. Providers of care, largely private physicians and hospitals (but also public hospitals), made significant decisions about public beneficiaries' access to care, the quality and quantity of individual services, and the prices to be paid. The result was high access and quality/quantity, but also high program spending, which has prompted a reassertion of public budgetary control. Newly activist program administration is using various mechanisms to promote economizing. Unable and unwilling to specify standards of public access or quality/quantity too overtly, administration instead seeks to squeeze prices—mainly through administrative price setting but also through competitive bidding and voucherlike arrangements. Under such new incentives, major choices that in many non-American systems would be public are here "reprivatized" to be resolved out of the limelight by beneficiaries, traditional providers, or new intermediaries like Competitive Medical Plans.

INTRODUCTION: TRADITIONAL ROLES OF PUBLIC AND PRIVATE SECTORS IN HEALTH CARE

The medical system in the United States is a peculiarly American creation, mixed and messy, with no single or even predominant ideological thrust.[1] The system delivers high-quality care to most (but not all) of the population, at high cost. One of its most mixed and messy aspects concerns the relative roles of the public and private sector.

This potpourri distinguishes the meaning of privatization in the American health-care context from its use in other sectors or other parts of the world. Elsewhere, privatization generally means either (1) selling a public asset or loss-making activity to a private buyer who will then market same, or (2) contracting out a public activity to a private contractor thought capable of

From *Journal of Policy Analysis and Management*, Vol. 6, No. 4 (Summer 1987): 648–66.

more efficient performance. That is, it means public economizing either through private financing and provision or through private production. In American health care, production of health services is already largely in the private sector, regardless of whether financing is public or private. As a result, the changes in the mix of public and private roles contemplated by many current economizing efforts do not fit within such neat definitions. This paper's main concern is the promotion of "competitive bidding" as a way of further refining the allocation of public functions to public and private actors.

Public and private roles intermingle both in financing for and in production of health care. Most providers are private, although public hospitals provide 23% of hospital admissions, and 40% of all hospital financing comes from taxes.[2] Publicly financed but privately produced *services* are the rule even for the elderly and the poor, the two population groups with the highest state and federal government involvement. Although such "public" *care* is privately produced (in the main), on the financing side the *insurance* (or administrative oversight) for that care is furnished by government bureaus directly, along with the tax finance that pays for the insurance.

We pause here for an aside on nomenclature. By financing we mean providing funds, almost wholly through third-party-payment insurance (or insurancelike government programs). Delivery, an infelicitous word for a personal service, means the actual rendering of medical care. These distinctions correspond to the traditional differentiation in public finance: public provision of a service, with eligible recipients and maximum quantity determined politically and with taxes as a source of finance, in contrast to public production of a service, with management and service delivery by public employees.

It is important to note, however, that beyond health-care financing and delivery lies another important function that does not fit so well within the traditional dichotomy of provision/production. This function is the production of insurance, to use the word in its broad sense of any third-party-payment program rather than in the narrow sense of a contract assuming some specified risk. Insurance today involves increasingly active administration or management of benefits and payment for personal medical care services. The production of insurance requires specifying and monitoring not only the prices paid but also the quality furnished by private-sector service producers.

Thus various bidding, voucher, and incentive schemes can either be viewed as a way of privatizing part of the insurance production or as a way of determining quality and price for already privatized services. Full control by the insurer over quality and price presumably occurs when the payer and the producer become one, as, for example, in the Veterans Administration system.

Recent trends suggest that this mixed market is likely to stay that way. The fraction of health-care spending financed or provided by the public sector has been remarkably stable over the past 10 to 15 years, with the public share fluctuating only marginally around the level of about 40%. The production side has experienced some movement, notably a modest fall in the market share of nonfederal public hospitals. Some privatization in the common sense of contracting out public-hospital functions has also occurred through management contracts and occasionally with transfer of ownership as well.

According to conventional wisdom, these firms raise prices somewhat to make the institutions profitable.[3] The decline in market share of the public hospitals has been almost entirely offset by an increase in the share of investor-owned firms. The share of not-for-profit firms has been almost constant.

NATURE OF THE PUBLIC ROLE

The Rationale for Public Intervention

The most persuasive normative rationale for public provision of health care is a consumption "externality"; that is, individuals feel altruistic concern about the health or level of medical-care consumption of their fellow citizens, mainly those with fewer resources than themselves. Seeing the public role as altruism resembles the conception of health care as a "merit good" or a "natural right" to which people are entitled. The difference is that merit goods and rights come with an expectation about the level of care, whereas, unlike rights, altruistic impulses can come in varying degrees of strength and are appropriately varied in quantity and quality when price or cost varies.[4]

This central rationale of altruism tells us only that direct, unsubsidized purchase by isolated individuals will not lead to socially appropriate levels of care for everyone. It calls instead for a subsidy of some type, but not necessarily for publicly owned (or nonprofit) firms actually engaged in production. One conventional reason for public production (or heavily regulated private production) involves the presence of natural monopoly caused by economies of scale. This phenomenon does not generally have much importance in health care, where economies of scale for hospitals and other providers exist only up to moderate sizes.[5]

For health care, a rationale for other than private profit-maximizing production must come instead from the difficulties that the altruistic subsidy payer (whom we will call the donor) typically experiences in *monitoring* the subsidized services delivered. Specifically, the donor may find it costly or impossible to specify or manage exactly what is being delivered and to whom those services are delivered; thus the recipients (eligibility) and the benefit package (especially quality and quantity) must be specified to make a subsidy operational, but it may not be easy for the donor to monitor them directly.

If quality, quantity, and eligibility are not monitored perfectly, the for-profit firm may be able to increase profits by reducing quality or eligibility, then converting the resulting cost savings into profits. (Its profit-maximizing behavior with regard to quantity depends largely upon whether the payment unit consists of each separate service or a whole bundle of services.) Here, both not-for-profit and government-owned providers may play a role. Such providers may be expected to have less incentive than a for-profit to convert quality to profits, more incentive to gather and disseminate information concerning deserving recipients, and more incentive to select deserving recipients from among those persons who present themselves for subsidized care. (Note that this does not mean that public-spirited people are indifferent to earning net revenues; the issue is the length to which they will go to do so, and under what circumstances). Furthermore, in the publicly owned firm, the combination of *inputs* can be easily monitored even if the outputs cannot, so that input use may serve as a proxy for output quality. All of these theoretical predictions about quality apply at any specified level of revenues from sales and philanthropy. Moreover, if entry is free, and if firms (for-profit, not-for-profit, or governmental) will enter as long as they can cover costs at some level of quality, the resulting competitive equilibrium will probably be the same regardless of firm ownership.[6]

In this sense, nonprofit firms can act as proxies for donors: The manager of such a firm acts as agent for a donor-dominated board of trustees, and the manager of a governmental hospital acts as agent for the politicians and taxpayers. In this capacity not-for-profit managers may be acting more efficiently in a social sense than would the manager of a for-profit firm receiving the same subsidy.

Applying the Basic Rationale to Medical Care: Theory and Practice

One uncontroversial assumption about medical care in general is that quality is very hard to monitor. The political process handles the quality issue somewhat differently from the eligibility/quantity issue. Eligibility for federal subsidy has been largely determined by categorical and observable characteristics of individuals—age, income, presence of dependent children, disability—although decisions about actual use of care were left to providers and the eligible patients themselves. A massive infusion of federal funds and a growing federal presence followed the eligibility expansions of Medicare and Medicaid, the latter involving states as well.

Taken together, these two programs virtually wiped out the private demand for subsidies to elderly people. More recently, however, federal cutbacks have shifted part of the burden to private employers, creating newer demands for more public aid. For a time, Medicaid also greatly attenuated the demand for subsidies to the nonelderly poor; again, more recently state Medicaid programs have also been cutting back.[7]

In contrast to eligibility, quality levels for public programs have been specified much less precisely. Traditional practice simply encouraged high quality (and quantity) by paying providers for their incurred costs or provider-set charges. Combined with competition for patients and physicians, the result was high quality but also high costs. One historic rationale for the structure of these programs as third-party-payment entitlement programs was to lessen beneficiaries' dependence on private charity or public providers and to "mainstream" them into the same mixed public-private system used by well-insured private patients.

Yet certain problems arose in these approaches to eligibility and quality. On the quality/costs side, the problem was high costs. On the eligibility side, the recession of the early 1980s and state cutbacks in Medicaid programs led to an increase in the number of persons with no insurance, public or private. As of the spring of 1984, between 35 and 40 million people under the age of 65 lacked health insurance—almost one person in six.[8] Some commentators hold that privatization is a solution to the problem of high costs, while others hold that one type of privatization is a cause of the second problem of coverage shortfalls.

PUBLIC PRODUCTION

Role of the Public Hospital

In 1984, state or local governments operated 1,645 short-term general hospitals that contributed about 18% of the general bed supply and 2%–3% of admissions. Historically, public hospitals grew out of almshouses for the poor, and most paying patients were treated in their own homes. More recently, the typical public hospital has been constituted and operated much like other hospitals, with the notable difference that part of their mission is to serve as a "provider of last resort" for those without financial resources. Perhaps unfairly, public hospitals are stigmatized as having lower quality than private ones; this is not at all clear from objective evidence. The typical public hospital, in fact, receives most of its funding from paying patients, including those eligible for Medicaid. As a rule, however, the net deficit of such hospitals has traditionally been funded by a public jurisdiction.

The early expansive conception of Medicaid programs held that it was better not to rely solely on public hospitals for charity care, but rather to "entitle" people to third-party coverage at whatever hospital they and their physician choose. The idea was to avoid two-tier or dual-track medicine by mainstreaming Medicaid eligibles. Under this approach, public hospitals were meant to compete on quality and other grounds for patients and doctors. They would either successfully make themselves attractive to insured patients or wither away. During the 1970s public hospitals' market share did indeed decline, but in the 1980s third-party payment for indigent health care may instead be withering away.

In this more recent context, the traditional role of the public hospital seems to be reemerging, generally under state law giving a county or city responsibility. For example, this occurred in California a few years ago when the state drastically cut the scope of its state-only portion of Medicaid. Thus, covering the "medically indigent," formerly a state obligation (with no federal role), was made a direct obligation of county governments. County governments were given block-grant funding, fixed amounts of support with which to fund care in a manner of their own choosing. The block grants were smaller than the amount expected to have been spent under the previous state Medi-Cal program. Most California counties have used this money to fund provision of direct production of care in county hospital systems. Others have attempted to contract with private hospitals for production of services for the medically indigent population.

Many other efforts are under way nationwide to find some way of handling the growing burden of care for the indigent who are not covered by Medicaid. So many different approaches are being tried, particularly at the county level, that it is impossible to attempt to catalogue them all here.

We can note, however, that providing care through a public facility (rather than entitling public beneficiaries to third-party payment at the facility of their choice) can be a relatively efficient way to pay for the level of indigent care that society now seems willing to contribute. Categorical public funding for the poor covers only a defined fraction of the low-income population. The remainder of the poor differ greatly in the need for a subsidy (a majority of the working poor have private health insurance). In fact, the majority of the uninsured are not poor.[8] Under these circumstances, it may be preferable to permit the rationing decisions to be made by the providing organization. Such decisions would involve both deciding who can receive below-cost care and how much care they will receive.

Public facilities are especially suited for rationing public care to deserving eligible patients, particularly if they are given their subsidy as a fixed budget rather than as a blank-check promise to fund whatever net deficit results from their activities. This approach makes two key assumptions: Public hospitals will in fact act as providers of last resort, giving care to all in medical need, and they will diligently collect payment from those able to pay, thus concentrating the limited available social contributions on those in true financial need.

PUBLIC PROVISION: THE PAST AND CURRENT PROBLEMS

How has public production of insurance (or of insurance administration) typically functioned, and why it has been thought to be deficient? It is safe to say that both Medicare and Medicaid have been seen as excessively costly, at least as traditionally administered. Hospitals, it has been felt, are excessively costly because the cost-based nature of payment did not discourage inefficiency or reward economy. Physician services have been regarded as excessively costly because the basic method of determining prices to be paid probably yielded some rents, even after some limited efforts to curb them. And quantity of all types of service was probably excessive, because payment was made as a generous fee-for-service basis without offsetting controls on utilization. The Health Care Financing Administration (or HCFA, the federal agency for Medicare and Medicaid) and the states, in short, did not produce efficient administration. It is small consolation to note that private insurers were not obviously more successful.

Although this traditional form of health-benefits administration can be viewed as complete public provision, there is another way of looking at it. HCFA and the state Medicaid plans basically left unspecified what level of quality was to be achieved, what quantity of services was to be delivered, and (within broad limits) what price was to be paid for those services. In a sense, the administrative function of determining the levels of these factors was left to the private-sector providers (and their patients). This "partial privatization" did not seem to work well, certainly not from a public-spending vantage point. Another way to look at what happened is that, having decided to rely on private production of medical services, government needed some form of privatization but was incapable of writing full specifications (or was unwilling to do so).

The result was contracting out without a contract. In effect, by putting only a weak limit on maximum prices, quality was permitted to float upwards (driven by competition)—even for investor-owned hospitals. But so did unit price and volume of services, and thus total expenditures as well.

ENTER BIDDING

Politicians and public administrators thus have recently faced a growing quandary: They want to reduce public medical spending, or at least its rate of growth, and they strongly suspect that prices are too high. But they do not know what price is right. Bidding offers one appealing way of dealing with overpricing per unit of service that comes from "rents" (unduly high profits) or differential inefficiency (across firms). The great virtue of bidding is that it allows the buyer to achieve a price close to the efficient cost of production even though the buyer starts with absolutely no information about production costs.

Bidding also can achieve sudden shifts in payment levels after each pricing round; most administrative processes dare to make only incremental adjustments. Using bidding as a way of paying for publicly provided services does, in effect, return the function of price administration to the public sector. In a way, it brings to life a previously dormant public function, that of actually determining and limiting prices; under prior practice, public administrators merely ratified privately set prices.

If a reasonably large number of bidders compete, the winning bid generally will represent a price near the lowest cost for producing the service in question. And when the "service in question" can be defined precisely in bid specifications, bidding would generally be regarded as an appropriate way of producing services *and* administration. It would permit services to be privatized, administration to be "publicized," and all to be right with the public/private world.

But the essence of the argument about privatization is that the quality of both care and administration is difficult to specify in advance or monitor after the fact. Not only do public officials find it technically difficult or impossible to specify quality for most medical services, but they also find it politically unattractive to specify explicitly anything less than the best available—even where some measures of quality are feasible.

What happens when one tries bidding with incomplete specification of quality (including access)? The theoretical prediction on this is straightforward: If quality is not monitored well but business goes to the lowest bidder, quality will be set as low as permitted by the quality-monitoring mechanism. Given that level of quality (whatever it is), the bid price will be close to minimum costs of production. Predictions are somewhat different if winning a bid depends on quality (even if measured imperfectly) as well as price. Nevertheless, it is quite likely that such a mechanism would yield quality levels below those that prevail if quality could be specified and monitored. Bidding will yield care of low-quality efficiently produced at some low price. In contrast, simply announcing some higher price will permit (but not require) higher quality.

The observation that quality is likely to fall under bidding does not settle the matter, of course. Several scenarios are possible. It may well be that, even under the old system, there were no substantial systematic rents and inefficiencies—just very high-level, expensive quality of low marginal value. But it is extremely difficult for a public bureau to specify any limited quality level, much less to propose to reduce existing quality; political rhetoric demands highest possible quality. The virtue of bidding from this perspective, then, is that it may be a more politically attractive way of moving to a lower point on the cost-quality tradeoff frontier. Indeed, for the public servant, bidding in this regard is virtually a no-lose proposition. If price and quality are cut, the governmental agency can blame the bidder and take the credit for defending "highest possible quality." A good bit of the argument for and against bidding models in health reflects, one suspects, not technical aspects of administration or monitoring, but differences in the preferred combinations of cost and quality.

Still another scenario tries to avoid some of the defects of conventional bidding models by departing a bit from the classical, winner-take-all bidding model. One approach is to permit several winners in a price-bidding arrangement, with no guaranteed quantity for each. (We will examine an example of this below.) Such a scheme does two things. With several winners, there are usually several sites. With a service like medical care, access is part of quality, and thus having multiple winners may improve access. Second, if clients can choose among the winners, the resulting quality competition will serve to put a limit—somewhere—on covert reductions in quality, at least as it is perceived by the client.

What does all of this conceptualization suggest about bidding in health care? It clearly says that where there are many sellers, where quality can be specified in advance, and where access is not a problem, bidding makes sense. Laboratory tests of portable, storable specimens might furnish an example: Many sellers exist in most geographic areas and for most tests, and further entry is easy. Tests can occur far from the doctor's office or other site where a tissue, fluid, or other specimen is taken, which allows economies of scale (and further eases entry).

The difficult cases are those in which the provider of financing and the consumer of services have problems monitoring quality appropriately. Compared to the ideal, bidding will not work well in this case. But where does this leave us? Does this mean that no alternatives to the old system exist? One could advocate that Medicare set up its own tertiary-care hospitals, or that it take over some set of such hospitals; but no one has seriously suggested either alternative.

What has been contemplated instead are ways to alter the process of payment and bidding to make it a more suitable (or less deficient) method of administering payment. Some of these changes amount to conversion of large parts of the insurance administration function to the private sector.

MEDICAID'S EXPERIENCE WITH BIDDING

Traditional Medicaid rules, like those for virtually all conventional insurance programs, required "free choice of provider" for beneficiaries. Bidding requires limiting the number of winners, often only to one, and hence clearly violates this principle. Because of this conflict, public medical programs until recently have experimented only marginally with bidding. Promoted by strong budgetary pressures, however, many state Medicaid programs since the mid-1970s have effectively limited providers' rates as well as free choice by beneficiaries through a number of actions resembling bidding.

Drugs and Appliances

Numerous Medicaid programs in the early 1980s began using bidding-like arrangements for selected medical care services. These programs usually involved "volume purchasing" of such items as eyeglasses, hearing aids, laboratory and x-ray services, durable medical equipment, and prescription drugs.[9] As of late 1982, nine states had 14 different programs of this sort in operation. In addition 17 more had proposed, or were considering, approximately 40 different volume-purchasing programs. Note that all these goods and services are relatively standardized items whose provision often occurs in conjunction with a separate purchase of a professional service. In such cases, the true consumer is a professional purchasing on behalf of a patient rather than patients themselves.

Even these programs faced political and legal difficulties because of their conflict with free choice of provider under Medicaid. But federal legislation in 1981 legitimized bidding for drug and equipment suppliers. Where consistent with federal legislation, HCFA has generally attempted to facilitate and encourage arrangements for volume purchasing. State officials generally claim substantial savings from such arrangements. Initial claims of success deserve to be double checked because the assessment methodology is unclear and because all those involved have strong motivation to report large savings.

Bidding arrangements for similar goods and services under Medicare have generally been avoided. HCFA has proposed a bidding demonstration for the purchase of laboratory services, but it has not yet been implemented.[10]

California and Arizona

Recent state programs in California and Arizona have gone much further, approximating more traditional forms of bidding for major personal medical services—the former for hospital inpatient care and the latter for larger aggregations of care, up to capitation for all covered medical services. These two Medicaid experiments, carried out under waivers of federal Medicaid rules, provide the best workshop to date for observing bidding principles in action for publicly funded medical care.

The California reform, enacted in 1982 and implemented immediately, drastically altered prior practice, with the explicit goal of achieving large savings. The reform changed the payment unit for inpatient hospital care (other services were excluded) from traditional cost reimbursement per service to an all-inclusive per-diem amount, regardless of diagnosis, intensity of care, or length of stay. Hospitals were then asked to submit advance bids to fix their rate prospectively. Although widely known as "bidding" and although the enabling legislation allowed either formal bidding or negotiations, the actual process is one-on-one contract negotiation, reportedly chosen to save time. Indeed, the person initially put in charge was called "special negotiator." Informally and nearly universally, the negotiator quickly became known as the "czar."

Within each Medi-Cal service region the czar and his staff sought bids. After reviewing past cost reports, they suggested acceptable levels to hospitals without promising that any particular level would win. It is said that, regardless of the first bid, the standard negotiating ploy was to respond, "knock $50 off and we will consider it." Prices once accepted were binding for up to two years, although they could be changed with 90 days notice from either side.

Savings were expected from two interrelated effects. First, inpatient days were to be shifted from high-cost providers to low-cost ones. Second, the price paid to each contracting hospital was expected to be lower than it would otherwise have been. Apparently, the latter effect has predominated. Relatively few hospitals wanting contracts were excluded or have since been dropped. Ultimately, the hospitals whose bids were accepted in the first year had accounted for 85% of previous Medi-Cal expenditures, so there was relatively little exclusion. One preliminary assessment of the first year notes that 6 of the 11 contracting hospitals surveyed had reduced rates because of contracting; only two had significant increases over prior payment levels.[11] State estimates indicate that per-diem payments fell 15% or 16% between the beginning of contracting and September 1983. Rates had previously been increasing at about 7% per year.

As yet, no full assessment has been made of the program's precise effects on the volume of days, style or quality of care, or ease of patient access. The estimated effects on total program spending are therefore somewhat tentative.

Arizona's new Medicaid program provides the most thoroughgoing example of the use of formal bidding for public medical services. The state had never had a Medicaid program because of political opposition to the loss of control over spending under federal requirements. Granted a waiver to design its own program to cover all Medicaid services except long-term care, the state implemented a massive effort to stimulate bids in every county. Bidders could cover all medical services or just some specified subsets of services (inpatient, outpatient, and so on). Bidders could put quantity limits on their submissions, and each winner was to be paid its own bid. Having multiple winners in each county was intended to promote competition in the interest of quality and to act as a guarantee against failure by any one winner.

The state had set explicit overall budgetary limits, which were exceeded by the bids received. A round of negotiation and "voluntary" bid reductions therefore became necessary. The fullest assessment of this initial implementation concludes that the necessity for post-bid adjustment in fact increased bids and raised the price paid by the state.[12] The speed with which the entire process had to be implemented—somewhat less than a year—posed numerous administrative difficulties. Both the state administration and the private administrator in charge of overseeing the bids (a position itself filled through competitive bidding) were subject to numerous political complaints and hints of scandal.

To date, no one has made a full evaluation of the costs and quality impacts of the Arizona experience. It seems to be a political success, but the prepaid plans have not yet been expanded to include the intended private participants. The program did succeed in winning bids in every county, and numerous prepaid plans now exist, whereas previously there had been few or none in most counties.

Despite their problems, the California and Arizona experiences indicate that forms of bidding can work in health care in the sense of being feasible, at least for a low-income, dependent population. That is, meaningful specifications can be written (even for the complex set of full, capitated services); providers can be motivated to submit attractive bids, and services can be delivered roughly as promised. Both state's systems have relied heavily on negotiation rather than pure bidding, and both were implemented when the political necessity of reduced prices was apparent. For the near future, the conditions of the states' budgets, rather than the theoretically obtainable minimum costs for a specified bundle of services, will probably determine the level of state payouts. Whether the programs will subsequently move back towards the bidding ideal or rather move in the direction of further negotiating and political price setting remains to be seen. Also unclear is the programs' ability to monitor and enforce quality standards and to maintain long-term incentives for prudent purchasing by the states.

ALTERNATIVES TO BIDDING, LEFT AND RIGHT

Rate Setting and Administrative Pricing

Given that classical, winner-take-all bidding offers no panacea as a method of privatizing government-financed medical care, one alternative in an economizing age is to turn "left," strengthening government authority and extending its control over private production decisions. Two important options merit brief mention here, hospital rate setting and administrative pricing.

Public regulation of hospital prices and budgets has long been a potential public strategy. At the federal level, it probably reached its zenith with President Carter's ill-fated hospital cost-containment bill, which was twice defeated in Congress. Hospital rate setting survives as a major state strategy, particularly for Medicaid spending, but also for other payers. In the early 1980s, there was a brief vogue for "all-payer" systems that also covered Medicare payments (with federal permission); four states had such systems at one point, but two have subsequently withdrawn. Rate setting seems to work in the sense that it reduces the rate of increase in hospital spending; effects on quality are less well established.

Government can also set prices administratively, simply announcing a rate for each more or less specified service that its program(s) will pay. Providers must then "take it or leave it," and beneficiaries are limited to those "taking it." Until recently, the major example of this approach in the Medicare program was the fixed payment for outpatient maintenance kidney dialysis needed by End-Stage Renal Disease patients. The major new initiative of this type is Medicare's Prospective Payment System by Diagnosis Related Groups (DRGs). To oversimplify: Medicare during 1983 essentially set initial prices for some 470 DRG payment units, each a fixed prepaid amount for a hospital stay. In practice, almost every hospital virtually had to accept its new rates, which were substantially below the payments that would have resulted under the old cost-reimbursement scheme. The annual rate of change and any shifts in the relative DRG prices have become major political issues. As for state rate setting, the method's fiscal impact (favorable) is far clearer than its quality/access impact.

Vouchers and Incentives

A different method of dealing with both quality and cost moves "right," giving patients direct access to funds and the ability to choose where to spend them. This approach differs markedly from administrative price setting and from conventional bidding (with or without some patient choice among winners), both of which emphasize payer-provider interactions. The "voucher" idea is the best example of a patient-oriented scheme, but other variations exist on the same theme (one of which we will discuss in detail).

The best known example of a medical-care voucher is the all-inclusive annual voucher. Such an arrangement gives patients an amount of purchasing power that is pegged to the costs of the conventional public insurance program. It permits them to spend the funds on any insurance arrangement that provides at least as much coverage. Sometimes the patient is permitted to supplement the voucher, and occasionally (though rarely) he is allowed to receive as cash any shortfall between the payment required by the firm receiving the voucher and the value of the voucher itself. Such arrangements give the "consumer" a role similar to that in a conventional, competitive market, even though the public resources are earmarked for health care. Redefining the unit of payment in this arrangement away from the specific service at a specific provider and toward the patient may well have a greater impact than the voucher per se. By moving the locus of incentives, the shift should change behavior.

Vouchers will work best if all the necessary ingredients for a competitive market, *except* purchasing power, are present. In particular, there should be competition among sellers, some number of sellers accustomed to capitation-voucher style of payment, and good information about the quality and prices among at least some of the buyers. Finally, public policy must be willing to respect the preferences of beneficiaries for things other than the total amount of expenditure. If preferences vary markedly among beneficiaries, vouchers to allow choice make more sense than a single plan for all.

Although these conditions obviously do not hold for medical care, there are nevertheless some substantial advantages to any voucher approach, whether it is for capitation or for individual services. One advantage is that vouchers permit beneficiaries to consider both costs and quality in allocating the resources allotted to them. They have an opportunity to make themselves as well off as they can. As a second major advantage, the ability of beneficiaries to switch sellers puts pressure on sellers to keep price down and quality up. Rents will be squeezed out, at whatever level of quality is achieved. As Frank Sloan notes, vouchers "engage the consumer in cost containment."[13]

Particularly if certain firms that provide care can be certified as providing quality that does not fall below some socially acceptable level, giving consumers vouchers has attractive properties. Most proponents of vouchers assume that quality assurance will require the organization receiving the voucher to be a Health Maintenance Organization (HMO) or similarly organized "competitive plan" that actually delivers care; private conventional insurance arrangements are not yet an option under Medicare. The elderly can take 95% of what Medicare would have spent to the local HMO and be regarded as well served, but they are not (yet) allowed to take it to conventional "Medigap" insurance plans such as those pitched by Art Linkletter or Lorne Greene. This means that, despite the rapid growth rate of HMOs, their small market share in many markets will limit the potential for using vouchers.

One's attitude toward vouchers then depends very much on the importance one attaches to the lower cost and greater freedom associated with vouchers as compared to the possibility that some less-adept consumers will be worse off. Making the mesh in the safety net finer to prevent such a fall is possible, but it increases both costs and the number of other beneficiaries who will become entangled in the webbing. Vouchers also *change* the type of private firm that determines the quantity of care the patient will receive. And with the change in type of firm comes a change in its incentives.

After a series of fairly positive demonstration results from HMO-type voucher arrangements, Medicare recently permitted all Medicare beneficiaries to elect membership in an HMO or Competitive Medical Plan (CMP). (HMOs are organizations that both finance and arrange for delivery of medical care for a prepaid capitation amount. Early HMOs were mainly prepaid group practices; those meeting the rather restrictive standards of the federal HMO Act have been able to receive start-up grants and certain regulatory advantages, including ability to participate in Medicare. CMP is a broader term, encompassing many alternative delivery arrangements that accept prepayment and imposing far fewer standards for qualification.) This new CMP option carries the portability of the classic voucher, but it does not permit the beneficiary to gain financially from selecting a low-cost seller. Quasi-financial incentives exist, however, because plans may choose to cut patients' coinsurance obligations under Medicare or add otherwise uncovered benefits.

One argument in favor of vouchers that allow insurance choices other than HMOs and CMPs is that many employers now routinely make such choices available to their employees, and Medicare would just be following suit for retired employees. As a case in point, the federal government offers a startlingly large variety of plans to its employees, although it does, of course, exercise some quality control (and engage in some cross subsidization). It seems somewhat disingenuous for federal policymakers to argue that federal workers are capable of making such choices, but citizens on Medicare or Medicaid are not.

Patient Choice With Incentives

In 1983, the federal government proposed a creative voucher-like plan for dialysis services for patients with End Stage Renal Disease (ESRD). Patients were to get rebates for choosing less expensive kidney dialysis units for their care. This proposal led to the so-called "competitive bidding" demonstration, which was tried in Denver, Colorado and Riverside, California for a brief period in 1985. The basic idea was that HCFA (the Health Care Financing Administration) would ask kidney dialysis units to "bid"—that is, to say at what price they would provide dialysis. If they could provide it at a price below the prevailing Medicare rate, then their patients would receive most of the difference in cash.[14]

Although this idea was called "competitive bidding," its key element was a renewed emphasis on patient choice: *Patients* would make a choice and *patients* would benefit or suffer from their choices. They would not be penalized for choosing a nonbidding dialysis unit, but they would be rewarded for choosing any less expensive ones that emerged through the bidding. Their physicians, usually nephrologists, presumably would help inform this choice. Physician payment rules were not to be changed in any way (i.e., physician payment was separate and unaffected by the payment for dialysis services), but a patient exodus from a unit would naturally hurt physicians practicing there.

As an example, suppose the going Medicare rate was $130 per dialysis in a given area. One or more providers might think that they could provide dialysis at a price of $120 because they were efficient or could run a large-scale unit once they attracted more patients. If so, the model allowed them to offer their patients 70% of the $10 difference. By offering this reward to patients, the low-priced units could attract more new patients than they could without the new inducement and could thereby operate for lower cost per unit of care. Without a formal government-approved rebate, units were not free to offer direct financial incentives; lowering their price merely lowered their receipts from the government (and for a few uninsured patients, the coinsurance obligation).

Thus, bidding was necessary to create price differences among which patients could choose, but the central element of the proposed demonstration was indeed patient choice under a voucher-like arrangement. Only the reward of attracting more patients gave providers an incentive to bid. The demonstration therefore might better have been called the "patient-choice model," but the term bidding was politically important at the time. The proposal had a number of attractive features, notably that patients were given new incentives but "held harmless." Competition among units helped to protect quality, and, by itself calling for bids, the government was helping patients get lower prices than any individual patient with a voucher could achieve. Conversely, the model did not offer strong incentives for dialysis units to bid.

Introducing these concepts to the ESRD program, however, proved radical. The HCFA proposal was met with a firestorm of resistance, particularly from Denver nephrologists. Despite this resistance and after considerable administrative delays and changes, HCFA pressed ahead with its demonstration of a patient-choice model. (The largest change was to make ineligible all lower-income recipients, those receiving Supplemental Security Income (SSI) assistance.) To the surprise of the ESRD community and especially Denver nephrologists, one dialysis unit did make a bid—and for a strikingly low amount, creating an $8 rebate per treatment for eligible patients. (Patients normally receive three treatments per week.) No new patients seemed to come to the bidding Denver unit as a result of the rebate. As was the bidder's right, the bid was withdrawn after six months.

The biggest but not the only reason for lack of patient movement in Denver seems to have been active resistance by the nephrology community. The bidding unit lacked even the wholehearted support of its own staff nephrologists. Other factors included HCFA's making many patients ineligible to receive a rebate and the failure of both HCFA and the bidding unit adequately to explain patients' options to them. (No bid was made in Riverside, mainly because units there were so far apart that little movement was feasible regardless of incentives offered.)

Although the model was promising and its implementation did not really provide a fair test, HCFA has evidently decided not to continue this or other bidding demonstrations in ESRD. They preferred instead to test capitation payment directly to providers, without patient vouchers.

BIDDING VERSUS OTHER ECONOMIZING "PRIVATIZATIONS"

Medical care differs from other goods and services in many dimensions, so it should come as no surprise that it also differs with regard to privatization and bidding. In our view, there are two important differences: one empirical and one normative. The empirical difference is that, although public finance raises and allocates 40% of funds for medical services, the private sector produces the lion's share of those services. The main normative difference, at least for many of the services where privatization is an issue, is that the recipients of the publicly financed services are generally different from those who pay the taxes to support them. As a consequence, virtually any issue of productive efficiency becomes interwined with questions of redistribution on a state or national level—how much will or should be distributed from (largely) nonpoor, nonaged taxpayers to the poor and elderly who benefit from the major public programs?

The first difference means that we are not considering turning over to the private sector a service that historically has been produced by government. It is already largely private. However, there has historically been a role, recently somewhat in eclipse but now reemerging, for publicly owned hospitals or clinics in producing care for the poor who are not or cannot be designated as categorically eligible for other programs. Because taxpayers are not willing to pay enough for Medicaid to cover all of the needy, an alternative is to use the public hospital both as a way to deliver care to needy but categorically ineligible people, and as a way of determining which people are needy for how much care. If the hospital is given a fixed budget, with political and market accountability, it should produce such care in a reasonably efficient way and to ration it in a way that is roughly consistent with taxpayer desires.

In effect, the public hospital produces a unique service not so much in the medical care itself, but in determining eligibility, amounts of care, and quality of care for public clients. The location of production of this crucial *administrative* function—whether in a government bureau or in a private firm—is at the heart of the normative question of bidding, vouchers, and the like for Medicare and Medicaid beneficiaries.

Specifically, the major normative question faced by the programs for tax-supported provision of medical care is whether the administration of the "insurance policy" that pays (private) hospitals and doctors will itself remain in the public sector, operated by the Health Care Financing Administration and state Medicaid "insurance firms." Proposals for bidding and vouchers both amount to transferring part of the administrative function to private firms, sometimes incorporated with the production of medical care (as in an HMO) and sometimes still separated. So, in a different way, do rate setting and administrative pricing. Where does this leave our topic of privatization in health care? The increasingly important "middle" function at the boundary between provision and production—administration or management of insured spending—is being split between the public and private sectors in a new way.

Medicare and Medicaid program management has now moved to economize by rejecting the traditional "privatization" of complaisant cost paying and passive acceptance of provider and patient decisions on the quantity and quality of services. Instead the management encourages "*de*privatizing" one aspect of administration—setting prices or limiting spending. Reasserting control over quantity and quality is equally important, but this newly discovered function has typically been "*re*privatized" with a vengeance, always under new rules and often literally under new management. Administrative authority is often being delegated to a different set of private firms, including a (limited) set of winning bidders, HMOs, Preferred Provider Organizations (PPOs), or case managers. Public managers typically resist specifying quantity or quality, partly for want of technical capacity, partly out of political reluctance to specify reductions. The basic pattern is "privatize the pain, publicize the gain."

What role do bidding and similar arrangements play in this economizing scenario? The three central elements in administration of insurance are price, quantity, and quality. Medical bidding deals directly with the first. In today's climate, government has two feasible options for controlling medical prices for public beneficiaries, namely administrative price setting and bidding or bidding-like processes. Allowing providers to set public prices or simply accepting prices charged to private parties seems unacceptable.

Administered prices can be set more or less arbitrarily (depending on legal and political constraints), and the market response to them is unpredictable. This strategy is thus bipartite (set the price and observe the outcome) and iterative (do it again). Generally, this approach seems most suited for making small, incremental changes, at least so long as "free choice of provider" requirements govern program design. Larger cuts would be possible if one acceptable result was much more limited access, in the sense of fewer participating hospitals. The approach also appears to be best suited for a large purchaser.

Bidding, in contrast, seems best suited for achieving large or sudden changes as opposed to incremental ones, where there is good reason to suspect rents or inefficient production *and* where a significantly reduced number of providers or other dimensions of quality or amenity is politically acceptable. Without the credible threat of exclusion from the program, bids will be unlikely to go too much lower than current prices (or those achievable through across-the-board administered pricing).

Government deals with quantity primarily through its choice of the payment unit for which the prospective price is bid or set. The traditional fee-for-service method encourages productivity (and overproduction if the price is too high). Capitation, one of the newest darlings of public budgeteers, promotes parsimony (regardless of price) and potential underproduction. Final decisions on usage continue to be left to (now prepaid) providers and to patients. Direct public controls on usage are relatively rare compared with private-sector insurance, although Medicaid programs have more such provisions than Medicare. Medicare's Professional Review Organizations (PROs) may prove an exception, even though they were created to deal with prepaid underservice rather than with "improper" utilization.

The final major specification of insurance administration is quality (in our broad sense of the word, including convenience and amenities as well as medical competence and demonstrated effect on health). Even more than for quantity, determinators of quality are being "reprivatized." Government cannot or will not directly specify what it wants for its various classes of beneficiary here. Indeed, quality is almost a residual—what emerges after other specifications have played themselves out in the medical marketplace. Government indirectly sets quality through the price level it chooses and the extent of competition it allows.

Given a specific price and extent of competition, the major administrative design issues are who shall make such determinations in government's stead and how. The three candidates are beneficiary/patients, conventional providers, and new firms (including HMOs, "gatekeeper" primary-care physicians who manage care, and capitated private insurers). Capitation vouchers or patient financial incentives give patients the primary role. Conventional providers will set quality levels where, for instance, Medicare prepays hospital stays and hospitals decide how to produce the necessary services. Patient choice obviously still matters where multiple capitated providers exist, although less "shopping" may occur with fewer patient financial incentives. If bidding or some other method has restricted patient choice among competitors, providers obviously will be freer to reduce quality.

Finally, new firms may make the relevant choices: The prepaid, contracted with, or bidding provider may not be a conventional physician practice or a hospital; instead, it may be some new organizational entity that contracts with the ultimate providers of care. Such entities include the now familiar HMO, HMO-like Competitive Medical Plans, more conventional third-party insurers, primary-physician gatekeepers, and third-party administrators of otherwise insured plans. For each of these, government specifies benefits in only a general way, much as in traditional public insurance practice. But the major new difference is that the payment to cover those benefits is fixed in whole or in part, thus causing the private firm to assume risk and to make tradeoffs between quality and cost (and possibly profit as well).

CONCLUSION

No dominant solution exists in the public sector's search for medical economy through reshuffling of functions. No strong empirical evidence suggests that the public sector is either more or less efficient than the private sector in the paper-shuffling part of the administrative function.[15] The public sector seems determined to reclaim price setting. Current "privatization" efforts crucially affect the set of agents who determine what is to be paid for medical care, what quality is to be furnished to public clients, and what quantity they are to receive. In our view, the major impact of such transfers is likely to be on quality, broadly defined. But in order to make any judgment about the desirability of a public-to-private transfer, the hardest thing is to specify what quality level society really wants for the elderly and the poor. In many ways, bidding or vouchers can be a politically acceptable way for taxpayers to cut the quality they provide to these populations, reduce the taxes they pay, and do both not just with a clean conscience, but also with a healthy sense of outrage against venal hospitals and doctors. (Drastic cuts in hospital payment rates under Medicare's DRGs are not entirely dissimilar.)

But to offer any critical analysis, the analyst needs to know what is wanted. The political advantages of passing the buck that often lie at the heart of these changes make that a difficult task, and consequently it is not possible to come to a definitive judgment.

Many choices of methods are really subservient to a hidden agenda rather than a clear exposition of public interest or role. For example, one may favor hospital rate setting in order to hide the costs of a covert program of assistance to uninsured hospital patients. Alternatively, one may favor competitive bidding of the brutal, limiting sort if one wants to cut quality and access to care but does not want to say so directly.

Setting social goals overtly probably would help us match tools to their task. But deciding what one truly wants is always difficult, especially in medical care where quality is so hard to specify or measure and where political judgments vary so greatly from area to area and from one beneficiary group to another. Moreover, it is a virtual political taboo to begin overt discussion of less than highest feasible quality. Having chosen to finesse unpleasant decisions about quality and access by focusing solely on price, we need to be prepared to take our medicine.

Research on which this paper draws was funded by a grant from the Health Care Financing Administration, which is gratefully acknowledged. The opinions are solely the authors'.

RANDALL R. BOVBJERG and PHILIP J. HELD are Senior Research Associates, the Health Policy Center of The Urban Institute, Washington, D.C.

MARK V. PAULY is Robert D. Eiler Professor of Health Care Management and Economics, Wharton School and Executive Director, The Leonard Davis Institute of Health Economics, University of Pennsylvania.

NOTES

1. U. E. Reinhardt, "Uncompensated Hospital Care," in Frank A. Sloan, James F. Blumstein, and James M. Perrin, Eds., *Uncompensated Hospital Care: Rights and Responsibilities* (Baltimore: The Johns Hopkins University Press, 1986), pp. 1–15.

2. American Hospital Association, *Hospital Statistics:* (Chicago: AHA, 1985), Table 2A, p. 8.

3. Government Accounting Office. "Public Hospitals: Sales Lead to Better Facilities but Increase Patient Cost" Monograph No. GAO/HRD 86-60, (Washington, D.C.: General Accounting Office, 1986); B. H. Gray, Ed., *The New Health Care for Profit: Doctors and Hospitals in a Competitive Environment* (Washington, D.C.: National Academy Press, 1983).

4. M. V. Pauly, "Efficiency in the Provision of Consumption Subsidies," *Kyklos*, 63(1) (1970): 33–57; M. V. Pauly, *Medical Care at Public Expense* (New York: Praeger, 1970).

5. T. N. Grannemann, R. S. Brown, and M. V. Pauly, "Estimating Hospital Costs," *Journal of Health Economics*, 5(2) (1986): 107–127; P. J. Held and U. E. Reinhardt, *Analysis of Economic Performance in Medical Group Practices* (Princeton: Mathematica, 1979).

6. Newhouse, J. P. "Toward a Theory of Nonprofit Institutions: An Economic Model of a Hospital," *American Economic Review* (March 1970): 64–74.

7. Rosenblatt, R. "Dual Track Health Care—The Decline of the Medicaid Cure," *University of Cincinnati Law Review*, 44 (1975): 643ff; J. Holahan and J. Cohen, *Medicaid: The Trade-off between Cost Containment and Access to Care* (Washington, D.C.: The Urban Institute Press, 1986).

8. M. B. Sulvetta and K. Swartz, *The Uninsured and Uncompensated Care* (Washington, D.C.: National Health Policy Forum, George Washington University, June 1986).

9. C. Hanson and L. Bartlett, *Volume Purchasing of Goods and Services in State Medicaid Programs* (Washington, D.C.: State Medicaid Information Center, October 1983).

10. S. H. Bell and L. L. Orr, *Durable Medical Equipment Competitive Bidding Demonstration* (draft) (Washington, D.C.: Abt Associates, 1986); Z. Dyckman, *A Descrip-*

tion of Competitive Bidding Services for Clinical Lab Services (draft) (Washington, D.C.: Center for Health Policy Studies, November 1983).

11. L. Johns, R. A. Durgan, and M. Anderson, *Selective Contracting for Health Service in California: Final Report* (Washington, D.C.: Lewin & Associates, Report to National Governors Association, March 5, 1985).

12. J. B. Christianson, D. G. Hillman, and K. R. Smith, "The Arizona Experiment: Competitive Bidding for Indigent Medical Care," *Health Affairs* (Fall, 1986): 88–103.

13. F. A. Sloan, "Issuing Medical Vouchers," in Robert J. Blendon and Thomas W. Moloney, Eds., *New Approaches to the Medicaid Crisis* (New York: F&S Press, 1982), pp. 159–175.

14. Health Care Financing Administration. "Draft Protocol for ESRD Competitive Bidding Demonstration," *Contemporary Dialysis & Nephrology*, 5 (Feb. 1984): 31–36, 43, 46; R. R. Bovbjerg, P. J. Held, and L. Diamond, "Provider-Patient Relations and Treatment Choice in the Era of Fiscal Incentives: The Case of the End-stage Renal Disease Program," *Milbank Memorial Fund Quarterly* 65(2): forthcoming (1987).

15. M. V. Pauly, *The Role the Private Sector in National Health Insurance* (Washington, D.C.: Health Insurance Institute, 1978).

27

The Regulation of Nursing Homes: A Comparative Perspective

Patricia Day and Rudolf Klein

T
WO PHENOMENA ARE COMMON TO NEARLY ALL
developed market economies. The first is the growth of long-
stay institutional care for the elderly, in line with demographic
trends. The second is the use of State regulation of private interests
to protect the frail, incapacitated, or dying elderly in these institutions.
The question of how best to safeguard the interests of one of the most
vulnerable sections of the population is as universal as the underlying
demographic trends which have helped to prompt it. In this exploratory
article, we examine some of the issues involved in the regulation of
standards of quality of care—an approximate measure—from a comparative perspective. We do so by looking at the experience of the
United States and Britain. Despite the differences in the context and
scale of the nursing home industries in the two countries, they share
a common concern about the problems of regulation. In the United
States, there has been a long and continuing history of scandal about
the treatment of patients and concern about fraudulent use of the
public purse; the reports of the Institute of Medicine (1986) Committee
on Nursing Home Regulation and of the Senate Special Committee
on Aging (U.S. Congress 1986) are only the most recent in a long
line of documents exposing the inadequacies of the system of regulation.
In Britain too, the growth of the nursing home industry in recent
years has led to increasing debate about the adequacy of the regulatory

From *The Milbank Quarterly,* Vol. 65, No. 3 (1987): 303–47.

system for protecting the elderly although, until recently, there has been no concern about costs (Day and Klein 1987a).

The aim of this article is to explore whether there are any common themes that can be distilled from an analysis of how the two regulatory systems work in practice. The nursing home industries in the United States and in Britain contrast sharply in their scale and method of finance; individual nursing homes differ markedly in their size and management structure—even the definitions of what is meant by nursing home care are not the same in the two countries; finally, the legal framework and technologies and scope of regulation in the two countries are very different. Yet, as the evidence examined in this article shows, there are striking similarities in the problems encountered and in the styles of enforcement adopted in response. There is, in practice, a remarkable convergence in the regulatory *process* despite all the dissimilarities between the two systems and the contrast beween the formal regulatory *models* used. From this it follows, to anticipate our conclusions, that the debate in both the United States and Britain about how best to improve their regulatory systems could usefully examine what is common to them both: the special characteristics of nursing homes and the logic of the regulatory process itself. If there are regulatory failures (as there are, in both countries) the reasons, we argue, are to be found less in the nature of the systems of formal control than in an inadequate appreciation of the social environment of nursing home care. In turn, this implies that future policy should move toward a model of regulation which can encompass both formal and informal, legal and social control.

Risks and Benefits of Comparison

To compare the regulatory strategies of countries which differ so fundamentally in their health care systems as the United States and Britain is to risk the ire of specialists on either. Inevitably, a somewhat oversimplified picture wll emerge. Why then incur the risk? The reason for doing so stems from the logic of comparative studies (Ashford 1978; Marmor 1983). Such an approach helps us to avoid the danger of ethnocentric overexplanation or policy area overdetermination. That is, it allows us to guard against the temptation to explain everything in terms of the characteristics of a particular national system or of a particular service within that system.

Our analysis is therefore shaped by a series of questions. Are there some issues common to all regulatory systems, across countries and across industries? Are such issues furthermore common to all industries within any given country, such as Britain or the United States, thus reflecting characteristics of the political and economic environment rather than those of a specific industry? Or are the issues of regulation in the case of nursing homes different from those which arise in the case of other industries within the same political system? And, if so, is there something special and unique about the nature of nursing homes and the care of the elderly, which makes regulatory issues in this policy area international, cutting across nations and differences in the political and economic environment? Only by asking such questions can we disentangle which problems of regulation are general, which are country-specific, which stem from the particular nature of nursing home care, and which derive from the context (political, organizational, and financial) in which the nursing home industry operates.

This article, moreover, adopts a comparative approach in a double sense. It compares both between and within countries. Its origins lie in a study by the authors of the regulatory process in Britain where only recently has there been the kind of rapid expansion in nursing homes that characterized the United States in the post-Medicaid era. It was this that led them to the United States to see what lessons could be learned from the American experience by comparing the two systems of regulation. There is a considerable body of literature that suggests there is a distinctly American model of regulation and that this is legalistic and adversarial, whereas the British and European model is informal and consensual (Kelman 1984; Majone 1982; Moran 1986; Vogel 1983; Wilson 1984). None of these studies deal with the nursing home industry. If their findings also held for the nursing home industry, it would seem reasonable to conclude that regulatory models reflect general national characteristics rather than those specific to the industry being regulated. Conversely, if their findings did not hold for the nursing home industry, it would seem reasonable to concentrate on the special characteristics of that industry when discussing regulatory issues.

To compare, however, the American and British models of regulation—i.e., the formal characteristics of the two systems as set out in legislation and official regulations—does not necessarily tell us how they work in practice. Regulatory style—i.e., the way in which regulation is actually carried out by inspectors and surveyors—may be equally important. In the case of our British study, our concern was precisely to examine how national policy was implemented at the local level (Day and Klein 1985). This seemed an even more appropriate concern in the United States, given the diversity of social, political, and economic conditions and the evidence that regulatory practices vary from state to state (Institute of Medicine 1986). Accordingly, we carried out brief studies in two states, Virginia and New York, chosen because they represent different civic traditions or political cultures. While Virginia's political style, it has been argued, is distinctive "in its sense of honor and gentility" (Patterson 1968, 202), these are hardly the words that would be used to describe New York's. In this, our assumption was that if these two states had more in common with each other than either had in common with Britain, then indeed it would be possible to talk about an American model in practice as well as in design. Furthermore, it would follow that the problems of American regulation could correctly be ascribed to the characteristics of the United States regulatory system, and the way in which the nursing home industry is financed and organized. In contrast, if it emerged that there were problems or issues cutting across both countries and states, it would be reasonable to seek to ascribe these, in part at least, to the characteristics of nursing homes and their inhabitants.

In all this, our article represents only a first, rough cut at the subject, and this for a variety of reasons. First, we deal with only one dimension of regulation: i.e., the regulation of standards or quality of care. We do not deal with the regulation of either quantity or prices. This is because the regulation of standards is the only dimension common to both the United States and Britain. For the biggest difference between the regulatory systems of the two countries is, as we shall see, precisely that Britain does not try to limit entry into the nursing home market through certificate of need or similar procedures or to control charges. Second, our article represents a tourist's view of the American scene; it seeks to convey the shock of surprise which a new landscape produces on the outsider, and to pick out those features which perhaps have lost their ability to surprise the inhabitants, but does not attempt to provide a complete or detailed map. Lastly, we do not attempt to assess the two systems in terms of their outcomes, i.e., which one is more successful in maintaining quality and preventing abuse. Not only is quality itself an elusive and difficult notion, which is precisely why the regulation of standards is problematic. But it is also the product of a complex, ill-understood process in which social, organizational, and economic dynamics may be just as important as the regulatory system, and, at present, we lack the understanding needed to separate out the contributions of these factors.

In line with the logic of our inquiry, we start by reviewing briefly some of the wider literature dealing with regulation. This is not only helpful in identifying what is special about nursing homes as such but also in alerting us to issues of regulation that cut across countries and industries. From that we move on to sketching out the very different role and scale of the nursing home industry in the United States and Britain, before examining their regulatory models and processes in detail.

Theory and Practice of Regulation

What can be learned from the general literature of regulation? It is a literature that is as wide-ranging as regulation itself in modern societies. It deals with the regulation of drugs and processed foods, with clean air and the pollution of water. But it is a literature primarily concerned with quality in its varying aspects, from the quality of the air we breathe to the quality of the working environment. From it can be filleted out three themes that help to organize the discussion of regulation, whether of nursing homes or any other industry. They are: general models of regulation, problems of implementation, and differences in national styles. In what follows, this section briefly picks out the main points generated by the literature, in order to provide benchmarks for the subsequent discussion of what (if anything) is special about the regulation of nursing homes.

To start with, there is general agreement (Hawkins and Thomas 1984), that there are two "contrasting systems, styles or strategies" of regulation. On the one hand, there is the *compliance model*. Here the emphasis is on preventing problems, on encouraging the investment of time and money to improve the situation; the inspector sees his or her role as being to cajole, negotiate, and bargain. Legal prosecution is seen as a last resort. The social relation between the regulator and the regulated is valued as a means of assisting in the discovery of future problems. On the other hand, there is the *deterrence model*. Here the emphasis is on punishing wrongdoing. The style is accusatory and adversarial. Recourse to formal legal proceedings is almost automatic. Effective punishment of rule breaking, it is assumed, will lead to improved behavior in future. In practice, most regulatory systems tend to be a blend of the two strategies; the distinction is helpful, however, in identifying the bias of any particular system.

Complicating the picture is the fact that the rules being enforced may be ambiguous or imprecise. Assumptions about what is desirable are conflated with assumptions about what is feasible. The resulting aggregation of scientific, technical, economic, and political criteria is not only ad hoc but also logically inscrutable (Majone 1982). From this it follows that the notion of an offense is problematic: the "facts" do not speak for themselves, but are interpretative judgments made by the regulator (Hawkins 1984). In turn, the judgments may depend on the way in which the regulators see the behavior of the regulated (Kagan and Scholz 1984). It is the context that gives meaning to any breach of the rules. If the organization or firm being regulated is seen as an amoral calculator, prepared to risk breaking the rules in order to maximize profits, then an aggressive deterrent strategy is likely to be pursued. Any breach of the rules will be interpreted not as an accidental slip-up, but as a deliberate attempt to get round the system. Conversely, if the firm is seen to be organizationally incompetent, then the regulator is likely to see himself or herself as a consultant. Any breach of the rules may well be attributed to organizational failure, rather than as the product of deliberate intent. Lastly, if the firm is seen as a political citizen, responding to what is perceived as the reasonableness of specific rules, or the lack of it, then the regulator is likely to try persuasion and bargaining.

All this emphasizes the role of discretion in regulation. Inspectors and surveyors are examples of "street level" bureaucrats (Lipsky 1980) whose personal values or style may not necessarily be the same as those of their employing agency. If inspectors and surveyors often see themselves as wheeler-dealers, whose skill lies in getting cooperation by means of bluff and persuasion and whose ability to gain compliance may depend on their skill in dispensing technical advice (Bardach and Kagan 1982), this may be at odds with the managerial philosophy of a regulatory agency that sees its role as enforcing the letter of the law.

The tension between compliance and deterrence models becomes more apparent still if account is taken of another characteristic of most systems of social regulation. This is that, unlike the criminal law, they are not primarily concerned with individual acts but with organizational behavior over time. Individual acts (e.g., the emission of noxious fumes at one particular point in time) matter chiefly insofar as they indicate an organizational failure (e.g., maintaining inadequate control over production processes). The point is well made in a British study of water pollution control:

> In the more familiar areas of behaviour embraced by the traditional criminal law, compliance usually means refraining from an act. But in pollution control compliance often requires a positive accomplishment, sometimes with major economic implications. Time and money have to be spent in one form or another, in planning, buying, building and maintaining compliance. The result of all this is that pollution control staff must display patience and tolerance, rather than legal authority, for their goal is not to punish but to secure change (Hawkins 1984, 197).

From this it follows that regulation can usefully be analyzed in terms of ongoing social relations between regulators and regulated, rather than as a one-time legal process.

So, from an American perspective, Reiss (1984, 33) argues that in simple societies social control, or regulation, is exercised through the capacity to observe, monitor, and directly intervene in behavior. In complex societies, however, "where one cannot directly observe, yet seeks to control," regulation is built on "trust relationships." To stress the importance of trust is indeed to bring together many of the points made in this section. If one of the characteristics of regulation is "an all-pervasive uncertainty" (Hawkins and Thomas 1984, 8)—uncertainty about the precise definition of standards, uncertainty about how much time to allow for improvements to be made, uncertainty about whether to interpret a breach of the rules as a symptom of chronic failure or as a one-time accident—then it is perhaps inevitable that much depends on the "trust relationship' between regulators and regulated. And this will be particularly so in the case of institutions like nursing homes where, for most of the time, it is impossible to observe directly what is happening, where change can be rapid and uncertainty is high on all the counts listed above.

But before turning to the specific case of nursing homes, one final theme remains to be explored. This is the difference, already touched on, in the national regulatory styles of the United States and Britain. The United States differs from Britain, and indeed from most other Western societies, in the sheer extent of regulatory activities. Where other countries rely on direct forms of public intervention, such as the public provision of health facilities or public ownership of the railroads, the United States tends to rely instead on the public regulation of private activities. America passed its antitrust legislation, a triumph of market ideology, in 1890 and 1917; Britain waited until the 1960s before passing its Monopolies Act in a halfhearted attempt to encourage the kind of competitive behavior taken for granted in the United States. This may be why the debate about deregulation in the United States has the same highly charged, ideological tone that the debate about the privatization of nationalized industries has in Britain (Wilson 1984, 204–5). In contrast, regulation in Britain, as in most West European countries (Majone 1982) and particularly Sweden (Kelman 1984), is a low-profile activity. It tends to be politically uncontentious. In turn, there appears to be a consistent difference in the regulatory styles of the two countries, cutting across the industries being regulated:

> If one compares the British and American approaches to insurance regulation, equal employment, banking regulation, consumer protection, occupational health and safety, or securities regulation, a clear pattern emerges: in each case Americans rely heavily on formal rules, often enforced in the face of a strong opposition from the institutions affected by them, while the British continue to rely on flexible standards and voluntary compliance—including, in many cases, self-regulation (Vogel 1983, 101).

Explanations for this divergence vary. Some stress differences in the political cultures of the two countries; in the United States businessmen are seen as predatory competitors in a way that is not the case in Britain (Vogel 1983). Others put more emphasis on differences in political institutions and the extent to which they promote cooperation between industry and government (Wilson 1984). But from the perspective of our interest in nursing homes, it is the unanimity about the consistency of the pattern that matters. If Britain's approach to regulation seems to conform to the compliance model, America's appears to be nearer the deterrence model. If the style of British regulation is consensual and informal, America's is adversarial and legalistic. If the former stresses cooperation, the latter produces conflict. So we would expect the regulation of nursing homes to conform to this pattern.

There is, however, a tension between differences in the national styles of regulation and growing convergence in the characteristics of the industries being regulated. As Moran (1986, 201) concludes in his study of the regulation of financial markets in the two countries, "National political cultures impose their own regulatory styles; the increasing structural similarities in markets encourage regulatory convergence." If, in fact, the social control of nursing homes raises common issues which cut across national systems of provision—issues specific to the characteristics of the industry—then we might also expect to find some similarities in the processes of regulation. So we might expect that the regulation of nursing homes could turn out to be, like the regulation of financial markets, a study in convergence stemming from shared characteristics and shared problems.

The Two National Systems Compared

The health care systems of the United States and Britain reflect their societies. Both these very different societies have, if to varying degrees, accepted the notion of State responsibility for the availability of medical care (Fox 1986). But the way in which this commitment has been implemented is very different. In the United States, a heterogeneous society with an ideology hostile to direct State involvement (King 1973), this generally means private provision publicly financed. In Britain, a far more homogeneous society with a long tradition of paternalism in social policies, this generally means public provision publicly financed. In turn, the formal structures of regulation in the two countries reflect this fundamental difference. That of the United States has followed money, and developed largely to protect public funds; that of Britain, set up much earlier, has its origins in professional self-interest. The United States system is designed to regulate comprehensively quantity and prices, as well as quality; that of Britain is concerned only with quality. In what follows, we shall elaborate on each of these points.

Historically, the provision of long-stay institutional care for the elderly in the two countries has a similar origin. In each case, nineteenth-century public poorhouses and mental hospitals provided shelter and accommodation for the sick needy and destitute, including the poor elderly, who did not qualify for voluntary or religious care. But in the twentieth century the pattern of development has increasingly diverged, especially over the last 40 years or so. In the United States, the growth of long-stay institutional care for the elderly has been a largely unintended by-product, first, of income maintenance policies (Waldman 1985) and, in the 1960s, of medical insurance programs (Vladeck 1980). The type of provision has followed the availability of public funds, although of course the United States could have chosen to follow a different pattern of development. And since the demands funded by national and state governments under the Medicare and Medicaid programs are for *medical* care, the market responded by dramatically expanding the number of nursing home places. In turn, as we shall see, the nature of the funding shapes the way in which the function of nursing homes is perceived and the regulatory system is designed, since it is medical need that unlocks access to public finance.

In contrast, the British system of long-stay institutional care for the elderly still reflects its nineteenth-century origin. It has evolved, without any real break, out of the Victorian Poor Law—and indeed some of the nineteenth-century institutions are still in use. The Poor Law's function of caring for the infirm elderly is now divided beween the long-stay hospitals of the National Health Service (NHS) and the residential homes run by local authorities, while private and voluntary nursing and residential homes have developed to meet demands not met by either of the former. In theory, NHS hospitals respond to medical need, while local authority homes respond to social need, but in practice the distinction is blurred. The emphasis of public policy has continued to be on public provision, with private provision having a residual role. Indeed, the number of nursing home beds fell between 1938 and 1960 (Woodruffe and Townsend 1961). It was only in the 1980s that, as an unintended consequence of a change in the regulations governing welfare payments (Day and Klein 1987b), public finance started to be available on any scale for funding people in private nursing or residential homes. Partly as a result of this, although partly also reflecting the increased prosperity of many of Britain's elderly, there followed a boom in private provision. While access to public provision is rationed according to criteria laid down by the service providers (i.e., family circumstances, housing conditions, the availability of alternative community services, as well as medical requirements), access to private provision financed by social welfare payments is conditional only on satisfying a financial means test. There is no requirement that public finance should be conditional on demonstrating either social or medical need. In analyzing the regulatory systems of the two countries, however, we shall concentrate exclusively on the regulation of nursing homes, ignoring the regulation of residential and other forms of institutional provision. For these are the most nearly comparable to skilled nursing facilities in the United States, i.e., they deal with the upper range of dependency (Bartlett and Challis 1985; Bennett 1986; Torbay District Health Authority 1985) and care is the responsibility of qualified nurses.

The regulatory models of the two countries reflect, in turn, the history, finance, and pattern of long-stay institutional care. In the United States, public regulation has followed public money (Ruchlin 1979; Institute of Medicine 1986, appendix A). As the federal government's financial involvement grew with the introduction of Medicare and Medicaid in the 1960s, so it introduced its own standards to supplement the state licensure rules. The regulatory system is thus designed as much to protect the public purse against fraud or graft as the consumer against ill-treatment or exploitation. It is a regulatory model shaped, moreover, by the assumptions that nursing homes are an extension of hospitals (Butler 1979) and their function is to provide medical care; that the protection of the public purse requires that they not be used by those who don't need such care; and that providers are supplying appropriate care at an appropriate price. In sharp contrast, the concerns of the British regulatory model are much narrower. It is a system that developed long before the very recent involvement of public funds in the financing of nursing home care and that, like the pattern of long-stay institutional care itself, is an example of historical continuity. In essence, Britain's regulatory model was devised in 1927, when the Nursing Homes Regulation Act was passed (House of Commons 1926; Abel-Smith 1964). Its passage reflected not worry about public funds or even public alarm about standards but professional pressure. It was the College of Nurses which fought for regulation in order to protect its members against competition from unqualified staff or staff with qualifications other than nursing; some so-called nursing homes appear to have been used as brothels. From this follows one of the main characteristics of the British regulatory system even today. Nursing homes are statutorily defined as places where a qualified nurse is in charge. It is an emphasis which partly reflects the fact that the British nursing elite have traditionally had a higher social status than their United States counterparts, and partly that British nursing homes, unlike American ones, are seen not as an extension of the hospital but as providers of a different kind of environment and care. It is a model which, moreover, has proved remarkably resistant to change. Despite increasing anxiety about the infusion of public funds through the social security system (Audit Commission 1986), despite the growing salience of private health care as a political issue (Klein 1979; McLachlan and Maynard 1982), and despite occasional scandals in private nursing homes, there has as yet been no move to extend the scope of regulation beyond quality to the control of quantity and value for money. In this respect the present regulatory system remains, despite a flurry of legislative activity in the early 1980s, firmly based on the foundations of the 1927 Act.

Another contrast between the United States and British formal regulatory systems derives, predictably enough, from the fact that while the former has a federal constitution, the latter has not. In the United States, the regulatory function is divided between the states, responsible for the licensure of nursing homes, and the federal government, responsible for laying down the conditions of eligibility for federal funds. In Britain, it is central government, i.e., the Department of Health and Social Security (DHSS), that is responsible both for legislation and administration of the system. In practice, however, regulation is more devolved in Britain than in the United States. For example, the federal government reviews the way in which the states exercise their regulatory responsibilities. Further, the federal conditions of participation (Institute of Medicine 1986, appendix B) spell out in considerable detail what is required of nursing homes. In contrast, the DHSS delegates the regulatory role to the 192 English District Health Authorities (DHAs) which form the bottom tier of the National Health Service's (NHS's) administrative structure (the structure of the NHS differs in the component countries of the United Kingdom and, to avoid confusion, we concentrate on England in what follows). It is DHAs which are responsible for licensing and inspecting nursing homes, for laying down staffing and other requirements, and if need be, for withdrawing their licenses. In all this, appeal lies not to the DHSS but to an independent tribunal set up in 1985. The DHSS itself appears to be disinterested in the way the regulatory system works; most conspicuously, it has no way of systematically finding out whether the 192 DHAs are, in fact, applying the same requirements or standards.

Moreover, the DHSS regulations are considerably less specific and less concrete than the federal conditions of participation in spelling out what those requirements or standards should be. There are some specific legal requirements, notably for record keeping and twice-yearly inspections. But, beyond that, the DHSS has not specified how the general aims of legislation—"to protect the public through ensuring that adequate standards of care and accommodation are provided" (Department of Health and Social Security 1981)—should be translated into concrete requirements for the physical layout, staffing levels, or operating methods. It delegated this task to the National Association of Health Authorities (NAHA), a nongovernment body, which in 1985 produced a set of model guidelines for DHAs (National Association of Health Authorities 1985). The standards set out in this set of guidelines have no statutory force but simply provide, in the words of the document, "a series of benchmarks against which each District Health Authority is invited to assess and set its own requirements." In comparing the federal and British regulatory systems, we shall be treating the NAHA guidelines as part of the latter, while also noting that their informal and quasi-voluntary nature may be one of the defining characteristics of the British regulatory system. In the case of the United States, too, national requirements are incorporated in a national survey instrument. At the time of our field studies, this was the 69-page federal form HCFA-1959 (now being replaced by the Patient Care and Services protocol for surveyors). In contrast, there is no equivalent national survey form in Britain and the NAHA's checklist for surveyors is a mere 9 pages long. By comparison with Britain, the United States, therefore, emerges (predictably) as being more legalistic and (surprisingly) as more centralized in its approach to regulation, the centralization of funding accompanying the centralization of regulatory control.

A final contrast between the two models stems not from differences in funding but from the fact that the United States lacks a cohesive system of public provision for health care in general, as well as for long-stay institutional care for the elderly in particular. In Britain, unlike the United States, the development of the regulatory system consequently reflects the implicit assumption that public provision is the norm. It is the public sector that regulates the private sector while itself is immune from regulation. It is the public sector that, furthermore, is supposed to set the standards against which private provision is assessed, and whose "publicness" in itself guarantees quality. It is an assumption that in recent decades has been severely challenged by a series of scandals (Martin 1984), and that has led to the creation of public sector inspectorates. The Health Advisory Service (1986), created in the 1970s, inspects services and institutions for the elderly across the public sector, while the more recently created Social Services Inspectorate (1985a) reviews services and institutions provided by local authorities. But while the reports of the inspectorates have underlined the fact that problems of looking after the elderly cut across public and private provision (Day and Klein 1987a) and that both sectors are equally scandal prone, they have not so far generated any explicit code of practice or standards for the public sector.

In summary, then, the United States formal model of nursing home regulation is more comprehensive, more explicitly legalistic, and more centralized than the British one—a conclusion that is a mixture of the predictable and the unexpected, reflecting differences in national regulatory traditions and in the funding of long-stay institutional care for the elderly. But how similar or different are the actual regulatory requirements as spelled out in the national legislation, codes, and conditions? To answer this question, as a preliminary to examining how the systems actually work at the subnational level in the two countries, we compare the actual provisions of the Skilled Nursing Facility (SNF) condition of participation (Institute of Medicine 1986, appendix B) and those of the DHSS regulations as supplemented by the NAHA (1985) guidelines; we use the SNF rather than the Intermediate Care Facility (ICF) conditions since it is skilled nursing facilities which offer the nearest functional equivalent to British nursing homes. To analyze the requirements, we use the familiar distinction between structural, process, and outcome criteria (Donabedian 1966) as our framework. And, as we shall see, the sheer difficulty of defining what is meant by quality in nursing home care—a difficulty epitomized by the insistence of both American and British systems that "adequate" care be provided and their shared problem of defining what is meant by adequacy—tends to produce convergence, even while organizational and financial differences tend to drive them apart.

Structural or Input Requirements

Among the most striking characteristics of the two sets of formal requirements are their common insistence on spelling out in great detail how nursing homes should be designed, and the extent of agreement about what desirable standards are in terms of the physical environment. In each case, there is the same emphasis on fire precautions. In each case, there is a requirement to have standby emergency electricity generators. In each case, too, there is a minimum standard for the size of patient rooms; for single occupancy room, it is 107 square feet in Britain as against 100 square feet in the United States.

But similarities yield to contrasts when it comes to staffing inputs, which are shaped by the very different perception of the function of nursing homes in the two countries. Both countries require a registered nurse to be in charge of nursing services in each home; both, too, require that a qualified nurse should be on duty at all times, though not necessarily a registered nurse. Both countries, furthermore, recoil from specifying nurse-patient ratios because, as the British guidelines argue, there is too much variation in the characteristics both of the facilities themselves and of patients. In the case of British nursing homes, however, it is only the nursing inputs that are specified. Indeed, it is precisely the fact that a qualified registered nurse is in charge that legally defines a nursing home as such, as already noted. In contrast, the American requirement is for a "qualified administrator" to be responsible for the facility as a whole. In addition, the federal standards insist on a much larger degree of staff specialization—hence, such requirements as that there should be a "full-time qualified dietetic supervisor," which would condemn quite a large proportion of the much smaller British nursing homes to bankruptcy. Above all, the American requirements, unlike Britain's, demand a medical input, as much to protect the public purse as the patients themselves. Not only must each nursing home appoint a medical director; equally, each patient has regularly to be visited by a physician responsible for certifying and recertifying the need for medical treatment. In contrast, patients in British nursing homes are merely registered, like all British citizens, with a general practitioner; it is up to the patients themselves, or those in charge of the nursing home, to decide when to call in a doctor. No assumption of a need for medical treatment is built into the British requirements.

Process Requirements

The divergence between the United States and British approaches to codifying standards becomes more marked still when it comes to the way in which they set about defining how nursing homes should be run. Even here, however, there are some common elements. In both cases there are the same stresses on certain administrative routines, such as record keeping and following set procedures for prescribing and dispensing drugs. But, more generally, the American approach is to insist in considerable detail on a pattern of routines and procedures, while the British approach is to promote a style of care by enunciating some fairly general aims. The differences follow, in fact, a systematic—and, by this stage in the analysis, familiar—pattern. While the American requirements suggest a rule-bound approach, the British ones tend to be informal and persuasive; while the former reflect a medical model of care, the latter tend to be based on a nursing model.

So the British guidelines point out that "the environment should, as far as possible, be domestic in character, and enable patients to retain their individuality and self-respect." Further, they emphasize that "it is important that the organisation and the attitude of staff reflect the need for patients to achieve and maintain maximum independence." But the implications of these general pointers for the actual running of the home are not spelled out; indeed, in the DHSS's circular to health authorities—setting out the latter's responsibilities—only two brief paragraphs are devoted to the way in which care should be organized, as against five paragraphs devoted to fire precautions (Department of Health and Social Security 1981). There could hardly be a greater contrast with the United States requirements, with their insistence on a managed package of care, starting with a patient care plan and a detailed specification of the social and rehabilitation services that must be available. If the emphasis in British regulations is on maintaining the independence of the patient, in the United States regulations it appears to be on mobilizing medical, rehabilitative, and other resources on his or her behalf. If the former tend to stress the maintenance of a homelike atmosphere by the nursing staff, the latter stress the availability of technical services and use an energetic language of goal setting and the purposeful planning of care by multidisciplinary teams.

A further difference in the process requirements is the much greater emphasis in the federal conditions on protecting the rights of patients. If the emphasis on medical certification and review suggests a fear that public funds will be ripped off by nursing homes, the emphasis on patient rights suggests a fear that the residents will be exploited. The British guidelines have a laconic reference to the need to make sure that each nursing home has a room where patients may make any complaints to an inspector; they also have a requirement that patients should have access to a public telephone. But general exhortations about privacy, self-respect, and individuality apart, there is nothing like the federal requirement that each facility should have "patients' rights policies," including the *right* to be "treated with consideration, respect and full recognition of their dignity and individuality." Nor is there anything remotely resembling the extensive federal requirements to protect patients' funds against abuse. In the American case, the assumption appears to be that consumers need to be protected against predatory producers, while the British regulations reflect an implicit respect for the property right of providers. Add to this the traditional British suspicion of the language of individual civil rights and a reluctance to embody these in legally enforceable rules, and the differences in the styles of the nursing home regulations fall into the larger pattern of Anglo-American divisions.

Outcome Requirements

Here, at last, we come to complete convergence between the two national systems. Neither federal regulations nor the British guidelines have any formal criteria or requirements expressed in terms of desired outcomes for the patients themselves. In this respect, as in others, practice diverges from theory. The regulatory requirements as enshrined in national codes or conditions are at best only a rough and ready, and at worst a misleading, guide to what happens in the actual practice of regulatory enforcement. In the resolution, both systems do take account of outcome in various ways, as we shall seek to demonstrate in the following sections where we examine the implementation of national policies in the two countries.

Political and Cultural Variations on National Themes

Q. How many Virginians does it take to change a light bulb?

A. Three. One to change the bulb, two to talk about how good the old one was.

Q. How many New Yorkers does it take to change a light bulb?

A. Thirty-seven. One to change the bulb, and a 36-member law firm to sue for damages under product liability.

Q. How many Englishmen does it take to change a light bulb?

A. Only one, but he won't do it because the bulb has always worked in the past.

From a comparison of national regulatory systems, our analysis moves on to examining how formal models are translated into policy practice. The evidence so far suggests that there are indeed systematic differences between the American and British national nursing home regulatory models, and that these are in line with what might be expected from the general approach to regulation in the two countries. Political culture in the largest sense—i.e., including the use of the law—matters. But do differentiations in political culture help to explain variations in regulatory strategies not only across but also within nations? And are such variations sustained through the policy implementation process, from the drawing up of codes to their enforcement in individual nursing homes? To answer the first of these questions, we compare the regulatory systems of New York and Virginia with those of Britain's District Health Authorities. In doing so, we will largely be telling the story of New York's exceptionalism. To answer the second of the questions, we turn in the following sections to a comparative examination of enforcement and implementation styles. In doing so, we shall find that while indeed variations in political culture continue to explain divergences in regulatory *strategies,* the common characteristics of the nursing home industry compel convergence in regulatory *practices* as we move nearer to the working level of inspection and enforcement.

In selecting the state of New York and the Commonwealth of Virginia for our American case studies, we deliberately chose to contrast a confrontational and abrasive political culture with a more consensual and conservative one. We could, of course, have picked our pair on other, deliberately simplified criteria; moreover, if the aim of our study had been to try to identify which characteristics of that protean and ambiguous concept—political culture—are linked to specific aspects of regulation, we would have had to use a much larger sample. For our purposes, however, this pairing allows us to ask whether Virginia has more in common with New York (with which it shares a national framework of regulation and finance) or with Britain (with which it shares some traditions of political culture). In the case of Britain, we use a composite portrait of English DHAs, rather than a pair picked out to match New York and Virginia, and this for reasons highly revealing of Britain's political culture. Not only are DHAs recently invented administrative artifacts, created by central government in 1982, and so lacking in any political identity, let alone culture. But also, despite the comparative vagueness and looseness of the national regulatory framework within which DHAs work, there is *less* variation in the models of regulation used locally than between New York and Virginia (Day and Klein 1985). Most DHAs have adopted the NAHA guidelines as the basis of their own codes, even though nursing home owners tend to complain about differences in interpretation on points of detail. In a relatively homogeneous and deferential country, with strong professional networks and shared attitudes among regulators, governments can promote common practices in the execution of national policies by using informal social pressures rather than formal rules and procedures.

The history and style of the regulatory systems in our three study areas follows the pattern of the differences in their political cultures. New York has a long history of headline nursing home scandals, especially following the rapid post-Medicaid expansion of the 1960s (Vladeck 1980). The image of the nursing home owner as a predatory, amoral calculator neatly fits the New York experience. In contrast, Virginia has no such legacy of well-publicized horror stories. Nursing homes, like other businesses, are part of the political landscape rather than, as in New York, targets on which politicians can sharpen their reputation for being defenders of the weak against the strong and possibly corrupt. In Virginia, the nursing home industry is strongly represented in the legislature, and the ownership of nursing homes is seen both as a service to be regulated and as a property right; regulators tend to adopt a political bargaining style. In New York, the industry is seen as an adversary, to be treated with aggressive suspicion lest anyone think that the regulators are getting into bed with the regulated—the recurring American nightmare (Wilson 1980). In all these respects, the British system tends to resemble the Virginian in style. It is a system which, as we have seen, developed in response to professional pressures rather than public scandals, and which has had a low political profile.

All these differences are, however, not only consistent with variations in political culture but also are related to the particular nature of the nursing home industry in our three study areas, and it would be foolhardy to speculate on the precise contribution of these factors to our findings. Thus, New York (see table 1) has more nursing homes and beds than Virginia and the whole of England put together; furthermore, a high proportion of its facilities are in densely urban areas where all service industries, whether transport or education or health care, have problems reflecting the local environment and labor market, a point to be elaborated on later. Virginia has less than a quarter of New York's beds, and the growth of facilities in the metropolitan belt around Washington is a relatively recent development. In England, only 14 out of the 192 DHAs have more than 500 beds (Larder, Day, and Klein 1986), and even the DHA with the most beds has only one twentieth of Virginia's total.

The size of the industry, in turn, affects the size of the regulatory bureaucracy. Thus, New York (see table 1) has a regulatory staff of 300 or more than eight times as many as Virginia. This is a much bigger difference than would follow from the relative sizes of the industry and points to the independent influence of political culture. In England, by way of contrast, regulation is a cottage industry; the total estimate of about 100 regulators represents the full-time equivalents of mainly part-time contributions from NHS staff engaged in other duties (Department of Health and Social Security 1985). Only a handful of DHAs have full-time regulators. Neither Virginia nor England, therefore, faces New York's problem of internal control within the regulatory agency. Neither, consequently, is as preoccupied with self-regulation within the regulatory bureaucracy; both tend to

TABLE 1
Anglo-American Comparisons: Basic Statistics on Nursing Homes and
Regulatory Systems

	U.S.	Virginia	New York	England
Population				
Total	229m	5.4m	17.6m	46.8m
Age 65 & over	25.5m	0.5m	2.14m	7m
(as % of total)	(11.1%)	(9.3%)	(12.1%)	(15%)
Age 85 & over	2.44m	0.045m	0.222m	0.5m
(as % of total)	(1.1%)	(0.8%)	(1.2%)	(1.1%)
Nursing Homes				
Number (1981)	13,326	163	570	820 (1983)
No. of beds (1983)	1,450,000	23,000	96,000	28,000 (1984)
No. of beds per 1,000 age 65 & over (1983)	55.8	40.8	43.1	4.0 (40.1)*
Rate of bed expansion 1981–1983	3.5%	11.4%	2.4%	35% (1982–1984)
% < 60 beds	NA	26%	15%	83%
% for-profit	70%	66%	51%	29%*
% public	8%	10%	10%	58%*
% voluntary	22%	24%	39%	13%*
Regulatory Staff				
Number	2,700	37	300	100
No. of nursing homes per regulator	4.9	4.4	1.9	8.2
No. of beds per regulator	537	622	320	284

* These figures refer to *all* institutions for the elderly in England.
Sources: The U.S. data is derived from tables in Institute of Medicine 1986; Harrington et al. 1985; and personal communications from relevant agencies. The English data are derived from Larder, Day, and Klein 1986, and Day and Larder 1986.

rely on informal social pressures to maintain internal discipline, cohesion, and consistency among agency staff, whereas New York has developed a highly sophisticated system of self-evaluation and statistical information as part of a continuing attempt to control its own officers.

New York, above all, is unique among our three cases for having developed its own methodology of regulation, and for the fact that this is outcome oriented (Axelrod and Sweeney 1984). The starting point for each facility inspection is a review of patients to identify "Sentinel Health Events" (SHEs). These are negative outcome indicators, i.e, conditions which, given good quality care, need explanation and justification. SHEs include contractures, decubitus ulcers, accidents, indwelling catheters, the use of restraints, and poor grooming. Patient observation is also emphasized (New York Office of Health Systems Management 1982). If the incidence of SHEs is above the statistical norm for facilities, there then follows a more detailed investigation of all relevant cases. This information, in turn, feeds into the conventional survey procedure, as does the information from the complaints system. The two forms of review are seen as complementary (Axelrod and Sweeney 1984, 2). The SHE process "is a review of the quality of care rendered to patients. It is patient-centered in that it evaluates quality from the vantage point of the individual patient's experience in a facility, as opposed to the survey which measures the facility's capability to render care and service." The history of this inspection methodology is, in itself, revealing of the New York style. First, the impetus to change came from public scandal and public pressure in the 1970s. Second, the methodology was developed on the basis of a special study carried out by an academic institution. Third, it was introduced only after field trials and prolonged staff training sessions. Fourth, it involved the creation of a new data processing system. Fifth, it has been subjected to a detailed evaluation (New York Office of Health Systems Management 1982). In this it illustrates the highly professional, self-critical, and intellectually sophisticated New York approach to regulation, as well as perhaps a general regulatory paradox. This is that the greater the risk of *unavoidable* public scandals, the greater will be the care taken by the regulators to demonstrate their own organizational and technical competence and integrity.

New York's outcome-centered methodology of regulation has been stressed because, in other respects, the formal regulatory requirements in our three case studies provide few surprises. They largely follow the national models outlined in the previous section, with variations in emphasis rather than of principle, the variations following the by now predictable pattern of New York and England at the two poles, with Virginia in the middle. So, for example, New York's awesomely heavy tome of codes, rules, and regulations (New York 1983) contrasts with Virginia's slim volume setting out the state's licensure rules and regulations (Virginia 1980); the latter is not so very different from the notes of guidance published by the average English DHA. Again, the state requirements in New York tend to be more stringent, more numerous, and more precise than those in the federal code, whereas in Virginia the requirements generally follow the federal conditions, although allowing nursing homes licensed or under construction before 1980 to operate with lower physical standards. As against New York's 63-page SHE protocol, with its elaborate instructions to surveyors about how to collect the information and about sampling methodology, Virginia has a 3-page checklist for a "quality assurance walk through," which asks surveyors to observe, for example, whether the staff have a "happy/hurried/defensive communication with residents" and whether patients are "happy/glum, open/afraid to talk" and so on; a checklist which was promptly and enthusiastically adopted by the regulatory staff of an English DHA when shown to them by the authors.

In all these respects, Virginia tends to lean toward English practice, in the sense that its requirements are less stringent and its procedures less mechanistic than New York's. But, as might be expected from the discussion of national frameworks in the previous section, in two crucial respects Virginia is much closer to New York than it is to England. First, both Virginia and New York have patient-centered systems, predictably so given that one of the main concerns of the American regulatory system is to make sure that public money doesn't buy the wrong kind of care for the wrong type of patient at the wrong price. Although Virginia has nothing like New York's outcome-oriented system, it does have an extensive data system that provides information about all Medicaid patients (Virginia 1985) and is designed to ensure that patients do not get inappropriate institutional care where other forms of support might be better. In Britain, there is *no* system for collecting data about nursing home clients (Day and Klein 1987a). DHAs have no way of telling routinely how old the nursing home patients are, what their medical condition is, how their stay is being financed, or whether they are getting any form of treatment from anyone. DHA surveyors will look at the individual patients during their visits, and some have even begun to devise their own homemade forms of assessment. But there is no standard assessment form which allows changes over time to be recorded.

Second, and again predictably, the regulatory guidelines of English DHAs differ from both New York's and Virginia's in their concentration on input, rather than process or outcome requirements. The emphasis, in line with the national model, is on specifying the size of rooms, laundry and catering facilities, the number of bathrooms and lavatories, and so on. The registration staff of each DHA also "lay down the number of registered nurses, enrolled nurses and nursing auxilliaries to be on duty at any time of the 24 hours" (Southport District Health Authority 1985); there are wide variations in staffing levels since these are fixed not in the guidelines but left for each nursing home to take account of its physical layout and patient mix (Day and Larder 1986). But there is not the assumption, reflected in both New York's and Virginia's process requirements, that producing treatment plans or activity programs for individual patients can be taken as an indicator of quality. Instead, the assumption implicit in DHA guidelines is that the appropriate institutional environment, as reflected in inputs or structure, will lead to quality of care "by creating an atmosphere which will promote individuality and personal preference in matters of daily living," and by ensuring that patients "live in comfortable, clean and safe surroundings" and are treated "with respect and sensitivity to their individual needs and abilities" (Oxfordshire District Health Authority 1985). In short, the state and DHA requirements accurately reflect the biases of the two national systems and their different perceptions of the function of a nursing home. To caricature only a little, in England the emphasis is predominantly on interpreting quality in terms of patient comfort and the atmosphere of the home; in the United States it is on seeing quality in terms of energetic (preferably medical or technical) intervention.

Models of Regulatory Enforcement

New York's exceptionalism is once again evident when we move to analyzing the models of enforcement in our three study areas. New York is the epitome of the hairs-on-chest, no-nonsense enforcement model in line with what might be expected from its adversarial political structure. It provides an example of a deterrence model of enforcement, to return to the vocabulary of the general literature on regulation. In contrast, Virginia resembles England in relying on a compliance model. If Virginia's case is anything to go by, therefore, differences in political culture within countries appear to be more important than differences between nations when it comes to the enforcement of nursing home regulations; the neat Anglo-American antithesis turns out to be too simple by half. And even the New York model turns out to be blurred, its sharp edges blunted, in the day-to-day practice of regulation, as we shall see when we move on to the implementation of the enforcement models.

New York is quite explicit in adopting a deterrence model of enforcement. Interviews with the agency officials at the top of the organizational hierarchy produced a unanimous and emphatic insistence that "we are policemen, whose job it is to enforce the regulations. . . . There is no room for the nice consultant telling facilities how to do a good job." The role of the inspectors, as they saw it, was "to go in, define the problem, give a ticket to the nursing homes and expect them to put it right." It was not the job of the inspectorate, they stressed, to identify or even discuss solutions to the problems: "We go in to determine whether they are managing properly, not to manage it." The agency philosophy is that as long as the product is right, it is not the business of the inspectorates to tell the facility how to run itself: hence, of course, the insistence on measuring outcomes as a proxy for the quality of the product. Conversely, if the product is not right, it is the responsibility of the nursing home management to take the appropriate action: "We don't tell them how to correct problems." So, defects in outcomes are not related to inadequacies in inputs. Agency policy, for example, is not to prescribe staffing levels as a way of remedying inadequacies, partly because staffing levels in New York are traditionally generous, partly because of the implications for reimbursement rates. The formal, keep-your-distance approach is also evident in the way in which New York surveyors write their reports. Surveyors can only record a deficiency if it is in the code. So, for instance, nursing surveyors may think that wrong or inappropriate techniques are being used. But if there is no specific reference to this in the code, such judgments cannot be allowed into the survey deficiency reports. Hovering over every report writer is the specter of a lawyer who will challenge any deficiency report that is not sustained by the code. In summary, then, the New

York model is characterized by its outcome or product orientation, by its assumption of a hands-off and hostile relation between regulators and regulated, and by its emphasis on legal process.

If New York is an example of a state where a sophisticated regulatory bureaucracy polices what is seen as a potentially predatory industry, Virginia is an example of a state where a small regulatory team is involved in a complex social and political relationship with its nursing home industry. The tone of voice in the interviews with Virginia's regulators was not so different from that found when talking to regulators in English DHAs. In both cases, the emphasis was on drawing the industry into a cooperative partnership. The Virginian tone is nicely caught in the state's introductory notes of guidance to facilities with Medicaid patients: "The goal of Virginia's Medical Assistance Program is to provide medical care for Virginia's needy citizens. You, the provider, play an important part in the success or failure of the Program to achieve this goal. . . . On behalf of the Citizens of the Commonwealth your participation is greatly appreciated" (Virginia 1982). Similarly, the notes of guidance devised by the English DHAs are addressed to nursing home proprietors and, in particular, to newcomers to the industry. They are designed to be helpful to prospective proprietors, some of whom know little about nursing homes, as well as setting out the formal rules and regulations.

Virginia, like England, offers an example of the compliance model in action. Within the relatively small regulatory agency itself, control is largely a matter of informal relations among the people working in it. Similarly, there is a deliberate emphasis on building up trust relationships with the facilities, with no apparent sense that this may risk regulatory capture by the industry. In the words of one member of the agency staff, "We see ourselves as part of a team rather than just merely as enforcers." Teams of surveyors are kept together for three or four years so that they can "build up good working relationships" with nursing homes. If there are real worries about conditions in a nursing home, the survey team may make repeat visits and give advice: "We become resource persons." The close relations with providers do not exclude unannounced surprise visits, sometimes at night. But they do set up the expectation that the provider will comply voluntarily by producing a plan of correction, that argument and advice will be the main weapons of enforcement and that legal processes will be involved very rarely. In summary, the reliance is on persuasion rather than the law, although there is an awareness that this strategy may be more effective in the traditional rural areas of the state than in the metropolitan belt around Washington, in particular. In all this, Virginia is as determined as New York to enforce its standards, but does so in a more relaxed style and with a clear idea of the need to restrict the activities and power of both government and business.

The DHA enforcement model in England is remarkably similar to Virginia's. If anything, it is even more informal because of the small and scattered nature of the regulatory staff. This means that there is no distinct regulatory agency and, therefore, no explicit regulatory philosophy. Most English regulators are nurses, and tend to see themselves as professional colleagues of the nurses in charge of homes. They perceive their role as being largely to improve professional practices, such as the management of incontinent or demented patients, and to this end most of them organize study days and training sessions designed to bring nursing home staff into the mainstream of professional thinking about "good practices." They see themselves as providing support, education, and advice. The general assumption is that if things go wrong in a nursing home it is just as likely to be the result of ignorance, isolation, or incompetence as of predatory commercialism or deliberate exploitation. If a nursing home is in trouble the resulting series of visits by inspectors is therefore as likely to be designed to prop up staff morale and to improve care as to spot infractions of the rules. There are few inhibitions about demanding improvements in staffing. It is a model of enforcement which, as in Virginia, does not imply laxity of standards or tolerance of shortcomings but simply a different kind of diagnosis about why things go wrong—human frailty as much as human greed—and about what treatment is needed—from that implicit in New York's model.

The Virginian style is also reflected in the letters sent out to facilities after inspections of care. There is little sense of an invisible lawyer crouched over the surveyor's shoulder, and the comments about inadequate treatment of patients are not limited to specific infractions of the codified rules and regulations as in New York. So, in one case, the agency points out (in a 6-page letter detailing deficiencies) that "residents were observed clad only in their night clothes without underwear, bath robes or lap robes" and that one patient, 4′ 2″ tall, was in a regular height bed with no step stool provided to assist her getting into bed, though she was reported to have "falls" and that "four residents needed shampoos or hair care." As in New York, the formal assumption is that it is not the agency's role in these cases to suggest how such deficiencies should be put right or to specify, for example, what the staffing levels should be, no doubt for very much the same reasons: i.e., lest such instructions be used to justify extra financial claims. But, as we shall see when we turn to the style of implementation, the formal model is not always carried through into practice in either New York or Virginia. Nor, for that matter, is it in England. There, as noted, the emphasis of the formal regulatory approach is on institutions rather than on individual patients, on inputs rather than on processes, let alone outcomes. Yet, as in Virginia, the letters that are sent out after inspections frequently make general remarks about individual patients or the environment in which they live. So they will, for example, note "that an elderly lady sitting in the garden was not provided with a blanket despite a request that this should be done" or that "there was a distinct smell of urine in parts of the home." In short, the convergence in the comments of surveyors provides a strong hint that, whether they are working in England or Virginia, they are reacting much the same way to much the same phenomena. And if this is so, does this further suggest that, whatever the formal differences between the models of regulation used, there may be a more general convergence in the way in which they are implemented in the two countries—even in New York? This is the question addressed in the next section.

Implementation of Regulation in the Field

There are a number of reasons for not taking regulatory models at face value as guides to what actually happens in the field. Whatever the agency philosophies, codes, and strategies, these still have to be translated into practice in a series of day-to-day encounters between the regulators and the regulated. This raises more than the general problem of street-level bureaucracy (Lipsky 1980), i.e., the difficulty in *any* organization of getting its field staff to implement agency policy. There is also an inevitable tension between the objectives of the agency and the desires of the staff to carve out areas of autonomy for themselves where they can use their own discretion and apply their own skills. But such tensions will be particularly evident in regulatory agencies in general (Bardach and Kagan 1982) and in those dealing with nursing home regulation in particular.

First, if all street-level bureaucrats tend to carve out areas of discretion for themselves, this is likely to be a particularly strong drive in the case of nursing home surveyors. Most of these see themselves as professionals in their own right. This is particularly so for the nurses who form the largest single group of surveyors in New York (120 out of 300) and the majority in Virginia and England, and the social workers who are strongly represented in Virginia especially. And if they see themselves as professionals, we would expect them to assert their own discretion and to insist on using their professional judgment. Second, given the characteristics of nursing homes, surveyors cannot avoid using their discretion. Things simply do not speak for themselves; they have to be interpreted. This is a problem, as we have seen, common to all regulatory agencies; even in the case of water pollution inspectors have to make judgments about when something should be treated as an unavoidable or at least a pardonable accident rather than a deliberate offense (Hawkins 1984). But in the case of nursing homes, which are about the management of often very difficult people rather than about the management of pipes and machinery, such judgments are obviously even more frequent and crucial. As with water pollution, too, the surveyor's moral judgment of the provider will play a part. As regulators everywhere are agreed, nursing homes are peculiarly volatile institutions, where a sudden change of staff may produce a radical alteration in the quality of care provided. Inevitably, therefore, surveyors have to interpret such a change. Is it the result of circumstances outside the control of the nursing home manager? Is he or she doing his or her best to put matters right? Or does the change reflect the provider's incompetence or preoccupation with cutting costs? Depending on the answer, different strategies are likely to be pursued.

Lastly, we would expect nursing home regulatory staff to be particularly ill at ease with, and subversive of, a deterrent model of regulation. Not only does such a model rob them, in theory, of opportunities for discretion and professional judgment; equally it deprives them of the job satisfaction involved in using this expertise to give advice. But nursing homes, quite apart from their volatility, are examples of institutions where one cannot always observe yet seek to control (Reiss 1984). Any system of collecting statistics and of inspection, however frequent and however reinforced by the investigation of complaints, may be at odds with the rhythm of change within nursing homes. Therefore, whatever the model of regulation adopted by the agency as its official policy, it will be rational for individual inspectors to try to build up informal trust relations wth nursing homes (even though, once they have judged the provider to be a predator immune to persuasion or education, they may throw the book at him). For most of the time, and perhaps for most nursing homes, any regulatory system depends on self-regulation and on the social pressures, from agency staff and others, which compel such self-regulation.

For all these reasons, stemming partly from the nature of the regulatory task itself and partly from the special characteristics of nursing homes, we would therefore expect to find convergence in the way in which the different models in our three study areas are implemented. And this is precisely what we do find. Even the "hard case" of New York, with its explicitly adversarial, legalistic, and deterrence model of regulation, turns out in practice to adopt a style of implementation that is not nearly so different from that of Virginia or England as the differences in their official philosophies and codes would imply. In what follows, we rely on impressionistic data collected in the course of a short visit and cannot present anything like a complete picture of how the New York system works. But we can and do identify examples of policies and practices that are incompatible with the official model and that suggest that the pure deterrence model may, in fact, be unimplementable whether in New York or anywhere else.

New York, as we have seen, is the epitome of a no-nonsense deterrence model based on a sophisticated technology of regulation. It is not only an agency that prides itself on explicitly repudiating the consultancy, advisory compliance model. It is also an agency that has developed a technology for measuring the achievement or otherwise of the required standards, i.e., its system of outcome indicators. The two are, of course, linked. If there are hard indicators of outcome, and if the provider's failure can be deduced from such measures, then there is no need to engage in negotiation about the meaning of what is going on in nursing homes or of bargaining about how, where necessary, to put things right. In an ideal deterrence model the facts and statistics do speak for themselves, yielding automatic verdicts and penalties; they deter precisely because they do not allow argument or excuses. There will, therefore, be a constant drive, as in New York, to develop an ever more sophisticated technology of measuring what goes on in nursing homes in order to avoid argument about its interpretation and to stop excuses. Such techniques, it is argued, are a way of overcoming the problems of discretion, subjectivity, bargaining, and political judgment; there is actually a technological fix for our problems, and even the difficulties of implementation can be overcome by devising what in effect is a self-steering system.

But can they? The experience of New York suggests otherwise. As already argued, one of the characteristics of the New York agency is the energy applied to internal self-regulation. And one of the reasons for this is its acknowledged difficulty in preventing its field staff from playing a consultancy role. "We have continuously to remind them that they shouldn't be consultants," one agency officer pointed out. So one of the objectives of the New York training program for surveyors is precisely to prevent such recidivism. Even in the view of the nursing home industry itself, however, neither agency directives nor training fully succeed in this aim. In the words of one nursing home manager, "The relationship is 60% consultative, 40% a police approach. If we were in a strict police relationship, surveyors could close down 95% of the nursing homes in New York. The regulations are so complex that you could find nit-picking reasons for closing down just about every institution in the state." It was the same nursing home manager who pointed out that, contrary to the official view, plans of correction were usually worked out in negotiations with the agency staff: "We would know just through interactions with survey people what they want, even if they didn't put it on paper. There is lots of informal bargaining about plans of correction and scope for arguing about how best to put something right."

Similarly, New York is far more flexible in its use of penalties for infractions than a deterrence model would suggest. The state has an elaborate tariff system for calculating fines for different categories of violations (New York 1983, section 742.1), ranging from 100 to 1,000 dollars a day. But the tickets are not handed out automatically; nor are the fines, once imposed, collected automatically. In 1984, for example, a total of $549,000 in fines was imposed. But only $331,000 was collected. As the state agency officials explained, the use of fines and other penalties is part of a finely graded enforcement strategy. Just as fines are preferred to imposing sanctions such as a ban on admissions, let alone closing down facilities, so fines in turn are seen as a form of suspended sentence designed to improve behavior: "Our preference is to get *compliance* [emphasis added] rather than to fine." Moreover, in deciding when and what sanctions to impose, moral judgments are made: "Enforcement is used on those facilities which historically have not conformed, and have got a pattern of infractions, or where conditions are so horrific that something must be done quickly." What is more, enforcement is inescapably a matter of political judgment in New York as elsewhere. It involves a judgment about the tradeoffs between encouraging a surplus of nursing homes (which makes deterrent measures such as closures easier) and the financial costs of so doing (New York's virtual ban on new developments is certainly a factor in inhibiting enforcement). It involves judgments, too, about the likely reactions in the community and by trade unions to threats of closures; inevitably so, given that nursing homes are a source of benefits not just to their ostensible clients, the patients (if indeed they are), but to their employees and to the community where they generate economic activity. In summary, enforcement—like in-spection—cannot be seen as a mechanical process, where the trick is to choose the right instruments and design the appropriate machinery, but as a social and political process.

Lastly, it is clear that even the technological centerpiece of the New York regulatory system, the Sentinel Health Event (SHE) system for measuring negative outcomes, does not eliminate the need for discretion and professional judgment. The model of regulation implicit in the SHE system, as enshrined in official agency philosophy, is that if outcomes are satisfactory, there is no need to worry about either inputs or processes. There is no need, for example, to worry about staffing levels, the constant preoccupation of regulators in England. If care is delivered by a team of robots but outcome indicators are satisfactory, no matter. In fact, however, the actual use of the SHE instrument suggests a rather more complicated and less mechanistic pattern of behavior. For SHEs are only outcome *indicators*. They do not purport to measure actual outcomes. They simply send up signals that things are happening which should not be happening in well-run establishments. In other words, they are ways of alerting surveyors to start looking at inputs and processes in those institutions which have been identified as being at risk. They are a device, and were intended as such, for concentrating agency resources where there is most cause for concern. They do not dispose of the need for taking an interest in inputs or processes, nor for the need for professional judgments by the inspectors.

Indeed, the inspectors interviewed, whether in New York, Virginia, or England, showed a remarkable consistency in the way they described their actual methods of inspection, irrespective of the official model of regulation. Often they used the same words to describe a process of quickly summing up the general atmosphere and smell of a nursing home before getting down to the specific regulatory requirements demanded of them by federal, state, or DHA codes and guidelines. And the reason they did so was because most of them were nurses, and spoke as nurses trained to observe the same things. If political cultures pull regulatory models in different directions, professional culture pulls regulatory practice together again.

In any case, an inspection visit is a complex social event which may not fit into the tidy categories of a regulatory model. For example, a model of regulation based on specific codes and precise instruments assumes that an inspection is like a scientific expedition, and that the main requirement is to provide the appropriate tools of investigation. But the reality of regulation is of a group of surveyors arriving in an untidy situation where they rely on their personal and professional sensors to pick up cues and hints which may signal deeper discontents. In short, we need a different model of knowledge (Lindblom and Cohen 1979) to explain what surveyors actually do, one which acknowledges tacit and experiential knowledge.

Again, the official models in Virginia and England are based, as we have noted, on observing, respectively, process and inputs. In practice, the distinction breaks down. Is the lack of a blanket for an elderly patient a deficiency in inputs (not enough provided by the facility) or in process (callousness on the part of staff) or in outcome (all patients should be warm)? The surveyor, and it is usually a female nurse in all of our three study areas, who enters a facility and immediately sniffs the air and looks at whether patients are sitting comfortably, is taking in all three dimensions of quality. She is searching for hints and signals, not for evidence that will stand up in a court. The latter will come at a subsequent stage in the inspection. If the signals are unfavorable, no matter whether they are prompted by a sophisticated statistical analysis as in New York or by a visual and olfactory trawl, the systematic check follows. And, it is tempting to conclude from this, the real difference in the three systems lies not so much in *what* the inspectors are concerned about but *how* they rationalize and record their concerns. In New York, and in Virginia to a lesser extent, the nature of the regulatory system compels a detailed classification and detailed justification of their findings in terms laid down by a detailed legal code; not surprisingly so in a country with a written constitution, which emphasizes due process and legal justification. In contrast, in England, there is no such framework compelling inspectors to systematize their findings; again, not surprisingly so, in a country without a legal constitution, no tradition of legal redress against the executive, and with a small-scale system of nursing homes.

In tracing through national regulatory models to the front line of implementation, we have ended up with a more complex, finely shaded picture than that covered by the conventional antitheses between deterrence and compliance, legal and informal, American and British approaches to regulation. The evidence suggests that while the varying characteristics of the political and social environment tend to drive the models of nursing home regulation apart, with each nation or state imposing its own distinctive stamp on the system, the characteristics of the nursing home industry as well as shared problems in the regulatory task itself tend to bring them together again during the process of implementation. So while there is divergence in the formal regulatory models, there is often convergence in the methods used. A top-down analysis of national policies tends to stress the former; a bottom-up analysis of what happens at the front line tends to bring out the importance of the latter. The convergence is, of course, not complete. New York remains different in many respects, such as the degree of involvement by the courts; perhaps it could not be otherwise, given the scale of its regulatory activities, which dictates a degree of bureaucratic formalism absent in both Virginia and England. There were also indications that regulatory practices are more relaxed and informal in up-state as against down-state New York, providing a reminder that the characteristics of the nursing home industry are themselves not a fixed factor but may vary both within and between states and countries in some respects. The degree of convergence found does suggest, however, that, to return to the question we set ourselves at the start of this article, there are indeed problems and issues cutting across countries and states, stemming from the nature of nursing homes everywhere, which must be tackled by all regulatory systems.

Finally, our analysis suggests that it is important to distinguish between two related but distinct dimensions of regulation. The first is concerned with the *techniques* of regulation, or the degree to which the definition of standards and the measurement of their achievement is developed. The second is concerned with *styles* of enforcement, or the familiar distinction between deterrence and compliance strategies. The two are linked, as we have seen. Reliance on sophisticated techniques goes hand in hand with a deterrence stance, as in New York. Less highly developed techniques go hand in hand with a compliance stance, as in Virginia and England. Nor is this surprising. The logic of developing sophisticated techniques is precisely to limit, as we have seen, surveyor discretion by a system of automatic signaling followed by the automatic imposition of penalties. The emphasis is on quantification, bureaucratic rules, and legal processes. Conversely, if techniques are less highly developed, more reliance will inevitably be put on the judgment and observations of surveyors. The emphasis is on the social processes between the regulators and the regulated, and their shared social environment. In our concluding discussion of the policy implications of our findings, we shall, therefore, distinguish between the *technological* and the *social-interaction* models of regulation in an attempt to capture both these dimensions. This seems a more satisfactory, because more comprehensive, way of distinguishing between regulatory models than the conventional but more limited distinction between deterrence and compliance strategies that draws attention only to enforcement styles.

Some Implications for Policy

Our finding that the actual, day-to-day process of nursing home regulation tends to converge, despite differences in national context, methods of finance, and regulatory philosophies, can yield a variety of policy conclusions. So one possible implication might be that the technological model needs to be further developed; if it does not work quite as expected, this might be because it is still too crude a piece of machinery. An alternative view might be that the social-interaction model, since descriptively it seems to capture reality rather well, should provide the basis for policy prescription and future developments. And yet a third conclusion might be that regulatory strategies should seek to combine aspects of both models. In what follows, we explore the implications of pursuing these lines of argument. Since there is no systematic documentation of comparative standards in nursing homes in our three study areas or anywhere else, our discussion must, inevitably, remain tentative. And even if we did know more about comparative standards, this would not necessarily tell us anything about the impact of the regulatory systems as distinct from that of the environments in which nursing homes operate and of the methods used to finance them. Lastly, it might be argued that the problem of achieving desirable standards is not one of devising and operating an improved machinery of regulation but, in England as in the United States, one of inadequate finance; given the failure of successive studies, however, to find a consistent relation between inputs and outputs in nursing home care, it is unrealistic to assume that ploughing in more resources would make debate about the regulation of quality redundant. We shall, in any case, limit our own analysis to those issues which apply whatever the level of payments and whatever the system of finance; our exclusive concern, as we stressed at the beginning, is with the regulation of quality, as distinct from quantity or price.

Let us start with the case for developing the technological model of regulation. This rests on two crucial assumptions. It implies, first, that good care is something that can be defined and measured over time, and, second, that its production can be guaranteed given competent management. Like the medical model of care, it incorporates a belief in scientific method: in definable techniques and procedures leading to desirable (and measurable) outcomes. But on both counts there are reasons for skepticism at the very least, about the scope for applying the technological model to the regulation of the particular circumstances of nursing homes (just as there may be skepticism about applying the medical model to nursing home care). First, defining quality and measuring its achievements has inherent problems, both technical and conceptual. Clearly, as everyone agrees (Institute of Medicine 1986), the ideal technical instrument of regulation would be routine measures of outcome reliable enough to speak for themselves and to allow no argument; New York's SHEs are, after all, only indicators based on negative outcomes and merely represent a first step. If only this technical problem could be cracked, it may be argued, the technological model would surely work. However, and again there is general agreement in the literature, taking the first step is going to be very difficult (Challis 1981; Hawes 1983; Kurowski and Shaughnessy 1985). Equally, we would argue, even the most technically sophisticated measures of outcome are never going to speak for themselves without ambiguity and without debate—i.e., that quality of care will never be automatically deducible from outcome measurements. Not only is the notion of quality itself contestable, in that it is liable to change over time and that it is culture-specific. More important still, most desirable outcomes are, in fact, continuing processes, crucially so for those nursing home patients (the majority) who are there to die. For these patients the way they are treated on their way to the grave—with kindness, courtesy, and consideration—will always be more important than whether or not they arrive there a little fitter or later. This is why a system of regulation which assumes, like the American one, that patients in nursing homes, like patients in hospitals, are there to be made well may lead to perverse results.

The other reason why the technological model of regulation is flawed and why its principles will inevitably be betrayed by practice, as we found, derives from the assumption that the right techniques of providing care will assure the right results. This is to ignore the basic dynamics of nursing homes as institutions which can create intolerable situations both for their patients and for their staff. To quote Vladeck (1980, 29):

> The typical nursing home is a pretty awful place. It is a pretty awful place *even when* it is clean and well-lighted, staffed to minimally adequate levels, and provides decent food, adequate medical attention, and a full slate of activities. It is awful because the circumstances, medical and social, of the people living there are extremely difficult to do much about, and because the presence of an adequate supply of individuals motivated, educated, and trained to work effectively in such circumstances is extraordinarily rare.

Not only is looking after the elderly a difficult, sometimes appallingly demanding task. But it is also a task that is largely left to the least trained and worst paid members of staff, the nursing aides. To quote Vladeck again (1980, 20): "Few jobs in this society are worse than those of aides in nursing homes. . . . And it is generally a job without much gratification. Aides bear the brunt of nursing home residents' grievances. Few aides ever see any of their patients get better. Fewer still ever advance up the occupational hierarchy within the nursing home." In other words, it is the marginal people in the labor market looking after the marginal people in society.

The problems of nursing homes stem, therefore, not from the way in which the United States industry is financed or structured (although these may be aggravating factors) but from the very nature of these institutional dynamics. Here the experience of England provides clinching evidence. Over the years there have been numerous cases of poor conditions and poor treatment in various institutions for the elderly and other vulnerable groups. But these problems are as likely to erupt in the public as in the private sector. So, for example, there has been a series of scandals about the quality of care provided in NHS long-stay hospitals (reviewed in Martin 1984), just as there continues to be cause for concern about the quality of care provided in inner-city residential homes for the elderly run by local authorities (Social Services Inspectorate 1985b; Clough 1987). The crucial factor, then, is not the for-profit motive; staff, even in publicly owned institutions, may well pursue their own interests—maximizing their own autonomy, rather than profit—to the detriment of patients. It is that providing institutional care is inherently difficult and precarious. And it is precisely because of these characteristics of institutional care for the elderly that the technological model of regulation invariably proves impossible to sustain in practice. If maintaining good quality care (however defined or measured) is a continuous battle, in which defeats are inevitable and occasional scandals all too likely, then regulation in turn must be a continuous process.

The strength of the social-interaction model of regulation precisely is that it accurately reflects the facts of institutional life. If constant scrutiny is required, if the process of maintaining or improving quality is a continuing battle in which the regulators seek to make allies of the regulated, then this cannot be achieved by improving the techniques of regulation alone. If the social-interaction model is to be used as the basis for policy prescription, however, as distinct from merely being used to provide an accurate description of what goes on in Virginia, England, and (to an extent) even in New York, then it is important to draw out the full implications. For what we are discussing here is not simply the interaction between the regulators and the regulated. We are also arguing that the quality of life in nursing homes is influenced as much by the social environment as by the tutelage of the regulatory agency, and that the trick in successful control of standards may lie as much in getting this whole relationship right—as in improved regulatory strategies—in developing, as it were, an ecological approach to regulation. So, for example, if instability is one of the problems of nursing homes, if regulatory staff cannot hope to know what is happening on a day-to-day basis, then the appropriate solution may be to find ways of increasing the visibility of what goes on in nursing homes by exposing their activities to more eyes for more of the time. This indeed is already more common practice in the United States than in England and is endorsed in the Committee on Nursing Home Regulation recommendations (Institute of Medicine 1986, chapter 6) for promoting consumer involvement in, and generating more information about, the activities of nursing homes; interestingly, however, this strategy is dealt with in one chapter while three chapters are devoted to proposals for improving the technology of regulation.

The logic of pursuing the full implications of the social-interaction model, of adopting what we have called an ecological strategy, suggests asking a series of even wider questions. For instance, we have stressed the inherent problem posed by working conditions in institutions, the sheer awfulness at times of looking after demented or dying elderly, and the consequent difficulties of attracting and keeping appropriate staff. There are a variety of possible responses. One may be, as in Virginia, to insist on training for unskilled staff; alternatively, reimbursement schedules could be changed in order to enhance pay and status. But yet another option could be to look at the balance between a given community and its nursing homes, to ask how many beds can actually be adequately staffed given the nature of the local labor market. Similarly, it might be sensible to ask what institutional size, combined with what kind of institutional layout, is most compatible with providing good quality care. The questions cannot, of course, be divorced from the issue of how good quality care is defined. In England the objective is largely, as we have seen, to create a homelike atmosphere, an aim also echoed in Virginia; in turn, this has created a consensus among English regulators that it is difficult to provide an adequate quality of life in institutions with more than 30 to 40 beds. If the objective is to provide active interventionist care, then this will inevitably mean bigger institutions; however, it still raises the question of just how big these institutions can become before quality of life suffers. Again, it may be worth exploring the issue of what the appropriate scale of regulatory activity should be. Just as it is possible to have agencies which are too small to develop regulatory expertise (as in many English DHAs), so there may be a point where large agencies become dysfunctional. Need regulation necessarily be a state function if this means, as in New York, the creation of a large, somewhat introspective, bureaucracy in order to deal with an enormous industry? If a social-interaction model of regulation like Virginia's or England's is reinforced by strong community and professional networks, if control is to be exercised through the visibility of nursing homes to the local population, then this obviously cannot be reproduced in a state which has to regulate twice as many beds as the other two put together. But it could be reproduced if regulation were devolved to lower and smaller tiers of government, although obviously there is a balance to be drawn between regulatory agencies which are overbureaucratic because overlarge and those which are overindulgent because they are not strong enough to resist local pressures.

Adopting the social-interaction model, and an ecological approach to regulation, also implies adopting a pluralist stance. The model suggests that the design of regulatory systems should match the social, political, and economic circumstances of their environment. What is appropriate in Virginia will not necessarily be appropriate in New York; what is appropriate in up-state New York will not necessarily be appropriate in the Bronx and Brooklyn. So divergences from the national norm, the wide spread in practices revealed by just about every survey of regulatory enforcement in the United States, need not necessarily be a sign of original sin, of deviations from some golden norm of good practice. Instead, the somewhat different way in which federal policies have been adapted in the implementation process can be seen as a learning process (Majone and Wildavsky 1978), in which the national framework is adapted to local circumstances. Conversely, this interpretation, if accepted, would suggest that the drive toward greater conformity in regulatory practices between states, the demand for ever tighter federal standards and more precise federal instruments of assessment, may be something of a search for technologist's gold.

To make this point is to bring the argument to our last option, which is to acknowledge that a working model of regulation will inevitably have to have a number of different dimensions. An effective system—that is, one which protects the individual patient as well as bringing the nursing home into line—must combine techniques *and* social interaction, relations with the community *and* the ecology of the nursing home industry. For if the weakness of the pure technological model is that it cannot be implemented in practice, the weakness of the pure social-interaction model is that it can all too easily slide into relativism. Is adaptation to the local environment to be the only test of the effectiveness of a regulatory system? What differences in standards and enforcement procedures between states are tolerable? If a mechanical legalism is the occupational disease of a technological approach to regulation, sloppy subjectivism is the danger inherent in the social-interaction model; so, for example, in England there is a clear case for the development of techniques of measurement and the codification of some standards in order to discipline the judgment of surveyors (Day and Klein 1987a). Our analysis does not, therefore, dismiss the need for improving the techniques of regulation. Our argument, rather, is that these should be used as tools in the complex process of regulation, formal and informal. Techniques, such as outcome measures, may discipline subjective judgments, just as they feed into a wider social dialogue. But they cannot be a substitute for either; regulators going down that narrow path are likely to find themselves between a rock and a hard place. Nursing homes are society's means for putting the cloak of institutional invisibility around some of its most intractable and nasty problems, and if we treat them solely as a technical issue instead of arguing about them, we will create a more worrying situation than any yet uncovered.

References

Abel-Smith, B. 1964. *The Hospitals in England and Wales, 1800–1948.* Cambridge: Harvard University Press.

Ashford, D.E. 1978. *Comparing Public Policies.* Beverly Hills: Sage.

Audit Commission. 1986. *Making a Reality of Community Care.* London: Her Majesty's Stationery Office.

Axelrod, D., and R.D. Sweeney. 1984. *Report to the Governor and the Legislature on the New Surveillance Process for New York State Residential Health Care Facilities.* Albany: New York State Department of Health.

Bardach, E., and R.A. Kagan. 1982. *Going by the Book.* Philadelphia: Temple University Press.

Bartlett, H., and L. Challis. 1985. Private Nursing Homes for the Elderly: A Survey Conducted in the South of England. Bath:

Centre for the Analysis of Social Policy, University of Bath. (Mimeo.)

Bennett, J. 1986. Private Nursing Homes: Contributions to Long-stay Care of the Elderly in Brighton Health District. *British Medical Journal* 293:867–70.

Butler, P.A. 1979. Assuring the Quality of Care and Life in Nursing Homes: The Dilemma of Enforcement. *North Carolina Law Review* 57 (6):1317–82.

Challis, D.J. 1981. The Measurement of Outcome in Social Care of the Elderly. *Journal of Social Policy* 10 (2):179–208.

Clough, R. 1987. *Independent Review of Residential Care for the Elderly within the London Borough of Camden.* London: Borough of Camden.

Day, P., and R. Klein. 1985. Monitoring Standards in the Independent Sector of Health Care. *British Medical Journal* 290:1020–22.

―――. 1987a. Quality of Institutional Care and the Elderly: Policy Issues and Options. *British Medical Journal* 294:384–87.

―――. 1987b. Residential Care for the Elderly: A Billion-pound Experiment in Policy-making. *Public Money* 6 (4):19–24.

Day, P., and D. Larder. 1986. *Nursing Manpower in Private and Voluntary Nursing Homes for the Elderly.* Social Policy Paper no. 8. Bath: Centre for the Analysis of Social Policy.

Department of Health and Social Security. 1981. *Registration and Inspection of Private Nursing Homes and Mental Nursing Homes.* Circular no. HC (81) 8. London.

―――. 1985. *Review of the Costs Incurred by Health Authorities in the Registration and Inspection of Private Nursing Homes and Hospitals.* Report no. 10/85 of the NHS Management Service. London.

Donabedian, A. 1966. Evaluating the Quality of Medical Care. *Milbank Memorial Fund Quarterly* 44:166–206.

Fox, D.M. 1986. *Health Policies, Health Politics.* Princeton: Princeton University Press.

Harrington, C., R.J. Newcomer, C.L. Estes, and Associates. 1985. *Long-term Care of the Elderly.* Beverly Hills: Sage.

Hawes, C. 1983. Quality Assurance in Long-term Care. A Briefing Paper for the National Academy of Sciences Institute of Medicine Committee on Nursing Home Regulation, Washington. (Mimeo.)

Hawkins, K. 1984. *Environment and Enforcement.* Oxford: Clarendon Press.

Hawkins, K., and J.M. Thomas. 1984. *Enforcing Regulation.* Boston: Kluwer-Nijhoff.

Health Advisory Service. 1986. *Report on Services for Elderly People Provided by the Brighton Health Authority and the Social Services Department of East Sussex County Council.* Sutton, Surrey.

House of Commons. 1926. *Report from the Select Committee on Nursing Homes (Registration)*. HC 103. London: Her Majesty's Stationery Office.

Institute of Medicine. 1986. *Report of a Study by the Committee on Nursing Home Regulation*. Washington: National Academy Press.

Kagan, R.A., and J.T. Scholz. 1984. The Criminology of the Corporation and Regulatory Enforcement Strategies. In *Enforcing Regulation*, ed. K. Hawkins and J.M. Thomas, 67–95. Boston: Kluwer-Nijhoff.

Kelman, S. 1984. Enforcement of Occupational Safety and Health Regulations: A Comparison of Swedish and American Practices. In *Enforcing Regulation*, ed. K. Hawkins and J.M. Thomas, 97–119. Boston: Kluwer-Nijhoff.

King, A. 1973. Ideas, Institutions and the Policies of Governments: A Comparative Analysis. *British Journal of Political Science* 3 (3):291–313.

Klein, R. 1979. Ideology, Class and the National Health Service. *Journal of Health Politics, Policy and Law* 4 (3):464–90.

Kurowski, B.D., and P.W. Shaughnessy. 1985. The Measurement and Assurance of Quality. In *Long-term Care*, ed. R.J. Vogel and C.H. Palmer, 103–33. Aspen: Aspens Systems Corporation.

Larder, D., P. Day, and R. Klein. 1986. *Institutional Care for the Elderly: The Geographical Distribution of the Public/Private Mix in England*. Social Policy Paper no. 10. Bath: Centre for the Analysis of Social Policy.

Lindblom, C.E., and D.K. Cohen. 1979. *Usable Knowledge*. New Haven: Yale University Press.

Lipsky, M. 1980. *Street Level Bureaucracy*. New York: Russell Sage Foundation.

Majone, G., and A. Wildavsky. 1978. Implementation as Evaluation. In *Policy Studies Review Annual* 2:113–27. Beverly Hills: Sage.

Majone, G. 1982. Prevention and Health Standards: American, Soviet and European Models. *Journal of Health Politics, Policy and Law* 7 (3):629–48.

Marmor, T.E. 1983. *Political Analysis and American Medical Care*. Cambridge: Cambridge University Press.

Martin, J.P. 1984. *Hospitals in Trouble*. Oxford: Basil Blackwell.

McLachlan, G., and A. Maynard. 1982. *The Public/Private Mix for Health*. London: Nuffield Provincial Hospitals Trust.

Moran, M. 1986. Theories of Regulation and Changes in Regulation: The Case of Financial Markets. *Political Studies* 34 (2):185–202.

National Association of Health Authorities. 1985. *Registration and Inspection of Nursing Homes: A Handbook for Health Authorities*. Birmingham.

National Audit Office. 1985. *National Health Service: Control of Nursing Manpower*. London: Her Majesty's Stationery Office.

New York. 1983. *Official Compilation of Codes, Rules and Regulations. Title 10: Health. Vol. C*. Albany: Department of State.

New York Office of Health Systems Management. 1982. Facility Surveillance Group: PMR/IPR Manual. BLTCS-03. Albany. (Mimeo.)

Oxfordshire District Health Authority. 1985. *Registration and Conduct of Nursing Homes: Guidelines*. Oxford.

Patterson, S.C. 1968. The Political Cultures of the American States. *Journal of Politics* 30 (1):187–210.

Reiss, A.J. 1984. Selecting Strategies of Social Control over Organisational Life. In *Enforcing Regulation,* ed. K. Hawkins and J.M. Thomas, 23–35. Boston: Kluwer-Nijhoff.

Ruchlin, H.S. 1979. An Analysis of Regulatory Issues and Options in Long-term Care. In *Reform and Regulation in Long-term Care,* ed. V. Laporte and J. Rubin, 81–125. New York: Praeger.

Social Services Inspectorate. 1985a. *Inspection of Local Authority Care for Elderly Mentally Disordered People*. London: Department of Health and Social Security.

———. 1985b. *Inspection of Residential Care for Elderly People and for Children in the London Borough of Southwark*. London: Department of Health and Social Security.

Southport District Health Authority. 1985. *Notes of Guidance on the Registration and the Conduct of Nursing Homes*. Southport.

Statutory Instruments. 1984. *The Nursing Homes and Mental Nursing Homes Regulations*. Department of Health and Social Security SI no. 1578. London: Her Majesty's Stationery Office.

Torbay District Health Authority. 1985. *Strategic Development Study into Services for the Elderly*. Interim report. Torquay: Torbay Health Authority.

U.S. Congress. 1984. *Long-term Care in Western Europe and Canada: Implications for the United States*. An information paper prepared for use by the Special Committee on Aging, United States Senate, 98th Congress, 2nd Sess., S Prt 98–211 34–708. Washington.

———. 1986. Nursing Home Care: The Unfinished Agenda. Washington.

Virginia. 1980. *Rules and Regulations for the Licensure of Nursing Homes in Virginia*. Richmond: Department of Health.

———. 1982. *Nursing Home Manual*. Richmond: Virginia Department of Health.

———. 1985. *Virginia Medical Assistance Program Long-term Care In-*

formation and Monitoring System. Richmond: Department of Medical Assistance Services. (Mimeo.)

Vladeck, B.C. 1980. *Unloving Care: The Nursing Home Tragedy.* New York: Basic Books.

Vogel, D. 1983. Co-operative Regulation: Environmental Protection in Great Britain. *Public Interest* 72:88–106.

Waldman, S. 1985. A Legislative History of Nursing Home Care. In *Long-term Care: Perspective from Research and Demonstrations,* ed. R.J. Vogel and C.H. Palmer. Aspen: Aspen Systems Corporation.

Wilson, G.K. 1984. Social Regulation and Explanations of Regulatory Failure. *Political Studies* 32 (2):203–26.

Wilson, J.Q. 1980. ed. *The Politics of Regulation.* New York: Basic Books.

Woodruffe, C., and P. Townsend. 1961. *Nursing Homes in England and Wales: A Study of Public Responsibility.* London: National Corporation for the Care of Old People.

Acknowledgments: The research on which this article is based was supported by grants from the Nuffield Provincial Hospitals Trust and the Milbank Memorial Fund. The research in the United States was made possible only by the generosity of members of Virginia's Deparments of Health, Medical Assistance Services, and for the Aging and New York's Office of Health Systems Management in giving their time to the authors. A particular debt of gratitude is also owed to Judith Miller Jones and David Tilson for opening doors, both intellectual and other, and to Ralph Hall, Bill Scanlon, and Jim Tallon, among the many academics, legislators, regulators, and nursing home managers who provided insight and information. The article has also been greatly improved by comments on the first draft by Judy Feder, Ted Marmor, Carl Schramm, and, above all, Dan Fox.

Address correspondence to: Prof. Rudolf Klein, School of Humanities and Social Sciences, University of Bath, Claverton Down, Bath BA2 7AY, England.

Educational Policy: Perspectives on Reform

There are perhaps few areas where the rhetoric of the counterreform movement of the Reagan administration was more evident than in the area of education. Throughout the 1980s, the president and other senior officials hammered constantly about the problems of American education and the need for a "return to basics." In the last years of the decade, there was no one more vocal or strident in his comments on the "softness" and "mediocrity" of American education than the secretary of education, William Bennett. Whether he was decrying the changes in the core curriculum for undergraduates at Stanford University, the role of teacher unions in what he thought to be the hindering of new merit-pay plans, or in his blasting of many current programs targeted specifically to various minority groups, specifically bilingual education, school desegregation, and affirmative action, he let it be known what he thought of the reform efforts of earlier years. Secretary Bennett was the point man for an administration offensive to change the perspectives on American thinking about education as well as redefining the federal role in education.

The issue now is one of what impacts the counterreform period has had on American education. The question is whether these changes will "stick" or whether with a move away from such a vigorous challenge to the system, some of the apparent change will rapidly disappear. These questions are addressed by all four of the authors in this section. One of the interesting outcomes of reading these papers is that there is no consensus on just what exactly it is that the Reagan administration actually accomplished. Some would suggest the changes were substantive and institutional, others see the changes as more in rhetoric, while still others are not convinced that any real change occurred at all. But the criteria for such an assessment are what count. If the criterion is one of the continued existence of federal programs, the outcomes seem to be generally business as usual. If the criterion is one of "returning power to the states," then there has definitely been some change. And if, instead, one uses the criterion of redefining the intent of education, then there has been some change as well. Each of these criteria is addressed by one or more of the authors to follow.

Regardless of the degree of change (or not) in the substantive aspects of American education, there is one area where those authors who speak to the matter do agree—there has been a significant change in the language used for discourse about education. Terms like "equity," "access," and "commitment to public education" have given way to discourse over "excellence," "achievement," "parental choice," "prayer in school," and "why can't our system do what the Japanese educational system can do?" Again, the question is whether this shift in the nature of the dialogue may portend a more profound change—one that no longer looks at the schools as vehicles of change for liberal social agendas, e.g., integration, pluralism, cultural diversity and pride, or creating institutional access for low-income and minority groups. At this time, it is simply too soon to tell what staying power this alternative perspective—one that emphatically rejects the previous social agenda—will have during the 1990s.

The first paper in this section, by David Clark and Terry Astuto, does an outstanding job of tracing the events of the counterreform period during the Reagan administration. Their concern is precisely with what has been discussed above—what changes have, in fact, occurred specifically at the federal level. They detail, on a year-by-year basis, the various initiatives and proposals of the administration to get its agenda accepted and implemented. What characterizes the efforts of the administration over the eight years was a consistency of purpose that did not waiver. The ideological perspective that came with all those who assumed power on January 21, 1981 (or shortly thereafter), did not change, even as the individual actors on the stage changed. Clark and Astuto frame the Reagan administration agenda for the federal role in education as the "three D's," disestablishment, diminution, and devolution. In all three, they believe there has been significant success. They conclude by noting, "these changes are likely to continue beyond the Reagan years."

The second of the papers, by Michael Cohen of the National Governors' Association, essentially takes over where the first paper ends. Cohen uses the counterreform efforts of the 1980s as the backdrop for asking what the implications are for restructuring the educational system in the 1990s. His concern is with state and local policy agendas. He views continued educational reform as an imperative, given what he terms "three inescapable conclusions." His conclusions involve (1) the economic needs for an educated work force; (2) the need to reach all students; and (3) the massive public investment in education and the need for its careful management. Predicated on these three givens, Cohen then proceeds to develop his analysis for both state and local governmental levels as to the challenges they face in public education and how these might be met in the decade of the 1990s. Working from the level of the school building through the school district to the state level, the author specifies for each a set of needed changes that he argues will require a fundamental restructuring of the educational system.

Cohen believes that the challenges are such that simply "tinkering" with the current system will not suffice. Underlying his proposals is the basic belief that decisions and responsibilities should be pushed as far down into the system as possible. Those closest to the students should have considerably more say in the methods of instruction, content, and structure of the school. If it is at the school-building level where the primary responsibility for education rests, then there too is where the authority and accountability should also rest.

With the winds of the Reagan administration at their backs, many supporters of private and parochial education thought federal support was soon to be. After all, Ronald Reagan had run for president stressing the need for support of private and parochial schools, supporting parent choice through the creation of voucher programs, and generally to let the market place of educational opportunities work its will to produce the options most parents would want. Tuition tax credit plans were widely discussed and proposals were formulated. Even the National Governors' Association had come out in support of increased choice among public alternatives. But a 1984 Supreme Court decision, *Aguilar* v. *Felton,* put a considerable damper on these hopes. This decision ruled that public school personnel could no longer go onto the premises of private or parochial schools to offer remedial services. Based on the criteria of unacceptable government entanglement in religion, the ruling had considerable fallout on the relations between the public and private sectors. No longer could those in parochial education expect the same level of federal help in the education of disadvantaged children. Bruce Cooper traces the outcomes of the decision and assesses the options available to those who would want federal support for parochial education. It is an unresolved policy issue— one the Reagan administration could not sort out, in spite of the level of interest and ideological commitment to do so.

In the attack on the educational system, one sector that has come in for particularly scathing reviews is teacher education. Countless reports, task forces, and policy papers have recommended that the present system be overhauled. Whether it be the weaknesses in the curriculum, the lack of an emphasis on strong substantive preparation in one field, the lack of enough "real-world" experience to help prepare the new teachers for what they will face, or the unwillingness of schools of education to certify any students who have not been through their entire prescribed curriculum, the general consensus is that United States teacher education programs are substandard and unequal to the tasks at hand. Willis Hawley explores one of the policy recommendations that has frequently emerged in the debate on what to do. Often the recommendation has been given that the teacher education program be lengthened from four years to five. This recommendation has powerful supporters and is seriously being considered in a number of states.

Hawley argues that careful assessment needs to be given to this proposal, for it may produce exactly the opposite of what is intended. Instead of more and stronger candidates who are better trained, the end result may well be, Hawley argues, weaker candidates, fewer in number and no better trained than at present. Hawley is particularly blunt on this last point. He states, "Moreover, there is absolutely no evidence that extended preparation programs make teachers more effective as they enter the profession." Here again is a potential instance of political pressure moving policies along faster than does the conceptual development of that same policy. The five-year teacher preparation programs may be but another example of "ready, fire, aim."

28

An Assessment of Changes in Federal Educational Policy during the Reagan Administration

David L. Clark and Terry A. Astuto

Introduction

Have the actions and achievements of the Reagan administration produced a significant, enduring change in federal educational policy? The
answer to this question depends upon the criterion used to frame the
response. Jack Jennings (1985), long-time counsel for education for the
Committee on Education and Labor, House of Representatives, noted
little change:

> The smoke of debate [over the federal role in education] should not obscure the
> reality that the prospects for the survival of federally funded education programs
> are greater today than at any time since Reagan took office. The President
> forcefully challenged the very existence of these programs during his first term.
> But he failed to achieve his goal. In the process of opposing the President's
> onslaught, Carl Perkins was able to forge a new bipartisan consensus in Con-
> gress on the importance of these programs in the total effort to improve U.S.
> education [p. 567].

Denis Doyle and Terry Hartle (1985) maintained a view similar to
Jennings, arguing:

This is an updated and revised version of a chapter, "Federal Education Policy in the United
States: The Conservative Agenda and Accomplishments," in William L. Boyd and Don Smart,
eds., *Educational Policy in Australia and America: Comparative Perspectives* (Philadelphia:
Falmer Press, 1987). Used by permission of Falmer Press.

What the administration achieved was accomplished in the first six months of the term. . . . Many of its most important goals—tax credits, school prayer, regulatory reform, abolishing the department—are increasingly unlikely. By any score card it has lost more battles than it has won. . . . In basic outline the federal role in education looks very much as it did under Presidents Nixon, Ford, and Carter [pp. 148–49].

Eileen Gardner (1984), in *Mandate for Leadership II: Continuing the Conservative Revolution,* assigned mixed grades to the administration's first-term performance. While lamenting losses in Congress over tuition tax credits, vouchers, school prayer, and the reform of student financial aid, Gardner cited the beginning of a successful revolution, i.e.:

The Commission on Excellence in Education rallied the nation which has begun the long, arduous journey back to world preeminence in education. Thanks to the Commission, far reaching reform has been generated without additional federal money or mandates. The response to the report on excellence and the Chapter 2 Block Grant is prophetic: Americans are proving themselves capable and willing to take on the responsibility for educating their children through state and local initiatives—initiatives that were stymied by the growing federal control [p. 54].

Laurence Iannaccone (1985) viewed the changes as of both significance and duration:

Whatever the political outcome of the 1986 midterm and 1988 national elections may be, President Reagan and Secretary Bell have accomplished their goals for changing the locus of the educational policy making process, its value-driven policy premises and redefining the mission of the schools. These were 1) to return educational policy making to the states and local districts ("where it belongs" in the words of Secretary Bell, April, 1981); 2) to establish this philosophy of government for a generation and 3) to emphasize basic skills and academic achievement as the central mission of the public schools [p. 5].

However accurate or valid these assessments may be judged to be, they employed different criteria for change. Jennings used the continued existence of federal programs in education as the criterion. Doyle and Hartle addressed the question at a more global level; the basic outline of the federal educational role was the criterion. Gardner used a set of specific policy preferences in education espoused by political conservatives, e.g., school prayer, tuition tax credits, increased standards. Iannaccone judged success against what he argued was the most important overarching goal of President Reagan's domestic policy, i.e., "to transfer many domestic programs to the states" (1985, p. 4), and a specific educational goal, i.e., a focus on basics and academic achievement. The thesis we shall argue differs markedly from the interpretation of Jennings and of Doyle and Hartle; extends beyond the concerns covered by Gardner; and is generally consistent with the interpretation of Iannaccone.

The thesis of this paper is twofold: (1) A major redirection of federal educational policy has occurred during the Reagan administration. The essence of that policy has been altered in basic ways. If there is a new bipartisan consensus, it is a consensus in support of a different federal role in education. (2) The scope of the redirection will be broadened and many of the changes will become institutionalized during a new era of federal educational policy. The change that has occurred had its roots in years preceding the Reagan administration, although its lifeblood was furnished by that administration, and will continue to dominate educational policy development for decades.

So that the reader can fairly assess our thesis and the evidence we present in support of its validity, we should make our criteria clear. Firstly, our criteria encompass the substantive content of the policy preferences in education being discussed and acted upon at federal, state, and local levels. These substantive criteria bridge both what education should be about, e.g., concentration on basics and character education, and how education should be conducted, e.g., parental control and choice as well as individual and institutional competition. Secondly, our criteria include procedural issues that deal with the role of governmental levels in policy development and administration, e.g., disestablishment of the Department of Education, devolution, and deregulation.

Before turning to the changes in direction in educational policy during the two terms of the Reagan administration, we shall offer a cursory retrospective (ca. 1980–1981) of where the change began. Our argument is that some of the changes have been profound and dramatic. Since it is often easy to adjust over time to even dramatic changes, our cause is served by reminding the reader of the starting point.

In 1980, under the heading "The Teachers' Coup," the *New Republic* commented:

> Veteran power brokers have been pushed aside by a relative newcomer to the hurly-burly of capital politics—the National Education Association. In the last four years the NEA has helped elect a President, single-handedly forced a Department of Education down Congress' throat, and lobbied successfully for dramatic increases in federal spending on education [Chapman, 1980, p. 9].

Teacher training institutions were afraid that the new teacher centers (referred to routinely as NEA's proprietary legislation) would usurp the teacher education function of the university.

The new Department of Education (ED), under the leadership of Shirley Hufstedler, was administering 150-plus categorical programs with a staff of over 6,000 employees, and growing. Almost every one of those programs had its own staff, its own legislative authority, its own budget, its own advisory committee and consultants, as well as regulations, a system of evaluation, special constituencies of parents, businesses, and educators, and protective legislative authors and sponsors in Congress. ED was big business before the department ever hit the ground and there was no reason to suspect that it would not become bigger.

Anyone involved with ED at all remembers the Teacher Corps, the State Capacity Bulding Program, the National Diffusion Network, the Joint Dissemination Review panel. ED was out where the teachers were, involved vigorously in the dissemination and diffusion of new ideas.

The department focused on equity for the handicapped, for ethnic minority groups, for women. Any proposal submitted to ED for research, training, or technical assistance had to reflect equity concerns in both the content and the staffing of the project. Perhaps that is an appropriate way to conclude this retrospective, i.e., by identifying the dominant lexicon of terms that controlled the discussion and emphases of the era: (1) equity; (2) needs and access; (3) social and welfare concerns; (4) the common school; (5) regulations, enforcement, and monitoring; (6) federal initiatives and interventions; (7) diffusion of innovations.

These are little-used terms in Washington today and the new lexicon is especially interesting because an essentially conflictual set of terms has emerged that fits the new educational policy discussions in Washington, i.e.: (1a) excellence, standards of performance, individual competition; (2a) ability, selectivity, minimum entrance standards; (3a) economic and productivity concerns; (4a) parental choice, institutional competition; (5a) local initiative, deregulation, limited enforcement; (6a) state and local interests and initiatives; (7a) exhortation, information-sharing.

Finally, to place the change in perspective, substitute President Reagan's comments on education in his 1984 or 1988 State of the Union address for President Carter's comments in his State of the Union address in 1980. The educational community would have imagined it had been struck by a thunderbolt. In fact, President Reagan's comments in 1984 were barely newsworthy when he said:

> But we must do more to restore discipline to the schools; and we must encourage the teaching of new basics, reward teachers of merit, enforce standards, and put our parents back in charge. I will continue to press for tuition tax credits to expand opportunities for families, and to soften the double payment for those paying public school taxes and private school tuition. Our proposal would target assistance to low and middle income families. Just as more incentives are

needed within our schools, greater competition is needed among our schools. Without standards and competition there can be no champions, no records broken, no excellence—in education or any other walk of life. And while I'm on the subject—each day your members observe a 200 year old tradition meant to signify America is one nation under God. I must ask: If you can begin your day with a member of the clergy standing right here to lead you in prayer, then why can't freedom to acknowledge God be enjoyed again by children in every school room across this land [State of the Union, 1984, p. 91].

Or, recall Reagan's remarks in 1988, which were obviously a retrospective, congratulating his own administration on holding the line on expenses, raising test scores, focusing on the basics, increasing student work time, diffusing merit pay plans, reducing high school electives and, most important of all, returning control of schools to the states, to wit:

And speaking of the family, let's turn to a matter on the mind of every American parent tonight—education. We all know the sorry story of the '60s and '70s— soaring spending, plummeting test scores—and that hopeful trend of the '80s when we replaced an obsession with dollars with a commitment to quality, and test scores started back up. There is a lesson here that we all should write on the blackboard a hundred times—in a child's education, money can never take the place of basics like discipline, hard work and, yes, homework. As a nation we do, of course, spend heavily on education—more than we spend on defense—yet across our country, governors like New Jersey's Tom Kean are giving classroom demonstrations that how we spend is as important as how much we spend. Opening up the teaching profession to all qualified candidates; merit pay, so that good teachers get A's as well as apples and strong curriculum, as Secretary Bennett has proposed for high schools—these imaginative reforms are making common sense the most popular new kid in America's schools. How can we help? Well, we can talk about and push for these reforms. But the most important thing we can do is to reaffirm that control of our schools belongs to the states, local communities and, most of all, to the parents and teachers [State of the Union, 1988].

Contrast these statements with the lexicon of federal educational policy terms numbered 1–7 above. Something big has happened. A major change has taken place. The significance of the change remains to be debated in later sections of this chapter.

Accomplishments of the Reagan Administration in Federal Educational Policy: The First Term

Federal policy changes are difficult to portray. On the one hand, specific policy actions or speeches create a sense of crisis that too much is happening too quickly. Conversely, general policy shifts move at such a glacial pace that the movement is barely noticeable. However, a consistent set of policy actions and assertions provides evidence of the administration's accomplishments in redirecting federal educational policy. As depicted in table 28.1, the policy actions of the first term focused primarily on the restructuring of the federal role in education.

1981—Budgetary Reductions

In 1981 the educational policy of the Reagan administration was dominated by procedural considerations. Washington insiders referred to the five Ds, i.e., disestablishment (elimination of the Department of Education), deregulation, decentralization, deemphasis (reduction of the position of education as a priority on the federal agenda), and most important, diminution (reduction of the federal budget in education). Although the administration's education agenda was precise, it lacked a substantive dimension. The components were (1) derivative from broader social policy preferences, e.g., reduce the social program budget, eliminate regulations, foster the new federalism, and (2) reflective of structural concerns about the federal role in education, e.g., stop throwing money at the problems of education and get the feds off the backs of state and local policymakers who are better able to deal with educational problems.

The early achievements of the administration reflected those procedural emphases. Educationists were jolted by the first significant reductions in the federal education budget in a quarter century. There was, in fact, not even an interesting debate about the cuts. The administration insisted that reductions in the overall federal budget were imperative, the cuts had to come from the social programs portion of the budget, and education was required to take its share. That meant cutting whenever and wherever it was possible. Before the dust settled, the cumulative reductions in the fiscal year (FY) '81 and FY '82 budgets had amounted to roughly 20 percent.

The federal education budget turned out to be a more vulnerable target than its defenders had anticipated. Educationists discovered anew that the budget issue facing them was not simply the size of next year's increase. The 1981 budgetary losses created a mindset that has persisted, i.e., the expectation for less. In the intervening years, educationists have accepted the notion that a program that does not lose money from year to year has been successful in defending its position. If diminution is a policy preference, that lesson is a necessary first step.

The big news in 1981 seemed to be only the budget. As it turned out that was not quite the case. Secretary Bell also established the National Commission on Excellence in Education, and its chairperson, David P. Gardner, signaled a central theme that would persist and reappear two

TABLE 28.1
Changes in Federal Educational Policy: The First Term

Year	Hallmark(s)	Actions	Effects
1981	Rescissions Reductions	Cumulative education budget cuts of over 20 percent	Establishing the expectations for less (diminution)
1982	Block grant Deregulation	Implementation of Education Consolidation and Improvement Act Revocation of regulations Constraint on enforcement of regulations	Dismantling the categorical programs (disestablishment, decentralization) Constraining ED from the design of educational interventions (disestablishment, decentralization) Moving accountability to the state level (deregulation, decentralization)
1983	Report of the National Commission on Excellence	Publication of *A Nation at Risk* Support for the design of career ladders for teachers and other forms of merit pay Encouragement of upward adjustment of standards National Forum on Education	Moving from a focus on equity to excellence Focusing improvement strategies on adjusting standards (decentralization) Reducing the role of the educationist in school improvement Increasing educational policy activity at the state level (decentralization)
1984	Awards and recognition	Secondary School Recognition Program Academic Fitness Awards Excellent Private Schools Program National Distinguished Principals Program	Developing consensus on direction of reform Highlighting reform already underway (disestablishment, decentralization) Recognizing established performance

years later when he commented, "the absence of [such] a standard [of achievement] tends to translate into a situation where there's less pressure [to achieve] and lowered expectations on the part of students to take more difficult courses or a wider range of them" (Ingalls, 1981, p. 11).

The administration did not assert publicly an agenda of specific substantive goals in 1981, but the comments made in interviews by representatives of the administration were clear—and set the stage for many of the more specific policy preferences of later years, to wit:

• Public education is failing, mediocre at best, wholly ineffective at worst.
• The federal presence in education has made a bad situation worse. Federal intervention has removed the action from the state and local levels where the problems must be solved.
• Federal regulations are an unnecessary burden on state and local educational officials. They are contributing to the mediocrity of the field.
• Federal involvement in education has been misdirected, i.e., emphasizing social and welfare concerns rather than educational performance.

1982—The Block Grant

The key event of 1982 was implementation of the Education Consolidation and Improvement Act (E.C.I.A.)—a thrust toward decentralization. The education block grant delivered on the statement in the 1980 Republican Platform text calling for replacement of the "crazy quilt of wasteful programs with a system of block grants that will restore decision making to local officials responsible to voters and parents" (p. 2034). The block grant was less than the administration's aspirations. Vocational education and special education escaped inclusion in the block. But a vital change occurred. The flow toward increased federal involvement in educational policy was reversed. The addition of new categorical programs was made significantly more difficult; the likelihood that existing programs would be added to the block grant was made more likely. From 1958 to 1982 the conservatives were fighting a vigorous but losing battle, categorical proposal by categorical proposal, to thwart the extension of federal involvement in education. Now the liberals found themselves pressed to save existing categorical initiatives with little chance of adding new ones. The significance of the block grant was in reversing this trend, which simultaneously removed ED from the business of inventing and sponsoring legislation supporting federal-level interventions in education. The block grant can be viewed as an enabling step toward the president's concept of the new federalism as it might be applied to education.

Less dramatic, but complementary to the block grant, was the effort to disentangle the federal government from the web of regulatory require-ments attached to the categorical programs. The disentanglement was accomplished through revocation and nonenforcement. In the former category, Secretary Bell announced the revocation of thirty sets of rules associated with nineteen of the categorical programs that had been in-cluded in the block grant. In the latter, enforcement was constrained, for example, by preventing the department's Office of Civil Rights from using Title VI to require bilingual instruction in the public schools.

Halfway through the first Reagan administration an unexpected realiza-tion dawned on the educationist community. The conventional wisdom held by previous administrations toward education had operated on the assumption that the education lobby, individually and collectively, was a force with which the executive branch needed to be concerned. But this administration had almost entirely ignored that lobby. With the exception of Secretary Bell, leaders in ED were noneducationists—appointed with-out reference to or consultation with the educational community. The administration went out of its way to snub the largest lobby of all, the National Education Association. Consultation with the education commu-nity about planned changes in education was replaced by press confer-ences to announce the changes. And the consequences to the administra-tion of this unorthodox behavior appeared to be minimal. In fact, the educationist lobby had begun to accommodate to the new rules of the game and had settled in for a rear-guard action protecting critical elements of the federal role in education. Whatever else one could say about the beginning of the Reagan administration and however successful individual lobbies and lobbyists had been in protecting their interests, the initiative lay in the hands of an administration that wanted to chart a new course in federal educational policy.

1983—The Reform Reports

The obvious reason for the appearance of the plenitude of reform reports on education in 1983 and 1984 is that there was a groundswell of concern about education two to three years earlier. A more realistic explanation is that the reports were the fallout from a period of uncertainty about where education was headed at the national level. The reversal of the normal course of events that seemed likely from President Reagan's early state-ments about education encouraged the establishment of commissions, committees, task forces, and teams to examine where the field was and where it was headed. Surely that is an appropriate explanation for the National Commission on Excellence in Education. The commission was one of the few steps the new secretary of education could take without conflicting directly with one or another of the administration's positions about deemphasizing, diminishing, and decentralizing the federal role in education.

There were a number of curious effects from the publication of *A Nation at Risk*. One of the original five Ds, i.e., deemphasis, suffered a setback. The president discovered that involvement in educational policy can be fun and rewarding. Most important from the administration's viewpoint, the involvement was possible without compromising seriously the criteria of diminution, decentralization, deregulation, or even disestablishment. The follow-up on the commission report was centered in the state capitals. No major new federal initiatives were required. Exhortation and suasion actually worked as the keystone to the federal role in the field. The report itself and the follow-through on the report had four effects that confirmed biases of the administration:

1. By title and content, the report switched the attention of educational reformers and policymakers from equity to excellence. The argument of the report was essentially that excellence begets true equity.
2. *A Nation at Risk* baldly omitted the educationist community from most of the reform recommendations. No one reading the report would have expected educationists to be the key actors in the reform movement.
3. The report suggested a school-improvement strategy based on modified standards and requirements. This contrasted sharply with the complex school-improvement efforts of ED built around such technical-assistance strategies as the National Diffusion Network or the Research and Development Exchange.
4. The locus of action for reform was switched from the national level to state and local levels. While recognizing a federal role in education, the recommendations focused on standards and requirements under the control of state and local policymakers.

1984—Awards and Recognition

The president had a relatively busy "education year" in 1984, although expectations for education policy in an election year are always modest. The year was kicked off in December 1983 with a National Forum on Education in Indianapolis. The forum was an activity of consensus-building to validate the Excellence Commission's report and to encourage the states to be about the business of educational reform. The primary activity of ED was to keep education visible through a variety of awards programs for teachers, principals, students, and schools—awards to celebrate the existence of excellent performance in education wherever it existed. The strategy worked well to defuse education as a campaign issue but, equally important, its effects on educational policy were to: (1) highlight reform moves already underway; (2) imply that the tactics in education employed by the administration to date were already bearing fruit; (3) encourage state policymakers to press ahead with such popular reform topics as career ladders for teachers, increased graduation requirements, competency tests for teachers, and lengthened school calendar years and school days.

Summary of the Reagan First Term

The policy actions that occurred during the first term defined the components of the "new federalism" in education and provided evidence of the administration's success in redirecting federal educational policy. Early cuts and continued cost containment in the education budget advanced diminution and established the expectation for less. Deregulation, through both elimination and nonenforcement of regulations, signaled the end of the era of close federal inspection of educational programs. The block grant fostered decentralization. Educational policy activity increased markedly in the states. Equally important, generating and sustaining interest in new federal categorical programs became virtually impossible.

The overarching procedural policy preferences were devolution and diminution. On the one hand, authority and responsibility for educational policy was transferred substantially from federal to state and local levels. Education senators and representatives were replaced by education governors. Concurrently, the economic aims of the administration were fostered, e.g., reducing expenditures, reallocating budgetary priorities.

In addition to these procedural educational policy preferences, the administration foreshadowed a set of substantive preferences. Improvement strategies following *A Nation at Risk* focused on adjusting standards and establishing conditions for competition among students, teachers, and schools through, for example, advocacy of merit pay and comparisons of student achievement. By tying into the predispositions of the American people about education and by emphasizing in the media the president's view of education, the administration convinced or agreed with a large segment of the populace that:

• the core problems of the schools are discipline, drugs, standards, and teachers;
• school improvement can be achieved by establishing and adhering to higher standards and requirements for admission to educational curricula, progress through the schools, and exit from the schools;

- problems of education cannot be solved at the federal level, and efforts to do so have failed;
- parents should control the choice of schools their children attend and should be involved in their children's education;
- localities should be in control of their own schools;
- moral values, prayer, and character education need to be returned to the schools;
- a cabinet-level department of education is not needed;
- the federal government should be less rather than more involved in education;
- schools would be better if they were not a public monopoly;
- achievement levels in public schools should be made public and compared across school systems, within and across states;
- teachers would be better teachers if they earned salary increases by merit;
- most students do not work hard enough in school;
- most students graduate from high school with insufficient preparation to earn a living or to go on to college;
- school curricula should concentrate on the basics, and include more "hard" subjects and fewer electives.

The most interesting feature of these opinions about education is not whether they were latent in the 1960s and 1970s or whether they have grown in the 1980s, but that they now fit the policy agenda being advocated by the president and the secretary of education. As one looks ahead at the possible policy changes in education, there is, at least currently, substantial support among the American people for the administration's policy preferences.

Accomplishments of the Reagan Administration in Federal Educational Policy: The Second Term

Actions to support the procedural policy preferences continued during President Reagan's second term. The president persisted in advocating elimination of the Department of Education. Budget reducations were proposed in the administration's budgets for FY '85, '86, '87, and '88. State and local responsibility for educational policy and program development was included routinely in the president's speeches, and active education governors were praised for their efforts, e.g., specific reference to Governor Kean in the 1988 State of the Union address. But the "new" activities of the second term focused on further clarification of the administration's substantive policy preferences and refinement of the policy mechanisms appropriate to the modified federal role, i.e., diffusion, exhortation, and encouragement.

1985—Secretary Bennett and the Three Cs

The key move by the administration in education in 1985 was the appointment of William Bennett as secretary of education. For the first time the president had a management team in place that was *(a)* committed to all aspects of the administration's platform in education, *(b)* free of commitment to any previous administration's positions and to the professional associations in education, and *(c)* able to articulate the administration's position to the media and to the public.

Secretary Bennett used exhortation and suasion to refine and direct the substantive focus of the second Reagan term through his advocacy of the Three Cs—content, choice, and character (see table 28.2). The Reagan administration had pushed content earlier under slightly different labels— concentration on basics and on the new basics, i.e., science, mathematics, and computer skills. State legislatures picked up the theme by requiring more high school graduation credits in science and mathematics, subjects where enrollment in advanced courses had declined. Half of the states established scholarship and forgivable-loan programs to encourage high school students to enter teaching; most of these programs concentrated on mathematics and science.

Bennett expanded the focus on content beyond the basics to a dialogue about what is to be taught. He criticized the lack of a coherent design in the curricula of many schools and offered the advice that schools should alter their programs to emphasize the "core studies [that] constitute the nucleus of our schools' common curricula," stressing mathematics, science, English, and history (Hertling, 1985a, p. 10). Beyond a focus on the basics, the secretary noted his intention to finance activities to upgrade textbooks and teaching materials and "the development of projects that would allow the public to identify essential knowledge—literary works or historical events that should be familiar to every child" (Hertling, 1985b, p. 10).

Finally, the administration emphasized the link between education and the economy. Discussions about vocational education were framed in terms of the direct link between education and employability. Similarly, the secretary's attacks on bilingual education argued the need to open up opportunities for employment and advanced education to bilingual students who need English proficiency.

The additions to the "new basics" agenda by Secretary Bennett raised the possibility that the administration might confront opposition that would challenge the general consensus supporting basics in education. Past efforts to upgrade textbooks and teaching materials have triggered ideological debates. A truly national debate over essential knowledge would

TABLE 28.2
Changes in Federal Educational Policy: The Second Term

Year	Hallmark(s)	Actions	Effects
1985	A new management team The Three Cs	Appointment of Bennett and Finn Additions to and enlargement of the substantive agenda: voucher bill, grants programs in character education and content improvement State-level legislation raising standards, emphasizing science and mathematics	Increasing the visibility and influence of the secretary as an advocate of the president's program in education Articulation and supporting the substantive emphases of the administration's agenda Continuing the flow of actions and initiatives in educational policy to the states
1986	Populist diffusion National level gubernatorial leadership in education Year of the Elementary School	Publication of *What Works* series: teaching and learning, drugs Publication of *Time for Results* Publication of *First Lessons*	Legitimating and popularizing the administration's substantive agenda of educational reform Extending the state's role in educational reform to the national level Establishing a long-range agenda for state-based national reform in education
1987	Old targets, old attacks AIDS and Supreme Court nominees	Proposed budget reductions Attacks on educationists and the condition of learning Secretary's position on AIDS and involvement in the Supreme Court nomination	Reiterating the procedural and substantive policy preferences of the administration Expanding the public visibility of the secretary's office
1988	Accountability Consolidation Achievements	Focus the revision of federal programs to reward success; press the theme of accountable institutions and individuals in education Reiterate education themes in election-year rhetoric Claim asserted gains in educational reform during the Reagan administration	*Interregnum* Press advantage against entrenched educationists Support the 1988 presidential campaign with evidence of progress in education Bridge post-1988 with a continued emphasis on the Reagan education agenda

probably stimulate dissension if the consequence appeared to have practical implications for local schools. In fact, however, the focus on content was contained within areas of public consensus or indifference, and ED supported individuals and groups at state and local levels who shared the general concern for an emphasis on traditionally defined curricular content. The first round of grants made by Secretary Bennett covered mathematics, history, substance abuse, text structure, and nuclear education.

The second of Secretary Bennett's Three Cs was choice. Choice actually covered three distinct interests of the administration: (1) parental control over where children attend school; (2) parental influence on what is to be taught, by whom, and how; and (3) parental involvement in the schooling process for their children. However, the cornerstone of this policy preference is the creation of conditions under which parents can choose their child's school. Secretary Bennett argued that this is extending to the poor the privilege held by the more affluent who exercise the privilege by choice of neighborhood or choice of a private school.

The necessary condition for parental choice of schools has been defined by the administration as some form of educational vouchers or tuition tax credits. Vouchers and tuition tax credits for students eligible for Chapter 1 funds were included in the administration's FY '86 budget proposal. In November 1985, following the *Felton* decision, ED drafted a new voucher bill, the Equity and Choice Act of 1985 (TEACH); Undersecretary Bauer noted that it would be one of the department's top priorities. Secretary Bennett was active in supporting and encouraging state-level initiatives for voucher plans. Roughly half of the secretary's first round of discretionary grant awards were made to agencies studying choice and parental involvement in schooling.

Secretary Bennett's third C was character. In describing the use of the secretary's discretionary funds to foster this goal, Bennett indicated that he wanted to fund projects that foster "wholesome" student character. Schools should encourage "such qualities as thoughtfulness, kindness, honesty, respect for the law, knowing right from wrong, respect for parents and teachers, diligence, self-sacrifice, hard work, fairness, self-discipline and love of country" (Hertling, 1985b, p. 10). Illustrating the types of character-related projects that could receive funds, he mentioned: (1) use of history, literature, and other academic subjects to promote character development; (2) establishment of clear goals and policies that "respect and support values from the students' homes," and encourage attendance, academic excellence, and an orderly, drug-free environment (Hertling, 1985b, p. 10). President Reagan was usually more direct in his definition, emphasizing "good old-fashioned discipline" and "organized school prayer." In the broadest sense, the administration's position defined traditional American values as derivative from the work ethic and the country's Judeo-Christian heritage. Despite the obvious possibilities for controversy surrounding federal grants in this area, the actual first round of eleven awards in March 1986 included mainline grantees from the education establishment (National School Boards Association and the American Federation of Teachers), three universities, the National Humanities Institute, and the Boy Scouts.

1986—Diffusion with Populist Appeal

Chester Finn, assistant secretary for the Office of Educational Research and Improvement (OERI), outlined the federal role in educational research:

> The Federal government is uniquely equipped to support and encourage education research, data collection, and dissemination of knowledge about effective educational practices. The Federal government can economically and efficiently establish uniform procedures and definitions for statistical purposes. Likewise, the Federal government has a unique ability and interest in disseminating knowledge about successful educational practices [Finn, 1986, p. 1].

This view of the federal role in educational research is consistent with the mechanism popularized in 1986 for influencing educational policy. Instead of relying solely on exhortation through the bully pulpit, the administration disseminated its message through written materials with popular appeal. *What Works* (U.S. Department of Education, 1986) represented the kind of dissemination effort proposed by Finn. In identifying the target audience for *What Works,* Finn observed: "It is not particularly aimed at our association muckety-mucks. It's much more for school board members, your 3rd grade teachers, the parent of your 7th graders" (Hertling, 1986b, p. 8). Bennett concurred with Finn's view, observing that both *What Works* and *Schools without Drugs* (U.S. Department of Education, 1986) were "directed at parents, teachers, and local decision makers and not national policy makers and education 'experts.' We're talking to the people we're supposed to be talking to" (Hertling, 1986b, p. 10). Bennett added that these efforts are consistent with the federal government's responsibility "to supply accurate and reliable information to the American people" (Hertling, 1986b, p. 10).

Dissemination with populist appeal served the administration's policy bent in several ways. First, widely distributed written information focusing on common-sense solutions and "how to's" serves as a powerful complement to general exhortation by federal officials. The intended user is the general public, those people the administration believes can be counted on to improve the nation's schools. Policy action at the state and local levels is encouraged: "I share Secretary Bennett's oft-stated conviction that the American people, equipped with reliable information, accurate data, and solid research findings, can be counted on to fix their own schools and post-secondary institutions" (Finn, 1986, p. 8).

Equally important, the written documents provided a belief system about school improvement and reform consistent with the administration's position of advocacy. For example, *What Works* began with citation of the evidence supporting the effect of the parents and the home on the education of children, "parents are their children's first and most influential teachers" (p. 7); moved on to the classroom where the first research finding again emphasized parents, "parental involvement helps children learn more effectively" (p. 19); emphasized findings on basic skills, reading, writing, mathematics, science, study skills, and homework (pp. 21–42); and concluded with evidence on the characteristics of effective schools, e.g., school climate, discipline, rigorous courses (pp. 44–62). *Schools without Drugs* advised parents to "teach standards of right and wrong and demonstrate these standards through personal example" (p. 13) and advised schools to develop and enforce clear policies and rules and "implement a comprehensive drug prevention curriculum for kindergarten through grade 12, teaching that drug use is wrong and harmful and supporting and strengthening resistance to drugs" (p. vii). Examples of successful local programs were described. The message of ED's dissemination efforts was consistent with the substantive interests of the administration, i.e., content, choice, and character.

Finally, the information provided through this dissemination vehicle painted a simplified view of reform and school improvement, a view that suggested that improvement can and will occur without federal programs if only the people know what needs to be done and why. For example, in introducing *What Works,* Reagan wrote (p. iii):

> *What Works* provides practical knowledge to help in the education of our children. . . . I am confident that with the benefit of such knowledge and renewed trust in common sense, we Americans will have even greater success in our unstinting efforts to improve our schools and better prepare our children for the challenges of today's world.

Similarly, Bennett wrote in the foreword (pp. v–vi):

> Most readers will, I think, judge that most of the evidence in this volume confirms common sense. So be it. Given the abuse common sense has taken in recent decades, particularly in the theory and practice of education, it is no small contribution if research can play a role in bringing more of it to American

education. Indeed, the reinforcement these findings give to common sense should bolster our confidence that we, as a people, can act together to improve our schools.

Outside Washington, another important event occurred in 1986 that reinforced the changing federal role in educational policy—the release of *Time for Results: The Governors' 1991 Report on Education* (National Governors' Association). This report included recommendations about leadership and the management of schools, use and maintenance of school facilities, improvement of the teaching workforce, increasing college quality, using technology, fostering parent involvement and choice, and strategies for addressing the needs of "at risk" students. In describing the governors' interest in education, Governor Kean said: "Education is good politics. Nobody is able to run for governor this year without an education agenda in either party" (Olson, 1986, p. 36).

The federal role in education has always been marginal in a quantitative sense (roughly 8 percent of elementary and secondary school expenditures; about 20 percent of higher education cost because of the student aid programs). Qualitatively that investment, though small, has been critical to achievements in the areas of equity and access for minority groups and women. Education is lost in the midst of the federal budget. But it is a big-ticket item at the state level, amounting frequently to from one-third to one-half of a state's budget. With an expanding state interest in education and an accompanying leveling off and decline of federal initiatives and involvement, devolution is alive and well in Washington. *Time for Results,* together with the increased activity of the state legislatures in educational policy and program development, served to legitimate the federal interest in devolution and established a long-range agenda for state-based national reform in education.

Secretary Bennett designated 1986 as the Year of the Elementary School. In September the secretary released *First Lessons,* a form of report card on the status of elementary education. Neither the designated year nor the report card seemed to capture the public's imagination or redirect attention to what Bennett described as a neglected area of education.

1987—Old Targets, Old Attacks

For the first time since at least the publication of *A Nation at Risk,* education drifted into a state of public indifference at the national level. The administration began the year with a quixotic attack on the education budget that was never taken seriously. The primary targets were vocational education (a recommendation to eliminate all federal funding), financial aid to college students (a $3.7 billion reduction), and the federal school-lunch program (18 percent cut). The rationale for the cuts was programmatic and fiscal:

> As in the past ED officials endorsed many of the cuts on policy grounds, arguing that the bulk of the targeted programs are too expensive or ineffective, or that they allow recipients, such as college students, to reap the benefits without shouldering their fair share of the costs. But this year, the same officials freely admitted that many of the cuts were driven by the Gramm-Rudman-Hollings Act [Montague, 1987a, pp. 1, 26].

In response to attacks on the proposed budget from Congress and the educationist community, Bennett echoed the long-standing beliefs of the administration about the condition of education: "The fixation with money . . . gives them [the education bureaucracy] an excuse not to do what they are supposed to do. . . . American education is not underfunded. It's underproductive, overregulated, and underaccountable" (Crawford, 1987, p. 13).

President Reagan continued his by now anticipated message on education. In his 1987 State of the Union address he said, "the 100th Congress of the United States should be remembered as the one that ended the expulsion of God from America's classrooms" (Montague, 1987b, p. 18). He continued to press for prayer and choice and values and disengagement of the federal government from education:

> It's just this simple. . . . Students with strong values will do well in school. . . . Education suffered when the federal government tried to give too much direction to local schools. . . . Some seem to think education is best directed by administrators in Washington. I say the American people know better than anyone in Washington how to fix their own schools [Rodman, 1987, p. 53].

Programmatically, ED held the line and pressed old interests. The administration's attack on bilingual education resulted in a Congressional compromise that future funding increases would go primarily for "English only" teaching methods. A limited, voluntary voucher was included in Chapter 1 plans. ED's research priorities were announced: parental choice in schooling; character education; literacy; effective education; education of at-risk students; foreign language instruction; management and organization of schools; early childhood learning; educational finance.

Secretary Bennett was visible in 1987 even if the program of ED was not. He entered vigorously into the battle against AIDS, assuming controversial positions on mandatory testing, involuntary disclosure of AIDS test results to spouses, and a program of AIDS education stressing sexual abstinence. To add to this controversy, the secretary became involved in the latter stages of the withdrawal of Douglas Ginsburg as President Reagan's Supreme Court nominee. Whether the secretary should or should not be involved in such matters is irrelevant to this analysis. That his involvement overshadowed the other events of the year in education seems relevant.

1987–88—An Interregnum

By June 1987 Secretary Bennett had abandoned the hopeless task of cutting the education budget, noting "we're revising our strategy. . . . It's time for this Administration to get the credit it deserves for being a major force in educational reform" (Montague, 1987a, p. 1). By September he was foreshadowing an administration priority for 1988:

> We will talk a lot this year about accountability, accountability, accountability. . . . We will try to get our programs at the federal level to focus on accountability and try to urge actions at the state and local level to have more accountability. . . . Where there's success, let's build on it, let's replicate it, let's reward it. Where there's failure, let's not [Miller, 1987, p. 1].

Throughout the year Bennett took available occasions to place the blame for shortfalls in the educational reform movement on educationists in general and the National Education Association (NEA) in particular. As usual, his language left little doubt about where he stood on "Education Reform and the 1988 Election," which happened to be the title of his speech before the National Press Club. He labeled the NEA the "most entrenched and aggressive opponent of education reform" in the nation (Olson, 1987, p. 1). He suggested that each candidate for the presidency in 1988 should be asked, "On which issues will you stand with the NEA, and on which will you stand with the American people?" (Olson, 1987, p. 18).

We do not anticipate any major initiatives by the administration in 1988, but we do expect that Secretary Bennett will pursue the theme of accountability (this may be reflected in some program changes in ED); attacks on the education establishment; retrospective claims of accomplishments in educational reform by the administration from 1981 to 1988; and continued advocacy of the most popular education positions of the Reagan administration. In short, we expect the secretary to attempt to provide the Republican candidate for the presidency with a strong record on which to stand and to encourage the party to press on with the Reagan program in education in 1989 and beyond.

Conclusion

The educational policy agenda of the Reagan administration was easy to track and compile. Whether one analyzes a radio address on education by President Reagan, State of the Union messages, or statements by Secretaries Bell or Bennett, the same issues were discussed and the same positions were advocated. The administration promoted a set of procedural policy preferences that defined the nature of the federal role in education:

- disestablishment, i.e., a reduced federal role in education;
- diminution, i.e., reduced federal spending in support of education;
- devolution, i.e., transfer of authority and responsibility for educational policy and program development from the federal to state and local levels.

The administration also promoted a set of substantive policy preferences in areas in which the president has had a strong personal interest:

- institutional competition, i.e., breaking the monopoly of the public school to stimulate excellent performance;
- individual competition, i.e., recognizing excellence to stimulate excellence;
- performance standards, i.e., increasing minimum standards for teachers and students to increase achievement;
- focus on content, i.e., emphasis on basics to ensure performance in critical instructional areas;
- parental choice, i.e., parental control over what, where, and how their children learn;
- character, i.e., strengthening traditional values in schools.

The administration's educational policy agenda was accompanied by a deemphasis on, or disappearance of, policy preferences in education held by the federal government prior to 1980. The federal role that emerged from 1955 to 1980 promoted the creation and adoption of interventions to improve the American educational system by opening it up to least-well-served clientele, establishing school-improvement strategies and tactics, funding areas in which states and localities were deemed laggard or fiscally incapable of response, and monitoring and evaluating the success of those endeavors after they had been undertaken.

At the least, one can argue that this pre-1980 role was stalled and contained by the Reagan administration. The only exception of consequence that emerged was the mathematics and science legislation, and its funding was halved after one year of operation. The national reports on

706   Policy Issues for the 1990s

the condition of education in 1983 and 1984 set the stage for a response of
the magnitude of the National Defense Education Act of 1958 or the
Elementary and Secondary Education Act of 1965. And the response
occurred *at the state level*. The federal response was, appropriately for
this administration, exhortation and encouragement and dissemination of
"what works."

The driving wheel behind the categorical programs of the 1960s and
1970s was equity for minorities, the poor, the handicapped, and women.
That is no longer the case. Social and welfare concerns, including equity,
are not major forces in national-level decision-making about education.
This is not intended to be an argument that they are ignored, simply that
they are no longer pivotal considerations. For the present, different priorities are in place in Washington that emphasize excellence in performance,
competition, selectivity, economic concerns, choice, local initiatives, and
the support of traditional values. That is a different direction.

The educational policy preferences of the Reagan administration all
showed progress during the two terms of the administration; and the
cumulative effect has been to modify the basic federal role in education,
to stimulate continued growth and independence of the state governments
in educational policy development, and to foster the substantive interests
of the administration in competition, increased performance standards,
traditional values, parental choice, and a focus on the basics in education.

To answer the question with which we began: Yes, the years of the
Reagan administration have produced a significant, enduring change in
federal educational policy. Given the overarching domestic and fiscal
policy preferences at the federal level, these changes are likely to continue
beyond the Reagan years.

References

Bennett, W. J. 1986. *First Lessons: A Report on Elementary Education in America.*
    Washington, D.C: U.S. Department of Education. September.
Chapman, S. 1980. "The Teachers' Coup." *New Republic*, October 11, p. 9.
Crawford, J. 1987. "Bennett Attacked on ED Budget Plan." *Education Week*,
    February 11, pp. 13–14.
Doyle, D. P., and T. W. Hartle. 1985. "Ideology, Pragmatic Politics, and the
    Education Budget." In J. C. Weicher, ed., *Maintaining the Safety Net: Income
    Redistribution Programs in the Reagan Administration*. Washington, D.C: Amer-
    ican Enterprise Institute for Public Policy Research, pp. 119–53.
Finn, C. E., Jr. 1986. Statement before the Subcommittee on Select Education,
    U.S. House of Representatives, Washington, D.C: February 19.
Gardner, E. M. 1984. "The Department of Education." In S. M. Butler, M. Sanera,
    and W. B. Weinrod, eds., *Mandate for Leadership II: Continuing the Conserva-
    tive Revolution*. Washington, D.C: The Heritage Foundation, pp. 49–62.

Hertling, J. 1985a. " 'Coherent Design' Missing in Curricula, Says Bennett in Call for Common Core." *Education Week*, March 20, p. 10.
———. 1985b. "Bennett to Spend Discretionary Funds on 'Content, Character, and Choice.' " *Education Week*, June 12, p. 10.
———. 1986a. "Secretary's Grants Finance Efforts to Boost '3C's.' " *Education Week*, March 19, pp. 1, 13.
———. 1986b. "ED Report Stresses 'Common Sense.' " *Education Week*. March 12, pp. 10, 12.
Iannaccone, L. 1985. "Excellence: An Emergent Educational Issue." *Politics of Education Bulletin 23*, no. 3, pp. 1, 3–8.
Ingalls, Z. 1981. "Gardner Brings a 'Traditional View' to New Federal Review of Education." *Chronicle of Higher Education*, September 9, p. 11.
Jennings, J. 1985. "Will Carl Perkins' Legacy Survive Ronald Reagan's Policies?" *Phi Delta Kappan* 66 (April): 565–67.
Miller, J. 1987. "Combative Bennett Charges into Final Year: Says He Will Stress 'Accountability' of Educators for Results." *Education Week*, September 16, pp. 1, 16.
Montague, W. 1987a. "$14 Billion Spending Plan Would Eliminate Funding for Vocational Education." *Education Week*, January 14, pp. 1, 26.
———. 1987b. "Democrats, Bennett Spar after Reagan's Address." *Education Week*, February 4, pp. 1, 18.
———. 1987c. "Skepticism Greets Bennett Decision to Seek End to Push for Spending Cuts." *Education Week*, June 17, pp. 1, 13.
National Commission on Excellence in Education. 1983. *A Nation at Risk: The Imperative for Educational Reform*. Washington, D.C: U.S. Government Printing Office.
National Governors' Association. 1986. *Time for Results: The Governors' 1991 Report on Education*.
1980 Republican Platform text. 1980. *Congressional Quarterly Weekly Report*, July 19, pp. 2030–56.
Olson, L. 1986. "Governors Draft 5-Year Blueprint to Press Reforms." *Education Week*, September 10, pp. 1, 36.
———. 1987. "Speech Terms NEA 'Most Aggressive' Foe of Reform in Nation." *Education Week*, September 16, pp. 1, 16.
Rodman, B. 1987. "President Hits Road to Spread Message on School Agenda." *Education Week*, April 1, pp. 1, 53.
State of the Union address. 1984. *Weekly Compilation of Presidential Documents*, January 30, pp. 87–94.
———. 1988. Transcript reprinted in *New York Times*, January 26, p. A16.
U.S. Department of Education. 1986. *What Works: Research about Teaching and Learning*. Washington, D.C.: Superintendent of Documents, U.S. Government Printing Office.
———. 1986. *Schools without Drugs*. Washington, D.C.: Superintendent of Documents, U.S. Government Printing Office.

29

Restructuring the Education System: Agenda for the Nineties

Michael Cohen

Introduction

Since the early part of the 1980s, education has been the dominant issue on state policy agendas. Since the enactment of Mississippi's Education Reform Act in 1982, virtually every state has substantially increased funding for education and, at the same time, enacted new policies, programs, and regulations to raise performance standards for students, teachers, and schools. Yet despite these efforts, the need for education reform continues, and the work of the recent past must be extended into the future. This is because American society is undergoing profound changes, largely as a result of the combined effects of demographic changes affecting families, the workforce, and the schools, as well as changes in America's competitive position in the world economy.

This has been the fundamental message of reports issued in 1986 by both the Carnegie Forum on Education and the Economy and the National Governors' Association. Both Carnegie and NGA start with the recognition that the education system must continue to adapt to changes in the broader social and economic environment. More specifically, the need for continued education reform is rooted in three inescapable realities. First, the economic well-being of the states and their citizens is increasingly

This chapter was originally published by the National Governors' Association (NGA), Center for Policy Research. It is reprinted here with permission of the NGA.

dependent upon a well-educated and highly skilled workforce. Second, the health of our economy as well as the stability of our democracy requires schools and colleges to effectively educate *all* students. The continuing high proportions of students at risk of academic failure deprives our economy of needed manpower, and threatens our democratic institutions. As a result of academic failure far too many of our citizens are condemned to unproductive and unfulfilling lives. Third, public education is a big public business. On the average, states invest approximately 37 percent of their annual budgets in education and fund slightly more than 50 percent of the costs of elementary and secondary education. With a commitment of resources on this scale, and in light of competing demands for scarce state resources, improving both the efficiency and the productivity of the education system must be a continuing concern for governors and other state policymakers.

In the early part of the decade state education reform initiatives focused on raising performance standards and providing the resources to achieve higher levels of performance. In many cases, the steps—such as increased high school graduation and testing requirements for students, competency testing and new evaluation requirements for teachers, and new accreditation standards for school districts—were intended primarily to boost the performance levels of the lowest achievers.

Although important, these steps have not completed the task of improving education. In fact, we have just begun. We must go well beyond raising the floor of educational performance. We must also dramatically raise the ceiling of educational accomplishment. At the same time, we must significantly increase the proportion of students, from all backgrounds, who are performing at or near the highest level.

The Challenge for Public Education

The challenges facing the education system today are fundamentally different from those addressed before, even in recent years. As recently as a decade ago, the overriding demand on schools was to increase the number of students who mastered basic skills such as reading and computing. In the future, maintaining a high standard of living will increasingly require a workforce with greater intellectual competence and flexibility. These traits must be broadly distributed throughout the workforce; they will be important for line workers as well as for senior-level managers and executives.

More specifically, students will need a substantial knowledge base as well as higher-order cognitive skills. Such skills include the ability to communicate complex ideas, to analyze and solve complex problems, to identify order and find direction in an ambiguous and uncertain environment, and to think and reason abstractly. Because workers in the future will experience rapid changes in both work technologies and jobs themselves, students also will be required to develop the capacity to learn new skills and tasks quickly. This will require a thorough understanding of the subject matter students study and an ability to apply this knowledge in creative and imaginative ways, in novel contexts, and in collaboration with others.

Even dramatic improvements in the proportion of students who master routine basic skills can only result in a widening mismatch between the skills of the workforce and the skill demands of the workplace. Consequently, the demand on schools is now shifting from simply increasing the number of graduates with basic skills to both increasing the proportion of students who graduate and improving the intellectual capabilities of graduates.

Currently, only a small percentage of high school graduates have acquired and mastered the knowledge and higher-order skills they will need. Because most high school graduates acquire only a rudimentary set of basic reading and computation skills, they are ill-equipped to handle even moderately complex tasks in the workplace. For example, the 1984 National Assessment of Education Progress showed that slightly more than 60 percent of 17-year-old students lack the ability to find, understand, summarize, and explain relatively complicated information, including information about topics they study in school. Often, they do not have the reading comprehension skills needed in higher education or business environments. The same assessment showed that typically only 15 percent to 25 percent of eleventh-graders could respond adequately to a writing task, depending upon the nature of the particular task. The overwhelming majority of eleventh-graders could not write a brief passage well enough to accomplish their writing objective.

While these low average performance levels are distressing enough, they mask large and persistent achievement gaps among subgroups of students. Students who are black or Hispanic, or who come from poor families or rural or disadvantaged urban areas, consistently perform less well than do others. For example, the average reading proficiency of black and Hispanic 17-year-old students is roughly the same as that of 13-year-old white students. And though some 45 percent of white 17-year-olds have acquired adept reading skills, the same is true for only 16 percent to 20 percent of black and Hispanic students.

Further, roughly 15 percent to 20 percent of 18- to 19-year-olds nationally (and nearly 40 percent in some urban areas) have not completed high school, and presumably are considerably less skilled than most of their age cohort. These dropouts are drawn disproportionately from the ranks of poor and minority youngsters. This suggests that the achievement gaps between minority and majority youth are even larger when the entire cohort of school-age youth, rather than just current students, is considered.

These achievement gaps are not new; they have been of concern for some time. What gives this issue more urgency today is that the percentage of students who are at risk of poor academic performance or dropping out altogether—those drawn from poor and minority backgrounds—represent an increasing share of both the school population and our future workforce. Thus, society cannot continue to write off this segment of the population; the future well-being of this country is fundamentally dependent upon their educational success.

In short, the nature, level, and distribution of student outcomes must change significantly. The holding power of schools must improve so virtually all students at least complete high school. The proportion of students who master higher-order thinking skills must increase dramatically. In addition, it is not enough to raise the *average* performance levels; the proportion of students from poor and minority backgrounds who acquire higher-order skills must increase substantially as well.

Further, the required gains in outcomes are proportionately greater than the likely increases in education expenditures, even if funding increases continue at the pace of the past several years. Since 1983–84, there has been real growth in education expenditures of more than 25 percent, and the state share of elementary and secondary expenditures now exceeds 50 percent nationally. Investments also must be made in early childhood, higher education, and worker retraining programs, among others, to respond to the same economic and demographic challenges.

Consequently, the productivity of the education system must increase dramatically. Schools need to educate more students to considerably higher levels of achievement, and need to use their resources more effectively in doing so.

Restructuring the Education System: Critical Issues

Few would argue that so sweeping a challenge can be adequately addressed through incremental changes in schooling practices. Indeed, by calling for a fundamental restructuring of the education system in reports such as *A Nation Prepared, Time for Results,* and *Children in Need,* political, business, and education leaders have recognized that the traditional structure and organization of schools are not well suited for the new demands they face. Typical instructional arrangements are more appropriate for teaching students basic skills than for helping them acquire more complex cognitive skills. And, as presently organized, staffing arrangements and scheduling practices leave relatively little time for teachers to prepare for instruction, review student work, or engage in substantial and personalized interaction with students. There is even less time and opportunity to develop collegial working relations among faculty, which are important for both professional development and school improvement. Consequently, school improvement efforts initiated within the existing school structure, such as effective schools programs, may demonstrate some success in increasing basic reading and math skills, but they cannot approach the productivity gains ultimately required.

This section discusses specific issues at the school building, local school district, and state levels that must be addressed and resolved in order to move from the rhetoric to the reality of restructured schools.

Two key assumptions provide the starting point for the following analysis. First is the assumption that the primary rationale for restructuring schools lies in the need to improve the productivity of the education system in general, and, in particular, student acquisition of higher-order thinking skills. It should be acknowledged, however, that others advocate restructuring schools primarily to enhance other values, namely either teacher professionalism or parental and student choice. In this analysis, those issues are treated largely as instrumental considerations rather than necessarily desirable ends. The extent to which either one is promoted is dependent upon the contribution it makes to the overriding goal of improving productivity.

The second assumption is that improving educational productivity requires a restructuring of the entire education system, and not just the schools. The structure and process of governance and control at the state and local levels must be adjusted in order to accommodate and support necessary changes in the organization and management of instruction in schools and classrooms. Accomplishing this first requires an analysis of needed changes in instruction, and then an examination up and through the education system to identify further changes at the school, district, and state levels that also must be made.

Currently, most discussions about restructuring schools involve some mix of ideas about greater school site management and autonomy, more flexibility and variability in the organization of schools, greater teacher participation in school decisionmaking, and the decentralization of decisionmaking and deregulation of schooling. While each of these ideas, and others, properly belong in a discussion of restructuring schools, rarely if ever are they grounded in any clear way to improved school productivity or student acquisition of skills. Until such connections are made, it will be difficult to build political or policy support for initiatives to restructure schools, and even more difficult to know how to go about the process.

School-Level Issues

Helping all students acquire higher-order skills requires a curriculum that engages students in rigorous and challenging work. Particularly for students from disadvantaged backgrounds, who are prone to academic failure and dropping out, the curriculum also must be structured to provide opportunities for frequent success, to enhance each student's sense of self-worth and competence. Further, schools must provide an environment in which students receive personal attention, so they feel that someone cares about them personally and consequently are able to form a positive attachment to the school.

The primary issues to be resolved at the school site level have to do with identifying structural and organizational features of schools that need to be altered in order to accomplish this. Put somewhat differently, educators and policymakers alike need a map, or a vision, of what restructured schools might look like. This is especially critical when one considers that much of the work, and even more of the decisionmaking, that will go into restructuring schools will be done by educators at the school site level.

What features of schools need to be altered? A starting point are those conditions of instruction known to be related to student learning. These include educational goals, the structure of knowledge, instructional tasks and activities, instructional group size and composition, and instructional time.

Educational goals.   What students learn is at least partly a function of what schools are expected to teach them. To a considerable extent, instructional goals are determined by state and local school boards and the tests used to assess school and student performance. Because these measures continue to emphasize basic skills and minimize higher-order skills, instructional goals and student learning will fall short of what is needed. Therefore, state and local school boards must establish clear goals reflecting higher-order skills and invest in the development of assessment devices that both reflect and measure those goals.

Structure of knowledge.   The way knowledge is organized into school curricula has a significant impact on what students learn. For example, in many high school science courses, the curriculum emphasizes breadth of coverage in favor of depth of coverage. Consequently, students may be exposed to what are little more than vocabulary lessons in 34 different units of physics, rather than concentrating on a half dozen or so in a way that would enable them to learn how physicists approach and solve problems.

As another example, elementary reading instruction is typically organized around discrete skills for decoding, vocabulary, or comprehension. The assumption is that skills are hierarchical in nature, and the curriculum must first help students master the simpler "basic" skills before they proceed to acquire "higher-order" skills. Therefore, youngsters who do not master the basic skills along with their peers are provided remedial instruction, generally in the form of additional drill and practice in the basics.

A growing body of research in cognitive psychology and related fields suggests that this mode of operation may be quite flawed. In fact, studies demonstrate that skilled readers, even at the early elementary grades, are able to comprehend what they read not simply because they have acquired the basics, but because they intuitively and automatically rely on what we think of as higher-order skills. As they read, they actively draw on their own knowledge, and ask questions and make inferences about the printed text. According to this emerging view, improving reading skills of poor readers requires far less in the way of drill and practice on the basics, and far more in the way of experiences which cultivate students' thinking and reasoning skills.

Instructional tasks and activities. To a considerable extent at the secondary level, and somewhat less in elementary grades, instruction takes the form of lecture and recitation during which an entire class is focused on the same content and engaged in the same activities. This method effectively forces all students to move through the curriculum at the same pace, regardless of differences in their rates of learning. It encourages teachers to use questioning strategies that emphasize brief and unambiguously correct answers, and limits student engagement in active learning. Alternative activity structures that emphasize student choice over a selection of activities or cooperative small-group work on long-term projects can be more responsive to differences in student interests and achievement levels. At the same time they can provide opportunities for all students to become meaningfully engaged in reasonably complex and demanding learning tasks and gain practice working cooperatively with others.

Instructional group size and composition. There is considerable evidence that student achievement is affected by the size and composition of each learning group. Grouping practices—class size, student assignment to classes, the creation of instructional groups within classes—make a difference in student achievement. This is also true of tracking practices in secondary schools. They determine the social environment in which a student learns, the curriculum, the pace of instruction, and a host of other learning conditions. Further, the way instructional groups are typically formed in elementary schools—25 student in a class, 3 to 5 ability groups per class—are neither the only forms of grouping nor necessarily the most effective. There is strong evidence that suggests that alternatives, such as heterogeneous groups combined with cooperative reward structures and peer tutoring, can work well. One can imagine a variety of arrangements that can be more effective, such as large lecture classes for some material, balanced by small-group projects for other material; individual student work on computers or other technologies; or extensive use of peer tutoring, which creates instructional groups with only two students and capitalizes on rather than eliminates variation in student achievement and ability levels.

Instructional Time.   Time is a critical structural feature of schooling. It is perhaps the most important instructional resource. As a structural feature, time defines the basic structure of schools and of instruction. The school year, the school day, the schedule, the curriculum, graduation requirements, and even the progression of students from one learning opportunity or setting to the next, are all defined by fixed blocks of time and set by state or local policy or regulation. Consequently, time is treated as a fixed resource. All students are expected to learn at the same rate and complete their learning at the same time. Yet we know that students learn at varying rates. Within classrooms, treating time as a fixed resource means that some students are routinely bored while waiting for their classmates to catch up. Others repeatedly must move on to the next unit before mastering the current material. Inevitably these students fall further and further behind their peers. Across courses and grade levels, treating time as a fixed resource means that some students experience the cumulative loss of opportunity to master needed skills. Consequently, by the time students complete or otherwise leave school, there is tremendous variability in their levels of knowledge and skills. In contrast to this are outcomes-based education and mastery learning, in which student performance standards are treated as fixed but the amount of time and number of opportunities students have to reach standards vary.

This is not a complete list of instructional conditions that affect student learning, but it does illustrate several points. First, it is possible to identify key dimensions of the structure of instruction that affect pedagogical practice and student learning. Second, for each of these dimensions, there is a basis in research and experience that can serve as a starting point for the design and implementation of new structural arrangements. Third, it is virtually impossible to change just one component at a time; they are integrally tied together. Any substantial change to one requires—and permits—changes in the others at the same time. Therefore, improving school productivity and student learning demands that schools be restructured substantially.

Enough is known from the effective schools research to demonstrate that improvements in the technical features of the organization of instructional and other school resources are necessary but not sufficient steps to realize the desired gains in student achievement. Schools, after all, are social institutions, and their culture, norms, expectations, and mechanisms for involving teachers and students in their work are critical to their success. Further, circumstances among schools, even within a single district, vary considerably. Schools vary in their mix of students and staff, in the characteristics of the communities they serve, and in their past attempts at innovation and improvement. From this point of view, schools require considerable autonomy to allow for the most sensible fit between particular forms of instructional organization and current practices, existing staff capabilities, and student and community needs. Therefore, inventing a new set of structural arrangements to be applied uniformly in all schools would not suffice. Rather, schools must be able to form and adjust their own structures and processes, as needed.

This approach has several implications. First, decisions about the most productive form of instructional organization need to be made close to the action—by teachers and principals at the school site level. Second, if decisions about instructional organization are to be made at the site level, other related decisions must also be made at the site level. These include, for example, staffing arrangements, decisionmaking processes, staff and organizational development needs, and curriculum selection and development. Allowing schools the leeway to make decisions in these areas requires that resources devoted to these activities are allocated to the school site as well.

New instructional and organizational arrangements will mean new roles for teachers and new staffing arrangements. For example, creating smaller instructional groups, variable time for student mastery and progress, or interdisciplinary curricula cannot readily be accomplished in schools in which the teacher's role is defined by sole responsibility for particular subject matter or large groups of students. Rather, these new instructional arrangements will require greater use of team teaching and other forms of collaboration and coordination. Similarly, increased planning, decisionmaking, professional development, and school improvement responsibilities for school staff also will require new roles for and frequent interaction among teachers.

It will be critical to find time for teachers to assume these new roles and responsibilities. This will not be easy within the current school structure.

At present, schedules for teachers largely match the school day of students (though the teaching day is generally somewhat longer), and, despite the allotment of "preparation" time for teachers, rarely are there significant blocks of time during which teachers can interact with one another or with small numbers of students. Consequently, additional staff time, as well as new ways of organizing teachers' use of existing time, must be found.

In all probability, some of this time can be obtained only with additional resources for more staff, for a longer school day or year, or both. However, it may also be possible to find more effective ways to use existing staff resources, such as preparation periods, in-service training time, or the time of administrators such as department chairs or assistant principals. Further, it will be important to look for ways to use less expensive resources, such as paraprofessionals, volunteers, peer tutors, and instructional technologies, whenever possible, so each teacher's time can be used most productively.

School District Issues

The school district creates the context in which schools operate. In most instances, this context places primary emphasis throughout the system on the degree to which school practice complies with district policy. When the policies determine the allocation of instructional time, the amount of homework to be assigned, the number and length of teacher preparation periods, the curricular and instructional materials to be used, and the number and timing of "in-service days" and the like, some of the most important instructional decisions are being made at the district level. Teachers and building administrators then assume the role of implementing a set of procedures designed elsewhere.

At the heart of the reassessing of the local district role should be an effort to create an orientation toward performance, rather than procedure, in which the district provides the enabling tools and resources, rather than the constraints. The primary orientation of school staff should be to make judgments about how to select, organize, and use available resources to achieve desired ends. In such an arrangement, interaction between the central office and individual schools would mainly focus on whether schools are achieving district goals, rather than whether they are following district guidelines.

Local district functions must be carefully examined and revised if needed change is to occur. The precise nature of these changes remains to be seen; it is reasonable to expect that new arrangements will differ widely depending upon district size and other characteristics. Nonetheless, it is possible to identify several broad issues that must be addressed by all school districts.

First, many functions typically performed at the central-office level, on a uniform basis for all schools, should be either delegated to or shared with individual school buildings. In most districts, responsibility for goal setting, curriculum development, textbook selection, grouping and tracking policies, personnel policies, and resource allocation are typically lodged with the school board and are uniform across all schools within the district. Legal authority for such policy decisions appropriately belongs with the school board. However, the standardization of these practices across all schools, without regard to variations in local building circumstances, is often incompatible with the discretion required at the school site in order to improve educational productivity. Consequently, districts and schools need to sort out which responsibilities and authority can be assigned to the individual school and which must remain at the central-office level.

Moving in this direction will require districts to carefully balance competing pressures for centralized control and local autonomy. For example, though it is desirable for individual school buildings to have sufficient flexibility to select instructional materials well suited for their particular students and well matched to their instructional strategies, it is also desirable for students—especially in large districts—to be able to move from one neighborhood and school to another without finding entirely different textbooks and other instructional materials. Therefore, mechanisms will need to be established that both promote diversity and retain some common features among schools. Establishing districtwide goals and performance measures for which each building is accountable could be one such approach. However, developing assessment tools that faithfully reflect shared goals and at the same time permit varied curriculum materials will prove to be enormously difficult. Therefore, districts will have to consider a number of strategies and arrangements to assure the proper balance.

For example, schools could be responsible for establishing annual goals within the context of district goals. Schools could have the authority to determine their own instructional policies, to decide how best to group students for instruction, to organize instructional time, to select and use textbooks and other instructional materials, and to control the resources required to perform these functions. The local school board and central office, in turn, might require the school to submit annual goals and plans for accomplishing them. The district would be responsible for reviewing and approving the plans, for providing technical assistance and training to support the school planning process, for monitoring implementation, and for evaluating its effectiveness. This arrangement would require that responsibility, authority, and resources move down in the system to the school building, with the district responsibility shifting to supporting and evaluating building efforts.

School decisionmaking and governance patterns must change as well. Creating greater discretion at the school site level also should involve broader participation in decisionmaking, so that both teachers and parents participate meaningfully in shaping the school's program.

As indicated above, giving teachers greater discretion with respect to the organization of instruction is a key component of school restructuring. This does not mean more autonomy for teachers behind the closed door of the classroom. Teachers are interdependent. In order for schools to be effective, teachers must make decisions collegially. This is especially true when the task involves creating more flexible instructional arrangements and new roles for school staff; these are decisions that must be worked out among the staff as a whole. The challenge for school districts is to create structures in which school-level decisionmaking can proceed effectively and efficiently, and in which teachers can play a significant role in administrative and management decisions that have important instructional consequences. At the same time teachers must retain a primary focus on classroom teaching, so their energies are not dissipated trying to manage the entire school.

One of the primary benefits of school site discretion is the ability of the school, within the context of state and local goals, to shape a unique and coherent school mission and culture that responds to the needs of its particular clientele. Providing greater discretion and empowering teachers to make decisions at the school level requires that parents and community members also be given a greater voice in school decisionmaking. The issue here goes well beyond the benefits of parental involvement for the academic performance of their children. Rather, it recognizes that the public—especially but not exclusively parents—must have a way of shaping decisions over the focus and mission of a school. In public agencies such as schools, fundamental value questions are not appropriately resolved exclusively by the professional staff. While local school boards have historically performed this function, their capacity to serve as the *exclusive* structure for lay participation will be diminished if a greater share of decisionmaking is moved from the school district to the individual school building.

Consequently, school districts will need to establish school-level governance structures, such as school site councils composed of teachers, administrators, parents, and community members. Districts must determine the scope of authority for these structures and help work out ways that increased professional participation and greater community involvement can be mutually reinforcing.

Greater school site autonomy and enhanced influence for teachers and parents are only part of the changes required in the school district role. When more autonomous schools take on truly distinctive cultures and orientations, both students and staff will need greater choice in the school they want to attend or the building in which they work. In this way the appropriate match of staff strengths, client preferences and needs, and school mission can be achieved. Therefore, districts also may want to consider altering traditional practices for assigning students and staff to schools. Rather than assigning students based on where they live, districts could permit students and their parents to select the school of their choice. Similarly, staff also could have greater choice over the school in which they work, to permit a better fit between each teacher's own style, skills, and philosophy and the school in which he or she works. Greater choice for both students and staff should create more widespread commitment to and support for the school's mission.

The nature of local district personnel policies and practices must change as well. Internship and induction programs for beginning teachers must be established to provide support and help them master both classroom and schoolwide roles. Teacher evaluation systems, which currently assess how well teachers demonstrate specific behaviors and instructional practices, should instead focus on how well they are able to make appropriate instructional decisions and judgments in order to accomplish results with their students.

The role of the collective bargaining process in promoting school restructuring needs to be examined as well. Evidence on the impact of collective bargaining suggests that unions have served to increase the extent of bureaucratic control by making teaching work more rationalized, more highly specified and inspected, and by increasing the number and specificity of rules determining work roles and conditions. However, there are recent experiments, such as in Dade County, Florida, and Rochester, New York, in which the collective bargaining process has been used to promote greater flexibility at the school site. And in Toledo, Ohio, the teachers' union used the bargaining process to introduce rigorous peer review procedures in which senior teachers review and evaluate probationary teachers.

These are illustrative of the range of current policies and practices that will need to be reviewed in order to promote school restructuring. Equally important is a reconsideration of local control and leadership. Over the past decade and a half, local school board authority has been eroded as a result of federal legislation, court actions, collective bargaining agreements, and, most recently, state initiatives. And, as a recent study by the Institute for Education Leadership shows, local school boards frequently spend the bulk of their time on crisis management or operational details, and infrequently engage in systematic planning, policy development, or oversight. Generally, local school boards lack strong connections to local government, political cultures, and business and civic groups.

These conditions, together with the demands of restructuring schools, point to the need for developing new conceptions of local control and leadership. Successfully restructuring the education system and providing greater discretion to individual schools must occur in a policy framework that establishes long-range goals, attracts and retains high quality personnel, assures that resources are adequately targeted to students with greatest need, and generally makes success at the school site level possible. Further, it requires ongoing oversight and assessment to determine whether goals are being accomplished and policies are having their intended effect.

Strengthened local leadership involves more than a proactive policymaking approach. It also requires the development of mechanisms for strengthening ties to the local community and strong advocacy for education and youth. In addition, it requires the capacity to broaden the constituency and support base for education, promote widespread community understanding of the needs of the education system, marshal needed resources for the schools, and establish linkages with parents and members of the community at large to support and strengthen the instructional program.

State-Level Issues

Changes at the school and district levels will require changes at the state level in at least three broad areas: setting educational goals, stimulating local innovation, and rethinking state accountability systems.

Setting educational goals. States must assume larger responsibilities for setting educational goals and defining outcomes standards. This is a critical precondition to providing greater discretion and flexibility at the local school site level. Accomplishing this will require state action on several fronts.

State boards of education can begin by establishing long-range educational goals that adequately reflect the knowledge and higher-order skills graduates will need. Currently, few states seriously attempt to establish long-range educational goals. Historically, if educational goals were established at all, they were too vague to guide policy development or establish performance standards for schools and forgotten soon after they were established. In many states, descriptions of desired student outcomes either take the form of vague prescriptions for youngsters to reach their full potential, or highly specified and lengthy lists of instructional objectives reflecting subject matter course requirements. There must be a middle ground.

States should institute a long-range-planning and goal-setting process, to establish educational goals to meet the broad societal needs schools must serve. Desired outcomes must focus educators' attention and efforts on teaching the most important knowledge and skills, while giving them the freedom to make curricular and instructional decisions about how best to accomplish these outcomes.

Setting appropriate goals is an important first step. However, in order to have an impact on educational practice, goals must be linked to state testing and assessment programs. In many states, this will require replacing existing minimum competency tests, which focus exclusively on basic skills, with newly developed instruments for assessing higher-order skills.

In developing new assessment tools and procedures, several issues should be addressed. First, assessment systems can have powerful effects on curriculum and instruction, especially if student performance has such serious consequences as promotion or graduation. If tests are designed to be "taught to," as is the case with advanced placement tests, they can be powerful tools for shaping the local curriculum and making it more rigorous. They can also provide useful feedback to educators and incentives to students.

In order to work this way, the tests should be linked to a specific program of study, rather than assessing knowledge of a broad curricular domain. Further, tests must measure the depth of knowledge and higher-order skills required of students. If they continue to reflect only minimum competencies, they are likely to restrict what teachers attempt to do and thus lower education standards and performance for all but the weakest students.

Second, assessment tools geared to higher-order skills may take different forms from most existing state testing programs. Continued reliance on multiple choice or short answer questions is simply not adequate. Rather, assessment tools are needed that require students to synthesize, integrate, and apply knowledge and data to complex problems. They should present tasks for which no one answer is right, but for which a range of solutions may be possible. These may take the form of essays, projects, or other demonstrations of competence, such as those called for in Ted Sizer's Coalition of Essential Schools. Scoring systems that rely on expert judgment rather than simply checking for the correct answer are an essential part of these assessment tools.

Third, while states should develop assessment tools that effectively shape local curriculum and student preparation, they should also seek to ensure that the same measures don't overly restrict local curricular choices and instructional approaches, or else the benefits of increased school site autonomy also will be restricted.

Fourth, states need to be wary of the danger that any particular outcome measure can have powerful and unintended effects on schooling by overly narrowing the focus of educators to only those outcomes that are measured. This danger can be mitigated in part by making sure that what is measured is truly valued, so attention is given to the most important educational outcomes. It can also be mitigated by developing a system of indicators that accurately reflect the multiple goals held for schools. Not only do we want *average* improvement gains, we also want to ensure substantial gains for the lowest achiever students. Although we want to improve cognitive skills, we also need to reduce the dropout rate. And not only do we value students' presence in schools, we also value their self-esteem, the degree of satisfaction they and their parents feel about their schools, and the willingness of students to pursue a variety of learning opportunities beyond formal schooling.

Stimulating local innovation.   Improvement in education productivity and the professionalization of teaching will require new school structures that allow more varied instructional arrangements, greater collegial interaction among teachers, and greater teacher involvement in decisionmaking. Although the need for restructuring is clear, notions of how schools could be restructured are not yet well developed. New concepts for restructuring must come through carefully supported local efforts, where new ideas can emerge from and be tested against the realities of schools and classrooms. Consequently, states must provide leadership by:

- articulating a vision of restructured schools;
- encouraging local experimentation with various school structures;
- reducing unnecessary administrative and regulatory barriers to experimentation with promising approaches;
- providing ongoing implementation support and technical assistance to schools and districts trying new approaches;
- linking rewards and sanctions for schools to their performance;
- researching and disseminating results to other schools.

In many states, this will require a significant upgrading of the state education agency's technical assistance and research capabilities.

Rethinking state accountability systems.   Successfully restructuring schools will require states to rethink the nature and mix of the accountability mechanisms upon which they rely. States will need to fashion systems that focus on educational outcomes and that provide strong incentives for improved results throughout the system by linking performance with tangible consequences in the form of rewards and sanctions.

Historically, states have regulated local educational practices largely by setting standards for inputs into the education system, e.g., per pupil expenditures, availability of instructional resources, staff qualifications, program offerings, and the like. States rarely attempted to influence directly the nature of educational practices by regulating teaching methods or curriculum content. Nor have they collected or used information on educational outcomes—student performance—as part of their regulatory or accountability system. With rare exception, states have not applied sanctions for failure to meet state standards, though they have had statutory authority to withhold funds or force consolidation for districts that did not comply. In short, states have relied on a set of bureaucratic regulations of educational inputs largely to provide legitimacy to an otherwise unregulated system.

Within the past decade, states have begun to tighten and strengthen their accountability strategies. Beginning in the mid-1970s, states have incorporated minimum competency testing into their policy frameworks. Thus, they began to specify and measure outcome standards. However, the standards were often set relatively low, focusing exclusively on basic-skills performance. Typically, states did relatively little beyond collecting and reporting test scores, relying on their publicity to stimulate and inform local improvement efforts.

Second, several states have begun recently to incorporate the findings of the effective schools research into their regulatory systems, establishing standards for such education practices as staff development, goal setting, principal leadership, and the like. Thus, in addition to regulating inputs and inspecting results, many states also have begun to regulate educational practice.

Third, there is renewed interest among states in developing appropriate sanctions for poor performance or noncompliance with state standards. For example, Arkansas linked its revised accreditation standards to school district consolidation, forcing school districts that failed to meet standards to dissolve and consolidate with a neighboring district. And both South Carolina and New Jersey have developed procedures for the state to intervene in the management and/or governance of local districts that fail to meet state standards. In New York State, schools with the lowest academic performance are required to participate in a school improvement program with state-sponsored technical assistance.

These developments in state accountability systems have occurred at a time when state attention has been focused largely on improving the quality of the lowest-performing schools and districts in the state. In the past, state efforts were devoted to raising the floor of educational perform-ance. As states turn their attention to raising the ceiling of educational performance, they will need to rethink their approach to holding schools and districts accountable. More specifically, they will need to address several broad issues.

First, states must link the accountability system to the assessment system, so accountability focuses primarily on how well schools produce desired results, framed in terms of school goals.

Second, states must fashion systems that focus on both the school building and the school district simultaneously. Holding individual schools accountable for performance recognizes that schools are the primary units for providing instruction and the basic building blocks for reform. It is consistent with the overall call for promoting greater school site autonomy and acknowledges the often substantial differences in performance among schools within the same district. However, because schools operate under the resource constraints, direction, policy guidance, and support system of the local school district, accountability systems must be designed to hold both schools and districts accountable for their performance.

Third, states will need to set appropriate performance standards for schools. There are three different standards of comparison the state can use to judge the adequacy of school performance—absolute standards, comparative standards, and improvement standards.

When *absolute* standards are employed, the performance of each school or district is compared with some fixed, predetermined standards. For example, the state might require 85 percent of the students in every school to pass state tests, or it might set a goal of no greater than a 5 percent dropout rate for each school. Such an approach enables the accountability system to reflect state goals and targets equally throughout the system. However, it also means that the accountability system will serve largely to distinguish upper-middle-class schools from those serving predominately poor students, since school performance and student body composition will be highly correlated.

In contrast, a *comparative* approach would judge a school's perform-ance only against those serving similar student bodies. Such an approach offers several advantages. It is likely to be perceived as legitimate by educators, because it recognizes that socioeconomic and other resource factors influence school performance. Schools that serve predominately poor and minority students will have opportunities for success, because they are essentially competing against one another. At the same time, it reduces the likelihood that schools serving more affluent students will be complacent, because they, too, will be measured against similar schools.

Thus, the low-performing schools that seldom have opportunities to be recognized for success will find it possible to receive recognition for their efforts. Schools in affluent communities, for whom recognition can often be a function of their clientele rather than their effectiveness, will be challenged by the efforts of other schools with equally advantaged student bodies. However, this approach also has several disadvantages. It sets lower standards for schools with large concentrations of poor students. If these standards remain low, ultimately it will work to the disadvantage of the most-at-risk students.

When *improvement* standards are used, a school's performance is judged against its own previous performance. Any school that shows significant gains, regardless of its starting point, is viewed as successful and deserving of reward. This approach makes it possible for virtually all schools to be successful (except those at the very top with little room for additional improvement). It increases the likelihood that low-performing schools will be viewed as successful simply because progress is easier to achieve when one starts at the bottom.

These three standards of comparison are not mutually exclusive. Each offers unique advantages and disadvantages. If carefully combined, they ought to provide rewards for outstanding performance and powerful incentives for continued improvement throughout the system.

Fourth, once standards are set, states need to link rewards to performance. Although rewards may take a variety of forms (such as recognition or flexibility), there is reason to believe that discretionary dollars for the school building should be an important feature of any reward system. The reason is not that additional dollars will motivate school staff to work harder. Rather, additional resources can powerfully underscore both the intrinsic satisfaction and the external recognition that come with success. In addition, the school's decision about the use of additional resources can foster shared problem-solving among school staff.

Finally, for schools that persistently fail to show improvement or meet performance standards, states must develop appropriate forms of intervention. State intervention strategies may involve a sequence of steps, including requirements for schools and school districts to develop and implement improvement plans, providing assistance in the development and implementation of such plans, specifying the steps the school or district must take in order to meet standards, or ultimately, some more forceful intervention, such as consolidation or state takeover of the district.

In moving toward performance-oriented accountability systems, states will need to review existing approaches to regulating educational inputs and practices. Greater emphasis on outcomes and performance must be balanced with the value of input regulations for ensuring equality of educational opportunity, especially for students residing in rural, small, or poor districts. It also will need to be balanced against the potential of carefully crafted educational process and practice standards to effectively structure and inform local planning and school improvement efforts.

Beyond the need to sort out various regulatory arrangements, states also need to consider other possible accountability mechanisms. For example, a system that relies heavily on diversity and autonomy among local school sites can accommodate, if not capitalize on, market mechanisms of control. Although this approach can take a number of forms, the underlying principle involves providing opportunities to students and their parents to enroll in the school or educational program of their choice. The assumption here is that if enrollment and funding levels are linked, schools have an incentive to make themselves as attractive as possible. Variability in educational programs among schools can allow for careful matching between school and student preferences and needs, presumably boosting productivity in the process.

Another approach to accountability relies on professional mechanisms of control. A professional control model essentially turns decisions about appropriate educational practice to a self-regulating profession. It presumes that a well-developed knowledge-base informs the training, certification, and evaluation of teachers, and that working conditions allow highly trained professionals to exercise judgment and employ the most appropriate instructional practices. One attraction of increased professional control is its potential to attract and retain highly talented individuals in the profession.

Within the education system, few mechanisms are already in place that can form the basis of a professional system of control. The National Board for Professional Teaching Standards, established by the Carnegie Forum on Education and the Economy, is intended to be such a mechanism. It will enable the profession to establish standards for the certification of high levels of teaching competence. There are proposals to create comparable boards at the state level for the licensure of beginning teachers as well. In most states, licensure responsibilities currently reside in lay state boards of education, which are expected to act on behalf of the broad public interest. States must carefully examine whether both licensure and certification ought to be determined by the profession or whether licensure more appropriately belongs in the hands of agents of the public.

To stimulate continuous school improvement, states must analyze carefully and determine the most appropriate mix of professional, market, outcome, process, and input systems of accountability. They also must develop an appropriate set of incentives and sanctions attached to accountability mechanisms. The task for states is not to select the single best approach. Rather, the fundamental task for states is to sort out which mix of control strategies, rewards, and sanctions will contribute most effectively to productivity improvements according to each particular state's circumstances.

Conclusion

The preceding analysis has argued that the challenges facing the education system are fundamentally different from those it has confronted in the past, largely because of significant changes in the economic and social fabric of the country. Responding to these new challenges will require a fundamental restructuring of schools, especially of the way instruction is provided and staff roles and responsibilities are defined. However, needed changes in schools cannot occur without corresponding changes in the way that local districts and states operate. States and districts alike must find ways to create a pervasive emphasis on performance and results throughout the education system. Local districts will need to find ways to shift greater decisionmaking authority and responsibility to the school site level to create mechanisms for enhanced professional and parental involvement in decisionmaking, and to provide resources and other forms of support and assistance to individual schools. States, in turn, must significantly strengthen their efforts to set educational goals and assess performance, to stimulate local diversity and experimentation, and to provide rewards and sanctions linked to school performance. Only by making concordant changes at the school, district, and state levels will the education system be able to respond to the challenges of the coming decade.

References

Applebee, Arthur; Judith A. Langer; and Ina V. S. Mullis. *The Writing Report Card: Writing Achievement in American Schools.* Princeton, N.J.: Educational Testing Service, 1986.

Bossert, Steven T.; David C. Dwyer; Brian Rowan; and Ginny V. Lee. "The Instructional Management Role of the Principal." *Educational Administration Quarterly* 18 (1982).

Carnegie Forum on Education and the Economy. *A Nation Prepared: Teachers for the 21st Century.* Report of the Task Force on Teaching as a Profession. Washington D.C.: Carnegie Forum on Education and the Economy, 1986.

Cohen, Michael. "Designing State Assessment Systems." *Phi Delta Kappan,* April 1988.

————. "Instructional, Management, and Social Conditions in Effective Schools." In A. Odden and L. D. Webb, eds., *School Finance and School Improvement: Linkages for the 1980s.* Cambridge, Mass.: Ballinger Publishing Co., 1983.

————. "State Boards in an Era of Reform." *Phi Delta Kappan,* September 1987.

Corcoran, Thomas B. "The Role of the District in School Effectiveness." In *Increasing Educational Success: The Effective Schools Model*. Committee on Education and Labor, House of Representatives. Washington, D.C.: U.S. Government Printing Office, 1987.

Danzberger, Jacqueline P., et al. *School Boards: Strengthening Grass Roots Leadership*. Washington, D.C.: Institute for Educational Leadership, 1986.

Darling-Hammond, Linda. "The Toledo (Ohio) Public School Intern and Intervention Program." In A. E. Wise, et al., *Case Studies for Teacher Evaluation: A Study of Effective Practices*. Santa Monica, Calif.: Rand, 1984.

David, Jane. "The Puzzle of Structural Change." Paper prepared for Symposium on Structural Change in Secondary Education, National Center on Effective Secondary Schools, 1987.

Kerchner, Charles T. "Union-Made Teaching: The Effects of Labor Relations on Teaching Work." In Ernest Z. Rothkopf, ed., *Review of Research in Education 12*. Washington, D.C.: American Education Research Association, 1986.

Meyer, John W., and Brian Rowan. "The Structure of Education Organizations." In M. W. Meyer and Associates, *Environments and Organizations*. San Francisco: Jossey-Bass, 1978.

NASBE Task Force on State Board Leadership. *The Challenge of Leadership: State Boards of Education in an Era of Reform*. Alexandria, Va.: National Association of State Boards of Education, 1987.

National Assessment of Educational Progress. *The Reading Report Card: Progress toward Excellence in Our Schools*. Princeton, N.J.: Educational Testing Service, 1985.

National Governors' Association. *Jobs, Growth & Competitiveness*. Washington, D.C.: National Governors' Association, 1987.

―――. *Results in Education: 1987*. Washington, D.C.: National Governors' Association, 1987.

―――. *Time for Results: The Governors' 1991 Report on Education*. Washington, D.C. National Governors' Association, 1986.

Purkey, Stuart C., and Marshall S. Smith. "Effective Schools: A Review." *Elementary School Journal* 83, no. 4 (1983).

Raywid, Mary Anne. "Restructuring School Governance: Two Models." Draft paper prepared for the Center for Policy Research in Education, 1987.

Resnick, Daniel P., and Lauren B. Resnick. "Standards, Curriculum and Performance: A Historical and Comparative Perspective." *Educational Researcher*, April 1985.

Resnick, Lauren B. *Education and Learning to Think*. Washington, D.C.: National Academy Press, 1987.

Smith, Marshall S., and Stuart C. Purkey. "School Reform: The District Policy Implications of the Effective Schools Literature." *Elementary School Journal* 85, no. 3 (1985).

Stern, Joyce D., ed. *The Condition of Education: A Statistical Report 1987 Edition*. Washington, D.C.: Center for Education Statistics, U.S. Department of Education, 1987.

30

The Uncertain Future of National Education Policy: Private Schools and the Federal Role

Bruce S. Cooper

Introduction

The setting was the Carl Perkins Hearing Room, the US House of Representatives 10 March 1987. The atmosphere was tense and the stakes were high. Two key witnesses were testifying before the House Subcommittee on Education: the Bishop of Covington, Kentucky, the Most Reverend John A. Hughes, a speaker for Catholic and other religious schools, was at one end of the table; and at the other end Dr Richard R. Green, Superintendent of the Minneapolis public schools, spokesman for the American Association of School Administrators (AASA), the national superintendents' group, as well as other public school associations. Their concern was nothing short of the future of federal aid to education; their topic, the re-authorization of Chapter 1, the nation's largest and most important law for federal support to education.

In past years, Bishop Hughes and Dr Green would have appeared before this subcommittee arm-in-arm, united in advocating a common bill for the continuance of the $3.4 billion program, which had between 1965 and 1985 pumped more than $40 billion of federal aid into the poorest schools, in the poorest neighborhoods, to give remedial help to the neediest, lowest achieving children in reading, writing, and mathematics. Today, however, the two leaders were arguing from conflicting ideological positions and for different programs, signaling a division in the once cohesive lobby for federal aid to education and an apparent collapse of the coalition which had successfully protected Title I/Chapter 1 since 1965.

Bishop Hughes, chair of the Committee on Education of the United State Catholic Conference, spoke first, 'on behalf of 2.8 million children who attend the 9245 elementary and secondary Catholic schools, as well as for the millions of people, parents, and others who support them' (*Testimony on HR 950*, p.1). The Bishop broke ranks with the public school groups when he uttered the unutterable: advocating a kind of limited 'voucher' to parents for the 300,000 or so poor, low achieving children eligible for Chapter 1 services in Catholic and other religious schools, if the public schools were unable to provide services themselves. He stated in his testimony:

> First, we recommend that school districts be allowed to provide a *parental grant* as an option within the Chapter 1 program. This would provide parents of Chapter 1 students alternative methods of obtaining supplemental educational services best suited for their children. The school district could provide such a compensatory education grant equal to the Chapter 1 per pupil expenditure within the district if equitable services could not be provided in any other way. (p. 3, emphasis added).

Though the good bishop was careful not to say the no-no word 'voucher' – he instead used terms such as 'parental grant' and 'compensatory education grant' – reactions from the public school spokesman, Dr Green, and from the Democratic subcommittee chair, Augustus G. ('Gus') Hawkins of California, were swift and sure: Green stated in no uncertain terms

Reprinted with permission from *Journal of Education Policy*, Vol. 2, No. 5 (1987): 165–81.

that private schools were 'divisive' and should receive no public aid through the parents. Representative Hawkins, leaning back in his chair, high atop the hearing room dias, said that no 'voucher bill' would ever be reported out of 'his committee'. All that HR 950, the bill on the table, was prepared to offer private, parochial school pupils was a $30 million add-on grant to help *public schools districts* with extra capital costs for serving these private school students off the premises of the parochial schools, as the courts now require. In the words of Superintendent Green:

> We are pleased to endorse the new $30 million authorization in Section 117(d) to help local districts pay for the capital expenses they have had to incur in providing services to private school students. We believe this provision will significantly help districts comply with the Supreme Court's *Aguilar* v. *Felton* ruling (Testimony, March 10, 1987, p.3).

So, the schism between public and private school groups had appeared. The stage was now set for a new era in school policy and politics: school faction against school faction. After more than two decades of relative comity and stability, the basic framework of educational politics had changed (Cooper and Poster 1986). The rules of the game, and the coalitions that played by these rules, were severely altered, though contests between advocates of public aid to private, religiously-affiliated schools and those against any public aid to non-public schools were almost as old as the nation itself (Cooper 1985, Levin 1983).

This chapter analyzes the events leading up to this conflict between public and parochial school advocates. Why had the relative calm between 1965 (when President Lyndon B. Johnson signed into law the Elementary and Secondary Education Act, with its all-important Title I, later called Chapter 1) and 1985 been broken? How had the US Supreme Court's ruling on 1 July 1985, in *Aguilar* v. *Felton*, a decision forbidding public school teachers from entering parochial schools to deliver these Chapter 1 services to eligible students, disrupted the relationship between public and private school interest groups? And, based on this new relationship, what is the future of federal aid to education, as illustrated in the 1987 legislation for the re-authorization of Chapter 1: one continuing Chapter 1 as is (as indicated by HR 950) and the other introduced by the Reagan administration, advocating locally-issued, optional vouchers to parents for their eligible, but unserved children in church-related schools.

Background

The politics of conflict resolved

The relationship between private schools and government finance has a long and complex history, one relevant to the future of national education policy in 1987 and beyond. Prior to 1965, public aid to parochial schools had been a major stumbling block to the passage of a law for federal aid to schools. Whenever a federal assistance bill was introduced in the late 1940s through the early 1960s, supporters of private, sectarian schools demanded a fair share of the money for their schools and their children. A coalition against federal aid to parochial schools emerged, comprised of the public school establishment, the civil liberties groups (e.g., Protestants and Other Americans United for the Separation of Church and State, and the American Civil Liberties Union), and the American Jewish Congress (see Eidenberg and Morey 1969: 204).

And 1965, when President Lyndon Johnson introduced the Elementary and Secondary Education Act, was no different. The key spokesperson for the Catholic schools, the Rt. Reverend Frederick G. Hockwalt of the National Catholic Welfare Conference, refused to support the bill unless aid was included for children in his schools. Direct funding would not work: politically it was too divisive; constitutionally it would certainly have violated the First Amendment doctrine of the 'separation of Church and State'. What was President Johnson to do?

The formula worked out in ESEA was a stroke of genius and the well-known Johnsonian 'art of the possible'. He insisted on the following: (1) that parochial school students receive *services*, not funds, under the same guarantees and eligibility requirements as students in public schools; (2) that the concept of 'child benefit' be substituted for direct aid to private schools; and (3) most importantly, that the funds be given totally and directly to the public schools, which would then hire additional public school staff to serve the private schools. The same approach was used in the 'sharing' of materials, books, audio-visual equipment, in Title II of the same law: these items would be 'owned' by public schools and 'loaned' to private schools which had eligible students. In all, then, the Title I/Chapter 1 law explicitly guaranteed equitable services for all 'entitled' children, in both public and private schools. Without the dual concepts of 'entitlement' whereby all needy children were eligible for services, and 'child benefit', whereby federal resources went to private school children, not private schools, it is very unlikely that the Title 1 program would have been enacted into law.

Once passed, a twenty-year history of co-operation between local school districts and parochial schools emerged. In 97% of the cases, eligible Title I/Chaper 1 children were served on the premises of their private schools: public school teachers were given a religiously 'neutral' room in the parochial school where they could give remedial help in reading and mathematics to students. It was simple, safe, and convenient – since Chapter 1 children could easily leave their regular classroom (in what often was called a 'pull-out' program) and enter the remedial center for help. Everyone seemed happy: public schools got extra money, extra staff, and primary responsibility for the program in parochial schools; private school students received much-needed help, located in their schools; and private schools received indirect help, via their children's education. Political leaders, too, found a welcome base of support in the Democratic strongholds, the major cities where many Catholic schools, serving poor children, were located. It was no wonder that Chapter 1 was re-authorized so handily between 1965 and 1985 with such strong, unified political support from both political parties and public and private schoold groups.

The Court, Constitution, and conflict

On 1 July, 1985, however, the US Supreme Court, in the *Aguilar* v. *Felton* decision, ruled that the hard-won accommodation between public and private, sectarian sectors was no longer legal. According to a 5–4 decision of the judges, public school teachers could no longer come onto the premises of the parochial school to offer the remedial help, because such involvement was 'excessively entangling'. The Supreme Court found that the Chapter 1 program failed the triparte test of constitutionality created earlier in the *Lemon* v. *Kurtzman* decision. According to *Lemon*, statutes must (1) have 'secular purposes', (2) 'neither advance nor inhibit religion', and (3) not foster 'an excessive government entanglement' [403 US 602, 612–13 (1971)]. But in order for authorities to know that criteria one and two are being met – that the program was neither advancing nor inhibiting religion and was 'secular' in purpose, public official had to monitor and observe the Chapter 1 program. The inspectorial function, then, violated the third test, the 'excessive entanglement' prohibition. To fulfill the first two requirements, they must violate the third, a judicial Catch-22. As reported in the Court decision about New York City schools, public school supervisors

> took specific steps to be sure that its Chapter 1 classes were free of religious content. It instructed its personnel to avoid all involvement with religious activities in the schools to which it was assigned; it directed them to keep contact with private school personnel to a minimum; and most important, it set up a supervisory system involving unannounced classroom visits (*Aguilar*, p.10).

Programmatic fall-out: In the two academic years (1985–86 and 1986–87) since the Court's ruling, school districts have found it difficult to impossible to continue serving Chapter 1 children off the premises of the parochial schools legally, conveniently, economically, and equitably. Recent surveys (US Department of Education 1987) show that the most common form of off-site service is to transport private school children to public schools. This approach has not been favored by many parents and private school leaders – since it is highly disruptive, time-consuming, and inconvenient.

Other attempts by school districts have included using mobile classroom vans which rotate around the district, parked at the curbside of the private school to take on Chapter 1 children in groups of 4 to 8 students. This method is easier for the children (they only have to walk a few yards), but it has proved very expensive (vans cost between $45,000 and $105,000 each per year to rent or buy, operate, maintain, store, insure, and fuel), difficult to move through city traffic, and labor intensive (they require a teacher, guard, and driver, plus a maintenance crew). Parents have complained that the vans show up late, or not at all, tie up traffic, and block access to the schools. (Large city parochial schools may have six to ten of these monsters parked at the doorstep, eliminating virtually all the teachers, parking spots, blocking access to the doors, and confusing delivery trucks, fire trucks, and garbage vans.) One Catholic school administrator mentioned that the 'wrong van' showed up, which did not have the children's workbooks and records – so the teachers had nothing to 'teach with'.

Other districts have tried hooking Chapter 1 schools together electronically, using television or computers. These methods have the advantage of being within the private school, available, and simple; they do pose problems of use, however, since parochial schools must provide the staff and expertise in the building to utilize the technogical forms of Chapter 1 services. Perhaps Chapter 1 children also need a personal approach, not a canned program beamed in from the central board of public education. Problems of software development, use of technology, and where to fit the remedial services into the school program still exist. Only about 8% of the districts are attempting to use technology to overcome the strictures of *Aguilar*.

In all, then, the aftermath of the Court decision has been disasterous for the Chapter 1 remedial program. Attendance has dropped on average from between 27 to 46% in various districts, as parents remove their children or as districts cannot put together a workable program, due, for example, to the inability to purchase enough vans (hence, the request of the federal government in HR 950 for more funds for capital costs).

Legal and political fall-out: Besides the obvious educational difficulties created by the off-site requirement, the *Aguilar* decision now threatens the basic, legal tenets which have supported federal aid to education in the USA for over 20 years. First, the 'child benefit' theory is in question. The Court now holds that children can only benefit from an environment other than the one which their parents have selected, the religious setting, if these pupils are to receive the resources which the government has guaranteed and argued these students need to survive.

For many, leaving the comfort, security, and ethos of their school – for a ride to an alien public school where they are 'outsiders' and seen as 'deprived' – is a significant imposition.

For some religious families, such as the Orthodox Jewish students in the Chapter 1 program, the public school, with its co-educational program, is a violation of beliefs and norms. Hence, the key concept of 'child benefit' has now been significantly modified: it now means that students can only benefit away from their chosen school, effectively killing the tenet for them.

Second, making it impossible for some children to receive their much-needed and legally-prescribed federal services, just because of their choice of school, violates the basic concept of 'entitlement'. Now only public school children are 'entitled' to Title I/Chapter1, because it is conveniently available to them in their schools. Private school children must lose the service or give up school time to attempt to receive remediation. What other groups will be next to loose their entitled rights? Without this stipulation, the basis of federal aid for compensatory education is eroded and threatened, starting with the private school student.

Third, and perhaps most seriously, the Court decision, and its aftermath for the parochial school students of the nation, have threatened the very First Amendment rights of religious freedom which the courts are supposedly protecting. Now, since *Aguilar*, children must give up their religious choice, in order to get the programs their parents want. In effect, the Supreme Court has given greater emphasis to the 'Establishment clause' (the 'separation of Church and State' doctrine) and much less to the 'Free Exercise' portion of the Bill of Rights. For the hundred thousand or so children who are denied Chapter 1 remedial help since the Court decision, one could argue that they have also lost their religious liberty and choice. For they are penalized educationally for exercising a religious conviction: that being in a Catholic, Jewish, or Protestant setting is important to them. They, unlike other children, must now chose beween getting much-needed educational services or exercising religious freedom.

So while the government recognizes the sanctity of religion in other sectors, and provides at public expense chaplains for the armed services, for the US Congress itself (which opens each session with a prayer), for hospitals run by religious foundations, and so forth, the Court has now determined that families will be deprived of useful, equitable educational assistance if they also want a religious experience for their offspring. Thus, in its effort to prevent the government's involvement in the 'Establishment of religion', through federal aid to parochial schools, the Court may be running rough-shod over the other half of the First Amendment, the preservation of 'free exercise' of religion, an irony from a court so intent on the preservation of fundamental liberty in the US.

The political fall-out from *Aguilar* occupies us in the remainder of this chapter. The nature of federal politics of education, now and in the future, will likely witness a return to the past: the era between the second World War and 1965 when ESEA was first legislated. Our analysis will show basically two styles of political behavior: (1) prior to 1965, when school politics was ideological, fiercely divisive, and crippling to the enactment of new legislation; and (2) between 1965 and 1985, when groups buried their ideological differences (though not very deeply, we have discovered), calm and compromise were possible, and an accommodation was carefully accomplished.

The first style, the all-or-nothing conflict so common before 1965 and ESEA, was prevalent as early as 1948 when President Truman pressed for a general aid to education bill in his State of the Union Address and when the Senate in that same year easily passed the bill by a vote of 58 to 15. But the issue of aid to parochial schools emerged with full and divisive force in the House. Representative John Lesinski (Democrat, Michigan) chaired the House Education and Labor Committee and appointed Graham Barden (Democrat, North Carolina) to head the Subcommittee on Education. The so-called Barden bill was significantly different from the Senate version, denying any kind of aid to private and parochial schools. Lesinski, a Catholic, 'vowed that this "anti-Catholic bill" would never clear the full committee... The colloquy between Barden and Lesinski', according to Eidenberg and Morey (1969) 'ignited a religious controversy which had been smoldering for years' (p. 20). Francis Cardinal Spellman, prelate of New York, had even stronger feelings, calling the Barden bill 'a craven crusade of religious prejudice against Catholic children'. When even Mrs Eleanor Roosevelt backed Barden and his law prohibiting federal aid to parochial schools, the Cardinal wondered why this pillar of Democratic principles should 'repeatedly plead causes that are anti-Catholic'.

The presentations in Congress in 1987 have much in common with these earlier conflicts. As we shall see, the bills under consideration divide, rather than unite, the ideological sides in this debate. The key difference, perhaps, is the ultimate irony that the Republican administration is pleading the case for Catholic and Jewish schools, while the Democrats – long thought to be the party of the immigrant, the ethnic poor, and the urban voter – are backing the bill which will, in effect, make it impossible for children in Catholic and Jewish schools to receive the resources they are guaranteed and need. Does this foreshadow a shift in party alliances, with the Democrats speaking for the school establishment (teachers and administrators associations), while the Republicans defend the rights of parochial school families, many of whom are Black, Protestant, White, Catholic and Jewish?

The interest groups

Key to our understanding of the future of federal aid to education is an analysis of the positions of the key actors in the battle for re-authorization. As just discussed, the clarity of purpose and the unity of action which had characterized Chapter 1 and Title I for the last 22 years (since 1965) appear lost. Interest groups now stand in conflict with one another, rather than as valuable allies in a unified effort to gain Congressional re-authorization. Here is an overview of the key lobbying groups: their power, interests, and actions.

Religious school groups

Roman Catholic: Perhaps the group with the most to lose, or gain, in this current battle in Congress are children attending Roman Catholic schools. These pupils receive about 90% of all Chapter 1 services within the non-public school sector, since the Catholic church operates the largest number of private schools for low income students. Their support for Chapter 1/Title I has been strong and constant over the years. The leaders of the Catholic school organizations were relatively successful in (1) pressing bills in Congress which benefit their children; (2) working closely with local school boards in developing high-quality, on-site programs prior to the court ruling: and (3) overcoming the resistence of some key districts and states which have laws and policies against giving aid to non-public school students.

In particular, Catholic lobbyists have successfully obtained clauses in the Chapter 1 laws and re-authorizations which forcefully guarantee equitable services to all low income, low achieving students regardless of their choice of schools. Even HR 950, which is likely unworkable under the 'off-site' requirement of the *Aguilar* decision, has a stipulation in Section 117(a) that expenditures 'for educationally deprived children in private schools shall be equal to expenditures for children enrolled in public schools'. And like earlier versions, this bill has a 'bypass provision' to ensure that the federal government can get funds to private school students, even when this effort is resisted or forbidden by local or state laws and policies.

Following the court decision, the Office of the General Counsel of the US Catholic Conference (USCC), the political arm of the Catholic bishops, has followed the impact of the change on Catholic schools. It has urged its schools to continue pressing for their hard-won rights and equitability. It has counselled patience and co-operation with local authorities in working out various off-site programs. When it became clear, however, that these off-the-premises approaches were failing, there was no clear alternative, other than some form of voucher.

Yet, the USCC has failed to mount a powerful movement to change Chapter 1 after *Aguilar*. In part, the leadership of Catholic education has been ambivalent because no simple, clear alternative presents itself – as expressed in Bishop Hughes's testimony discussed at the opening of this chapter. Besides pressing for a 'parent certificate', the Bishop also supported, in the next paragraph, the expansion of HR 950 by $30 million for capital costs. It appeared that USCC was covering its bets, whether the Democratic or Republic administration's bill was passed. In part, Chapter 1 does not appear to be important enough for the hierarchy of the church to play for keeps. No Msgr Hockwalt, the leader of the Catholics during President Johnson's drafting of ESEA in 1965, has emerged to talk tough to the Congress. After all, HR 950 includes language and provision for private school students – though its method of delivery, via public school staff has proved less than equitable.

Jewish school groups: Another religious group has joined in support of federal aid to education. The Jewish community, long a stalwart in backing aid to public schools alone, has now begun to speak in favor of federal funding of Chapter 1 for children in private, Jewish schools. In part, this turnabout has occurred with the opening of Jewish day schools by all the main branches of American Judaism. The Orthodox community, with by far the largest number of day schools (often called *yeshivas*), receives some $3 million yearly in federal aid to its nearly 5000 needy children in 75 schools. The Conservative Jewish schools have many fewer schools and almost no pupils who qualify for Chapter 1. And even the Reform Jewish community, at its 1986 Biennial meeting of the Union of American Hebrew Congregations, has passed a resolution urging the UAHC to support local Jewish communities in their efforts to open Reform Jewish all-day schools, but only after the resolution renewed the deep commitment of the Jewish community to public schools.

The strongest Jewish advocacy group for Chapter 1 children in Jewish schools is Agudath Israel of America, a political organization representing the interest of the Orthodox community. Agudath Israel stands strongly alongside the USCC and its Catholic children in backing vouchers and other efforts to gain a fair share of federal funds for children in private schools. But unlike the Catholics, the Jewish groups find themselves backing these programs, like Chapter 1, because by Orthodox belief Jewish boys and girls should not go to school together; co-education, a universal quality of public education, is unacceptable to these families. Thus, Agudath Israel backs Jewish education because it is the only alternative. And since these schools accept all Jewish children, regardless of family size and income, the need for government-sponsored services is great.

Like the Catholics, the Jews find the 'off-site' provision of programs less than satisfactory; thus, Agudath Israel stands firmly with the Catholic interest groups in supporting some form of modified family certificate or 'voucher'.

Public school groups

Teachers' unions: Teachers' associations, particularly the National Education Association (NEA), have found any proposal to grant funds to parents, any kind of voucher, an attempt, in the union's eyes, to steal public funds from the much-maligned public schools. Recently, when President Reagan and Secretary of Education William J. Bennett proposed a Chapter 1 voucher, the response from the head of NEA was fast and negative. Mary H. Futtrell, NEA President, proclaimed her organization's opposition to any effort to divert public money to parents:

> Sadly, the current administration has chosen the opposite course: It has abandoned needy children, systematically slashing Chapter 1 funds . . . Substituting vouchers for what remains of Chapter 1 signals a further retreat. The intent of the Administration's proposal is not to improve but to impoverish public schools, to weaken the very institutions that have most helped the most needy. Vouchers are a hoax, a guise for funneling public monies to private schools. When this strategy is defended on the grounds that it will unleash the potential of 11 million disadvantaged children, the hoax becomes hypocritical, odious, and cruel. (Futtrell 1986: 14).

Even though public school teachers have been teaching in private schools under Chapter 1 for over 20 years, the idea of continuing this service in some other way, perhaps through some direct form of aid, is now strenuously opposed by the unions.

Administrators' groups: The public school administrators association, such as AASA represented by Dr Green in the opening scenario, have lined up against attempts to fund families of private school students under Chapter 1. The Association of California School Administrators opposes the choice-making of parents inherent in various voucher schemes, arguing that parent choice is 'selfish' concern for the child at the expense of the society:

> Parent choice proceeds from the belief that the purpose of education is to provide individual students with an education. In fact, educating the individual is but a means to the *true end* of education – which is to create a viable social order to which individuals contribute and by which they are sustained. 'Family choice' is, therefore, basically selfish and anti-social in that it focuses on the 'wants' of a single family rather than the 'needs' of society. (ACSA 1979: viii, emphasis added).

One should be weary of people expounding the 'true end' of education. Also, since when is a concern among parents that their children be well-behaved, safe, and effectively educated in reading, writing, reasoning, mathematics, and basic decency a 'selfish and anti-social aim'? After all, what more could a society expect from children than to be knowledgeable, skillful, competent, and respectful young people, even in a private schools, goals which must be a vital concern to all parents and society as well.

Other groups, too, have opposed vouchers and other approaches to privatization in education, even when limited to Chapter 1. It seems clear that 'educators' – teachers, administrators, school boards – feel that they have the most to lose by shifting funds to parents, even when these guaranteed services cannot be delivered to parochial schools except at great cost and inefficiency.

The political parties

Too little attention is payed to the role of partisan groups in determining federal school policies in the USA. Quite clearly, the Democratic Party supports enlarged federal involvement in education, though it reflects the basic concerns of the teachers and administrators, not parochial school parents and leaders. The Republicans came into office under the banner of reduced federal involvement and a disbanded US Department of Education. Yet, in the early years of the Reagan presidency, the administration did much to focus attention on education as a national issue and has presented a number of interesting concepts.

Once Republican policy-makers and groups such as the American Enterprise Institute, CATO, and the Heritage Foundation realized that education was a good outlet for their efforts to privatize education, fund the individual, and press for vouchers, conservatives began to expand their role in education. From *What Works* (US Department of Education 1986) to *Investing in Our Children* (Doyle and Levine 1985), from *Excellence in Education: The States Take Charge* (Doyle and Hartle 1985), to *A Nation Prepared?* (Carnegie Forum 1986), the importance in education of the Republic administration and its beliefs has expanded.

Yet, interestingly, on the Chapter 1 issue the Republican administration seems powerless to press its Chapter 1 voucher. In part, this is the result of the rising power of Democrats in Congress, the weakened state of the president after 'Irangate', the lack of unified lobbying among Catholics and Jews, and the lack of understanding among lawmakers concerning the changing issues in aid to parochial schools.

Some practical politics

The future of Chapter 1, the major compensatory education law, will likely be settled before this volume is published. In fact, Congress appears to be moving rapidly with hearings completed in the House and the Senate now in process (spring 1987). A range of suggestions has been made for restructuring Chapter 1 during re-authorization. At least six options have been considered, as shown in figure 1. They are arranged in a continuum from total privatization, with a national/local voucher for all children in school, to the total 'nationalization' of Chapter 1, wherein parochial school students would be dropped from the federal law – an option favored by many teachers' associations and the groups supporting the total separation of Church and State (e.g., PEARL, National Coalition for Public Education And Religious Liberty, the group responsible for initiating the *Aguilar* v. *Felton* case in the first place). Recently, PEARL has filed another suit which argues that it is unconstitutional for public school districts to 'handle' any funds for parochial school students, which would make Chapter 1 services unavailable under HR 950 to any private school pupils via the public schools (vouchers, anyone?).

These six options for aid to private school students are analyzed below in light of a five-part test: legality, feasibility, practicality, acceptability, and educational advisibility:

1. *Legality under the Constitution*: Is the option going to pass Court muster as non-entangling?
2. *Political feasibility*: Would such a proposal pass Congress and the White House, given current and future political beliefs?
3. *Practicality*: Could local education authorities or other agencies implement such a proposal, given issues of educational quality and efficiency?
4. *Acceptability to parents*: Would families and private school leaders find the plan useful to them?
5. *Educational advisibility*: Would the alternative lead to a quality educational program for children in non-public schools?

Option 1: Total privatization of education

At one extreme on the continuum, the US might overcome the problem of funding non-

Figure 1.   Policy options for the future of Chapter 1

Options	Example	Brief Analysis
Option 1: Total voucherization	New Hampshire, 'Alum Rock' experiment	Unlikely: requires joint action of states, and local government
Option 2: Chapter 1: Manditory local voucher	TEACH bill	Died in committee: strong 'compensatory' and 'privatization' qualities: allows choice among schools and private/public sectors
Option 3: Chapter 1: Local option voucher	(a) Wednesday Group's CHOICE bill (b) Reagan administration's Compensatory Educational Certificates bill, subtitle A	Died last session: parental choice and 'Individualized Instructional Plan' In 100th Congress: strong opposition from Democrats and public education lobby; private school concern about options to locals
Option 4: Chapter 1: By-pass to parents	Vitullo-Martin/Cooper Proposal: already done in by-pass states e.g., Missouri, Virginia	Difficult during Congressional re-authorization; legal questions
Option 5: Chapter 1: Re-authorize with small increase for private school off-site costs	Hawkin's Bill (HR-950)	Status quo: continues off-site approach: strong Democratic/teacher union support; loses parochial school groups
Option 6: Chapter 1: Remove denominational private school students from law	Pre-1965 approach	Strong support from PEARL, some public school groups; not likely

public and public schools by 'going private', through a universal school voucher or tax credits (negative tax credits for the poor). Such a plan would create a large, regional 'market' in education, where parents could select among a variety of public and private schools and the government funds 'would follow the child' to the schoolhouse door.

Such ideas have been around since the 1960s (Jencks 1970). (They actually can be traced back to the 1820s when states funded schools which were sponsored by a variety of local denominational, eleemosynary, and public schools.) New Hampshire in 1974 came close to passing a statewide voucher scheme, whereby all education would be available with a grant from the state. Many communities in the upper tier of New England (Vermont, New Hampshire, and Maine) already allow parents to opt out of their 'local' schools, to any available school of choice, even schools located across state borders in other states.

These total privatization plans (vouchers, tax credits, transfer credits) would likely pass the first test, *constitutionality*. In fact, the US Supreme Court in *Mueller* v. *Allen* ruled that Minnesota's state tuition tax deduction program was legal, since families could apply for tax relief from school costs whether their children attended a public or private school. It was non-entangling since it did not involve public schools administering a denomination program; and it neither 'established' nor 'prohibited' religion, since it was evenhandedly available for a portion of costs to attend either public or private schools.

On the second test, *political feasibility* total privatization fails miserably: there is no chance of passage at the national level at this time. Ever since economist Milton Friedman (1955) proposed the voucherization of education, the idea has raised the deepest enmity of school professionals.

Practicality and *acceptability* seem high, however. Such a plan could easily be implemented, with checks being issued to families of school-age children, through some kind of local voucher authority which could act as a distributor, clearinghouse, and fair advertising agency. The experience of the Alum Rock limited voucher plan (see Rand Corporation 1981, Lines 1985) seems to show that it can be done. Other nations, such as Holland and Denmark, both with official state religions, have given families wider choice at public expense. And public interest in vouchers remains high, with various polls showing that parents would enjoy the chance to choose their children's school. Black parents, for example, prefer choice under a voucher by 64% in favor, 23% against, as indicated in a Gallup Poll in 1983.

The ideas seems to pass most of the criteria: total privatization is likely legal, probably workable, certainly intriguing. Whether it would lead to improve education quality is not known. But politically, such an extreme is a bombshell and has virtually no chance of passing.

Option 6: Drop private school students from the law

The opposite extreme from total privatization through a general school voucher would be to drop private school students from federal aid programs completely (see figure 1). Such a move would please PEARL and other groups which object to any involvement of 'church and state'. Such a strong move would however, run counter to the whole history of Title I/Chapter 1, which depended on support from lawmakers from heavily Catholic and Jewish areas. Such drastic medicine would also radically change the 'entitlement' quality of the compensatory education laws which guaranteed help to children who qualify (poor, low achieving) regardless of what kind of schools they select.

To drop the private school pupils from the major federal aid program would be dramatic indeed. It would mean that the First Amendment concerns about 'entanglement' would completely overpower the right of 'free exercise', though if Chapter 1 remains as is (as under the pending bill, HR 950), the net effect may be the same: parochial school students may be excluded *de facto* since the off-site provision is too inconvenient, costly, and unworkable.

Chapter 1 Vouchers

If total voucherization (total privatization of education) is not possible, and if it is unlikely that private school students will be excluded entirely, what about using Chapter 1 as an opportunity to give parents more choice over what kinds of *remedial* education their offspring might get? The Chapter 1 voucher has a certain appeal; three such bills have been introduced in Congress since the *Aguilar* decision. These plans vary in two important ways: first, these proposed policies differ as to whether they include all Chapter 1-eligible children or just those attending non-public schools. Second, they vary as to whether they are manditory or optional at the local level. Three bills, TEACH, CHOICE, and a Compensatory Education Certificate (CEC) law all created Chapter 1 vouchers. The first, TEACH, required that all Chapter 1 children receive a voucher; CHOICE and the CEC law allowed local districts the option to issue them to nonpublic school families.

Option 2: Manditory voucherization of Chapter 1

The Equity And CHoice Act (TEACH) proposed in 1985 the total voucherization of Chapter 1 and required that local education authorities issue these grants to all Chapter 1-eligible pupils in private schools. Based on the local average expenditure for Chapter 1 in the public schools, ranging from about $400 to $1300 per child per year, these TEACH vouchers would be awarded by the local district to private school families.

Under the principle established in *Aguilar* granting vouchers to parents might likely be legal, since public schools themselves have no direct contact with denominational ones: no supervision is required, other than to see that the grant is in an educational setting. According to TEACH, the voucher could be cashed in three different settings: (1) a public school in same district where the child was currently enrolled: (2) a public school in another school district, allowing children to apply the voucher toward the costs of going to an out-of-district public school: or (3) a private school for use in remedial education or tuition.

In terms of the five-part criteria for evaluating Chapter 1 programs, the manditory Chapter 1 voucher stands much like other privatization measures. It is probably workable, acceptable to many parents, and educationally sound, though until it is tried on a wide scale, it is hard to be precise. But, TEACH is unacceptable politically; it died in the House Education subcommittee in 1985 for most of the same reasons as a general voucher bill would: too threatening to the forces that support the public schools. Constitutionally, TEACH would likely pass a legal test, under the *Mueller* decision, though if the PEARL case now pending were to be decided in PEARL's favor, then the fact that local school districts handled the TEACH voucher money would be 'entangling' and a violation of the 'separation' principle.

The politics of TEACH illustrates the new politics of education in the US. Supporters (though weak) stand up against a powerful array of teachers' unions, civil liberties groups, and other liberal public interests. Perhaps a voluntary Chapter 1 voucher, controlled by the local education authorities, to be discussed next, might be more acceptable.

Option 3: A local option voucher (LOV)

Two more recent bills – one proposed last session by a group of Republican Congressmen called the Wednesday Group, the other introduced in 1987 by the Reagan Administration with a 'compensatory Education certificate' (CEC) – appear to overcome some of the problems of other voucher plans, though its chances of passage seem dim.

The CHOICE Bill: The CHOICE legislation (CHildren's Opportunity [or Option] for Intensive Compensatory Education Act of 1986) has five principles at its heart. First, it targets Chapter 1 services 'on those children who are most in need: educationally disadvantaged low-income students'. Second, it stresses 'comprehensive' and 'effective' services: third, the law would 'significantly increase the participation of parents' in the educative process. Fourth, it expands the service options by including 'special instruction services by a range of public, private elementary and secondary schools and universities'.

Fifth, it assures continued 'enforcement of civil rights laws'. If a locality cannot serve private school students well, it can use 'the issuance of educational vouchers' (Section 555.a) for poor, underachieving school children, much as Chapter 1 has since its inception.

New to CHOICE, however, would be the use of Individualized Instructional Plans (or IIPs), much like children in special education receive. Even private school students are included:

> Representatives of private schools shall be consulted with respect to the development of such a plan if the child is primarily enrolled in a private elementary or secondary school, or if the child is currently receiving special instructional services from a private school through the issuance of an educational voucher. [Sec.556,f.(3)]

Parents would then be invited to participate in setting their children's compensatory education program, whether they attended a public or a private school. Similar to earlier laws, CHOICE allowed a bypass, whereby states that constitutionally prohibit the issuing of vouchers to parochial schools could seek a direct grant from the US Department of Education, as is now the case in Missouri, Oklahoma, and Virginia. As Republican Congressman Thomas Petri, one of the bill's sponsors explains, the proposed law 'offers a variety of alternatives', which assures that 'the spirit of free enterprise and competition is alive and well'.

On the five-part test, CHOICE would likely be acceptable to parents and private schools, would be workable, and does overcome the constitutional problem of having public schools serve private ones. The direct involvement in drawing up the Individualized Instructional Plan may be a legal problem, though PL 94–142 does require direct involvement of parents, private school, and public school (though the private school inclusion in this law is under challenge in some states for its possible illegality). And like TEACH, the CHOICE bill was not successful in Congress and is now dead (see figure 1). It faced the same political difficulties as all the other voucher schemes, whether manditory or local options.

Republican Administration's Compensatory Education Certificates: In March 1987, as Chapter 1 reauthorization began, the Reagan administration introduced its own law in contrast to the Democratic bill HR 950. The administration's law contained an optional, local voucher provision in its American Excellence Act of 1987 (AEA). Much like CHOICE, the AEA law makes a strong point of including children who attended parochial schools, including a Compensatory Education Certificate (CEC). This law, then, allows LEAs to fund local private schools pupils and their families through a grant, as a way around the problems posed by the *Aguilar* decision.

Similar to TEACH, this bill permits families, once they receive their CEC, to use it in their local private or public school, or outside the district in a public school or university program for remediation. In the words of the proposed law

> the Act would authorize and LEA to provide these certificates if it determines that doing so (1) would be more effective in meeting the needs of eligible children than direct services provided by the LEA, or (2) needed to provide services required under Chapter 1.

This bill has several advantages over earlier voucher proposals. It leaves the decision on issuing a CEC to the local school board, thus allowing the district to decide. Some cities, such as New York City, might decide that it is cheaper and easier to give the parents the voucher, rather than to pay exhorbitant amounts for vans, buses, computers hook-ups, costs which come out of both the public school and private school portion in equal proportions ('off the top').

Legally, this kind of grant might be acceptable, since there are no public employees on the premises of the parochial school. It would be workable, sound, and efficient, though politically, as our opening scenario indicates, the bill faces tough going. There are some questions as to whether LEAs would give away these resources, and how parents might use them. But such practical matters pale beside the obvious political problems which this proposal – however interesting and elegant – seems to pose.

Why the Republican Party has not gone out strongly for it, joined by the Catholic and Jewish school leaders, is difficut to say. Obviously, the political consensus around Chapter 1 is disrupted; but no clear avenue has been opened for replacing Chapter 1 services on the premises. Republican lawmakers likely do not want to offend the powerful local public school interests; Catholic and Jewish leaders eem somewhat disorganized and are unwilling to attack Chapter 1 publicly. But, once the bill reaches the floor of the House and Senate, some of the issues may become clearer and opposition to HR 950 (to be discussed next) may emerge.

HR 950: Chapter 1 reauthorization law: House Democrats and moderate Republicans seem to be supporting this bill, entitled the 'Special Educational Needs Act of 1987' the reauthorization of Chapter 1. From a private school perspective, the proposed law is basically a continuation of the program, as is, with the requirement for the range of off-site programs, with a small addition of funds ($30 million) for capital costs associated with the leasing or buying of property, mobile vans, and educatinal radio, television, and computers).

From research already completed (Vitullo-Martin and Cooper 1987), it seems quite clear that HR 950 will not recover the parochial school youngsters who have left the program, either because it was too inconvenient or simply was not available to them locally. The bill, while it acknowledges the problems created by *Aguilar*, fails to respond in an effective way; instead, it gives the local districts more money. This approach is consistent with previous practices in Chapter 1, where public school interest groups are more interested in receiving and controlling the millions of federal dollars. The idea of losing control of even a small portion of the funds is anathema to a system which has become used to federal funding, and will hardly give up. (LEAs would rather spend millions on vans, renovation of buildings, costly transportation, and educationally unsound programs thant give up a penny to private school parents for their children.)

Thus, in terms of our five criteria, HR 950 fulfills the political feasibility, in that it appears to have storng political support from the Democrat-controlled Congress and from the powerful public school lobby. In terms of legality, at this time continuing off-site will pass constitutional concerns. But, on grounds of educational quality, convenience, acceptability, and practicality, we have already seen that moving children off-site is not working. The latest figures from Agudath Israel on its participation rates among children in Jewish schools, for example, show that among the 4403 eligible for service under Chapter 1 in 1987, and 926 (or 21%) are actually being served: 745 children in the 72 mobile vans leased by the boards of education, 81 in neutral sites, and 100 in public schools locations. One wonders, too, about the educational quality of a program that so separates the remedial function under Chapter 1 from the regular education effort of the non-public schools.

Option 4: National bypass provision

As shown in figure 1, part 4, one other approach to the future of federal aid to non-public schools would be to use the provision for bypass in the current or future laws (e.g., HR 950) to allow unserved children in parochial schools to receive the Chapter 1 program. Under such an approach (see Vitullo-Martin and Cooper 1987), the US Secretary of Education could 'invoke bypass' for communities which were not providing equitable services and parents or groups of parents could become the 'third party agent' for direct funding.

This method has already been used in 105 school districts between 1970 and 1986 when LEAs were unwilling or unable (usually because of a state constitutional prohibition against public aid to private schools) to serve parochial school students. The process, as in the past, is being stipulated in the current reauthorization legislation, and could be used imediately in locations where the *Aguilar* decision has made off-premises programs unworkable or unavailable. It could be extended to the entire nation, since overall the data show a sharp decrease in both the quantity and quality of services for children attending religiously-affiliated schools. It would be legal and would have the effect of voucherizing Chapter 1 without a long and bitter Congressional fight over the issue.

Summary

It seems quite clear that the future of federal aid to education, particularly to denominational schools, is changed and uncertain. The rules of the game have shifted from consensus and co-operation among school interest groups, to open conflict over the nature of future programs. Whereas the US Catholic Conference and Agudath Israel of America had joined the American Association of School Administrators, the National Education Associateon, and the American Federation of Teachers, in supporting a common bill for re-authorizing Chapter 1 since 1965, when the Elementary and Secondary Education Act was drafted, these groups are now divided.

Public school groups want business as usual: a continuation of the current scheme. Private school interests see the unworkability of using the existing approach of having public schools serve private, sectarian students, and want a change. What had been a joint belief in *equity* for all underprivileged, low achieving students under the concepts of 'entitlement' and 'child benefit' has now been transformed to a battle over *choice* and vouchers. What was once a calm, consensual process has become a highly ideological, sometime vitriolic debate, with a superintendent of schools telling a Congressional subcommittee that private schools are of questionable value, as divisive. Sounds like the 'good old days' of anti-Catholic, anti-Jewish, anti-private schools, so common as the public schools were gaining their size, power, and hegemony in the US.

The future of Chapter 1, and by implication, all federal aid to education, revolves around whether one accepts the *status quo* that (1) private schools are adequately being served under the current Chapter 1 formula – letting public schools deliver services to parochial schools; and (2) that a few, very minor adjustments, like a small amount of new funds, will make Chapter 1 work fine as is. Or one may believe that some major restructuring of the program is necessary, along the lines of direct funding to families through a parental certificate or bypass provision.

The extremes

The future of federal aid could take one of two extremes: to restrict federal aid to public schools only, or to attempt broad forms of privatization through family choice and empowerment. Either extreme is highly ideological, divisive, and difficult, though there are strong groups at either end.

The middle way

At the center are basically two competing futures. Either allow LEAs to grant certificates to unserved, eligible families so the parents can buy the guaranteed services; or continue to ask public school staff to provide the services the services through extra funding (the *status quo* with a few extra dollars). It appears at the time of writing this essay that HR 950 has the best chance of passage in the autumn of 1987 or early in 1988.

The only likely means of changing the Chapter 1 program to serve private school students is a strong stand by private school groups, working closely with Republicans who favor privatization and some Democrats who fear a reaction from their largely Catholic and Jewish constituents. But, in the spring of 1987, after the first round of hearings in the House and Senate, little political pressure has been exerted. Funding and serving children in parochial schools is too small an issue right now to bring the legislative process to a halt, as Msgr Frederick G. Hockwalt, spokeperson for the US Catholic Welfare Council, successfully did in 1965, until Congress paid attention to the needs of children in non-public schools. The Catholic associations do not seem to have the will, or the power, right now. Perhaps, privatization and choice, 'Republican issues', have obscured the needs of children in basically Democratic regions: New York City, Philadelphia, Chicago, and so forth.

Whatever future that the nation accepts in 1987–88 for federal aid to education, it seems clear that we have entered a new era, one with less stability, less clarity of policy outcome, and greater risks. Ironically, just as the nation is coming to accept the value of religion and religious education, of the rights of families to chose the kinds of education for their children, and the apparent successes of parochial schools in helping children who suffer from poverty and ignorance, we find the national political system punishing the least privileged simply because they exercise a religious choice in education. While we recognize the remedial needs of these students, that they should and must have this help if they are to *succeed in life*, we may now continue an aid structure which forces them to chose between a religious program or remedial services – a cruel, lose/lose dilemma.

Many Catholic and Orthodox Jewish schools hang on by a thread, charging low tuition to the urban poor, and struggling to stay open. Now, the withdrawal of these 'guaranteed' federal services, either by law or by making them practically inaccessible, may be the last straw for some. Many inner-city denominational schools will likely close in the next few years: they will read the message from Congress that they are not worth saving (that meeting public school interests is more important politically to a nation than funding the children who need the help, wherever they go to school).

Thus, much is at stake: the future of religious rights and liberties, freedom of choice in education, and the relations between government and schools, society and religion. The opportunities are great at this cross-roads, but so are the risks. For at a time when issues are changing and controversial, coalitions unstable and unpredictable, and former allies aligned in opposition to one another, the future of national education policy is truly uncertain.

References

ASSOCIATION OF CALIFORNIA ADMINISTRATORS (1979) *Background Material on the Family Choice Inititaive* (Sacramento: ACSA).

CARNEGIE FORUM ON EDUCATION AND THE ECONOMY (1986) *A Nation Prepared? Teachers for the 21st Century* The Report of the Task on Teaching as a Profession, (New York: Carnegie Corporation).

COOPER, B.S. and POSTER, J. (1986) 'Commentary: Breakdown of a coalition', *Education Week* 21 May, p. 28.

COOPER, B.S. (1985) 'Refighting the private school wars', *Politics of Education Bulletin*, 12, pp. 14–16.

DOYLE, D.P. and COOPER, B.S. (1986) 'Funding the individual? An essay on the future of Chapter 1', paper presented to the National Conference on Alternative Strategies in Compensatory Education, Washington, DC, 18–19 November and forthcoming in a book.

DOYLE, D.P. and HARTLE, T.W. (1985) *Excellence in Education: The States Take Charge* (Washington, DC: The American Enterpise Institute).

DOYLE, D.P. and LEVINE, M. (1985) *Investing in Our Children: Education Relations* (Washington, DC: The American Enterprise Institute).

EIDENBERG, E. and MOREY, R.D. (1969) *An Act of Congress: The Legislative Process and Making of Education Policy* (New York: W.W. Norton).

FRIEDMAN, M. (1955) 'The role of government in education', in R.A. Solo (ed.) *Economics and the Public Interest* (New Brunswick, NJ: Rutgers University Press), pp. 123–153.

FUTTRELL, M.H. (1986) 'Commentary' *Education Week*, 6 January, p. 14.

JENCKS, C. (1970a) *Education Vouchers: A Report on Financing Elementary Education by Grants to Parents* (Cambridge, MA: Center for the Study of Public Policy).

LEVIN, H.M. (1983) 'Educational choice and the pains of democracy', in T. James and H. Levin (eds.), *Public Dollars for Private Schools: The Case of Tuition Tax Credits* (Philadelphia: Temple University Press), pp. 17–38.

LINES, P.M. (1985) *Peaceful Uses for Tuition Vouchers: Looking Back and Looking Forward* (Denver: Education Commission of the States).

RAND CORPORATION (1981) 'The education and human resources council', *A Study of Alternatives in American Education, Vol VII* (Santa Monica, CA: Rand Corporation).

VITULLO-MARTIN, T. and COOPER, B. (1987) *The Separation of Church and Child: The Constitution and Federal Aid to Religious Schools* (Indianapolis: Hudson Institute).

US DEPARTMENT OF EDUCATION (1986) *What Works: Research About Teaching and Learning* (Washington, DC: USDE).

US DEPARTMENT OF EDUCATION. (1987) 'Preliminary findings from the national assessment of Chapter 1 about the participation of private school students', Fast Response Survey System, ECIA Chapter 1, (Washington DC: USDE).

31

The Doubtful Efficacy of Extended Teacher Preparation Programs: An Invitation to More Basic and Less Costly Reforms

Willis D. Hawley

Introduction

The Growing Interest in Extended Programs

As the attacks on teacher education have increased, the reform strategy that has gained the most adherents seems to be the proposal to require teacher candidates to have at least five years of preservice education rather than the four now typically needed in order to be certified.

The five-year teacher preparation movement, which encompasses many programmatic variations, has powerful proponents. Among them are a special task force of the American Association of Colleges of Teacher Education (AACTE), the majority of the members of the National Commission on Excellence in Teacher Education, and the Carnegie Forum on Education and the Economy. The Holmes Group, which includes the deans of schools of education at most of the nation's research universities, publicly calls for would-be teachers to complete five years of college *and* an internship before entering full-time teaching. Many leading schools of

This article is a revised version of "The Risks and Inadequacy of Extended Programs." In E. C. Galambos, ed., *Improving Teacher Education: New Directions for Teaching and Learning* (San Francisco: Jossey-Bass, 1986), pp. 27–36. I am indebted to Phillip Schlechty for his ideas on the functioning of Professional Development Centers.

education (e.g., Chicago, Stanford, and Teachers College, Columbia) now offer teacher training opportunities only at the postbaccalaureate level.

The remarkable thing about this movement to increase the years of preservice education for prospective teachers is that it has been proceeding apace without serious opposition despite the probability that it will decrease both the number and the quality of teacher candidates at a time when we expect a severe teacher shortage. Moreover, there is absolutely no evidence that extended preparation programs make teachers more effective as they enter the profession.

One reason that extended programs have not been subject to more criticism is that they come in so many shapes and sizes. For purposes here, we are concerned with any strategy that *requires* students to take a minimum of five years of *college-based* coursework (which could include practice teaching) before they are allowed to teach at full salary.

The Logic of Extended Programs

The case for extended teacher preparation programs rests fundamentally on criticisms of undergraduate programs rather than on documented benefits for postbaccalaureate preservice teacher education. Among the attacks on undergraduate programs that appear most to influence demands for this proposed reform are the following:

1. Education courses often lack intellectual rigor.
2. Teacher education faculty are not as well prepared academically as other university faculty—they are neither up-to-date practitioners nor scholars in their fields.
3. There is too much to know about teaching to be learned in four years of college given the other things students must learn in order to be well-educated professionals.
4. The relatively low status of teaching is the product, at least in part, of the fact that the preparation for many other professions begins in earnest after students have a bachelor's degree (law and medicine are usually cited as examples).
5. It is difficult to prepare teachers to be practitioners in undergraduate colleges that do not recognize the importance of career-related education.

If, for the sake of expediting this discussion, one were to grant each of these problems with undergraduate teacher preparation, would it follow that more preservice education is an effective solution? On the face of it, extended programs do not address the first two criticisms at all and, as will be argued in more detail below, are likely to be ineffective or very limited responses to the others.

A Time for Experimentation and Systematic Evaluation of Reform Alternatives

Strategies for improving teacher education are not limited to incremental changes in conventional four-year programs and the adoption of extended programs. There are at least two other general alternatives: basic reforms of undergraduate programs and more radical reforms involving the sharing of the responsibility for teacher preparation with the teaching profession. While the evidence on teaching effectiveness continues to grow, knowledge about how teachers become effective is in short supply. For this reason, and because all proposals for teacher education reform are problematic, this is the time for experimentation and research. In short, it is premature to settle on one best way to prepare teachers, especially when the new model being advocated most aggressively has high costs and uncertain outcomes.

Much of the debate over four- versus five-year teacher preparation programs consists of unsubstantiated claims and assumptions (see, e.g., *Journal of Teacher Education,* 1981, and the Holmes Group, 1986). To some extent, speculation about the probable impact of future policies is inevitable, but it is possible in this case to be more analytical about the costs and consequences of teacher education improvement strategies than we have been thus far.

The problem in making policy is to choose the most cost-effective strategy that can be implemented. If the ultimate goal of teacher education reform is to enhance the learning of elementary and secondary school students, the problem faced by policymakers—in government and in institutions of higher education—who are considering the mandating or funding of extended programs is to determine not only whether to invest in one or more promising strategies for improving teacher education but to decide whether such an investment of money and energy seems to be among the most promising ways to enhance student learning in schools.

The Risks of Mandating Extended Programs

There are two types of risks that would be incurred if extended programs were required of all teacher candidates: (1) the costs of becoming a teacher would increase and, absent *significant* improvements in teacher compensation and working conditions, the quality and quantity of candidates in the applicant pool would decline; (2) the costs of implementing extended programs would deny resources to other, more productive educational reforms.

Impact of Extended Programs on the Applicant Pool

In calculating public and individual costs, we are assuming that new policies would become effective in 1990. All estimates, therefore, use the latest data available (cf. Stern, 1988) and extrapolate recent trends to arrive at the 1990 estimates.

The cost of a five-year teacher preparation program *to individuals* is of two types. First, the cost of tuition and fees. In the 1990–91 academic year, these annual costs will be about $2,000 at four-year public colleges and universities. The tuition cost to students of adding a fifth year at private colleges and universities is four to five times this amount.[1]

A second type of cost to individuals is earnings foregone. Let us assume that first-year teachers will earn salaries and fringe benefits worth about $21,500.[2] Thus, requiring a fifth year of collegiate education prior to entry into the profession will increase the overall cost of becoming a teacher at a public college or university by $23,500 for the average individual. The costs of becoming a teacher would be much higher, of course, for students attending private institutions.

These are very substantial costs to add to the current cost individuals must pay to become a teacher, much higher costs than those alluded to by advocates of five-year programs (see AACTE, 1983). To be sure, the advocates of five-year preservice teacher preparation recognize that there are costs, but they seldom count earnings foregone and, when they do, they often argue that, over time, the five-year teacher will make up the amount by higher salaries. This second argument has two parts. First, it is asserted that the fifth year of study will qualify individuals for a higher place on the salary scale than the bachelor's-degree-only teacher, so that the money lost will be earned back in a short time. But this is not the case. Typically, a master's degree would add about $1,600 to a teacher's annual earnings. While not all five-year programs would lead to a master's degree (cf. AACTE, 1983), let us make that assumption to give the argument for five-year programs the benefit of the doubt.

Second, assuming that the four-year teacher begins to pursue a master's degree in year two of service and completes the degree in three years, going to school part time, the four-year teacher would "catch up" with the five-year teacher over a period where the net income advantage of the five-year teacher was about $6,400. But the five-year teacher "lost" more than $26,500 in earnings foregone during the extra year he or she was in college.

These estimates make the unlikely assumption that the individual would not have to borrow money to pursue a fifth year of study. With a 9 percent interest rate on a $5,000 student loan, the five-year teacher will pay about $2,500 in interest over a five-year repayment period.[3]

Furthermore, arguments that some of the $23,500 of additional costs of becoming a teacher can be amortized over time may be unpersuasive to teacher candidates, *many* of whom are not sure they want to teach for a very long time. Moreover, if you don't have the $23,500 to invest, the idea that there is a reasonable return on investment (an incorrect assumption in any case) is irrelevant. Historically, teaching has drawn its candidates from those college students least likely to be able to make such an investment.

In summary, if we increase the costs of becoming a teacher, the attractiveness of the profession will decline unless these costs are offset by benefits, intrinsic and extrinsic, not now available. Those who will drop out of the pool will come disproportionately from the ranks of those who are brightest, have the best interpersonal skills, are the most imaginative, and for other reasons have broader career options. This proposition is a fundamental assumption made by labor economists and is akin to the idea that we cannot expect to increase the quality of our teachers unless we raise teachers' salaries significantly, an argument often made by advocates of extended programs.

There are those who argue that since teachers are not motivated by money, those who now teach will not take these new costs into account. But the market is now in equilibrium in this regard; that is, we attract those students whose altruism leads them to discount economic benefits. If we raise the economic costs, we shall have to raise the intrinsic rewards teachers get from teaching or a decline in the quality and quantity of teacher candidates will result. Extended programs do not alter the intrinsic rewards of teaching. Of course, if we did increase the benefits of being a teacher, without increasing the costs of becoming a teacher, we could enhance the quality of the applicant pool. This reality is evident in the recent increases in numbers and quality of teacher candidates that follow nonincremental increases in teacher salaries.[4]

It would be possible, of course, for the public to subsidize the individual's costs of becoming a teacher so that extended programs would not decrease the quality and size of the teacher candidate pool. We shall turn to this potential cost of extended programs in the next section, but let us here draw attention to two reasons other than the economic one just cited why eliminating undergraduate teacher preparation programs, as many proponents of extended teacher preparation advocate, is likely to decrease the quality and quantity of those entering the teaching force. First, national studies demonstrate that college students become increasingly materialistic and concerned with their own welfare as they progress through their undergraduate studies. It can reasonably be argued that undergraduate teacher education programs can attract idealistic students to the profession by providing them with early opportunities to experience the intrinsic rewards of teaching, have the support of like-minded peers, and be socialized by their professors. Ralph Tyler (1985) has recently reminded us that there is much to learn from the past in this regard. Tyler draws attention, for example, to the findings of the Commission on Teacher Education, which concluded in its 1944 report that attracting altruistic and able youngsters into teaching was significantly fostered by providing freshmen and sophomores opportunities to be involved in classrooms from the time they entered college. Experiences with teacher education early in college can also provide students who are really not interested in or suited to teaching with opportunities to change directions at relatively low cost— often at no cost. (The majority of youngsters who say they want to teach, at age eighteen, do not complete a teacher preparation program.) The person who completes the fifth year of studies in preparing to teach who then changes her or his mind, or is found to be unqualified, will have made a big investment for which there is no direct return. (Thirty percent or so of those who complete teacher preparation programs choose not to teach, though this percentage could decline if entry costs were higher.) Society's investment in such persons, which would include taxes not paid, is also nonproductive vis-à-vis school improvement.

Another likely consequence of eliminating teacher certification for persons who do not have a year of postbaccalaureate study will be a substantial reduction in the role now played by liberal arts colleges in the preparation of teachers. One recent study of private institutions in Ohio found that only one-third were certain that they would continue to prepare teachers if five-year programs were mandated in that state (Cyphert and Ryan, 1984). It is not clear what the overall impact of this will be on the quality of teacher preparation because the ability of such schools to offer a full and up-to-date curriculum in education varies widely. But it is virtually certain that the number of young teachers educated at selective and high quality colleges like Swarthmore, Dartmouth, Oberlin, and the University of the South (Sewanee) will decline because such students will be less likely than those with fewer options to explore a teaching career. The same point seems applicable to universities that do not have schools of education but now offer programs of undergraduate teacher certification. Such universities include Brown, Emory, Rice, Tulane, and Washington (St. Louis). All of this means that the role played by private colleges and universities in the education of the nation's teachers will decline.

Aside from the practical consequences of pushing such high-status colleges and universities out of the teacher education business, the symbolic importance of their involvement in the preparation of teachers should not be overlooked. It is not inconsequential that Harvard has recently returned to the business of undergraduate teacher preparation, even though very few teachers will be Harvard graduates.

The Reform Movement and the Economic Costs of Extended Programs to Taxpayers

Some advocates of extended teacher preparation are aware that such programs are likely to have a negative effect on the size and quality of the teaching force. This recognition has led some would-be reformers to the advocacy of significant governmental subsidies for extended programs. How much would it cost to *maintain* the quality of the teacher candidate pool? Conventional economic analysis would say that we would need to eliminate the added costs of entry to retain the same quality of entrant (cf. Manski, 1985). If one follows this logic, and if one accepts the National Center for Education Statistics (NCES) estimates that we could require as many as 170,000 new teachers a year in the mid-1990s,[5] the annual costs of *subsidies* for extended programs to the taxpayers would be over *$5 billion*.

If subsidies are paid by states, this will place a particular constraint on the teacher labor market because, as is now the case for financial incentive programs for math and science teachers, beneficiaries will almost certainly have to teach in the state providing the funding. This, in turn, will discourage competition for teachers across states reducing the pressure for higher teacher salaries. In times of teacher shortages, interstate competition for teachers is a powerful impetus to increased teacher salaries, as the current pattern of changes in teacher compensation in the southern states indicates.

But whether government subsidies are available or not, extended programs will increase the costs to the taxpayers. Requiring students to attend college for five rather than four years means that we shall require that 25 percent more services must be provided in the form of courses, facilities, and student services. This cost will be reduced in the short run to the extent that students fill out their additional year by attending courses and using facilities that would otherwise be underutilized. In the long run, however, savings in the public's cost for higher education that could be obtained as a result of the decline of the college-age population would be lost because fifth-year teacher candidates would take up space that could otherwise be used, faculty would be kept on who would not otherwise be needed, and institutions of higher education would be discouraged from seeking new markets—some of which might not be as highly subsidized as is upper-division undergraduate education.

James B. Conant, in his criticism of extended teacher preparation, focused, in part, on the utility to society of this investment: "The issue between four-year and five-year continuous programs turns on the value one attaches to free electives. And if a parent feels that an extra year to enable the future teacher to wander about and sample academic courses is worth the cost, I should not be the person to condemn this use of money. But, I would, as a taxpayer, vigorously protest the use of tax money for a fifth year of what I consider dubious value" (Conant, 1953, p. 204).

Data that would allow a good estimate of the cost to the taxpayer, not counting the costs of aforementioned subsidies to individuals, are not available. One can conservatively estimate the average publicly subsidized cost of one year of college for each student who graduates from teacher-education programs to be approximately $5,250.[6] If we take into account the role of private colleges and universities, which would diminish substantially if the costs of reentry teacher education were significantly increased, the preparation of teachers would cost the taxpayers about $500 million more than if all teachers entered the profession after four years of college.[7] (There would be a proportional cost to private colleges and universities.) If the fifth year counted toward a master's degree, then taxpayers would pay higher teacher salaries for beginning teachers and this cost would be about $6,400 per teacher.[8] Add another billion dollars a year.

If we were to add the institutional costs of extended programs at public colleges and universities, the costs we would have to add to maintain the quality and size of the teacher candidate pool (recognizing that most observers feel the pool is now inadequate), and the increased salary costs, the annual cost of implementing extended teacher programs nationwide would be over $6 billion.

The numbers and assumptions upon which these calculations rest are not beyond question. But if extended programs were not to result in a decline in the quality and quantity of teacher candidates, there seems to be little doubt that the cost would comprise a very sizable share of the funds available for educational improvement. Does anyone believe the society will make a multi-billion-dollar investment in preservice teacher education? Does anyone really believe that it should, given that these funds might be used to increase teacher salaries, or improve the skills of those already teaching, or reduce class sizes for children with special needs?

Will Extended Teacher Education Programs Improve the
Quality of Teaching?

Assumptions underlying the Case for Extended Programs

If we recognize that there are considerable risks and high costs to requiring that teachers have five years of college before they teach, we should expect advocates of extended programs to make a persuasive case that the change they propose will significantly improve the quality of teaching. As noted above, no evidence to this effect has yet been offered. Of course, the proponents of extended programs assert that teachers so prepared will be more knowledgeable and skillful. This argument appears to rest on one or more of the following assumptions about extended programs: (1) there will be gains in the attractiveness of the profession; (2) students will learn more in extended programs about teaching and how to teach; (3) teachers trained in extended programs will be better prepared in their teaching fields; (4) taking more liberal arts courses will make students more effective teachers; (5) what students learn in college about teaching will be reflected in their classroom performance on the job.

Let us briefly examine each of these assumptions.

Assumption 1: *There will be gains in the attractiveness of the profession.* Advocates of extended programs have argued that requiring teachers to have an additional year of schooling before they are allowed to teach will actually increase the quality of those entering the profession because extended programs will improve the status of the profession, which in turn will lead to an increase in teachers' salaries. Improved status and higher salaries will attract able students.

Generally speaking, however, earnings and educational attainment are not closely related once college graduation is assured, especially for women. One can only speculate about the public's willingness to pay teachers more competitive salaries *because* they have higher degrees. The current market differential for a master's degree is only about $1,600. Teacher salaries declined in the 1970s while increasing proportions of teachers earned master's degrees. (Indeed, teachers are twice as likely as other college graduates to have a master's degree.) Moreover, public funds necessary to implement extended programs would diminish the resources available for teacher salary increases.

The salary and status arguments are interrelated, of course. Does the requirement of more education for entry lead to higher status for a given profession? To be sure, advanced education is correlated with occupational prestige. But many jobs require no more than a college degree for entry and have higher status than does the job of school teaching, including engineering, journalism, and many jobs in business. Education is only one component of occupational prestige (Treiman, 1977) and its contribution seems related, at least in part, to assumptions about the degree to which higher education separates the intellectually able from the less able and transmits knowledge and skills beyond the reach of most people. One reason teachers do not have higher status is that there are so many of them. Ten percent of all college graduates are needed each year to staff the schools; more people are inducted into teaching annually than are inducted into the armed forces.

The tenuous link between postbaccalaureate education and social status for teachers is nicely illustrated by looking at cultures different from our own. Japan, for example, probably accords its teachers higher status than does any other industrialized country. Yet fewer than 4 percent of Japanese teachers have a master's degree and almost all started to teach upon graduation from college. The relatively low status of teachers in the United States tells us more about the value we place on good teaching and public servants in general than it does about the relationship between social status and the years of college completed after one receives a bachelor's degree.

One way to test the argument that extended programs will lead to higher salaries and higher status is to look at what has happened in California, the one state that has required completion of a fifth year of college before would-be teachers can be fully certified. First, teachers' salaries in California have been similar to those in many nonsouthern states for several years. In 1985–86 beginning teachers' salaries in California took a nonincremental jump to go above the national average. But to attribute this salary increase to a requirement that was established more than two decades ago would be wrong. It is much more reasonable to assume that the recent increase in teachers' salaries in California (not so remarkable when the cost of living is taken into account) is the result of concern over the quality and quantity of those who have chosen to teach in that state, given its fifth-year requirements. Many cities in California cannot fill open teacher positions; teaching candidates have ranked very near the bottom of thirty occupations with respect to measures of verbal and quantitative abilities (Kerschner, 1983); and close to one-third of the teachers statewide are hired with temporary credentials because not enough students seek full certification before entry. In short, the lesson to be drawn from California's long experience with extended programs is that they do not increase the status or attractiveness of the teaching profession.

Assumption 2: *Students will learn more in extended programs about teaching and how to teach.* A major argument for fifth-year programs is, of course, that teachers so educated will know more about teaching. There are two ways in which this might happen. First, teacher candidates might take more professional coursework. Second, teacher applicants in extended programs will take more sophisticated and more demanding courses.

One-year postbaccalaureate certification programs generally limit students to fewer education courses than they might take in an undergraduate program. Of course, students might be required to take undergraduate electives in preparation for the fifth year. Such requirements, however, would further complicate entry to the profession because they would further extend the time required to prepare to teach for those who decide to teach after graduation from college or late in their college career.

If teachers' *initial* training in extended programs would result in a master's degree, the total amount of *formal* professional education the typical career teacher receives probably will be less than it is now. For example, the typical high school teacher certified upon graduation from college will have taken about sixty semester hours of professional coursework by the time he or she receives the master's degree. The person who receives the master's degree upon completion of a one-year postbaccalaureate training program will take half this much coursework. This argument will not be persuasive to those who discount the value of professional education courses, but such persons are presumably not among the advocates of five-year programs.

It might be argued that the "graduate" courses embodied in extended programs will be more intellectually demanding and thus students will learn more about how to teach. Graduate courses required of master's degree candidates in education are not known to be more demanding than undergraduate education courses. And why should they be? They will be taught by the same faculty members. So far as we know, twenty-two-year-olds are not better learners than twenty-one-year-olds. On the other hand, persons pursuing a master's degree or a fifth year of study are likely to be more productive learners if they actually have taught in classrooms because they can then use their experience to frame questions and to organize information. In other words, good teaching involves an enormously complex and demanding set of intellectual tasks. Learning how to perform those tasks is likely to be easier if teachers have a clearer idea about what the process of teaching actually involves.

In summary, it seems difficult to argue, either on the basis of existing evidence or on logical grounds, that extended teacher education programs, in themselves, will improve what teachers know about teaching. It may be, however, that extended programs that require undergraduate education courses could provide teachers with more pedagogical knowledge than four-year programs that insist on a strong liberal arts curriculum and intensive study of the subjects or subject the student will teach. Whether this will make such teachers more effective is a different issue.

Assumption 3: *Teachers trained in extended programs will be better prepared in their teaching fields.* Extended programs that require undergraduate education courses will not open up much room in the curriculum for subject-matter courses. To the extent that they do, or that postbaccalaureate-only programs do free up time for subject-matter courses, this will permit persons training to be elementary school teachers to take more math, science, English, or social studies courses. But extended programs should have little impact on the number of courses in their subject field that secondary teachers take. The reason for this is that in most education schools, secondary teacher candidates already complete a disciplinary major or its equivalent.

Of course, the content of the courses they take is more important than the numbers, but this point is not relevant to the debate over the length of preservice teacher education. Moreover, there is reason to believe that the amount of coursework in the subject being taught does not contribute to effective teaching (Druva and Anderson, 1983; Ashton, Crocker, and Olejnik, 1987). This last point seems counterintuitive, but it may suggest that once one has ten or so courses in one's field, it is not the number of courses, but whether or not one understands fundamental principles and the structure of the discipline or body of knowledge involved (see Leinhardt and Smith, 1985; Shulman, 1987).[9] It seems doubtful that most undergraduate course sequences in any particular field produce these understandings among the students who take them (see Atkin, 1985). At most colleges and universities, especially those that educate the greatest number of teachers, undergraduate education seems to be something of a random walk during which course selection is often based on convenience and the desire for free time (see Galambos, Cornett, and Spitler, 1985). As a recent report of the Association of American Colleges concludes, the typical curriculum "offers too much knowledge with too little attention to how knowledge has been created and what methods and styles of inquiry have led to its creation" (Select Committee, 1985, p. 24).

Assumption 4: *Taking more liberal arts courses will make students more effective teachers.* Some advocates of extended programs, in particular those who argue that teacher preparation programs should begin after undergraduate education has been completed, believe that this reform will make teachers better educated and thus more effective.

Let us assume that undergraduate teacher candidates will take, in addition to the education-related courses they must pass to be certified (some of these are liberal arts courses, in most states), an academic major *and* satisfy general education or distribution (liberal arts) requirements. (Thus most students seeking certification in secondary education will take about three-fourths of their courses outside of education departments and colleges.) If no increases in the number of education courses accompanied the implementation of extended programs, requiring five years of college for teacher preparation would mean that students would be freed to take eight to ten electives in lieu of education courses. There is, however, absolutely no evidence that such a change would make students better teachers. The extent to which taking more liberal arts courses would improve teaching would seem to depend importantly on the difference between the intellectual content of the electives and the education courses a student would take. No doubt there are education courses that are undemanding and devoid of the concerns for theory and method of inquiry that characterize the *best* liberal arts courses, but many students seem to choose their electives on the basis of how undemanding they are (Galambos, Cornett, and Spitler, 1985). And, if it is true that many liberal arts courses are more rigorous than many education courses, this speaks to the need to change the content of education courses.

Assumption 5: *What students learn in college about teaching will be reflected in their classroom performance on the job.* The movement toward extended teacher education programs (at least among teacher educators) is motivated in large measure by the rapid growth in knowledge about effective instructional practices and teaching behaviors. The argument, of course, is that there is now more to know about how to teach effectively than ever before and that teachers should know this information and be able to use it before they enter the classroom. This argument assumes that what teacher candidates learn before they become teachers is often put to good use in the classroom. There is, however, reason to doubt this presumption. Recent research on how teachers learn to teach indicates that much of what teachers learn in the preservice stage of their career is undone or substantially mitigated during the first year or two of teaching and, perhaps, by the "practice teaching" experience (Evertson, Hawley, and Zlotnik, 1985). The implication of this reality is that increasing the amount of information and skills teachers learn in college is an inefficient—and perhaps futile—strategy unless ways are devised to enhance the ability of teachers to use what they have learned on the job. Some advocates of extended programs, such as the Holmes Group, have recognized this problem and have advocated the use of intensively supervised paid internships to facilitate induction to the profession. These internships, however, when *added* to the extended program, will significantly increase the costs of entry for individuals or the public costs of preparing new teachers.

Summary: The Costs and Benefits of Extended Programs

Extended programs, absent government subsidies, will in effect charge teacher candidates an additional $23,500 for the privilege of becoming teachers. This will significantly reduce the quality and quantity of those entering the profession at a time when the nation is facing the prospect of shortages of qualified teachers. To argue that this would not happen is the same as arguing that we do not need to improve teachers' salaries in order to increase the quality of teacher candidates. The costs to teachers of extended progams and their impact on the candidate pool could be shifted from individuals to governments with resultant increases in the attractiveness to teachers and decreases in funds available for other educational improvements. If public funds were used to keep the costs to teacher candidates at their current levels, the cost to the taxpayer could be over $4.5 billion annually. And, as we have seen, even if governments do not subsidize postbaccalaureate training of individual teachers, taxpayers will have to pay significantly more for higher education than they do now if teachers are required to take a fifth year of college coursework.

Of course, many reforms will cost money and the question that needs to be asked is: What are the potential contributions of extended programs to the improvement of teaching and how likely is it that these contributions will be realized?

It is possible that requiring a fifth year of college for preservice teachers would increase the status of teachers and thus lead to higher salaries, both of which would attract teachers to the profession in needed numbers who are more able academically. But the one statewide effort to achieve these objectives—that is, California's—has not been successful. The absence of a systematic relationship between teachers' status and their education in other countries also undermines this assumption. Occupational prestige comes from many sources, educational attainment being but one of these. Moreover, it seems reasonable to believe that the status attributed to education is related in large part to perceptions that postbaccalaureate education is selective and rigorous, characteristics that are not commonly believed found in most departments and schools of education. Further, to the extent that higher costs of entry reduce the attractiveness of teaching to more academically able students, the prestige of the profession is likely to decline.

The best case to be made for the extended programs that do not require undergraduate coursework in education seems to rest on the proposition that substituting liberal arts courses for preservice education courses will make teachers more effective. The contributions to effective teaching that extended programs requiring undergraduate coursework in education could make rests on the doubtful assumption that what can be learned from more preservice education courses will be reflected in changes in the teacher behavior on the job. Adding undergraduate requirements to post-baccalaureate teacher preparation programs, a necessity if elementary school teacher candidates were to meet certification standards, would further restrict access to the profession.

In short, the possibility that extended programs will reduce the quality and quantity of teachers is high and the likelihood that they will improve teacher performance is not great. This does not mean that we should not experiment with extended teacher preparation programs but it does mean that such trials should be carefully evaluated. Furthermore, if the risks of extended programs seem high and the benefits uncertain, other strategies for improving teacher education should be explored more aggressively than they have been. Two such alternatives to both the status quo and the extended college-based programs are the reform of undergraduate programs and postbaccalaureate internships. These two strategies would complement each other and, taken together, would almost certainly be more cost effective than extended programs.

Improving Teacher Education without Resorting to Extended Programs

Reforming Undergraduate Teacher Education

The idea that five years of preservice education will enhance the quality of teaching is another manifestation of the propensity of social reformers to respond to weaknesses in political institutions by creating new structures rather than reforming the ones found to be inadequate. It is the American way of change but it usually is ineffective because it does not address fundamental problems.

Ideally, significant proposals to change undergraduate teacher preparation would address two conflicting beliefs held by different advocates of five-year programs. On the one hand, such reforms must address the concern of professional educators and education professors that the new teacher will have the knowledge and the skills necessary for effective teaching. On the other hand, they must respond to the belief that a substantial liberal arts undergraduate education is necessary if our teachers are to be well educated. The way out of this conundrum seems to have four stepping stones.

1. *Recognize that teachers cannot learn all or even most of what there is to know about effective teaching in one year or a year and a half of college.* Acceptance of this proposition has important implications for how we structure the teaching profession, a point we shall return to below. No

teacher educator would disagree with this assertion but many are unwilling to make the tough choices about what is to be learned and *how*. Moreover, the content and modes of instruction embodied in teacher education need to take into account the fact that what is known now will be replaced—in short order if recent history is any guide—with new, more powerful knowledge. Current research provides some clues about the knowledge that is most essential to effective teaching (see Hawley and Rosenholtz, 1984; and Brophy and Good, 1985). If we were to ensure that teachers had continuing opportunities to increase their professional expertise, we could focus on pedagogical courses that contributed to teacher effectiveness. This would surely reduce the content of most current curricula, thus making room for the learning of more productive capabilities and skills, and the theories that undergird them.

2. *Prepare teachers to be learners on the job.* If we adopt the view that pre-entry teacher education should focus on essential professional knowledge and skills, and we recognize that our knowledge about teacher effectiveness will change and inevitably be incomplete, we need to help prospective teachers to be good at learning and applying new information to the solution of the complex and varied problems most teachers confront. Learning on the job would be facilitated most significantly if teachers were better able to *(a)* manage their classrooms and the teaching-learning process, *(b)* use theory as a tool for learning and inventing, *(c)* engage in systematic inquiry about the complicated instructional problems with which they must deal, and *(d)* engage in collegial learning. Most teachers get little of these types of basic education for teaching (Joyce and Clift, 1984). Survival in a land whose mysteries can be understood only by trial and error and consultation with the local guardians of folklore lead many teachers to abandon what effective practices they did learn so as to accommodate to rather than overcome the difficulties they face (Hawley and Rosenholtz, 1984, chaps. 2 and 4; Fullan, 1982). As Joyce and Clift argue: "The real issue is whether the product of teacher education is . . . someone who controls the processes of applying new knowledge to practice" (1984, p. 6).

3. *Make teacher education more intellectually rigorous.* Much of the critique of teacher education is based on the assumption that it is less demanding academically than most other college or university courses of study. The validity of this assumption varies, of course, but it seems all too true. The easy and well-traveled paths to academic rigor are tougher grading policies and increased requirements. More fundamental strategies include the incorporation of new research and significant theory in the curriculum, insistence that students be held to high expectations (in much the same way that good school teachers are taught to relate to their

students), and attention to the development of student skills of critical inquiry and clarity of expression. All of these goals can best be achieved when they are pursued by all of an undergraduate's teachers. Indeed, the distinction usually made between liberal arts education and "professional" education seems unnecessary and inappropriate as Judd (1930) noted more than fifty years ago. Why, for example, could not courses on classroom management grapple with philosophical issues of equity, equality, and justice so that the works of Rousseau, Rawls, and de Tocqueville were on the same reading list as the writings of Emmer, Evertson, and Slavin?

4. *Transfer the responsibility for initial on-the-job training to school systems.* Outside the fields of medicine and education, colleges and universities typically do not provide significant preservice clinical or practical education to either undergraduate students or professional students. In teacher education programs, the so-called practice teaching experience often replaces three to five courses and, in general, does little—at best— to facilitate students' transfer of their course-based learning to effective use in the classroom (for a succinct review of relevant research, see Evertson, Hawley, and Zlotnik, 1985). Eliminating practice teaching from the undergraduate curriculum could focus attention on the need for opportunities to apply knowledge in the context of specific courses. Some of this could take place in schools and much of it could be realistic and complex through the use of computer-driven, video-disk-supported problem-solving exercises.

Simply transferring the responsibility for clinical training to school systems would not facilitate the transfer of knowledge to the actual practice of teaching, but it seems doubtful that much of what the typical teacher now brings to his or her first full-time job would be lost. However, the burden on school systems and the desirability of linking what is taught in college to what is taught on the job suggest the need for a new mechanism for training teachers, such as an internship or what the Holmes Group calls a Professional Development Center.

Reforming the Education of Teachers by Establishing Professional Development Centers

There is growing agreement among researchers, teachers, and teacher educators that something must be done to make induction into the teaching profession a more rewarding experience so that teachers build upon rather than abandon what they learned in preservice education. Not only do the current forms of induction into teaching (including practice teaching) often result in unlearning of college-acquired knowledge and skills, they often result in a failure to experience fully the intrinsic rewards of teaching, so that new teachers are discouraged from persisting. Between 20 and 25 percent of new teachers leave teaching before they begin their third year. This high rate of attrition results in high costs to school systems, to taxpayers (who must pay for training replacements for the teacher drop-outs), and to the children who must break-in the large number of new teachers that the nation's schools recruit each year.

The problem of entry to teaching is as great for students who graduate from extended programs as it is for those who enter teaching upon receipt of their baccalaureate degree. Thus, an absolutely essential aspect of any teacher-education reform program is the provision to teachers of significant support as they make the transition from college to independent responsibility for classroom teaching. Depending on how such support is provided, it would be feasible to transfer practice teaching—and perhaps specific methods courses—out of the undergraduate curriculum (or graduate curriculum, for that matter) and to make these part of the induction experience.

The way in which both college-based teacher preparation and teacher induction could be improved is through the establishment of teaching schools or Professional Development Centers (PDCs), which would provide teacher candidates with opportunities for clinical learning and practice that are significantly different from those now available to either education students or new teachers.

PDCs would be the joint responsibility of schools of education and school systems and would be staffed by faculty from both who were selected because of teaching abilities and their existing or potential expertise as teacher educators. PDCs, like teaching hospitals, would serve an array of clients (students) so that the elite laboratory school model for teaching training of the past would not be replicated.

Regular teachers who were especially selected and trained would teach classes, and teacher candidates would assist them, eventually taking full but supervised responsibility for teaching. Specific methods courses would be taught in the PDC during the first part of the academic year, and more advanced subjects would be taught later in the year, perhaps in module formats.

Not every school system would have a PDC. Access to state funds needed to support PDCs over and above the district's per-student expenditures would be competitive and provided on a per-student-teacher basis. In states with career ladder or mentor teacher plans, some teachers reaching the highest step could become teacher educators, so that already appropriated funds could be used to provide partial support for the programs. The PDCs would educate teachers for any school system just as colleges and universities do now. Reciprocal agreements among states could avoid restrictions on the labor market for teachers. Public and private colleges and universities would be allowed to compete, in collaboration with school systems, for the resources necessary to administer a PDC.

In addition to the classroom teachers staffing the school, college and university faculty as well as senior master teachers would be assigned to the PDC. Classroom teachers could be rotated through the school and, as teacher candidates assumed more responsibility, would be freed to undertake research or other enrichment activities, including preparation for leadership roles in staff development throughout the school system. This is not the place to lay out the details of how a PDC would be organized and financed. It would surely cost more per teacher trained than four-year preparation programs. But it would cost less than extended programs. Whatever stipends were necessary to maintain or increase the quality of the pool of candidates would be no greater than those needed for extended programs—and might be less, since services would be provided to the school system involved.

Is this proposal not just another form of an extended program? Not really. It substantially alters the character of the learning-to-teach experience that teacher candidates now have in extended programs. In particular, a PDC would deal with the weakest characteristics of conventional teacher education, clinical training and induction to the profession. Extended programs by and large do not address these problems in satisfactory ways. As noted, the Holmes Group has recognized that extended programs are not likely to be successful unless they are followed by a PDC experience.

The training that a teacher received in a PDC should be seen as the beginning of a career throughout which there would be recurrent opportunities for professional growth, including graduate study. Moreover, it seems reasonable to believe that teachers would benefit more from graduate study after they have taught than before they entered the profession.

Conclusion

Neither the improvement of undergraduate teacher education nor the establishment of Professional Development Centers will ensure effective teaching, but they are, especially if implemented together, likely to be more cost-effective ways of improving the quality of teaching in our schools than are extended college- and university-based teacher preparation programs.

Extended programs will be very costly and their benefits uncertain. Moreover, they seem to dodge or implicitly deny some important criticisms of teacher education, including the lack of curricular rigor, the relative absence of scholarly credentials within the education professorate, and the problem of induction.

It may be that the more one accepts the "more is better" argument of extended-program advocates and the more one considers the implementation problems, the more one is likely to argue for even more extensive preservice programs. The Holmes Group, as noted, has come to this conclusion and its members are not alone (see Joyce and Clift, 1984; and Benson, Losk, and Stoddart, 1984). The Holmes Group, in wrestling with implementation problems facing extended programs and with the need to alter substantially both the intrinsic and the extrinsic rewards of being a teacher, seeks to resolve these problems by establishing two classes of teachers, one educated at major research universities for extended periods (preservice is just the beginning), and the other educated less rigorously and less extensively at other colleges and universities. In order to encourage the "best and brightest"—or some approximation thereof—to bear the costs of entry and to forgo other occupational options, the Holmes Group would provide access to more prestigious and higher paying roles only to graduates of programs like the ones it advocates. Differences in classes of teachers would, in effect, create an occupational caste system among teachers not unlike the physician-nurse or physician-technician distinctions in the medical professions. Initial eligibility for advanced professional status would be defined by academic ability not by teaching performance. The irony of all this is that the public and private flagship universities would likely lose any claim to a leadership role vis-à-vis those colleges and universities that would end up training the bulk of the nation's teachers.

Perhaps this overstates the negative consequences of extended programs. But reasons to doubt the contributions that extended programs will make to improved student learning are rooted in (1) current criticisms of teacher education, (2) the experience of California in prescribing five-year programs, (3) conventional assumptions about the relationship between increased costs of occupational entry and a decreased supply of academically able teacher candidates, and (4) sensible conclusions about the limits of public funds available for educational reform. The case for extended programs rests on precarious analogies to other professions that are very differently organized and financially supported and the expert judgment of teacher educators from research universities. The advocates of extended programs are not alone among would-be reformers in their claims that intuition and common sense should determine public policies. But sharing this commitment with other wishful thinkers does not equate one's dreams with the welfare of children.

One might characterize the claims for extended programs as bad theory and bad policy analysis. But this would be imprecise. Proposals for extended programs are wholly devoid of policy analysis. And if the types of theory most relevant to arguments for reforming teacher education are those relating to how teachers learn and how organizations change, one will find no such foundations used to construct the case for extended programs.

Murray Edelman has characterized changes in public structures that do not address the fundamental problems that created the demand for change as symbolic politics (Edelman, 1964). One consequence of symbolic politics is that the illusion of substantive change so created induces quiescence because demands for change have the appearance of being met. The establishment of extended programs may be an example of symbolic politics. None of this need be planned and is not meant to question the motives of those who advocate extended programs. But before we plunge into a commitment to extended programs, it seems sensible to insist that their proponents demonstrate how their proposals would change teachers' capacities and behaviors in ways that will improve student learning.

The truth of the matter is that we know relatively little about how to educate effective teachers. It speaks volumes that there is almost no research on the effectiveness of alternative ways to educate teachers. Before initiating major system-wide changes in the *requirements* students must meet in order to teach, it seems prudent to experiment with different strategies and curricula and to evaluate their relative effectiveness. This will require collaboration among state education departments, colleges and departments of education, and school systems. It is ironic that a knowledge-based industry like education has been so little interested in using research to determine how better to perform its function.

At a time when there is so much doubt about the usefulness of teacher education, we need to be deregulating, encouraging innovations, and evaluating the efficacy of alternatives. No doubt, some ways of preparing teachers are better than others. So far as we know, there is no one best way. Perhaps there never will be.

Notes

1. This estimate is based on an extrapolation of data provided in Stern (1988), table 1.1. Tuition grew about 6 percent annually from 1980–81 to 1986–87. Room and board costs are assumed to be constant for college graduates still in school and those teaching.
2. National data on beginning teacher salaries are not available. This estimate assumes fringe benefits worth about 20 percent and uses $18,000 as the average

beginning salary (not counting summer earnings) for 1987–88. Percentage increases are estimated to be 6 percent per year.
3. Much of this cost to the individual obtains whether a loan is needed or not because the money that was needed for college could have been invested.
4. The relationship between changes in teacher salary levels and the supply of teachers has been documented. In the 1970s the purchasing power of teachers declined, but from 1984 to 1987, salaries in constant dollars rose rapidly (Stern, 1988, chart 1:20). This fluctuation is reflected in the drop in the number of teacher education students during the 1970s and early 1980s (Stern, 1988, chart 1), and the more recent rise in enrollments in teacher education (Galluzo et al., 1988, and Hawley et al., 1988). The relationship between salaries and quality of candidates has not been well documented but can be seen in data from southern universities (cf. Hawley et al., 1988). Several reports on teacher education have identified low teacher salaries as a fundamental problem in attracting academically able persons to teaching (cf. Carnegie Foundation, 1986).

   I estimate that we shall need to educate at least 200,000 prospective teachers a year to meet the demand. In its most recent estimates of demand (which have been revised downward from earlier estimates) the National Center for Education Statistics (NCES) projects that the annual number of new hirees will rise from 128,000 in 1988–89 to 174,000 in 1995 and then level off (Stern, 1988, chart 1:18).
5. The 200,000 estimate of the demand may be high but we shall have to educate more teachers than we have openings because many teacher candidates (recently the number has been about 30 percent) will decide not to teach. Making the subsidies contingent on service (e.g., forgivable loans) will reduce the attractions of the subsidies (cf. Spero, 1985) and this will affect the quality of the pool. Those who argue that the estimates by NCES are high must reckon with the fact that in 1983, when projections used less conservative assumptions than they do now, 212,000 teachers were hired during a year that NCES estimated that the number of *new* teachers needed would be 164,000 (Plisko and Stern, 1985). Of course, the difference could be accounted for by interdistrict transfers and hirees from the "reserve pool," but we do not know about this.
6. This figure is derived by taking the annual per-student expenditure for public four-year colleges in 1985 (1983, p. 113), and projecting that to 1990 with 6 percent annual increases and then subtracting the average tuition in public universities. The subsidized cost for private education is about the same, although most of the money does not come *directly* from public revenues. I used the costs per student at "comprehensive universities" rather than at those that offer the doctorate. The per-student costs at doctoral institutions are almost twice the costs at comprehensive universities. The net increase estimated also takes into account the probability that 50 percent of all teachers receive a master's degree with part-time study and estimates the part-time cost to be half that of the full-time cost.
7. I am assuming that 85 percent of the teachers would be educated in public institutions and that some of the added costs of full-time students would be reduced by the costs to part-time students (who do not usually add very much to overhead costs).
8. This calculation assumes a 33 percent attrition rate of entering teachers four years later and assumes that extended programs have been implemented for at least four years. There are no solid data on attrition rates nationally, but this estimate seems sensible (cf. Grissmer and Kirby, 1987).

9. While the number of courses teachers take seems to contribute little to their effectiveness, how well teachers know the subjects they teach—as measured by tests of subject-matter knowledge and grade-point average—appears to account for a small amount of teacher effectiveness and to be associated with more sophisticated teaching behaviors (Ashton, Crocker, and Olejnik, 1987).

References

American Association of Colleges of Teacher Education (AACTE). 1983. *Educating a Profession: Extended Programs for Teacher Education*. Washington, D.C.: American Association of Colleges of Teacher Education.

Ashton, P.; L. Crocker; and J. Olejnik. 1987. "Teacher Education Research: A Call for Collaboration." A paper presented to the Southern Regional Consortium of Colleges of Education. Nashville, Tenn.

Atkin, J. M. 1985. "Preparing to Go to the Head of the Class." The Wingspread Journal, no. 3.

Benson, C.; D. Losk; and T. Stoddart. 1984. *The Education of Educators: Preparing and Retaining Excellent Teachers*. Public affairs report. Berkeley: Institute of Governmental Studies, University of California.

Brophy, J. E., and T. Good. 1985. "Teacher Behavior and Student Achievement." In M. Wittrock, ed., *Handbook of Research on Teaching*. (3rd ed.) New York: Macmillan.

Carnegie Foundation, 1986. *Taskforce on Teaching as a Profession*. New York: Carnegie Forum on Education and the Economy.

Conant, J. B. 1953. *The Education of American Teachers*. New York: McGraw-Hill.

Cyphert, F. R., and K. A. Ryan. 1984. "Extending Initial Teacher Preparation: Some Issues and Answers." *Action in Teacher Education* 6, nos. 1–2, pp. 63–70.

Druva, C. A., and R. D. Anderson. 1983. "Science Teacher Characteristics by Teacher Behavior and by Student Outcome: A Meta-Analysis of Research." *Journal of Research in Science Teaching* 20, no. 5, pp. 467–79.

Edelman, M. 1964. *The Symbolic Uses of Politics*. Urbana: University of Illinois Press.

Evertson, C.; W. D. Hawley; and M. Zlotnik. 1985. "Making a Difference in Educational Quality through Teacher Education." *Journal of Teacher Education* 36, pp. 2–12.

Fullan, M. 1982. *The Meaning of Educational Change*. New York: Teachers College Press.

Galambos, E. C.; L. M. Cornett; and H. D. Spitler. 1985. *An Analysis of Transcripts of Teachers and Arts and Science Graduates*. Atlanta: Southern Regional Education Board.

Grissmer, D. W., and S. N. Kirby. 1987. *Teacher Attrition: The Uphill Climb to Staff the Nation's Schools*. Washington, D.C.: The Rand Corporation.

Hawley, W.; A. Austin; and E. Goldman. 1988. *Changing Teacher Education in the South*. Atlanta: Southern Regional Education Board.

Hawley, W. D., and S. J. Rosenholtz. 1984. "Good Schools: What Research Says about Improving Student Achievement." *Peabody Journal of Education* 61, no. 4, pp. 1–178.

Holmes Group, The. 1986. *Tomorrow's Teachers*. East Lansing, Mich.: The Holmes Group.

Journal of Teacher Education. 1981. Entire issue deals with four- versus five-year teacher education programs. Vol. 32.

Joyce, B., and R. Clift. 1984. "The Phoenix Agenda: Essential Reform in Teacher Education." *Educational Researcher* 13, no. 4, pp. 5–18.

Judd, C. H. 1930. "The School of Education." In R. A. Kent, ed., *Higher Education in America.* Boston: Ginn, pp. 157–91.

Kerchner, C. T. 1983. *Flood Times and Aging Swimmers: An Exploration into the Supply and Demand for Teachers.* Claremont, Calif.: Claremont Graduate School.

Leinhardt, G., and D. Smith. 1985. "Expertise in Mathematics Instruction, Subject Matter Knowledge." *Journal of Educational Psychology* 77, pp. 241–71.

Manski, C. 1985. "Academic Ability, Earnings and the Decision to Become a Teacher: Evidence from the National Longitudinal Study of the High School Class of 1972" (Working Paper no. 1539). Cambridge, Mass.: National Bureau of Economic Research.

Plisko, V. W. 1984. *The Condition of Education:* Washington, D.C.: U.S. Government Printing Office.

Plisko, V. W., and J. D. Stern, eds. (1985). The condition of education: 1985 edition. Washington, D.C.: U.S. Government Printing Office.

Select Committee of the Association of American Colleges. 1985. *Integrity in the College Curriculum: A Report to the Academic Community.* Washington, D.C.: Association of American Colleges.

Shulman, L. S. 1987. "Knowledge and Teaching: Foundations of the New Reform." *Harvard Education Review* 57, no. 1, pp. 1–22.

Spero, Irene K. 1985. "The Use of Student Financial Aid to Attract Prospective Teachers: A Survey of State Efforts." Testimony before the Subcommittee on Postsecondary Education, Committee on Education and Labor, U.S. House of Representatives, July 31.

Stern, J. D. 1988. *The Condition of Education: 1988 Edition.* Washington, D.C.: U.S. Government Printing Office.

Treiman, D. J. 1977. *Occupation Prestige in Comparative Perspective.* New York: Academic Press.

Tyler, Ralph. 1985. "What We've Learned from Past Studies of Teacher Education." *Phi Delta Kappan* 66, pp. 682–84.

Employment and Training Programs: Why Is Success So Elusive?

It is not for a lack of trying that the current employment and training programs in the United States are so modest in their accomplishments. Indeed, the past twenty years have witnessed a continual parade of new and retooled programs to assist youth, dislocated workers, minority groups, the handicapped, refugees, and others to find their way into the world of work. Many seem to have an exceptionally difficult time in finding their way along this path. That this is so, given the time and effort of well-intentioned and knowledgeable persons, speaks to the difficulties that the United States is experiencing in developing and executing effective programs.

The papers in this section all address one or another aspect of the present situation—both in policy and in programmatic dimensions. While no one of the papers makes all the points to follow, there is some consensus spread among the authors on the following conclusions. First, the United States has great difficulty in developing coherent policies and programs because of deep, unresolved ideological conflicts over the causes and consequences of unemployment. Ideological positions conflict on what motivates those without work to want to work, on what effects public assistance has on those without work, on whether those without work have character flaws (e.g., lazy, unmotivated, undisciplined, etc.) or are the "victims" of a changing economy, and whether or not government has an obligation to change the circumstances of those without work. Because of such schisms, the possibilities and probabilities of being able to forge coherent policies are greatly diminished, perhaps to the point of being nil. There continues to be widespread disagreement on the origins of unemployment and whether the remedy is a public or a personal responsibility. The ideological checkmating that occurs narrows the policy options. Thus in the absence of clear direction and agreement, the realistic option is to do little.

A second conclusion, and derived from the first, is that the United States has not committed itself to putting a permanent organizational structure in place systematically to assist those making the transition from not working to working. Whether this be, for example, apprenticeship programs for youth or job retraining centers for adults, the country has no infrastructure in place. The system that does exist is a patchwork quilt, subject to wide fluctuations in funding, constant shifts in priorities, ever redefined target populations, and continual questions about its existence in the first place. The result is that in some places and under some circumstances, some persons receive help. The serendipitous nature of such a system is self-evident. It also reflects the current American ambivalence in stark terms.

Third, the country suffers in the implementation of those programs that are supported because of several key reasons. There is a lack of cumulative staff expertise in the management of many such programs, since the programs are on "soft money" and those who come to manage them frequently do not stay long. The transitory nature of the programs garners transitory staff. This also reinforces short-term approaches and attempts at "quick fixes," for who is likely to be around or where would the money come from to take an in-depth and long-term approach to the issue? The revolving door of staff expertise and stable support means that the country muddles along with an ad hoc employment and training system that is never very far up the learning curve.

Finally, there is no agreement on just who are the key actors and institutions that ought to be involved. Stated differently, just whose problem and responsibility is it, anyway? Many in the private sector argue that the responsibility lies with the education system and its mandate to train students to the point where they are able to enter the labor market. The schools often argue that they are doing their part; it is the private sector that refuses to assist in skill development or to provide the opportunities for on-the-job training. The arguments go round and round. Some analysts push for independent agencies to carry the responsibility, others push massive joint efforts where all the key actors are at the table, and still others argue for supporting those without work to start their own businesses, be they youth or adult. There is so little agreement on which institutional strategies merit support that leadership does not emerge. Instead, many groups just go for their "piece of the action" and leave the puzzle scattered about.

Allan Rosenbaum, the author of the first paper in this section, provides an analysis of what he terms "employment and training policy in a time of transition." The transition he documents is that of the shifting American economy and the increasing sense of its fragility. Many analysts believe that the United States economy is not well positioned at present in international competitiveness. Compound this with the ambiguous nature of American employment and training policy (made even more tentative by the Reagan counterreform efforts), and the end results are decentralization and marginal efforts at best. Those who are facing the brunt of the changes and transformations underway within the United States economy are essentially asked to face those changes unsupported by the government. Rosenbaum traces the urge toward decentralization and the roles that the state and local governments are increasingly expected to play. He questions the capacity of the states to develop, on their own, programs that reach down to those groups most impacted by the economic dislocations taking place.

Translating program conception into program reality is the focus of the second paper by Martin Levin and Barbara Ferman. Their concern with program implementation leads them to concentrate on what can be learned from successful youth employment programs in eight cities—in contrast to all we have learned about what not to do. While they concede that adequate funds are a necessary component to successful program development and implementation, they also are firm in their view that sufficient funding is not enough to ensure success. The actual management, direction, and nurturing of individual programs also has to be considered. They are concerned with what they term "governmental learning" and how such learning is retarded in the present environment, to the detriment of better program management.

Sar Levitan and Frank Gallo turn their attention to one of the few national employment and training efforts that can claim some consistent success—the Job Corps. Established in 1964, the Job Corps has now a quarter-century of experience in developing, refining, and continually monitoring the model they use in working with "at-risk" and unemployed teenagers and young adults. The authors provide extensive descriptive information on the Job Corps, documenting the costs, modes of financing, target populations, residential-centered programming, and various training and educational components. The end result is a comprehensive description of a strategy that measures rather well against multiple performance criteria. The Job Corps is an expensive program. But it also stands as an important case study of what can be accomplished with sustained commitment and funding.

Considerable attention has been paid in the past two decades to the West German strategy for assisting youth in making the transition from school to work. Stephen Hamilton has recently completed a detailed study of the German apprenticeship approach and reports on his findings in the next paper in this volume. The West German commitment to providing apprenticeships to all youth who desire them is impressive—and it is a commitment that is continually met, year after year. What the West German model demonstrates, and from which the United States could well learn, is the underlying conviction that youth succeed when they know that opportunities exist. Training programs developed in the absence of opportunities to apply and further develop what has been learned are, in the end, little more than shams. Hamilton makes the point that while the United States has done an exceedingly admirable job of providing opportunities for the approximately 50 percent of youth who wish to go on for further education, the system is almost nonexistent for the other 50 percent who are leaving school to enter the world of work. For those staying in school, the transition to employment takes place later and then with the assistance of placement officers, guidance counselors, campus recruiters, etc. Such a system is not there for eighteen-year-old school leavers seeking to enter employment.

Finally, there is the piece by James Bovard, which, in strong and unequivocal terms, calls into question the employment and training policies of the United States government over the past twenty years. Bovard is not impressed by United States efforts, to say the least. His very first sentence makes clear where he stands: "Federal job-training programs have harmed the careers of millions of Americans, failed to impart valuable job skills to the poor, and squandered billions of dollars annually." He believes there have been fundamental errors in the assumptions and approaches of United States training efforts. All the tinkering one might do with existing programs will not correct the basic errors and lack of demonstrable impacts for those who seek help. The basic fallacy, according to Bovard, is the assumption that the private sector lacks the incentives to train people for jobs. Accepting this fallacy leads policymakers and program developers to alternative strategies—strategies that are programmed to fail. This drives Bovard to conclude, "Bad training is worse than no training at all."

32
Employment and Training Policy and American Political Ideas: Old Problems and Emerging Programs

Allan Rosenbaum

Neither public policy nor government programs are shaped within a vacuum. Rather, they are developed within a broad contextural framework. That framework includes not only past history, established law and a variety of institutional and social structures, but also a broad set of beliefs about which the society has established a general consensus. In the essay that follows, an attempt is made to examine first, the emergence and development of employment and training programs and policy in the United States, and, second, how that pattern of development has been affected by basic American beliefs about the roles of the public and private sector in the economy, the question of fragmentation and coordination in American government and issues of state and local versus Federal power.

AMERICAN POLITICAL BELIEFS AND EMPLOYMENT AND TRAINING POLICY

Relative to other areas of domestic social policy, the field of employment and training is a comparatively youthful one. Policy and program initiatives in such fields as education, welfare and even parks and recreation can, at the national, state or local levels of government, be traced to at least the turn of the century, if not before. Employment and training policy in the various program forms in which we know it today can trace some roots back to the New Deal and others to the Employment Act of 1946. However, a large part of present governmental activity in this area of public policy was not initiated until the early 1960s with the passage at the federal level of the Area Redevelopment Act, which included modest funding for "manpower training." This legislation, which had been vigorously advocated by a former University of Chicago economist turned U.S. Senator, Paul Douglas, served as precursor to a host of subsequent new and/or expanded federal initiatives.

It is perhaps both ironic and predictable that the United States should move very slowly in the initiation of public efforts to deal with issues of employment and training policy. On the one hand, it is surely arguable that having an employable and employed workforce is central to the preservation and growth of both the nation's economic and political systems. Furthermore, throughout the second half of the nineteenth century and the first half of the twentieth century, recurring recessions, not to mention full-scale depressions, certainly served to create a constituency of citizens in need of such services.

On the other hand, even a brief examination of American political and economic history and theory provides an understanding of why public officials have been slow to create policy and programs in this area. No idea is a more central part of American political and economic theory than the belief that the nation's well-being is best served by the absence of government involvement in its economic activities (Lowi, 1969). The existence of employment and training programs as a government activity strikes directly at the core of this belief system. The support of a massive

Reprinted with permission of *Policy Studies Review,* Vol. 6, No. 4 (May 1987): 695–704.

education establishment does not challenge basic beliefs, because not only is education necessary to sustain the existence of a democratic political system--a point made by political theorists as diverse as Jean-Jacques Rousseau and John Dewey--but, it is also in the interest of the economic system to have an educated and disciplined labor force that can readily learn the skills necessary to perform work successfully (Simon, 1987).

Even the support of a welfare system does not strike as centrally at the heart of the nation's most cherished myths as does the establishment of employment and training programs. This is because welfare programs in the United States historically have been premised on the proposition that the individual's need for assistance is a result of their own personal limitations, not those of the economic system (Handler, 1972). These limitations have ranged from those over which the individual has no con-trol--being widowed with young children--to those over which the indi-vidual has much control--self-indulgence and shiftlessness.

Only in the 60s, did we begin to witness a significant recognition, as reflected in national policy, that welfare dependency might be a function of systemic as well as personal causes (Steiner, 1966). This, of course, was when discussions of employment and training policy really entered the mainstream of the nation's political dialogue. The complementary develop-ments were not coincidental. Rather, they required as a precondition an acceptance in American political ideas of the recognition that sustaining economic well-being in a complex society might require at least some meas-ure of ongoing government involvement.

Employment and training policy is, thus, different from most social policies in that at its basic core is the premise that the private sector marketplace in and of itself cannot sustain the economic well-being of the nation. Central to each new element of employment and training policy is the belief that there are Americans who wish to and could be productive members of the workforce who either lack the skills to be absorbed into or are being ignored by the private sector. That very fact represents perhaps as direct a challenge to the prevailing American economic and political mythology as any ideas about social policy that have been serious-ly put forth in this country. Consequently, it is a fact that has been dealt with cautiously and reluctantly. Societies are never anxious to address issues that raise questions about the most fundamental elements of their belief systems.

In light of the American political tradition, it is not altogether surpris-ing that massive economic dislocation, indeed national crisis, was the necessary precursor to even a very modest initiation of employment and training policy. It was in the midst of the Great Depression that Congress passed the Wagner-Peyser Act, thus creating a public Employment Service which is the oldest extant element of America's present employment and training system. The ostensible purpose of the public Employment Serv-ice, then, as now, was to assist the nation's unemployed in finding em-ployment, preferably in the private sector.

THE AMERICAN WAY: WHEN IN DOUBT, DECENTRALIZE

The considerable ambivalence of America's political leadership to national employment or economic policy, and the considerable strength of the na-tion's localist and decentralized tradition, are seen in the structure of the Employment Service that was established (Martin, 1964). Despite the fact that the federal government was then flexing its domestic policy and programmatic muscles in a way that had neither been witnessed, or even conceived of, at any previous time in American history, the passage of the Wagner-Peyser act did not really create a national employment service. Rather, it created a series of federally funded and guided, but state governed and managed, employment services. Thus, a pattern of political and institutional development was initiated in the policy arena that was not only reasonably compatible with the American political belief system (Grodzins, 1963), but which has continued to influence new initiatives in this area of public policy right through to the present.

Two years after it enacted Wagner-Peyser, the Congress approved the Social Security Act of 1935. This landmark legislation set up the nation's unemployment insurance system. Once again the system that was established was a decentralized one, designed to be administered and managed by the nation's state governments. As in the case of Wagner-Peyser, this occurred neither because state governments were regarded as needed financial participants or an especially effective administrative unit. Indeed, at this time many, if not most, state governments faced grave fiscal crises of their own and were hardly models of either good management practice, civic responsibility or institutional integrity. The strong state reliance was simply a matter of achieving a programmatic structure that could most comfortably fit the nation's political and economic traditions.

While the basic structure of the Unemployment Insurance system has remained relatively constant, the federally mandated functions of the Employment Service began, especially during the 60s and the 70s, to expand. Now, not only are various specialized programs administered by the Employment Service, but many participants in other federal programs, such as Unemployment Insurance and some Food Stamp recipients, must register with their local Employment Service Offices. Thus, the role and activities of the Employment Services has grown substantially over time. With that growth came a substantial expansion of federal influence over the system.

During the past few years, the organization of the Employment Service, as it is structured by federal legislation and policy, has begun to be changed in such a way as to decrease federal control and increase state control of it. Not only has the Wagner-Peyser Act been amended by the Congress but, in addition, the Job Training Partnership Act (JTPA), which Congress enacted in 1982, included a number of provisions that affected the operation of the Employment Service. Furthermore, in keeping with the general goal of the Reagan administration to lessen federal involvement in state and local governments' activities (a goal that is certainly highly consistent with American political tradition), federal oversight of and technical assistance to the state agencies administering Employment Service programs has decreased significantly. One prominent manifestation of this is that the number of federal employees responsible for administering the Employment Service at the Washington office of the Department of Labor has declined during the Reagan administration from about 300 to 50.

The creation of a public Employment Service and an Unemployment Insurance system, especially highly fragmented ones, represents, by contemporary standards, only the most modest of government intervention in the functioning of the economy. The national crisis represented by the Great Depression inevitably produced much more significant interventions in the economy in the form of such public employment programs as the

Civilian Conservation Corps and the Works Progress Administration. Despite the fact that the self respect and economic security of millions of Americans were sustained by these policy initiatives and even today tens of millions of Americans continue to enjoy and utilize the recreational, cultural and public works legacies of these programs (Simon, 1987), they were both ended and discredited with remarkable rapidity, once the advent of World War II made that politically feasible.

The end of World War II did, however, bring forth a renewal of concern about the capacity of the American economic system to function effectively absent governmental intervention and, consequently, gave rise to agitation in some quarters for a more active federal role in employment policy. The passage of the GI Bill, however, served to dissipate this need by facilitating a massive expansion of the nation's state and privately guided higher education system through the enrollment of hundreds of thousands returning veterans. This, in turn, facilitated the gradual absorption of huge numbers of potential new entrants into the nation's work force in a way that limited the need for government intervention into the private economic sector and, in so doing, was compatible with American political ideology.

Consequently, it was possible that the one major economic adjustment act of the era--the Employment Act of 1946--could be a piece of legislation that is remarkable primarily in terms of the fact that, despite its title, it does not really create any programs which are designed to address issues of employment or unemployment. Rather, the legislation represents what Murray Edelman (1971) might characterize as a symbolic rather than a substantive response to a problem or what Theodore Lowi (1969) might describe as an attempt to create policy without law or administration. Both approaches are, of course, in this arena highly compatible with the underlying American pattern of beliefs.

A NEW ERA--A CHANGING WORLD VIEW

It was the social and economic events of the 60s--the civil rights movement, the increasingly youthful population, new labor saving developments in industrial technology and a changing and growing economy--that helped to generate a level of growth in the area of federally supported employment and training programs that was unmatched since the days of the Great Depression. Spurred on by the process of gearing up for a "war on poverty," new programs, one after another, began to take their place amidst a sometimes confusing array of initials and acronyms which were the byproduct of intensified federal efforts to meet the new and the old economic and employment problems facing the nation.

During the second half of the 50s, following the Korean War, unemployment had risen steadily, accompanied by a rising concern about workers displaced because of economic changes over which they had little control. The prevailing concern was for those who were being "automated" out of jobs due to technological development in industry--such as that which was occurring in the coal mines of Appalachia and the textile mills of New England. Thus the Area Redevelopment Act of 1961, primarily aimed at reducing unemployment in depressed areas by attracting industry to them, contained a small job training component. This was greatly enlarged upon with the passage by Congress of the Manpower Development and Training Act (MDTA) of 1962. Also in this period, Congress passed the Vocational

Education Act of 1963.   It expanded training opportunities through the initiation of Area Vocational Centers and other programs.   Most significantly, however, it represented the federal government's first efforts at refocusing the nation's education and training activities upon the hard core poor.

Fears of large scale displacement of workers by automation were somewhat dissipated by the low unemployment during the period of rapid economic growth which lasted into the late 60s.   However, the contrast between the prosperity of the country at large and the plight of millions who seemed trapped in an ongoing cycle of poverty served to shift the emphasis of employment and training programs to those caught in the double bind of economic and educational deprivation.   The influence of the civil rights movement in both changing American ideas and focusing attention on the need for employment and training services by the poor cannot be overestimated.   What were then known as "manpower programs" were seen by both civil rights activists and public administrators as an important lever to bring about a more equitable economic distribution.   Attention also began to be focused upon the "social dynamite" of unemployed youth.

As a result of concerns of this sort, the landmark Economic Opportunity Act of 1964 contained several major employment and training programs-- initially the Job Corps and Neighborhood Youth Corps for youth and, in later amendments to the Act, Operation Mainstream, New Careers and Special Impact.   In addition, the MDTA was amended in 1963, 1965, 1966, and 1968 to expand training and supportive services for youth and the poor in general and to encourage the development and utilization of newly organized "skills centers."   In 1967, the Work Incentive Program (WIN) was added as an amendment to the Social Security Act which was designed to remove those provisions of the public assistance regulations which tended to discourage welfare recipients from taking jobs.

In 1968, still another major development in employment and training policy was initiated--involving the private sector in program development and management.   The MDTA program authorized funding for two distinct types of training and retaining: Institutional (carried out at training facilities) and On-the-Job Training (OJT) (carried out by private employers at the actual work site).   Experience with early employment and training initiatives had resulted in two important findings.   First, successful training for the severely disadvantaged unemployed cost a good deal more than had been allowed for under most federal programs; and, second, better performance was experienced in training enrollees who were guaranteed a job at the end of the programs.   This latter realization gave impetus to the formation of the National Alliance of Business (NAB) to administer the "JOBS" program which would contract with private employers to subsidize training aligned to specific job openings.   Following upon this, in 1969, the Public Service Careers (PSC) program, modeled after JOBS, was initiated to provide subsidies for training to governmental agencies that would provide a pretraining commitment for jobs in the public sector.

During this period, other new programs emerged out of the growing awareness of the essentiality of supportive services in successful programs for the disadvantaged.   A variety of experimental programs such as the "Jobs Now" program in Chicago demonstrated the value of "high support" services including "job coaches" to follow a trainee throughout the several stages of his or her training and initial work experience.   Increasingly, the more successful program designs reflected an awareness of the need for additional supportive services: day care, aid to first payday pay, transportation expenses, health care and the like. Such services were found to be vital complements to the job training and basic education programs which most successfully equipped the unemployed or under-employed person with a marketable skill.

In addition to these new programs, the 60s were characterized by expanding appropriations for vocational education, vocational rehabilitation, apprenticeship training (especially for minority workers) and adult educa-tion. Nevertheless, at the end of the 60s, unemployment began to rise steadily as the disastrous economic impact of the Viet Nam War began to be felt. In December, 1970, a $9.5 billion bill which would have created over 300,000 employment openings in the public sector over four years was passed by both houses of the U.S. Congress but vetoed by the President. The creation of jobs in the public sector--either on a permanent basis or timed with economic fluctuations--had, however, by this time emerged as a major issue in employment and training policy. The reason for this was the growing sense that the most serious issue of national employment policy was not insufficient aggregate demand but rather structural unemployment that resulted from a growing segment of the population who lacked the training and skills to compete successfully in the private sector economy.

THE IRRESISTIBLE URGE--PROGRAM COORDINATION

As the 60s were ending, a major issue that has continued to concern both students and practitioners of employment and training policy had just begun to emerge. This was the issue of program coordination. Increas-ingly, administrators became concerned about fragmentation and a lack of coordination among a variety of programs aimed at essentially common goals. In 1967, the Senate Subcommittee on Employment, Manpower and Poverty noted that "a constant theme" of its field hearings and consultant studies was "the lack of effective coordination among federal programs." The result was several efforts to establish some coordination among the varied federal programs. These included the establishment of the Coop-erative Area Manpower Planning System (CAMPS) at the national, regional, state and metropolitan levels, as well as the Concentrated Employment Program (CEP) which attempted to promote the concept of a one-stop service center of supportive placement and orientation services. In some degree, this idea drew its inspiration from the Model Cities program which had been established by LBJ in the mid-60s.

That coordination should emerge as an issue of major concern in em-ployment and training policy is not very surprising. With the post-World War II growth of government programs, coordination has become a much sought after goal in the provision of public services in the United States. That this should be so is not very surprising. One of the most brilliant and durable social inventions of the American founding fathers was the notion of fragmenting government as a means of helping to preserve both local control and individual liberty. Inevitably, however, a government that is fragmented, whether by level, branch, or function, is going to require coordination. This will especially be the case when financial resources are in short supply and the demand for a service comes from many individuals at many times and in many places.

Consequently, it is not surprising that questions are frequently raised about the extent to which employment and training activities, as well as social services in general, are effectively coordinated. In a fragmented system reform, advocates will always see increased coordination as a means to greater efficiency and economy. In general, such a belief is probably an accurate one. Whether that is always the case, however, is by no means clear. Efforts to coordinate the work of two or more agencies or governmental units require the expenditure of limited resources--sometimes a lot of them. Thus, the absence of totally satisfactory coordination of public services may, in at least some instances, not necessarily be a bad thing.

Even in the 80s, with very restricted public funds, there can be no doubt that there are duplications and overlap in local employment and training services. Such a situation may be a beneficial one, however, for any of several reasons. First, in many instances, there is a large enough demand for certain services to justify the need for more than one organization to provide similar efforts. Second, it may be that one or another group is not doing an adequate job and thus, alternative options are useful. Third, it is likely that competition among them strengthens the performance of such organizations.

NEW INITIATIVES--NEW PROBLEMS

One of the most significant consequences of the emergence of the multiplicity of federal employment and training program efforts was the growth in number of projects which the U.S. Department of Labor had contracted for from local, state, public and private agencies. By one estimate, the Department of Labor had, by the early 1970s, entered into 40,000 contractural agreements with such organizations for the implementation of specific employment and training activities. That fact combined with the Nixon administration's advocacy of consolidating individual grant in aid programs into more generalized block grants led to the enactment of the Comprehensive Employment and Training Act (CETA) in 1973. The primary provisions of that legislation represented a return to the more traditional approach of providing employment and training services that had been initially embodied in the Employment Service and the Unemployment Insurance program--federal funding of program activity that is implemented and managed by state and, in this instance, local governments.

The CETA legislation had also built into it a provision for the creation of what would ultimately become a substantial public sector jobs creation program. Indeed, even prior to the adoption of CETA in 1973, the Emergency Employment Act of 1971 had been passed, which provided in excess of two billion dollars for a program of public sector jobs. Many of the existing employment and training programs were combined into Title I of CETA, while Title II incorporated the public employment program that had been established in the Emergency Employment Act of 1971. In 1977, Title IV of CETA was significantly expanded with the adoption of the Youth Employment Demonstration Projects legislation in 1977. The result was that by FY 1980 over two million people were employed in public sector jobs under the CETA program's public employment section; and, an additional half-million individuals were enrolled in the youth program that had been established under Title IV.

As unemployment remained high during the course of the latter 70s and early 80s, the public sector employment provisions of the CETA program came to dominate the activities of state and local employment and training

organizations.   Not surprisingly, given the pattern of development that
has characterized employment and training policy in the United States and
the nature of the American political belief system, these programs became
the subject of increasing controversy and criticism.   An endless array of
newspaper reports continually pointed to corruption and administrative
failures in these programs.   In fact, over time, the administration of these
programs did improve and a number of studies found them to be rather
effective (Haveman & Palmer, 1982).   Nevertheless, the criticism of these
programs continued unabated into the first year of the Reagan administration.

One result of this criticism of CETA programs was the enactment in
1982 of the Job Training Partnership Act.   This legislation, which currently drives a substantial portion of the nation's employment and training
system, made several significant changes.   First, it eliminated the public
service jobs activities that had been supported by the federal government.
Second, it substantially enhanced the role of private sector business in
shaping employment and training programs through Private Industry Councils at the local level.   Third, it gave state government officials an important role in the development and oversight of employment and training
programs, although it did leave the ultimate responsibility for their administration with local agencies, specifically, service delivery areas which are
ultimately responsible to local governments.

Perhaps the most significant consequence of the enactment of the JTPA
legislation was to be found in its symbolism of a major change in roles in
the implementation of employment and training policy.   JTPA sent a very
strong and clear message to the employment and training community that
the federal role was to be decreased significantly with the states and
private sector substantially increasing their influence over such programs.
That development, vigorously advocated by the Reagan administration and
its congressional supporters, was greeted with considerable enthusiasm in
many quarters of the employment and training community.   There are,
however, some aspects of this change that might cause one to pause and
consider long-term consequences.   Perhaps, the most important of these
has to do with the role of state governments in the shaping of public
policy.

A close look at the public policy record of many state governments
seems to reflect a middle and upper class policy bias (McConnell, 1966)
that should cause at least some concern about either the willingness or the
capacity of such governments to adequately address the employment and
training needs of individuals from the working and lower classes.   A
detailed analysis of this phenomenon is clearly the subject for another
paper but a few comments will serve to illustrate the point.   A first place
to look to find evidence would be tax policy; the adjustment of which,
most observers acknowledge, remains the single most effective way to
shape the distribution of income and economic resources within a modern
industrial state (Paukert, 1968).

Over the past six years, the Reagan tax reforms have, whether intended or not, had a decidedly counterequalitarian impact on the federal tax
system.   Prior to that, however, during the 50 years from 1930 to 1980,
there can be no question that the federal tax system was at least mildly
progressive (requiring paying a higher tax rate by the more wealthy), and
state and local state systems, when combined, were decidedly regressive
(requiring the paying of a higher actual rate of taxes by lower as opposed

to middle and upper income individuals) (Pechman, 1969). Thus, state governments were certainly contributing to the preservation of economic inequality through their tax policy.

State and local performance in the area of elementary and secondary education is equally revealing. In a landmark study published in the early 1970s, Christopher Jencks found that the American education system was structured in such a way that the children of the top 20 percent of the nation's population (in terms of income) benefited from a rate of public educational expenditures that was twice as much as that spent on the children of bottom 20 percent of the nation's population (in terms of income distribution) (Jencks, 1972). At the conclusion of the 1970s, after almost a decade of judicially initiated state efforts to equalize education expenditures among the rich and poor, the actual disparity in public, state and local spending for education between the well-to-do and the children of the poor had not decreased, but rather increased (Brown, 1978).

As a final point in this regard, one might reflect for a moment upon the role of the states in the provision of two important public services, higher education and welfare assistance. Generally speaking, the American public higher education system, which has been driven by the nation's state governments, is regarded as one of the true wonders of 20th century public policy--an achievement envied by virtually every nation in the world. While certainly an important channel of opportunity for some of the nation's poor, higher education has always primarily been used and benefited by the middle and upper classes (Windham, 1970). In contrast, the American system of welfare assistance has greatly lagged behind that of most of the industrialized western world in its development. While American political beliefs are no doubt the most important explanatory factor, the absence of the aggressive state support of such programs is certainly a contributory one.

Actually, the issue of the state versus federal role in the shaping of public policy has been one of the perennial issues of political and constitutional concern throughout the nation's history. Thus, it is, perhaps, appropriate in this time of focusing upon the bicentennial of the Constitution to turn to its writing for a final observation on this topic. During the course of the past century, the nation has come to accept the notion that a primary goal of authors of the Constitution was to significantly limit federal policymaking power and guarantee the reservation of basic powers to the states. Ironically, the reality was quite the reverse.

As the distinguished, and thoroughly conservative, historian Forrest McDonald has pointed out, not only did the founding fathers come together in Philadelphia to attempt to enhance the power of a then floundering national government, but an even greater concern was to rein in and bring under control state governments which, in the brief period from the Revolutionary War until the Constitutional Convention, had emerged as oppressive bodies which were dramatically increasing local taxes and writing discriminatory regulatory law (McDonald, 1987). It is, perhaps, useful for both practitioners and students of employment and training policy to think twice as they rush to line up in support of the Reagan administration's proposals for the continued devolution of the nation's employment and training, employment service, and unemployment insurance activities from the federal level of government to the states.

REFERENCES

Brown, L.L., et al. (1978). *School finance reform in the seventies: Achievements and failures.* Washington, DC: USDHEW.

Edelman, M. (1971). *Politics as symbolic action: Mass arousal and quiescence.* Chicago: Markham.

Grodzins, M. (1963). Centralization and decentralization in the American federal system. In R.A. Goldwin (Ed.), *A nation of states: Essays on the American federal system.* Chicago: Rand McNally.

Handler, J. (1972). *Reforming the poor: Welfare policy, federalism and morality.* New York: Basic Books.

Haveman, R.H., & Palmer, J.L. (1982). *Jobs for disadvantaged workers.* Washington, DC: The Brookings Institution.

Jencks, C., et al. (1972). *Inequality: A reassessment of the effect of family and schooling in America.* New York: Basic Books.

Lowi, T.J. (1969). *The end of liberalism.* New York: W.W. Norton Company.

Martin, R. (1964). *Grass roots.* Birmingham: University of Alabama Press.

McConnell, G. (1966). *Private power and American democracy.* New York: Alfred A. Knopf.

McDonald, F. (1987, May 6). *The intellectual world of the founding fathers.* The 16th National Endowment for the Humanities Jefferson Lecture, Washington, DC.

Paukert, F. (1968). Social Security and income redistribution: Comparative experience in Social Security and economic development. In Lampman (Ed.), *Transfer and redistribution as social process.* Madison, WI: Institute for Research on Poverty.

Pechman, J. (1969, Fall). The rich, the poor, and the taxes they pay. *The Public Interest.*

Simon, P. (1987). *Let's put America back to work.* Chicago: Bonus Books.

Steiner, G. (1966). *Social insecurity.* Chicago: Rand McNally.

Windham, D. (1970). *Education, equality and income redistribution.* Lexington, MA: D.C. Heath.

33

The Political Hand: Policy Implementation and Youth Employment Programs

Martin Levin and Barbara Ferman

Outstanding studies in the past decade have illuminated the sources of ineffective implementation and thus have suggested what not to do. To learn more about what to do, we analyzed a broad range of cases of effective implementation of youth employment programs in eight cities. The goal was to build an impressionistic model of the conditions contributing to effective implementation. We found that executives in the successful programs often acted as "fixers," repairing the implementation process and protecting and correcting their programs, especially through coalition building and constant intervention in administrative detail. Some executives created patterns of interest convergence among the relevant actors, using incentives to turn mild interests into active support. They thus provided the public sector's missing "political hand," analogous to the market's "invisible hand."

In the early 1970s, the implementation problems of the Economic Development Administration (EDA) and the Office of Economic Opportunity (OEO), as well as other programs such as Model Cities, New Towns-in-Town, and federal aid to education, were considered to be largely the result of overly ambitious social engineering by liberal Democrats. It was often said that these liberal plans were immodest and that the liberals themselves were both too optimistic and uninterested in the actual details of implementing their "bright ideas."

By the end of the 1970s decade, experience suggested that such diagnoses of the problems of implementation probably missed the mark. Domestic policies of conservative Republican administra-

* We wish to thank Frank Levy, Tom Glynn, Gene Bardach, Aaron Wildavsky, and Martin Shapiro for their invaluable comments on an earlier draft. Support for the preparation of this article came from the James Gordon Foundation of Chicago and the Office of Youth of the Department of Labor.

From *Journal of Policy Analysis and Management*, Vol. 5, No. 2 (Winter 1986): 311–25. Copyright 1986 by the Association for Public Policy Analysis and Management. Reprinted by permission of John Wiley & Sons, Inc.

tions—often with rather modest goals—also foundered at the implementation stage. This was true for both the swine flu vaccination program and the Community Development Block Grant program.

It seems that more is needed than good intentions or even good program designs to achieve effective policies. In the past two decades, implementation has been identified as the knottiest aspect of policymaking. One critical source of these difficulties, it is now clear, is the fact that in the heterogeneous society and fragmented political system that characterize the United States, there are numerous possibilities for disagreement, delay, and resistance. Thus, the legislative successes of yesterday often become the implementation problems of today.

YOUTH EMPLOYMENT In the past few decades, youth unemployment has become a serious national problem. The existence and persistence of high teenage unemployment rates, especially the disparities between teenage and adult rates, and between the rates of white and black teenagers, are now well known. Also well known is the fact that a relatively small proportion of youths—approximately 10%—accounts for almost half the unemployment of the youth group as a whole; this is a subset that is unemployed for long spells, six months or more.[1] Some suggest that the size of this relatively small subpopulation in the totals means that the problem is less serious than is usually supposed; others take the opposite view.[2] Whatever side one espouses, it is clear that any programs to reduce youth unemployment ought to be shaped by considerations of how to improve the lot of this specific subset.

Programs such as those authorized by the 1977 Youth Employment Demonstration Project Act (YEDPA) are especially suited to targeting specific groups. The implementation of nine of these programs in eight cities provides a rich basis for observing the role of the political hand in the implementation process. At its inception, YEDPA represented a new federal initiative to alleviate youth unemployment. In the first 18 months of its operation beginning in 1978, YEDPA expanded to a program that served some 450,000 youths at an expenditure of $1.7 billion. Projects under YEDPA focused on both developing new jobs and providing youths with the training, experience, and placement assistance to fill jobs. The training involved remedial reading, practical arithmetic, and on-the-job experience. All of the nine projects we analyzed included efforts to develop sound work habits and discipline. The youths in the nine YEDPA programs were aged 16 to 21, with family incomes not over about $9400 (the benchmark figure actually varied somewhat by region). Over 80% of the youths in the YEDPA came from low-income families, and 51% were black or Hispanic. In some programs, most were still in school, and in others most were not. Whether in school or not, most youths in these programs were difficult to work with—they showed poor academic development, lack of discipline, and poor work habits.

LEARNING WHAT
WORKS

Like many social programs, YEDPA had implementation problems. But the nine YEDPA programs analyzed here differ from
most of these other programs in a number of ways. First, the implementation obstacles YEDPA faced were somewhat different
from those of other programs. In general, there are three major
types of implementation obstacles: resistance—some actors resist
implementation because they feel it is not in their interests; imperfect convergence of interests—some actors create delay or threaten
to delay in order to expand their benefits; disorganized interests—
others create obstacles simply because they are unclear where
their interests lie or are unable to organize themselves to respond
to their convergent interests. The first two types of obstacles are
common to most programs. The obstacles of disorganized interests, on the other hand, are often overlooked in implementation
analyses even though they are more formidable than is typically
recognized. The problems of this sort encountered by the YEDPA
programs provided a fine opportunity to examine the dynamics of
disorganized interests.

Another way in which these YEDPA programs differ from most
others is that they provide more insights than the analyst usually
encounters regarding what works. Several outstanding studies in
the past decade have illuminated the sources of ineffective implementation.[3] Because these studies concentrated on programs
whose performance appeared inadequate, their chief virtue is in
telling one what not to do. The YEDPA study, on the other hand,
was motivated in large part by the desire to learn more about what
to do; the goal was to build an impressionistic model of the conditions contributing to effective implementation.

In seven of the nine programs studied, we concluded that implementation had been effective; the two remaining programs seemed
on the borderline. These seven satisfied three broad criteria for
effective implementation. First, was the program able to hold delay to a reasonable level? Second, was it able to hold financial
costs to a reasonable level? Third, was it able to meet its original
objectives without significant alteration or underachievement of
these objectives?

Among the factors that played an important role in overcoming
the obstacles to effective implementation were the actions of the
executives in these nine programs, especially their actions as "fixers." As "fixers," they were constantly repairing and adjusting the
machinery used for executing their programs, constantly putting
together coalitions to support, protect, and sometimes expand
those programs.[4] Some of these executives also created patterns of
interest convergence among the relevant actors, using incentives
to turn mild interests into active support. They thus provided the
public sector's missing "political hand," analogous to the market's
"invisible hand," and facilitated a public use of private interest.
There also was the growth of a local policy infrastructure in these
cities that resulted in local actors contributing positively rather
than negatively to the implementation of federal programs. This
seems to be a significant change from the 1960s.

But there are significant limits to how effective the implementation can become. Thus, program executives should develop an anticipatory and "dirty-minded" perspective: the ability to anticipate and predict implementation difficulties and to be attuned to conflicting interests and their likelihood of delaying, even outright resisting, implementation. A "dirty-minded" implementor, for example, might have better predicted the major implementation difficulties that the swine flu vaccination program would face and would have suggested precisely the actions and thoughts that those in charge of that program did not take.

To the extent that these nine YEDPA programs were effectively implemented, their performance seemed to be explained by the existence of some specific structural conditions in the environment in which they operated and some specific behavioral patterns on the part of their managers. The behavioral patterns have already been mentioned: an ability of managers to build piece by piece and to play the role of fixer. The environmental conditions are described and explored below. The distinction between structural and behavioral elements is useful. But like any such concept, it tends to simplify reality—all of these conditions interact significantly and tend to constitute a package of interrelated and interdependent elements. An executive pursuing the fixer strategies, for instance, would have little success in some environments. But, as will be argued below, talent is more scarce than either money or good ideas, especially at the executive level. Thus, favorable structural conditions are a secondary factor, supplementing or conditioning the effects of the behavioral patterns. At times, they can help produce favorable results even when highly talented executives are not available.

THE STUDY'S METHODOLOGY   The aim here, as suggested, is to build an impressionistic model of the conditions that contribute to effective implementation. Therefore, these nine programs were selected from a larger pool of about 100 programs for which there was preliminary evidence of effective implementation.[5] They were selected because they were among the most effectively implemented and because they represented a diversity in size, region, and ethnicity of the youths in the program. The nine included programs in Pittsburgh, New Haven, Portland (Oregon), Syracuse, Albuquerque (two programs), San Antonio, Newark, and Baltimore.

For each of these nine programs, in addition to collecting statistical and documentary data, we conducted over a dozen interviews with a variety of actors. The interviews were systematic, although open-ended, and each lasted 45 min to 2 h. Drafts of all nine case studies were submitted to several actors in each program, including each program executive, in an attempt to check our findings and incorporate feedback. We have benefited from their suggestions. In the case of only one individual—apparently motivated by the fear of political fallout in Washington—did they differ from our conclusions. And this difference eventually was resolved to that actor's satisfaction.

Within these limits of our data, which are quite common to policy analysis in general and implementation studies in particular, we are confident of our generalizations. Nevertheless, while our data are strongly suggestive of the conclusions reached, in most instances they cannot demonstrate them conclusively. We have not followed the usual social science practice of using pseudonyms for the cities analyzed. We hope this will ameliorate any evidentiary issues by encouraging other researchers to check our findings by analyzing these programs themselves.

STRUCTURAL CONDITIONS FOR EFFECTIVE IMPLEMENTATION

Programs often are stillborn because nobody views them as being in their direct interest. Lacking such interests, the characteristic inertia of the governmental process tends to block effective implementation.

YEDPA was a good idea with a good program design. But the support of those who were concerned about youth employment, such as civil rights groups and local political leaders, was insufficient to implement these nine programs. They needed the support of those with more immediate interests in the programs, such as city governments and their agencies and private companies that received free labor, as well as the schools that were directly involved in executing the programs.[6]

The Political Hand

In some cases, groups that would benefit from the programs were not aware of those prospective benefits. The challenge for the executives was to create a convergence of interest. They used incentives and inducements to develop interests; they turned mild interests into active support. This seems to have contributed greatly to effective implementation.

For instance, New Haven, Portland, and San Antonio public housing authorities were in a position to receive free labor to support their programs for conserving and rehabilitating old structures, provided they took certain preliminary measures. One was to designate worksites for the program. The programs also needed general support from construction unions, as well as more direct contributions that included providing crew supervisors and apprenticeship positions for the youths who graduated from the programs. In turn, the programs offered unions an opportunity for preapprenticeship training at reduced costs, a referral service that helped unions satisfy affirmative action requirements, and the possibility of some additional jobs for union journeymen at a time when some in that category were unemployed.

Interest convergence is a pattern in which private (or individual) and public interests come to coincide. This resembles the (ideal) pattern of individuals in a private market. But in public sector activities like the implementation of a complex public program, there is no "invisible hand" to lead interests to coincide. Indeed, the inherent tension between private and public interests is a constant obstacle to socially desirable actions in the public sector. These YEDPA executives' actions in creating interest convergence in effect provided the public sectors' missing *"political hand"*[7] and created a *public use of private interest.*

One is reminded of Barnard's classic statement on the function of the executive, "to facilitate the synthesis in concrete action of contradictory forces, to reconcile conflicting forces, instincts, interests, conditions, positions, and ideals."[8] Others have suggested that the executive's principal tool in that process is communication aimed at mediating between groups and educating groups to their interests.[9] Through this ability for role taking, the executive becomes a medium for communication. These YEDPA executives communicated (as well as created) the incentives to those actors who merely had latent or potential positive interests to gain from YEDPA.

Using the Local Policy Infrastructure In pursuing their role, YEDPA executives seem to have been helped by the existence of a recently developed policy infrastructure at the local level in these cities. The individuals and organizations comprising this infrastructure were oriented toward innovation and social progress. Many were alumni of Great Society programs and their foundation spinoffs; others came from post-Great Society innovative programs of the Federal Departments of Labor and Housing and Urban Development. The accumulated experiences of many federal social programs taught a great deal to both individuals and institutions. The individuals represented a new generation of activist bureaucrats. They functioned in a real sense as "organizers," and likening them to community or labor organizers captures a good deal of their political background and personal predilection. But they played a larger role because they were also skilled bureaucrats.

The term "infrastructure" is used to emphasize the rich organizational—rather than merely personal—legacy found in these cities. Numerous community-based organizations, new public agencies, and special programs within public agencies have developed and have become experienced, effective, and relatively prosperous. They know how to develop monetary and political support. For example, the Mexican–American Unity Council (MAUC) is a community development corporation that operates San Antonio's YCCIP. It was formed in 1967 and became involved in a broad range of community development projects, including major roles in the financing of large downtown construction projects. It is a politically influential organization, locally through alliance with activist priests, and nationally through its director's contacts with federal bureaucrats.

The growth in local infrastructure produced complex organizational and personal networks linking persons and organizations and gave them overlapping interests. The networks are built on past relationships and trust. This greatly facilitates securing the joint action and program assembly necessary for effective implementation. For instance, the assistant director of the prime sponsor in Pittsburgh and the program's director worked together as Neighborhood Youth Corps counselors in the late 1960s and early 1970s. Personal trust and cooperation developed over the years enabled them to avoid the suspicion that has existed between prime sponsor and schools in other cities, and which has led to implementation delays.

These policy infrastructures are an important social development of the last two decades, and using them could aid the implementation of a wide variety of other programs. A good deal of organization and many outstanding administrators remain from adult CETA and earlier manpower programs. YEDPA benefited greatly from the positive and negative lessons of the adult CETA programs. For example, the negative publicity that surrounded CETA nationally encouraged YEDPA prime sponsors and RDOL's to adopt stringent cost-monitoring devices. Without CETA (or any of its predecessors such as the Neighborhood Youth Corps and the Manpower Demonstration Training Act), YEDPA's implementation would almost certainly have been slower and less effective. There would have been more learning on-the-job and fewer program managers with the experience needed to anticipate implementation pitfalls and thus be better able to develop ways of avoiding, coping, or overcoming them.

Modest and Straightforward Design Although effective implementation depends on good local administration, that is not sufficient in itself. Even when a local program has a talented executive, implementation may founder simply because of the complexity of the program design. Thus, the modest, straightforward, and even simple designs of these YEDPA programs seem to have contributed markedly to effective implementation.

These designs maintained YEDPA's focus on the goals of job development, experience, training, and placement. YEDPA programs were not intended to redistribute political power or create political autonomy in low-income neighborhoods, as the Office of Economic Opportunity and Model Cities sought to do. By keeping to modest, specific goals, YEDPA's implementation was able to avoid the implementation pitfalls that have beset other social programs since the mid-1960s. For instance, the bulk of YEDPA expenditures have gone for youth wages and benefits. In fact, there was a formal and rigorously enforced regulation in the two largest categories of programs that 65% of each program's budget must go directly for youth wages and benefits. By contrast, the complex design and implementation processes of many earlier social programs often were major contributors to ineffective implementation and poor outcomes. The indirect design of EDA described in Jeffrey Pressman and Aaron Wildavsky's classic study of Oakland is a good example. They subsidized the capital of business—rather than their wage bill—on the promise that they would later hire low-skilled minority persons.[10]

Anticipating Pitfalls Even with modest designs, all of these nine programs experienced many implementation difficulties. But the implementors took several steps to anticipate these pitfalls. Thus, they were better able to develop ways of avoiding or coping with them.

First, often they did not attempt to start from scratch. Many YEDPA programs were built (Portland, Pittsburgh, and Newark) or modeled (San Antonio and New Haven) on previously successful ones. For instance, Pittsburgh's was built upon previously successful programs that had been designed for less disadvantaged youths. This enabled Pittsburgh to avoid most of the ordinary implementation difficulties: key actors—at both the worksites and the schools—had already worked together successfully for seven years.

Second, in several of these programs, internal evaluation and reassessment led to the detection and correction of serious implementation problems. In effect, they created a second phase for these programs that could be effectively implemented after initial problems were detected. The test of a good policy or a good program is not the absence of error but the ability to detect errors and then correct them.[9] In Baltimore, for example, after the first few months of operation there appeared published reports, citizen complaints, and mayoral inquiries that made it clear to the heads of the prime sponsor and the program that there were serious implementation problems (i.e., significant administrative difficulties—such as breakdown of the payroll systems for youths—resulting from the overcentralization of a large program). They assembled a task force of their top staff to review operations and develop recommendations. The subsequent changes (greater decentralization; in particular, the responsibility for supervision, counseling, and payroll was shifted to smaller units) greatly improved implementation. A similarly successful reassessment and reorganization was undertaken in San Antonio.

BEHAVIORAL Fixer strategies are crucial to effective implementation. The pro-
CONDITIONS gram assembly process will not run by itself. It has to be put together piece by piece. It should be guided by a strong executive.
Fixers Actors and interests have to be cajoled, convinced, and persuaded into joint action. Adjustments and adaptations have to be made. Coalitions have to be built. Numerous compensating actions were taken by these program executives in response to intentional omissions at the design and formulation stages (designers felt that it was not politically or financially feasible to include them earlier). One occurred in Albuquerque's WORP where planners knew it would be difficult for program youths to use the city's small public transportation system to get to the distant worksite, but needed to avoid an expensive transportation item in their proposal lest they lose out to less costly competitors. After the program was funded and many youths began to get fired because they could not get to their jobs on time using public transportation, the program executive renegotiated the grant to obtain transportation funds. Other

compensating actions were in response to inadvertent omissions, which are endemic: at the earlier stages nobody can fully anticipate the difficulties and resistance that may surface in implementation.

Coalition building is a central element of the fixer strategy. The most significant element of coalition building pursued by these YEDPA executives was the creation of the patterns of interest convergence described above. There were also other instances of coalition building by these fixers. In San Antonio, the prime sponsor director created a coalition behind the YCCIP program by developing support for it from local construction unions and from the Six Parish Coalition (a group previously formed by activist priests to organize barrio residents).

Other recent studies also point to the major contributions to effective implementation made by program executives. For instance, studies of the "Effective Schools" movement, successful black schools, and a broad range of London schools all indicate that the role of the schools' staffs as shaped by the "program executive"—the Principal—is much more important in achieving improved academic performance and improved behavior than educational innovations such as new teaching techniques, special programs, and new facilities.[12]

Bridging Agents Several program executives made major contributions to effective implementation by acting as "bridging agents." This role consisted of securing joint action among various interests through the executive's standing and membership in more than one of the relevant implementation camps. One bridging agent assembled Albuquerque's "THE" program by bringing together the hotel industry (providing worksites, jobs, and training) and the public schools. She was head of vocational training in the public schools, and her husband was a hotel executive and leader in the local hotel industry. The idea for "THE" came from her husband's constant complaint that he could not find enough trained people to work in his hotel. She also had a number of important contacts in the hotel industry that facilitated "THE's" initial implementation.

Similarly, the person who conceived, designed, and was *de facto* director of the Syracuse program had extremely helpful positions in several camps: he was a black officer at the Air Force base worksite (and head of its social action training program) who had been active in a broad range of black community affairs in the city and once worked in its Human Rights Department with a current executive in the prime sponsor's office. Like other bridging agents, the officer also had knowledge of labor shortages in the worksites to which he was close. And he thought that the base's labor shortage could be ameliorated by the YEDPA youths.

LIMITS TO ACTION Talented program executives, especially those able to act as "fixers," were a key to the success of implementation in these nine cases. But there seem to be significant limits to their availability.

Effective executive action in implementation requires the ability to carry it out, the resources, and the incentives. Ability is scarce. Even in a period of tight budget constraints, talent usually is more scarce than money, especially at the executive level. As James Q. Wilson has argued,

The supply of able, experienced executives is not increasing nearly as fast as the number of problems being addressed by public policy . . . Anyone who opposed a bold new program on the grounds that there was nobody around able to run it would be accused of being a pettifogger at best and a reactionary do-nothing at worst. Everywhere, except in government, it seems, the scarcity of talent is accepted as a fact of life . . . The government—at least publicly—seems to act as if the supply of able political executives were infinitely elastic, though people setting up new agencies will often admit privately that they are so frustrated and appalled by the shortage of talent that the only wonder is why disaster is so long in coming.[13]

Even when there is a potentially strong executive for implementation with the ability, he or she must have sufficient resources for the task. But often the able person does not. Nevertheless, a significant number of persons have the ability and resources, yet many of them do not have sufficient incentives. Indeed, the scarcity of these incentives seems to be the most significant limit. Most incentives for executives to become active in implementation run in the wrong direction, and the few positive incentives are weak. The electoral imperative is the biggest disincentive. American public officials feel their first job is to get themselves or their bosses re-elected (or elected in the first place). This creates a short-run orientation and pressure for fast action. The constraint is the next election, which typically is in less than four years (less than two years for Congressman and many state legislators). All this goes against the grain of working on implementation or even developing an interest in it. Instead, potential implementation leaders opt for the dramatic; it need not be a dramatic achievement. A dramatic disclosure or proposal may be sufficient for one's electorate or superior. By contrast, implementation of an older proposal (even if effective) is not dramatic or fast; often it is downright dull.

These pressures also create incentives for symbolic politics rather than substantive activity. To convey a symbol—or effort, position, or commitment—it often may be sufficient for the official to take a stand, make a proposal, or sometimes initiate a program. Often this satisfies the electoral imperative without actually having to lead the implementation effort. In the extreme, officials "proclaim and abandon": they are more interested in a podium for policymaking rather than actual policy adoption and implementation.

THE POLITICAL HAND AND INTEREST CONVERGENCE Another replicability problem is that positive incentives for innovative social programs often are not present. Sometimes the innovation is supported by organizations and actors who favor it on

general material or ideological grounds, but are not direct beneficiaries. This leads to less than total commitment. Even more commonly, the major beneficiary of the program is that most amor-
phous group—citizens and taxpayers as a whole. The public
interest is notoriously difficult to organize, especially to press for
something as unglamorous as policy implementation that follows
high-visibility legislative struggles. The difficulty is compounded
when benefits are widely dispersed.

Thus, a pattern of interest convergence must usually be developed. For too long we have either acted as if a "political hand"
would appear spontaneously or simply bemoaned its absence in
the public sector. But interest convergence is at best difficult to
develop, probably even more difficult in policy areas other than
youth employment. Indeed, the positive contributions of local
unions that we found probably are not typical of other cities and
other unions. Moreover, the development of interest convergence
seems to be very dependent on the actions of a "fixer," and these
people are scarce.

There are, however, other conditions that are likely to be replicated in other policy areas.

LOCAL POLICY INFRASTRUCTURE Current local conditions surrounding the implementation of
YEDPA seem to be significantly more favorable than they were 15
or even 10 years earlier. Implementation difficulties then often
seemed to be caused by local actors; at worst there was active
resistance, and at best an inability to make programs work. By
contrast, today local conditions and actors tend to provide an extra boost to the implementation of federal programs. Employment
and other social programs of the 1960s and 1970s provided many
lessons—positive as well as negative—and helped develop local
infrastructures which have contributed toward effective implementation. It seems likely that this learning and infrastructure
development also occurred in other policy areas and in other cities. For instance, Paul Hill's analysis of federal education programs found that the development of informal networks of state
and local officials facilitated the implementation of Title I.[14]

MODEST DESIGNS AND MODEST GOALS Modest, straightforward program designs also seem to be replica-
ble, as are modest program goals. Since some conditions depend
on able program executives to activate them and since talented
executives are scarce, such modest designs and goals are especially
important because average executives can carry them out.

To practical persons, our emphasis on the importance of talented executives and simple, modest program designs may seem
obvious matters of common sense. But experience shows that program designers in particular, and staff people in general, tend to
overlook both of these issues. Intellectuals of all political stripes
overemphasize bright ideas as the most important element in
achieving effective policies. Whether they are staff people in Wash-

ington or designers at City Hall, they tend to look at elegant designs as sufficient in themselves and to forget about what is going to happen at the front line. However, these YEDPA cases and a host of other studies show that programs do not start up automatically.

Overlooking the importance of a simple design is part of this same tendency. Program designers often confuse complexity with superiority and forget that average administrators will be carrying out their complex designs.

THE IMPLEMENTORS' CREDO: "DIRTY MINDEDNESS" Given that modest and simple program design facilitates effective implementation, the operational questions of what an executive actually should do still remain. These YEDPA cases suggest the importance of executives approaching their task with the view that implementation will be difficult. Several of these YEDPA executives tried to anticipate pitfalls in three ways. First, they gave high priority to the task of internal evaluation and reassessments to detect and correct errors, and in doing this, they performed the very important function of implementation of error correction.

Second, several of these program executives acted as if they had what has been called a "dirty mind": the ability to anticipate and predict implementation difficulties and to be attuned to conflicting interests and their likelihood of delaying, even outright resisting, implementation.[15] Most importantly, the "dirty-minded" implementor is aware that most implementation difficulties cannot be anticipated fully (What else can we expect but the unexpected?) and that a program's implementation cannot even come close to being free of error.

This awareness leads to the third way in which these several programs executives tried to anticipate implementation pitfalls— scenario writing. While accepting the fact that implementation difficulties can never be anticipated fully, a shrewd and dirty-minded implementor will try to improve and formalize his anticipation as much as possible. Scenario writing can help do this. Scenario writing involves the imaginative construction of future sequences of actions, the resulting conditions and reactions, and in turn, the further conditions and reactions that are developed by all actors and organizations involved in the implementation process. At its best, it should sensitize the program executive to the obstacles that lie ahead. It brings the likely flaws and problems to the forefront.[16] Thus, it forces designers and program executives to try to take account of them.

ADAPTABLE AND REALISTIC IMPLEMENTORS YEDPA's modest and straightforward design was important. But a major element of its success was the flexibility and improvisation that it allowed program executives. Previous experience seems to have been more important than preconceived plans for program details. These YEDPA cases suggest the importance of a strategy of flexibility and improvisation for policy implementation, as opposed to fixed battle plans. Elegant designs, especially when devel-

oped from the top (the federal level in this case) may be less important for success than the conditions and personnel at program
sites. The advantages of a strategy of improvisation over fixed battle plans suggest some ways to train better implementors. First,
the training should be directed toward changing implementors'
expectations: make them more realistic about the high probability
of error and ineffective implementation. Second, in the face of
these more realistic expectations, we ought to train implementors
to be more adaptable so that they might be better able to cope with
these constant difficulties. They should be trained to view implementation as a process of avoiding pitfalls. In part, this can be
done by reacting to circumstances. As Edmund Burke put it so
well, "Circumstances give in reality to every political principle its
distinguishing colour and discriminating effect. The circumstances are what render every civil and political scheme beneficial
or noxious . . ."[17]

CURRENT   This emphasis on adaptable implementors is a necessary balance
CIRCUMSTANCES AND   to the earlier stress on the importance of anticipatory approaches
REALISTIC   in general and scenario writing in particular. But of course both
EXPECTATIONS   strategies are needed. The specification of the conditions under
which one should be preferred seems to depend largely on the
context.

Fifteen years ago the lessons that needed to be emphasized were
different than our focus on caution, modesty, and anticipatory
strategy. In 1967, in his "strategy for economic development," Albert Hirschman in effect argued against modesty and foresight. He
suggested that imbalance, ignorance of all the conditions at hand,
and hence all the limitations, and even a touch of foolhardiness
were needed to give initial impetus to the development. He urged
executives to ignore the overly cautious conclusion that usually is
developed by focusing on the obstacles to implementation. He also
urged them to overextend their reach and not to be constrained by
knowledge of implementation difficulties in economic development. By contrast with the lessons of the present study, Hirschman
felt that foresight and knowledge of these conditions and obstacles
too often tended to discourage people and immobilize the process.[18]

However, circumstances are a paramount policy consideration.
Hirschman in part seems to have been reacting against the circumstances of the 1950s and 1960s—the call for "balanced development" with much emphasis on planning for contingency and little
on the need for risk taking. By contrast, we are responding to the
circumstances in domestic social policy of the past two decades:
insufficient modesty, overly complicated program designs, and little appreciation of the virtue or necessity of simple design. For two
decades, the predominant view has been that a good program design, or in some cases merely good intentions and substantial funding, would be sufficient to bring about effective implementation. It
has been a period with insufficient focus on the importance of the

task of implementation qua implementation. In particular, there has been insufficient focus on the importance of talented executives (and all the component characteristics and strategies) in achieving effective implementation or on the problem of the scarcity of executive talent.

Perhaps the message of more realistic expectations about implementation difficulties is needed less during the Reagan administration—a time of social policy retrenchment. But even assuming continued retrenchment for the next several years, this does not alter the need for realism about implementation. Indeed, we would speculate that significant budget cuts in domestic programs probably will mitigate the development of realistic expectations about implementation. And they will retard the process of "governmental learning" in which organizational memories about the nature of policy implementation can be developed.[19] As suggested, funding is an important and necessary element for effective implementation, but as countless studies indicate, it is not a sufficient element. In this period of budget cuts, it seems likely that there will be a tendency to blame program deficiencies largely on these cuts. There probably will be the commensurate tendency to overlook more general implementation difficulties, inadequacies, and the whole issue of institutional capacity. We speculate that the view will develop, as has developed during other recent periods of budget cuts (the Ford and Nixon administrations, the New York City fiscal crises, Propositions 13 and 2½), that "if only the money would be restored, we could accomplish almost everything that we intended." And thus there will be a tendency to forget about the other continuing generic problems of policy implementation that exist even with adequate funds.

MARTIN LEVIN is with the Department of Politics, Brandeis University. BARBARA FERMAN is with Barnard College of Columbia University.

NOTES   1. Clark, Kim and Summers, Lawrence, "The Dynamics of Youth Unemployment," in *The Youth Labor Market Problem: Its Nature, Causes and Consequences*, Freeman and D. Wise, Eds. (Chicago: University of Chicago Press, 1982), pp. 194–234.

2. For example, see the opposing views of, on the one hand, Martin Feldstein and David Ellwood ("Teenage Unemployment: What is the Problem?" in Freeman and Wise) and, on the other, Clark and Summers, and the various supporting views that each cite.

3. Pressman, Jeffrey and Wildavsky, Aaron, *Implementation*, 2nd ed. (Berkeley: University of California Press, 1979); Bardach, Eugene, *The Implementation Game* (Cambridge: MIT PRess, 1977); Derthick, Martha, *New Towns In-Town: Why a Federal Program Failed* (Washington: The Brookings Institution, 1973); Hargrove, Erwin, *The Missing Link* (Washington: The Urban Institute, 1975); Murphy, Jerome, "Title I of ESSEA: The Politics of Implementing Federal Education Reform," *Harvard Educational Review*, 41(1) (1971): 35–63; Berman, Paul, "The Study of Macro- and Micro-Implementation," *Public Policy*, 26(2) (1978): 157–184; Binstock, Robert, and Levin, Martin, "The Political Dilemmas of Intervention Policies," in Binstock, Robert, and Shavas,

Ethel, *Handbook of Aging and the Social Sciences* (New York: Van Nostrand Reinhold, 1976); Ingram, Helen, "Policy Implementation Through Bargaining: The Case of Federal Grants-in-Aid," *Public Policy, 25*(4) (1977); 499–526; Mazmanian, Daniel, and Sabatier, Paul, *Effective Policy Implementation* (Lexington, MA: Lexington Books, 1981); Nakamura, Robert, and Smallwood, Frank, *The Politics of Implementation* (New York: St. Martin's, 1980); Radin, Beryl, *Implementation, Change, and the Federal Bureaucracy* (New York: Columbia University Press, 1975); Williams, Walter, *The Implementation Perspective* (Berkeley: University of California Press, 1980).

4. Bardach, Eugene, *The Implementation Game*, chap. 11.

5. These 9 were selected from a larger pool of about 100 programs for which there was preliminary evidence of effective implementation. These 100 programs were selected on the basis of the following published studies and interviews with Department of Labor officials in Washington and program officials and prime sponsors from all areas of the country. Wurzburg, G., et al., "Initial Youth Employment Demonstration Projects Act Experience at the Local Level," National Council on Employment Policy, Washington, DC, 1978; Wurzburg, G., et al., "The Unfolding Youth Initiative Employment Policy"; Ball, J., et al., "The Youth Entitlement Demonstration Program: A Summary Report on the Start-Up Period of the Youth Incentive Entitlement Pilot Projects," Manpower Demonstration Research Corporation, New York; Ball, J., et al., "An Interim Report on Program Implementation," Manpower Demonstration Research Corporation, New York, 1979.

6. See our forthcoming book, *The Political Hand* (New York: Pergamon, 1985), for a more detailed discussion.

7. We are indebted to Eugene Bardach for suggesting this analogy.

8. Barnard, Chester, *The Functions of the Executive* (Cambridge: Harvard University Press, 1938), p. 243).

9. Mead, George, *Mind, Self, and Society* (Chicago: University of Chicago Press, 1934).

10. Pressman and Wildavsky, *Implementation*.

11. Wildavsky, Aaron, "The Past and Future Presidency," *The Public Interest, 41* (Fall 1975): 56–76.

12. Sowell, Thomas, "Patterns of Black Excellence," *The Public Interest, 43* (Spring 1976): 26–58; Rutter, M., et al., *Fifteen Thousand Hours: Secondary Schools and Their Effects on Children* (Cambridge: Harvard University Press, 1979).

13. Wilson, James, "The Bureaucracy Problem," *The Public Interest, 6* (Winter 1967): 3–9.

14. Hill, Paul, "Enforcement and Informal Pressure in the Management of Federal Categorical Programs in Education," Rand Corporation, Santa Monica, CA, 1979.

15. Bardach, Eugene, "On Designing Implementable Programs," in *Pitfalls of Analyses and Analyses of Pitfalls*, E. Quade and G. Majone, Eds. (New York: Wiley, 1978).

16. Bardach, Eugene, *The Implementable Game*.

17. Edmund Burke, quoted in Kristol, Irving, "Decentralization for What," *The Public Interest, 11* (Spring 1968): 10–21.

18. Hirschman, Albert, "The Principle of the Hiding Hand," *The Public Interest, 6* (1968): 10–23.

19. Etheridge, Lynn, *Government Learning* (New York: Pergamon, 1985).

34

The Job Corps: Investing Pays Off

Sar A. Levitan and Frank Gallo

A product of the Great Society's antipoverty efforts, the Job Corps is the nation's oldest continuous federal youth training program. Its high costs have prompted continuing scrutiny, but by the early 1980s the program's accomplishments were acknowledged across the political spectrum. The Job Corps' statutory goal is "to assist young individuals who need and can benefit from an unusually intensive program, operated in a group setting, to become more responsible, employable, and productive citizens."

The program operates residential centers in the belief that removing poor youth from their debilitating environment is a necessary precondition to improving employability. The model reflects the view that poor individuals are trapped in an intergenerational "culture of poverty" which can be best combated through intensive services to youth. Having profited from experience, the Job Corps' effectiveness has improved since the program was established in 1964, but its basic structure has changed little under JTPA. It remains a federally-administered program. Throughout its history, the corps has provided extremely disadvantaged youths with basic education and vocational training, followed by job placement assistance after leaving a center.

Several states operate year-round youth corps programs which are similar to the Job Corps, spending approximately $100 million annually to assist some 15,000 enrollees. The $44 million California Conservation Corps, which operates both residential and nonresidential camps, is the largest state effort. State and local youth corps pursue a broad variety of educational and vocational goals. Al-

From *A Second Chance: Training For Jobs* by Sar Levitan and Frank Gallo. W. E. Upjohn Institute. Copyright, W. E. Upjohn Institute, 1988.

though many state and local programs do not restrict eligibility to poor youth, enrollees are primarily disadvantaged.[1]

Administration and Financing

As of mid-1987, the Job Corps funded 105 centers. Businesses and nonprofit organizations administered 75 centers under contract, while the federal Departments of Agriculture and the Interior operated 30 civilian conservation centers (CCCs), modeled upon the New Deal's Civilian Conservation Corps. CCCs emphasize construction and natural resource projects and are located on public lands, primarily in national parks and forests. Contract centers operate in both urban and rural locales.

Nearly three-quarters of Job Corps centers and training slots are located in the South and West (table 6.1).[2] Because many eligible youth do not live in close proximity to Job Corps centers, only a little over half of enrollees are assigned to centers in their home states.[3] The law limits nonresidential trainees to no more than a tenth of participants, and approximately this proportion of nonresidents are enrolled each year. Currently no center is strictly nonresidential.

Table 6.1
Relatively few Job Corps centers are located in the Northeast and Midwest (1987).

	Number		Distribution		
	Contract centers	Civilian conservation centers	All centers	Training slots	Low income 16-21-year-olds (1980)
South	35	12	45%	49%	37%
West	16	11	26	24	21
Midwest	11	5	15	14	23
Northeast	13	2	14	13	20

Sources: U.S. Department of Labor and Abt Associates, Inc.

The training capacity of the centers varies widely, from 100 to 2600 slots. Centers which can train over 500 corpsmembers at a time constitute a fifth of all centers but serve almost half of total enrollees (figure 6.1). All of the 30 civilian conservation centers and a quarter of the contract centers have a capacity of less than 250 slots, reducing their ability to operate administratively efficient training programs. The six largest private contractors operate 48 centers and train three-fifths of enrollees.

	Distribution		
			Average center
	Centers	**Training slots**	**capacity**
Civilian conservation centers	29%	16%	213
Six largest private operators	46	58	490
Other private operators	26	27	407

The major source of program instability has been widely fluctuating funding support and attempts by Presidents Nixon and Reagan to abolish the corps, resulting in capacity enrollment ranging from 25,000 to 40,000. In inflation-adjusted 1986 dollars, Job Corps funding reached over $1 billion in 1966, but dropped to $300 million in the mid-1970s (figure 6.2). Financing rose initially following President Carter's inauguration but declined again, subsequently increasing when the administration made reducing youth unemployment a major domestic priority. Since 1981, constant

Figure 6.1
Twenty-one centers train nearly half of all corpsmembers.

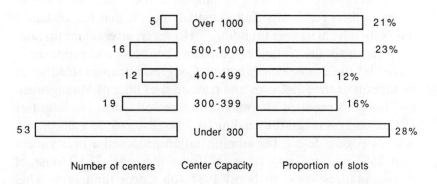

5	Over 1000	21%
16	500-1000	23%
12	400-499	12%
19	300-399	16%
53	Under 300	28%

Number of centers   Center Capacity   Proportion of slots

Source: U.S. Department of Labor, Employment and Training Administration

dollar funding for the Job Corps has ranged from $600 to $680 million. Center enrollment capacity has closely followed the available funding.

Figure 6.2
Job Corps appropriations have fluctuated
since the program began.

Source: U.S. Department of Labor, Employment and Training Administration

On its 20th anniversary in 1984, President Reagan gave the program a glowing endorsement, stating, "Your vital program has provided hundreds of thousands of deprived youths with basic educational and vocational training to prepare them for their future in the workplace. This is in keeping with the American spirit of helping others reach their full potential, a spirit that has sustained our Nation from its very founding."[4] However, several months later the Reagan administration executed an about-face and proposed in early 1985 to eliminate the program. Congress remained steadfast in its support of the Job Corps and rejected the Office of Management and Budget's repeated attempts to reduce Job Corps funding. For 1987, Congress raised the funding by 7 percent to $656 million and, acknowledging defeat, the administration proposed a nearly identical $652 million budget for the following year. The House of Representatives voted to boost 1988 Job Corps funding to $783 million.

The administration's efforts to eliminate or scale back the Job Corps, while unsuccessful, nevertheless diminished the program's cost-effectiveness. The program's utilization rate, a measurement of average center enrollment compared to capacity, declined from over 99 percent in 1983 and the first half of 1984 to about 95 percent in 1984-5, increasing costs by about $600 per corpsmember service year. Job Corps director Peter Rell testified before a congressional committee that the efforts to end the program were "the major reason" behind recruitment difficulties, because young people were wary of enrolling in a program which might imminently close.[5]

Labor Department staff reductions further impaired federal administration. From 1980 to 1987 federal Job Corps personnel diminished by over a third, from 294 to 190. Three business Job Corps operators protested the effects of the personnel cuts on the program's effectiveness, and one, RCA, criticized the "drastic decrease in the level and quality of technical assistance." The business representatives also noted that the Labor Department's annual program reviews, designed to improve center operations, have become more cursory.[6] These criticisms were substantiated in a leaked internal Labor Department memorandum on the Job Corps which concluded, "It seems clear from all indications that we are not doing a fully adequate job of monitoring." The memo also acknowledged that the Department "practically eliminated" training and technical assistance contracts which had supplemented departmental staff assistance to centers.[7]

Job Corps costs are far higher than those of other JTPA programs, primarily because of the expenses associated with operating residential facilities (figure 6.3 and table 6.2). The cost per training year (the cost of serving a corpsmember for a year) declined steadily between the start of the program and the late 1970s, as two administrations deferred needed capital improvements and permitted health care and allowance expenses to fall behind the cost-of-living. Rectification of these problems and the expansion of the program raised corps costs slightly until the early 1980s.[8] From 1982 to 1985 inflation-adjusted costs per training year declined by 2 percent.

Figure 6.3
The Job Corps' high costs are primarily due to residential expenses (1985).

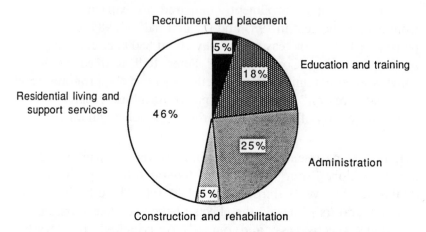

Source: U.S. Department of Labor, Employment and Training Administration

Despite cost reductions over the past two decades, continued high costs — $15,800 per training year in 1985 — have prompted efforts to improve cost efficiency and repeated attempts to close or contract-out the civilian conservation centers, which are more costly. Excluding expenses over which centers have little control (e.g., allowances, construction, recruitment and placement), costs per training year in 1984 ranged from $8300 to $20,000 across centers. The differences were primarily attributable to salaries and economies of scale.[9]

Center capacity	Cost per training year
Under 300	$10,751
300-700	10,185
Over 700	9,394

Even after controlling for size, CCC costs per training year were 40 percent more than at contract centers because of higher vocational training and residential living costs. Higher staff costs account for more than half the differential. The costs of union instructors constitute 65 percent of the difference in training

Table 6.2.
Job Corps Costs (1985)

	Cost	Distribution	Cost per training year
	(millions)		
Total*	**$602.1**	**100.0%**	**$15,731**
National administration	$ 3.5	0.6%	$ 92
Recruitment and placement	32.0	5.3	835
Residential living and support	278.9	46.3	7,286
Salaries	79.2	13.2	2,070
Enrollee allowances	72.8	12.1	1,902
Food	33.1	5.5	866
Energy, utilities, and telephones	28.9	4.8	756
Medical and dental	22.0	3.7	575
Leases and maintenance	16.6	2.8	434
Clothing	13.7	2.3	357
Recreation	5.0	0.8	132
Miscellaneous	7.5	1.2	195
Education	29.1	4.8	760
Salaries	25.4	4.2	663
Miscellaneous	3.7	0.6	96
Vocational training	73.8	12.2	1,928
Salaries	53.2	8.8	1,391
Work experience projects	11.4	1.9	298
Miscellaneous	9.1	1.5	238
Equipment (including educational and vocational)	7.2	1.2	189
Center administration	148.4	24.6	3,877
Salaries	81.0	13.4	2,117
Contractor profit	12.3	2.0	321
Miscellaneous	55.1	9.1	1,439
Construction, rehabilitation, and acquisition	29.3	4.9	765

Source: U.S. Department of Labor, Employment and Training Administration

*Due to different reporting sources, these totals differ slightly from data cited earlier.

expenditures, and higher residential costs are explained by civil service salaries and costlier food expenditures (56 and 32 percent of the difference, respectively).

CCC enrollees experienced better labor market success than contract center corpsmembers in 1984:

	Placement rate	Hourly wage rate
Civilian conservation centers	84%	$4.47
Contract centers	71	3.91

However, a comparison of relative training expenses (excluding equipment) in 1982 indicates that the superior performance of CCCs may not be commensurate with the costs.[10] Moreover, CCC enrollees are probably slightly more advantaged.

Job Corps Enrollees

Recruitment and Screening

Unlike other JTPA components, the Job Corps has sought consistently to limit enrollment to poor youths who face impediments to employment. The Job Corps' high costs, the nature of the target population, and the difficulties inherent in a residential program necessitate a careful selection process. The law requires that applicants must be

- 14 to 21 years old (although in practice only 16-21-year-olds are accepted);

- economically disadvantaged and in need of education, training or counseling to secure meaningful employment, meet Armed Forces requirements, or succeed in school or other training programs;

- living in an environment that would "substantially impair prospects for successful participation in other programs providing needed training, education, or assistance;" and

- "be free of medical and behavioral problems so serious that the individual could not adjust to the standards of conduct, discipline, work, and training which the Job Corps involves."

Several of the standards involve highly subjective judgments, requiring staff to single-out individuals who have employment handicaps severe enough to necessitate exceptional assistance but not so debilitating as to preclude success. The screening process is of crucial importance in minimizing the number of enrollees who drop out of the corps. Early leavers receive little benefit and drive up already high residential costs.

Until the early 1980s, most recruitment and screening was performed by public employment offices, but the Labor Department subsequently instituted a more competitive system. All contracts are awarded through competitive bids and provide a fixed price (typically $160 to $240) for each recruit. Currently state and local government agencies, private profit and nonprofit groups, and Job Corps centers augment the recruitment efforts of public employment offices.

Although the corps often pays recruiters a premium for enlisting women, it continues to experience difficulties attracting women to the program. Parental reluctance to allow their teenage daughters to enroll in a residential program, as well as the fact that prospective female corpsmembers are more likely to be single parents, probably contribute to problems in recruiting women. Congress, in 1982, ordered the department to "immediately take steps to achieve" 50 percent female enrollment, but the proportion of women instead fell from 38 to 32 percent during the succeeding four years.

A persistent criticism of recruiters centers on their lack of effort to determine if applicants could be better served by alternative programs. Congress intended the Job Corps to be a last resort for youth whose living environment impairs their employment and education prospects. In 1979, the U.S. General Accounting Office concluded that the program's screening was so lax that "nearly any disadvantaged youth can qualify." GAO noted that an inadequate eligibility determination procedure had characterized the corps since its inception.[11] More recent investigations indicate that the problems GAO enumerated continue.[12] However, while it is clear that Job Corps screening has not satisfied the letter of the law, the characteristics of corpsmembers indicate that recruiters generally enforce the law's intent.

Characteristics

The Job Corps' clientele has remained remarkably similar over the years. The average corpsmember reads at the 6th grade level. Almost three of four have never held a full-time job. Four of five are high school dropouts, and nearly half of their families receive welfare (table 6.3).

Female enrollees generally have completed more schooling than males. One of four female enrollees has completed the 12th grade, compared to about one of fifteen men. One of six female and one of twenty male enrollees are nonresidents. Nonresidential corpsmembers have completed slightly more years of schooling than residential enrollees, but their entry reading levels are nearly identical. Eighteen percent of nonresident enrollees are Hispanic, compared to 8 percent of residents.

The clientele of civilian conservation centers differs markedly from that of contract centers, and is probably less disadvantaged. Half of CCC enrollees are white, compared to only a quarter of contract center enrollees. Only one in ten CCC participants is female. Although CCC corpsmembers are slightly younger and have consequently completed less schooling, their entry reading levels are on average a grade higher than contract center participants.[13]

Given the subjectivity of the Job Corps' eligibility requirements, it is possible only to estimate the number of potentially eligible individuals. About one million of the approximately four million disadvantaged 16-21-year-olds are high school dropouts. An additional but unknown proportion are deficiently educated graduates. Like other job training programs, the 100,000 annual enrollees represent a fraction of those potentially eligible. However, due to the program's residential nature only a minority of the eligible youth wish to enroll.

Table 6.3
Most corpsmembers are minority high school dropouts with severely deficient reading skills (1985).

Characteristics	Percent
Sex	
Male	68.2%
Female	31.8
Age at entry	
16	19.5
17	20.3
18	20.0
19	17.6
20	12.5
21	8.5
Over 21	1.6
Race	
Black	56.9
White	28.2
Hispanic	8.9
Indian	3.9
Other	2.1
Highest grade completed	
1-7th grade	4.7
8th grade	13.5
9th grade	22.8
10th grade	22.1
11th grade	16.5
12th grade or more	20.4
Entry reading level	
Under grade 3	7.7
Grades 3-4	23.8
Grades 5-6	30.9
Grades 7-8	23.9
Above grade 8	13.7

Source: U.S. Department of Labor, Employment and Training Administration

Upon arriving at a center, the new corpsmember receives a week-long orientation explaining the educational and vocational programs, residential rules, health services and recreational activities. Most of the centers assign a veteran corpsmember to each new enrollee to facilitate his or her transition to center life. The average enrollee remains at a center for seven months, but a third leave within three months (figure 6.4).

Figure 6.4
A major problem of the Job Corps is that half the enrollees remain in the centers for less than six months (1985).

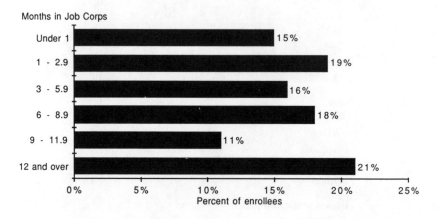

Months in Job Corps

Under 1	15%
1 - 2.9	19%
3 - 5.9	16%
6 - 8.9	18%
9 - 11.9	11%
12 and over	21%

0%   5%   10%   15%   20%   25%
Percent of enrollees

Source: U.S. Departmentof Labor, Employment and Training Administration

Education

Centers organize the educational and vocational programs by dividing the day in half for each track, alternating weeks, or using both methods depending upon the occupational training course.[14] In 22 centers examined, 10 used a split-day schedule, 6 alternated weeks, and 6 used a combination schedule. The split-day schedule is more advantageous to enrollees, who have problems under the alternating week schedule in sustaining their attention for a full day of educational instruction and retaining course material during the off week. Centers which alternate weeks of educational and vocational instruction do so primarily to accommodate commuting vocational instructors.

Basic Education

Over four-fifths of corpsmembers have completed the 9th grade, but only 14 percent read at that level. However, entry-level abilities range from the functionally illiterate to those who can read fairly well. Therefore, instructors first administer standardized tests to determine at what level corpsmembers should begin their reading and math program. In addition to the placement test, the Labor Department recently required centers to administer adult basic education tests to all new enrollees to uniformly gauge educational gains.

To accommodate divergent reading abilities, Job Corps reading instruction is individualized. Enrollees move through a series of short, competency-based lessons, progressing to the next lesson only after passing a test to ensure proficiency. Individuals proceed at their own pace and are assisted by instructors when they need help. Basic course materials are standardized, but the Labor Department encourages centers to test innovative and experimental approaches, and the Job Corps has pioneered in developing instructional materials for youth and adults who failed in or were failed by the schools.

Lack of confidence and motivation typically compound corpsmembers' reading difficulties. Although the program deemphasizes competition between enrollees, staff report that poor readers often feel stigmatized by other corpsmembers. Centers are not equipped to deal with learning disabilities, and individuals with severe disabilities are usually terminated from the program. Many enrollees are more interested in occupational training than education, and participants' interest and progress often lag when they do not see the relevance of schooling to their careers. Consequently, educational and vocational instructors often work together to resolve occupational training problems attributable to poor reading skills.

The Job Corps' reading program is remarkably successful in comparison to traditional schooling techniques, although the centers have been slow to utilize computer-assisted instruction, probably because of financial impediments. Recent achievement tests indicate that corpsmembers on average gain about two months of reading achievement for every month of instruction. Thus enrollees not only perform dramatically better than they had in school, but outpace average student performance. The average corpsmember, enrolled in the program for seven to eight months, probably progresses from a 6th grade reading ability to a 7th or 8th grade level. Although the Labor Department has required centers to maintain records of participants' reading gains, a 1985 study found that reporting was so inadequate that "no reliable data" existed to assess reading improvement.[15] However, since that time the department has revised its instructions, requiring centers to use a uniform standardized test to assess corpsmember educational progress.

Some centers offer courses in English as a second language, primarily for the Hispanic, Vietnamese, Cambodian and Laotian corpsmembers who account for about a tenth of enrollees. These individuals usually remain in ESL programs until their English is adequate for educational and vocational training, which typically takes six months to a year. The Labor Department does not report the average length of stay for ESL enrollees, but it is probable that many do not remain long enough to complete an occupational training course.

Most new enrollees' math skills do not extend much beyond basic addition and subtraction. Instructors estimate that 40-60 percent of new corpsmembers have difficulty with fractions, measurements, percentages and decimals. The math program offers individualized and self-paced instruction designed to make corpsmembers proficient in consumer math. Unlike the program's other education courses, the math curriculum is based primarily on commercially published texts rather than on Job Corps materials, although some supplementary exercises have been developed specifically for the program.

Math instructors generally encounter few problems teaching from the standardized curriculum, although, as in the reading program, teachers commonly use supplementary materials. Math education is linked to some degree with vocational training, particularly in labs where students practice measurement exercises. Teachers also work informally with vocational instructors when corpsmembers face training difficulties attributable to deficient math skills.

High School Equivalency and Beyond

Enrollees who attain 8th or 9th grade reading proficiency enter the high school equivalency degree program. The Job Corps has designed a special curriculum for the program, although many instructors supplement this material and a fifth of the instructors questioned were so dissatisfied with the curriculum that they did not use it at all.

Evaluations of the Job Corps demonstrate that attainment of an equivalency degree has a significant impact on later employment success and educational achievement.[16] However, only about a seventh of the enrollees take the General Education Development (GED) test. Ninety percent of those who take the test pass it.

Several factors partially explain the limited number of corpsmembers who take the test. A fifth of new enrollees in 1985 had completed the 12th grade. Most of these individuals probably already possessed a diploma or equivalency degree, and in fact only 4 percent took the GED while in the corps. A third of enrollees leave the program within three months, and it takes about that much time to complete GED instruction. However, even of those who had not completed the 12th grade and stayed in the Job Corps longer than six months, less than a third take the GED test. Not even half of those staying over a year take the test. One study examined the correlation between entry reading level and GED attainment for corpsmembers who had completed grades 9 through 11 and remained in the program for over six months. The distribution follows:

Entry reading level	Obtained GED
Less than 7th grade	16%
7th to 8th grade	46
9th grade or higher	65

Although the Job Corps' GED program has improved considerably in recent years — the proportion of enrollees obtaining equivalency degrees has doubled since the late 1970s — more emphasis on securing equivalency degrees for corpsmembers is necessary.[17] The limited number of long-term participants who receive certificates suggests that the record can be further improved. In late 1986, the

Job Corps instituted a GED performance standard to promote the high school equivalency program.

Corpsmembers who complete their vocational program and attain a high school diploma or equivalency degree may receive postsecondary education or training through the corps' advanced career training program. Begun in 1979 to encourage lengthier program stays and provide a career ladder for outstanding achievers, the Labor Department canceled the program in 1981 but revived it three years later. Currently, 30 centers contract with a variety of private vocational schools and community colleges to train about 2 percent of corpsmembers at an annual cost of $1.5 million.

Health and Consumer Instruction

In addition to math and reading courses, Job Corps centers provide health and "World of Work" education. The latter program offers training in job search skills and consumer education, typically beginning at the same time as the math and reading classes and lasting 30 to 40 hours over a two- to eight-week period. Because the World of Work program is typically completed within a few months of enrollment, most centers offer a 5-15 hour refresher course for corpsmembers preparing to leave the center.

Although the curriculum is standardized, the health education program offers group rather than individualized instruction designed to help enrollees make informed decisions about their health needs. The program usually begins within a month and a half after corpsmembers arrive at the center, and provides 27 lessons for an average of 32 hours instruction.

Instructors

Job Corps teachers' salaries and benefits are inferior to working conditions in local schools. Entry-level teacher salaries at the centers are 15-20 percent below starting wages at area schools, although corps instructors face a longer workday and a 12-month working year. However, centers report few difficulties in recruiting competent instructors because many teachers are attracted by a program that offers a strict disciplinary system and the challenge of teaching students who failed in or were failed by the established educational system. An oversupply of qualified teachers in recent years has also benefited the program.

As government civil service employees, teachers at civilian conservation centers are better paid than contract center instructors, but civil service procedures delay processing of hiring new teachers by as much as two to six months. The lowest paid CCC instructor makes about as much as the highest paid teachers at contract centers. The latter usually leave after three to five years for a better paying job, while many CCC instructors have over 10 years tenure.

Vocational Training

Job Corps enrollees' work histories are commensurate with their limited educational achievements. Seventy percent have never held a full-time job, and another 12 percent have previously worked full time but not within six months of enrollment. Half of those who had held full-time jobs earned the minimum wage or less.

Shortly after enrolling, each corpsmember participates in a three- to five-day vocational orientation program and learns about the training opportunities at the center. However, fewer than half of the centers provide new enrollees with some hands-on exposure to various trades, and instructors believe that a more intensive orientation is necessary to allow enrollees to make informed vocational choices. Vocational assignment is generally determined by corpsmember preference, and four of five corpsmembers are assigned to their first vocational choice.[18]

The Job Corps offers training in about 120 occupations, although each center typically offers only 8-10. Four of five corpsmembers are trained for one of eleven occupations:

clerk typist or secretary	9.3%
cook or baker	9.1
welder	8.8
nurse's or medical assistant	8.8
auto repair	8.7
carpenter	8.2

general or sales clerk	8.0
custodial or maintenance	6.7
mason	6.5
painter	3.4
electrician	3.0

The remainder of the training opportunities represent a wide variety of occupations. About half of these require relatively few skills, such as keypunch operator, warehouseman and receptionist, while the others are more skilled jobs, such as accountant or appliance repair person.

Occupational enrollment reflects traditional gender patterns. Most women are trained to be clerk typists, nurse's aides, cooks, or clerks. Greater variety is generally available to men, in addition to the listed occupations. The Labor Department's comprehensive review of the program's offerings in 1983 concluded that Job Corps trades correlated well with occupational demand projections. The review panel recommended 12 new offerings, including computer and health-related trades, and several of these occupations were added by 1987. High initial investment costs inhibit new vocational offerings.

Center operators provide most of the training. In addition, the Washington Job Corps office selects national contractors, usually labor unions, to provide some training. Each service provider offers training for distinctly different occupations. For example, almost 80 percent of national contractor training is for construction trades, provided primarily by carpenters', masons' and painters' unions. In 1982 contract center instructors provided training for 75 percent of the 32,000 enrollees who spent over three months in the program, national contractors taught 16 percent, and civilian conservation center instructors trained the remaining 9 percent of enrollees. CCCs rely heavily on national contractors to provide training, while the contract centers commonly use in-house staff. Both kinds of centers also use local subcontractors for a small proportion of training.[19]

Like Job Corps education courses, much of the vocational training program is individualized and self-paced, consisting of a series of competency-based lessons. The adequacy of facilities and equipment varies from center to center, with the larger centers being generally better equipped. Some of the smaller centers have out-dated or insufficient equipment, most commonly for construction, clerical, automotive and welding courses. In 1980, the Job Corps began a major overhaul of its vocational program to establish standardized courses which stress the basic skills necessary to perform in each occupation. Industry and training experts as well as Job Corps personnel designed the courses, which were then tested at selected centers. Implementation of the new system, which will encompass all major occupational offerings, is scheduled to be completed in 1988.

Although hands-on experience is considered an important ele-ment of the Job Corps' vocational program, opportunities for learning while doing are not uniformly available across occupa-tions. Corpsmembers training in the construction, automotive, and industrial production trades tend to receive the most hands-on experience in actual or simulated settings, while health, clerical and sales training is more classroom oriented.

The centers generally have little difficulty recruiting and retaining vocational instructors, but face somewhat greater problems than the education program experiences. Salaries of CCC and national contractor instructors are at least comparable with similar private sector jobs, which results in extremely low turnover. Although the wages offered by contract centers are not as generous, they too experience minimal recruitment and turnover problems because the steady work hours offered by the program attracts instructors.[20]

The Residential Living Program

The most unique feature about the Job Corps is its residential nature.[21] The program's designers believed that providing a struc-tured and supportive living environment was essential to break the "cycle of poverty" trapping many impoverished youngsters, but this theory is by no means universally accepted. Disentangling the elements which account for the Job Corps' success is no easy task. The most recent net impact study of the program included only residential enrollees because, when the study began in 1977, very few enrollees lived outside the centers. Moreover, differences between the two types of enrollees preclude simple comparisons of postprogram outcomes.

A demonstration project underway in mid-1987, called Jobstart, is designed to replicate the Job Corps approach in a nonresidential setting. Seventeen- to 21-year-old dropouts from impoverished homes with limited reading skills were randomly assigned to either Jobstart training or a control group in late 1985 and 1986. Jobstart involves 15 sites, 11 administered by local JTPA Title II agencies and 4 by Job Corps centers. All sites are to provide at least 5.5 months of instruction, significantly less than the Job Corps' average in recent years of seven to eight months, which may complicate assessments of the project.[22]

Operating a residential program poses a severe challenge for both Job Corps staff and participants. Corpsmembers must adjust to living in a new environment away from home while pursuing a disciplined education and training program, an especially difficult challenge for troubled youngsters lacking self-confidence. Many corpsmembers fail again, and either drop out or are dismissed from the program.

Corpsmembers receive living allowances of $40 to $100 monthly based on duration of enrollment as well as performance.

Monthly allowance	Duration	Proportion of enrollees (November 1986)
$ 40	Entry to 2 months	32%
$ 60	2-6 months	32
$ 80	After 6 months	14
$ 90	Merit allowance	7
$100	Merit allowance	14

Success or failure in the program often hinges upon whether new enrollees can adjust to group living. Housing accommodations in various centers range from a barracks to college-type dorm rooms. Anywhere from 2 to 42 enrollees sleep in a single room, although 8 or less is typical. Staff and corpsmembers share housekeeping chores. A staff of resident advisers (RAs) living in the dorms is responsible for acclimating enrollees to center life and minimizing behavioral problems, including drinking and fighting. The RAs play a crucial role in maintaining discipline. Center officials report that a drop in the number of RAs below a critical threshold is associated with unacceptable levels of misbehavior.

Extensive counseling also helps corpsmembers adjust to center life. Homesickness is a universal problem, and enrollees also receive individual and group counseling for a wide variety of personal, educational and vocational difficulties. Most contract centers schedule regular group counseling sessions fairly often, usually every week, which are supplemented with monthly individual counseling. In contrast, at CCCs most counseling is provided informally by RAs. Formal counseling is generally used only when a corpsmember requests it or a teacher or RA makes a referral.

Job Corps staff consider the recreational program a vital tool in channeling the energy of enrollees into acceptable activities. Corpsmembers themselves plan and operate most recreational activities — which include team sports, dances, parties, and center stores or snack bars — to ensure that they are appealing.

All centers have elected corpsmember governments, varying from moribund bodies to those extensively involved in almost all facets of center activities. Not surprisingly, corpsmember governments are most interested in recreational programs and food service. The Labor Department also requires each center to encourage leadership potential. More gifted corpsmembers are enrolled in a leadership training course lasting from 6 to 40 hours, and then assigned work as aides in classrooms, recreational facilities, offices and shops. In return for extra responsibilities and work, the individual receives special privileges such as living in an honor dorm, use of recreational facilities outside normal hours, and passes to leave the center.

Corpsmembers receive comprehensive health care to ensure that medical problems do not inhibit their progress in the program. Each center has a full-time nurse or medical technician, and those centers without a staff doctor establish consulting arrangements with outside physicians. In addition to routine medical services, almost all centers operate alcohol and drug abuse and pregnancy programs. Job Corps staff at various centers estimate that 1-10 percent of female participants arrive pregnant at centers, and a small proportion become pregnant while enrolled. Pregnant corpsmembers generally remain in the program until the seventh month of pregnancy.

Life at the centers is fairly regimented. Attendance is carefully monitored, and enrollees must obtain passes to leave the center for any reason. Staff conduct periodic inspections of both living and storage areas, and about half the centers routinely search all packages coming in or out of the facilities to keep out alcohol and drugs. If a crime is committed, most security officers try to handle the matter internally unless it involves a serious offense. Centers which rely on informal procedures have some difficulty levying consistent sanctions for like offenses.

Almost all centers use trained security personnel. Demands on these employees vary greatly between centers, with some expected to provide counseling while others merely follow formal security procedures. Because salaries are not competitive with local security agencies, the Job Corps experiences difficulty in recruiting and retaining qualified security personnel.

Running the residential program is a demanding job requiring a diversity of skills. The staff is primarily composed of residential advisors and counselors, although the duties associated with each of these positions vary greatly across centers. There is approximately one residential staff member for every eleven enrollees, a ratio which varies little among centers.

RAs at some centers (especially CCCs) do a great deal of counseling, while others primarily perform custodial work. In contrast to most positions at Job Corps centers, RAs and related jobs such as dorm attendants are subject to fairly high turnover. Salaries are generally low, and many RAs are college students or else take the position as a second job. Almost half the centers examined in 1984 experienced an average annual RA turnover rate of 35 percent.

Job Corps counselors are better paid but face diverse duties. Counselors are supposed to advise corpsmembers on their educational and vocational goals as well as personal problems. In addition to their therapeutic duties, counselors also typically manage the performance evaluation panels which monitor corpsmember progress. Professional qualifications are minimal considering the demands placed on counselors. Only 1 of 23 centers examined in 1984 required a master's degree — a bachelor's degree in psychology or sociology was usually acceptable. To assist counselors, the national office requires each center to hire a mental health consultant to be available for a few hours a week to advise or train counselors and to accept referrals of particularly difficult cases.

The Dropout Problem

Ensuring that as many new entrants as possible complete the program is critical to the success of the Job Corps. Over the years, the Job Corps has greatly diminished the proportion of early leavers, but the problem remains serious. The Job Corps is a voluntary program, and enrollees are free to leave when they wish. The average stay in the centers is 7.2 months, but a third of participants leave within 3 months, half of these within the first month. By minimizing early departures and providing more intensive training, the Job Corps has nearly doubled average training duration since the program began (figure 6.5). Program completers now stay, on average, over a year in the Job Corps.

Figure 6.5
The average stay in the Job Corps has increased significantly.

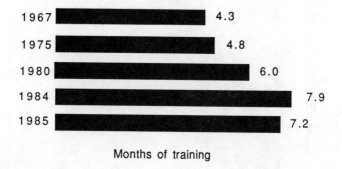

Months of training

Source: U.S. Department of Labor, Employment and Training Administration

Despite the improvements, only a third of enrollees completed the program in 1985 (table 6.4). Women are more likely to leave for

Table 6.4
Most corpsmembers do not complete their training program (1985).*

	Male residents	Male nonresidents	Female residents	Female nonresidents	Total	Average stay (months)
Terminations	37,600	3,300	16,100	3,500	60,500	7.2
Average stay (months)	6.8	10.5	7.3	8.2	7.2	–
Reasons						
Completed program	28.7%	53.7%	34.6%	40.2%	32.3%	13.5
Quit	49.1	37.5	48.3	52.1	48.5	3.9
Resigned	30.1	20.2	28.8	25.2	29.0	4.6
AWOL	19.0	17.3	19.5	26.9	19.5	2.9
Left for disciplinary reasons	16.2	4.5	8.3	1.4	12.6	5.3
Medical	1.9	.8	4.5	1.9	2.5	4.1
Withdrawal of parental consent	2.2	.7	2.6	.3	2.1	2.1
Administrative	1.5	2.1	1.2	2.1	1.5	3.9

Source: U.S. Department of Labor, Employment and Training Administration

*Details do not total 100 percent because reasons for 0.5 percent of terminations are unrecorded.

medical reasons (primarily due to pregnancy) and less likely to depart for disciplinary infractions than men. Nonresidents are much more likely to complete the program than residents, partly because they do not face the pressures and regimentation of center life. In 1985, 35 percent of residents compared with 25 percent of nonresidents remained less than three months in the Job Corps. Residents are more likely to depart for disciplinary reasons because most serious incidents occur after hours when nonresidents have left for the day.

Corpsmembers who leave without notice usually stay in the program for less than three months and constitute the bulk of the early leaver problem. Corpsmembers have indicated the following principal reasons for early departures:[23]

- homesickness;
- an inability to adjust to the Job Corps' structure and rules;
- insufficient pay;
- poor screening by recruiters; and
- enrollees' inability to make decisions about their interests and goals.

Interviews with center staff confirm many of these impressions. Staff view homesickness as the most important reason for dropping out within the first month, and an inability to adjust to center life as the principal explanation for those leaving in the second or third month. Lack of privacy, racial and ethnic animosities, regimentation, and bullying or assaults are the most common adjustment problems.

Younger corpsmembers are more prone to drop out early, and the likelihood decreases with age. During 1984, 34 percent of 16-year-olds compared with 23.5 percent of 21-year-olds left the program within three months. Similarly, only two-fifths of the youngest corpsmembers stay over six months, compared to three-fifths of the 21-year-olds. Job Corps administrators have long known that younger enrollees are prone to drop out, and over the years the average age of the corpsmembers has increased: a little over a decade ago nearly two-thirds of enrollees were under 18, compared with 40 percent currently. To improve the cost efficiency of the Job Corps, a persuasive case can be made for excluding 16-year-olds from the program.

Whites — who are a minority in the centers — are much more likely than ethnic or racial minorities to leave the Job Corps within three months:

Whites	38%
American Indians	32
Hispanics	31
Blacks	25
Asians	8

The likelihood of whites dropping out is increased for those assigned to predominantly black centers. Over a quarter of the whites assigned to centers with over 70 percent black enrollment leave within the first month, compared to 16 percent of the whites assigned to other centers. Interestingly, the white dropout rate does not differ for the two types of centers in the second and third month of enrollment, which may indicate that white dropouts are uncomfortable in a black environment rather than that racial tensions constitute a persistent problem.

Enrollees at civilian conservation centers are more likely to stay in the program over three months than those at contract centers. The size and location of a center, corpsmember gender, and whether enrollees are assigned to their preferred occupational training program apparently have little impact on the dropout problem.[24]

The Labor Department and center operators have reduced the numbers of early leavers through various techniques. Recruiters are expected to carefully screen potential enrollees for serious medical and behavioral problems, and the Labor Department audits recruiters who refer too many unsuitable applicants. The referral of clearly ineligible applicants to centers is apparently not a serious problem. The 2.5 percent of corpsmembers terminated for medical reasons had been in the program for an average of four months, making it unlikely that many of these medical problems predated admittance to the Job Corps. Similarly, since the 1.5 percent of enrollees terminated for administrative reasons (including ineligibility as well as a failure to make sufficient progress) had also typically been in the program for four months, it is doubtful that many were admitted due to poor screening. Moreover, some screening errors are attributable to false information provided by applicants who conceal mental health problems or criminal records from recruiters. Legal restrictions often prevent recruiters from independently verifying this kind of information.

While recruiters apparently enlist few ineligible applicants, they often fail to fully explain the program to applicants, which significantly contributes to the dropout problem, according to both center staff and corpsmembers. A recent evaluation found significant variations between recruitment agencies in the accuracy and completeness of information they possessed concerning individual centers. The recruiters were generally knowledgeable about center training programs, but often lacked information about center living conditions, recreational programs, health facilities, and the surrounding community. Many recruiters had not visited the centers for which they solicited applicants, and were therefore dependent upon the centers' promotional literature, hardly an unbiased source. Some recruiters did not even possess copies of the corpsmember handbooks produced by each center.

Job Corps centers use various approaches to minimize the number of dropouts. Center staff commonly phone prospective enrollees to ensure that they have been informed about center living conditions, know what training opportunities are available, and are genuinely committed to the program. Many centers have a big brother or sister program to help orient new enrollees, and several make dormitory assignments with an eye toward ensuring racial balance and minimizing bullying. Counseling staff try to spot problems which might lead to early departures, and minimize homesickness by permitting calls and visits home.[25]

Postprogram Experiences

Placement assistance

Upon leaving a center, corpsmembers are provided job search assistance and a readjustment allowance. Until 1985, public employment offices provided most of the job search assistance in about four-fifths of the states, but by competitively bidding placement contracts the national office has expanded the role of alternative

organizations. Job Corps centers, a state human resource department, private corporations, Wider Opportunities for Women (a
community-based organization), and the United Auto Workers
now augment the employment service network. All agencies are
now paid a fixed fee for every job placement, replacing the previous
practice of reimbursing for all expenditures whether or not a
placement resulted.

Upon a corpsmember's departure, the Job Corps center notifies
the responsible placement agency that the former enrollee is due to
arrive in the area. Contact is facilitated because corpsmembers can
only pick up their readjustment allowance at the agency office, and
over 90 percent of terminees are located. Corpsmembers who stayed
in the program at least six months receive $75 for each of the first
six months, and $100 for each month over six. Terminees who
remained in the corps more than nine months are paid $100 for each
month they were enrolled.

Since they are judged partially by their alumni placement record,
some centers offer placement assistance, complementing the work
of the placement agencies over which they have little control. The
remote locations of civilian conservation centers generally render
placement efforts impractical, but some contract centers use their
work experience program to generate jobs for graduates. National
contractors are especially successful at using their local contacts to
place corpsmembers.

Longer Training Pays Off

Placement agencies report that program completers are relatively
easy to place, while early leavers require considerable assistance.
The Job Corps performance standards reflect this fact. Two of the
standards assess center success in retaining participants. A third
standard gauges the success of long-term enrollees (over six months'
time) in finding work or continuing their education. The Labor
Department has established a range of acceptable performance
rather than a target figure (table 6.5).

Although the national average performance was within the
acceptable range for the three targets, a third of the centers had
overall unacceptable ratings for the year ending in June 1986.
Despite the Labor Department's tough talk on sanctions, no more

than four contracts were terminated due to poor performance. Thus the standards have been used more as guidelines and have probably had limited influence on center operations.

Table 6.5
One of three centers failed to meet the performance standards.

	90+ day retention rate	180+ day retention rate*	180+ day positive termination rate	Total centers	Unacceptable rating
Performance standards					
1985	65-75%	75-83%	80-90%		
1986	64-75	73-80	80-92		
1985 outcomes	66	76	86	105	35
Range	46-94	62-90	63-97	-	-
Program operator					
Agriculture Department	70	77	89	18	3
Interior Department	65	75	90	12	3
Management & Training Corp.	65	77	88	13	2
Singer	71	77	85	11	2
RCA	64	73	87	10	8
Teledyne	67	75	84	7	3
Res-Care, Inc.	63	75	84	5	3
Minact	63	73	80	4	3

Source: U.S. Department of Labor, Employment and Training Administration
*Proportion of 90+day enrollees who remain over 180 days.

The department issued a fourth performance standard in late 1986 designed to encourage attainment of high school equivalency diplomas. Unlike the other benchmarks, the GED standard is applied individually to each center and is based on a regression model which considers the age and reading level of participants, as well as other enrollee and center characteristics. The target gauges equivalency attainment among enrollees who enter the program with at least a fourth grade reading level and are old enough to take the GED test. A model standard of 30 percent GED attainment was chosen based on 1984 performance, and each center must meet the model-adjusted target plus or minus 9 percentage points, but the adjustments cannot lower the standard below a 10 percent GED attainment rate. Using 1986 enrollee and center characteristics, the model produced performance targets ranging from 10 to 38 percent across centers.

A fifth performance standard assessing educational gains was to be issued during 1987. Centers are now required to administer a standardized test to corpsmembers on three "national test days" every year. The department will use the test results to establish minimal educational improvement goals for each center.

The Job Corps' national office has used performance standards in a more creditable manner than other JTPA programs. Performance standards have been applied to accomplishments over which centers have more direct control, such as length of training and educational progress. The corps' performance standard system is also based on more reliable data than that collected in other JTPA programs because centers record, for example, the entry reading levels of enrollees. The fact that a third of the centers failed the 1985 benchmarks indicates a need for either greater enforcement or a recalibration of the standards. Even the performance of the major contractor with the worst record (RCA) was not much different from that of the average center. Other JTPA performance systems could benefit by adopting some of the Job Corps' practices.

The Job Corps' definition of a successful placement is similar to the Title IIA program's positive termination outcome, but without the deficiencies that mar that standard. Corpsmembers who acquire a part-time or full-time job or an on-the-job training position of at least 20 hours a week; enroll full time in a school, training or apprenticeship program; or join the military or national guard within six months of termination are considered successfully placed. Other JTPA programs generally count placements within a three month postprogram period.

The Job Corps' placement reporting practices have raised troubling questions. Until the early 1980s, the program only reported outcomes for corpsmembers it was able to locate. Currently, the corps assumes that unlocated corpsmembers have the same rate of placement success as the recorded group of individuals who receive no assistance from placement agencies. However, this assumption is questionable because performance standards discourage placement agencies from submitting records for individuals not placed. A more serious problem is the failure of the national office to verify reported placements. The Labor Department's inspector general found that about one of four reported placements were spurious in 1982.[26] No similar audits of reported performance have been performed during the past five years.

For the year ending in June 1986, using the corps' estimation procedure, 74 percent of terminees were successfully placed. If only those individuals who were located are counted, the positive termination rate rises to 81 percent, while discarding the estimation technique but including unlocated individuals lowers the rate to 66 percent. Four-fifths of those placed obtained jobs or joined the military, and the remainder entered school. Male enrollees and program completers fare best in the labor market (table 6.6). Former female corpsmembers are more likely to drop out of the labor force to assume family responsibilities, which reduces their positive termination rate. Reported Job Corps outcomes are very similar to the outcomes for the relatively more advantaged youth in the Title IIA program.

Table 6.6
Program completers achieve the best postprogram results (1985).

	Positive termination rate*	Hourly wage
Total	74%	$4.17
Male	77	4.28
Female	68	3.90
Termination Reason		
Completed program	83	4.55
Disciplinary reasons	72	3.89
Resigned	73	3.90
AWOL	69	3.85
Medical	49	3.66
Administrative	64	3.70
Removal of parental consent	71	3.80
Length of Stay		
0-89 days	67	3.80
90-179 days	71	3.92
180+ days	80	4.34

Source: U.S. Department of Labor, Employment and Training Administration

*Data reflect authors' adjustment of Labor Department statistics to account for unlocated terminees.

Enrollees who train to become carpenters, masons, and painters are generally most successful at finding relatively high paying jobs within six months after leaving the corps (table 6.7). The relatively superior outcomes for trainees in these construction trades is probably attributable to two factors. First, a sizable proportion of construction training is offered by national union contractors who have an established employment network for Job Corps graduates. Second, union construction programs tend to select older and relatively more qualified corpsmembers.[27]

The likelihood of completing training or positively terminating from the program does not vary much by training occupation. Job placement and wage rates exhibit more variation; occupations with large numbers of women fare worst in the labor market. Except for clerk typists and secretaries, trainees who remain for longer periods in the program tend to find better paying jobs. Overall, only a third of employed terminees find work in their field of training.

Longer Term Impact

The Job Corps underwent a careful assessment during the late 1970s and early 1980s. The findings convincingly demonstrate the program's worth in improving enrollees' employment prospects, and the evaluations have protected the Job Corps from serious budget cuts despite White House efforts in the 1980s to discredit the program's established record.

A comprehensive study examined the experiences of a random sample of 1977 corpsmembers over a four-year period and a comparison group of youth with similar characteristics. The similarity of the two groups was confirmed by the fact that the experiences of the early Job Corps leavers paralleled those of the comparison group.

The positive impacts of the program, which persisted throughout the four-year follow-up period, were striking. Former corpsmembers had significantly greater employment and earnings, more education, better health, and less serious criminal records than the comparison group. The corpsmembers were also less likely than the comparison group to receive cash welfare payments, food stamps or unemployment insurance. Former enrollees received on average half the amount of cash benefits obtained by members of the

Table 6.7.
Construction trainees achieve greatest labor market success in the short term (1985).

	Trainees	Duration (months)	Completed training	Positive termination rate	Job placement rate	Hourly wage	Job matches training occupation	Percent males
Total	**50,588**	**7.2**	**35%**	**81%**	**66%**	**$4.17**	**35%**	**68%**
Male dominated occupations								
Cook or baker	4,613	6.1	39	80	65	3.84	51	62
Welder	4,442	7.2	37	83	69	4.23	25	93
Auto repair	4,403	6.2	35	85	71	4.13	28	95
Carpenter	4,156	7.5	36	85	74	4.68	46	93
Custodial or maintenance	3,383	6.5	40	83	69	4.13	39	87
Mason	3,280	7.5	33	83	72	4.53	42	95
Painter	1,727	6.9	36	82	71	4.48	41	87
Electrician	1,527	6.9	41	87	76	4.28	44	92
Female dominated occupations								
Clerk typist or secretary	4,692	7.1	41	79	59	3.97	36	21
Nurse's or medical assistant	4,440	6.2	41	78	61	3.76	42	23
General or sales clerk	4,059	6.6	43	79	62	4.01	36	24

Source: U.S. Department of Labor, Employment and Training Administration

Note: Table excludes unlocated terminees.

comparison group. Despite the program's persistent difficulties in securing high school equivalency degrees for enrollees, former corpsmembers were much more likely to have earned diplomas or equivalency degrees than nonparticipants, and more had enrolled in college.

Counting civilian jobs and military enlistments, former corpsmembers worked an average of one and a half weeks more in the first follow-up year than the comparison group, and three to five weeks more in the second through the fourth years. The civilian employment rate was 6 percent higher for corpsmembers. Annual earnings, in 1977 dollars, were $262 higher than nonenrollees' earnings in the first year and $405 to $652 higher in the next three years, about 15 percent higher than the comparison group. Participants' higher earnings were primarily attributable to increased working time rather than to higher wages. The evidence was mixed as to whether the Job Corps' positive employment impact was fading toward the end of the four-year follow-up.

Imputing dollar values to Job Corps benefits — admittedly an inexact science — analysts concluded that the program yields $1.46 for every $1 invested. From a societal perspective, benefits exceeded costs by over $2300 per corpsmember in 1977 dollars ($4200 in 1986 dollars), and the program's investment in the average enrollee was paid back in just three years. Most of Job Corps' benefits were derived from the increased economic output and decreased criminal behavior of corpsmembers.[28]

Interestingly, the program's benefits were not apparent during the year after corpsmembers left the centers, as the alumni had some difficulty readjusting to the outside world, indicating that short-term results may not be a reliable barometer of long-term employment success. Somewhat surprisingly, the study found that general or sales clerk trainees fared best in the long run. Adjusting for participant characteristics, individuals trained as clerks, welders and electricians had the highest earnings, while former corpsmembers in the other principal vocational programs earned at or below the average for all corps alumni (table 6.8). Former painter trainees, who exhibited nearly the best results in the short term, fared poorly in the long run. On the other hand, the former clerk trainees with the highest long-term earnings performed below average in the immediate postprogram period. The findings, while they do not make intuitive sense and bear further investigation, provide further support for cautiously interpreting performance measures based on short-term results.[29]

The evaluators also examined the impact of the program from the perspective of corpsmembers and the taxpayers who foot the bill. Not surprisingly, program participants reap most of the benefits from the Job Corps. However, taxpayers also gain from reduced social program and criminal justice costs, and from the labor value of the projects corpsmembers contribute while enrolled. Overall, the cost-benefit ratio for taxpayers is only slightly negative, 98 cents for every dollar invested.

Although benefits persisted during the four-year follow-up period, the analysts assumed that the benefits of the Job Corps diminished after time. However, if the benefits continue throughout

Table 6.8.

Corpsmembers trained as clerks achieve the best long-term labor market success compared with a control group.

	Increased earnings (1977 dollars)
Average	$ 655
Men	
General or sales clerk	1251
Welder	1186
Electrician	1150
Carpenter	695
Auto repair	605
Mason	546
Cook or baker	242
Custodial or maintenance	235
Painter	-651
Women	
General or sales clerk	1708
Clerk typist or secretary	495
Nurse's or medical assistant	189

Source: Mathematica Policy Research, Inc.

former enrollees' working lives, the program's cost-benefit ratio would be much more favorable, $2.11 for every dollar invested — over $10,000 per corpsmember in 1986 dollars.[30]

Although the evaluation of the Job Corps reviewed the experiences of enrollees who entered the program a decade ago, there is no reason to believe the corps is less effective today. In fact, the current program is probably more effective because the proportion of early dropouts has declined and average training duration has increased.

A Quarter Century of Progress

Despite some anxious moments, the Job Corps has survived the Reagan administration attacks relatively unscathed. Nonetheless, staff cuts at the federal level and reduced resources for research and development threaten the corps' ability to experiment with new approaches to serve severely disadvantaged youth. Contrary to fashionable deprecations of Washington, the Job Corps' achievements are due both to national leadership as well as the dedicated center staff which the program has consistently attracted. Since its inception, the Job Corps has collected the information necessary to pinpoint problems and taken steps to enhance its educational, vocational, and residential programs. Other JTPA components could benefit greatly by adopting these practices.

Efforts to boost training quality and provide a greater proportion of enrollees with high school equivalency degrees are now underway. Additional funding would permit expanded use of computers in instruction, which showed considerable promise in a late 1970s study. However, given the program's high costs, efforts to improve cost efficiency should also continue. Increasing individual center capacity would undoubtedly reduce unit costs. While reductions are possible, as long as the Job Corps operates residential facilities it will remain an expensive program, albeit cost-effective in the long run.

Notes

1 Human Environment Center, *Conservation and Service Corps Profiles* (Washington: Human Environment Center, November 1986), pp. 1-5; Public/Private Ventures, *The California Conservation Corps* (Philadelphia: Public/Private Ventures, June 1987) and *Youth Corps Profiles* (Philadelphia: Public/Private Ventures, December 1986).

2 Abt Associates, Inc., *An Assessment of Funding Allocation Under the Job Training Partnership Act* (Cambridge, Massachusetts: Abt Associates, Inc., August 31, 1986), p. 103.

3 Office of Job Corps, *Vocational Education Offerings Review: Documentation Report No. 1* (Washington: U.S. Department of Labor, September 1983), p 10.

4 U.S. House of Representatives, *Congressional Record,* March 5, 1985, p. H 1029.

5 Peter Rell, Job Corps director, in U.S. Congress, House Committee on Education and Labor, Subcommittee on Employment Opportunities, *Job Corps Center Closings and Slot Reductions* (Washington: U.S. Government Printing Office, May 15, 1986), Serial No. 99-116, p. 55.

6 Representatives from RCA, Singer and Teledyne, in U.S. Congress, House Committee on Government Operations, Manpower and Housing Subcommittee, *Administration of the Job Corps Program by the Employment and Training Administration of the Department of Labor* (Washington: U.S. Government Printing Office, September 26, 1984), pp. 4-5, 45.

7 Memorandum from Roberts T. Jones, Office of Job Training Programs, August 1, 1984, in U.S. Congress, House Committee on Government Operations, Employment and Housing Subcommittee, *The Job Corps: Do Its Benefits Outweigh the Costs?* (Washington: U.S. Government Printing Office, May 23, 1985), pp. 11-14.

8 Robert Taggart, *A Fisherman's Guide* (Kalamazoo, Michigan: W.E. Upjohn Institute for Employment Research, 1981), p. 49.

9 Macro Systems, Inc., *Job Corps Process Analysis: Final Report* (Silver Spring, Maryland: Macro Systems, Inc., October 1985), p. 11:3, Exhibit 11:2.

10 U.S. General Accounting Office, *Job Corps* (Washington: GAO, July 1986), HRD-86-121BR, pp. 7-9, 11, 14; Office of Job Corps, *Vocational Education Offerings Review: Documentation Report No. 4* (Washington: U.S. Department of Labor, September 1983), p. 7.

11 U.S. General Accounting Office, *Job Corps Should Strengthen Eligibility Requirements and Fully Disclose Performance* (Washington: GAO, July 9, 1979), HRD-79-60, pp. 1, 13.

12 U.S. Department of Labor, *Semiannual Report of the Inspector General, October 1, 1984-March 31, 1985* (Washington: U.S. Department of Labor, 1985), pp. 12-13; Macro Systems, Inc., *Job Corps Process Analysis: Final Report* (Silver Spring, Maryland: Macro Systems, Inc., October 1985), pp. 3:12-23.

13 Office of Job Corps, *Vocational Educational Offerings Review: Documentation Report No. 1* (Washington: U.S. Department of Labor, September 1983), p. 16.

14 Except where other sources are cited, this section is based on Macro Systems, Inc., *Job Corps Process Analysis: Final Report* (Silver Spring, Maryland: Macro Systems, Inc., October 1985), Chapter 4.

15 Phone conversation with John Amos, Office of Job Corps, July 26, 1987; Macro Systems, Inc., *Job Corps Process Analysis: Final Report* (Silver Spring, Maryland: Macro Systems, Inc., October 1985) p. 4:23.

16 Mathematica Policy Research, Inc., *Evaluation of the Economic Impact of the Job Corps Program: Third Follow-Up Report* (Princeton, New Jersey: Mathematica Policy Research, Inc., September 1982), p. 123.

17 Robert Taggart, *A Fisherman's Guide* (Kalamazoo, Michigan: W.E. Upjohn Institute for Employment Research, 1981), p. 125.

18 Macro Systems, Inc., *Job Corps Process Analysis: Final Report (Silver Spring, Maryland: Macro Systems, Inc., October 1985), pp. 5:9-11, 20-5.

19 Office of Job Corps, *Job Corps Vocational Offerings Review: Final Report* (Washington: U.S. Department of Labor, October 1983), pp. 21-4, 26-7; Macro Systems, Inc., *Job Corps Process Analysis: Final Report* (Silver Spring, Maryland: Macro Systems, Inc., October 1985), pp. 5:12-14, 28-30.

20 Macro Systems, Inc., *Job Corps Process Analysis: Final Report* (Silver Spring, Maryland: Macro Systems, Inc., October 1985), pp. 5:5-6, 19-20, 26-8, 31.

21 This section is based on Macro Systems, Inc., *Job Corps Process Analysis: Final Report* (Silver Spring, Maryland: Macro Systems, Inc., October 1985), Chapters 6-8.

22 Patricia Auspos and Marilyn Price, *Launching Jobstart* (New York: Manpower Demonstration Research Corporation, January 1987).

23 U.S. Department of Labor, Employment and Training Administration, *Review of Selected Aspects of the Job Corps Program,* July 1982, pp. 41, 44.

24 Macro System, Inc., *Job Corps Process Analysis: Final Report* (Silver Spring, Maryland: Macro Systems, Inc., October 1985), pp. 9:3, 7-16.

25 Macro Systems, Inc., *Jobs Corps Process Analysis: Final Report* (Silver Spring, Maryland: Macro Systems, Inc., October 1985), pp. 3:26-9, 30-2, 7:6-7, 9:5-7; U.S. Department of Labor, Employment and Training Administration, *Review of Selected Aspects of the Job Corps Program,* July 1982, p. 42.

26 Rodriguez, Roach & Associates, P.C., *Special Review of Screening and Placement* (Washington: U.S. Department of Labor, August 12, 1983), pp. 21, 47-8.

27 Robert Taggart, *A Fisherman's Guide* (Kalamazoo, Michigan: W.E. Upjohn Institute for Employment Research, 1981), p. 268.

28 Mathematica Policy Research, Inc., *Evaluation of the Economic Impact of the Job Corps Program: Third Follow-up Report* (Princeton, New Jersey: Mathematica Policy Research, Inc., September 1982), pp. 111, 118, 121, 130-1, 157, 177-9.

29 Mathematica Policy Research, Inc., *Relative Effectiveness of Job Corps Vocational Training by Occupational Groupings* (Princeton, New Jersey: Mathematica Policy Research, Inc., March 1983), pp. 8-12.

30 Mathematica Policy Research, Inc., *Evaluation of the Economic Impact of the Job Corps Program: Third Follow-up Report* (Princeton, New Jersey: Mathematica Policy Research, Inc., September 1982), pp. 241, 248, 251, 253.

35

Apprenticeship as a Transition to Adulthood in West Germany

Stephen F. Hamilton

One means of gaining an ecological perspective on adolescent development is to examine another country's institutions for youth. While the United States has no institution that effectively bridges school and work, half of West Germany's 16–18-year-olds are apprentices, learning a career in the workplace while attending school only one day a week. Apprenticeship enables youth who do not enroll in higher education to move directly into primary-labor-market careers at a time when their counterparts in the United States are leaving full-time schooling to begin a period of low-skill and low-paid work in the secondary labor market. Although West German apprenticeship cannot be transplanted to the United States, it has implications for our educational system and labor markets. First, it demonstrates that the marginal attachment of youth to employment results from constraints on opportunity rather than from youthful irresponsibility. Second, it suggests that the preparation of youth as skilled workers requires a heavy investment and extensive employer participation. A more appropriate function for secondary vocational education might be to use work-related activities as a means to teach academic subjects. Third, it proves the value of out-of-classroom learning, particularly for those youth who do not perform well in classrooms.

An ecological approach to the study of adolescent development is attractive because it recognizes the complexity of multiple interactive influences that are visible when everyday life is carefully observed. However, such verisimilitude is not necessarily the key criterion for selecting a theoretical framework. Science has traditionally progressed by means of reductionism, treating complex phenomena as if they were simple to derive general laws that are valid regardless of the vagaries of, for example, friction in physics.

Bronfenbrenner (1979) has made a convincing case that reductionism has not served the social sciences well. He urges an approach that

Reprinted with permission of *American Journal of Education*, Vol. 95, No. 2 (February 1987): 314–45. Copyright 1987 by the University of Chicago.

systematically includes variation rather than controlling it out. Un-fortunately, trying to apprehend the world's complexity can quickly exhaust the social scientist's theoretical and methodological resources. One must select a restricted segment of that complexity to study while retaining consciousness of how much has been left out.

The study reported here uses the transition from school to work as a window on the ecology of adolescent development. It also applies a second method of apprehending an ecology—namely, cross-cultural comparison—which highlights one ecology's distinctive aspects by comparing it with another. The original motivation for the study and the theme of this report is that apprenticeship provides an institutional bridge from school to work for West German youth who do not enroll in higher education.

In the absence of any comparable institution, that transition in the United States is marked by a floundering period for adolescents, char-acterized by a succession of low-paying jobs requiring few skills and offering few opportunities for advancement. Frequent movement from one job to another results in high frictional unemployment. Only in their early to middle twenties do substantial numbers of young people without college degrees begin to enter careers.

Our educational system is only loosely tied to the labor market. Secondary-school credentials count for little, and vocational training fails in most cases to prepare high school students for careers. Ap-prenticeship combined with part-time vocational schooling enables West German youth to enter careers as skilled workers by the age of 18. Although their system has flaws and is not exportable as a whole to the United States, it (1) reveals that the labor market behavior that we attribute to youthfulness is more correctly attributed to the structure and operation of our educational system and labor markets and (2) identifies some promising approaches to improving institutional supports for the transition from school to work in the United States.

An Apprentice Auto Mechanic

Karl Oettinger works in a modern, well-equipped garage that is part of a Honda and British Leyland dealership in a large West German city. Eighteen years old, Oettinger is nearing the end of his three-year apprenticeship. He has been promised a job in the company on completion of the examination that will qualify him as a skilled worker or journeyman. To prepare for the examination (scheduled to be administered three months subsequent to our conversation), he is taking an evening course that he pays for himself. He is already working independently rather than under the direction of a journeyman.

I spent a morning observing Karl at work and talking with him. He was one of eight auto mechanics and 12 white-collar apprentices whom I observed at work and in school and interviewed. I shall describe his situation in some detail because it illustrates some of the features of apprenticeship that contrast most sharply with the modal transition from school to work of young people in the United States who do not enroll in postsecondary education.

Karl is talkative, enthusiastic, and energetic, a bright, likable young fellow. During the three and one-half hours that I visited him, he serviced two Hondas, gave me a guided tour of the dealership, and engaged in long discussions of his work, his plans, his family, and his fondness for the United States.

Karl's first task was routine maintenance on a new Honda, including an oil change, tune-up, and checks of tire pressure, fluid levels, and headlight focus. He explained in detail why he was doing what he did, offering a brief disquisition, for example, on the proper level of acidity in a battery's electrolyte. His second assignment was also regular maintenance, but this time on a five-year-old Honda that required a valve adjustment and a retightening of the head, the latter, he explained, to correct distortions caused by differential temperatures in light metals.

Throughout the morning Karl repeatedly expressed pride in his employer and in himself, noting, for example, as he signed the tags recording date and mileage for adding oil and testing antifreeze, that some other mechanics were reluctant to take responsibility for their work.

Karl's pride and self-assurance were also evident in his plans for the future. He volunteered that after four or five years he would go back to school to become a master, a difficult challenge but better in the long run than remaining a journeyman for 40 years. After that, he said, he might study further to become an engineer. Later he told me he would most like to work on designing engines but that the chances of getting such a job were as remote as winning the lottery.

When I asked about these plans during the formal interview two weeks later, Karl explained that something new had come up in the meantime. He had been doing some part-time sales work evenings and weekends, and now his boss had offered him a job as a salesman, which would mean a higher salary and a company car for his private use. He had not yet decided but was "99 percent certain" that he would take it. This position would give him advancement opportunities in sales and management, but he said that he would complete his apprenticeship and take his examination anyway because he might still want to become a master and engineer and because if something unforeseen happened he would always have his qualification as a mechanic.

This sudden shift of an apprentice mechanic into sales is not at all typical. Most salespersons must complete a very different kind of apprenticeship accompanied by schooling appropriate to commercial occupations. Karl Oettinger's atypical case illustrates very dramatically, however, three points about West German apprenticeship. The first is that it provides direct entry into careers at an age when young people in the United States are either still in school or just beginning to seek full-time employment—most of them in the secondary labor market, which is defined by the absence of career possibilities. The second point is that apprenticeship rather than full-time schooling is the foundation for youths' transition into adult working life. Third, although apprenticeship can legitimately be criticized as being overly narrow, it is the entry point into a range of career opportunities, not a narrow channel. I shall develop these points in the following pages, but first I need to add more information about Karl Oettinger in order to present a balanced portrait of him and to heighten the contrast between West Germany's and our own provisions for young people like him.

One might infer from the foregoing description that Karl is a compliant young man who has "bought into the system," an adolescent organization man or, worse, another example of German deference to authority. In fact, Karl expressed a critical view both of his training and of the auto mechanic's occupation. His chief complaint about his training was that he had learned primarily routine maintenance on Hondas. Furthermore, he went on, "My occupation is in a crisis." Auto mechanics are trained to locate, disassemble, and repair defective components, but the cost of labor has become so high that it is usually less expensive simply to throw out the old part and install a new one. "We are becoming nothing more than parts changers," he complained.

He was even more critical about his vocational schooling. The curriculum, he said, is not coordinated. Brake systems are studied from a theoretical perspective in one class while specific instructions for repairing them are given in another class at another time. He did not enjoy his classes in German and social studies either but allowed that those subjects were important and useful.

Karl's behavior in school was even stronger evidence that his attitude was not simply acquiescence to established authority. He was anything but a model student. While I visited his class, he got out of his seat several times, carried on a constant conversation and an occasional wrestling match with his deskmate, argued with his teacher, and copied two in-class exercises from someone else's paper. He was not malicious or incorrigible, just a goof-off. Yet, in the workplace he was a model of industry and responsibility.

There is a difference between being a good worker and being a good student that Karl's case illustrates dramatically. By making extensive and systematic use of the workplace as a learning environment, the West German educational system recognizes and capitalizes on that difference, providing opportunities for youth who would fail or just get by in the United States's school-bound system.

The West German Educational System

Apprenticeship is one part of a secondary educational system that is also distinguished from secondary education in the United States by its differentiation into three levels of schools. The differentiation comes early, and it is strong. All children attend the *Grundschule* or elementary school in their neighborhood.[1] They begin in the first grade at age 6.[2] At the end of grade 4 or 6 (there is variation among states), those judged capable of entering universities are separated from the others and enrolled in *Gymnasien*, college-preparatory secondary schools.

This judgment is based on school grades, teacher recommendations, and, in special cases, an examination. Parents may be able to insist that their children be enrolled in a *Gymnasium* but not that they remain there if they are found incapable of doing the work during an orientation period. That work is substantial. The curriculum is heavily academic, and the work load is demanding. In metropolitan areas *Gymnasien* specialize in, for example, math and science, music, modern languages, or classics. The *Gymnasium* continues through grade 13 and concludes with an examination. Passing that examination confers the *Abitur*, which qualifies its holders to enter a university.[3]

Those elementary school pupils who do not enter a *Gymnasium* either remain in the *Hauptschule* or main school or, if they are more academically able, enroll in a *Realschule,* which confers the *mittlere Reife* on completion of grade 10. Two paths are open to young people after either type of secondary schooling: full-time vocational school or apprenticeship combined with part-time vocational school. (See fig. 1 for a schematic representation of these various educational paths.)

The full-time vocational schools differ in their entrance requirements, duration, and options for graduates. Variations among states and occupations add to the complexity. Some are open to both *Hauptschüler* and *Realschüler. Realschüler* are qualified to enter others immediately, while *Hauptschüler* must first complete additional full-time schooling. Some graduates of full-time vocational schools move directly into employment, while others enter higher education. Apprenticeship is also an option following completion of full-time vocational schooling.

It is possible to become an apprentice without receiving passing grades and receiving a completion certificate. Efforts to impose such academic prerequisites have been opposed on the ground that school failures also need a place in the educational system. Nevertheless, employers favor applicants for apprenticeships who have obtained completion certificates, and they prefer *Realschüler* over *Hauptschüler.* As a result, apprenticeship in some occupations is virtually limited to holders of the *mittlere Reife* or higher credentials. *Hauptschüler* are limited predominantly to manual occupations, while *Realschüler* are qualified to enter technical and lower-level managerial occupations. *Hauptschüler* may be trained as carpenters, auto mechanics, office assistants, and sales clerks, but *Realschüler* can choose from those options plus occupations such as laboratory technician, precision mechanic, secretary, and personnel manager.

Educational reform efforts over the past two decades have focused on democratizing what has been criticized as an elitist system. One approach has been to reduce the barriers between the different levels of schools, primarily by introducing more uniformity into the curricula

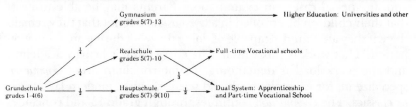

Fig. 1.—West German schools. Grades in parentheses indicate variations among states. Fractions are approximate proportions enrolled, ignoring comprehensive schools and special schools. Arrows indicate only major paths.

of grades 5 and 6. As a result, some upward movement does occur, but downward movement is far more prevalent. The most dramatic reduction in barriers has been the expansion of "the second educational path" (*der zweite Bildungsweg*), which enables a small group of dedicated and energetic people who did not attend *Gymnasium* to earn entrance to a university through a combination of night school and advanced trade training. *Fachhochschulen,* institutions offering higher vocational education at a level comparable to many college-level programs in the United States, have provided another path for those without the *Abitur*. Whereas the *Gymnasium* was once virtually the only route to higher education, by 1981, 28 percent of those entering higher education came from other kinds of schools, including evening *Gymnasien* and comprehensive high schools (Bundesminister für Bildung und Wissenschaft 1983, p. 145).

The most controversial approach to democratization and the centerpiece of reform efforts through the 1970s was the introduction of comprehensive high schools (*Gesamtschulen*). With the exception of a few states with strong leftist political traditions (e.g., West Berlin, Bremen, Hessen), this movement lost momentum by the end of the decade (Mitter 1980), with only 16 percent of secondary school pupils enrolled in comprehensive schools, half of which are actually the three traditional types of schools under one roof (Körner 1981).

However, the strongest democratizing trend has not been in school structure but in enrollment patterns. While the *Hauptschule* was formerly the predominant form of schooling, enrolling more than 70 percent of eligible youth in 1960, it now enrolls less than half, with the remaining half divided fairly evenly between *Realschulen* and *Gymnasien*, once relatively elite institutions (Bundesminister für Bildung und Wissenschaft 1983, p. 36). Males are no longer in the majority in these secondary schools.

The Dual System

Das duale System is the combination of apprenticeship with part-time vocational schooling that provides a transition from full-time school into careers for those youth not enrolling in full-time further education. About half of 16–18-year-olds are apprentices (Bundesminister für Bildung und Wissenschaft 1983, p. 80).

Apprenticeship

Apprentices and their parents sign contracts with employers, the terms of which have been determined by collective bargaining and are standard within each occupation. Apprentices receive modest stipends, normally in the range of \$150–250 per month (Münch and Jung 1980, pp. 49–52), approximately half a beginning skilled worker's wages, and they are entitled to a minimum of 18 days of paid vacation. Apprentices who complete their training and pass the qualifying examination are certified to be skilled workers and, as such, are entitled by law to earn the wages set by collective bargaining for their occupation. A survey of youth completing full-time schooling in 1977 found that 58 percent of those who had completed apprenticeships were employed by their training firm one year later. Only 4 percent were unemployed (Stegmann 1983, pp. 32, 34; see also Williams 1981).

The following statement, the opening paragraphs of the 1984 annual *Report on Vocational Education* issued by the Federal Minister for Education and Science (Bundesminister für Bildung und Wissenschaft 1984), contains so much that is both characteristic of West German apprenticeship and distinct from that of the United States that it repays detailed explication: "1983 was a record year for vocational training in the dual system. Never before in the Federal Republic of Germany have so many youth found an apprenticeship as in 1983. This is the result of a joint effort of all participants in the vocational training system—the companies, employers' organizations, labor offices, chambers, unions, and public administration. Such a unified joint effort is also necessary in 1984 in order to assure future training and vocational opportunities for youth, to strengthen the competitiveness of the economy, and to fulfill the social obligations of the society" (translated by the author).

The report opens with self-congratulation for the number of apprentice placements and exhortations to continue increasing that number. Chancellor Helmut Kohl made a campaign promise that all applicants would be able to find an apprenticeship, making the shortage of places a hot political issue even though it can be attributed to the conjunction of large numbers of youth attaining school-leaving age—the cohort born in the baby boom of the 1960s—and a sluggish economy owing to worldwide recession. Other causes include tighter laws governing apprenticeship programs and advancing automation (Winterhager 1980).

The third sentence accurately enumerates the diverse actors in the dual system. The *companies* are ultimately responsible for apprenticeship. They provide the bulk of the places and bear the costs of apprentice training, including apprentices' stipends. *Employers' organizations* and *unions*, though naturally adversarial, have well-established functions and relations in the politics of vocational education. In addition to their voluntary membership in employers' organizations, all German companies are required to join and finance *chambers*. There is a chamber with sections for small businesses engaged in specific trades, such as house painters, bricklayers, bakers, and barbers. There is a chamber of industry and commerce for all sorts of large businesses. Among their functions, chambers set and enforce standards for apprentice training, in part by writing and administering the qualifying examinations apprentices must take to enter their occupations as skilled workers. *Labor offices* are operated by the federal government. They are the sole agencies authorized to offer occupational guidance and placement counseling; schoolteachers are legally denied that role. *Public administration* provides apprenticeship places in such enterprises as the post office, the government-owned railroad, and the military.

The fourth sentence, while urging continued unified (*solidarische*) joint effort, lists the functions of apprenticeship. Providing training and vocational opportunities for youth is familiar enough, but strengthening national competitiveness and fulfilling social obligations are broader purposes. West Germany depends very heavily on manufactured exports for its prosperity, and apprenticeship training is considered essential to the high-quality products that maintain competitiveness. The notion that employers have social obligations to fulfill by training apprentices may seem quixotic, but apprenticeship is viewed as an entitlement of young people as much as schooling, and employers are seen as obligated to provide that part of vocational training.

By far the largest numbers of apprentices are in industry and commerce and handwork or crafts. Industry and commerce comprise manual and technical and clerical/managerial occupations in larger firms. In 1983 47.3 percent of all apprentice contracts were in the domain of industry and commerce. Handwork absorbed 36.5 percent of all new apprentices in the same year. Almost all of the remaining apprentices were to be found in agriculture (3.6%), civil service (3.8%), and as professionals' helpers (8.1%) (Bundesminister für Bildung und Wissenschaft 1984, p. 25).

The path from training to career can be quite simple and direct, as it is when a young person is trained by a company in a specific occupation and then hired by that company to perform in that same occupation. However, there are other paths as well. In addition to the more than 400 training occupations, successful apprentices may move into more than 20,000 other skilled occupations, some requiring further training (Deutscher Industrie- und Handelstag 1982, p. 7).

Not all companies train apprentices. The Deutscher Industrie- und Handelstag (1982, p. 8) estimated that 10 percent of the firms engaged in industry and commerce and 40 percent in the crafts or handwork sector are training firms. The difference between the two sectors is revealing of the differential costs of apprenticeship to companies. The net costs of apprenticeship training to employers is a topic of debate between employers and unions, the employers insisting that they invest substantial sums and unions arguing that some employers exploit apprentices as a source of cheap labor. Although now outdated, average net costs estimated in the early 1970s probably accurately reflect current proportional outlays: DM 6,692 per apprentice per year for industrial and commercial firms with more than 1,000 employees, DM 5,050 for such firms with less than 1,000 employees, and DM 2,582 for handwork firms. Other occupational sectors all had lower net costs (Münch 1979, p. 91). It is safe to say that large industrial and commercial firms make substantial investments in training apprentices while smaller firms invest less and handwork firms invest less than half as much, which accounts in large part for the difference in proportions of the firms offering training: because it costs less for handwork firms to train, more of them do.

Why would private companies make any investment at all in training young people who have no obligation to use their training in the same company? One part of the answer is contained in the reference above to the social obligations of the society. Apprenticeship is so deeply embedded in the West German society and economy that the private sector is seen as obligated to provide training. Perhaps the most vivid demonstration of that presumed obligation was the passage in 1976 of a law empowering the federal government to levy a new payroll tax if sufficient apprenticeship places were not provided, the money raised thereby to be spent on alternative, primarily school-based, vocational training programs for those young people unable to find apprenticeships (Taylor 1981). Although the tax has never been levied, the number of apprenticeship places was increased, suggesting that the threat was effective.

Despite its foundation in tradition, an abstract obligation does not explain why some companies choose to train apprentices while the majority do not. Self-interest is also involved. One way in which training apprentices serves a company's self-interest is that the public is aware of the machinery for controlling the quality of apprenticeship training. A company that trains apprentices is, as a result, implicitly certified as doing high-quality work. Manufacturing firms describe their apprenticeship programs in their glossy annual reports. Plumbing firms and cabinetmakers' shops display signs in their windows announcing that they train apprentices.

But the most direct form of self-interest lies in what apprentices can do for an employer. This, in turn, varies according to the sector and the size of the firm. Large industrial and commercial firms invest in training because they expect to employ the people they train and to recoup in productivity what they have invested. These firms typically train approximately the number of young people they expect they will need to fill their upcoming vacancies. They are highly selective about who becomes an apprentice. Apprentices who fail to meet expectations are simply not hired when their training is done.

Apprenticeship in large industrial and commercial firms is qualitatively different from that in other types of firms, and not solely because of the company's larger investment. That investment buys full-time, highly qualified trainers and training facilities set apart from production. For example, the instructional shop of a large factory-owned automobile repair shop that I visited occupies an entire building. It is equipped with more than 30 workstations for approximately 20 apprentices and a large supply of tools and machines including drill presses, lathes, and welders. A separate room almost as large as the shop is used for classroom instruction and doubles as a recreation area. Apprentices spend their first seven or eight months learning basic metalworking techniques in the instructional shop before they begin to work in the repair shop. They return at regularly scheduled intervals throughout their apprenticeship to learn advanced techniques.

Large firms also offer many more options for placements than do small ones. Apprentices can move from one department to another in order to obtain the widest possible exposure to the firm. Apprentices are there primarily to learn; if they can learn best by contributing to productive work, all the better, but the work done need not substantially offset the costs of training until after training has been completed.

Smaller firms are less desirable and therefore less selective in choosing apprentices. They have fewer openings and are less able to predict what openings will be available in two or three years when apprentices complete their training. They cannot employ enough apprentices to make a full-time trainer economically viable or to maintain facilities reserved for training. The number of departments and the associated range of experiences open to apprentices are more limited. The work apprentices do is relatively more important. They may be pressed into service to fill vacancies caused by illness, vacations, or retirements and be kept at the same tasks longer than their learning needs would dictate.

The advantage of large firms should not be interpreted as being a universal law. Smaller firms are increasingly cooperating, with government financial assistance, to create multifirm instructional shops. An apprentice in a small commercial firm may learn more functions in greater depth because the firm as a whole is comprehensible and because she or he is able to work in all facets of its operations. One white-collar apprentice I interviewed in a large firm made this point by saying that he could learn much more by working with the buyer in his father's firm, who buys everything needed by the firm, than by working in the section of the purchasing department of his training firm that buys nothing but synthetic parts. Trainers in the large firms I visited made the same point—that while large firms could in general offer a better apprenticeship, some small firms give excellent training.

Limitations on the quality of apprenticeship owing to size of firm are particularly noticeable in the handwork sector, which continually trains more apprentices than can be hired as skilled workers. Ironically, it is this shrinking sector that has absorbed the largest portion of the increased number of apprentices. Industry and commerce's share of apprentices fell from 52.1 percent in 1973 to 45.6 percent in 1982, while handwork's share rose from 35 to 39.7 percent. Industry and commerce absorbed 70,000 more apprentices, but handcraft added 200,000 (Bundesminister für Bildung und Wissenschaft 1983, p. 84). The reason for this distortion may be traced to the lower costs of training and the emergency represented by the shortage of places. Small firms have found it easier to add apprentices than have large firms. The consequences of this would be more severe if large employers did not welcome applicants trained in handwork: they are seen as skilled, careful, reliable, and trainable. They move in large numbers, therefore, into semiskilled and skilled positions in industry and into the service sector (Bundesminister für Bildung und Wissenschaft 1984, pp. 55–66), where jobs are not only more plentiful but also generally higher paying.

Despite this and other problems, some of which are described below, West German apprenticeship usually impresses U.S. observers with its quality (Reubens 1980; Limprecht and Hayes 1982). Its continued vitality is indicated by the increasing tendency of *Gymnasium* graduates to become apprentices. In 1970 only 1.3 percent of those qualified to enter universities became apprentices in officially recognized programs. By 1978 5.5 percent did so, and the proportion has remained in that range because of limited openings in the universities and poor job prospects for university graduates (Stegmann and Kraft 1983; Bundesminister für Bildung und Wissenschaft 1984, pp. 67–70). Studies of the occupational achievements of men trained as skilled manual workers—a category including fully 70 percent of male employees who have served apprenticeships—indicate that apprenticeship leads to secure gainful employment in a range of occupations including but not limited to the training occupation (Hofbauer 1981; Lempert 1983).

Part-Time Vocational Schools

Part-time vocational schools (*Berufsschulen*) accompany apprenticeship as the second half of the dual system. Enrollment in them fulfills the compulsory schooling requirement, which extends to age 18. The traditional schedule places apprentices in school for one or one and one-half days each week. In recent years, block instruction—that is, full-time schooling for five or six weeks at a time two times a year—has become more popular. The vocational teachers and most of the apprentices I interviewed favored block instruction; but employers have resisted it, especially small employers, because it means dismissing all of their helpers for the same extended period of time.

Vocational schools teach both occupational courses and general courses such as social studies and German. Mathematics is taught in courses specifically related to an occupation, such as those providing instruction in accounting for commercial apprentices and in the calculations used in machine shops for apprentice metalworkers. Vocational schools for manual workers give practical instruction in workshops. Like *Gymnasien*, vocational schools can be highly specialized in large cities but must be more general in less-populated areas. Youth in rural areas must either accept apprenticeship in an occupation for which both an apprenticeship place and a school are conveniently located or move to a metropolitan area for training.

My observations in two vocational schools—one for lower-level managerial employees in industrial firms (*Industriekaufleute*) and the other for auto mechanics—led me to see the qualifying examination as the focal point for most of what happens in such schools. (See also Sardei-Biermann 1984; Dittmann-Kohli, Schreiber, and Möller 1982.) This examination covers all of the major subjects taught in the schools. It is written, administered, and graded by the appropriate chamber. The regulations governing the examinations specify that the chambers' examination committees include a majority of employer representatives, along with vocational school teachers and employees' (i.e., union) representatives. This arrangement strongly links the vocational schools' curricula with employers' views of what employees should know.

The written portion of the examination is in multiple-choice format. It is dominated by factual material and by fixed procedures, which must be learned by rote. Commercial apprentices also have an oral examination in which they can demonstrate their social graces, their thinking skills, and some of the specific knowledge they have gained on the job. Auto mechanics, like other manual apprentices, have a practical as well as a written test. They are given tools, materials, and a blueprint and must construct a metal device within a set time and have it evaluated for precision and craftsmanship.

One teacher blamed the examination for the absence of pedagogical variety in her classroom. Because the amount of class time had recently been reduced without changing the examination and course content, she explained, there was no time for small-group work or discussion. In this and in other classes I observed, teacher lecturing predominated, often supplemented either by mimeographed handouts summarizing the points to be memorized for the examination or by notes written on the blackboard, which pupils were instructed to copy. Pupil participation was limited to supplying answers to problems or to playing "guess what is in the teacher's head" in response to more open-ended questions.

But this pattern of teacher-centered instruction cannot be attributed solely to the examination. It is the prevailing pattern in West German elementary schools (Hopf, Krappmann, and Scheerer 1980, p. 1130). And it is prevalent in U.S. schools despite various reform efforts (Cuban 1982; Goodlad 1984). In technical subjects, given the examination's importance to both pupils and teachers, the teachers' role as information giver makes some sense. State education ministries give teachers a very detailed curriculum to follow, and the examination questions are drawn from that material. However, the justification for teacher lectures is much weaker in the general courses such as social studies and German.

I observed a social studies teacher who discussed current events such as disarmament negotiations and the reasons for the U.S. dollar's rising value against the West German mark in an informative and critical manner, providing insights from his personal experience and urging his pupils to look for the connections among things because without seeing the connections one cannot understand events. But he did this in a teacher-centered manner: he urged his pupils to think but did not give them a chance to practice doing so; he gave them information but retained control of that information and interspersed it liberally with his own opinions.

The same class's shop (*Fachpraxis*) teacher gave an impressive demonstration of how engaging vocational instruction can be. He had only 10 pupils, because the class was divided in two for shop instruction.

The lesson was on master brake cylinders. Using a diagram drawn on the blackboard, the teacher explained a cylinder's principal parts and their functions. Pupils participated steadily with both answers and questions. The teacher's questions called for both short and extended answers—for example, the name of a part and an explanation of what it does. After half an hour, the teacher moved the class to a table in the back of the room. With the pupils surrounding the table, he quickly disassembled a real master cylinder with a slice cut out to reveal its internal workings. As he removed the parts, he named each one and placed it on the table. He called attention to a small part, saying that they should know it for the examination.

Next the teacher presented a dual master cylinder, also sliced open for demonstration, explaining that it was from a truck. The pupils joined in identifying the parts and describing their functions. One asked about the function of a screw-on cap with a spring. The teacher turned the question back to the pupils, who made several guesses until he showed them that it was a second valve. The first cylinder had only one. Finally, he brought out a smaller master cylinder, saying that it was a recent model whereas both of the others were old. As one pupil began casually reassembling the first cylinder, the teacher encouraged him to complete the job and all watched him do so.

This class had more pupil participation than any other I observed. It made excellent use of the fact that the pupils had been instructed about brake systems and had worked on them before. The teacher was clearly the authority, but he expected his pupils to have some knowledge too and gave them a chance to show it.

Both my own interviews with apprentices and several West German studies (especially Sardei-Biermann 1984) indicate that apprentices view the vocational school much as academically less able U.S. students view high school—that is, as an unavoidable nuisance. My respondents described some instruction as valuable for employment and citizenship, but mostly they described themselves as taking in what the teacher said and remembering it long enough to pass an exam. Many joined Karl Oettinger in criticizing the lack of coordination between school instruction and apprenticeship tasks.

From School to Work/From School to Career

Under normal labor market conditions, West German youth move directly from school, via apprenticeship and part-time vocational school, into careers. (Fifteen months of military or alternative service intervene for males.) Career entry at age 18 or 19 is the norm for those youth who do not enroll in higher education. Most high school graduates and dropouts in the United States, in contrast, go to work in the secondary labor market, where they take low-paid, low-skill jobs, often in small firms, with little job security, few opportunities for developing skills, and no career ladder.

The expansion of the service sector in the U.S. economy has created a growing number of secondary-labor-market jobs. Given low entry requirements and low pay, the penalties for quitting or being dismissed are low. In fact, the best chance for increasing one's earnings is finding a new job. Therefore, mobility is high, leading to high rates of frictional unemployment. This growing secondary labor market is filled with young people, women, minorities, and dropouts working as custodians, store clerks, gas station attendants, and in fast-food restaurants.

The secondary labor market provides work, but not careers, for youth. Primary-labor-market employers discriminate against youth, not on the grounds of credentials but on the grounds of their age and presumed instability. The same young people who are viewed as being poor risks at age 18 are hired at age 22 as factory workers, salesmen, manager trainees, and in other career entry positions with no additional schooling and no new specific job skills (Barton 1976; Osterman 1980).

There is a self-fulfilling prophecy in operation here. Employers view youth as unreliable and therefore employ them only in jobs in which tenuous attachment to a particular employer and to the labor market is structurally encouraged. A 20-year-old has no reason not to quit his job and take three months off if the job he can get when he returns is no worse than the one he has now. He should certainly be advised to change employers if he has a chance to earn 20¢ an hour more, since his employer will lay him off or cut his hours at the first sign of a drop in sales.

Eighteen-year-old new car salesmen, auto mechanics, personnel officers, TV repairmen, travel agents, and policemen in West Germany are inherently no more responsible than their age-mates in the United States, and they have less formal schooling. But they have a clear, direct, and functional path into careers that is absent in the United States. The supposedly irresponsible labor market behavior of U.S. youth does not result from their youthfulness but from the structure of our educational system and labor markets.

The second point of contrast between the United States and West Germany resides in our strong reliance on schools as the principal institution, other than the family, supporting the transition to adulthood. During the 1970s, the most frequently repeated criticism of U.S. secondary schools was that their isolation from the larger community had detrimental consequences for adolescents' development. The classic statement of this critique was made by the Panel on Youth of the President's Science Advisory Committee (1974), but numerous other blue ribbon panels of scholars, educators, and social critics issued similar statements. A healthy variety of promising programs consistent with these recommendations sprang up around the country, but they remained interesting innovations, never threatening the traditional structure of secondary education or changing the modal patterns of transition to adulthood. (See, e.g., National Commission on Resources for Youth 1974; Conrad and Hedin 1982; Hamilton 1980.)

By the middle of the 1980s, the political climate has changed so dramatically that the issue of youth's isolation is ignored and their problem at the transition to adulthood has been redefined as being one of inadequate schooling. Recent reports on secondary education have paid little attention to disadvantaged youth, the youth labor market, problems of socialization and development, or the reports of the previous decade. The presenting problem is that young people are performing poorly on tests of academic skills. Declining test scores are tied, without benefit of empirical testing or explicit theory, to declining productivity and competitiveness in the U.S. economy. The solution, we are told, is to give youth more demanding courses and keep them in school for more time.[4]

The West German dual system is important as a counterexample, challenging the unstated assumption that schools are the only or even the best settings for learning. A German word, *Schulmüdigkeit,* meaning school weariness, identifies a problem that their system recognizes, while ours blames the victim. Classroom instruction has failed to engage the interest and improve the performance of a substantial proportion of youth and will continue to fail if it is only intensified. Out-of-school learning is a viable alternative, as has been demonstrated by evaluations of alternative schools, experiential learning programs, drop-out prevention programs, and vocational education (Hamilton 1986; McDill, Natriello, and Pallas 1986).

Vocational education clearly demonstrates U.S. reliance on schools. Although it sometimes includes cooperative education and on-the-job training, it is predominantly school based. Furthermore, it is largely ineffective as preparation for employment. There are exceptions to this pessimistic generalization. Some exemplary schools and programs move young people into related skilled and semiskilled occupations. The most uniform positive results by this criterion are in clerical training. Employers do hire young women with clerical skills immediately out of high school, and those skills transfer quite well. But the larger picture is not so bright.

Compared to graduates of the general track, vocational graduates have little if any advantage in the labor market, in terms of either status, amount of employment, or earnings (Berryman 1982; Grasso and Shea 1979; Reubens 1974; Meyer and Wise 1982; O'Toole 1979; National Institute of Education 1981; Wilms 1984). In a sympathetic review of research on the employment-related effects of secondary vocational education, Mertens (1983) demonstrated the value of distinguishing (1) among students with more and less intensive vocational schooling, (2) among different vocational fields, and (3) between long-term and short-term effects. However, her conclusion—that vocational education is good for some young people some of the time—is faint praise. Surely the inclusion of marginal programs and students with no commitment to their training occupation masks the impact of effective programs, but the weight of the research evidence fails to support the claim that vocational education effectively educates young people for vocations.[5]

The contrast with West Germany is stark. Not only is vocational training the norm for upper-secondary-school youth, but that training qualifies participants as skilled workers. Few vocational education programs in U.S. secondary schools even aspire to that level of skill training. From the perspective of the level of training offered, U.S. apprenticeship programs are more comparable. But the comparison only highlights how much larger and more central apprenticeship is in West Germany. According to Reubens (1980), who has done the most extensive multinational studies of apprenticeship, U.S. apprenticeship is concentrated in a few trades, primarily construction related. Small pay differentials between workers with and without completed apprenticeship training are a disincentive to apprenticeship completion in the United States. Perhaps most dramatically, apprentices comprised 5.7 percent of the labor force in West Germany in 1977, when they were 0.29 percent of the U.S. labor force (Reuben 1980, p. 12). Considering that apprenticeship in the United States is limited to predominantly male occupations in the trade sector, is unconnected with public schools, is frequently inaccessible to minority and disadvantaged young people, and that practically all apprentices are older than 20, it is simply not a viable pathway from high school to career entry or adulthood.

Federally funded youth employment programs are another candidate for the role of U.S. institutions comparable to the West German dual system. Of the great variety of programs and program approaches tried between the War on Poverty and the Youth Employment and Demonstration Projects Act, the only one that still exists and can confidently be held up as exemplary is the Job Corps. In general, work experience and employment training programs for in-school youth have shown few enduring positive results (Mangum and Walsh 1978; see also Taggart 1982; Hahn and Lerman 1983; Betsey, Hollister, and Papageorgiou 1985). The Job Corps's relative success suggests that effectiveness demands a narrow focus (in its case, on the most disadvantaged youth) and intensive treatment, including removal from the home environment, remedial academic instruction, explicit attention to desirable worker attitudes and behavior, job skill training in classrooms and instructional shops, on-the-job training, and job placement. Sadly, most youth employment programs have not lasted long enough to accumulate the practitioners' wisdom and evaluators' findings that underlie Job Corps practices; no others have had comparable resources to devote to each participant. Even with all these advantages, the Job Corps has a high drop-out rate, its benefits accruing to those who remain the longest (Levitan and Johnston 1975).

By far the most common introduction to employment for U.S. youth is part-time and summer employment during enrollment in high school. The expansion of the service sector of the economy and the dispersal of commercial establishments throughout suburban areas have made part-time jobs accessible to the majority of high school students. Ironically, while the Panel on Youth of the President's Science Advisory Council (1974) and others were urging increased opportunities for youth to encounter the world of work, youth were increasingly taking advantage of those opportunities in fast-food restaurants and shopping centers. The larger irony, however, is that careful examination of the impact of such work experience on adolescent development has not supported the expectation that it would be primarily favorable. An extensive study by Greenberger, Steinberg, and their students (summarized in Steinberg 1984) has clearly demonstrated that part-time work has considerable costs as well as benefits.

A major limitation to such work experience is that it is in the secondary labor market, where skills and skill training are minimal. Another is that youth jobs do not necessarily expose youth to the presumably benign influence of adults. One's workmates tend to be one's schoolmates rather than benevolent adult mentors. Furthermore, working tends to create new opportunities for undesirable behavior such as stealing and lying, to increase cynicism about unethical acts, and to produce stress that increases use of alcohol, tobacco, and marijuana. Most seriously, when work hours per week exceed 15–20, school performance begins to suffer. Steinberg (1984) concluded his review with the interpretation that work experience with the most favorable developmental consequences combines the role of worker with that of student (or family member), something apprenticeship does by design.

Limitations of the West German System

Although I have tried to present a balanced portrayal of the dual system, noting difficulties in connection with the integration of apprenticeship experience with the *Berufsschule* curriculum and the quality of training offered by small firms, my emphasis has consciously been on the strengths of the system. However, if the dual system is to suggest ways in which U.S. policies and practices might be altered, we must attend to its limitations as well as its strengths.

First, however, I shall address the objection most quickly raised against the West German system by Americans—that it is hopelessly undemocratic. In all societies, schools contribute to the process of sorting young people into a hierarchy of occupations and social strata. The perennial question in U.S. educational sociology is whether and to what extent our schools foster social equality or reproduce prevailing inequalities. The question persists because the issues of value and method are too complex to allow any final resolution. The same issues hamper any effort to compare two nations' educational systems with respect to their egalitarianism. I shall, therefore, offer only a brief argument intended to challenge the assumption that the U.S. system is fundamentally more democratic than the West German.

Comprehensive high schools in the United States, though founded in a democratic ethos, are, in reality, class-stratified institutions. The separation of students into different ability groups and curricula establishes an in-school hierarchy that reflects to a large extent socioeconomic differences among students (Rosenbaum 1980). The cliques that organize students' social interactions outside the classroom maintain such strong divisions that, as one close observer described it, students identified with different social groups might as well not even exist for each other (Cusick 1973). They inhabit different social worlds despite attending the same school. When residential segregation by class and race is added to this pattern, comprehensive high schools in metropolitan areas become socioeconomically distinct, each being dominated by students from the social class and racial and ethnic group of the surrounding community. The presence of private and parochial schools exacerbates this segregation.

In West Germany, although enrollment in college-preparatory *Gymnasien* and in the lowest-level secondary schools, *Hauptschulen*, is highly related to parents' education and occupation (Trommer-Krug 1980), *Realschulen*, the middle-level secondary schools, enroll a representative cross section of society (Führ 1979). The children of blue-collar workers (*Arbeiter*) are more likely to become blue-collar workers themselves than are the children of white-collar workers (*Angestellten*), but one longitudinal study of a large sample found the difference to be only, respectively, 60 percent versus 50 percent (Stegmann 1983, p. 22). What is more, youth from the lower- and middle-level secondary schools who complete apprenticeship and vocational schooling can step immediately into careers, unlike graduates of either the general or the vocational tracks in U.S. comprehensive high schools.

Recall Karl Oettinger for a moment, completing at age 18 his twelfth school grade, albeit in a part-time school, and his third year of apprenticeship, choosing between a position as a skilled mechanic and one as a new car salesman. Imagine a comparable young man in the United States, hard-working, savvy, and personable but no more than a mediocre student. Approaching high school graduation, he could look forward to three or four years of floundering about in the secondary labor market before finding a career entry position. What definition of democracy or equal opportunity places him at an advantage over Karl Oettinger? If schools are judged, as Lightfoot (1983) proposes, by how well they meet the needs of the least advantaged, then West Germany's system of secondary education is better and more democratic than ours.

Nevertheless, the strongest criticism of the dual system over the past decade has come from the left side of the West German political spectrum, from those who favor a system that provides more options instead of channeling youth. The Social Democrats (SPD) have advocated increasing reliance on schools for this purpose and have opposed employers' control over youth and the educational system. Reform efforts in West Germany might be characterized as moving in an American direction, toward delayed career choice, comprehensive high schools, more schooling and less on-the-job training (von Dohnanyi 1978). (For data on education and inequality in West Germany and information about recent reform efforts, see Williamson 1977).

One aspect of the channeling of youth that seems especially undesirable from the U.S. perspective is the need for early career decisions. Heinz and his associates (1985) have documented the impact of a tight labor market on this process by interviewing young people repeatedly over three years as they moved from the *Hauptschule* into employment. Respondents began with quite modest career aspirations but abandoned those as dream careers as they learned from parents, friends, older siblings, and labor office advisers that they were not good prospects. Seeking apprenticeship placements, they considered a wide range of possibilities, depending more on what was available than on their personal interests. The key idea at this stage was that having some apprenticeship is always better than having none. Those who found training places eventually shifted their occupational aspirations from their original interests to finding a job in the field for which they were being trained. Most poignantly, they steadfastly maintained that the field in which they happened to find an apprenticeship was in fact the field they most wanted to enter, conveniently forgetting the aspirations they had previously shared with the investigators.

The investigators denied that the process they described can be considered one of choice. Choice, they argued, is for young people who are successful in school. The young people they studied do not really make choices but adapt themselves to what is available, precisely the argument advanced by Osterman (1980) with respect to working-class youth in the United States (See also Beekhuis and Friebel-Beyer 1983.)

The narrowness of apprenticeship training can be illustrated by listing occupational titles—for example, ceramic tile layer, coppersmith, tax advisor's assistant, pastry shop sales clerk. Occupations that are essentially identical are distinguished for training purposes depending on whether the placements are in large firms under the jurisdiction of the chamber of industry and commerce or in small firms under the jurisdiction of the handwork chamber. One consequence of narrow specialization is that career changes are difficult. I interviewed an apprentice auto mechanic who had decided in his third year that the work was not creative enough. He had arranged to switch to auto body repair as a result, which would require an additional three years of apprenticeship and *Berufsschule,* with no recognition for the courses and experience he had already accumulated.

The number of training occupations has been reduced by 100 over the past 10 years. Reformers working along these lines have also tried to identify broader occupational fields and to introduce an intermediate step in the process of career entry, in which young people learn about the broader field—metalwork, for example—before choosing a specific career.

The basic vocational education year (*Berufsgrundbildungsjahr*) is the principal institutional result of this effort. Young people who complete this year-long introduction to a broad field are eligible to move into conventional apprenticeships with credit for one year of training, shortening their time as apprentices and increasing their stipend. Although the original proposal was for a school-based program, employers succeeded in introducing an employer-based option that is more like conventional apprenticeship. Traditional apprenticeship has proved so strong that, except in those regions and occupations in which all employers have agreed to support this innovation, employers regard it as an inferior arrangement—and young people consequently accept it only when an ordinary apprenticeship cannot be found (Sonntag and Frieling 1983; Wachtveitl and Witzel 1983).

Employers' control is the pivotal issue in West German debates about the dual system. Employers openly state that they wish to retain control in order to assure that vocational training meets their needs; but their control has some advantages for apprentices as well, assuring that only knowledge and skills deemed useful are taught. Employers can also match the numbers of apprentices to their anticipated need for skilled employees. For example, as the printing industry changed over to computerized processes, it simply stopped training new apprentices. In an interesting reversal of U.S. employers' attitudes toward youth, West German employers prefer to hire young people so they can instill desired attitudes and behavior in them.

It is precisely this potential for employers to mold compliant young minds into an uncritical work force that, since the end of World War II, has motivated proposals for more schooling (Taylor 1981). Particularly with regard to traditionally male manual occupations, critics charge that the true function of on-the-job training is not teaching skills but inculcating discipline. They buttress their case by pointing to the prevalence of repetitive and unskilled tasks assigned to apprentices in small shops and to apprentices' subordination to adult authority (see, e.g., Seidenspinner 1974).

However, since the reform movement of the 1970s, economic sluggishness and the election of a conservative government have directed attention to other issues. Youth unemployment is the most pressing of these. It was once tempting to describe apprenticeship as an antidote to youth unemployment. As recently as 1980, West Germany's rate (for ages 15–24) was a mere 3.9 percent (up from 0.4 percent a decade earlier) compared to the U.S. rate of 13.3 percent (for ages 16–24). But by 1984, the rate for the United States was unchanged while West Germany's had risen to 10.1 percent (OECD Department of Economics and Statistics 1985, pp. 470–471, 480–481). The relation between economic demand for labor and demographic supply of potential workers appears to be a more powerful determinant of youth unemployment than skill training or other policies (Reubens, Harrison, and Rupp 1981).

Unemployment is viewed as an even more critical issue in West Germany than in the United States. The state is expected to assure that jobs are available to all who are willing to work, in part to obviate radical political activity of the kind that led to the rise of the Nazis. Labor laws protecting most workers from layoffs, combined with the gatekeeping function of the apprenticeship system, assure that youth bear the brunt of unemployment. Unemployment occurs in two waves: the first at the point when school-leavers are ready to enter into apprenticeship and the second at its termination, when trained workers are ready to begin full-time employment. Because public policy has been directed primarily at assuring an adequate supply of apprenticeship places—or, failing that, suitable school-based alternatives—the group that experiences the highest rates of unemployment includes youth in their early twenties, who have exhausted their educational options but are not needed by the economy. In comparison to the U.S. system, in which unemployment is highest among teenagers and declines steadily thereafter with age, apprenticeship can be said to postpone unemployment. The West German birthrate fell drastically after the baby boom. The supply of new workers entering the labor market is predicted to drop below demand by 1990, and the next crisis is expected to be a shortage of skilled workers. Hence the commonly expressed notion that West Germany is "stockpiling" skilled labor. It remains to be seen how young people will emerge from their years in storage.

Persistent high levels of unemployment before and after apprenticeship have added to the numbers of youth who fail to obtain training. Lacking attractive prospects for training or employment, youth who might otherwise be marginal apprentices remain outside the system or fail to complete their program. They are somewhat comparable to high school dropouts in the United States, though their future prospects are probably even dimmer because, in a system that prepares youth for specific jobs, those without the required training for one have almost no opportunities at all. The greater respectability of skilled workers in West Germany as compared to the United States is accompanied by very low status for unskilled (*Ungelernte*) or informally trained (*Angelernte*) workers. The former are at the bottom of the social hierarchy, have severely limited earning power, and face a lifetime of insecure employment. The latter lack the security and mobility of skilled workers with training certificates.

The proportion of untrained youth is difficult to determine precisely. In 1979, 6.2 percent of 15–17-year-olds were classified as *Jungarbeiter*, that is, employed youth not in full-time school or apprenticeship (Münch and Jung 1980, p. 133). Some of these eventually become trained, but others (4–5 percent) who begin apprenticeship fail to complete it. The size of the untrained group, therefore, can be estimated at between 5 and 10 percent of the youth population.

A third current concern with apprenticeship, in addition to unemployment and the youth who are left out, is the fit between traditional training and technological change. Karl Oettinger raised this issue with respect to auto mechanics. I questioned a *Berufsschule* director about it after noticing a poster in his office encouraging young people to consider a list of training occupations that included organ builder and glass-laboratory-instrument maker but nothing related to computers. He explained that it takes approximately 10 years to create a program for a new occupation. On the other hand, employers regard traditional apprenticeship as a solid base for further training in more advanced technology. For example, I interviewed a young woman who was completing her apprenticeship as a white-collar office worker and would then begin an additional year-and-a-half training program in electronic data processing. Her employer, a large manufacturing firm, also had a special five-year program that qualified apprentices in two fields, electronics and precision mechanics, to prepare them for repairing industrial robots.

Implications for the United States

What can we learn from West Germany? First, as noted above, that the floundering period is avoidable. It results from the structure of our educational institutions and labor markets, not from immaturity or incapacity on the part of youth. The floundering period does not appear to inflict irreparable harm on the employment prospects of youth; because it is normative, most grow out of it. Only the hardcore unemployed continue to experience past their mid-twenties such tenuous attachment to the labor force. Yet the floundering period can be a terribly difficult time for youth and their parents because of our society's individualism. We blame unemployed and underemployed young people for the failures inflicted on them by our institutions.

There are other costs associated with the floundering period as well. If the Business–Higher Education Forum (1983) is correct in maintaining that improved academic achievement is essential to maintaining and improving national economic productivity and competitiveness, then it must be a waste of productive potential to relegate a large cohort of youth to jobs in which they are neither highly productive nor engaged in increasing their skills.

The second lesson from West Germany is that our vocational education system could be substantially improved—but in two different ways. We could attempt to upgrade its technical quality so that graduates would be truly skilled workers. West Germany as a model suggests that the only way this goal could be achieved would be with substantial cooperation from employers and vastly increased resources. Most vocational high schools are simply not equipped to train skilled workers. Alternatively, we could leave the task of training skilled workers with employers and postsecondary schools and alter the purposes and practices of secondary vocational education to make it more like what was once called manual training. Manual training, as I am using the term, means teaching generic employee virtues such as punctuality, neatness, and ability to follow instructions; training in fundamental manual skills to increase dexterity and precision; and supplementing classroom instruction in academic skills by requiring their application in realistic situations.

The second alternative seems more feasible and promising. Surveys of employers consistently indicate that they expect to train their employees in specific job skills (Lund and McGuire 1984; Wilms 1984). What employers say they want from schools are reliable employees who can read, write, and calculate; learn new information and skills; and work hard. This is the perception that has motivated the neglect of vocational education in recent reform proposals. But this neglect, as vocational educators have been quick to point out, ignores the function of vocational education as an alternative mode of learning for many young people who do not learn well in classrooms. Simply demanding more and more rigorous academic instruction and performance is more likely to drive such youth out of school than to make them more employable (National Commission on Secondary Vocational Education 1984).

For this set of youth, in view of the failure of most vocational programs to prepare them for occupations, it makes sense for those programs to increase the emphasis on learning academic material rather than specific job skills. Such material need not be limited to the most basic, either. There is geometry to be learned in calculating the lengths and angles of roof joists, physics in understanding how tempering hardens steel, and biology in relation to sanitary practices, to name only a few examples. Vocational programs appear to provide a more comfortable environment than academic classrooms do for students whose academic performance is marginal (Claus 1984; Berryman 1982). It would be consistent with the spirit of recent reform proposals to take advantage of this positive aspect of vocational education but make it more academically demanding and more effective at inculcating generic skills.[6]

The third lesson is that improving education requires more than increasing class time and improving classroom curriculum and instruction. After two decades of attention to the powerful influence of families, neighborhoods, economic conditions, and race on school performance and after the development of numerous successful experiential learning programs, it seems gratuitous even to make this statement. It is needed, first, because these influences have been virtually ignored by most of the recent reform recommendations and, second, because nothing that has been done in the United States has approached the magnitude of West Germany's use of out-of-classroom learning. There are opportunities for learning in workplaces and other community settings that cannot be matched in classrooms. We need to explore what additional opportunities can be created in this country without either turning over the education of youth entirely to employers or limiting that education to narrow occupational training.

One of the challenges is to determine what incentives employers have or could be offered to provide education to young people who will not necessarily become their own employees. Such programs as Experience-Based Career Education, the Career Intern Program, and Executive High School Interns have answered that question, but on a relatively small scale—as have numerous local experiential learning programs, which are not necessarily career related. Youth-directed projects have the potential for expanding the number of experiential learning possibilities and giving participants experience in planning, problem solving, and decision making that can make them better citizens as well as better workers (Hamilton, Basseches, and Richards 1985). What the West Germans have done that is potentially beneficial to all but particularly beneficial to youth who are not academically adept is to introduce a large dose of adult-world reality into secondary education.

Just as the West Germans admire and have tried to learn from our bold attempt to provide advanced secondary schooling for all, we should try to learn from their differentiated but vocationally appropriate treatment of youth who do not enter higher education. Perhaps the ideal to be sought in both of our democratic societies is a combination of the vision enunciated by Willard Wirtz (1975), in which education and work would alternate through the life span rather than define distinct life stages, and the vision of Wolfgang Lempert (1981), in which all young people would earn the qualifications required for both skilled employment and university entrance. Perhaps both Wirtz and Lempert are simply offering contemporary details to flesh out the vision of democratic education that has never been enunciated better than by John Dewey (1916/1966, 1938/1963).

Notes

An earlier version of this paper was presented at the 1985 meeting of the American Educational Research Association in Chicago. Among those who made constructive comments on previous drafts are Mary Halligan Shann, Walter Heinz, Peter Katzenstein, Wolfgang Lempert, and an anonymous reviewer.

1. Private schools may be found in large cities, but less than 5 percent of school-age children are enrolled in them—and mostly in *Gymnasien,* not elementary schools (Bundesminister für Bildung und Wissenschaft 1983, pp. 24, 34).

2. Kindergartens are equivalent to U.S. nursery schools, enrolling 3–5-year-olds and usually being located outside of public schools.

3. Because university students have already received a broad liberal arts background in *Gymnasium*, equivalent to at least a year—and perhaps two—in U.S. colleges, university courses are much more specialized. Future medical doctors and lawyers, for example, begin their courses of study immediately. Therefore, a university course of instruction may comprise four to eight years. Universities charge no tuition. Government loans are granted to low-income students; parents who are financially able to do so are required by law to provide living expenses for their children while they are enrolled. When applications exceed the universities' resources and anticipated needs for trained professionals, as they do routinely in such fields as law and medicine, students are admitted in a sequence determined by their *Gymnasium* grades, final examination scores, and admissions tests (the *Numerus clausus;* see Spence 1981).

4. There are, to be sure, exceptions to this generalization among the many reports and studies, but this is an accurate characterization of the recommendations that have captured the attention of the White House and the general public. See Education Commission of the States (1983) for a summary and Howe (1983) for a critical analysis.

5. Proponents of vocational education cite a different set of studies indicating a more favorable impact on postgraduation employment and earnings; see, for example, National Center for Educational Statistics (1984, p. 17), Gustman and Steinmeier (1982), and Rumberger and Daymont (1984).

6. The limited contribution of vocational education to academic learning has been demonstrated by Rock (1985), who found that vocational graduates' performance on achievement tests was only marginally better than dropouts'.

References

Barton, P. E. "Youth Transition to Work: The Problem and Federal Policy Setting." In *From School to Work: Improving the Transition*. A collection of policy papers prepared for the National Commission for Manpower Policy. Washington, D.C.: Government Printing Office, 1976.

Beekhuis, W., and R. Friebel-Beyer. "Weiterbildung: zwischen Chance zur Selbstentwicklung und Zwang zur Arbeitsplatzsicherung." In *Von der Schule in den Beruf: Alltagserfahrungen Jugendlicher und sozialwissenschaftliche Deutung*, edited by H. Friebel. Opladen, West Germany: Westdeutscher Verlag, 1983.

Berryman, S. E. "The Effectiveness of Secondary Vocational Education." In *Education and Work*. 81st yearbook of the National Society for the Study of Education. Edited by H. F. Silberman and K. J. Rehage. Chicago: University of Chicago Press, 1982.

Betsey, C. L., R. G. Hollister, Jr., and M. R. Papageorgiou, eds. *Youth Employment and Training Programs: The YEDPA Years*. Washington, D.C.: National Academy Press, 1985.

Bronfenbrenner, U. *The Ecology of Human Development: Experiments by Nature and Design*. Cambridge, Mass.: Harvard University Press, 1979.

Bundesminister für Bildung und Wissenschaft. *Berufsbildungsbericht 1984, Grundlagen and Perspektiven für Bildung und Wissenshaft*. Bad Honnef, West Germany: Bock, 1984.

Bundesminister für Bildung und Wissenschaft. *Grund- und Strukturdaten, 1983/ 84.* Bad Honnef, West Germany: Bock, 1983.

Business–Higher Education Forum. *America's Competitive Challenge: The Need for a National Response.* Washington, D.C.: Business–Higher Education Forum, 1983.

Claus, J. F. *An Ethnographic Investigation of Attitude Development in Vocational Education: The Importance of Ethnographic Meaning.* Paper presented at the annual meeting of the American Educational Research Association, New Orleans, 1984.

Conrad, D., and D. Hedin, eds. *Youth Participation and Experiential Education.* New York: Haworth Press, 1982.

Cuban, L. "Persistent Instruction: The High School Classroom, 1900–1980." *Phi Delta Kappan,* 64, (1982): 113–18.

Cusick, P. A. *Inside High School: The Student's World.* New York: Holt, Rinehart & Winston, 1973.

Deutscher Industrie- und Handelstag. *Berufsausbildung in der Bundesrepublik Deutschland: das duale System.* Bonn: Deutscher Industrie- und Handelstag, 1982.

Dewey, J. *Democracy and Education.* New York: Free Press, 1966. (Originally published 1916.)

Dewey, J. *Experience and Education.* New York: Collier, 1963. (Originally published 1938.)

Dittmann-Kohli, F., N. Schreiber, and F. Möller. *Lebenswelt und Lebensbewältigung: theoretische Grundlagen und eine empirische Untersuchung am Beispiel von Lehrlingen.* Zentrum I, Bildungsforschung, Sonderforschungsbereich 23, Forschungsberichte 35. Konstanz: Universität Konstanz, 1982.

Education Commission of the States. *A Summary of Major Reports on Education.* Denver: Education Commission of the States, 1983.

Führ, C. *Education and Teaching in the Federal Republic of Germany.* Bonn-Bad Godesberg, West Germany: Inter Nationes (Munich: Carl Hansler Verlag), 1979.

Goodlad, J. I. *A Place Called School: Prospects for the Future.* New York: McGraw-Hill, 1984.

Grasso, J., and J. R. Shea. *Vocational Education and Training: Impact on Youth.* Berkeley, Calif.: Carnegie Council on Policy Studies in Higher Education, 1979.

Gustman, A. L., and T. L. Steinmeier. "The Relation between Vocational Training in High School and Economic Outcomes." *Industrial and Labor Relations Review* 36 (1982): 73–87.

Hahn, A., and R. Lerman. *The CETA Youth Employment Record: Representative Findings on the Effectiveness of Federal Strategies for Assisting Disadvantaged Youth.* Waltham, Mass.: Center for Human Resources, Heller School, Brandeis University, 1983.

Hamilton, S. F. "Experiential Learning Programs for Youth." *American Journal of Education* 88 (1980): 179–215.

Hamilton, S. F. "Raising Standards and Reducing Dropout Rates." *Teachers College Record* 87 (1986): 410–29.

Hamilton, S. F., M. Basseches, and F. A. Richards. "Participatory-democratic Work and Adolescents' Mental Health." *American Journal of Community Psychology* 13 (1985): 467–86.

Heinz, W. R., H. Krüger, U. Rettke, E. Wachtveitl, and A. Witzel. *"Hauptsache eine Lehrstelle": Jugendliche vor den Hurden des Arbeitsmarkts.* Weinheim, West Germany, and Basel: Beltz, 1985.

Hofbauer, H. "Berufswege von Erwerbstätigen mit Facharbeiterausbildung." *Mitteilungen aus der Arbeitsmarkt- und Berufsforschung* 14 (1981): 127–38.

Hopf, D., L. Krappmann, H. Scheerer. "Aktuelle Probleme der Grundschule." In *Bildung in der Bundesrepublik Deutschland: Daten und Analysen.* Vol. 2. Edited by Max-Planck-Institut für Bildungsforschung, Projektgruppe Bildungsbericht. Reinbek, West Germany: Rowohlt, 1980.

Howe, H. "Education Moves to Center Stage: An Overview of Recent Studies." *Phi Delta Kappan* 65 (1983): 167–72.

Körner, A. "Comprehensive Schooling: An Evaluation—West Germany. *Comparative Education* 17 (1981): 15–22.

Lempert, W. "Ausbildung zum Facharbeiter: Startbahn oder Parkplatz, Aufzug oder Abweg?" *Berufsbildung in Wissenschaft und Praxis* 12, no. 3 (1983): 77–83.

Lempert, W. "Perspectives of Vocational Education in West Germany and Other Capitalist Countries." *Economic and Industrial Democracy* 2 (1981): 321–48.

Levitan, S. A., and B. H. Johnston. *The Job Corps: A Social Experiment That Works.* Baltimore: The Johns Hopkins University Press, 1975.

Lightfoot, S. L. *The Good High School: Portraits of Culture and Character.* New York: Basic Books, 1983.

Limprecht, J. A., and R. H. Hayes. "Germany's World-Class Manufacturers." *Harvard Business Review* 60, no. 6 (1982): 137–45.

Lund, L., and E. P. McGuire. *The Role of Business in Precollege Education.* Research Bulletin no. 160. New York: The Conference Board, 1984.

McDill, E. L., G. Natriello, and A. M. Pallas. "A Population at Risk: Potential Consequences of Tougher School Standards for Student Dropouts." *American Journal of Education* 94 (1986): 135–81.

Mangum, G., and J. Walsh. *Employment and Training Programs for Youth: What Works Best for Whom?* Washington, D.C.: U.S. Department of Labor, 1978.

Mertens, D. M. "The Vocational Education Graduate in the Labor Market." *Phi Delta Kappan* 64 (1983): 360–61.

Meyer, R. H., and D. A. Wise. "High School Preparation and Early Labor Force Experience." In *The Youth Labor Market Problem: Its Nature, Causes, and Consequences,* edited by R. B. Freeman and D. A. Wise. Chicago: University of Chicago Press, 1982.

Mitter, W. "Education in the Federal Republic of Germany: The Next Decade." *Comparative Education* 16 (1980): 257–65.

Münch, J. *Das duale System: Lehrlingsausbildung in der Bundesrepublik Deutschland.* Bonn: Deutscher Industrie- und Handelstag, 1979.

Münch, J., and E. Jung. *Jugendarbeitslosigkeit und Berufsbildung: sozialer und materieller Status von Jugendlichen beim Übergang von der Schule zum Beruf in der Bundesrepublik Deutschland.* Berlin: Europäisches Zentrum fur die Förderung der Berufsbildung (CEDEFOP), 1980.

National Center for Educational Statistics. *High School and Beyond: A National Longitudinal Study for the 1980s: Two Years after High School: A Capsule Description of 1980 Seniors.* Washington, D.C.: U.S. Department of Education, 1984.

National Commission on Resources for Youth. *New Roles for Youth in the School and the Community.* New York: Citation Press, 1974.

National Commission on Secondary Vocational Education. *The Unfinished Agenda:*

The Role of Vocational Education in the High School. Reprinted in *Education Week* 4, no. 13 (November 28, 1984): 9–13.

National Institute of Education. *The Vocational Education Study: The Final Report.* ERIC Document Reproduction Service no. ED 205 831. Washington, D.C.: National Institute of Education, 1981.

OECD Department of Economics and Statistics. *Labor Force Statistics, 1963– 1983.* Paris: Organisation for Economic Cooperation and Development, 1985.

Osterman, P. *Getting Started: The Youth Labor Market.* Cambridge, Mass.: MIT Press, 1980.

O'Toole, J. "Education Is Education and Work Is Work—Shall Ever the Twain Meet?" *Teachers College Record* 81 (1979): 5–21.

Panel on Youth of the President's Science Advisory Council. *Youth: Transition to Adulthood.* Chicago: University of Chicago Press, 1974.

Reubens, B. G. *Apprenticeship in Foreign Countries.* U.S. Department of Labor R&D Monograph 77. Washington, D.C.: Government Printing Office, 1980.

Reubens, B. G. "Vocational Education for All in High School." In *Work and the Quality of Life,* edited by J. O'Toole. Cambridge, Mass.: MIT Press, 1974.

Reubens, B. G., J. A. C. Harrison, and K. Rupp. *The Youth Labor Force, 1945–1995: A Cross-national Analysis.* Totowa, N.J.: Allanheld, Osumun, & Co., 1981.

Rock, D. A. *The Impact on Achievement Gains of Dropping Out of School.* Paper presented at the annual meeting of the American Educational Research Association, Chicago, 1985.

Rosenbaum, J. E. "Social Implications of Educational Grouping." In *Review of Research in Education.* Vol. 8. Edited by D. C. Berliner. Washington, D.C.: American Educational Research Association, 1980.

Rumberger, R. W., and T. N. Daymont. "The Economic Value of Academic and Vocational Training Acquired in High School." In *Youth and the Labor Market: Analyses of the National Longitudinal Survey,* edited by M. E. Borus. Kalamazoo, Mich.: W. E. Upjohn Institute for Employment Research, 1984.

Sardei-Biermann, S. *Jugendliche zwischen Schule und Arbeitswelt: zur Bedeutung der Schule für den Übergang in den Beruf.* Munich: Deutsches Jugendinstitut, 1984.

Seidenspinner, G. *Lehrlinge im Konfliktfeld Betrieb.* Munich: Juventa, 1974.

Sonntag, K., and E. Frieling. "New Ways of Vocational Training in the Federal Republic of Germany: An Empirical Research Comparing Training Systems." *International Review of Applied Psychology* 32 (1983): 289–306.

Spence, J. "Access to Higher Education in the Federal Republic of Germany: The *Numerus clausus* Issue." *Comparative Education* 17 (1981): 285–92.

Stegmann, H. "Jugendliche und die Ausbildung für einen Arbeiterberuf." In *Arbeitsmarkterfahrungen und Berufsorientierungen Jugendlicher,* edited by W. Kruse, G. Kühnlein, and U. Müller. Munich: Deutsches Jugendinstitut, 1983.

Stegmann, H., and H. Kraft. "Abiturient und betriebliche Berufsausbildung: Nachfrage nach Ausbildungsplätzen, Übergang in eine betriebliche Berufsausbildung und späteres Studium." *Mitteilungen aus der Arbeitsmarkt und Berufsforschung* 16 (1983): 28–38.

Steinberg, L. "The Varieties and Effects of Work during Adolescence." In *Advances in Developmental Psychology.* Vol. 3. Edited by M. Lamb, A. Brown, and B. Rogoff. Hillsdale, N.J.: Erlbaum, 1984.

874   Policy Issues for the 1990s

Taggart, R. "Lessons from Experience with Employment and Training Programs for Youth." In *Education and Work*. 81st yearbook of the National Society for the Study of Education. Edited by H. F. Silberman and K. J. Rehage. Chicago: University of Chicago Press, 1982.

Taylor, M. E. *Education and Work in the Federal Republic of Germany*. London: Anglo-German Foundation for the Study of Industrial Society, 1981.

Trommer-Krug, L. "Soziale Herkunft und Schulbesuch." In *Bildung in der Bundesrepublik Deutschland: Daten und Analysen*. Vol. 1. Edited by Max-Planck-Institut für Bildungsforschung, Projektgruppe Bildungsbericht. Reinbek, West Germany: Rowohlt, 1980.

von Dohnanyi, K. *Education and Youth Employment in the Federal Republic of Germany*. Berkeley, Calif.: Carnegie Council on Policy Studies in Higher Education, 1978.

Wachtveitl, E., and A. Witzel. "Anpassungsbereitschaft und Enttäuschungsfestigkeit: Realismus von Jugendlichen im Prozess der Eingliederung in den Arbeitsmarkt." In *Arbeitsmarkterfahrungen und Berufsorientierungen Jugendlicher*, edited by W. Kruse, G. Kühnlein, and U. Müller. Munich: Deutsches Jugendinstitut, 1983.

Williams, S. *Youth without Work: Three Countries Approach the Problem*. Paris: OECD, 1981.

Williamson, W. "Patterns of Educational Inequality in West Germany." *Comparative Education* 13 (1977): 29–44.

Wilms, W. "Vocational Education and Job Success: The Employer's View." *Phi Delta Kappan* 65 (1984): 347–350.

Winterhager, W. D. "Berufsbildung und Jugendarbeitslosigkeit: Einschätzung der Situation." In *Bildung in der Bundesrepublik Deutschland: Daten und Analysen*. Vol. 2. Edited by Max-Planck-Institut für Bildungsforschung, Projektgruppe Bildungsbericht. Reinbek, West Germany: Rowohlt, 1980.

Wirtz, W. *The Boundless Resource: A Prospectus for an Education/Work Policy*. Washington, D.C.: New Republic Book Co., 1975.

36

The Failure of Federal Job Training

James Bovard

Federal job-training programs have harmed the careers of millions of Americans, failed to impart valuable job skills to the poor, and squandered billions of dollars annually. For 25 years, government programs have warped work ethics, helped disillusion generations of disadvantaged youth, and deluged America with fraudulent statistics. After spending over a hundred billion dollars on manpower programs[1] we have learned little or nothing: today's programs merely repeat the mistakes of the early 1960s. Federal programs have reduced the incomes of millions of trainees and have helped create a growing underclass of permanently unemployed Americans.

In the last 25 years, we have had more than 50 different federal training programs—yet unemployment rates have kept increasing; indeed, they have soared among groups targeted by government jobs programs. Every few years the names of the programs are changed and the politicians and Labor Department swear that success is just around the next budgetary bend, but little or nothing improves.

Amazingly, the federal government has stayed in the training business for a quarter of a century without any major success to show for it. America has been served an alphabet soup of failed jobs programs—from MDTA (Manpower Development and Training Administration), to CETA (Comprehensive Employment and Training Act), YEDTP (Youth Entitlement Demonstration and Training Program), JTPA (Job Training Partner-

From *Cato Institute Policy Analysis*, No. 77 (August 1986). Reprinted with permission of the Cato Institute.

ship Act), AYES (Alternate Youth and Employment Strategies), STEADY (Special Training and Employment Assistance for Disadvantaged Youth), STIP, BEST, YIEPP, YACC, SCSEP, HIRE, ad infinitum.[2]

Federal training failures have been masked by endless statistical shams. The Department of Labor has strained for 25 years to expand the definition of "success"—from counting Job Corps trainees as employed simply by confirming that they had a job interview, to counting as permanently employed people who spend one day on a new job, to counting as a major achievement teaching 17-year-olds to make change from a dollar. DOL's abuse of statistics epitomizes the welfare state's disregard of the evidence of its failure. A 1979 *Washington Post* investigation concluded, "Incredibly, the government has kept no meaningful statistics on the effectiveness of these programs—making the past 15 years' effort almost worthless in terms of learning what works."[3] Since 1979, DOL has perfected its ostrich act and now knows almost nothing about how its training programs are operating on the state and local levels.

Auspicious Beginnings

The father of modern government training and employment programs was President Franklin D. Roosevelt with his Works Progress Administration (WPA), the largest program of the New Deal. When Roosevelt announced this relief program, he declared, "All work should be useful in the sense of affording permanent improvement in living conditions or of creating future new wealth." FDR's standards for WPA have been mocking government employment programs ever since. WPA, commonly known as "We Poke Along," distributed paychecks to over 3 million people and is generally credited with giving leaf raking a bad reputation for an entire generation. By 1938, even FDR was embarrassed by his pet program.

The modern era of manpower law opened with the Area Redevelopment Act of 1961, a statute based on the "right" of geographical areas to equal economic development. The Area Redevelopment Administration (ARA) was established to direct federal money and training funds to depressed areas and was expected to play a substantial role in achieving full employment. Like subsequent federal training programs, ARA was based on the idea that jobs should come to people, rather than people going to jobs. ARA was thus the first of many training programs that discouraged individual adjustment.

Many of ARA's targeted unemployed did not want to learn a new trade. As its first annual report noted, "One of the most serious obstacles was the fact that job opportunities in redevelopment areas were limited because of the long-term economic decline which characterizes those areas."[4] In

ARA's first year, only 6,492 trainees enrolled—and fewer than 1,300 got jobs in fields related to their ARA training. Since unemployment exceeded 5 million when ARA was enacted, ARA's impact was negligible.

The Area Redevelopment Administration's goal was to "create jobs" and give training; but the General Accounting Office (GAO) found that the agency typically overreported the number of jobs created by 128 percent,[5] did not use available information to evaluate the number of new jobs supposedly created,[6] and routinely gave millions of dollars to locales that no longer had high unemployment.[7] By 1965, the ARA had sufficiently discredited itself to be renamed the "Economic Development Administration."

In 1962, Congress passed the Manpower Development and Training Act (MDTA) to provide training for workers who lost their jobs due to automation or other technological developments. MDTA was hailed by "manpower experts" as the great hope for American workers.

But, though MDTA expanded throughout the 1960s, its success was confined largely to political speeches and statistical charades. In 1964, GAO revealed that the Manpower Development and Training Administration defined as permanently employed any trainee able to hold any job for a single day. In a 1972 report, *Federal Manpower Training Programs— GAO Conclusions and Observations,* GAO concluded that federal manpower programs were failing on every score—that youth programs were not reducing the high-school dropout rate, that valuable job skills were not being taught, that little effort was being made to place trainees in private jobs, that DOL monitoring of contractors was inadequate, and that little follow-up of trainees was occurring.[8] GAO noted, "According to DOL, there is an overriding concern with filling available slots for a particular program rather than with developing the mix of services that the person needs."[9]

A Congressional Budget Office report on MDTA concluded, "The impact of training on wage rates has been minimal; the wage rate increases of participants are not substantially different from those of nonparticipants."[10] A 1967 poll by the Manpower Research Council found that 80 percent of the members of the American Society for Personnel Administration felt that "the federal government's manpower and training administration has not helped them find qualified employees; and the largest percent of this group said this was because training was given in the wrong skills."[11]

As GAO noted in a later report, "The Federal Government has been very responsive to employment and training problems but tends to respond to such problems by creating separate programs."[12] New federal training programs were created by the bushel: by 1967, there were 30 of them. Congress attempted to resolve the confusion by creating the Concentrated

Employment Program, but to no avail. A GAO report on CEP found that in East Harlem, the program sought to enroll 1,400 trainees but placed only 6 people in jobs. In Central Harlem, CEP was more successful: it sought to enroll 1,400 and succeeded in placing 31 trainees in jobs.[13] A 1973 GAO report on the District of Columbia Manpower program found 17 different agencies with 91 different programs, with no coordination. GAO concluded that "no one knows how many people are being trained; for what occupations they are being trained, or the impact on the demand for skilled workers." GAO noted that the same problems existed "in any urban area in the nation."[14]

In 1973, faced with a confusing hodgepodge of floundering training programs, Congress passed the Comprehensive Employment and Training Act (CETA). In the preface to the new law, Congress conceded that "it has been impossible to develop rational priorities" in job training. Existing federal programs were widely perceived as failures, and CETA was supposed to be the cure for all that ailed job training. However, most of the contractors and subcontractors under MDTA were simply given new, often more lucrative grants and contracts under CETA. The same agencies and nonprofit organizations repeated the same mistakes under a new acronym.

CETA began as a training and employment program, but job creation took precedence during the 1974–76 recession. Although the recession was over when President Jimmy Carter took office in 1977, Carter nonetheless ordered the creation of 350,000 additional public service jobs by year's end. Local government officials complained to Congress that the Labor Department was pressuring them to hire more people than they wanted; DOL officials threatened to withdraw all funds if localities did not spend "another million by Friday."

CETA spent $30,000 to build an artificial rock for rock climbers to practice on, gave $500 a month to a communist agitator in Atlanta to, in his words, "organize for demonstration and confrontation," and paid for a nude sculpture class in Miami in which aspiring artists practiced Braille reading on each other.[15] The usual racketeering abounded. In Philadelphia, 33 Democratic party committeemen or their relatives were put on the CETA payroll. In Chicago, the Daley political machine required CETA job applicants to have referral letters from their ward committeemen and left applications without such referrals piled under tables in unopened mail sacks.[16] In Washington, D.C., almost half the City Council staff was on the CETA rolls.

CETA was often used to increase demand for other government services. In Florida, CETA recruits went door-to-door to persuade people to sign up for food stamps. In Maryland, CETA workers offered free rides to the welfare office. In New York, CETA workers ran a phone service to inform people what unemployment compensation benefits they were entitled to.[17]

At one point, CETA was paying over 10,000 artists and spent over $175 million on art projects. This was not because CETA expected an increase in the demand for artists or because any inadequacy was identified in existing methods of training artists. CETA spent millions on the arts simply because it thought that the arts were a nice thing and that taxpayers should have more of them, whether they liked it or not. In Montgomery County, Maryland, the richest county in the nation, CETA paid nine women $145 a week to attend ballet school. In Poughkeepsie, New York, CETA workers busied themselves attaching fake doors to old buildings to beautify the city.[18]

But, perhaps worse than wasting the public's money, CETA squandered part of the lives of its participants. A study by SRI, a Labor Department contractor, concluded that "participation in CETA results in significantly lower postprogram earnings" and that "all program activities have negative effects for men."[19] A study by the Urban Institute concluded that CETA produced "significant earnings losses for young men of all races and no significant effects for young women."[20] Studies by the Policy Research Group and the Center for Employment and Income Studies concluded that CETA had "negative overall effects" on employment.[21]

CETA spent $53 billion—yet only 15 percent of its recruits got unsubsidized jobs in the private sector.[22] In 1982, when CETA was winding down, GAO found that 50 percent of laid-off CETA workers were unemployed and that 55 percent of those were receiving one or more forms of government handouts. Only 25 percent had permanent, full-time jobs.[23]

The Job Corps

In the early 1960s, as the first wave of baby boomers joined the job market, youth unemployment rose sharply. Secretary of Labor Willard Wirtz proposed solving the youth-unemployment problem by requiring all youth to stay in school till age 18.[24] When Wirtz's proposal was not accepted, the "experts" decided that there was a grave school-to-work transition problem and that massive federal intervention was the only solution. Since 1961, government jobs programs for youth have prospered while the youth themselves have fared increasingly worse.

The Job Corps, created in 1964, was the flagship of President Lyndon Johnson's War on Poverty. Johnson claimed that the poor were trapped in a cycle of poverty and that only the government, by taking charge of poor youths' lives, could save them. Johnson's view must have surprised the millions of poor immigrants to America who had raised themselves out of poverty. Designed to remove youths from their home environment and give them a new start, the Job Corps was to be mother, father, and spiritual adviser to its young charges. It is a classic example of a federal agency getting a good reputation at birth and retaining it regardless of how badly it fails in succeeding years.

In a major 1969 study, GAO concluded that "post Job Corps employment experience . . . has been disappointing."[25] Job Corps terminees did not do materially better than other eligible youth who had applied to enter the program and then chose not to participate. A GAO survey discovered that in the cases of 362 corps members who left the program in 1967 and were reported to be employed immediately thereafter, 22 percent of their "employers" indicated that the Job Corps terminees had never worked for them. Only 25 percent of employed terminees were working in areas in which they had received training.

Nor has the Job Corps's record improved. An unpublished study conducted by the Operations Research Institute in 1972 found that Job Corps recruits were much more likely to be unemployed after their training than before.[26] GAO discovered in 1979 that recruits who dropped out of the corps within the first 30 days had higher average earnings afterward than those who stayed in up to six months.[27]

The history of the Job Corps is largely a history of the abuse of statistics. When few of the early recruits went on to get jobs—the original purpose of the corps—policymakers decided that it was also a "positive" outcome if terminees went back to school. However, since many recruits were in school before signing up, it is difficult to see how going back to school could rank as a major accomplishment. When the number of terminees getting jobs continued to be abysmally low, definitions were further stretched to count only those recruits who had completed a vocational training course—about one-third of all Job Corps recruits. If a member of this group had held a job for a single day after leaving the corps, he was counted as "employed" as a result of the training program. GAO found that one corps center counted graduates as employed simply by confirming that they had had a single job interview scheduled. DOL, with prize-winning *chutzpah*, claimed the Job Corps had a success rate of over 90 percent throughout the 1970s.

One of the main effects of the Job Corps has been to redistribute crime from inner cities to suburban and rural training centers. Many localities have sued the federal government to bar placing corps centers in their domain. In the 1960s, it was common for judges to tell youths convicted of crimes, "Go to jail or go to the Job Corps." Job Corps centers are renowned for the stabbings, rapes, and thefts that are often perpetrated by the trainees. Sen. Mike Mansfield (D-Mont.) complained, "It was not my intention to support the establishment of three reformatories in my state."

Two-thirds of Job Corps recruits drop out of the corps before they complete the vocational training course. This is understandable, considering the quality of the training the corps provides. GAO found that "interests and aptitudes are seldom determined and used in assigning youths to centers and specific training."[28] The vocational training provided usually gives recruits only the illusion that they have valuable skills. The medical lab-technician program places fewer than one in five trainees in related jobs. The mail clerk program places fewer than one in six trainees. The corps is still training people to be railway clerks, even though railroads appear to be a dying industry. The corps only recently began a limited program in word processing, even though word processing has long been one of the fastest growing job fields.[29]

Even when the training is good, it is often not geared for the youth's locale. Most Job Corps recruits train hundreds of miles from their home towns; this may be a good way to break dependencies or bad associations, but it means that they are not getting skills that are in demand where they live. As usual with government training programs, corps members receive training in skills that are the easiest for the government to provide, rather than those in greatest demand.

Job Corps officials insist that they have a hard task because 85–90 percent of their recruits are high school dropouts. But Job Corps recruiters actually encourage youths to drop out of high school and join the corps. Corps members receive a stipend of up to $100 a month to learn what they were often previously learning in public schools. Many who drop out of school are already in vocational education programs, programs that are sometimes better than what the corps offers. Recruiters are paid on a per-head basis, however, so they entice youths to leave school and join the corps.

Summer Youth Employment Programs

In 1964, it was decided that government should hire any low-income teen who couldn't find a job on his own. Soon, with the usual bureaucratic imperialism, local governments were vigorously dissuading teens from even looking for private jobs, begging them to come learn to be a "government worker."

Federally funded summer jobs programs have warped hundreds of thousands of youths' work ethics and helped blight a whole generation of inner-city children. The General Accounting Office concluded in 1969 that some workers "regressed in their conception of what should reasonably be required in return for wages paid."[30]

Ten years later, GAO found that "almost three of every four [urban] enrollees were exposed to a worksite where good work habits were not learned or reinforced, or realistic ideas on expectations in the real world of work were not fostered."[31] And, according to government training experts, the situation hasn't changed much since then.

Summer jobs programs have always been laughable—basically a federal slush fund for mayors. The only real requirements for program operators are to pay minimum wages and not to lose the money.

The Neighborhood Youth Corps was established in 1965 to give poor urban youths "meaningful" work experience and to encourage them not to drop out of school. But, as the General Accounting Office reported repeatedly, the program had no effect on dropout rates and did not prevent a huge increase in youth crime rates.[32] And "meaningful work experience" has always been defined by government social workers or political appointees—not exactly sage judges of value.

Like other jobs programs, summer youth programs have required frequent name changes to retain their credibility. In 1972, the Neighborhood Youth Corps was rechristened the "Summer Program for Economically Disadvantaged Youth" (SPEDY); in 1977, the name was changed again, to the "Summer Youth Employment Program."

To call SYEP a "jobs program" is a serious abuse of the language. In Washington, D.C., teens busy themselves this summer building a model cardboard city or attending a "Basketball Reading Incentive Camp."[33] Many are routinely sent home with pay hours before their "work day" ends and have complained about being required to listen to endless lectures about South Africa and nuclear power.[34] In Baltimore, teens will be paid for passing out toys and for chauffeuring cats and dogs to old folks' homes.[35] In Phoenix, SYEPers last year enjoyed themselves painting pictures of cars on the sides of buildings.[36] Across America, being in the general vicinity of a broom or rake constitutes a "real job" for SYEP.

SYEP often looks like a full-employment program for social workers. Job training descriptions abound with such terms as "self-enrichment," "self-exploration," and "getting to know yourself." In Martha's Vineyard, Massachusetts, one job program "attempts to facilitate interactions between students who have had little previous exposure to each other . . . in a co-teaching enriched work experience."[37] In Richmond, "participants will attend weekly meetings designed to help youths organize their thoughts, values, and life goals through exercises in self-awareness and community awareness. Participants will be counseled into making a decision on possible employment situations."[38]

"Job shadowing"—following a regular employee around and watching him toil—is a favorite SYEP job description. Many SYEP jobs apparently consist largely of "job readiness training." At J. Sargent Reynolds Community College in Richmond, the program's goal is "to provide a comprehensive pre-employment experience for 20 participants age 16 to 21."[39] These may be good things—but they have nothing in common with doing a day's work for a day's pay.

If these youths had nowhere else to go, SYEP might not be such a scourge on their characters. But local governments are becoming aggressive employers of first resort for young people. The motto of the Washington, D.C., program is "Go with us—Grow with us in 1986." The New Hampshire Job Training Council is getting the rock band Aerosmith to perform at their annual kickoff to drum up interest among youth. Phoenix is trying to get Jesse Jackson to come and dignify the program with his presence. These desperate gimmicks are understandable, since many localities cannot find enough youth to fill federally funded positions.[40]

In the private sector, a youth keeps a job by producing enough to earn his pay. In the public sector, administrators earn brownie points by firing as few teens as possible. According to one SYEP expert, the only time some youths show up at work is to get their checks.

Jim Moore, director of Phoenix's Employment and Training Division, observes that SYEP "is more for the good of the participant than for the business or organization that's using these kids."[41] In Baltimore, ads urge businesses to "buy a kid a job" for the summer. This may sound humane, but pampering kids with "feel good" experiences is no way to prepare them for jobs that are often tedious and difficult, and require an actual contribution to the firm's output. Such programs as SYEP are a prime contributor to illusions and unrealistic expectations among some young blacks about the world or work and may have actually increased long term unemployment. Columnist William Raspberry noted, "We are raising a generation of kids who don't know the meaning of work" and cited summer jobs programs as one of the culprits.[42]

SYEP leaves many youths worse off than they otherwise would be. A study of SYEP by Harvard professors Jon Crane and David Ellwood funded by the Department of Health and Human Services concluded that "roughly 40% of SYEP jobs simply displace private employment" for minority youth.[43] This is especially bad since, as Vice President Mondale's Task Force on Youth Unemployment reported in 1980, "private employment experience is deemed far more attractive to prospective employers than public work."[44]

SYEP is popular with politicians partly because it is a pork barrel. In Washington, D.C., the city is covered with leaflets proclaiming, "The

Mayor has a Job for You.'' Politicians get to take credit for what kids would have done for themselves anyway.

The National Academy of Sciences, in a major report issued in November 1985, concluded that none of the government employment and training programs for young people, except the Job Corps, significantly improved long-term earnings or employability.[45] Though SYEP has sometimes been justified as "fire insurance"—a bribe to deter youth from looting and so on—NAS concluded that SYEP did not reduce criminal activity among participants.

NAS examined a variety of trial programs for low-income youths created during the Carter administration and found that none—from guaranteeing teens jobs after completing school, to providing special job-placement assistance, to subsidizing wages—showed evidence of significant success. Though over $2 billion was spent on youth-employment "experiments" from 1977 to 1981, NAS concluded that the vast majority of "evaluations" had little or no scientific worth. NAS observed, "Virtually all of the YEDPA project evaluations had only three-to-eight month postprogram followups" of participants,[46] thus making it impossible to evaluate the program's long-term effects.

NAS noted, "Though it is widely recognized that of all youth employment problems those of school dropouts are the most serious, there appears to be a tendency for employment and training programs to avoid serving this group."[47] In San Francisco, only 3 percent of SYEP participants in 1985 were school dropouts. In Baltimore this year, the mayor announced that only students with good attendance records would be eligible for summer government jobs. This policy makes a travesty of targeting the program to the neediest, least-capable job seekers.

NAS did note "mutually negative attitudes by SYEP participants and program personnel toward each other." In Washington, SYEP recruits often complained about long, boring, and repetitive orientation sessions. NAS noted that "relatively few trainees have positive evaluations of the programs."[48] Sen. Lawton Chiles (D-Fla.) complained in 1979 that youths in summer jobs programs "get such a strong message of cynicism and corruption that it cannot fail to carry over into their attitudes about work, crime and society."[49]

Government jobs programs saturated black inner cities in the late 1970s. In 1978, up to half of all black teenagers who were working had jobs with government programs. In subsequent years, some of the sharpest declines in employment and labor-force participation were shown by the group most heavily targeted by government jobs programs. The employment-to-population ratio for out-of-school black females aged 20–24 nosedived from 63.4 percent in 1978 to 48.5 percent in 1981. The employment-to-population ratio for black males aged 16–24 fell from 67.8 percent in 1978 to 57.8 percent in 1981. The inactivity rate—the percentage of the population neither employed nor in school—for black males aged 20–24 almost doubled between 1978 and 1983, from 15.9 percent to 27.0 percent. For black females aged 18–19, the inactivity rate increased by over 50 percent between 1978 and 1983.[50] Some of the declines can be accounted for by the reductions in government employment programs. But much of it may be due to bad habits and unrealistic attitudes picked up from government programs.

The Job Training Partnership Act

The Job Training Partnership Act is the Reagan Administration's contribution to job training. President Reagan frequently cites its 68-percent job-placement rate for "economically disadvantaged" trainees as proof of the success of a public-private partnership. Former labor secretary Ray Donovan called JTPA "one of the greatest achievements in the history of government social policy,"[51] and current labor secretary Bill Brock calls it "a model for human resource programs."[52] But JTPA's success is a mirage: instead of serving the hard-to-employ, JTPA is largely a welfare program for business.

As a Congressional Quarterly study noted, "By wiping the slate clean . . . changing the law's name and modifying its governance structure—JTPA provided a new lease on life for federal job training strategies."[53] Most JTPA contractors also provided services under CETA. Once again, the main thing that has changed is the program's name.

JTPA is more private-sector oriented than CETA was, but it is still a creature of politics and bureaucracy. JTPA programs are advised and sometimes directed by local Private Industry Councils (PICs). The PICs are free to establish job-training programs as they choose. They only need to meet standards set by the Labor Department for job placements, average wages, cost per placements, and total expenditures on youth.

JTPA's success figures are virtually worthless. The national 68-percent placement rate is concocted from 50 state measurements with no consistency or uniformity. JTPA's placement figures are "largely one-day-on-the-job" figures, according to Gary Walker, a New York consultant who has evaluated the program for the Ford Foundation and others.[54] (A 1979 GAO report found that 78 percent of those who got jobs through government training programs in the Tidewater area of Virginia either quit or were fired within six months.[55]

Perhaps even more misleading, JTPA's placement rate refers only to "graduates." In some states, people who drop out of training programs are treated as if they never existed. This sleight-of-hand makes JTPA look significantly more successful than it is.

The Reagan administration claims that JTPA serves primarily the hard-to-employ. But up to twice as many people are eligible for JTPA as were for CETA. JTPA's guidelines are so broad that over 42 million people have been eligible for government-subsidized training since October 1983. (Fewer than 2 million have signed up.) Under CETA, recruits had to be unemployed or underemployed. Under JTPA, someone can quit his current job and enter government-paid training for another one.

Nor are JTPA recruits the hard-core disadvantaged that politicians portray. JTPA is serving a lower percentage of high school dropouts (23 percent) than did CETA. Roughly a fifth of JTPA recruits have some college or post-high school education.

JTPA primarily transfers the cost of job training from the private to the public sector. The National Alliance of Business published a booklet titled, "Bottom-Line Benefits: Increasing Profits Through Targeted Tax Credits and Job Training Incentives." JTPA pays employers 50 percent of a worker's wages for up to six months if the employee is receiving on-the-job training. Little monitoring is done to ensure that businesses actually train the worker. The Private Industry Councils are encouraging businesses to use JTPA for their routine training expenses, and boast that participating companies have lowered their operating expenses.

"Customized training"—designing a training program for the specific training needs of an individual company—is a popular JTPA activity. In Cincinnati, JTPA is paying for in-house training program costs previously assumed by General Electric.[56] In Spring Hill, Tennessee, JTPA will help pay training costs at General Motors' new Saturn plant. In New Jersey and Maryland, special programs have been set up to train people to work at McDonald's restaurants.[57] The local PICs brag that the programs have a high placement rate, but McDonald's would have had to train people anyway. The only difference was who paid for the training.

Where JTPA is not paying for training that would have occurred anyway, it often pays for training for jobs that don't exist. In the mining region of Minnesota, unemployment reaches 80 percent in some towns. With the decline of the American steel industry, demand for iron ore will remain depressed, and new industries are unlikely to enter the area. Yet JTPA is pouring in money to retrain the locals and help them search for nonexistent jobs. As a Labor Department study noted, "Relocation is part of the program that is not very popular among the training staff."[58] *Work America*, a bi-monthly newspaper published by the National Alliance for Business, one of the largest government contractors involved with JTPA, observed, "Operating a job training program when there are very few jobs is similar to producing a product which has no available market."[59] Like agricultural subsidies that keep unsuccessful farmers on the farm, job training subsidies encourage people to stay in depressed areas with little or no hope of ever finding work.

A recent five-part series in the *Pittsburgh Press* concluded that JTPA "is mired in a bureaucratic tangle that throws millions of dollars into dead-end training programs." There were the usual myriad stories of waste, fraud, and abuse. One employer defended himself: "Just because a businessman has an on-the-job training contract and his two sons are his only employees, where's the conflict of interest? Is it wrong to upgrade the skills of your children?" One participant in an electronic training program complained, "There was never enough equipment to work on and most of the equipment was from 1969." One woman who wanted to attend morticians' school was "frustrated by JTPA bureaucrats who said she needed psychological counseling because her career goal was morbid." Another trainee complained, "They give you directories of companies and have you call Vice Presidents to get around the personnel office, but all that happens is that you get transferred to the personnel office anyway."

In Pittsburgh, 96 percent of JTPA funds were being spent on classroom instruction—even though classroom instruction is known to be the least effective training method. But it is much easier to stick clients in a classroom than to place them in private jobs, so employment and training bureaucrats often favor endless classroom training.[60]

JTPA's most bizarre feature is its "employment-generating activities." The PICs are using tax dollars to advertise and procure federal contracts. Illinois used JTPA funds to set up Procurement Outreach Centers around the state to help local businesses chase federal contracts. The National Alliance of Business thought this program was so clever that it gave Illinois an award for the program.[61] Indiana has a similar program.[62] In Sacramento, JTPA paid for advice on loan packaging, taxes, and employer-employee relations for small businesses.[63]

JTPA's youth programs are as bad as CETA's. Sen. Dan Quayle (R-Ind.), the chief author of JTPA, claims that "JTPA has a job placement rate . . . for the young people around 70 percent." But according to the Labor Department, less than 40 percent of JTPA youths get jobs—even for a single day. JTPA inflates its apparent success rate by combining job placements and other "positive terminations"—including returning to school and development of "youth competencies." The PICs can count as "youth competencies" almost any activity that teenagers choose short of suicide. "Youth competencies" usually refers to "employability skills"—such as "world of work awareness," "making change" from a dollar,[64] and demonstrating "effective non-verbal communication with others."[65]

This allows programs to measure their success by the number of certificates they hand out, rather than by the number of people who get jobs.

Cream-skimming—taking the most employable applicant, rather than the most needy—is pervasive. Consultant Gary Walker's study noted that in one area PIC paid for a local private job-training school that "reportedly turned down 25 eligibles for every one accepted; in another, a bank teller program screened 118 JTPA eligibles to get 19 enrollees."[66] JTPA is largely training only very trainable people. Some locales are even actively recruiting trainees on college campuses.

The average wage for JTPA hirees is $4.62 an hour—barely half the national average hourly wage of $8.64 and not exactly a banner achievement, since most JTPA recruits have high school degrees. After adjustment for inflation, JTPA's average wage is no better than that received by CETA graduates—$4.44 an hour in 1983.[67]

If the National Weather Service operated like JTPA, it would claim credit for the sun rising each morning. JTPA has done little or nothing for people that they could not have done for themselves, or have done through existing government education programs. The only place that JTPA has surely increased the net amount of job training is in rural and depressed areas, where there are few jobs. If job training would not have been offered in places without a federal subsidy, it is doubtful that the skill is really in demand.

If the college-trained and most capable recruits were left out of the average, the typical JTPA wage would probably be around $4.00 an hour. Employers would have had to hire and possibly train people for those jobs regardless of JTPA. JTPA—at best—simply helps some low-income people get jobs in lieu of other low-income people getting the same job. One government training expert noted that JTPA serves "the best of the economically disadvantaged."[68] Since JTPA provides subsidies to employers who hire primarily the most able low-income people, the least skilled job seekers may be made worse off in the labor market by JTPA's activities.

Other Jobs Programs

Other federal jobs programs have been equally ineffective. The Trade Adjustment Assistance program has consumed more than $3 billion in taxpayer revenue since 1975—supposedly to help industrial workers who have lost their jobs because of imports start new careers. But according to an American Enterprise Institute study, "From mid-1975 to March 1983, only one of every 23 TAA recipients entered training, only one of 244 received a relocation allowance, and only one of 222 received a job search allowance."[69] Cato Institute economist James Dorn notes, "TAA has hampered adjustment by supporting anti-competitive union wage rates."[70] TAA usually is little more than generous compensation for pricing oneself out of a job at the bargaining table. The vast majority of TAA payments have gone to laid-off United Auto Workers and United Steelworkers members, and have implicitly underwritten these unions' demands for wages far above world-market levels.

The National Academy of Sciences study of youth employment programs observed that such programs isolate disadvantaged youth, thus possibly making it harder for them to fit into the real job market. According to a recent study by Brookings Institution scholar Gary Burtless, special federal treatment of disadvantaged job seekers may actually make it more difficult for them to find work. Burtless examined the Targeted Jobs Tax Credit, which provides generous tax credits to employers for hiring "economically disadvantaged" job seekers. Burtless found that TJTC eligibles who told potential employers of their "dependent" status were far less likely to be hired than those who never mentioned that they were on federal aid and that the employer could get a tax credit for hiring them. The stigma attached to this program thus apparently far outweighs any good the program does.[71]

Conclusion

Many, if not most, of the participants in federal jobs and job-training programs would be better off today if the programs had never existed. Aside from wasting scores of billions of dollars, government manpower programs distorted people's lives and careers by making false promises, leading them to believe that a year or two in this or that program was the key to the future. People spent valuable time in positions that gave them nothing more than a paycheck or a certificate, while they could have been developing real skills in private jobs with a future.

As Sar Levitan, perhaps the leading expert on government job programs, admitted in 1973, training programs "affect the distribution rather than the degree of unemployment."[72] Bill Spring, a Carter administration domestic policy expert, declared, "We can't provide jobs through training. But we can try to equalize the weight of unemployment on various groups."[73] In a nutshell, federal training programs aim to help some workers take better jobs from other workers. For this we spent a hundred billion dollars?

The fallacy underlying all job training programs is that the private sector lacks the incentive to train people for jobs. This is like assuming that farmers don't have an incentive to buy seed, or that auto manufacturers lack incentive to seek out parts suppliers. Businessmen naturally prefer that all the factors of production—including labor—be readily available. But where there is a shortage of skills and a demand for services, there is an incentive to train.

Amazingly, the federal government has shown little or no interest in honestly evaluating the results of its jobs programs. Especially under JTPA, the Department of Labor has made ignorance an art form. DOL claims to have little or no information on the local JTPA or SYEP programs—not even annual reports or local newsletters. As one training expert who wished to remain anonymous observed, "DOL doesn't know what's going on—and they don't want to know what's going on. That way, they can't get blamed."

Federal job training programs are always run with a "social work" mentality—trying to create a pleasant experience for the participants, rather than to prepare them for the real world. But, Uncle Sam's "No stress, no strain" work environment is no favor for trainees.

The primary beneficiaries of federal jobs programs have been the legions of social workers, consultants, and "manpower experts" that have made a good living off these flounderings for 25 years. In some cases, the interest of the government bureaucrats is directly opposed to that of the trainees they are supposed to serve. The federal government finances a nationwide Employment Service designed to refer job seekers to jobs. The service is widely seen as incompetent; two local studies found that welfare recipients got significantly more jobs when the federal Employment Service referred them to private employment agencies.[74] But according to a recent GAO study, job seekers are not referred to private agencies largely because government employees are afraid that they would eventually be displaced.[75] Low-income people thus stay unemployed simply to help ineffective bureaucrats keep their jobs.

As with so many government programs, federal training programs have aimed to produce impressive statistics rather than real achievements. Cream-skimming has always pervaded federal training programs—always trying to get the most qualified recruits who need the least help.

Federal job training programs will almost always be either unnecessary or worthless. Either the government will be training people for jobs that the private sector would have trained them for anyhow—or the government will be training for jobs that don't exist. Federal training programs have tended to place people in low-paying jobs, if trainees got jobs at all. So if the programs have any effect at all, it is simply to help some low-income people get jobs instead of other low-income people.

The surest way to create jobs would be to reduce unemployment compensation, food stamps, and other federal benefits for able-bodied non-workers. Other reforms that would help would be to abolish the minimum wage, lower taxes to stimulate economic growth, and reduce paralyzing regulation on local business creation.

Bad training is worse than no training at all. The federal government has tried every imaginable manpower scheme in the last quarter century, and has failed dismally every time. The sooner government stops making false promises and giving people false hope, the sooner low-income people can begin learning real skills in the private sector.

Notes

1. In constant 1983 dollars. Gary Burtless, "Manpower Policies for the Disadvantaged: What Works?" *Brookings Review* (Fall 1984).
2. The unidentified acronyms stand for, respectively, the Skills Training Improvement Program, Basic Essential Skills Training Program, Youth Incentive Entitlement Pilot Projects, Young Adult Conservation Corps, Senior Community Service Employment Program, and Help through Industry Retraining and Employment Program.
3. John M. Berry and Art Pine, "19 Years of Job Programs—Question Still Is 'What Works?' " *Washington Post,* April 24, 1979.
4. Area Redevelopment Administration, *A Report of Occupational Training Related Activities under the ARA for the Fiscal Year Ending 6/30/62.*
5. General Accounting Office, B-146910, June 3, 1964.
6. General Accounting Office, B-153449, May 3, 1965.
7. General Accounting Office, B-153449, June 25, 1964.
8. General Accounting Office, *Federal Manpower Training Programs—GAO Conclusions and Observations,* February 17, 1972.
9. Ibid., p. 49.
10. Congressional Budget Office, *CETA Reauthorization Issues,* 1978, p. 15.
11. *Congressional Record,* 1967, p. 2524.
12. General Accounting Office, *Federally Assisted Employment and Training: A Myriad of Programs Should Be Simplified,* May 8, 1979, p. iv.
13. General Accounting Office, *Concentrated Employment Program in New York City Has Not Met Its Employment Objectives,* September 7, 1972.
14. General Accounting Office, *Federal Programs for Manpower Services for the Disadvantaged in the District of Columbia,* January 30, 1973.
15. R. K. Bennett, "CETA: $11 Billion Boondoggle," *Reader's Digest* (August 1978).
16. *Washington Post,* July 1, 1975.
17. James Bovard, "Tales from the CETA Crypt," *Inquiry,* August 3, 1981.
18. Ibid.
19. Quoted in *Youth Employment and Training Programs* (Washington: National Academy of Sciences, 1985), p. 177.
20. Quoted in ibid.
21. Quoted in ibid., p. 178.
22. Albert Angrisani, assistant secretary of labor, letter to the editor, *New York Times,* August 31, 1982.
23. General Accounting Office, *Implementation of the Phaseout of CETA Public Service Jobs,* April 14, 1982.

24. *National Review,* April 7, 1964.
25. General Accounting Office, *Review of Economic Opportunity Programs,* March 18, 1969.
26. Sar A. Levitan and Benjamin H. Johnson, *The Job Corps: A Social Experiment that Works* (Baltimore: Johns Hopkins University Press, 1976), p. 96.
27. General Accounting Office, *Job Corps Should Strengthen Eligibility Requirements and Fully Disclose Performance,* 1979.
28. Ibid.
29. Senate Committee on Labor and Human Resources, *Job Corps Amendments of 1984,* February 8, 1984.
30. General Accounting Office, *Review of Economic Opportunity Programs,* 1969.
31. General Accounting Office, *More Effective Management Is Needed to Improve the Quality of the Summer Youth Employment Program,* February 20, 1979.
32. General Accounting Office, *Review of Economic Program,* 1969; *Management of the Neighborhood Youth Corps Summer Program in the Washington Metropolitan Area,* 1972; *Federal Manpower Training Programs,* 1972.
33. *Guide to the Mayor's 1986 Summer Youth Programs* (Washington). Department of Employment Services, Government of District of Columbia, 1986).
34. Margaret Engel, "Summer Jobs In D.C. Short on Training," *Washington Post,* August 4, 1986, p. C1.
35. *Baltimore Bluebook of Summer Jobs, 1986* (Baltimore, 1986).
36. Program Director Jim Moore, telephone conversation, April 26, 1986.
37. James Bovard, "Summer Jobs Should Do More Than Keep Youths off the Street," *Wall Street Journal,* May 7, 1986.
38. "A Guide To Richmond Summer Job Projects" Richmond Private Industry Council, Richmond, Va., 1980.
39. Ibid.
40. Bovard, "Summer Jobs."
41. Jim Moore, telephone conversation, April 26, 1986.
42. William Raspberry, "Kids Who Don't Know How to Work," *Washington Post,* December 2, 1977.
43. Jon Crane and David Ellwood, *The Summer Youth Employment Program: Private Job Supplement or Substitute,* March, 1984. U.S. Department of Health and Human Services, Grant No. 92A-82.
44. Vice President's Task Force on Youth Unemployment, 1980.
45. National Academy of Sciences, *Youth Employment and Training Programs,* 1985.
46. Ibid., p. 3.
47. Ibid., p. 3.
48. Ibid., p. 364.
49. Quoted in J. Cameron, "How CETA Came to Be a Four-Letter Word," *Fortune,* April 9, 1979.
50. National Academy of Sciences, pp. 42, 47.
51. Ray Donovan, *New York Times,* July 22, 1984.
52. Cited in James Bovard, "Son of CETA," *New Republic,* April 14, 1986.
53. Donald C. Bauer and Carl E. Van Horn, *Politics of Unemployment,* (Washington: Congressional Quarterly Press, 1985).
54. Bovard, "Son of CETA."
55. GAO *Federally Assisted Employment and Training: A Myriad of Programs.*
56. Neal Peirce and Robert Guskind, "Job Training for Hard-Core Unemployed

Continues to Elude the Government," *National Journal,* September 28, 1985, p. 2200.

57. "McDonald's Pilot Program Makes McCareers," *Work America* February 1985; and Ellen Bierlow, "Going for the Gold-Collar Worker," *Washington Post,* June 12, 1986, p. D5.

58. *Dislocated Worker Projects under Title III of JTPA,* (Department of Labor, April 1985).

59. "Rural America and The Job Training Partnership," *Work America,* April–May 1985, p. 3.

60. Paul Maryniak, " 'Real Help' Elusive in Job Training Partnership," *Pittsburgh Press,* April 13–17, 1986.

61. "National Awards for 1985," *Work America,* August 1985.

62. National Alliance of Business Database accession number P000612.

63. National Alliance of Business Database accession number P000212.

64. Pittsburgh-Allegheny Co. PIC Newsletter, November 14, 1984.

65. Department of Labor, *An Introduction to Competency-Based Employment and Training Programming under the JTPA,* 1985.

66. Bovard, "Son of CETA."

67. Ibid.

68. Off-the-record comment to author.

69. *Reauthorization of Trade Adjustment Assistance* (Washington: American Enterprise Institute, 1983).

70. James A. Dorn, "Trade Adjustment Assistance: A Case of Government Failure," *Cato Journal* 2, no. 3 (Winter 1982): 865–905.

71. Gary Burtless, "Are Targeted Wage Subsidies Harmful? Evidence From a Wage Voucher Experiment." *Journal of the Institute of Socioeconomic Studies,* Fall 1985.

72. Sar Levitan, *Manpower Policy* (Philadelphia: Temple University Press, 1973), p. 31.

73. Kathy Sawyer, "War on Youth Unemployment: Dispiriting News from the Front," *Washington Post,* March 8, 1980.

74. General Accounting Office, *More Jobseekers Should Be Referred to Private Employment Agencies,* March 1986.

75. Ibid.

Poverty and Dependency

In November 1987 David J. Garrow wrote the following as part of a book review in the *Washington Post:* "The last two decades have witnessed a spiraling and ongoing economic decline in America's black inner-city neighborhoods. By virtually any social or economic yardstick—employment, schools, crime, or housing—conditions today are dramatically worse than they were in the early 1960s."

Each of the papers in this section work to understand a part of the answer to the question of why the worsening conditions Garrow described have come to be. The question is vexing. Indeed, not everyone accepts the basic premise of the statement. There are many who believe great strides have been made and that the country is in far better condition—contrary to Garrow—than it was in the early 1960s. Thus the question is not one of understanding why there has been decline but, rather, what has facilitated the success the country has experienced. Others, who accept the basic premise of a decline in the economic vitality and life of inner-city neighborhoods, present quite disparate assessments of why this is so. The end result is understood. Why and how the conditions have become as they are is hotly disputed. That debate is reflected in articles included in this section.

Several articles here also carry the argument one step further. They pose the question: "What is to be done?" In doing so, two basic emphases emerge. One line of analysis stresses the need to eliminate poverty, making sure that citizens in the country do not fall below a particular economic floor. (Some of this same line of reasoning was evident earlier in the Health Policy section where the emphasis was on lifting the elderly above the poverty level via increased benefits from Social Security.) The goal of those who stress poverty elimination via additional economic resources frequently presume those resources will come from government.

The alternative line of analysis addresses the problem that reliance on government funds is presumed to generate dependency on those funds, thus reducing one's willingness to be self-reliant and an economically contributing member of the society. Welfare dependency was of particular concern to those in the Reagan administration. Their critique of the "War on Poverty" and the growth of the welfare systems of the 1960s and 1970s was that such programs destroyed initiative, undermined the integrity of the family, and spawned a welfare culture that was becoming intergenerational. In short, strictly focusing on income levels and government transfers was destructive of personal and economic independence.

One area where there seems to be some common ground is in the recognition that the current welfare system is badly flawed and needs serious repair. Whether the emphasis is on eliminating poverty or minimizing dependency, both perspectives agree that what the United States has now is cumbersome, bureaucratic, counterproductive, and destructive. A fundamental rethinking about United States welfare policy is now past due. Efforts to restructure the welfare system are presently underway in the U.S. Congress.

Moving from welfare to workfare is high on the agenda of those who are now exploring alternatives to the present system. Creating an approach where those in poverty are aided to build marketable skills for the labor market is seen to be a long-term approach to reducing both poverty and dependency. Thus this strategy is finding support among both liberals and conservatives—though each comes to support the effort for different reasons. The liberals are high on notions of human-capital formation, job-training programs, education, and skill-building that comes from direct government assistance to poor persons in the program. Conservatives come to support workfare because it addresses the dependency issue, stresses participation in the market, and is thought to build individual motivation through experiencing the benefits of having employment. This convergence presents one of those interesting policy situations where a potential political consensus could emerge—substituting a workfare system for a welfare system is the way the United States ought to go in the 1990s. The logic of such a system as well as its limitations are discussed in several of the following articles.

There are those scholars, however, who argue that what has happened in the United States, since 1960, to the population in poverty is so profound and now so driven by systemic economic and corporate forces that looking to more government programs of any type to reverse the present situation is simply not sufficient. What has happened, these scholars argue, is the emergence of a structural underclass that is outside the mainstream of American life, trapped in the core of the older cities, and seemingly unreachable by conventional social programs. Trying to do more of what has already been tried with this group is thought doomed to failure. New strategies and new perspectives will be needed if the problems of the underclass are to be addressed in fruitful ways. Central to that reexamination is the notion of moving away from viewing public assistance as an "entitlement" to viewing government assistance as part of a reciprocal agreement where public support comes in exchange for an obligation on the part of the recipients to change their life circumstances. Several articles here deal specifically with the nature of the underclass as well as the policy strategies available to deal with these conditions.

The first article in this section, by Judith Gueron, reports on efforts made over the past years by the Manpower Demonstration Research Corporation (MDRC) to understand the current conditions of the American welfare system and systematically to test alternative strategies for reform. The particular focus of this paper is on the potential of reforming welfare through creation of various work opportunities and experiences. The data for the study came from a five-year project in which a number of individual states were each evaluated for three years. Three key questions are posed in the study and addressed in this paper. The questions focus on the feasibility of imposing obligations as a condition of receiving welfare, of attempting to understand what workfare programs look like in actual practice, and whether or not such initiative makes a difference. The paper closes with answers to these questions and their implications for reform of the current welfare system.

Michael Morris and John Williamson focus specifically on the trade-off in welfare policy between concerns over eliminating poverty and those of minimizing dependency. Their view is that trade-offs between these twin concerns are quite likely. This is in contrast to those who would suggest that the use of workfare would be a solution simultaneously to both concerns, i.e., increasing both self-sufficiency and income. The analysis presents a fruitful topology of current policy options for addressing poverty from those on the conservative right to the liberal left. In assessing these policy options, the authors focus on two important findings. First, "the antipoverty impact of government transfer programs is significantly greater than the antipoverty impact of dependency-reduction programs." Second, the more assumptions a program has to meet in order to be successful, the less the likelihood of success. Generally, dependency-reduction programs have longer assumption chains than do income-transfer programs and thus are more vulnerable to failure.

Neil Gilbert addresses one critical component of the current welfare debate that seems to be increasingly neglected. He asks, specifically, what is to become of the children. Gilbert moves from the general proposition that child-rearing is at any time and for any two-parent family a difficult and challenging task to the particular concern that current debates take no account of what the policy options mean for single parents (frequently read "teenage parent"). It is the latter group who have to cope with child-rearing under much more duress.

Gilbert is concerned that current debates treat the parent only as an economic agent providing financial support to self and the children. Parenting is a more complex and demanding task. Ignoring the social-emotional needs of the single parent as well as of the children is extremely short-sighted. The notion of "social obligations," he argues, is broader than only financial considerations. The broader view encompasses the social obligation to treat children well, provide them a nurturing home, the time and attention of a parent, and a home free of the grinding grip of poverty. The fact that United States society has turned away from a special concern with children has led to little sympathy for those who are care givers, particularly when they are the single parents of those children. He is particularly emphatic that there may well be trade-offs between having the time to parent and the time to work that teenage parents can meet only by choosing one over the other. For Gilbert, choosing the latter is the poorer choice.

Posing the question "Who are the working poor?" Charles Murray provides an answer. His analysis keeps peeling away at the numbers of the groups typically presumed to be the working poor to the point where he believes that the majority of those considered to be "working poor" are "living lives that they choose to live." He believes that while persons may statistically be classified as poor, they personally will not consider themselves such. Further, he suggests that idiosyncratic decisions not to participate in the labor market, to add nonworking persons to one's household, or to live in rural areas will all influence the statistical outcome while not necessarily meaning that the person is truly poor. The conclusion he draws is that fewer of the poor are "victims" than they are persons living out their own choices.

Finally, Richard Nathan addresses the circumstances and implications of the emergence of an urban underclass in the United States. Nathan rejects the arguments of those who believe that the conditions of the poor and the reasons for persons' being in poverty are no different now than they have been in the past. It is his view that there has emerged a "real and new condition in the society with which we must come to terms." This new condition is structural, and while there may still be debates over why and how this change occurred, Nathan believes that the country has got to focus its attention now on how to deal with these new realities. The conditions of the underclass are economic, behavioral, and geographic.

Further, they have now taken on a persistence that will not easily give way to short-term, low-intensity social programs. Rather, the country faces the challenge to demonstrate a concerted political effort both to spend the necessary funds to reach this group and then to exert the will to target the funds where they can be most beneficial. Neither of these two impulses is presently in evidence in the United States. Whether or not the 1990s will be different will tell if and when the United States begins to do something about what Nathan calls "America's most challenging social problems."

37

Reforming Welfare with Work

Judith M. Gueron

This country has long debated the question of how to design the welfare system—particularly the federally supported Aid to Families with Dependent Children (AFDC) program, which provides cash assistance to families headed primarily by female single parents. The debate has intensified as welfare reform once again has become a presidential priority. A pressing issue before Congress is whether welfare programs should continue to be broad entitlements or whether, instead, they should become "reciprocal obligations," whereby work—or participation in an activity leading to work—is required in return for public aid. Although other features of welfare reform have been aired recently, they have not yet been thoroughly discussed or studied.

Fortunately, the body of knowledge on work approaches has grown considerably during the last five years. In 1982 the Manpower Demonstration Research Corporation (MDRC) began a five-year study examining eight state initiatives that attempt to restructure the relationship between welfare and work. The evaluations in five states have been completed.[1]

This paper first sets the context for the discussion by outlining the issues surrounding the AFDC program and the evolution of the debate about reforming welfare with work. It then summarizes the major findings of the MDRC study. In conclusion, it suggests some of the implications of these findings for welfare policy and discusses important unanswered questions.[2]

From *Reforming Welfare with Work,* Occasional Paper 2, Ford Foundation Project on Social Welfare and the American Future. Copyright 1987, Ford Foundation. Reprinted with permission of the Ford Foundation.

Background:
The AFDC Program and the
Pressure for Reform

The current AFDC program is one way of balancing the competing values and objectives of social welfare policy: to reduce poverty (especially among children), to promote family stability, to encourage mothers and fathers to support themselves and their families, and to minimize costs. Today's debate about the program echoes a central dilemma that was identified as long ago as the English Poor Laws: Is it possible to assist the poor without, by that very act, giving people incentives for behavior that perpetuates poverty and dependency? This question, in turn, rests on ideas about who the poor are and what has caused their condition.

Although the debate about AFDC has long recognized that the multiple objectives of the program cannot all be maximized and that any welfare system involves trade-offs, at issue is whether the existing AFDC program represents the best balance possible, given current values and knowledge.

Of particular concern in AFDC policy are questions about whether it reduces the incentives for people to work and whether it promotes a "culture of poverty" (for example, teenage pregnancy and multigenerational dependency). The arguments are simple:

- Most people have to work for income. Welfare recipients have an alternative.

- In addition, the very rules of AFDC and all other income-conditioned programs serve to "tax" the income gained by people who do work: these rates are often very high. As a result, the structure of the AFDC program makes work less attractive and encourages dependency.
- Although AFDC has been criticized for not providing sufficient income, any attempt to increase welfare grants to levels that provide a decent standard of living for adults and children will only increase the disincentives for recipients to take low-paying jobs.
- Since AFDC eligibility is open primarily to women heading households and since benefits depend on the number of children, the very design of the program may discourage family formation and allow fathers to avoid supporting their children.

Unfortunately, it is easier to describe the arguments than to quantify the extent to which poverty or female-headed families actually result from welfare programs rather than from other social or economic forces.

It is also difficult to devise alternative policies that perform better. There are a number of reasons why reform has proven elusive. First, the debate surrounding the appropriate policy connection between work and welfare has frequently been highly charged, dealing as it does with central issues of income redistribution, social justice, and individual responsibility. Since there is no consensus on the relative importance of the different policy objectives, efforts at reform that succeed better in meeting one objective—but only at the expense of reducing another—usually encounter strong opposition. Second, the lack of reliable data on the alleged negative effects of welfare makes it difficult to assess the actual trade-offs involved in different reform options.

There is also persistent disagreement on the causes of poverty and welfare dependency, with different diagnoses suggesting different cures. Some blame the disincentives embodied in welfare programs themselves, while others stress the limited education, skills, and work experience of the poor. Some highlight health problems or negative attitudes toward work, and still others point to the labor market, with its lack of opportunities for employment and advancement. The importance of these non-welfare factors suggests that changing the AFDC rules will be only one step in any attack on poverty.

In the past twenty-five years, three basic approaches have been taken to reform welfare in order to better reconcile the central values listed above. The first would change the rules for determining welfare eligibility and the size of benefits in order to increase the financial incentives for choosing work instead of welfare (that is, it would encourage recipients to increase their work effort voluntarily). The second would transform the AFDC entitlement into a "bargain," in which an AFDC grant carries with it some reciprocal obligation to accept a job, to search for work, or to participate in work experience, education, or training activities in preparation for work. This second approach has been mandatory, in that an individual can lose AFDC benefits for failing to cooperate with the program requirements. A third strategy has been to rely less on AFDC cash grants and more on alternatives that provide other incentives: for example, child-support enforcement, changes in tax policy that increase the rewards for work, and the direct provision of training or jobs.

The discussion below outlines why the welfare reform debate has increasingly shifted toward the second approach—work solutions—and presents the evidence on the feasibility and effectiveness of this strategy. (Throughout, this paper focuses on welfare programs directed to families, not to the aged or disabled.)

The AFDC Program

Public assistance programs in the United States have tried to make sharp distinctions between those considered able to work and those judged appropriate for public support. Working-age men have been included in the former category—and they have received only limited support in the welfare system. The aged and severely disabled are classified in the latter category. There has been more controversy about poor single mothers, with a recent major shift in the relative emphasis given to ensuring the well-being of children and encouraging their parents to support themselves by working.

When the AFDC program was adopted as part of the Social Security Act of 1935, it was regarded primarily as a means to provide assistance to poor children. The initial assumption was that only a small group of poor mothers would receive benefits on behalf of their children: widows and the wives of disabled workers who—like other women—should have the opportunity to stay at home and care for their children. The issue of work incentives did not arise since these were cases of hardship, not choice. The focus was on child welfare, and encouraging mothers to enter the work force was not seen as a route toward that goal.

In recent years, several factors have led to a change in public perceptions about the appropriateness of employment for welfare mothers— including mothers of very young children.

First, in the 1960s and early 1970s AFDC caseloads and costs grew rapidly, as did the proportion of the caseload headed by women who were divorced or never married. Second, the employment rates of all women— including single parents and women with very young children—increased dramatically, leading many to reconsider the equity and appropriateness of supporting welfare mothers who could be working. Third, although recent research confirms that most people use welfare only for short-term support, it also points to a not insignificant group for whom AFDC serves as a source of long-term assistance. The growing concern about the presumed negative effects of such dependency on adults and children has prompted intensified efforts to reach this group.

All of these developments have raised questions about whether the design of the AFDC program is not part of the problem.

Strategies for Reforming AFDC

All AFDC reform efforts have grappled with the challenge of providing adequate income while maintaining incentives for work and self-sufficiency, and doing both at a reasonable cost. Years of debate have confirmed the impossibility of simultaneously maximizing all of these objectives and have also identified some of the trade-offs that the different approaches imply.

During the period from the mid-1960s to the early 1970s, many attempts to increase the employment of welfare recipients centered on building financial incentives for work into the AFDC program itself. As a first step, the 1967 amendments to the Social Security Act reduced the rate at which welfare grants decreased (the implicit marginal "tax" rate) when recipients went to work.

Then interest shifted and the debate centered on the advantages of replacing AFDC with a universal, noncategorical, negative income tax. This was proposed in the Nixon Administration's Family Assistance Plan, which would have guaranteed a minimum income to all Americans, not only single-parent families but also the working poor. It was hoped that this expanded coverage would lessen the incentives for family dissolution and, at the same time, would not seriously reduce work effort. However, some have argued that the findings from several of the federally sponsored income-maintenance experiments suggest that more generous financial incentives to work would have increased the size of the beneficiary population and actually reduced, rather than increased, overall work effort.[3] For many people, this new evidence eliminated the possibility of welfare reform by means of a comprehensive negative income tax system.

As a result, the welfare reform proposals of both the Carter and Reagan administrations have included some form of a comprehensive work obligation, under which "employable" welfare recipients would have to accept a job or participate in a work-related activity. These plans relied on mandatory requirements to provide an incentive—through the threat of a loss of welfare benefits—for welfare recipients to work.

An early harbinger of this policy shift was the enactment of the Work Incentive (WIN) Program. Introduced as a discretionary program in 1967, WIN became mandatory in 1971; that is, in order to receive AFDC benefits, all adult recipients without preschool children or specific problems that kept them at home would have to register with the state employment service, to participate in job training or job-search activities, and to accept employment offers. In theory WIN imposed a participation obligation, but the program was never funded at a level adequate to create the precondition for a real work test: a "slot" for each able-bodied person.

Under pressure to increase the work effort and reduce the AFDC rolls, both the Carter and the 1981 Reagan proposals called for a redefinition of the welfare entitlement. The two designs had striking similarities that are usually overlooked. Both suggested that the right to welfare benefits be linked with an obligation to work: that is, employable AFDC recipients who failed to locate jobs would be required to work as a condition of receiving public aid.

There were, however, important differences in the amount and the form of that aid. The Carter proposal guaranteed welfare recipients full-time public service employment (PSE) jobs and paid them wages. In contrast, the Reagan Administration's universal "workfare" plan mandated that recipients work in exchange for their welfare grants, with no compensation beyond the public assistance check (except for the limited reimbursement of working expenses). In all states except those with the highest grants, the workfare formulation would lead to part-time work and continued low income.[4] (Here and elsewhere in this paper, the word "workfare" is used to describe a mandatory work-for-benefits program, and not the evolving broader definition that encompasses any form of work-related obligation or option.)

The special appeal of restating the AFDC "bargain" this way lies in its seeming to reconcile the conflicting welfare policy objectives, at the same time as it may provide a direct attack on the causes of poverty and dependency. The claimed advantages of this approach include:

- *Strengthening work incentives and bringing AFDC into line with prevailing values.* By design, such programs provide the strongest work incentives, since benefits are conditioned on meeting a work requirement. Welfare recipients would have an obligation that parallels the one faced by other citizens and that fits with mainstream American values and the belief in the work ethic—values shared by the general public and by welfare recipients.
- *Improving the employability of welfare recipients.* It was hoped that work programs would increase human capital, indirectly by instilling a sense of responsibility or the work ethic, and directly by developing skills by means of well-structured work experience. To ensure that this occurred, some states have extended the range of mandatory activities to include education and training.
- *Providing social benefits.* To the extent that workfare and public service employment strategies create additional positions and meaningful work, they also promise to provide useful public services.
- *Reducing the welfare rolls.* Mandatory work approaches, it was hoped, would reduce welfare dependency by deterrence and assistance. Because of the new requirements, some individuals might not apply for welfare and others might leave the rolls more quickly. Some might refuse work assignments because of conflicts with unreported jobs and then be "sanctioned;" i.e., removed from the rolls. Others, benefiting from new skills or from a work record, might find it easier to obtain unsubsidized jobs.
- *Psychological benefits and public support.* Supporters also have argued that forging a direct connection between welfare and work bestows greater dignity on recipients, has positive effects on the worker and his or her family, and increases public support for the AFDC program.

Critics challenged the ability of both the Carter and Reagan proposals to satisfy these claims. Given the existing service delivery system and the nature of the welfare population, they questioned whether a large-scale participation and work requirement could be enforced in a manner that met acceptable standards of fairness. For example, how would these programs differentiate between recipients who should be excused from any obligation for good cause, and those who should be penalized for noncompliance? This dilemma was particularly challenging, given the widespread recognition that there was no easy and straightforward formula to determine the "employability" of female household heads, which would depend on diverse and changing factors such as health and the availability of child care.[5] Many also questioned whether a sufficient number of useful jobs could be created that would provide employment skills and yet not displace regular workers, and, if not, whether jobs for welfare recipients would become punitive or "make-work."

Critics also thought that workfare or public service employment would not speed the transition to unsubsidized work because the economy did not generate enough regular jobs, and program services were of limited value in helping recipients obtain available ones. Moreover, some questioned the assumption that people would move off the rolls to avoid a work obligation, seeing no need to create a work ethic that was already there. As a result, they argued that the additional costs of administering a work program would exceed any potential welfare savings. Finally, critics maintained that public employees and other groups would not accept the supplementation of the work force by unpaid or low-paid public assistance recipients.

Although many of these criticisms were directed both at the Carter and the Reagan proposals, welfare advocates for the most part preferred the Carter public service employment approach to the Reagan workfare model. In addition, advocates favored expanding the list of required activities to include education and training and wanted to increase the level of support services. Such measures appeared to shift the balance away from obligation toward opportunity.

Ultimately, the high cost of the Carter Administration's proposal— the Congressional Budget Office put a price tag of more than $15 billion a year on the Program for Better Jobs and Income—led to its rejection. The Reagan Administration's 1981 version was treated more favorably. Although Congress did not mandate a national program, the states could choose to implement workfare. The states that did so have often made further changes that have transformed it from a straight work requirement—in which recipients "pay back" society—to one that aims as much to assist people in leaving welfare as to have them fulfill an obligation while they are on welfare.

Lessons from the 1980s:
An Evaluation of State
Work/Welfare Initiatives

In passing the Omnibus Budget Reconciliation Act of 1981 (OBRA), Congress reflected a growing consensus on the need for welfare recipients to work and to become more self-supporting and, at the same time, uncertainty about the feasibility and effectiveness of the proposal for universal workfare. The legislation gave states a chance to experiment, albeit within the context of sharply reduced funding.

The Community Work Experience Program (CWEP), a provision of OBRA, made it possible for the first time for states to choose to make workfare mandatory for AFDC recipients. States also were authorized to fund on-the-job training programs by using a recipient's welfare grant as a wage subsidy for private employers. In addition, primarily through a new option known as the WIN Demonstration Program, they could change the institutional arrangements for delivering employment and training services and were allowed greater flexibility in the mix of these services. In many states, the OBRA possibilities seemed to trigger a new resolve on the part of state administrators to make WIN participation requirements more meaningful than they had been in the past.

In 1982, the Manpower Demonstration Research Corporation began a five-year social experiment to examine the new state work initiatives. MDRC's Demonstration of State Work/Welfare Initiatives is a series of large-scale evaluations in eight states and smaller-scale studies in three additional states. Major funding for the study was provided by the Ford Foundation, matched by grants from other private foundations and the participating states, which, in general, received no special operating funds.

As a result, the project is not a test of centrally developed and funded reform proposals, but of programs designed at the state level in the new environment of OBRA flexibility and constrained funding. And, because these initiatives are often the state's WIN Demonstration Program, the study for the first time provides rigorous answers on the effectiveness of the WIN Program in its 1980s WIN Demonstration incarnation.[6]

To ensure that the project produced findings of national relevance, the states selected are broadly representative of national variations in local conditions, administrative arrangements, and AFDC benefit levels— which, for a family of three in 1982 in the participating states ranged from a low of $140 per month in Arkansas to a high of $526 in California. Demonstration locations include all or part of several large urban areas—San Diego, Baltimore, and Chicago—and a number of large multicounty areas spanning both urban and rural centers in the states of Arkansas, Maine, New Jersey, Virginia, and West Virginia. (Table 1, on pages 16 and 17, summarizes the key features of the eight state programs and the different groups studied in each state.[7])

The study tests not one program model but a range of strategies, reflecting differences in state philosophies, objectives, and funding. Some states have limited their programs to one or two activities; others offer a wider mix. A few programs are voluntary, but most require participation as a condition of receiving welfare benefits.

In designing their programs, many states chose job-search activities and unpaid work experience. The job-search strategy is based on the assumption that many welfare recipients are currently employable but have not found jobs because they do not know how (or are not sufficiently motivated) to look for them. Job search does not train people for specific jobs but encourages and teaches them how to seek employment.

Two versions of mandatory unpaid work experience exist in six of the states. In the first, the CWEP or workfare version, work hours are determined by dividing the AFDC grant by the minimum wage. The work requirements can be either limited in duration or ongoing—that is, they last as long as the recipients remain on welfare. In the second version—usually called WIN Work Experience because it was first used in the national WIN Program—the number of hours worked is unrelated to the grant level and participation is generally limited to thirteen weeks.

Contrary to some expectations, the states in the study—reflecting the larger national response to OBRA—did not choose to implement universal workfare. Mandatory job search was more widely used. Among the demonstration states, only West Virginia (with its unusual labor market conditions) followed the model originally offered to the states as an option in the 1981 legislation: workfare with no limit on the length of a recipient's participation. The West Virginia program, however, was directed primarily to men receiving assistance under the AFDC program for unemployed heads of two-parent families (AFDC-U). The state placed less emphasis on workfare for women receiving AFDC.

Other programs (in Arkansas, San Diego, and Chicago) established a two-stage sequence consisting of job search followed by a work obligation (usually limited to thirteen weeks) for those who had not found unsubsidized jobs in the first phase. Virginia required job search of everyone and offered short-term workfare as a later option among other mandatory services. Baltimore operated a range of educational and training services (including job search and unpaid work experience), with participants' choices tailored to their needs and preferences. Two states—New Jersey and Maine—implemented voluntary on-the-job training programs with private employers, using the diversion of welfare grants as the funding mechanism.

The programs varied in scale. Although most were large, none covered the full AFDC caseload. Five operated in only part of the state. Most were targeted to women with school-

Table 1

Key Characteristics of State Work/Welfare Initiatives

State/City(a)	Program Model and Nature of Requirement to Participate(b)	Study Area(c)	Target Group
Arkansas	Mandatory program. Job-search workshop followed by individual job search and 12 weeks of work experience in public and private nonprofit agencies.	Pulaski South and Jefferson Counties	WIN-mandatory AFDC applicants and recipients including women with children aged 3 to 5.
San Diego, California	Mandatory program. Job-search workshop followed by 13 weeks of CWEP in public and private nonprofit agencies.	County-wide	WIN-mandatory AFDC and AFDC-U applicants.
Chicago, Illinois	Mandatory program. Individual job search followed by activities, including 13 weeks of work experience.	Cook County	WIN-mandatory AFDC applicants and recipients (including recently approved cases).

Maine	Voluntary program. Pre-vocational training, 12 weeks of work experience and on-the-job training funded by grant diversion.	Statewide	AFDC recipients on welfare for at least six consecutive months.
Baltimore, Maryland	Mandatory program. Multicomponent including job search, education, training, on-the-job training, and 13 weeks of work experience.	10 out of 18 Income-Maintenance Centers	WIN-mandatory AFDC and AFDC-U applicants and recipients.
New Jersey	Voluntary program. On-the-job training funded by grant diversion.	9 of 21 counties	WIN-mandatory and voluntary AFDC recipients.
Virginia	Mandatory program. Job search followed by 13 weeks of CWEP, education, or training.	11 of 124 agencies (4 urban, 7 rural)	WIN-mandatory AFDC applicants and recipients.
West Virginia	Mandatory program. CWEP—unlimited duration—in public and private nonprofit agencies.	9 of 27 administrative areas	WIN-mandatory AFDC and AFDC-U applicants and recipients.

Notes:

(a) In Arkansas and Maryland, a full evaluation was conducted in the indicated counties and a process study was done in other counties.

(b) In San Diego, Chicago, and Virginia there were two different experimental treatments.

(c) In addition to the study areas, Virginia and West Virginia implemented the program statewide and Arkansas, Illinois, and Maryland in selected other areas.

age children—the only group traditionally required to register with WIN—who typically represent about one-third of the adults heading AFDC cases. Some worked only with subsets of this mandatory group—for example, people who had recently applied for welfare and were new to the rolls—while others included both new applicants and those who were already welfare recipients. In addition, three programs required people receiving welfare through the AFDC-U program to participate.

The states also had different objectives. Some placed relatively more emphasis on developing human capital and helping welfare recipients obtain better jobs and long-term self-sufficiency. Others stressed immediate job placement and welfare savings. The states also varied in the extent to which they emphasized and enforced a participation requirement. Although most planned to increase participation above the levels achieved in WIN, few clearly articulated a goal of full or universal participation.

Interim Findings from the State Work Initiatives

The MDRC study is structured as a series of three-year evaluations in each state. Because the research activities were phased in at different times, the study extends over five years. Final results are now available from five of the programs—those in Arkansas, San Diego, Virginia, West Virginia, and Baltimore—and partial results are available from most of the others.[8]

The study addresses three basic questions. Each is discussed below, with the focus on overarching lessons, not on the full range of program-specific findings.

Is it feasible to impose obligations—or participation requirements—as a condition of welfare receipt? Pre-1981 welfare employment programs—both the WIN Program and several special demonstration programs—were generally unable to establish meaningful work-related obligations for recipients. A major question at the outset of the MDRC study was whether the existing bureaucracies would have greater success.

In some cases, the answer is "yes." In most of the states studied, participation rates are running above those in previous special demonstrations or in the WIN Program. Typically, within six to nine months of registering with the new program, about half of the AFDC group had taken part in some activity, and substantial additional numbers had left the welfare rolls and the program. Thus, for example, within nine months of welfare application in San Diego, all but a small proportion— 9 percent of the AFDC and 6 percent of the AFDC-U applicants—had either left welfare, become employed, were no longer in the program, or had fulfilled all of the program requirements. In some of the other states, the proportion of those still eligible and not reached by the program was as high as 25 percent, indicating a somewhat looser enforcement of the participation requirement. Overall, this represents a major management achievement and reflects a change in institutions and staff attitudes.

However, given the financial constraints under which states have been operating, one should not exaggerate the level of the services recipients have received or the intensity or scope of their participation obligation. By far the major activity has been job search, a relatively short-term and modest intervention. Education and training activities have been limited, and workfare, when it was required, has almost always been a short-term obligation—usually lasting thirteen weeks.

In part, this response reflects limited funds. The programs were relatively inexpensive, with average costs per enrollee ranging from $165 in Arkansas to $1,050 in Maryland. Had the typical obligation been longer or more intensive, it would have been necessary to raise the level of the initial investments in services. States have thus far managed to deliver services with generally modest funding. However, if resources remain low or are further depleted—or if the programs expand in scale—there is a risk of returning to the pre-1981 WIN approach of formal registration requirements and little real programmatic content.

What do workfare programs look like in practice, and how do welfare recipients view the mandatory work requirements?

Much of the workfare debate hinges on the nature of the worksite experience: that is, whether the positions are of a punitive and "make-work" nature or whether they produce useful goods and services, provide dignity, and develop work skills. MDRC addressed these questions by means of in-depth interviews with random samples of workfare supervisors and participants in six states. Results suggest that:

• The jobs were generally entry-level positions in maintenance, clerical work, park service, or human services.
• Although the positions did not primarily develop skills, they were not make-work either. Supervisors judged the work important and indicated that participants' productivity and attendance were similar to those of most entry-level workers.
• A large proportion of the participants responded positively to the work assignments. They were satisfied with the positions and with coming to work, and they believed they were making a useful contribution.
• Many participants nevertheless believed that the employer got the better end of the bargain, or that they were underpaid for their work. In brief, they would have preferred a paid job.

These findings suggest that most states did not design or implement workfare with a punitive intent. This may explain results from the worksite survey that indicated that the majority of the participants in most states shared the view that a work requirement was fair.[9] These results are consistent with findings from other studies that show that the poor want to work and are eager to take advantage of opportunities to do so. As one of MDRC's field researchers observed: these workfare programs did not create the work ethic, they found it.

Although this evidence is striking, it should not be used to draw conclusions about the quality of the programs or about the reactions of welfare recipients should workfare requirements be implemented on a larger scale, be differently designed, or last longer than the typical thirteen-week assignment in the states studied.

Do these initiatives make a difference? Do they reduce the welfare rolls and costs and/or increase employment and earnings? How do the programs' benefits compare to their costs? Experience suggests that these are very difficult questions to answer. Prior research shows that, contrary to popular conceptions, half of all welfare recipients normally move off the rolls—often to a job—within two years.[10] Thus, if a study points to the achievements or cost savings of a program based only on the performance of its participants—for example, based on job placements—it will overstate the program's accomplishments by taking credit for those who would have found jobs on their own. The challenge in assessing program achievements, or "impacts," is to distinguish between program-induced changes and the normal dynamics of welfare turnover and labor market behavior of this population. Accurate assessment requires data on what people would have done in the absence of the program: that is, data describing the behavior of a control group.

In eight of the states in MDRC's study, the research is structured to meet the major objection leveled at many earlier evaluations: that their control groups did not correctly mimic the behavior of the participants or that they had no control group at all. The human resources commissioners in these eight states acted with notable foresight. In an unusual display of commitment to high standards of program evaluation, they cooperated with the random assignment of more than 35,000 individuals to different groups, with some participating in the program (or several program variations) and some placed in a control group, receiving limited or no program services.

It is very rare to be able to conduct an evaluation with this degree of reliability. In fact, never before has a major part of the nation's employment and training system been assessed on this scale, using an "experimental" methodology based on random assignment. Typically, researchers have had to contend with studies that yield a great deal of data but produce little evidence about what the program has actually accomplished. Often, "results" merely show what would have happened to participants in the normal course of events. In contrast, a study using random assignment sets a demanding standard for what can be registered as change and accurately pinpoints the real achievements of the program.

Assessing the impact and the benefit-cost results to date is very much like looking at a glass and characterizing it as half full or half empty. Depending on one's perspective, there are real accomplishments or there is a basis for caution. In either case, the findings are complex and require a careful reading. The balance of this section presents the positive view and then discusses potential limitations on what the programs can achieve.

First, the results dispel the notion that employment and training interventions do not work. In light of the findings for these work/welfare initiatives, it is no longer defensible to argue that welfare employment initiatives have no value. Using a variety of approaches, four of the five programs studied thus far produced positive employment gains for AFDC women. The one exception was the workfare program in West Virginia, where the state's high unemployment and rural conditions severely limited job opportunities.

Table 2 (pages 24-27) compares the behavior over time of people in the "experimental" group (who were required to participate in the program) and people in the "control" group (who were not).[11] The results are for the primarily female AFDC group. As shown in the table, the program of mandatory job search followed by short-term workfare for AFDC applicants in San Diego increased the employment rate by 6 percentage points (from 55 percent to 61 percent) during the fifteen months of follow-up. Average total earnings during the same period—including the earnings of those who did not work as well as those who did—went up by $700 per person in the experimental group, representing a 23 percent increase over a control group member's average earnings. Roughly half of the gains in earnings came about because more women worked, and half because they obtained longer-lasting jobs or jobs with better pay or longer hours. The employment gains persisted, although at a somewhat reduced level, throughout the nearly eighteen months of follow-up.

In contrast, the program had minimal or no sustained employment effects on the primarily male group receiving AFDC-U assistance (not shown in Table 2).

As also indicated in Table 2, there were roughly similar employment gains in Arkansas, Maryland,[12] and Virginia, although the states varied dramatically in the subgroups of the AFDC rolls that they served and in the average earnings of the control groups.

The findings are quite different in West Virginia, where the relatively straightforward workfare program led to no increases in regular, unsubsidized employment. Although there are many possible explanations—including the design of the program or the characteristics of the women served—the most likely one—a weak state economy—was foreseen by the program's planners, who did not anticipate any employment gains. In a largely rural state with the nation's highest unemployment rate during part of the research period, a welfare employment initiative could provide a positive work experience without translating this into post-program unsubsidized employment gains.

West Virginia's program is a useful reminder that there are two sides to the labor market. Welfare employment programs focus on the supply side. In extreme cases, when the demand is not there, the provision of work experience and a change in the terms of the welfare "bargain" may simply not be enough to affect employment levels. Welfare recipients can be encouraged or required to take regular jobs, but the jobs must be available. The results to date suggest that demand constraints may be particularly acute in rural areas.[13]

The second positive finding is that the programs also led to some welfare savings although, compared to the effects on employment and earnings, the results were less consistent. In San Diego, over 18 months, average welfare payments per person in the experimental group were $288 below the average paid to members of the control group—a reduction in welfare outlays of almost 8 percent. Similar reductions occurred in Arkansas and Virginia but not in Baltimore and West Virginia. However, there was no evidence that, once people

Table 2
Summary of the Impact of AFDC Work/Welfare Programs
in San Diego, Baltimore, Arkansas, Virginia, and West Virginia

Outcome(a)	Experimentals	Controls	Difference	Decrease/Increase
San Diego—Applicants				
Ever Employed During 15 Months	61.0%	55.4%	+5.6%***	+10%
Average Total Earnings During 15 Months	$3802	$3102	+$700***	+23%
Ever Received AFDC Payments During 18 Months	83.9%	84.3%	-0.4%	0%
Average Number of Months Receiving AFDC Payments During 18 Months	8.13	8.61	-0.48*	-6%
Average Total AFDC Payments Received During 18 Months	$3409	$3697	-$288**	-8%
Baltimore—Applicants and Recipients				
Ever Employed During 12 Months	51.2%	44.2%	+7.0%***	+16%

Average Total Earnings During 12 Months	$1935	$1759	+$176	+10%
Ever Received AFDC Payments During 15 Months	94.9%	95.1%	−0.2%	0%
Average Number of Months Receiving AFDC Payments During 15 Months	11.14	11.29	−0.15	−1%
Average Total AFDC Payments Received During 15 Months	$3058	$3064	−$6	0%
Arkansas—Applicants and Recipients				
Ever Employed During 6 Months	18.8%	14.0%	+4.8%**	+34%
Average Total Earnings During 6 Months	$291	$213	+$78*	+37%
Ever Received AFDC Payments During 9 Months	72.8%	75.9%	−3.1%	−4%
Average Number of Months Receiving AFDC Payments During 9 Months	4.96	5.49	−0.53***	−10%
Average Total AFDC Payments Received During 9 Months	$772	$865	−$93***	−11%

Table 2 (continued)

Summary of the Impact of AFDC Work/Welfare Programs
in San Diego, Baltimore, Arkansas, Virginia, and West Virginia

Outcome(a)	Experimentals	Controls	Difference	Decrease/Increase
Virginia—Applicants and Recipients				
Ever Employed				
During 9 Months	43.8%	40.5%	+3.3%*	+8%
Average Total Earnings				
During 9 Months	$1119	$1038	+$81	+8%
Ever Received AFDC				
Payments During 12 Months	86.0%	86.1%	-0.1%	0%
Average Number of Months				
Receiving AFDC Payments				
During 12 Months	7.75	7.90	-0.14	-2%
Average Total AFDC				
Payments Received				
During 12 Months	$1923	$2007	-$84**	-4%
West Virginia—Applicants and Recipients				
Ever Employed				
During 15 Months	22.3%	22.7%	-0.4%	-2%
Average Total Earnings				
During 15 Months	$713	$712	$0	0%

Ever Received AFDC Payments During 21 Months	96.8%	96.0%	+0.8%	+1%
Average Number of Months Receiving AFDC Payments During 21 Months	14.26	14.46	−0.21	−1%
Average Total AFDC Payments Received During 21 Months	$2681	$2721	−$40	−1%

Source: Final reports from programs in San Diego, Baltimore, Arkansas, Virginia, and West Virginia.

Notes: These data include zero values for sample members not employed and for sample members not receiving welfare payments. The estimates are regression-adjusted using ordinary least squares, controlling for pre-random assignment characteristics of sample members. There may be some discrepancies in calculating experimental-control differences due to rounding.

* Denotes statistical significance at the 10 percent level; ** at the 5 percent level; and *** at the 1 percent level.

(a) The length of follow-up varied by outcome and state. Employment and earnings were measured by calendar quarters. To assure that pre-program earnings were excluded from the impact estimates, the follow-up period began after the quarter of random assignment. In contrast, AFDC benefits were tracked for quarters beginning with the actual month of random assignment. As a result, the follow-up period for AFDC benefits was at least three months longer than that for employment and earnings.

had applied for welfare, they were deterred from completing the application process by the obligation to participate in a work program.

A third encouraging piece of information is that the programs were often most helpful for certain segments of the welfare caseload. For example, employment increases were usually greater for women receiving AFDC than for men in two-parent households (AFDC-U), and for those without prior employment compared to those with a recent work history. Although women and those without recent employment were still less likely to be working and more likely to be on welfare than their more advantaged counterparts, the employment requirements and services of the workfare programs helped narrow the gap.[14]

When benefits were compared to costs, results were generally positive. An examination of the programs' effects on the government budget shows that, not surprisingly, such initiatives cost money upfront, but, in general, the investment pays off in future savings in five years or less. In San Diego, an average dollar spent on the program for AFDC women led to estimated budget savings over a five-year period of over $2. Programs in Arkansas and Virginia also had estimated budget savings, but in Baltimore and West Virginia, there were some net costs.[15]

The research also offers some unusual findings about the distribution of benefits across federal, state, and county budgets, a question not often addressed in benefit-cost studies. In San Diego, where a detailed study was conducted, all three levels of government gained, based on the particular funding formula and matching arrangements that were in place. However, the federal government bore more than half of the costs and enjoyed the greatest net savings. Indeed, had there been no federal funds—or had there been substantially less federal funding—the state and county would have had no financial incentive to run these programs.[16] The findings highlight the importance of continued federal support to encourage states to undertake welfare employment initiatives that may ultimately prove cost-effective to operate.

Another way to look at program benefits and costs is to examine them from the perspectives of the groups targeted for participation—i.e., those who might have earned more as a result of the program, but who also might have lost money because of reductions in welfare and other transfer payments, such as Medicaid and Food Stamps. In most cases, the AFDC women came out ahead, the exceptions being in Arkansas, a state with very low grants, where almost any employment led to case closings; and West Virginia, where there were no gains in earnings. For men on AFDC-U, the story was very different. There were overall losses, not gains, from the programs, as reductions in welfare and other transfer payments exceeded increases in earnings.

What about the empty side of the glass? In what way do the results suggest caution? It is important to note that, although the programs produced changes, the magnitude of those changes was relatively modest. Across states, increases in quarterly employment rates were between 3 and 9 percentage points, excluding West Virginia where there were no employment gains. (Quarterly rates are not shown in Table 2.) Earnings in the four other states increased from \$110 to \$560 a year (including persons who did not find employment and had no earnings). Thus, while it is worthwhile to operate these programs, they will not move substantial numbers of people out of poverty.

Issues and Lessons

Results to date from the work/welfare study suggest a number of major lessons.

It is feasible, under certain conditions and on the scale at which the demonstration programs were implemented, to tie the receipt of welfare to participation obligations. However, just as striking as the increases in participation these programs have achieved is the nature of the obligation. In most cases, it has been confined to job search, with workfare used only in a limited way for a relatively small number of people. This is due, in part, to funding constraints and to the sequencing of job search before work experience. It is also true that, when more funds have been available, states have often chosen to enrich the range of mandatory options rather than to impose a longer workfare requirement. The recent initiatives in California and Illinois include not only greater obligations but an expanded array of services beyond job search and workfare to such options as education, preparation for employment, and training.

A number of quite different ways of structuring and targeting these programs will yield effective results. Overall, the results do not point to a uniform program structure that merits national replication. Instead, one of the notable characteristics of these state welfare initiatives has been their diversity—in populations served, local conditions, and program design. A key explanation for the successful implementation of these initiatives may indeed be that states were given an opportunity to experiment and felt more ownership in the programs than they did in the earlier WIN Program, which was characterized by highly prescriptive central direction.

In cases in which states chose to operate mandatory workfare, the interim results do not support the strongest claims of critics or advocates. Despite critics' fears, workfare as implemented in the 1980s has been more often designed to provide useful work experience than simply to enforce a *quid pro quo*—although both objectives may be present. As a result, the work positions quite often resemble quality public service employment jobs, structured to meet public needs and to provide meaningful work experience. Under these conditions—when the jobs are considered worthwhile and the obligation is limited, as it is in most states—welfare recipients generally do not object to working for their grants.

On the other hand, the interim findings do not support the more extreme claims of proponents. The work positions developed few new skills. Although the San Diego findings provide some evidence that adding workfare after job search may increase a program's effectiveness, the West Virginia results are a cautious reminder that, at least in certain conditions, what is needed is not only workfare positions but regular jobs.[17] Furthermore, there was no evidence in San Diego that the work mandate, as it was administered, deterred individuals from completing their welfare applications or "smoked out" large numbers of AFDC women who held jobs with unreported income.

Thus, arguments for and against workfare—and participation obligations more broadly defined—may involve not so much a choice between those who want to reduce welfare costs and those who fear that the programs are coercive as an opportunity to change the values, politics, and perceived fairness of the welfare system. These issues remain prominent in state debates on policy options, in which questions of values are often as central as questions about likely savings. Some argue—as did the West Virginia welfare commissioner in 1982—that even if workfare costs more to begin with, its design is preferable because it fits with the nation's values and improves the image of welfare. In contrast, others continue to emphasize that what is needed is not requirements but jobs, as well as investments in training, education, and child care that will help people find the kinds of work that confer economic security in the long run.

The programs led to relatively modest increases in employment, which in some cases translated into even smaller welfare savings. Nonetheless, the changes were usually large enough to justify the programs' costs, although this finding varied by state and target group. For those accustomed to grandiose claims for social programs, the outcomes for these initiatives—as well as for other welfare employment programs—may look small. With gains that are not dramatic and only limited savings, the programs do not offer a cure for poverty or a short-cut to balancing the budget. This may prompt critics to reject these approaches, claiming that 3 to 9 percentage point gains in employment or 8 to 37 percent increases in earnings are unsatisfactory. There are, however, several reasons to conclude otherwise.

First, there is always a strong temptation to search for a simple solution to a complex problem. The welfare debate is filled with this kind of rhetoric. Now, faced with the reality of limited gains, it may be tempting to seek another "solution," for which there is no similar evidence. Yet, given the fact that reliable findings on the effects of social policies are rare, the striking feature of these programs is their consistently positive outcomes in a wide range of environments, with the sole exception of the very unusual circumstances in West Virginia. There is no comparable evidence on an alternative strategy.

Second, since the study measured changes for samples that were representative of large groups in the welfare caseload, results in the range of 5 percentage points take on added importance. The outcomes are also expressed as averages for a wide range of individuals, some of whom gained little or nothing from the program (including those who never received any services) and others who gained more. Thus, even relatively small changes, multiplied by large numbers of people, have considerable policy significance.

Third, the lessons from the demonstration suggest ways to make these programs more effective and provide evidence that some groups—for example, those without recent work histories—benefit more substantially than others.[18] Fourth, it is possible that the short-term effects may underestimate the longer-term gains, especially if attitudes toward AFDC shift as the concept of reciprocal obligations becomes more accepted. (On the other hand, there is evidence that, in some cases, effects that are initially positive may decay over time.)

Finally, the benefit-cost findings suggest that, within a relatively short time, program savings often offset costs, a balance that represents about as much as any social program has been able to achieve. While previous smaller-scale tests of special programs have produced cost-effective results, this study provides the first solid evidence of such outcomes in a major ongoing service delivery system. The ability to effect change on a large scale is an important new achievement.

Unanswered Questions

Although these state initiatives provide a wealth of information about the implementation and effectiveness of alternative approaches to reforming welfare with work, they leave unanswered a number of questions about the design and scale of programs.

The results summarized in this paper are for programs that have participation obligations of limited intensity, cost, or duration. They primarily required job search and short-term work experience. One unanswered question is whether more costly, comprehensive programs— providing either more services or longer obligations—would have greater effects.

Several states are using or plan to provide more intensive services or requirements, including educational remediation and training, and to complement these with extensive child-care services. Two examples are the Greater Avenues for Independence (GAIN) legislation in California and the Employment and Training (ET) Choices program in Massachusetts. Another more intensive approach is Supported Work, a program offering paid transitional work experience under conditions of close supervision, peer support, and generally increasing responsibilities.[19] Supported Work was tested as a voluntary program and found effective for women with histories of long-term welfare dependency. Although the incremental return to larger investments is not clear, the persistence of dependency for many, even after job search or short-term workfare, provides a rationale for states to offer more intensive services, while evaluating them to see whether they lead to long-term rewards.

A second open question concerns the broader implications of an ongoing participation requirement on family formation, the well-being of children, and attitudes toward work. It is important to note that child care was not a major issue in these programs, since their requirements were mostly short-term and limited mainly to women with school-age children. However, the availability and quality of child care would be much more important if either of these conditions changed, or if the programs made even larger differences in the rate at which women moved out of the home and into permanent jobs.

A third unanswered question is whether relatively low-cost mandatory programs will prove effective for the most disadvantaged groups of welfare recipients, those facing major barriers to employment (e.g., those with substantial language problems or educational deficiencies). Although there is evidence that the programs have a stronger impact on recipients who have some obstacles to employment—as opposed to the more job-ready who will find employment on their own —additional study is required to determine whether there is a threshold below which more intensive assistance is needed.[20]

A fourth unanswered question concerns the feasibility of operating larger-scale universal programs, and whether they would have the same results. The pre-1980 work mandates often foundered on legal, political, and bureaucratic obstacles, but the more recent large-scale initiatives in the MDRC study were implemented more smoothly.[21] It is not clear, however, whether work programs can be extended to an even greater share of the AFDC caseload (including the majority of AFDC women with younger children) without compromising quality, encountering political or administrative resistance, or raising broader issues such as whether welfare recipients would displace regular workers either during or after the program.[22]

Also, as the West Virginia findings suggest, in rural areas with very weak economic conditions, workfare serves as a jobs program, not as a transition to unsubsidized employment. A major unanswered question is the more precise relationship between the effectiveness of the programs and economic conditions, and whether this relationship is affected by the scale of the program.

In addition, all of the results were measured only over the short term. Whether these results persist, increase, or decay is important in judging the potential of the work/welfare approach.

Finally, while there is substantial information on the effectiveness of these programs, it remains unclear whether the achievements come from the services provided or from the mandatory aspect of the programs.[23] Although the distinction between mandatory and voluntary programs is sometimes not as great as one might think—since most nominally mandatory programs seek voluntary compliance and involvement—some differences exist and their importance remains uncertain.

General Conclusions About
Work/Welfare Programs

$\mathbf{A}$t the outset, this paper outlined the multiple goals of welfare policy and the continuing search for a balance that might more successfully provide income without distorting incentives for work or family formation. MDRC's five-year experiment testing limited work requirements has provided some new evidence to inform this debate. As expected, the lessons are complex.

The continuing interest in work solutions, even in states with very weak labor markets, is testimony to the important political and value issues inherent in the debate. Issues of equity, concerns about a system that may send the wrong signals or encourage long-term dependency, the stigma associated with public assistance, and the widespread unpopularity of the welfare system—all of these have pushed states to add some type of an obligation to AFDC. However, the interest in such programs continues to be tempered by funding constraints and an understandable unwillingness to set up ones that stress obligations at the expense of providing opportunities that help people move off the rolls or of assuring the well-being of children.

The results of recent research suggest that introducing a stronger work emphasis into the AFDC program ultimately will not cost but save money—although it will cost money in the short run. Thus, the claims of both critics and advocates described earlier contain a measure of truth. In the past, social programs have been oversold and then discredited when they failed to cure problems. In contrast these findings provide a timely warning that welfare employment initiatives will not be a panacea but can provide meaningful improvement. The extent of the changes, however, suggests that the major arguments may continue to center around politics and values as well as the different ways to increase the programs' effectiveness.

The modest nature of the improvements also indicates that welfare employment obligations can be only part of a "solution" to poverty. Other reforms—for example, changes in the tax laws and expansion of the earned income tax credit to increase the rewards for work, educational reforms, training and retraining, increased child-support enforcement, and job-creation programs—are important complements if welfare is not only to be made more politically acceptable but also to succeed in reducing poverty substantially.

The fact that there is support for work programs—within the general public and the welfare population—argues for a welfare reform approach that promotes and also rewards work. Workfare, narrowly defined, does the former, but to the extent that it does not deter dependency or assist many people off the welfare rolls, it may not provide enough added income and adequately combat dependency. What this suggests is that there be both requirements within the welfare system and added opportunities and rewards for leaving welfare. "Sticks" may be a part of the solution, but "carrots" are also merited if work is to be more an alternative to than a punishment for being poor.

Notes

1. The research for the study of state work/welfare initiatives has been supported by the Ford, Winthrop Rockefeller, and Claude Worthington Benedum foundations, the Congressional Research Service of the Library of Congress, and the states of Arizona, Arkansas, California, Florida, Illinois, Maine, Maryland, New Jersey, Texas, Virginia, and West Virginia. The research and the conclusions reached by the author, however, do not necessarily reflect the official positions of the funders.

2. The author wishes to acknowledge with gratitude the helpful comments made on an earlier draft of this paper by Gordon Berlin of the Ford Foundation and Robert Reischauer of the Brookings Institution, as well as those made by members of MDRC staff, including Michael Bangser, Daniel Friedlander, Barbara Goldman, and James Riccio.

3. That is, the findings showed that the impact of changing the AFDC income floor and tax rate for persons currently eligible was relatively small, but the impact on the number eligible for assistance was large. As a result, work reductions—which were modest for the current caseload— could become larger when combined with the work reductions of persons newly eligible. Moreover, a substantial share of the additional cost of extending AFDC to two-parent households would simply go toward replacing reduced earnings rather than raising income.

4. Both plans are sometimes called two-track approaches, since AFDC recipients would be divided into those required to work (e.g., women with children six years and over) and those not expected to work (e.g., women with responsibilities for young children).

5. See, for example, the discussion in Gould-Stuart, 1982.

6. For a more detailed discussion of the design of the study and the interim findings, see Gueron, 1986.

7. In Table 1, "AFDC" refers to welfare cases that are usually headed by a single parent, usually a woman; "AFDC-U" refers to cases headed by two parents (with the principal earner unemployed) and where the targeted participant is usually male. All AFDC-U case heads are required to register with the WIN program (i.e., are "WIN-mandatory") as are most AFDC case heads with children at least six years of age. "Applicants" are individuals who were studied from the time at which they applied for welfare, and some of whom subsequently became welfare recipients (but continue to be called applicants in this study). "Recipients" are individuals who were receiving welfare benefits when the study began. (In some states, the study was limited to those recipients who had just become WIN-mandatory; in other cases the program covered the full range of recipients.)

8. The final reports now available are: Friedlander et al., 1985a; Friedlander et al., 1985b; Friedlander et al., 1986b; Goldman et al., 1986; and Riccio et al., 1986. Interim findings from the studies are included in the following reports: Auspos, 1985; Ball, 1984; Goldman et al., 1984; Goldman et al., 1985; MDRC, 1985; Price, 1985; Quint, 1984a; Quint, 1984b; Quint and Guy, 1986. In a number of these states, data are currently being collected that will extend the follow-up for a longer period of time.

9. The same survey was recently conducted with participants and supervisors in New York City's workfare program. Although in general the results were similar to those in the other six states, it appears that participants in New York City, Chicago, and Baltimore shared less favorable views about

mandatory work obligations than those in the other areas. Nevertheless, the majority of participants in these cities perceived these obligations as being fair. See Hoerz and Hanson, 1986, p. 32.

10. Bane and Ellwood, 1983; and Ellwood, 1986.

11. People were assigned to the experimental or control groups when they applied for welfare, were required to register with the WIN program, or had their WIN status reviewed. As discussed above, not all experimentals actually participated in program activities or (if they were new applicants) received welfare payments. In addition, although controls could not receive special program services, they were eligible for other employment and training services in the community and sometimes for regular WIN services. For a further explanation of cross-state differences in sample composition, control services, or experimental participation patterns, see the detailed final reports on each state.

12. In Maryland, the length of follow-up was notably short, given the longer duration of program services for some participants. To ensure that the study did not mistake the program's accomplishments, additional work is now under way to determine whether the measured impacts increase or decay over a longer period.

13. The Virginia and Arkansas studies also showed lower or no employment gains in rural, as compared to urban areas. See Riccio et al., 1986; and Friedlander et al., 1985a.

14. A preliminary study suggests that this pattern of differences is not as clear for long-term recipients. See Friedlander and Long, 1987.

15. As indicated in footnote 12, the Baltimore results may change when data covering a longer follow-up period become available.

16. For San Diego the benefit-cost analysis showed that the benefits to the state and county exceeded their costs by $314 per experimental. For the federal government the comparable net benefit was $676 per experimental. Total costs were estimated at $636 per experimental, of which the federal

government paid $443, or 70 percent, and the state and county paid $193, or 30 percent. If most of the federal costs had been shifted to the state and county, their overall costs would have exceeded their share of program benefits, eliminating any incentive to operate the program. See Goldman et al., 1986 and unpublished data.

17. One unusual feature of the San Diego study was the simultaneous random assignment of AFDC applicants to a control group and to two experimental treatments: job search alone and job search followed by short-term workfare. The results showed that job search alone also had positive impacts (i.e., employment gains and welfare savings), but the findings were less consistent and the gains in earnings smaller than for the combined program.

This suggests that, under certain circumstances, employment impacts may be greater if individuals who do not find employment in job-search workshops are required to meet a short-term work obligation. For further discussion of the findings for the programs in San Diego and West Virginia, see Goldman et al., 1986; and Friedlander et al., 1986b.

18. In addition, data on changes in the distribution of income provide some tentative information on possible ways to improve such programs in the future. For example, the Baltimore initiative (a relatively more intensive program with not only job search, but also work experience, education, and training) was more likely to move some individuals into higher categories of earnings (i.e., earnings above a full-time, minimum-wage job) than the Arkansas program (a very low-cost version of job search).

Other results suggest that the level of welfare grants is also important, since in states with high grants, employment increases more often resulted in net gains in total income (i.e., earnings plus welfare payments). See Friedlander, et al., 1985b; Friedlander et al., 1985a; and Goldman et al., 1986.

19. MDRC, 1980.

20. See Friedlander and Long, 1987.

21. See Gueron and Nathan, 1985, for a summary of this earlier experience.

22. A study of another type of job guarantee—paid work experience for youths as opposed to unpaid workfare for welfare recipients—suggested a possible trade-off between job quality and displacement. See Ball et al., 1981.

23. Other studies, not reported in this paper, show that voluntary job-search and work-experience programs also are effective for AFDC women. See Manpower Demonstration Research Corporation, 1980, and Wolfhagen, 1983.

References

Auspos, Patricia; with Ball, Joseph; Goldman, Barbara; and Gueron, Judith. 1985. *Maine: Interim Findings From a Grant Diversion Program*. New York: Manpower Demonstration Research Corporation.

Ball, Joseph; and Wolfhagen, Carl; with Gerould, David; and Solnick, Loren. 1981. *The Participation of Private Businesses as Work Sponsors in the Youth Entitlement Demonstration*. New York: Manpower Demonstration Research Corporation.

Ball, Joseph; with Hamilton, Gayle; Hoerz, Gregory; Goldman, Barbara; and Gueron, Judith. 1984. *West Virginia: Interim Findings on the Community Work Experience Demonstrations*. New York: Manpower Demonstration Research Corporation.

Bane, Mary Jo; and Ellwood, David T. 1983. *The Dynamics of Dependence: The Routes to Self-Sufficiency*. Cambridge, Mass.: Urban Systems Research and Engineering, Inc.

Ellwood, David T. 1986. *Targeting "Would-Be" Long-Term Recipients of AFDC*. Princeton, New Jersey: Mathematica Policy Research, Inc.

Friedlander, Daniel; Hoerz, Gregory; Quint, Janet; Riccio, James; with Goldman, Barbara; Gueron, Judith; and Long, David. 1985a. *Arkansas: Final Report on the WORK Program in Two Counties*. New York: Manpower Demonstration Research Corporation.

Friedlander, Daniel; Hoerz, Gregory; Long, David; Quint, Janet; with Goldman, Barbara; and Gueron, Judith. 1985b. *Maryland: Final Report on the Employment Initiatives Evaluation.* New York: Manpower Demonstration Research Corporation.

Friedlander, Daniel; Goldman, Barbara; Gueron, Judith; and Long, David. 1986a. "Initial Findings From the Demonstration of State Work/Welfare Initiatives," *The American Economic Review* 76: pp. 224-229.

Friedlander, Daniel; Erickson, Marjorie; Hamilton, Gayle; Knox, Virginia; with Goldman, Barbara; Gueron, Judith; and Long, David. 1986b. *West Virginia: Final Report on the Community Work Experience Demonstrations.* New York: Manpower Demonstration Research Corporation.

Friedlander, Daniel; and Long, David. 1987. "A Study of Performance Measures and Subgroup Impacts in Three Welfare Employment Programs." New York: Manpower Demonstration Research Corporation.

Goldman, Barbara; Gueron, Judith; Ball, Joseph; Price, Marilyn; with Friedlander, Daniel; and Hamilton, Gayle. 1984. *Preliminary Findings From the San Diego Job Search and Work Experience Demonstration.* New York: Manpower Demonstration Research Corporation.

Goldman, Barbara; Friedlander, Daniel; Gueron, Judith; Long, David; with Hamilton, Gayle; and Hoerz, Gregory. 1985. *Findings From the San Diego Job Search and Work Experience Demonstration.* New York: Manpower Demonstration Research Corporation.

Goldman, Barbara; Friedlander, Daniel; Long, David; with Erickson, Marjorie; and Gueron, Judith. 1986. *Final Report on the San Diego Job Search and Work Experience Demonstration.* New York: Manpower Demonstration Research Corporation.

Gould-Stuart, Joanna, 1982. *Welfare Women in A Group Job Search Program: Their Experiences in the Louisville WIN Research Laboratory Project.* New York: Manpower Demonstration Research Corporation.

Gueron, Judith M. 1986. *Work Initiatives For Welfare Recipients: Lessons From a Multi-State Experiment.* New York: Manpower Demonstration Research Corporation.

Gueron, Judith. 1985. "The Demonstration of State Work/ Welfare Initiatives." *Randomization and Field Experimentation: New Directions for Program Evaluation,* No. 28, pp. 5-13.

Gueron, Judith; and Nathan, Richard. 1985. "The MDRC Work/Welfare Project: Objectives, Status, Significance." *Policy Studies Review* 4: pp. 417-432.

Hoerz, Gregory; and Hanson, Karla. 1986. "A Survey of Participants and Worksite Supervisors in the New York City Work Experience Program." New York: Manpower Demonstration Research Corporation.

Manpower Demonstration Research Corporation. 1985. *Baseline Paper on the Evaluation of the WIN Demonstration Program in Cook County, Illinois.* New York: Manpower Demonstration Research Corporation.

Manpower Demonstration Research Corporation. 1980. *Summary and Findings of the National Supported Work Demonstration.* Cambridge, Mass.: Ballinger Publishing Co.

Price, Marilyn; with Ball, Joseph; Goldman, Barbara; Gruber, David; Gueron, Judith; and Hamilton, Gayle. 1985. *Interim Findings From the Virginia Employment Services Program.* New York: Manpower Demonstration Research Corporation.

Quint, Janet; with Goldman, Barbara; and Gueron, Judith. 1984a. *Interim Findings From the Arkansas WIN Demonstration Program.* New York: Manpower Demonstration Research Corporation.

Quint, Janet; with Ball, Joseph; Goldman, Barbara; Gueron, Judith; and Hamilton, Gayle. 1984b. *Interim Findings From the Maryland Employment Initiatives Programs.* New York: Manpower Demonstration Research Corporation.

Quint, Janet; Guy, Cynthia; with Hoerz, Gregory; Hamilton, Gayle; Ball, Joseph; Goldman, Barbara; and Gueron, Judith. 1986. *Interim Findings From the Illinois WIN*

Demonstration Program in Cook County. New York: Manpower Demonstration Research Corporation.

Riccio, James; Cave, George; Freedman, Stephen; Price, Marilyn; with Friedlander, Daniel; Goldman, Barbara; Gueron, Judith; and Long, David. 1986. *Final Report on the Virginia Employment Services Program.* New York: Manpower Demonstration Research Corporation.

Wolfhagen, Carl; with Goldman, Barbara. 1983. *Job Search Strategies: Lessons from the Louisville WIN Laboratory Project.* New York: Manpower Demonstration Research Corporation.

38

Workfare: The Poverty/Dependence Trade-Off

Michael Morris and John B. Williamson

Conservative critiques of the American welfare state in the 1980s (e.g., Gilder, 1980; Mead, 1986; Murray, 1984) have helped, perhaps inadvertently, to crystallize a key dilemma for policymakers: Should poverty reduction or dependency reduction be assigned a higher priority in the formulation of poverty policy? At first glance this does not seem to be a choice that policymakers should have to make. Cannot both objectives be sought simultaneously? Indeed, isn't increased self-sufficiency the surest escape from poverty?

Our analysis indicates that the answer is, "Not necessarily." To the extent that this analysis is valid, it suggests that a fundamental reorientation of our thinking about the potentials and limits of poverty policy is called for. This would entail a reexamination of workfare, a strategy that is at the heart of the current welfare reform zeitgeist (e.g., Gueron, 1986, 1987; Kaus, 1986; Mead, 1986; U.S. General Accounting Office, 1987a). Specifically, what does workfare offer to those who have traditionally identified with liberal approaches to poverty policy? We believe that it offers both more—and less—than is commonly supposed.

Poverty Reduction versus Dependency Reduction

Poverty and dependency represent distinct, though potentially related, social phenomena. The former concept emphasizes the *level* of one's

From *Social Policy,* Vol. 18, No. 1 (1987): 13–16, 49–50. Copyright 1987 by Social Policy Corporation.

income, while the latter focuses on the *source* of that income. To the extent that an individual does not have enough income to maintain an "adequate" standard of living, one is poor. And to the extent that one's income, whatever its level, comes from government transfers, one is dependent. In theory, then, a society could be characterized by high levels of poverty and dependency, low levels of both, or be high on one dimension and low on the other.

Within a social policy context, conservatives have traditionally been much more interested in minimizing dependency than in eliminating poverty. Consequently, they tend to look askance at reductions in the poverty rate that are achieved through government transfers. Mead (1986), for example, asserts that "policymakers have not really solved poverty, only exchanged it for the problem of large-scale dependency." This is a very unsatisfactory exchange from the perspective of an ideology which holds that "economic independence—standing on one's own abilities and accomplishments—is of paramount importance in determining the quality of a family's life" (Murray, 1984). Thus, victories over poverty that are won at the expense of self-sufficiency give little cause for celebration. The key to well-being lies less in the standard of living one achieves than in *how* one has achieved it.

In fairness, it must be noted that most conservatives do not deny that poverty per se is a phenomenon worthy of policymakers' attention. They are quick to claim, however, that reducing dependency is the most effective and efficient route to reducing poverty. In this context, dependency-reduction interventions can attempt to increase the poor's human capital either directly or indirectly. Direct approaches include strategies such as job/skill training and educational assistance, while the lowering or termination of welfare benefits is frequently seen by conservatives as a powerful indirect strategy.

The conceptual model that links the *direct* approaches to reduced dependency is self-evident. In the case of the *indirect* approach, it is assumed that the decreased value or availability of government transfers will, in the long run, motivate individuals to gain the skills and experiences necessary to support themselves and their families at above-poverty-line levels (Murray, 1984). A belief in the character-building potential of poverty is clearly an important component of this line of reasoning (Miller, 1969).

It is true that not everyone could be counted on to respond to this indirect approach by developing the motivation needed for long-term upward economic mobility. The poverty of this recalcitrant, "underserving" subgroup would be deemed by the conservative perspective to be justified and functional for the society as a whole. (Conservatives generally acknowledge the necessity of providing government transfers to those whom they regard as being "deserving" or truly "needy" such as the mentally or physically disabled.) Most conservative analyses strongly imply, however, that the *overall* level of poverty in a society dominated by the indirect model would be lower than that currently observed in the United States (e.g., Murray, 1984). In the short run, of course, poverty would be expected to increase.

In contrast to conservatives, liberals generally place greater emphasis on reducing poverty than on minimizing dependency, at least in the short run (e.g., Ellwood and Summers, 1986). Dependency, while viewed as undesirable, is regarded as less debilitating and injurious to one's quality of life than unrelieved poverty. Consequently, liberals are much more likely than conservatives to endorse programs that provide direct economic assistance (AFDC, Food Stamps) but which, by their very nature, place participants in an economically dependent position vis-à-vis the government.

Liberals frequently claim, however, that the well-being that results from reduced poverty can, in the long run, increase the ability of many recipients to become nonpoor through their own efforts (Williamson et al., 1975). In essence, then, it is being asserted that programs which increase dependency in the short run can, in the long run, help reduce dependency.

When these liberal predictions are viewed in conjunction with the short- and long-run predictions offered by conservatives when advocating reductions in government transfers, an interesting pattern emerges. Liberals claim that the long-term impact of generous government transfers on dependency reduction will be positive, even though their short-term impact will be negative. In a parallel fashion, conservatives argue that the long-run impact of small or nonexistent transfers on poverty reduction will be positive, even though their short-term impact will be negative. Not surprisingly, neither liberals nor conservatives are willing to accept the validity of the long-term predictions made by the other. Indeed, this mutual skepticism is at the very core of the two groups' ideological incompatibility.

While liberals generally recoil at the indirect, termination-of-benefits approach to dependency reduction, they wholeheartedly endorse the training, educational, and other interventions associated with the direct strategy. In fact, it is they, and not conservatives, who have traditionally provided the greatest support for government-sponsored programs in these areas, as historians of the War on Poverty have noted (Friedman, 1977; Patterson, 1981).

What the preceding discussion suggests is that liberals and conservatives differ less in their long-term *objectives* concerning poverty and dependency reduction than in the *means* they prefer for reaching them. The following section brings empirical evidence to bear in an analysis of the competing claims made for the effectiveness of these means.

Options for Poverty Policy

At the far right of the ideological spectrum is the proposal to eliminate virtually all government transfers to the poor, an approach whose most notable spokesman in the past few years has been Murray (1984). A less conservative approach, and one that is increasingly drawing the attention of moderates and liberals, is workfare. The essence of this strategy is that able-bodied welfare recipients must work in return for their benefits. The nature of the work performed is less important than the fact that the recipient engages in labor. Thus, from this perspective there is nothing necessarily undesirable about individuals being assigned to menial, dead-end jobs as a condition for receiving assistance.

The value of workfare is seen as primarily residing in the social message it sends to both recipients and non-recipients: The expected state of affairs in society is that one's income is the result of one's labor, and this exchange should not cease to function just because one is receiving government transfers (Mead, 1986). To the extent that this message is strongly and consistently delivered through workfare, it is predicted that individuals will be more effectively socialized to engage in behaviors that can prevent or ameliorate their own dependency.

Workfare incorporates elements of both direct and indirect approaches to dependency reduction. The experiences and skills gained through workfare jobs, even low-skill ones, can directly increase participants' chances of obtaining unsubsidized employment. In addition, some individuals will refrain from applying for public assistance altogether because they wish to avoid the associated work requirements. The dependency of this subgroup on government transfers is thereby reduced. Moreover, it is likely that a portion of this subgroup will eventually find employment in the private sector.

From a policymaking perspective, it is important to note that inherent in the endorsement of the workfare approach is the acceptance, or at least tolerance, of a system of government transfers to which the work requirements are attached. In general, however, workfare advocates—especially conservative ones—are not enthusiastic about such transfers and prefer that they be kept low so that employees in the low-wage labor market are not tempted to leave their jobs to qualify for workfare.

A more liberal approach to the issues of work and self-sufficiency can be found in the education and training strategy, of which the War on

Poverty was a prime example. There is more of an emphasis here on ability development and skill-building than in the workfare model. In addition, issues of motivation and socialization are addressed in a less heavy-handed, sanction-oriented fashion than in workfare. Hence, the overall thrust of the education and training approach is less oriented to the social control of participants, and more focused on their voluntary self-development.

Given this background, it should not be surprising that the models of workfare that appeal most to moderates and liberals are those that include a heavy dose of education and training. Liberal support for harsher, less enriched versions of workfare is relatively weak. In this context it is noteworthy that liberals and conservatives frequently use a single label—workfare—to encompass a variety of programmatic approaches reflecting different ideological perspectives. Thus, there is in reality less consensus about how to accomplish welfare reform than the current popularity of the term "workfare" would suggest (U.S. General Accounting Office, 1987a).

Finally, at the far left of the policy spectrum is the comprehensive welfare state characterized by a guaranteed annual income at or near the poverty line. Poverty reduction is clearly accorded primary importance in this scenario. While this perspective views dependency reduction and self-sufficiency as worthwhile social objectives, it maintains that society's first obligation is to provide all of its citizens with a minimally adequate standard of living. Consequently, the issue of work requirements, which plays so prominent a role in workfare, receives much less attention here. It is not so much that welfare-state supporters believe that these requirements are trivial or inherently undesirable. Rather, they fear that preoccupation with the work issue will divert attention from, and ultimately undermine support for, the much more important goal of poverty reduction.

For each of the four major policy options, the predictions that supporters would make for the impact of that option on poverty and dependency are presented in Figure 38.1. Both the short- and long-term predictions take as their point of departure the current levels of poverty and dependency in American society. It is noteworthy that the long-term predictions for the four options are all in the same direction. To be sure, supporters of the various approaches would acknowledge that these long-term decreases would probably differ in magnitude from one strategy to the other. For example, there would almost certainly be more poverty in a society where the most conservative option prevailed than in one where the most liberal one did. And there would be more dependency in the latter than in the former. Indeed, those differences are consistent with the differing priorities—poverty reduction or dependency reduction—of those endorsing the

FIGURE 38.1
Four Approaches to Poverty Policy: Advocates' Predictions

Approaches		Predicted Impact	
		Short-term	Long-term
Dismantled Welfare State	Poverty	up	down
	Dependency	down	down
Workfare	Poverty	no change	down
	Dependency	down	down
Education and Training	Poverty	no change	down
	Dependency	no change	down
Generous Welfare State	Poverty	down	down
	Dependency	up	down

strategies. A review of the empirical evidence, however, suggests conclusions concerning the relative efficacy of the four approaches that go beyond the self-evident comparisons just drawn.

Differences in Poverty Efficacy

Countless studies have been conducted over the years to evaluate the impact of programs representing the poverty-reduction and dependency-reduction approaches. While it is beyond the scope of this article to examine this literature in detail, the findings encountered in such a review are consistent enough to be meaningfully summarized. The crux of this summary can be stated briefly: The antipoverty impact of government transfer programs is significantly greater than the antipoverty impact of dependency-reduction programs (Morris and Williamson, 1986). The former programs include those offering either cash or in-kind assistance such as Social Security, Aid to Families with Dependent Children (AFDC), Supplemental Security Income (SSI), Unemployment Insurance, Food Stamps, subsidized housing, and Medicaid and Medicare. The most prominent dependency-reduction efforts include job/skill training, educational interventions (e.g., compensatory education), and social services (e.g., counseling, family-planning services).

There are, of course, significant differences in the antipoverty performance of programs *within* the government-transfer and dependency-reduction categories. For example, many dependency-reduction interventions do have some positive economic impact, and it can even be argued that a few are highly effective such as the Job Corps, supported work for welfare mothers, and contraceptive services for adolescents (see Forrest et al., 1981; Hollister et al., 1984; Long et al., 1981). Where transfer programs are concerned, Social Security is by far the most effective, helping to reduce the poverty rate among the elderly from 35 percent in 1959 to 12 percent in 1985. AFDC, on the other hand, provides a level of support to participants that is painfully modest (Danziger et al., 1986; U.S. Bureau of the Census, 1986). Important as these within-group differences are, they should not obscure the basic point that, overall, transfer programs out-perform dependency-reduction ones in generating economic benefits for participants.

Critics of the transfer approach claim that estimates of its positive economic impact tend to be very inflated. They maintain that most estimates fail to take into account the influence that these programs have on the labor supply, birth rates, and other factors related to low-income status (e.g., Gwartney and Stroup, 1986; O'Neill, 1986; Plotnick, 1984). As Orr and Skidmore (1982) succinctly observe: "Any receipt of cash or goods that is not a reward for work by definition makes work less necessary, because the recipient can enjoy a given level of consumption while working less than would otherwise be the case." To the extent that individuals respond to this incentive structure by actually working less than they would in the absence of the transfer program, some of the poverty that is "alleviated" by the intervention has in fact been created by it.

The available evidence indicates that these behavioral responses to assistance are modest in magnitude (Morris and Williamson, 1986; U.S. General Accounting Office, 1987b), and certainly are far less than those suggested or implied by some of the more publicized conservative analyses (e.g., Murray, 1984). Thus, it is highly unlikely that more refined estimates of antipoverty impact would significantly alter the major conclusion that transfer programs are superior to dependency-reduction efforts in fighting poverty (see, however, Browning and Johnson, 1986).

Analyzing Poverty Assumptions

Why is it that transfer programs are found to have a greater antipoverty impact than dependency-reduction ones? One reason would seem to be methodological. The impact of most cash and in-kind programs on a participant's economic status is immediate and relatively easy to measure. The impact of most dependency-reduction programs is not. The economic benefits of the latter programs are usually not expected to be noticeable for some time. (Note the "no change" predictions for poverty in the workfare and education/training categories in Figure 1.) Indeed, in the case of educational interventions, it may be a decade or more before economic payoffs are supposed to occur. Assessing economic outcomes under these circumstances is an exceedingly difficult and imprecise task. As a result, evaluation studies may be underestimating the full impact of dependency-reduction programs on participants.

It is doubtful, however, that these methodological problems account for more than a small percentage of the differences in program efficacy that have been observed. A much more important reason would appear to be differences between the two strategies in the assumptions that must be met in order for them to have a significant antipoverty impact. Transfer programs tend to involve relatively short chains of assumptions, with the individual assumptions in these chains being relatively easy to satisfy. In contrast, dependency-reduction interventions usually require relatively long chains of assumptions, with individual assumptions being relatively difficult to satisfy. Both the length of the chains and the stringency of individual assumptions appear to contribute to the differential effectiveness of the two approaches.

Consider, for example, a transfer program such as Social Security. In order for it to have a significant economic impact on participants, two conditions must be met: the amount of assistance rendered must be non-negligible and this assistance must actually be received by participants (i.e., Social Security checks must be successfully delivered to them).

Compare these assumptions with those required by a dependency-reduction program such as skill training for employment:

1. Participants must possess or develop the motivation and ability necessary to learn the skills being taught.
2. The model of skill training that is used must be educationally sound.
3. Training must be at a sufficiently high level to qualify program graduates, in either the short or the long run, for jobs paying nonpoverty wages.
4. These jobs must actually be available in the communities where program graduates reside, or in communities they can move to.
5. Graduates must have the ability and motivation to hold onto these jobs once they obtain them.
6. The local, regional, and/or national economy must be vigorous enough to support the continued existence of these jobs.

It is clear that the length of the skill-training assumption chain is much longer than that of Social Security. This puts the skill-training intervention at a disadvantage since, all other things being equal, the greater the number of assumptions required by a program, the lower the probability that all of them will be met. (The only exceptions would be those unlikely cases in which the probability of success for every assumption was 100 percent). Thus, even if *each* of the assumptions associated with these two programs had the same high probability of success, say, 90 percent, the *overall* probability of skill training generating significant economic benefits for a given participant (53 percent) would still be much lower than the corresponding probability for Social Security (81 percent).

The vulnerability of lengthy assumption chains is perhaps most vividly demonstrated by the fact that five of the skill-training assumptions might have 100 percent probabilities of success, but the overall chances of the intervention succeeding would only be 20 percent if the sixth assumption had a 20 percent success probability. No chain is stronger than its weakest link, and long chains present more opportunities for weak links than strong ones.

The extended time frame required by most dependency-reduction interventions and the indirect route through which they are supposed to exert economic impact are primarily responsible for their relatively long assumption chains. To the extent that both of these features are inherent to the dependency-reduction strategy, it is unlikely that the assumption chains associated with most of these interventions can be appreciably shortened.

The *nature* of dependency-reduction assumptions is also problematical. These assumptions frequently call for changes in the participants' motivation, ability, values, beliefs, or attitudes. Achieving significant change on these dimensions through social-policy interventions has traditionally been a very difficult task. In other words, the probability of satisfying these assumptions tends to be low when compared with the chances of fulfilling the assumptions associated with transfer programs, e.g., successfully delivering a Social Security check.

Most dependency-reduction efforts also involve assumptions over which the program itself has no direct, or even indirect, control. These assumptions frequently focus on the ability of the labor market to provide employment to motivated job-seekers. If these assumptions had high probabilities of success in their own right, the fact that dependency-reduction interventions had little control over them would not be particularly problematical. For the most part, however, this appears not to be the case. It has long been recognized, for example, that local job markets frequently experience great difficulty in absorbing the graduates of skill-training programs. Indeed, this was one of the most common criticisms of training programs during the War on Poverty (e.g., Levin, 1977).

In contrast to the dependency-reduction approach, transfer programs tend to place much less emphasis—at least in the short run—on change-oriented assumptions and assumptions that are beyond their control. Thus, even if the assumption chains of the two types of programs were equal in length, there would still be reason to expect the transfer strategy to have significantly greater economic impact. Once again, it is unclear how these problematical assumptions could be removed from most dependency-reduction programs; they seem to be inherent to the approach.

Those who expect the transfer approach to reduce dependency in the long run must contend with the same assumption-related problems that affect the ability of the dependency-reduction strategy to reduce poverty: long assumption chains, change-oriented assumptions, and assumptions beyond the control of the intervention. It should not be surprising, then, that there is no strong empirical evidence demonstrating that transfer programs have a long-term positive impact on self-sufficiency. If anything, the evidence suggests that there might be a slight negative impact on self-sufficiency in the long run (Bane and Ellwood, 1983; Browning and Johnson, 1986; Hill et al., 1985).

None of the four approaches are likely to be effective at bringing about major reductions in both poverty *and* dependency. The only strategy that is likely to reduce poverty to negligible levels is the guaranteed-income approach. This is because it is the only one that avoids the lengthy, difficult assumption chains inherent to the dependency-reduction strategy. There is, however, a price to be paid for the poverty-reduction potency of the guaranteed-income approach: dependency for a substantial segment of the population. This is the inevitable trade-off that policymakers must confront. Put another way, if poverty is defined such that the only way to solve it is through greatly increased self-sufficiency, our analysis suggests that there is no realistic solution to the problem of poverty in the United States.

Workfare Reexamined

The conclusions we have presented call into question the unbridled enthusiasm that has greeted workfare in many quarters. Insofar as workfare simply attempts to reduce poverty through increased self-sufficiency, it is unlikely that a major impact on poverty will result. To be sure, workfare programs are not all the same (Gueron, 1986, 1987; U.S. General Accounting Office, 1987a). Some emphasize education and training to a much greater extent than others, and the available evidence on employment-oriented interventions suggests that these are likely to have a great anti-poverty effect (Morris and Williamson, 1986). The more fundamental point, however, is that even the most intensive and powerful workfare designs are severely constrained by numerous impact-dampening assumptions.

Does this mean that those who are primarily interested in poverty reduction should oppose workfare and focus instead on lobbying for more generous government transfers? Not necessarily. In the current political climate such a strategy would almost certainly be counterproductive. The general public strongly supports self-sufficiency-oriented approaches to poverty reduction (Lewis and Schneider, 1985), and the preliminary evidence indicates that most workfare participants view their workfare experiences positively (Gueron, 1986, 1987). Moreover, these preliminary studies suggest that workfare does have *some* antipoverty impact, though its magnitude appears to be very modest. And at a more ideological level, it does not seem unreasonable to us to expect able-bodied adults to work in exchange for the government transfers they receive. What is unreasonable is to expect this approach to substantially resolve the poverty problem among the welfare population (Ellwood, 1986; Gueron, 1987).

The most viable strategy for those advocating increased government transfers is to link that advocacy to support for workfare initiatives. To the extent that workfare is accompanied by generous benefit levels, significant poverty reduction can be achieved. Not surprisingly, this achievement will severely compromise the ability of workfare to decrease dependency, since generous benefits will increase the attractiveness of the program to many who would otherwise work in low-paying jobs in the private sector. Thus, we once again encounter the inevitable trade-off between poverty reduction and dependency reduction. If employers raised the wages of private, dead-end jobs in response to increased government transfers, the severity of this trade-off would be lessened. For this to happen, however, transfers would have to be increased by amounts that are probably too large to be feasible in political (and perhaps economic) terms.

To be sure, incorporating into workfare the intensive training components that have been found to be most successful in other employment-oriented interventions would contribute to the reduction of both poverty and dependency. It must be reiterated, however, that even high-quality training does not appear to have the potential to reduce poverty to the extent that can be achieved through generous benefit levels.

The Future of Reform

What are the chances that, at a national level, workfare can be tied to generous government transfers and meaningful training? Probably not very great. But they are certainly greater than the chances of welfare benefits being substantially increased in the absence of a workfare requirement. Viewed in this light, the current romance of policymakers and the media with workfare need not be just another in a long line of cruel hoaxes played on the poor. It can represent instead an opportunity for making significant progress against poverty.

The extent to which this opportunity is taken advantage of will be more a function of political dynamics than of financial feasibility. While there are certainly limits to any society's ability to simultaneously redistribute income to the lower class and maintain economic growth, the available evidence indicates the United States could redistribute significantly more income than it currently does without approaching these boundaries (Burtless, 1986).

A smaller percentage of the U.S. national income is spent on redistribution than in most other Western industrialized countries. Moreover, this relatively low level of redistribution does not appear to have led to a relatively high level of economic growth when the United States is compared with these nations. There is also no consensus among economists that, at a micro-economic level, the impact of U.S. tax/transfer system on individual work effort and savings has substantially compromised overall economic efficiency.

Thus, economic constraints do not appear to represent an insurmountable obstacle to the strategy we have proposed. Rather, it is society's preference for dependency reduction over poverty reduction in dealing with the lower class that stands in the way. Whether the antipoverty impact of social policy can be strengthened in the face of this reality represents one of the key challenges for the political left in the coming decade.

References

Bane, Mary Jo and David T. Ellwood, *The Dynamics of Dependence: The Routes to Self-Sufficiency* (Cambridge: Urban Systems Research and Engineering, 1983).

Browning, Edgar K. and William R. Johnson, "The Cost of Reducing Economic Inequality," *Cato Journal* (Spring/Summer 1986), pp. 85–109.

Burtless, Gary, "Public Spending for the Poor: Trends, Prospects, and Economic Limits," in Sheldon H. Danziger and Daniel H. Weinberg (eds.), *Fighting Poverty: What Works and What Doesn't* (Cambridge: Harvard University Press, 1986), pp. 18–49.

Danziger, Sheldon, Robert Haveman and Robert Plotnick, "Antipoverty Policy: Effects on the Poor and the Nonpoor," in Danziger and Weinberg, op. cit., pp. 50–77.

Ellwood, David T., *Working Off of Welfare: Prospects and Policies for Self-Sufficiency of Women Heading Families* (Madison: Institute for Research on Poverty, 1986).

Ellwood, David T. and Lawrence H. Summers, "Poverty in America: Is Welfare the Answer or the Problem?" in Danziger and Weinberg, op. cit., pp. 78–105.

Forrest, Jacqueline Darroch, Albert I. Hermalin and Stanley K. Henshaw, "The Impact of Family Planning Clinic Programs on Adolescent Pregnancy," *Family Planning Pespectives* (1981), pp. 109–116.

Friedman, Lawrence M., "The Social and Political Context of the War on Poverty: An Overview," in Robert H. Haveman (ed.), *A Decade of Antipoverty Programs:*

Achievements, Failures and Lessons (New York: Academic Press, 1977), pp. 21–47.

Gilder, George, *Wealth and Poverty* (New York: Basic Books, 1980).

Gueron, Judith M., "Work for People on Welfare," *Public Welfare* (Winter 1986), pp. 7–12.

———. *Reforming Welfare with Work* (New York: Manpower Demonstration Research Corporation, 1987).

Gwartney, James and Richard Stroup, "Transfers, Equality, and the Limits of Public Policy," *Cato Journal* (Spring/Summer 1986), pp. 111–137.

Hill, Martha S., Sue Augustyniak, Greg J. Duncan et al., *Motivation and Economic Mobility* (Ann Arbor: Institute for Social Research, University of Michigan, 1985).

Hollister, Robinson G., Jr., Peter Kemper and Rebecca A. Maynard (eds.), *The National Supported Work Demonstration* (Madison: University of Wisconsin Press, 1984).

Kaus, Mickey, "The Work Ethic State," *The New Republic* (July 7, 1986), pp. 22–83.

Levin, Henry M., "A Decade of Policy Developments in Improving Education and Training for Low-Income Populations," in Haveman, op. cit., pp. 123–188.

Lewis, I. A. and William Schneider, "Hard Times: The Public on Poverty," *Public Opinion* (June/July 1985), pp. 1–7, 59–60.

Long, David A., Charles D. Mallar and Craig V. D. Thornton, "Evaluating the Benefits and Costs of the Job Corps," *Journal of Policy Analysis and Management* (1981), pp. 55–76.

Mead, Lawrence M., *Beyond Entitlement: The Social Obligations of Citizenship* (New York: Free Press, 1986).

Miller, Walter, "The Elimination of the American Lower Class as National Policy: A Critique of the Ideology of the Poverty Movement of the 1960s," in Daniel P. Moynihan (ed.), *On Understanding Poverty: Perspectives from the Social Sciences* (New York: Basic Books, 1969), pp. 260–315.

Morris, Michael and John B. Williamson, *Poverty and Public Policy: An Analysis of Federal Intervention Efforts* (Westport: Greenwood Press, 1986).

Murray, Charles, *Losing Ground: American Social Policy, 1950–1980* (New York: Basic Books, 1984).

O'Neill, June, "Transfers and Poverty: Cause and/or Effect?" *Cato Journal* (Spring/Summer 1986), pp. 55–76.

Orr, Larry L. and Felicity Skidmore, "The Evolution of the Work Issue in Welfare Reform," in Paul M. Sommers (ed.), *Welfare Reform in America: Perspectives and Prospects* (Boston: Kluwer-Nijhoff, 1982), pp. 167–186.

Patterson, James T., *America's Struggle Against Poverty 1900–1980* (Cambridge: Harvard University Press, 1981).

Plotnick, Robert, "The Redistributive Impact of Cash Transfers," *Public Finance Quarterly* (1984), pp. 27–50.

U.S. Bureau of the Census, *Money Income and Poverty Status of Families and Persons in the United States: 1985*, (Current Population Reports, Series P-60, no. 154, 1986).

U.S. General Accounting Office, *Work and Welfare: Current AFDC Work Programs and Implications for Federal Policy*, 1987a.

———. *Welfare: Issues to Consider in Assessing Proposals for Reform*, 1987b.

Williamson, John B., Jerry F. Borren, Frank J. Mifflen, et al., *Strategies Against Poverty In America* (Cambridge: Schenkman, 1975).

39

The Unfinished Business of Welfare Reform

Neil Gilbert

A modern paradox is that despite time-saving household devices, an unprecedented degree of affluence, and the benefits of universal education, the family's ability to care for children seems to be diminishing. How can it be that more time, money, and knowledge coincide with less capacity for childrearing?

Several factors contribute to this improbable state of affairs. Between 1960 and 1979 the proportion of out-of-wedlock births multiplied more than threefold from 5.3 percent to 17.1 percent of all births. During the same period, the rates of divorce to marriage rose from 26 percent to 50 percent, adding substantially to the ranks of single parents. By 1985 single-parent families comprised almost 24 percent of all families with children. Estimates suggest that 70 percent of all children born today will spend some part of their first eighteen years in a single-parent household. These figures imply that it may not be the parents' aptitude for childrearing that is on the decline so much as their mere presence. There are simply fewer parents at hand to look after children.

The growth of single-parent families accounts for only part of this turn of events. Two-parent families have also experienced a remarkable decrease in the time and effort traditionally devoted to child care by mothers. The women's liberation movement has enlarged opportunities for wives to assume roles other than that of motherhood. These opportunities have been seized in increasing numbers. Whether in response to economic need or to personal desires for professional careers, between 1970 and 1983 the

From *Society*, Vol. 24, No. 3 (March/April 1987): 5–11.

rate of employment for married women with children under six grew from 30 to 50 percent. Most of these women work full-time.

While high rates of divorce, illegitimacy, and female participation in the labor force offer plausible explanations for what is coming to be known as the "child-care crisis," it is possible that the malady goes deeper. Some would say that the family's sense of moral obligation to nurture and protect its young has dwindled. Certainly, fewer children are being produced. Over the last two decades the birth rate for women fifteen to forty-four years of age declined by 42 percent, and since 1973 the rate of legal abortion has more than doubled. Many people, however, still wish to have children. This wish may be father to the deed, but the deed does not insure the father's acceptance of social and economic responsibility once the child has arrived, as evidenced by the fact that two-thirds of the single-parent families headed by women receive no child support from the absent father.

The mounting evidence of child abuse and neglect adds a dimension of wickedness to the child-care crisis that goes beyond the denial of parental duty. In 1982, more than 900,000 cases of abuse and neglect were reported nationwide, an increase of 123 percent since 1976, when the American Humane Association began collecting these data. The proportion of these maltreatment reports that was substantiated rose from 30 percent in 1979 to 41 percent in 1982. While higher rates of reporting and substantiation have made this problem more visible, the full extent of child maltreatment is difficult to gauge. Some evidence suggests, for example, that as many as two-thirds of abuse and neglect cases are not reported.

Although there are no reliable data to compare child abuse in the 1980s with periods prior to 1976, there are reasons to believe that the incidence of this behavior has increased over the last few decades along with the social isolation of family life. The decline of the extended family and the break-up of the nuclear family have reduced the kind of informal social controls imposed by the immediate presence of other adults. This is not to say that child abuse is provoked by the attenuation of informal social controls, but that the situational constraints against this behavior are less potent. The lower threshold of informal controls and higher degrees of social and economic stress experienced by single-parent families undoubtedly contribute to the higher incidence of child abuse in this group. Children in single-parent families are more than twice as much at risk of abuse than those in households in which both parents are present. The risk is even greater when the single-parent is a teenager.

Whether owing to economic and social forces beyond individual control, a moral retreat from parental obligations, or some combination therein, the diminishing level of family care during the early years of childhood has left the young more vulnerable to physical harm than at any period in recent decades. Since the mid-1960s, government has been called upon with increasing fervor to assist families in caring for children. Providing this assistance is a delicate business as the relationship between family and state is nowhere more sensitive than in the realm of child care. State interventions in this realm often miscarry, not for lack of good intentions, but because of the strains between the liberating and protective tendencies inherent in social policies. Particularly in matters of family life, social policy objectives are muddled by incompatible desires to protect children and to liberate parents. This predicament is illustrated in the program of Aid to Families with Dependent Children (AFDC), in which the conflicting tendencies of social policy are settled in ways that seldom contribute to the best interest of children, especially the growing number of children born of unwed teenagers.

Presumption of Competence

The AFDC program provides financial assistance to about 3.7 million single-parent families (a smaller segment of this program covers an additional 250,000 families in which both parents are present but unemployed) at an annual cost of roughly $14 billion. The average monthly AFDC payment to single-parent families is $334, with a range from $92 in Mississippi to $499 in California. These families are overwhelmingly female headed; approximately 53 percent were teenagers when their first child was born. In matters of both size and composition, this case load differs dramatically from the group the program was originally intended to serve.

When Aid to Dependent Children (ADC, later retitled AFDC) was established in 1935, its planners conceived the program mainly as a protective measure for deserving widows and their children, a small group expected to shortly disappear from the public assistance rolls through absorption into the social security system under the proviso for survivors' insurance. History proved the planners to be wrong. From the outlook of 1935, it would be unseemly to fault them for the liability to forecast the tremendous increases in divorce and out-of-wedlock births that swelled the AFDC roll to its current dimensions. Indeed, in the short run, developments were not as precipitous as the trends that emerged over the last two decades. Between 1940 and 1950 the rate of births for unmarried women was low and fairly stable, going from 3.8 percent to 4.0 percent of all births. From 1950 to 1979, there was a four-fold increase in these rates as they climbed from 4.0 percent to 17.1 percent of all births. Over that period, teenage mothers accounted for close to one-half of the out-of-wedlock births.

While the AFDC program has strayed considerably from the original course its planners envisioned, many programs evolve in unexpected directions, and such changes are not necessarily objectionable. The changing demographic composition of AFDC recipients raises a fundamental issue about the presumption of competence that initially justified the provision of cash grants to single mothers in this program.

In designing social welfare programs, policymakers have the option to provide benefits in various forms such as cash, vouchers, and in-kind goods and services. In-kind benefits give policymakers a measure of social control over the way that tax dollars are finally consumed by welfare recipients; this imbues social welfare provisions with a paternalistic character which supports public choice over the exercise of individual responsibility. Cash benefits allow recipients the freedom to decide exactly what goods and services should be purchased to satisfy their needs. Recipients of these benefits are presumed competent and responsible enough to exercise consumer choice in ways that are deemed socially desirable, or at least inoffensive to public sensibilities. When AFDC began, it was taken for granted that the deserving widows for whom the program was designed were reasonably competent as parents and managers of family affairs. Few people imagined that a high proportion of this program's cash benefits would be going to unwed teenage mothers, a group for whom the presumption of competence is open to question.

Although this question concerns only the teenage-mother segment of AFDC recipients, more than half of all the women on AFDC started as teenage mothers; at any time the number of children in this group (more than 250,000 in 1975) is not trivial, nor are the implications for their welfare.

Caring for a young child is normally a struggle, even with two parents at hand to share the physical and emotional demands of this experience. For a single parent the burden is truly formidable. If that single parent is a mother still in her teenage years, an unusually stormy period of human development, the demands of childrearing are often beyond capability, a point given bleak testimony by this group's excessive rates of child abuse and neglect. Even more unsettling are recent findings that the incidence of Sudden Infant Death Syndrome is 68 percent higher among children of teenage mothers than in the general population.

The formal distinction between adolescence and the age of maturity is largely one of normative judgment. While the line may be fuzzy, it is drawn by public bodies in many areas. Federal and state governments impose varied constraints on youths between fourteen and twenty-one, including regulations regarding voting, qualifying for a driver's license, consuming alcoholic beverages, securing parental consent for medical treatment, and enlisting in the armed forces. These limits are fixed because the community is not fully convinced that teenagers are able to perform responsibly in areas of social life in which incompetence or lack of impulse control can have serious consequences.

In sharp contrast to the qualms about normal teenage behavior that underlie age-specific regulation of drinking, driving, voting, and the like, when it comes to caring for children, public policy assumes a remarkably lax attitude toward teenage parents. Adolescents presumed insufficiently mature to drive an automobile safely (not an irrational belief in view of the unusually high accident rates among teenage drivers) are given public support under AFDC to nurture and socialize helpless infants, with virtually no conditions attached. Why is the parental competence of teenage recipients disregarded by AFDC policy, despite compelling evidence of calamity in this area?

Given the alarming rates of child abuse, neglect, and Sudden Infant Death Syndrome among this group, it is doubtful that public officials fail to question the parental competence of unwed teenagers on AFDC because of ill-placed confidence in their maternal abilities. More likely, it is the dread of state intrusion into the sacred realm of parent-child relationships that deflects critical judgments on this matter.

If AFDC policy is any indication, parental competence may be a more delicate issue than the question of one's general competence to deal with the ordinary affairs of daily life. Up through the early 1970s everyone on public assistance was required to accept periodic home visits from social caseworkers, who provided advice and counseling. These social services were linked to financial aid under the assumption that poor people were in some manner deficient, suffering from personal pathologies that could be alleviated through casework intervention. It was an assumption that grossly exaggerated both the curative powers of social casework and the pathology of the poor. The poor are a diverse lot, some of whom no doubt might benefit from social services. There is little evidence that most, let alone everyone, on public assistance—which includes the elderly, disabled, blind, and single-parent families—need these services. Critics charged that the obligation to accept social services in order to obtain financial aid humiliated clients and spread caseworkers so thin that their efforts could not be concentrated on those most in need. A more effective and efficient system, it was argued, would allow for the provision of services only when specifically requested by clients. This view eventually prevailed when, among other things, the public assistance rolls increased by over a million recipients in the four years after funds were made available to expand casework services under the 1962 Social Security Amendments.

The shift from a system of mandatory social services for all to a system of voluntary services on request was oblivious to the special needs of different groups. To admit that not every public assistance recipient requires social services simply by virtue of their economic status is not to say that none should be obliged to accept these services. This turnabout from mandatory to voluntary provisions forfeited the opportunity to mold the service component of AFDC around factors such as risk and vulnerability. While the move to a voluntary system released AFDC parents from the infrequent although continuous supervision and implicit social control of the family caseworker, it has left the children of teenage mothers exposed to care by those the community deems in many cases to be too imprudent to drive, drink, and vote. The voluntary system amounts to a case of public support for children to raise infants without supervision. Because these children are parents, much of the common sense exercised in age-related regulatory social policies is suspended in deference to parental rights and the sanctity of family life.

What can be done? It would be best to prevent the problem of out-of-wedlock teenage births. Toward this end, several remedial measures such as sex education, abortion, and family planning services have been widely implemented over the last two decades. For the most part, these efforts are directed toward young women, as they are at risk of pregnancy. There are other contributing parties to this risk, and in recent years special attempts have been made to reckon with them. Since the passage of Title IV-D of the Social Security Act in 1974, absent fathers of children on AFDC have come under increasing pressure to fulfill their child-support responsibilities. In Wisconsin, where an inventive scheme is underway to enforce child-support obligations through a payroll tax on absent fathers, the net of social responsibility is being cast even wider. Under the Abortion Prevention and Family Responsibility Act of 1985, the parents of minors who give birth out-of-wedlock can be held financially accountable for the expenses of raising their children's babies.

By firming up a long-standing, if currently shaky, set of social rules and expectations, these most recent measures reflect what James Q. Wilson describes as efforts to "induce private virtue through public policy." If minors who bear illegitimate children cannot be convinced to alter their behavior, at least they and their families can be held accountable for its consequences.

The idea is to discourage illegitimacy. The extent to which policies that enforce normative obligations associated with having children will actually prevent out-of-wedlock births among minors awaits the verdict of human experience. No doubt some teenagers will be persuaded to restrain their impulses and to behave with greater regard for the not-so-distant consequences of their sexual activity. Yet, short of abstinence, there are no evident solutions to the problem of teenage illegitimacy. Similar to the record of teenage driving, sexual activity at an early age appears innately afflicted by a high rate of accidents. Less than one-quarter of the pregnancies experienced by unwed teenagers are reported as intentional. This is a program that goes well beyond lack of knowledge. According to a national survey in 1979, almost every sexually active young woman knows about some method of contraception. Despite an increase in the consistent use of contraception, premarital pregnancy among adolescents has been on the rise, a trend that is but partially explained by a shift to less effective contraceptive methods. This perplexing trend only confirms that we are dealing with an exquisitely complex problem, one wrought of adolescent sexuality, the spontaneity and emotional exuberance of youth, and deep-seated needs for acceptance and affection, all operating in a highly permissive social context. These psychological, biological, and cultural forces exert a powerful influence on teenage behavior, an influence that seems to transcend the mundane incentives of social policy.

While adolescent illegitimacy rates are not immune to policy inducements, the degree to which teenagers' sexual imbroglios may be deterred by appeals to rational self-interest is not as formidable as policymakers might wish. Those youth who respond least to policies that aim to prevent illegitimacy through remedial services or normative sanctions are the group most lacking in the kind of judgment and self-control required to be competent parents. To the extent that preventive efforts are successful, they will reduce the incidence of teenage illegitimacy, leaving the AFDC roles with a smaller but more intensely problematic group of adolescent mothers. Ultimately, the question of what can be done must address ways to protect the vulnerable infants of unwed teenagers. It is an issue that inpugns the existing balance between freedom and social control in welfare policy and draws our attention to the unfinished business of welfare reform.

In the Interest of Children

Much of the current debate on the reform of AFDC centers upon the business of how to encourage and prepare welfare recipients for movement into the labor force. With California and Massachusetts leading the way, a spate of workfare programs—which entail training, job search requirements, day-care services, and opportunities for public employment if private jobs do not pan out—have been embraced by coalitions of liberals and conservatives. This emerging consensus on welfare reform is derived, in part, from the fact that a majority of mothers with school-age children are now entering the labor force, a trend that makes it awkward for even the most sympathetic welfare advocates to hold AFDC recipients exempt from the obligation to seek employment. There is also a growing concern about the moral symmetry of welfare, which stipulates that social rights to various forms of public aid should be squared with the civic responsibility to be self-supporting.

While workfare conveys an audible message about the fiscal responsibilities of welfare recipients, it is mute on the topic of maternal obligations. The purchase of after-school child care is offered as a natural, almost beneficent, substitute for the absence of working mothers, with the tacit assumption that nothing lost in the bargain is worth questioning. Although federal law permits the states to require parents with children as young as three to participate in workfare programs, most states have limited mandatory participation to those with children at least six years old. Hence, at the moment workfare reforms are of slight consequence to teenage mothers, except for the relatively few who elect voluntary involvement.

Workfare schemes peripherally address the care of children mainly in the context of creating after-school supports that might free their parents for regular employment. Preschool youngsters of teenage mothers are virtually untouched by this current wave of welfare reform. The lack of social protection for this high-risk group of children on AFDC becomes all the more conspicuous in light of the vigorous political drive to amend AFDC in other respects. Insuring this group's health and safety remains the unfinished business of welfare reform in the 1980s. It is a task that can be accomplished through several measures, ranging from the simple extension of current reforms to the imposition of a more exacting system of AFDC program requirements for teenage parents.

Beginning with the extension of current reforms, a case may be made for requiring the participation of teenage mothers in workfare programs. Taking their children's welfare as a primary objective, one can argue that these youngsters will actually be safer and receive better care in all-day preschool programs than at home. From this viewpoint, the placement of youngsters in day care is advanced as a benign experience, based on the interpretation of findings from a substantial body of research. This corpus of research on the effects of day care has been summarized by such firm assurances as "it typically does not harm," "children of working mothers do as well in school as those of mothers who stay at home," and "children of employed and nonemployed mothers do not differ on various child adjustment measures." These assurances are at once muffled by a host of qualifications which acknowledge: inconsistency of findings, lack of data on long-term effects, inability to measure subtle characteristics, and the significant, if undetermined, influences of numerous mediating variables—quality of care, number of hours in day care each day, mother's satisfaction, child's temperament, social class, age of children, father's involvement, mother's work schedule, child's sex, and number of children in the family, to mention the most obvious. Filtered through all these qualifications, summary statements equating the consequences of day care and home care emerge as empty generalizations.

There are some who argue that these generalizations are not simply meaningless, but dead wrong when it comes to most full-time care for children under six. It is widely believed that the bond of love formed between mother and child in these early years endows one's future with a capacity for human attachments and the regulation of aggression. As Selma Fraiberg reads the evidence, this bond is seriously impaired by placing youngsters in child-care facilities for eight to ten hours daily, Monday through Friday, which is the schedule that would apply to the preschool children of most AFDC mothers employed thirty to forty hours a week. At the time in life when love, trust, and self-valuation are shaped through human interaction, Fraiberg worries that children in day care may learn only the churlish manners and rough justice of the preschool playground. Or they may learn "that all adults are interchangeable, that love is capricious, that human attachment is a perilous investment, and that love should be hoarded for the self in the service of survival."

Voiced almost a decade ago, these concerns are echoed in the recent investigations by Deborah Fallows, whose long-standing sympathies for the women's movement are shaken by visceral reactions to the cheerless, desultory milieu in most of the day-care facilities she observed around the country. (There were exceptions, the best of which charged from $5000 to $8000 a year.) Ruminating on the everyday experience of a typical child in these settings, Fallows depicts an ordeal marked less by outright abuse than by benign neglect: "He didn't do badly—he roamed independently, joining in when he felt like it, taking off when he didn't. He got no individual attention, because none was offered. No one talked to him or hugged him, because there weren't enough adults to go around." It was a familiar scene of life at many centers where the main activity was filling time. If Fallows's observations are accurate, whatever the long-term effects of institutional child care, the immediate quality of daily existence afforded young children in these facilities rarely celebrates the joys of childhood.

These kinds of evidence do not entirely dispose of the argument for full-time day care. Even those who believe that most day care is a grim experience in the lives of young children must address the question of its impact on highly vulnerable groups such as the children of unwed teenage mothers, with an eye to the alternatives. Consider, for example, the claim by a child development specialist at the University of Virginia, that "children are usually better off with satisfied substitute care-givers and a happy part-time mother than with an angry frustrated full-time mother." While scarcely a scientific endorsement for the benefits of day care, this claim is certainly bleak testimony that, as elsewhere in life, the care of children can descend to limited choices between the lesser of two evils. Given the high rates of abuse and neglect by teenage mothers, and their generally deficient parenting skills, it is not illusory to see day care as a refuge from a potentially harmful home.

Extending workfare requirements to teenage mothers might still be seen as a reform beneficial to children, despite the general misgivings one might have about the effects of full-time day care for preschoolers. In this case we accept the advantages of bad over worse, a persuasive if not compelling choice when it comes to caring for children. There remains the question of what will happen when subsidized child care for those in the workfare program is discontinued, as planned after three to twelve months of employment. The preferred possibilities are that participants will be earning enough at that time to pay for this service or that they will be eligible to enroll their children in subsidized programs under other auspices; but additional outcomes are conceivable. A pilot project sponsored by the California Department of Social Services to train children for self-care, for example, offers a disquieting alternative. Under this scheme, latchkey children who were once perceived as a problem are transformed, with some training on household safety and what to do in an emergency, to an expedient solution for the problem of inadequate adult supervision. It is a disquieting alternative because in seeking to improve the conditions of self-care, this project imparts a normative sanction to the act of leaving children home alone. While self-care may be tenable for those fourteen years old, it borders on neglect for children six and seven years old. Self-care at its best is a risky and unsettling experience for most children in the early school grades.

The extension of workfare would reduce the demands on teenage AFDC recipients to tend to their children in the early years and would increase their obligation to provide financial support through employment in the marketplace. It is a trade that avoids the difficult question of how to improve teenage mothering in those early years which are so critical to their children's social and intellectual development.

While workfare sidesteps the issue, we can imagine several reform measures which would affirm the importance of early mothering and directly seek to influence behavior in this realm. In particular, three AFDC program changes likely to improve the quality of parental care by teenage mothers involve mandatory parent education, home health visitors, and in-kind provision of welfare assistance. These measure differ markedly from the extension of workfare in that they invoke social control leveled at the parent-child relationship.

Mandatory parent education is a simple unobtrusive reform measure, under which teenage mothers on AFDC would be required to take a course in child care and to demonstrate mastery of its content. Such courses are widely available to young mothers, although at the moment unconnected to eligibility for AFDC benefits. No one seriously questions the unwed teenage mother's rights to state support when she is unable to provide for her family. Should the community not expect that this right be accompanied by an obligation to acquire the skills and knowledge necessary to achieve an adequate standard of performance in the parenting role for which she is being subsidized? While parent education might well be required of all AFDC recipients, it is especially germane to teenage parents for whom the presumption of competence is most in question and the record of child care least assuring.

What happens if a mother either refuses to attend the course or is unable to demonstrate mastery of its content? To disqualify these parents for AFDC support leaves their children in double jeopardy, with mothers who are both destitute and inept. Under the circumstances, denial of eligibility would seem highly undesirable. The essential point of the requirement can be reinforced by combining it with other reform measures. The relatively few who through lack of attendance or ability are unable to pass a parenting course, for example, might be obliged to participate in a more intensive home health visiting service than those who can demonstrate adequate knowledge of parenting skills. Enrollment in workfare is another option that could be adopted in these cases on the assumption that for most of their waking hours during the week children would be as well cared for in day-care centers as by mothers who cannot pass a course in the basics of good parenting.

Home health visiting is a more intrusive measure than parent education. Although a function routinely performed by the National Health Service for all families with babies in Britain, most Americans are not terribly receptive to having state employees regularly enter their homes to check on how well their children are doing. Indeed, loss of a certain degree of privacy has been one of the personal costs typically associated with the receipt of public aid. Home visiting by social workers was a fundamental condition of eligibility for all AFDC recipients up through the mid-1970s, at which time this practice was discontinued, in part because it was unable to achieve a broad mandate to reduce dependency. Compared to these earlier social casework services, home health visiting would be more limited in both its purpose and coverage. While casework sought to treat and rehabilitate all those on public assistance, home health visiting concentrates on the physical well-being of the children of teenage mothers. The weekly or bimonthly visits would offer advice and support to young mothers as well as professional supervision of their child-care practices. At the same time that it strives to enhance the parenting skills of teenage mothers, this intense periodic monitoring may be the best form of protection the state can offer against abuse and neglect, short of high quality institutional care.

Moving beyond incremental reforms, such as parent education and home visiting, the provision of in-kind assistance is a sweeping measure that would substitute board and residential care facilities for existing cash grants to teenage mothers on AFDC. This shift to in-kind benefits challenges the presumption of competence that justifies awarding public assistance in the form of cash to minors.

The argument is that along with inadequate parenting skills teenage mothers lack the good judgment necessary to handle cash grants and to manage household affairs on their own. Following this train of thought, the Reagan administration has recently proposed that unwed teenage mothers should live at home with their parents in order to qualify for AFDC. In fact, the majority of first-time AFDC recipients do remain at home with their parents, at least during their first year of motherhood. Ongoing adult supervision is generally beneficial, but not in every case. One must assess the probable quality of that supervision for minors on AFDC and the living conditions under which it occurs. Among those who stay at home, many teenage mothers bring their newborn child into a poor, tense, already crowded household in which parental supervision, as it was, did not impede their teenage daughter's out-of-wedlock pregnancy. Among those who leave home, some are fleeing from an environment that would be detrimental to their children's well-being. In any event, teenage mothers might find a residential facility, along the lines of a college dormitory with a variety of child-care and educational services, an agreeable alternative to living at home with their parents.

A group home for teenage mothers is subject to both tightfisted and generous renditions, depending upon its primary purpose. If this approach to welfare provision is designed mainly to have a deterrent effect on potential AFDC recipients, it will surely resemble, as Charles Murray sees it, "a good correctional half-way house." Here regulations are stern, amenities meager, but the children are at least safe and well-nourished. This setting conjures up visions of the nineteenth-century poorhouse, an institution rarely distinguished by humanitarian tendencies. In a short-lived revival of the poorhouse, California's Sacramento County Welfare Department recently introduced a program under which people eligible for general assistance were given room and board at the Banyon Street Shelter in lieu of cash grants. Banyon Street was a squalid affair, endorsing conventional opinion that facilities of this sort are a punitive device intended to discourage application for public assistance.

What if deterrence were not the main objective? It is possible to imagine a residential facility designed to help mothers care for their children in a secure congenial setting—where the physical environment and social temper are in closer affinity to a college dormitory than to a correctional half-way house. Such a facility would have professional staff on hand to counsel teenage mothers on child-care practices and to organize cooperative efforts around the preparation of meals, babysitting, and other work needed to keep the residence running smoothly. These communal arrangements would present an opportunity to gain experience in household management and child care while allowing sufficient time for residents to enroll in educational programs that would prepare them for future employment. The analogy to a college dormitory should not be carried too far. Differences between a correctional half-way house and a college dormitory can be attributed as much to the character of their respective residents as to any pattern in their structures of institutional life. Whatever its planned affinity with a college dormitory, a group home for unwed teenagers would certainly possess a distinct social complexion and generate its own special problems of management.

The types of supportive services and basic amenities envisioned in a well-designed group home would be expensive, probably higher than the average AFDC grant in many states. In contrast to the high cost to the public, the immediate benefits of a secure nurturing environment in the early years of life are experienced only by the children served. Public benefits of such an investment are many years down the road, and even then they are not easy to measure. In addition to the high cost, there are those who might caution not to make these facilities too agreeable, lest they create an incentive for teenage pregnancy. For the moment, the danger of public spending to produce a residential environment quite that attractive to teenagers would seem remote.

Work, Children, and Social Obligations

With middle-class mothers going to work in unprecedented numbers, AFDC's original mission of public relief for families headed by females outside of the labor force is not as compelling in 1986 as it was half a century ago. The shift of women's labor from the household to the market economy has left less time and energy for raising children; never an easy process, childrearing has become more intricate as families struggle to balance workplace demands with parental responsibilities. Today, two-paycheck families earning well above the median income often experience uncomfortable strains in managing the daily chores of domestic life. While the domestic burdens of a two-wage-earner family pale in comparison to those of the working mother in a single-parent family, public sympathies for the special conditions of the latter have eroded under the increasing pressures of family life that are being felt throughout society. In an era when states are vigorously experimenting with work-oriented welfare reforms it is thus a little out of keeping to ask how the provision of welfare might be arranged to promote good parenting and the well-being of children. This question not only draws our attention to the plight of the community's most vulnerable members, it also raises an essential point about the nature of social obligations.

Recent discussions of welfare policy have turned from the classification of entitlements to the identification of social obligations and from cost-benefit outcomes to implications for normative behavior. In support of social obligations and normative behavior, the duty to earn one's way has dominated the agenda for welfare reform. But social obligations of family life extend beyond the parent's role as an economic provider. It is widely accepted that parents assume the profound responsibility to socialize and protect their children, to serve as a nurturing presence that cultivates human development. Seeing one's parents regularly going to work and supporting the family is a lesson in normative behavior well to be learned. Whether it is best taught to children at two, four, six, twelve, or fourteen years of age is an open issue. It is also an important issue because to earn one's way and at the same time responsibly discharge the other obligations of parenthood may not be possible in single-parent families when the children are very young and most in need of adult guidance and care. In the long run, the behavior of adults regarding a wide range of normative expectations is influenced more by how they are raised as children than by public policies designed to induce private virtues later in life.

The current discourse on welfare reform might benefit from a broader and more balanced conception of social obligations, one which includes concern for ways to improve the family's care of children. Measures such as parent education, home visiting, and the provision of benefits in-kind offer a start in this direction. None of these measures is entirely new. They are old schemes, drawn more finely to accommodate the interests of children with unwed teenage parents. By its very nature, such fine tuning of social policy offers only partial solutions to the stubborn problems of AFDC. The details of these reforms will need to be worked out along with broader questions, such as: Should the different measures be voluntary or compulsory? How can the measures be combined most effectively to reinforce each other? These are matters for states to experiment with and refine according to local preferences. As a package these reforms present an opportunity for a flexible, yet more exacting policy response in the delicate realm of family relations—a response that focuses on the early years of life, which is the best time to start caring for children.

40

In Search of the Working Poor

Charles Murray

THE AMERICAN DEBATE about poverty and public policy has always been grounded in the prevailing answer to the question, "Can any American who is willing to work hard make a decent living?" From the founding of the nation until the 1960s, the consensus answer among policymakers had always been "yes" with minor qualifications. During the 1960s, the policy consensus shifted to "no" and has remained there ever since. Poverty is largely structural, the new received wisdom has held; it is caused by barriers and culs-de-sac in the economy that will inevitably trap certain populations in poverty.

In recent years, the received wisdom has been given a twist, stated most clearly and with the best data in *Years of Poverty, Years of Plenty* by researchers at the University of Michigan using the Panel Study of Income Dynamics (PSID)—a longitudinal data base that began with a sample of some 5,000 American families in 1968 and has been continued through annual interviews since then.[1] The authors of *Years of Poverty, Years of Plenty* work to their conclu-

[1] Greg J. Duncan with Richard D. Coe, Mary E. Corcoran, Martha S. Hill, Saul D. Hoffman, and James N. Morgan, *Years of Poverty, Years of Plenty: The Changing Fortunes of American Workers and Families* (Ann Arbor, Michigan: Institute for Social Research, 1984).

sions from two new empirical findings made possible by a longitudinal data base. First, if we track the total income of American families over a long period of time, we find that a large proportion of the families experience a year or more in which that income falls beneath the poverty line. Second, we find that only rarely does the income of a poor family remain beneath the poverty line *every* year. To illustrate, if 0 represents a year of income below the poverty line and 1 represents a year of income above the poverty line, only a few poverty profiles of a decade will read 0000000000. Much more often, the profile of a low-income family over a decade will look something like 0101011101. Furthermore, the authors could find no way of clearly distinguishing these "temporarily poor" people from the population as a whole. "They were somewhat more likely to be black or to live in families headed by a woman," they report, "but on the whole, the main difference between them and the rest of the population was simply that they had experienced one or two particularly bad years."

The authors portray an America in which income rises and falls rapidly and steeply for unavoidable reasons. They conclude that poverty is not the lot of a permanent underclass, but for the most part a short-term situation into which many people fall and out of which they rise again. The authors close by quoting approvingly from an earlier study of the PSID:

> [W]e may have been oversold on the Protestant Ethic and have refused to see the extent to which people are the victims of their past, their environment, luck, and chance. It is after all difficult to believe that there are not some situations where individual effort matters—in seizing opportunities for better jobs, moving to new areas, or avoiding undue risks. But for public policy purposes and for arguments about the extent to which one could reduce dependency in our society by changing the behavior and attitudes of dependent members, the findings certainly do not encourage expectations that such changes would make much difference.

One key conclusion of the structural argument—that poor individuals are not responsible for their poverty—remains intact, but a new charge is added: The American economy leaves large sections of those not poor vulnerable to sudden attacks of poverty. The logical policy implication drawn from this conclusion has been that generous income supports make an appropriate buffer against a turbulent and chancy economic system; it is not good enough that people simply go out and try their best to make a living.

As I read this analysis, I suddenly realized that my own experience was fodder for the authors' quantitative case. In the late 1960s I had been making a living and supporting a family, then went to graduate school, then resumed making a living. My poverty profile from 1969 to 1978, the years used for the poverty analysis in *Years of Poverty, Years of Plenty*, was 1100111111. Or if one started my overall income profile at 1971 and ended it at 1978, the years that the authors use for their analysis of income mobility, I was one of the Horatio Algers who struggled all the way from poverty to the top quintile of the American income distribution. My history exemplified the numbers reported in *Years of Poverty, Years of Plenty*. But the interpretation drawn from those numbers was completely inapplicable to me. I had never been thrown out of work—I left the labor force voluntarily. My economic improvement following poverty reflected nothing more than a predictable income trajectory for young men with a new professional degree. Perhaps most importantly, I had never really been poor. It only looked that way. Mightn't such realities explain much of the chaos reported in *Years of Poverty, Years of Plenty?*

I recently had the opportunity to examine the PSID from this perspective, as reported in more technical detail elsewhere.[2] Here I summarize one of the main results of that inquiry, half hopeful and half disturbing. The hopeful half is that poverty in America is seldom the result of uncontrollable events involving the economic system. I will argue that the old wisdom—that anyone who is willing to work hard can make a decent living—has much more truth to it than has recently been acknowledged. The disturbing half is that our current popular understanding of the poverty population may be very wide of the reality. I conclude with a proposal for clarifying the situation.

Focusing on adults on their own who try to work

The discussion focuses on the American labor market as a way of escaping poverty. I assume that people 65 and over are not expected in the normal course of events to be in the labor market. (I discuss the physically disabled below.) Otherwise, I assume that any person of working age does in fact have the choice of the labor market open to him or her. So while in one sense this discussion ignores a dominant source of poverty (the female-headed household where the woman is not in the labor market), in another sense the findings are

[2] Charles Murray and Deborah Laren, *According to Age: Longitudinal Profiles of AFDC Recipients and the Poor by Age Group* (Washington, D.C.: American Enterprise Institute, September 1986), from which material in this article has been adapted. I am grateful to Greg Duncan, co-director of the PSID and lead author of *Years of Poverty, Years of Plenty*, for his encouragement and many substantive contributions throughout the effort.

at least pertinent to that population. The labor market is not an attractive short-term option to many such women (in some cases for very sound reasons), but the evidence about the labor market suggests that it is probably an excellent long-term one.

The data base I originally drew from the PSID consists of all persons in the PSID who in 1970 were either the head of household (excluding full-time students) or the spouse of a head of household and were between the ages of 20 and 64 inclusive—in other words, "adults on their own." The follow-up period is the subsequent ten-year period 1971-1980. In the following discussion, I will sometimes omit the adjective "working-aged" for purposes of convenience, but it always applies.

To represent each subject's poverty profile over the years 1970-80 in an easily scanned summary, the income for each of those eleven years was converted to a number ranging from "0," representing an income below the poverty line, to "9," representing an income of more than three times the poverty line. Each number from 1 to 9 represents an increment of 25 percent of the poverty line (e.g., "3" represents an income ranging from 151-175 percent of the poverty line). In effect, people with an income denoted by "9" are in the middle class (three times the poverty line for an average family of four in 1986 represented an income of more than $33,600).

Using this framework, I examined specific subpopulations of interest, in each case looking for patterns in case-by-case reconstructions. Three important notes about the presentation are that (1) all income figures are given in 1987 purchasing power, (2) all percentages refer to national proportions, using the PSID weighting system, and (3) the sketches used as illustrations are based on actual cases in public-use data tapes but have been converted to unrecognizable composites in compliance with the PSID's promises of confidentiality to its respondents.

The question: Given that a person is poor but in a household that is participating in the labor market, what happens over the next ten years?

The curious case of education

The obvious first way of disaggregating the dynamics was to examine poverty among populations with varying educational levels, and the attempt to do so brought forth the first notable finding. As of 1970, there was such a small problem of poverty among people with a basic education that it is difficult to analyze how it occurs and how it is escaped. Even with 4,702 cases in the data base, there is a scarcity of data. For example, one interesting source of patterns was thought to be college graduates. What happens to them after a spell of poverty? The answer is that poverty strikes so seldom that, among the 604 cases of working-aged adults in the PSID who were poor in 1970, only six, representing a national proportion of nine-tenths of one percent of the working-aged college graduates, were poor in 1970. None sank below the poverty line in 1980. One of the six, a person not in the labor market, experienced significant poverty in the intervening years. Only one other case exhibited even a single year of subsequent temporary poverty.

More surprisingly, the same obstacle—too few cases—impeded an analysis of poverty among that archetypical American family wage earner, the white high-school-educated male. The 604 cases of poor people in 1970 again included just six such cases, representing three-tenths of one percent of all such white males between the ages of 20 and 64. The situation is only slightly different for white women who had a high school degree or were married to someone with a high school degree. Only eighteen cases, representing 1.3 percent of that population, were poor in 1970. Of these women, only ten had worked at all in that year, and only two had worked more than fifteen weeks.

The small proportions of college and high school graduates who are involved in the analysis convey how easy it is to lose track of the poverty problem in our preoccupation with the people who *are* poor. Poverty does not strike throughout the American population like the flu; it is tightly concentrated. Even within populations we have become accustomed to thinking of as having serious economic problems with job insecurity (blue-collar workers with just a high school education, for example), the incidence of actual *poverty* (as distinguished from other kinds of economic problems) was extremely low, even during an economically lackluster decade.

This general observation applies most dramatically to the black population. In 1970, the Bureau of the Census showed that 30 percent of the black population was living below the poverty line. The PSID for that year showed 22 percent of working-aged black adults below the poverty line. These are extremely large proportions, as befits the central role that black poverty has played in the poverty debate. Contrast those figures with this one: Of working-aged black men in the PSID who had just a high school education, only 5 percent were poor. Even among black women, only 10 percent of those with a high school education were below the poverty line. I hasten to add that the black male figure should be interpreted as "married black males with a high school education," for the PSID carries only a few single black males in that category. Nonetheless, such findings (which have been reached by others with census data on the incomes of black married couples and black full-time workers) bear emphasizing. For many years now, the severe black poverty problem has had little to do with blacks with a basic education, married blacks, or blacks who remained continuously in the labor market. If in 1970 the black poverty rate had equalled that experienced by blacks who had finished high school, it would have been more than a percentage point lower than the overall poverty rate among American whites.

The more general statement is that poverty among the working-aged in 1970 was a phenomenon among people with less than a high school education, who constituted a remarkable 75 percent of working-aged adults below the poverty line.[3] That most poor people are ill-educated does not mean that most ill-educated people are poor. On the contrary, 90 percent of them were not poor in 1970, 90 percent were not poor in 1980, and 84 percent were not poor in either year. But three out of four people who were poor came from that group.

The curious case of disability

Another obvious dimension for analyzing poverty among the working-aged is physical disability. Disability itself is closely associated with poverty: 36 percent of the poor in 1970 reported that the head of household suffered a disability that affected both the kind and amount of work he or she could do. Among those poor who were not disabled, to what extent is subsequent poverty a function of subsequent health misfortunes? The answer is that, among those who had no disability in 1970 and had been in the labor market, 13 percent were reporting a major disability by 1980. This argues for the importance of disability in formulating policy toward the poor, and must be remembered as a qualifier when assessing the

---

[3] In subsequent years, Current Population Survey (CPS) data show that the proportion of people getting high school degrees has risen sharply, making possible indirect analyses of what caused the relationship between a high school degree and low poverty in 1970. (Was it self-selection? Education? Credentialing?) The short answer (again using CPS data) is that the proportion of persons with less than a high school education who are not in poverty (about 80 percent by the CPS's method of counting) remained fairly constant from 1975-1985, declining very slightly overall, while the percentage of the poor who come from the group fell rapidly. The implication is that it is about as easy as ever for the ill-educated to make a living above the poverty line, but that the persons now drawn into the high school degree pool are not acquiring the same level of protection against poverty that a high school degree used to represent—a combination of trends with intriguing implications that are too complicated to explore here.

reliability of the labor market. If you are poor and in the labor market, these data say, there is a one-in-eight chance that you will be impeded from remaining in the labor market over the next decade because of physical handicap.

But once again, an obvious question produced curious results. Almost nine out of ten persons who were both poor and disabled in 1970 (88 percent) also happened to come from that same ill-educated population that dominated the ranks of the poor. A variety of hypotheses explain why this might be so. For example, the ill-educated and poor tend to work at manual labor, and manual labor tends to produce physical ailments. Or they received inferior health care. Or the reason they got less than a high school education was related to mental or emotional deficiencies that also tend to produce (or not to prevent) physical disabilities. Or they said they were disabled to avoid the responsibilities of work or to get disability benefits.

Whatever the combination of explanations might be (and some good empirical work on the subject is needed), the initial concentration of physical disability among the ill-educated is compounded by what happened between 1970 and 1980. Of those among the poor who did *not* have a disability in 1970 but had acquired one by 1980, 81 percent of the newly disabled persons had less than a high school education. The net result is that the person with a high school degree or more who was physically disabled and poor in 1970 was rare (0.3 percent of adults with high school education or better), and the educated, poor, able-bodied person in 1970 who left the labor market because of a physical disability over the course of the decade was even rarer. As I discuss the dynamics of subsequent poverty among those who stayed in the labor market, the bare statement about disability is that of those who were able-bodied and in the labor market in 1970, almost 13 percent were reporting a major disability in 1980. The more complete statement is that this form of misfortune remains a curiously selective affliction of the ill-educated, and that something more complicated than the hand of fate is involved.

Trying to understand subsequent poverty among working people

The preceding discussion establishes that whenever we talk about working-aged people below the poverty line we are talking about an extremely small minority of the American population, and that this small minority is itself systematically concentrated among a particular subgroup. For most purposes, the case for the labor market is already made. We may try to imagine, for example, setting up goals for an economic system that was being devised from scratch. Only the most optimistic would set standards of success as demanding as those reflected in the numbers just presented. But there remains the periodic, temporary poverty that *Years of Poverty, Years of Plenty* emphasized, which was the initial subject of my inquiry. The conclusion I take from a reconstruction of cases in the PSID is that an unknown but large portion of people listed as being "below the poverty line" are not living in poverty. What appears to be "temporary poverty" is often no such thing, and the precipitous ups and downs are often statistical rather than a reflection of real changes in quality of life.

The Mississippi fallacy

How can one hypothesize that large numbers of people below the poverty line are not really poor, when (it is widely argued) the current poverty line is far too *low*? Three general factors are at work. Let me preface them by noting a general problem that has deformed our image of the poor.

When staff members from CBS News or the *New York Times Magazine* or a congressional investigating committee want to do a feature on poor people, they do not sample randomly from the population below the poverty line. Since their topic is real poverty, not official poverty, they quite sensibly search out people who fit the description of people who really are "living in poverty," and any Human Services Department in almost any county can readily give them a few vivid examples. Thus when poverty among the aged appears on the television screen, it tends to consist of a single elderly woman isolated in a tiny room in a big city. A poor child is an ill-clad waif playing amidst trash heaps. A poor rural person lives in a tar-paper shack—peculiarly often in Mississippi (hence the label for the fallacy). These people are indeed "typically" poor in the conceptual sense of impoverishment—misery is an essential part of our understanding of what genuine poverty should mean. But we tend to reify poverty on the basis of such images, and then assume that the poverty index identifies the same population—a logical leap that no one familiar with the problems of measuring poverty would make. Real, unquestioned poverty exists in the United States and in the cases of the PSID, and nothing that I am about to say is intended to belittle that reality. But when cases are pulled from the pool of people whose only qualification is that they are below the official poverty line, a much different distribution of portraits emerges.

The following cases are presented as illustrations. I continue to focus on the working-aged and the question of ability to make a decent living. Remember that all dollar figures are given in terms of 1987 purchasing power.

People in small towns and rural areas

The poverty profile for Mr. and Mrs. A is 00001011330. This husband and wife were in their mid-thirties in 1970. He had a grade school education; she finished junior high. That opening year, he worked full time, she worked 1,200 hours, and still they brought in an income of only $7,000. Mr. and Mrs. A had two years in the late 1970s when they escaped near-poverty, but that was a brief respite. They both worked in 1980, but they were once again poor.

Mr. and Mrs. A seem to be a classic case of the working poor: They plugged away, almost got out of poverty, had a few better years, but slid back into poverty even though they continued to work. Now consider part two of the profile, remembering that they both lived throughout this period in a rural area (meaning a town of fewer than 10,000 people or the countryside itself).

Following that first year in which they made only $7,000, Mr. and Mrs. A are shown by the poverty index as being constantly in poverty or near-poverty for the next seven years. But during those same years they brought home an average income of $16,000 (excluding the more prosperous years of 1978-79). In 1980, when they were again shown as having fallen into poverty, they made $14,000. Mr. B owned three working vehicles, including two trucks that he used as part of his business. Mr. and Mrs. A also owned their own home free and clear, a five-room house that the PSID interviewer gave the highest ratings for neatness and condition.

The case illustrates many of the ways in which reality can diverge from the image of poverty, but the one I want to stress here is that the income brought in by this "poor" family was not being spent in a large city but in rural America. These are very different worlds, and yet the definition of the poverty line is precisely the same for the people in both.[4] It is perhaps the most egregious of the several computational inadequacies of the poverty index. As anyone who has lived in both a small town and a city can testify, the differences in the costs of enjoying "a decent existence" are great.

A few of these differences are measurable in dollars. In Denison, Iowa, for example, a town of 6,700 chosen because it happens to represent the national average for housing rental in small towns, the median monthly rent for a residence in 1980 was $290 (in 1987 dol-

---

[4] Until 1980, thresholds for farm families were 85 percent of the threshold for nonfarm families. There has never been an adjustment for people living in small towns or in the countryside who are not farmers.

lars). In Manhattan, the equivalent median was $367. This represents a 27 percent difference in one of the key costs of living. Apart from that, the housing costs in Denison and Manhattan are likely to be different because people in small towns, including low-income people, own their own homes more frequently than people in big cities. Married couples (who in 1970 constituted 71 percent of the small-town and rural poor) own their own homes more frequently than single people (who constituted 56 percent of the large-city poor). A couple that in a small town has earned Mr. and Mrs. A's income for thirty years is likely to be paying no mortgage, while a couple earning the same income in Manhattan will probably still have to worry about rent.

But these adjustments and similar adjustments in food and other basic costs are still measured in dollars, and dollars fail to capture the real difference between Manhattan and Denison in the cost of living a decent life. What the average rent does not tell you is how big the rooms are, whether there is a yard for the children to play in, what the place looks like and smells like and how many rats inhabit it. Perhaps even more importantly, the average rent does not tell you what the street outside the front door is like, what the neighbors are like, what the schools are like, and whether you can safely go for a stroll after nightfall.

Among the entire population of the working-aged who were poor in 1970, 30 percent were living in towns of fewer than 10,000 people and another 15 percent were living in small towns (not parts of metropolitan areas) of 10,000-25,000 people.

Poor people with many children

The case of Mr. and Mrs. A could be repeated here as well: They had four children, which is one reason why their real income could be substantial and yet leave them in near-official poverty. Let us add to that a very different kind of sketch involving children:

> Ms. B has a poverty profile of 01022100101. She lives in an inner-city neighborhood, making between $10,000 and $13,000 a year. She remained in or near poverty because she had five children. Four of these children were already of working age in 1970 (ages 18-23) and the fifth was 15. At least three of the five were living with her at any one time throughout the decade. But none of the children worked regularly; indeed, they almost never worked. In addition, one of the daughters had a child of her own who was added to the household.

The poverty index is pegged to the number of people in the household. This makes sense: Children cost money, hence a flat "poverty income" is unrealistic. But it can also lead to nonsensical results. For example, it is possible for a person to have an income of $5,500 and be classified as "not in poverty," then over a period of years increase his income to $22,000—quadruple his real income—and in the poverty statistics be shown as one of those people who has slid from "not in poverty" to "in poverty."

Three points are to be made about poverty and number of children. One again has to do with the insensitivity of the poverty index to the difference between living in different types of communities. In the inner city, the marginal cost of a child is probably as great or greater than the index suggests. Few low-income people in a city have an apartment with extra space in which new children (or aged parents or indigent siblings) can be put without crowding the others. But it happens quite often in rural areas that a family with a low income lives in a house with extra rooms, or one in which a new child means nothing worse than converting a one-child bedroom into a two-child bedroom. Hardly anyone in a city has the option of holding down the family's food costs by starting a garden in the back yard, or buying food directly from the farmer; many people in small towns and rural areas have such options (and exercise them).

The failure of the poverty index to take differential cost of living into account also gives the large family in a small town an increasingly larger "discretionary surplus" as family size increases. Suppose (to use a simplified calculation for purposes of illustration) that the cost of a standard food basket is 25 percent higher in Manhattan than in Denison, that in Manhattan it costs $2,000 to feed a couple and $500 to feed each marginal child, and that a standard "food index" is based on the Manhattan costs. The "food index" thereby gives a two-person family in Denison a $400 bulge (money that the Denison family can spend on something else). But when there are six children, the food index has grown to $5,000—and the bulge has grown to $1,000, money that the family in Manhattan is spending on food but the family in Denison (which eats just as well) is devoting to other needs (which are also less expensive in Denison than they would be in Manhattan), and so on. The more children, the greater the discrepancy between the purchasing power of a poverty-level income in the big city and that in the small town.

The second point involves the child as a "revealed preference," in the language of some economists. If a family was making $13,100 last year, barely above the poverty line, then this year gets a raise to $14,100 and a new baby as well, the odds are good (one would like to think the odds are high) that the couple is celebrating both the raise and the baby, even as a researcher is marking them down as having fallen into poverty (because the poverty threshold with the extra child has risen to $14,969). Let us say that the next year they get another $1,000 raise and again are above the poverty line. Their poverty profile for the three years has been 101: they were "temporarily poor." But they chose to be poor—or more accurately, they chose to have a child, and unbeknownst to them became poor. Compare their psychological position to that of another family who had been making $13,100, didn't have a new baby, and got a $1,000 pay cut to $12,100, which remained there for still a third year. The way that the poverty thresholds happen to fall, they did not retreat (statistically) into poverty—their poverty profile for the three years is 111—but they are also very likely (with good reason) to feel as if they are going backwards, failing, and living more poorly in the second two years than they did during the first year.

The third, related point involves the explicability of poverty and the role of the economic and social system. The case of Ms. B is apt. A single adult who makes an income of $10,000 (for example) has it within her capacity to live a life that is not "impoverished." Low-income, yes; impoverished, no. Ms. B will be able to do it in the Denisons of America much more easily than in its Manhattans, but she *can* do it. In that sense, it is incorrect to say that a working person who brings home an income of $10,000 but nonetheless is beneath the poverty line "cannot make a decent living." The question rather is what society considers to be a reasonable family wage. Should any working person acting as the sole provider be able to support a spouse above the poverty line? A spouse and a child? A spouse and two children? Should he be able to do it at the age of 18? Should he have to expect to wait until he has "gotten settled" (a quaint, bygone concept) and is able to support a family? All these are questions that will be answered differently by different people. But (at some number of children that I will not try to specify) we should stop confusing the poverty of people who have continued to have children with the poverty of people who "cannot make a decent living" by working. And when Ms. B's children continue to live in the house year after year without contributing significantly to the family's coffers, the system is not failing. Ms. B is making choices—one may or may not think them wise, but they are recognizably her choices.

Among working-aged people below the poverty line in 1970, 34 percent had four or more children in the house. Of these, more than half had six or more.

Older people who retire early

Mrs. C's profile is 99999993100. Mrs. C, aged 55 in 1980, was widowed during the 1970s. In the two years after Mr. C's death, her income plunged from the $47,000-$50,000 range to below the poverty level, less than $4,000 per year, where it remained through 1980.

To this point I have been discussing subsequent poverty among those who were poor in 1970. Mrs. C's story, and the third perspective from which temporary poverty must be reassessed, involves those who are poor, able-bodied, and making no visible effort to escape their poverty.

According to the numbers, Mrs. C looks like a case study in how poverty has become feminized. She was married to a man with a middle-class income who died and left her without an income. She went from prosperity to poverty. But it turns out that Mrs. C has a college degree and used to work as an accountant. (Her own labor income in 1970 was $27,000.) She continued to work for one year after her husband died, then stopped. As of 1980 she was living in a small town, listed no disability, received no welfare or social security income, and, despite being only 55 years old, termed herself "retired." She continued to live in the paid-off family home in this small town, and, as far as one can tell from the variables in the PSID, continued to live the same life she had lived when her husband was alive.

Two aspects of life in one's fifties and thereafter make such outcomes not only possible but also fairly common. One is that the requirements for income drop sharply when the children are through school, the house is paid for, the car still works, and one has acquired all the sofas, lawn mowers, neckties, and toaster ovens —the material infrastructure of daily life—that one needs. The second is the accumulation of assets. A widow has a modest stock portfolio, for example; she sells a hundred shares of something when she needs extra cash, the portfolio grows enough to offset her occasional sales, and she keeps this up until she dies. The money from the hundred shares never gets reported as income.

The correction of such errors does not lie in improving the adjustment for cost-of-living for the elderly. I could also draw a composite from the PSID whose age, marital situation, and 1980 income are identical to Mrs. C's, but who is frequently ill, has no medical insurance, no inheritance, must rent an apartment in a large city, and is living in desperate poverty. There is no way to construct an across-the-board cost-of-living adjustment that will discriminate between the comfortable and the destitute.

Among those who were poor in 1980, not disabled, and had reached the 55-64 age bracket (that is, were still below the normal retirement age), 24 percent listed themselves as retired and 26 percent listed themselves as housewives not in the labor market. Of this group, 78 percent had not been poor in 1970. Thirty-eight percent had been making more than three times the poverty threshold in 1970.

Betting on the labor market

Can any American who is willing to work hard make a decent living? Even if we adopt a loose definition of "working poor," including not just people who worked nearly full-time but those who worked *at all* in 1970, the numbers suggest how difficult it is to remain in the labor market and nonetheless continue to be poor. These are the summary numbers:

Of the population of working-aged adults in 1970, 95 percent were not poor. In almost half of the remaining cases, the head of household either was not in the labor market or had a substantial physical disability. This leaves 2.7 percent of working-aged adults who could be classified as living in "working poor households," if we use an inclusive definition that accepts anyone in a household where the head of household worked at least one hour in the preceding year and was not substantially disabled. Of these:

• 49 percent lived in towns of less than 25,000 or in rural areas.

• 40 percent had at least four children in the house.

• 43 percent had 1970 cash incomes of at least $10,000 in 1987 purchasing power.

What happens to a population of able-bodied working poor persons during their subsequent working years? Of those who had worked, or were the spouse of someone who worked, and were of working age (under 65) throughout the follow-up period, by 1980:

• 23 percent were out of the labor market, split between those who reported permanent disability and those who reported being voluntarily out of the labor force. The rates of poverty were 65 percent of the permanently disabled, 53 percent of the retired and housewives.

• 77 percent were still in the labor market. (Of these, 85 percent were no longer poor, and 15 percent were still poor. 78 percent had not been poor at any time in at least the last four years.)

Among the still-poor 15 percent—those members of the working-aged population who had been able-bodied working poor in both

1970 and 1980, and were still in the labor market and poor in 1980 (who represent three-tenths of one percent of the total working-aged population):

- 26 percent lived in towns of fewer than 25,000 persons (almost all in towns of fewer than 10,000).
- 49 percent had at least four children in the house.
- 60 percent had 1980 cash incomes of more than $10,000 in 1987 purchasing power.

These last percentages are based on only thirty-six cases out of the original 4,702, so the percentages must be assumed to be unstable.

Making sense of the numbers

Poverty is the elephant of social policy, with social scientists playing the role of the groping blind men. We each describe a different appendage without really contradicting one another. In this case, I have asked a specific question regarding people who are in the labor market and reached the conclusion, using the same data base that was used to portray the America of *Years of Poverty, Years of Plenty*, that it is extremely rare for a person to get into the labor market, stick with it, and remain poor. It is quite common for the rare person who is both working and poor not only to escape poverty but to reach the median income range or higher within a few years and remain there securely. Suppose, however, I had made just one different assumption, that people who are not in the labor market are discouraged workers, out of the labor market only because they know there are no jobs (or only "dead-end" jobs). Presto: The portrait can be made to flip completely, and the nation becomes once more a country with structural poverty woven inextricably throughout the economy.

The sort of analytic ping-pong represented by these contradictory descriptions of the numbers must somehow be diverted into a more productive dialogue. The policy implications of the different interpretations are too important, and too contradictory, to be based on the shadowy quantitative sketches available to us. By the same token, however, qualitative summaries of case-histories leave far too much room for selective interpretation in such politically-charged topics, no matter how pure the good faith of the investigator. What is needed first is not more analyses, but better data.

Let me suggest a proposal, and not an impossibly expensive or time-consuming one. Suppose that someone took a nationally representative sample such as the PSID and identified in that pool all the persons who were officially below the poverty line. Suppose that a team of interviewers armed with an interview protocol based on open-ended conversation (many established techniques are available) went out and tape-recorded interviews with an appropriately selected sample of a few hundred poor people, who were asked the kinds of questions that the numbers cannot answer. Let me emphasize that I am not advocating ethnographic research, but rather using low-income people as accurate reporters of qualitative information about themselves. In addition to the conversational interview, the research team would collect the standard close-ended items about income, occupation, and demographics. Then suppose that the verbatim transcripts of these interviews, including all of the interviewer's questions and comments, cleansed only of material that would compromise the subjects' anonymity, were made available for scholarly use in the same way that the PSID is available.

Based on my reading of the PSID, I am predicting that such a data base will force major revisions in the received policy wisdom. We will have to slash the accepted count of poor people, if by "poor people" we mean "people without the material resources to live a decent existence." A more specific prediction is that the estimates of rural and small-town poverty among whites will drop sharply. It will be found that year-to-year income shifts seldom mean much—that the trajectory of "standard of living" is far smoother than the year-to-year income figures suggest. What about the disabled? No one knows what the figures concerning them really mean; this will be an opportunity to find out.

The overarching revision in the received wisdom will be in the image of the poor as victims. Some are victims, without question. But a great many people below the poverty line (I will go out on a limb and predict a majority) will be seen as living lives that they choose to live. The most numerous will be people who reveal that they don't consider themselves to be living impoverished lives, even though their income puts them below the federal poverty line. But the PSID data also indicate that most of those who do consider themselves to be poor have an option open to them for increasing their income—the labor market—that they are not using, or are using only sporadically. In still other cases, idiosyncratic decisions (like Ms. B's choice to let her adult, idle children live with her) will be at work.

No data will be able to resolve the question of personal responsibility versus environment or genes. But as matters stand, the policy debate is founded on images of people who are poor for reasons like the following: because they cannot work or cannot find work, because they work at jobs that never allow them to rise above the minimum wage, because they are plunged into poverty by unforeseeable disasters. These images, I am arguing, cannot withstand a rich qualitative data base about the officially poor. In any event, two undoubted goods will come from amassing such a data base. One will be to provide the policy debate with a frame of reference, so that we will come closer to arguing about people rather than abstractions. The other will be to remind social scientists and politicians alike of how little poverty has to do with income.

41

Will the Underclass Always Be with Us?

Richard P. Nathan

Ken Auletta added a word to the popular vocabulary with his series of *New Yorker* articles and book on the underclass. At first, people interested in social policy balked at the term, concerned that it would have an adverse labeling effect, stigmatizing the people in what the *Economist* in a March 15, 1986, article termed America's "huge and intractable, largely black underclass." I have written this article as an essay on the word *underclass* (what does it mean?); the condition (is it new; why has it developed?); and the response (how should we deal with this condition?). This is not a research paper; it is more of a personal statement with emphasis on the policy response to underclass conditions.

Using the Word

It is not a happy conclusion, and in my case it did not come easily, but I conclude that the word *underclass* is an accurate and functional term and that we should use it in diagnosing and prescribing for American social problems in the current period. One reason for this conclusion is purely practical. The word has caught on. Nothing social scientists could do would change matters very much. There is also a second and more important reason for this conclusion that the word is functional.

Regrettably, I conclude that the word *underclass* reflects a real and new condition in the society with which we must come to terms. It is a condition properly described by the term *class*. Sociologist Ralf Dahren-

From *Society*, Vol. 24, No. 3 (March/April 1987): 57–62.

dorf, in *Class and Class Conflict in Industrial Society,* defines class as a group emerging from societal conditions that affect structural changes.

My essential argument is that there has been a distinctive structural change in social conditions in the United States over the past two decades that is expressed by the term *underclass,* and that there is now a broad consensus among politicians and experts that this has occurred. The word is increasingly used in the media as a shorthand expression for the concentration of economic and behavioral problems among racial minorities (mainly black and Hispanic) in large, older cities. For those of us interested in urban and social policy, the time has come to shift our focus from diagnosis to prescription. There are still important research issues on our agenda relating to the causes and characteristics of the underclass, but there is no longer as much to be achieved by debate on underclass conditions compared to attention devoted to how we deal with these conditions. In particular, research by William Julius Wilson provides a convincing analysis of the "problems that disproportionately plague the urban underclass." Says Wilson, in an article in P. G. Peterson's *The New Urban Reality:*

> Included in this population are persons who lack training and skills and either experience long-term unemployment or have dropped out of the labor force altogether; who are long-term public assistance recipients; and who are engaged in street criminal activity and other forms of aberrant behavior.

Researchers, government officials, and organizations and foundations interested in social and urban policy should place more emphasis on the strategies that can be adopted, and can be expected to work, in dealing with this problem. While I present a description, which I think reflects a widely shared view on the nature of the underclass, my emphasis remains on the response to this critical new reality in American society.

Emerging Consensus

The existence of a distinctive underclass, in an ironic way, is a result of the success, not the failure, of American social policy. The successes of the civil rights revolution (surely not complete, but extraordinary nonetheless) have caused a bifurcation of the racial minority groups that were the focus of the civil rights laws of the fifties and sixties and the big-spending social programs from the mid-sixties into the seventies.

I remember my first visit to a southern state in the mid-fifties. Driving through a rural area, I saw signs that said "Colored" on run-down cabins and motels. My reaction was to think how remarkable it was that such

TABLE 41.1

Central City	1980 Population	Population Below Poverty in 1979	Population Below Poverty and Living in Poverty Areas
Newark, N.J.	326,105	106,895	94,988
Atlanta, Ga.	409,424	112,622	93,192
Birmingham, Ala.	280,004	61,658	45,222
St. Louis, Mo.	444,308	96,849	76,456
Montgomery, Ala.	173,334	33,556	27,780
Detroit, Mich.	1,182,733	258,575	189,002
Chicago, Ill.	2,965,648	601,410	429,940
Cleveland, Ohio	564,407	124,860	93,784
Philadelphia, Pa.	1,653,164	340,517	248,735
New York, N.Y.	6,963,692	1,391,981	985,770
Oakland, Calif.	333,263	61,609	37,409
Los Angeles, Calif.	2,907,573	477,976	290,786
Kansas City, Mo.	440,001	57,965	34,441
Houston, Tex.	1,578,359	199,763	90,181
100 LARGEST CENTRAL CITIES	47,507,225	8,125,233	5,191,114

Source for Tables 41.1–3: U.S. Census of Population, 1980: Subject Reports: Poverty Areas in Large Cities (PC 80-2-8D). Washington, D.C.: Government Printing Office, February 1985.

accommodations could already have what were then brand-new colored television sets. It did not take long for me to realize that these were segregated facilities.

Such outward manifestations of discrimination are gone now from our official language and the behavior of our leading and large institutions. This is not to deny that discrimination exists in more subtle forms; it is meant to call attention to the fact that the opportunity structure of our society has changed. Members of racial minority groups who are educated, talented, and motivated can assimilate in ways that a generation ago would have been thought inconceivable.

There are unanticipated results of social change. As avenues of opportunity have opened for upwardly mobile and educated members of racial minority groups to move to suburbs and better-off urban neighborhoods, the people left behind in the ghetto—the hidden city—are more isolated. The role models of an earlier day—a teacher, postman, civil servant— have left. There is no reason they should not have left; however, the result is that the dangerous inner-city areas festering in our land have become an increasingly more serious social and economic problem.

It is useful to put this point as a hypothesis: underclass conditions are multifaceted. They are economic, behavioral and geographically focused. This is not to say that we can easily put our social science calipers to the task of measuring the underclass. The underclass involves more than things we can measure with conventional economic and demographic indicators—such as low income, long-term unemployment, limited education, and the incidence of welfare dependency. The underclass condition is also attitudinal and behavioral. It involves alienation, and for the long-term welfare subgroup what Thomas Pettigrew, in V. T. Corello's *Poverty and Public Poverty,* calls a feeling of "learned helplessness." It is often manifest in crime and vandalism, which serve to further isolate underclass groups.

Although a great deal of research has been done on poverty and underclass conditions, there are bound to be differences in interpretation. The main point that needs to be made here is like the cautionary label on cigarette packs: "Be careful when you read the work of social policy experts." We need social policy experts, and there are important areas yet to be studied under the heading of the underclass. Nevertheless, it is possible to draw different conclusions from the same data. At the very least, thoughtful observers of this subject should look at the work of a range of experts rather than unquestionably accepting a single interpretation of the nature and reasons for underclass conditions—mine included.

Having given this warning, I feel more comfortable in summarizing my own conclusions. My view of the situation, based on what we know at present, is that the underclass is a distinctively urban condition involving a hardened residual group that is difficult to reach and relate to. This condition represents a change in kind, not degree, although it must always be added that we are talking about a relatively small subgroup among the poor. Census Bureau data are available for 1980 on the population by race in urban poverty areas in the nation's 100 largest cities. They show disturbingly high concentrations of black and Hispanic urban poverty. These data indicate that the black and Hispanic population of urban poverty areas accounts for between 6 to 15 percent of all persons in poverty in the United States, depending on the definition used for poverty areas. If we define urban poverty areas as census tracts with 20 percent or more poverty population, there were 4.1 million black and Hispanic poor persons in poverty areas of the 100 largest cities in 1980. This is 15.1 percent of all persons classified as being in poverty. If we use a more highly concentrated definition of poverty areas—40 percent or more of the population in poverty—6 percent of all persons in poverty reside in these areas. The concentration of poor black and Hispanic persons in poverty areas in selected cities is shown in the tables. Over the past decade, census data indicate that the concentration of poor blacks and Hispanics in poverty areas rose by some 40 percent in the most severe urban poverty areas, although the 1970 and 1980 data are not precisely comparable.

TABLE 41.2

Central City	Black & Hispanic Population Below Poverty in 1979	Black & Hispanic Population Below Poverty and Living in Poverty Areas	Percent Black & Hispanic Poor Living in Poverty Areas	Percent City Population That is Poor, Black or Hispanic, and Lives in Poverty Areas
Newark, N.J.	94,925	87,952	92.7%	27.0%
Atlanta, Ga.	95,628	85,043	88.9%	20.8%
Birmingham, Ala.	49,461	40,310	81.5%	14.4%
St. Louis, Mo.	69,018	63,731	92.3%	14.3%
Montgomery, Ala.	26,231	24,630	93.9%	14.2%
Detroit, Mich.	205,114	160,736	78.4%	13.6%
Chicago, Ill.	472,653	390,220	82.6%	13.2%
Cleveland, Ohio	83,334	73,563	88.3%	13.0%
Philadelphia, Pa.	229,140	204,940	89.4%	12.4%
New York, N.Y.	988,933	848,671	85.8%	12.2%
Oakland, Calif.	45,206	31,605	69.9%	9.5%
Los Angeles, Calif.	322,288	240,199	74.5%	8.3%
Kansas City, Mo.	31,655	25,646	81.0%	5.8%
Houston, Tex.	146,299	84,272	57.6%	5.3%
100 LARGEST CENTRAL CITIES	5,169,529	4,139,976	80.1%	8.7%

The politics involved in dealing with urban underclass conditions are difficult because, overall, the numbers of people affected are small, the people involved tend not to vote, they do not have powerful interest groups that support them, and the places in which these problem conditions are concentrated can be dangerous and threatening to outsiders.

This situation has important implications for government policy. That underclass conditions are so intractable and that they involve alienation and criminal behavior is one of the reasons underlying the current conservative-retrenchment mood of the nation on social policy. There has been a shift over the past decade not just on social spending and not limited to our belief about what we can achieve under social programs. This shift involves a perceptible and disturbing change in public opinion on race and civil rights issues. The way we came to believe we are supposed to behave toward the members of minority groups in the sixties and seventies has changed in the eighties. This often unspoken—although sometimes privately conceded—shift in opinion was partially caused by the increased severity of urban underclass conditions, and this situation in turn is manifest in heightened racial intolerance. In the long run, these developments, unless we respond to them wisely, could threaten the social and civil rights policy gains of the earlier and more hopeful period beginning in the mid-sixties that lasted throughout most of the seventies.

A Matter of Values

My third topic is a response to underclass conditions. My purpose is not to discuss specific programs, but rather to present ideas on the strategy for dealing with underclass conditions. Here, I have better news to report. New thinking is emerging in the current period about government social policies that represent a fortuitous development. It reflects a synthesis of conservative and liberal ideas on a basis that includes the best features of both. It is useful to view this development in historical perspective.

To a considerable degree, the motivating spirit of social policy in the United States in the Great Society period was a feeling of guilt about the conditions of a society that blocked, rather than facilitated, the movement of racial minorities into the social and economic mainstream. Associated with this spirit was a sense of discovery that the culture and ideas distinctive to racial minorities should be recognized and more widely appreciated. Soul food. Gospel music and the dress, language, and humor of blacks, in Tom Wolfe's wonderful satire, all came to be part of a new,

TABLE 41.3

Central City	1980 Population	Whites Below Poverty Level in 1979	Poor Whites in Poverty Areas	Percent White Poor Living in Poverty Areas
Newark, N.J.	326,105	10,959	6,337	57.8%
Atlanta, Ga.	409,424	16,058	7,600	47.3%
Birmingham, Ala.	280,004	11,858	4,676	39.4%
St. Louis, Mo.	444,308	27,085	12,191	45.0%
Montgomery, Ala.	173,334	7,240	3,122	43.1%
Detroit, Mich.	1,182,733	50,646	26,472	52.3%
Chicago, Ill.	2,965,648	117,218	33,851	28.9%
Cleveland, Ohio	564,407	40,401	19,416	48.1%
Philadelphia, Pa.	1,653,164	104,992	39,001	37.1%
New York, N.Y.	6,963,692	360,469	114,502	31.8%
Oakland, Calif.	333,263	11,439	2,971	26.0%
Los Angeles, Calif.	2,907,573	119,998	29,140	24.3%
Kansas City, Mo.	440,001	25,154	8,088	32.2%
Houston, Tex.	1,578,359	46,867	3,996	8.5%
100 LARGEST CENTRAL CITIES	47,507,225	2,658,750	902,278	33.9%

socially-motivated form of radical chic. White liberals especially reached out in well meaning ways to understand and identify with the black community.

This attitude carried over to government programs. Among the central ideas of Lyndon Johnson's war on poverty were compassion and power to the people. Again, Tom Wolfe captured the feeling of this concept in the popular literature. In his "Mau-Mauing the Flak Catchers," published in *Radical Chic and Mau-Mauing the Flak Catchers*, he wrote about going downtown to mau-mau the bureaucrats. "The proverty program encouraged you to go in for mau-mauing." Otherwise, the bureaucrats at City Hall and in the Office of Economic Opportunity, said Wolfe, wouldn't know what to do. "They didn't know who to ask." The answer in San Francisco, the locale of Wolfe's story, depended on "the confrontation ritual."

> Well . . . they used the Ethnic Catering Service . . . right. . . . They sat back and waited for you to come rolling in with your certified angry militants, your guaranteed frustrated ghetto youth, looking like a bunch of wild men. Then you had your test confrontation. If you were outrageous enough, if you could shake up the bureaucrats so bad that their eyes froze into iceballs and their mouth twisted up into smiles of sheer physical panic, into shit-eating grins, so to speak—then you knew you were the real goods. They knew you were the right studs to give the poverty grants and community organizing jobs to. Otherwise they wouldn't know.

As I read the tea leaves of social policy, this deferential attitude carried over into the Nixon-Ford period in the mid-seventies. It determined what was permissible in both the rhetoric and substance of social policy. The now widespread frustration with Great Society programs did not become a part of the popular mindset on social issues until the latter part of the seventies.

George Will makes an observation, in *Statecraft as Soulcraft*, that is helpful in understanding the new philosophy of social action that began to emerge in the late nineteen seventies. He notes that politicians, although they may not concede that this is so, are often involved in shaping and changing moral values.

> . . . statecraft is soulcraft. Just as all education is moral education because learning conditions conduct, much legislation is moral legislation because it conditions the action and the thought of the nation in broad and important spheres in life.

This idea is the key to the hopeful point that we appear to be moving toward a new formula for dealing with underclass conditions that corrects for the miscalculations and excesses, however well-intended, of the Great Society. Social policy is now evolving in a way that reflects an increased belief on the part of both liberals and conservatives that there should be a behavioral *quid pro quo*. There was reluctance on the part of people in the field of social policy from the mid-sixties through the mid-seventies to intrude on the culture and value system of the groups that in Lyndon Johnson's presidency were discovered as a new focus for social policy. Allowing people to do their own thing was felt to be (and there is a good argument for this) the right approach to helping the poor. The guaranteed-income or negative income tax idea reflects this view. The problem of the poor is that they do not have enough money; providing resources—preferably in the most flexible form, hard currency—was seen as enabling them to make their own choices.

Imperceptibly at first, a movement developed in the late seventies on the part of social policy intellectuals questioning these assumptions. There is a concept in economics that is helpful for this analysis: signaling. We may not be doing people a favor if we transmit signals about welfare rights and entitlements in a society that has a deep and strong Calvinist tradition that practically deifies the work ethic. The change that has occurred in our ideas about signaling under social programs is best seen by looking at the welfare field, and particularly at the most controversial welfare program for ablebodied, working-age poor people with children—the Aid to Families with Dependent Children (AFDC) program.

There have been three main theories of welfare reform for AFDC over the past twenty years, all of which have been publicly prominent. One theory is the guaranteed-income approach. Another is the employment approach (jobs are the answer). The third, for which Ronald Reagan was the principal spokesman in the seventies, is the devolutionary or block-grant approach to welfare reform. Its aim is to turn back responsibility for the welfare population to the states on the premise that states (and also local governments) are in the best position to provide services and make the fine-grained determinations necessary to enable (or better yet, push and require) working age, ablebodied poor persons to move into the labor force.

The synthesis I see emerging in the current period contains elements of all three approaches, although the dominant themes are work (the employment approach) and devolution (relying more heavily on the states). A single word captures the shift that is occurring: workfare.

In the seventies the word *workfare* was used in a narrow way to refer to the idea that people should work off their welfare grants, that is, that welfare recipients should be required to work, even in make-work jobs, in exchange for receiving their benefits. Liberals on social policy issues—

and this included most welfare administrators—heaped abuse on this idea, calling it "slavefare" and rejecting it out of hand. Efforts to tie welfare to work in a binding way were often undermined by the welfare establishment. This occurred, for example, in Massachusetts, where such an effort was made by Governor Edward King, and in California under Governor Ronald Reagan. Reagan's 1971 California welfare reform plan, which included an AFDC work requirement and a work-experience component, never got off the ground. At its peak, only 3 percent of the eligible population participated in work-experience programs.

Something happened on the way to the forum—in this case the U.S. Congress. Ronald Reagan as president won grudging acceptance from the Congress to include authority under the AFDC program in the 1981 budget act to allow states to test new employment approaches to welfare reform, including the workfare approach. What emerged out of the efforts to implement this legislation is what I call "new-style workfare." The history of the nomenclature is interesting.

The 1981 budget act included a provision permitting the states to experiment with what was termed in Washington CWEP, standing for "community work experience programs." The same acronym had been used in California in the seventies, only the "C" was for "California," and not "community" under this California program.

The big difference in the 1980s—and this is a critical point—is that liberals and the welfare establishment began to shift their ground politically and, at the same time, to shift their terms of reference. The term *workfare* is increasingly being used in a new way. It takes the form of obligational state programs that involve an array of employment and training services and activities: job search, job training, education programs, and also community work experience. Over two-thirds of the states are now developing new-style workfare programs along these lines. Research by the Manpower Demonstration Research Corporation in eight states, with 35,000 people assigned to program and control groups, shows promising— although not large and dramatic—results from these programs in terms of increased earnings and reduced welfare dependency. Whether this shift to new-style workfare is intellectual or tactical is had to say. My reading of new-style workfare is that the initial response of the welfare establishment and liberals among social policy experts was expedient and tactical, but that as events transpired conviction followed suit.

One reason for the increasingly positive response, particularly on the part of state government officials, to the new authority in the 1981 budget act reflects the opinion held by many observers of urban conditions: the critical need in distressed urban areas is jobs. In effect, new-style workfare creates jobs (short-term, entry-level positions very much like the CETA—

Comprehensive Employment and Training Act—public service jobs we thought we had abolished in 1981). At the same time, new-style workfare provides a political rationale and support for increased funding for education and training programs; it also discriminates under these employment and job preparation programs in favor of the most disadvantaged people. The latter effect (discrimination in favor of the most disadvantaged) corrects for the problem of "creaming" under employment and training programs, a practice which has been the subject of strong and justifiable criticism on the part of experts in the field of employment and training.

The California story for new-style workfare is particularly interesting. Under a conservative governor, George Deukmejian, a deal was struck between the governor and liberals in the legislature, notably Arthur Agnos, on legislation that involves a fundamental restructuring of the welfare system to shift its orientation from a payment and social service system to a new system strongly oriented toward training, education, job placement, and work—including in some cases the assignment of welfare family heads to obligatory work experience positions.

At first, the language was oblique. Work experience was called PREP in California, the letters standing for preemployment preparation. Increasingly the press and participants in the debate on this legislation came to call the whole program and process by one word, workfare. This newspeak of welfare reform in California—and also in many other states—now uses the term *workfare* to refer to the array of job-focused programs and child care and other services to reduce welfare dependency. New-style workfare is a blend of conservative and liberal themes. In finding this nice balance, there is reason to hope that politicians have detoxified the welfare issue. This shift is healthy and encouraging for social policy in the United States. The basic strategy involves state initiatives, institutional change at the state level, and the idea of obligation.

This is not to say that the obligational concept in social policy can be expected to take hold everywhere and expand rapidly. Successful policy change must have a foundation in values. It is in these terms—in terms of building a new foundation of values as a basis for policy change—that I see some grounds for a modest sense of hopefulness in the current period.

We make our greatest progress on social reform in the United States when liberals and conservatives find common ground. New-style workfare embodies both the caring commitment of liberals and the themes identified with conservative writers such as Charles Murray, George Gilder, and Lawrence Mead. It involves a strong commitment to reducing welfare dependency on the premise that dependency is bad for people, that it undermines their motivation to support themselves, and isolates and stigmatizes welfare recipients in a way that over a long period feeds into and accentuates the underclass mindset and condition.

The new message is a familiar one: "You have to go along to get along." You have to go along, that is, with a set of values about work, job skills, behavior in the workplace, and attitudes toward success in the economy. Society is behaving like a supportive parent. Rather than telling people, "there is something wrong with you, you need help," we do better by telling them, "you are as good as the next person, you should make it on your own." Confidence rather than deference is the essence of this new approach to social policy.

In the long run, the test of the society's will to move in this direction requires two things: money and a willingness on the part of governments at all levels to focus training, educational, and employment services on those who need them the most. This includes both female welfare family heads and unemployed young males in distressed urban areas. Fortunately, research shows that such a targeting policy—discriminating in favor of the most disadvantaged people—has positive results. Yet, even if we respond to this challenge, underclass conditions will not be alleviated quickly or easily. The task requires time, patience, and a willingness to experiment and adapt in social policy. To this question about the underclass: will it always be with us?, the answer is that, even with the best efforts, it will be with us for a long time. Nevertheless, I believe there is reason now for a more hopeful mood about our ability to make a dent in America's most challenging social problem which tests the very mettle of our democracy.

About the Editor

Ray C. Rist is deputy director of the General Government Division, United States General Accounting Office (GAO). He joined GAO in 1981. His extensive knowledge of evaluation design principles has helped construct the proper analytical framework for GAO jobs as diverse as reviews of defense programs, education, and employment. His work in the areas of program evaluation and policy analysis spans nearly twenty years and has involved him in countless studies at the local, state, national, and international levels.

Rist contributed to various academic and professional efforts prior to his joining GAO. From 1977 to 1981, he was national director of the Youthwork National Policy Study and professor at Cornell University. Also, Rist worked from 1974 to 1976 with the National Institute of Education (NIE) in several capacities on planning and implementing research and evaluation programs in the areas of school desegregation, bilingual education, school violence, and services for disadvantaged students. He left NIE in 1976 to accept an appointment as senior Fulbright fellow at the Max Planck Institute in West Berlin, Federal Republic of Germany. While there, he evaluated various social, educational, and economic policies regarding the "guest-worker" population in West Germany. From 1968 to 1974, he was a sociology professor, first in Illinois and then in Oregon.

Rist earned his Ph.D in sociology and anthropology in 1970 from Washington University (St. Louis). His list of book and article publications is extensive. His fourteen books have been published by, among others, Harvard University Press, M.I.T. Press, Transaction Books, Columbia University Press, and Klett-Cotta Press of Stuttgart, Germany. His most recent books are *Policy Studies Review Annual, Vol. 8* (Transaction Books, 1986) and *Finding Work: Cross-National Perspectives on Employment and Training Policy* (Falmer Press, 1987). He has lectured in more than twenty countries and served as a consultant to many international organizations.